International Finance

for

Multinational Business

edited by

Lee Charles Nehrt

Associate Professor of International Business
Graduate School of Business
Indiana University

International Textbook Company
Scranton, Pennsylvania

To my wife

Ardith Ann Nehrt

Preface

International business, as a field of study, was to be found in only a limited number of schools of business, prior to 1960. Since that time a dozen schools have initiated a program in international business. Momentum has been gained, and today we find that literally scores of business schools are attempting to start programs in this field. Two factors have frustrated many schools. One is a lack of qualified staff and the other is a shortage of textbook material.

International finance has not escaped these frustrations. But this was to be expected. For many years, international finance was primarily in the domain of the economists. That portion which concerned business schools was essentially aimed at the concept of international trade rather than the current concept of multinational business. As a consequence, the teaching of international finance in today's international business programs requires the use of a multitude of outside readings on aspects of international finance not covered by existing texts.

Former courses in international finance were concerned with the documents for financing foreign trade; the organization of commercial banks to handle these documents; the determination of exchange rates and the trading of foreign exchange; the function of exchange controls; and the operation of several institutions such as the International Monetary Fund, and the International Bank for Reconstruction and Development. The texts available reflected the above coverage.

In support of international business programs, however, a number of other areas of international finance are of primary importance. For example: What are the relationships between trends in the U.S. balance of payments and U.S. government policy on foreign investment? What are the flows and trends in foreign aid which affect the investment environment in the underdeveloped countries? What developments in the capital and money markets, of both industrialized and underdeveloped countries, affect the ability of companies to raise both investment and working capital for their overseas operations? How do U.S. and foreign tax laws affect profits and the transfers of funds? Or, what policies and methods of accounting and reporting should be followed to accurately reflect operating profits in countries where inflation and devaluations are prevalant and to permit the parent company to better conduct their financial planning for those sudsidiaries?

All of these factors are important to the executives of multinational firms as a basis for their decision-making for new investments and for determining the sources, timing, and amounts of funds to acquire or transfer within their world-wide operations.

The choice of readings to cover this greatly enlarged field of international finance presented the editor with a dilemma: A collection of scholarly articles of a timeless nature, addressed to these many aspects, would have been preferable, but they are sparce. A set of readings confined to such articles would not fulfill the functions of a book of readings. The decision was therefore made to collect articles from a wide variety of sources, relying on the more scholarly articles to the greatest extent possible, and filling in with the best available from other sources. The result, it is hoped, is a collection of readings which will essentially satisfy the needs of a course in international finance.

There are several aspects of international finance which are essential to a course but which are not contained in this set of readings. One of these missing elements is the explanation of documentation related to international trade. This may seem mundane, but a detailed understanding of the use of documents controlling the flow of credits and payments is a prerequisite to a comprehension of the balance of payments, foreign exchange trading, and foreign exchange controls. A second important element not included in this volume is the theory of the balance of payments. These two elements were omitted because of space limitations and because they can be found in all existing texts as well as in other sources.[1]

Another aspect of international finance missing from these readings is that of foreign banking systems. An entire course can be (and in some schools is) devoted to this subject. It is important for the international businessman to understand the banking systems of the countries in which he operates, so the subject cannot be ignored. The writer has found that for the purposes of a course in international finance, it is invaluable to include several sessions where students report on and discuss the banking systems of several chosen countries of interest, including an industrialized country, an underdeveloped country, and a socialist economy.

Another aspect of international finance not included in these readings, but which has greatly increased in importance in recent years, is that of medium-term trade credit. Increasing amounts of capital equipment exports are being financed on terms of from one to five years. This type of financing has become a vehicle for foreign investment financing and is an important ele-

---

[1] For example, The American Bankers Assn. has published a monograph entitled *A Banker's Guide to Financing Exports*; and the Intercollegiate Case Clearing House has a case on "The Theory of the Balance of Payments."

ment in the financing of economic development. It has led to the establishment of new institutions and to new relationships between governments, financial institutions and manufacturing companies. Very little has been written on this topic. The major work is a recently published monograph by this writer.[2]

The other major element missing from this volume, an element which is of key importance to a course in international finance, is the set of cases dealing with the operational problems of the field. The writer has found the following cases to be most useful:

1. Industrial Development Bank of Turkey
2. Goodrich International Rubber Company
3. Baccollim (Colombia)
4. P & M, Inc.
5. Tatung Engineering Company
6. Bell Campinas, S. A.
7. Pittsburgh City Bank
8. Ecuadorian Rubber Company

These cases are, of course, separately available from the Intercollegiate Case Clearing House.

With the additions noted above, it is hoped that this text will provide the necessary material for a modern course in international finance to meet the needs of today's multinational business community.

LEE CHARLES NEHRT

Bloomington, Indiana
November, 1966

[2] Lee Charles Nehrt, *Financing Capital Equipment Exports*, Scranton, Pa.: International Textbook Company, 1966.

Contents

Introduction 1

part A   THE INTERNATIONAL MONETARY ENVIRONMENT

   1. **Foreign Exchange: Theory and Practice** 7

      The Nature and Efficiency of the Foreign Exchange Market, *Jerome L. Stein* 9

      Interest Rate Differences, Forward Exchange Mechanism, and Scope for Short-term Capital Movements, *William H. White* 45

      Additional Readings 60

   2. **Central Banking: The Exercise of Monetary Policy**.. 62

      Foreign Central Banking: The Instruments of Monetary Policy, *Peter G. Fousek* 64

      New Central Banks, *Federal Reserve Bank of New York* .. 91

      Additional Readings 99

   3. **The U.S. Balance of Payments: Actual and Potential Effects on Multinational Business** 101

      Gold and the Balance of Payments, *The First National Bank of Chicago* 104

      The Balance of Payments in 1963, *Walter Lederer* 120

      How Real is The Drain on Dollars? *Business Week* 139

      Should We Devalue the Dollar? *Hendrick S. Houthakker* .. 145

      Devaluation is Not the Answer, *Robert Z. Aliber* 150

      Let's Get Rid of Our Cross of Gold, *Abba B. Lerner* 155

      Using the Free Market to Resolve the Balance of Payments Problem, *Milton Friedman* 161

      Flexible Exchange Rate? Not For Us! *Herbert Bratter* 171

      The Balance of Payments Payoff of Direct Foreign Investments, *Emile Benoit* 175

      Interest Equalization Tax: A Deceptive Tourniquet, *First National City Bank, New York* 184

      The President's Balance of Payments Program, *Federal Reserve Bank of New York* 189

      Additional Readings 199

4. **The International Monetary System: Its Operation
    and Suggested Reform** 201

    International Payments, Imbalances, and the Need for
    Strengthening International Financial Arrangements, *Report
    to the Joint Economic Committee* 204

    International Liquidity, *J. Keith Horsefield* 231

    The West is Risking a Credit Collapse, *Jacques Rueff* 240

    Annual Gold Review, *First National City Bank, New York* 247

    The London Gold Market, *Bank of England* 257

    Atlantic Monetary Arrangements, *The Chase Manhattan
    Bank, New York* 262

    The United Kingdom Financial Crisis, *The First National
    Bank of Chicago* 267

    Additional Readings 271

5. **Exchange Controls: Types, Uses, and Trends**........ 273

    Restrictions on the Movement of Funds Within Latin
    America, *Samir Makdisi* 276

    Exchange Measures in Venezuela, *W. John R. Woodley* ... 302

    Floating Vs. Pegged Exchange Rates: The Canadian Ex-
    perience, *Canada's 1964 Report of the Royal Commission
    on Banking and Finance* 328

part B   FINANCING TRADE AND ECONOMIC
           DEVELOPMENT

6. **Commercial Banking and Multinational Business**... 351

    Banking Across Frontiers, *The Economist* 353

    International Growth: Challenge to U.S. Banks, *George S.
    Moore* 363

    Foreign Bank Activity in the United States, *R. Gerald Fox* . 377

    Foreign Banks in London, *O. Petit* 384

    Commercial Banking Trends in Western Europe, *The Chase
    Manhattan Bank, New York* 389

    Whirling in a Latin American Spiral, *The Economist* 394

    What Course in Africa? *The Economist* 399

    Additional Readings 403

7. **Financing East-West Trade, and Trade Between
    Socialist Countries** 404

    United States and East-West Trade, *The First National
    Bank of Chicago* 407

    East-West Trade—Present Trends, *Moscow Narodny Bank
    Quarterly Review* 412

    The Soviet Union, the Comecon, and Western Trade, *Åke
    O. Liljefors* 419

    Trading With the People's Republic of China, *Board of
    Trade Journal, London* 428

China's Western Trade; No More Rhubarb, *The Economist* 434

The Finance of East-West Trade, *Investors Chronicle* 436

Some Aspects of the U.S.S.R.'s International Trade and Payments, *Oleg Kulikov* 441

Toward a Transferable Rouble?, *The Economist* 447

The International Bank for Economic Cooperation, *Moscow Narodny Bank Quarterly Review* 452

Additional Readings 456

8. **The International Financing of Economic Development** 457

Development Assistance Efforts and Policies, *OECD, Paris* 461

The International Bank for Reconstruction and Development, *Alec Cairncross* 492

Some Techniques of Development Lending, *IBRD, Washington* 506

Additional Readings 521

part C   *FINANCING FOREIGN INVESTMENTS AND OPERATIONS*

9. **Aspects and Trends in International Capital and Money Markets** 525

Recent Innovations in European Capital Markets, *Federal Reserve Bank of New York* 528

Eurodollars in Today's World Markets, *A. Robert Abboud* 539

Credit Creation Through Eurodollars? *Geoffrey L. Bell* .. 554

Western European Capital Markets and U.S. Capital Outflow Restriction, *John D. Hogan* 562

The European Capital Markets, *The Chase Manhattan Bank, New York* 577

The Unit of Account, *Weekly Bulletin of the Kredietbank* . 584

The European Stock Markets, *The First National Bank of Chicago* 589

Additional Readings 594

10. **Money and Capital Markets in Underdeveloped Countries** 595

A Philippine Case Study: Problems in Financing Economic Development: The Need for an Effective Capital Market, *H. K. Charlesworth and Richard W. Hooley* 597

Methods of Fostering a Capital Market, *Shirley Boskey* .. 608

The Development of Money Markets, *Peter G. Fousek* ... 616

The New Money Markets, *J.S.G. Wilson* 621

Money Markets of South-East Asia, *David Williams* 634

Additional Readings 642

11. **The Role of Development Banks in International Finance** **644**

Problems and Practices of Development Banks, *Shirley Boskey* 646

The Role of Private Institutions in Development Financing, *William Diamond* 687

The Poorer Nations Find a New Bootstrap, *Business Week* 694

Additional Readings 698

12. **Financing Direct Investments Abroad** **699**

Financing Overseas Expansion, *John G. McLean* 703

Edge Act and Agreement Corporations in International Banking and Finance, *Federal Reserve Bank of New York* 720

The Aid Guaranty Program, *Irving Trust Company, New York* 729

International Finance Corporation, *Machinery and Allied Products Institute, Washington* 734

Financing Foreign Operations: Spain, *Business International* 746

Financing Foreign Operations: CACM, *Business International* 753

The Peace by Investment Corporation, *Benjamin A. Javits and Leon H. Keyserling* 757

Additional Readings 766

part D OTHER FINANCIAL ASPECTS OF MULTINATIONAL BUSINESS

13. **Taxation of Multinational Business** **769**

U.S. Tax Policy: Basic Principles, *Thomas E. Jenks* 772

U.S. Tax Policy: Legislative Proposals, *Laurence D. Hollman* 777

Taxing U.S. Investments Abroad, *First National City Bank, New York* 785

Foreign Income Provisions of the "Revenue Act of 1962," and Where We Go from Here, *Thomas B. Curtis* 793

United States Taxation of International Business, *Edward B. Bartoli* 800

How Taxes Compare, *Business Week* 808

Choice Between Alternative Countries for the Location of an Enterprise, *European Taxation* 823

Tax Coordination Is the Next Step, *Carl S. Shoup* 836

Importing a Tax from Europe, *Business Week* 844

Additional Readings 848

14. **Accounting, Controlling, and Reporting in International Finance** **849**

Reporting Undistributable Foreign Earnings, *H. H. Oppenheimer* 851

Devaluation of Foreign Currencies, *John J. Miller* 870

Management Accounting Problems in Foreign Operations,
George C. Watt 878

Inflation and Foreign Investments, *S. R. Sapienza* 887

How ITT Manages Its Foreign Exchange, *John Verroen* .. 898

Additional Readings 907

Index **909**

Introduction

It is difficult, today, for students and practitioners of international finance in the United States to place the field in a proper perspective. The role now being played by this country, its banks and manufacturing companies, is fairly recent in the history of international finance. Prior to World War I, Great Britain was the center of the financial world, with the United States only on the periphery. Even between the first two world wars, most of the world's trade was still financed in sterling, and New York was only beginning to make its capital market available to the rest of the world. Prior to the 1940's, some of the oil and mining companies and a very few manufacturing companies had foreign investments. Also, only a small number of our commercial banks had attempted to establish a network of foreign branches or subsidiaries.

All of this has changed since World War II, and most of it in the short period of the last decade. The U.S. dollar is used as a basis for financing the majority of world trade and has become the bulwark of the whole international monetary system. New York became a prime source of long-term capital for foreign governments and firms. Not only the New York banks, but also the major inland banks have come to feel that a foreign branch is a status symbol which carries with it profits as well as prestige. And, the U.S. companies which have moved into direct foreign investments during the last decade are numbered in the thousands.

The recentness of this movement abroad means that most Americans have little appreciation of "the good old days" when England was the center of international finance; when the pound sterling was of unquestioned strength and when the United States, one of the other developing countries of the world, went to England with outstretched hand. The following quotes ring strangely on the ears of Americans today:

> It was highly embarrassing for an American to be in London in the winter of 1842–43. The securities which had gone into default (i.e., the securities of various states of the U.S.) had been purchased at a premium by large numbers of the governing classes (of London). And, the resentment which they felt at their mistaken judgements spread without delay to all persons and things American. The United States were held collectively responsible for the shortcomings of their numbers. Business letters to merchants of impeccable standing contained allusions to American credit. English houses took pains to let their clients know that they

1

owned no American stock. At least one American of irreproachable antecedence was barred admission to a London club, specifically because he belonged to a republic which did not fulfill its engagements. . . .

In the summer of 1842, agents of the U.S. Treasury appeared in London soliciting a loan to cover the shortage which the decline of import trade was causing in the customs receipts. They met a cold reception. "The people of the United States may be fully persuaded," thundered the *Times,* "that there is a certain class of securities to which no abundance of money, however great, can give value; and that in this class their own securities stand pre-eminent." Bankers echoed the refrain. "You may tell your government," said the Paris Rothschild to Duff Green, "that you have seen the man who is at the head of the finances of Europe, and that he has told you that they cannot borrow a dollar, not a dollar." The difficulty, as one finance company explained to the commissioners, was that American credit stood too low.[1]

It is helpful to reread these and similar reports periodically to remind oneself of how recently the United States has gained predominance. For, the financial executive in today's multinational corporation cannot function efficiently unless he can fully understand the financial environment *within* the many countries with which his firm is doing business.

This need greatly extends the reaches of the field of international finance. The term "international" no longer means simply "between nations," but must include the concept of "foreign" as well. International finance has always concerned itself with the institutions, practices, policies, and problems within the United States; it is now as necessary to be concerned with the same factors within foreign countries.

How does one put a handle on this vast area? What approach should one take toward an understanding of its intricacies? Three approaches are useful; the environmental, the functional, and the institutional.

The environmental approach describes and analyzes the environment in which business firms and financial institutions operate. The major category of environmental phenomena is governmental controls. The bases for these policies differ from country to country. In the United States and the United Kingdom, most governmental controls affecting international finance derive from attempts to stem balance of payments deficits. Germany has been concerned about balance-of-payments surpluses. France, Canada and Japan are motivated by nationalism. Most underdeveloped countries are reacting to combinations of balance of payments difficulties, nationalism, and the need to increase the rate of development. The result of all of this is an environment consisting of exchange controls, varying exchange rates, varying interest rates, internal credit restrictions, trade credit restrictions and promotion, restrictions on East-West trade, and a wide variety of tax policies.

[1] Hamilton Jenks Leland, *The Migration of British Capital to 1875,* New York and London: Alfred A. Knopf, 1927, pp. 104–106.

On the other hand, there are the environmental phenomena, many of which are structural in character, over which governments do not or cannot exercise controls. For example, there may be a lack of, or inefficient operation of, money markets, capital markets and other financial institutions; varying rates of inflation and hyper-inflation; shortages of loan and investment capital; and varying attitudes towards investments in industry within traditional and transitional societies.

The functional approach to international finance is much more direct. Taking the point of view of the companies and financial institutions, the functions of international finance are: the financing of international trade; the financing of international investment; the movement of capital between countries (including repatriation of profits and capital); and the total problem of financial planning for international operations. It must not be forgotten that, for the multinational corporation, these functions include the financing of investment and trade within foreign countries. All of these functions must, of course, occur within the environmental conditions referred to earlier. And, these functions are all facilitated by a wide variety of financial institutions.

Thus, the institutional approach is another manner of studying the field of international finance. These institutions can, first, be divided into domestic, international, and foreign. A further breakdown would divide the domestic and foreign institutions into public and private, while the private can be further subdivided into banking and nonbanking institutions. Some of these nonbanking institutions are even found on the company level, such as tax-haven corporations (which still function within the restrictions of the Revenue Act of 1962) and domestic subsidiaries for the financing of trade credit.

The institutions might be studied on a functional basis. For example, some institutions are concerned with financing international trade, others with financing international investments, while others act as sources of capital within foreign countries for the continuing operation of existing investments, etc. This does, however, encounter difficulties in that many institutions are multi-functional. Thus, in studying the institutions, one must of necessity study not only the functions which they perform, but also the problems with which they deal and the policies which they follow to cope with the environment in which they operate.

This book does not follow any of these three methods. First of all, the writer does not believe that any *one* of the three methods is sufficient. And, even if a choice had been made, the availability of readings was too sparse to permit parochialism. The first part of the book, therefore, deals with the international monetary environment, while the next two parts are concerned with the major functions of financing trade, investment and operations. The financing of economic development is included because it is the source of major capital flows, and because the lack of it is the cause of considerable difficulties in both trade and investment. On the other hand, the success of economic development, as discussed in the introduction to Chapter 8, increases the market for imports and enhances the attractiveness of the climate for investment.

The last part of the book, covers questions of taxation, accounting and controlling, which are not usually considered as part of international finance. The writer has found, however, that a major number of the decisions within a multinational corporation, which relate to financial planning and capital flows, are based on these questions. In addition, the writer has noted that many employees, when taking their first job in a multinational firm, are placed in the department of accounting and finance. This is considered an excellent training ground for feeling the pulse of the organization. The analysis of reports from foreign operations and their consolidation into the parent company's accounts provide a broad and rapid education. But, the employee is well advised to be familiar with those problems before arriving on the job.

THE INTERNATIONAL MONETARY ENVIRONMENT

chapter *1*
Foreign Exchange: Theory and Practice

With most countries, U.S. trade is financed almost entirely in dollars. With some, however, such as Canada and the West European countries, a significant percentage of the trade is conducted in foreign exchange. In addition to trade transactions, there is usually a need for foreign exchange when a U.S. company invests abroad. This is true for direct investment as well as for portfolio investment. The need to deal with foreign exchange arises again when the investments are liquidated or when the profits from the foreign investments are repatriated to the United States or are transferred to some other part of a multinational firm's operations. Dealing with foreign exchange is thus a necessity for every firm engaged in international business.

Dealing in foreign exchange usually involves a risk. Such a risk can, however, often be avoided or reduced, but such risk avoidance or reduction is usually accomplished at a cost. These, then, become the basic problems of a company's international financial analyst. He must help management to make decisions on the question of whether to accept a given foreign exchange risk or to pay the cost of covering the risk. Such decisions can often play as significant a role in the parent company's dollar profits (or losses) as the actual operations of the company's foreign subsidiaries.

It is, therefore, important that the international businessman understand the forces which affect foreign exchange prices. He should also be familiar with the market which permits him to move his funds from one currency to another, or to protect himself against exchange losses associated with an investment in a given currency.

Most foreign exchange transactions in the United States are handled by commercial banks. There are approximately twenty-five U.S. banks and twenty foreign banks, mostly in New York, which conduct nearly all of the foreign exchange transactions in the United States. The foreign exchange market has been described as a three-tiered market. There are, first, the transactions between the banks and their commercial customers who are the ultimate users and suppliers of foreign exchange. Second, there are the transactions between the commerical banks. These are carried out through foreign exchange brokers, of which there are now eight; all located in New York, and these are the transactions which "make the market." A supplemental portion of this second tier is the transactions of the Federal Reserve Bank of New York on behalf of the U.S. government as well as on behalf of foreign central banks. The third tier consists of transactions between the New York banks and banks or foreign exchange dealers abroad.

These New York banks serve as the foreign exchange center of the United States as a whole. In recent years, however, a number of banks located in other cities have improved their communications with New York exchange brokers or have actually established exchange trading facilities in a New York office. About a half-dozen such banks, outside of New York, are thus an integral part of the New York foreign exchange market.

In an historical perspective, it has been estimated that over the past seven years, the volume of foreign exchange trading through New York has tripled, to reach an annual rate of about $75 billion. On busy days, volume reaches $700 million to $800 million. In spite of this growth, however, the New York market continues to rank below those in London, Paris, and Zurich.

For a more detailed discussion of the institutional organization of the foreign exchange market and of its day-to-day operations, the reader is directed to a free booklet, issued by the Federal Reserve Bank of New York, entitled *The New York Foreign Exchange Market.*

The two readings included in this section are more concerned with the theory of the operation of foreign exchange markets. The first, by Jerome L. Stein, is generally recognized as a definitive study of the subject. It covers a discussion of the individuals or institutions which make up the market and analyzes the factors which motivate their actions. It then analyzes the determinants of the price of foreign exchange during normal periods and during periods of speculation.

The second reading, by William H. White, discusses in greater detail the relationship between interest rate differentials and the discount on forward exchange. In so doing, however, it covers the problem which faces every company involved in foreign exchange transactions; namely, that of evaluating the risk of loss. The author proceeds to utilize his analysis as a basis for recommending governmental policies which might affect the movement of hot money. This will be particularly important as a consideration for solutions to the U.S. balance of payments situation, discussed in Chapter 3.

THE NATURE AND EFFICIENCY OF THE FOREIGN EXCHANGE MARKET*

I. THE SCOPE AND SIGNIFICANCE OF THIS STUDY

One of the most important and least understood markets is the foreign exchange market. Through this institution, residents of different currency areas are enabled to trade with one another, and invest in one another's assets. Despite Great Britain's dependence upon international trade and London's historic role as banker for the world, the Radcliffe Committee hearings indicated that many economists and bankers do not fully understand the nature of the foreign-exchange market. The Committee was led to ask: "How well organized is the forward exchange market? Can we hear more about who is engaged in the market? Whom does it comprise?" The answers to these questions left much to be desired.

The Bank of England has varied the Bank Rate to affect, among other things, movements of short-term capital. Nevertheless, the Committee discovered that the Bank does not know the impact of Bank Rate policy upon the foreign exchange market and upon the international movement of short-term capital.[1]

Concern is being shown over the adequacy of the international monetary reserves of the United States relative to its short-term liabilities. As a result of gold outflows, the gold reserves of the United States are $16.5 billion (as of the end of May 1962), whereas its short-term liabilities to foreign countries exceed $18.9 billion. Since the dollar is a key currency, the low ratio of gold to short-term liabilities has been viewed with apprehension. Were a downward trend in this ratio to continue, many believe that foreign confidence in the dollar would be weakened and a serious financial crisis would occur.

One method of coping with the problem of international reserves would be to eliminate the need for official reserves, by leaving the foreign exchange market free to equilibrate the demand and supply of foreign exchange.

* Jerome L. Stein, published as a monograph by the International Finance Section, Princeton University, 1962.
[1] Committee on the Working of the Monetary System, Minutes of Evidence (London: HMSO, 1960) para. 3215–19 and 1479–90.

9

Central banks and official stabilization funds would abdicate in favor of private enterprise.

This proposal has found little favor with economists, and still less with members of the New York financial community. While the latter called a system of floating rates "a trader's paradise," many thought that such a system was socially undesirable. They maintain that a foreign exchange market completely free from government stabilization cannot be relied upon as the sole source of cushioning for current-account disequilibria. The Radcliffe Committee considered that experience between 1914 and 1925, and again between 1931 and 1939, had been sufficient to demonstrate the "inconvenience of a fluctuating pound." Many claim that the recent Canadian experience is inconclusive as a demonstration of the successful operation of a completely free market, since the central bank was in the market constantly to absorb the excess supplies and demands of U.S. dollars. On the other hand, there was little intervention in the Canadian sterling market, for this rate was highly volatile. For example, the price of sterling ranged from C 2.71\frac{11}{16}$ to C 2.75\frac{1}{2}$ during the period January 27, 1959 to February 13, 1959. From March 28, 1959 to May 26, 1959 the price ranged from C 2.69\frac{15}{16}$ to C 2.72\frac{5}{8}$. Numerous other similar instances can be cited. These marked price fluctuations suggest that more evidence is required before one may assert that a completely free exchange market is superior to a stabilized exchange market.

The small group of economists who favor a free exchange market adduce *a priori* reasoning to support their claim that a free market would efficiently cushion temporary current-account disequilibria. This group claims that "positive speculators' profits imply that they have stabilized the price."[2] Destabilizing actions by speculators are said to imply that they have lost money. Insofar as their operations are profitable, it is claimed that they have been a stabilizing influence. No evidence has been adduced by this group to show whether or not "speculators" did in fact make money. Moreover, the argument concerning the relation between stability and profitability has been shown to be incorrect, in the institutional context of the contemporary exchange market. When there is trading in both spot and forward exchange, and only the spot price is stabilized by the exchange authority, speculators can destabilize the price and yet make money.

Although little is known about the nature of the foreign exchange market, each group in the dispute holds its position with great confidence. The members of the first group glanced at economic history casually, and found large price movements during a period of free exchange markets. But these

    [2] Lester G. Telser, "A Theory of Speculation Relating Profitability and Stability," *The Review of Economics and Statistics,* Vol. XLI (August 1959); Milton Friedman, "The Case for Flexible Exchange Rates," in *Essays in Positive Economics* (Chicago 1953), pp. 157–203.

financial experts and economists failed to examine the question of cause and effect. Did the free exchange market unsettle an otherwise stable system; or did the era of a free market coincide with a period of great instability in the balance of payments? If the exchange markets had been stabilized during this period, what would have happened to the international reserves of the various countries? Could stabilized rates have been held at their pre-war levels during the period 1919–1925? None of these questions has even been raised by the opponents of free exchange markets. On the other hand, the members of the second group failed to adduce any evidence that the activity of risk-bearers in a free exchange market is such as to avoid ex-cessively large price fluctuations that result from random variations in the balance of payments, i.e., that result when the market has confidence in the stability of the current set of exchange rates. This is an empirical question, and the proponents of free markets have neglected to examine it adequately.

Recently, the U.S. Treasury, acting through the Federal Reserve Bank of New York, has intervened in the forward-exchange market. With the coopera-tion of the Bundesbank, it has sold D-mark futures, and with the cooperation of the Swiss National Bank it has sold Swiss francs forward, to reduce the forward premia. At the time, the President of the New York Federal Reserve Bank said operations in other European currencies were being considered in order to further strengthen central bank defenses against speculative capital movements.

Efficient intervention presupposes a thorough knowledge of the system of interrelationships known as the foreign exchange market. Otherwise, the indirect effects of a given policy may run counter to the objectives of the policymakers.

The present essay is devoted to a study of the interrelationships among the participants in the foreign exchange market. In Section II, we discuss the functions of the foreign exchange market, and present a general view of the roles of professional risk-bearers, interest-arbitrageurs, borrowers who hedge their foreign exchange liabilities and speculators. Section III gives a detailed examination of the methods of operation of professional risk-bear-ers and interest-arbitrageurs in the contemporary foreign exchange market; the complexities of the market are explicitly considered in this section. Section IV explains the reactions of the foreign exchange market to current and to anticipated disturbances. There is one pattern of price behavior that results from random variations in the balance of payments; and a different pattern of price behavior that results when the market thinks that changes in the exchange rates will occur in the near future. An examination of the data enables us to infer the nature of the disturbance: whether it was based upon random or anticipated fluctuations in the balance of payments. Finally, the price relationships that prevailed during recent speculative periods are shown to be compatible with the analysis developed in Section IV.

II. The Functions of a Foreign Exchange Market

A. The Efficiency of a Foreign Exchange Market

Although the basic balance of payments may be in equilibrium[3] over the year as a whole, at a given exchange rate, it is unlikely that the balance will be in equilibrium every day, week or month. The balance on current account varies during the year from a surplus to a deficit, particularly in countries producing primary products. In the United States, for example, the balance on current account during 1959 was $172 million; but there were surpluses in the first and last quarters, and deficits in the second and third quarters, of the year. A foreign exchange market which results in a situation whereby the basic balance is in equilibrium at every quarter, month, week, or day is an inefficient market. An analogy can be made between the fluctuations in the net supply of wheat and in the net supply of foreign exchange. Wheat is harvested a few times during the year. It is socially desirable that the consumption of wheat, or foreign exchange which is simply a command over imports, be spread out over the year. This spreading (or smoothing) out can only occur if there are institutions willing to sell foreign exchange during periods of shortage and buy foreign exchange during periods of surplus. A period of shortage occurs when our basic balance tends to be negative; and a period of surplus occurs when our basic balance tends to be positive. An efficient market exists if there are institutions willing to buy and sell foreign exchange for, and from, inventory during these periods. In effect, these institutions invest in foreign exchange during periods of surplus and disinvest during periods of shortage. Through variations in the inventories of these private institutions, i.e., the short-term capital account,[4] the supply and demand for foreign exchange will be equal every day, although the basic balance may be in equilibrium only over the year as a whole.

A year is an arbitrary period of time. At a given exchange rate, the basic balance may be in equilibrium over the current year. Suppose that a shortage or a surplus of foreign exchange is anticipated for the following year. An efficient exchange market should induce the economy to prepare

---

[3] The basic balance of payments is the sum of the current-account balance plus the long-term capital account plus unilateral transfers. The term equilibrium has many meanings, especially in the balance of payments literature. In the present chapter it is used to mean that the sum of surpluses and deficits over a given period of time is equal to zero.

[4] The short-term capital account refers to the *private* sector's *net* change in short-term claims against foreigners. The sum of the short-term capital account plus the net change in *official* claims against foreigners is identically equal to the basic balance. Since the analysis here is devoted exclusively to the private sectors, variations in the official or government claims against foreigners are excluded from the present analysis of how the foreign exchange market operates.

for future shortages or surpluses. If a shortage is anticipated, the economy should be induced to accumulate foreign exchange at present: i.e., to export short-term capital. On the other hand, if a surplus is foreseen, the economy should be induced to borrow (import) short-term capital during the current period. Again, an analogy can be made with wheat production. If a wheat shortage is expected, the economy should be induced to accumulate wheat inventories. That is, current production should exceed current consumption. On the other hand, if a surplus of wheat is expected, current consumption should exceed current production and wheat inventories (if they exist) should be reduced.

An efficient foreign exchange market cannot exist unless there are institutions which can be induced to accumulate foreign exchange during periods when there is a surplus in our basic balance, and decumulate stocks of foreign exchange during periods when there is a shortage in our basic balance. The terms "surplus period" and "shortage period" refer to a longer period of time, over which the basic balance is zero.

The institutions which can be induced to import or export short-term capital occupy a crucial role in determining the efficiency of the foreign exchange market. A general and simplified discussion of the variables which influence their behavior is the subject of this section. The phenomena of interest arbitrage, the switching of finance with the exchange risk covered, speculation in foreign exchange and the necessity of a set of professional risk-bearers are explained. The simple rules and conclusions presented here are modified in the next section to correspond more accurately to the complex world of our experience.

B. Short-Term Investment and Borrowing

1. RISK-AVOIDING SHORT-TERM INVESTORS.   Many institutions which invest in domestic Treasury bills and other domestic short-term securities can be induced to invest in foreign Treasury bills and other foreign short-term securities, and vice-versa. A comparison of the relative rates of return on domestic and foreign assets is one of the key considerations involved in the selection of an efficient portfolio. Suppose that the investor firmly expects to hold the bill until its maturity three months later. The expected return on an investment of $1 in U.S. Treasury bills is $1 multiplied by the Treasury-bill rate. The expected return on $1 invested in U.K. Treasury bills is not necessarily $1 multiplied by the U.K. Treasury-bill rate. There is no certainty that the American investor will be able to sell his sterling for the same price at which it was purchased. Whenever there is uncertainty concerning the rate of exchange, the expected return on foreign investment is not necessarily the same as the foreign interest rate.

Whenever forward markets exist, the risks of exchange-rate fluctuations can be reduced by shifting them to the professional risk-bearers. The investor in U.K. Treasury bills can get a quotation on a *swap* from a professional risk-bearer. The *swap* is a simultaneous purchase and sale of foreign exchange of different maturities, entered into with a given party. Thus the investor may be told, on March 28, 1962, that he can buy pounds for $2.81¾ and that he can sell his pounds three months later for $2.80⅛. The investor could contract a current (spot) purchase and a forward sale of pounds, on that date, at a cost of 2.307 percent per annum. A potential short-term investor would compare the Treasury-bill rates in the two countries with the cost of the swap, to determine relative returns on comparable assets. His expected return on a U.K. Treasury bill held to maturity would be equal to the U.K. Treasury-bill rate less the cost of the swap (2.307 percent). It is this rate of return, with the exchange risk covered, that can properly be compared with the rate of return on a U.S. Treasury bill. Whenever the foreign interest differential (i.e., the foreign rate less the U.S. rate) exceeds the cost of the swap, the rate of return on a foreign asset held to maturity exceeds the rate of return on a domestic asset held to maturity. Thereby an outflow of short-term capital is induced; that is, Americans are induced to accumulate interest-yielding foreign exchange.

On the other hand, when the foreign interest differential is less than the cost of the swap, an inflow of short-term capital is induced. For example, if on March 28, 1962, the U.K. Treasury-bill rate was 4.5 percent and the U.S. Treasury-bill rate was 2.7 percent, the expected return on a U.S. Treasury bill to maturity exceeded the return on a U.K. Treasury bill held to maturity, with the exchange risk covered. An institution which owns, or has access to, pounds could do the following on March 28, 1962: (i) buy dollars for pounds; (ii) invest in U.S. Treasury bills; and (iii) sell the dollars forward for pounds, to be delivered in three months. It would earn 2.7 percent on the Treasury bills and 2.307 percent on the swap, for a total of 5.007 percent. This exceeds the 4.5 percent return that it could earn on U.K. Treasury bills held to maturity; and it would have pounds at the end of three months for use in its main business. In this situation, an English branch of the American concern is induced to decumulate pounds, and an English concern is induced to supply pounds in the present.

Interest arbitrage is the phenomenon whereby firms tend to invest abroad with the exchange risk covered with a forward sale of the currency. The institutions engaged in this form of investment, the interest-arbitrageurs, are risk-avoiders.

2. RISK-AVOIDING SHORT-TERM BORROWERS. The same variables which induce short-term investors to invest in (say) New York, rather than in London, induce certain firms to borrow short-term funds in London rather than in New York. The choice among alternative sources of finance, with the ex-

change risk covered, is the dual to interest arbitrage discussed above. Its effects are exactly the same as those of interest arbitrage.

An American concern in need of funds for (say) three months may command such an outstanding international reputation that it can borrow as easily in London as it can in New York. Most likely, it will have branches in all major money markets. The prime-commercial-paper rate in New York may be 3.25 percent per annum, and in London it may be 4.63 percent per annum. If the concern in question borrows in London, its expected cost in dollars is uncertain if it sells the borrowed sterling for dollars, and fails to protect itself against the exchange risk. When the loan has to be repaid, the price of sterling may have risen above, or have fallen below, the price at which the borrowed sterling was originally purchased. The borrowing concern, if it chooses, can reduce the exchange risk by comparing the costs of borrowing in London and in New York with the exchange risks covered.

To borrow in London the firm must pay 4.63 percent per annum. If the sterling is sold for dollars and simultaneously repurchased for delivery in three months, the firm will make 2.307 percent per annum (given the rates quoted in section A above). Its net borrowing cost would be 2.323 percent (4.63 — 2.307 percent) per annum. On the other hand, if it borrowed in New York its cost would be 3.25 percent per annum. The foreign interest differential of 1.38 percent (4.63 — 3.25 percent) is less than the discount on the forward pound of 2.307 percent. Hence, if the debt will be repaid at maturity, it is cheaper to borrow abroad with the exchange risk covered than it is to borrow at home. Thereby a supply of pounds is produced in the foreign exchange market.

Whenever an inflow of funds into the United States is induced as a result of interest arbitrage, American firms are induced to borrow abroad rather than at home. This increases the supply of (spot) foreign exchange offered in the market. Foreign firms are discouraged from borrowing in New York and, as a result, the demand for foreign exchange is reduced. Conversely, whenever an outflow of funds from the United States is induced by interest arbitrage, foreign firms are induced to borrow in New York rather than in their own countries and, as a result, the demand for (spot) foreign exchange is increased. American firms are discouraged from borrowing abroad, and the supply of foreign exchange is reduced.

3. UNCOVERED POSITIONS. Institutions may invest in foreign short-term securities, or incur liabilities denominated in foreign currency, without protecting themselves against exchange-rate fluctuations. Suppose that the maximum decline in the price of foreign exchange, within its stabilization limits, is less than the foreign interest rate differential. Then an institution which thinks that devaluation is improbable within three months may not bother to sell forward exchange at a discount, when it purchases a foreign Treasury

bill or Bank bill. Thereby it saves the cost of the swap, which is the cost of an insurance premium, on an asset which will be held to maturity. Similarly the firm which borrows in the low-interest-rate money market need not purchase forward exchange, if it is at a premium, provided that the maximum rise in the price of foreign exchange is expected to be less than the interest differential. An institution which fails to secure forward cover (i.e., to offset its foreign-exchange asset with a forward sale, or to offset its foreign-exchange liability with a forward purchase) is not necessarily speculating. In the pre-1914 gold-standard era, short-term capital flowed among countries without forward covering, because the spread between the gold points was often narrower than the interest differentials and devaluation was considered most improbable. Speculation was not responsible for the failure to cover. The investors or borrowers did not consider the insurance worth the cost.

C. Risk-Bearing

1. PROFESSIONAL RISK-BEARERS. The risk-avoiders are the investors in foreign assets who want to protect themselves against the decline in the price of foreign exchange, and the institutions which have incurred liabilities in foreign currency and want to protect themselves against a rise in the price of foreign exchange. If there were no institutions willing to buy and sell forward exchange, then the risks of exchange-rate fluctuations would deter many from investing or borrowing abroad. An efficient foreign exchange market requires that there be short-term capital exports when our basic balance *tends* to be in surplus, and short-term capital imports when our basic balance *tends* to be in deficit. Over the entire period the basic balance should be in equilibrium; but, as already noted, it is inefficient to restrict monthly or quarterly imports to be exactly equal to the corresponding value of exports. If the risks of foreign investment and borrowing are great, there will be few institutions willing to accumulate foreign exchange during periods of surplus and sell foreign exchange during periods of shortage. The market would then be forced to restrict its imports of goods and services to the value of exports of goods and services. For primary-products producers, imports would be cheap and lavishly consumed shortly after the harvests, and imports would be scarce during the rest of the year.

Insofar as investors and borrowers can shift the exchange risks onto a set of professional risk-bearers, there will be a more abundant flow of short-term capital among countries. The professional risk-bearers quote prices for forward exchange and for spot exchange. For the reasons explained in Section IV, sometimes the forward exchange is at a premium and at other times it is at a discount relative to the spot exchange. In the example cited on page 14, the forward pound was at a discount (or the forward dollar was at a premium) of 2.307 percent per annum. An investor in sterling short-term assets who protects himself against the exchange risk pays an insurance premium of 2.307 percent per annum to the risk-bearer. On the other hand, the firm which borrows in London and protects itself against the exchange risk by selling forward dollars to (i.e., by purchasing forward pounds from) the professional risk-bearers, finds that it will gain 2.307 percent per annum by "purchasing" this insurance. The insurance cost, in a sense, is negative. (Cost here is defined to mean the difference between the forward price at which the foreign exchange is purchased and the spot price at which the borrowed foreign exchange is initially sold.)

In a world of exchange-rate uncertainty, the professional risk-bearers facilitate the international flows of short-term capital. In so doing they contribute to the efficiency of the foreign exchange market.

Moreover, their willingness to bear risk stimulates international trade and leads to more efficient international distribution and production of goods and services. Exporters may quote prices either in terms of domestic currency or in terms of the currency of the importers. In either case, one of the parties to the transaction incurs an exchange risk. By shifting the exchange risk to professional risk-bearers, the volume of trade can be increased. A vivid example of how the existence of risk-bearers can stimulate trade concerns German-Russian trade in the last quarter of the nineteenth century. The British exporters "never quoted in terms of a fluctuating currency," and Russian importers would have had to bear the entire exchange risk. German exporters were willing to quote in terms of rubles since a well developed forward market existed in Berlin. The German exporters were able to shift the exchange risks to the professional risk-bearers who purchased forward rubles. I think that partly as a result of this ability, of German exporters and importers to shift the risks to a group specializing in risk-bearing, one-third of Russia's foreign trade was with Germany. The inducement to engage in international trade and profit from international differences in price, is increased by the presence of professional risk-bearers who make markets in forward exchange.

2. SPECULATORS. Theoretically, the exchange market could be efficient if speculators were willing to purchase foreign exchange when the basic balance tended to be in surplus, and were willing to sell foreign exchange when the basic balance tended to be in deficit. Then the existence of the forward market would not be necessary to induce inflows and outflows of short-term capital. The speculators would perform the functions of foreign investors, borrowers and risk-bearers. To revert to the wheat analogy, the speculators would be the purchasers and storers of wheat in the post-harvest season, and the sellers of wheat out of stocks during the pre-harvest season.

The main body of speculators in foreign exchange are the exporters and importers who have claims or liabilities denominated in foreign currencies. Their main method of speculation is via the leads and lags in international payments. When there is an excess supply of foreign exchange the price tends to fall. If the speculators think that this decline is temporary, the importers who must make payments in foreign currency accelerate their purchases of foreign exchange. Thereby, they accumulate foreign exchange inventories in anticipation of a rise in price. They are both foreign investors and speculators. Similarly, the exporters who have received payment in foreign currency may lag their sales of foreign exchange receipts. They will continue to hold these foreign assets in anticipation of a price rise. The net effect of the leads and lags is to produce a short-term capital outflow, when a period of shortage is expected to follow the current period of surplus. The economy thereby stores foreign exchange for the anticipated period of shortage.

When a surplus in the basic balance is anticipated, the leads and lags operate in reverse and produce a capital inflow. Importers who have incurred liabilities in foreign currency speculate by lagging, or delaying, their payments. An attempt is made to maintain their foreign exchange liabilities in the anticipation of a decline in the price of foreign currency. This lag reduces the demand for foreign exchange. Importers who lag their payments are similar to the firms which borrow abroad and expect to repurchase the foreign exchange at a lower price than it was sold originally. Exporters speculate against a currency by accelerating the sales of their export receipts before the price falls. This increases the supply of foreign exchange prior to the appearance of the surplus. The net effect of the leads and lags in this example, is to produce a capital inflow in anticipation of a surplus in our basic balance. Thereby the economy is induced to increase its present rate of import consumption in view of an expected increase in foreign exchange receipts.

Although speculators are substitutes for interest-arbitrageurs, for borrowers who cover themselves against exchange risks, and for professional risk-bearers who make (*inter alia*) markets in forward exchange, they are imperfect substitutes. First, the total supply of international short-term capital would be reduced if potential investors could not shift the exchange risks to the professional risk-bearers. On the other hand, the existence of forward markets and professional risk-bearers does not reduce the supply of *speculative* capital. Second, when there is exchange-rate uncertainty, the existence of a forward market increases the volume of international trade. A contraction of international trade, which would occur if forward markets were reduced in scope by official restrictions and therefore made more risky, would reduce world national income and welfare. Hence speculators are not perfect substitutes for professional risk-bearers.

III. Professional Risk-Bearers and Short-Term Investors

The efficiency of the foreign exchange market is profoundly influenced by the activities of the professional risk-bearers and short-term investors. In this section, the professional risk-bearers and short-term investors are described in detail.

A. Professional Risk-Bearers

The large banks which buy and sell foreign exchange are the professional risk-bearers in the foreign exchange market. This responsibility is the function of the senior exchange trader, who is usually a vice-president of his bank. Exchange traders make primary markets. They quote "bid and ask" prices, and act as principals in almost all transactions. In "exotic" currencies—those which are infrequently traded—or in currencies of nations with highly unstable or capricious governments, the risks of acting as principals are too great. Then the traders act as brokers: they buy if they can find a customer and sell if they can find someone who has that currency to offer. There are brokers who are used in inter-bank dealings in the New York market, but they are quite distinct from the traders who work for the banks with foreign exchange departments. In the New York market, banks do not deal directly with each other but use the services of brokers. A two-point ($\frac{2}{100}$ of a cent) commission is charged for these services. Moreover, brokers keep traders informed of the prices in the market. There are many misconceptions concerning the source of profits for exchange traders. Their profits, when they exist, do not arise mainly from the spread between their bid and ask prices. When a trader makes a market, by quoting a bid and an ask price, he does not necessarily buy at the bid and sell at the ask. Position-taking involves risk. This is illustrated by the following incident.

On the Friday prior to the revaluation of the D-mark in 1961 (from 4.2 to 4.0 marks to the U.S. dollar) several banks found themselves oversold on D-marks. During the day, their customers and other banks purchased more D-marks than they sold to the banks in question. The bank traders expected to cover their sales by purchasing D-marks in Germany on Saturday morning. If they sold dollars at the Bundesbank's buying price for dollars (i.e., selling price for D-marks), they would have made profits on the transactions. Revaluation was "in the air": it had been expected for months. But *traditionally*, exchange-rate changes had been made after the close of business on Saturdays. So, they were confident that they could buy their marks on Saturday morning. Moreover, a high authority in the Bundesbank said, in a speech to a small group of bankers on Thursday, that revaluation would not occur. On Saturday morning, the traders placed buy orders with the German commercial banks. The German commercial banks went to the Bundesbank, which was the only buyer of dollars at that time. Contrary to previous practice, the Bundesbank refused to sell; and it revalued the mark. Instead of a trading profit, a loss was made on an uncovered short position.

1. LINES, POSITIONS AND INVENTORIES.   A trader has a *running position sheet* in each currency. This sheet contains the purchases and sales for a series of dates, and the sum of the net purchases over the entire series of dates. The bank's *position* is the sum of its net purchases and sales for the set of dates in its running position sheet. A position may be *long* or *short*, depending upon whether the bank is a net buyer or seller of foreign exchange over the set of dates.

Most traders have *lines*, which are the maximum long and short positions they can have in various currencies. The lines given to the trader depend upon (1) the capital of the bank: its ability to withstand losses. An intrepid trader can embarrass his bank financially. Positions are checked regularly by the senior trader, who usually is a vice-president, and by the executive vice-president, to prevent the trading department from assuming more risk than senior management deems prudent. The lines also depend upon (2) the volume of business in a given currency. The lines in sterling and the Canadian dollar will normally exceed the lines in the lira and the D-mark, because the volume of business in the first two currencies is so great. Moreover, as the volume of business in sterling has grown since 1958, sterling lines have also increased.

Every bank which maintains a market in a given currency has an inventory of that currency, or has to maintain at least one account in a bank in the country of that currency. Even when a bank has a short position in a currency, it will probably have an inventory of that currency. On a certain day, say January 9, a bank may have £1 million. But in the sterling position sheet of that date, there may be more future commitments to sell sterling than to buy sterling. Over the entire set of commitments, the bank may be a short-seller, although it currently owns £1 million of balances.

Balances or inventories are held for the convenience of doing business with customers, just as the retail merchant, manufacturer or wholesaler holds an inventory of goods.

2. THE MANAGEMENT OF POSITIONS.   A position is held to anticipate the requirements of customers and to anticipate the movements of the market, in such manner that profits will be made. For example, in 1957 the major traders did not share the customers' views that sterling would be devalued, or that the D-mark would be revalued. They did expect their customers and other banks (e.g., foreign banks) to offer sterling and demand D-marks. Consequently, they assumed long positions in D-marks and short positions in

sterling to anticipate the customers' requirements. By purchasing D-marks for a series of dates and selling sterling for a series of dates, (i) they were able to sell D-marks spot, near future and far future without being short and, (ii) they were able to buy sterling spot, near-future and far-future without being overloaded. If they had not assumed a short sterling position, the bank traders would not have been able to make attractive bids on the customers' offers to sell, or they would have been forced to unload quickly before the price of sterling fell in the market. The New York banks are in active competition with each other; and are anxious to offer the highest bid and lowest ask to secure the customer's business, and still make a profit. If a banker allowed his position to be thrust upon him, he would not have been able to compete actively for his customers' business. Each trader attempts to impress upon his customers his ability to give them the best prices in the market.

Positions are also taken to anticipate the market's reaction to future events. If a trader believes that, when the U.K. gold-reserves figures are published in the next few days, they will show a significant decline, he will take a short position in sterling. He expects the prices of spot and future sterling to decline when the market sees the published figures. Then, he could even out his short position at a profit.

Positions have to be managed, for the banks' customers and other banks are constantly thrusting positions upon them. The trader must decide what position he wants to take, in each currency, and must react accordingly.

3. LONG POSITIONS. Suppose that a bank is offered foreign exchange, for spot and future delivery, over a period of days. Several choices are open to the bank trader. (1) He may sell the exchange outright. (2) He may take a long uncovered position. (3) He may hedge the spot and near-futures by deliberately taking a short position in far-futures.

All banks cannot even out their spot positions, if they have been net buyers of foreign exchange as a result of a balance of payments surplus. Attempts by some banks to even out their positions will result in declines in the prices, and hence in trading losses for the selling banks. The bank trader will decide whether it is more advantageous for him to sell out at a loss or to adopt some combination of alternatives (2) and (3) above.

As the price of foreign exchange falls under the selling pressure, a trader who thinks that the price decline will only be temporary may consider maintaining a long position. His expected profit would be equal to the expected capital gain from the rise in the price, less any costs of tying up his working capital in foreign exchange balances. There is no unanimity among traders in price expectations, and there are significant differences among traders in the opportunity cost of tying up funds. These two considerations, plus the attitudes toward risk, account for differences in bank-trader behavior.

The position that a trader wants to assume, as reflected in his running position sheet, involves a whole series of dates. If spot is undervalued, the trader must compare the expected appreciation that is likely to occur with the opportunity cost of tying up bank reserves in foreign balances. There are two components of the opportunity cost of tying up funds: the domestic costs and the trading costs. If there is a brisk demand for funds in the New York money market, funds tied up in foreign exchange balances imply a loss of reserves. A loss of reserves means that the bank foregoes lending to customers at the prime rate, which in turn entails a loss of current income and customer confidence. Recourse can always be made to the Federal Funds market or to the discount window at the Federal Reserve Bank. However, commercial banks are reluctant to be in debt to the Federal Reserve Bank. At times, the discount rate is high: it was 4 percent in 1959 and 1960. Moreover, the Federal Reserve Bank may request that the bank repay its debt by selling off investments (at a loss) during a period of rising rates, or that it call in loans. When a rising demand for loans to domestic customers is expected, the opportunity cost of having reserves tied up in foreign exchange balances may offset the expected appreciation in the spot price.

Another deterrent to building up spot balances occurs when a trader has a limited amount of working capital. Then, he can only augment his balances in one currency by depleting his balances in another. Since a minimum inventory is often needed in each of the major trading currencies, he will be reluctant to deplete his inventories in another major currency for the sake of an expected capital gain. There are more efficient ways of making capital gains than by depleting inventories (see below).

Other bank traders (or the same trader at another time) may have lower opportunity costs of funds, so that the expected appreciation in the spot price exceeds the profit that can be made in alternative uses. For example, a commercial bank may have net free reserves and may be willing to take a risk of tying up its funds for a couple of weeks or months. Or, the bank trader may be employed by a "merchant bank" which does not accept deposits from the public; its main business is the acceptance of bills, foreign exchange transactions and underwriting. At a given time, this merchant bank may not be utilizing all of its capital in underwriting, and hence may be eager to earn money on an expected appreciation of the spot exchange. These traders would then be more willing to build up their foreign exchange balances.

If the trader believes that the cost of tying up funds in additional balances exceeds the expected appreciation in price, he has several alternative courses of action. It is assumed that banks have been net buyers of foreign exchange.

First, the trader could even out his spot position by selling the foreign exchange purchased. In a period of selling pressure, such a course of action leads to trading losses but it does not tie up his working capital. Second, if the prices of futures (futures and forward are synonyms in the New York market) have been falling at greater rates than have spot prices, the trader might find it advantageous to swap. A swap, as explained earlier, is a contract for a spot and a forward transaction in the opposite directions. It could also be a contract for the simultaneous purchase and sale of a near-future for a far-future (or vice versa). The trader may contract, for example, to sell spot for delivery in three days and purchase the same amount for delivery in ten days. Profit will be made on the swap if futures are at a discount. As a result of this swap the trader achieves several objectives.

(1) He does not tie up his working capital in foreign exchange balances.

(2) He nevertheless maintains a long position, in anticipation of the price rise.

(3) He realizes some trading profits from the swap.

The large banks, with active domestic-loan business, do *not* absorb the variations in the spot exchange that arise from the daily, weekly, monthly or quarterly surpluses (or deficits) in the balance of payments. Unless the spot exchange is considerably undervalued, their opportunity costs of funds are too high to induce them to build up their balances. When they have a position, it is in the futures market, not in the spot market.

If futures are at a premium, the bank trader may be deterred from taking a long position. The loss on the swap, of spot for futures, may offset the expected rise in price of the foreign exchange. In such an event, he might sell his spot outright and take a trading loss. The bank trader will simultaneously determine his desired position and the maturity of his position, i.e., the distribution of his net purchases among spot, near-futures and far-futures. The maturity of his position will depend upon the relation of current to expected prices. For example, during the month of July 1961, the major banks were not bearish on sterling. Their customers and foreign banks, however, expected a devaluation; and spot sterling fell to $2.78-$\frac{7}{16}$. Without the intervention of the Central Bank, it would have fallen lower. The discount on three-month sterling was as high as $3\frac{1}{8}$ cents; on July 12, 1961 future pounds could be purchased for 2.75\frac{5}{16}$. The senior traders expected drastic domestic measures to be undertaken within the United Kingdom and large-scale international support for the pound. A trader holding such views would take a long position, concentrated in near- and far-futures.

If the trader's timing were correct, he would come into possession of pounds at the time that the pound would be rising as result of these disinflationary measures. On July 25, 1961 the Bank Rate was increased; and sterling rose from 2.78\frac{7}{16}$ to 2.80\frac{5}{8}$ at the end of October.

A long position in far-futures would also have been profitable, and was, in fact, taken by those who were not bearish. Traders who purchased three-month-futures in July would have sold out at a 6\frac{5}{16}$ cent profit in October, without having any funds tied up in the interim.

There are risks inherent in the purchase of foreign exchange. Not only is there a risk of a possible default by the seller of exchange, but there is a risk that the price will fall rather than rise. The first risk is reduced by purchasing forward exchange only from institutions which have accounts with the bank, or whose financial integrity is above question. Thereby, the bank reduces the probability that the seller may be unable to deliver the exchange. Similarly the bank does not sell forward exchange to non-customers, or to those whose financial standing is questionable. The risk of a price fall cannot be eliminated except through the maintenance of an even position in each maturity. But it can be reduced through an appropriate hedge.

A hedge is the assumption of a selling (buying) commitment to offset a buying (selling) commitment. It is a method of bounding (i.e., limiting) possible losses. For example, suppose the bank sold a currency three-months forward. Assume further that the market believes that this currency will be revalued within six months and that consequently people want to buy futures. If the trader does not share this view, but does not want to maintain a short position, he may hedge. He would buy a near-futures contract to cover his sale of the three-month-futures. Since the market expects a revaluation within six months, the far-futures will be at a premium over the near-futures, regardless of interest rates in the two markets. The covering operation: the purchase of near-futures and the sale of far-futures will, therefore, be profitable.

If the currency is, in fact, revalued, the trader does not lose. His asset (near-futures) will appreciate just as his liability (sale of far-futures) will rise in terms of domestic currency. Moreover, he will probably profit from a revaluation which the market considers to be adequate. Prior to the revaluation, the forward premium will exceed the short-term interest differential in the two markets. The supply of forward exchange arising from interest arbitrage will be unable to cope with the speculative purchases. There will be, therefore, an "intrinsic premium"—which arises whenever the forward premium, on a percentage basis, exceeds the difference between the foreign and domestic short-term money rates. After an adequate revaluation, the forward-spot relationship will approximate the interest differential more closely. It is likely that interest rates will be higher in the country which has just revalued its currency. Hence, the forward will go to a discount under spot. If the trader reverses his position upon revaluation, by selling his near-futures and buying far-futures, he will emerge with a profit. His total profit will be the initial premium on far-forward plus the final discount on far-forward. No working capital has been tied up in this transaction.

These points are clearly illustrated by the events which occurred during the period of the revaluation of the D-mark (March 1961). In February and March short-term interest rates were higher in Germany than in the United States. In March the market yield on 3-month Treasury bills was 2.327 percent in New York, and 60-90-day Treasury bills were yielding 2.50 percent in Germany. Nevertheless, the forward mark was at a premium (i.e., the forward dollar was at a discount). The spot dollar was at 4.170-4.171 DM during the first few days of March, whereas the forward dollar was at 4.169 DM. Speculative bull pressure on the forward D-mark counterbalanced the sale of forward marks arising out of interest arbitrage. After revaluation, the forward mark went to a discount momentarily. On March 6, 1961 the spot dollar was 3.99 DM and the forward dollar was 4.00 DM. However, the market felt that the revaluation did not proceed far enough, and that the mark would appreciate again. The premium on forward marks reappeared and persisted certainly through the month of March. Since the revaluation was not considered adequate by the market, speculative buying of forward marks counterbalanced the sales of forward marks by the interest-arbitrageurs.

4. SHORT POSITIONS. Positions are sometimes assumed consciously, in anticipation of customers' needs or of the state of the market. At other times, positions are thrust upon banks by the unexpected actions of their customers and of other banks. Then the ingenuity of the trader is required to adjust his present position to his desired position.

When banks are short, they have contracted to sell more than they have contracted to purchase. Let us assume that a bank trader is bearish on a currency and wants to maintain a short position. How does he do it? The *least* common method of covering a short position in spot exchange is by borrowing from a foreign bank at the overdraft rate. There are three reasons why this method of covering is hardly ever used. First, there are restrictions (in force at the date of this writing—April 1962) upon the granting of overdrafts for this purpose in the United Kingdom and in France: the maximum overdraft period is 48 hours to cover commercial items in transit. Second, the overdraft rate is a penalty rate: it is "too high." In England this rate is between ½ and 1 percent above the Bank Rate (6 percent on November 4, 1961). In Canada, where there are no restrictions, the overdraft rate is high: 5¾ percent in October 1961. Third, banks are reluctant to be in debt to their foreign correspondents.

Suppose that a trader has sold spot exchange, for delivery in three days, and does not have it. What will he usually do, if he is bearish? First, he may use his foreign currency accounts to cover. The major banks hold considerable amounts of foreign currency balances for their customers. These deposits arise when a customer has foreign exchange which he will need in a short period of time. He signs a waiver releasing the bank from any exchange-rate or restrictions liability; and has on deposit a certain amount of foreign currency. It is agreed that he cannot write checks on this sum without going through the bank. Thereby, the bank has a sum of foreign exchange to cover short positions. When, and if, the trader's prognosis materializes, he can replenish at a profit the exchange that he sold.

Second, he has three days to deliver the exchange, and can buy it back on the second day. In this manner, he can cover his sale at a profit, if the rate falls very soon after his sale.

Third, he may enter into a swap. He can buy exchange for delivery in three days and simultaneously sell (to the same party) exchange to be delivered in 3 plus x days. If forward exchange is at a premium, he will make profit on the swap while he maintains his short position. Even if forward is at a discount, the swap is almost invariably cheaper than an overdraft. In recent years, the maximum swap cost for sterling has been $6\frac{1}{2}$ percent on an annual basis; whereas the overdraft rate has usually been substantially higher.

When a trader assumes a bearish position in a currency, his position will be in the near- and far-forward maturities. Then there is no need to cover until the contract matures; and there has been no cost involved in carrying the short position. When the contract matures, the trader can maintain his short position by entering into swaps, or by using his foreign currency accounts.

B. Short-Term Investors

Under this heading, the complexities of the contemporary foreign exchange market are explicitly introduced to present more realistically the phenomena of interest arbitrage and its dual: financing in various money markets with the exchange risk covered.

1. CONSIDERATIONS INVOLVED IN INTEREST ARBITRAGE. There is a floating money supply, estimated by some bankers at between one and two billion dollars, available to profit from differences in interest rates among centers. This supply comes from the large nonfinancial concerns which maintain foreign branches and foreign deposits, and from foreign (Swiss, German and French) banks. In recent years, there has been a greater participation in this market by American nonfinancial concerns.

Interest arbitrage is not devoid of risk, for there is the possibility that the funds may be needed before the maturity date of the short-term obligation. A nonfinancial corporation may encounter an unexpected opportunity for an advantageous purchase for cash, or some contingency may arise requiring a sudden expenditure. The 3-percent net earned on a Treasury bill or a bank bill may not compensate the corporation for its inability to liquidate its investment, except at a substantial loss. The breadth of the foreign center's short-term money market—the ability of the market to absorb large amounts of money without significant changes in the prices of bills—is as important a consideration as the reputation of the debtor. Only London, Montreal-Toronto, and New York possess such broad markets. Interest differentials in other countries do not exert the same attractions as interest differentials among the three centers cited above.

A second risk that the interest-arbitrageur incurs concerns the probability that an exchange loss will occur, or an exchange gain will not be realized, if the investment is liquidated prior to maturity. For example, in June 1961 the U.K. Treasury-bill rate was 4.50 percent, and the U.S. Treasury-bill rate was 2.33 percent, per annum. A 2.17-percent differential existed in favor of London. However, on June 15, 1961 the three-month forward dollar was at a premium of $1\frac{3}{4}$ cents on a price of $2.79⅛ per pound. On a per annum basis, the premium on the forward dollar was 2.51 percent. An investor with sterling balances who (i) purchased dollars on June 15, (ii) invested his dollars in U.S. Treasury bills, and (iii) sold his dollars forward (for pounds) for delivery on September 15, could have made 4.837 percent *if he held his asset to maturity.* If he kept his funds in U.K. Treasury bills he would have only made 4.50 percent.

But suppose the party in question needed pounds in August to meet some contingency. The U.S. Treasury bills would have to be sold at a slight loss, since the August rate was 2.39 percent. The three-month forward contract, calling for the delivery of dollars on September 15, would have to be repurchased; and spot pounds would have to be purchased with the spot dollars received from the sale of the Treasury bills. On August 15, 1961, one-month forward dollars were at a premium of $1\frac{3}{16}$ cents. This meant that he would have repurchased his forward dollars at a higher price than he would have sold his spot dollars. His *net* gain on swaps would have been equal to: (a) $1\frac{3}{4}$ cent profit on the swap on June 15, less (b) $1\frac{3}{16}$ cents loss on the swap on August 15, for a net gain of $\frac{9}{16}$ cent per pound for two months, which is equivalent to a gain of 3.38 cents for a year on a purchase price of $2.79⅛. This amounts to 1.21 percent per annum. Over the entire transaction, therefore, he would have made an *exchange gain* of 1.21 percent per annum plus an *interest return* of less than 2.33 percent per annum, for a total return of 3.54 percent per annum. This is less than the 4.50 percent that he could have earned had he kept his funds in U.K. Treasury bills. Interest arbitrage would have been profitable had he kept his funds invested for the entire three months. Insofar as he was forced to liquidate at the end of two months, he suffered a net loss. Risk is not absent from interest arbitrage.

Third, the interest-arbitrageur runs a risk—even if he is certain that he will not be forced to liquidate his investment prior to maturity—if the foreign currency is under pressure. This serious element of risk has been succinctly described by H.M. Treasury:

> (b) if sterling is under pressure and the pound is suspect, inward interest arbitrage would be unlikely to take place, irrespective of how profitable it might be. The reason is that the Exchange Control Act enables the Government to determine how foreign held balances may be dealt with. Consequently, foreigners who are content in the ordinary course to hold funds in London, are less willing to do so when sterling is weak, when

the reserves are falling and when defensive measures of some kind are expected. Under such circumstances foreigners are disposed to withdraw funds from London even if that may involve them at times in quite considerable cost. It is therefore quite unrealistic to suppose for one moment that the opportunity of a relatively small interest advantage would persuade them at such times to bring more money in.[5]

The phenomenon of borrowing abroad, with the exchange risk covered, is the dual to interest arbitrage. The risks involved in hedged foreign investment apply equally to hedged foreign borrowing. Neither one is an *automatic* response to international differences in interest rates.

The phenomenon of interest arbitrage extends to interbank borrowing as well as to financial investment by nonfinancial concerns. The Eurodollar market, for example, is concerned with this type of arbitrage. An institution borrows in a low-interest-rate market and lends in a high-interest-rate market. Usually, the exchange risk is covered.

For example, in the fall of 1960, there was a shortage of loan money in Japan. A penalty rate of 6.94 percent was charged by the Central Bank to banks borrowing in excess of their quotas. In New York, however, the Treasury-bill rate was 2.48 percent, approximately equal to the maximum interest rate on three-month time deposits. At the same time, private foreign institutions held $7.55 billion on deposit with United States banks.

The Eurodollar market developed to take advantage of such opportunities. For approximately $5\frac{1}{4}$ percent, a Japanese bank could borrow dollar deposits, owned by foreigners, for three months. It would sell the dollars spot and simultaneously buy them forward for three-months delivery. The yen proceeds would then be loaned out in Tokyo at a rate more than sufficient to pay the $5\frac{1}{4}$ percent and the cost of the swap. Not only was this transaction profitable for the Japanese; it was also profitable for the owner of the Eurodollars who made $2\frac{3}{4}$ percent more than the time-deposit rate in New York. In this way, interest arbitrage *tended* to equalize interest rates among countries.

2. THE FORWARD RATE AND THE INTEREST PARITY. The interest parities (i.e., the interest differentials on short-term securities between two countries) do not *independently* determine the forward rate (i.e., the percent premium or discount on forward exchange). First, the forward rate affects the international movements of short-term capital among countries and thereby affects the interest parities. For example, foreign official and nonofficial institutions owned $9.45 billion of U.S. Treasury bills and certificates in August 1961. This was almost 20 percent of the total value of Treasury bills and certificates owned by the public *and* by the Government agencies and trust funds.

---

[5] Committee on the Working of the Monetary System, *Principal Memoranda of Evidence*, Vol. 1, H. M. Treasury, p. 121.

Changes in the forward rate, which affect the relative profitability of foreign investment in Treasury bills, can produce a sizeable change in the bill rate. Second, in view of the risks cited above, the supply of funds available for interest arbitrage may be inadequate to equate the forward rate with the interest parity.

Concerns engaged in interest arbitrage consider three types of investment: internal investment (i.e., within their own business), domestic-portfolio investment (bills, commercial paper, etc.) and foreign-portfolio investment. Funds will be allocated among these alternative uses, on the basis of expected rates of return—net of risk. Sometimes the profit opportunities for internal investment by a firm are so great that there is little remaining for portfolio investment. At other times, e.g., in the interim between the flotation of a new issue and the internal investment of the funds, there is a surplus available for portfolio investment.

Funds for interest arbitrage by nonfinancial concerns are competitive with funds for domestic-portfolio investment. It is a mistake, however, to think of foreign investment as a perfect substitute for domestic-portfolio investment. To be sure, the ratio of foreign to domestic securities desired will increase as the profit on covered interest arbitrage increases. But, there is a maximum ratio of foreign to domestic securities that a nonfinancial corporation desires to hold. As this ratio is approached, firms are less eager to substitute foreign for lower-yielding domestic securities. There is always the fear that restrictions could be imposed upon the repatriation of foreign capital, if a crisis should develop. If the concern is large, it may fear that a sudden withdrawal of funds may upset the foreign-money or forward-exchange market. Finally, the stockholders and Board of Directors may be disturbed by a large ratio of foreign to domestic securities.

Consequently, there is not always a perfectly elastic supply of funds to eliminate any differential that may appear between the forward rate and the interest parity. The greater the distrust of the foreign currency, the smaller the supply of funds available for covered interest arbitrage. One should also remember that official restrictions on the flow of short-term capital may prevent the elimination of profits on covered interest arbitrage.

Two examples illustrate the failure of the market to equilibrate the forward rate with the interest parities. The first example concerns the United States and Canada, where the investment risks consisted entirely of the probability that the investments would have to be sold prior to maturity. The second example concerns the United States and England, where the presence of exchange restrictions accounted for the yield discrepancies.

During much of the time between 1952 and 1958 it was possible to make a profit of 1 to 2½ percent over the Canadian Treasury bill rate by buying U.S. dollars spot to invest in U.S. Treasury bills and covering by selling U.S. dollars forward. The failure of the market to eliminate this profit was attributable to a principle of increasing risk. Canadian banks and nonfinancial concerns did substitute some U.S. Treasury bills for Canadian Treasury bills, in view of the interest differentials and cost of the swap. However, Canadian and U.S. Treasury bills are not perfect substitutes. If a Canadian bank or nonfinancial concern must liquidate a U.S. Treasury bill prior to maturity, it incurs the *additional* risk that it will have to repurchase its original sale of forward U.S. dollars at a higher price than it sells its spot U.S. dollars. Since U.S. Treasury bills are riskier than Canadian bills, for Canadian concerns, there is a limit to the extent that they will substitute higher-yielding U.S. bills for lower-yielding Canadian bills. Hence the supply of funds for interest arbitrage is not perfectly elastic.

When there are exchange restrictions, the forward rate can exceed the interest parity. During the period July to September 1957, the forward dollar was at a 6-7-percent premium relative to the pound; whereas the London rate exceeded the New York rate by 1 percent. Even when the increase in the Bank Rate raised the interest differential to 3 percent in favor of London, it was still less than the premium on the forward dollar. Had there been no exchange restrictions, the outflow of short-term funds from England might have forced a devaluation.

It has therefore been demonstrated that the interest parities (i.e., the interest-rate differentials on short-term securities between two countries) do not independently determine the forward premium or discount. The determination of the forward rate is reached in a more complicated manner, as will be explained in the next section.

IV. MARKET ADJUSTMENTS DURING NORMAL AND SPECULATIVE PERIODS[6]

A *normal* period may be defined as one when there is confidence in the stability of a given set of spot and forward rates. When there is a difference between current and the normal set of prices, the market expects this difference to be eliminated within a short period of time. On the other hand, we define a *speculative* period as one when the market expects a change to occur in the normal set of prices, within a short period of time.

A normal period prevails when the balance of payments surplus or deficit is expected to be ephemeral at the given set of exchange rates. On the other hand, in a speculative period the balance of payments deficit or surplus is not expected to be temporary at the existing set of rates.

---

[6] This section is an application to the foreign exchange market of a theory of commodity markets developed in my article, "The Simultaneous Determination of Spot and Futures Prices," *American Economic Review,* Vol. 51 (December 1961). The foreign exchange market deals with a storable commodity: claims on foreigners.

There is a different pattern of market reactions during a normal period than during a speculative period. Examination of price movements will reveal whether the period was basically normal or basically speculative. With this information, it is possible to evaluate the efficiency of the foreign exchange market.

A. Price Regularities during a Normal Period

During a normal period, there will be an inverse relationship between the spot price of a foreign currency and its forward premium (a discount is a negative premium). When the spot price rises, the forward premium will fall (or the discount will widen). When the spot price falls, the forward premium will rise (or the discount will narrow).

During a normal period, variations are constantly occurring in (a) relative interest rates between countries, (b) the current-account balance, (c) the long-term capital-account balance, and (d) the volume of unilateral transfers. The market then adjusts to these variations.

Market adjustment to these variations must be such as to (1) equate the supply and demand for spot exchange, and (2) equate the supply and demand for forward exchange. Interdependence between these two markets is so great that if one market is in disequilibrium, the other market cannot remain in equilibrium. Tables 1–6 are constructed to summarize these equilibrium adjustments.

1. THE SUPPLY AND DEMAND FOR SPOT EXCHANGE. Suppose that there is a surplus in our balance of payments: item 1, Table 1. This surplus could have

TABLE 1

SPOT PURCHASES AND SALES DURING A NORMAL PERIOD:

SURPLUS IN THE BALANCE OF PAYMENTS

PURCHASES	SALES
(2) Leads and lags: importers accelerate purchases of exchange and exporters lag their sales of exchange in anticipation of a rise in the spot price.	(1) Surplus in the balance of payments (produces a decline in the spot price).
(3) Interest-arbitrageurs buy spot as forward premium rises, or forward discount falls.	
(4) Foreign concerns borrow in New York, and sell dollars for foreign currency. They cover the exchange risk.	
(5) Some institutions may take long uncovered positions.	
(6) The decline in the spot price tends to reduce (1).	

been produced in many ways: through a decrease in unilateral transfers, a rise in the long-term capital-account balance or in the current-account balance. Regardless of the way in which it was produced, an excess supply of spot exchange is generated, which the market believes to be ephemeral.

The spot price falls as a result of this surplus. As the market sells exchange to the large banks, which make the market, the traders bid lower prices. These lower bids are made with the anticipation that the traders will even out their spot positions. Their opportunity costs are too high to induce them to build up their foreign exchange balances in any significant degree.

As the spot price falls, relative to a set of normal prices, the leads and lags in payments develop. The importers accelerate their payments in foreign currency, before the price recovers to its normal level. Thus, some of the spot exchange is absorbed. Similarly, the exporters lag their sales of foreign exchange, and wait until the price recovers to its normal level. This reduces some of the excess supply of foreign exchange. A net demand for spot exchange is produced by the leads and lags (item 2, Table 1).

Interest-arbitrageurs provide a large demand for spot exchange (item 3, Table 1). As the spot price falls relative to the forward price, the forward premium rises or the forward discount falls. Given the money-market rates of interest in two countries,[7] the profitability of outward interest arbitrage increases with a rise in the forward premium, or with a decline in the forward discount. Interest-arbitrageurs then purchase spot exchange and invest their proceeds abroad with the exchange risk covered.

It is not true that the supply of funds available for interest arbitrage is always sufficiently (elastic) great to bring the forward premium (or discount) into equality with the Treasury bill-rate differential. From July 1960 to November 1961 the yield differential on three-month Treasury bills between London and New York, allowing for forward-exchange cover, ranged from 1.5 percent per annum in favor of London to 2 percent per annum in favor of New York. Moreover, the interest-rate differential is not an *independent* variable which determines the forward premium or discount. The sizeable flows of funds among the large money markets affect short-term interest rates. One reason why the New York Federal Reserve Bank seeks to hold foreign deposits in competition with the commercial banks, is the desire to synchronize its open-market operations with the investment activities of foreign central banks in the New York market. The latter are sufficiently great to influence the prevailing short-term money rates, and negate the effects of Federal Reserve operations.

---

[7] For expositional simplicity, we are considering two "countries": the United States and the rest of the world. If there is a balance of payments surplus, our currency will tend to appreciate relative to all other currencies. Otherwise, there will be opportunities for arbitrage. Hence the inducements to outward interest arbitrage will apply to all the other foreign money markets.

For these reasons, and those given above, we consider the forward premium (or discount) a dependent variable. During normal periods the forward premium is inversely related to the spot price.

There is reason to believe that the interest-arbitrageurs absorb a great fraction of the variations in the quantities of spot exchange. Although this outward flow of funds is extremely important in cushioning the effect of a balance of payments surplus, it has been accorded the derogatory title of a "hot-money movement."

As the forward premium rises on the foreign currency, the forward dollar goes to a discount. It becomes less costly to borrow in New York, with the exchange risk covered, than it was prior to the decline in the spot price of the foreign currency. Foreign firms can borrow in New York, sell the dollars for foreign currency, and simultaneously repurchase forward dollars. Since the discount on the forward dollar has increased (or the premium on the forward dollar has decreased), the net cost of this borrowing operation is decreased. Similarly, American firms will find it more expensive to borrow abroad, with the exchange risk covered, than before. The reason is that the premium on the forward foreign currency, i.e., the "insurance cost" of the hedge, has increased. The net effect is to increase the net demand for foreign exchange (Table 1, item 4).

A smaller source of absorption for the balance of payments surplus comes from the medium-sized banks. Insofar as they may have low opportunity costs of their funds, they may increase their foreign exchange inventories when the spot price declines (Table 1, item 5).

For the reasons mentioned in Part B below, the decline in the price of foreign currency may affect our basic balance of payments in the very short run. Some export sales may be cancelled, or some long-term foreign investments may be accelerated, as a result of the decline in the price of foreign exchange. This phenomenon (Table 1, item 6) tends to offset item 1.

Equilibrium in the spot market occurs when the quantity of foreign exchange offered as a result of a balance of payments surplus is equal to the quantity absorbed by the purchasers (items 2 through 6). The same procedure applies, *mutatis mutandis*, when a deficit occurs.

2. THE SUPPLY AND DEMAND FOR FORWARD EXCHANGE. Transactions (3) and (4) in Table 1 have duals in the forward market. Interest-arbitrageurs, who invest their funds abroad, or firms, which switch their borrowing to New York, not only purchase spot exchange, but simultaneously sell forward exchange to the same party. These are items 3 and 4, in Table 2. If they invest in an asset, or incur a liability, with a maturity of *h* days, they simultaneously sell their exchange forward for *h* days. As a result, a supply of forward exchange is produced. The selling pressure in the spot market is transmitted to the forward market.

PURCHASES	SALES
(6) Professional risk-bearers.	(3) Interest-arbitrageurs. (4) Firms which borrowed in New York and covered themselves against the exchange risk.

As interest-arbitrageurs and borrowers in New York sell futures, the price falls. Large banks, which are the professional risk-bearers in the foreign exchange market, seldom take positions mainly by augmenting their foreign exchange balances. When they take a position, it is in the futures market. An investment is made in futures, without tying up valuable reserves, in anticipation of a price rise. They are represented by item 6, Table 2. Their position is taken as a result of the difference between the current price of futures and the price that is expected to prevail at a later date Long positions are taken if the price expected to prevail at a later date exceeds the current price of futures. Short positions are taken if the price expected to prevail at a later date is below the current price of futures.

Equilibrium exists when the spot price has fallen and the forward premium has increased (or the discount has been decreased). As a result, (1) there is a greater amount of investment abroad by interest-arbitrageurs, and (2) a greater volume of claims against foreigners is held by other hedgers and by institutions with uncovered spot positions. Moreover, the price of futures falls to induce the large banks to assume the risks of accommodating the interest-arbitrageurs and other hedgers. The decline in the price of futures is an integral part of the process whereby risk is shifted to the risk-bearers. Since the forward premium has increased (or discount has decreased), the future price falls by less than the spot price.

B. Variations in Interest Rates during Normal Periods

A change in the interest-rate differential may be viewed by the market in several ways. First, it may not be accompanied by any strong expectations that there will be a change in the normal set of exchange rates. In this case, the change in the interest differential is a normal disturbance. That is, it occurs during a normal period. Second, the change in the interest differential may be heralded as a decision to alter the exchange rates, relative to its current levels. In such a case, the disturbance is speculative: it occurs during a speculative period. There are many situations when both views are held by different components of the market. Then the resulting price reactions will be the weighted sum of the reactions of the various components.

The reactions of the market to a change in interest rates during a normal period are developed here. In the movement to the new equilibrium, the movements of the spot price and forward premium will be in opposite directions.

1. THE SUPPLY AND DEMAND FOR SPOT EXCHANGE.   Assume that interest rates abroad rise relative to domestic interest rates, but that no significant changes are expected in the normal rates of exchange. Tables 3 and 4 summarize the equilibrium adjustments in the spot and forward markets.

TABLE 3

SPOT PURCHASES AND SALES DURING A NORMAL PERIOD:

RISE IN FOREIGN INTEREST RATES

PURCHASES	SALES
(1) Interest-arbitrageurs purchase spot exchange and invest their funds abroad. Price tends to rise. (Some of the outflow of short-term capital could be uncovered.) Borrowing shifts to New York with the exchange risk covered. Spot foreign exchange is purchased with the borrowed dollars.	(2) Leads and lags: importers lag their foreign exchange purchases and exporters accelerate their foreign exchange sales. (3) Short positions may be taken by some institutions. (4) Current-account or long-term capital-account surplus may rise.

An outflow of funds will result as foreign interest rates are increased. Owners of U.S. Treasury bills and time deposits will switch their funds to foreign bills and time-deposit accounts. Similarly, borrowing will shift to New York. Spot foreign exchange will be purchased with the borrowed dollars. The exchange risk will be covered. The attempts to buy foreign exchange will drive the price up, for the bank traders will raise their ask prices to obviate covering these sales at a loss. This phase of the process is illustrated by item 1, Table 3. As the spot price increases, the profitability of interest arbitrage decreases. Thereby, the net increase in demand for foreign exchange is reduced.

As the price rises, relative to the expected normal price, the leads and lags in international payments develop (item 2, Table 3). Exporters accelerate the sales of their foreign exchange receipts before the price reverts to its former level. Similarly, importers lag their purchases of foreign exchange in anticipation of a subsequent decline in price. The net effect is to increase the quantity of foreign exchange offered in the market.

It is possible that the rise in price may increase our current-account surplus in the very short run. When exchange-rate movements are great, import purchases may be cancelled by those who failed to secure forward cover. This would increase the net supply of foreign exchange (item 4, Table 3).

Such incidents did occur during the period of floating rates, 1919–1925. During 1919, for example, the monthly average price of sterling ranged from $3.91 to $4.76; and during 1920 it ranged from $3.30 to $3.95.

> . . . In July 1919, the decline in the sterling-dollar rate, which had until then been gradual, was sharply accelerated. The extraordinary levels at which money on call was being lent in New York, coupled with heavy offers of cotton bills, combined to weaken sterling in that month and in the absence of support the rate fell 20 points in one week, reaching 4.28 on July 17. Cables were almost immediately after received in London to the effect that an actual cancellation of an important export order in cereals had taken place in Philadelphia as a direct result of the decline in the exchange. Acute apprehension was felt that export orders would be greatly reduced and confusion reigned among American exporters.[8]

When exchange-rate movements are "sufficiently great," the long-term capital-account or the invisible current-account balance may also be affected with a negligible lag. A concern contemplating a sizeable long-term investment abroad may delay making the investment if the price of foreign exchange rises above its expected normal level. A half cent saved per unit of foreign exchange mounts up to a significant amount on a multimillion dollar foreign investment. Hence, the long-term capital account could be affected in the very short run by exchange-rate variations. Along similar lines, the timing of corporate dividends from foreign branches of American concerns may be influenced by the current exchange rate. Consequently, the invisible current-account balance may be influenced, with a short lag, by the difference between the current and expected normal exchange rates.

Some institutions may take short uncovered positions in foreign exchange, as a result of this price rise. They would (i) reduce their foreign balances, (ii) swap spot for a future maturity, or (iii) use their foreign customer accounts to make delivery. They expect to repurchase the foreign exchange when the price reverts to its lower level.

The price of foreign exchange will rise until item 1 is counterbalanced by items 2–4. In the final equilibrium the spot price will, of course, be higher than initially.

2. THE SUPPLY AND DEMAND FOR FORWARD EXCHANGE. Transaction 1, Table 3 has a counterpart in the forward-exchange market. Interest-arbitrageurs simultaneously sell forward when spot is purchased. In this manner they attempt to shift the risks of exchange-rate fluctuations onto the institutions which purchase futures. The major risk-bearing institutions in the futures market are the large banks which make the markets in all maturities. The

---

[8] William Adams Brown, Jr., *England and the New Gold Standard 1919–1926.* (London: P. S. King and Son, Ltd., 1929), pp. 57–58. W. A. Brown uses points synonymous with cents.

price of futures must fall below the normal expected price, in order to induce the banks to purchase these futures. Table 4 describes the equilibrium in this market.

TABLE 4

FORWARD PURCHASES AND SALES DURING A NORMAL PERIOD:

RISE IN FOREIGN INTEREST RATES

PURCHASES	SALES
(5) Large banks, which take positions in futures, lower bid prices.	(1) Interest-arbitrageurs and foreigners who borrowed in New York sell forward exchange to cover spot purchases.

The equilibrium adjustment produces a rise in the spot price and a decline in the forward premium (or rise in the forward discount). Thereby, (i) the rate of capital outflow is reduced, (ii) a demand for forward exchange is produced, and (iii) institutions increase their sales of spot exchange. *Mutalis mutandis*, the same argument applies for a decline in foreign interest rates during a normal period.

C. Speculative Periods

1. PRICE REGULARITIES.   The market consists of a variety of institutions with different price expectations or aversions to risk. During a speculative period, several important segments of the market expect prices to change and react accordingly. It is shown that, during a speculative period, the spot price moves in the same direction as the forward premium (or in a direction opposite to the forward discount). Equilibrium adjustments in the spot and forward markets, when the price of foreign exchange is expected to decline, are summarized in Tables 5 and 6.

Suppose that the traders in the large banks expect large-scale selling of a foreign currency by their customers and foreign banks. Such selling may be motivated by fears of devaluation. The traders who make the market will

TABLE 5

FORWARD PURCHASES AND SALES DURING A SPECULATIVE PERIOD:

EXPECT PRICE OF FOREIGN CURRENCY TO FALL

PURCHASES	SALES
(2) Interest-arbitrageurs purchase forward exchange as forward premium declines or discount rises. (3) Some institutions buy spot dollars and sell forward dollars, to profit from the price differential.	(1) Large banks sell in anticipation of the state of the market or of customers' requirements.

TABLE 6

SPOT PURCHASES AND SALES DURING A SPECULATIVE PERIOD:

EXPECT PRICE OF FOREIGN CURRENCY TO FALL

PURCHASES	SALES
(4) Leads and lags by those who think the price decline has proceeded "too far." (5) The current and long-term capital account will decline as a result of the fall in the spot price.	(1) Sales of spot by bears. Initial leads and lags also enter here. (2) Interest-arbitrageurs who sell spot foreign exchange and invest proceeds in United States. (3) The institutions which buy spot dollars with foreign exchange and simultaneously sell forward dollars.

then sell the foreign currency short, to avoid long positions or market losses when the selling orders materialize. Their actions are listed in item 1, Table 5 and item 1, Table 6, when they sell forward and spot, respectively.

Their short position occurs in the forward market predominantly, for the reasons explained in Section III. Initially, the major pressure is exerted upon the forward market; and the premium on the forward foreign currency declines or the discount rises. This means that the premium on the forward dollar rises, or the discount on the forward dollar declines. As a result, inward interest arbitrage is encouraged. Foreigners, or American concerns which maintain foreign balances, are induced to redirect their short-term investments from the foreign center to New York. The net yield on investments in New York, with the exchange risk covered, has been increased by the rise in the premium (or fall in the discount) on the forward dollar. Interest- arbitrageurs then sell spot foreign exchange (item 2, Table 6) and simultaneously purchase forward foreign exchange (item 2, Table 5) from the large banks. Similarly, American concerns are induced to finance themselves abroad with the exchange risks covered. They are subsumed under item 2.

In addition to the interest-arbitrageurs, some institutions may seize an opportunity to make profits by swapping. They would buy spot dollars and sell forward dollars (i.e., sell foreign exchange spot and repurchase futures) when the forward premium on the dollar exceeds their costs of carrying larger dollar balances. These institutions, so similar to the interest-arbitrageurs, are cited in item 3 in Tables 5 and 6.

Restrictions on the outward flow of short-term capital from foreign countries may reduce the importance of the above items in equilibrating the forward market. Were outward interest arbitrage prohibited effectively, item 2 would disappear in Tables 5 and 6. The forward price would continue to decline under the selling pressure. On the other hand, a large source of supply in the spot market would be eliminated. Insofar as the central bank supports the spot market, the drain on its reserves would be mitigated.

During speculative periods, the Bank of England has not supported the forward market. Its failure to intervene is motivated by a desire to let the bears suffer when the pound is *not* devalued. Bears who sold sterling futures, in a market with few buyers, sell at very low prices. If sterling is not devalued, they are forced to cover at considerably higher prices. Thereby, they "have been taught a lesson."

Such a policy is fraught with danger. The greater the forward discount, the more profitable is interest arbitrage out of the United Kingdom. Unless the restrictions on a capital outflow are highly effective, the substantial forward discount on sterling will make a covered short-term capital outflow highly profitable. The three-month Treasury-bill rate differential was in favor of New York by 5–6 percent per annum in July–September 1957—with the exchange risk covered. If capital does escape, the reserves will be depleted; and devaluation could be forced upon the exchange authorities.

Transmission of the bear pressure from the futures market to the spot market occurs via the activities of the interest-arbitrageurs. Another great source of selling pressure in the spot market arises from the leads and lags in international payments. This source of supply is subsumed under item 1, Table 6. During the third quarter of 1957, the leads and lags were estimated to have caused a reduction of £90–100 million in the United Kingdom's reserves.

Offsetting these selling pressures in the spot market are two factors. As the price of foreign exchange declines, expectations tend to be revised. The greater the decline in price, the more institutions change from bears to bulls. Each institution has initially expected the price of foreign exchange to fall to a certain price. When the current price declines below this price, the institution will accelerate its payments, and lag its receipts, in foreign currency. The initial leads and lags tend to be reversed as the price falls. Thereby, the initial supply of spot tends to be absorbed. This phenomenon is stated in item 4, Table 6.

Another offset to the initial bear pressure upon the spot market is the balance of payments (item 5, Table 6). For the reasons explained above, the current and long-term capital accounts may react rapidly to substantial changes in the exchange rate.

The price of spot exchange will decline, in a free market, until items 4 and 5 offset items 1, 2, and 3 in Table 6. When the spot market is being supported, the drain on reserves will continue until equilibrium is attained.

At the final equilibrium, the spot price and forward premium will be less than they were prior to the bear pressure. A lower forward premium (or higher forward discount) is necessary to equilibrate the forward market. A lower spot price is necessary to equilibrate the spot market. A similar argument explains why the spot price and forward premium will rise together during a bull speculative period.

2. SUPPORTING EVIDENCE FROM THE RECENT PAST. During 1961, there was a revaluation of the D-mark which the market considered to be inadequate.

Chart 1
Spot Price and Forward Premium on D-Mark
Relative to Sterling, March 1961

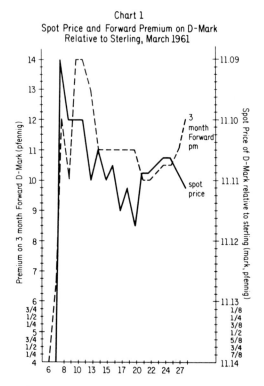

Later in the year, there was a run on sterling in anticipation of a devaluation. This run was reversed when the Bank Rate was raised and large stand-by credits were obtained from the International Monetary Fund. If the theories developed above are correct explanations of the workings of the foreign exchange market, then the positive relationship between the spot price and the forward premium should have occurred during the speculative periods.[9] This relation did in fact hold, as will be shown presently.

(i) The German Revaluation. After four years of debate, the Germans revalued the mark. On March 3, 1961, the official parity was 11 marks 76 pfennig to the pound, with effective stabilization limits 11.59¼—11.92¾. By Monday, March 6, the new parity was 11 marks 20 pfennig to the pound, with effective stabilization limits 11.0366—11.3646.

Quotations from *The Economist* (March 11, 1961) describe the speculative nature of the immediate post-revaluation period, which is graphed in Chart 1.

> Saturday's announcement came as a universal surprise in the markets. The Dutch decision followed in the early hours of last Monday; and later that day one European government after another, including some of the

[9] The positive relationship between the forward premium and the spot price exists both when the former is measured as a percent of the spot price and in absolute terms.

unlikeliest ones, proclaimed solemnly that they had no intention of revaluing their currency. Yet uncertainty remains, stemming in part from the limited extent of the German revaluation. Will it be enough? Is it the first and final, or just first? Doubts about this are being voiced in every financial centre in Europe. They cannot be set at rest by even the most awesome statements of intent—these have been as effectively devalued by Herr Blessing as they were by Sir Stafford Cripps in 1949. (p. 981)

Sterling has been under heavy pressure, particularly on Wednesday [March 8], when the flood of speculation that has swamped the exchange markets concentrated its full force against the pound, provoked by a suggestion in a German newspaper that it might be devalued, so to say, to meet the mark half way. (p. 985)

This bear pressure on the pound, or bull pressure on the mark, coincided with the substantial increases in the spot price of the mark and its forward premium, from March 6 through March 8.

According to the theory summarized in Tables 5 and 6, the bear speculation against the pound (i.e., the bull speculation in favor of the mark) (a) should have induced interest arbitrage from England to Germany and (b) should have induced German firms to borrow in London. Thereby interest arbitrageurs, and Germans who borrowed in London, should have demanded the forward pounds supplied by the professional risk-bearers or their customers. This must have occurred. At the end of February, U.K. Treasury bills yielded 1.31 percent per annum more than German Treasury bills; and day-to-day money yielded 0.38 percent per annum more in England. In March, U.K. Treasury bills yielded 1.98 percent more, and day-to-day money yielded 0.36 percent more, than they did in Germany. From March 6 to March 11, the forward-mark premium rose from 1.44 percent per annum to 5.05 percent per annum. Covered short-term investment in Germany was more profitable than investment in England. By the same token, a German firm borrowing in England, could save 5.05 percent per annum by hedging its sterling liability with a purchase of forward sterling. Not only was the flow of funds, from England to Germany, profitable but it seemed to have occurred on a large scale. There was a rise of $125 million in the Bundesbank's gold and foreign exchange holdings during the week ended March 7, and $206 million the following week. It may be assumed that a large part of the funds that moved to Germany was obtained by conversions from sterling and by transfers of dollar deposits from England.

Subsequently the fierce speculative attack on sterling abated. *The Economist* (March 19, 1961, p. 1091) wrote:

It is possible that the relief is no more than momentary, but the great thing is that speculative activity has been prevented from snowballing.

One possible reason for the temporary reversal of the heavy speculative pressure was the statement issued by the governors of the leading European central banks after their monthly meeting at the Bank for International Settlements during the week ending March 18.

> . . . A statement from the BIS is something of an event. This haven for central bankers (where, it is reputed, no Treasury official has set foot, and certainly no public relations officer) normally gets through its monthly weekend meeting without the public being aware that the governors have met at all. But last Monday [March 13] representatives of the central banks of Belgium, Britain, France, Germany, Italy, the Netherlands, Sweden and Switzerland said this to the world:
>> The governors are satisfied that the rumours which circulated last week in the market about possible further currency adjustments have no foundation and they wish it to be known that the central banks concerned are cooperating closely in the exchange markets.

One can picture quiet satisfaction among the central bankers over the elliptical second half of that statement.

During that week, there were clear downward trends in both the spot price and forward premium on the D-mark. Trends were not monotonic, for the markets were on edge. Operators in the London foreign exchange market estimated the week's turnover to be the heaviest since the days of speculative frenzy in the early 1920's.

As the speculative attack abated, the premium on the forward mark declined from 5.05 percent to 3.60 percent per annum from March 11 to March 22, 1961. The data are therefore consistent with the theory summarized by Tables 5 and 6.

(ii) The Decline and Rise of The Pound. Towards the end of June, 1961 a sterling crisis was portended. "The fate of the pound, therefore of world exchange arrangements as a whole," wrote *The Economist* (July 8, 1961), "is likely to be decided before the August holidays." The period June 26 to August 9, described in Chart 2, has three phases. During the first phase, June 26 to July 11, there was general speculative pressure against the pound. Many were most reluctant to hold sterling over the weekends: they would go short on Friday or Saturday and cover on Mondays. The Bank of England was in the market supporting the declining pound. Speculative pressure was concentrated in the forward market, where the dollar rose to a 4.49 percent premium on an annual basis. The selling of sterling futures started in Germany and was followed by sales from New York. Gold and foreign-exchange reserves of the United Kingdom declined by $132 million during June. During this speculative period, the positive relationship between the spot price of the dollar and its forward premium are apparent from Chart 2.

The supply of forward pounds was absorbed by the interest-arbitrageurs who invested in U.S. Treasury bills, and by American concerns which were induced to borrow in London with the exchange risk covered. In June, Treasury bills yielded 2.17 percent more in London than in New York. This differential was 2.86 percent in July. On bankers' acceptances, the differential in favor of London was 1.89 percent in June and 1.97 per cent in July. During

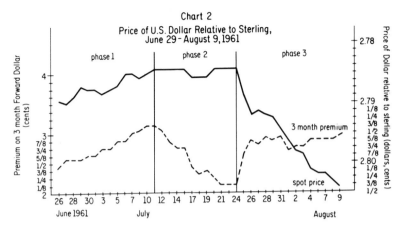

Chart 2
Price of U.S. Dollar Relative to Sterling,
June 29 - August 9, 1961

phase 1, from June 26 to July 12, the premium on the forward dollar rose from 3.495 percent to 4.489 percent. Outward interest arbitrage from London to New York was profitable. Thereby, a demand for the forward pounds was generated. This is precisely the mechanism described in Tables 5 and 6.

From July 11 to July 25, when the Bank Rate was suddenly increased, another set of events occurred. The large New York banks thought that the market was overly bearish on the pound. They therefore went long pound futures, while their customers and foreigners continued to sell spot pounds and future pounds. Pressure on the spot pound arose out of the leads and lags in international payments. This would explain the decline in the forward premium, while the spot pound was steady at 2.78⁷⁄₁₆. There was no doubt that The Bank of England was actively supporting the pound at that level; but there was no evidence of official support in the forward market.

Insofar as pound futures were being purchased, the stimulus for outward interest arbitrage from the United Kingdom diminished. The premium on the forward dollar declined from 4.3995 on July 12 to 3.0527 percent per annum on July 24.

On July 25, 1961, the third phase began. The Bank Rate was raised from 5 to 7 percent; and the Chancellor fortified the reserves by resorting to the International Monetary Fund. As Chart 2 indicates, spot sterling responded immediately to these measures (i.e., the spot dollar declined dramatically and steadily).

The Bank Rate rose from 5 to 7 percent, the discount rate on (3-month) Bank bills rose from $4\frac{3}{4}$–$\frac{3}{16}$ to $6\frac{1}{4}$–$\frac{3}{4}$, and Fine trade bills (3-months) rose from $5\frac{1}{2}$–6 to $7\frac{1}{4}$–8, percent per annum. Britain's credit from IMF consisted of an immediate drawing of nine currencies totalling $1.5 billion, and a stand-by arrangement for an additional $0.5 billion during the next twelve months.

The speculative bubble was pricked and the attraction of high interest rates produced the price relationships observed during a *normal* period. Since the professional risk-bearers in New York were not short sterling futures on July 25, the supply of interest-arbitrage funds from the United States to London raised the premium on the forward dollar. Informed market opinion realized that the rise in the forward premium on the dollar, during this period, was not a sign of speculation.

> Few operators . . . have felt ready to put money into London without covering themselves in the forward market; and as the forward discount works out at an annual rate of 3¾–4 per cent on New York . . . this virtually wipes out the interest differential. A sharp rise in the interest differential is naturally associated with a widening in the forward margin, and this movement on Wesnesday [July 26] could not therefore be attributed to a worsening of confidence. On Thursday forward rates were a little stronger, though dealings were not large.[10]

A speculative period, phase 1, gave way to a normal period, phase 3. In the first phase the spot-dollar and the forward premium on the dollar were positively related. During the final phase, when interest rates were increased in London, the negative relation appears. These incidents are compatible with the regularities predicted by the theory developed above.

Note: The editor has omitted a ten-page appendix (from the original publication) dealing with an empirical study of the ability of the professional risk-bearers to forecast the movements of the floating sterling-dollar rate between 1921–1925.

[10] *The Economist,* July 29, 1961, p. 472.

INTEREST RATE DIFFERENCES, FORWARD EXCHANGE MECH-ANISM, AND SCOPE FOR SHORT-TERM CAPITAL MOVEMENTS*

With the relaxation of exchange controls and the rapid rise in the volume of international trade over the last few years, there has developed both a very large supply of money, which is shifted from one international monetary center to another in search of higher interest rates, and a large volume of demand for money, which shifts in search of lower interest rates. Together, these shifts can subject a country whose interest rates become relatively low to rapid and large losses of gold and foreign exchange reserves. Even though the country's longer-run position is not unsound, such losses may provoke speculative flights of "hot money," which could place the exchange rate in jeopardy.

Failure to anticipate these results of a relaxation of exchange controls in an environment of stable exchanges is explained, in part, by a belief that the international shifts of short-term lendings and borrowings actually carried out would be limited to a small fraction of the amounts that lenders and borrowers desired to make. The cause of this limitation was found in a restricted availability of forward foreign exchange; and forward exchange is a necessary ingredient in a major part of the short-term lendings or borrowings that respond to differences in interest rates.

This paper will describe how the opportunity for large movements of short-term funds can be provided by the normal responses of exporters and importers to movements in the forward exchange rate. It will also note some implications of the situation for three alternative means of dealing with the legal range of variation of the exchange rate (widening the spread between capital movements: official operation in the forward market, widening the the "gold points"), and enlarging the narrower range within the gold points over which the exchange rate actually is permitted to move.

* William H. White, *IMF Staff Papers*, November, 1963, pp. 485–501.

45

ROLE OF FORWARD EXCHANGE IN SHORT-TERM CAPITAL MOVEMENTS

Movements of short-term capital in response to international differences in interest rates are normally dependent on protection against unfavorable movements in exchange rates. An extra interest yield of 1 percent on three-month Treasury bills of the United Kingdom would be entirely canceled out if the pound were to depreciate just ¼ percentage point before the funds invested in the bill could be repatriated.[1]

The accepted view has been that the amount of a currency which holders of foreign balances can contract now to buy at some date in the future, as a protection for exchange transactions, is normally rather inflexible. To obtain agreement from others to make a future sale of domestic currency is exchange for foreign currency temporarily held, the holder of short-term balances might have to pay not only the going exchange rate but also a premium. If arrangements to purchase large additional amounts of domestic currency were to be made, this premium would be pushed so high that it would more than cancel out any possible advantage secured from the higher short-term interest rate of the foreign country. Hence, it has been thought that the volume of "covered interest arbitrage" transactions normally could be no more than "small," and that most of any large volume of short-term capital movements observed would have to be explained by motives other than a desire for higher interest yields.[2] Precisely this reasoning has been offered

---

[1] For a thorough discussion of many aspects of the forward exchange market not covered here, see S. C. Tsiang, "The Theory of Forward Exchange and Effects of Government Intervention on the Forward Exchange Market," *Staff Papers*, Vol. VII (1959–60), pp. 75–106.

[2] Definitions of terms used in this discussion:

Forward exchange: A contract to buy (sell) foreign exchange at some stated future date, the exchange rate used being agreed to at the time the contract is made. (Contracts are commonly made for periods of up to six months in advance of the exchange transaction.)

Forward cover: An exchange contract used to offset the exchange rate risk incurred in the holding of assets denominated in a foreign currency or in an obligation to make (receive) a payment in foreign currency.

Spot exchange rate: The rate of exchange between currencies—the exchange rate in which transactions that are to be immediately carried out are arranged.

Forward premium on the pound: The percentage excess of the price of the pound for future delivery over the spot exchange price of the pound in terms of some other currency. (When the forward pound is at a discount, the pound's price in the forward market is cheaper than its price in the spot market.)

To aid understanding, the discussion of the forward exchange mechanism is being expressed in this paper in terms of sterling/dollar transactions. However, it is not implied that any of the situations described is especially characteristic of those two currencies.

in criticism of an increase in short-term rates carried out by the United States in July 1963 for the purpose of attracting short-term funds.[3]

VARIABILITY IN USE OF FORWARD COVER FOR CURRENT ACCOUNT PAYMENTS

Monetary relationships among the main money-market currencies were uncertain and disturbed during the whole period from before World War II until late in 1958. In these conditions, a theory of forward exchange markets was developed which assumed that all those who undertook nonspeculative short-term dealings in foreign exchange would normally obtain exchange rate protection. This view has persisted even since the main European currencies acquired external convertibility in 1958.

The new element in the foreign exchange market, which made necessary a revision of previous opinion, was the restoration of confidence in the maintenance of the official parities: importers and exporters—who have probably been the chief users of forward exchange contracts—became confident in 1959 that, for example, the dollar price of the pound sterling would not move (within the next three months) outside the legal limits of $2.78 and $2.82. The narrow movements in the forward exchange rate which would make forward exchange ¼ percent cheaper, or ¼ percent more expensive, than spot exchange thus became a matter of importance for the trader. Previously, he had felt that he had to conduct most, if not all, of his foreign exchange operations through the forward market, and to ignore the spot market almost completely. Movements of ¼–½ percent in the forward rate therefore had little influence on his exchange transactions—as little influence as equal spot rate movements are assumed, by the theory of international trade, to have on those exports and imports for which the spot exchange market is used. But once confidence was established in the limits of $2.78 and $2.82 for the pound (which restrict its range of variation to

---

[3] "The potential benefit to the dollar, however, cannot be measured simply by the relative change in interest rates. Since very few short-term funds these days cross national boundaries without being covered against the risk of an alteration in the exchange rate before they are repatriated, the cost of such forward cover must also be taken into account. Indeed, when there are no pressing fears of depreciation, the forward rate will normally adjust itself to the differential in money rates between the two centres, thus eliminating the incentive to transfer funds. . . . [this] calls into question whether the mere adjustment of interest differentials can be relied upon to exert any significant effect on the flow of short-term funds unless it is flanked by an active policy of influencing forward exchange rates as well. In short, even if European money rates do not rise at all, the rise in U.S. rates may have no real impact on the flow of funds to Europe unless the authorities intervene in the forward market—as they did successfully in 1961." From "America Tackles Its Deficit," *The Banker,* Vol. CXIII (August 1963), p. 525.

a mere 1.4 percent), the trader who was not interested in foreign exchange speculation would realize that, under some conditions, use of the forward market would be advantageous, and that under others, resort to the spot market at the time of payment would be preferable.

This is understood most easily if it is assumed that the trader has an idea that the most likely value for the spot rate three months hence is the same as the current spot rate. If, under these circumstances, a U.S. importer of goods from the United Kingdom were to pay a premium of 1 cent for forward pounds (e.g., $2.81½ when the spot rate is $2.80½) rather than wait to buy spot pounds when the payment is due, he would be buying insurance, against possible variations in the exchange rate, at a price equal to two thirds of the maximum possible loss against which he is insuring (1½ cents, since the spot pound could rise to only $2.82). However, rather than pay a premium of 1 cent for insurance against a loss whose maximum would be 1½ cents, many importers of U.K. goods would refrain from covering forward. The reasons for such a decision are especially persuasive because the purchase of forward cover would not only be an insurance against the loss caused by an appreciation of the spot pound but would also eliminate the *profit* which would accrue if the spot rate for the pound should fall below the existing rate of $2.80½. At the upper limit of $2.82, the U.S. importer could never gain by covering forward, and he probably would lose; at this price, therefore, his demand for forward pounds would be zero. At $2.78, by similar reasoning, he would buy forward cover for all his imports. (The preceding discussion applies equally if the import is to be paid for in dollars; the U.K. exporter, who expects to receive dollar payments, would then do the forward covering, and would make similarly large adjustments in his purchases of forward pounds in response to very small movements in the forward rate.)

Expressed in more general terms, the purchase of forward cover at a premium constitutes acceptance of an exchange loss now in order to eliminate the chance of a possible greater loss later. But once the size of the later loss has been restricted to a figure which could not jeopardize continuation of the trader's activities, the choice between the two losses becomes purely a matter of probabilities. And when the probabilities are against accepting a loss now, the trader who does accept it more nearly resembles a "speculator," for he is gambling on an unlikely outcome. In a sense, his behavior is even more speculative than that of the gambler: the gambler at least has the hope of a quick win which will permit him to stop betting before the unfavorable probabilities can assert themselves, whereas the trader knows that he must keep on betting for a period long enough to have the unfavorable probabilities take effect. Thus, when existing exchange parities are trusted, the usual view that traders are not interested in exchange rate speculation requires acceptance of the fact that the extent to which foreign exchange risks are covered does vary according to the cost of cover.

When the trader cannot select any spot rate, such as the current figure, as the most probable value for the spot rate three months hence, the only factors relevant to his decision are the current *forward* rate and the gold points. This requires a revision of the reasoning just presented. Assume, for example, that the trader normally considers that all spot rates between $2.78 and $2.82 have *equal* probabilities of being realized in three months. In that event, a trader having numerous, frequently repeated import transactions will know that he will gain by buying forward pounds at a price below $2.80 and lose if he buys at a price above $2.80. Given the uncertainties of his assumed probability distribution at any particular time, the trader will not feel justified in switching from full to zero use of forward cover as soon as the price of the forward pound rises above $2.80. Instead, he will make gradual adjustments as the excess of the forward rate above $2.80 increases. He will seek no forward cover for his imports when the forward rate is $2.82, but will seek complete cover when it is $2.78.

A reasonable inference from the preceding is that, if the action of interest arbitragers should cause the forward pound to depreciate by as little, say, as $\frac{1}{3}$ percent (e.g. from 2.81\frac{1}{2}$ to 2.80\frac{1}{2}$), traders would make very large net purchases of forward pounds, or large reductions in the net sales of forward pounds which they would otherwise be making. This means—in contrast to the popular view—that holders of short-term funds in other centers who might wish to take advantage of higher U.K. interest rates would find that a large volume of forward pounds could be sold for forward dollars at the sacrifice of relatively little of the extra interest earnings obtainable in the United Kingdom.[4]

The preceding discussion is made more explicit by Diagrams 1 and 2. Diagram 1 shows how the importers' and exporters' ("traders'") net de-

---

[4] Paul Einzig has said that some of the traders dealing in items with wide profit margins can afford to take the risk of going uncovered, especially since it keeps alive the chance of an exchange profit. But he apparently is not reporting anything like the systematic, strong reaction of traders to changes in the cost of forward cover which is implied by the reasoning offered above. Whereas Einzig says that traders in staple commodities operate on profit margins that are too narrow to permit the running of such risks (*A Dynamic Theory of Forward Exchange,* London, 1961, p. 65), the reasoning above implies that higher profits will be earned—on the average, at least—by using less exchange rate insurance, the more its cost rises toward the amount of the maximum exchange risk. Even if ownership capital would otherwise be inadequate, these extra profits should provide the intelligent commodity trader with a self-insurance fund adequate for survival of any plausible succession of exchange losses of, say, 1 percent.

Somewhat stronger belief that traders are sensitive to the cost of forward cover is indicated by the testimony which the Governor of the Netherlands central bank gave to the Radcliffe Committee in late 1958 (Committee on the Working of the Monetary System, *Minutes of Evidence,* London, 1960, p. 816). However, no similar view could be found anywhere else in the Committee's evidence, memoranda, or report.

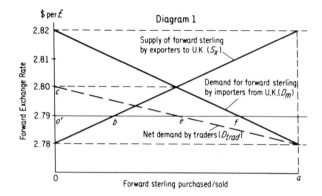

mand curve for forward sterling is derived from the volume of trade and the position of the forward exchange rate. The diagram is drawn on the simplifying assumption that exports and imports are equal, each being *oa* over a three-month period.

At the upper limit of £1 = $2.82, no U.S. importer who had confidence in the £/$ parity and gold points for the next three months would buy sterling in the forward market. If the forward pound fell to the lower limit of $2.78, all importers would buy forward sterling. This would imply—on the assumption that import payments are covered three months forward—that importers would (after a three-month transition period) be holding forward contracts equal to the value of one fourth of a year's imports. Exporters expecting to receive payments in sterling would *sell* all that sterling forward when the forward rate was $2.82, but none when the rate was $2.78.

The excess of the U.S. importers' forward purchases over the U.S. exporters' forward sales at any given rate is the traders' net demand for forward pounds, D_{trad}. Thus, in Diagram 1, the net demand at an exchange rate of £1 = $2.79 ($o'e$) is equal to the gross demand ($o'f$) minus the supply ($o'b$).

The traders' net demand curve is shown also in Diagram 2, on which the ordinate represents not the absolute number of forward dollars a pound but four times the percentage discount of the price of forward pounds below the price of spot pounds. Thus, if the spot price were $2.80, a forward price of $2.79 would be shown in Diagram 2 as a $1\frac{1}{3}$ percent discount:

$$\frac{\$2.79 - \$2.80}{\$2.80} \times 4 = \text{approximately } 1\frac{1}{3} \text{ percent}$$

We may now consider the supply of forward pounds offered by interest arbitragers—a supply which is assumed to be equal to the short-term funds that they transfer to the United Kingdom. (This discussion assumes that dollar balances are placed in loans denominated in sterling; the same rea-

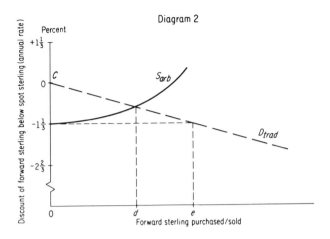

Diagram 2

soning applies, however, where—as with some Eurodollar deposits and loans by U.S. banks—the loan is fixed in dollars and the *borrower* is left to convert it into sterling and offer the forward pounds.) The curve S_{arb} in Diagram 2 represents the arbitragers' supply of forward pounds; it is drawn on the assumption that funds placed in the United Kingdom may be removed in three months. This curve is assumed to be very elastic at first but to become inelastic as more of the available liquid balances are transferred to the United Kingdom. If the discount on the forward pound below the spot pound is 1 cent (approximately $\frac{1}{3}$ percent), the purchase of spot pounds and subsequent repurchase of dollars through a forward contract would yield a loss of $\frac{1}{3}$ percent of the funds invested. Since the funds were invested for a period that might well be only three months (one quarter of a year), this loss would cancel out the benefit derivable from a U.K. interest rate that was higher by $1\frac{1}{3}$ percent per annum than the rate earnable on an alternative investment in the United States. In other words, if the short-term interest rate in the United Kingdom exceeds that in the United States by $1\frac{1}{3}$ percent, the arbitragers' supply of forward pounds falls to zero when 4 times the discount of the pound's forward value in terms of dollars below its spot value is $1\frac{1}{3}$ percent; reductions in the forward discount induce an increasing supply of forward pounds from arbitragers. When the three-month interest rate in the United Kingdom exceeds the U.S. rate by less than $1\frac{1}{3}$ percent, the *supply* of pounds by arbitragers falls to zero at a smaller discount on the forward pound than $\frac{1}{3}$ percent. The S_{arb} curve is then higher, and the volume of funds placed in the United Kingdom is, of course, smaller.

The superimposition of the D_{trad} curve on the S_{arb} curve of Diagram 2 raises certain problems. The independent variable in Diagram 2 is the discount of the forward rate relative to the spot rate, whereas the independent variable determining trader demand in Diagram 1 is the level of the forward rate relative to the gold points (or simply the absolute level of the forward rate). As described earlier, the trader's demand for forward exchange is probably a function of both these variables. It is permissible, therefore, to express D_{trad} as a function of the forward discount alone (Diagram 2) only if the level of the spot rate is constant. For example, an appreciation of the spot rate that was accompanied by an equal rise in the forward rate would leave the forward discount unchanged; Diagram 2 would therefore show no change. But, from the relationship shown in Diagram 1, it is known that a rise in the absolute level of the forward rate must reduce trader demand for forward cover even if the forward discount is unreduced. Therefore, the D_{trad} curve in Diagram 2 which refers to successively higher spot rates (and, hence, for any given forward discount, to higher forward rates) must be shifted increasingly to the left.

Spot rates may rise when British interest rates are increased for the purpose of attracting foreign funds. Any inflow of funds would tend to cause appreciation of the spot pound, and the D_{trad} curve would therefore shift to the left. But that leftward shift must reduce the possibilities for transfers of covered funds to the United Kingdom. Even if the D_{trad} and S_{arb} curves were very elastic—so that scope seemed to exist for large transfers of covered funds—the leftward shift of the D_{trad} curve might prevent significant transfers from occurring. That result is not the most frequent one, however. As was seen in 1960 when the official reserves of the United Kingdom increased (and decreased) by large amounts while the spot pound was held very close to $2.81, the possibilities for such counteracting movements of the spot rate may be limited.

Quantitative Importance

Dollar-sterling Trade

A rough idea of the possible amount of the short-term capital flows evoked by the opportunities for covered interest arbitrage can be derived from the amount of forward exchange that traders would normally be using and the variation in this amount that would be caused by a small change in the forward rate (spot rate constant). We may assume that there is general confidence that the exchange parity and limits will remain fixed for the next three months. If in these conditions forward sterling were quoted at its lower limit, $2.78, all importers having sterling payments to make in three months would buy corresponding amounts of forward sterling, and no exporters would sell forward. At the upper limit, $2.82, no importers would buy forward, but all exporters would sell forward pounds equivalent to the value of the receipts that they expect over the next three months.

The preceding implies that a movement in the rate for the forward pound from $2.82 to $2.78 would raise traders' net demand for forward sterling by the equivalent of three months' exports plus three months' imports—i.e., by approximately the value of one half of a year's exports. This range could not be fully exploited by interest arbitragers because, as described above, a $\frac{1}{3}$ percent change in the rate—one fourth of the distance from $2.82 to $2.78—would cancel out the advantages of a $1\frac{1}{3}$ percent interest rate differential. For purposes of discussion, it may therefore be taken that traders' adjustments would permit a covered arbitrage movement no greater than one eighth of a year's exports (one fourth of one half of a year's exports).

The opportunities for transfer of covered funds would be larger than this if the forward rate were initially not much more than $\frac{1}{3}$ percent above its lower limit of $2.78, for, as the actions of arbitragers pushed the forward pound close to $2.78, an occasional participant in the forward market—the speculator on small movements in exchange rates—would find it increasingly worthwhile to buy forward sterling. (At the worst, the spot rate would also be at $2.78 when the speculator's forward contract matured, in which case a very small loss would be incurred; but a higher spot rate could be expected, if it had not already been at $2.78 for an abnormally long time, and some exchange profit would be foreseen.) At the extreme, a forward pound rate of $2.78 would connote an infinitely elastic D curve, and there could be no further depreciation of the forward pound to limit any transfers of covered funds to London that are initiated by a rise in U.K. interest rates.[5]

Because the importance of the possibilities for covered arbitrage can be demonstrated without reference to the special case of a forward pound close to $2.78 at a time when exchange parities are not under suspicion, the previous finding that arbitrage movements are limited in practice to one eighth of a year's exports will be retained for purposes of discussion. (Of course, the $2.78 rate is not an unreasonable assumption if interest

[5] Under these conditions the scope for arbitrage could be further enlarged by arbitragers' forgoing forward cover. Those who are as willing as the traders to trust the exchange parities would see no advantage in selling the pound forward at a price little above its lower limit of $2.78. (See John Maynard Keynes, *Treatise on Money*, II, London, 1930, pp. 323–26.)

This and the speculative factor have been offered as explanations of the co-existence after mid-1960 of large arbitrage transfers and a yield on U.K. Treasury bills (net of the cost of cover) that remained 1 percentage point higher than the yield on U.S. bills (John H. Auten, "Foreign Exchange Rates and Interest-Rate Differentials," *The Journal of Finance*, Vol. XVIII, March 1963, pp. 17–18). But because that explanation must assume substantial speculative purchases of forward sterling when the price falls only 0.6 cent below $2.80, and when a deepening U.S. recession could have promised a weaker spot pound, the trader reactions proposed in the present study seem to be a better explanation.

rates in the United Kingdom are already substantially above those in the United States when a further increase in U.K. rates is being considered, since that excess would imply the existence of a substantial forward discount on sterling.)

Nonsterling Trade

It is clear that this fraction of one eighth can be safely applied to all commercial transactions directly between the two countries concerned. But bilateral trade between money-market countries is usually a small fraction of their total trade. Only one sixth of total U.S. import and export trade has been with the United Kingdom (and the rest of the sterling area). It is important, therefore, to determine how much of arbitragers' desired forward transactions may be absorbed by trade with third countries. When U.K. interest rates rise and the forward pound is made to depreciate by, say, 1 percent, consistency requires that the *sum* of the forward pound's depreciation in terms of francs and the forward franc's depreciation in terms of dollars total the same 1 percent. In a first approximation, each will depreciate by $\frac{1}{2}$ percent if the slopes of the two bilateral D_{trad} curves ($£/F$ and $F/\$$) are equal. In that case, the amount of forward cover made available for arbitragers through this trilateral channel is that associated with a $\frac{1}{2}$ percent change in forward rates, rather than a 1 percent change: those conducting the trade between the United States and France will buy only the extra amount of forward francs which the $\frac{1}{2}$ percent depreciation of the forward franc relative to the dollar induces them to buy, and those conducting trade between France and the United Kingdom will buy only that extra amount of forward pounds which is made desirable by the $\frac{1}{2}$ percent depreciation of the pound relative to the franc. (Since the two D_{trad} curves were assumed to have equal slopes, it follows that arbitragers desiring to sell pounds forward for forward dollars are enabled to sell approximately the same gold-value amounts of forward pounds in exchange for forward francs as they sell forward francs in exchange for the forward dollars they seek.) If, to simplify further, the slope of the U.S.-U.K. D_{trad} curve were the same as the other two, it would follow that half as much cover for arbitrage transfers would be obtained through the indirect, trilateral channel as through the direct channel of U.S.-U.K. trade. (Only one third as much could be obtained through quadrilateral channels if these were used.) A full description of the multilateral mechanism would go beyond the scope of this paper.[6]

---

[6] Some of the relevant factors are the following: The slope of the other bilateral D_{trad} curves may be raised above that of the U.K.-U.S. curve because of less well organized forward exchange markets; a 3 percent permitted range of variation for the spot exchange rates between European currencies (more, where Switzerland is involved) in contrast to the $1\frac{1}{2}$ percent range for rates against the dollar (see dis-

Where depreciations of the forward exchange values of several currencies are involved, the probability is created that some forward currency will be pushed close to its lower gold point. In that situation, the possibilities for arbitrage provided by a dollar of trilateral trade would be almost as large as those created per dollar of direct U.K.-U.S. trade. At the extreme, if, before the rise in U.K. interest rates, the forward franc was already at its lower limit in terms of the dollar, the speculative demand for forward exchange (described above as infinitely elastic when the forward rate was at the lower gold point) would prevent any further depreciation of the forward rate, and all the assumed 1 percent forward depreciation would be concentrated in just one exchange market—on the $£/F$ rate. U.S. trade with France would therefore provide just as much cover for funds placed in London as U.S. trade with the United Kingdom.

Because of this consideration, it will be assumed for illustration that each dollar of U.S. trade with nonsterling countries can provide cover for one half to three fourths as much arbitrage as does a dollar of U.S. trade directly with the United Kingdom. If it is assumed that the average of U.S. commercial export and import trade with the sterling area is about $3 billion and the corresponding figure for trade with the rest of the world is, perhaps, $15 billion, then the $18 billion total of U.S. commercial exports is equivalent, for present purposes, to $10½–14¼ billion of exports to the sterling area. On the assumption that the arbitrage movement can be as much as one eighth of such exports when short-term interest rates in the United Kingdom rise 1⅓ percentage points above U.S. rates, it follows that scope exists for the transfer within a few months of $1.3–1.8 billion of covered funds from the United States to the United Kingdom.

The significance of this amount of capital outflow may be increased by the presence of an accompanying outflow of *un*covered medium-term funds. If there is confidence in the spot exchange parities, such outflows could occur, for an exchange loss of even 1 percent on uncovered arbitrage funds

cussion of widening the spread between the gold points below); and less confidence in the maintenance of the exchange parities of such countries.

The opportunity for covered transfer from the United States to the United Kingdom is further reduced where there are arbitrage funds in France that also will be attracted to the United Kingdom. If the associated sales of forward pounds in exchange for francs proved sufficient to account for a ¾ percent depreciation of the forward $£/F$ rate, only ¼ percent more would have been left for the use of the arbitragers who wanted to leave New York; and, as above, this would have to be divided between the two bilateral forward markets. Hence, the trilateral channel would provide cover for only a little over one fourth as much arbitrage as the 1 percent depreciation of the forward $£/\$$ rate would provide through the direct, bilateral channel.

A factor which may increase the scope for trilateral arbitrage is central bank purchases of home forward currency to limit the severity of its depreciation.

would no more than neutralize the advantage of a 1 percentage point higher interest yield on one-year foreign securities.

MEASURES FOR RESTRAINING INTEREST ARBITRAGE TRANSFERS

Since 1958, international movements of short-term funds searching for maximum interest yields have once more become a problem for countries with active money markets, and the question arises whether drastic measures will be needed to limit capital transfers. The fact that very large proportions of the capital transfers are dependent on forward cover suggests the possibility of limiting these capital movements by measures much less drastic than either changes in domestic interest rates not required by internal conditions, or exchange control.

Central Bank Participation in the Forward Market

A generation ago, Keynes proposed official intervention in the forward market in order to adjust interest rates in accord with internal requirements, free from the counteracting influence of covered interest arbitrage. For example, in conditions like those represented in Diagram 2, the United States could have prevented the outflow of covered funds responding to higher short-term interest rates abroad by selling enough forward sterling to force it to a ⅓ percent discount below the spot rate. This would have meant the sale of forward sterling equal to the amount that would otherwise have been sold by arbitragers (*od* in Diagram 2) plus an additional amount necessary to satisfy the enlargement of traders' demand for forward sterling which the cheapened price would elicit (*de*).[7]

If the country thus intervening in the forward market had a strong exchange position or expected its position to strengthen, the incurring of such large forward exchange liabilities by the central bank would create no problem. If, however, the main reason for resisting an outflow of capital was that it might endanger the country's exchange position, the advantages of such intervention are more doubtful. By restraining arbitragers from buying the foreign currency spot, the intervention does, it is true, conserve official exchange reserves (*od* in Diagram 2), but it does so at the expense of rais-

---

[7] The cheapening of the forward price of pounds may cause some diversion from the spot to the forward market of speculation that would occur in any case; but this can be disregarded because it would merely substitute a rise in short-term official liabilities for a fall in official reserves. If the cheapening goes far enough to bring the pound close to its lower gold point, it will also cause the speculative purchases of forward pounds described earlier, and purchases of that kind should be taken into consideration.

ing official short-term foreign exchange liabilities by a larger amount ($od + de$).[8]

The debate on the merits of prolonged intervention in the forward market will not be resumed here.[9] It is appropriate at this point only to show how the picture is altered by the new factor of traders' enhanced sensitivity to forward rate movements. The foregoing analysis suggests that the potential covered interest arbitrage movements are much larger than has been commonly supposed, so that the need for deterrents is greater; but where the adequacy of reserves is the motive for intervention, the cost of the deterrent is also greater than has been hitherto believed. If the D_{trad} curve of Diagram 2 were the much steeper one previously supposed to exist, the distance de would be much smaller, i.e., the excess of the immediate rise in official short-term (forward) liabilities over the saving in official exchange holdings would be smaller. Insofar as the weakening of the official "net" foreign exchange position is considered as weighing against official intervention in the forward market, then the foregoing demonstration of increased flexibility in traders' use of the market weakens the case for official intervention. In one sense, this demonstration implies a reduced *need* for intervention. This is so where the motive for intervening is fear that wide movements in the forward rate will elicit destabilizing speculation on the

[8] It should be noted that the creation of extra forward contracts with traders merely formalizes a part of the authorities' existing obligation to provide importers with foreign exchange in three months' time; importers merely arrange now to purchase foreign exchange in three months' time that they would otherwise have had to purchase in three months without prearrangement. From this consideration, the additional short-term liabilities can be considered as neutralizing a much smaller amount of foreign exchange assets.

[9] Two new viewpoints on that question may be of interest. Einzig argues that prolonged official efforts to hold down the premium on forward foreign exchange when the home currency position is weak are undesirable because they could require the central bank to assume a volume of forward liabilities larger than its gold and exchange holdings. That excess would be of no concern (psychological factors aside) insofar as the buyers of forward exchange lacked surplus liquid assets and therefore would be unable to hold abroad the exchange acquired when the contract matured. (If they did hold liquid funds, they would presumably acquire spot exchange if forward exchange remained expensive.) However, he finds that foreign-owned domestic companies are an important special case; they would not buy spot exchange to protect themselves against a possible devaluation but would buy large amounts of forward exchange, provided that the premium paid was not too high. They could do so, even though illiquid, because the companies' inventories and other assets could be liquidated if it became necessary to provide local currency to carry through the forward contract. (See Paul Einzig, "Some Recent Developments in Official Forward Exchange Operations," *The Economic Journal*, Vol. LXXIII, June 1963, pp. 248–50, 252–53.)

But the only condition under which they would want to restrict their domestic operations to gain funds for financing the acquisition of foreign balances would be when the central bank was forced to *stop* holding down the premium on forward exchange at a moment when devaluation seemed likely. And for even that situation to be relevant, it must be assumed that the foreign-owned firms would not have become interested in holding spot foreign exchange at the expense of their regular business

exchanges. The flatter D_{trad} curve implies a narrower range of variation for the forward rate and hence less risk of destabilizing speculaltion.

Aside from their effects on the exchange reserves, covered arbitrage movements may be deemed undesirable because of their effects on internal money markets and on money supply conditions. This should not be an important problem for the United Kingdom, the United States, or countries that have equivalent means of "sterilizing" gold inflows and outflows by changing the supply of Treasury bills, etc. In the money markets of other countries, however, short-term capital movements may be disruptive. For such countries, the demonstration that these movements can be larger than previously supposed strengthens the case for official intervention.

Widening the Spread between Upper and Lower Intervention Points

A widening of the "spread" between the gold points has sometimes been proposed as a means of discouraging speculative capital movements, if doubts develop about stability of the exchange rate. This device also has advantages with respect to the nonspeculative movements of covered arbitrage funds. The means by which the widened spread reduces the scope for arbitrage transfers that reflect changes in interest rate differentials is illustrated by Diagram 1. The maximum change in traders' net use of forward cover occurs when the price of forward sterling changes by the full distance between the lower and upper gold points, $2.78 and $2.82, respectively. If the range between these were doubled (the lower and upper points being $2.76 and $2.84), the same change in traders' net use of cover would de-

---

operations except for having been first drawn into it by the possibility of speculating cheaply in the forward market.

The case for prolonged official sales of forward exchange seems likely to survive this criticism.

Another criticism of prolonged official intervention in the forward market (Jerome L. Stein. "The Rationality of Official Intervention in the Forward Exchange Market," *The Quarterly Journal of Economics,* Vol. LXXVII, May 1963, pp. 312–16) can be interpreted as merely a warning to the confused central bank that would want to attract short-term capital by selling the *home* currency forward, when the (annual rate of) forward discount on the home currency was already smaller than the excess interest yield obtainable on domestic Treasury bills; such sales would, of course, increase the discount on the home currency and thereby discourage the movement of short-term funds into the country. Bent Hansen objected to that form of prolonged official participation which would seek successive *additions* to the stock of arbitrage funds held in a low-interest-rate country which was experiencing persisting current-account deficits. Once the domestic arbitrage funds held abroad and the easily attractable foreign funds were attracted, the remaining supply would be inelastic, and further transfers could be secured only by very large additional official sales of forward exchange (Bent Hansen, "Interest and Foreign Exchange Policy," *Skandinaviska Banken Quarterly Review,* Vol. 39, October 1958, p. 121). It is possible that the recent rapid growth of the stock of arbitrageable funds has greatly reduced the importance of this objection.

velop only over twice as great a movement in the forward rate. Consequently, the slope of the traders' net demand curve would also be doubled, and a given change in the forward discount would provide half as much opportunity for covered interest arbitrage. If the slope of the D_{trad} curve of Diagram 2 is doubled, but the zero point (c) unchanged, then (as a first approximation) the capital movement will be cut almost in half: the steeper D_{trad} curve will intersect the S_{arb} curve a little to the right of $\frac{1}{2}$ *od*. If the capital movement had already taken place, widening the spread would cause a return flow to the United States of almost $\frac{1}{2}$ *od*.[10] (This analysis may require some qualification to allow for the effect, noted earlier, of associated movements of the current *spot rate*.)

Widening the Spread between de facto Intervention Points

Permitting the spot exchange rate to rise close to its present upper limit of $2.82 should greatly reduce the possibilities for covered arbitrage in the United Kingdom. As described above in the interpretation of the diagrams, the higher the absolute level of the forward pound that is associated with any given forward discount, the smaller is traders' demand for forward pounds. At a forward rate as high as $2.81, the proximity to the upper gold point would become a matter of interest even to those traders who rely chiefly on the size of the forward discount when deciding on how much forward cover to use. They might find the forward pound cheap at a 1 cent discount below the spot pound; but the spot pound itself would tend to seem abnormally high; and, when measured against a more likely figure for the spot pound three months hence, the forward price of $2.81 would tend to seem to be no discount at all. Therefore, when the spot pound had risen to $2.82, the D_{trad} curve for a forward rate of $2.81 would probably be closer to the negative value of Diagram 1 than to the positive value shown in Diagram 2 for the equivalent discount (one U.S. cent, or $1\frac{1}{3}$ percent, annual interest-rate basis). At the least, it can be assumed that trader demand for forward sterling would be very small.

Thus it is probable that permitting the pound to appreciate close to its upper gold point ($2.82) would create a major deterrent to covered short-

---

[10] The zero point could move in either direction. It is actually the two curves underlying the D_{trad} curve, D_m and S_x, which undergo the doubling of slopes. These curves can be conceived of as remaining *un*changed at a point midway between the gold points, with the steepening of slopes taking the form of a rotation around each midpoint. If the two curves intersect at that level (D_{trad} = zero at $2.80), the zero point on D_{trad} does not shift. But if the intersection point, and c, are above $2.80 (as when imports are larger than exports), widening the spread will *raise* the intersection point and c; that means that the part of the D_{trad} curve lying above $2.80 is shifted to the right. If the forward rate is above $2.80, the widening of the spread causes funds to move *from* New York to London; in the more likely case of a forward rate not much below $2.80, it would cause only a small movement to New York.

term capital movements. This procedure would have the advantage of avoiding the problems of a widened official spread, and would probably also be a greater deterrent to capital movements.

De facto, the United Kingdom has intervened at a spot rate of about $2.81, expanding and contracting the official gold and dollar reserves by large amounts while the rate was at that level. (Under severe pressure, it has permitted the pound to drop to as low a rate as $2.79.) This behavior suggests a desire to keep the spot rate within one cent of par where possible, and hence a reluctance to widen either the *de facto* or the official intervention points. If covered interest arbitrage movements should constitute a serious problem, the merits of a widened *de facto* range of variation within the existing gold points might be found to outweigh its disadvantages.

ADDITIONAL READINGS

Aliber, Robert Z., "Counter-Speculation and the Forward Exchange Market," *Journal of Political Economy*, December, 1962, pp. 609–613.

Auten, John H., "Counter-Speculation and the Forward Exchange Market," *Journal of Political Economy*, February, 1961, pp. 49–55.

———, "Foreign Exchange Rates and Interest Rate Differentials," *Journal of Finance*, March, 1963, pp. 11–19.

———, "Monetary Policy and the Forward Exchange Market," *Journal of Finance*, December, 1961, pp. 546–558.

Brehmer, Ekhard, "Official Forward Exchange Operations," *IMF Staff Papers*, November, 1964, pp. 389–412.

Coombs, Charles A., "Treasury and Federal Reserve Foreign Exchange Operations," *Federal Reserve Bank of New York Monthly Review*, September, 1964, pp. 162–172.

Cutilli, Bruno, "The Role of Commercial Banks in Foreign Exchange Speculation," *Banca Nazionale del Lavoro Quarterly Review*, June, 1963, pp. 216–231.

Einzig, Paul, "The Relation Between the Practice and Theory of Forward Exchange," *Banca Nazionale del Lavoro Quarterly Review*, September, 1962, pp. 227–239.

Feavearyear, Sir Albert, *The Pound Sterling*, London: Oxford University Press, 1963.

Goldstein, Henry, "Counter-Speculation and the Forward Exchange Market," *Journal of Political Economy*, October, 1963, pp. 494–500.

Gray, H. Peter, "The Marginal Cost of Hot Money," *Journal of Political Economy*, April, 1964, pp. 189–192.

Grubel, Herbert G., "A Neglected Aspect of Forward Exchange Theory and Policy," *Journal of Finance*, September, 1963, pp. 537–548.

Hawtrey, R. G., *The Pound at Home and Abroad*, London: Longmans, 1961.

Holmes, Alan R., and Schott, Francis H., *The New York Foreign Exchange Market*, Federal Reserve Bank of New York, 1965.

"How the U.S. Plays Its Hand in Foreign Exchange," *Morgan Guarantee Survey*, December, 1962, pp. 3–12.

McMillan, Claude, "The Swap as a Hedge in Foreign Exchange," *California Management Review,* Summer, 1962, pp. 57–65.

Stein, Jerome L., "The Optimum Foreign Exchange Market," *The American Economic Review,* June, 1963, pp. 384–402.

Tyng, Ed., "Trading Billions in Foreign Exchange," *Burroughs Clearing House,* June, 1962, pp. 40–41.

chapter **2**
Central Banking:
The Exercise of Monetary Policy

The art or practice of central banking seems, at first, to be somewhat distant from the interests of the international businessman. It quickly becomes apparent, however, that as central banks are the keepers of countries' foreign exchange reserves, they soon touch upon vital areas of interest. Relating to the U.S. balance of payments, the decision of whether or not to turn dollars in to the U.S. government for gold immediately affects the U.S. gold outflow and the resultant governmental policies, as discussed in the following chapter. The international monetary system, as a whole, has been kept in operation through the close cooperation of central banks, as will be seen in Chapter 4. Also, where a country is having major balance of payments problems, the operations of the exchange controls, as described in Chapter 5, are in the hands of the central bank. The two readings in this chapter, however, are not concerned with the above mentioned facets of central banking. The subject here, is the possible effects of central bank policy on a multinational corporation in its operations *within* foreign countries. To what extent do the monetary policies of a country and the manner in which they are administered, affect the operations of a subsidiary?

The central bank discount rate, and its role in affecting the general level of interest rates, is only the beginning of the impingement of central bank policy. It is, certainly, of primary concern among the industrial countries as a major determinant of the flow of funds between countries. It also affects the cost of borrowed capital within countries, though less so in the underdeveloped countries where there is often little relationship between the central bank discount rate, the "legal" interest rate, and the cost of borrowed money.

Hence, in an underdeveloped country, it is the central bank's credit policies rather than its discount rate which is of more importance to an operating subsidiary. These credit policies may affect the general level of credit, as a means of attempting to control inflation. Or, they may be very selective, to encourage some industries and discourage others, as a means of achieving a desired direction in economic development.

The international businessman should understand why central banks institute different policies, so as to be able to predict them and take prior preventive measures (if possible). He should also understand how the central bank administers these monetary and credit policies, if he is to operate under and around them.

The first paper in this chapter discusses the policies of central banks, the institutional framework within which they operate, and the effects of such policies, depending upon the power of the individual bank and the level of advancement of the economy in which it is operating. The second paper illustrates the newness of most of the world's central banks, and the variety of relationships between central banks and governments as well as between central banks and the financial communities which they control or attempt to control.

FOREIGN CENTRAL BANKING: THE INSTRUMENTS OF MONETARY POLICY*

I. INTRODUCTION

By now almost every country in the free world has turned to monetary and credit control to help safeguard and promote its economic health. In the first postwar years such active reliance on monetary management had been rare indeed, but after the outbreak of the Korean conflict in 1950 central banking came to the fore in more and more foreign countries, and gradually the revival of credit policy became world-wide. In the process, the older monetary instruments have been altered and new ones developed, thus changing the outward appearance of central banking but not its basic concepts.

In the immediate postwar years these very concepts were questioned, and most foreign countries kept central banking relegated to, at best, a minor subsidiary role in overall economic policy. This subordination of monetary policy reflected the ideological, economic, and theoretical climates then current, which combined to create a strong hostility to general credit controls. However, although inflation continued to be the dominant problem, other circumstances gradually changed. The enthusiasm for centralized planning and detailed controls waned, the destruction and dislocation of the war were overcome, the war-inherited surplus liquidity largely disappeared, and the combination of fiscal policy and direct controls was found wanting. On the theoretical side, a reassessment of the ideas of the 1930's restored to monetary policy a considerable share of its earlier and perhaps then exaggerated importance.

Monetary and credit policy operates specifically through five interrelated factors: the availability of credit relative to demand, the volume of money, the cost of borrowing, the prices of capital assets, and the general liquidity of the economy. Naturally enough, the economic and financial structure of a country will be crucial in determining the importance of these factors, and thus the scope for effective monetary control. A barter economy obviously will not lend itself to such influences. In an economy where the market sector is still fairly narrow and nonmonetary transactions are

* Excerpted from a monograph, with the same title, by Peter G. Fousek, Federal Reserve Bank of New York, New York, 1957.

still widespread, the reach of monetary policy will necessarily be limited. Many of the less developed economies, moreover, are so greatly dependent on foreign trade that monetary fluctuations are often externally induced and the field for domestic monetary measures is correspondingly restricted. In addition, some of these economies may at times be undergoing such a chronic and cumulative inflation that other measures may have to be taken to eliminate the basic causes of the disequilibrium before credit controls although at all times necessary, can play their full part.

Even when a country is well advanced along the road of economic development, its financial structure still may not easily lend itself to effective monetary management. The banking system itself may not be open to the influence of central bank operations, since it may be well supplied with liquid reserves or may be in a position to draw quickly and inexpensively on funds in more developed foreign centers. Other financial institutions, for their part, may be rather rudimentary, may serve purely local needs, and may be only very loosely integrated. Moreover, a country's banking system and other financial institutions may be highly developed, but its organized money and capital markets may still be very thin. Such institutional impediments to monetary policy are present in most foreign countries, and although they are being gradually overcome their existence has speeded the adoption of new techniques by most central banks abroad.

This development of new techniques has greatly changed the role of the discount rate. In the days when central banking was confined to a few countries with well-developed and closely connected financial systems, the discount rate was *the* instrument of credit control. Today it is one of several, and discount rate changes have come in many countries to be used mainly to reinforce other monetary measures. Furthermore, a new dimension has been added to discount policy in the form of more or less direct limitations on the availability of central bank credit. At the same time, open market operations have become recognized as ideally the most effective monetary policy tool. In most foreign countries, it is true, they cannot be used in the same effective manner as in the United States primarily because of the absence of developed money and capital markets. But such operations are so flexible and powerful an instrument for influencing bank reserve positions, and thus the availability of bank credit and the liquidity of the whole economy, that many foreign countries are striving to create the market conditions which will make them possible; moreover, they are modifying the traditional operating techniques in order to obtain some of the benefits of open market policy even while their financial markets remain relatively thin. Changes in commercial bank cash reserve requirements, are also a powerful tool for tightening or easing bank reserve positions, but they are a much blunter instrument than open market policy. Nevertheless, their use abroad has greatly increased, and in a number of countries they are regarded as a substitute for open market operations; in some countries, in fact, they have become the main weapon of monetary policy.

These then are the three principal central banking instruments, but foreign countries have also developed new tools to overcome the weaknesses that these instruments exhibit in their institutional structures. Certain countries have established special reserve requirements, often called minimum liquidity ratios, which in addition to cash include government securities among the reserve-eligible assets and thus immobilize a portion of commercial bank government securities portfolios. These minimum ratios have been used both to meet special situations, such as war-inherited excess liquidity, and to strengthen the older credit control weapons. Other control devices that have a direct impact on the volume of bank loans or on particular bank operations—as opposed to the indirect and generalized effect of the traditional tools—have ranged from informal suggestions by the authorities that commercial banks restrain their lending to formal loan ceilings and other detailed administrative instructions covering bank assets and liabilities.

In addition to using quantitative methods to control the overall amount of bank credit, foreign countries have relied on selective controls more extensively than has this country in order both to channel funds into preferred fields and to restrict the extension of credit for particular purposes. This difference is partly explained by the difficulty of curbing credit expansion with the traditional instruments in the institutional and economic setting of those countries; it is also due to the inadequacies of their financial structures which as yet are not fully able by themselves to distribute credit into the most economic uses.

But whatever the institutional setting, no country uses an individual credit control instrument in isolation. Obviously, to put pressure on bank reserves through central bank open market sales, and at the same time permit free access to the "discount window" at a rate excessively below market rates, would achieve little. Thus, in the United States, open market operations—the primary instrument—are supplemented by discount policy and reserve requirement policy. Such a distribution of emphasis on the various central bank instruments, however, is only rarely possible abroad. Instead, in some of the financially more developed countries, open market operations serve in a subordinate manner to reinforce discount policy and reserve requirement changes. In others, discount rate changes are combined with direct restrictions on access to the "discount window" and with minimum liquidity ratios. Among the financially less developed countries, variations in reserve requirements are sometimes buttressed by ceilings on commercial bank borrowing at the central bank or by differential discount rates; in a few cases, the impact of reserve requirement changes on bank reserves may at times be supplemented by transfers of Treasury deposits between the central bank and the commercial banks. Elsewhere, discount policy in all its ramifications is used in conjunction with special devices such as import-predeposit requirements and bank-portfolio ceilings. Clearly, the variations are almost innumerable and depend, not only on a country's economic and financial structure, but also on the other economic policies in force and on the urgency of the problems to be solved.

In the last few years, however, a definite movement toward a primary reliance on the general quantitative instruments has been discernible among the central banks of the financially more developed countries abroad. In the financially less developed countries, direct and selective credit controls often still predominate, but even there the emphasis on general quantitative controls is increasing.

This text is devoted to a description of the development of central banking techniques abroad during the postwar period through October 1957. It is not intended as an evaluation of the results of monetary policy in the various foreign countries. This much, nevertheless, may here be stressed: central banking cannot carry by itself the burden of needed economic readjustments. Many foreign countries have conducted monetary and credit policies in a determined and timely manner; those, however, that have done so in conjunction with appropriate budget and debt management policies have succeeded best in steering their economies along the path of balanced expansion.

II. Discount Policies and Techniques

Discount rate changes have been in the forefront of the postwar revival of monetary policy abroad. These changes in the cost of credit supplied by central banks to commercial banks and other borrowers have had a threefold significance. First, they have reflected the central bank's appraisal of economic trends; secondly, they have provided evidence of official determination to resist inflationary or deflationary pressures, expressed both internally and through foreign exchange difficulties; and, thirdly, they have served to influence—generally together with other monetary policy changes—the cost and availability of credit.

Although discount policy was the first important method of credit control to be developed, its importance tended to wither away during the 1930's, mainly because of the severe falling-off in the demand for capital and credit during the depression years, and the resulting accumulation of surplus reserves by the commercial banks which accordingly had no need to borrow from their central banks. Since World War II, however, discount policy has re-emerged as a major instrument of credit control, although without its former pre-eminence and considerably changed in form. With the development of other central banking tools, it has come to be used mainly in conjunction with other instruments; and, as central banking has spread, it has been adapted to environments differing considerably from those where it was first instituted. Even in countries with developed financial systems, its scope and application have been materially altered.

Access to Central Bank Credit

Discount policy may conveniently be defined as the varying of the terms, and of the conditions in the broadest sense, under which the market may have temporary access to central bank credit through discounts of selected short-term assets or through secured advances. It is governed by two basic and sometimes conflicting functions of central banks: the obligation to act as lenders of last resort, and the duty to regulate the total volume of commercial bank credit.

During the early stages of discount policy, the European central banks, largely following the example of the Bank of England, gradually adopted relatively simple rules to guide their operations in the field. However, with the passage of time, these rules have become more elaborate and both the kinds of borrowers and the forms of central bank credit have changed substantially.

Although many of the older central banks, such as the Bank of France, are still permitted to lend to nonbank as well as bank borrowers, their lending to the nonbank public is generally much less than in the past; moreover, the charters of the newer central banks, such as the Central Bank of the Philippines, have in most cases prohibited accommodation to the nonbank public, except in some areas where commercial banking facilities were inadequate. The principle has thus become increasingly accepted that central banks should not, in general, engage in ordinary commercial banking and should confine such transactions to special emergency periods and circumstances. When a central bank has a large commercial banking business, the resulting transactions have often conflicted with its functions as the bankers' bank and the controller of credit. In some countries central banks have found it difficult to exercise ·self-restraint in such operations, particularly since they are not confronted with the problem of liquidity to the same extent as are commercial banks. Moreover, the cooperation of commercial banks, which is so important for the central bank's success, has sometimes been difficult to obtain when the central bank was competing with them.

In addition to commercial banks, official development-credit institutions have become sizable borrowers at the central banks in a number of Asian and Latin American countries. Furthermore, government securities dealers or discount houses borrow, in the form of advances or of repurchase agreements, from the central banks in some countries that have relatively developed money markets; in the United Kingdom, indeed, it is the discount houses and not the commercial banks that borrow at the Bank of England, and the commercial banks instead of borrowing from it rely on reducing their call loans to the discount houses to meet short-term drains in their cash reserves.

The strict rules that used to limit the eligibility of bills for discounting and of securities as collateral for advances, as well as the maximum period of such advances, have by now been considerably relaxed, as it has increasingly come to be realized that eligibility rules as such are not a protection against the overexpansion of credit. Most foreign countries no longer limit central bank discounts to the commercial bill of exchange in the strict sense of the term, but permit the discounting of a wide variety of other paper. Similarly, the admissible collateral for central bank advances now often includes not only all types of government securities but various other securities as well. While central bank advances continue to be of short maturity in a number of countries, the maximum legal maturity period of both discounts and advances has in most countries been increased from the three months that used to be the rule to as much as one year in the case of ordinary borrowing. For special purposes, such as agriculture, industrial development, housing construction, and exports, longer periods than for ordinary borrowing are permitted in a number of countries, primarily those with less developed financial systems. Moreover, some of the newer central banks are legally empowered, in emergency circumstances, to extend the maturity of their credit operations and to lend against practically any collateral.

The tendency of commercial banks in a great many countries to seek central bank accommodation in the form of short-term advances against collateral rather than discounts has pushed the earlier discount-eligibility rules still further into the background. More than one half of the foreign central banks, for which such data are available, now lend a greater amount in the form of advances than of discounts. This trend reflects primarily the decreased importance of the commercial bill of exchange in many countries and has been facilitated by the enlarged commercial bank holdings of government securities, which provide ready collateral for central bank lending. Advances have tended to become the preferred method of borrowing also because the funds are frequently needed only for short periods and because this form of borrowing is more convenient.

Another major element of discount policy is the rate that the central bank applies to its discounts and advances. Under earlier central banking practices, the discount rate was the rate for the discounting of prime commercial bills, with a somewhat higher rate for advances against collateral; at times, however, some central banks also charged a higher rate for discounts of less acceptable paper. Today, in contrast, many central banks publish a schedule of numerous different rates for their discounts and advances.

At the moment, a single rate is in effect in only a few foreign countries, primarily Italy, New Zealand, and the United Kingdom. Several central banks (e.g., those in West Germany and Switzerland) have retained the early practice of having two main rates, with a rate on advances somewhat higher than the rate applicable to discounts. A few other central banks (e.g., in Austria and Denmark) set—besides the discount rate—several rates for advances, varying with the collateral.

About half of the foreign central banks maintain discount rate scales, with two or more rates according to the purpose of the loan; this practice is particularly prevalent in Asia and Latin America. The lower rates of these discount rate scales apply most often to discounts of agricultural paper, but frequently also to loans to official development-credit institutions and in some countries to discounts of, or loans against, Treasury bills. In addition, a number of central banks, as discussed below, charge rates higher than their basic rates when the borrowers exceed certain limits. It should also be noted that a few central banks do not charge interest on the basis of any published rates, but instead charge rates according to circumstances and the general state of the market. This is done in Sweden, where the central bank a few years ago discontinued publishing the rates on its lending to the banks; the bank has continued to publish the official discount rate, but this rate does not determine the cost of commercial bank borrowing from the central bank and is primarily an indicator of monetary policy. A similar practice exists in Australia, where the central bank actually has never published an official discount rate or any other rates for its loans to the banks.

The Discount Rate and the Cost of Credit

Discount policy seeks to affect both the cost and the availability of bank credit, and its influence depends in the first place on the extent of commercial bank borrowing from the central bank. In a number of countries (particularly Canada, Switzerland, and some countries in Asia and Latin America) commercial bank recourse to central bank credit is ordinarily very small. At the other extreme is a much larger group (notably Austria, Belgium, France, Japan, and a number of Latin American countries) where the commercial banks' borrowing from the central bank generally exceeds their deposits at the central bank, often by several times, and is sometimes as large as one third of the total commercial bank loans to the private sector of the economy. This great variation in commercial bank recourse to central bank credit is due to a number of factors. In certain countries, notably France, it has been the custom for the central bank to rediscount commercial paper for the commercial banks at any time, and not merely when the banks have exhausted all other sources for replenishing their funds; there may, however, be credit "lines" for individual banks limiting the amounts they can borrow without penalty. In another group of countries, the commercial banks have generally found little need to borrow from the central bank because during most of the postwar period they remained very liquid as a result of World War II finance (as in the Netherlands) or of balance of payments surpluses (as in Switzerland). In some of the less developed countries, the commercial banks tend to avoid recourse to the central bank except in extraordinary circumstances, since they prefer to operate with ample reserves.

In countries where commercial bank recourse to central bank credit is usually large, the direct influence of the discount rate tends to be great both on market yields and on the rates charged by the commercial banks. Even in those countries where such recourse is generally small, however, discount rate changes may have wide repercussions. In the first place, money market rates react quickly in a market that works on a narrow margin and from time to time depends on central bank accommodation. In addition, in foreign countries where effective open market operations are possible or where variations in commercial bank cash reserve requirements are an available tool of monetary policy, the central bank can affect the cost of commercial bank credit by bringing about changes in the amount that the commercial banks have to borrow and by varying the rate that it charges for its accommodation.

In many foreign countries, moreover, the influence of the discount rate on the cost of credit does not depend on direct market effects alone. The discount rate has a considerable psychological importance, since discount rate changes are often an indication of a general interest rate movement expected or desired by the central bank. As a result, in a number of foreign countries, a more or less fixed relationship has been established between the discount rate and commercial bank interest rates and also various other rates. The foremost instance of this practice is in the United Kingdom, where there is a fixed margin, which is not necessarily the same for all levels of the discount rate, between this rate and the rates charged by the commercial banks on their advances and call loans, as well as the rates paid on their deposits. Similar arrangements, even though less precise, exist in most other European countries and in the Union of South Africa. In other countries where such practices have not developed, the tendency nevertheless has been for commercial bank lending rates to be adjusted in line with changes in the discount rate. Moreover, many of the newer central banks in Asia and in Latin America and some central banks elsewhere have authority to control commercial bank rates directly by imposing maximum rates, and thus can in effect change these rates along with the discount rate;

however, many of these countries have made relatively little use of such powers.

Discounting and the Availability of Credit

The banking system, by borrowing from the central bank and thus adding to its reserves, can offset the central bank's attempts to limit the reserve base in order to restrain the availability of credit. Where there is a traditional reluctance on the part of the commercial banks to remain indebted to the central bank for long, this problem is greatly reduced. But such a tradition is now rather rare outside the United States, with the result that various ways have been devised to strengthen the central bank's control over the amount of its discounts and advances.

Under the earlier central banking tradition as it evolved in the United Kingdom, the discount rate was set high enough to be a "penalty rate," and as such tended to discourage borrowing from the central bank. Originally, a penalty rate was defined as a rate higher than the rate charged on the commercial paper presented for rediscount. However, with the decline in the importance of commercial paper this definition ceased to have general applicability. At present the consensus seems to be that a discount rate is a penalty rate when it is above the rate on the pivotal assets through which the commercial banks adjust their portfolios; these are the assets (most often Treasury bills, but in some countries call loans to government securities dealers) that the banks would sell first during periods of reserve pressure. In this sense, there are only a few foreign central banks today whose discount rate can be called a penalty rate. In the United Kingdom the discount rate is maintained at a penalty level as a matter of general, long-standing policy. In Canada it is kept so through a special arrangement that went into effect in November 1956, when the Bank of Canada announced that thenceforth until further notice its minimum lending rate would be set each week at $\frac{1}{4}$ percent above the average treasury bill tender rate. The bank, after explaining that this was the simplest method of ensuring that its rate would always be a penalty rate, stated that the new method was intended also to make it clear to the public that "interest rates are determined in the market by the interplay between the supply of, and the demand for, loanable funds." A somewhat similar arrangement exists in Finland, where the central bank charges the commercial banks rates that are at specified margins above the rates charged by the commercial banks themselves on the paper presented for rediscount. In New Zealand, the discount rate is at present also a penalty rate in this strict sense, since it exceeds by 2 percentage points the average rate of 5 percent that the commercial banks are at present allowed to charge on their loan operations.

Instead of applying penalty rates, many foreign countries have turned to other means of limiting the recourse of commercial banks to central bank credit. A number—including in recent years Belgium, Colombia, West Germany, the Netherlands, and Uruguay—have at times tightened the eligibility requirements for commercial paper presented for rediscount. In the Netherlands the central bank has warned the commercial banks that recourse to central bank credit cannot be considered a facility that can be made use of continuously, while in Switzerland the central bank has stated that, although it is always ready to meet the banks' short-term marginal requirements, it must refuse to supply them with funds for financing longer term transactions. Many other countries have endeavored to restrict the amount of commercial bank borrowing from the central bank in more direct ways. Thus, in some, among them Italy and the Philippines, the monetary authorities on occasion have declined to increase, or have actually cut back, their loans to the commercial banks. In Mexico, the central bank has been even more restrictive and has permitted the commercial banks to rediscount only in the event of a decline in deposits. Other countries, e.g., Denmark and Finland, have at times warned the commercial banks as a group that no further accommodation would be available to them if they continued their credit expansion. Many of the newer central banks (e.g., those in Guatemala and Korea) are actually empowered, or even are required, by statute to influence general credit conditions, when credit creation becomes excessively rapid, by declining to lend to the commercial banks regardless either of the eligibility of the paper submitted for discount or of the creditworthiness of the borrower.

Specific ceilings on commercial bank borrowing from the central bank have become increasingly common in recent years, and now exist in a number of countries, including Austria, Belgium, Colombia, Costa Rica, France, West Germany, Nicaragua, and Peru. These ceilings are often based on the commercial banks' capital funds, and usually exempt some categories of commercial bank borrowing from the central bank, since the authorities have not always found it possible to limit central bank lending rigidly. In France, for example, the discount ceiling does not apply to discounts of medium-term bills, such as export or construction bills, the outstanding volume of which is smaller than the volume of regular short-term bills and may be restricted in other ways. Similarly, in West Germany, the discount ceiling does not cover advances from the central bank, which are much less important and more costly than discounts; however, the ceiling is lowered by such short-term borrowing by banks abroad as does not serve the financing of imports or of transit trade of goods. In some of these countries, notably France and West Germany, the size of the discount ceilings has on occasion been changed in accordance with the requirements of monetary policy. In addition, in Chile, Colombia, Finland, France, Japan, and Peru, discount limits are or have been utilized, in conjunction with progressive discount rates that increase with the amount borrowed. In Chile, for example, the rate charged for commercial bank borrowing from the central bank rises to 11 percent, or almost double the basic rate, for borrowing in excess of 90 percent of a bank's capital and reserves but below 100 percent; for borrowing above 100 percent it equals the average rate of interest charged by the borrowing bank in its lending operations during the preceding month. In France, rediscounts above the primary ceiling are made at 2 percentage points above the basic rate, and rediscounts above the secondary ceiling at a still higher rate determined by the governor of the central bank. A different type of progressive rate has been employed in Pakistan, where the progression depended on the duration of the borrowing rather than on its amount.

In Canada, the central bank has instituted a special procedure that increases the penalty effect of the discount rate, which as noted above is set at a fixed amount above the Treasury bill rate. In the first place, each advance of the central bank to the commercial banks is made for a fixed period of seven days (the Bank of England similarly makes advances to the discount houses for a minimum period of seven days). Secondly, the central bank charges rates above its basic rate according to both the amount and the duration of the borrowing. Thus, higher rates are charged on a second advance to one bank in any calendar month, or on a renewal of an advance, or on an advance in excess of a certain amount specified for each bank.

Aside from using the discount instrument to influence the overall volume of credit, a number of foreign central banks, particularly in Latin America and Asia, have come to use it mainly as a tool of selective credit control, either by prescribing different criteria for rediscounts of different types of bills or by fixing rates that vary according to the purpose of the loan. By and large, however, the effectiveness of the selective use of the discount instrument is open to doubt, especially because a bank may borrow against one kind of paper but lend the proceeds to its customers against another kind.

The Revival of the Discount Rate Instrument

The postwar revival of the discount rate instrument abroad was slow at first, but gradually gathered momentum as more and more countries found monetary controls to be a vital part of anti-inflationary policies. By 1955, in fact, most European and British Commonwealth countries with well-developed monetary and banking systems had again turned to discount policy, and many were using this monetary tool quite emphatically. With the wider recourse to the discount rate instrument, these countries have tended to raise or lower their discount rates more or less at the same time, as may be

Chart 1
Central Bank Discount Rates in Selected Countries

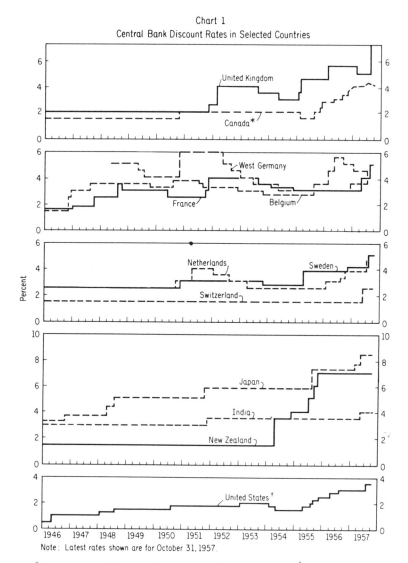

Note: Latest rates shown are for October 31, 1957.

*Since November 1, 1956 the Canadian rate has been fixed each Thursday at $\frac{1}{4}$ percent above the latest average tender rate for Treasury bills. From that date on, it is shown here at the end of each month.

† Federal Reserve Bank of New York discount rate. Preferential rate for advances secured by Government securities maturing or callable in one year or less in effect through April 24, 1946.

seen from Chart 1. While a few countries raised their rates in the immediate postwar years, the first general phase of discount rate increases lasted from mid-1950 through mid-1952; these increases were followed by declines which, in some countries that had raised their discount rates relatively early, began in the second half of 1951. The second upward movement started in mid-1954, became more pronounced after the Bank of England rate increases at the beginning of 1955, and was still continuing in the fall of 1957. During this period, it is true, there have also been four discount rate reductions—three in West Germany beginning in September 1956, and one in the United Kingdom in February 1957—but the United Kingdom raised its rate again in September 1957. Even though changes have generally been less numerous than during the pre-1914 period or even during the 1920's, there have been from January 1955 through October 1957 no less than forty-eight[1] increases in twenty countries with more developed financial systems (practically all the countries of Western Europe, several in the British Commonwealth, and Japan). While there have been relatively fewer rate changes than before the war, the magnitude of individual changes has remained about within the same range and has generally been greater than in the United States; discount rate increases of one percentage point have been quite common, and there have been some as large as two percentage points. As the monetary restraint policies began to take effect, rate increases became less frequent, dropping from nineteen in 1955 to sixteen in 1956 and to five in the first half of 1957. Subsequently, however, eight discount rate rises were announced during July–October 1957; this greater frequency of rate increases reflected both a strengthening of monetary restraint policies in countries that had resorted to tighter money later than others and a renewal of inflationary and exchange-reserve pressures elsewhere. In many of these countries, rates have reached the highest level since the early 1930's and in some cases have risen to all-time peaks.

In most countries with well-developed financial systems, moreover, discount rates have ceased to be mere symbols and have again become important monetary control instruments. This renewed effectiveness has been largely due to the absorption of the war-inherited excess liquidity of the banking systems through the postwar increase in production and prices.

Monetary policy measures, too, have reduced banking liquidity, thus making the banking systems more dependent on central bank credit and increasing the effectiveness of the discount rate. For example, special reserve requirements were established in Belgium in 1946, in Italy in 1947, and in France in 1948 to meet the postwar problem of exceptionally large bank holdings of government securities. In late 1948 West Germany, and in 1952 New Zealand, first resorted to increases in their cash reserve requirements. In Norway and Sweden reserve requirements were made effective in 1955; in addition, a more realistic pricing of long-term government bond issues helped bring about a tightening of capital market conditions. The funding

---

[1] This excludes discount rate increases in the United States, which are not under discussion here, as well as the weekly changes that have taken place in the Bank of Canada discount rate since November 1956 when its current method of setting the rate, as described above, went into effect.

of short-term government debt—the conversion of short-term into long-term debt—also was an important method of reducing bank liquidity in certain countries, notably the United Kingdom in 1951 and the Netherlands in 1954.

In many countries a more flexible use of open market operations, following upon the abandonment of rigid supports of government securities, also helped greatly to enhance the importance of the discount rate since it returned to the central bank a large measure of control over credit creation. When the Bank of England, for instance, raised its discount rate in November 1951 for the first time since 1939, signaling a return to monetary flexibility, the bank simultaneously ceased supporting Treasury bills at a fixed rate.

In addition, the improvement in the balance of payments positions of most countries since the war has led to a greater freedom for international capital movements, and short-term funds have again come to be attracted by interest rate differentials among the major financial centers. As a result, marked discount rate increases or decreases by leading to changes in market interest rates have at times been able, although to a much lesser extent than before the war, to exert an influence on the movement of short-term capital between countries, thus contributing to a reduction in foreign-exchange-reserve strains. In fact, several countries have in recent years made changes in official discount rates with the avowed purpose of correcting an undesirable flow of funds.

The movements in interest rates that accompanied the various policy changes in individual countries, and which tended increasingly to reflect the underlying supply and demand conditions, are shown for a number of countries in Charts 2 and 3.

Chart 2
Treasury Bill Rates in Selected Countries

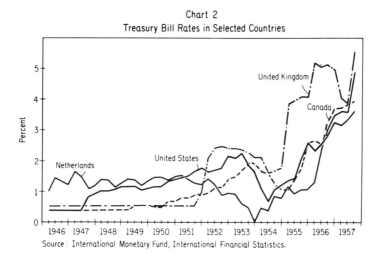

Source: International Monetary Fund, International Financial Statistics.

Chart 3
Long-Term Government Bond Yields in Selected Countries

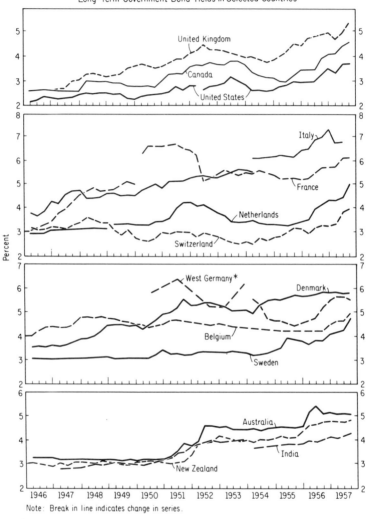

Note: Break in line indicates change in series.

*Yield of mortgage bonds of private banks.

Source: International Monetary Fund, International Financial Statistics.

The countries with less developed financial systems, on the other hand, have changed their discount rates rather infrequently. Monetary policy is necessarily less effective in these countries since a part, sometimes substantial, of their economies is still outside the money stream; in addition, the less developed state of their financial systems narrows the scope for discount policies and other quantitative monetary instruments. Moreover, in many of these countries, especially in Asia and the Middle East, the reserves of the commercial banks are usually so ample as to preclude the need for regular use of the central bank "discount window." Foreign-owned commercial banks operating in these countries generally prefer to replenish their reserves when necessary by borrowing abroad, either at their head offices or in the market. Where discount policy has frequently taken the form, not of simple discount rate moves, but rather of direct limitations on the amounts of central bank lending as well as of changes in selective discount rate scales.

The Present-Day Role of Discount Policy

The present-day economic setting imposes various limitations on the effectiveness of the discount rate weapon abroad. The higher income tax rates, the increased practice of financing investment by ploughing back profits, and the reduced importance of the commercial bill have injected additional impediments to the ready responsiveness of private demand for bank credit to interest rate changes. In certain countries, the growth of nationalized industries and other officially controlled enterprises has largely insulated major sectors of the economy against changes in the cost and availability of credit. Still another limitation on discount policy—although much less widespread than in the earlier postwar years—is the more than ample bank liquidity, which persists in various countries and results in central bank accommodation being little used and in the discount rate being out of touch with the market. Moreover, some foreign central banks have still not gained full control over the reserve base of the banking system, since they continue to allow free access to their credit facilities through a "back door" at a low rate (often by standing ready to purchase Treasury bills at a pegged rate) rather than through the "discount window." Furthermore, in many countries, the money and capital markets are not yet closely integrated, with the result that impulses imparted to short-term rates by discount rate changes are not necessarily reflected in long-term rates. Finally, international capital movements remain more restricted than before the war and less sensitive to interest rate changes, with the result that the impact of discount rate changes on the international flow of short-term capital is smaller, although it has been enlarged somewhat in the last few years.

Despite these and other obstacles to the efficient working of discount policy today, the discount instrument still has a significant role to play in influencing the cost and availability of credit. Particularly important are the question of timing and the relation of discount policy to other credit control tools. In recent years numerous foreign countries have resorted to discount rate adjustments at a relatively early stage and often at the first signs of change in economic conditions, rather than later under emergency conditions when their lateness would generally make them ineffective. Most countries, moreover, have effected discount rate changes, not in isolation, but in conjunction with other monetary policy measures. With the revival of active monetary policy, discount rate changes have in many foreign countries regained their powerful psychological influence. Traditional arrangements relating bank interest rates to the discount rate have been reestablished and have led to the almost immediate reaction of these rates to discount rate movements. As flexibility has gradually returned in the major money centers and the newer money markets have been broadened, changes in discount rates have tended to be transmitted fairly rapidly to other market rates. In some foreign countries discount policy has also come to be used, not only to influence interest rates, but also to influence directly, by such means as discount ceilings, the amount of commercial bank borrowing from the central bank. Even though it has lost its pre-eminence, simplicity, and directness, and is still rather subordinate in countries with less developed financial systems, the discount instrument remains an essential credit control tool.

III. Open Market Operations

Open market operations of some form are conducted by the central banks of most countries that have, or are developing, active money and capital markets. The nature and extent of such operations, and their relative importance among the tools of monetary control, vary widely. In the United States, open market operations—i.e., the purchase and sale of Government securities (and bankers' acceptances) as directed by the Open Market Committee of the Federal Reserve System—have become the chief instrument of credit control, providing a flexible means of influencing the volume of bank reserves and thereby helping to maintain appropriate credit conditions.[2] Outside the United States, however, open market operations are a full-fledged credit policy instrument in only a few countries, notably the United Kingdom and Canada. Elsewhere, such operations are generally limited in scope; they are not always undertaken at the central bank's initiative; they are in some instances conducted directly with banks or other investors; and they may be conducted in securities other than government obligations or bankers' acceptances. Nevertheless, although institutional difficulties are encountered in many foreign countries, open market operations are rapidly gaining in importance abroad.

---

[2] For a description of techniques in the United States, see Robert V. Roosa, *Federal Reserve Operations in the Money and Government Securities Markets,* Federal Reserve Bank of New York, July 1956.

Legal and Institutional Setting

Before the 1930's, only a few foreign central banks had statutory authority to conduct open market operations, but today practically all are empowered to deal in government and government-guaranteed securities. Many foreign central banks also have authority to purchase and sell bankers' acceptances and commercial bills. In a few countries, moreover, they can undertake operations in special mortage bonds (e.g., in Bolivia, El Salvador, and Norway), while in certain others they can operate in all nongovernment bonds (e.g., in Australia, Denmark, and Japan). Finally, a number of central banks, particularly in the financially less developed countries, have power to issue their own securities for monetary policy purposes.[3]

In many countries, however, the purchase of government securities by the central bank is circumscribed by legislation as to the total amount, the ways in which the purchases may be effected, and the maturity of the securities that may be purchased. Limits on central bank holdings of government securities, whether acquired in the market or directly from the government, sometimes are stipulated in absolute amounts (as in Belgium) or are related to the central bank's capital and/or demand liabilities (e.g., in Pakistan and Venezuela). Such provisions are generally designed to limit governmental recourse to central bank credit. For the same reason, the legislation of a number of countries prohibits direct purchases of securities from the government, while in Cuba the central bank is normally permitted to buy only government securities that have been outstanding for more than one year. Similarly, some central bank laws provide, in effect, that open market operations may not be carried out to help finance government deficits, and specify that such operations may take place only in order to "regulate the money market" (e.g., in Austria and France) or for "monetary policy purposes" (e.g., in Chile, Korea, and the Philippines). In addition, certain central bank laws enjoin the central bank from purchasing securities during inflationary periods (e.g., in Ceylon, Cuba, Korea, and the Philippines).

In some cases there are legal restrictions on the maximum maturity of government securities that can be included in central bank portfolios. Such restrictions either provide that the securities must be short term but without defining the maturity (e.g., in Venezuela), or actually specify maximum maturities, ranging from two years (in Switzerland) to five years (in Mexico) or even ten (in Guatemala). In other countries, such as Ceylon, the legislation requires the central bank in conducting open market operations to have regard to the need for maintaining adequate holdings of short-term

---

[3] For example, in Ceylon, Chile, Cuba, the Dominican Republic, Ecuador, Egypt, El Salvador, Honduras, Korea, Mexico, Paraguay, and the Philippines.

securities in order that the bank may more readily contract its credit if necessary.

Legal limitations on the government securities holdings of central banks, however, are less frequent today than some years ago. In 1941 they were relaxed in South Africa and in 1953 in Switzerland; they were removed completely in 1936 in New Zealand, in 1945 in the Netherlands, in 1948 in India, and in 1954 in Canada. In some countries, such as Denmark, Norway, Sweden, and the United Kingdom, such legal restrictions have never existed.

Statutory authority alone is, of course, not sufficient to enable a central bank to conduct meaningful open market operations. A suitable institutional framework is required, and in many foreign countries the lack of such a framework is a serious barrier to the development of open market operations as an effective instrument of monetary policy. The most important and most frequent obstacle is the lack of broad and active money and capital markets; such markets enable the central bank to sell or buy government securities in appropriate amounts to exert the desired effect on commercial bank reserves, and at the same time absorb these transactions without wide price fluctuations. In the absence of a developed money market, moreover, the commercial banks tend to operate with ample excess reserves, and their cash ratios tend to fluctuate widely (since the banks have no other ready way of adjusting their positions). Under such circumstances, central bank securities sales, for example, may merely reduce the banks' excess reserves and may thus fail to restrict the availability of credit from the commercial banks.

A somewhat less common and less serious difficulty is the risk that changes in commercial bank reserve positions brought about by open market operations may in some instances be offset so readily by changes in borrowing from the central bank through discounts and advances as to leave the availability of credit from the commercial banks largely unaffected. This risk is minimized, of course, insofar as commercial banks are reluctant to incur indebtedness or remain long in debt; in many countries, moreover, as pointed out in Section II, either central bank discount rates are maintained as "penalty rates" in order to reduce the incentive to borrow from the central bank, or else such borrowing is limited directly by formal or informal discount ceilings.

Finally, in some foreign countries the central banks lack a sufficient volume of securities suitable for open market operations, or the market holdings of securities eligible for central bank purchase are very small.

It is thus not surprising that open market operations are rarely used abroad in the same continuous and broad manner as in this country; only in the United Kingdom and Canada does the institutional framework permit the employment of open market operations as a full-fledged credit policy instrument. In West Germany, it is true, central bank sales of short-term government securities have been very large in recent years, but the lack of a broad market appears to have rendered the bank's operations relatively passive; nevertheless, the purpose of the bank's open market operations—the absorption of the large liquid funds accruing to the banking system from the foreign exchange inflow—seems to have been achieved to a high degree. In other countries, such operations have generally been carried out in more limited ways: to even out daily money market fluctuations (as in France) or to offset seasonal and other changes in bank liquidity (as in the Netherlands). Central bank open market operations have also served in many foreign countries merely as a means of supporting government securities prices; such operations, however, have in recent years been abandoned or have been made more flexible in most European and British Commonwealth countries, with the result that other monetary measures such as discount rate increases have been strengthened. In countries with less developed financial systems, central bank open market operations have been used primarily as part of the overall effort to broaden the countries' capital markets.

The United Kingdom

In the United Kingdom, the institutional conditions for effective open market operations have long been present. The London money and capital markets are among the most developed in the world, and the commercial banks operate with stable cash ratios. Direct borrowing at the central bank is not available to the commercial banks, and the borrowing done by discount houses tends to be limited by the penalty effect of the discount rate, which remains consistently above most money market rates.[4] Finally, the Bank of England has usually had an ample securities portfolio for its operations, and its purchases and sales are known to be supplemented by the operations of the large government funds.

The Bank of England's open market operations, which originated in the last century, were developed more fully in the 1920's and 1930's. During World War II and the early postwar years, however, the bank kept the Treasury bill rate rigidly pegged, and thus supplied funds to the market at the latter's initiative. It was only in November 1951 that the Treasury bill

---

[4] Since the commercial banks do not borrow at the central bank, they adjust their positions by calling in their loans to the discount houses. Changes in the volume of borrowing from the central bank, therefore, may not have the same direct and immediate influence on the availability of bank credit as in some countries, where the banks borrow directly from the central bank and where such borrowing affects their own willingness to extend credit because they are anxious not to remain in debt to the central bank for long.

rate was finally "freed" and the bank's control over the availability of credit thereby strengthened.

In general, the bank appears to confine its open market operations to short-term securities, although on occasion it intervenes also in the medium and long-term market. Partly because data on changes in the detailed composition of the bank's holdings are not published, it is difficult to determine the importance of the bank's longer term operations. In any event, it seems to be agreed by observers that during recent years the bank has conducted operations in longer term securities only in order to smooth out undue deviations from what the authorities have taken to be the underlying trend of securities prices. There has been little, if any, suggestion by market observers that the bank was attempting to lead the market, or to determine the actual level of prices and rates for government securities of any maturity category. It should also be pointed out that the "government broker"—one of the principal brokers in the government bond market—operates in medium and long-term government securities on behalf not only of the Bank of England but also of the government departments, as well as of the broker's own private customers. The bank's transactions in the short-term securities market are executed by another firm, its "bill broker"— one of the London discount houses. This broker normally effects transactions for the Bank of England with all of the other discount houses and also with the commercial banks. Because of the need to even out or offset the frequent and large swings in Treasury cash transactions, as well as other disturbances in the money market, the bank's operations are continuous and thus enable it to maintain close technical surveillance over the market.

The bank's operations clearly have a direct bearing on money market conditions. For instance, when the bank desires to increase the pressures on the availability of funds, it may (by shrinking its purchases or making sales or not renewing maturing issues) "leave the market short of cash," thus forcing it "into the bank"—that is, forcing the discount houses to borrow at the discount rate, which as noted is a penalty rate. Such borrowing at the Bank of England tends in turn to induce the discount houses to buy fewer and sell more short-term securities, thereby raising the rates of interest on these securities and exerting a restraining influence on the money market as a whole. The frequency with which the market is forced "into the bank", and of course the amount of such borrowing, can thus importantly affect the cost and availability of credit. Nevertheless, the Bank of England's operations have met with certain difficulties during the inflationary periods of recent years, since the Treasury faced large cash deficits and resorted to substantial issues of Treasury bills placed in great part with the banking system. As the governor of the bank pointed out in October 1956:

> Unfortunately, at some periods during more recent years, it has not
> proved possible to match the total requirements of Government and

public bodies by the sale of long-term securities. Floating debt has again at times become excessive, bank deposits too high, and technical pressures more difficult to maintain.

Continental Europe

On the European Continent, central bank open market operations have so far remained limited in scope, primarily because of the lack of broad and active money and capital markets. In West Germany, the operations of the central bank in their present form began only in 1955 when the bank was confronted with a growing need to reduce the liquidity of the banking system because of the large inflow of gold and foreign exchange, and yet had only a negligible securities portfolio. In order to obtain suitable securities, the bank reached an agreement with the government for the transforming of certain nonmarketable securities held by the bank (the so-called "equalization claims" created during the 1948 currency reform) into short-term marketable securities with maturities of up to two years. However, in the absence of a broad short-term market the bank's operations are rather passive: it restricts itself to changing from time to time its published selling rate (the buying rate being above the latter, in some cases by varying margins) for the securities it deals in, and the actual transactions then depend on the decisions of the banks and the public authorities with which the central bank deals. Nevertheless, the central bank's open market sales have been very large since the second half of 1956, as it has endeavored to offset the effects of the heavy inflow of foreign exchange. On several occasions in 1957, after net sales of such securities had almost reached the authorized limit, the bank negotiated agreements with the government to transform further amounts of nonmarketable into marketable securities, thus raising the original limit of 2 billion Deutsche marks to 7 billion. The central bank has also, on occasion, operated in the long-term bond market (as a rule, though, for the issuers' account).

In the Netherlands, the central bank has been facing somewhat similar problems in its open market operations. Up to 1952, it is true, there had been an additional obstacle to open market sales, in that the Treasury was continuously selling short-term securities on tap at fixed rates regardless of its immediate financing needs, thus draining the market of superfluous funds. However, in mid-1952 such sales were suspended when an understanding was reached between the bank and the Treasury, whereby open market operations would henceforth be carried out by the bank while the Treasury in principle would limit its sales of short-term securities to the amount of such securities maturing. Since then, the central bank has entered the market from time to time, both as a seller and as a buyer; on occasion it has replenished its securities portfolio by transforming the Treasury's book debt, inherited from the Occupation, into marketable securities with maturities of up to five years. The book debt, however, has been greatly reduced, and, since the bank's current securities portfolio is also relatively small, the bank's ammunition for open market sales is limited. The thinness of the market—despite the operations of government securities dealers—has likewise tended to restrict the scope of open market operations. Up to the end of 1955 the bank had confined itself to announcing from time to time its willingness to sell, or to buy, at specified rates that were changed only infrequently. These rates, however, were often out of touch with the market. To remedy this weakness of its open market operations and thus strengthen its influence on the market, the bank since late 1955 has conducted open market sales at rates determined through bids from the market. In addition, as of the end of 1956 the bank instituted repurchase agreements with the commercial banks on short-term government securities; these agreements are negotiated, with the bill brokers as intermediaries, at rates set by the bank on the basis of bids received in a competitive tender.

In France, where banks and discount houses participate in a fairly well-established money market, the central bank's operations have been limited to smoothing out the periodic disturbances in the flow of funds in the market. The bulk of the central bank's transactions, outright as well as under repurchase agreements, is in Treasury bills issued with maturities of up to two years, and takes place through a special broker. The limited scope of the bank's operations, as its governor stated in the annual report for 1954, has had two causes: first, the government, confronted with a large deficit, has been obliged to borrow heavily from the commercial banks through Treasury bills, sold continuously at fixed rates and with net yields substantially above the discount rate; secondly, the Bank of France has been under legal obligation to buy at its discount rate all Treasury bills three months or less from maturity offered to it by the banks. This obligation, however, was removed in mid-1957, and the Bank of France thus obtained greater freedom for its open market operations.

In the Scandinavian countries, open market operations have been conducted largely in longer term government securities. In Denmark, where the central bank had already been operating in the bond market in the interwar period, the bank is known to be fairly active and to exert an important influence on government bond prices. During most of the postwar years, however, it has not supported long-term yields rigidly, but instead has conducted its transactions mainly on the basis of general monetary policy considerations. During the last few years the changes in the central bank's open market portfolio have been small, and its day-to-day operations in the bond market have apparently been chiefly conducted with the purpose of evening out incidental swings in market supply and demand. In Norway, the central bank does not appear to have engaged in open market operations until the early 1950's, and its transactions have been principally on the buying side. In 1955 it replaced its former rigid supports by more flexible purchases, and in 1956 it actually reduced its portfolio. Since the bank's securities portfolio is limited, it has proposed to the Finance Ministry the conversion of a part of the government's book debt, stemming from World War II, into short-term bonds that would thus become available to the bank for sale in its market operations. In Sweden, the operations of the central bank have been a major factor in the bond market during the postwar years. Up to October 1954, they had been geared to the government's cheap money policy; at that time, however, the bank announced, as part of its monetary restrained policy, that it not only would abstain from supporting government bonds but also would, if necessary, sell securities in the market in order to increase the effect of its credit restraint measures. Since then the central bank has been in the market both as a seller and as a buyer, and apparently has not supplied the banks with the full amount of reserves that would have been needed to meet all credit demands.

In other European countries, central bank open market operations are currently negligible. Thus, in Belgium, there was in October 1957 no flexible money market in which the central bank could effectively operate, although such a market was under consideration. As regards the long-term market, official operations there are conducted by the Fonds des Rentes, a fund administered by the central bank and the Treasury and established in 1945 to regulate government bond prices; the central bank itself does not operate in that market. Because of the government's large budget deficits, the government has remained heavily in debt to the central bank; as a result, the unutilized margin of the government's legal credit ceiling at the central bank (which applies both to direct borrowing and to indirect borrowing through the bank's securities purchases) has been so small that there has been little leeway for open market purchases; and open market sales have been thwarted by the heavy borrowing of the government and its agencies in the market to help meet the heavy deficts. These factors, according to the 1955 annual report of the central bank, have deprived it of an important field of action, whereas it would be desirable, as the bank has since pointed out, that the bank be able to influence the liquidity of the economy by selling and buying government securities in the market.

In Switzerland, where the economy has been very liquid during most of the postwar years, it is the smallness of the central bank's securities portfolio that has prevented the bank from engaging in major open market sales. For this reason, the bank at times has made limited sales of gold coins to the public to absorb the excess liquidity of the banking system; however, reliance has been primarily placed on gentlemen's agreements—notably for the maintenance of minimum cash reserves—between the authorities and the banks and other financial institutions. In addition, the accumulation of large cash balances by the Treasury and the issuance by the Treasury of special securities have helped to absorb excess liquidity.

Other Countries

In some countries of the British Commonwealth, central bank open market operations, while not very extensive, have helped to broaden the capital markets and at the same time have exerted some influence on the banking systems. In the Union of South Africa, the stated primary aim of the central bank's open market policy has been to maintain orderly conditions in the government bond market and establish appropriate relationships between the rates for different maturities. The bank quotes buying and selling prices for government securities, based on a pattern of rates that it decides on from time to time according to circumstances and monetary policy aims. Thus, in September 1955, besides increasing the discount rate, the bank announced that it would operate in the bond market in order to bring the yields on short and long-term government issues up to certain levels. In Australia, the central bank's operations in support of government bond prices have until recently been relatively rigid, and have at times involved very large additions to bank reserves. However, in the spring of 1956, as part of the government's restraint measures, the bank reduced its support of the bond market to "a more normal" level, and long-term yields rose by ½ per cent. It should also be noted that the bank has attempted to improve the marketability of government bonds by being a ready buyer of such bonds in small amounts and by facilitating transactions in the market when large buying or selling orders were involved.

In India, heavy bond-support operations by the central bank were abandoned as far back as November 1951. The bank then announced that, instead of maintaining the long-term rate by buying any government securities offered to it, it would refrain, except in special circumstances, from buying securities to meet the banks' seasonal needs; these would thenceforth have to be met mainly through the "discount window." This change in open market policy was intended to make effective the newly increased discount rate, and to assure that a seasonal contraction would take place when the peak of the seasonal needs for funds was over. The central bank's securities transactions, which take place either directly with the banks or through brokers, have also been intended to help the bank secure a better distribution of their securities portfolios, as well as at times to prepare the market for new government loan issues. In Ceylon, the central bank's operations, although relatively small, have been chiefly designed to help regulate the banking system's liquidity. On occasion, however, the bank has aided in stabilizing the market during the issue of government loans. In February 1956, when the bank's portfolio was almost exhausted but the economy unusually liquid, the bank issued its own one and two-year securities—the first instance of an issue of central bank bonds in many years. In February 1957 the bank again issued its own securities, this time of six and eighteen months maturity. In Pakistan, the central bank informs its broker that it is prepared to buy or sell securities, and leaves it to the market to make use of the facilities thus offered. In this way, it has been able to relieve periods of stringency while guarding against wholesale unloading of securities, and at the same time has provided a more or less consistent demand for securities.

In Japan, after a long lapse, the central bank again turned to open market operations in late 1955 in a setting of greatly increased bank liquidity. The bank's sales, however, remained small, and the bank agreed to suspend them several days prior to the maturity dates of the particular securities. Moreover the bank stood ready, for a short period after the sales, to repurchase at the same price the securities that it had sold. It similarly stands ready to repurchase also the securities sold by the Treasury under a 1956 arrangement of placing new securities directly with the commercial banks and other financial institutions rather than with the central bank.

In other countries of Asia as well as in Latin America, the scope of central bank open market operations has remained even more limited because of the extreme thinness or virtual absence of capital markets. In these countries such operations have generally consisted of purchases only, and on the rare occasions when sales were made, care has usually been taken not to depress securities prices. Moreover, the purchases have often been intended to supply needed funds directly or indirectly to the government or the various government agencies. In some cases, purchases appear to have been undertaken not to influence the availability and cost of credit as such but to support government securities prices in order to encourage the growth of a market. In a number of these countries, it is true, central bank operations have helped to widen the ownership of government securities, but official commitments to support government bonds have also often tended to impede efforts directed at preventing too rapid an expansion in the money supply. The need to develop a market has been formally recognized in the newer central bank statutes by provisions calling for the establishment of securities stabilization funds (e.g., in the Dominican Republic, Ecuador, Honduras, and the Philippines). These funds have been designed to increase the liquidity of government securities by preventing or moderating sharp price fluctuations. Their operations, however, have generally remained very small. In the face of thin capital markets, the authorities in these financially less developed countries have at times resorted to central bank repurchase guarantees for newly issued government securities, as in Cuba. Often they have also employed measures of a special nature in order to reduce banking liquidity, broaden the markets, and aid in the financing of government deficits. Thus, a number of these (e.g., Cuba, Honduras, Indonesia, Mexico, and the Philippines) have established reserve requirements that permit, or in some cases require the commercial banks to hold a part of their required reserves in the form of government securities. In Cuba, in addition, the commercial banks are obliged to invest in government securities an amount equal to a certain percentage of their deposits in order to be eligible to accept official deposits. In Paraguay, Guatemala, and Ecuador, the authorities have introduced special laws requiring insurance companies and other financial institutions to invest in government and other officially favored securities.

The Growing Importance of Open Market Operations

The endeavor of many foreign countries to develop facilities for central bank purchases and sales of securities in the market reflects a widely recognized need to improve the flexibility and strengthen the impact of monetary and credit controls. It is also clear that there are many institutional obstacles to be overcome in most countries. Despite the advance that has been achieved in a number, the open market instrument still is very rarely the major credit control tool. In most foreign countries, where it is used, it generally serves to supplement in a subordinate manner other instruments such as discount policy and reserve requirement changes. Nevertheless, in the last few years the sale of government securities by central banks, in order to mop up excess liquidity, has become in many cases an important instrument of monetary management. Furthermore, insofar as central banks abroad are still supporting government securities prices, such operations have come to be effected more flexibly and at interest rates that reflect more realistically the basic supply and demand conditions prevailing in the money and capital markets.

The growing experience of foreign central banks with open market operations is demonstrating that many of the obstacles to their effective use can be overcome. The lack of a suitable central bank securities portfolio is, as a rule, the easiest to remedy; when a central bank has no book claims on the government that can be transformed into marketable securities, it may obtain the power to issue its own securities in order to secure the needed ammunition. A much more serious obstacle is to be found in the lack of appropriate fiscal and debt management policies; however, there is growing realization in many countries of the need for balanced budgets and for covering unavoidable deficits through noninflationary means, and a number of countries have been adjusting their policies accordingly. The absence of sufficiently broad money and capital markets is another fundamental problem. In the less developed countries, the broadening of financial markets is largely dependent or continued economic growth and diversification. But even among these countries, as well as among the more developed ones, central banks have already contributed significantly to the development of such markets, both by helping to create a proper institutional framework and by nourishing the further growth of these markets.

NEW CENTRAL BANKS*

Sixteen new central banks have opened their doors since the beginning of 1959—the Central Bank of the States of Equatorial Africa and of Cameroon, the Central Bank of the States of West Africa, the Bank of Morocco, and the Central Bank of Nigeria in 1959; the Bank of Sudan, the Bank of the Republic of Guinea, and the Somali National Bank in 1960; the Bank of Jamaica, the Malagasy Bank of Issue, and the Bank of the Republic of Mali in 1962; the Central Bank of Algeria and the Central Bank of Cyprus in 1963; the Bank of Lebanon, the National Bank of Rwanda, the Bank of the Kingdom of Burundi, and the National Bank of the Congo (Leopoldville) in 1964. The central banks of Morocco, Nigeria, Sudan, and Guinea were described in a previous article in this *Review*;[1] the other twelve new central banks will be discussed here.[2]

The Central Bank of the States of Equatorial Africa and of Cameroon serves the newly independent states of Cameroon, the Central African Republic, Chad, Congo (Brazzaville), and Gabon. (This bank will be referred to as the Equatorial African central bank.) The Central Bank of the States of West Africa serves Dahomey, Ivory Coast, Mauritania, Niger, Senegal, Togo, and Upper Volta. (This bank, which will here be termed West African central bank, also served Mali until 1962.) Both of these institutions were organized under French auspices before the independence of the countries concerned.

* *Monthly Review,* Federal Reserve Bank of New York, July, 1964, pp. 133–137. (Dorothy B. Christelow had primary responsibility for the preparation of this article.)

[1] See "International Developments," this *Review,* October 1960, pp. 181–83. The article also treated the Bank of Ghana, established in 1957, and the Central Bank of Malaya and the Central Bank of Tunisia, established in 1958.

[2] Another group of new central banks—not here discussed—will begin operations in the near future. These include central banks for Sierra Leone, Jordan, and Trinidad and Tobago. Furthermore, with the coming into being of the Federation of Malaysia in 1963, the Central Bank of Malaya became the Central Bank of Malaysia, with responsibility for the entire new country. Conversely, the breakup of the Federation of Rhodesia and Nyasaland into three countries will lead to the emergence of three separate central banks to replace the Bank of Rhodesia and Nyasaland. One of these, the Reserve Bank of Rhodesia (for Southern Rhodesia), has already opened its doors. While its powers and functions resemble those of the predecessor institution in most respects, it has been given the added power to require banks to maintain cash reserves against advances rather than against deposits.

In another group of countries—including Ethiopia, Iceland, Iran, Nicaragua, and the United Arab Republic—where the central banks had exercised both central banking and commercial banking functions, these institutions have in recent years been converted into central banks proper and their commercial banking operations transferred to existing or newly established commercial banks. These central bank reforms and conversions are also outside the scope of this article.

After becoming independent in 1960–61, these countries signed agreements with France (during 1960–62) under which all (except Mali) have continued to use the facilities of the existing central banks, whose organization and powers have been considerably modified to conform to the changed situation.

All but two of the countries served by the twelve new central banks had a monetary authority or currency board prior to the establishment of the new banks; the exceptions were the Malagasy Republic and Lebanon, where the note-issuing privilege had in each case been held by a commercial bank. While all the new central banks retain some of the attributes of the institutions they replace, they have generally been given a wide variety of additional monetary control powers.

The countries served by the new central banks vary considerably with respect to the degree of their financial and economic development. In some of the new states many economic transactions take place outside the monetary sphere, while in others such as Lebanon and Jamaica the banking systems are highly developed. The share of currency in the total money supply—a rough inverse measure of the use of banks in a country—varies from roughly 30 percent in Lebanon and Jamaica to around 40 percent in Cyprus and Senegal, 50 percent in Somalia, and reaches about 65 percent in Mali and Upper Volta. (The United States figure is about 20 percent.)[3] There is also considerable variation in the degree to which financial institutions other than commercial banks have taken root. On the other hand, almost all the countries concerned display certain common characteristics: they are notably dependent on international trade; foreign capital has played or is expected to play a considerable role in their economic development; and foreign commercial banks are a major element in their banking systems.

The objectives of the new central banks as set out in their statutes are to assure the external and internal stability of the currency and to foster a monetary environment conducive to economic development. To this end, all the central banks are given the exclusive right of note issue, the obligation to act as fiscal agent and banker for the government, the power to buy and sell gold and foreign exchange, and the authority to discount, purchase, and sell specified types of financial obligations. In addition, most of the new banks have at least some of the following powers of control and supervision over commercial banks: to establish minimum cash reserve requirements, to set limits on lending and deposit rates, to prescribe the asset distribution and the total volume of credit outstanding, to examine the books and to require statistical reports, and to set minimum capital requirements.

---

[3] The uniform definition of the money supply used for this comparison is that of the International Monetary Fund in its *International Financial Statistics:* currency outside banks, demand deposits, post office checking deposits, and private-sector deposits with the central bank where these exist; government deposits are excluded.

Central Bank-Government Relations

All the new banks are owned by the respective governments (except that the French government still holds all the capital of the Equatorial African central bank and half the capital of the Malagasy bank). In most cases, the presiding officer and the boards of management are appointed by the respective governments for a fixed period and are subject to reappointment. The exceptions are the three central banks whose member countries—all former French colonies—belong to the African Financial Community. The West African central bank's administrative council includes a minority appointed by the French government, and its presidency rotates every two years among council members representing the member states. Half the council members of the Malagasy Bank of Issue are appointed by France, and the president is chosen by the council, subject to the approval of the governments of the Malagasy Republic and France. The French government also appoints one half the members of the governing council of the Equatorial African central bank and, in addition, the President of the French Republic appoints the president of that institution.

Many of the new central bank statutes include further provisions to assure the harmonization of central bank action with the government's general economic policy. Some statutes provide that government officials or their representatives are to be members of the central bank's policy-making body. In Lebanon, two high government officials are minority members of the central bank's governing board; in Algeria, the law is sufficiently flexible to allow the chief of state to appoint government officials to a minority or majority position on the governing board. In Mali, five of the ten-member governing board represent government departments and two represent the national assembly. Other statutes provide for government approval or supervision of certain aspects of central banking. In Cyprus approval by the finance minister is required, if commercial bank reserve requirements are to be raised above a certain level. In Jamaica, the finance minister may "from time to time after consultation with the governor give to the bank in writing such directions of a general nature as appear to the minister to be necessary in the public interest." In Somalia, a committee consisting of the prime minister and key cabinet members is designated to supervise the operations of the central bank. In Burundi, major policy decisions of the central bank must be approved by the finance minister. In the Congo, a representative of the ministry of finance attends meetings, but is not a member, of the bank's governing board.

At the same time, a majority of the statutes limit central bank financing of their governments; the limitations typically apply to direct financing (i.e., through short-term advances or direct purchases of securities) and to indirect financing (i.e., through open market purchases or discounting of gov-

ernment securities offered by banks or others). Algeria, the West African
countries, and Malagasy all limit the total volume of government indebtedness that may be held by the central banks to a specified proportion (varying
from 10 percent to 15 percent) of ordinary government revenues during the
previous fiscal year. In the Congo, direct and indirect advances may each
equal 20 percent of average government receipts over a past three-year
period. Cyprus and Jamaica set more complex limits. Thus, in Cyprus the government's total direct and indirect indebtedness to the central bank may
amount to 20 percent of annual revenues plus 6 percent of the bank's sight
liabilities plus the government securities the bank took over from a note
security fund. In Jamaica, in addition to central bank short-term advances up
to 15 percent of annual government revenue, 50 percent of the assets backing the currency may be in securities of the Jamaican government; moreover,
the bank may hold government securities in amounts up to seven times the
bank's capital (which itself may be increased by the bank's board of governors with approval of the Jamaican House of Representatives). The Burundi
bank's limit is an absolute amount. The Somali National Bank is limited only
with respect to direct short-term advances to the government, while the Bank
of Lebanon and the National Bank of Rwanda are subject to limits that may
be exceeded in circumstances of "exceptional gravity." The remaining two central banks (namely, the Bank of the Republic of Mali and the Equatorial
African central bank) are not limited as to the total government indebtedness
they may hold.

DEVELOPMENT OF THE FINANCIAL SECTOR

All the new central banks have been given a general mandate for promoting economic development—often including special responsibilities for developing financial institutions, credit instruments, and domestic money markets. For this reason, these banks tend to have at their disposal legal powers
going beyond the traditional tools of rediscounting and open market operations, which themselves can of course also be used to promote certain types
of credit instruments and to encourage specific types of loan transactions by
increasing the liquidity of the instruments involved.

Thus, central bank powers to prescribe the distribution of assets in commercial bank portfolios may be of considerable importance: the Bank of
Jamaica has the power to prescribe a minimum ratio of domestic assets to
total commercial bank deposit liabilities; the central banks of Cyprus and the
Congo have the broader power to prescribe the purposes for which commercial bank advances and investments may be made; and the Rwanda cen-

tral bank is empowered to enter into agreements with commercial banks in this same regard.

Furthermore, where the existing financial sector is relatively small, it may be deemed advisable—indeed necessary—for the central bank to be able to deal directly with the borrowing and depositing public. This power has been a feature of the early years of many established central banks. Limited direct central bank contact with the borrowing public through discounting and advances on government securities is provided by all the statutes discussed here, except those for Lebanon and Cyprus. And the Algerian and West African central banks may accept noninterest-bearing deposits from the public in certain cases, although such deposits have in fact been small.

Broader powers have been given the central banks of Jamaica, Somalia, Mali, and Burundi—namely to discount for and make advances to, as well as to accept deposits from, nonfinancial customers. The Bank of Jamaica, to be sure, has indicated its intention to abstain from such commercial banking operations. But, in Somalia, the central bank's claims on the private sector are about two-thirds as large as similar commercial bank claims, while its rediscounts for commercial banks are negligible. The Mali central bank's claims on private borrowers are approximately four times as large as those of commercial banks, and it also discounts heavily for the commercial banks. In many countries where the central bank has not been given such broad powers to deal directly with the public, as well as in some of the countries where the central bank has such powers, separate government development banks tend to perform some of the same functions.

The specific types of paper eligible for discounting, rediscounting, loan collateral, or outright purchase are in themselves of considerable importance in the process of financial development, as already noted. In addition to discounts of and loans against government securities, all the central banks here discussed may discount or loan against first-class paper drawn to finance trade, industry, and agriculture. The maximum allowable maturity of the underlying paper is 90 days in Lebanon, but more usual limits range from 180 days to one year.

A number of statutes also provide for longer term commitments on the part of central banks to assist in the growth of negotiable securities markets and to finance economic development. Following the French tradition, the Central Bank of Algeria, the Equatorial African and West African central banks, and the Malagasy bank may extend credit to commercial banks and other financial institutions for as long as five years in order to finance industrial exports, housing, or other projects included in national development plans. Cyprus permits central bank investment in first-class, fixed-maturity, fixed-interest securities in amounts up to 5 percent of the bank's liabilities (exclusive of government deposits). The central bank of Mali has taken over the functions of the government-owned Popular Bank of Mali for Development. The Bank of Jamaica may, with the approval of the finance minister, buy and sell shares of companies specially authorized by the government to develop a local money or securities market or to improve "the financial machinery for financing of economic development." The Burundi bank may commit amounts equal to the sum of its capital, reserves, and amortization accounts to the purchase of long-term obligations issued or guaranteed by the government and, with agreement of two thirds of the bank's governing board, of long-term obligations of other borrowers and shares in newly organized government-sponsored financial institutions.

CREDIT CONTROL

The new central bank statutes suggest the existence of several distinct although overlapping approaches to the problem of general monetary control. In those countries that were formerly French colonies, primary reliance is placed on variation in central bank credit to banks and other financial institutions, mainly through changes in the discount rate and through variable ceilings on the overall volume of such credit. The West African central bank and the Equatorial African central bank determine the discount rate and the credit ceilings for each state, while national monetary committees are responsible for the distribution of credit among the commercial banks and other eligible credit institutions in the individual states. It is therefore possible for these central banks to pursue differential credit policies in the individual member states, as circumstances may require, although the freedom of payments among these countries would tend to complicate such differential policies and, in fact, makes a concerted economic and monetary policy highly desirable. In all these former French colonies, commercial bank reliance on central bank credit is very heavy: the central banks tend to refinance from 30 percent to 60 percent of bank credit outstanding, there being of course considerable variation from country to country and over time. Changes in the commercial banks' external indebtedness to their French head offices or parent banks or to other French banks can, to be sure, offset changes in central bank credit to some limited extent. The statute creating the Burundi central bank, which commenced operations very recently, suggests a similar approach to credit control, although the concept of setting ceilings on the availability of central bank credit does not appear in the Burundi statute.

The new central banks in Lebanon, Somalia, Jamaica, Cyprus, Rwanda, and the Congo rely for purposes of credit control largely on a combination of variations in commercial bank reserve requirements, the rediscount mechanism, and open market operations, plus a varying array of direct controls. One reason for the addition of direct controls to the traditional central bank arsenal in less developed money markets is usually the problem of dealing with potentially large inflows of funds from abroad. These inflows can be offset by changes in required reserve ratios only within the limits set by law, while large central bank sales of commercial paper or government securities might prove unduly disruptive or altogether impossible in thin financial markets.

The statutes of five of the six central banks discussed in the foregoing paragraph specify the range or upper limit of permissible variations in reserve ratios. In Jamaica, the ratio may be varied from 5 percent to 15 percent of deposit liabilities. The upper limit in Cyprus, Rwanda, and the Congo is 20 percent of deposit liabilities, with an additional 10 percentage points permitted in Cyprus in exceptional circumstances. In Lebanon, the maximum required reserve ratio is 25 percent for demand deposits and 15 percent for time deposits. As for direct controls, the Bank of Jamaica may set limits both upon the overall volume of commercial bank credit outstanding and upon specific types of credit; the Cyprus and the Congo banks have the same power with respect to commercial banks and other designated financial institutions; and the Rwanda bank may accomplish the same end through agreements with commercial banks and other financial institutions. The Lebanon bank may set variable liquidity ratios and other asset-liability relationships for commercial banks and other financial institutions. The central banks of Cyprus and the Congo also may set commercial bank lending and deposit rates.

Central banks which make substantial use of their powers to deal with the nonbank public—those in Somalia, Mali, and Burundi—possess an additional instrument of monetary control. By altering the volume of central bank credit to the nonbank public, these banks have a direct means of influencing the liquidity of the nonbank sector as well as that of the bank sector of the economy.

INTERNATIONAL FINANCIAL RELATIONS

Many of the statutes specify the form in which the central banks' international reserves are to be held, as well as the minimum level to which these reserves may fall. These provisions are, of course, influenced by the special relation to a major currency area a country may have.

Jamaica and Cyprus are members of the sterling area and as such have generally tended to hold the bulk of their reserves in short-term sterling assets in London. Funds are freely transferable within the sterling area, while the sterling balances held by the area's monetary authorities are convertible into other currencies in accordance with each country's exchange regulations and general sterling-area policy. In Jamaica, the central bank law requires that reserves be held in the form of gold, sterling notes and coin, balances or money at call with banks in the United Kingdom, United Kingdom Treasury bills, or other securities issued or guaranteed by a government or territory of the British Commonwealth. The provisions in the central bank statute of Cyprus specify only that the bank's foreign assets are to consist of gold and such foreign exchange and foreign securities as the governing board shall from time to time designate. The statutory minimum level of foreign exchange reserves at the Jamaica central bank is stated in terms of its relation to the currency circulation. This reflects the practice of the former British-administered currency board which this new bank succeeds; but, whereas the currency board generally aimed at maintaining 100 percent sterling cover for currency outstanding, the new central bank statute provides for 50 percent cover in gold or eligible foreign exchange assets. In Cyprus, reserves must be 30 percent of currency and central bank sight liabilities. These two statutes make no specific provision as to how and when the banks are to act to maintain these ratios.

Algeria, Mali, the countries of Equatorial and West Africa, and the Malagasy Republic are members of the French franc zone. With some exceptions, zone members hold most of their foreign exchange reserves in the form of French franc liquid assets. Algeria and Mali, whose central bank laws do not specify the form or size of their international reserves, may also hold gold and nonfranc foreign exchange. The countries served by the Equatorial African, West African, and Malagasy central banks, however, maintain their foreign exchange reserves in the form of "operations accounts" at the French Treasury, or they may hold French government securities. These members of the African Financial Community (CFA) have in exchange been given the guarantee of unlimited conversion of CFA currencies into French francs. The technical arrangement involves automatic overdraft facilities when a country's operations account shows a deficit. These accounts may be debited by CFA central banks for the purchase of nonfranc currencies by residents of CFA countries in conformance with these countries' exchange regulations, which generally resemble those of France.

French willingness to assure convertibility of CFA francs is related to the French voice in the management of the three above-named banks and to certain additional safe-guards. For example, the statute for the West African central bank provides that an increase in the bank's discount rate and a reduction in rediscount ceilings must be considered when foreign exchange reserves remain for thirty days below 20 percent of sight liabilities (currency and deposits combined); if the ratio falls below 10 percent for the same period of time, these measures must be adopted immediately. Also, an agreement between the West African Monetary Union (the group of states served by the West African central bank) and the French Treasury provides that, if the operations account of the area as a whole is in debit for sixty consecutive days, the central bank's discount rate must be raised by 1 percentage point. For an individual country with a net debtor position in the operations account, the discount ceiling must be reduced by 20 percent, while for a country whose operations-account credit amounts to less than 15 percent of its currency outstanding, the ceiling is to be reduced by 10 percent.[4]

The remaining five new banks—in Lebanon, Somalia, the Congo, Rwanda, and Burundi—are members of neither the sterling area nor the French franc zone, although the three last-named countries were members of the Belgian monetary area until 1960. The Lebanon bank is required to hold gold and foreign exchange reserves equal to 30 percent of its currency and sight liabilities or 50 percent of the currency issue, whichever is larger. The Somali bank must hold a reserve of gold and convertible currencies equal to 100 percent of currency outstanding. Neither statute provides for special action in the event these ratios are not maintained. The Congo bank must maintain gold and foreign exchange reserves equal to 40 percent of currency and sight liabilities, but this requirement may be suspended by the governing board of the bank for the first five years of the bank's operations. The Rwanda bank is to hold foreign exchange reserves in the form of gold, accounts with foreign central banks, or in readily marketable securities, but is under no obligation to maintain them at any specific level. The Burundi statute does not mention international reserves, although the bank has sufficient powers to acquire and maintain foreign exchange reserves.

CONCLUDING REMARKS

The broadening of the financial structure as a prerequisite for sustained economic development is one of the prime tasks of virtually all these new central banks. Such a broadening must in a number of cases necessarily accompany the effective exercise of central bank credit control. The tools given these institutions will, therefore, have to be used not only to encourage price and balance of payments stability, but also to promote the growth of sound and diversified financial institutions and to foster confidence in money and banks—efforts which will in turn aid economic growth in general. It may thus be expected that all the banks here discussed will gradually broaden their potential for judicious and flexible use of central banking instruments.

ADDITIONAL READINGS

Bank for International Settlements, *Eight European Central Banks,* New York: Praeger, 1963.

[4] It will be understood that ties concerning central banking are only one aspect of the continuing financial cooperation between France and her former African colonies. Thus, besides grants, the French also make loans, through the Caisse Centrale de Coopération Économique (CCCE), to CFA-area development banks, public corporations, and private enterprise. The CCCE is financed by French Treasury advances. It also serves as note-issuing authority for Saint-Pierre-et-Miquelon and in this connection maintains an operations account at the French Treasury.

deKock, M. H., *Central Banking,* London: Staples, 1961.

Hawtrey, R. G., *The Art of Central Banking,* London: Frank Cass & Co., 1962.

Lord Cobbold, "Some Thoughts on Central Banking," *Journal of the Institute of Bankers,* February, 1963, pp. 17–26.

Meek, Wilbur T., *The Central Bank of Venezuela; Structure, Functions and Operations,* Department of Research, School of Business, Louisiana Polytechnic Institute, 1961.

Roosa, Robert V., *Federal Reserve Operations in Money and Government Securities Markets,* Federal Reserve Bank of New York, New York, 1956.

Sen, S. N., *Central Banking in Underdeveloped Money Markets,* Calcutta: Bookland Private Ltd., 1961.

chapter 3

The U.S. Balance of Payments:
Actual and Potential Effects on
Multinational Business

The deficit in the U.S. balance of payments is not a recent phenomenon. As shown in the first reading, this deficit has been with us continuously since 1949. In the early 1950's, however, most foreign countries were still recovering from the exhaustion of their foreign exchange reserves; this was the period of the dollar shortage, and the U.S. Government, along with the rest of the international financial community, felt that it was a good thing for the United States to maintain a deficit so as to replenish the foreign exchange reserves of other countries. The United States did not even mind the concomitant gold outflows, because of the enormity of her gold reserves. In 1958, however, there was a huge gold outflow, causing concern among some of the experts. When substantial gold outflows continued, more people became concerned, and by 1960 the question of stopping the deficit in the U.S. balance of payments became a topic of importance, but still primarily to government officials.

The decade of dollar outflow had had a favorable influence on the U.S. business community. It put dollars in the hands of foreign purchasers and thus brought about convertibility in many countries, helped to significantly increase total world trade, and still was accompanied by a surplus in the U.S. balance of merchandise trade.

The continued gold outflow, however, caused government officials to look for possible solutions, which were of concern to U.S. companies. Since one of the suggested (and attempted) solutions was an increase in interest rates in the United States, all businessmen, regardless of their involvement in international trade or investment, became interested in the causes and possible solutions. The first two readings in this chapter give a detailed analysis of the situation, which is needed as a basis for any intelligent discussion of the problem.

The complexity of the situation, on the other hand, is illustrated by the problem of measuring the deficit. There are different ways of keeping accounts of a country's balance of payments, and the method employed by the United States may not be the best. It depends, of course, on what one wishes to measure, and on the use one wishes to make of the results. This problem is discussed in the article, "How Real is the Drain on Dollars?"

One of the first potential solutions mentioned (though usually only behind closed doors) when a country is having balance of payments difficulties, is that of devaluation: Should the United States devalue the dollar? The potential ramifications to such a step are endless. If the possible primary, secondary, and tertiary steps of such a move are followed, in detail, this alone involves an understanding of a significant portion of the entire field of international finance. The two articles, "Should we Devalue the Dollar?" and "Devaluation is not the Answer" are only a beginning of the discussion on this question.

As noted before, the outflow of dollars has had many desirable side effects. The concomitant outflow of gold is causing more immediate concern. Why not get rid of our cross of gold? This possible solution is discussed in the article by Abba Lerner. A further step in the same direction would be to let the value of the dollar float, to adopt a policy of flexible exchange rates, and to let the play of free market forces determine the value of the dollar. The Canadian experience with this policy is described in detail in the later section on Exchange Controls, but the possible application of this solution to the U.S. situation is discussed in two articles in this chapter. Milton Friedman states a positive view to such a policy and Herbert Bratter takes the negative.

The international businessman in the United States became more directly concerned with U.S. Government policy when it began to restrict his actions. The Revenue Act of 1962, along with its effect on the tax burden of U.S. companies and on their foreign investment planning, is discussed in a later section on taxation. Supposedly, the taxation of foreign-earned income was designed to reduce U.S. private investment in developed countries. Critics claim that its potential effect is to reduce foreign investment in underdeveloped countries as well. Does this have a positive influence on the U.S. balance of payments? No conclusive study of this question has been conducted, but the problem is ably discussed in the article by Emile Benoit.

The U.S. Government took another step to reduce the outflow of dollars through the adoption of an "interest equalization tax," whose primary purpose was to impede the floatation of dollar bonds in the New York capital market, by West European and Japanese governments or companies. There were, however, many overflow effects from this tax. Its overall effect could be negative, instead of positive. It affects not only the investment bankers of Wall Street, but also commercial banks, capital equipment exporters, and, ultimately, all U. S. firms with foreign operations. This question is discussed in the article, "Interest Equalization Tax: A Deceptive Tourniquet."

The U.S. Government continues to shy away from measures which "directly" restrict the flow of funds, measures which could be interpreted as exchange controls. There is, however, a broad field for the exercise of government power in the issuance of "guidelines" and in the use of "moral suasion." To the outside world, such measures can appear innocuous, while at the same time, they are effective. To the banks and companies involved, however, they can be insidious, for they involve simultaneously a divulgence of additional "company confidential" data to government, and an implicit threat. The bank or company which disregards such "guidelines" is never sure when, or in what form, the government might seek to "punish the offender." The first moves by the government in this direction, are documented in the reading, "The President's Balance of Payments Program."

GOLD AND THE BALANCE OF PAYMENTS*

The receipts and expenditures that make up our balance of payments result from a great number of transactions. It is the combined effect of all these transactions and not just a few that generate the payments deficits. Despite the fact that the causes of the deficits cannot be clearly pinpointed, it is useful to dissect the balance of payments into its main component parts. The salient features of our strengths and weaknesses thus become apparent.

The U.S. balance of international payments has shown a deficit every year since 1950 with the exception of 1957. Between 1950 and 1956 the deficits averaged $1.5 billion and were of no real concern.

Indeed, they served the beneficial function of eliminating the "dollar gap" of the early postwar period without being accompanied by an unmanageable

TABLE 1

U. S. BALANCE OF PAYMENTS, 1947-1962

Billions of dollars; receipts [+], payments [-]

CURRENT ACCOUNT:	– Annual Average–			1956	1957	1958	1959	1960	1961	1962
	1947-49	1950-52	1953-55							
Merchandise exports.	+13.8	+12.5	+13.1	+17.4	+19.4	+16.3	+16.3	+19.5	+19.9	+20.6
Merchandise imports.	– 6.8	–10.4	–11.0	–12.8	–13.3	–13.0	–15.3	–14.7	–14.5	–16.2
Trade balance.	+ 7.0	+ 2.1	+ 2.1	+ 4.6	+ 6.1	+ 3.3	+ 1.0	+ 4.8	+ 5.4	+ 4.4
Service and investment income (net)*.	+ 1.0	+ 1.2	+ 1.4	+ 1.7	+ 2.1	+ 1.6	+ 1.5	+ 1.3	+ 1.8	+ 2.5
Balance on current account.	+ 8.0	+ 3.3	+ 3.5	+ 6.3	+ 8.2	+ 4.9	+ 2.5	+ 6.1	+ 7.2	+ 6.9
PRIVATE CAPITAL ACCOUNT:										
U. S. Long-term investment.	– 0.8	– 1.0	– 1.0	– 2.6	– 3.3	– 2.6	– 2.3	– 2.6	– 2.5	– 2.6
U. S. Short-term investment.	..	– 0.1	– 0.3	– 0.5	– 0.3	– 0.3	– 0.1	– 1.3	– 1.5	– 0.5
Foreign long-term investment (net).	+ 0.1	+ 0.2	0.3	+ 0.7	+ 0.5	..	+ 0.9	+ 0.3	+ 0.7	+ 1.0
Balance on capital account (net).	– 0.7	– 0.9	– 1.0	– 2.4	– 3.1	– 2.9	– 1.5	– 3.6	– 3.3	– 2.1
U. S. GOVERNMENT ACCOUNT:										
Current Military Expenditures.	– 0.6	– 1.3	– 2.7	– 2.9	– 3.2	– 3.4	– 3.1	– 3.0	– 2.9	– 3.0
Net Capital Transactions†.	– 5.6	– 3.1	– 2.0	– 2.4	– 2.6	– 2.6	– 2.0	– 2.8	– 2.8	– 3.0
Balance on government account (net).	– 6.2	– 4.4	– 4.7	– 5.3	– 5.8	– 6.0	– 5.1	– 5.8	– 5.7	– 6.0
ERRORS AND OMISSIONS:	+ 0.8	+ 0.4	+ 0.6	+ 0.5	+ 1.2	+ 0.5	+ 0.4	– 0.6	– 0.6	– 1.0
OVER-ALL BALANCE:										
Surplus (+) or deficit (–).	+ 1.9	– 1.6	– 1.6	– 0.9	+ 0.5	– 3.5	– 3.7	– 3.9	– 2.4	– 2.2
BALANCING ITEMS:										
Gold outflows (+); inflows (–).	– 1.5	+ 0.4	+ 0.5	– 0.3	– 0.8	+ 2.3	+ 0.7	+ 1.7	+ 0.9	+ 0.9
Convertible foreign exchange sales (+); purchases (–).	..	..	..	..	..	..	..	..	– 0.1	..
Foreign liquid dollar holdings increases (+); decreases (–)‡.	– 0.4	+ 1.2	+ 1.1	+ 1.2	+ 0.3	+ 1.2	+ 3.0	+ 2.2	+ 1.6	+ 1.3
Total.	– 1.9	+ 1.6	+ 1.6	+ 0.9	– 0.5	+ 3.5	+ 3.7	+ 3.9	+ 2.4	+ 2.2

* Includes pensions and private remittances and excludes military expenditures.

† Government grants and capital outflows less repayments on U. S. loans.

‡ Includes foreign holdings of all short-term assets, plus U. S. government notes and bonds.

*From a booklet by the same title published by The First National Bank of Chicago, 1963.

TABLE 2

U. S. BALANCE OF INTERNATIONAL PAYMENTS

(Billions of dollars)

	1960	1961	1962
RECEIPTS:			
from export of merchandise	$19.41	$19.91	$20.57
from export of services	7.89	8.15	9.25
from repayments on U. S. Gov't loans	.63	1.27	1.27
from foreign investments in the U. S.	.20	.73	.97
Total	$28.13	$30.07	$32.06
LESS-			
EXPENDITURES:			
for import of merchandise	$14.72	$14.51	$16.19
for services, and military bases abroad	8.60	8.41	8.81
for pensions and private remittances	.85	.88	.92
for gov't foreign investment and aid	3.38	4.05	4.27
for private foreign investment: Long-Term	2.54	2.48	2.58
Short-Term	1.31	1.47	.47
net transactions unaccounted for:	.65	.63	1.00
Total	$32.06	$32.43	$34.24
DEFICIT: (Receipts minus expenditures)	$ 3.93	$ 2.36	$ 2.18
Accounted for by:			
increase in foreign ownership of bank balances, government securities, and other investments	2.23	1.62	1.27
outflow of gold from U. S.	1.70	.86	.89
convertible foreign currencies; sales (+); purchases (−)		−.12	.02
	$ 3.93	$ 2.36	$ 2.18

drain on the U.S. gold stock. The small surplus of 1957 reflected the abnormal increase in U.S. exports precipitated by the Suez crisis. Then, starting with 1958, the deficit reached troublesome proportions, averaging $3.2 billion during the next five years. Furthermore, the payments deficits were accompanied by a surge in the outflow of gold which in the years 1958 through 1962 totaled $6.8 billion, representing a 30 percent decline in the U.S. gold stock held at the end of 1957.

Some improvements in the balance of payments were registered during the past two years, but these remained minor if debt prepayments by foreign governments are excluded. In 1961 the improvement resulted mainly from a widening of the favorable balance in merchandise trade, and a decrease in short-term capital outflow which was mostly reflected in the account "errors and omissions." In 1962 the small improvement was due mainly to a further decline in short-term capital outflow.

Throughout the postwar period, our merchandise balance of trade has been favorable; that is, our exports have exceeded our imports. However, the export surplus has not been large enough to offset other international expenditures. Furthermore, since a considerable part of the surplus may be traced to

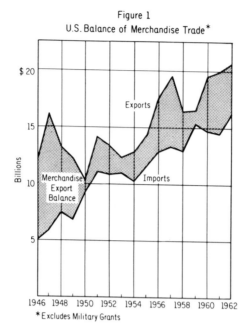

Figure 1
U.S. Balance of Merchandise Trade*

*Excludes Military Grants

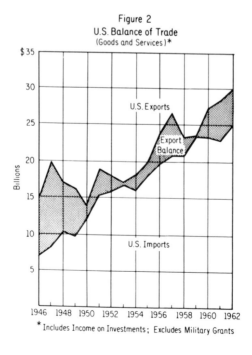

Figure 2
U.S. Balance of Trade
(Goods and Services)*

* Includes Income on Investments; Excludes Military Grants

aid-generated exports and to our own private capital flows, our performance in unassisted exports is not as satisfactory as would appear at first glance.

When payments and receipts for goods, services and income on investments are considered, our export surplus narrows considerably in every instance during the past ten years except for 1962. Moreover, were income on investments excluded, there would be an unfavorable balance on goods and services in 1953, 1954, 1955, 1958, and 1959.

The surplus in our balance of trade has not been sufficient to finance fully our growing private and government outlays. Thus, the deficits. In the five years, 1958–1962, the deficits totaled $15.7 million, almost 1½ times as alrge as the combined deficits of the previous twelve postwar years.

Between 1950 and 1957, the deficits caused little loss of gold. In fact, there were additions to U.S. gold holdings in four of the eight years and the net outflow for the period amounted to only $1.7 billion. Gold was used in settlement of only 16 percent of the combined deficits for the period. Starting with 1958, the increases in the payments deficits were accompanied by substantial transfers of gold. During the past five years, about 41 percent of the aggregate deficit was settled by gold, a yearly average outflow of over $1.3 billion.

Despite the decline in our holdings, the United States still has about 40 percent of the total monetary gold of the free world. By applying the customary measurements—for example, the ratio of total reserves to annual imports —our reserve position still appears strong and adequate. However, no matter how ample the gold stock, it cannot sustain for long the kind of depletion we have witnessed in recent years. Thus, the drain must be stopped if the dollar is to continue to perform the vital and strategic function of a key reserve currency in international trade and finance.

The most disturbing development of the persistent deficits in our balance of payments has been the combination of the decline in our gold reserves and the increase in foreign dollar claims. These claims, consisting principally of deposits in U.S. banks and U.S. Government obligations for which gold ultimately may be demanded, have risen from about $10.5 billion in 1950 to $27.6 billion at the end of 1962.

The effects of the international gold movements and the accumulation of dollar claims against the United States can be seen in the rapid build-up of these holdings by foreign nations.

Part of the explanation for the deterioration of our relative position in gold holdings lies in the comparative rates of gold production. At the same time that we were losing gold through international transactions, world gold production was rising at a rapid rate while that of the United States was declining moderately. International liquidity, however, does not increase by the full extent of gold production since much of the gold finds its way into private hands rather than into the reserves of governments. In the years 1948, 1951,

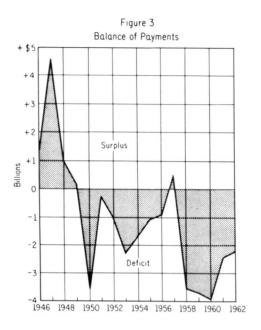

Figure 3
Balance of Payments

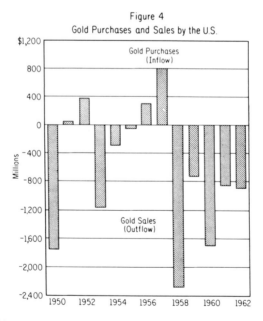

Figure 4
Gold Purchases and Sales by the U.S.

1952 and 1960, private holdings increased considerably more than official
holdings. In general, the years characterized by political or financial stress are
those which also witness a greater relative accumulation of gold in private

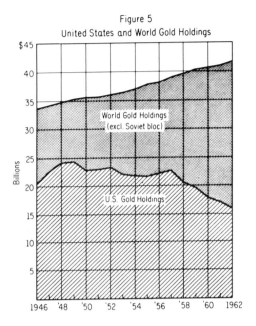

Figure 5
United States and World Gold Holdings

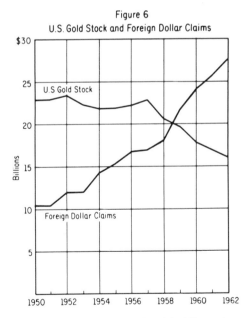

Figure 6
U.S. Gold Stock and Foreign Dollar Claims

hands. Normally, however, increases in official holdings far outstrip the additions of the private sector.

Foreign governments and international organizations account for the

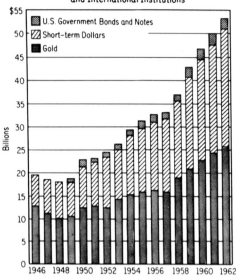

Figure 7
Gold and Dollar Claims of Foreign Countries
and International Institutions

largest part of dollar claims against the United States. The willingness of foreigners to hold dollars is based on the belief that they will be able to convert their dollars into gold and that the prevailing price or conversion rate of $35 for one ounce of gold will not be altered. Only official holders—governments and central banks—can convert their dollar holdings into gold.

Foreign private holders of dollars, on the other hand, cannot buy gold from the United States. However, when their short-term dollars greatly exceed the amount they need as working balances in conducting international transactions, they will normally convert dollars into their local or other needed currencies. In this way, foreign dollar holdings may shift from private to official hands, and from a potential claim to a possible direct claim against our gold.

More than one-half of our $50 billion liabilities to foreigners at the end of 1961 was short-term. These short-term liabilities consist mainly of time deposits at commercial banks, bankers' acceptances, U.S. Government securities, commercial paper and demand deposits in American banks, which serve as working balances for day-to-day business purposes. Long-term foreign investments in the United States, on the other hand, consist largely of holdings of corporate stock and of direct investments in foreign controlled corporations.

Throughout the postwar period the expansion of U.S. investments abroad has more than offset the growth of our liabilities to foreigners. Our capital movements abroad, however, in contrast to foreign investments in the United

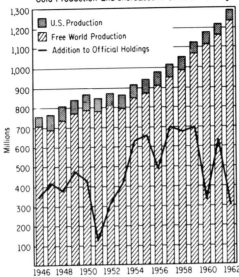

Figure 8
Gold Production and Increases in Official Holdings

TABLE 3

WHO HOLDS WHAT?

Dec. 31, 1962 (Billions of dollars)

GOLD HOLDINGS BY:	
U. S.	$16.1
International institutions (IMF)	2.2
Foreign governments and banks	23.2
World total (excl. Russia)	$41.5
SHORT-TERM DOLLAR HOLDINGS BY:	
International institutions	$ 5.1
Foreign governments and banks (Official)	11.9
Private	7.9
World total (excl. Russia)	$24.9
FOREIGN GOLD AND DOLLAR HOLDINGS BY SELECTED AREAS:	
Western Europe	$29.6
(France . . . 3.7)	
(W. Germany . . . 6.4)	
(Italy . . . 3.6)	
(United Kingdom . . . 4.6)	
Canada	4.4
Latin America	3.4
Asia	5.0
(Japan . . . 2.5)	
Other	1.8
Total	$44.2
International Institutions	8.3
Grand Total	$52.5

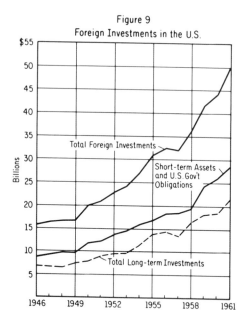

Figure 9
Foreign Investments in the U.S.

States, have emphasized long-term investments. Private long-term investments accounted for 65 percent of the $77 billion total of U.S. investments abroad at the end of 1961. Thus, while our international solvency continues to be reassuring, our assets far exceeding our liabilities, the dollar comes under occasional pressure because of the decline in our liquidity position. The latter is governed by the relation between U.S. gold stock and short-term dollar liabilities to foreigners—i.e., foreign holdings of short-term dollar assets.

Throughout the postwar period, Canada, Western Europe and Latin America have been the leading recipients of U.S. foreign private investments. Starting with 1958, the year when the European Common Market became operative, American private investments in Western Europe have been sharply accelerated. By 1961 total U.S. private investments in Western Europe surpassed those in South America; thus Western Europe became second only to Canada as the most popular area for U.S. private investments abroad.

An important component of our foreign investments is the direct investment by American industry—i.e., branches abroad of U.S. companies and investment in foreign corporations in which U.S. companies have important managerial interests. Both petroleum and manufacturing have evidenced strong growth, but since 1958 manufacturing has attracted the greatest attention as funds flowed to Europe.

During the past few years the movement of short-term investment from the United States has been a major cause of the deficits in our balance of payments. This flight of short-term capital has in part resulted from higher in-

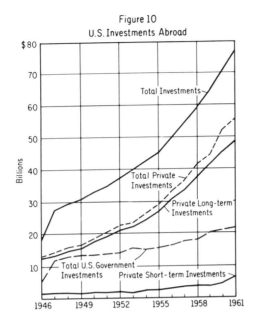

Figure 10
U.S. Investments Abroad

terest rates abroad as compared with those available in the United States on similar short-term investments; partly it has represented the extension of short-term credit to foreign borrowers; and partly it has been motivated by speculation in the foreign exchange market.

Interest rates in other leading countries have been typically higher than in the United States. As a consequence, there is a tendency for U.S. short-term capital to move abroad seeking higher yields. In an effort to discourage such funds from leaving the country, the monetary authorities in the United States in recent years have attempted to put a floor under short-term rates. This policy is credited in part for the diminution of short-term capital out-flows during the past two years. Such a policy, however, presents a dilemma during periods of business decline when domestic conditions might call for easier credit and lower interest rates.

While our export prospects are not particularly reassuring, our import requirements are rising steadily. Our economy is increasingly dependent on our ability to import a long list of raw materials. Furthermore, imports of machinery and vehicles have climbed considerably since the middle 1950's. Purchases from abroad of vegetables, foods and beverages, on the other hand, have shown a slight decline in recent years.

Although total exports have risen substantially in the post-war period, the rate of growth in recent years has been modest. The major categories of our export trade, after reaching a peak in 1957, have remained virtually stationary since then.

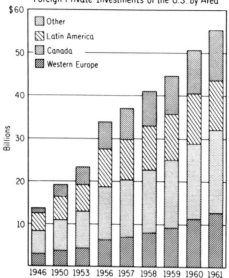

Figure 11
Foreign Private Investments of the U.S. by Area

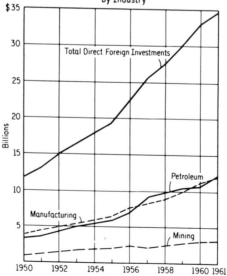

Figure 12
Value of U.S. Direct Foreign Investments
by Industry

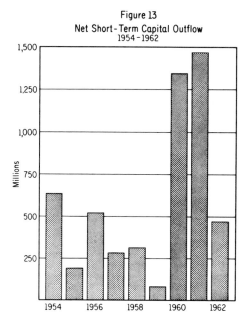

Figure 13
Net Short-Term Capital Outflow
1954-1962

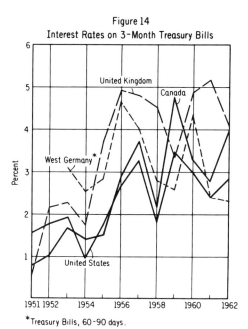

Figure 14
Interest Rates on 3-Month Treasury Bills

*Treasury Bills, 60-90 days.

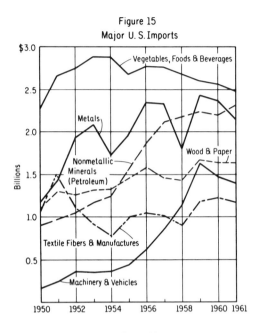

Figure 15
Major U. S. Imports

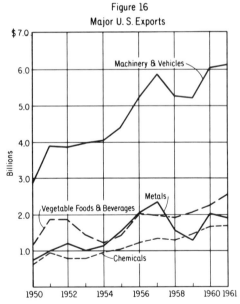

Figure 16
Major U. S. Exports

Our ability to export ultimately determines the international position of the dollar. The challenge from foreign competitors in export markets has come in many areas. The inroads made by small foreign cars in a number of countries including the United States has been particularly apparent. As technology abroad improves further, American business can expect that competition will both broaden and intensify.

SUMMARY

The United States economy today is more seriously affected by international economic forces than at any time in recent peacetime history. While many factors have contributed to this development, three, revealed by the foregoing charts, appear most significant.

First, our foreign payments have exceeded our receipts or income from abroad for many years, resulting in a persistent and sizable deficit in our balance of payments.

Second, the deficit has resulted in a substantial reduction in our gold reserves and a parallel but sharper rise in gold and short-term dollar holdings of foreign nations.

Third, the mobility of private capital has accelerated.

Our imports, overseas investments, military expenditures abroad and foreign aid have expanded more rapidly than our receipts from exports. Starting with the decade of the 1950's, the trade supremacy of the United States has been increasingly challenged. There is evidence that our competitive position in certain markets has deteriorated, especially in the trade of manufactured products. To a considerable extent, this reflects the reconstruction and rehabilitation of the war-torn industrial economies of continental Western Europe, the United Kingdom, and Japan with modern plants and the latest technology.

The second development—the decrease in our gold reserves and the increase in foreign gold and dollar holdings—evidences the growing role of the United States as banker and financier for the free world. Today, the entire structure of the international monetary and reserve mechanism of the free world is built on the fixed relationship between gold and the dollar and the readiness of the United States to buy or sell gold at $35 per ounce. The continuation of the present system requires, above all, the unshakable confidence of the trading nations of the world in the ability and determination of the United States to maintain the value of the dollar and its convertibility into gold at the fixed price of $35 an ounce.

The United States, like any bank, has demand liabilities in excess of liquid reserves. Under these circumstances, the United States has no other alternative but to pursue policies that will engender confidence in the dollar.

The foregoing charts also indicate the mobility of short-term capital in recent years. While the reasons for this development are varied, perhaps the most important has been the achievement of external currency convertibility by the major trading nations of Western Europe and, to a lesser degree, Japan. This enabled their banking and business enterprises to increase foreign balances in the United States and elsewhere and to trade them actively.

The movements of funds were stimulated by interest rate arbitrage due to the wide differential in yields between the United States and foreign countries on comparable short-term investments; by the changes in the value of several leading currencies—the mark and the guilder; and also by speculation. The experience of the past few years has demonstrated dramatically the extent to which the market for capital has become international in character. The sudden, massive international transfer of capital funds has led to the introduction of a number of techniques and procedures during the past two years to cushion the effect of this movement of funds and to defend the dollar.

The Treasury and Federal Reserve System have resumed active intervention in the foreign exchange market. To facilitate this task the Federal Reserve Bank of New York, acting as agent for the Treasury and the Federal Reserve, negotiated a series of reciprocal credit arrangements or swap facilities with leading foreign central banks. The U.S. Treasury started the practice of borrowing currencies from foreign official agencies through the issuance of obligations denominated in the foreign currency concerned. As in the case of the currency swap, the foreign authority is assured of repayment in its own currency and feels protected against any possible devaluation of the dollar. Normally, therefore, the country involved is willing to hold more dollars than otherwise and feels less compelled to exchange dollars for gold, thus alleviating the pressure on our gold stock. The United States also entered into an agreement with nine other major countries by which the lending resources of the International Monetary Fund were increased by $6 billion, two-thirds of which were provided by countries other than the United States. Finally, international cooperation has led to the formation of a "gold pool" by which the monetary authorities of the leading countries are providing gold from their reserves for sale on the London gold market. This makes available a supply of gold which complements that of the United States in helping to prevent large fluctuations in the price of gold and serves to discourage excessive speculation.

These innovations provide our monetary authorities with powerful means to cope with any sudden pressure against the dollar. However, they clearly do not constitute a solution to a continuation of the deficit in our balance of payments.

As a nation, the United States must demonstrate to the world its determination to balance its international payments. Accomplishment of this objective requires that we either increase our foreign receipts or reduce our outlays abroad. Actually, a balance probably will be restored by some combination of the two. Various steps have been taken already. The government has made significant efforts to reduce its economic and military expenditures abroad. It also has sought to distribute the burden of foreign aid more equitably among the nations of the West and has taken steps to tie the outlays for foreign aid programs more closely to purchases of U.S. goods and services. U.S. officials have encouraged prepayments of loans by foreign governments and have fostered agreements with Western European nations for the purchase of military equipment and services from the United States. The results of these efforts have been helpful, but there obviously are severe limitations as to how far and how long we can use such measures.

An expansion of our exports of goods and services can contribute importantly to the solution of our balance of payments problem. This means utilizing our basic strengths, which consists of managerial ability and ingenuity, the skills of an expanding labor force, a highly efficient productive plant, and a wealth of natural resources. These must be combined so that our products are competitive in the markets of the world.

Markets abroad represent a challenge and a profit opportunity that unfortunately far too few American businessmen have pursued. The challenge of foreign competition must be met on all levels—cost of production, quality, attractiveness to foreign buyers, packaging, merchandising, distribution—in short, producing the right products, at the right prices, and with the right quality to meet the desires of foreign buyers. Only in this manner will our sales abroad be expanded sufficiently.

One of the most important changes favoring our exports has been the removal by the major trading countries of Europe, and lately to a lesser extent also by Japan, of the quantitative restrictions on imports from the dollar area, with the notable exception of agricultural products. Moreover, the Trade Expansion Act of 1962 has set the stage for a liberalization of international trade. However, a new element of concern is the current trade policy of the European Economic Community. Because of it, for example, the outlook for the sales of our agricultural products abroad is clouded.

Redressing the deficit in our international payments so as to maintain the value of the U.S. dollar, the keystone of the monetary and payments structure of the entire free world, is a matter worthy of the most careful thought, requiring the aggressive, determined, coordinated efforts of government, labor and business.

THE BALANCE OF PAYMENTS IN 1963*

The outstanding development in our foreign transactions during 1963 was the sharp decline in the adverse balance from the first to the second half of the year. For the year as a whole, the improvement from the preceding year was considerably smaller. The changes are most evident in the balances on the "regular" types of transactions, including goods and services, Government grants and capital flows, movements of U.S. private capital and private foreign investments (other than changes in liquid assets) in the United States. After adjustment for seasonal variations, the balance on these transactions shifted from about $2,300 million in the first half of 1963 to $1,000 million in the second half (revised from the preliminary release). The total for the year was $3,300 million, as compared with $3,570 million in 1962, $3,040 million in 1961, and between $3,500 and $4,200 million during the years 1958 to 1960 (Table 1, line A13).

SPECIAL TRANSACTIONS

If "special" Government transactions are added to the regular types of transactions, the improvement in the balance from the first to the second half of 1963 is also evident, although the quarter-to-quarter changes are affected by the large changes that occurred in "special" transactions. If sales of nonmarketable medium-term Government securities which are convertible by the foreign holders into cash at short notice—first issued in 1963—are included with liquid liabilities, the seasonally adjusted balance changed from about $2,170 million in the first half to about $490 million in the second half of 1963 (Table 1, line C1). If these securities are considered a medium-term capital inflow (although of the "special" type) the balance shifted from $1,670 million to $290 million (Table 1, line C2). The annual balance under the first classification of these securities was $2,660 million, and under the second, $1,960 million. The balance on "regular" plus "special" types of transactions in 1962 was about $2,190 million and in 1961 $2,370 million.

In addition to the sale of nonmarketable medium-term securities, the special transactions include advances by foreign governments in excess of

---

*Walther Lederer, *Survey of Current Business,* March, 1964, pp. 14–23.

TABLE 1

ANALYSIS OF U.S. BALANCE OF PAYMENTS, SEASONALLY ADJUSTED, EXCLUDING MILITARY GRANT AID

(Millions of dollars)

	CALENDAR YEAR		1962				1963			
	1962	1963	I	II	III	IV	Ir	IIr	IIIr	IVp
Transactions other than changes in official monetary assets and in liquid liabilities (including nonmarketable, medium-term convertible Government securities)										
I. U.S. PAYMENTS (DEBITS) RECORDED	33,254	35,544	8,246	8,316	8,214	8,478	8,463	9,753	8,373	8,955
1. Imports of goods and services	24,964	26,118	6,119	6,222	6,282	6,341	6,270	6,453	6,694	6,701
2. Merchandise	16,145	16,962	3,942	4,030	4,127	4,046	4,014	4,182	4,392	4,374
3. Military expenditures	3,028	2,880	754	748	732	794	748	725	708	699
4. Other services	5,791	6,276	1,423	1,444	1,423	1,501	1,508	1,546	1,594	1,628
5. Remittances and pensions	736	812	191	182	176	187	211	211	195	195
6. Government grants and capital outflows	4,281	4,532	1,075	1,078	1,045	1,083	1,053	1,355	1,010	1,114
7. (Transactions involving no direct dollar outflows from the United States)	3,211	3,650	806	830	804	771	812	1,088	829	921
8. (Dollar payments to foreign countries and international institutions)	1,070	882	269	248	241	312	241	267	181	193
9. U.S. private capital	3,273	4,082	861	834	711	867	929	1,734	474	945
10. Direct investments	1,557	1,799	199	506	359	493	501	488	209	601
11. Long-term portfolio	1,209	1,641	357	329	188	335	512	620	294	215
12. Short-term	507	642	305	−1	164	39	−84	626	−29	129
II. U.S. RECEIPTS (CREDITS) RECORDED	32,093	33,379	7,688	7,901	8,327	8,177	7,715	8,344	8,534	8,786
1. Exports of goods and services	29,790	31,603	7,206	7,610	7,550	7,424	7,452	7,903	7,921	8,327
2. Merchandise	20,479	21,902	5,022	5,262	5,270	4,925	5,010	5,494	5,559	5,839
3. (Financed by Government grants and capital)	2,345	2,733	595	574	585	591	590	827	641	675
4. Military sales	660	632	113	190	141	216	181	203	p92	156
5. Income on investments, private	3,850	4,067	904	940	946	1,060	1,059	969	993	1,046
6. Income on investments, Government	472	498	109	144	105	114	123	124	125	126
7. Other services	4,239	4,504	1,058	1,074	1,088	1,109	1,079	1,113	1,152	1,160
8. Repayments on U.S. Government loans, scheduled	617	649	155	184	130	148	151	156	178	164
9. Repayments and selloffs, nonscheduled	666	325	....	53	471	142	25	34	241	25
10. Foreign private capital other than liquid funds	155	392	172	15	3	−35	−27	266	136	17
11. Government liabilities	865	410	155	39	173	498	114	−15	p58	253
SELECTED BALANCES (NET CREDITS +, DEBITS −)										
A. Regular types of transactions, seasonally adjusted:										
1. Merchandise trade, excluding military	4,334	4,940	1,080	1,232	1,143	879	996	1,312	1,167	1,465
2. Military sales and expenditures	−2,368	−2,248	−641	−558	−591	−578	−567	−522	p−616	−543
3. Incomes on investments	3,327	3,369	773	839	806	909	904	806	809	850
4. Other services	−467	−576	−125	−125	−90	−127	−151	−146	−133	−146
5. Goods and services	4,826	5,485	1,087	1,388	1,268	1,083	1,182	1,450	1,227	1,626
6. (Excluding exports of goods and services financed by Government grants and capital outflows)	1,943	2,149	348	689	550	356	447	437	464	801
7. Remittances and pensions	−736	−812	−191	−182	−176	−187	−211	−211	−195	−195
8. Government grants and capital outflows, less changes in associated liabilities, less scheduled loan repayments	−3,517	−3,789	−907	−850	−850	−910	−871	−1,200	−786	−932
Domestic and foreign private capital:										
9. Direct and long-term portfolio	−2,495	−3,053	−361	−769	−557	−808	−1,022	−905	−391	−735
10. Short-term	−623	−637	−328	−50	−151	−94	66	−563	53	−193
11. Miscellaneous Government nonliquid liabilities	−3	(x)	(x)	−3	3	−1	(x)	1	2	−3
12. Errors and unrecorded transactions	−1,025	−495	−27	−37	−469	−492	−135	+121	−386	−95
13. Balance on regular types of transactions (seasonally adjusted)	−3,573	−3,301	−727	−503	−934	−1,409	−991	−1,307	−476	−527
14. Less: Net seasonal adjustments	....	....	−113	−129	+337	−95	−181	−94	+364	−89
15. Balance on regular types of transactions before adjustment	−3,573	−3,301	−614	−374	−1,271	−1,314	−810	−1,213	−840	−438

TABLE 1 (Continued)

	CALENDAR YEAR		1962				1963			
	1962	1963	I	II	III	IV	Ir	IIr	IIIr	IVp
B. Special Government transactions (not seasonally adjusted):										
1. Nonscheduled receipts on Government loans	666	325	....	53	471	142	25	34	241	25
2. Advances on military exports	470	359	142	-2	107	223	20	-5	p105	239
Sales of nonmarketable, medium-term, nonconvertible securities:										
3. Dollar securities	....	31	....	....	....	....	58	¹19	-45	¹-1
4. Foreign currency securities	251	-74	....	....	....	251	5	-29	-50	....
Sales of nonmarketable, medium-term, convertible securities:										
5. Dollar securities	....	150	....	....	....	....	125	....	25	....
6. Foreign currency securities	....	552	....	....	....	....	225	152	150	25
C. 1. Balance A+B excluding net receipts from sales of nonmarketable, medium-term, convertible Government securities (including seasonal adjustment of items in A)	-2,186	-2,660	-585	-452	-356	-793	-883	-1,288	-225	-264
1a. Excluding seasonal adjustment (equals line 52, table 2)	-2,186	-2,660	-472	-323	-693	-698	-702	-1,194	-589	-175
2. Balance A+B including net receipts from sales of nonmarketable, medium-term, convertible Government securities (including seasonal adjustment of items in A)	-2,186	-1,958	-585	-452	-356	-793	-533	-1,136	-50	-239
2a. Excluding seasonal adjustment (equals line 52a, table 2)	-2,186	-1,958	-472	-323	-693	-698	-352	-1,042	-414	-150
D. Increase in short-term official and banking liabilities and in foreign holdings of marketable U.S. Government bonds and notes (decrease -)	653	1,580	46	486	-188	309	320	918	187	155
1. Foreign private holders including banks and international and regional organizations (excluding IMF)	200	603	699	24	-458	-65	394	142	38	29
2. Foreign official holders	453	977	-653	462	270	374	-74	776	149	126
E. Decrease in U.S. monetary reserve assets (increase -)	1,533	378	426	-163	881	389	32	124	227	-5
1. IMF position	626	30	237	44	331	14	-46	2	59	15
2. Convertible currencies	17	-113	-114	-324	104	351	-33	6	-28	-58
3. Gold	890	461	303	117	446	24	111	116	196	38

r Revised.   p Preliminary   (x) Less than $500,000.
1 Certificates sold abroad by Export-Import Bank.

deliveries on military contracts, and repayments of foreign debts to the U.S. Government in advance of contractual schedules. Advances by foreign countries on military contracts exceeded deliveries during 1963 by $360 million with most of the difference accruing in the second half of the year. Data on deliveries in that period are still preliminary however, mainly with respect to timing between the third and fourth quarters. For the year 1963 as a whole receipts from net advances were about $110 million less than in 1962. (Table 1, line B2.)

Repayments on foreign loans in advance of contractual schedules were relatively large in the third quarter when France and the Netherlands made large payments. The figures in the other quarters represent mainly sales by the Export-Import Bank of foreign notes prior to their maturity. For the year 1963 as a whole nonscheduled receipts were $325 million, compared with $666 million in 1962. (Table 1, line B1 and Table 2, line 41.)

Except for the sale of nonmarketable medium-term convertible securities, which amounted to $702 million during 1963 (with $502 million in the first half of the year and $200 million in the second), net receipts from special transactions in 1963 were $640 million, compared with about $1,380 million in 1962. While these receipts improved the balance as measured by changes in monetary reserves and liquid liabilities, the decline from 1962 to 1963 demonstrates the advisability of separating these transactions from the other or "regular" types in analyzing developments affecting the balance of payments.

CHANGES IN RESERVES

A major change in 1963 affecting our international financial position stemmed from the fact that foreign countries kept much more of their net receipts from transactions with the United States in liquid dollar assets. Accordingly, U.S. reserve assets, including the gold tranche in the IMF (which measures our nearly automatic drawing right) declined substantially less than in 1962. The total decline in reserve assets during 1963 was $378 million, compared with $1,533 million in 1962, and going back 4 years, between a low of $600 million in 1961 and a high of $2,275 million in 1958. The decline during 1963 in gold holdings alone was $461 million, by far the smallest amount since 1957.

The reduction in foreign purchases of U.S. gold can in part be attributed to strengthened cooperation between the monetary authorities of the principal countries involved in international financial transactions. This cooperation since 1961 has gradually become more effective in dampening the impact of various adverse political and economic developments on international gold and capital markets. Larger sales of gold in 1963 by the Soviet Union to finance increased purchases of foodstuffs by the Soviet bloc countries were another factor reducing foreign demand for U.S. gold. The total amount of gold added to foreign reserves from sources outside the United States, which include Soviet sales as well as new gold production less private purchases in the free world is estimated to have been about $930 million in 1963, as compared with less than $400 million in 1962 and $740 million in 1961. (See Table 2, Memorandum item III.)

The rise in foreign holdings of liquid dollar assets in 1963 was about $1,580 million. In addition to this foreign central banks purchased the $700 million of nonmarketable, medium-term convertible U.S. Government securities. In 1962 the total rise in foreign holdings of liquid dollar assets was about $650 million. The rise in 1963 is believed to have been accentuated by the accumulations of dollar proceeds from gold sales by Soviet bloc authorities in private foreign banks, in anticipation of dollar payments for increased imports of foodstuffs.

Line	TYPE OF TRANSACTION	ALL AREAS 1962 Year	III	IV	1963 Year	I	II	IIIr	IVp	WESTERN EUROPE 1962 Year	III	IV	1963 Year	IIIr	IVp	EASTERN EUROPE 1962 Year	III	IV	1963 Year	IIIr	IVp
1	Exports of goods and services	31,329	7,322	8,185	na	7,651	8,777	7,680	na	10,792	2,476	2,888	na	2,517	na	162	30	25	211	40	69
2	Goods and services transferred under military grants, net	1,539	218	305	na	447	675	p215	na	626	108	144	na	p114	na						
3	Goods and services excluding transfers under military grants	29,790	7,104	7,880	31,603	7,204	8,102	7,465	8,832	10,166	2,368	2,744	10,676	2,403	2,974	162	30	25	211	40	69
4	Merchandise, adjusted, excluding military	20,479	4,888	5,146	21,902	4,945	5,675	5,184	6,098	7,106	1,683	1,784	7,598	1,739	2,142	131	23	18	171	27	55
5	Transportation	1,749	446	441	1,848	410	468	496	474	871	225	216	864	229	213	14	4	4	19	3	10
6	Travel	921	286	188	941	187	265	289	200	104	31	24	114	33	26	(x)	(x)	(x)			
	Miscellaneous services:																				
7	Private	1,475	370	393	1,511	372	373	373	393	572	139	151	603	145	152	8	2	2	11	3	3
8	Government, excluding military	184	49	49	204	49	51	50	54	58	15	14	56	14	14	(x)	(x)	(x)	(x)	(x)	(x)
9	Military transactions	660	127	209	632	164	241	p78	149	539	94	180	517	p57	117						
	Income on investments:																				
10	Direct investments	3,050	646	1,059	3,158	778	695	659	1,026	520	106	217	538	101	151						
11	Other private	800	201	213	909	210	226	227	246	183	45	49	209	53	58			(x)		(x)	
12	Government	472	91	182	498	89	108	109	192	213	30	109	177	32	101	9	1	1	10	7	1
13	Imports of goods and services	24,964	6,466	6,312	26,118	5,919	6,553	6,955	6,691	8,830	2,229	2,236	9,181	2,407	2,396	95	28	20	99	32	21
14	Merchandise, adjusted, excluding military	16,145	3,960	4,181	16,962	3,915	4,223	4,305	4,519	4,537	1,073	1,203	4,717	1,166	1,317	79	21	17	81	23	19
15	Transportation	2,055	543	477	2,154	468	595	586	505	1,139	316	243	1,250	348	300	4	1	1	3	(x)	1
16	Travel	1,905	737	378	2,071	315	536	805	415	615	247	103	680	276	115	7	5	(x)	8	7	
	Miscellaneous services:																				
17	Private	436	114	108	434	103	107	114	110	254	63	63	260	66	65	(x)	(x)	(x)	(x)		
18	Government, excluding military	400	143	99	421	91	84	150	96	88	23	25	105	30	27	4	1	1	6	2	1
19	Military expenditures	3,028	732	794	2,880	748	725	708	699	1,606	368	433	1,483	361	363	1	(x)	1	(x)	(x)	
	Income on investments:																				
20	Private	656	151	186	796	188	188	183	237	400	91	117	465	102	147			(x)	(x)	(x)	
21	Government	339	86	89	400	91	95	104	110	191	48	49	221	58	62				(x)		
22	Balance on goods and services	6,365	856	1,873	na	1,732	2,224	725	na	1,962	247	652	na	110	na	67	2	5	112	8	48
23	Excluding transfers under military grants	4,826	638	1,568	5,485	1,285	1,549	510	2,141	1,336	139	508	1,495	-4	578	67	2	5	112	8	48
24	Unilateral transfers, net (to foreign countries(-))	-4,178	-826	-975	na	-1,086	-1,397	-872	na	-1,102	-205	-257	na	-224	na	-35	-9	-9	-36	-9	-9
25	Excluding military transfers	-2,639	-608	-670	-2,719	-639	-722	-657	-701	-476	-97	-113	-428	-110	-109	-35	-9	-9	-36	-9	-9
26	Private remittances	-491	-117	-143	-548	-130	-141	-132	-145	-148	-34	-42	-146	-43	-47	-27	-7	-8	-26	-6	-7
	Government:																				
27	Military grants of goods and services	-1,539	-218	-305	na	-447	-675	p-215	na	-626	-108	-144	na	p114	na						
28	Other grants	-1,903	-434	-466	-1,907	-440	-515	-462	-490	-208	-36	-40	-153	-36	-30	-6	-1	-1	-7	-2	-1
29	Pensions and other transfers	-245	-57	-61	-264	-69	-66	-63	-66	-120	-27	-31	-129	-31	-32	-2	-1	(x)	-3	-1	-1
30	U.S. capital, net (increase in U.S. assets (-))	-4,368	-496	-1,359	-5,733	-1,436	-2,399	-316	-1,582	-592	120	-44	-1,413	100	-370	-42	-6	6	-57	5	-14
31	Private, net	-3,273	-521	-1,083	-4,082	-974	-1,683	-250	-1,175	-1,258	-309	-298	-1,595	-151	-415	3	-4	6	-26	2	-15
32	Direct investments, net	-1,557	-324	-538	-1,799	-501	-498	-154	-646	-808	-211	-160	-800	-96	-188						
33	New issues of foreign securities	-1,076	-133	-461	-1,294	-506	-518	-184	-86	-195	-15	-7	-272	-19	-34						
34	Redemptions	170	58	34	150	31	52	24	43	17	8	4	18	3	5						
35	Transactions in outstanding foreign securities	-55	-15	49	43	-48	-64	56	99	-8	3	2	60								
36	Other long-term, net	-248	-34	33	-540	-11	-124	-119	-286	-86	-8	-34	-486	-82	-243	2	-2	1	-17	2	-11
37	Short-term, net	-507	-73	-200	-642	61	-531	127	-299	-186	-77	-139	-541	41	-15	1	-2	5	-9	(x)	(x)
38	Government, net	-1,095	25	-276	-1,651	-462	-716	-66	-407	666	429	254	182	251	45	-45	-2	(x)	-31	3	1
39	Long-term capital	-2,133	-486	-660	-2,184	-563	-620	-438	-563	-288	-59	-63	-304	-54	-79	-2	(x)	(x)	(x)		(x)
40	Repayments on U.S. Government loans, scheduled	617	115	213	649	126	131	163	229	232	42	111	209	66	89	13	2	(x)	14	8	1
41	Repayments and selloffs, nonscheduled	666	471	142	325	25	34	241	25	666	471	142	277	233	4						
42	Foreign currency holdings and short-term claims, net (increase (-))	-245	-75	29	-441	-50	-261	-32	-98	56	-25	64		6	31	-56	-4	(x)	-45	-5	(x)
43	Foreign capital (lines 44-48), net (increase in U.S. Liabilities (-))	1,020	162	505	802	73	237	180	312	778	125	380	636	154	223	(x)	(x)	(x)	(x)	(x)	(x)
44	Direct investments in the United States	132	6	8	86	-18	36	56	12	62	16	-8	111								
45	Other long-term investments	139	-16	12	301	9	167	56	69	102	-38	-15	190	38	51	(x)	(x)	(x)	(x)	(x)	
46	U.S. private short-term commercial and brokerage liabilities	-116	13	-55	5	-18	63	24	-64	-115	-1	-43	46	28	-43	(x)	(x)	(x)	(x)	(x)	
47	U.S. Government liabilities other than interest-bearing securities	614	159	289	453	37	-19	p139	296	478	148	195	338	p115	205	(x)	(x)	(x)	(x)		
48	U.S. Government nonmarketable medium-term nonconvertible securities	251		251	-43	63	-10	-95	-1	251		251	-49	-95	-1				(x)		
49	U.S. Government nonmarketable medium-term convertible securities				702	350	152	175	25				577	175	25						
50	Increase in short-term official and banking liabilities and in foreign holdings of marketable U.S. Government bonds and notes (decrease (-))	653	-188	309	1,580	r320	r918	187	155	-717	-683	-64	661	84	34	1	(x)	4	11	-4	6
51	Increase (-) in monetary reserve assets, including gold, convertible currencies, and IMF position	1,533	881	389	378	32	124	227	-5	1,127	500	183	287	129	-68						
52	Reduction in monetary reserve assets and increase in liquid liabilities including U.S. Government medium-term convertible securities (lines 49-51)	2,186	693	698	2,660	702	1,194	589	175	410	-183	119	1,525	388	-9	1	(x)	4	11	-4	6
52a	Excluding increase in U.S. Government non-marketable medium-term convertible securities (lines 50 and 51)	2,186	693	698	1,958	352	1,042	414	150	410	-183	119	948	213	-34	1	(x)	4	11	-4	6
53	Errors and omissions and transfers of funds between foreign areas (receipts by foreign areas (-)), net	-1,025	-389	-742	-495	15	141	-306	-345	-1,456	-104	-850	-1,815	-528	-313	9	13	-6	-30		-31
	Memorandum items:																				
I	Increase in reported total foreign gold reserves and liquid dollar holdings.[2]	2,514	661	877	3,523	840	1,350	749	584	493	-334	255	2,052	442	332	1	(x)	4	11	-4	6
II	Through estimated net receipts from or payments (-) to, the United States.[3]	2,128	681	680	2,591	687	1,178	574	152	-1,046	-287	-731	-290	-140	-322	10	13	-2	-19	-4	-25
III	Through other transactions.[4]	386	-20	197	932	153	172	175	432	1,539	-47	986	2,342	582	654	-9	-13	6	30	0	31

r Revised.   p Preliminary.   na Not available.   (x) Less than $500,000.

1. Transactions with shipping companies operating under the flag of the Bahamas, Honduras, Liberia and Panama are included in "unallocated."
2. Changes in reported total gold reserves of foreign banks and governments (including international organizations but excluding the countries of the Soviet bloc), net of convertible currencies held by U.S. monetary authorities, plus liquid claims on the United States plus net changes in their IMF position through U.S. dollar transactions.

	CANADA						LATIN AMERICAN REPUBLICS						JAPAN						ALL OTHER COUNTRIES[1]						INTERNATIONAL INSTITUTIONS AND UNALLOCATED[1]						Line
	1962			1963			1962			1963			1962			1963			1962			1963			1962			1963			
	Year	III	IV	Year	IIIr	IVp	Year	III	IV	Year	IIIr	IVp	Year	III	IV	Year	IIIr	IVp	Year	III	IV	Year	IIIr	IVp	Year	III	IV	Year	IIIr	IVp	
	5,386	1,287	1,388	5,549	1,350	1,535	5,263	1,287	1,334	na	1,278	na	1,859	425	473	2,214	559	629	7,548	1,741	1,985	na	1,857	na	319	76	92	310	79	75	1
		81	13	17	na	p9	na												832	97	144	na	p92	na							2
	5,386	1,287	1,388	5,549	1,350	1,535	5,182	1,274	1,317	5,238	1,269	1,371	1,859	425	473	2,214	559	629	6,716	1,644	1,841	7,405	1,765	2,179	319	76	92	310	79	75	3
	3,889	908	982	4,096	983	1,105	3,291	806	817	3,221	771	849	1,507	337	383	1,798	449	519	4,555	1,131	1,162	5,018	1,215	1,428							4
	107	29	28	102	28	25	235	59	61	277	76	74	96	24	23	108	29	28	284	73	73	324	91	86	142	32	36	154	40	38	5
	430	135	80	368	124	67	307	88	70	347	94	80	13	5	3	20	6	5	67	27	11	92	32	22							6
	175	45	48	173	44	47	287	77	72	268	70	70	94	23	25	97	24	25	255	63	74	277	87	75	84	21	21	82	20	21	7
	3	1	(x)	2	(x)	1	36	10	10	45	11	12	6	2	2	7	2	1	81	21	23	94	23	26							8
	26	6	4	18	p3	4	16	3	6	17	p1	2	24	5	4	24	p5	10	42	13	13	45	p9	15	13	6	2	11	p3	1	9
	476	93	173	477	89	199	762	171	212	787	187	206	26	7	7	22	7	5	1,234	265	430	1,317	271	460	32	4	20	17	4	5	10
	280	70	73	313	79	87	135	35	36	149	36	38	78	19	21	107	26	30	76	19	21	85	21	23	48	13	13	46	12	10	11
	(x)	(x)					113	25	33	127	23	40	15	3	5	31	11	6	122	32	34	153	36	44				(x)			12
	4,609	1,324	1,153	4,856	1,381	1,230	4,387	1,038	1,109	4,545	1,147	1,171	1,890	516	488	2,066	554	554	4,481	1,129	1,141	4,724	1,229	1,190	672	202	165	647	205	150	13
	3,445	881	899	3,651	931	982	3,456	788	874	3,531	871	922	1,358	382	350	1,497	413	393	3,187	796	816	3,410	885	862	83	19	22	75	16	24	14
	102	26	27	104	29	25	146	39	42	146	38	33	70	18	16	77	20	17	176	45	40	161	40	34	418	98	108	413	111	95	15
	492	275	80	513	280	85	477	130	115	540	148	128	50	13	15	52	14	16	264	67	65	278	80	71							16
	49	14	12	57	15	13	119	34	29	102	30	28	4	1	1	4	1	1	10	2	3	11	2	3							17
	4	1	1	5	1	2	73	18	20	81	21	20	7	2	2	11	2	3	124	30	33	140	38	35	100	68	17	73	56	8	18
	304	75	74	278	64	58	76	20	19	82	23	22	376	94	97	370	90	88	665	175	170	666	170	168	(x)						19
	178	42	48	191	46	51	31	7	8	52	13	15	10	2	2	31	8	8	36	9	10	42	10	12	1	(x)	1	15	4	4	20
	35	10	12	57	15	14	9	2	2	11	3	3	15	4	5	24	6	7	19	5	4	16	4	5	70	17	17	71	18	19	21
	777	−37	235	693	−31	305	876	249	225	na	131	na	−31	−91	−15	148	5	96	3,067	612	844	na	628	na	−353	−126	−73	−337	−126	−75	22
	777	−37	235	693	−31	305	795	236	208	693	122	200	−31	−91	−15	148	5	96	2,235	515	700	2,681	536	989	−353	−126	−73	−337	−126	−75	23
	−23	−7	−7	−29	−7	−7	−353	−77	−96	na	−97	na	−30	−7	−9	−28	−8	−6	−2,479	−495	−546	na	−511	na	−156	−26	−51	−136	−16	−80	24
	−23	−7	−7	−29	−7	−7	−272	−64	−79	−380	−88	−97	−30	−7	−4	−28	−8	−6	−1,647	−349	−402	−1,682	−419	−393	−156	−26	−51	−136	−16	−80	25
		−1	−1	−5	−1	−1	−78	−16	−29	−104	−18	−18	−21	−5	−6	−20	−5	−5	−215	−54	−55	−244	−59	−64	−2		−2	−3		−3	26
																															27
							−81	−13	−17	na	p−9	na							−832	−97	−144	na	p−92	na							28
							−176	−44	−46	−255	−66	−74	−3	−1	−1	−1	−1	(x)	−1,356	−326	−329	−1,358	−341	−308	−154	−26	−49	−133	−16	−77	29
	−23	−6	−6	−24	−6	−6	−18	−4	−4	−21	−4	−5	−6	−1	−2	−7	−2	−1	−76	−18	−19	−80	−19	−21							30
	−634	−161	−293	−771	36	84	−727	−120	−226	−531	−101	−148	−572	−75	−141	−888	−93	−184	−446	−236	−457	−1,942	−264	−710	−355	−18	−204	−131	1	−40	31
		−164	−294	−773	32	84	−227	1	−127	−154	−50	−123	−516	−58	−119	−833	−97	−387	−407	37	−169	−644	13	−344	−234	−24	−82	−57	1	25	32
	−312	−51	−150					32	18	−22	50	−124	−53	−5	−26	−89	−17	−22	−348	−42	−117	−521	−49	−228	−68	−33	−63	−14	−4	20	33
	−457	−41	−294	−736	−79	−25	−102	(x)	−83	−35	−23		4	3	1			(x)	31	4	18	3	6	17	2	2	12	3	2		34
	96	38	23	106	15	30	5	3	(x)	1	(x)		−23	−11	−4	−20	−5	1							−98	10	−20	−55	2	3	35
	78	3	37	96	28	29	−13	−2	−11	11	2	5	−103	−33	−36	−137	−39	−69	14	55	6	39	7	15	−1			−1	(x)		36
	−36	−5	8	−17	−25	−11	−41		105	44	18	33	−240	36	−37	−55	4	3	55	19	−102	36	−113		(x)	(x)	(x)	(x)			37
	−3	−108	98	47	131	165	−111	23	−116	−97	−97	−37	−56	−17	−22	−55	4	3	−1,039	−273	−288	−1,298	−277	−366	−121	6	−122	−74		−65	38
							−500	−121	−99	−377	−51	−25	−98	−23	−29	−93	−9	−3	−1,004	−286	−299	−1,157	−289	−267	−121			−121	−77	−65	39
							−620	−118	−148	−553	−86	−149																			
	3	1	2	4			179	35	47	216	34	103	39	3	7	61	12	6	152	31	48	144	40	30	2	2		5	3		40
							33	4	21										15	4											41
	3	1	2	4			−59	−38	2	−73	−3	(x)	3	3	(x)	−23	1	(x)	−187	−18	−37	−300	−32	−129	−2	4	−1	−2	−3	(x)	42
	116	4	39	21	−2	23	105	29	47	14	17	−20	10	14	−10	−56	−12	−12	−42	−15	8	107	16	14	53	5	41	80	7	84	43
	43	13	7		6		−20	−12	−2	24	5	9	−25	3	−3	−3	−2	−3	4	1	(x)										44
	59	12	23	15	(x)	8	−21	−2	−9	35	11	−1	1	(x)	(x)	1	(x)	(x)	−19	8	8	36	(x)	5	17	4	5	24	7	6	45
	19	9	8	−10	3	8	16	10	4	−27	3	−10	−15	8	−18	−27	−13	−5	−21	−14	−6	23	3	−14	(x)	1	(x)	(x)	(x)		46
	−5	−4	1	−1	p−1	1	104	21	49	26	p15	−7	(x)	1	−1	−5	p−2	−4	1	−7	9	39	p12	23	36		36			78	47
				1		(x)				(x)												5									48
				125																											49
	522	596	−8	−68	−16	−129	124	−116	182	659	147	129	505	134	138	259	76	69	42	−15	20	196	−96	123	176	−104	37	−138	−4	−77	50
	−193	3	249	(x)	−17	17	−175	−9	−84	−32	16	3							90	44	9	24	25	5	684	343	32	99	74	38	51
	329	599	241	57	−33	−112	−51	−125	98	627	163	132	505	134	138	259	76	69	132	29	29	220	−71	128	860	239	69	−39	70	−39	52
	329	599	241	−68	−33	−112	−51	−125	98	627	163	132	505	134	138	259	76	69	132	29	29	220	−71	128	860	239	69	−39	70	−39	52a
	−565	−398	−215	29	37	−293	150	44	−48	−423	−113	−67	118	25	37	565	32	237	768	105	122	616	202	−28	−49	−74	218	563	64	150	53
	281	619	260	166	−13	−70	−114	−169	86	648	158	175	505	134	138	259	76	69	420	110	64	378	−25	126	928	301	70	9	115	−54	I
	−236	201	26	86	4	−405	99	−81	50	204	50	65	623	159	175	824	108	306	900	134	151	836	131	100	753	153	269	455	119	88	II
	517	418	234	80	−17	335	−213	−88	36	444	108	110	−118	−25	−37	−565	−32	−237	−480	−24	−87	−458	−156	26	175	148	−199	−446	−4	142	III

3. For "All Areas" equals balance (with reverse sign) of line 23 (less net sales of gold by domestic sources to (+) or purchases from (−) the monetary gold stock of the United States) plus lines 25, 30, 43, and 53. Domestic sales to (+) or purchases from (−) the monetary gold stocks were in millions of dollars: 1962 III, −12, IV, −18, 1963 I, −15, II, −16, III, −15, IV, −23.

4. Line I minus line II for all areas represents gold obtained by foreign central banks and governments outside the United States.

Source: U.S. Department of Commerce, Office of Business Economics.

An important development in 1963 was the substantial gains in gold and dollar holdings of several of the less developed countries. As a group these countries accounted for more than $1 billion of the total foreign gain in liquid dollar assets and gold purchases from the United States, while the developed countries accounted for about $1.6 billion (including the $700 million of nonmarketable medium-term convertible securities). In 1962, the less developed countries as a group had only a minor increase in reserves.

Among these countries, major increases in dollar and gold holdings were registered by Argentina, Mexico, Venezuela, and Spain.

Major Changes In Foreign Transactions

The major changes in the "regular" types of international transactions are shown in Table 3.

Among the changes from 1962 to 1963 the following appear most significant:

(1) The $1.4 billion rise in merchandise exports considerably exceeded the $800 million rise in imports. About $400 million of the rise in exports and, therefore, in the trade balance was directly financed by Government grants and capital outflows, and in this period at least did not contribute to dollar receipts from abroad. (To the extent that exports are financed by dollar loans, principal and interest will be received in subsequent periods, while some of the loan repayments received in the current period may be considered payments for exports in earlier periods.)

(2) A reduction was achieved in military expenditures.

(3) Net income on foreign investment increased as it did in most of the postwar years, but only by $40 million as compared with $365 million in 1962 and $680 million in 1961.

(4) Net outflows of private capital rose by about $570 million. A part of that rise may have been associated, however, with the rise in exports, although data to measure the relationship between exports and private capital flows are not available.

(5) Government grants and capital outflows rose by $250 million, but goods and services supplied under these programs from the United States and other expenditures in the United States rose by about $440 million so that direct dollar outflows were about $190 million less than in 1962.

(6) The balance on unrecorded transactions (and errors in the estimates) continued to be on the debit side during the year as a whole, but it was about $530 million less than in 1962. The decline may be due, in part, to better coverage in 1963 of the figures on capital flows and in part to a decline in capital movements, both long- and short-term, which usually fail to be recorded. It would be incorrect, however, to assume that errors and omissions are limited to the data on capital flows.

TABLE 3

MAJOR CHANGES IN INTERNATIONAL TRANSAC-
TIONS SEASONALLY ADJUSTED

(Millions of dollars)

(+ indicates changes resulting in an improvement of the balance of payments)

	1961-62	1962-63	First to Second Half 1963	Third to Fourth Quarter 1963
Merchandise exports..	+566	+1,423	+894	+280
Merchandise imports...	−1,648	−817	−570	+18
Balance..............	−1,082	+606	+324	+298
Income on investments:				
Receipts................	+478	+243	+15	+54
Payments..............	−113	−201	−66	−13
Balance..............	+365	+42	−51	+41
Military expenditures and sales (net)........	+164	+120	−70	+73
Travel (net)..............	−137	−146	−52	+1
Government grants and capital outflows......	−225	−251	+284	−104
Of which direct dollar outflows........	(+46)	(+188)	(+134)	(−12)
Domestic and foreign private capital excluding foreign holdings of liquid dollar assets....	+389	−572	+1,158	−590
Unrecorded transactions..	−120	+530	−467	+291
Total transactions listed above.......................	−646	+329	+1,126	+10
Other transactions.........	+116	+57	+169	−61
Changes in balance on "regular" transactions	−530	+272	+1,295	−51

The major factor in the improvement of the balance from the first to the second half of 1963 was the decline in capital outflows. The changes from the third to the fourth quarter were largely offsetting. The rise in net credits on goods and services was offset by a rise in net debits on private capital outflows, Government grants and capital movements, while net debits on unrecorded transactions declined.

MERCHANDISE TRADE

The rise in U.S. exports of agricultural goods from 1962 to 1963 accounted for about $560 million of the $1.4 billion increase in merchandise exports (excluding goods sold and transferred under military programs). Starting in the second quarter and accelerating later in the year, it comprised about $220 million, or one-fourth of the increase in total exports from the first to the second half of 1963, and for about $175 million, or nearly two-thirds, of the rise from the third to the fourth quarter. Wheat and other grains accounted for about $235 million of the $560 million rise over the previous year in all agricultural products. All of that increase occurred in the second half of the year.

Adverse weather conditions leading to short crops in large parts of Europe and Asia contributed to the increase in foreign imports. A part of these imports were obtained from the United States. When these imports were obtained from other countries, such as Canada, Australia, and Argentina, their higher earnings enabled them to increase their imports, some of which have already or may in the future come from the United States.

Weather conditions abroad provide only a partial explanation of the rise in agricultural exports, including some of the increase in grain shipments. The expansion in cotton sales particularly in the fourth quarter of the year (which more than compensated for a decline during the first half of 1963) was due to changes in Government sales procedures which make it easier for U.S. exporters to compete in international markets. Increased sales of tobacco reflect largely a recovery from the preceding year, when sales were temporarily reduced. While sales of these products may not continue to rise as fast as they did in the latter part of 1963, the new level does not appear to be too high relative to the longer run export trend which may be anticipated.

Agricultural exports also reflect the rising standard of living abroad, particularly in the other industrialized countries. A major part of the export rise to these countries was in dairy products, vegetable oils and oilseeds, and various animal feeds.

About $150 million of the 1962–63 rise in agricultural exports (from about $1,250 million to about $1,400 million) was financed by Government grants and capital. Such exports were relatively large in the first half of 1963 but fell off in the second half. During that period the rise in dollar sales was, therefore, even larger than in total agricultural exports.

Dollar sales of agricultural products in 1963 which were due to temporary conditions may be estimated roughly at about $100–$150 million. Most of these shipments occurred in the last quarter of the year.

About $150 million of the 1962–63 export rise resulted from higher shipments of fuels, mostly coal. The rise in coal exports was accentuated by weather conditions and interruptions in coal production in Europe last spring, but is also due to a reduction in import restrictions as European requirements rose relative to production and inventories rapidly declined. U.S. coal is competitive in European markets provided low cost transportation facilities are available. To a large extent U.S. coal is used there in steel production.

Coal exports did not continue to rise after the middle of 1963, but the gains achieved by that time were maintained.

Exports of nonagricultural materials and of finished manufactures, with the exception of commercial aircraft and "special category" goods (largely military and electronic equipment), rose in response to the acceleration in business activity in the other industrialized countries, although domestic demand, which competes with foreign demand for our industrial output, also increased. Exports to Western Europe and Japan appear to have increased somewhat more than one would expect on the basis of past relationships. In the case of Europe, the additional exports appear to have been—in part at least—consumer goods. Such exports rose over 1962 by about $60 million, as compared with the previous year's rise of $10 million. Nevertheless, they continued to comprise only a rather small percentage of total exports to that area, and remained a rather insignificant part of the rapidly rising consumer demand abroad.

The major part of the rise in exports to Western Europe, most of which was presumably associated with the rise in production in that area, was in various industrial materials, and in machinery.

Exports to Japan also expanded earlier and initially faster than may have been expected on the basis of past relationships, but this relative advance narrowed again toward the end of 1963 as production in Japan accelerated.

Directly and indirectly the major turns in export to Japan also appear to be influenced by major changes in Japanese reserves. Downturns in reserves have in the past resulted in restrictions on imports and slowdowns in output, while growing reserves have facilitated relaxations of import restrictions and accelerations in economic activity.

A major factor in the export rise, particularly in the second half of the year, were expanding purchases by Canada. This increase may reflect the effects of the elimination of special import restrictions imposed during the Canadian exchange crisis in the middle of 1962 as well as the rise in Canadian business activity, and the increased incomes derived from the rise in sales of agricultural products.

Substantial increases in exports to Australia and South Africa were also achieved, reflecting increases in the receipts of these countries from higher imports and investments by the United States and other industrialized countries. Shipments to the other countries in Asia, particularly India and Pakistan reflected higher Government aid, as well as higher returns on their exports.

In contrast to the rising exports to other parts of the world, business with Latin America stagnated through most of the year but some acceleration occurred in the last quarter. The major increase at that time was to Venezuela but there was also a rise in sales to some of the mineral exporting countries, and—with the major exception of Brazil—to some of the coffee exporters. The recent strengthening in prices for their exports should provide a basis for a further expansion in their imports from the United States.

Merchandise Imports

Although imports did not rise in the last quarter of 1963 the increase for the year as a whole was just over 5 percent, not much less than the 5.4 percent rise in GNP. In past periods of expanding business activity imports frequently have risen somewhat more than domestic output.

The largest relative rise in imports was in manufactured consumer goods, including automobiles. For the year as a whole it amounted to 11.5 percent, more than twice the rate of increase in all imports, and more than double the rate of rise in total consumer expenditures on goods other than food, gasoline and oil. Imports of capital equipment also moved up faster than total imports. These two groups of manufactured goods comprise more than 40 percent of the total import rise.

A sharp rise occurred also in steel imports, which advanced by about $150 million or 28 percent. Imports of other industrial materials and fuels rose only by 1.7 percent or less than one-third the rate at which domestic business activity expanded.

Imports of foodstuffs, which are much less sensitive to fluctuations in domestic production and incomes, expanded mainly because of rising prices, particularly for sugar. World coffee quotations started to rise about mid-September 1963, but through the end of the year had relatively little effect on import values. The price rise accelerated sharply, however, during the first 2 months of 1964. Imports of cattle, meat products and fish, which totaled close to $1 billion, were only slightly higher than in 1962 and the upward trend in previous years was almost stopped.

Among the countries which benefited most from the rise in imports were Japan and Hong Kong (with U.S. imports rising by more than 10 percent), Canada (6 percent), and Australia, and New Zealand (14 percent). The increase from Europe was only about 4 percent, and from Latin America not much over 2 percent, and most of that was in imports from Argentina.

Military and Services Transactions

A major improvement of the balance of payments was achieved through a reduction by about $150 million in defense expenditures abroad. Nearly half of that decline was due to lower payments for fissionable materials, as the backlog on deliveries, contracted for in earlier years, gradually declined. The reduction in other expenditures is also significant, however, because it was achieved in spite of rapidly rising costs abroad, particularly for services, and increased salaries for U.S. personnel during the latter part of the year.

Deliveries on foreign orders for military equipment, according to preliminary figures, did not rise, however, although the backlog of orders continued to expand. In the second half of 1963 advance payments by foreign countries for military equipment exceeded deliveries by about $360 million. As these receipts change considerably from one quarter to the next, and the build-up of such liabilities cannot be expected to continue at the current rate, they are entered in the analysis table (Table 1, line B2) as special transaction. In Table 4, however, instead of deliveries and changes in liabilities cash receipts are shown (line B2). Total cash receipts in 1963 were about $150 million less than in 1962, and approximately offset the decline in cash expenditures.

Travel expenditures continued to rise during the year. Receipts from abroad increased only by $20 million. The major reason that this rise was not larger was the decline in Canadian travel in the United States following the devaluation of the Canadian dollar in May 1962. Receipts from other countries increased by about $80 million or about one-sixth.

INCOME ON INVESTMENTS

The balance on investment income, as was pointed out earlier, increased from 1962 to 1963 only by about $40 million, the smallest amount since 1959. The decline in net receipts was the result of a slowdown in the rise in income on direct investments to hardly more than $100 million for the year as a whole (and an actual decline during the latter part of the year) and a substantial acceleration in income payments.

It is still true that the outflow of U.S. capital is mostly for long-term investments, which yield more than we pay on the inflow of foreign funds, a large part of which are held in liquid assets. However, the rise in domestic interest rates on time deposits and Government securities has affected not only the new foreign funds flowing in subsequent to that rise, but also, rather promptly, payments on all such foreign assets held here. This rise was the major reason for the increase in payments of income on foreign investments.

Receipts from all private U.S. investments abroad advanced further to a new high of $4.1 billion in 1963, but the rate of growth was lower than in the past few years and receipts in the fourth quarter of 1963, according to preliminary data, were slightly less than in the corresponding quarter of the previous year.

Income received from direct foreign investments accounted for about three-quarters of the total. Partial data now available indicate that branch profits in 1963, derived mainly from the petroleum and mining industries, were growing at a steady rate, but that dividend distributions from manufac-

TABLE 4

U.S. BALANCE OF PAYMENTS BY MAJOR COMPONENTS,[1] SEASONALLY ADJUSTED
(Millions of dollars)

	CALENDAR YEAR		1962				1963			
	1962	1963	I	II	III	IV	Ir	II	IIIr	IVp
Goods and Services, Government Assistance and Long-Term Capital Accounts[2]										
A. 1. Nonmilitary merchandise exports	20,479	21,902	5,022	5,262	5,270	4,925	5,010	5,494	5,559	5,839
2. Less those financed by Government grants and capital	2,345	2,733	595	574	585	591	590	827	641	675
3. Merchandise exports, other than those financed by Government grants and capital	18,134	19,169	4,427	4,688	4,685	4,334	4,420	4,667	4,918	5,164
4. Nonmilitary merchandise imports	−16,145	−16,962	−3,942	−4,030	−4,127	−4,046	−4,014	−4,182	−4,392	−4,374
5. Balance on trade excluding exports financed by Government grants and capital	1,989	2,207	485	658	558	288	406	485	526	790
6. Nonmilitary service exports	8,651	9,069	2,071	2,158	2,139	2,283	2,261	2,206	2,270	2,332
7. Less those financed by Government grants and capital	538	603	144	125	133	136	145	186	122	150
8. Service exports other than those financed by Government grants and capital	8,113	8,466	1,927	2,033	2,006	2,147	2,116	2,020	2,148	2,182
9. Nonmilitary service imports	−5,791	−6,276	−1,423	−1,444	−1,423	−1,501	−1,508	−1,546	−1,594	−1,628
10. Balance on services other than those rendered under Government grants and capital	2,322	2,190	504	589	583	646	608	474	554	554
11. Balance	4,311	4,397	989	1,247	1,141	934	1,014	959	1,080	1,344
B. Other major transactions:										
1. Military expenditures	−3,028	−2,880	−754	−748	−732	−794	−748	−725	−708	−699
2. Military cash receipts	1,143	980	254	189	255	445	204	192	p193	391
3. Government grants and capital–dollar payments to foreign countries and international institutions	−1,070	−882	−269	−248	−241	−312	−241	−267	−181	−193
4. Repayments on U.S. Government loans, excluding fundings by new loans	1,182	798	128	211	578	265	127	153	403	115
5. U.S. direct and long-term portfolio investments abroad	−2,766	−3,440	−556	−835	−547	−828	−1,013	−1,108	−503	−816
6. Foreign direct and long-term portfolio investments in the United States	271	387	195	66	−10	20	−9	203	112	81
7. Remittances and pensions	−736	−812	−191	−182	−176	−187	−211	−211	−195	−195
8. Changes in Government liabilities[3]	248	−43	(x)	−3	1	250	63	−9	−93	−4
9. Balance	−4,756	−5,892	−1,193	−1,550	−872	−1,141	−1,828	−1,772	−972	−1,320
C. Balance on Goods and Services, Government Assistance and Long-Term Capital Accounts	−445	−1,495	−204	−303	269	−207	−814	−813	108	24
D. Recorded U.S. private short-term capital outflow less foreign short-term credits to the United States (excluding foreign liquid dollar holdings)	−716	−670	−354	−112	−156	−94	66	−596	53	−193
E. Unrecorded transactions	−1,025	−495	−27	−37	−469	−492	−135	121	−386	−95
F. Sales of nonmarketable, medium-term, convertible Government securities	....	702	....	....	....	....	350	152	175	25
G. Balance C + D + E	−2,186	−2,660	−585	−452	−356	−793	−883	−1,288	−225	−264
H. Balance C + D + E + F	−2,186	−1,958	−585	−452	−356	−793	−533	−1,136	−50	−239
Memorandum items: Reconciliation with table 1 of Government grants and capital outflows:										
1. Government grants and capital outflows, total	4,281	4,532	1,075	1,078	1,045	1,083	1,053	1,355	1,010	1,114
2. Less: Expenditures on merchandise in the United States	2,345	2,733	595	574	585	594	590	827	641	675
3. Expenditures on services in the United States	538	603	144	125	133	136	145	186	122	150
4. Refunding of Government loans	71	165	25	16	18	12	43	33	15	74
5. Government loans to repay private loans	93	33	26	62	5	....	33	....		
6. Military credits	17	22	3	9	−2	7	3	10	p5	4
7. Increase in Government liabilities associated with Government grants and capital	147	94	13	44	65	25	31	−1	46	18
8. Equals: Dollar payments to foreign countries and international institutions under Government grants and capital (excluding changes in restricted accounts)	1,070	882	269	248	241	312	241	267	181	193

1. Excludes military transfers under grants. (x) Less than $500,000. r Revised. p Preliminary.
2. Short-term capital movements between parent companies and their foreign affiliates are reported as part of direct investment.
3. Excludes liabilities associated with military transactions, with Government assistance operations, and with sales of nonmarketable, medium-term, convertible Government securities.

turing and other affiliates did not increase in 1963 and may have diminished. The failure of dividends from these subsidiaries to rise may suggest that a larger part of their earnings was reinvested abroad. Data to confirm this are not yet available, however.

The quarter-to-quarter changes in income on direct investments are frequently the result of the timing of dividends by a few large subsidiaries in continental Europe. If these were smoothed out, the drop in the fourth quarter of 1963 from the fourth quarter of 1962 would be eliminated, but for the year as a whole there would still be a gain of only about 3 percent in total direct investment receipts, compared to about 10 percent in 1962.

Income from U.S. holdings of foreign securities and from short- and medium-term loans increased by about $100 million in 1963, about the same as in 1962. This gain is based largely on additional investments averaging $2 billion per year in 1962 and 1963.

PRIVATE CAPITAL MOVEMENTS—GENERAL DEVELOPMENTS

The outflow of U.S. capital, which had started to rise in the last quarter of 1962, continued that increase in the first half of 1963, reaching a total of about $2,660 million in that period. The rise was largely in new issues of foreign securities, but direct investments were also up and so were long- and short-term bank loans, as well as investments of corporate funds in foreign, particularly Canadian, banks. To stem the outflow of capital, the President proposed in the middle of July the enactment of an interest equalization tax on purchases of foreign securities to be effective generally as of the following day for purchases of outstanding securities and for purchases of new issues which were arranged after that date. In addition the ceiling on interest rates on time deposits was raised, and the discount rate was increased; these measures made it possible for the rates on short-term Treasury bills and on private negotiable obligations with comparable liquidity to go up.

The capital outflow dropped to about $1,420 million during the second half of the year—although this period still included the sales of some new issues which had been arranged for earlier. The decline was mainly in the third quarter, however. In the fourth quarter capital outflows—after allowance for seasonal changes—increased again to about $950 million, which was about as high as the quarterly average during the years 1960 to 1962. About $390 million of the $470 million rise between the two quarters was in direct investments.

For the year as a whole the net outflow of U.S. private capital was about $4,080 million, $810 million more than in 1962 but still less than in the previous peak year of 1961.

Inflows of foreign private funds for investment in other than liquid

assets were about $240 million up from 1962, as a result of increased pur-
chases of U.S. securities. Inflows of foreign capital for direct investments in
the United States were somewhat smaller than in 1962.

Both U.S. investments in foreign securities (new issues) and foreign purchases of U.S. securities were increased in the second quarter by about $100
million as a result of transactions closely linked to each other.

The debit balance for the combination of U.S. capital outflows and foreign capital inflows was about $3,690 million, or $570 million higher than
in 1962.

MAJOR TYPES OF CAPITAL TRANSACTIONS

U.S. direct investments abroad for the year as a whole were about $1,800
million, as compared with $1,560 million in 1962. The outflow was relatively
large in the first half of the year. In the third quarter the outflow dropped
sharply, but that decline was nearly compensated by a rise in the fourth.

The large shift in direct investment capital outflows from the third to the
fourth quarter even after seasonal adjustment reflected a change from a
short-term cash inflow from continental Europe in the third quarter to an outflow in the fourth. Another factor was a large cash outflow to Venezuela,
considerably higher than in the fourth quarter of 1962. The change may be
associated with tax payments and seems to be reflected in official dollar balances held by that country.

Direct investments in the fourth quarter were also raised by a higher
rate of permanent investment in manufacturing and petroleum companies,
including about $40 million spent to acquire existing European companies.

Although direct investment capital flows varied sharply between quarters,
the overall rise in 1963 would correspond to the projected increase in plant
and equipment expenditures of the foreign enterprises, as reported by the
U.S. parent companies early in the year.[1]

Net purchases of foreign securities, both newly issued and outstanding
(excluding the special transaction in the second quarter mentioned above)
were not much higher in 1963 than in 1962. During 1963, they declined,
however, from about $900 million in the first half (which was nearly twice
the 1962 rate) to about $100 million in the second. Purchases of newly
issued securities dropped—after seasonal adjustment—from a quarterly average
of $430 million in the first half of the year to $218 million in the third quarter and $115 million in the fourth.

Transactions in outstanding securities shifted from net purchases of about
$110 million in the first half of 1963 to net liquidations of $150 million in
the second half. The net liquidation of foreign equity securities in the fourth

[1] *Survey of Current Business,* October 1963, p. 15.

quarter was about $100 million, with continued net selling of Canadian stocks and sizeable selling of European stocks in contrast to large net purchases through August. The shift from net purchases to net sales probably was stimulated by the relatively buoyant situation of the U.S. stock market, as well as by the interest equalization tax proposal.

There was also a substantial shift from 1962 to 1963 in investments by nonfinancial corporations of funds in foreign time deposits and other short-term receivables. In 1962 their holdings of such assets increased by $266 million while in 1963 they were reduced by $70 million (Table 5). New in-

TABLE 5

SHORT-TERM PRIVATE CAPITAL, 1962 AND 1963, BY COUNTRY AND TYPE

(Millions of dollars)

	CALENDAR YEAR		CHANGES[1] (DECREASES (-)) 1962				1963				AMOUNT OUTSTANDING END OF DECEMBER 1963
	1962	1963	I	II	III	IV	I	II	IIIr	IVp	
Total short-term capital outflow line 37, Table 2......	507	na	326	-92	73	200	-61	531	-127	na	na
Total reported by U.S. banks......	277	700	171	-99	-90	295	-78	398	-107	487	5,817
Major financial centers, total......	-31	61	-48	-143	16	144	-47	207	-175	76	1,253
United Kingdom......	44	8	-22	-8	12	62	-24	-9	9	32	230
EEC and Switzerland......	19	-26	-29	-28	-3	79	-42	109	-84	-9	416
Canada......	-94	79	3	-107	7	3	19	107	-100	53	607
By type:											
Commercial and financial claims payable in dollars......	37	41	51	-137	31	92	-28	102	-81	48	807
Foreign currency deposits and claims....	-68	20	-99	-6	-15	52	-19	105	-94	28	446
Other countries, total......	308	639	219	44	-106	151	-31	191	68	411	4,564
Japan......	205	396	251	-20	-47	21	11	117	-7	275	2,137
Latin American Republics......	81	95	-1	28	-50	104	-72	38	89	40	1,586
Other......	22	148	-31	36	-9	26	30	36	-14	96	841
By type:											
Commercial and financial claims payable in dollars......	302	624	230	37	-111	146	-37	191	66	404	4,475
Foreign currency deposits and claims....	6	15	-11	7	5	5	6	(x)	2	7	89
Total reported by nonfinancial concerns......	266	-70	155	44	163	-96	17	121	-20	-188	2,087
Major financial centers, total......	174	-139	127	17	145	-115	-10	97	-10	-216	1,229
United Kingdom......	17	-25	-4	-28	67	-18	-46	5	22	-6	216
EEC and Switzerland......	59	12	51	26	-23	5	(x)	5	-1	8	344
Canada......	98	-126	80	19	101	-102	36	87	-31	-218	669
Claims payable in dollars......	105	na	112	25	63	-95	20	133	-41	na	na
Foreign currency deposits and claims......	69	na	15	-8	82	-20	-30	-36	31	na	na
Other countries, total......	92	69	28	27	18	19	27	24	-10	28	858
Claims payable in dollars......	79	na	24	3	24	28	27	5	-11	na	na
Foreign currency deposits and claims......	13	na	4	24	-6	-9	(x)	19	1	na	na
Brokerage balances, total......	-36	na	......	-37	......	1	......	12	......	na	na

r Revised.   p Preliminary.   na Not available.   (x) Less than $500,000.

1 Excludes Exchange Stabilization Fund holdings.

2 Changes adjusted for variations in coverage and therefore do not necessarily correspond to changes computed from reported amounts outstanding.

3 Fourth quarter 1963 estimated on the basis of partial preliminary reports; amount outstanding at the end of 1963 estimated on the basis of figures for the end of September 1963 plus the preliminary data on movements during the last quarter of 1963.

vestments in such assets were still large during the first half of 1963, but the movement was reversed sharply during the second half when over $200 million of such assets were liquidated. Both the outflow in 1962 and early 1963 and the subsequent inflow affected mainly U.S. dollar assets held in Canada. This change in movements during 1963, which exceeded the usual seasonal shifts of funds, may be related to the higher earning opportunities for relatively liquid investments in the United States following the rise in interest payments on such assets in the middle of the year. Longer term corporate loans were also reduced, particularly in the fourth quarter, when more than $150 million of credits appeared to have been shifted to U.S. commercial banks.

The largest rise in capital outflows in 1963 was in bank credits, both in medium-term credits with a contractual maturity of over one year and in short-term loans some of which are made on a revolving basis and de facto are frequently extended for periods exceeding 1 year. The total for the year (without the apparent shift of outstanding loans from commercial concerns) was about $1,280 million, of which about $580 million were medium-term loans. In 1962 total bank credits were less than $400 million, including not quite $120 million in medium-term credits.

The rise in medium-term bank credits started in the second quarter of the year (before the interest rate equalization tax was proposed) but it accelerated during the second half even after taking account of the more than $150 million apparently shifted from commercial concerns. The short-term bank credits followed the same pattern (particularly if a very short-term loan to Europe of about $100 million extended at the end of June and repaid early in July is disregarded). With these adjustments and allowance for seasonal variations, bank credits in the first half of 1963 were about $500 million and in the second half about $780 million.

The net increase in medium-term bank loans for the fourth quarter was $459 million ($415 million after seasonal adjustment), nearly all in December, but this included the credits apparently taken over from commercial firms. The loans were extended to several European countries, as well as to a number of Latin American countries, and Japan.

Short-term credits by U.S. banks shifted abruptly from a net liquidation of about $100 million in the third quarter to net extensions of $490 million in the fourth. A major part of the shift was seasonal and it also resulted from large credits provided to Japan. In the fourth quarter these credits were $275 million, and followed over $100 million in credits extended during the second quarter (see Table 5). Other credits were mainly to Latin America and other less developed countries. Some increase occurred also in credits to Canada (offsetting in part the return flow of corporate funds), but new lending to the major financial centers in Europe continued to be relatively small.

TABLE 6

CHANGES IN SHORT-TERM OFFICIAL BANKING LIABILITIES AND IN FOREIGN HOLDINGS
OF MARKETABLE U.S. GOVERNMENT BONDS AND NOTES

(Millions of dollars)

	CALENDAR YEAR		1962				1963			
	1962	1963	I	II	III	IV	I	II	IIIr	IVp
Total (decrease −) (line 50, Table 2)	653	1,580	46	486	−188	309'	320	918	187	155
By foreign holder:										
Foreign central banks and governments, total	453	977	−653	462	270	374	−74	776	149	126
As reported by U.S. banks	1,054	511	−472	737	412	377	−178	595	19	75
Other	−601	466	−181	−275	−142	−3	104	181	130	51
Foreign commercial banks	−147	434	442	−243	−214	−132	384	75	−36	11
International and regional institutions (excluding IMF)	213	−225	213	−2	−107	109	−64	−48	−19	−94
Other foreigners and undetermined	134	394	44	269	−137	−42	74	115	93	112
By type of liabilities:										
Deposits in U.S. banks	−69	1,127	145	73	−638	351	423	451	56	197
U.S. Government obligations:										
Bills and certificates payable in dollars	1,819	−642	242	659	767	151	−422	212	−153	−279
Bonds and notes (marketable)	−728	671	−283	−214	−192	−39	128	240	215	88
Nonmarketable certificates payable in foreign currencies	2	−18	29	....	75	−102	....	−23	−25	30
Other	−462	....	−115	−115	−115	−117	....	....	....	....
Bankers acceptances, commercial paper, time deposit certificates and other liabilities	100	431	23	90	−87	74	191	32	87	121
Other banking liabilities payable in foreign currencies	−9	11	5	−7	2	−9	(x)	6	7	−2

r Revised.　　p Preliminary.　　(x) Less than $500,000.

SUMMARY

The improvement in the balance of payments during 1963 reflects in part favorable changes in the more basic economic relationships between this country and the rest of the world, measures taken by the Government, and some developments which may have only temporary significance.

The change in these relationships seems to have been reflected mainly in merchandise trade, and perhaps some of the capital movements. It seems to be based on the rapid rise in living standards in most of the other industrialized countries and some improvement in investment opportunities here. The rise in exports seems to have been somewhat more than what could be expected from past experience. The additional exports—particularly to the other industrialized countries—appear to have been in agricultural and to a lesser extent in consumer goods. At the same time our other exports, particularly in industrial materials and machinery, rose as foreign business activity expanded.

In addition to these developments we had the benefit of exceptionally high exports of agricultural goods which may be attributed to strictly temporary factors.

Imports, while also expanding, moved up somewhat slower than in earlier periods of rising business activity, but the lesser rise was mainly in imports from the less developed countries, some of whom spend a relatively large part of their exports earnings in the United States. The longer run balance of payments effect of the relatively slower rise in imports, therefore, may not be as large as the relatively slow import rise itself may suggest.

Government measures to reduce expenditures and increase receipts abroad resulted in a drop in military expenditures and an increase in foreign orders for military equipment which should be followed by an increase in shipments.

The large change during the year was, of course, in capital outflows, particularly in net purchases of foreign securities. During the first half of the year these transactions included large amounts of Canadian issues which were not expected to continue at that rate. There were also indications, however, that new issues of other countries would continue to rise. The proposed interest equalization tax provided a barrier to such new issues and also resulted in a change from net purchases to net sales of other foreign securities. This change, however, may also have reflected improved investment opportunities in domestic securities. An important shift also occurred in the flow of corporate funds—not related to direct investments—from net acquisitions of foreign assets in 1962 and the first half of 1963 to relatively large liquidations during the latter part of the year. This shift may reflect the rise in interest rate on relatively liquid assets in the United States.

Even with these improvements, the outflow of U.S. capital—which basically reflects the larger supplies relative to demands here than abroad— remained large, particularly through direct investments and bank loans, which increased substantially during the year.

The renewed rise of capital outflows in the fourth quarter appears to reflect deeper lying economic relationships as well as temporary diversions from longer-run trends. The exceptionally sharp rise in direct investments may be in the latter category, and this may also apply to part of the rise in bank loans. On the other side, however, was the exceptionally large return of funds from Canadian banks. This would suggest that, omitting temporary fluctuations, capital movements in the fourth quarter may have been somewhat but not much below the actual figures, but perhaps by as much as one-third under the rate in the first half of the year.

Abstracting from the temporary developments, and from the "special" Government transactions that have been reviewed, it would seem, that the balance during the latter part of 1963 was improved and probably broke out of the range of adverse balances between $3 to $4.5 billion experienced between 1958 and the first half of 1963. This improvement, while significant, was not quite as large, however, as the actual transactions may suggest.

HOW REAL IS THE DRAIN ON DOLLARS?*

Which way should the U.S. figure its balance of payments deficit?
In 1963 . . .
Goods and services produced a surplus of. *$5.5-billion*
But foreign aid, long-term capital flows, and
other drains added up to. *$8.1-billion*
Result: an outflow of. *$2.6-billion*
Does this measure the deficit?
. . . or should you add short-term capital. . . . .*$ .7-billion*
To give a total of. *$3.3-billion*

The Western world's central bankers will be huddling in Tokyo next week for the annual meeting of the International Monetary Fund, and on the surface there will be an atmosphere of good will and accomplishment.

U.S. delegates will be as cheerful as any, as they try to convince European bankers that this nation is making progress solving its balance of payments deficit. At home, however, a hot argument is brewing over just how much of the dollar drain is real and how much is a statistical illusion that could be eliminated by the stroke of a pen.

I. NEW CHAPTER

The meeting will mark a turning point in the postwar saga of international finance. For the first time, almost all the delegates will admit to inadequacies of the present system of settling international payments. Central bankers will get the machinery going for an increase in IMF members' quotas —the amounts to be anted into the IMF's pool of gold and currencies, which determine members' borrowing rights—to answer credit demands of expanding world trade. Both IMF and the Group of Ten—the 10 leading industrial nations of the free world—already have come out for quota increases, so few surprises should be in store.

Hidden Discord

Yet the common agreement on quotas tends to obscure rather than resolve some major differences between IMF nations on the need to reform the

* *Business Week*, September 5, 1964, pp. 43–46.

monetary system—let alone how to do it [BW Aug.15'64,p.24]. More than that, European nations still are embittered by U.S. failure to close its balance of payments gap more quickly. Europeans believe the outflow of U.S. dollars at this stage is fueling inflation abroad.

The United States doesn't share this view, but this country's payments deficit remains more than a nagging headache. Considerable progress has been made since the dark days of 1963 when the second-quarter deficit ran at an annual rate of $5-billion. But this year's second-quarter rate was still $2.8-billion, and skimpy figures for the third quarter show little improvement, if any.

Darker View

At worst, some Washington officials early this year predicted a 1964 deficit of about $2-billion, compared to the $3.3-billion figure of 1963. Now, the outlook—barring further new action—is for a deficit of more than $2.5-billion.

Exports appear to have leveled off, while imports are rising, cutting into the traditionally big U.S. surplus in merchandise trade. Meanwhile, capital outflows have held persistently high. The rise in bank lending abroad fully offset the cutback in portfolio investment that followed the proposal last year of the now-enacted "equalization" tax on U.S. purchases of foreign securities.

In the second quarter, U.S. bank loans abroad—both short and long—held near the record level of $700-million set in the first quarter. Significantly, short-term bank lending, exempt from the new tax on foreign securities, rose dramatically.

One Answer

In Tokyo, U.S. delegates doubtless will argue that if foreigners want to see the U.S. deficit lessen, they could quit coming to U.S. banks for money. Back home, however, a committee of nonofficial experts is preparing a dry statistical report that could—on paper, at least—greatly ease Administration worries about bank lending. The job is being done by the Review Committee for Balance of Payments Statistics, headed by Edward M. Bernstein, former research director of IMF. The group was organized a year ago to study possible new ways of measuring the U.S. deficit.

The 200-page Bernstein report will not be issued for another month—already it has been postponed several times because of infighting between the Commerce Dept. (which applies the strictest interpretation to our payments figures) and the Council of Economic Advisers (which favors a more relaxed course). Treasury leans to the CEA side.

Even after publication, the Bernstein report will have to be aired in Congressional committees. While it will offer several ways of looking at the deficit, its tone will favor adoption of measures that will definitely make the U.S. deficit look less gloomy than current reckoning.

Among these choices, the leading contender—the one Treasury likely will fight for—is to stop treating bank loans as an outflow of funds.

New Approach

This sounds like simple juggling with figures. But it is more than that.

As the St. Louis Federal Reserve Bank explains: "The definitions of liquid resources and liabilities . . . have been criticized for being too conservative and hence overstating our deficit and the threat it poses to defending the dollar." It continues: "Practices followed in measuring the U.S. international liquidity position are not free from criticism." More important, the bank concludes that public understanding "may best be served by not attempting to evaluate the position of a nation in the world economy on the basis of one arbitrary figure." In other words, the bank implies that an exaggerated deficit may lead to unduly restrictive fiscal or monetary policy at home as some critics contend happened in the early 1960s.

II. ACCOUNTING PROCEDURES

Under the U.S. system of keeping its books, this country's balance of payments accounts are aimed at showing how transactions with the rest of the world have affected the country's ability to meet financial claims made upon it.

In theory, this is done by simple double entry bookkeeping. Items that enhance U.S. liquid assets go on one side; those that draw them down go on the other. The deficit is the difference between the two totals. It is reflected in the net increase in U.S. short-term liabilities to foreigners (bank deposits, foreign-owned Treasury bills) plus the new reduction in U.S. gold stocks. Together, these represent the net decline in ability of the United States to pay bills on short notice.

Currently, the U.S. deficit is figured several ways:

The balance of regular transactions is the starting point. It was established by the Commerce Dept., official keeper of the payments accounts, as the most rigid measure of liquidity of assets and of claims against the U.S gold stock. This measure excludes net receipts from special government transactions—such as debt prepayments by foreign governments and advance payments for purchase of U.S. military goods. Commerce argues that because these are ad hoc, negotiated transactions, they cannot be considered part of the payments trend.

The overall deficit includes such special government transactions—on the grounds that many of them are recurring. Further, they could be expected to pick up when foreign countries run surpluses in their payments.

The basic balance is the sum of the net transactions for goods and services, long-term capital movements, and government account. Net movements of short-term capital and the errors and omissions item are regarded as a means of financing the deficit. Thus, while a net outflow of U.S. short-term capital increases the "overall" deficit, it has no impact on the basic deficit.

The Roosa deficit, often used by Treasury and loosely named after Treasury Under Secy. Robert V. Roosa, does not count sales of U.S. "convertible" bonds (the so-called Roosa bonds) to foreign governments as part of the deficit. But Commerce does, because those bonds are convertible into short-term securities.

The Bernstein group has studied a number of additional methods for figuring the balance of payments. Two of the more important of these include:

The "official settlements" deficit. This would count the increase in liquid liabilities to nonofficial foreigners as just another item in drawing up our balance—not as a means of financing the deficit.

The argument for this theory is that the only direct claims against U.S. gold stocks are those held by foreign central banks, since only central banks can convert dollar holdings into gold. Nonofficial claims are held by commercial banks and corporations that need to maintain working balances to finance trade. Thus, the reasoning goes, these dollars are not likely to be turned over to central banks.

Derailing this method is the fact it leaves the U.S. balance up to the whims of foreign bankers. For instance, if a foreign commercial bank shifts its dollars to its central bank for strictly business reasons, the change would then increase the U.S. deficit. Moreover, the French central bank often forces commercial banks in France to turn in dollars when it wants to show a better surplus.

The monetary reserves deficit, the rosiest of all concepts, has never been seriously considered in the United States. This method would put the deficit at only the decline in actual monetary reserves—gold, foreign exchange holdings, and the nation's reserve assets held by IMF.

Out of all these ways to figure the deficit, the Bernstein group has a wide choice. But it is leaning toward a new multiple-choice arrangement that would include what is being called, for lack of a better name, the "total net liquidity" deficit—which would exclude private short-term loans as a drain.

III. CHANGING THE EMPHASIS

As Treasury sees it, private short-term capital outflows essentially represent liquid assets that can be quickly recalled to the United States. In 1963, they totaled some $720-million—of which roughly $700-million was attributed to bank loans abroad. The rest came from short-term lending abroad by industrial corporations, most of which are protected by hedging operations in the foreign exchange market.

From the U.S. point of view, the beauty of this concept is obvious: It would drastically reduce the payments' deficit. Indeed, using this method, U.S. payments would have been in surplus in the first quarter and shown only a small deficit in the second quarter.

But getting this method adopted for popular use is quite another matter.

Clearly, it opens the door for policymakers who want to make our payments position look good. The Administration, for instance, could encourage banks to make short-term loans rather than long-term loans—which would still show as a drain. Should corporate loans still be counted as a drain, the Administration could also encourage corporations that lend to foreign subsidiaries to deposit the money in a U.S. bank first and let the bank make the loan.

Back to Basics

The shift in how to treat bank lending is questioned on still more fundamental grounds: A hot dispute is in process over how liquid the assets are.

Of the $6.5-billion in "short-term claims of U.S. banks on foreigners" at the end of June, over $1-billion was held for customers largely as collection claims for bad debts. Of $4.9-billion out in loans, some $3.4-billion represented loans to Japan and Latin America. Only $300-million was in cash or near-cash holdings of the U.S. banks involved.

The U.S. Government, moreover, has no control allowing it to mobilize bank assets, and under ordinary banking practice the majority of foreign loans would not be counted as liquid assets.

Making A Case

Even so, arguments can be made for the proposed shift—or at least some portion of it. When a U.S. bank makes a foreign loan, it usually requires a compensatory balance. Also, when a U.S. corporation or bank deposits money in Canada, the Canadian bank usually reinvests the dollars in the United States almost immediately. Treasury officials also point out that when a U.S. corporation or bank makes a seven-day deposit in London (a fairly common occurrence), the British bank is not likely to put the money to long-term use.

It may be, then, that the new "total net liquidity" approach will replace the Roosa deficit as one of the three main ways to measure the U.S. deficit.

In fact, Treasury hopes so. But it still recognizes—as it deals with European central banks in Tokyo—that the chief problem is confidence in the dollar. The cold fact is that foreign central banks a few years ago grew tired of holding dollars—and adding to them. But this has changed a good deal over the past few years, though the French and some others still complain. And the drain on our gold stock has subsided considerably.

SHOULD WE DEVALUE THE DOLLAR?*

During the last five or six years the American economy has faced two major problems. The first and most serious is a mild but persistent recession; the second is an equally persistent balance of payments deficit, manifested in a steady loss of gold.

It is clear by now that neither of these problems is wholly due to short-term influences. As to the general economy, it seemed in late 1959, and perhaps even in late 1961, that nothing more serious had happened than another recession like those of 1948–49 and 1953–54. It turned out, however, that the recovery of 1958–59 stopped well short of full employment and was quickly followed by another downturn. The recovery of 1961–62 has so far been even less impressive; as this article went to press another downturn appeared to be on the way. We can say, therefore, without exaggeration, that the economy is even now in a recession.

The long-term nature of the balance of payments problem has become increasingly evident. The gold outflow continues, despite a variety of government measures, such as the tying of foreign aid to purchases in the United States, the shifting of military purchases from abroad to this country and the maintenance of high, short-term interest rates. These restrictive measures may yet succeed in their immediate goal, but even if they do, the underlying problem will not have been solved; it will merely become less visible. We shall say more about that later on.

The combination of a mild depression and a balance of payments deficit is further proof that long-term factors are at work. In the short run a recession will normally lead to an improvement in a nation's payments position because the demand for imports will decrease. While the U.S. economy has been in the doldrums, the world economy has in fact been booming. How is it possible, then, that the United States has faced both a mild depression and an international payments deficit?

Many reasons have been advanced for the balance of payments deficit, some valid, others not. Inflation, once a popular explanation, can be ruled out, for the United States has had less inflation than other developed countries. Foreign aid has also been cited frequently, but actually it is smaller now than in the late 1940s and early 1950s, when there was no balance of payments problem. Moreover, a large part of foreign aid (perhaps as much

* Hendrik S. Houthakker, *Challenge*, October, 1962, pp. 10–12.

as 80 percent) is now directly tied to American exports, so that a reduction in aid would not lead to an appreciable reduction in the deficit, while it would lead to a reduction in domestic employment. It could also be pointed out that France, which spends proportionately more on foreign aid than the United States, has a surplus on foreign account. Whatever one may think about the merits of foreign aid, it is hardly responsible for the dollar problem.

Another popular explanation is more to the point if correctly stated. Wages in the United States are much higher than wages abroad. This fact by itself means little or nothing; otherwise the United States could not export anything at all. What matters is not the hourly wage rate but unit labor costs—the wages paid in producing one unit of output. Since American workers, in general, produce much more per hour than their foreign counterparts, high wage rates do not necessarily lead to high labor costs. Indeed, as a first approximation we can say that wages are high in the United States precisely because productivity is high.

Of course, the above argument does not apply to each individual branch of industry. The productivity of U.S. workers in banana growing, for instance, would not be high enough to offset the climatic advantages enjoyed by Central America; consequently, bananas are imported, and for similar reasons cotton and tobacco are exported. Climatic and other geographic differences are important mostly in agriculture, mining, and tourism. In manufacturing, one of the most important factors determining competitiveness is the amount of capital which must be invested.

The high productivity of American labor is due in part to intensive use of labor-saving equipment. Where the scope for such equipment is limited (as in shipbuilding), American industry is unable to compete without government aid; but where the scope is great (as in coal mining), the United States can be an exporter. Differences in the cost of capital may also be a complication, but actually such differences are too slight to have much effect. Labor is not the only factor of production, but it is far and away the dominant one where international trade in manufacturers is concerned.

The complications just mentioned are important in determining the pattern of trade, but they do not invalidate the basic proposition that American wages reflect American labor productivity: with his high wages, the American worker can buy the goods which he produces. It would seem, therefore, that high wages cannot impede overall exports. But, unfortunately, this is not the whole story.

If foreign trade were conducted by barter, and if imports and exports of goods and services were the only international transactions, unit labor costs would have to be approximately equal everywhere in the long run; otherwise there could be no equilibrium. Neither of these conditions prevails in reality. Let us consider them in turn, assuming for the moment that commodity imports and exports are the only foreign transactions.

Under a system of international barter there would be no need for exchange rates. This need arises as soon as each country has its own money. Under the classical gold standard the general price level in each country is supposed to move in such a way as to preserve the approximate equality of labor costs in the long run (in the absence of international financial transactions. Flexible exchange rates will preserve this equality even without changes in domestic price levels.

Under the present system of international payments (embodied in the Bretton Woods agreement and supervised by the International Monetary Fund), however, there is in practice only one method of long-term international adjustment, namely devaluation or revaluation, a drastic step which most countries (and especially the United States) have been very reluctant to undertake.

It is true that each country could try to adjust its domestic price level in order to maintain a competitive position, but this is not an attractive method. The need to adjust the domestic price level was precisely the reason why the classical gold standard was abandoned. Changes in the price level, especially in a downward direction, are likely to be accompanied by changes in income and employment, whose magnitude may be out of all proportion to the international disequilibrium that causes them. In fact, the downward rigidity of prices may be such as to put the whole burden of adjustment on income and employment. Hence, nearly all countries now try to insulate their domestic economies from foreign developments. This means that under the Bretton Woods system international equilibrium is much harder to achieve than under the classical gold standard or under flexible exchanges. The position of the United States is a case in point.

American wages are not too high in relation to the productivity of labor if we reckon everything in dollars. American wages may well be too high if we calculate them in pounds sterling, or German marks, or any other currency. This could not happen under barter or (in the long run) under flexible exchanges, but it can easily happen under the Bretton Woods system, where official exchange rates are essentially arbitrary. The general price level in the United States is high compared to the general price level in Germany when prices are converted at official exchange rates.

Thus recent figures from the German Statistical Office indicate that an average basket of commodities bought for $1 in the United States would cost only 3.11 marks in Germany, while the official exchange rate is four marks to the dollar. We may say, therefore, that the dollar was over-valued with respect to the mark by 22 percent. This is especially significant because the German mark itself is now somewhat overvalued with respect to most other currencies. Except for the revaluation of the German mark by five percent in 1961, the degree of overvaluation has not changed much recently and is not likely to disappear by itself within the next several years.

Similar calculations (now somewhat out of date) have also been made by the Organization for European Economic Cooperation (OEEC), with similar results. Still another calculation, using somewhat different methods, was undertaken by Deborah Paige of the University of Cambridge and Gottfried Bombach of OEEC. On the basis of data on industrial output rather than on consumption, they found that, in terms of commodities, the pound sterling in 1957 was *worth* about $3.90, as against an official rate of $2.80, indicating an overvaluation of the dollar with respect to sterling of about 28 percent.

The latter figure can be verified by a long-range comparison. In 1937, when the sterling-dollar exchange rate was free to seek its natural level, the pound sterling was quoted at $5. Twenty years later the general price level in Britain had risen by about 183 percent and in the U.S. by about 129 percent. This would give a 1957 value for the pound of about $4.04, not very different from the Paige-Bombach figure ($3.90) derived by an altogether different method. Between 1957 and 1962 the overvaluation of the dollar was reduced by a few percentage points, which would bring the percentage of overvaluation with respect to the pound in line with the German figure.

Crude as these calculations inevitably are, they leave no doubt that the U.S. dollar is overvalued with respect to most currencies (the only important exception being the Canadian dollar). As a result, American exports are discouraged and imports into the United States encouraged. It is true that American exports have developed favorably in the last few years, but this is due to the tying of foreign aid to the purchase of American goods and to "sales" of farm surpluses for local currencies, which remove these exports from foreign competition. Such measures, coupled with the shifting of military expenditures to the United States, amount, in effect, to a partial devaluation of the dollar.

We now have to bring in the complicating factor of international financial transactions. In the present context only long-term capital movements, or continued movements of short-term capital, are relevant. If these lead to a net outflow of funds, the need for competitiveness in exports is greater and the danger of overvaluation correspondingly more severe. For a country that habitually imports capital, on the other hand, an overvalued currency is advantageous.

In the case of the United States there has been a steady outflow of long-term capital, due in large measure to private investment abroad. (There has also been a steady inflow of short-term capital, but this is hardly a stabilizing factor. The accumulation by foreigners of a basically overvalued currency is a grave threat to the international financial system.)

American business has tended more and more to invest abroad rather than in the United States because of the difference in unit labor costs. The need to finance this foreign investment in its turn calls for increased current net exports and consequently for still greater competitiveness. If the overvaluation of the dollar were removed by devaluation or otherwise, investment abroad would become less attractive and the need for a large export surplus reduced. In the present circumstances, domestic investment, and consequently employment, remain well below attainable levels.

With this remark we return to our starting point, the general condition of the economy. Overvaluation of the dollar discourages foreign demand for U.S. output. Since foreign demand is small relative to domestic demand, the resulting depression is only mild. However, if the foreign demand were higher, we would be in a far better balance of payments position. There is no doubt that if U.S. levels of income are kept down far enough, the gold outflow can be stopped without devaluation. Both the Eisenhower and the Kennedy Administrations have been reluctant to counteract recessions or stimulate recoveries to any great extent, because the appropriate fiscal and monetary policies would have had an adverse influence on the balance of payments. In effect, therefore, national income has been kept down to preserve the price of gold at an arbitrary level of $35 per ounce, which was fixed a generation ago.

In its last Annual Report (January, 1962), the Council of Economic Advisers estimated that at the end of 1961 actual gross national product was about $28 billion below the annual level obtainable at full employment; this figure has not changed much since then. Prof. Jaroslav Vanek of Harvard University, in a paper written for the Joint Economic Committee, has calculated that a devaluation of 15 percent would raise GNP by $15 billion or $20 billion per annum and reduce the unemployment rate by two or three percent. These figures show the magnitude of the stakes.

International transactions are relatively unimportant to the American economy. By keeping the gold price fixed, the balance of payments has become a wholly disproportionate constraint on economic policy. Fixed exchange rates are convenient from a banker's point of view, but it is time to ask whether this convenience is worth the high price in income and employment.

DEVALUATION IS NOT THE ANSWER*

The United States has for many years run a deficit in its international accounts, paying out more for imports, overseas military expenditures, foreign aid and foreign investments than it earns back from exports, overseas business profits and other sources. The result is an increase in foreign-owned dollars, which can be exchanged for U.S. gold.

However, devaluing the dollar, as Prof. Houthakker suggests [*Challenge*, October, 1962] offers no miraculous cure for our balance of payments problem. A careful assessment of the nature of our present plight will show this quite clearly.

Houthakker stated that the U.S. dollar is overvalued in relation to all other major currencies except perhaps the Canadian dollar. He derives this conclusion from a comparison of living costs in various countries—an approach full of pitfalls.

For instance, according to the logic of this argument, if a package of goods costs less in Ireland than in Germany, it follows that the Irish pound is undervalued in relation to the mark. Similarly, if the same package of goods costs less in Japan than in Ireland, it means that the Irish pound is overvalued in relation to the Japanese yen.

The inadequacy of this approach is exemplified by the economic history of the postwar era. In the late 1940s and early 1950s the cost-of-living yardstick would have shown that the U.S. dollar was considerably more overvalued than at present. But, at the same time, there prevailed an acute worldwide dollar shortage. Describing the situation, Sir Geoffrey Crowther, Editor of *The Economist*, wrote: "It is difficult to believe that there can ever have been another case of a country where the demand of the rest of the world for its products was so urgent and its demand for the products of the rest of the world so indifferent."

Since then the cost of living has risen much more rapidly in Western Europe than in the United States. According to the logic of Prof. Houthakker's argument, this ought to have worsened the dollar shortage. But, instead, the dollar shortage has disappeared, and France, West Germany and some of the other West European nations accumulated large dollar reserves. The cost-of-living yardstick is just too incomplete.

Seventeenth-century economists first advanced the theory that the na-

* Robert Z. Aliber, *Challenge*, December, 1962, pp. 25–27.

tional cost of living should determine exchange rates. Of course, relative price levels greatly influence exchange rates. But the rates are also partly determined by the flow of private capital, government expenditures abroad, foreign investment earnings, and so forth.

Even if international transactions were limited to imports and exports, the cost-of-living yardstick would be inadequate. The cost-of-living test could show prices somewhat higher in the United States than in other countries, but our commercial exports could still exceed our commercial imports. For example, in 1962 U.S. exports will approximate $21 billion while imports will run at about $16 billion. Perhaps $3 billion worth of U.S. exports will be government-assisted—such as overseas shipments of surplus farm commodities and foreign aid. But *still* purely commercial exports will exceed imports in value by more than 10 percent. The U.S. commercial trade surplus would be even larger if our country promoted exports as aggressively as, for instance, West Germany and Japan.

Fundamentally, the large U.S. commercial trade surplus results from two factors. First, a great many products such as refrigerators, coal, phonograph records, construction machinery, poultry and corn are produced more cheaply in the United States than abroad. Second, the United States holds a technological lead in the design of such items as large jet aircraft and complex computers. The competitiveness of U.S. prices for many products, and design superiority in others, made it possible for exports to exceed imports from Western Europe by 45 percent in 1961.

Most supporters of dollar devaluation would probably agree that the free exchange market provides a far better test of the value of a nation's currency than the cost-of-living comparisons made by statisticians. In their view, the dollar is overvalued because in almost every year since 1949 the United States has run a balance of payments deficit. But it does not automatically follow that just because a nation has a payments deficit its currency is overvalued, nor conversely that a balance of payments surplus proves that a currency is undervalued.

That deficit countries have overvalued currencies and surplus countries have undervalued currencies is not an analytical proposition but, rather, a definitional one.

A nation's balance of payments surplus may stem from a great many factors. Switzerland, for instance, has run up large balance of payments surpluses, partly because of the inflow of money from Latin America, the United States, Britain and West Germany. However, at the same time, Switzerland has run large deficits in all its basic accounts except short-term capital flow. France's balance of payments surplus dates from 1958, when Gen. de Gaulle returned to power and instituted tight monetary policies. The coincidence with De Gaulle's return to power is so striking that one can only wonder what will happen when the Fifth Republic gets a new leader.

There are not many countries which actually have undervalued currencies. For a time during the 1950s it appeared that the West German mark and the Italian lira were *somewhat* undervalued, but this is no longer the case. In March, 1961 the Adenauer government upvalued the mark by five percent, which may have been partly responsible for the switch from a surplus to a deficit in the West German balance of payments. Presumably, the upvaluation ought to have exerted a downward pressure on domestic prices by encouraging imports and discouraging exports. However, prices have increased sharply in Germany and it appears they will continue to do so. For example, since the spring of last year the West German cost of living has risen by six percent while industrial wages have increased by about 15 percent.

Similarly, the value of the Italian lira has been whittled down by recent developments. Slowly, Italy's surplus manpower is being absorbed by the rapidly expanding industries of Northern Italy, West Germany, France and Switzerland. At the same time, the equalization of the wages received by women and the reduction of the workweek suggest that both wages and prices will continue to rise while Italy's payments surplus may be further reduced. For example, since early 1961 Italy's wholesale prices have risen by 2.9 percent while hourly factory wages have risen by about 10 percent. During the first seven months of 1962 Italy had a total balance of payments surplus of only $2.4 million, compared to a surplus of $577 million in 1961.

Full employment, or even overfull employment, prevails in Western Europe and this enhances the pressure for higher wages and a shorter workweek. Over the coming years West European prices will probably continue to rise more rapidly than U.S. prices. At the same time, the rate of U.S. investment in Europe is likely to slow down. Consequently, the price and cost factors which in the last several years have led to the large U.S. payments deficit will diminish and the U.S. competitive position relative to Europe should become more favorable.

The excessive 1949 devaluation of leading West European currencies in relation to the dollar gave the Europeans a cost advantage in many areas, but they were unable to take full advantage of the circumstances because of their limited production capabilities. In recent years, as West European output increased and exports expanded, they relaxed many of their restrictions on the import of U.S. goods. This facilitated the expansion of U.S. exports to Western Europe and helped maintain a satisfactory U.S. payments balance. By 1959 the West Europeans had removed most of their quantitative restrictions on the import of American goods which had been adopted for balance of payments reasons. So, this means of keeping payments in balance was no longer available.

This is why the large U.S. payments deficit occurred at about the same time that most European currencies were freed from extensive exchange controls. Since then a more rapid rise in European prices and costs has tended to assist the necessary international adjustment. At the same time, the large balance of payments deficit has forced the United States to initiate overdue remedial measures. The payments deficit focused attention on the need for a more adequate export credit program, more generous depreciation allowances and tax reforms. It has also convinced the U.S. Government to exert pressure, especially on West Germany, Italy and the Netherlands, to extend aid to underdeveloped countries and to force greater scrutiny of U.S. military expenditures abroad.

United States defense expenditures abroad in recent years have amounted to about $3 billion annually. These sums have exceeded the deficit in U.S. payments. In the early postwar years U.S. expenditures abroad were welcomed as a means of relieving the pressing dollar shortages of most European nations; indeed, the size of the expenditure was partially tailored to the size of their dollar shortage. Even though the dollar shortage has disappeared, it has been difficult to alter the size of these expenditures. If in the future our North Atlantic Treaty Organization allies assume a larger share of the common defense program, the "overvalued" dollar might become an "undervalued" dollar.

The fact remains that from 1958 to 1961 the United States had a cumulative payments deficit of nearly $14 billion. Yet many of the adjustments necessary to reduce and eliminate the U.S. payments deficit have now taken place or are under way.

If we disregard shifts in short-term funds, the United States may show a small surplus in its basic balance of payments in 1963. Assuming that the gross national product increases by $25 billion next year, imports might rise another $600 million or $800 million over the current level. But this will largely be offset by larger exports, reduced outflow of capital and income from foreign investments.

Consequently, if the United States were to devalue its currency in terms of gold, almost every other industrial nation would undoubtedly do likewise by a similar amount. Many British economists, in fact, feel that the pound sterling would have to be devalued to an even greater extent. This points out one of the paradoxes of the current international payments structure. It is that there can be deficit countries with "overvalued" currencies without there being surplus countries with "undervalued" currencies, for the sum of payments deficits greatly exceeds the sum of the payments surpluses. For example, in 1961 aggregate worldwide deficits in basic accounts exceeded surpluses by more than $1.2 billion (the previous year the disparity was $1.5 billion). This imbalance would have been much greater if short-term capital movements were included. In its 1962 annual report, the International Monetary Fund, in a masterful understatement, noted that: "The excess of deficits thus implies that the country figures tend to err more frequently in the direction of overstating deficits or understating surpluses." The U.S. payments deficit would have been much smaller if it used computation methods similar to those employed by countries which have shown a surplus.

United States monetary authorities have not been able to formulate policies solely on the basis of rational considerations. They have, of necessity, been concerned with the problem of keeping foreign-owned short-term dollar assets in the United States. If U.S. short-term interest rates became too low, foreign capital, as well as some American-owned funds, would be encouraged to move abroad. Such an outflow of funds would be especially troublesome if it occurred at a time when the United States was running a large payments deficit.

The aim of U.S. monetary policies has been to prevent the outflow of short-term capital. Monetary policy has not been used to keep income and imports down. Its restraint on the growth of income and imports has been incidental rather than deliberate. Instead, the emphasis in reducing our balance of payments deficit has been given to selective measures like tying foreign aid to purchases in the United States and the reduction in overseas military spending.

A conflict between the attainment of domestic economic aims and a satisfactory international financial position has not arisen because of a deficit in our basic accounts, but rather because the dollar is used as the principal reserve currency. If we devalued the dollar by increasing the price of gold, we would not strengthen the position of the dollar as a reserve currency. Paradoxically, if other countries followed the lead of the United States and increased the price of gold in terms of their currencies, then our international financial position would improve even though the value of other currencies in terms of the dollar remained unchanged.

But surely our domestic and international objectives can be harmonized without a general increase in the price of gold.

LET'S GET RID OF OUR CROSS OF GOLD*

The $9 billion decline in the U.S. gold stock since 1948 is the least damaging result of our balance of payments problem. Indeed, it is a good thing for us to get useful goods and services in exchange for an idle stock of yellow metal. The evil is that in our hysteria over the gold outflow, we have resorted to damaging restrictionist policies, giving the lie to our declared devotion to freedom of trade.

Tying our foreign aid to compulsory purchases of American goods, keeping the wives of servicemen from joining their husbands abroad, cutting tourists' custom-free imports, and imposing a tax on foreign lending may not seem so serious. But the fear that domestic prosperity will worsen our balance of payments (because prosperous citizens spend more on imports) is now a primary justification for policies permitting a high level of unemployment (costing about $50 billion a year) and for our puny rate of economic growth (threatening our position of leadership in the world).

We suffer the foregoing evils, fearing that a continued gold outflow will force us to devalue the dollar sooner or later in terms of gold. Such a development would not only be a great shock to world trade and international finance, but a breach of faith with foreign holders of dollars.

A devaluation of the dollar in terms of gold is the same thing as a rise in the dollar price of gold. But why is gold so valuable and threatening to become still more valuable? The answer is that we have pursued a long-term policy of supporting the price of gold—i.e., we have been ready in the past to buy any amount of gold at the fixed price of $35 an ounce. Thus we have established a system based on the worldwide confidence that an ounce of gold will always be worth at least $35, and possibly more.

We are thus in a fix of our own making, but, unlike Sinbad the Sailor, we can easily throw off our Old Man of the Sea. To develop a more rational international monetary system permitting reasonable solutions for our balance of payments problem, we have only to put an end to our support price for gold. Our payments problem is terrifying, dangerous, and insoluble only as long as we are burdened with our cross of gold.

The mechanics of our payments problem are essentially simple. We have been getting about $20 billion worth of foreign currency in payment for our exports, and using up only about $16 billion to pay for our imports (so

* Abba P. Lerner, *Challenge*, April, 1964, pp. 22–24.

that we have been running a $4 billion *balance of trade surplus*). But for reasons of international policy, we have been paying out an additional $7 billion on military account, for foreign aid and for capital investments. We have thus had in 1963 a $3 billion *balance of payments deficit*, and have covered part of it with our gold (while borrowing abroad to cover the rest).

Our balance of payments deficit is thus the same thing as an excess demand on our part for foreign currency. Our demand is for $23 billion worth (to pay for our imports, military expenses, foreign aid and capital investment), while only $20 billion worth is being supplied in payment for our exports. The natural cure, just as for any other excess demand, say for tin, is a rise in price. A rise in the exchange valuation of foreign currency would make our purchases from abroad more expensive in terms of dollars and we would buy less. Our exports would become cheaper for foreigners and they would step up their buying. The increase in our exports and decrease in our imports would provide the extra foreign currency needed.

Whether we call the increase in the dollar price of, say, West German marks an appreciation of the mark or a depreciation of the dollar is quite important psychologically. An "appreciation" of the mark makes the Germans feel proud. A "depreciation" of the dollar undermines American confidence in the dollar.

In the days of old, gold came to be the unquestioned standard of value for excellent reasons. Gold was not only the most convenient form for holding wealth, but currencies like the U.S. dollar owed their value to the guarantee of redemption in a fixed quantity of gold. But gold is no longer suitable as backing for the world's monetary supply because of two important developments.

In the first place, the U.S. economy has grown tremendously in magnitude and the dollar is used much more than gold in international payments transactions. Thus gold is valuable because it can be exchanged for dollars rather than the other way around.

In the second place, the world gold supply has not expanded sufficiently to satisfy the need for international money (usually called "international liquid reserves"). In spite of the enormous growth of gold substitutes (such as dollars and other "key currencies") to help meet the demand, gold has been and still remains in short supply.

As a result, a country losing gold frantically seeks to stem the outflow. But while the United States has resorted to damaging restrictive measures to cut its deficit, other countries which have acquired the gold lost by the United States have shown little inclination to implement *expansive* measures that might check the gold inflow. It has been argued that the world gold stock and gold substitutes are adequate to satisfy all rational international requirements, but as long as the central banks *behave as if* there is a shortage, *a shortage exists.*

Given the scarcity of gold, the "natural" cure would be a depreciation of the dollar and an upward valuation of foreign currencies. As long as we continue to work with gold, the only way to raise the dollar price of foreign money is by raising the dollar price of gold—that is, by *devaluation*.

But for a variety of subjective and objective reasons, the United States is unwilling to devalue the dollar. Also, it is doubtful whether the devaluation would have the desired result. Other countries would probably nullify our move by raising the price of gold in their own currencies in a *competitive devaluation*. Furthermore, a devaluation would lead to a much greater outflow of our gold. The outflow would accelerate because foreigners would no longer be willing to hold dollars as a "gold substitute."

But if devaluation is impractical, it might seem that restrictionism offers the only way out of our current predicament. We can reduce imports and our capital investments abroad by *taxing* imports and foreign lending or by running our economy at still lower gear, with still more unemployment, so that our people will not be able to spend so much on imports (and, incidentally, on domestic products, too). But restrictionism can reduce the deficit only until other countries retaliate with *competitive restrictionism*. There's no way out as long as we continue to submit to the tyranny of gold.

The Gordian knot can be cut only by going on the offensive. Instead of trying to *defend* the dollar, we can *attack* and depose gold. We possess the means to free ourselves from the tyranny of gold. We need simply announce that we will no longer buy gold, and plan to sell all the reserves we possess. We could dump our entire gold supply, $15 billion worth, on the market. We could sell our gold gradually, or we might simply stop trying to check our gold outflow and thank the buyers for giving us useful goods in exchange for our gold.

At the same time, we could increase the general acceptability of the dollar for international liquid reserves by combating inflation more energetically —i.e., by maintaining the purchasing power of the dollar and by extending a purchasing power guarantee (in additional dollars) to all foreign holders of dollars. In other words, the guarantee would assure foreigners that the purchasing power of their dollar holdings would not be eroded even if U.S. prices increased, despite the federal government's vigorous anti-inflation policy.

The plan could be much strengthened by the inclusion of sterling and the Canadian dollar. A large fund—say $10 billion—should then be set up in these currencies to cover any temporary imbalances between their accounts.

International confidence in gold would necessarily be shaken by the policy which I have outlined. Of course, the value of our own gold stock would also diminish. But the purely nominal markdown of the bookkeeping valuation of a stock of metal would constitute only a negligible consideration compared with the real economic loss we are currently enduring from our low level of employment and slow economic growth.

The decline in the dollar value of the international liquid reserves, insofar as these consist of gold stocks held by the monetary authorities of the world, would increase the need for other forms of international liquid reserves. Dollars (and sterling), fortified by the purchasing power guarantee, would be available to fill this gap. Countries wishing to replenish their reserves would try to increase their holdings of dollars (and sterling) by selling more to us and buying less from us. This would mean an increase in our deficit, but it would be covered by our supplying dollars to satisfy their need for international reserves.

The final result would be the establishment of an automatic dollar (or dollar-sterling) standard, working just like an ideal gold standard. An ideal gold standard is one in which the supply of gold is never too scarce or too plentiful, but increases sufficiently whenever a scarcity of gold tends to raise its value, and decreases sufficiently whenever an abundance of gold tends to lower its value, so as to keep its value stable.

The purchasing power guarantee would enable any country to obtain a stable unit of international reserves at any time by producing and selling a constant amount of goods as specified in the purchasing power guarantee. It would be just as if, under the gold standard, every country had gold mines and could always produce an ounce of gold by devoting a constant amount of effort toward digging and refining it.

There would, of course, be losers—South Africa and the Soviet Union, as gold-producing countries, and such speculators as had placed their trust in gold.

The European central banks could conceivably prevent a gold devaluation by buying up at $35 an ounce all the gold that was offered for sale. But to do this they would have to mobilize $15 billion or $16 billion, plus additional funds which might be needed to buy up the gold thrown on the market by other countries and by frightened gold hoarders.

Even if those who wanted to protect gold succeeded in preventing its price from declining, there would be no depreciation of the dollar, i.e., no *increase* in the price of gold, unless they tried to buy up *more* than the entire amount of gold dumped on the market; and they would not want to do that even if they could. Their success in protecting the value of gold would prevent us from setting up a better international monetary system. But by releasing our great stock of gold we would still have relieved the gold shortage, and by our purchasing power guarantees (making the dollar a better substitute for gold) we would have relieved the gold shortage still further, perhaps even completely curing the current shortage in international liquid reserves and therewith the U.S. balance of payments crisis.

The difficulties and dangers of devaluation have led to a search for palliatives. If our deficit is temporary and will be followed by an equally large surplus, we need no policy. We need only *borrow* enough to tide us over till better days come.

Our false sense of optimism has been buttressed by a flood of authoritative pronouncements. Spokesmen for the Federal Reserve System and other central bankers have solemnly declared that international reserves are adequate. The International Monetary Fund points to its own unused loan funds. The U.S. Treasury concentrates on developing ingenious new ways of borrowing money and arranging stand-by credits. The Brookings Institution, even though it recognizes the inadequacy of international liquidity, hopes that if we can borrow enough to tide us over some difficult years, an expansionary U.S. domestic policy will diminish the deficit by inducing capital to remain in (or come to) the United States for investment, and that European and Japanese inflation will improve our competitive position.

But only the talk is optimistic. We are actually following a makeshift policy of *borrowing* to reduce the gold outflow, and *restricting* employment, imports and capital outflows to reduce the deficit. This defensive "Maginot Line" strategy cannot insure victory. The resulting economic slack may *increase* the deficit by driving capital abroad, and any relief from our restrictions may be negated by foreign retaliation. Meanwhile, we could gradually lose all our gold, exhaust all our borrowing possibilities and be forced to devalue the dollar after all. Our only hope lies in breaking the siege by mounting a daring attack.

Thus far the possibility of going to the attack has not been seriously considered, so thoroughly have we been brainwashed into unquestioning acceptance of gold's sovereignty. This contention is beautifully demonstrated by an article, "Reforming the International Monetary System," written by Under Secretary of the Treasury Robert V. Roosa for the October, 1963 issue of *Foreign Affairs*.

Under Secretary Roosa grouped reform proposals into three categories. The first is a return to a "full gold standard," with a doubling or tripling of the price of gold. This is rejected for the good reason that the gigantic devaluation with which it must begin would destroy the confidence on which it must rest. The second proposes "that each currency fluctuate in price against the others." It, too, is rejected since it is unpopular with monetary authorities and threatens competitive devaluations. The opposition of monetary authorities is an obstacle rather than an objection to the policy itself, and competitive devaluation is meaningful only *in terms of gold*.

Only the third category of reform, built on "gold supplemented by various forms of credit," Roosa concludes, constitutes "a promising avenue for constructive advance." Interestingly, *all three* approaches are considered only in the context of the continued sovereignty of gold. Our "fourth" approach, to begin by crashing the gold barrier, is not even considered in this authoritative survey!

Questions will, of course, be raised on aspects of the plan which need to be spelled out in greater detail than is possible in this article. One question concerns the nature of the purchasing power guarantees. Another concerns the short-term effects of the expected drop in the price of gold. And, of course, powerful resistance could prevent the proposed plan from being carried out.

But the plan I have suggested has important advantages: by revolting against the tyranny of gold and dethroning it by simply ceasing to support it, we can set up a dollar or dollar-sterling standard that would automatically provide all the international liquid reserves needed for world prosperity and economic stability, just like an ideal gold standard.

USING THE FREE MARKET TO RESOLVE THE BALANCE OF PAYMENTS PROBLEM*†

Discussions of U.S. policy with respect to international payments tend to be dominated by our immediate balance of payments difficulties. I should like today to approach the question from a different, and I hope more constructive, direction. Let us begin by asking ourselves not merely how we can get out of our present difficulties but instead how we can fashion our international payments system so that it will best serve our needs for the long pull; how we can solve not merely this balance of payments problem but the balance of payments problem.

A shocking, and indeed, disgraceful feature of the present situation is the extent to which our frantic search for expedients to stave off balance of payments pressures has led us, on the one hand, to sacrifice major national objectives; and, on the other, to give enormous power to officials of foreign governments to affect what should be purely domestic matters. Foreign payments amount to only some 5 percent of our total national income. Yet they have become a major factor in nearly every national policy.

I believe that a system of floating exchange rates would solve the balance of payments problem for the United States far more effectively than our present arrangements. Such a system would use the flexibility and efficiency of the free market to harmonize our small foreign trade sector with both the rest of our massive economy and the rest of the world; it would reduce problems of foreign payments to their proper dimensions and remove them as a major consideration in governmental policy about domestic matters and as a major preoccupation in international political negotiations; it would foster our national objectives rather than be an obstacle to their attainment.

To indicate the basis for this conclusion, let us consider the national objective with which our payments system is most directly connected: the promotion of a healthy and balanced growth of world trade, carried on, so far as possible, by private individuals and private enterprises with minimum intervention by governments. This has been a major objective of our post-

* Milton Friedman, *Financial Analysts Journal*, March–April, 1964, pp. 21–25.

† Editor's note: The text of this paper is a statement presented by **Professor** Friedman on November 14, 1963, before the Joint Economic Committee on **the** occasion of its Hearings on Balance of Payments.

war international economic policy, most recently expressed in the Trade Expansion Act of 1962. Success would knit the free world more closely together, and, by fostering the international division of labor, raise stanards of living throughout the world, including the United States.

Suppose that we succeed in negotiating far-reaching reciprocal reductions in tariffs and other trade barriers with the common market and other countries.[1] Such reductions will expand trade in general but clearly will have different effects on different industries. The demand for the products of some will expand, for others contract. This is a phenomenon we are familiar with from our internal development. The capacity of our free enterprise system to adapt quickly and efficiently to such shifts, whether produced by changes in technology or tastes, has been a major source of our economic growth. The only additional element introduced by international trade is the fact that different currencies are involved, and this is where the payment mechanism comes in; its function is to keep this fact from being an additional source of disturbance.

An all around lowering of tariffs would tend to increase both our expenditures and our receipts in foreign currencies. There is no way of knowing in advance which increase would tend to be the greater and hence no way of knowing whether the initial effect would be toward a surplus or deficit in our balance of payments. What is clear is that we cannot hope to succeed in the objective of expanding world trade unless we can readily adjust to either outcome.[2]

Suppose then that the initial effect is to increase our expenditures on imports more than our receipts from exports. How could we adjust to this outcome?

One method of adjustment is to draw on reserves or borrow from abroad to finance the excess increase in imports. The obvious objection to this method is that it is only a temporary device, and hence can be relied

---

[1] To simplify exposition I shall hereafter refer only to tariffs, letting these stand for the whole range of barriers to trade, including even the so-called "voluntary" limitation of exports.

[2] Many people concerned with our payments deficits hope that since we are operating farther from full capacity than Europe, we could supply a substantial increase in exports whereas they could not. Implicitly, this assumes that European countries are prepared to see their surplus turned into a deficit, thereby contributing to the reduction of the deficits we have recently been experiencing in our balance of payments. Perhaps this would be the initial effect of tariff changes. But if the achievement of such a result is to be *sine qua non* of tariff agreement, we cannot hope for any significant reduction in barriers. We could be confident that exports would expand more than imports only if the tariff changes were one-sided indeed, with our trading partners making much greater reductions in tariffs than we make. Our major means of inducing other countries to reduce tariffs is to offer corresponding reductions in our tariff. More generally, there is little hope of continued and sizable liberalization of trade if liberalization is to be viewed simply as a device for correcting balance of payments difficulties. That way lies only backing and filling.

on only when the disturbance is temporary. But that is not the major objection. Even if we had very large reserves or could borrow large amounts from abroad, so that we could continue this expedient for many years, it is a most undesirable one. We can see why if we look at physical rather than financial magnitudes.

The physical counterpart to the financial deficit is a reduction of employment in industries competing with imports that is larger than the concurrent expansion of employment in export industries. So long as the financial deficit continues, the assumed tariff reductions create employment problems. But it is no part of the aim of tariff reductions to create unemployment at home or to promote employment abroad. The aim is a balanced expansion of trade, with exports rising along with imports and thereby providing employment opportunities to offset any reduction in employment resulting from increased imports.

Hence, simply drawing on reserves or borrowing abroad is a most unsatisfactory method of adjustment.

Another method of adjustment is to lower U.S. prices relative to foreign prices, since this would stimulate exports and discourage imports. If foreign countries are accommodating enough to engage in inflation, such a change in relative prices might require merely that the United Stakes keep prices stable or even, that it simply keep them from rising as fast as foreign prices. But there is no necessity for foreign countries to be so accommodating, and we could hardly count on their being so accommodating. The use of this technique therefore involves a willingness to produce a decline in U.S. prices by tight monetary policy or tight fiscal policy or both. Given time, this method of adjustment would work. But in the interim, it would exact a heavy toll. It would be difficult or impossible to force down prices appreciably without producing a recession and considerable unemployment. To eliminate in the long run the unemployment resulting from the tariff changes, we should in the short run be creating cyclical unemployment. The cure might for a time be far worse than the disease.

This second method is therefore also most unsatisfactory. Yet these two methods—drawing on reserves and forcing down prices—are the only two methods available under our present international payment arrangements, which involve fixed exchange rates between the U.S. dollar and other currencies. Little wonder that we have so far made such disappointing progress toward the reduction of trade barriers, that our practice has differed so much from our preaching.

There is one other way and only one other way to adjust and that is by allowing (or forcing) the price of the U.S. dollar to fall in terms of other currencies. To a foreigner, U.S. goods can become cheaper in either of two ways—either because their prices in the United States fall in terms of dollars or because the foreigner has to give up fewer units of his own currency to acquire a dollar, which is to say, the price of the dollar falls. For example, suppose a particular U.S. car sells for $2,800 when a dollar costs 7 shillings, tuppence in British money (i.e., roughly £1 = $2.80). The price of the car is then £1,000 in British money. It is all the same to an Englishman—or even a Scotsman—whether the price of the car falls to $2,500 while the price of a dollar remains 7 shillings, tuppence, or, alternatively, the price of the car remains $2,800, while the price of a dollar falls to 6 shillings, 5 pence (i.e., roughly £1 = $3.11). In either case, the car costs the Englishman £900 rather than £1,000, which is what matters to him. Similarly, foreign goods can become more expensive to an American in either of two ways—either because the price in terms of foreign currency rises or because he has to give up more dollars to acquire a given amount of foreign currency.

Changes in exchange rates can therefore alter the relative price of U.S. and foreign goods in precisely the same way as can changes in internal prices in the United States and in foreign countries. And they can do so without requiring anything like the same internal adjustments. If the initial effect of the tariff reductions would be to create a deficit at the former exchange rate (or enlarge an existing deficit or reduce an existing surplus) and thereby increase unemployment, this effect can be entirely avoided by a change in exchange rates which will produce a balanced expansion in imports and exports without interfering with domestic employment, domestic prices, or domestic monetary and fiscal policy. The pig can be roasted without burning down the barn.

The situation is of course entirely symmetrical if the tariff changes should initially happen to expand our exports more than our imports. Under present circumstances, we would welcome such a result, and conceivably, if the matching deficit were experienced by countries currently running a surplus, they might permit it to occur without seeking to offset it. In that case, they and we would be using the first method of adjustment—changes in reserves or borrowing. But again, if we had started off from an even keel, this would be an undesirable method of adjustment. On our side, we should be sending out useful goods and receiving only foreign currencies in return. On the side of our partners, they would be using up reserves and tolerating the creation of unemployment.

The second method of adjusting to a surplus is to permit or force domestic prices to rise—which is of course what we did in part in the early postwar years when we were running large surpluses. Again, we should be forcing maladjustments on the whole economy to solve a problem arising from a small part of it—the 5 percent accounted for by foreign trade.

Again, these two methods are the only ones available under our present international payments arrangements, and neither is satisfactory.

The final method is to permit or force exchange rates to change—in this case, a rise in the price of the dollar in terms of foreign currencies. This solution is again specifically adapted to the specific problem of the balance of payments.

Changes in exchange rates can be produced in either of two general ways. One way is by a change in an official exchange rate; an official devaluation or appreciation from one fixed level which the government is committed to support to another fixed level. This is the method used by Britain in its postwar devaluation and by Germany in 1961 when the mark was appreciated. This is also the main method contemplated by the IMF which permits member nations to change their exchange rates by 10 percent without consultation and by a larger amount after consultation and approval by the Fund. But this method has serious disadvantages. It makes a change in rates a matter of major moment, and hence there is a tendency to postpone any change as long as possible. Difficulties cumulate and a larger change is finally needed than would have been required if it could have been made promptly. By the time the change is made, everyone is aware that a change is pending and is certain about the direction of change. The result is to encourage a flight from a currency, if it is going to be devalued, or to a currency, if it is going to be appreciated.

There is in any event little basis for determining precisely what the new rate should be. Speculative movements increase the difficulty of judging what the new rate should be, and introduce a systematic bias, making the change needed appear larger than it actually is. The result, particularly when devalution occurs, is generally to lead officials to "play safe" by making an even larger change than the large change needed. The country is then left after the devaluation with a maladjustment precisely the opposite of that with which it started, and is thereby encouraged to follow policies it cannot sustain in the long run.

Even if all these difficulties could be avoided, this method of changing from one fixed rate to another has the disadvantage that it is necessarily discontinuous. Even if the new exchange rates are precisely correct when first established, they will not long remain correct.

A second and much better way in which changes in exchange rates can be produced is by permitting exchange rates to float, by allowing them to be determined from day to day in the market. This is the method which the United States used from 1862 to 1879, and again, in effect, from 1917 or so to about 1925, and again from 1933 to 1934. It is the method which Britain used from 1918 to 1925 and again from 1931 to 1939, and which Canada used for most of the interwar period and again from 1950 to May, 1962. Under this method, exchange rates adjust themselves continuously, and market forces determine the magnitude of each change. There is no need for any official to decide by how much the rate should rise or fall. This is the method of the free market, the method that we adopt unquestioningly in a private enterprise economy for the bulk of goods and services. It is no less available for the price of one money in terms of another.

With a floating exchange rate, it is possible for governments to intervene and try to affect the rate by buying or selling, as the British Exchange Equalization fund did rather successfully in the 1930s, or by combining buying and selling with public announcements of intentions, as Canada did so disastrously in early 1962. On the whole, it seems to me undesirable to have government intervene, because there is a strong tendency for government agencies to try to peg the rate rather than to stabilize it, because they have no special advantage over private speculators in stabilizing it, because they can make far bigger mistakes than private speculators risking their own money, and because there is a tendency for them to cover up their mistakes by changing the rules—as the Canadian case so strikingly illustrates—rather than by reversing course. But this is an issue on which there is much difference of opinion among economists who are agreed in favoring floating rates. Clearly, it is possible to have a successful floating rate along with governmental speculation.

The great objective of tearing down trade barriers, of promoting a worldwide expansion of trade, of giving citizens of all countries, and especially the underdeveloped countries, every opportunity to sell their products in open markets under equal terms and thereby every incentive to use their resources efficiently, of giving countries an alternative through free world trade to autarchy and central planning—this great objective can, I believe, be achieved best under a regime of floating rates. All countries, and not just the United States, can proceed to liberalize boldly and confidently only if they can have reasonable assurance that the resulting trade expansion will be balanced and will not interfere with major domestic objectives. Floating exchange rates, and so far as I can see, only floating exchange rates, provide this assurance. They do so because they are an automatic mechanism for protecting the domestic economy from the possibility that liberalization will produce a serious imbalance in international payments.

Despite their advantages, floating exchange rates have a bad press. Why is this so?

One reason is because a consequence of our present system that I have been citing as a serious disadvantage is often regarded as an advantage, namely, the extent to which the small foreign trade sector dominates national policy. Those who regard this as an advantage refer to it as the discipline of the gold standard. I would have much sympathy for this view if we had a real gold standard, so the discipline was imposed by impersonal forces which in turn reflected the realities of resources, tastes, and technology. But in fact we have today only a pseudo gold standard and the so-called discipline is imposed by governmental officials of other countries who are determining their own internal monetary policies and are either being forced to dance to our tune or calling the tune for us, depending primarily on accidental political developments. This is a discipline we can well do without.

A possibly more important reason why floating exchange rates have a bad press, I believe, is a mistaken interpretation of experience with floating rates, arising out of a statistical fallacy that can be seen easily in a standard example. Arizona is clearly the worst place in the United States for a person with tuberculosis to go because the death rate from tuberculosis is higher in Arizona than in any other state. The fallacy in this case is obvious. It is less obvious in connection with exchange rates. Countries that have gotten into severe financial difficulties, for whatever reason, have had ultimately to change their exchange rates or let them change. No amount of exchange control and other restrictions on trade have enabled them to peg an exchange rate that was far out of line with economic realities. In consequence, floating rates have frequently been associated with financial and economic instability. It is easy to conclude, as many have, that floating exchange rates produce such instability.

This misreading of experience is reinforced by the general prejudice against speculation; which has led to the frequent assertion, typically on the basis of no evidence whatsoever, that speculation in exchange can be expected to be destabilizing and thereby to increase the instability in rates. Few who make this assertion even recognize that it is equivalent to asserting that speculators generally lose money.

Floating exchange rates need not be unstable exchange rates—any more than the prices of automobiles or of government bonds, of coffee or of meals need gyrate wildly just because they are free to change from day to day. The Canadian exchange rate was free to change during more than a decade, yet it varied within narrow limits. The ultimate objective is a world in which exchange rates, while free to vary, are in fact highly stable because basic economic policies and conditions are stable. Instability of exchange rates is a symptom of instability in the underlying economic structure. Elimination of this symptom by administrative pegging of exchange rates cures none of the underlying difficulties and only makes adjustment to them more painful.

The confusion between stable exchange rates and pegged exchange rates helps to explain the frequent comment that floating exchange rates would introduce an additional element of uncertainty into foreign trade and thereby discourage its expansion. They introduce no additional element of uncertainty. If a floating rate would, for example, decline, then a pegged rate would be subject to pressure that the authorities would have to meet by internal deflation or exchange control in some form. The uncertainty about the rate would simply be replaced by uncertainty about internal prices or about the availability of exchange; and the latter uncertainties, being subject to administrative rather than market control, are likely to be the more erratic and unpredictable. Moreover, the trader can far more readily and cheaply protect himself against the danger of changes in exchange rates, through hedging operations in a forward market, than he can against the danger of changes in internal prices or exchange availability. Floating rates are therefore far more favorable to private international trade than pegged rates.

Though I have discussed the problem of international payments in the context of trade liberalization, the discussion is directly applicable to the more general problem of adapting to any forces that make for balance of payments difficulties. Consider our present problem, of a deficit in the balance of trade plus long term capital movements. How can we adjust to it? By one of the three methods outlined: first, drawing on reserves or borrowing; second, keeping U.S. prices from rising as rapidly as foreign prices or forcing them down; third, permitting or forcing exchange rates to alter. And, this time, by one more method: by imposing additional trade barriers or their equivalent, whether in the form of higher tariffs, or smaller import quotas, or extracting from other countries tighter "voluntary" quotas on their exports, or "tieing" foreign aid, or buying higher priced domestic goods or services to meet military needs, or imposing taxes on foreign borrowing, or imposing direct controls on investments by U.S. citizens abroad, or any one of the host of other devices for interfering with the private business of private individuals that have become so familiar to us since Hjalmar Schacht perfected the modern techniques of exchange control in 1934 to strengthen the Nazis for war and to despoil a large class of his fellow citizens.

Fortunately or unfortunately, even Congress cannot repeal the laws of arithmetic. Books must balance. We must use one of these four methods. Because we have been unwilling to select the only one that is currently fully consistent with both economic and political needs —namely, floating exchange rates—we have been driven, as if by an invisible hand, to employ all the others, and even then may not escape the need for explicit changes in exchange rates.

We affirm in loud and clear voices that we will not and must not erect trade barriers—yet is there any doubt about how far we have gone down the fourth route? After the host of measures already taken, the Secretary of the Treasury has openly stated to the Senate Finance Committee that if the so-called interest equalization tax—itself a concealed exchange control and concealed devaluation—is not passed, we shall have to resort to direct controls over foreign investment.

We affirm that we cannot drain our reserves further, yet short term liabilities mount and our gold stock continues to decline.

We affirm that we cannot let balance of payments problems interfere with domestic prosperity, yet for at least some four years now we have followed a less expansive monetary policy than would have been healthy for our economy.

Even all together, these measures may only serve to postpone but not prevent open devaluation—if the experience of other countries is any guide. Whether they do, depends not on us but on others. For our best hope of escaping our present difficulties is that foreign countries will inflate.

In the meantime, we adopt one expedient after another, borrowing here, making swap arrangements there, changing the form of loans to make the "figures" look good. Entirely aside from the ineffectiveness of most of these measures, they are politically degrading and demeaning. We are a great and wealthy nation. We should be directing our own course, setting an example to the world, living up to our destiny. Instead, we send our officials hat in hand to make the rounds of foreign governments and central banks; we put foreign central banks in a position to determine whether or not we can meet our obligations and thus enable them to exert great influence on our policies; we are driven to niggling negotiations with Hong Kong and with Japan and, for all I know, Monaco to get them to limit "voluntarily" their exports. Is this a posture suitable for the leader of the Free World?

It is not the least of the virtues of floating exchange rates that we would again become masters in our own house. We could decide important issues on the proper ground. The military could concentrate on military effectiveness and not on saving foreign exchange; recipients of foreign aid could concentrate on how to get the most out of what we give them and not on how to spend it all in the United States; Congress could decide how much to spend on foreign aid on the basis of what we get for our money and what else we could use it for and not how it will affect the gold stock; the monetary authorities could concentrate on domestic prices and employment, not on how to induce foreigners to hold dollar balances in this country; the Treasury and the tax committees of Congress could devote their attention to the equity of the tax system and its effects on our efficiency, rather than on how to use tax gimmicks to discourage imports, subsidize exports, and discriminate against outflows of capital.

A system of floating exchange rates would render the problem of making outflows equal inflows unto the market where it belongs and not leave it to the clumsy and heavy hand of government. It would leave government free to concentrate on its proper functions.

In conclusion, a word about gold. Our commitment to buy and sell gold for monetary use at a fixed price of $35 an ounce is in practice the mechanism whereby we maintain fixed rates of exchange between the dollar and other currencies—or, more precisely, whereby we leave all initiative for changes in such rates to other countries. This commitment should be terminated—as the corresponding commitment for silver already has been. The price of gold, like the price of silver, should be determined in the free market, with the U.S. Government committed neither to buying gold nor to selling gold at any fixed price. This is the appropriate counterpart of a policy of floating exchange rates. With respect to our existing stock of gold, we could simply keep it fixed, neither adding to it nor reducing it; alternatively, we could sell it off gradually at the market price or add to it gradually thereby reducing or increasing our governmental stock piles of this particular metal. Personally, I favor selling it off (which would involve removing the present gold reserve requirement for Federal Reserve liabilities) and simultaneously removing all present limitations on the ownership of gold and the trading in gold by American citizens. There is no reason why gold, like other commodities, should not be freely traded on a free market.

FLEXIBLE EXCHANGE RATE? NOT FOR US!*

One proposed "remedy" for the U.S. balance of international payments deficit is that the United States abandon the fixed link between the dollar and gold at $35 per ounce and allow exchange rates to fluctuate. This proposition, which has been termed by Dr. Henry C. Wallich, a member of President Eisenhower's Council of Economic Advisers, as "calamitous" advice, prompted Senator Paul Douglas to raise the question with Chairman Martin of the Federal Reserve Board. As a result the staff of the Board has prepared for the Joint Economic Committee a discussion of the pros and cons of such a monetary policy as set forth by proponents and opponents. To this reader the cons seem heavily to outweigh the pros.

In requesting the staff report from the Board, Senator Douglas explained: "Instead of having fixed exchange rates, why should it not be a good thing for the western world to adopt a fluctuating exchange rate? Then you wouldn't have to worry about your balance of payments or gold reserves. You would have exchange rates fluctuate according to the relative balance of imports and exports, claims and debits, and you would get an automatic adjustment."

He made it clear that he thinks flexible rates have merit. Banking authorities "who have in recent years turned their back on a flexible international system of exchanges," Sen. Douglas said, "have contributed a great deal . . . to the difficulties that the world is now in."

Examining the theoretical consequences of the move suggested by the Senator, the 25-page survey transmitted by Chairman Martin in April points out that the change would entail "sweeping consequences for international economic relations and through them for the domestic economies of the free world." World monetary relationships, as reconstructed since World War II, are based on a system of fixed par values for practically all currencies.

Stated in a nutshell: the advocates of flexible exchange rates argue that such a system would provide each major country with a mechanism for prompt and sensitive adjustment of international payments, greatly reducing if not eliminating the constraints imposed on domestic financial policies by fixed exchange rates.

At present when there is a payments deficit, foreign countries pile up dollar balances with which they may buy gold at the fixed price of $35; and

* Herbert Bratter, *Banking*, June, 1962, pp. 48, 126, 128.

as they take gold away from here the reserves which underlie the U.S. credit structure are reduced and the central bank is under pressure to compensate for the gold loss by pursuing offsetting policies, regardless of what it otherwise might wish to do.

GOLD PRICE REACTION

But with flexible exchange rates, the foreigners acquiring dollars because of a U.S. payments deficit would find the dollar price of gold rising. They could take away less gold than today and the Fed would be under less necessity to compensate for gold losses.

Meanwhile, goods exported from the United States would tend to decline in value measured in foreign currencies, owing to the depreciation of the dollar exchange rate. This would tend to stimulate U.S. merchandise exports and retard U.S. imports and so work for stabilization of our balance of international payments.

Thus, payments adjustments would be more efficient and less likely to have adverse side effects than adjustments under the present system. The foreign exchange rate is a price that should be allowed to perform the normal functions of a price: to balance supply and demand in the foreign currency market. This would bring relatively prompt adjustment in the balance of payments. So reason the proponents of full flexibility.

The latter realize, however, that a completely flexible system of exchange rates is unrealistic; that some official intervention in the markets to smooth out temporary fluctuations must be envisaged. This raises questions. Would a country's authorities steady exchange rates with gold or with other currencies? Would central banks hold each other's currencies? What would be the rules of the game; how avoid competitive depreciation? For these and other questions the proponents have theoretical answers.

As set forth in the Board's staff memorandum, a critical evaluation of the above-summarized case leads to seven main conclusions.

SEVEN CONCLUSIONS

(1) The rigidities of the present economic system are not so pervasive that modern economies cannot, within reasonable periods, adjust to temporary disequilibrium in the balance of international payments under a system of fixed exchange rates.

(2) A system of flexible exchange rates would not free participating countries from having to watch their balance of payments and monetary reserves. In fact, because of the uncertainties of exchange rate fluctuations and

instabilities, they would have to pay more attention to them than under a system of fixed exchange rates.

(3) Whatever advantages may be claimed for flexible exchange rates, they would be more than offset by disadvantages if the system were applied to currencies widely used as a means of international payments and as international reserve assets.

(4) Flexible exchange rates would involve a serious risk that destabilizing forces generated by exchange rate fluctuations would become uncontrollable.

(5) Flexible exchange rates would make international trade and investment transactions more uncertain and hence more costly.

(6) By impeding the international division of labor, the system would retard economic growth throughout the free world.

(7) The limited supply of gold and the risks of keeping monetary reserves in foreign currencies of fluctuating value would hamper the intervention needed to make a modified system of flexible exchange rates workable. Reaching agreement on effective rules of the game would also be difficult.

World business need not be seriously affected if the exchange rate for a minor currency fluctuates. It would be quite another matter if the dollar— a world "key currency"—fluctuated freely in relation to other currencies and to gold. With the end of the dollar as a world yardstick of values a scramble for gold might occur, with wild gyrations in its price. A marked decline in the dollar might well stimulate fears of further decline and speculation would feed on itself. Commodity prices then would soar; a serious inflation of prices would set in. This could easily become a self-propelling spiral. Foreign borrowing here would be stimulated and foreign capital here would be repatriated with the decline in confidence in the dollar.

ECONOMIC EFFECTS . . .

Fluctuating exchange rates would affect international price relationships, interfere with international investments, and encourage protectionism, which in turn would slow economic growth internationally.

No responsible government could long permit the adverse effects of freely fluctuating exchange rates without taking preventive or corrective action. Sooner or later it would have to take such action, thus proving the claimed advantages of flexible rates to be illusory, the memorandum states.

. . . AND POLITICAL EFFECTS

The Fed memorandum deals only with theoretical economic effects of a shift to flexible exchange rates. Apart from these, opponents of the shift hold, the political effects on the free world would be disastrous. A fluctuating dollar would end U.S. leadership of the free world, as the dollar would cease to be the leading key currency. The disruption of the existing payments system would greatly disturb the economic and political cohesion of the noncommunist world. If other leading currencies also were set free to float with alternating currents, the world's limited supply of gold would be left as the sole settler of international accounts and monetary reserve material.

U.S. official foreign exchange policy continues to cling to a firm link with gold at $35 an ounce. There is not the slightest sign of a shift to a floating rate of exchange.

THE BALANCE OF PAYMENTS PAYOFF OF DIRECT FOREIGN INVESTMENTS*

The Administration has proposed to raise the effective taxes on certain U.S. companies by taxing the profits of their foreign subsidiaries as earned and before their receipt by the United States taxpayer. A major announced purpose is to reduce the outflow of U.S. foreign investment, at least to the developed areas, in order to strengthen the U.S. balance of payments.[1]

Many interesting and controversial questions are raised by this proposal —in law, equity, public administration, and economics. For example: Is it legally sound to tax an American corporation for the profits earned by a foreign corporation which it has not received and may, in some cases, never receive? Is it equitable and good policy to subject U.S.-owned foreign subsidiaries to heavier taxes than are paid by foreign-owned companies with which they are primarily in competition—and which have equally free access to American capital markets? To what extent would the proposed tax changes actually reduce new capital outflows or speed up dividend transfers back to the U.S. parent companies? Are the proposed changes necessary to eliminate tax evasion through undervaluation of exports to foreign subsidiaries and of transfers of intangibles (patents, know-how and goodwill) to them, and also to prevent excessive tax avoidance by the use of devices for obtaining capital gains treatment of foreign earnings? Will the new legislation create new problems of administration? To what extent does direct foreign investment reduce the volume of new investment at home and what are its effects on employment and output in a period when restrictive mone-

* Emile Benoit, *Michigan Business Review*, July, 1962, pp. 9–14.

[1] "Concluding that deferral damages the balance of payments, it (the Treasury) decided that the time was most appropriate to end a tax preference that could no longer contribute to national objectives. Deferral should not have been ended right after the war, as the United States was then concerned to aid in European reconstruction by promoting an outflow of private American capital. It should not be ended now for the less developed countries as the United States is now concerned to promote development in those countries. But there can be no justification for continuing deferral for the developed countries, and there is every reason to anticipate that ending it now would strengthen the balance of payments." *Statistical Data and Economic Issues Involved in Treasury's Testimony on Tax Deferral,* submitted by the Secretary of the Treasury to the House Ways & Means Committee under letter of June 29, henceforth referred to as "The Treasury Memorandum." See *Hearings on the President's 1961 Tax Recommendations,* p. 3522.

tary-fiscal policies are keeping domestic demand below full utilization levels? *But it is with the balance of payments aspect of the problem only that this paper is concerned.*

The assumption that foreign investment burdens the balance of payments has appeared to some as self-evident, since foreign investment appears as a payment or debit item in the balance of payments. However, the purely conventional character of the balance of payments accounts, and the considerable degree of interrelation of the various items, both concurrently and over time, should be kept in mind.

Mr. Walther Lederer, Chief, Balance of Payments Division, U.S. Department of Commerce, in a speech before the American Statistical Association in New York City on December 28, 1961, discussing the balance of payments, stated as follows:

> First of all, it is important to understand that balance of payments compilations are done on the principle of double entry accounts, in which each transaction is shown as a credit as well as a debit item in exactly the same magnitude.
>
> Consequently, the total of all transactions also results in an equality of the total credit and debit entries. The balance of payments is always in balance. This concept generally is not followed in the collection of the data and it is often forgotten in the interpretation of the account itself.
>
> Second, the transactions included in the balance of payments presentations are not limited to those involving international payments in 'money,' usually consisting of gold, dollars, or other freely usable currencies, during any single period. The data cover all transactions involving transfers of resources, both real and financial.

Failure to keep these points in mind has, in the past, given rise to the argument that the elimination of foreign aid—a debt item—could cure our balance of payments deficit. It was quickly pointed out by economists, however, that a large segment of our exports—which are credit items—are directly related to the provision of such aid and would rapidly disappear in the absence of such aid. Thus, the elimination of aid would by no means improve our payments position to the full extent of the aid cut.

Similarly, much direct foreign investment is closely tied to the export of capital equipment and, in addition earns dividends (also, sometimes royalties and fees) which represent receipts in the balance of payments, offsetting the capital outflow. Earnings remitted to the United States from direct foreign investment have exceeded net capital outflows into such investment in every year between 1950 and 1960, and to a total amount of $8.5 billion. Even Europe, taken alone shows a surplus of earnings over outflows between 1950 and 1959.

The export content of direct foreign investment varies considerably. In some cases, the capital outflow and the export of capital equipment may be identical in amount, and the parent company's capital contribution to the subsidiary may even take the form of a direct shipment in kind of capital equipment. The more common case involves a deposit of funds to the account of the subsidiary, in either a foreign or a U.S. bank. The subsidiary will then make prompt dollar payments to the parent corporation in other dollar equipment supplies, to the extent that American equipment is procured. Only insofar as the funds placed at the disposal of the subsidiary exceed the latter's purchases in the United States does the transaction constitute a burden to the U.S. balance of payments.

What percentage of U.S. direct foreign investment eventuates in exports of capital equipment is not definitely known, although a Commerce Department study of 1957 estimated that about a quarter of U.S. machinery exports were to foreign subsidiaries of U.S. companies. Clearly, the equipment-export content of foreign investment will vary significantly from one time and place to another. The amount of exports of capital equipment and other sorts generated by direct foreign investment is now the subject of a number of studies. The 1957 Commerce Department study noted that exports of industrial components and industrial materials to U.S. subsidiaries amounted to about a billion dollars.

A private study by 19 leading companies of their foreign investments showed exports of capital equipment and materials for further processing to their foreign subsidiaries of $677 million over the 4 years 1957 through 1960, plus $812 million of net exports to foreign subsidiaries for resale, plus $691 million of other exports attributed to the existence of the foreign investments.[2]

In addition, these companies remitted a total of $289 million in dividends and earned $117 million in royalties and management fees and other service fees. Thus, the total earnings on their investments in this period, together with the net export sales directly and indirectly generated by them—deducting imports of finished goods from the subsidiaries—totaled $2.6 billion, enormously exceeding the actual outflow of new capital funds into the investments which totaled only $148 million in the corresponding period. While part of this $2.6 billion might have been gained in exports and royal-

---

[2] This study to which the present writer served as technical consultant covered the direct foreign investment of the following companies: American Machine & Foundry Co.; Armco International Co.; Cabot Corporation; Continental Can Co.; Corn Products Co.; Eastman Kodak Co.; General Electric Company; Goodyear International Corp.; H. J. Heinz Company; Merck Sharp & Dohme International; Monsanto Chemical Co.; Otis Elevator Co.; Pfaudler Permutit Co.; Pfizer International, Inc.; Ritter Company, Inc.; Taylor Instrument Companies; Texas Butadiene & Chemical Corp.; The Proctor and Gamble Co.; Union Carbide Corp. The study was presented by Mr. H. J. Heinz, II, for the Industry Committee on Foreign Investments to the House Ways and Means Committee on June 8, 1961. Hearings on the President's 1961 Tax Recommendations, Volume 4, No. 70510, pp. 3185 ff.

ties even without foreign investment, this would be true of only a small part of the total.

Questions were later raised concerning the representativeness of these results. The sample, which was originally announced as "upwards of 5 percent" of direct foreign investments by U.S. manufacturing companies (in fact, it turned out to be closer to 8 percent) was clearly untypical in the average maturity and size of its foreign investments, so that the returns earned and the exports generated might be exceptionally high. Even if untypical, however, the absolute amounts of the exports reported by this limited sample, were impressively large. The study did not specifically segregate the investments in subsidiaries in developed countries but, since four-fifths of U.S. foreign manufacturing investment is in the developed countries and 95 percent of it takes the subsidiary form, substantial relevance may be presumed.

The trend of these data was paralleled by a later Commerce Department Study of 155 companies representing about 80 percent of the direct foreign investments of U.S. manufacturing companies.[3] This study showed net exports to or developed by subsidiaries totalling $4.2 billion in 1959 and 1960 after deducting imports from subsidiaries other than for foodstuffs and pulp and paper, which would presumbably have been imported in any case. These are amounts which dwarf any alleged shortfalls of dividend reflows relative to investment outflows. In this study, the data from Europe and Canada were segregated.

A fundamental issue is raised by the possibility that some of the investment-induced exports may be offset, however, by export-displacement from the competition of U.S. foreign subsidiaries. There is no solid statistical basis for evaluating this factor, but there are good business and economic reasons to think it has limited significance. Aside from cases where changes in relative costs preclude continued exclusive reliance on exports, there are many other cases where high transportation costs, import or foreign exchange controls, administrative regulations, or other barriers to U.S. exports make or threaten to make it impossible to supply given markets by means of exports. American manufacturers testify almost invariably that they seek to hold a given foreign market by exporting to it as long as they can hope to do so, thereby avoiding the additional costs and risks of establishing an overseas foreign operation. Wherever the U.S. producer has a product with such a strong market position that it need fear no local competition, he will generally continue to export the product from his U.S. plant, thus economizing on overhead and avoiding the commitment of capital and managerial resources to a foreign operation. Therefore, when a U.S. foreign subsidiary is established, it very rarely displaces a U.S. export that could actually have

[3] Conveyed by letter of June 22 to the Undersecretary of Commerce, The Honorable Edward Gudeman, to the Honorable Wilbur D. Mills, Chairman, Ways and Means Committee.

been saved, or creates new competition from foreign-based producers that would otherwise have been avoided.

Furthermore, a good share of U.S. imports from subsidiaries (which are subtracted from exports to subsidiaries to determine the net export-creating influence of foreign investments) may not increase U.S. total imports, but simply displace other imports: e.g., imports of small British Fords probably displaced more Volkswagens or Renaults (with which they were in effective competition) than U.S. produced cars, which basically catered to a different category of demand. As a further mitigating factor, some imports from U.S. subsidiaries may indirectly serve to increase U.S. exports—since, in a number of cases, imports of components from foreign subsidiaries have reduced the costs of American products and increased their export-competitiveness. Moreover, substantial amounts of imports from U.S. subsidiaries are entirely noncompetitive with U.S. production.

Finally, any loss of exports to subsidiaries may be offset by the indirect stimulus to U.S. exports which arises from the contribution of U.S. direct foreign investment in raising production, income and consumption abroad and, hence, foreign imports. Additional U.S. exports generated in this way would be sold to all sectors of a foreign economy and would consist in part of foodstuffs and raw materials rather than manufactures. They would not necessarily be sold through U.S. subsidiaries and would be difficult to identify. An unpublished study by the Stanford Research Institute is reported to have estimated the indirect increase in U.S. exports from this source at $2.8 billion in 1957[4] part of which would, of course, overlap with the increased sales to U.S. subsidiaries.

In principle, then, it is difficult to come to any other conclusion than that, over a period of years, a successful or profitable U.S. direct foreign investment may contribute handsomely to the balance of payments, by: (1) earning dividends (2) earning royalties and fees (3) financing exports of capital equipment, components and materials, etc. (4) building up a foreign marketing potential capable of expanding sales of the products both of the parent and of the subsidiary, and (5) raising foreign income and thereby imports of U.S. products.

The difficult and relevant question that remains is, how long these favorable balance of payments effects take. This question cannot be answered by comparisons between the outflow of capital investment over any short period of years and the reflows from dividends, interest, royalties, fees, and induced exports during that same period of years. This is because part of the reflows during the period investigated are attributable to the investment made in an earlier period, and part of the potential returns to the investment would not be fully manifested during the reference period. The shorter the reference

4 The Treasury Memorandum—Hearings, P. 3526.

period, and the more uneven the flow of investment and the rate of earnings, the more serious the distortion that is introduced by any such comparison.[5]

Let us define the balance of payments payout period or "b/p payout" for short, as the time required for capital outflows into a direct foreign investment to be offset by reflows from dividends, interest, royalties, fees, and induced exports. This is not identical with the usual "profit" payout from the point of view of the individual investor. On the one hand, the investor may feel that his investment has earned back its original value even though much of it remains in foreign currency and has not been transferred into dollars. On the other hand, the bulk of the dollars invested may be spent on the imports of dollar machinery (not necessarily sold by the investor) thereby providing a quick balance of payments payout, despite the possibly low rate of profit earned and consequently the slow profit payout for the investor.

As we have seen, the first attempts to measure b/p payoffs were deficient both in leaving out the reflows from investment-induced exports, interest, royalties and fees, and in trying to establish a relationship between total investment outflows and related reflows *within the same time period,* without consideration of the appropriate time lags.

As an alternative approach, light has been sought by the construction of simplified models, based on reasonable or plausible or historically-based assumptions concerning such matters as rates of investment, profits, dividends, etc.

A chart embodying the first model prepared by the Treasury, based on an assumed foreign tax of 20 percent a profit rate of 20 percent, full retention of earnings for 5 years and reinvestment of half of earnings thereafter, showed reflows equalling the initial investment in 10 years.[6] It was later recognized

---

[5] The Treasury initially tried to develop a case that direct foreign investment burdened the balance of payments by this type of comparison of capital outflows and earnings reflows over a fixed span of years. Because the reflows have greatly exceeded the outflows over the last decade, such a case could be made only by concentrating attention on Europe and Canada separate from the rest of the world and for the limited period 1957 through 1960—a period marked by unusual acceleration of investment and distorted by the exceptional $370 million re-purchase of the British Ford interest in 1950. The Treasury, however, appears now to have abandoned this methodologically unsound approach and to be placing its main emphasis on the development of models, as will be described.

[6] Statement by Secretary of the Treasury Dillon to House Ways and Means Committee, May 3, 1961. The Secretary's testimony did not draw attention to this basic b/p payout period, but instead drew the conclusion that "it will be 17 years before cumulative remittances to the United States equal those that would have occurred if the deferral privilege had not existed." This conclusion rests on controversial assumptions about the extent to which tax avoidance is an important motive for reinvestment of foreign earnings—a topic which falls outside the scope of this paper. We merely note, in passing, that even in Europe, where the proportion of new ventures is very high and profit prospects particularly bright, U.S.-owned companies have been reinvesting 53.3 percent of earnings and transferring 46.7 percent of earnings

by the Treasury that this model was defective in omitting reflows attributable to royalties and fees, and to investment-generated exports. A more sophisticated model, including these reflows, was later developed by the Treasury, using historically-based parameters related to actual experience in 1959 and 1960.[7]

We present below a model of the b/p payout of a $1,000 direct investment in Europe, based on the Treasury's parameters. The most significant aspects of the model, in our opinion,[8] are:

1. By the seventh year of the investment, cumulative reflows exceed the initial investment.

2. The average excess of the initial investment over cumulative reflows during this seven-year period is $478. Alternatively, this may be viewed as an investment outflow of $1,000 which has taken 47.8 percent of seven years (i.e., about 3⅓ years) before returning enough dollars to offset the initial outflow. The balance of payments payout period of such an investment is, then, 3⅓ years. Incidentally, this sort of period corresponds to the subjective impressions of the investment payout period held by businessmen now participating in direct foreign investments in Europe.

3. In seven years, the initial dollar investment will have increased by nearly three quarters because of reinvested earnings. This constitutes an additional potential reflow by further enhancement of earnings and by gradual repatriation of capital through sale of equity to local interests —or by forced liquidation, at a discount, in the event of a national emergency.

4. Thus, by assuming an average short-term dollar indebtedness of $1,000 for 3⅓ years, the U.S. economy gains a long-term dollar resource which in seven years is worth $1,780, not counting the original investment which has, by then, been fully repaid in reflows.

5. Within a decade, the original $1,000 investment (which has long since been repaid) is producing dollar reflows of $300 a year, and building up potential reflows of $189 a year. Thus, actual and potential reflows

---

as dividends to the United States. This compares with an average of 40 percent reinvestment and 60 percent distribution for the average U.S. domestic corporation. This relatively minor difference would, in the circumstances, appear to be readily explainable by ordinary business considerations, without the need to invoke tax avoidance as playing an important role.

[7] Presented in testimony of Secretary of the Treasury Dillon to the Senate Finance Committee on April 2, 1962.

[8] Regrettably, the Treasury did not present a straightforward balance of payments payout analysis, but directed attention to the longer time period required for inflows to equal outflows *assuming a continued increase of 10 percent a year in capital outflows*. A continued increase of this magnitude over a long period of years has no historical parallel and is implausible from a business viewpoint, and is also confusing in that the reflows from the first year are continuously being offset by the new capital outflows, thereby lengthening the period before cumulative outflows are balanced by inflows. Investment this year does not make it inevitable to invest 50 percent more 5 years from now, and the payoff on this year's investment should not be reduced by balancing reflows from this year's investment against new investment made 5 years from now.

together would then be building up at a rate, *in each year,* equivalent to nearly half of the original investment. Moreover, the cumulative total of reflows plus the capital value of the investment (representing potential reflows) would amount to about 4 times the original investment.

BALANCE OF PAYMENT PAYOUT MODEL FOR
$1,000 DIRECT FOREIGN INVESTMENT IN EUROPE

	Capital Invested (Original $1,000 plus Reinvested Earnings)	*Reinvested Earnings (8.95% of Capital Invested)* *	*Reflows (14.5% of Capital Invested)†*	*Cumu- lative Reflows*	*B/P Payout Position (Ini- tial Capital Outflow minus Cumulative Reflows)*
	1	2	3	4	5
1.	$1,000				$1,000
2.	1,089	$ 89	$145	$145	855
3.	1,186	97	158	303	697
4.	1,292	106	172	475	525
5.	1,408	116	187	662	338
6.	1,634	126	204	866	134
7.	1,780	146	237	1,103	(103)‡
					478 Average
8.	1,939	159	258	1,038	
9.	2,112	173	281	1,319	
10.	2,361	189	306	1,625	

* Based on earnings at 16.8% of the value of direct investment in the previous year, times 53.3% of earnings reinvested.

† Based on dividends at 7.85% of direct investment value (earnings at 16.8% of investment value times 46.7% of earnings distributed as dividends) plus royalties and fees at 2.5% of previous year's direct investment value, plus investment-generated exports at 4.1% of previous year's direct investment value.

‡ Surplus of reflows.

Source: Based on parameters developed by U.S. Department of the Treasury, as explained in memorandum accompanying testimony of Secretary of the Treasury Dillon to Senate Committee on Finance, on April 2, 1962.

The model has primarily a heuristic significance. The estimates upon which it is based are certainly not good enough to serve as a basis for major changes in national policy. In particular, it is far from clear that the average of 1959 and 1960 (an average that hides markedly dissimilar trends in the two years) provides any safe basis for long-term projections. Such as they are, however, the data seem to support the notion that direct foreign invest- ment provides strong support to the balance of payments rather than burden it, except in the fairly short run.

Improved data might strengthen this favorable presumption. (1) The model now omits certain categories of investment-generated exports, namely: (a) exports by U.S. firms to American subsidiaries other than their own;

(b) exports through selling subsidiaries unless sold on a commission basis[9] and (c) exports generated by the expansionary effect of U.S. investment but not sold through U.S. subsidiaries. (2) The model assumes no reflows in the first year. Many U.S. investments gave rise to substantial U.S. equipment exports in the first year, as well as promotional and management fees. (3) The model makes no allowance for the effects of increased utilization of foreign loan funds to provide improved leverage for the U.S. equity funds invested. Access to foreign loan funds becomes increasingly easy as U.S. firms operate successfully over a period of years and become better known to foreign banks. Increased utilization of leverage financing raises the scale of operation and, hence, of profitability and reflows, without requiring additional dollar capital investment.

[9] The appropriateness of excluding 100 percent of the exports in this category seems debatable because, in many cases, a manufacturing operation is now required to cover part of the overhead expense of the selling organizations which are rapidly becoming indispensable for maintaining export sales. A local production operation is needed because some of the items in a line of products cannot be as economically produced in the United States, or require substantial modifications to meet local requirements. When parallel manufacturing and sales subsidiaries exist, then sales are generally done through the sales subsidiary, and whether a commission is charged or not is purely a matter of accounting conventions, without substantive significances.

INTEREST EQUALIZATION TAX:
A DECEPTIVE TOURNIQUET*

Last month, the House of Representatives passed a bill providing for a tax on purchases of foreign securities by Americans. The bill now awaits hearings in the Senate Finance Committee. Although it is generally expected that the legislation will be passed, it may be worthwhile to have yet another look at a measure which even its advocates regard as undesirable as permanent legislation and which, in any event, is due for reconsideration by December 1965.

In spite of this lack of enthusiasm, the Administration continues to urge the approval of the tax on the ground that failure to pass it might cast doubts upon U.S. willingness to reduce the large and stubborn balance of payments deficit. This effort places the main burden of redressing the deficit on cutting private investment abroad though such investment creates opportunities for U.S. exports and builds up valuable income-producing assets. Furthermore, it constitutes a departure from the principles of free international movement of capital—principles that the United States urges other nations to restore and respect because they make for a flourishing world economy.

The levy, it may be recalled, bears the title of "interest equalization tax" and is designed principally to check purchases of newly issued foreign bonds through raising interest costs by 1 percentage point for borrowers from the so-called "developed" countries. The legislation, which was proposed last summer when the balance of payments turned sharply for the worse, is to be applicable retroactively to July 19, 1963 (August 17 for securities listed on national exchanges).

While the tax is not law, it has—not unexpectedly—created so many uncertainties with regard to costs of raising funds in the United States that it has shut off practically all foreign bond purchases by Americans. Like the Emperor's new clothes in the fable, the tax does not exist but nobody can challenge its image.

RANGE OF POSSIBLE RESULTS

There is no sure way of estimating the possible results of the proposed tax. Judging by capital shortages throughout the world and by restrictions

* *Monthly Letter of Business and Economic Conditions,* First National City Bank, New York, April, 1964, pp. 45–47.

in London and Continental capital markets, borrowers will undoubtedly continue to seek long-term money in the United States. To provide statistical background, Table 1 sums up purchases by Americans of foreign bond issues over recent years by grouping borrowers according to their tax status under the contemplated legislation.

TABLE 1

NEW ISSUES OF FOREIGN SECURITIES PURCHASED BY
AMERICANS, GROUPED ACCORDING TO SELLER'S STATUS
UNDER THE PROPOSED TAX

(Millions of dollars)

Exempt from tax	1956-60 Avg.	1961	1962	1963 Jan.-June	1963 July-Dec.	1963 Year
Canada	$346	$237	$457	$632	$104	$736
Latin America	24	18	102	12	23	35
Israel	50	58	60	35	33	68
World Bank*	133	12	84	0	0	0
Subtotal	553	325	703	679	160	839
Subject to tax						
Western Europe. . . .	50	57	195	219	53	272
Japan	7	61	101	108	57	165
Australia, New Zealand, South Africa	30	80	77	18	0	18
Subtotal	87	198	373	345	110	455
Total	640	523	1,076	1,024	270	1,294
Redemptions.	127	123	170	83	67	150
Net total	513	400	906	941	203	1,144

* Includes in 1962, issues of the Inter-American Development Bank.
Source: U. S. Department of Commerce, Survey of Current Business.

By far the biggest borrower at long term in the U.S. market is Canada. Within 48 hours following the Administration's announcement of the proposed tax last July, Canadian officials asked for, and obtained, a general exemption for new issues on the grounds of special economic relationships between our two countries. This is to be done under a clause in the proposed legislation giving the President authority to provide exemption from the tax "where required for international monetary stability." As officially stated, only Canada today qualifies for exemption on these grounds—with the understanding that Canada will not increase its official monetary reserves through the proceeds of borrowings in the United States. As Canada will return to our capital market on an exempt basis, the whole scheme has lost much of its potential usefulness as a means of significantly reducing the volume of foreign bond issues.

Less-developed countries are also to be exempt from the tax; but— with the notable exception of Israel—they have raised long-term money in our market only sparingly. The World Bank and the Inter-American Development Bank are also exempt.

This leaves only developed countries other than Canada—i.e., mainly

Western Europe and Japan—as the area where the tax deterrent might decrease bond sales significantly. Such issues—floated mostly by governments and semi-official institutions—have gained U.S. investors' acceptance only in recent years. Admittedly, the future cannot be predicted solely on the basis of past experience. While the volume of such borrowings will, in all likelihood, recede from the high level of the first half of 1963, it is doubtful whether the net effect of the proposed tax will be substantial enough to warrant taking such a potentially harmful and unsettling step.

The proposed legislation also imposes a 15 percent tax on U.S. purchases of foreign stocks and other outstanding securities. Such purchases have never been a serious factor in our international payments.

CONTROL AND REGULATION

As originally conceived, the measure represented an intellectual attempt at interest equalization between our capital market and the principal centers abroad. It was to increase costs to foreigners of capital in the U.S. market without any need for U.S. financial authorities to interfere with market processes through controls over, or even the screening of, capital issues. Yet, as embodied in the actual draft legislation, the measure depends more upon controls over the transactions that are exempt from the tax than upon the tax itself. Of the 71 pages of H.R. 8000 as approved by the House, 50 pages are devoted to the listing of exemptions.

Some of these exemptions are to be provided for in the law. Thus, recognition is given to the importance of financing U.S. exports by exempting securities or commercial bank loans that mature in three years; recognition is also given to the foreign exchange earning power of overseas investments by American corporations by exempting direct investments. Many exemptions are, however, left to the discretion of the President and the Treasury Department. Thus, the tax, as proposed, would apply to 22 "developed" countries selected by the Administration. For example, Portugal would be exempt, but not Spain; Finland but not Norway; the Philippines but not Hong Kong. The selection is subject to change by Executive Order. Canada's exemption, noted above, also rests on the discretionary power of the President.

The exemption proposed for commercial banks is designed to make sure that credit "in support of normal and recurrent business operations abroad will not be unnecessarily impeded," to quote Treasury Secretary Dillon. The "possibility of abuse of this exemption" prompted the Treasury to seek and obtain an amendment to the legislation endowing it with specific authority to obtain from banks detailed reports of their foreign lending activity. The implied threat of taking away the exemption is expected to obtain voluntary compliance with official views.

The real effect of the proposed tax is thus control and regulation. Not surprisingly, some people have suggested that there is a better way to obtain the desired result—a voluntary capital issues committee acting on guidelines established by appropriate governmental agencies to screen foreign plans for borrowing in our market.

Those who regard a capital issues committee as a lesser evil than the proposed tax are aware of the drawbacks common to both: experience shows that "temporary" taxes as well as "temporary" controls tend to become permanent; even if things do not go well, the medicine is all right but just more of it is needed. In addition, one expedient often carries with it a whole sequence of further expedients, each with less justification than the last. The alleged advantage of the capital issues committee is its informality and flexibility.

The difficulty is that a capital issues committee would have to ward off the countless outside pressures which would be brought to bear on it as it performs the thankless task of deciding just how much portfolio investment abroad is sustainable. Such a committee, which would have to make judgments against the background of the country's delicate and complex international relations, could scarcely win many friends and might earn many enemies.

More fundamentally, tinkering with controls may well have unwanted consequences. As the former President of the New York Federal Reserve Bank Allan Sproul noted:

> We need to avoid experimenting with direct controls, whatever they may be called, which in times of strain may be interpreted as a forerunner of stronger controls of capital outflow, or even of all dealings in foreign exchange, which in turn would heighten the danger of anticipatory withdrawals of foreign funds from our markets.

Investors abroad seek and trust bonds denominated in U.S. dollars. A considerable part of foreign dollar bonds issued in the United States has been sold to nonresidents. Since mid-1963, issues that otherwise would have been floated in New York have been carried through in European markets but it is the label "U.S. dollar" that makes them acceptable to investors. The smaller shrinkage of the purchasing power of the dollar and its greater freedom of use compared with many other major currencies have not remained unnoticed.

THE BROADER CONTEXT

In this whole context, it needs to be recognized that borrowings in the United States are attractive because long-term interest rates abroad, except in Switzerland, are higher than in our market. This is the result of the very abundance of U.S. savings, together with the reluctance of the Administration to condone higher costs and lesser availability of credit. Yet, given the conditions in which the U.S. economy finds itself this year, interest rates may well tend to rise of their own accord. This would tend to slow up new borrowings, including new issues of foreign bonds. Now that tax relief has been given, materially higher interest rates need not darken the prospects of sustained business expansion. They need not restrain investment and output so long as profit incentives and profit expectations are encouraging.

It is neither necessary nor desirable to erect a wall around a particular sector of the U.S. capital market. Whenever Canada, Japan and those Western European nations which are not dollar-rich sell bonds in the United States, the proceeds are used—directly or indirectly—to buy U.S. goods and services. Usually, there is a direct connection: trade follows credit.

The business community makes a strong contribution to our balance of payments. This is unmistakably evidenced by the surplus on merchandise account and the excess of remitted income over the net outflow of private capital for long-term investment abroad. U.S. Government policies to redress the balance of payments deficit should encourage this contribution—not hamper it, as does the proposed tax.

The interest equalization tax may well prove to be a deceptive tourniquet. Its enactment should serve as yet further evidence of the tendency for a persistent balance of payments deficit to corrupt the principles of a free international capital market. Government policy should serve not to postpone but to expedite action to deal with the payments deficit effectively and resolutely.

THE PRESIDENT'S BALANCE OF PAYMENTS PROGRAM*

Last month's Review *contained several official statements and documents relating to the initial measures taken to implement the President's program for quickly achieving a substantial improvement in our balance-of-payments position. One of these documents was a letter by Chairman Martin to nonbank financial institutions, giving guidelines for their foreign lending and investing. Two additional sets of such guidelines have since been issued and are reprinted below. One consists of the Federal Reserve System's guidelines for commercial banks. The other constitutes the Commerce Department's program for nonfinancial business concerns.*

CIRCULAR NO. 5628—MARCH 5, 1965, GUIDELINES FOR FOREIGN LENDING ACTIVITIES OF COMMERCIAL BANKS UNDER THE PRESIDENT'S BALANCE OF PAYMENTS PROGRAM

To All Banks in the Second Federal Reserve District:

The following statement was issued by the Board of Governors of the Federal Reserve System and released for publication in morning newspapers, Monday, March 8:

The Board of Governors of the Federal Reserve System today issued a set of fourteen guidelines for commercial banks to follow in complying with the President's program to improve the nation's balance of payments position, in part through voluntary efforts to restrain foreign lending and investment. It was recognized that, in restraining the growth of loans to foreigners, banks will be foregoing some of the gains that would otherwise have accrued to them. Nevertheless, the Board stated, if a voluntary program is to be effective, the national interest must come first in decisions on future specific loan transactions.

The guidelines for foreign lending operations specify that absolute priority should be given to all bona fide export credits. With respect to nonexport credits, banks are expected to give the highest priority to loans to less developed countries and to avoid restrictive policies that would place an un-

* Extracted from *Monthly Review*, Federal Reserve Bank of New York, April, 1965, pp. 89–95.

due burden on Canada, Japan, and the United Kingdom. To meet these priorities, the guidelines contemplate that nonexport credits to other advanced countries will be cut back to the extent needed to achieve the goal of the President's program.

The objective of the program is that outstanding bank credit to nonresidents of the United States not rise above the amount outstanding at the end of 1964 by more than 5 percent. Banks which find themselves in excess of the target are expected to reduce their foreign loans as quickly as possible and, in the most extreme case, to bring their lending back to the target level within the next twelve months.

The guidelines cover the method of calculating the base for an individual bank against which the rise of 5 percent in outstanding loans can be measured. They also clarify how those banks already in excess of the target as a result of year-to-date operations will be expected to bring their operations within the policy objectives. The guidelines spell out, among other topics, the relationship of trust departments to the program, the handling of financial transactions for customers, the position of Edge Act corporations, the operations of foreign branches of United States banks and of United States branches of foreign banks.

Following is a partial text of the guidelines:

Preface to Guidelines

The following guidelines have been designed by the Board of Governors of the Federal Reserve System for use in implementing President Johnson's program for the voluntary curtailment of foreign credit by banks. They will be in effect until modified or supplemented. However, they may be changed from time to time in the light of new circumstances and in the light of the experience gained as the program goes forward. The guidelines should be helpful to individual banks as they play their own particular part in the achievement of the President's over-all balance of payments program, and each bank should feel free at any time to discuss its problems with the Federal Reserve Bank of its District.

It is clear that banks, in undertaking a voluntary role in the program, are being called upon to make sacrifices. In restraining the growth of their loans to foreigners they will be foregoing some of the gains that would otherwise have accrued to them. But, if a voluntary program is to be effective, decisions on future specific loan transactions must be made primarily with an eye to the national interest rather than profits. The achievement of the President's goal will be in the long-term interest not only of the nation, but also of the individual institutions which are now being called upon to forego immediate advantage or gain.

Banks in Excess of 5 Percent Target

It is clearly recognized that some banks may currently be above the 5 percent target because of loans made prior to February 11, 1965, or may subsequently be brought above the target as a result of (a) binding commitments entered into before February 11, or (b) the extension of bona fide export credits, or (c) the extension of credits at the specific request of an agency of the United States Government. A bank in such circumstances would not be considered to be acting in a manner inconsistent with the program; however, it should reduce its claims on foreigners to 105 percent of the base as quickly as possible. Even in the most extreme case, this reduction should be accomplished within the next twelve months.

Such a bank will be invited periodically to discuss with the Federal Reserve Bank of its District the steps it has taken and proposes to take to bring about the reduction of its claims on foreigners consistent with these guidelines.

Banks with bona fide commitments are clearly not being asked to refuse to honor such commitments, even if honoring them involves a temporary excess of lending above the target. However, banks would be expected to seize every opportunity to withdraw or reduce commitments, including credit lines, that are not of a firm nature, and to ensure that drawings under credit lines are kept to normal levels and usage. At time of renewal, all credit lines should be reviewed in light of their consistency with the voluntary foreign credit restraint program. Proposed extensions or renewals of existing bona fide commitments should be reviewed in the same manner.

Loan Priorities

Within the 5 percent guideline, absolute priority should be given to bona fide export credits. Credits that substitute for cash sales or for sales customarily financed out of nonbank or foreign funds are not entitled to priority.

With respect to nonexport credits, banks should give the highest priority to loans to less developed countries and should avoid restrictive policies that would place an undue burden on countries such as Canada and Japan, which are heavily dependent on United States financing, and on the United Kingdom, which is suffering from balance of payments difficulties.

Given the probability of some expansion of the end-of-1964 volume of loans for financing exports and the priorities established for the less developed countries, as well as the need to avoid restrictive practices with regard to Canada, Japan, and Britain, it is expected that nonexport credit to the other advanced countries will be cut back to the extent needed to achieve the goal of the President's program.

Without attempting to specify all types of loans that will need to be restricted, it is obvious that credits to developed countries that can be cut back with benefit to our balance of payments and with the least adverse side-effects include: credits to finance third-country trade; credits to finance local-currency expenditures outside the United States; credits to finance fixed or working capital needs; and all other nonexport credits to developed countries that do not suffer from balance of payments difficulties.

Bank Sales of Foreign Assets to United States Residents

In general, banks should not expand their lending abroad by selling to United States residents (including United States banks) claims on foreigners existing as of the base date and replacing such assets with other loans to foreigners. Sales to United States residents of foreign securities owned on the base date, which would be free of the interest equalization tax, or of loan participations, could assist an individual bank to stay within the 5 percent target, but would clearly not benefit the United States payments position. Therefore, in the event of any such sales, the bank's base should be reduced by an amount equivalent thereto.

Banks With No Foreign Loans Outstanding On December 31, 1964

In general, banks with no previous foreign lending experience would be expected not to make foreign loans during 1965. However, bona fide export loans to foreigners may be made in reasonable amounts, provided this financing does not represent a shift from previous United States or foreign sources of financing. Banks making foreign loans for the first time should take precautions to ensure that their activities do not become a means through which credit is extended to foreign borrowers who have been denied credit by established lenders cooperating in the voluntary program.

Banks Whose Previous Foreign Business Has Consisted Almost Entirely of Export Financing

The few banks falling in this category would ordinarily be expected to keep within the 5 percent ceiling. Since they would have no maturing non-export loans to provide funds for additional export credits and would therefore need to rely upon nonrenewal of maturing export loans, reasonable amounts in excess of the target from time to time would not be considered in conflict with the program. But every effort should be made by such banks to keep their lending within the ceiling. They should take care to ensure that export loans do not represent a shift from previous United States or foreign sources of financing.

Trust Departments

Managing officers of trust departments should be made familiar with the voluntary restraint effort. They should bear the purpose of that program in mind in making any acquisitions of foreign obligations for trust accounts. For example, they should not exercise their authority under any trust account to acquire foreign obligations which, in the absence of the restraint program, would have been acquired by the bank for its own account. Pension funds, including those administered by banks, have been furnished separate guidelines, as part of the program to restrain foreign credits of nonbank financial institutions.

Financial Transactions for Customers

While banks must, of course, follow instructions given to them by their customers, it is expected that, in buying foreign investments for customers, they will be guided by the principles inherent in the President's balance of payments program. They should not encourage customers to place liquid funds outside the United States. Banks should not place with customers foreign obligations which, in the absence of the restraint program, they would have acquired or held for their own account.

Foreign Branches

It is assumed, of course, that United States banks having branches, as well as subsidiaries and affiliates, in foreign countries will not utilize them to avoid the foreign credit restraint program for United States banks.

Foreign branches have independent sources of funds in the countries in which they are located and from third countries, in many cases through the attraction of Eurodollar deposits. The balance of payments program is not designed to hamper the lending activities of the foreign branches insofar as the funds utilized are derived from foreign sources and do not add to the dollar outflow. Concern arises only in those cases where the resources are derived (directly or indirectly) from the United States.

Total claims of the head office on overseas branches, including permanent capital invested in, as well as balances due from, branches, represent bank credit to nonresidents for purposes of the program.

Problems of Edge Act Corporations

Edge Act and agreement corporations are included in the voluntary credit restraint effort. The foreign loans and investments of such a corporation may be combined with those of the parent bank for the purposes of the program, or separate targets may be set for the parent bank and the subsidiary.

An Edge Act corporation that has not yet undertaken any significant volume of loans and investments may take as a base, alone and not in combination with its parent, its paid-in capital and surplus, up to $2.5 million, even though an equivalent amount of foreign loans and investments had not yet been made as of December 31, 1964.

United States Branches and Agencies of Foreign Banks

Branches and agencies of foreign banks located in the United States are requested to comply with the principles of the program of credit restraint applicable to domestic banks.

Substitution of Export Credit for Credit for Other Purposes

Banks should be on the alert to avoid granting credit to domestic customers if the result would be to aid the latter in making foreign loans or investments inconsistent with the program. Even export credit to foreigners, if it supplants credit previously obtained from foreign sources and thus frees the foreign funds for other uses, may be detrimental to the United States payments position.

This is obviously a difficult area and one in which there is considerable room for possibly damaging substitution of domestic for foreign financing, and for substitution of export credits to foreigners for other credits to foreigners. In general, success will depend on the ability of banks to identify loans that are inconsistent with the program and on the application of the Department of Commerce program with respect to foreign credit and investment by nonfinancial firms.

Management of A Bank's Liquid Funds

Banks that have placed their own funds abroad for short-term investment purposes, including United States dollar deposits outside the United States or the acquisition of non-United States money market paper, should refrain from increasing such deposits and investments and should, in a reasonable and orderly manner, seek to reduce them. Since such funds are ordinarily placed outside the United States solely to provide a slightly higher rate of return, they are strong candidates for reduction under the program.

This guideline applies equally to deposits and investments payable in foreign currencies and to those payable in United States dollars.

This guideline does not call for a reduction in necessary working balances held with foreign correspondents, although such balances are also considered claims on nonresidents for the purposes of the program.

ALFRED HAYES,
President.

CIRCULAR NO. 5633—MARCH 18, 1965, PROGRAM OF DEPART-
MENT OF COMMERCE FOR BUSINESS CONCERNS UNDER THE
PRESIDENT'S BALANCE OF PAYMENTS PROGRAM

*To All Banks and Other Financial Institutions
in the Second Federal Reserve District:*

The President's program to improve the nation's balance of payments
position, in part through voluntary efforts by American industrial concerns to
effectuate reductions in their capital outflow, has been implemented with
respect to such concerns by the Department of Commerce. In a letter to the
chief executive officers of over 600 industrial concerns, which was released
on March 17, Secretary of Commerce John T. Connor set forth the program
proposed by the Department of Commerce.

For your information, the following documents are printed on the following pages:

Press release of the Department of Commerce, dated March 17, 1965;

Letter of the Secretary of Commerce;

You will note from the letter that the Secretary of Commerce expects
corporations planning substantial investments abroad to take care to minimize
the balance of payments effects of such investments. He states that the Department of Commerce or the appropriate Federal Reserve officials, when the
System's program for banks is involved, would be glad to discuss such situations with the concerns. The Secretary also points out that repatriation of short-
term financial funds invested abroad should be done with caution in the case
of balances in countries subject to balance of payments problems, and suggests that it would be desirable for companies with large balances to consider consulting with the appropriate Federal Reserve Bank on this problem.

ALFRED HAYES,
President.

Press Release of the Department of Commerce Dated March 17, 1965

Secretary of Commerce John T. Connor today called upon American business executives engaged in international operations to "make an extraordinary effort" to help improve the nation's balance of payments position.

The Secretary issued his call in a letter to 600 corporate executives,
enlisting their personal support in a voluntary program to produce "significant reductions" in the balance of payments deficit.

The Secretary said the list of 600 companies did not necessarily encompass all firms engaged in international business, and he extended an open
invitation to other firms with sizable international activities to participate.

Such firms should write him if they feel they can make a substantial contribution to the voluntary program.

In his letter, the text of which he made public today, the Secretary asked each company to set up a balance of payments "ledger" for 1964, showing selected debits and credits, to consider how their 1964 results could be improved for 1965 and 1966, and to give him their personal estimates of the dollar amount of prospective improvement for 1965.

"We have been thinking in terms of an average improvement in balance of payment terms, in 1965 of 15 to 20 percent over the 1964 results," Secretary Connor said. "We realize, however, that any such target will be inappropriate for many corporations—either on the low or high side—but the important thing is to make an extraordinary effort. . . . only you are in a position to set up a reasonable but meaningful objective for your own company, in the light of your operating facts and problems."

The Secretary also asked for 1963 and 1964 figures for short-term assets held abroad "because of the unique opportunity" to shift such assets and register an early improvement in the balance of payments.

He requested that first reports be submitted by April 15th, and quarterly reports through 1965 and 1966.

He said he had decided against a formalized system of prior notification of new investments and expansions abroad, including financing, expressing the belief that the estimates and reports being requested would prove to be adequate.

"We, of course, expect that care will be taken to minimize the balance of payments effects of large investments," the Secretary said, "and either we, or the appropriate Federal Reserve officials when their program is involved, would be glad to discuss such situations should you so desire."

In his letter, the Secretary stated that individual reports and estimates would be kept confidential and periodic summaries of the data collected would be compiled for use by the government and for release to the public.

In the category of "special problems," the Secretary mentioned the national objective of increasing private investment in less developed countries,[1] and said he did not wish the program to inhibit the flow of such investment.

A second "special problem" dealt with the repatriation of short-term financial funds, the Secretary requesting the exercise of caution in countries having balance of payments problems.

On a third "special problem" involving Canada, the Secretary said he did not anticipate cutbacks in direct investments. He asked, however, that

---

[1] The "developed countries" are: Australia, Austria, Belgium, Canada, Denmark, France, Germany (Federal Republic), Hong Kong, Italy, Japan, Liechtenstein, Luxembourg, Monaco, Netherlands, New Zealand, Norway, Republic of South Africa, San Marino, Spain, Sweden, Switzerland, United Kingdom. This list is subject to some modification at a later date.

firms "take particular care to assure that short-term funds put at the disposal of subsidiaries in Canada serve only to meet operating needs."

Secretary Connor closed his letter to the corporate executives stating, "President Johnson is confident, as am I, that you will cooperate with us in this extremely important program of serious concern to you and to our country. We urgently need your help."

Letter of the Secretary of Commerce

The President has asked me to handle the voluntary cooperation program with American industry which is a key part of our overall effort to improve our nation's balance of payments situation. Since the success of this program depends entirely on full cooperation and help from the heads of the United States corporations doing a significant amount of business internationally, I am writing to you to enlist your personal support.

The Advisory Committee for this industry program, chaired by Mr. Albert L. Nickerson, Chairman of the Board of Socony Mobil Oil Company, is composed of outstanding leaders from the business community who have been active in direct overseas investments and international trade. That Advisory Committee met with me on February 26, and strongly urged that our program be set up on as informal and personal a basis as possible, with a minimum of formal reporting requirements and other "red tape." All members of the Advisory Committee have given me their judgment that the leaders of American industry will respond quickly and favorably to that kind of approach and that, as a result of such leaders taking personal responsibility for this effort, our voluntary program will produce significant reductions in the balance of payments deficit. The Advisory Committee is particularly in favor of a flexible approach that enables each company head to work out his own program, based on the operating facts of his own business, rather than limit the means of meeting each company's objective by having the government prescribe some formula of general application.

That advice makes sense to me, and the form of the program that we had been planning has been modified along the lines suggested.

Consequently, I ask for your help specifically as follows:

1. Please set up for your company a balance of payments "ledger" for the year 1964 which shows the selected debits and credits. I enclose a summary work sheet to indicate the needed figures, and some instructions to help your technical people in preparing it for you.

2. After looking at your 1964 results—and we realize in most cases a significant favorable balance will be shown—please consider how that 1964 result can be improved for the years 1965 and 1966. We have been thinking in terms of an average improvement in balance of payments terms, in 1965 of 15–20 percent over the 1964 results. We realize, however, that any such target will be inappropriate for many corporations—either on the low or

high side—but the important thing is to make an extraordinary effort. There-fore, we have concluded that only you are in a position to set up a reasonable but meaningful objective for your own company, in light of your operating facts and problems. The nine suggestions listed on the enclosed press release do not exhaust the list of possibilities that you and your associates can put together in devising an approach meeting the national purpose, yet tailored to your particular circumstances. In short, I am asking you to establish, *and then let me know,* your best *personal* estimate of how much of an improve-ment in terms of net dollars you think your company can make over all in 1965, compared with 1964, by taking all feasible steps to help the nation deal with this serious problem.

3. It would also be helpful for us to have a few of your summary figures for the year 1964 showing credit and debit items separately. The work sheet referred to in paragraph 1 would be appropriate for your 1964 report and should be returned to us. It may also be helpful in calculating your 1965 target. We understand that for many firms or industries, such as petroleum operations or contract construction, there may be a need to include in their "ledger" other information on foreign transactions in order to show a realistic balance of payments performance. In such situations, we would welcome any supplementary figures you wish to supply, and will take them into con-sideration in reviewing your results.

4. Because of the unique opportunity to shift short-term assets and make an early improvement in the balance of payments, I would also like to have your figures at the end of 1963 and 1964 for short-term assets held abroad either directly or through United States banking or other financial institutions. In addition, we would like to have figures on such assets held in developed countries by your subsidiaries and branches.

5. I would like to receive your first set of figures by April 15, if this is possible, and I hope it is.

6. Thereafter, I am asking you to send me quarterly reports through the years 1965 and 1966 showing the data in paragraphs 2, 3, and 4 above and revisions, if any, in your overall goal for the year. You should also give your personal evaluation of points or problems you consider to be of particu-lar significance.

7. While prior notification regarding substantial new investments or ex-pansions abroad, including information indicating how they would be fi-nanced, would be helpful, we have decided against a formalized program asking for such information. It is our hope that the overall estimates and reports that I am requesting will prove to be adequate, and that the results will be clear enough to obviate the need for prior notification of new in-vestments. We, of course, expect that care will be taken to minimize the balance of payments effects of large investments and either we, or the ap-propriate Federal Reserve officials when their program is involved, would be glad to discuss such situations should you so desire.

8. We shall be very glad to talk on the telephone or meet with you to discuss this or any other aspect of this voluntary program of interest or concern to you as it moves along.

Your company's report and estimates will be treated by us as strictly "Confidential" and shown only to those few government officials who are working with us directly in this program. We do plan to put together a periodic summary of the reports in aggregate terms for consideration with the Advisory Committee and for reports to the President, the Cabinet, and the public.

There are a few special problems which I would like to call to your particular attention.

First, we regard the national objective of increasing the contribution by private enterprise to growth in less developed countries of such importance that we do not wish this program to inhibit the flow of these investments.

Second, while relatively rapid progress in repatriating short-term financial funds invested abroad, wherever appropriate, would be helpful, we request that this be done with caution in the case of balances in countries subject to balance of payments problems. We are naturally concerned not to cause difficulties on the exchanges and it would be desirable for companies with large balances to consider consulting with the appropriate Federal Reserve Bank on this problem.

Third, we do not anticipate cutbacks in Canadian direct investments, but firms should take particular care to assure that short-term funds put at the disposal of your subsidiaries in Canada serve only to meet operating needs in Canada. Opportunities should be explored for obtaining at least a portion of working capital requirements from the Canadian market. In this process, we hope that short-term investments in Canada by parents or subsidiaries clearly in excess of working requirements will not be increased. No doubt opportunities will arise to reduce these balances, particularly those denominated in United States dollars, but this should be done only in a gradual and orderly way.

I am sure you are aware of the vital importance of improving the United States balance of payments position. Such improvement is essential to international monetary stability, to this nation's economy, and to continued business progress. The capability of this nation to manage its international fiscal affairs is being carefully watched around the world.

President Johnson is confident, as am I, that you will cooperate with us in this extremely important program of serious concern to you and to our country. We urgently need your help.

ADDITIONAL READINGS

Boot, F. R. and Boot, J. C. G., "Pay Interest on Gold," *The Banker*, October, 1963, pp. 677–680.

Coombs, Charles A., "Treasury and Federal Reserve Foreign Exchange Operations," *Federal Reserve Bank of New York, Monthly Review,* March, 1965, pp. 42–50.

"Defending the Dollar: Latest Moves by LBJ," *U.S. News and World Report,* February 22, 1965, pp. 47–50.

Ellsworth, P. T., "From Dollar Shortage to Dollar Glut," *Michigan Business Review,* March, 1960, pp. 10–14.

"Foreign Capital Borrowing in the United States," *Federal Reserve Bank of Cleveland, Economic Review,* January, 1964, pp. 2–6.

"Foreign Long-Term Borrowings in the United States," *Federal Reserve Bank of Chicago, Business Conditions,* September, 1963, pp. 5–10.

Gemmill, Robert F., "Interest Rates and Foreign Dollar Balances," *Journal of Finance,* September, 1961, pp. 363–376.

"Longer Life Likely for Dollar Gap," *Business Week,* October 10, 1964, pp. 162–165.

MacDougall, Sir Donald, *The Dollar Problem: A Reappraisal,* International Finance Section, Princeton University, 1960.

Raynolds, David R., "The U.S. Balance of Payments," *Financial Analysts Journal,* November–December, 1963, pp. 11–16.

Reimann, Guenter, *The Future of the Dollar,* International Reports, Inc., New York, 1963.

Roosa, Robert V., "Balance of Payment Adjustment and International Liquidity," *Journal of Finance,* March, 1964, pp. 1–15.

Salant, Walter S., (et al.), *The U.S. Balance of Payments in 1968,* Brookings Institution, Washington, 1963.

U.S. Government, *Higher Interest Rates on Time Deposits of Foreign Governments,* Hearings, Committee on Banking and Currency, House of Representatives, 87th Cong., 2nd Sess., July 10–18.

Ward, Richard, "The Balance of Payments and the Foreign Exchanges," *The National Banking Review,* June, 1964, pp. 559–568.

chapter **4**

The International Monetary System: Its Operation and Suggested Reform

International trade and investment thrives on an efficient and stable international monetary system. The present system, which came into being after World War II, has, during the past five years, been subjected to periodic stresses and strains. These stresses and strains in themselves, bring about governmental policies which act as hinderances to the flow of trade and investment. A failure of the system would cause major disruptions in the operations of multinational businesses. The function of the international monetary system is not, therefore, of interest solely to international economists and government officials. The international businessman is vitally interested in its day-to-day operation and in the prognosis for its continued proper functioning.

The international monetary system has evolved over the centuries, and gold has long been a basis of its operation. The records of Egyptian Pharaohs of 3,000 B.C. show that gold was being dispatched to India to pay for merchandise, but there were difficulties caused by the wide variation in weight, and fineness of gold rings and bars. Greek merchants struck the first gold coins (as far as is presently known) around 750 B.C.

The ancient Greeks believed in sound money; this is, that a coin should contain a specific amount of gold without change over a long period of time. But the Romans had less scruples along this line, and when several of the Emperors found themselves pinched for money, they diluted the gold coins with base metals, resulting in domestic inflation and a disruption of international payments. The longest record for sound currency was during the Byzantine Empire. In 325 A.D. the Emperor Constantine introduced a gold piece called the "bezant," which contained 65 grains of gold. For 800 years this was the key currency throughout the Eastern world and was maintained without devaluation during all that time.

Meanwhile, during the Middle Ages, Europe's economy closely resembled a barter economy. When economic activity revived after the end of the Middle Ages, the currency situation improved. The large inflow of precious metal from the New World facilitated this process. An important event occurred in 1561 when Queen Elizabeth I of England, in a surprise move, removed all debased coins from circulation and in their place issued silver coins of uniform quality and weight. There was, thereafter, no tampering with the value of coined sterling. During this same period, gold coins predominated in other countries. By the early 1800's England had adopted what was essentially a gold standard, while other countries, such as France, were on a bimetallic standard, where currency was defined in terms of both gold and silver.

During the 1870's, most of the major European countries adopted the gold standard, and the United States joined the group in 1879. From that decade until World War I, almost all the major countries of the world were on the gold (specie) standard. (Their currencies were convertible into gold at the initiative of any holder, and exports and imports of gold were unrestricted.) This was the period known as the "golden age of the gold standard."

At the beginning of World War I, however, most Western nations suspended the gold standard. The United States was the first country to return to it, in 1919. England, for example, did not return until 1925 and France in 1928. But the countries generally discontinued the coinage of gold. Instead, the gold was bought and sold by the central banks at a fixed price, meanwhile serving as a monetary reserve for foreign payments. This was known as the gold bullion standard. Some countries, at that time, went on the gold exchange standard, under which the monetary unit was defined not in gold, but in terms of the currency of another country which was on the gold standard.

The international financial crisis came in 1931 when the leading bank of Austria had difficulties, resulting in a run on it followed by a general, large-scale withdrawal of foreign balances from Austria. Soon thereafter, the failure of a large German bank led to a bank panic in that country, and to a withdrawal of funds by foreigners. The pressure then shifted to England where the banking system was vulnerable because it had large frozen balances in Germany and Austria. On September 19, 1931, the Bank of France decided that the situation was hopeless and that it should salvage as much as possible. It therefore gave orders to each of six New York banks to sell a million pounds sterling. This broke the price of sterling and on September 21, the British government suspended the responsibility of the Bank of England to sell gold, and this marked its departure from the gold standard.

The United States legally abandoned the gold (specie) standard in March, 1933. In January, 1934, it reduced the gold value of the dollar and went on a gold bullion standard. Six nations, known as the "gold bloc," still adhered to the true gold standard; France, the Netherlands, Belgium, Switzerland, Italy and Poland. The central banks of these countries cooperated to check speculations on their currencies. This gold bloc broke up, however, in 1936 when France, Switzerland and the Netherlands devalued their currencies. Thereafter, only the United States and a few other countries were on the gold bullion standard. Most nations were on inconvertible paper standards under which groups of currencies were kept at a parity with each other but not at a constant value in terms of gold or silver. With the coming of World War II, practically all countries including the United States, went off any type of gold standard.

Such, then, was the setting out of which evolved our present international monetary system. And, such is the way in which the present system might break down, if the International Monetary Fund proved to be inadequate and if cooperation between the central banks of the leading countries ceased.

The following readings do not describe the details of the operations of the International Monetary Fund, the center of the present system. The first reading does, however, describe the present international monetary system in general terms and then goes on to discuss its inadequacies and various possible corrective measures.

It will be seen, in the first reading, that a central factor in any discussion of the system is the question of adequacy of international liquidity. The second reading, by J. Keith Horsefield, is a detailed analysis of this question, to establish a basis for any further intelligent discussion of the overall system.

One of the leading critics of the present system is Jacques Rueff. His article, "The West is Risking a Credit Collapse," is a statement of his thesis that the world should return to the gold standard.

As factual back-up to the articles by Horsefield and Rueff, the next two articles, "Annual Gold Review" and "The London Gold Market," provide the reader with essential data on the availability and distribution of gold in the world, and on the institutional framework through which the world price of gold is determined.

Following these is an article on recent developments in the international monetary system . . . on the arrangements which have been made among the countries of the Atlantic community to bolster the system until more basic changes might be agreed upon.

Finally, an article on the United Kingdom's 1964–65 financial crisis is essentially a case study of a near failure of the system, including the causes of the crisis and the steps taken within the system to save the situation. This was not a simple problem of a potential devaluation by some foreign country. A number of other countries are in the sterling area; still other countries which have close trade relations with the sterling area may have found it necessary to follow with their own devaluations. How far such a snowball effect might have carried is difficult to predict, but interesting and instructive to speculate.

INTERNATIONAL PAYMENTS IMBALANCES AND THE NEED FOR STRENGTHENING INTERNATIONAL FINANCIAL ARRANGEMENTS *

INTRODUCTION

The system of international trade and payments among the industrially advanced countries of the free world has undergone a sweeping transformation during the past dozen years. The key changes have been the lifting of restrictions on external payments, resulting in nearly complete currency convertibility, and the removal of import quotas on most manufactured goods and raw materials, though they are still applied to coal, oil, and many agricultural products.

This marked progress toward liberalization of free world trade and payments conforms to a longstanding objective of our foreign economic policy, and it has contributed substantially to the realization of vital U.S. economic and political goals. By exposing previously sheltered national industries to outside competition, it has stimulated management to improve organization, adopt more efficient technology, and develop better products and thereby it has spurred economic growth both here and abroad. By weakening the excessive market power of concentrated industries and strong industrial unions, it has helped to reduce the danger of a recurrence of sellers' inflation. Finally, it has bolstered free world unity by removing the discriminatory bilateral and regional arrangements of the era of inconvertibility and quotas.

The record is not an entirely favorable one, however. Quotas on certain imports remain and interfere with trade. The European Common Market, which represents an ambitious step toward trade liberalization and economic and political integration for its members, has brought about increased discrimination against American and other nonmember exports. And up to the present the United States has borne a disproportionate share of the costs of programs for joint security and economic development.

*Report to the Joint Economic Committee, 87th Cong., 1st Sess., U.S. Government Printing Office, Washington, 1961.

Nevertheless, the dominant tendency in the free world over the last dozen years has been toward more liberal trading and payments arrangements amongst its advanced economies. Persistence of this trend would make a great contribution to both free world growth and stability, and to its political and economic unity. It is essential that everything possible be done to encourage further progress.

But it is now becoming clear that even past achievements are threatened by the failure of the free world to create an efficient international monetary mechanism. The difficulties which some of the countries of the free world face as a result of its inadequacy are likely to force them toward more restricted and discriminatory trade, to a lower rate of growth, to a reduced contribution toward economic development and joint military security, and away from meaningful economic integration. In short, the economic objectives of the free world are in jeopardy because its international monetary mechanism is inadequate.

One manifestation of the difficulty is the succession of payments crises, which most recently have affected Britain and the United States. But these are only the most spectacular items of evidence. The demands in several countries to raise tariffs, to protect one sector or another of the economy from foreign competition, to reduce commitments to aid underdeveloped economies, to lower the contribution for military defense, are others. And Britain's recently adopted policy of high interest rates, which cannot but discourage economic growth, is still another. These retrograde pressures are the consequence of arrangements under which a country's international reserves may easily become inadequate.

The Subcommittee on International Exchange and Payments of the Joint Economic Committee is naturally concerned when there is any serious threat to major economic objectives of the free world. It is for this reason that it undertook an investigation of the international monetary mechanism, evaluating it for possible weakness, and considering proposals to strengthen it.

ANALYSIS

A. Description and Evaluation of Present System

1. Nature of the Present System

The gold exchange standard. Countries keep their international reserves in two forms. First of all, they hold gold, which of course can be used on specified terms to make international payments. Secondly, they may hold either one or both of the so-called reserve currencies—sterling or dollars, and these are also generally acceptable as means of international payment. Finally, all members of the International Monetary Fund have unrestricted rights to a certain amount of the Fund's holdings of currencies, and in addition, conditional rights to larger amounts. The Fund's holdings of gold and convertible currencies establish the maximum amounts that member countries together can now get; their unrestricted rights, in total, are a great deal lower.

Quasi-fixed exchange rates. Under the terms of the Bretton Woods Agreement under which the International Monetary Fund was established, member countries set the price of gold (or dollars) in their own currency and this pattern of gold and dollar prices with unrestricted gold movements determines the structure of exchange rates. But the structure can be modified by the unilateral action of any one country if the change is not greater than 10 percent; or if the change is to be larger, by the agreement of the Fund. Thus the structure of exchange rates can be regarded as fixed, until it is changed; and at certain dates, September 1949, for example, or to a lesser extent in the spring of 1961, the changes have been significant.

Role of reserves. The reserves of gold and reserve-currencies, supplemented by what each country can hope to get from the Fund (and other sources), permit it to make payments which exceed its receipts. If a country's reserves are sufficient it is thus able to finance a level of payments that is higher than its receipts; or in other words, its reserves permit it to finance a deficit in its balance of payments.

When trade is relatively free, and currencies are convertible without restriction into others, deficits (and, of course, surpluses) must be anticipated. This follows because under such conditions payments will not invariably be scaled down so as to be no higher than receipts; moreover, funds can be readily transferred from one country (and currency) into another. And with the gradual growth in the level of trade and spread of convertibility, the likelihood that some countries will have large deficits, and others large surpluses, grows.

Summarizing then, the West's international monetary mechanism is a gold exchange standard, with gold and the key currencies serving as the major reserves; with quasi-fixed exchange rates for the various currencies; and with the need for reserves dominated by the likelihood of large deficits in any country's balance of international payments.

2. The Weaknesses of the Present System

(A) MAJOR COUNTRIES NEED LARGE RESERVES. Reserves are needed to allow a country to finance deficits until they can be dealt with by acceptable methods. There are several reasons why, under the circumstances of the present day, reserves must be a good deal larger than earlier.

Growth in liberalized trade raises need for reserves. First of all, as we have already noted, with progress towards liberal trade and currency convertibility and with a gradual growth in the level of trade the likelihood of deficits is increased and thus the requirement for reserves is raised. But this is only a part of the picture.

Structual disequilibria raises need for reserves. A second reason stems from a change in the factors underlying payments deficits. Typically, in the past, they were a consequence of the uneven timing or severity of the business cycle in the various countries. A country in which demand was inflated, relative to others, would experience a payments deficit, as its purchases increased by more than its sales. The cure for a payments deficit caused by domestic inflation is to halt the inflation, and normally this should and can be done quickly. A country in which demand was relatively depressed would experience a payments surplus. The cure for its domestic and international imbalance consists in prompt domestic monetary and fiscal policies to end the decline. But in recent years, payments imbalances have not been of this type. They have had their origin in dynamic factors which have created structural disequilibria among the various economies and these have shown themselves to be relatively persistent. Shifts in the pattern of demand (from silk to the synthetic fibers, for instance), shifts in technology, or the rapid development of industry in newly competitive economies may cut into one country's export markets, and foster another's. The proper, though not the easiest or the quickest, adjustment for the deficit country is then to build up a new area of concentration, as Britain did when she shifted resources from coal and textiles to engineering; or as Japan did when she shifted from silk to a broad range of manufactures. But these adjustments take a great deal of time, and for this reason the duration of deficit may be great. The reserves needed to finance deficits during the adjustment will accordingly be high.

Government commitments and need for reserves. There is a third reason for expecting the need for reserves to be high. The United States and some of the other advanced countries of the West have accepted responsibility to assist the underdeveloped economies. Such assistance has normally required them to make large international payments. We have also been required to make large additional payments in connection with the common military effort. There is as yet no agreement among the members of the Atlantic Community regarding an equitable sharing of these burdens. Until there is, the United States has had to stand ready to meet these pressing needs, which can grow abruptly without regard to our Reserve position.

Hot money and need for reserves. Finally, with convertibility, and no sure guarantee that exchange rates will remain fixed, there are powerful speculative motives for the international transfers of funds; transfers may also be influenced by changing differentials in interest rates. And the volume of funds which their holders can seek to move from one country to another is almost limitless. To refer to short-term capital exports from the United

States as an example, they are not limited to the $10 billion of short-term dollar assets held by official institutions in other countries, or to the $17¼ billion of such assets in the possession of both private and official holders abroad. They could be increased many times over by efforts of Americans to transfer their liquid assets to other countries, as was demonstrated in the fall of 1960 when Americans acquired large amounts of short-term assets abroad when rumors of devaluation suggested speculative gains from doing so.

Unfortunately recent experience of currency crises and changes in exchange rates such as the upward revaluation of the mark and guilder have undoubtedly made funds far more volatile than they were earlier. Hence the need for reserves to finance such hot money exports must be much higher than before. The overall need for reserves has surely increased sharply in recent years.

(B) SUPPLY OF RESERVES IS LIKELY TO BE INADEQUATE.

Composition of reserves. The total supply of reserves is equal to the amount of gold in official holdings, the amount of reserve currencies so held, and the amount of credit that countries can count upon unconditionally, or at least when their need for it is most intense. The first component is equal to the cumulative amount mined minus that part which has gone into commercial and artistic channels or private hoards. The addition to total reserves through official holdings of reserve currencies cannot exceed the cumulative total of British and American payments deficits and will fall short by (1) British and American losses of gold to foreign countries, plus (2) the amount of dollars and sterling absorbed in private balances. Credit availability includes some of the resources of the IMF together with credit made available on an ad hoc basis through central bank mutual support operations, as in the spring of 1961.

Overall reserves inadequate if any (major) country's reserves inadequate. There has been a good deal of discussion as to whether the total amount of reserves (including credit commitments) is adequate. It seems to us that much of this debate misses the point, for whether the total supply is greater than the total amount needed, or not, does not really tell us whether reserves are in fact adequate. There may well be an excess of reserves, in the aggregate, while at the same time some countries may find their holdings too low. And unfortunately then the deficiencies of these latter countries are not offset by the excesses of others. Indeed, so long as there is any deficiency of reserves in any country, there is an overall deficiency, in any meaningful sense.

More on inadequacy of reserves. If now we seek to determine whether the volume of reserves is adequate or deficient, we must note that no mechanism exists either to keep the total in line with the total of needs, or to keep the reserves of each country in line with its own needs. And while we cannot, in the abstract, decide whether the total is high enough or not, we can agree that it would be a remarkable coincidence if each country's reserves were adequate. More than that, we can detect a good deal of evidence, in recent exchange crises for example, which points to inadequacy in one country or another at the present time.

One of the strengths of the domestic economy consists in its ability to adjust output to changing demand. When more automobiles are wanted, more will be produced. The same responsiveness can be found in the domestic monetary system. When more domestic reserves are "needed" by the banking system, more will normally be made available through the central banks, or, if the deficiency is felt by only some banks, then through the sale of financial assets by them to other banks whose reserves are excessive. But there seems to be no mechanism which insures the appropriate response of supply to changes in the need for international reserves. In this critical sector, chance, as it helps determine how much gold can be profitably mined, and the combination of forces that influence the balance of payments of the key currency countries, plays the predominant role in affecting the supply. The demand for reserves plays little part. There is, thus, an ever-present danger that a country's reserves will fall below the level it needs, and that its corrective actions will be injurious to the economic well-being of the free world.

Future prospects for reserves.   The prospects that reserves will fall below the amount needed is even more alarming when we look ahead. The reserves of the free world, under present arrangements, will only grow by an increase in the West's official holdings of gold and reserve currencies. In recent years, a significant fraction of newly mined gold has gone into private hoards, or into the Soviet Union's reserves, and it is widely believed that the addition to free world monetary reserves from this source will not come to more than 1 percent a year. Increases in official holdings of the reserve currencies depend in the first instance upon the payments deficits of Britain and the United States; however, they are in fact likely to be smaller for two reasons:

(i) Private holdings of reserve currencies may continue to rise, as they have over the last few decades. They are the more likely to rise, the greater is the confidence in these reserve currencies.

(ii) And if confidence is wanting, official institutions may be reluctant to continue accumulating reserve currencies. Thus, if there is no lack of confidence, official holdings of reserve currencies would be bound to rise by less than the payments deficits of the key currency countries; while if there is not full confidence, the results might be the same, though for different reasons.

Between 1952 and 1960, the cumulative payments deficit of the United States came to $16.6 billion. Gold production (excluding that of the Soviet

Union) came to $8.9 billion. The greatest possible increase in reserves of the advanced economies of the free world in these circumstances could have been as much as $25.5 billion. But in fact there were various drains—gold into private hoards, or into other official reserves, and an accumulation of reserve currencies in private hands, offset by small sales of Soviet gold to the West—and as a result, total gold and reserve currency in the West's official monetary institutions rose by no more than $10 billion, an increase of 29 percent in 8 years—or about 2.5 percent a year.

Generally, under the gold exchange standard, there are likely to be increasing difficulties in securing a large enough growth in reserves. Clearly, the output of gold itself is inadequate, for if it were not, a simple gold standard would have sufficed. But the increase in holdings of the reserve currencies runs into this difficulty—the higher the stocks already held, the more reluctant the holders are to acquire more, except when the gold stocks of the reserve-currency countries are rising about as quickly; and this reluctance would probably be reinforced by the reluctance of the reserve-currency countries to increase their short-term liabilities too rapidly without increasing their gold holdings.

(c) SPECIAL DIFFICULTIES FOR RESERVE-CURRENCY COUNTRIES. The United States and Britain are placed in special jeopardy by the operations of the present gold-exchange standard. In order that the reserves of the other advanced economies of the West be adequate, their official institutions must hold large amounts of short-term dollar and sterling assets. These holdings must be convertible into gold or other currencies on demand; moreover, there cannot even be serious doubt about convertibility for if there were, holders would rush to transfer their assets into gold or into a preferred currency.

This means that the gold holdings of the reserve-currency country are especially liable to sharp and severe drains. And when it is remembered that foreign official holdings of short-term dollar assets now come to about $10 billion, while the total U.S. gold stock (including the amount required as reserves against the liabilities of the Federal Reserve Banks) comes to $17¼ billion, the position is seen to be somewhat hazardous. Moreover, recorded private foreign holdings of such dollar assets amount to $7¼ billion, and if a suspension of convertibility should be feared, their owners would presumably join the rush, by transferring their dollar assets to a central bank which can demand gold. Finally, and even more important, given these possible claims upon the U.S. gold stock, wealth owners in the United States showed in 1960 that they can become uneasy at times over the possibility that the dollar might have to be depreciated either against gold, or against another currency; indeed they might be unduly fearful of this possibility. Hence, they would be ready, any time they feared a relative fall in the price of the dollar, to transfer their assets into another currency, and the amount of funds subject to transfer for these reasons could be enormous.

The position of sterling is in some respects even more difficult, for although the holders of a large part of outstanding sterling balances have agreed informally to keep a large part of their reserves in this form, the British gold stock is much smaller.

Thus, the probability of large hot money movements from the reserve-currency countries is especially high, simply because a detonator in the form of foreign holdings of the reserve currency is an inevitable feature of the mechanism of the gold exchange standard. And given this high probability of extensive shifts of short-term funds, the reserve-currency countries need to have especially high reserves. If they lack them, they become exposed to all the dangers described below.

In the light of these considerations, it is not surprising that the United States and Britain do not want to rely upon the growth of dollars and sterling assets held as reserves by other countries. Nor is it surprising that these other countries should on their part want to limit their holdings of dollars and sterling, preferring instead, after a certain point has been reached, to accumulate gold. But when this point has been reached—when the resistance of either the debtor or creditor countries or both to further increases of short-term debt becomes evident—then the gold-exchange standard is no longer fully viable. If that situation does not already exist, it seems, unfortunately, to be not far away.

The special weakness of the gold-exchange standard is that it does not provide adequate reserves. Any of the major economies may be exposed to this inadequacy; the reserve-currency countries are particularly liable to suffer its consequences.

3. Ways in Which Inadequate Reserves Can Hurt the Free World

A country's international reserves permit it to pay out more than it receives on international account, the deficit being financed from its reserves. When its reserves are "inadequate," it is compelled to adjust its payments to its receipts more speedily than is desirable. Adjustments of this type may harm the deficit economy without contributing to the removal of the factors really responsible for the deficit; they are even more likely to injure other free world economies both as trading partners and, in some cases, as recipients of aid.

(A) TRADITIONAL CAUSE OF DEFICIT AND ADJUSTMENT—INFLATION OR DEPRESSION.   In tradition, a deficit in a country's balance of payments is the result of domestic inflationary pressures relative to the situation abroad. The cure for such a deficit would be then either to reverse the inflationary forces in the deficit economy, or if the other "surplus" economies were in depression, to bring about expansion in these latter economies. Monetary and fiscal measures would normally restore equilibrium, and the equilibrium attained would be desirable not only in the international sphere, but also from the standpoint of domestic stability. Moreover, the restoration of equilibrium should be achieved rapidly.

This cause now less important. Most payments imbalance in recent years have, however, not resulted from such forces. The advanced economies have on the whole been successful in preventing either excessive inflation or depression, and there have been few instances when one economy was considerably more active, or less active than the others. The uneven timing of the business cycle accounts for only a minor part of the payments deficits and surpluses which have characterized the last decade. And it seems likely that this source of payments imbalances will be of secondary importance in the future.

Other causes of imbalances persist. A country can, however, be exposed to a payments deficit (or surplus) which has a quite different origin. Neglecting those which are either seasonal or episodic (like Suez) in character, for they raise no special difficulties, there are two which demand close consideration.

(B) DEFICITS CAUSED BY HOT MONEY. One has been already discussed. Movements of short-term funds, looking either to higher yields, or to the possibility of speculative profit from anticipated changes in exchange rates or in the price of gold, can bring about a very large deficit (or surplus) in a country's payments position. And with the possibility of so large a deficit, there is a need for reserves to be very large, too.

Appropriate methods for correcting deficits caused by hot money. An important feature of deficits caused by movements of "hot money" is that they may take place not only when the economy is subject to extraordinary inflationary pressures but also when it is faced with deflationary forces. If they stem from a relatively low level of interest rates, they could be stopped by raising them, but to do this when the economy is depressed means forgoing domestic prosperity. In such circumstances, the better policy would be to permit the capital export to continue while efforts are made to improve the coordination of monetary policy among the major countries. But in order to provide enough time for this coordination to take effect, large deficits may have to be financed for some time from preexisting reserves. If the reserves were not large to begin with, there might be no opportunity for these methods, and instead domestic interest rates would have to be raised, driving the economy still deeper into depression.

If the export of short-term funds is a result of speculative expectations of a rise in the price of gold, or devaluation of the exchange rate, the best cure is to show convincingly that these expectations are groundless. This can be done most effectively when reserves are adequate. When they are inadequate, it may not be possible to do this and the deficit country may have to take other steps to close the gap, such as to raise tariffs, or interest rates, to restrict convertibility, or to restrict aid for economic development. We shall postpone briefly the consideration of these methods since they may also be forced upon a country which lacks adequate reserves when its deficit is the result of dynamic factors.

(c) DEFICITS CAUSED BY DYNAMIC DEVELOPMENT. In a world of rapid change, equilibrium in any country's balance of payments is not to be expected under conditions of liberalized trade and payments; on the contrary, relatively large and persistent surpluses and deficits are a natural and necessary accompaniment of such vigorous growth and change. Among the economically advanced countries, it is, generally speaking, those countries whose growth in productivity has been most rapid which have shown large payments surpluses (i.e., Germany, Italy, France); countries in which the gains in productivity have been retarded (the United States, Great Britain) have had deficits.

Desirable corrections of such deficits. The process of correcting these underlying imbalances without reversing the trend toward liberalization and without retarding growth has two aspects. From the side of the surplus countries, these surpluses partly reflect the fact that the growth of aggregate domestic purchases of goods and services plus foreign investment and aid are not keeping pace with rising productivity. In other words, these countries are not living up to their growing means. The resulting margin of excess productive capacity finds its outlet abroad, resulting in balances of payments surpluses and a piling up of gold and foreign exchange reserves.

One requirement for constructive adjustment process is that surplus countries live up to their growing means. The correction of the balance of payments surpluses of countries experiencing rapidly rising productivity must occur in part through more rapid increases in domestic consumption or capital formation (including, of course, what is imported from other countries), and in part through greater foreign investment, government aid to underdeveloped countries, and acceptance of a larger share of the costs of common defense. Although some of these adjustments are in part automatic, for example through wage increases such as are now occurring in Germany, they require much time for their realization; in part the adjustment hinges upon appropriate government action and this, too, is likely to lag as is shown all too clearly by the no-more-than-modest progress achieved so far in increasing the share of defense costs and development aid borne by the countries whose GNP has shown the largest increases. Meanwhile, delays and lags result in the stubborn persistence of surpluses; countries whose reserves have reached or exceeded the point of redundancy may feel no urgency about taking corrective action. Since surpluses for some countries must have their counterpart in deficits for others, deficits also tend to be persistent.

The other element in the process of correcting structural imbalances requires action by deficit countries. Deficit countries must act to accelerate their growth in productivity, in order to strengthen their position both in foreign markets and in competition with foreign goods in their domestic markets. Measures to raise productivity necessarily take time to bear fruit; the governmental measures which are appropriate to stimulate growth of productivity are often the opposite of those which would be applied to achieve an immediate improvement in balance of payments. For example, increased investment in modernization of plant and equipment may require lower interest rates and tax incentives; both the lower interest rates and the increase in domestic spending may temporarily worsen the balance of payments until their effects in higher productivity begin to be felt. Moreover, the experience of the European Common Market shows that reduction of trade barriers (and, perhaps even more, the announcement in advance of intended future reductions) is a powerful spur to technical advance. But the immediate, impact effect of a reduction in trade barriers will be to increase the balance of payments deficit through larger imports. Thus, the kinds of measures necessary to accelerate growth of productivity and improve the competitive position of deficit countries take time to bear fruit. And, as we shall see, most of the measures capable of bringing about quick improvement in the balance of payments—import restrictions, tight money, deflation—impair economic growth and intensify the underlying structural imbalance, so that the improvement in the payments position will be short lived.

Harmful effects of other methods of adjustment. Deflation: The country might, for example, raise interest rates and adopt other deflationary measures in order to curb its imports and so reduce payments. But a payments deficit of the kind we are now considering is a reflection of a loss of markets, and so is likely to occur when the economy is depressed. To apply further deflationary pressures at such a time would clearly not contribute to domestic equilibrium. More than that, they would scarcely encourage the investment-inducing facilities and techniques that would be needed to raise productivity and so ease the structural problem.

Trade restrictions: The deficit country might, of course, adopt other policies. It could, for example, raise tariffs to restrict imports in order to reduce its payments abroad. But while such measures might ease its international position, and even secure some relief from depression, the gains would be at the expense of other economies. And since other economies could also be expected to pursue their own advantage, they might retaliate and thus render the measures taken by the deficit country ineffective. What is more, even if the measures did succeed, the free world would lose from the raising of tariff barriers for it would not only reduce international specialization and so lower current productivity but it would also weaken competition and so discourage future technological advance.

Exchange rate adjustment: A devaluation of the exchange rates might also be recommended as a measure for reducing a payments deficit speedily. Provided that other countries did not retaliate, such a move would probably prove effective, and at the same time help to restore domestic prosperity; though perhaps at the cost of an adverse shift in the terms of trade. But the gains of the devaluing country would be offset by losses for the others. And there would be a further loss for the whole Western alliance simply because any change in the exchange rate would surely stimulate speculation on further changes, and thereby increase the likelihood of large movements of short-term funds.

Reducing aid for development or military programs: The deficit country could reduce payments by reducing the size of its programs for aiding underdeveloped economies, or for joint military security. But while these measures would contribute to the restoration of that country's international equilibrium, it would clearly be opposed to the other interests of the free world.

While the conventional weapons, just described, for dealing with a payments deficit can be condemned on certain grounds, some of them are appropriate when the source of the difficulty is not structural imbalance or hot money movements. Moreover, they are likely to produce their effects quickly. It is this latter feature that would encourage a country without adequate reserves to use the conventional measures whether they are appropriate or not. And when the cause of its difficulties is structural, rather than cyclical, they are not simply inappropriate in the sense that they do not strike directly at the cause, but they are likely to interfere with the needed dynamic adjustments, and in addition to harm the free world by slowing its growth, exposing it to the dangers of inflation, and reducing its contribution to economic development and military security.

But this is the threat which the West must face unless its reserves are adequate. At frequent intervals, some of the major countries will be under pressure to deflate when they should do the opposite, raise tariff barriers, cut foreign aid, and perhaps to depreciate simply because their reserves will be too low to allow them to adopt the other, slower-working policies that could restore equilibrium and in addition contribute to the West's economic health.

The reserve-currency country exposed to additional dangers. We have already drawn attention to the special jeopardy in which a reserve-currency country may find itself when foreign holdings of its short-term obligations are high. But this means that it may be unduly subject to political and economic pressures imposed by its creditors. By threatening to convert holdings of dollars or sterling into gold, or another currency, an important creditor can exert an influence which may be difficult to resist, unless the reserve-currency country has ample reserves.

In short, then, inadequate reserves may force important sectors of the Western World to adopt policies damaging to its major economic goals. In the interests of maintaining international equilibrium, economic growth may have to be slowed, developmental aid reduced to too low a level, efforts to enhance joint security curtailed, and competitive pressures against sellers' inflation may have to be relaxed unless reserves are generally adequate. And since the weakness of the current international monetary mechanism consists essentially in its failure to provide adequate reserves, the importance of making the appropriate modifications in it becomes manifest.

B. Requirements of An Effective International Monetary Mechanism

On the basis of the foregoing analysis, it is now possible to state the requirements of an effective international monetary mechanism.

1. Adequate Supply of Supplementary Reserves

An effective international monetary mechanism would channel an assured, dependable, and truly adequate supply of supplementary reserves from surplus countries with sufficient or redundant reserves to deficit countries with insufficient reserves. This means, first, that supplementary reserves must be dependably available in sufficient amount to permit any sudden destabilizing, speculative outflows of short-term capital to be met without strain. Secondly, supplementary reserves must be available in sufficient amount to permit the adjustment of structural imbalances in the underlying balance of payments to be gradual and constructive rather than hasty and destructive. When deficits are structural in origin, swift adjustment can be achieved only by methods which would undermine free world economic growth and reverse the trend toward liberalization of trade and payments. Gradual adjustment can be achieved by means which promote both growth and closer economic integration. Within a single country structural imbalances in interregional payments are avoided chiefly through equalizing capital movements, involving large and continual shifts in ownership of financial assets from deficit to surplus regions. This occurs automatically and without attracting notice. At the international level, uncertainty regarding currency values and other institutional barriers prevent capital movements from automatically filling this role. Consequently, in an integrated free world economy this job must be done by reserves and supplementary credits.

2. Scope of Membership in Supplementary Reserve Arrangements

In the case of most underdeveloped countries, the demand for imports is too insistent, in relation to limited export earnings, to permit much accumulation of reserves. These countries live on a hand-to-mouth basis; their purchases abroad in excess of the amounts provided from export earnings are tied closely to the amount of aid which the economically advanced countries are willing to extend, supplemented by IMF drawings and special credits to meet temporary payments difficulties. Since long-term foreign aid, supplemented by IMF and other short-term credits, tends to supplant reserves in financing the balance of payments of underdeveloped countries, their problems are rather sharply distinguishable from those of the economically advanced countries which accumulate sizable reserves and use them in meeting international payments. The IMF's resources in gold and key currencies are well adapted to the needs of underdeveloped countries; a new mechanism for providing needed supplementary reserves should be directed particularly toward fulfilling the mutual support needs of the economically advanced countries. This is particularly the case since any adequate supplementary reserve arrangement must be linked to close coordination of the economic policies of its members. The type of coordination needed is possible only among countries of similar institutions, similar stage of development, similar problems, and similar instruments of economic control.

3. Need for Coordination in Economic Policy

An effective mechanism for providing adequate supplementary reserves must be accompanied by much closer consultation and coordination of national economic policies than now exists. Such coordination would include (1) monetary and fiscal policies, (2) tariff and commercial policies, and (3) aid to underdeveloped countries and defense-burden sharing.

Coordination is necessary, in the first place, to provide assurance to the creditor countries that the supplementary reserve facilities are not being drawn upon by the debtors to enable them to sustain domestic inflationary policies. A country whose balance of payments deficit is the result of domestic inflation must be called upon to take prompt restrictive monetary and fiscal action instead of continuing to run a deficit. Second, through such a coordinating body, a country whose balance of payments is in surplus owing to cyclical deflation would be pressed by other members to adopt expansionary domestic policies. The effect would be to minimize the possibility, already slight, of long-sustained inflationary or deflationary tendencies in one or a few countries, although moderate and temporary cyclical divergencies are unavoidable.

Apart from inflation and deflation, international consultation and coordination should be developed for the purpose of concerting programs to adjust structural imbalances in international payments in ways which will accelerate economic growth. Such programs will cover the whole range of economic policies, rather than merely financial policy, and should include the principal industrial countries of the Atlantic Community plus Japan. Matters of commercial policy, including tariffs, export rebates, regional discrimination, and agricultural protection, would be involved. While reciprocal concessions by the United States are necessary for further trade liberalization, the special responsibility of the surplus countries to assume the leading role should be strongly pressed. Trade liberalization is a potent means of promoting structural adjustment, and tariff reductions by surplus countries are greatly preferable to upward revaluation of their currencies. A further objective of such policy coordination should be to reduce the present wide disparity among members of the Atlantic Community in the percentage of GNP contributed to common defense and foreign aid. Consultation and coordination among the leading industrial and trading countries with respect to economic policies bearing upon the balance of payments can be most appropriately organized under OECD, although the membership of the particular bodies dealing with these problems should include Japan and need not include certain of the smaller OECD members.

4. Restoration of Confidence in the Stability of Currencies and Exchange Rates

A basic factor accentuating present international payments difficulties is the atmosphere of uncertainty and skepticism regarding the stability of exchange rates. This is a consequence of our present system of quasi-fixed parities. If capital flowed to instead of away from countries whose payments were in deficit, present difficulties would be greatly eased.

The present speculative atmosphere cannot be cured merely by official declarations. Under today's conditions it is widely known that there may be no acceptable alternative, under some circumstances, to currency revaluation or devaluation as a means of correcting a large and persistent payments imbalance. Countries with deficits will not accept severe, prolonged deflation to achieve external balance, nor will surplus countries submit to sharp inflation. An adequate supplementary reserve arrangement, however, combined with appropriate coordination of national economic policies, would make it possible to reconcile the requirements of domestic stability and growth with balance of payments adjustment, without resorting to exchange rate adjustments. Domestic measures to combat recession would not need to be constrained by balance of payments difficulties.

A major policy objective should be to build up confidence in the permanence of the structure of exchange rates by avoiding any future changes in currency parities among the principal industrial and trading countries of the free world.

C. Proposals for Handling Problem of Reserves

If international reserves were as abundant as the plans that have been designed to deal with the problem, it would no longer be pressing. Ranging from an all-out return to gold coinage and no nonsense about paper money, to the development of claims on an international organization to replace gold in settling international payments, they at least attest to the sense of urgent need with which economists view the matter. It is not, however, the function of the subcommittee to choose one out of the many schemes that have been described, and recommend that the United States back it alone. Instead, with many of the schemes possessing attractive features, it seems wise to present our recommendations in terms of certain features which a number of the schemes possess. However, in order to provide a more concrete sense of some of these features, they will be presented in the context of short descriptions of some of the plans for reform.

1. Various Plans Described

The plans that are to be considered here range from a mere continuation of the present practice of making ad hoc central bank arrangements to extend credit in order to meet particular "hot money" crises as they arise, to the creation of an international central bank.

(a) AD HOC MUTUAL SUPPORT ARRANGEMENTS. Representatives of the major central banks or perhaps the various national treasuries could strengthen existing arrangements by providing for agreements for mutual support among the principal trading and financial countries. Such arrangements would deal primarily with short-term capital movements and in particular would protect the reserve centers (and their creditors) against the damaging effects of withdrawals of short-term funds. They might also be used, of course, to protect currencies against strains arising from other causes.

Such arrangements might take a wide variety of forms. Without going into detail, it will be enough to set out some of the dimensions of variations:

(a) Amount of support commitment.

(b) Duration of support.

(c) Conditions of support: Is there any dependable, advance commitment, or must the conditions be separately negotiated for each new situation, including satisfying lenders as to credit-worthiness of the borrower, satisfying them that the borrower is taking proper steps to rectify the basic cause of the strain, and so on?

(d) Intergovernmental or intercentral bank arrangements.

(e) Bilateral or multilateral arrangements.

(f) Form of support: Agreement to hold borrower's currency, or loan lender's currency (or possibly gold or a third currency).

(g) Exchange risk: If support takes form of holding borrower's currency, the currency holdings might be subject to a gold or exchange rate guarantee. Or a similar result could be accomplished by making the support take the form of a swap transaction; e.g., at a time of heavy pressure against the pound, the Swiss National Bank buys and holds sterling, but contracts to sell it 3 months forward to Bank of England at a specified rate of exchange.

It will be apparent that arrangements of this kind do not change the basic structure. Reserves would still consist of gold and reserve currencies. But particularly if the arrangements are intended to relieve a key-currency country, a commitment of this type is tantamount to a commitment to hold, and indeed to extend holdings of the reserve currency. From this standpoint, then, it could be regarded as a device for supplementing reserves at least temporarily.

(B) THE BERNSTEIN PLAN.   The Bernstein plan has earned strong support Like the arrangements described above, it provides for no change in the form in which reserves are kept and the role of the key-currency countries would not be altered. It contains two elements:

(i) *The integration of Fund quotas with members' own reserves.* Access to Fund resources would be entirely free, rather than restricted and discretionary, within the limits laid down in the articles of agreement: in the normal case, a member could draw 25 percent of its quota per year up to the point where total drawings were equal to 125 percent of its quota. Drawings in excess of 25 percent a year or 125 percent of quotas would require a waiver. Members would then treat their quotas as virtually an addition to their own reserves and would presumably meet deficits by drawing on the Fund pari passu with drawing on reserves.

(ii) *Increasing Fund resources in members' currencies.* Free access to Fund resources on this basis would not be possible today. One of the weaknesses of the Fund is that its holdings of the currencies of some of its members are limited unduly and may easily be exhausted. The reserve currency countries have contributed disproportionately to the Fund's resources; other Western European countries not enough. Consequently, the Fund is poorly equipped to deal with a shift of funds from one of the reserve centers to continental European countries. For example, while at the end of 1960 the Fund held $3.4 billion of U.S. dollars (including $800 million of Treasury bills in its so-called gold investment account), and $1.5 billion worth of pounds sterling, it held only $500 million of deutsche marks and $600 million of French francs. It is ironical, indeed, that a large portion of the recent British drawing upon the Fund had to consist of dollars. If the United States should wish to make use of its drawing rights, it is difficult to know what currencies the Fund could provide.

One way of strengthening its position would be to increase all members' quotas. But while this would increase Fund holdings of all members' currencies (including many for which it has no use), it would also increase members' drawing facilities correspondingly. Moreover, the objection might be raised that such a step was taken as recently as 1959.

Bernstein (and others) have also suggested that certain of the Fund's members agree to lend the Fund additional amounts of their currencies should its holdings of these currencies fall too low. These standby credits need be negotiated only with the leading countries whose currencies are most likely to be in demand, though there is no reason why other Fund members with convertible currencies should not join. Currency borrowed in this way would be employed to meet needs caused by destabilizing short-term capital movements from one financial center to another, rather than to finance deficits in a member country's underlying balance of payments. In order to keep such transactions separate from ordinary Fund transactions, Bernstein proposes that they take place through a subsidiary reserve settlement account.

The Bernstein plan and the mutual support arrangements discussed above could be combined. For example, one witness suggested to the subcommittee that central bank mutual support operations might be the first line of defense, running for, say, 3-month periods. If support were needed beyond that period, the Fund would be brought in as a second line of defense to replace the central bank commitments for mutual support.

(c) THE ZOLOTAS PLAN, AND OTHERS LIKE IT. Similar proposals which would give the Fund standby borrowing facilities, but under article VII rather than through a separate subsidiary, have been made by Professor Zolotas, Governor of the Bank of Greece, by Maxwell Stamp, as an alternative plan B to his more ambitious and preferred plan (described below); and by Per Jacobsson in his annual report to ECOSOC, April 1961.

(d) THE FRANKS-RADCLIFFE COMMITTEE PROPOSALS. Sir Oliver Franks and the Radcliffe Committee have proposed that the International Monetary Fund be authorized to accept deposits from its members, which they would treat as reserves. These deposits could be created either by the Fund's lending operations, or by deposit with the Fund by its members of reserves now held in the form of dollars, sterling, or gold. Under this arrangement, the present reserve base would be supplemented by deposit balances with the Fund. Triffin, whose full proposals will be discussed below, has also urged this step as a desirable transition toward his full plan. His idea in proposing it is (a) that countries might be more willing to hold gold-guaranteed deposits with the Fund than unguaranteed sterling or dollars, and thus the structure of reserves would be rendered more stable, and (b) that the acceptance of voluntary deposits by the Fund would be a steppingstone toward the full Triffin plan.

(E) THE STAMP PLAN. Maxwell Stamp has proposed that the Fund issue certificates up to a specified amount in any period, e.g., $3 billion a year, to an international agency to aid economic development. This agency would allocate the certificates to developing countries, and the latter would spend them at will. No country, however, would be required to accept the certificates. Countries which did agree to accept them would find their exports stimulated.

(F) PAYMENTS UNION FOR DEVELOPED ECONOMIES OF FREE WORLD. The success of the operations of the European Payments Union has suggested still another series of proposals which, if implemented, would give rise to a new form of reserve to supplement gold and the reserve currencies. The members of the OECD (and Japan and possibly Australia and New Zealand) would form a clearing or payments union. Deficits and surpluses of the members on ordinary account would be settled at an agreed ratio (e.g., half or two-thirds) in gold or foreign exchange acceptable to the payee. The remainder would be settled in the form of debits and/or credits on the books of the clearing union. Destabilizing short-term capital movements, however, would be settled entirely in debits or credits in the union. Credit balances in the union would, of course, be a form of reserves. This scheme could be regarded as providing an automatic, though often only partial, credit offset for any deficit, thus reducing the amount of reserves needed.

(G) THE TRIFFIN PLAN. Under the plan proposed by Triffin, claims against the International Monetary Fund, or other international institutions, are used as national reserves in place of the dollars and sterling now held as reserves. The essential elements are:

(a) Countries would agree to discontinue holding any reserves in the form of national currencies.

(b) Countries would agree to hold a minimum portion of their reserves in the form of deposits with the International Monetary Fund. (Triffin has suggested 20 percent as the initial percentage.)

(c) The International Monetary Fund would be authorized to expand its deposits by loans and "open market operations" subject to some appropriate limitation on the rate of expansion. Triffin has suggested that this expansion, together with the increase in monetary gold stocks, be limited to an annual increment in total reserves at some agreed rate, say 3 percent.

Thus the present International Monetary Fund would be converted into an international central bank, holding deposits and able to create credit. (The present IMF is a fund, not a bank. It can lend only the pool of currencies and gold represented by members' subscriptions.) The international central bank's deposit liabilities as well as its assets would be subject to a gold guarantee (or, strictly, a maintenance of gold value guarantee), as the present Fund's assets and liabilities are.

These are the bare essentials. There is room for considerable variation in their implementation. The point of prime importance is the transition from the present arrangement to the operation of the Triffin plan. Countries would initially acquire IMF deposits required to meet the minimum requirement by transferring to the IMF gold or foreign currencies they now hold as reserves, and by exchanging their present credit balances with the IMF for new deposits. To the extent that they do not choose to convert existing foreign exchange reserves into IMF deposits, they would liquidate them, by conversion into gold. (Triffin provides a minor exception for "working balances" in key currencies, and another exception for that portion of balances now held in sterling which is not convertible into gold.)

The transition from the present arrangements to the Triffin Fund-Bank would profoundly affect the international financial position of the reserve-currency countries. Their liabilities to other central banks and governments would be eliminated. In part, they would be replaced by liabilities to the Fund-Bank (maybe entirely in case of pounds). In part, they would be canceled against gold payments (perhaps only for the dollar).

Thus the Fund-Bank would acquire large amounts of dollars and sterling turned in by members. Triffin has calculated that if members who hold dollars and sterling prefer to retain their gold and deposit reserve currencies to meet their minimum deposit requirement (as of December 31, 1958), the Fund-Bank would acquire about $5 billion worth of reserve currencies. In addition, if members chose to deposit the rest of their dollars and sterling, and thereby acquire Fund-Bank deposits in excess of their minimum requirements, the Fund-Bank would get an additional $10 billion worth of dollars and sterling. Triffin has proposed that these dollar and sterling holdings, which would amount to $5 to $15 billion, should be subject to amortization at some maximum agreed rate, say 5 percent a year. With the Fund's maximum holdings of dollars amounting to about $10 billion, at the 5 percent rate, the Fund-Bank's dollar holdings would be subject to liquidation at a rate of no more than $500 million a year. If instead only $4 billion were turned in to the Fund-Bank, the United States would have to pay off the remaining $6 billion of foreign official dollar balances in gold immediately.

Certain aspects of the Triffin plan are subject to modification. The Fund's "open market operations" might be directed to the purchase of Government obligations of advanced countries or instead to bonds issued by the International Bank for Reconstruction and Development. Likewise, the requirement for minimum deposits and the arrangements for the transfer and subsequent amortization of existing holdings of reserve currencies could of course be modified.

(H) RAISING PRICE OF GOLD. Finally, it has been proposed that the problem could be handled most easily by means of a general increase in the price of gold. This would, of course, mean an increase in the monetary value of the existing reserves of the major gold-holding countries and it might, by increasing the ratio of gold reserves in the key-currency countries to their demand liabilities to foreigners, increase the readiness of these other countries to acquire dollars and sterling for reserve purposes.

Such a step would, however, have other effects which would have to be kept in mind. It would give a subsidy to the largest gold producers—South Africa and the Soviet Union. The incidence of windfall gains would be highly arbitrary, and it would "penalize" countries which had been willing to keep their reserves in the form of dollars and sterling, while favoring those which had insisted upon holding gold. Finally, it would provide a large windfall gain to private gold hoarders and probably stimulate speculative interest in gold. It might lead in the future to very large movements of funds out of the major currencies into gold in anticipation of further increases in its price, thereby vastly increasing the future need for reserves. In those Middle Eastern and Asian countries where gold hoarding has been endemic and has interfered with productive uses of saving, it would serve to enhance gold's prestige as a means of storing wealth.

2. Evaluation of Proposals

Adequacy of reserves. Supplementary reserves must be available in sufficient amounts to permit large outflows of short-term capital to be financed without strain, and to permit gradual and constructive adjustments to structural imbalances. Moreover, these reserves must be where they are needed and responsive in amount to growth in the need for them over time.

On this score most of the plans are reasonably satisfactory though with some it would be necessary to renegotiate the arrangements from time to time.

(1) The proposal for agreements among central banks for mutual sup-

port would not in itself provide any immediate increase in reserves. However, the increased borrowing facilities would permit an increase in liquidity for certain purposes. They would not provide for a steady future increase in reserves, except as countries might be more willing to add to their dollar (or sterling) holdings because these reserve currencies would be strengthened by the support arrangements.

(2) The Bernstein plan would provide for an immediate increase in reserves, through "integration" of Fund quotas with national reserves. However, it does not provide for an increasing level of reserves over time, although Bernstein is concerned about a future inadequacy of liquidity. In any case, since it secures a fairly large immediate increment, it could perhaps be counted on to meet the growth requirements for the next few years. Later, to quote the author, "it should be possible to have a more frequent review and revision of the quotas."

(3) The Zolotas plan would have similar effects.

(4) The Frank-Radcliffe suggestions would reduce the need for liquidity by limiting the use of the relatively unstable reserve currencies and bringing the new form of reserve under a gold guarantee. They would, however, do nothing to secure future relief.

(5) The Stamp plan does not bring about an increase in liquidity at once, though if it were put into effect reserves would be increased at a predetermined rate over the years. By providing for such an increase, it may be argued that the present "need" for liquidity would be reduced.

(6) The proposal to organize a Payments Union under the OECD would, if implemented, bring about an immediate increase in liquidity (or reduction in the need for it). In order to secure further accommodations in the future, it would be necessary to reduce still further the fraction of payments to be made in gold. It might perhaps be possible to agree, at the time the plan was being negotiated, for a schedule of future changes in the ratio. Moreover, with membership limited to the advanced economies, it might be easier to get the changes required than it would be in a more inclusive organization.

(7) Finally, the Triffin plan would not provide at the outset for any sharp increase in reserves. Triffin regards the present level of reserves as "on the low side," but his concern is mainly with the adequacy of future increments. His plan would secure a more or less automatic annual increase in reserves within agreed limits.

Supply of reserves must be dependable.   In view of the great harm that a crisis can do to confidence even if it is successfully surmounted, it is desirable that the new arrangements be geared to avert crises by coming into operation early enough, rather than simply to counter them once they have developed. On this score, the strongest plans are the Triffin scheme, the Bernstein plan—provided that drawing rights on the Fund are automatic—and the plan for an OECD-sponsored Payments Union. But the others, which have a greater element of discretion about them, can also prove effective if those in authority are informed and concerned to act in time.

In this connection it is desirable to stress the point that any of these plans will prove more effective if it provides opportunity for frequent consultation.

As an additional aspect of the requirement for an adequate and dependable supply of reserves, special arrangements may be desirable to meet the needs of the reserve-currency countries. Certainly any plan worth consideration should reduce the instability inherent in the present mechanism, with its use of reserve currencies. In principle, this could be done either by strengthening the reserve currencies themselves, as for instance by introducing gold guarantees, or by supplying a substitute for reserve holdings of dollars and sterling. The various plans all contribute in some degree to these ends, with the standby arrangements for mutual support probably providing the most uncertain solution, mainly because they are likely to be held from view.

Finally, the amount of reserves needed can be reduced if the claims to finance "hot money" movements can be held down. Most of the plans make no special provision for the treatment of short-term capital flows, except as they modify the role of the key currencies, or strengthen them against speculative doubt. But perhaps the major destabilizing factor to be faced in the future will be outflows of short-term capital. The plan for an OECD Payments Union provides for an automatic and complete reverse flow of capital as an offset to such capital exports, and thus is likely to grapple most effectively with this danger.

Scope of the arrangements. Some of the arrangements call for an extension of the role of the International Monetary Fund; others look to the OECD, or a group of the major economies, for their administration and operation. There are clearly arguments for both extremes. For simplicity, administrative ease, and the merit of grouping those countries whose problems are similar and which are already tackling other problems together, we see an advantage in a separate grouping of the economically advanced countries, whether it functions under the aegis of OECD or IMF. It would appear to be possible to implement the Triffin plan, or any of the others outlined above, on such a basis.

RECOMMENDATIONS

In accordance with policies announced by the President's balance of payments message of February 6, 1961, the United States has adopted a number of temporary measures to help reduce a basic deficit which was estimated to have been about $2 billion in 1960. While this deficit was completely eliminated in the first quarter of 1961, the balance was in part achieved by an unusually depressed level of imports, which is expected to go up as the momentum of U.S. recovery increases. Therefore, to assure long-term equilibrium in the U.S. balance of payments, a number of unilateral and multilateral programs are now underway. The most important are removing all obstacles to a continuing expansion of U.S. exports and travel to the United States, reallocating mutual defense costs, and sharing the burden of aid and future commodity stabilization arrangements for developing countries.

By international diplomacy and through such international organizations as NATO and OECD, the United States should make increased efforts to persuade other free world countries to bear a larger share of the costs of military security and foreign aid, both of which are substantial items in U.S. payments to other countries.

Export expansion will depend on the efforts of American business to offer attractive products, at competitive prices, to markets which have many other sources of supply. Growth of productivity through restoration of full employment and accelerated investment in industrial modernization would give growing competitive strength in export markets. The Government can assist in these efforts by providing information and by assuring adequate credit and insurance facilities. But the United States must also take the initiative in making certain that the formation of large regional trading areas does not discriminate unduly against U.S. and other exports to these areas. While boom conditions in the Common Market may help U.S. exports, it is of particular importance to secure a low European Common Market external tariff and a liberalized commercial policy on agricultural products and coal. Otherwise, a new source of payments imbalance will be introduced, with serious consequences not only for the United States but for the entire free world, particularly as the Common Market expands its membership to include other European countries. Consideration should in fact be given to forming a Free World Common Market, rather than further to encourage the growth of regional groups which divide the free world.

The subcommittee recognizes that these fundamental efforts to prevent continued deficits in the U.S. balance of payments, and to bring about conditions for better payments equilibrium among the free world countries are difficult and will take time. They will not succeed if weaknesses in our international monetary institutions permit transitional problems to be aggravated into crises. If we fail to correct the deficiencies in the present monetary mechanism, the economic growth and stability of the free world, including the countries which in recent years have enjoyed the most rapid growth, will be seriously impaired. Progress toward economic integration through liberalization in trade and payments will be halted and perhaps reversed by a new wave of restrictions. The repercussions on the political strength and unity of the Atlantic Community and on the economies of underdeveloped countries will be severe.

Accordingly, the subcommittee makes the following recommendations:

I. Action to Maintain Confidence In the Dollar As a Principal Reserve Currency

As recommended under Sec. II, a supplement to the present international monetary system is necessary. In addition, the United States should discourage destabilizing outflows of short-term capital, speculation against the dollar, and speculation in gold by the following action:

A. By the United States Unilaterally

(*1*) Pursue vigorously our economic goals of maximum employment, production, and purchasing power. By increasing our export competitiveness, and by maintaining confidence in the basic health of the American economy, attaining these goals will help protect the dollar.

(*2*) Vigorously oppose any further devaluations or revaluations of any of the principal currencies, besides reaffirming our opposition to an increase in the price of gold.

(*3*) Discourage the flight of short-term capital by pursuing a Federal Reserve policy of purchasing all maturities in the open market, and by not resuming the "bills only" policy.

(*4*) Eliminate the present 25-percent gold cover against Federal Reserve notes and deposits, so that official and nonofficial holders of dollar liabilities will have no doubt that the entire U.S. gold reserve stands back of the dollar in international transactions.

B. By the United States in Cooperation with Other Countries

Through the OECD, IMF, and GATT, encourage other countries to rely for anti-inflationary action less on high interest rates—which tend to induce short-term flights of capital—and more on restrictive fiscal measures, liberalized imports, and the removal of the remaining restrictions on payments.

II. Action to Improve Present International Arrangements Through a Supplementary Credit Agreement Within the IMF Among the Principal Industrial Countries

Such an agreement might take various forms. Whatever the form, the minimum requirements of any agreement are:

A. Parties to the Agreement

The parties to the agreement should be the principal West European countries, the United States, Canada, and Japan.

B. Nature of the Agreement

Each member should enter into an agreement with the IMF under which the member stands ready to purchase up to a specified amount of IMF interest-bearing obligations, denominated in its own currency, carrying the maintenance of value provisions of the articles of agreement and having maturities up to 4 or 5 years. The amount should be adequate, particularly in currencies other than the dollar and the pound. Funds would be borrowed by the IMF from participating countries having adequate or redundant reserves and strong balances of payments and lent to other participants experiencing payments deficits. Countries owning these IMF obligations should be permitted to use them in international payments, along with their gold and foreign exchange reserves.

C. Availability and Duration of Credit

Credits should be made promptly as needed. The size of the credit in relation to the deficit should, by agreement, be governed by the nature of the deficit: if the deficit is caused by "hot money," the bulk of the outflow should be financed by the credit; if the deficit is "structural" (i.e., of the type which requires correction through accelerated industrial modernization), credit might be granted to cover a significant fraction of the deficit over a period of several years; if, however, the deficit is caused by inflationary policies on the part of the deficit country, credit should be given for only a short period and only if the deficit country agrees to take adequate remedial measures.

D. Coordination with OECD

Financing operations under the IMF supplementary agreement should be closely related to the policy-coordinating functions of OECD in the fields of fiscal, monetary, and commercial policies, and aid to underdeveloped countries. Through OECD, payments imbalances due to inflationary or deflationary tendencies in particular countries can be promptly recognized; coordinated programs for achieving a generally low level of long-term interest rates to promote growth should be devised; commercial policies and aid policies provide important instruments for accelerating growth and correcting structural imbalances.

The subcommittee believes that such a supplementary IMF agreement should be negotiated this fall, so that it may be presented to Congress for legislative ratification early in 1962, preferably prior to the reciprocal trade legislation which will also be before Congress in early 1962. If in these negotiations it appears impossible to reach an agreement under the aegis of the IMF, a payments union under OECD is an alternative.

III. PROMPT STUDY OF FUTURE RESERVE NEEDS

The subcommittee recommends that the various agencies of the executive branch maintain, on a systematic and continuing basis, an analysis of the extent to which free world international reserves may be inadequate. In this analysis there should be taken into account factors such as the rise in the gross national product and foreign trade of member countries; the amount and distribution of existing reserve media—gold, dollars, and sterling; and the availability of "near reserves," such as the power to borrow from the IMF or any other institution.

INTERNATIONAL LIQUIDITY*

The Annual Report of the Fund for 1963–64, published in August 1964, contained two chapters dealing with the problem of International Liquidity. Simultaneously, there was published a statement on the same subject by the Ministers and Governors of ten major industrial countries, to which was annexed a report by their deputies. Drawing upon these papers, and also upon the Fund's Staff Papers, *Vol. XI (1964), pages 177–247, the Chief Editor of the Fund explains the nature of the problem with which they deal and current interest in this subject.*

What is meant by international liquidity? We may start by explaining what is *not* meant by the term. It does not refer to the means by which international trade is normally financed. Importers pay for imports by drafts on their banks, or by bills of exchange which are discounted at banks—that is, they make payment with the currency of the importing country. Exporters often borrow from their banks to finance the goods that they are selling abroad until they receive payment for them in their own currency. International trade (like domestic trade) is thus financed not by any *international currency* but by domestic banking systems, normally using the currencies of the exporters and importers concerned. Since at least two currencies are involved, however, there has also to be some means of exchanging the one for the other.

Clearly it is very important that adequate credit should be forthcoming to ensure that international trade flows freely. If exporters were not able to borrow from their banks to tide them over until payments were received from importers, the volume of exports might diminish. If importers could not tender drafts on their banks to make payments, imports might have to be cut off. And it is equally important that there should be adequate facilities for the exchange of foreign currencies for the domestic currency.

Various methods are used to ensure that credit is forthcoming. Some governments assist exporters by guaranteeing their receipts, or by providing them with credit. It is quite usual for international trade to be financed in a country that is neither the exporter nor the importer (usually one of the main industrial countries). In effect, the exporter borrows in that country any finance he may need before he receives payments, and the importer repays that country instead of the exporter. Or, the importer may borrow there the means to pay the exporter at the time the import is bought.

* J. Keith Horsefield, *The Fund & Bank Review*, Dec. 1964, pp. 170–177.

Types of International Liquidity

So far as exporters and importers are concerned, therefore, international trade usually involves only the domestic currencies of their own countries and of any third country in which the transactions may be conducted. But, as has been mentioned, there has also to be a mechanism for the exchange of one currency for the other. To a large extent this process is carried out in foreign exchange markets, where supplies and demands are matched. Some flexibility is added by commercial banks possessing variable quantities of other countries' currencies. But these arrangements often leave a balance of unsatisfied demand for some one or more currencies, and this demand travels up from the foreign exchange markets to the monetary authorities. These monetary authorities, if they are to be able to provide other countries' currencies, must themselves possess (or be able to borrow) amounts either of those currencies or of some others which can readily be exchanged for them. Thus, if a country has an import surplus, the monetary authorities may have to provide part of the foreign exchange needed to pay for imports.

For example, a Latin American country may import goods from the Federal Republic of Germany payable in deutsche mark in excess of its deutsche mark earnings from exports. If the excess payments in deutsche mark for trade are not matched by an inflow of deutsche mark on other accounts, the importing country's central bank will have to fill the gap by selling deutsche mark, which it may have acquired in the exchange market against U.S. dollars earned from transactions with other countries. Similarly, if the transaction is financed in New York, the U.S. bank will either itself provide the deutsche mark or will pay the exporter in dollars which he can exchange for deutsche mark in Germany; but the bank will expect to be paid in dollars by the Latin American importer, or by his central bank. If the Latin American country cannot produce or borrow the dollars or deutsche mark needed for such transactions as these, its imports will have to be curtailed, and the volume of international trade will shrink.

"International liquidity" is the term given to the world supply of reserves of gold or of currencies which are freely usable internationally, such as dollars or sterling, plus facilities for borrowing these. If international liquidity is adequate, countries will be in a position to let international trade flow freely; if there is a shortage of it, many will find it necessary to cut imports. In the one case, world trade is likely to expand; in the other, it will shrink. (If there is too much liquidity, there may be a risk of inflation—but that is another story.) It will be seen that international liquidity comprises, in large part, national currencies; but to form part of international liquidity these must be held in the reserves of countries other than those that have issued them. Dollars form no part of the international reserves of the United States, but they do form part of international liquidity insofar as they are held by other countries.

The second typical form of international liquidity—the ability to *borrow* reserves—is equally important. Trade can flow freely to any country which can pay for its imports by borrowing foreign exchange from somewhere else. That "somewhere else" may be another government, or private institutions in another country (such as a New York bank), or an international institution, such as the International Monetary Fund or the European Fund (organized by the European Economic Community), or one of the institutions financing development, such as the International Bank for Reconstruction and Development. We shall for the present consider only borrowing rights that place reserves unconditionally at the disposal of the borrowing government (just as the possession of actual reserves would). The alternative—"conditional" liquidity—is explained in the final section.

WHY IS INTERNATIONAL LIQUIDITY BEING STUDIED?

Before we go further it is pertinent to ask why it has been found desirable to make inquiries into international liquidity at all. We have seen that the main function of international liquidity is to smooth the path of world trade, and the growth of trade since World War II suggests that international liquidity has been adequate for its function. Except in 1958, international trade has grown steadily year by year since 1952. In the five years 1959 through 1963 the total flow of trade increased by over 40 percent, from $107 billion to $155 billion. Since 1950 the value of world trade has nearly tripled.

Moreover, one at least of the worries about international liquidity which was being felt soon after the War has since largely disappeared. At that time something like 70 percent of all the gold in international reserves was held by the United States, and it was difficult for the rest of the world to see how a more even distribution was to be achieved. For the United States to lose gold, it would have had to run deficits in its balances of payments, instead of the large surpluses which (because of its strong competitive position) it was at that time achieving. This situation was the reflection of the so-called dollar shortage, which some economists feared might almost be permanent. In actuality, since about 1949, and especially since 1957, the United States has had a series of deficits in its balances of payments. In this way a much better distribution of reserves has been brought about, as creditor countries have been paid in gold or dollars. In particular, the reserves of most European countries have benefited greatly, even though the reserves of the United States have remained large. Thus, even though the reserves of less developed countries have not grown, there is not at the present time a general shortage of international liquidity. Moreover, the international monetary system has been strengthened both by the increase in the facilities of the Fund and by the intensification of international cooperation on monetary matters.

There are, however, a number of reasons why it is desirable that the question of international liquidity be studied now. First, it is over 20 years since such discussions were held (they led then, at Bretton Woods, to the founding of the Fund and the Bank), and 20 years is a long time in a world where trade and commerce are expanding so fast. A second reason is that a large number of suggestions for improving the system have been put forward in recent years—some founded on fears that liquidity, however adequate now, might come to be insufficient, leading to another world slump. It seemed wise to investigate the environment of these fears, and also the schemes proposed, some of which, indeed, have been propounded at the Annual Meetings of the Fund, notably by the Governor for Greece, Mr. Xenophon Zolotas, and (in 1962) by the Governor for the United Kingdom, Mr. Reginald Maudling. A third reason is that the flow of dollars by which the reserves of most of the industrialized countries were reinforced during recent years cannot clearly continue indefinitely, and this has prompted consideration of what should be done when it ceased.

The questions that are being asked, therefore, may be summarized as follows. Can we be sure that there will be enough international liquidity available in the foreseeable future to prevent difficulties arising for lack of it? And if there is any doubt of this, what can be done to provide for additional liquidity?

The first of these questions divides again into two, neither of which is easy to answer: how much international liquidity can we expect there to be? and, how much shall we need?

Amount of International Liquidity

At the end of 1963, the aggregate of all countries' official reserves (excluding the U.S.S.R. and associated countries) was equivalent to $69.2 billion, an increase of about 16 percent since 1958. Of this total, gold held in reserves was worth $40.2 billion, liquid claims on the United States $13.7 billion, similar claims on the United Kingdom $6.5 billion, the "IMF gold tranche position" of member countries nearly $4.0 billion, and other items $4.8 billion. By "liquid claims" is meant bank deposits and short-term and marketable long-term securities. The "IMF gold tranche position" is made up of the amount that countries may draw from the Fund without increasing its holdings of their currencies beyond their quotas, and is equal for each country to the excess of its quota in the Fund over the Fund's holdings of its currency. This amount member countries may draw practically automatically and with a minimum of delay. (The reliability of the gold tranche position as a reserve asset was enhanced in August last by a decision of the Executive Directors of the Fund that drawings within the gold tranche will not in future have to be discussed by the Board, unless some Director asks for this to be done or the Managing Director feels that it should.)

The gold tranche position varies from country to country, since in the first place the quotas themselves, of course, differ; and secondly, the gold tranche at any given time is affected by Fund transactions in the member's currency. When a country joins the Fund, it normally pays 25 percent of its quota in gold, and 75 percent in its own currency. The Fund's initial holding of that currency is then 75 percent of the quota, and the country's gold tranche position is (100—75) percent, i.e., 25 percent, of the quota. However, when such a country draws on the Fund, the Fund's holdings of its currency increase, with the result that its gold tranche position diminishes by the same amount. If such a country draws from the Fund the equivalent of 25 percent or more of its quota, its gold tranche position falls to nil. On the other hand, if some other country draws from the Fund the currency of the member in question, so that the Fund's holding of its currency diminishes, then its gold tranche position correspondingly increases. Thus, at the end of July 1964, when the Fund's holdings of deutsche mark had declined to 12 percent of a quota of $787.5 million, Germany's gold tranche position was about $690 million.

How have the various elements in the total of reserves contributed to the 16 percent increase from 1958 to 1963? Gold held in reserves increased by $2.1 billion, claims on the United States rose by about $5.1 billion while those on the United Kingdom fell by about $0.2 billion, the IMF gold tranche positions increased by over $1.4 billion, mainly as a result of the general increase in quotas in 1959, and the other items rose by $0.8 billion. Thus, of the total increase of $9.3 billion, nearly 60 percent comprised increases in holdings of dollars.

How International Liquidity Grows

The gold added to reserves outside the Soviet area has come from two sources—new production and sales by countries in that area. The value of newly mined gold has been rising steadily since World War II. In 1963 it amounted to $1,360 million. The amount sold by Soviet bloc countries varies from year to year. In 1963 it was unusually large because these countries sold gold to pay for exceptional imports of wheat from Western countries; their sales may have reached $550 million. But of the total of $1,910 million of gold available from these two sources less than half found its way into reserves. Gold worth over $1 billion was used in industry or added to private hoards. Even this was a better result than was achieved in several recent years; in both 1960 and 1962, for example, the amount of gold added to reserves was a little over $300 million.

The second main type of reserves comprises the currencies of the major industrial countries, and especially dollars and sterling. Reserves held in the form of sterling have been rather stable over the postwar period. In contrast, the U.S. deficits over a long period of years have added substantially to the dollar holdings of other countries, and as long as these deficits continue the dollar claims of the rest of the world are likely to increase, adding to international liquidity. On the other hand, should the U.S. position change from deficit to surplus, international liquidity might contract, as it also would if countries decided to reduce the proportion of dollars or sterling in their reserves.

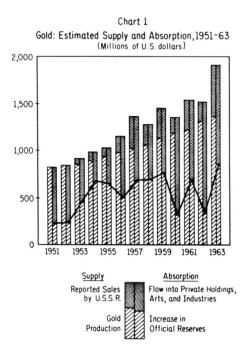

Chart 1

Gold: Estimated Supply and Absorption, 1951–63
(Millions of U.S. dollars)

The extent to which reserves are held in currencies is affected by the policies and practices of particular countries. If (to take an extreme instance) every country which became a creditor in international trade insisted on being paid in gold, there would be no scope for the use of currencies as reserves, and international liquidity would be restricted to reserves held in gold. At the other extreme, if every creditor country were always willing to accept payment in the currencies of its debtors, and refrain from exercising its right to obtain gold for these claims, international liquidity could expand indefinitely. In practice the position which is reached is somewhere between these two extremes. Most of the larger countries habitually seek to convert a proportion of the additions to their reserves into gold. The United States for a long time held only gold in its reserves, but since 1960 it has held small quantities of the currencies of other major countries.

Gold tranches with the Fund also vary with the international payments situation because (as has been explained) their size depends partly on how much countries have drawn from the Fund. For instance, the United Kingdom drew the equivalent of $1,500 million from the Fund in August 1961. Of this total, $500 million was obtained by the Fund by selling gold; the remaining $1,000 million immediately increased the gold tranche positions and hence the reserves of all the nine countries whose currencies had been drawn, although their conventional reserves decreased to the extent that the currencies drawn were converted into dollars or gold. At the same time the reserves of the United Kingdom rose by $1,500 million less the reduction in its gold tranche position. When the United Kingdom repaid its drawing, some of these effects were reversed.

It is clear from this example that changes in the total amount of unconditional liquidity (including gold tranche positions) available to national monetary authorities that arise from Fund transactions are in part accidental. They depend on a number of circumstances, such as whether the drawing country and the countries whose currencies are drawn are within the gold tranche position, whether the currencies made available are converted into other currencies by the drawing countries, and whether repayments take place in the same currencies as the corresponding drawings. Inasmuch as drawings are made principally by countries in credit tranches (that is to say, countries whose gold tranche has been used up), while the countries drawn upon are usually within the gold tranche, the net effect of Fund drawings tends to be in the direction of an expansion of unconditional liquidity. At the same time increases in gold tranches that result from a growth in Fund quotas do not add to total unconditional liquidity because gold paid over to the Fund will come from the members' reserves. At best, gold tranche positions will increase correspondingly. If, of course, by a change in Fund policies quasi-automatic rights were given for larger sums than the gold tranche positions, international liquidity would be correspondingly expanded.

The inquiries into international liquidity which have been proceeding have, therefore, covered such matters as the supply of gold, the means of increasing the proportion of the supply of gold which finds its way into reserves, the role of currencies as international reserves, and possible new ways in which the Fund could contribute to liquidity.

NEED FOR INTERNATIONAL LIQUIDITY

How much international liquidity is needed? There is no simple answer to this question. On the one hand, if no country ever had a surplus or deficit in its balance of payments, there would be no need for international liquidity at all; and even if there were temporary or seasonal imbalances, the need would be relatively small in relation to the volume of trade and other transactions. On the other hand, if half the countries in the world persistently ran large deficits in their balances of payments, and the other half large surpluses, there would be a cumulative need for international liquidity to fill the gap. The test of adequacy is that the international system works smoothly, without abrupt changes, and it is possible to say that, other things being equal, the larger the volume of international trade and other international transactions may be, the more international liquidity will be needed. But that does not carry us very far toward a quantitative assessment of the need.

We have also to consider its distribution; however large the volume of international liquidity, it would be inadequate if it were concentrated in one country (as witness the position after World War II, when a large part of all monetary gold was in the United States). Similarly, even though there is not at this time a general shortage of international liquidity, the reserves of many countries are nevertheless woefully inadequate. Also, a given quantity of international liquidity can be more efficiently or less efficiently used, according to the efficiency of the international monetary system itself.

STRENGTHENING INTERNATIONAL LIQUIDITY

The first fruits of the inquiries which have been going on appeared in two reports published in August last. The Annual Report of the Fund devoted two chapters to the subject of international liquidity. Simultaneously, there was issued a statement by the Ministers and Governors of the ten industrial countries associated with the Fund in the General Arrangements to Borrow,[1] to which was annexed a report by their deputies. The provisional conclusion reached in both reports was that international liquidity was adequate for the time being, but that if nothing were done a shortfall in international liquidity might develop. What can be done to obviate this, and so avoid hampering the growth of world trade?

One line of action would be to concentrate on strengthening international reserves. It is desirable, for instance, to secure for these reserves the largest possible part of new gold becoming available. Measures to strengthen confidence in the currencies which are widely held as part of international liquidity, such as dollars and sterling, would also be valuable in themselves.

A second way of helping to ensure the adequacy of international li-

[1] Belgium, Canada, France, the Federal Republic of Germany, Italy, Japan, the Netherlands, Sweden, the United Kingdom, and the United States—often referred to as the "Group of Ten."

quidity is to moderate the need for it. One method of doing this would be to seek to ensure that countries' own policies are such that they do not tend to run large deficits, or by the international coordination of economic policies. Equally important are precautions against the loss of confidence in any country's currency, such as might induce speculative movements of short-term capital, since these might call for international liquidity on an abnormal scale.

A third way might be to supplement the international liquidity described above by adding to reserves the right to borrow foreign currencies *conditionally*. There are various types of conditions which might apply to borrowings. Perhaps the most significant relates to the policies which a country must pursue to be qualified to borrow; thus, drawings from the Fund beyond the limit of the first credit tranche require "substantial justification," and are likely to be favorably received only when "they are intended to support a sound program aimed at establishing or maintaining the enduring stability of the member's currency at a realistic rate of exchange."

This third possibility is, in fact, the one on which attention has so far been concentrated. Not only is the structure of the Fund such that additional conditional liquidity, in the form of rights to draw on the Fund, can readily be made available, but there are positive merits in adding to liquidity in this conditional form—in a form which relates the supply of liquidity to an established and justified need for it.

This is the basis of the recommendation made in both the reports mentioned above for a general increase in the quotas of members of the Fund. This would be supplemented by special increases for those countries whose quotas are at present smaller than their relative importance in world trade would justify.

Beyond this, both the Fund and the Group of Ten countries are continuing their inquiries, and in particular are considering whether some other way of increasing international reserves may be necessary as well, and what would be the best method to proceed toward this end.

THE WEST IS RISKING A CREDIT COLLAPSE*

A grave peril hangs over the economy of the West. Every day its situation more and more resembles the one that turned the 1929 recession into the great depression. The instability in our monetary system is such that a minor international incident or a small economic or financial disturbance could set off worldwide disaster. There is a great deal of concern about this instability, though rarely expressed in terms as stark as I have used, and a number of measures have been suggested for dealing with it. But instead of going to the roots of what is wrong, these would rather prolong for several months or years the erring ways that are responsible for the danger.

The West has no task more urgent than to recognize the disease that infects it, and by curing it, to re-establish in the free world a monetary system that generates lasting stability.

The nature of the disease is apparent in this fact: during the decade 1951–60, while the United States was piling up balance of payments deficits totaling $18.1 billion, some $13 billion accumulated in foreign hands in the form of sight deposits or short-term investments in the U.S. money market. This $13 billion constitutes a claim on the U.S. gold reserve that could be called at any time—with catastrophic consequences.

This came about because, in the countries that were creditors to the United States, the central banks were content to accept dollars in settlement instead of demanding payment in gold. American attention is usually focused on the gold that has flowed overseas in recent years; there is great relief at present that the flow has at least temporarily come to a halt. But, paradoxically, the danger we are in was brought about not because the United States lost gold, but because it lost so *little* gold. During the decade U.S. gold reserves fell by only $5.3 billion. If the United States had settled its balance of payments deficits entirely in gold, its reserves would have dropped—all other things being equal—by $18.1 billion, and today they would amount to a mere $4.7 billion. By all the evidence, such an unthinkable drop in reserves would not have been tolerated. Action would have been taken much earlier to stop the deficits.

Thus a first conclusion suggests itself: The American balance of payments deficits were allowed to persist for the last ten years only because the United

* Jacques Rueff, *Fortune,* July, 1961, pp. 126–127.

States was not really required to settle its debts abroad. From the monetary point of view, it was as if the deficits had not happened.

It remains to explore how such a strange situation arose, what its consequences have been, and what new consequences it will entail if we let it continue. In this analysis, I am not overlooking the fact that the U.S. balance of payments deficit has been aggravated by the gifts and loans that the Americans bestowed, with a generosity unprecedented in history, upon the nations that suffered from a shortage of foreign exchange after the ordeals of the war. But the method of giving is no less important than the purpose of the gift, particularly since it is liable to affect deeply the stability, even the very existence, of both the giver and the receiver.

Furthermore, the situation I am about to analyze was neither created, nor even expressly desired, by the United States. It is the product of a prodigious collective error, an error that will go down in history as cause for stupefaction and scandal.

THE LOSERS GET THEIR MARBLES BACK

For more than a century, except for a few periods, the solidarity and relative stability of the civilized world were based on the monetary convertibility that was assured by the gold standard. Since all national currencies could be exchanged for a specified weight of gold, they were exchangeable at a fixed rate among themselves. What gave the arrangement its solidity was the fact that no country could create money except against gold or its own national credit (i.e., government bonds).

The United States retained gold coinage and full gold redeemability of currency until 1933; thereafter the use of gold was restricted to international payments. During World War I, Europe suspended the gold standard and afterward returned to a gold-bullion standard, which meant that redeemability was limited to a set minimum quantity of gold—one kilo (about thirty-five ounces); hence there was no more gold coinage.

The European powers made one other historical change in the gold standard and this is the one that chiefly concerns us here. Back in 1922, long before the United States went off the gold standard, the International Economic Conference in Genoa passed its famous Resolution 9, which recommended adoption of an international convention embodying "some means of economizing the use of gold by maintaining reserves in the form of foreign balances." This recommendation brought into existence the "gold *exchange* standard," which was gradually grafted on the old gold standard throughout most of the Western World. The gold exchange standard collapsed in the great depression of the Thirties but came to life again after World War II. It dominates the monetary picture today.

Under this standard, central banks consider themselves authorized to create money not only against gold or government bonds, but also against any foreign currency that is considered as good as gold. After World War I, these so-called "key currencies" were the pound sterling and the dollar; after World War II, only the dollar (though within the sterling area the pound has a status similar to that of the dollar).

The country with a key currency is in the deceptively euphoric position of never having to pay off its international debts. The money it pays to foreign creditors comes right back home, like a boomerang. When foreign central banks received dollars or dollar credits as a result of the American balance of payments deficits, they were not compelled to demand the gold to which their dollars entitled them. Instead, they left a large portion of these dollars on deposit in the United States where they were generally loaned to American borrowers. The central banks welcomed this new arrangement all the more enthusiastically because it substituted in their accounts revenue-producing assets for entirely unproductive gold bullion or coins. The functioning of the international monetary system was thus reduced to a childish game in which, after each round, the winners return their marbles to the losers.

THE BUILT-IN STABILIZER IS REMOVED

In this way the gold exchange standard wrought a vast revolution. It imparted to countries whose money had international prestige the marvelous secret of the deficit without tears. In those countries the discovery of this secret has profoundly affected popular psychology because it has minimized or suppressed the internal consequences that a balance of payments deficit would have produced under the automatic gold standard. In the United States the gold exchange standard had the effect of encouraging the generous program of foreign aid, and a blithe disregard of the deficit that ensued. The giver had the pleasure of giving, and the receiver the joy of receiving. The result is the monetary situation with whose disastrous implications we are now faced.

The replacement of the gold standard by the gold exchange standard has had three basic consequences:

First of all, under the gold standard a country with a balance of payments deficit would lose gold, and this loss would act as a restraint on internal purchasing power. This would tend to counteract the deficit, by releasing a greater part of the national product for export and inhibiting imports. But under the gold exchange standard, the volume of internal purchasing power is not at all affected by the deficit. By disconnecting the internal volume of purchasing power from the external balance of payments, the gold exchange standard removes one of the regulating influences that used to operate under the gold standard. A nation's balance of payments is no longer self-adjusting; its equilibrium can be assured only by rigorous credit policies or authoritarian management of foreign trade. Experience has demonstrated that while it is not impossible, it certainly is very difficult for monetary authorities to decree the contraction of credit that the gold exchange standard tends precisely to avoid. As for government regulations limiting foreign purchases, restricting the amount of foreign exchange tourists can take with them, or preventing the movement of short-term capital, these have to my knowledge always failed.

THE DOUBLE PYRAMID OF CREDIT

The second consequence of the gold exchange standard is a veritable duplication of credit bases in the world. This is the result of the boomerang effect noted before: the dollars that go abroad as a result of U.S. balance of payments deficits return to the United States as sight deposits or short-term investments.

More specifically, the process works this way. When the United States has an unfavorable balance with another country (let us take France as an example, it settles up in dollars. The Frenchmen who receive these dollars sell them to the central bank, the Banque de France, taking their own national money, francs, in exchange. The Banque de France, in effect, creates these francs against the dollars. But then it turns around and invests the dollars back in the United States. Thus the very same dollars expand the credit system of France, while still underpinning the credit system in the United States.

This process would have little or no effect if the balance of payments of the various nations were in equilibrium. But it becomes a powerful instrument of worldwide inflation when there are large international movements of capital from countries with key currencies. This was tragically illustrated by the events that led up to and followed the 1929 depression. The financial reconstruction of Germany after the Dawes plan in 1924 and of France after Premier Poincare's reforms in 1926 caused a massive flow of capital from the United States and Britain into those two countries. With both Germany and France operating under the gold exchange standard, this influx of capital gave the 1929 boom its unprecedented dimensions and its dreadful climax.

Similarly, movements of capital from the United States to Germany and France in 1958, 1959, and 1960 accounted for the abnormal rise in share prices in financial markets on both sides of the Atlantic. When capital flows from one country to another, the effect can be expansionist in the latter without being recessive in the former. With nothing tending to brake the boom, all the countries operating under the gold exchange standard find themselves carried along on a wave of inflationary economic and stock-market expansion. This explanation of inflation is in no way incompatible with the "cost-push" theory, which attributes inflation to the fact that wages are rising faster than productivity.

There is no doubt that the constant rise in overall purchasing power legitimizes wage demands and eliminates any obstacle to their being granted by employers.

THE DANGER OF COLLAPSE

The third and most serious consequence of the gold exchange standard is the deceptive character of the credit structure it brings about. The $17.5-billion U.S. gold reserve is doubly committed. Some $11.5 billion of it is pledged as the reserve that must be maintained, under law, against Federal Reserve currency and deposits. Meanwhile all of the reserve constitutes a guarantee against about $20 billion now held by foreigners in short-term or sight assets.

It is not the value of the dollar that is cast in doubt. The real cause for concern is that the gold exchange standard, working at a time of large international movements of capital, puts a double mortgage—and a very high one—on the U.S. gold stock. If foreign holders of dollar assets were suddenly to demand full payment in gold, they could topple the whole U.S. credit structure.

Of course, they are not likely to do this. But the simple fact that they have the right to do it obliges us to remember that the collapse of the house of cards built on the gold exchange standard in Europe was what turned the 1929 depression into a catastrophe. In 1961, with due allowances, the same circumstances have converged upon us again. Unless dealt with, they could produce the same effects all over again.

HOW TO LIQUIDATE THE DANGER

There are two things to be done:

First, we must introduce a new monetary system that does not tend to favor prolonged balance of payments deficits in countries with key currencies.

Second, we must liquidate the unstable and dangerously vulnerable situation resulting from the duplication of the credit structure, built on the gold reserves of those countries with key currencies.

The new monetary system must make it impossible for creditor nations to generate new internal purchasing power on their foreign balances while the purchasing power in debtor nations remains undiminished. *This means putting an end to the practice whereby central banks create money against the foreign exchange they receive and then lend this foreign exchange back to its country of origin where it also forms part of the money base.* The gold standard takes care of this by requiring central banks to issue money only against gold or national credits. Other multilateral arrangements might attain the same end, but being voluntary, they would be precarious and uncertain, whereas the discipline of the gold standard is unconditional and inevitable.

The evolution of the European Payments Union, by the progressive "hardening" of its means of settlement—i.e., the increase in the fraction that member countries had to pay in gold when settling their accounts with other members—is a good example of how we can advance along the road toward the gold standard.

There is unfortunately only one way to rid ourselves of the risks that are the West's legacy from fifteen years' operation of the gold exchange standard. This is to pay off in gold all the dollar assets held by central banks outside the United States. Only such a drastic step can banish the danger of sharp deflation or collapse that is inherent in the double-credit structure now based on the U.S. gold reserves.

The difficulty is that this would suddenly deplete the U.S. gold reserve below what must legally be held in reserve against Federal Reserve notes and deposits. This problem is less serious than it looks, for the reserve requirement can be changed by law, and besides the government has other resources at its disposal to bolster its reserves, such as its ability to draw on the International Monetary Fund. Moreover, if the liquidation of the gold exchange standard is not undertaken in panic—and this is precisely what must be avoided— it can be carefully organized to take place gradually.

TRIFFIN'S INTERNATIONAL MONEY

There is, however, another snag. Eliminating the dollar holdings of foreign central banks would reduce the total world volume of liquid money, possibly to a level below what is necessary to finance daily transactions. Such a consequence cannot be permitted.

Various suggestions have been made for avoiding it. One of the best known, that of Professor Robert Triffin of Yale, proposes that central banks put some of their foreign exchange reserves into the International Monetary Fund, where they would become a real international money. The fund would be given the power to counter shortages in international liquidity by creating its own currency at a rhythm fixed to accord with the needs of expanding trade. Pending the results of a detailed study, Professor Triffin tentatively indicates that the rhythm of new fund issues should be such as to assure a 3 to 5 percent annual increase in the stock of gold and foreign exchange held by central banks.

The Triffin plan is very similar to one Lord Keynes put forth in 1943 in a document called "Proposals by British Experts for an International Clearing

Union." It is ingenious because it would appreciably decrease the liquidity needs of individual central banks. But in the complex system Professor Triffin imagines, the new international currency would be only partially convertible into gold, and in certain circumstances it might have to be made absolutely unredeemable in gold. In addition, as the authority responsible for issuing the international currency, the fund would assume the power to influence indirectly the balance of payments of member states. The main reason, however, why the Keynes plan was rejected in 1943 was the fear that it was inflationary. This is still a valid reason for turning down similar proposals today.

The abhorrence of an inflationary solution to the liquidity problem has led some commentators to advocate a rise in the price of gold. They note that the price of gold has been fixed at its 1933 level—$35 an ounce—although in the meantime the general price level in dollars has almost doubled. There is no doubt that raising the price of gold in dollars (and therefore in all currencies whose rate is based on dollars) would increase the nominal value of gold reserves and thus facilitate the liquidation of the deceptive credit structure brought about by the gold exchange standard.

It would be imprudent, however, to derive from simple calculations an estimate of how much to increase the gold price or even to state conclusively that an increase is unavoidable. For one thing, methods of international payment could be improved so that a smaller volume of cash balances would be required to meet the needs of daily settlements.

All these considerations show that the liquidation of the gold exchange standard poses difficult questions for political art and monetary technique. These questions demand deep study and discussion. In preparing for this discussion it is worth observing that the problems to be resolved are not exclusively or even essentially American. Their solution can be found only in a profound modification of the system now in force for the settlement of international payments, hence of the very rules governing central banks.

If the gold exchange standard is principally responsible for prolonging the U.S. balance of payments deficits, it must be remembered that it was not the United States which established this standard, but the Genoa Conference of 1922, at which the United States was not even represented.

What one international conference did, only another international conference can undo. But it is essential that the undoing occur without delay. A monetary crisis would compromise the financial rehabilitation that has at last been accomplished in all the Western countries. It would expose their economies to a grave recession, and the threat of another 1929. In any event, whether in panic or in cool deliberation, the problem of the gold exchange standard will inevitably be resolved. If the governments of the West take the initiative in time, they will spare their peoples the disorder and suffering of a new world crisis.

ANNUAL GOLD REVIEW *

This annual review once again sets into perspective worldwide gold trends, developments and policies. The broad background for the world gold picture at the threshold of 1965 is provided in a series of charts extending as far back as 1934, the year in which the United States established its present $35 gold price.

Over the past twelve months, world gold output has risen to the highest level ever recorded. Of these supplies—augmented by sales of Russian gold, which were again sizable last year though distinctly smaller than in 1963— about $1 billion, or practically as much as in each of the preceding four years, appears to have gone into private uses and holdings. During the closing months of 1964, amidst pressures on sterling and apprehensions that the pound's difficulties might affect the whole international monetary system, fresh supplies of gold seem to have been fully absorbed by private demand.

Additions to official monetary stocks over the past twelve months have been something like $700 million or some $175 million less than in 1963. Most of the gold has moved into the reserves of the leading nations of Western Europe, which have also acquired gold from the U.S. Treasury; the U.S. stock has, however, undergone the smallest decline since 1957.

The concluding part of this commentary is concerned with the sterling crisis and its manifold implications. To help support sterling and relieve strains on the international currency structure, eleven leading nations swiftly extended late in November new $3 billion credit lines to the United Kingdom. Not enough time has yet elapsed to judge, by their effects, the measures taken to right Britain's balance of payments and strengthen sterling. The tender plant of confidence must be revived.

Our international monetary system, which has served the world well, is neither assured nor foredoomed. It is workable provided the leading countries maintain strong currencies and healthy balances of payments in an environment of reasonably free international trade and investment. These are also the indispensable prerequisites for any world monetary system.

OUTPUT AT RECORD LEVEL

In 1964, world gold output (excluding the U.S.S.R., other Eastern European countries, Mainland China, etc.) rose for the eleventh consecutive year

* *Monthly Letter of Business and Economic Conditions,* First National City Bank, New York, January 1965, pp. 7–11.

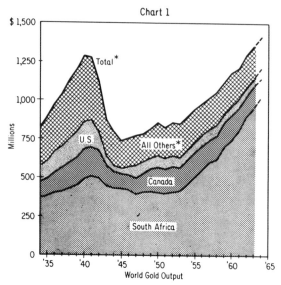

Chart 1

* Excluding the U.S.S.R.,other Eastern European countries, Mainland China, etc.

Source: Unless otherwise stated, the data for the charts and the tables in this article are derived from publications of the International Monetary Fund and the Federal Reserve Board. Data for 1964 in the first three charts are preliminary estimates made by this Bank.

(Chart 1). At approximately 40 million ounces, equal to $1.4 billion, last year's output was about 4 percent above 1963. It was some 67 percent higher than in 1953, before the post-war rise in output began, and 10 percent above 1940 when production had reached its previous peak following the worldwide wave of currency devaluations of the 1930's.

As in each year since 1953, the rise in gold output was attributable almost entirely to further gains in South African production, which accounts for about 70 percent of the world total. Over the past decade, South African output has increased almost one and a half times, principally because of the development of new mines and improved techniques. In the judgment of a body representing the South African mining industry, production there will have nearly reached its peak in 1964 or 1965 and may soon be expected to level off gradually, and subsequently to decline as older and marginal mines which cannot employ modern techniques may be closed down.

Elsewhere in the world, production during 1964 continued a downward trend. In Canada, the world's second largest gold producer, output slipped off further. In the United States, the third largest producer, it remained stationary at about $50 million, approximately one third of the prewar production.

Russia's gold caused considerable stir last year. The U.S.S.R., it may be recalled, was forced to import large quantities of wheat from Australia,

TABLE 1

ESTIMATED GOLD PRODUCTION IN 1964

	Millions of Dollars	Percent 1963	Change 1953	From: 1940
South Africa	$1,025	+ 7%	+ 145%	+ 108%
Canada	131	– 6	– 8	– 30
United States	51	– –	– 26	– 70
Australia	34	– 6	– 11	– 41
Ghana	32	– –	+ 23	+ 3
Southern Rhodesia	20	– –	+ 11	– 45
Philippines	15	+ 14	– 12	– 62
All others*	107	+ 4	– 11	– 65
Total*	$1,415	+ 4	+ 67	+ 10

* Excluding the U. S. S. R., etc.

Canada, France, West Germany and the United States in late 1963 and early 1964 and shipped out gold to pay for it. Judging from British gold import statistics, Russia exported to the United Kingdom during the last four months of 1963 gold valued at $213 million (for the entire year, the total was $281 million). During the first six months of 1964, Russian exports amounted to $272 million; no exports were recorded during July–October.

Russia's gold exports do not, of course, coincide with sales but the total of sales in London and in other markets was put tentatively by British sources at $350 million for the first ten months of 1964; as much as $550 million was similarly sold in the entire year 1963. At the 1963 level, Russian sales would appear to have been considerably in excess of output, variously estimated at $150–425 million a year (the latter figure comes from the U.S. Bureau of Mines). Should Russian gold sales in the West, in the absence of a new food emergency, return to some $250 million a year, as during 1957–1962—and assuming that the higher estimate for output is nearer the mark than the lower one—Russia should be able to add to its gold reserves; estimates of the Russian gold stock by Western observers range from $2 billion to as much as $10 billion. Last year, the Soviet authorities announced a drive for increased gold output and a reduction in costs of production.

PRIVATE GOLD ABSORPTION PERSISTS

New gold supplies from enlarged output, together with Russian sales, amounted last year to something like $1.8 billion; for 1963, the figure worked out to $1.9 billion.

Last year, roughly $1 billion of new gold was absorbed in private uses and holdings. During the first eight months, private demand, although persistent, was relatively moderate; but beginning with September it became much more active and, during the last four months of 1964, it probably

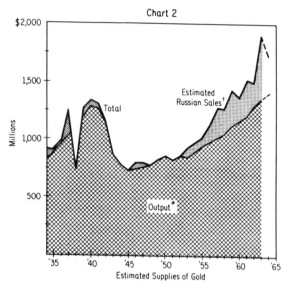

Chart 2

Estimated Supplies of Gold

* Excluding the U.S.S.R.,etc.

† From 1934 through 1947, imports by the United States and other countries, as published in the Federal Reserve Bulletin, September 1954, page 938 ; thereafter, estimated sales to governments and central banks, as published by the Bank for International Settlements in its annual reports. Data for 1938 have been adjusted to include outflow to the U.S.S.R. of $520 million of gold stated by the Bank of Spain to have been sent there.

absorbed all available new supplies. The greater demand seems to have been influenced by events like China's atomic explosion and the political changes in Russia; but the pressures on sterling, which culminated in a crisis late in November, and the uncertainties about currencies in general may well have been even more important.

There is no statistical basis for separating uses of gold in the arts and industry from other private uses. In the United States, gold consumption in 1963, the latest year for which data are available, amounted to about $100 million (net) or, on the average, the same volume as during each of the five previous years; this compares with an annual average of $50 million during 1953–57.

The pressures of private demand for gold are evidenced to only a small extent in fluctuations of the London price of gold. Last year, the price, expressed in terms of the U.S. dollar, moved from $35.08 per ounce during January–August to nearly $35.13 in December, the highest level since the Cuban crisis in October 1962. This is minimal in comparison with the $40 momentarily reached in October 1960.

For the past three years, supply-demand conditions in the gold market have made it possible to hold the price practically stable through interven-

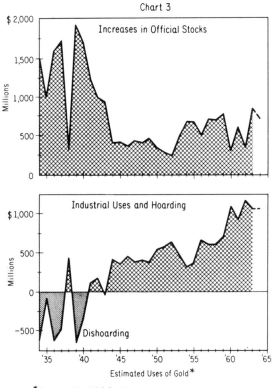

Chart 3

* Excluding the U.S.S.R., etc.

tions of the so-called London gold pool. This pool was established by the financial authorities of the leading nations in October 1961 to counteract undesirable fluctuations in the price of gold on the London market. It operates through interventions by the Bank of England acting as agent, with the United States taking a 50 percent share in the arrangement. In the beginning, the pool tended to sell gold but starting with late 1962 it purchased gold on balance, with net gains distributed among the participants. Much of the $624 million of gold the United States purchased from the United Kingdom during the twelve months ended September 1964 was presumably acquired from the pool.

REDUCED FLOWS INTO OFFICIAL STOCKS

During the first nine months of 1964, for which reasonably full accounting can be made at this time, $700 million was added to official gold reserves. During the last quarter, with widening pressures of private demand evidenced by the rise in the London gold price, probably little gold found its way into official stocks. For this reason, it may be fair to presume that last year's addition to official stocks was smaller than the $875 million in 1963.

TABLE 2

OFFICIAL GOLD STOCKS, OCT. '63 – SEPT. '64

(Millions of dollars)

	Changes through Transactions with:		Gold Stock
	U. S.	Other*	Sept. '64
United Kingdom	–624	420	2,302
Germany (Fed. Rep.)	225	163	4,149
France	404	129	3,564
Switzerland	30	0	2,532
Italy	–200	13	2,104
Netherlands	0	20	1,601
Belgium	0	28	1,395
Austria	87	0	592
Spain	2	0	576
Portugal	0	15 [‡]	497 [§]
Canada	0	215	990
South Africa	0	–54	589
All foreign countries [†]	–93	1,087	24,951
Int'l Monetary Fund	0	122	2,426
United States	--	9	15,643
World	–93	1,218	43,020

*Residual figures, including gold from new production, Russian sales, etc.

[†] Excluding the U. S. S. R., etc.

[‡] August 1963 – July 1964.

[§] July 1964

Note: The table covers all countries holding official stocks of $500 million or more.

U.S. gold acquisitions from the London gold pool and a sizable purchase from Italy largely offset U.S. sales to France, Germany and a few other countries during 1964. Demands for U.S. gold were also eased as a result of a reduction in the balance of payments deficit, as conventionally defined, to $2–2.5 billion, compared with $3.3 billion in 1963. The relative stability in the U.S. gold stock also reflects U.S. drawings from the International Monetary Fund of currencies like German marks or French francs; these are sold to nations that want to make repayments to the Fund but cannot do it in U.S. dollars because the Fund's dollar holdings are at their statutory maximum. These operations, initiated in early 1964 and totaling $525 million for the year, have the twofold effect of reducing the supplies of dollars in the hands of foreign governments and central banks and of ensuring that they would not purchase gold from the United States to repay the Fund. Finally, the U.S. gold position has been helped by sales of special nonmarketable U.S. Treasury securities to foreign governments and central banks ($547 million during January–October) ; these tend to reduce official foreign holdings of short-term dollars eligible for conversion into gold.

The U.S. Treasury gold stock on December 23 stood at $15,388 million— $125 million less than at the beginning of the year. It amounted to a healthy, but not excessive, two-fifths of the world monetary stock, as against three-fifths ten years ago and more than one-half before World War II.

The Federal Republic of Germany and France, the second and third largest gold holders, added about $920 million to their reserves during the twelve months ended September 1964 ; this is equivalent to most of the gold that found its way into world official stocks during the period.

Continuing purchases of gold by foreign governments and central banks attest to the desire of those responsible for administering national monetary reserves to protect them against the hazards of depreciation. For the longer run, in the view of the finance ministers of the leading nations, gold will remain "the ultimate international reserve asset." Although gold cannot "prudently" be expected to meet all needs for international liquidity in the future, its contribution will remain essential.

TESTING TIME FOR INTERNATIONAL LIQUIDITY

The $700 million of new gold added to world monetary gold stocks over the past year represents an increase of about 1.7 percent—compared with 2.2 percent in 1963. In each of the preceding five years, 1.4 percent was, on the average, added to world monetary gold stocks. Reserves in the form of dollars and sterling also increased ; these provide, under our gold exchange standard, means of economizing on gold. Today, gold accounts for about three-fifths of the total gold and foreign exchange reserves of governments and central banks, as shown in Chart 4.

Most of the nations of Continental Europe have ample reserves. Among other industrial nations, Japan, while possessing sizable reserves, has been under some pressure. The less-developed countries, as a rule, hold relatively small reserves. This is not, however, a problem of the world monetary system since additions to reserves of these countries would soon be spent on increased imports ; their basic problem is the lack of long-term capital for development.

Britain's gold reserves are undoubtedly too low for a country whose currency is used to finance about one-third of the world's trade and whose

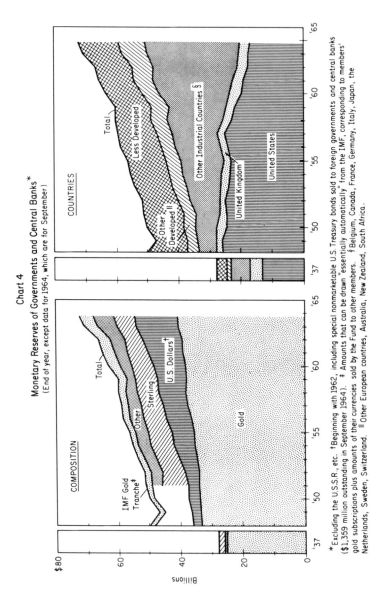

Chart 4
Monetary Reserves of Governments and Central Banks*
(End of year, except data for 1964, which are for September)

*Excluding the U.S.S.R., etc. †Beginning with 1962, including special nonmarketable U.S. Treasury bonds sold to foreign governments and central banks ($1,359 million outstanding in September 1964). ‡ Amounts that can be drawn essentially automatically" from the IMF, corresponding to members' gold subscriptions plus amounts of their currencies sold by the Fund to other members. §Belgium, Canada, France, Germany, Italy, Japan, the Netherlands, Sweden, Switzerland. ‖Other European countries, Australia, New Zealand, South Africa.

short-term liabilities to other governments and central banks are large. The British Government, it may be noted, is holding an important portfolio of foreign securities, mostly in U.S. dollars, worth $1 billion or more; on the other hand, most of the official sterling liabilities are to governments of other sterling-area countries. Even so, Britain's reserve position is not intrinsically strong.

Following the sterling devaluation in 1949, Britain safely rode through the sterling crises of 1951, 1957 and 1961. In 1964, Britain's balance of payments again worsened, mainly because of greatly enlarged imports. Amidst a widespread feeling of uncertainty, people felt compelled to speed up sales and defer purchases of sterling; these so-called leads and lags, along with withdrawals of non-resident funds, explain much of the recent weakness of sterling.

To help support sterling, Britain had recourse in September and October to short-term credits from central banks; reportedly, it used the bulk of the $1 billion drawing on the International Monetary Fund in early December to repay this indebtedness.[1] In late November, Britain secured additional credit lines totaling $3 billion, of which $750 million was in the form of an enlarged swap credit arrangement with the Federal Reserve and $250 million came from the U.S. Export-Import Bank. According to London sources, most credits are for three months from the time of drawing; some of these facilities were used in December.

This is the biggest financial operation of its kind. At the same time, however, the British economy remains under international scrutiny. Time has been bought at great cost to the United Kingdom and its trading partners. For the longer run, as the Bank of England noted last month, "improvement depends upon the success of longer-term measures to raise productivity . . . , to control costs, and to secure economies—all within a context of control over the pressure of demand. But . . . success will not come without an unusual readiness on the part of all concerned to discard long-standing attitudes and traditions of thought."

THE U.S. DOLLAR TODAY

People who speak in terms of a threatening gold deficiency for the United States often cite the fact that the Treasury gold stock, at $15.4 billion, is now less than the $27½ billion of U.S. liabilities to foreign countries and

---

[1] Because its holdings of currencies needed by Britain were not large enough, the Fund for the first time had to borrow some portion of these monies—$405 million—from its members; this was done under the so-called General Arrangements to Borrow, which in 1962 provided for supplementary resources to the IMF totaling $6 billion. To acquire additional currencies other than U.S. dollars, the Fund also sold $250 million of gold.

international financial bodies. Of this total, international institutions hold about $5 billion; since their purpose is to help overcome monetary crises and speed up economic development, they would not cash their claims into gold. Foreign governments and central banks, holding somewhat over $12 billion in short-term dollars, have a stake in the maintenance of the present monetary system and would be expected to avoid unreasonable demands for gold so long as we work to limit our balance of payments deficit. The balance of $10 billion represents short-term liabilities to foreign banks, traders and investors; these consist, to a large though not ascertainable extent, of working balances and are not eligible for conversion into gold unless previously sold to central banks.

The United States has a surplus in its foreign trade that, after allowing for exports financed by government-aid programs, is running at an annual rate of close to $4 billion. The trade surplus is augmented by sizable receipts on services, above all income from private investments abroad.

The balance of payments deficit has been reduced to little more than a half of the average of almost $4 billion during the peak years 1958–60, and the gold outflow, then worrisome, is much smaller. Even in the days of its largest deficits, the United States invested abroad more than it "borrowed." For a respectably long period of time, it has maintained a vigorous business expansion in an environment remarkably free of distortions that have traditionally triggered a recession. The business expansion—helped as it has been by the tax cut—has made the United States an even more advantageous place to invest. U.S. industrial efficiency is still the byword of the world. The domestic purchasing power of the dollar has registered a much smaller shrinkage than that of any other major currency.

Because of the clouds on the international financial horizon, there is today an even greater need for realism in U.S. economic and financial policies. It is in recognition of this need that the Federal Reserve discount rates have been raised twice within the past eighteen months. It is for this reason, too, that there remains the need to keep monetary expansion under watchful scrutiny, to curtail the rate of increase in Federal expenditures and to preserve the stability of unit costs.

THE LONDON GOLD MARKET*

BACKGROUND

London is the largest and most important gold market in the world. Its origins lie not too clearly defined in the history of the development of London as a financial centre. The firm of Mocatta and Goldsmid was founded in 1684, ten years before the granting of the Bank of England's Royal Charter. It was not until the nineteenth century, however, that London achieved its eminence, both for the refining and marketing of gold bullion and also for the exchange and disposal of gold coins of various countries. That eminence was in fact achieved before the discoveries of gold in Australia and South Africa, which made London's position ultimately even stronger.

CONSTITUTION

In the English way, the London gold market has no written or formal constitution. Like so many other institutions which are now a normal part of London's daily life, it has developed in response to changing needs and demands over the years and has adapted and modified its rules and procedures as it went along.

There are at present five members of the London gold market: Johnson, Matthey & Co., Ltd., Mocatta & Goldsmid Ltd., Samuel Montagu & Co., Ltd., N. M. Rothschild & Sons, and Sharps, Pixley & Co. Two, (Montagu and Rothschild) are merchant banks, one (Mocatta) is wholly owned by a merchant bank, one (Sharps, Pixley) is a pure broker, and the fifth (Johnson Matthey) is a metallurgical firm of international repute. Two of the members (Johnson Matthey and Rothschild) melt, refine, assay, and process gold. Rothschilds act as chairman of the market and have done so since the market was constituted in its present form after World War I, and the daily gold price fixing takes place on their premises.

All authorised banks under the Exchange Control Act, 1947, are also authorised to deal in gold. But in practice dealings are largely concentrated in the hands of members of the gold market, plus one or two others. The significance of membership of the market is that it confers the right to be present at the daily price fixing which is described below.

*This is an excerpt from an article appearing in the Bank of England's *Quarterly Bulletin* for March 1964.

In an active market, gold changes hands in considerable quantities; and for this to be done efficiently there must be a recognized specification for bars which are regarded as "good delivery." The requirements of the London market list of good delivery bars are that the bar has been melted and stamped by one of the forty or fifty refiners or mints situated all over the world which have been approved by the market. It must also carry a similarly acceptable assay shown either by an impressed stamp or by an assay certificate which must accompany the bar. The bar must assay at least 995, that is to say, at least 995 parts in 1,000 must be pure gold, and it must contain between 350 and 430 troy ounces of fine gold (the fine gold content is the product of the gross weight multiplied by the assay).

Changes are made from time to time in the London market list of acceptable melters and assayers by way of either addition or deletion. The former occur only after stringent tests have been made on sample bars by two London refiners independently which have satisfied the members of the market that the bars produced by a melter can be relied upon to conform to London's standards. Deletions happen very seldom but have occurred, for example, as the outcome of war. History and the technical expertise to be found here have resulted in the London market's standards being the basis of acceptability for gold bars in most countries in the world. One exception is the United States, where the authorities will accept, without melting and assaying, only unmutilated United States Government-stamped bars when tendered in the exact form in which originally issued.

Bars of sizes smaller than the good delivery bars described above are also produced by British refiners to meet the requirements of customers on the Continent of Europe and in other places throughout the world. Dealings in all kinds of gold coins also take place.

The London Fixing Price

The daily fixing of the gold price, which takes place at Rothschilds beginning at 10:30 each morning, is the only daily international gold price fixing of its kind in the world. There is no fixing on Saturday or on New Year's Day; but on all other working days a representative of each of the five members of the gold market attends in person at the "fixing room" at Rothschilds, a member of which firm takes the chair. Each of the five persons present is in communication, by direct telephone, throughout the course of the fixing with his own trading room, where, again, there may be direct communication by telephone or telex with operators in foreign centres who may be interested in dealing at the fixing if the price is right. The chairman will suggest a price, in terms of shillings and pence down to a farthing; this price will be chosen at the level where it is thought that buyers and sellers are likely to be prepared to do business. When the tentative price is proposed, all present declare the nature of their interest at that price, *i.e.,* as sellers or as buyers (or having no interest either way) with the sellers stating their amount but without, at this stage, the buyers declaring their actual requirements. If all present should declare themselves as buyers and no selling interest appears, business clearly cannot be done and the price is then moved up; conversely if all are sellers and there is no buying interest the price is moved down. At the new tentative price interests are again declared and this goes on until there are the possibilities of business, that is to say until there are both buyers and sellers in evidence. At this stage the extent of the buying interest is declared and a count is taken. If, for example, there are buyers of 400 bars and sellers of 250 bars those present must decide whether the 250 bars will be shared out amongst the buyers or whether the price shall be bid higher. Anyone has the right to bid a higher price or, if the selling interest is uppermost, to offer at a lower price. Finally a point is reached where buyers and sellers come together at a price, and that is the fixing price of the day.

It may be sensed from the foregoing that there is a subtle difference between the attitude towards the seller and that towards the buyer. This difference stems from a tradition that, while a large buyer may have to face a sharp increase in price if he wants to see his demands satisfied in full at the first time of asking, the market should always be slightly biased in favour of endeavouring to absorb all new production or other gold which may be offered at the fixing.

OPERATIONS ON THE LONDON MARKET

Operations on the London market are not confined to the amount of gold changing hands at the fixing price in the fixing room. It frequently happens that any one or all of the five members of the market have in hand both buying and selling orders to be executed at the fixing price; if so each member will offset buying orders against selling orders and will only go into the fixing room to transact the net balance of purchases or sales. There is no obligation for any member to declare or fulfil all his orders in hand at the fixing; he may, if he judges it to be more advantageous, execute part at the fixing and postpone the balance until later. A good deal of business is frequently done after the fixing has taken place at prices which may vary considerably during the course of a day. The amount turned over at the fixing can represent as much as 90 percent of the day's business or as little as 10 percent. Some international dealers prefer to operate at the fixing; others prefer to wait until the fixing has taken place and they can see what is the trend of the price for the day before doing their business. Operations whether at the fixing or afterwards are ordinarily for delivery of gold loco London and for payment two working days later. A commission of ¼ per mille (minimum ten shillings) is charged on all deals at the fixing. Transactions effected at times other than the fixing, transactions for value dates other than the normal two working days ahead, and those in currencies other than sterling are a matter of negotiation and may be dealt in at net prices without commission being charged separately. There is no organised or regular market in gold for forward delivery as there is in foreign exchange, though forward operations do take place, often for large amounts: those are, however, a matter of negotiation each time. While ordinary transactions are in gold for delivery loco London, deals can be arranged in the London market for delivery in other centres; (conversely a good deal of international business transacted in other centres or on the international telephone is in gold for delivery loco London).

The factors operating in the London market are broadly the following:

On the Supply Side

New production
Central bank sales
Other sales (including from time to time important amounts on
 Russian account)
Dis-hoarding

On the Demand Side

Central bank purchases
Purchases for industry and the arts
Hoarding purchases

The line of distinction between industrial and artistic consumption on the one hand and hoarding on the other is one which is not very clearly defined since increased demand for gold jewellery can, varying from one country to another, be either a disguised form of hoarding or a normal concomitant of inflation or just a result of a rising standard of living.

Hoarding is a term of art. In certain countries in the East, gold is the traditional manner of storing wealth, while in conservative-minded agricultural communities in various parts of the world it is a normal method of saving. Furthermore, in a number of countries throughout the world, a holding of gold has come to be regarded as a status symbol. In other countries, particularly on the Continent, gold may be held as an alternative to cash for balance-sheet purposes. So hoarding has come to mean all demand for gold which does not derive from central banks for reserve purposes or from industry and the arts in the stricter and literal sense of those terms.

The Bank of England's Part

The Bank of England are not physically represented at the fixing. But they are able, like any other operator, effectively to participate in the fixing by passing orders by telephone through their bullion broker and at the fixing they use exclusively the services of the chairman of the market, namely, Rothschilds. The Bank operate for a number of different parties; they are first the managers of the Exchange Equalisation Account, which may be a natural buyer or seller of gold: secondly, they are the agent for the largest single regular seller of gold in the world, namely, the South African Reserve Bank, which is responsible for the disposal of new production in South Africa: thirdly, they execute orders for their many other central bank customers: fourthly, the Bank aim, as in the case of the foreign exchange and gilt-edged markets, to exercise, so far as they are able, a moderating influence on the market, in order to avoid violent and unnecessary movements in the price and thus to assist the market in the carrying on of its business.

OTHER MARKETS

There are gold markets in other places. Leaving aside Paris, which is a domestic market, and Bombay which, since gold dealings were banned at the end of 1962, is no more than a black market, markets of varying importance exist in Switzerland, Belgium, Beirut, Aden, Cairo, Kuwait, Bahrain, Dubai, Bangkok, Saigon, Macao, Hong Kong, and in a number of other places as well, including more recently Johannesburg. During the period when the London gold market was closed (from September 1939 to March 1954) most of the international gold traffic was centred in Switzerland, Beirut, and Tangier—which has now lost its international status and no longer has an organised gold market—or in the East. The effect of reopening the London gold market in 1954 was to introduce a greater degree of stability into international dealings and to moderate fluctuations in the price of gold.

ATLANTIC MONETARY ARRANGEMENTS*

When the free world's financial community assembled for its annual meeting in Tokyo this year, the spotlight was again on the International Monetary Fund. And rightly so. Because for almost two decades now, the Fund has done an increasingly effective job in promoting monetary cooperation, and the recent Tokyo decision to raise Fund quotas by 25 percent clearly reaffirmed the Fund's central role as guardian of world financial stability.

But while the world-wide Fund holds center stage and commands the spotlight, a strong supporting cast of supplementary organizations has begun to play an increasingly important role. Thus, over the past few years, the industrial countries of Western Europe and North America have developed several new forms of monetary cooperation. Among them are the London Gold Pool, the Group of Ten, and a rejuvenated Bank for International Settlements.

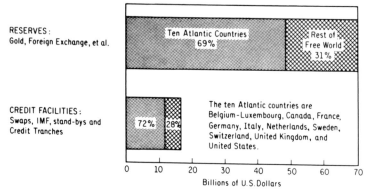

Ten Atlantic Countries Hold Seventy Percent of the Free
World's Official Reserves and Credit Facilities

Source: Ministerial Statement of the Group of Ten
Data as of December 31, 1963

One reason for the new, specifically Atlantic, arrangements is the many significant changes in the Atlantic countries' financial environment. Thus, the foreign trade of Western Europe and North America has more than doubled

*Report on Western Europe, The Chase Manhattan Bank, New York, August–September, 1964, pp. 1–2.

262

over the last decade. The world-wide dollar shortage, which caused concern only a few years back, has been replaced by a succession of large U.S. payments deficits. And, since 1958, the introduction of convertibility and the emergence of the Eurodollar market have greatly increased Atlantic capital movements.

A second, equally significant reason for Atlantic regionalism in monetary affairs is Western Europe's recent shift from international debtor to creditor. After World War II, when continental Europe depended on U.S. capital for its reconstruction, the IMF leadership fell quite naturally to the United States. Over the last decade, however, a number of European countries have run up substantial dollar holdings, thus becoming lenders of short-term funds to the United States. This shift in international debtor-creditor relationships has quite naturally led to a desire on the part of the new creditor countries to share

**MULTIPLE MEMBERSHIPS IN BIS, GROUP OF TEN, AND IMF
FACILITATE MONETARY COOPERATION AMONG ATLANTIC COUNTRIES**

Country	BIS	Gold Pool	Group of Ten	IMF
Common Market Countries*	Member	Member	Member	Member
Sweden	Member	Member	Member	Member
Switzerland	Member	Member	Associate	–
United Kingdom	Member	Member	Member	Member
Canada	–	–	Member	Member
United States	Member	Member	Member	Member
Japan	–	–	Member	Member

*The Common Market countries are Belgium-Luxembourg, France, Germany, Italy, and the Netherlands.

more largely in the control of the international payments system. In the Group of Ten and the BIS, the Western European countries have found means to reassert their financial role and international influence.

BIS—MEETING PLACE FOR CENTRAL BANKERS

The Bank for International Settlements, located in Switzerland, is best known for its monthly meetings of central bankers. Their purpose is the promotion of close cooperation and joint consultation among the leading financial countries. Thus the BIS meetings are regularly attended by central bank representatives from Belgium, Britain, France, Germany, Italy, the Netherlands, Sweden, Switzerland, and the United States. Because of the monthly meetings, the Bank's influence is considerable, and, in a sense, it has become the nerve center of Atlantic monetary cooperation.

The BIS was originally set up in 1930 to facilitate German reparations payments, but expanded its activities after World War II. Its members include most European countries and the United States. Today it serves as agent for the European Monetary Agreement, for the OECD, for the World Bank (IBRD), and for the European Coal and Steel Community. In addition, the Bank uses from time to time its $2 billion resources to stabilize foreign exchange markets.

A further basic task of the BIS is to keep a watchful eye on financial developments. The emergence of international money and capital markets puts a premium on comparative financial analysis, and recent BIS studies have dealt with some knotty problems. For instance, recent studies include a comparative analysis of eight European central banks, a thorough review of Europe's capital markets, and, in this year's annual report, an evaluation of the Eurocurrency markets.

Another aspect of the Bank's work is the mundane task of collecting financial statistics, one of the Bank's most important contributions. A case in point has to do with the movement of Eurocurrencies at the present time. Since an official statistic showing the Eurocurrency positions of the various countries is still lacking, not enough is known as to how and where these short-term funds are employed.

Furthermore, there is the necessary task of so-called credit surveillance—namely, keeping track of how balance of payments surpluses or deficits are financed. Since relevant statistics are not available in all instances, some countries have suggested that central banks supply the BIS with such information. A confidential exchange of the data may avoid excesses or shortages in credit extended to countries in payments difficulties.

THE GOLD POOL—PROP IN CRISIS

The Bank for International Settlements proved its worth in 1961 when heavy speculation was threatening the London gold market. To counter the speculative attack, the central bankers of the leading financial countries established a mutual gold pool at one of their monthly BIS meetings. The arrangement called for the central banks to pool part of their gold reserves under the Bank of England's management. With the additional gold at hand, the Bank of England had massive intervention powers, and the market soon stabilized at around $35 per ounce, the official price of gold.

This successful instance of financial cooperation among the Atlantic countries gave added support to the concept of regional monetary arrangements. For the advantages were obvious. The regularity of the BIS meetings assures a steady forum for discussion, the smallness of the group facilitates decision making, and the aggregate financial leverage of the Atlantic central banks maximizes the group's effectiveness. Thus the Atlantic countries found it only natural to organize in 1962 as the Group of Ten for the purpose of enlarging world liquidity.

THE GROUP OF TEN

The Group of Ten was formed to conclude with the Fund a "General Agreements to Borrow." Under this unprecedented agreement the International Monetary Fund acquired for a three-year period additional resources to the tune of $6 billion. This huge stand-by credit was made available as each member of the Group contributed a stand-by quota in its own currency. The IMF may relend these funds, subject to the lending country's approval, to any member country in payments difficulties.

This arrangement of the Group of Ten has a highly significant bearing on the future of the world monetary system. For the first time since its formation, the Fund has become able to render substantial support, albeit with restraints, to the U.S. dollar and the pound sterling. For while the International Monetary Fund has had ample resources to bridge the payments gaps of most countries, it had not been able to bail out the key currencies.

Yet, in a way, the terms of the "General Agreements to Borrow" are more significant for the future of the international payments system than the size of the stand-by credit itself. Last year, when the leading financial countries of Western Europe, North America, and Japan organized as the Group of Ten, most countries recognized the additional liquidity needs—actual or contingent —of the world monetary system. The obvious remedy would have been a substantial increase of Fund quotas. However, the Fund's members rejected this approach, and the Group of Ten was formed instead.

The main reason for by-passing a substantial quota increase at that time, was that some of the leading financial countries, notably France, were not prepared to increase permanently and substantially the Fund's discretionary lending powers. Therefore the agreement was limited to three years and will have to be renegotiated in 1966. And this is why the agreement stipulates that the Fund may provide assistance under the stand-by arrangement only if specifically approved by those countries whose currencies are involved. In this way the lending countries retain control over the Fund's disbursements, a scheme that obviously departs sharply from the Fund's multilateral nature. By itself, it is a clear indication of the different viewpoints that exist among the leading countries.

Most nations have always been reluctant to yield a large measure of their national sovereignty, particularly sovereignty over their own currency.

And as long as disagreements persist on how both to expand and control international liquidity, the leading financial nations seem unlikely to delegate a substantial degree of monetary control to a world-wide body. Here the Group of Ten and the BIS, together with other regional and bilateral arrangements, may offer an alternative system that operates by consensus rather than through directive and that makes a minimum infringement on national sovereignty.

THE UNITED KINGDOM FINANCIAL CRISIS*

The last quarter of 1964 will undoubtedly be remembered as one of the most critical periods in Britain's post war years as events precipitated a major international financial crisis.

Upon assuming office in October, the new Labor Government introduced a sweeping and, in some respects, controversial program. In an attempt to correct a widening balance of trade deficit, the government imposed, as temporary immediate steps, a surcharge of 15 percent on imports other than foodstuffs, unprocessed tobaccos and basic raw materials, and provided for a tax rebate of 1.5 percent on exports. In addition, the new policy called for a strict review of government expenditures for so-called "prestige" projects. In this connection, the government made known to France its wishes to reexamine their joint project for building the supersonic Concord airliner.

These measures were followed, on November 11, by an emergency budget containing provisions for new and higher taxes and the promise of enlarged social welfare benefits. The tax on gasoline was increased by 7 cents a gallon —an amount that is estimated to net the government $260 million a year. The standard rate of income tax is to be raised next April by 2.5 percent adding an additional $336 million yearly to government tax revenue. Moreover, the government announced its intentions to reform corporate and capital-gains taxes.

With the reform, the new corporation and capital-gains taxes—yet to be formulated—reportedly will follow a pattern similar to that prevailing in the United States. A capital-gains tax already exists in Britain, but only for gains made within six months, which are taxed at the standard income tax rate. There is no tax at all on capital gains on assets held longer than six months. The new capital-gains tax is expected to yield nearly $280 million a year to the government. Other tax measures designed to replace the present income and profits taxes, are said to involve a substantial increase in the tax paid by the recipients of dividends, but some reduction in taxes on retained business profits.

Along with the new and reformed taxes, the government disclosed that it would provide a massive $966 million a year increase in pensions and other social security benefits. The program, as reflected in the first budget of the

* *International Economic Review*, The First National Bank of Chicago, January 1965, pp. 1–5.

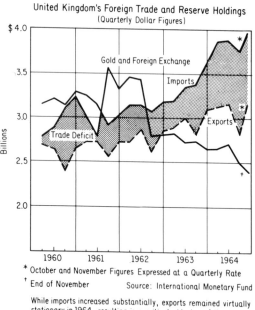

United Kingdom's Foreign Trade and Reserve Holdings
(Quarterly Dollar Figures)

* October and November Figures Expressed at a Quarterly Rate
† End of November   Source: International Monetary Fund

While imports increased substantially, exports remained virtually stationary in 1964, resulting in a critical widening of the trade deficit.

new Labor Government, contains—with the exception of the increase in the gasoline tax—postdated measures which, in effect, are to raise taxes to finance bigger social benefits.

The pound sterling weakened and the discount on pounds for future delivery widened sharply, suggesting a growing lack of confidence in the pound. The international financial community was worried about the payments deficit that had arisen because exports had not kept pace with rising imports, and also because of the capital outflow from the United Kingdom. Those who owned sterling deposits became uneasy about holding them longer. They were skeptical about the effectiveness of the proposed measures and feared a sudden devaluation of the pound. Moreover, several foreign governments bitterly attacked the import surcharge, and GATT (the General Agreement on Tariffs and Trade) condemned it.

The 15 percent import surcharge is affecting the trade of most countries with the United Kingdom. The impact is particularly severe on the suppliers of manufactured goods. The new tariff applies to about 60 percent of British imports from the Common Market, 48 percent of those from the United States, 36 percent from EFTA countries, and 13 percent from those of the Commonwealth and from the rest of the world.

The United Kingdom was accused of breaking the rules of the European Free Trade Association, the organization of seven countries that it had, in fact, created. For the EFTA countries the surcharge meant that in many cases Britain had unilaterally more than offset all the tariff cuts that had been made within the Association since its inception in May, 1960. Norway, Portugal, Switzerland,and Sweden are particularly hard hit. Among the EEC countries, the Netherlands and Belgium suffer the most. The surcharge also negatively affects the U. S. balance of payments both directly, through American exports to the United Kingdom, and indirectly, through the detrimental impact this measure has on some common trading partners. The United Kingdom is the third largest customer of the United States after Canada and Japan. Of a total $15 billion American commercial exports, $1 billion went to Britain in the first 9 months of 1964.

In the United States, both the Treasury and the State Departments issued statements indicating American understanding of Britain's problems and of the need to take steps to redress the deficit. However, there was no effort to disguise the fact that American exports to Britain would be adversely affected.

Throughout the first weeks of November the Labor Government maintained that it would not raise the bank rate as it might slow the pace of business activity in the United Kingdom. However, pressure on sterling continued to build up and on Friday, November 20, it reached major speculative proportions. The Bank of England was obliged to enter the market as a substantial buyer of sterling. This support action cost the British an estimated $56 million in reserves. On Monday, November 23, the Bank of England raised the bank rate to 7 percent from 5 percent. The pressure was so great that even this "crisis level" interest rate was insufficient to daunt the speculators. The rate move had come too late to restore by itself international confidence in the pound.

The bank rate, like the discount rate in the United States, is the key interest rate yardstick in the country and had been last raised to 7 percent in 1961. An interesting feature about the latest move is that the rate had not been changed on a Monday since 1931, when Britain went off the gold standard. Traditionally, the Bank of England announces its changes of the bank rate on Thursday. Following the British move, the United States raised its discount rate to 4 percent from 3.5 percent, while Canada increased its rate to 4.25 percent from 4 percent.

What finally stopped the speculation against the pound was an unprecedented $3 billion rescue package made available to the United Kingdom on November 25. The $3 billion short-term loan, which is repayable within 3 to 6 months, includes $250 million from the Export-Import Bank of the United States and a $750 million "swap" arrangement with the Federal Reserve Bank of New York. The latter represents a $250 million increase over an existing arrangement between the United States and the United Kingdom to use each other's currency during support operations in the foreign exchange market. The other participants included the central banks of Austria, Belgium, Canada, France, West Germany, Italy, Japan, the Netherlands, Sweden, Switzerland and the Bank for International Settlements, a quasi-official institution with

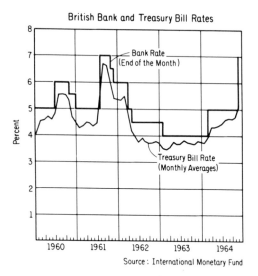

British Bank and Treasury Bill Rates

Bank Rate
(End of the Month)

Treasury Bill Rate
(Monthly Averages)

Source: International Monetary Fund

The increase in the rate on Britain's treasury bills hopefully
will attract short term capital from abroad alleviating the
pressure on the nation's balance of payments.

headquarters in Basle, Switzerland, which deals only with central banks. The $3 billion package was made available in various currencies consisting mainly of U.S. dollars, German marks, and French francs.

The immediate intent of the multinational operation was to demonstrate to the international financial community that the United Kingdom would and could defend the pound against speculation and that devaluation could be avoided through international cooperation.

The British Treasury disclosed that during last November the U.K.'s official reserves dropped $109 million, shrinking Britain's foreign exchange reserves to $2,344 million, the lowest level in seven years. It is generally understood, moreover, that even these figures hid the true dimensions of the drain. It was a major international financial crisis comparable in importance to the one in 1949 which led to the devaluation of the pound from $4.03 to $2.80. The decisive factor today has been international cooperation on a scale that could not even have been conceived in 1949.

On December 3, the United Kingdom drew $1 billion from the International Monetary Fund to replenish its depleted reserves and to pay back about $560 million, which it had previously borrowed from the Federal Reserve System and European central banks. With this drawing, Britain has not used up all of its credit with the IMF, but would still be in a position to obtain the equivalent of some $1.4 billion from the Fund. Finally, a few days later, the Bank of England, following up the previous month's increase in the bank rate, called on British banks and other financial institutions to be more selective in their lending policies.

In announcing its program, the Labor Government pointed out that in 1964 Great Britain faced the biggest balance of payments deficit in its history —between $1.96 billion and $2.24 billion. While the final figures will probably show a narrower deficit, about one-half of the imbalance, unlike that of the United States, stems from a large deficit in Britain's balance of trade. The other half shows up in the capital account.

In the short-term, the 15 percent surcharge on imports should be quite effective. This is due at least in part to the fact that British imports had increased considerably just prior to the introduction of the October measures, mostly in anticipation of just such an action. In addition, the rise of the bank rate should have the effect of limiting the rate of capital outflow. This, however, may not show immediate results. Due to technical factors, involving the repatriation of overseas balances for end-of-year balance sheet considerations, funds tend to flow out of London in December irrespective of the interest advantage. Therefore, the interest rate differential in favor of London is expected to show its first tangible effects in the first part of 1965.

Ultimately, in order to correct its balance of payments deficit, the United Kingdom must expand its exports. To do so requires that they be priced competitively. In addition, domestic consumption probably will have to be curtailed somewhat in order to limit imports and to make goods available for export.

Some headway has been made along these lines. Particularly commendable have been government's efforts to achieve a workable income policy under which wage and price rises would be held within the limits of productivity advances. On the other hand, it is evident that the higher import charges are protectionist, in fact, if not by intention, and will tend to promote inefficiency. If maintained for long, they will have a potentially troublesome negative influence on the competitiveness of British industry. As the new administration has suggested, a lasting solution to Britain's balance of payments difficulties is a complex process of modernization combined with an all out promotion of export trade. Within the context of the present international financial cooperation, the government may have a unique opportunity to push ahead on this front.

ADDITIONAL READINGS

Aliber, Robert Z., *The Management of the Dollar in International Finance*, International Finance Section, Princeton University, 1964.

Altman, Oscar L., "The Changing Gold Exchange Standard and the Role of the IMF," *Banca Nazionale del Lavoro Quarterly Review*, June, 1963, pp. 151–173.

———, "The Management of International Liquidity," *IMF Staff Papers*, July, 1964, pp. 216–247.

"A New Chapter in Silver History," *Monthly Letter of Business and Economic*

Conditions, First National City Bank, New York, December, 1963, pp. 137–140.

Angell, James W., "The Reorganization of the International Monetary System," *The Economic Journal,* December, 1961, pp. 691–708.

"A Practical Approach to Strengthening Int'l Liquidity," *Monthly Letter of Business and Economic Conditions,* First National City Bank, New York, September, 1964, pp. 104–107.

Bloomfield, Arthur, *Monetary Policy under the International Gold Standard: 1880–1914,* Federal Reserve Bank of New York, 1959.

Carter, Wm. A., "World Gold Production and the Money Supply," *Journal of Finance,* September, 1963, pp. 494–510.

Cuthbertson, J. R., "Gold Revaluation Without Tears," *The Banker,* January, 1963, pp. 15–22.

Dunning, John, "Capital Movements in the Twentieth Century," *Lloyds Bank Review,* April, 1964, pp. 17–42.

Fleming, J. Marcus, "Developments in the International Payments System," *IMF Staff Papers,* November, 1963, pp. 461–484.

———, "The Fund and International Liquidity," *IMF Staff Papers,* July, 1964, pp. 177–215.

Friedman, Irving S., "The International Monetary System," *IMF Staff Papers,* July, 1963, pp. 219–245.

Grubel, Herbert G. (ed.), *World Monetary Reform, Plans and Issues,* Stanford University Press, 1963.

Hansen, Alvin H., *The Dollar and the International Monetary System,* New York: McGraw-Hill, 1965.

"Introduction to the Fund," *The Fund & Bank Review,* June, 1964, pp. 3–14.

Katz, Samuel I., *Sterling Speculation and European Convertibility, 1955–1958,* International Finance Section, Princeton University, 1961.

Kumar, Rajendra, "The Working of the Present-Day International Gold Standard," *The Bankers' Magazine,* November, 1962, pp. 330–335.

Machlup, Fritz, *Plans for the Reform of the International Monetary System,* International Finance Section, Princeton University, 1964.

Malkiel, Burton G., "The Rejection of the Triffin Plan and the Alternative Accepted," *Journal of Finance,* September, 1963, pp. 511–536.

Meade, J. E., "The International Monetary Mechanism," *The Three Banks Review,* September, 1964, pp. 3–25.

Posthuma, S., "The International Monetary System," *Banca Nazionale del Lavoro Quarterly Review,* September, 1963, pp. 239–261.

Roosa, Robert V., "Reforming the International Monetary System," *Foreign Affairs,* October, 1963, pp. 107–122.

Sayers, R. S., "Cooperation between Central Banks," *The Three Banks Review,* September, 1963, pp. 3–25.

Tew, Brian, *The International Monetary Fund: Its Present Role and Future Prospects,* International Finance Section, Princeton University, 1961.

"The International Monetary System: As It Might Be," *Federal Reserve Bank of Atlanta Monthly Review,* February, 1964, pp. 1–6.

Triffin, Robert, *The Evolution of the International Monetary System, Historical Reappraisal and Future Perspectives,* International Finance Section, Princeton University, 1964.

chapter *5*
Exchange Controls: Types, Uses, and Trends

The terms "exchange controls" or "exchange restrictions" refer to governmental actions which limit the freedom of banks, companies, or individuals to buy and sell foreign currencies (foreign exchange). Such controls usually exist because the demand for foreign exchange is greater than the supply. If the controls were not imposed, the value of the country's currency would depreciate in terms of other currencies. One of the major purposes of exchange controls, therefore, is to prevent a depreciation of the currency. Similarly, since the anticipation of depreciation would cause people to wish to invest in other currencies, exchange controls are imposed to prevent capital flight. The very imposition of the controls, however, necessitates a rationing by some governmental authority of the available foreign exchange among the competing demands. Such rationing will thus give preference to the importation of goods or services which are essential to a country's economic growth or to some other national objective; or, it may give preference to individuals who yield the greatest political influence or give the biggest bribes to the officials concerned.

On the other hand, exchange controls are also used to prevent the importation of goods which are being produced (perhaps inefficiently) domestically. The controls thus function as a means of protection of an infant industry or of agricultural production.

These types of governmental controls of foreign exchange are of fairly recent origin in the history of international finance. There were limited and isolated attempts at exchange control during World War I, but these ceased at the conclusion of the conflict. The full-grown use of comprehensive exchange controls dates from 1931, when Germany was forced to leave the gold standard. Rather than allow her currency to depreciate, Germany maintained the value of the currency by imposing exchange controls. She was followed by a number of other Central European countries.

When war broke out in 1939, international trade was interrupted and practically all countries found it necessary to enforce rigid systems of exchange controls. The end of the war found many countries with a need for increased imports to rebuild their economies, but with a diminished supply of goods available for export. Consequently, although the United States was able to immediately dismantle its wartime exchange controls, most countries continued them.

A major objective of U.S. and International Monetary Fund policy was a rapid restoration of convertibility. Consequently, in 1946 the United States extended a credit of $3.75 billion to the United Kingdom to help achieve early convertibility of sterling. In accordance with their commitments under this loan agreement, the British made sterling convertible in 1947. But the country's economy, as well as the currency itself (at the then-prevailing exchange rate of $4.03 per pound sterling), was not yet strong enough for such a move, and convertibility had to be suspended five weeks after it was undertaken.

The movement toward convertibility began in December, 1951, when Canada abolished exchange controls and the United Kingdom permitted her banks to resume trading in foreign exchange. To be sure, this trading by British banks was at fixed rates and there were restrictions as to who could buy the sterling; yet, it was a positive step. A further step was made in 1953 when the United Kingdom, France, the Netherlands, West Germany, Denmark, Switzerland, and Sweden agreed to allow commercial banks to carry out arbitrage transactions in the currencies of these countries. Then, as dollars continued to flow into Europe, the Belgian franc, for all practical purposes, became transferable by 1955 and the West German mark reached a similar status by 1956.

The year 1958 marked the milestone in the movement toward convertibility and the dismantling of exchange controls. This coincided, naturally enough, with the large deficit in the U.S. balance of payments and with the accompanying tremendous gold outflow. The so-called "dollar shortage" disappeared and, under the leadership of the United Kingdom, fourteen European countries introduced nonresident convertibility, meaning that their currencies were freely transferable by nonresidents, where these currencies were obtained by current-account transaction. During the following several years, these countries gradually extended convertibility for current-account transactions to their own residents, but controls over capital account earnings remained largely in force.

Article VIII of the International Monetary Fund Agreement requires member countries to avoid multiple exchange rates, discriminatory currency practices, and restrictions on current transactions. Article XIV, on the other hand, permits members to maintain exchange controls which were in effect. But, once a country had accepted the obligations of Article VIII, it cannot reinstate such controls without the prior approval of the Fund.

A major step toward convertibility was made in February, 1961, when nine European countries (Belgium, France, Germany, Ireland, Italy, Luxembourg, the Netherlands, Sweden, and the United Kingdom) accepted the obligations of Article VIII. In addition, by that date, there were eleven Western Hemisphere countries which had bound themselves to the provisions of this article. Several additional countries have since joined the list each year, but nearly all continue to maintain controls over capital account funds.

Today, most of the countries in the world continue to exercise extensive controls over foreign exchange. The international monetary system has moved a long way toward the free movement of foreign exchange, compared with the situation which existed in 1950, but it has a long way to go.

Multinational business is quite obviously vitally affected by the existence of exchange controls and the manner in which they are operated. This is true from the standpoint of the effect of the controls on exports and imports of goods and services. It is equally, and more vitally true with regard to controls over the investment of capital and over the repatriation of capital and earnings.

The first reading is concerned with the exchange controls in effect in Latin America. It provides a background to the development of the controls now in operation and an understanding of the types of controls and the variations with which they are applied in different countries.

The second reading, by W. John R. Woodley, concentrates on the exchange control system of one country. Venezuela is not necessarily a typical country, but this study does provide a case history of the deterioration of a country's economy and of its balance of payments, which led to the need to impose exchange controls. It shows the difficult steps which the government had to take to establish a workable exchange control system. It then illustrates the monetary, fiscal and exchange policies which had to be undertaken to eliminate the underlying balance of payments deficit so as to achieve the elimination of multiple exchange rates and the eventual dismantling of the exchange control system. An understanding of this problem, by an international businessman, is necessary to his evaluation of any given country's exchange control system, and a determination of whether it will move toward a more rigid or less rigid system of controls.

There has been a continuing argument, in international financial circles, about the desirability of pegged exchange rates. It is largely the desire to maintain a given rate of exchange, and to avoid an abrupt devaluation, that exchange controls are imposed. Why not allow the exchange rate to float freely, attaining the level determined by the supply and demand at any given time? This question was touched upon by two readings in Chapter 3, though only in relation to the United States. But, the dollar is the world's leading currency and most other currencies have their value related to that of the dollar. To let the dollar float is thus an entirely different question from that of whether or not any of a hundred other countries should use the floating exchange rate rather than exchange controls. The third reading is a study of the Canadian experience with a floating exchange rate. It raises two interesting questions: (1) Is the Canadian experience transferable to other countries? and (2) what would the effects be on international trade and investment if a large number of countries chose to let their currencies float?

RESTRICTIONS ON THE MOVE-MENT OF FUNDS WITHIN LATIN AMERICA*

This paper was prepared in response to a request from the Latin American Center for Monetary Studies (CEMLA). It was discussed at CEMLA's Seventh Operational Meeting, held in Mexico City, September 3-4, 1962.

The main purpose of this paper is to describe major restrictive practices[1] affecting directly or indirectly the movement of funds within Latin America, and to indicate briefly their objectives and their effects on trade and payments. It begins with a summary in Section I. A brief review of major postwar developments in the Latin American restrictive systems is included in Section II. This is followed by the main section—Section III—where five types of restrictive device are discussed in detail : import surcharges, advance deposits, multiple exchange rates, quantitative restrictions, and regulation of capital transfers.[2]

The movement of funds within Latin America is subject, to a large extent, to the same restrictions that are applied to extra-area trade and payments; preferential treatment, where accorded, is described below in the appropriate context. In what follows, observations regarding the desirability of economic measures for the implementation of free trade area policies in individual countries are based on the situation at about the middle of 1962. Future developments in the various restrictive systems and in economic conditions in the countries concerned will, of course, also be affected by internal and external factors not related to the efforts to integrate trade.

I. SUMMARY

A number of Latin American countries have now achieved relatively free foreign exchange markets ; most of the other countries have gradually elimi-

* Samir Makdisi, *International Monetary Fund Staff Papers,* March, 1963, pp. 186–214.

[1] Excluding tariffs, export taxes, and a few other restrictions. Unless otherwise noted, this report reflects the situation in June 1962. Moreover, only a few references are made to Cuba's restrictive system, since information about that country is limited.

[2] Bilateralism has been virtually eliminated from intra-Latin American trade.

nated and/or simplified their multiple currency practices and other restrictive devices.[3] Cuba is the leading exception; practically all Cuban foreign trade and payments are now subject to restrictions or controls. Recently, a few countries have found it necessary to reintroduce exchange controls. But, generally, the trend toward liberalization has been achieved not at the cost of an increase in indirect controls but rather in conjunction with the implementation of stabilization programs. In those instances where intensification of some trade restrictions has accompanied the elimination of payments restrictions, the ultimate objective has been to maintain protection for domestic industries—a policy which has not negated all, or even most, of the benefits achieved by overall payments liberalization.

The movement of funds within Latin America is, to a large extent, still subject to the same restrictions that are applied to extra-area trade and payments. However, preferential treatment has resulted from (1) the first round of negotiations of the Latin American Free Trade Association (LAFTA), i.e., exemptions from import surcharges and advance deposits and, in one or two countries, from licensing, have been extended to a relatively small number of intra-LAFTA trade items; (2) the elimination of restrictions by the Central American group of countries on a large number of items originating (but not necessarily traded) within the group; and (3) exemptions from surcharges extended by a few countries, e.g., Argentina and Paraguay, to all or a substantial portion of their imports from neighboring countries, and exemptions from advance deposit requirements extended by Brazil to all imports from LAFTA countries. Recent reforms in some of the exchange control countries, whereby restrictive devices were simplified and the official rates of exchange made more realistic, help in facilitating the implementation of LAFTA.

Quantitative restrictions are, perhaps, the most important restrictive device now applied. The countries which apply these restrictions—Brazil, Chile, Colombia, the Dominican Republic, Mexico, and Venezuela (Table 1)—account for more than half of intra-Latin American trade. In Mexico, import items subject to permits are estimated to cover about one half of the country's imports in terms of value. Originally, licensing was used there mainly to conserve foreign exchange, but later it was increasingly utilized for protective purposes as well. In Venezuela, the role of the official free market was greatly expanded in April 1962, tending to lessen the restrictiveness of the import system. Prohibitions and import licensing, along with tariffs, however, comprise an important protective device. In Brazil, a substantial degree of quantitative restriction applies to imports of manufactured products which are included in the "Special Category." In Colombia, prohibitions and prior licensing for protective and payments purposes have had an important restrictive effect

---

[3] See F. d'A. Collings, "Recent Progress in Latin America Toward Eliminating Exchange Restrictions," *Staff Papers*, Vol. VIII (1960–61), pp. 274–86.

TABLE 1

LATIN AMERICAN COUNTRIES (EXCLUDING CUBA):

TYPES OF RESTRICTION MAINTAINED IN JUNE 1962

Import Surcharges	Advance Deposits	Major Multiple Rates	Quantitative Restrictions	Arrangements for Capital Transfers
Argentina	Brazil	Brazil	Brazil	Chile
Brazil	Chile	Chile	Chile	Colombia
Chile	Colombia	Colombia	Colombia	Dominican Republic
Costa Rica	Ecuador	Ecuador	Dominican Republic	Ecuador
Guatemala	Nicaragua	Uruguay	Ecuador	El Salvador
Paraguay	Paraguay	Venezuela	Mexico	Nicaragua
Uruguay	Uruguay		Nicaragua	Venezuela
			Venezuela	

on the country's trade and payments, greater reliance being placed on pro-hibitions than on licensing. A large number of import items was included in the prohibited list in 1960, while over half of the actual imports were subject to licensing. In Chile, exchange controls were temporarily reintroduced in January 1962 when quantitative restrictions were increased. Prohibitions now play an important protective and restrictive role, although until that date they had been steadily decreasing since 1956, when import licensing was abolished. Ecuador and Nicaragua also apply licensing controls, but the ap-plication is liberal and is mainly intended to enforce advance deposit require-ments.

In most Latin American countries, multiple exchange rates are not as im-portant a feature of the restrictive system as they were in earlier years. How-ever, they are still important in Brazil, Chile, Colombia, Uruguay, and Venezu-ela, and of lesser significance in Bolivia, Costa Rica, Ecuador, Nicaragua, and Paraguay. In Colombia and Venezuela, these practices serve a variety of ob-jectives: securing fiscal revenue, diversifying the composition of exports, sub-sidizing essential imports, and relieving possible pressure upon the central bank's reserves. Some of these purposes are also served in Chile by multiple rates, in conjunction with other controls. In Brazil and Uruguay, the applica-tion of exchange taxes on export proceeds, and in the former country the making of quarterly contracts to sell exchange for specific imports, give rise to several effective rates. In Brazil, multiple rates are used to redistribute revenue within the coffee and cocoa industries and to avoid short-term fluctu-ations of prices of a few essential imports in the face of possible changes in the exchange rate. In Uruguay, exchange taxes (retentions) serve as an im-portant source of fiscal revenue. In all the countries that apply multiple rates (with the exception of Chile, which reintroduced them recently), the restrictive system has been greatly simplified in recent years. Various reforms have brought the official rates closer to the prevailing market rate of exchange.

Advance deposits on imports are now required in Brazil, Chile, Colombia, Ecuador, Nicaragua, Paraguay, and Uruguay. Exemptions have been granted by Brazil, Chile, Paraguay, and Uruguay to imports of items appearing in their respective LAFTA concession lists; and Nicaragua has extended exemptions to imports from the Central American group. Generally speaking, deposit requirements have not proved to be a very effective device in restricting imports. They are much more effective when they accompany domestic stabilization measures. Like surcharges, they have proved to be a flexible tool, i.e., administratively they may be easily introduced or eliminated; their impact seems to be largely on extra-area imports. However, a number of countries which introduced them for restrictive purposes have had to retain them to avoid the inflationary impact of their release.

The use of import surcharges has usually been limited to a relatively small number of countries. Along with advance deposits they have often been utilized to ease the process of transition from strict exchange controls to a liberalized exchange system. They are now applied in Argentina, Brazil, Chile, Costa Rica, Guatemala, Paraguay, and Uruguay. The overall incidence of surcharges is, at present, probably highest in Argentina, where they seem to have hindered the efficient development of certain domestic industries. Except in Guatemala, the incidence of surcharges is relatively high on "nonessentials," and relatively low on other imports. Many essentials are exempt. Argentina and Paraguay also exempt imports from neighboring countries. All the countries mentioned above (except Costa Rica and Guatemala) have, in addition, extended exemptions to imports of items in their respective LAFTA concession lists. The application of these surcharges favors intra-area trade. The current policy of incorporating surcharges into the tariff schedule helps to avoid the adverse effects that could arise from the frequency of changes in the surcharge rates.

In those Latin American countries where regulations on capital transfers are applied (Chile, Colombia, the Dominican Republic, Ecuador, El Salvador, Nicaragua, and Venezuela), foreign investments are usually guaranteed the remittance of profits and principal. In a few countries, transfers of domestically owned capital funds are permitted, but in others they are subject to restrictive licensing or are prohibited. However, where capital remittances through the free market are permitted, the possibilities of transfer available to residents may in fact be greatly limited if the free and official rates differ significantly. Special privileges have not been extended to Latin American capital. But as part of the implementation of the objectives of LAFTA, intra-regional capital transfers should perhaps be encouraged. The maintenance of monetary stability, along with the elimination of restrictions on capital movements, would help the repatriation of Latin American capital, and also would encourage future intraregional capital movements, all of which would contribute toward building a firmer basis for Latin American economic integration.

II. DEVELOPMENTS IN THE LATIN AMERICAN RESTRICTIVE SYSTEMS

In the last decade or so, there have been four major developments in the Latin American restrictive systems:

(1) An increase in the number of countries which have established free foreign exchange markets. Thus, at the beginning of 1962, 12 countries[4] had virtually no exchange controls, compared with 8 in 1950.

(2) Gradual elimination and/or simplification of multiple currency practices. At the beginning of 1962, 6 countries[5] relied to an important extent on multiple rates, compared with 12 in 1950.

(3) Gradual elimination of bilateral payments agreements, particularly among the Latin American countries themselves. In June 1962, the number of intra-Latin American payments agreements had fallen to 2, from 16 in 1955.

(4) Continued limitation of imports through quantitative restrictions or otherwise.

The underlying trend toward freer exchange systems has not been maintained consistently throughout the postwar period. At the beginning of the 1950's, the Latin American exchange systems might have been divided into three groups. The first would have included the Dominican Republic, El Salvador, Guatemala, Haiti, Honduras,[6] Mexico, and Panama—countries that had already established relatively free foreign exchange markets, i.e., had removed direct exchange controls on both current and capital payments. These countries imposed few quantitative and cost restrictions, such as licenses and surcharges; in one or two, quotas were imposed, while others relied to a small extent on bilateral agreements. The second group would have comprised Peru, Uruguay, and Venezuela, where the main features of the systems were multiple rates, surrender requirements, and import licensing; capital transfers

---

[4] Inclusive of (1) El Salvador, which on May 1, 1961 introduced temporary controls over capital transactions, while leaving current transactions unrestricted, (2) Uruguay, which applies export retentions giving rise to varying rates for exchange received by exporters and maintains surrender requirements, and (3) Costa Rica, which requires the surrender of export receipts, with the exception of those earned by the foreign-owned banana companies. (These companies, however, sell exchange to cover local requirements, paying a 10 percent tax.)

[5] One of these, Chile, reintroduced multiple rates in January 1962 after having maintained a uniform rate of exchange since mid-1959.

[6] Honduras required the surrender of export receipts and maintained a small spread between the official and selling rates. Otherwise, it did not impose any exchange restrictions.

and payments for invisibles were largely unrestricted. Peru, however, did conclude several bilateral agreements. The third group, comprising Argentina, Bolivia, Brazil, Chile, Colombia, Costa Rica, Ecuador, Nicaragua, and Paraguay, maintained comprehensive exchange controls, characterized by multiple rates, surrender requirements, and control of capital transfers, in addition to quotas, licenses, export taxes, and, in some countries, advance deposits.

Early in 1962, Argentina, Bolivia, Costa Rica, Paraguay, Peru, and Uruguay were added to the first group. Furthermore, most of the remaining countries, while retaining multiple rates and/or other exchange and trade restrictions, had nonetheless achieved noticeable progress in simplifying and/or liberalizing their exchange systems. These developments at the national level have been reinforced by multilateral moves to reduce restrictions on intra-Latin American trade. They began with the ratification in December 1960 of the General Treaty on Central American Integration,[7] and in May 1961 of the Treaty of Montevideo[8] (which established the Latin American Free Trade Association). In 1959–60 intra-LAFTA trade accounted for roughly 40 percent of intra-Latin American trade, and trade among the Central American group of countries accounted for about 4 percent.

The present review excludes Cuba, where the trend of developments in the restrictive system has differed from trends elsewhere in the Latin American region. All Cuban foreign trade is now under direct state management, and all exchange transactions are carried out through the National Bank.[9] All exchange proceeds must be surrendered to the Bank, whose approval is required for exports and transfers abroad of foreign exchange, checks, securities, or other monetary instruments.

[7] This Treaty (signed by El Salvador, Guatemala, Honduras, and Nicaragua) requires the immediate removal of all tariffs and other charges on a large portion of commodities originating in the member countries. The remaining commodities (which in fact include many of the items actually traded) will be liberalized within five years. They are included in special lists. Restrictions on the first group of items, i.e., those not included in the special lists, have already been removed. The countries concerned have also agreed to equalize external tariffs, integrate their industrial projects, and establish a central bank for economic integration. All these agreements are being implemented. On August 2, 1961 a Preferential Trade Agreement was signed by Costa Rica, Nicaragua, and Panama, providing for free or preferential treatment of trade among the contracting parties; it also provides for exemption from quantitative restrictions other than those agreed by the parties concerned. All three countries have now ratified this agreement.

[8] The Treaty of Montevideo requires each contracting party to negotiate annually with the other contracting parties tariff reductions equivalent to at least 8 percent of the weighted average of the tariff in force for third countries. Tariffs include customs duties and any other surcharges having equivalent effect, whether of a fiscal, monetary, or exchange character. The first annual negotiated concessions became effective on January 1, 1962 for the seven original members (Argentina, Brazil, Chile, Mexico, Paraguay, Peru, and Uruguay). Colombia's negotiated concessions became effective in April 1962, while Ecuador negotiated with the other members in August 1962.

[9] Law 930, February 23, 1961.

III. Major Restrictive Devices

Import Surcharges

Surcharges constitute an important restriction in Argentina, Chile, and Uruguay, and, to a lesser degree, in Brazil, Guatemala, and Paraguay.[10] Except in Guatemala and Paraguay, the bases for determining variations in the rates levied are the degree of essentiality of the import and the competitiveness of the import with domestic production; the less essential and the more competitive the import, the higher the surcharge it bears. Many essentials are exempted. As a source of revenue, surcharge payments are important in Argentina where in 1958–61 they accounted for roughly 18 percent of government receipts; they are less important in the other five countries.

In Argentina, surcharges were applied, in conjunction with the 1959 exchange and stabilization program, to ease the process of transition toward a liberal and unified exchange system. Since then, changes have been made in the rates applicable to various import categories, resulting in a net reduction in their overall incidence.[11] Surcharges remain, however, an effective restrictive device, and with respect to certain categories they are still high. They are payable on the c.i.f. value of all imports other than certain essential goods, e.g., the principal metals, rubber, and newsprint.[12] The rates prevailing until December 31, 1961 were as follows: 20 percent on numerous raw materials, drugs, iron and steel bars, etc.; 40 percent on semiprocessed articles or raw materials produced domestically; 100 percent on spare parts, tools, and industrial machinery manufactured domestically but not in sufficient quantities; 150 percent on processed articles produced domestically, the import of which is not essential, and on industrial machinery manufactured domestically; and 200 percent on nonessential products and luxuries, e.g., whisky, transistor radios, textiles, and ready-made clothing of cotton and wool.[13] However, on January 24, 1962 surcharges were increased on various groups of imports, excluding items which appear on the Argentine LAFTA concession list. Imports of specified machinery, which until then were exempt from surcharges, were subjected to a 40 percent surcharge. Moreover, imports of a large number of goods which are either produced domestically or are considered of a nonessential nature were subjected to an additional temporary 100 percent surcharge, to be eliminated at the end of 1962. Furth-

[10] In connection with the exchange reform of September 3, 1961, Costa Rica imposed a temporary import surcharge of 15 percent on imports of specified less essential goods, and of 30 percent on luxury goods, pending the promulgation of a new tariff.

[11] Excluding temporary additional surcharges levied during 1962.

[12] Until January 4, 1962 imports of fuels were also exempted. On that date they became subject to a 20 percent surcharge.

[13] The 200 percent surcharge includes a temporary 50 percent surcharge.

ermore, on April 9, 1962 an emergency 20 percent additional surcharge was imposed on practically all imports; the few exceptions included items on Argentina's LAFTA concession list.

The total effect of the Argentine surcharges has been somewhat reduced, however—at least until the recent temporary changes—as several import items have been exempted from surcharge. For example, certain imports originating in neighboring countries and in Peru, a relatively small number of items appearing on the Argentine LAFTA concession list, and imports of machinery and materials for certain industries, are (or were) exempted from the surcharges. In addition, either surcharges of less than 100 percent paid on imports of certain raw materials and semifinished items which are subsequently incorporated into exports are repaid after six months or the imported item is granted alternative preferential treatment. The importance of these exemptions is partly indicated by the fact that in 1959–61 roughly two-thirds of Argentine imports were exempted from surcharges.[14]

In Chile, the authorities have similarly made use of surcharges, together with advance deposits, since 1959, when the exchange markets were unified and import prohibitions eliminated.[15] There are now 13 different surcharges, ranging from 0.1 percent to 200 percent, payable at the time of clearance of the goods through customs. They are applicable on all permitted imports except goods imported by large mining companies, agricultural spare parts, certain capital goods, and imports from LAFTA of some items which appear on the Chilean LAFTA concession list.[16] Needed imports, such as metallic minerals, natural products, antibiotics, pharmaceutical specialties, and industrial oils, are subject to the lower ranges of the surcharges, i.e., 0.1 percent to 20 percent; less "essential" or more competitive imports, e.g., skins, wheat flour, some fabrics, varnishes, aluminum sheets, tin and lead scraps, paper, motorboats, and office machinery, are subject to the higher ranges.

In Uruguay, surcharges were first applied in 1956, when reforms initiated that year provided a free certificate market for imports and exports. They were retained, along with advance deposit requirements, when the exchange and monetary reforms of December 17, 1959 resulted in the elimination of other import restrictions and in the establishment of a freely fluctuating market rate. Essential imports, such as sugar, salt, coffee, timber, iron and steel, industrial raw materials, paper, and imports from LAFTA of certain items that appear in the Uruguayan LAFTA concession list are exempted.[17]

---

[14] Of course, the more effective the rates, the greater is the reduction in the import of commodities subject to surcharges, so that the proportion of imports exempted is not a completely satisfactory indicator of the importance of the exemptions granted.

[15] A dual market, with increased restrictive measures, was reintroduced in January 1962.

[16] In January 1962, the list of prohibited imports was reintroduced and made to include many "nonessentials" and "luxuries."

[17] Other items in the concession list are subject to reduced rates.

Other imports subject to surcharges require registration with the Bank of the Republic, accompanied by an assurance from the bank handling the import financing that the necessary foreign exchange will be available at the time of customs clearance. The surcharges are collected by the Bank and levied as follows: 40 percent on goods not produced domestically; 75 percent on competitive imports;[18] and 150 percent on luxuries.

In Brazil, imports of goods in the "Special Category" classification are made on the basis of licenses issued to holders of "promises of licenses," which are purchased at auctions. The prices paid for these promises represent surcharges on imports. They usually fluctuate freely, but on January 30, 1962 a minimum of Cr$662.60 per U.S. dollar was fixed.

Guatemala maintains a 100 percent surcharge on imports from specified countries with which it has a trade deficit. The list of these countries is periodically changed. Should a country of the Central American group be included in it, the surcharge will not be applicable to items which do not appear in the special lists.[19] The surcharge is waived if goods are imported on Guatemalan ships.

In Paraguay, surcharges payable on the c.i.f. value and collected by the Central Bank were first used in 1959, on a limited scale. They are now levied on all imports except (1) those originating in Argentina, Bolivia, Brazil, and Uruguay, (2) those items included in the Paraguayan concession list which are specifically exempted from such payments,[20] and (3) government imports. With these exceptions, wheat and petroleum imports are subject to a 15 percent, and other imports to a 24 percent, surcharge.

The use of surcharges has usually been restricted to a relatively small number of Latin American countries, but in 1959–61 the countries then applying surcharges accounted for roughly 40 percent of intra-Latin American trade. Surcharges have protected domestic products and have been readily utilized for temporary balance of payments purposes, as evidenced by the experiences of the countries under consideration.[21] As noted above, they are relatively high when imposed on "nonessential" imports, i.e., goods either produced domestically or considered luxuries by the authorities. They are relatively low on "essential" imports, e.g., needed raw materials, food items,

[18] Uruguayan industrial output comprises mainly textiles, processed foodstuffs, and construction materials. Major agricultural produce includes wheat, linseed, oats, barley, corn, and rice.

[19] These lists include items to be liberalized within five years; see footnote 7.

[20] See footnote 17.

[21] The use of surcharges has been partly motivated by the decreasing effectiveness of customs duties. Two factors are responsible for this decreasing effectiveness: (1) trade agreements that have either bound existing rates or caused them to be reduced; (2) the administrative impracticability of changing tariffs as a short-term regulator. As a result, where duties are specific or where the basis for taxation of imports is in an overvalued official rate of exchange, tariffs have tended to be less effective as the general price level has increased.

and capital goods not available locally, many of which have, in fact, been exempted. The degree of incidence varies from one country to another, being currently highest in Argentina.

As to the impact of surcharges on the trade and payments of the countries applying them, and consequently on intra-Latin American trade and payments, three brief observations will be made. First, it is probably true that, except in Guatemala, the incidence of surcharges is greater on extra-area than on intra-area trade. The following factors may be mentioned in support of this statement: (1) the majority of the imports exempted from surcharges or attracting low rates originate within Latin America, e.g., food items and raw materials; (2) imports from neighboring countries are exempted in Paraguay, and a large number of such items are exempted in Argentina; in addition, the countries considered here are LAFTA members whose reciprocal concession lists include the elimination of surcharges on a number of items traded within LAFTA;[22] and (3) many items subject to high surcharges are largely imported from outside Latin America, e.g., textiles, alcoholic beverages, and machinery that competes with local production in Argentina; textiles and construction materials in Uruguay; tin bars and ingots, textiles, and wheat flour in Chile. These facts suggest that (with allowance for exemptions granted) the systems of surcharges in the countries which apply them discriminate in favor of intraregional and against extraregional trade.

Second, in Argentina, and to a lesser extent in Uruguay, the high surcharges on imports competing with domestic products seem to have hindered the efficient development of domestic production by shielding inefficient plants. In Argentina, for example, highly protective rates appear to have retarded the mechanization of agriculture and the efficient development of certain industries. In Uruguay, the incidence of surcharges is not so great as in Argentina, but the problem of inefficiency exists, as evidenced by the keen competition from the United States and Europe which local industry is facing in spite of relatively high surcharges. Such competition is beneficial to the extent that it forces local producers to become more efficient. The case for lowering surcharges in Argentina may be strengthened by the implementation of LAFTA: regional integration may assist local industries, by widening the market for their products and allowing them to reap the economies of scale, thereby enabling them to withstand foreign competition with an even lower degree of protection.

---

[22] The number of concessions negotiated in 1961 among LAFTA members, however, is smaller than might at first appear. According to one source (*The Review of the River Plate,* CXXXI, April 30, 1962, p. 151), if the Brussels Nomenclature were adopted, the number of items receiving concessions would be reduced from more than 2,500 to roughly 1,400, including a large number of agricultural goods already subject to bilateral agreements. In addition is the fact that a large number of the industrial goods included in the concession lists are not traded at all.

Third, it is desirable to differentiate between the balance of payments and trade objectives of trade policy, and to confine the application of surcharges to the latter. The utilization of surcharges for balance of payments purposes, and hence the frequency of changes in their applicable rates because of changes in the payments situation, can have a disrupting influence on the flow of intraregional trade, particularly now that a free trade area is being implemented. For example, additional temporary surcharges, when imposed by the countries under review, do not apply to intra-LAFTA trade, and this may cause a shift from extra-LAFTA to intra-LAFTA sources of supply, when available. But this shift may also be temporary if, when the additional surcharges are eliminated, importers in these countries find it profitable to resort to their original extra-area sources of supply. Producers in the other LAFTA countries, as well as importers in the countries which apply surcharges, are thus faced with an element of uncertainty arising from the application of a frequently changing policy regarding surcharges on extra-area imports. This uncertainty may be reduced when the separate levies on imports are incorporated into the new tariff schedules currently being worked out.[23]

Advance Deposits on Imports

Advance deposits for some or all imports are presently required in Brazil, Chile, Colombia, Ecuador, Nicaragua, Paraguay, and Uruguay. The essential features of this device are common to all seven countries, i.e., importers are required to deposit in local currency a certain proportion of the cost of the import before the item is imported, and this deposit is released sometime later, usually after the import has arrived. From the point of view of the importer, this amounts to a requirement that some part or all of the bill for imports be paid in advance, and thus it clearly has some inhibiting effect upon imports and the consequent flow of import payments. The extent of this restrictive effect differs widely among countries, depending upon the essential features of the requirements in force. Also, other incidental effects of this device have been widely different in Latin America.

Ecuador may be selected as an example of a country employing advance deposits in a relatively uncomplicated form. Private importers are required to deposit in sucres either 25, 50, or 100 percent (depending upon the item imported) of the c.i.f. value of all imports at the time when the import license is applied for.[24] This deposit is held by the Central Bank until the

---

[23] The disadvantages of instability in trade policy are not, of course, confined to the application of surcharges, but relate to other restrictions as well. In the majority of the countries under consideration, however, surcharges are an important tool in their trade policies.

[24] This applies to all nongovernment imports except those under the Agricultural Surplus Agreement with the United States, which are exempt from advance deposit requirements. Licenses are usually issued freely.

time of customs clearance, when it is released against payment for the goods. This implies that the minimum period during which the deposit is sterilized is equal to the time taken in shipment of the goods, but in practice this period is usually longer. Importers in Ecuador are also required to pay consular fees and import taxes when applying for the import license, thus augmenting the amount that must be put down before the import is shipped.

In Colombia, the advance deposit requirements are essentially similar to those in Ecuador. A nominal advance deposit of 1 percent is required for certain specified imports. Advance deposits on other items range in five categories, from 5 percent to 100 percent,[25] with a special requirement of 500 percent for imports of gold and silver coins. The advance deposit must be paid in local currency at the time that the import is registered; as a rule, it is returned 90 days after the merchandise is cleared through customs or, if the import is received in installments, at the time of the last shipment. However, Colombia's exchange system requires that payment for imports be made through the purchase of exchange certificates; when the advance deposit is to be used for this purpose, it may be released 45 days after customs clearance.

Nicaragua requires an advance deposit of 100 percent of the c.i.f. value of imports on Lists II and III (i.e., all except those in the most essential category), payable at the time of application for the import license and released when payment for the goods is effected. For List III imports (i.e., the least essential category), the import license is not issued until 30 days after the deposit is made. Thus, for List III imports, the deposit usually remains sterilized for the time the goods are in transit plus 30 days, while for List II imports the usual period is equal to the time the goods are in transit. Certain items specified in the Industrial Development Law, government imports, essential imports on List I, and imports from the Central American group which do not appear in the special lists are exempt from the advance deposit requirements.

In Uruguay, an advance deposit of 100 percent is required for only those goods subject to the highest surcharge (150 percent). But exemptions from this requirement were granted to items in the Uruguayan LAFTA concession list. The advance deposit must be made with the Bank of the Republic at the time of registration of the import; it is returned 9 or 12 months later, depending upon the item imported.

In Paraguay, an advance deposit of a flat 100 percent of the f.o.b. value is required for imports of certain specified commodities. As most commodities do not require import licenses, the deposit may be made at any time before the goods arrive in the country. If the deposit is made after the date of shipment, it is returned after a minimum of 180 days; if before, after a min-

---

[25] For the period April 5 to June 30, 1962, these requirements were temporarily raised to range from 20 percent to 200 percent.

imum of 120 days. For certain items imported from Spain through the Spanish free zone in Paraguay, the deposit is held only for 90 days. Imports from Argentina, Bolivia, Brazil, and Uruguay, and imports of items included in the Paraguayan LAFTA concession list, are exempt from the advance deposit requirements.

In Chile, advance deposit requirements were formally re-established on June 18, 1962, the rates being 10, 100, 200, and 1,000 percent of the c.i.f. value of the imports, depending upon their essentiality. Exemptions, however, have been extended to imports from LAFTA countries, imports by the Government and by the large copper, iron, and nitrate organizations, and imports through "free port" zones. The deposits must be made at the time when imports are registered at the Central Bank, and are retained for 90 days.[26] This system replaced the one introduced in January 1962 whereby the prepayment of surcharges on all permitted imports had an effect similar to import deposit requirements.[27]

In Brazil, importers can acquire exchange for the payment of imports only after they close an exchange contract with an authorized bank. Within five days an advance deposit equal to 100 percent of the exchange contract must be paid to the Bank of Brazil. For 30 percent of the deposit, importers receive 150-day Bank of Brazil notes bearing 6 percent interest. Imports originating in countries which are members of LAFTA, as well as a considerable number of specified imports, are exempt from the deposit requirement.

The preceding survey shows that two of the countries under consideration (Brazil and Paraguay) have suspended deposit requirements on a large portion of their Latin American imports. Two others (Chile and Uruguay) have waived this requirement on imports of items that appear on their respective LAFTA concession lists. Furthermore, in all seven countries relatively high advance deposit rates are applied to "nonessential" items and low rates to "essential" items. These considerations suggest, as for surcharges, that the incidence of advance deposit requirements discriminates in favor of intraregional and against extraregional trade. In any event, advance deposits have not proved to be a very effective restrictive device except where very large deposits have been required. In countries where advance deposits are employed in conjunction with a number of other more direct controls over imports, it is difficult to assess the impact of the deposit requirements. In other countries, the effect of the advance deposit depends on the possibilities

[26] They must be made in 5 percent or 7 percent U.S. dollar bonds issued in accordance with Article 7 of Law No. 14171 or Article 79 of Law No. 13305 (see International Monetary Fund, *International Financial News Survey*, Vol. XIV (1962), p. 252).

[27] For a brief period (December 27, 1961 to January 15, 1962), during which all exchange operations were suspended, an advance deposit of 10,000 percent was required for all imports. This amounted virtually to a prohibition of imports.

open to importers of borrowing the amount to be deposited; on the interest rates charged for such borrowings; and on the period of time during which the deposit remains with the authorities.[28] Experience in many Latin American countries has shown that the inhibiting effect upon imports of this device is fairly erratic, and it usually affects the small importers more than the large ones whose credit standing is good.

In several countries, advance deposits were first imposed in an attempt to reduce imports, but have had to be retained because of their monetary effects. When an advance deposit requirement is first imposed, there is usually a withdrawal of liquidity from the economy—provided, of course, that the deposits are sterilized in the central bank.[29] Once the system is fully established, however, there will be no net deflationary effect if imports and the deposit requirements remain constant, because the making of new deposits is matched by the release of old ones. Thus, a number of countries which imposed severe advance deposit requirements in connection with the introduction of new stabilization programs hoped to receive an initial deflationary thrust at the time it was most needed, but they later found that the deposit requirements could not be eliminated without reinjecting liquidity into the economy. Several of the countries which presently impose advance deposit requirements would perhaps eliminate them immediately if it were not for this factor. In Ecuador, for example, where the advance deposit requirements are relatively modest, the total amount of advance deposits held by the Central Bank in March 1962 was about S/ 130 million ($7.2 million at the official rate), or equivalent to 3–4 weeks' total import payments. Release of this amount without compensating measures to absorb the resultant increase in liquidity might seriously affect the monetary situation. In Paraguay, at one time, these funds rose to almost one-third of the money supply.

It must be recognized that part of the reason for the widespread prevalence of advance deposits in Latin America in the past has been that the device may be introduced quickly through administrative processes, and that its balance of payments and monetary effects are somewhat disguised and are not likely to be a subject of popular opposition. However, the declining use of this device at present seems to indicate that experience with it has brought about a growing realization of the disadvantages outlined above.

---

[28] For example, an importer in Ecuador making a 100 percent advance deposit, which will be returned to him in 3 months, may obtain funds at about 10 percent per annum. The cost of borrowing the funds therefore adds 2.5 percent to the final cost of the import, which is far less than the consular fees and import taxes applied to imports in Ecuador. See Eugene A. Birnbaum and Moeen Qureshi, "Advance Deposit Requirements for Imports," *Staff Papers,* Vol. VIII (1960–61), pp. 115–25.

[29] If the importer borrows the sum to make the advance deposit from a bank or other lending institution, the impact on the money supply will be still greater if these institutions do not have excess reserves.

Multiple Currency Practices[30]

Among the Latin American countries, important multiple currency practices are maintained at present by Brazil, Chile, Colombia, Uruguay, and Venezuela, and, to a lesser extent, by Ecuador. In all except Brazil and Uruguay there is a dual market system, including some mixing rates. In Brazil the application of exchange taxes and other practices give rise to several effective rates; and in Uruguay retentions on export proceeds give rise to several effective buying rates.[31]

Where dual markets exist, preferential rates commonly cover essential imports, government transactions, major exports, and registered capital movements, while the free market covers all other transactions. Chile reintroduced a dual exchange system in January 1962; an official rate now applies to imports (on the permitted list), exports, government transactions, and certain invisibles, and a free (brokers') fluctuating rate applies to other transactions.[32] The latter rate covers about 20 percent of all exchange transactions, averaging in the period January–June 1962 roughly 28 percent below the official rate.

Ecuador has fixed exchange rates applicable to most exports, imports and related invisibles, other essential invisibles, official transactions, and registered capital. All other transactions are settled in the free market.[33] The official rates, estimated to cover about 80 percent of all exchange operations, were depreciated in July 1961 after having been maintained unchanged for several years.[34] The free rate has also tended to depreciate, leading to a greater spread between it and the official rates.

Colombia has an "auction" rate applicable to all imports, government payments, students' remittances, and 80 percent of freight payments, and a

---

[30] As defined by the International Monetary Fund, "an effective buying or selling rate which, as a result of official action, e.g., the imposition of an exchange tax, differs from parity by more than one percent, constitutes a multiple currency practice." See International Monetary Fund, *First Annual Report on Exchange Restrictions* (Washington, March 1, 1950), p. 144. Thus, the following countries, where small exchange taxes are imposed or a limited volume of exchange transactions takes place at rates slightly different from the official one, have minor multiple currency practices: Bolivia, Costa Rica, Nicaragua, and Paraguay.

[31] Brazil maintains a free market rate which has tended to fluctuate with a spread—amounting to about 3 percent—between the selling and buying prices. Uruguay also has a fluctuating rate, although the central bank intervenes in the exchange market.

[32] The official buying and selling rates are E° 1.051 and E° 1.053 per U.S. dollar, respectively, compared with an average free rate in January–June 1962 of E° 1.483 per dollars.

[33] Minimum surrender prices for banana exports, which do not coincide with their f.o.b. export price, give rise to mixing rates. In April 1962 the effective rate for banana exports was S/ 18.47 per U.S. dollar, compared with the fixed buying rate of S/ 17.82 and a free rate of S/ 22.09 per U.S. dollar.

[34] The buying and selling rates are S/ 17.82 and S/ 18.18 per U.S. dollar, respectively, compared with the previous official rates of S/ 15.00 and S/ 15.15 per U.S. dollar, respectively.

fixed "certificate" rate applicable to major exports and to the capital trans-actions of the petroleum and metal-extracting industries. All other transactions take place at the free market rate. The two official rates, however, have changed in recent years, tending to depreciate, while the free rate has also depreciated, although not consistently. The exchange rate structure is further complicated by the application of a remittance tax, amounting to 10 percent of the free market rate, on capital registered before June 17, 1957, and by the establishment of minimum surrender prices for coffee and banana exports, all of which give rise to several effective rates.[35]

Venezula has a controlled market rate, and official and unofficial free rates. There are, in addition, special rates which apply to petroleum com-panies.[36] The controlled market rate applies mainly to about 20 percent of imports and to capital and commercial debts already registered with the Cen-tral Bank. The official free rate applies to about 80 percent of import pay-ments, proceeds from minor exports, and a number of invisible and capital transfers. All other transactions are effected through the unofficial free mar-ket. The rates applicable to transactions of the petroleum companies are con-siderably higher than the free rates.

Brazil has a fixed buying rate of Cr$355, and a fixed selling rate of Cr$365, per U.S. dollar. The exchange rate structure was practically unified with the elimination in July 1961 of import preferential rates. The rates then prevailing tended to fluctuate until January 1962 when the decision was made to maintain them at Cr$310 buying, and Cr$318 selling, per U.S. dollar. These rates, however, proved to be relatively appreciated, creating a shortage of exchange for financial remittances, owing to the very low level of reserves. Subsequently, the rates were depreciated to their present level.[37] Important multiple currency rates are created by the taxes levied on the export pro-ceeds of coffee and cacao. Thus, whereas the fixed buying rate is Cr$355 per U.S. dollar, the 15 percent exchange tax on cacao exports results in an effec-tive buying rate for this commodity of Cr$301.75 per U.S. dollar. As for the proceeds from coffee exports, their effective rate depends upon the price and quality of coffee exported.[38] The Bank of Brazil also makes quarterly

[35] To illustrate: at the end of 1961, the "auction" rate averaged Col$6.70 and the free rate Col$8.85 per U.S. dollar, but because of the remittance tax, the effective selling rate for capial registered before June 1957 was Col$7.58 per U.S. dollar.

[36] The scope of the official free market was widened in April 1962. Prior to that date, the controlled rate was applied to the larger portion of transactions, in-cluding essential imports, registered capital, exports of iron ore, government receipts, and certain invisibles. The petroleum rate is now Bs 3.09 per U.S. dollar, compared with an official free rate of Bs 4.54 and a freely fluctuating rate of Bs 4.58 in April 1962.

[37] In May 1962 the rates were depreciated to Cr$350 buying, and Cr$359 selling, per U.S. dollar, and on July 2, 1962 they were further depreciated to Cr$355 buying and Cr$365 selling.

[38] Exporters of coffee must surrender to SUMOC (Superintendency of Money and Credit) through the Bank of Brazil foreign exchange equivalent to $23 per bag of coffee exported.

contracts to sell exchange for imports of wheat, petroleum, and petroleum derivatives at special rates which, under inflationary conditions and with freely fluctuating market rates, tend to be more appreciated than the market selling rate. In addition broken cross rates result from transactions in bilateral currencies.

In Uruguay, a free market was established as a result of the 1959 exchange reform. Since October 1960 the rates in this market have remained stable, being maintained by the central bank at about Ur$11.00 buying, and Ur$11.03 selling, per U.S. dollar. The Exchange Reform Law of December 17, 1959, however, specifies that proceeds from wool exports must be subject to retentions of between 25 percent and 50 percent of their f.o.b. value, while proceeds from other major exports must be subject to retentions of between 5 and 50 percent.[39] These retentions give rise to several effective buying rates. For example, on the basis of a retention on greasy wool of Ur$30.00 per ten bags (effective since December 9, 1960), the effective rate for this export becomes Ur$8.44 per U.S. dollar. Minor exports, on the other hand, receive the full market value rate, to encourage them and to help to diversify the composition of exports.

The importance of multiple currency practices has been greatly reduced in Latin America, as is evidenced by the dwindling number of countries which rely on them to any great extent. One major cause is that the Latin American countries have found that the utilization of multiple rates is, by and large, ineffective, and sometimes undesirable, in attaining the objectives they are supposed to achieve, e.g., balance of payments equilibrium and protection of domestic industries.

The countries other than Brazil and Uruguay which maintain multiple rates do so as part of a more comprehensive exchange control system, and hence the effect that these rates exert is merged in the overall effect of other controls. The elimination of direct restrictions usually (but not necessarily, as illustrated above) results in the abandonment of multiple currency practices. For example, when Argentina and Paraguay unified their exchange markets,[40] this was one step in a comprehensive exchange reform and stabilization program aimed, among other things, at eliminating direct controls. Other countries have had similar experiences. Nevertheless, some observations may be made regarding the specific role of present multiple currency practices in the countries under review.

First of all, it is clear that in Ecuador the significance of multiple rates has been reduced as a result of the reforms which simplified the country's exchange system. The free market is still maintained, to facilitate the movement of unregistered capital and thus to relieve the authorities of pressures upon their international reserves resulting from possible capital outflows. Re-

---

[39] Retentions are portions of exchange proceeds, from the sale of exports, withheld by the Government without compensation.

[40] In 1958 and 1957, respectively.

cently the spread between the two rates has averaged about 18 percent, and to that extent multiple currency practices discriminate against those payments that have to be made in the free market, e.g., certain invisibles and the outflow of unregistered capital.

Chile's reintroduction of multiple rates—as part of its new exchange control system—is an attempt to relieve balance of payments pressures by moving out of the official exchange market the payments for certain imports and invisibles. Preference to specified imports has thereby been granted. The spread between the official and free rates—averaging in January–April 1962 roughly 38 percent—gives those imports which pass through the official market especially favorable treatment. Thus, the effect of the present Chilean multiple rates is not only to conserve the country's international reserves but also to influence the composition of imports and, as a result, the composition of consumption and investment.

Colombia and Venezuela, on the other hand, have made use of multiple currency practices to achieve a variety of objectives. In Venezuela, for example, fiscal revenue is a major consideration. Colombia establishes, for ma-exports, minimum surrender prices which, if higher than their f.o.b. export price, as has been true of coffee exports in the last few years, result in additional foreign exchange for the authorities, i.e., exporters have to purchase foreign exchange in the free market to cover the difference between the two prices.[41] Furthermore, Colombia has attempted to diversify its exports by applying a relatively depreciated rate to proceeds from bananas and other minor exports. Export proceeds from bananas, for example, are subject to minimum surrender prices lower than their f.o.b. export price, which amounts to a depreciated export rate for them, whereas proceeds from other minor exports are subject to rates approximating the free market rate.[42] In practice, however, progress in diversifying exports has been slow. The free market has also provided an outlet for speculative capital movements, relieving pressure exerted upon the authorities on account of capital outflow. In Venezuela, the multiple rate system has been used to subsidize "essential" imports, such as consumer goods and raw materials, by applying to them relatively appreciated rates, while the existence of the free market has served as an outlet for nonapproved capital transactions. But the reform of April 1962, whereby the official and unofficial free rates now cover the bulk of outgoing payments, has greatly reduced the importance of these two functions.

In Brazil and Uruguay, export retentions[43] serve as a means to redistribute revenue: in the former the receipts are earmarked for local industries (coffee, cacao), and in the latter receipts feed the Retention Fund (estab-

---

[41] In January 1962, the coffee export rate was Col$6.345 per U.S. dollar, compared with a fixed certificate rate of Col$6.56 per U.S. dollar.

[42] In January 1962, for example, the effective export rate for bananas was Col$8.12, compared with Col$6.345 per U.S. dollar for coffee exports.

[43] See footnote 39.

lished in 1959). In 1960, for example, export retentions in Uruguay accounted for about 90 percent of this Fund's resources, which were used by the Government to finance various subsidies: milk and public utilities.[44] The use of special rates in the two countries is not intended as a restrictive measure. Uruguay has already freed all exchange operations; and, although it maintains surrender requirements, these mainly serve to enforce export retentions. The Brazilian exchange taxes might have been replaced by export taxes but for the country's constitution, which prevents the Federal Government from levying export taxes. The special rates determined quarterly for wheat and petroleum imports, however, serve to stabilize, on a short-run basis, the prices for these commodities in the face of possible fluctuations in the market exchange rate. Normally, if the market rate is rising, these rates tend to be appreciated relatively to that rate, involving a subsidy to wheat and petroleum.

Present multiple currency practices do not discriminate between countries which are, and countries which are not, in Latin America. Furthermore, their discriminatory effect on categories of imports has not only declined but has become a minor consideration. In a number of countries where a free market exists, the basic aim of the authorities is not necessarily to discriminate against those transactions carried out at the free rate, but to relieve the pressure upon the country's international reserves. The decline in the use of exchange controls has deprived multiple currency practices of much of their former significance.

Quantitative Restrictions: Licensing and Prohibitions

The increase in the number of countries which have established relatively free foreign exchange markets has had, inter alia, the effect of decreasing the importance of trade and exchange licensing in restricting intra-Latin American trade. This trend has been further emphasized by steps taken to simplify the restrictive systems in those countries maintaining exchange controls. Nevertheless, quantitative restrictions constitute an important restrictive device in at least some of the countries presently using exchange controls, which together accounted in 1959–60 for over half of the intraregional trade. The coverage and effects of these restrictions vary greatly from one country to another, as indicated below.

The countries which now maintain quantitative restrictions may be divided into three groups: those which do not maintain exchange restrictions but rely on trade licensing (Mexico and a few others);[45] those which have

[44] The Montevideo transport companies, State Telephone and Electric Power Agency, State Airlines, and State Railways.

[45] Other countries where licensing is applied but where its coverage is limited and its restrictive effect unimportant are Guatemala, Haiti, and Honduras.

not yet unified their exchange markets but have in the last few years simplified their restrictive systems (Brazil, Colombia, Ecuador, and Nicaragua); and those which, after having eliminated exchange restrictions and/or unified their exchange markets, have found it necessary to reintroduce direct controls (Chile, the Dominican Republic, and Venezuela).[46]

Among the countries maintaining free foreign exchange markets, Mexico is the only one where, in addition to tariffs, licensing plays a major role in foreign trade policy. The emphasis on licensing has grown since 1950, and by the late 1950's the number of items subject to permits is estimated to have covered close to one half of Mexican imports (in terms of value). Importers are required to apply to the Ministry of Industry and Trade for prior licenses, the issuance of which is subject to quantitative restrictions. In the first round of LAFTA negotiations, however, exemptions from this requirement were extended to a small number of imports originating within LAFTA. Import controls have also been used to stimulate the export of certain local products: importers of specific products (automobiles, iron and steel pipes, watches, synthetic fibers, etc.) are licensed only if the importer guarantees the export of specified commodities to the same value—a practice that since 1956 has been primarily aimed at fostering cotton exports.

The original purpose of licensing in Mexico was partly the conservation of foreign exchange resources and partly protectionism; but later it was increasingly utilized for the latter purpose. Thus, among the criteria used in licensing have been the availability of domestically produced equivalents and the competitiveness of the proposed imports in the domestic market. This policy of import controls received further emphasis in 1961: a law promulgated on January 2 of that year empowered the Government to take measures affecting the total value of imports and their composition. Moreover, the recent policy of the Ministry of Industry and Trade has been that licenses are granted for imports of certain goods produced, or to be produced, locally only if they are compensated by exports in the same class of commodity; i.e., the licensed importer of a given product is required to export some variant of that import made locally.[47] Import licensing in Mexico is thus clearly an important tool of protectionism;[48] on the whole its restrictiveness, while important, varies in accordance with the degree of encouragement given to local industries and with the balance of payments situation of the country. As the implementation of LAFTA proceeds, the effects of liberalization on the Mexican domestic market will become more tangible. However, their initial influence on the country's domestic industries and its pay-

[46] In 1961, El Salvador reintroduced control temporarily over capital transactions.
[47] See *Noticias*, XVII, No. 43 (October 24, 1961), p. 4.
[48] It is also a flexible tool. Changes in import controls are accomplished by administrative decree, usually without advance notice, and generally become effective upon promulgation.

ments position is not likely to be very important, partly on account of the small portion of foreign trade which is conducted with LAFTA countries.

In the countries maintaining exchange controls all, or the greater portion of, exchange proceeds are channeled to the Government through surrender requirements.[49] The proceeds are then allocated for import and other payments. A large part of imports is subject to varying degrees of restrictive licensing, and in some cases to outright prohibitions or exchange quotas. Ecuador, Nicaragua, and Venezuela have the least restrictive systems. In Ecuador, prior licensing is required for substantially all imports exceeding a value of US$100. But licenses are freely issued, provided that import taxes are paid and advance import deposit requirements fulfilled. Payments for most invisibles made at the official rate require an exchange license from the Central Bank. The exchange system in Ecuador has been greatly simplified by reducing the number of multiple rates, liberalizing imports previously prohibited, and gradually eliminating discriminatory features in trade policy and bilateral agreements. The reform, including a devaluation, in August 1961 should make the country better able to achieve balance of payments equilibrium and eventually to unify the existing dual markets without the necessity of resorting to direct controls.

In Nicaragua, registered importers must apply for import licenses from the Central Bank, which usually issues them only after the advance deposit requirements have been fulfilled; payments for invisibles at the official rate are subject to authorization. Imports from other members of the Central American group are now exempt from quantitative and other restrictions unless they are included in the special lists which cover items to be liberalized within five years. As in Ecuador, the reform of the Nicaraguan system, especially that undertaken in 1959, when differential rates for exports and other multiple currency practices were abolished, has reduced the importance of direct controls. In both Ecuador and Nicaragua, surrender requirements mainly serve to channel the flow of exchange to the official market, while licensing is intended to enforce deposit requirements.

[49] Brazil requires the surrender of all export proceeds either to authorized banks or to the Bank of Brazil. The former are required, in turn, to surrender to the Bank the foreign exchange offered to them for sale. In Chile, large mining companies must pay their income taxes in U.S. dollars; all other export proceeds must be repatriated within 90 days, and, together with certain invisibles, must be sold to authorized banks at the official rate of exchange. Colombia requires the surrender of the proceeds of major exports to the Bank of the Republic at the fixed "certificate" rate; the proceeds from manufactured exports where the import content exceeds 50 percent of the f.o.b. value have similarly to be surrendered. The Dominican Republic requires the surrender of 90 percent of the exchange to authorized banks which, in turn, surrender it to the Central Bank. Ecuador and Nicaragua both require the surrender, at the official rate, of all export proceeds, including most invisibles. In Venezuela, the authorities acquire the larger portion of the country's exchange earnings by applying to exchange sold by the petroleum companies an appreciated (controlled) rate; in addition, the proceeds of exports of iron ore and other noncombustible minerals have to be surrendered at the same rate.

In Venezuela, certain imports are prohibited, those financed at the controlled rate (i.e., essentials) require exchange licenses and in some cases import licenses as well, and many of the imports financed through the official free market require an import license. Since April 1962, the list of essential imports eligible for exchange at the controlled rate has been greatly reduced, from approximately 75 percent of total imports to about 20 percent, so that the official free market rate now covers the larger portion of outgoing payments. Although the Venezuelan exchange and import systems have not been basically altered by the changes of April 1962[50] these changes indicate a move toward a unified market with reduced reliance on quantitative restrictions. Prohibitions and import licensing, however, comprise, with tariffs, an important protective device. Many imports competing with local products, e.g., processed foodstuffs, textiles, and soap, are either prohibited or allowed to enter only if domestic production is considered insufficient.

In Brazil and Colombia, the application of quantitative restrictions has important restrictive effects on trade and payments. In Brazil, imports are divided into two groups: a general category including mainly essential commodities, raw materials, and equipment and a special category including all other imports. Importers of goods included in the special category must obtain a "promise of license" at public auctions held in the stock exchanges of the country, except for items in the Brazilian LAFTA concession list when imported from LAFTA countries. SUMOC (Superintendency of Money and Credit) offers periodically a global value for these imports, and prospective importers bid against each other for the very limited amounts of available "promises of licenses." The holder of a "promise of license" is entitled to import licenses to a value equal to that of the promise. The Bank of Brazil also makes quarterly contracts to sell exchange for imports of wheat, petroleum, and petroleum derivatives, according them special rates. The quantities imported under these arrangements are determined by calculating the difference between estimated domestic demand and estimated domestic production.

Quantitative restrictions in Brazil exert an important influence. Through the special category arrangement outlined above, a substantial degree of restriction applies to imports of manufactured products competing with local production. Protection apart, the purpose of the Brazilian import control is to limit exchange disbursements, in view of the country's low international reserves. In this connection, it should be noted that the Brazilian authorities have maintained appreciated rates of exchange, fearing that more depreciated rates might lead to adverse repercussions. If the rates were at a more realistic level, and unless extraordinary circumstances arose, the authorities might be able to reduce controls over foreign exchange operations, and the country might be able to achieve external stability without such strict import controls. The adoption of such realistic rates is perhaps the more important

[50] See footnote 36.

in view of Brazil's membership in LAFTA: it would strengthen the competitive position of Brazilian manufactured exports, limit the country's import payments, and thus facilitate the country's liberalization efforts within LAFTA.

In Colombia, some imports are freely imported, some are prohibited, and others require prior licensing. Prohibitions and prior licensing have had an important restrictive role, greater reliance being placed on the former than on the latter. A useful indicator of this restrictiveness is the fact that in 1960 a large proportion of the import items were included in the prohibited list, while over half of the permitted imports were subject to prior licensing.[51] The protective aspect of both measures is evident from the prohibition of a number of imports competing with domestic production, e.g., agricultural products, certain textiles, toys, and some consumer durable goods, and in the licensing of others only to the extent that local production is not considered sufficient or that curbs on domestic monopolistic practices by local producers are desired. Reductions in import payments have also aimed at creating a surplus in the balance of payments, in the face of diminishing export (coffee) earnings, in order to service the country's foreign indebtedness. The law authorizes the Government to discriminate against imports from countries with which Colombia has a payments deficit, but in practice licenses have been issued, by and large, on a nondiscriminatory basis. The concessions granted to LAFTA in the first round of negotiations have been confined to exemptions or reductions in import duties.

Chile and the Dominican Republic reintroduced exchange controls in 1962 and 1961, respectively, and at the same time increased quantitative restrictions. In both countries these measures were motivated by balance of payments considerations, though the main causes behind the deteriorating payments situation were different: budgetary deficits, among other factors, in Chile, and the adverse repercussions of political events, including capital flight, in the Dominican Republic.[52] In Chile imports are classified as either prohibited or permitted. Importers of goods in the latter category are not required to obtain a license and are entitled to foreign exchange (at the official rate) which cannot be secured until 90 days after the date of the bill of lading covering the goods. Many other goods, however, considered luxuries or competitive with local production, are now prohibited, unless they are imported through the "free" zones and financed through the brokers' market; exceptionally, automobiles and trucks, if not prohibited, are subject to quotas. The list of prohibited imports was reintroduced in January 1962

---

[51] These restrictions reduced import registrations from a monthly average equivalent to US$52 million in 1955 to US$36 million in 1960. In 1958, import registrations were even lower (US$22 million).

[52] According to one source, capital flight in 1961 reached an estimated $70 million (U.S. Department of Commerce, *International Commerce*, July 23, 1962, p. 38).

and now includes a large proportion of Chilean imports. Reliance on prohibitions had virtually disappeared in 1959, having steadily diminished since 1956, when import licensing was abolished.

The Dominican Republic first introduced licensing in 1960, prior to which there were no controls over trade and payments. In that year, prior licensing was required for all import items whose c.i.f. value exceeded $1,000, and in January 1961 licensing was extended to cover all imports. The criteria for allocating licenses do not seem to be definite or clear, though protectionist as well as payments considerations are taken into account. Each license application is decided upon individually by the authorities concerned. If approved, foreign exchange is provided by the Central Bank which, in any event, must approve all outward payments. The restrictiveness of the import control system is partly indicated by the drop in Dominican imports, as revealed by official figures, from $125 million in 1959 to $90 million in 1960, and $69 million in 1961.[53] But, as in other exchange control countries, the effect of import controls was weakened by contraband trade.

Regulation of Capital Transactions[54]

The main use of regulations pertaining to capital transfers is in the countries maintaining both official and free exchange rates. In addition, the Dominican Republic and El Salvador reintroduced in 1961 control over capital transactions. In other countries, capital transfers are not regulated. Where regulations are applied, registered (approved) foreign investments are usually accorded favorable treatment: repatriation is allowed freely, and investors are exempted from payment of certain duties and taxes. Further, registered investment transactions take place through the official market, in contrast to unregistered investment, which not only has no guarantees but also— in countries where there is a free market—has to be effected through that market. Transfers of domestically owned capital funds are free in a few countries, while in others official authorization is required.

To illustrate: in Chile, which reintroduced capital controls in January 1962, all firms now require permission from the Central Bank to make or receive capital remittances; unlike individuals, they may not deal in the brokers' market without specific approval. Large mining companies may still freely remit interest, dividends, and amortization on invested capital after meeting taxes and local currency requirements. Similarly, foreign investments in approved enterprises can obtain a number of guarantees, as stipulated by Decree Law No. 258 of 1960, such as the right of withdrawal and the nonpayment of certain duties.

[53] In the period February 9–December 31, 1961, 76 percent of licenses applied for were granted.
[54] This section covers mainly regulation of capital representing foreign investments.

Colombia extends transfer guarantees to all capital investments registered before June 17, 1957. Amortization payments and profit remittances in connection with these investments are allowed, but may be made at the depreciated "auction" rate after the payment of a 10 percent remittance tax in dollars purchased in the free market. Capital entering the country after June 17, 1957 is unregistered and must be transferred at the free market rate. Special arrangements—by law and contract—apply to the capital imports and profit remittances of petroleum companies.

Ecuador allows remittances of registered capital, at the official rate, up to a total of 15 percent per annum. Unregistered capital is free to enter and leave through the free market in unlimited quantities. Foreign capital, in the form of exchange, sold by foreign companies to cover local requirements, has to be surrendered at the official rate if such capital is registered. All foreign investment, in the form of capital goods intended for the development of national production, may be exempt from taxes and may be freely re-exported.

Nicaragua maintains control over registered foreign capital invested prior to March 11, 1955: remittances at the official rate are subject to individual approval by the Central Bank and may not exceed 10 percent annually. Foreign investments registered after March 1955 are guaranteed free repatriation and free transfer of earnings at the official rate. Capital transfers by residents through the official market are not permitted.

Early in April 1962, Venezuela increased further the use of the free markets for capital transactions. All capital transactions are now made through the official and unofficial free markets, except foreign capital and debts already registered with the Central Bank; these continue to be effected at the controlled rate. Foreign capital is no longer being registered, and future investors cannot have access to the controlled market.

In the Dominican Republic, capital inflow is free but capital remittances are subject to the approval of the Central Bank. In El Salvador, the entry of capital in the form of foreign investment requires advance approval of, and registration by, the Ministry of Economy. Foreign investments in the form of loans are registered also by the Exchange Control Department. Registration guarantees annual remittances of net profits up to 10 percent of the registered capital, and repatriation of the proceeds from the sale of the assets of the enterprise up to the amount of the registered investment. All new exchange receipts arising out of capital transactions must be surrendered, and all capital remittances require exchange licenses, which are not normally granted to residents.

It is readily seen that approved foreign investments are accorded special treatment in the majority of the countries under review. But domestic capital transfers are subject to restrictions, if not to outright prohibitions, in some of the countries (Chile, the Dominican Republic, El Salvador, and Nicaragua), while in others no restrictions are applied provided the transfer is through the free market. (In Colombia, there is also the provision that a 10 percent remittance tax must be paid.)

The possibilities available to residents of those countries which nominally permit domestic capital transfers need to be examined in the light of existing conditions, since these possibilities may, in fact, be more limited than is suggested by the legal provisions. This applies, for instance, if capital exports take place through a free market and the difference between the official and free rates is significant. In such circumstances, even though the principle of free capital exports remains unimpaired, residents can avail themselves of the privilege only if they are inclined to pay a considerably higher exchange rate.

The inducements extended to foreign capital are in line with similar measures in other parts of the world guaranteeing the repatriation of foreign investments. Capital inflows from outside the region can assist in economic development in Latin America. But encouragement of long-term and short-term intraregional capital movements, which in the past have been of little importance, would be useful. It is of interest that no special privileges are extended to Latin American capital. In fact, the effectiveness of the encouragement extended by certain countries to foreign-owned capital is limited in practice to investors resident in those Latin American countries which have eliminated exchange restrictions, or which apply controls liberally vis-à-vis their residents. In those countries where exchange controls are strictly applied, it is difficult to transfer domestic capital abroad.

Clearly the movement of capital is very much influenced by a variety of economic and noneconomic factors. Capital outflow, which has been important in Latin America, is occasionally motivated, for example, by noneconomic considerations, by fear of depreciation, and by the anticipation of a move by a government to restrict the freedom of current and capital remittances. As indicated previously, the maintenance of a free market in some countries where official and free markets coexist serves to relieve the pressure upon the reserves of the central banks. The cause of this pressure is sometimes an overvalued rate of exchange or reduced export earnings, but often it is uncontrollable capital flight. In the absence of the last, the two markets could have been easily unified in some countries. It is evident that the mere elimination of restrictions on intraregional and extraregional capital transfers is not necessarily useful. In fact, it may be even detrimental unless it is accompanied, among other factors, by an atmosphere of confidence in the economic policy of the government. Now that LAFTA is being implemented, these considerations assume increased importance: the maintenance of monetary stability, along with the elimination of restrictions on capital movements, would encourage the repatriation of capital and would also encourage future intraregional capital movements, all of which would contribute toward building a firmer basis for Latin American economic integration.

EXCHANGE MEASURES IN VENEZUELA*

This paper describes steps taken by the Venezuelan Government to meet the balance of payments crisis which developed from 1958 to 1960. The remedial policies were applied over a lengthy period of time and with considerable variation in the emphasis placed on them, and it was not until early in 1964 that the reform of the exchange system was virtually completed. The results achieved reflected the characteristics of Venezula, particularly the balance of payments advantages and the strong tax base in an economy dominated by the petroleum industry. Nevertheless, the experience of the Venezuelan authorities provides a case study of the complexities and difficulties of exchange control devices and multiple exchange rates. It also illustrates the successful operation of monetary, fiscal, and exchange policies in overcoming balance of payments difficulties. In addition, examination of this experience casts some light on the economic effects of measures taken to control the balance of payments.

Origin of the Payments Difficulties

The extent of Venezuela's balance of payments difficulties is indicated by the decreases in exchange reserves, which were $383 million in 1958, $465 million in 1959, and $309 million in 1960. The main causes of this drain on the reserves were the rapid expansion of domestic credit (beginning in 1958) to finance the budget deficit and a crisis of confidence which reduced investment and other economic activity. The expansion of domestic credit was very large in 1958 and 1959. Most of this increase was due to the use by the Government of its deposits in the Central Bank. These had accumulated in 1956 and 1957 as the bolívar counterpart of the foreign exchange proceeds from the sale of oil concessions. In 1958 and 1959, when these deposits were drawn down to meet government expenses, including large amounts due to foreign contractors for public works projects that had already been completed, there was a substantial decrease of foreign exchange

*W. John R. Woodley, *International Monetary Fund Staff Papers*, November, 1964, pp. 337–364.

reserves. Part of the credit expansion was, however, offset in 1958 by the increased bolívar holdings of the public. In 1959, the government deficit was substantially smaller, and the expansion of bank credit to the Government was not large. Expansion of credit to the private sector continued. However, the liqudity held by the public did not expand, which meant that the expansion of credit was matched almost exactly by a decrease of foreign exchange reserves. In 1960, the decrease of reserves, although smaller than in the two previous years, was still large. A major crisis of confidence forced the commerical banks to contract credit rapidly, and there was a substantial flight from both money and quasi-money.

The Venezuelan economy had grown rapidly during most of the 1950's, being stimulated by an expanding oil sector. Tax revenue from oil permitted the Government to spend steadily increasing amounts. In addition, the Caracas metropolitan area grew because of the development of new industries, many of which were subsidiaries or branch plants of U.S. firms. The balance of payments crisis was marked by a decline in construction activity, with resulting unemployment in the metropolitan area, and by a slowing down, if not a cessation, of net foreign investments in the economy. Visible unemployment increased, mainly because the migration to metropolitan areas continued, although probably at a reduced rate.

In view of the deteriorating domestic developments and the rapid decrease of exchange reserves, the Venezuelan authorities decided late in 1960 that steps had to be taken to correct the situation. The budget deficit appeared to be the root of the problem, and various measures to correct it were examined. On the expenditure side, the decision to repay government debt as it fell due and the high rate of unemployment made substantial economies difficult. For revenues, the tax on petroleum companies had been increased shortly before, and other sources of internal taxation did not appear promising. In this situation, the Government turned to the exchange system. For many years, the Central Bank had purchased—at a rate of Bs 3.09 per U.S. dollar—more than 90 percent of the country's total foreign exchange earnings from the oil companies. This exchange was sold to the commercial banks for resale to the public at a rate of Bs 3.35 per U.S. dollar. Foreign exchange was available freely, as no restrictions were applied to capital or current transactions. The proposal was made by the Ministry of Finance and the Central Bank to have most exchange purchases of the Central Bank continue at the Bs 3.09 rate, but to introduce an exchange tax which would raise the effective Central Bank selling rate from Bs 3.35 to Bs 4.05 per U.S. dollar. The increased revenue from the widening of the exchange spread would be used to finance the government deficit and to permit continuation of the public works schemes. Ultimately, the Government rejected this proposal. As an alternative, the exchange rates were left unchanged, and a system of exchange controls was introduced by decree in November 1960.

INTRODUCTION OF EXCHANGE CONTROLS

The essential feature of the November 1960 decree was that the foreign exchange sold by the Central Bank at the official rate of Bs 3.35 per U.S. dollar was to be allocated on a priority basis. It was to be limited to "normal payments needs," i.e., payments by the Government and autonomous institutions and payments for imports and associated invisibles, technical services, expenses of students abroad, family remittances, current earnings of capital invested in Venezuela before November 8, 1960, and existing commercial debts, together with the servicing and repatriation of foreign capital invested in Venezuela after the decree, if such capital were registered with the Central Bank. The decree also permitted the Central Bank to approve any other payments, but it was expected that capital outflows would not be allowed. The decree made no mention of any exchange rate other than Bs 3.35, but one section provided that capital brought into the country and not registered with the Central Bank could be serviced and repatriated only through a free market.

The Central Bank implemented this decree by granting monthly allocations of exchange to the commercial banks, leaving the banks to distribute the exchange among their customers. The amount of exchange allocated to the commercial banks was based upon estimated exchange receipts. These quotas proved less than adequate to meet the demands on the banks, and the unofficial rationing of available exchange that developed was far from satisfactory in the light of the social priorities of the Government. The excess demand which spilled over into the free market resulted in a rapid decline in the price of the bolívar. The Central Bank intervened in the free market to keep the rate at about Bs 4.25 per U.S. dollar. This intervention, while successful for a few months in mintaining the rate, was finally stopped because of the excessive cost to the exchange reserves. When Central Bank intervention in the free market ended, the rate moved to as high as Bs 4.70 per U.S. dollar.

RELIANCE ON THE "OFFICIAL FREE" MARKET

The continued decrease of foreign exchange reserves, and the deterioration of the exchange rate on the free market, led the Government to revise the exchange system by a decree of March 17, 1961. This provided for the introduction of an "official free" market and transferred to the new market purchases of exchange for about 25 percent of imports and associated invisibles, some capital remittances, immigrant remittances, and travel purposes. Limits on the amounts that could be purchased through this market were imposed by instructing commercial banks not to exceed specified amounts for the several purposes. In order to stabilize the selling rate in this

market at Bs 4.58 per U.S. dollar the Central Bank stood ready to sell unlimited amounts of exchange to the commercial banks at this price minus a
spread of Bs 0.015 per U.S. dollar.

The main exchange payments left at the Bs 3.35 rate by the March
1961 decree were those for essential imports (about three fourths of total
imports), most government transactions, student allowances, registered commercial debts, and servicing of registered capital. In place of the former system of quotas of foreign exchange distributed by the commercial banks, the
exchange control office licensed individually all exchange transactions at the
official rate.

It became evident early in 1962 that this exchange rate structure was
not adequate as a protection against a further drain on exchange reserves.
The drain continued on a small scale in 1961; in addition, the recovery in
the economy which was anticipated for 1962 was expected to involve an increase
in imports. In view of this, a new decree was issued on April 2, 1962, modifying the relative importance of the selling rates. The major change was the
transfer of all but 20 percent of imports and of virtually all capital repatriation and servicing to the "official free" market. As a result of this reclassifi-
cation, the weighted average of the exchange rates for all payments increased
from about Bs 3.7 to about Bs 4.1 per U.S. dollar. A subsequent decree, issued on January 18, 1964, moved all imports to the "official free" market,
but provided that certain essential commodities, amounting to perhaps 10
percent of imports, would benefit from a subsidy of Bs 1.15 per U.S. dollar.

At the same time that the effective exchange rate for imports was de-
preciating, quantitative restrictions were being introduced and used to an increasing extent to provide protection for domestic industry. Significant use
of quantitative restrictions began in mid-1959, when imports of a number
of food products were made subject to licensing. Subsequently, imports of
less essential consumer goods and a variety of locally produced manufactured
goods were restricted. Other forms of incentive to local industry, such as special credit facilities, lease-purchase agreements, and exoneration from import duties, were also used more extensively.

The revisions of the exchange system and the use of quantitative restrictions were accompanied by substantial changes in fiscal policy. The government deficit financed through the banking system was reduced from Bs 297
million in 1960 to Bs 219 million in 1961; and budget surpluses of Bs 333
million in 1962 and about Bs 200 million in 1963 were achieved. Following
the sharp decline in 1960 in bank credit to the private sector, there was a
small increase in 1961 and only moderate expansions in 1962 and 1963.
The Central Bank permitted little use of rediscount facilities. The public's
holdings of liquid assets (money and quasi-money) remained almost constant over the three-year period.

It is difficult to link these changes in monetary and exchange policies
directly to changes in economic activity. In 1962, after two years of stability,

the gross national product rose by about 6 percent, and in 1963 by a smaller amount—probably 3 or 4 percent. The major factors on the demand side accounting for the increases in 1962 were larger exports, an increase in construction (which more than offset a decline in plant and equipment expenditures), and higher personal consumption. Probably the key element accounting for the resumed growth was the expanded output of petroleum. This had direct and indirect effects, the latter being particularly important in financing increased government expenditures on current operations.

PROBLEMS OF ADMINISTERING THE CONTROLS

When the exchange controls were introduced in November 1960, it was expected that they would be used only to limit capital payments. The forecasts of the balance of payments made at that time indicated that foreign exchange was adequate to meet current payments if the loss of capital could be stopped. In the period from November 1960 to March 1961, the technique of granting monthly allocations of exchange to the commercial banks for sale at the Bs 3.35 rate provided no way of determining the extent to which exchange sales by the commercial banks were for legitimate current payments and the extent to which they were for capital transactions. As exchange was short, the banks were under heavy pressure to provide exchange to favored customers. The inadequacy of exchange led the stock market to take the initiative in organizing a market for unofficial exchange transactions. While such a market was unofficial, it was tolerated by the authorities, who shortly began to intervene in it to prevent further depreciation of the bolívar.

After the March 1961 decree, which provided that certain transactions would pass through an "official free" market, the problem for the exchange control authorities was to separate transactions at the Bs 3.35 rate from transactions at the "official free" market rate, which was then about Bs 4.58 per U.S. dollar. No serious attempt was made to restrict capital transactions through the "official free" market. The Central Bank notified the commercial banks that exchange sales for certain purposes, e.g., support to family members living abroad, foreign travel, and capital remittances, were to be limited to specified amounts. The commercial banks were made responsible for assuring that exchange sold for imports was used for legitimate import transactions. The Central Bank, however, did not attempt to enforce these limits, and there was no effective separation of the "official free" market and the free market organized by the stock exchange. The effective exchange rates on the two markets remained virtually the same during the entire period from March 1961 until the end of 1963.

The large difference between the Bs 3.35 rate for some imports and other current transactions and the free market rate of Bs 4.58 provided a strong incentive for attempts to obtain exchange at the Bs 3.35 rate. The major difficulties for the authorities were to prevent overinvoicing of imports and the misrepresentation of other current transactions, to fix current earnings on foreign capital invested in Venezuela, and to define and administer the repayment of existing commercial debts.

With regard to the overinvoicing of imports, the exchange control authorities required the submission of regular commercial documents and obtained price information from abroad to ensure that the commercial documents presented were genuine. Great difficulties were encountered in attempting to make effective checks. For example, pricing practices in the pharmaceutical industry came under close examination. Subsidiaries of U.S. companies represented that their import prices, because they included allowances for research costs and licenses, were substantially higher than prices quoted by suppliers in Czechoslovakia and Italy. When the exchange control authorities offered to license amounts based on the lowest prices quoted abroad, suppliers complained about discrimination against imports from higher-priced markets. Also, the time that the exchange control authorities took to make decisions on these matters resulted in a number of complaints about delays in payments. It is, of course, impossible to assess accurately the effectiveness of the attempts at preventing overvaluation, but the exchange control authorities were never convinced that they were doing an adequate job.

A similar type of problem arose after the decrees of April 1962 and January 1964 with regard to imports transferred from the Bs 3.35 rate to the free market rate. The decrees provided that payment for imports already shipped or ordered could be made at the Bs 3.35 rate, even though payments for new imports would henceforth be made at the free market rate. This failure to use the normal cutoff practice (i.e., specifying that exchange sales after the date of the decree would take place at the free market rate) resulted in considerable confusion and in attempts by importers to obtain exchange at the Bs 3.35 rate for imports arriving in the country some months after the effective date of the decree. This problem was further accentuated by a decree of May 1963, which permitted certain importers of capital equipment to purchase exchange at the Bs 3.35 rate. A government commission was set up which approved sales of exchange for such imports if it was shown that the investment was being planned at the time of the April 1962 exchange decree. These sales not only gave preferential treatment to the importers involved; they also reduced the tax yield from the exchange spread between the Bs 3.09 buying rate and the "official free" market selling rate.

Up to March 1962, remittances of profits on foreign investments were permitted at the official rate, but the exchange control authorities limited such remittances to 12 percent of invested capital. To provide a basis for restricting remittances to the prescribed amount, it was necessary to define invested capital, to distinguish it from commercial debt, and to isolate the "foreign" element. A procedure was set up for registration of foreign capital, and all firms were required to fill out a questionnaire and to provide supporting balance-sheet data. This involved a tremendous problem of documentation and interpretation for the authorities, and it was several months before the capital registry began to show signs of order. The main conceptual problem which arose in the registration procedure was the definition of foreign capital. Foreign companies argued that reinvested profits, which could in fact have been freely remitted abroad in earlier years and then returned to Venezuela, were a legitimate part of invested foreign capital and that remittances of profits on such capital should be permitted. Some of the exchange control authorities believed, however, that foreign capital should consist only of foreign exchange actually remitted to Venezuela, and that the companies should produce records certifying actual exchange transactions before becoming eligible for remittances of profits on invested capital. The difference in definition was particularly important for such companies as public utilities, which were capital intensive and which had a long history of reinvesting current earnings to finance the expansion of facilities. The debate over this issue continued for so long, and the issue proved to be so intractable, that it was one of the factors that led to remittances of profits being transferred to the free market in April 1962. Companies which had not reinvested earnings in Venezuela to any important extent, and which therefore were not involved in the argument about the definition of capital, did manage during this period to remit dividends on earnings up to the prescribed amount.

Associated with the question of the registration and servicing of invested capital was the payment of existing commercial debts. The exchange control decrees of November 1960 and March 1961 provided for the payment at the Bs 3.35 rate of legitimate commercial debts existing at the time of the decrees. When registration of commercial debt was carried out, it became evident that the dividing line between legitimate commercial debt and working capital, particularly of subsidiaries of foreign firms, was not a clear one. Companies which had been financed by parent companies overseas for such things as trade inventories argued that the financing represented ordinary commercial debt and that it should be repaid to the parent concern at the official rate. Similarly, a large number of companies tried to make the case that commercial credit lines normally available to them could no longer be arranged and that payments had to be made more rapidly than before.

Another problem that emerged for the exchange control authorities was that Venezuelan debtors and the commercial banks tended to use the exchange controls as an excuse for not remitting payments. Importers represented to foreign suppliers that exchange was not available or that the exchange control was causing inordinate delays. Some commercial banks also received the bolívar counterpart of foreign exchange from importers but delayed application to the exchange control in order to use the local currency for working capital purposes. Delays in payments caused particular difficulties since, in some cases, the export transactions were insured by the export insurance agencies of the trading partners. When the insurance claims came due, the agencies investigated the reasons for the delays in the payments. This led the exchange control authorities in some instances to urge the prompt payment of commercial arrears.

The difficulties discussed above were important factors in persuading the authorities to shift most transactions to the free exchange market in April 1962. As noted previously (p. 305), payments at the Bs 3.35 rate were then restricted to about 20 percent of total imports, and virtually no repatriation of capital or remittances of servicing of capital were permitted at this rate. This greatly eased the task of the exchange control authorities, but it did not eliminate difficulties arising from the overvaluation of imports. The decree authorized the exchange control authorities to introduce a system of *aforos*—specified values of the imported articles—and to limit issuance of exchange control licenses to the *aforo* values. The introduction of this device was little more than a formal elaboration of the existing practice. The April 1962 decree also resulted in increases in imports of items for which exchange could be purchased at the Bs 3.35 rate, in anticipation that subsequent unification of the exchange rates would involve higher costs for these items. The exchange control authorities made only minimal efforts to curb such imports, in the belief that the best treatment of the problem was to let market forces eliminate excessive importing. This policy was made possible by the strengthening of the balance of payments and the easing of fears of a further exchange crisis. In April 1962, also, the "official free" and parallel free exchange rates moved from Bs 4.58 to Bs 4.54.

While the exchange control authorities had difficulties in controlling the servicing and repatriation of capital at the Bs 3.35 rate up to the time of the April 1962 decree, virtually no impediments were imposed on the export of capital through either of the free markets. Purchases of exchange at the "official free" market required the completion of a form that specified the purpose of the transaction. In practice, very few of these applications were rejected, and even when a particular bank rejected them it was not difficult for the purchaser to find another bank ready to make the sale. In addition, there was the unofficial free market, where transactions took place without any supervision from the exchange control authorities and which was generally regarded as a capital market. The fact that the exchange rates in the two free markets were practically identical throughout the period is solid evidence that there were no effective barriers between the two markets. Thus, the restriction on capital movements was not the exchange licensing imposed by the authorities but rather the existence of the free market rate. The change from Bs 3.35 to Bs 4.5 in the exchange rate for capital transactions had some effect on restraining outflows of capital, both by increasing the cost of exporting capital and by reversing expectations regarding the future course of the rate. More important factors were the wearing off of the first shock of the Cuban crisis, the increasing optimism about the domestic political situation, and the greater degree of monetary stringency resulting from the previous loss of foreign exchange reserves and the stricter fiscal policy.

After the revision of the exchange system in April 1962, the balance of payments situation began to improve, and it was very strong during the initial months of 1963. By the summer of 1963, it was evident that the payments difficulties had been solved, at least temporarily. The Venezuelan authorities still believed, however, that the system of exchange rates was not adequate and that further reform was required. The various exchange rates existing at the end of 1963 are shown in Table 1.

TABLE 1

VENEZUELA: EXCHANGE RATES AT DECEMBER 31, 1963

(in Bolívares per U.S. dollar)

BUYING	SELLING
3,046259 (Petroleum Company Rate) Local currency requirements of petroleum companies in excess of the Central Bank's foreign exchange sales during the given year.	
3.09 (Petroleum Company Rate) Local currency requirements of petroleum companies up to the limits of the Central Bank's foreign exchange sales during the given year.	
3.33 (Controlled Market Rate) Local currency requirements of exporters of iron ore and other non combustible minerals, and exports of coffee and cacao in a proportion depending on world prices.* Some re-exports. Government receipts.	3.35 (Controlled Market Rate) Payments for essential imports and related invisibles. Advanced students' expenses. Essential government payments. Registered capital.
4.525 ("Official Free" Market Rate) Other export receipts, including those earned by some government agencies. Some invisibles. Capital.	4.54 ("Official Free" Market Rate) All other imports and related invisibles. Travel expenses, other students' expenses, family maintenance, etc. Other capital.
4.525 (Free Market Rate)[†] Receipts other than those classified at the Bs 3.33 and petroleum company rates.	4.525 (Free Market Rate)[†] All payments other than those permitted at the controlled market rate.

*Special rates may apply to a proportion of the proceeds of exports of cacao, coffee, and certain processed cacao and coffee products, depending on the world prices for these commodities. These rates result from mixing between the Bs 3.33 controlled market rate and special buying rates of Bs 4.25 and Bs 4.75 per U. S. dollar. Exporters of these items have the alternative of selling their proceeds in the free market.

† There is no spread between the buying and selling rates, but brokers usually charge a commission of Bs 0.02 per U. S. dollar.

DISADVANTAGES OF MULTIPLE EXCHANGE RATES

The exchange reform of January 18, 1964 eliminated most of the multiple currency practices. The principal reason for the reform was to create confidence, both internally and externally, in the bolívar by convincing the public that the rate would remain constant at the newly established level. It was believed that the balance of payments had been brought under control, and that this could be demonstrated by simplifying the exchange rate structure and removing the remaining restrictions on payments through the free market. In addition to this overriding consideration, the existing multiplicity of rates had had a number of undesirable effects.

The foreign-owned oil companies operated substantially free from the exchange regulations. Exchange earnings did not have to be surrendered, and import payments, remittances of profits, and repatriation of capital were not subject to licensing by the authorities. The companies were, however, required to purchase bolívares from the Central Bank at a rate of Bs 3.09 per U.S. dollar in order to meet local costs, consisting mainly of income tax and royalty payments, wages paid to local employees, and the price of goods and services purchased domestically. The petroleum companies, when making local payments, operated on the basis of the Bs 3.09 rate; but they found that the dollars freely available to them were generally valued in the Venezuelan economy at Bs 4.5 per U.S. dollar. Thus, there was a strong economic incentive to avoid bolívar expenditures and to spend as much as possible in foreign exchange.

This effect had originally been of considerable importance in causing the oil companies to import supplies rather than to purchase them from domestic sources. Up to 1959, however, when the differential was only between Bs 3.09 and Bs 3.35, the companies had made deliberate attempts to purchase locally even when imports were cheaper, in order to create good will with the Government and to reduce the need to carry inventories of both imported and domestically produced goods. Since the firms which normally supplied materials to the oil companies frequently had branch plants or local distribution agencies, the problems of maintaining inventories and regular supplies could be shifted from the oil companies to these suppliers by the practice of purchasing within Venezuela. When the exchange rate differential increased to 48 percent, this policy of buying domestically became much more expensive. The problems were most acute in respect of purchases from local distributors of foreign-owned companies and from U.S. subsidiaries engaged in production in Venezuela. For example, the oil companies could purchase trucks in the United States with U.S. dollars valued at Bs 3.09, but the purchase of the same vehicle from the local distributor in bolívares had to be paid for at prices which included the distributor's markup on a landed cost valued at

Bs 4.5 per U.S. dollar. If, however, the oil companies shifted all purchases abroad and endangered local production facilities and employment, the Government might respond with quantitative restrictions on imports to protect the local producer. Moreover, if the companies imported products directly, the supplying firms might well go out of business, thus complicating the situation if the exchange rate for the oil companies should subsequently be moved to a level that encouraged local purchases with the advantages of inventory-maintenance by distributors. A similar type of issue arose for the oil companies with regard to paying for service contracts (e.g., for business machines, accounting services, and drilling and exploration work) in bolívares acquired at the Bs 3.09 rate, when the foreign-owned companies providing the services would accept payment abroad in U.S. dollars at an implicit rate of Bs 4.5.

The distorting effects of the Bs 3.09 rate for all local purchases by the oil companies became critical for the Government when the iron and steel mill, a state entity, began in 1962 to produce steel pipe which was satisfactory for use by the oil companies. The steel mill quoted prices for its steel pipe in bolívares and in U.S. dollars which were equivalent at the Bs 4.5 exchange rate. The dollar price for this pipe was about equal to the cost of the imported pipe. The companies found, however, that the bolívar price, which they had to pay with bolívares obtained at the Bs 3.09 rate, was not competitive with the dollar price for the imported product. In these circumstances the Government agreed that the normal rules should not apply, and that sales by the steel mill to the oil companies could be regarded as exports by the former and imports by the latter, payable in U.S. dollars.

The Bs 3.09 rate also created difficulties when the oil companies broadened their product lines by importing plastics, synthetic rubber, fertilizers, and insecticides from their overseas affiliates. Since the companies valued their dollars at Bs 3.09, imports were sold at a price reflecting this exchange rate. Other importers of these products, however, had to pay the free market exchange rate of Bs 4.5, and thus their bolívar prices were substantially above those quoted by the oil companies. In effect, the difference in the exchange rate meant that only the oil companies could sell the products involved, and that the source of supply was determined by the location of the oil companies' affiliates. This prompted complaints from some governments of discrimination against their exports.

Another difficulty faced by the oil companies was that their employees receiving dollar salaries could benefit substantially by evading the requirement that they meet their local living expenses by converting their dollar salaries at the rate of Bs 3.33 per U.S. dollar. Supervision by the companies of expenditures by their employees to ensure that reasonable amounts of exchange were being converted at the Bs 3.33 rate was a difficult task, and was undoubtedly uneven among the various companies. The technique used was to record the amount of exchange converted by each employee monthly, and to check these amounts against a scale of reasonable costs of living. Various exceptions were provided, to take account of such things as the liquidation of capital assets by employees and incomes earned by other family members.

Another problem which was of long-run concern was that the Corporación Venezuelan de Petróleo (CVP), a state-owned corporation, was gradually entering into the production and distribution of petroleum. To the extent that this company was able to export and produce dollar revenues in excess of its import needs, the Bs 3.09 rate handicapped its expansion. Moreover, sales of crude oil from the state-owned company to the foreign-owned companies encountered the difficulties that the latter were bound to pay in bolívares, which cost them Bs 3.09 per U.S. dollar, while prices in such contracts were traditionally set in U.S. dollars. The same problem arose when the state-owned company wanted to enter into service contracts with the foreign companies. Nevertheless, it was difficult for the Government to provide one exchange rate for the nationalized company and another less favorable rate for the foreign-owned companies. While the operations of the CVP were small at this time, the Government's policy was to encourage its growth. The Government had the alternative of contributing larger amounts to the capitalization of the company, but this was regarded as less satisfactory than having the company finance a good part of its growth with self-generated funds.

In addition to creating distortions in the oil companies' operations, the exchange system caused problems because some payments were made at the Bs 3.35 rate. Controlled market exchange was made available for the following: (1) essential payments by the Government, its entities, and autonomous institutions, except for imports not included in the list of controlled market imports; (2) the f.o.b. value, port of embarkation, of essential imports as listed in decrees issued by the Minister of Finance; (3) payments of commercial and some other debts of a similar nature registered with the exchange control authorities by May 5, 1961; (4) payments for imports which were transferred to the free market by the decree of April 2, 1962, but which had entered the country by that date or were shipped prior to April 13, 1962; (5) amortization and servicing of foreign debts incurred and registered with the Central Bank between March 19, 1961 and April 2, 1962; (6) remittances of up to $250 a month to students abroad (postgraduate students, up to $350 a month); and (7) payments for freight and insurance within specified limits on essential imports.

The major reason for specifying that payments for some commodities would be made at this rate was the desire to give preferential treatment to certain payments. The most important of these from the Government's point of view were payments for imports of a few foodstuffs, pharmaceuticals, industrial chemicals, and agricultural supplies and machinery. At the time of

the April 1962 decree, when about 60 percent of total imports were transferred from the Bs 3.35 rate to the "official free" market, the Government
calculated carefully the possible impact on the price level and estimated that
it would not amount to more than 3–4 percent. At that time it argued that
the major items important in the cost of living, particularly wheat, flour, and
pharmaceuticals, were not affected by the decree. However, the use of the
Bs 3.35 rate for these transactions handicapped domestic production, particularly of foodstuffs. Production of agricultural products for the metropolitan
market, such as fruits, vegetables, eggs, and poultry, had been rising rapidly,
and a number of U.S. pharmaceutical companies had established branch
plants, but there was little chance that Venezuelan production would be able
to compete with imports at the Bs 3.35 rate. An additional problem created
by the classification of payments at this rate was that, to avoid domestic
currency losses on exchange operations, the Central Bank had to be able to
purchase exchange at Bs 3.35 or less. When plans were made to give the oil
companies a more favorable buying rate, either imports had to be shifted
from the Bs 3.35 rate or special funds had to be found to finance exchange
sales at this rate.

Another unsatisfactory aspect of the exchange rate structure was the
existence of two free exchange markets. The "official free" market was separated from the other free market by restrictions on the amounts that commercial banks could sell for certain purposes; however, these restrictions were
not enforced, and in practice funds moved back and forth between the two
markets quite freely. This arrangement involved few practical difficulties apart
from the duplication of facilities, but it placed the Central Bank in the position of having in existence exchange controls which were not enforced and
which were probably unenforceable. Another objectionable feature of these
arrangements was that certain exchange transactions were forced outside of
normal banking channels to the stock market.

The Revision of January 1964

The various difficulties in connection with the exchange system, which are
outlined above, resulted in the introduction of new measures on January 18,
1964. The most important part of this decree was that the exchange rate for
Central Bank purchases of foreign exchange from the oil companies was adjusted from Bs 3.09 (Bs 3.04 in certain circumstances) to Bs 4.40, and for
purchases from exporters of iron ore, from Bs 3.33 to Bs 4.40. This adjustment involved hard decisions—first, concerning an appropriate level of the
exchange rate and, second, concerning the tax treatment of oil and iron ore
companies. These issues are discussed at length below. The decree also involved (1) a special subsidy exchange rate for coffee and cacao, (2) the

transfer of a number of imports from the Bs 3.35 rate to a rate of Bs 4.50, (3) certain adjustments in the arrangements for making the import rate of Bs 4.50 effective, and (4) special arrangements to subsidize basic imports.

Up to the time of this decree, exporters of coffee and cacao were eligible for special subsidy arrangements, but these arrangements had little practical effect because external prices of these products had risen in the period since the legislation was originally passed. The new decree revised the subsidy and provided new arrangements designed to prevent the return in bolívares to exporters from falling below specified amounts. The support scheme called for the Central Bank to purchase exchange from the exporters at Bs 4.485 per U.S. dollar, and to pay a subsidy equal to the amount necessary to bring the local value of the export proceeds up to the minimum support prices. For coffee, the minimum prices for each bag of 46 kilos were as follows: washed fine coffee, Bs 148; standard washed coffee, Bs 138; good washed coffee, Bs 128; natural good coffee, Bs 117; and current natural coffee, Bs 111. At the time of the decree, coffee prices in New York, adjusted to an f.o.b. Venezuela basis and converted at the Central Bank buying rate of Bs 4.485 per U.S. dollar, were washed fine coffee, Bs 193; standard washed coffee, Bs 184; good washed coffee, Bs 157; natural good coffee, Bs 148; and current natural coffee, Bs 139. A comparison of these prices indicates that the New York prices would have had to fall about 20 percent before the price support scheme would come into effect.

The situation in regard to cacao was considerably different. The support prices were as follows: for extra fine cacao, Bs 145; for first-grade fermented cacao, Bs 133: and for second-grade current cacao, Bs 121. The New York prices at about the time of the decree, adjusted to an f.o.b. Venezuelan port basis and converted at the rate of Bs 4.485, were extra fine cacao, Bs 224; first-grade fermented cacao, Bs 99; and second-grade current cacao, Bs 94. Thus, on the basis of the export prices prevailing at the time of the decree, the Central Bank would have been required to pay a subsidy of about one third on all exchange proceeds derived from exports of first-grade fermented cacao and second-grade current cacao. Exports of these two grades amounted in 1962 to less than $9 million.

Commercial banks were permitted to purchase foreign exchange from sources other than the Central Bank, i.e., from minor exports, current invisibles, and importers of capital, at the exchange rate set by market forces (about Bs 4.48 in the first days of the decree).

Prior to the new decree, about 15 percent of Central Bank sales were being made at the Bs 3.35 rate. The new decree made government payments, including debt service, subject to a rate of Bs 4.485, which applied also to Central Bank sales of exchange to commercial banks. In addition, a number of imports were transferred to the Bs 4.5 rate. It was estimated that the increased bolívar costs of budget expenditures would add about 4 percent to ordinary budget expenditures. The imports and invisibles transferred from the Bs 3.35 rate amounted to about 5 percent of total imports.

As explained above, prior to the decree there had been an "official free" market and a parallel free exchange market; in each market, the selling rate was Bs 4.54 per U.S. dollar. The new decree abolished all restrictions on commercial bank sales at the Bs 4.5 rate. This rate was to be made effective by permitting the Central Bank to sell unlimited amounts of exchange to commercial banks at the rate of Bs 4.485 per U.S. dollar and requiring the commercial banks to sell such exchange at Bs 4.5. It was expected that, as a result of the abolition of restrictions on payments through the "official free" market, the commercial banks would be able to obtain a dominant role in the sale of foreign exchange, and that the free market organized by the stock exchange would disappear. In the first few weeks after the exchange decree, the volume of transactions on the stock exchange fell sharply, and it appeared likely that this market would, at a minimum, become much less important.

The new decree provided for the subsidization of imports by permitting importers of certain products to obtain a rebate of Bs 1.15 per U.S. dollar on foreign exchange used to pay for the products. The most important of these products, together with the value of their imports in 1962, were milk powder, $37 million; wheat, $23 million; tinplate, $15 million; natural and synthetic rubber, $8 million; wood pulp, $7 million; small tractors for agriculture, $5 million; and penicillin, $4 million. In addition, some other pharmaceuticals, beans, fish meal, peanut oil, certain fungicides and insecticides, water pumps, and agricultural sprays were made eligible for subsidy. On the basis of 1961 and 1962 trade data, it appeared likely that these imports would amount to about 10 percent of total imports, apart from those by the oil companies. The decree provided that exchange licenses had to be obtained for these products prior to their shipment to Venezuela; but the intention of the authorities was to use the licenses only for preventing overvaluation of imports, since any attempt to restrict the supply would result in frustrating the price-maintenance purpose of the provision.

The items selected for subsidy reflected a variety of interests. Such products as milk, wheat, and pharmaceuticals were left at the Bs 3.35 rate to avoid an impact on the most sensitive cost of living items. Rubber and tinplate were left at this rate because they were components of products manufactured domestically and sold at controlled prices. In addition, a deliberate attempt was made to prevent any discouragement to agriculture by avoiding price increases for a variety of materials and equipment.

The provision of exchange for these imports at an effective rate of Bs 3.35 meant a cost to the Central Bank estimated at about Bs 150 million a a year. To finance this, the Central Bank had available the proceeds from the differential between its buying rate of Bs 4.40 and its selling rate to the commercial banks of Bs 4.485, which was expected to produce about Bs

80–90 million a year. The rest of the cost was uncovered, however, and its financing by the Central Bank would involve credit expansion of an equivalent amount. The Central Bank planned at the time of the decree to meet the bookkeeping problems involved in the financing by gradually revaluing the foreign exchange assets carried on its balance sheet at an exchange rate of about Bs 3.09 per U.S. dollar. Since the reserves were in excess of $700 million, the profit on this revaluation would provide financing for a number of years.

THE LEVEL OF THE RATE

The decree of January 18, 1964 provided for only a minimal adjustment of the exchange rate for most foreign payments, i.e., from Bs 4.54 to Bs 4.5 per U.S. dollar. The decision to establish the exchange rate at this level had been reached during several months of discussion, and it involved a number of considerations. The more general issues, particularly those related to imports, are reviewed here; those pertaining to petroleum are discussed in the next section.

The balance of payments record of Venezuela indicated that the exchange rate should be in the range from Bs 4.0 to Bs 4.5 per U.S. dollar. However, the choice within this range was difficult, and, as is typical of most exchange rate decisions, any precise rate was hard to justify. However, the range between Bs 4.0 and Bs 4.5 was large enough for meaningful discussions of the different effects of the two extremes to be possible.

The development of the balance of payments during 1962 and 1963 suggested that an exchange rate of Bs 4.0 might be appropriate. During these two years there was a considerable accumulation of foreign exchange reserves, even though the average selling rate for Central Bank exchange was between Bs 3.9 and Bs 4.1 per U.S. dollar. Reserves at the end of 1963 were equal to more than seven months of imports. They appeared to be more than sufficient by any of the usual tests of the adequacy of exchange reserves, and they permitted considerable leeway in meeting foreseeable balance of payments contingencies. In view of the development needs of the economy, there seemed little merit in a further accumulation of reserves, involving the diversion of resources from development to precautionary purposes.

Another consideration that had to be taken into account in setting the exchange rate was the significance that should be attributed to the current account surplus, per se. The traditional theory is that the current account position is what is relevant to the exchange rate, and certainly it would seem unusual in a developing country to set an exchange rate with the intention of trying to create or continue a sizable current account surplus.

Although the balance of payments in 1962 and 1963 was strong, there were good reasons for doubting that this strength could be regarded as normal. Imports had fallen by 26 percent from 1959 to 1960 and by a further 10 percent from 1960 to 1961. In 1962 and 1963, they remained relatively stable at the 1961 level despite a growth in gross national product of nearly 6 percent in the former year and of 3–4 percent in the latter. Nevertheless, it appeared that, as production continued to rise and as the capacity in existing plants was more fully utilized, imports could be expected to be more responsive to increases in domestic activity. This was particularly true in view of the fact that the major decline in imports was concentrated in investment goods. It seemed likely that the development needs of the economy and the lack of domestic sources of supply for the more sophisticated capital goods would lead to increases in imports for investment purposes.

At the same time that imports had been depressed, exchange receipts from the petroleum industry had been exceptionally large. Placing the income tax on a pay-as-you-go basis in 1961 produced an extra year's income tax receipts, which were spread over 1961, 1962, and 1963. Exchange receipts also benefited from the exceptionally large rise in oil exports from 1961 to 1962. The increase, which amounted to almost 10 percent, was substantially in excess of the growth in the world demand for petroleum in that year. While Venezuelan output might be expected to expand proportionately to the rise in total world demand for petroleum products, it could not be hoped that the relative size of the increase from 1961 to 1962 would be repeated. The increase in output during 1963 was considerably smaller than the rise in world demand, suggesting that the extraordinary increase from 1961 to 1962 was having an impact on the oil companies' decisions on allocating production among various fields. The view of the Venezuelan Government, expressed in conferences of the Organization of Petroleum Exporting Countries, that growth in output should be restrained in the interests of obtaining maximum prices for petroleum, also suggests a conservative bias in balance of payments forecasts.

Another factor which suggested that the balance of payments was abnormally strong in 1962 and 1963 was the deflationary impact of the large budget surpluses. In part, these surpluses were due to extraordinary income tax receipts, which were not likely to be repeated. Moreover, budget expenditures seemed likely to expand, both to meet social needs and to finance capital investment in infrastructure and industry. The main curb on development expenditures in 1962 and 1963 appeared to be imposed by administrative difficulties. It seemed reasonable to expect that development planning would improve and that projects acceptable to all parts of the Government would begin to be agreed more rapidly. The financial conservatism that stimulated budgetary surpluses in order to repay government debt, especially that owed abroad, also appeared likely to be less dominant as the foreign debt burden was reduced to minimal amounts.

Assessment of an appropriate rate was also complicated by the fact that the nature of the capital outflow from Venezuela was not clear. The balance of payments statistics for 1960 contained a large item for "errors and omissions," with the comment that this might be substantially of a capital nature, while the statistics for 1961 and 1962 showed large outflows of capital. Immigrants' remittances were undoubtedly an important part of the total, and there can be no doubt that any increase in the assets of Venezuelans in the upper income groups or of the sizable immigrant population was used in part to increase dollar balances abroad. In these circumstances, it appeared only reasonable for the exchange rate to be set on the basis of financing a considerable outflow of funds, whether these funds were, in fact, "errors and omissions" on current account items, immigrants' remittances, or normal transfers of assets abroad by Venezuelan residents. Experience with attempts to enforce capital controls from 1961 to 1963 indicated that direct restrictions were not likely to stop the payments involved.

In view of the factors outlined above, the Government concluded that the strength in the balance of payments was exceptional during 1962 and 1963, and that an exchange rate of Bs 4.4 or Bs 4.5 per U.S. dollar would not be more than adequate to meet the foreign exchange needs of the economy. It seems probable that this decision was conservative and that some margin for expansion in the economy was provided. The Government was anxious, however, to ensure that there would be no early resumption of exchange rate instability.

In addition to balance of payments considerations, a number of factors associated with the development policies of the Government were taken into account in establishing the exchange rate. The decree of March 1961 provided that all exports other than petroleum and iron ore were to receive the benefit of converting exchange proceeds at the free market rate. This very substantial improvement in the exchange rate for exporters—from Bs 3.33 per U.S. dollar to Bs 4.52—opened up some possibility of exporting manufactured products, and in the subsequent two years there were some small exports of manufactured products. The development plan called for substantial investments in other industries using Venezuelan natural resources, such as a steel mill, a fertilizer plant, a petrochemical complex, and an aluminum industry. It was hoped that, with an exchange rate near Bs 4.5, exports of these products would be possible. Exports of iron ore had been decreasing sharply for a number of years. Although the exchange rate was only of limited significance in the total operations of the iron ore companies, a substantial adjustment of the rate was expected to stimulate increased production from resources situated in Venezuela. As far as the oil industry was concerned, it was assumed that the exchange rate had little real effect on output or on the volume of sales abroad, since its effect was limited mainly to local costs of operations, which were not a large proportion of the total. Nevertheless, simplification of the exchange arrangements could not fail to be a favorable factor in influencing oil companies' decisions about investments in Venezuela.

No recent systematic data are available to permit comparisons of actual prices in Venezuela and abroad. Casual comparisons, as well as the experience of U.S. firms in Venezuela, indicate that prices in Venezuela, even converted at the Bs 4.5 rate, are close to those prevailing in the United States. The high degree of protection for industry and agriculture provided by the Venezuelan authorities in the form of quantitative restrictions, tax incentives, special credits, and tariff exonerations also suggest that Venezuelan costs were clearly out of line with those abroad as long as the exchange rate was Bs 3.35. The need to align Venezuelan prices with those prevailing abroad was rendered particularly important by the consideration being given by the Venezuelan authorities to entry into the Latin American Free Trade Association.

The Venezuelan authorities also placed some emphasis on the need for a rate of Bs 4.5 in order to reduce the pressure for quantitative restrictions. The policy with regard to those restrictions was formulated and implemented chiefly by the Ministry of Commerce and Industry, and was designed to encourage domestic production and to solve the unemployment problem, especially in Caracas. As industries began to develop behind the protection, the effects of those measures, particularly on prices, began to become evident. Most of the new industries were confined to the assembly of imported components, so that little foreign exchange was conserved. Prices, however, were marked up substantially, and the Government found difficulty in devising some technique for limiting profit margins in industries protected by the quantitative restrictions. The Government worked out informal price agreements with a number of firms, and the income tax successfully recaptured a substantial amount of the profits earned by those firms. Nevertheless, by the end of 1963 there was a growing concern that the protection granted had been excessive, and some means were being sought to reduce it.

Another factor influencing the choice of the Bs 4.5 rate was that it was close to the rate in the free market, and most of the economy had already adjusted to it. There was a general belief that the exchange rate system had been modified too frequently from 1960 to 1963, and that there were positive virtues in making any further modifications as small as possible. The selection of the rate of Bs 4.5 instead of Bs 4.0 meant that importers, domestic producers, and exporters did not have to make another adjustment to a change in the rate, and that the serious strains always involved in moving to a lower price level could be avoided.

CONSIDERATIONS REGARDING THE PETROLEUM INDUSTRY

As noted previously, petroleum exports have long played a dominant role in the balance of payments of Venezuela, accounting for more than 90 percent of export earnings. The operations of the oil companies also have important direct and indirect effects on employment and business activity. More than half of government tax receipts come from income taxes and royalties paid by the oil companies. Moreover, the exchange spread between the Bs 3.09 rate for purchases of exchange from the oil companies and the Central Bank selling rate produced in 1963 an exchange profit which amounted to about 15 percent of total tax revenues. Consequently, the possible effects of a change in the exchange rate for the oil industry were assessed very carefully by the Government. As part of his annual report for 1961, the Minister of Finance published a review of the possible impact of such a change, and the Ministers of Finance and of Mines and Hydrocarbons, together with the Central Bank, reviewed these studies during 1962 and again at the end of 1963. In the preparation of these studies, the companies were asked for data on their earnings and costs divided between their dollar and bolívar components. From these data, estimates could be made of the effects of a change in the exchange rate.

A number of points became evident as these studies progressed. First, a large number of companies were involved, and they varied considerably in size and type of operation. Since it was difficult and time consuming to obtain a division of company operations between dollar and bolívar expenditures, the most practical course appeared to be to concentrate on a few of the larger companies and to inflate the data to arrive at estimates for the industry as a whole. On the other hand, the position of the individual oil companies varied quite widely with regard to such procedures as local refining and marketing, the importance of exploration, and the size of capital budgets. This meant that the effect of a change in the exchange rate would vary for the different companies. Second, the year selected as the base for the study made some difference; therefore the results would be of only limited use for predictions, especially if it were assumed that a change in the exchange rate would itself have effects on the operating practices and investment policies of the companies. Third, the issues involved were complex, thus making difficult the public relations aspect of the politically sensitive question of relations with large foreign companies. Fourth, the effect of changing the exchange rate might well be offset or substantially modified by major changes in the international market for petroleum or by decisions by the international companies operating in Venezuela to alter the relative emphasis they put on various sources of supply.

The main questions for which answers were sought were the impact of a change in the exchange rate on the balance of payments, on the budgetary receipts of the Government, and on the net earnings of the oil companies. Table 2, which is based on the two largest oil companies' financial records for 1963, inflated to provide an indication of the oil sector as a whole, provides tentative answers to these questions. Columns (1) and (2) show the effects of the Bs 3.09 rate and the Bs 4.40 rate on the data expressed in dollars, while columns (3) and (4) show the same receipt and expenditure items expressed in bolívares at the two exchange rates.

The revenues from petroleum exports remain the same in dollar terms;

TABLE 2

VENEZUELA: EFFECTS ON THE OIL COMPANIES OF THE CHANGE IN THE

CENTRAL BANK'S BUYING RATE FROM Bs 3.09 - US $1 TO Bs 4.40 - US $1

	Million Dollars		Million Bolivares	
	Bs 3.09 = US $1 (1)	Bs 4.40 = US $1 (2)	Bs 3.09 = US $1 (3)	Bs 4.40 = US $1 (4)
Income				
Export sales	2,405	2,405	7,430	10,582
Local sales	157	110	486	486
Total	2,562	2,515	7,916	11,068
Costs				
Royalties	545	545	1,683	2,398
Other indirect taxes	9	6	28	28
Bolivar salaries	259	182	801	801
Dollar salaries	48	48	149	211
Other bolivar costs	126	89	390	390
Other dollar costs	245	245	757	1,078
Depreciation	306	306	944	944
Total	1,538	1,421	4,752	5,850
Gross Earnings				
Income tax	476	557	1,471	2,452
Net earnings	548	537	1,693	2,766
Total	1,024	1,094	3,164	5,218
Capital Investment				
Bolivar salaries	13	9	41	41
Dollar salaries	4	4	14	18
Other bolivar costs	61	42	187	187
Other dollar costs	75	75	232	330
Total	153	130	474	576
Dollar Sales to Central Bank	1,332	1,320	4,115	5,811
Tax Receipts by Government	1,030	1,109	3,182	4,878

Source: Derived by Mr. Gustavo Escobar, of the Ministry of Mines and Hydrocarbons, Venezuela, from tables prepared by the two largest oil companies.

thus, as a result of the exchange rate change, they increase by about 40 percent in bolívar terms. In the table, however, it is assumed that prices of petroleum products for the domestic market remain unchanged and that total sales remain constant in bolívares. Consequently, the dollar equivalent of these sales declines by about 30 percent. Since local sales are responsible for only about 6 percent of the companies' total proceeds, the companies could absorb substantially reduced profit margins on these sales without serious consequences for their overall financial position. Nevertheless, the petroleum companies, if free to establish prices without being influenced by the Government's attitude, would presumably increase the local price of petroleum products to take account of the lower value of bolívar earnings and the higher bolívar counterpart of costs incurred in dollars.

Among costs, royalties accrue to the Venezuelan Government in the form of barrels of petroleum valued at Gulf Coast posted prices and converted into bolívares at the rate applicable to the oil companies. In the table, these are shown as remaining constant in dollar terms and as rising by more than 40 percent in bolívares. The same assumption is made for dollar salaries and for other dollar costs. After the exchange rate adjustment, most of the companies reduced dollar salaries on the ground that the equivalence between dollar and bolívar salaries (the former for foreign and the latter for local employees) could be maintained only if dollar salaries were reduced to compensate for the larger number of bolívares that could be purchased with the dollars after the exchange rate change. Salaries were reduced, however, by less than 10 percent, because the companies applied the adjustment to only that proportion of salaries spent domestically, and they also provided an allowance for the higher income taxes arising because dollar salaries being converted into bolívares at the new rate were subject to higher marginal rates of taxation.

The costs shown in the table which are expected to remain constant in bolívar terms, and thus to fall by about 30 percent in dollars, are indirect taxes, bolívar salaries, and other bolívar costs. Most of the indirect taxes are taxes on imports which are specific taxes fixed in bolívar terms. Bolívar salaries for local employees are not expected to change because of a three-year labor contract agreed in mid-1963, and of the maintenance of equivalence between bolívar and dollar salaries by the reduction of the latter. It is assumed that the domestic price level would not change significantly as a result of the exchange rate adjustment, and therefore that the cost of items purchased in bolívares would remain constant. No attempt is made to adjust these items to take account of the probability that the oil companies would purchase more in bolívares and less in dollars as a result of the adjustment in the exchange rate. Even if substantial allowance is made for this type of substitution, the final results of the calculation are not modified greatly.

Depreciation allowances, which include depletion and the charging off of concession costs, are shown separately and are adjusted differently from the other cost items in the table. Depreciation allowances in Venezuela are calculated on the basis of historical costs, and at least the larger companies keep separate records in dollars and in bolívares, the exchange rate being the one in existence at the time the investment was made. For the purpose of calculating the earnings of the companies included in the table, it is assumed that depreciation remains constant in dollar terms. The depreciation allowances shown in bolívares are those accepted for income tax purposes by the Venezuelan tax authorities; as these are based on historical costs, they are not adjusted for the exchange rate change. Since the depreciation allowances remain constant in dollars and in bolívares, the implicit exchange rate between the two has obviously not been adjusted to the new level.

The gross earnings of the companies are shown as the difference between costs and total income. Since the income tax is graduated and a number of the smaller companies were being taxed at less than the maximum rates, the higher revenue figures in bolívares resulting from the exchange rate change produce a slightly higher effective tax rate. The income tax estimate in the table is made on the basis of the bolívar figures, and the resulting tax is converted into dollars at the Bs 4.4 rate. (If the tax rate is applied to gross earnings as shown in the dollar column, the results are not the same because the depreciation allowances shown in dollars are considerably higher at the Bs 4.4 rate than the depreciation allowances permitted for tax purposes.) Net earnings in dollars as well as cash flow (defined here as net earnings plus depreciation) are expected to remain virtually constant. Net earnings in bolívares rise about 63 percent, but cash flow, if calculated in bolívares and then converted at the two exchange rates, remains about constant.

Capital investment is also shown in the table in order to obtain some idea of the impact of all activities carried out by the oil companies. No change in the investment level is assumed, the table showing constant amounts of either dollar or bolívar expenditures, as the case may be, before and after the change in the exchange rate.

The final line of the table shows the tax payments made by the companies to the Government. (Taxes paid personally by employees are not included.) The increase of almost $80 million (about 7 percent) is due to the increase in income tax payments, resulting partly from the smaller companies being subject to higher marginal tax rates and partly from the fact that the value for tax purposes of depreciation allowances fixed in bolívares declines quite sharply. Tax receipts in bolívares increase by 53 percent. Royalties change proportionately to the exchange rate change. Receipts from indirect taxes remain constant in bolívares, while those from income tax rise more than proportionately to the exchange rate change, again because of the slightly higher tax rate and the reduced significance of depreciation allowances for tax purposes.

The increase of about Bs 1.7 billion in bolívar receipts shown in the table is not, of course, a net gain for the budget. The exchange profit produced by the previous system amounted to about Bs 1.1 billion, so that the rise in revenues is about Bs 600 million. Increased costs for the budget arising from debt service payments and imports may also amount to about Bs 150 million. Consequently, the net increase in government proceeds for the budget is of the order of magnitude of Bs 450 million. If the cost to the Central Bank of subsidizing imports at the Bs 3.35 rate (about Bs 150 million, of which Bs 80–90 million is financed from the exchange spread) as well as the higher costs of the imports by government agencies were taken into account, the net gain for the government sector of the economy would be further reduced. Nevertheless, the improvement of Bs 450 million in the budget position should permit some increase in development expenditures without involving government borrowing from the banking system.

The penultimate line in the table, "Dollar Sales to the Central Bank," is an attempt to estimate the balance of payments impact of the new measure. This item is an estimate of sales of dollars by the petroleum companies to the Central Bank to obtain bolívares mainly for tax purposes but also to meet bolívar expenditure (the sum of royalties, other direct taxes, bolívar salaries, and other bolívar costs for current and capital expenditures, plus income tax). It shows that the exchange rate change is expected to have a minimal impact on the balance of payments, dollar sales to the Central Bank declining by a negligible amount. The calculation does not, however, take account of the effect of the change in the relative prices of dollars and bolívares. To the extent that the new exchange rate has the effect of reducing or increasing economic activity, the impact on the balance of payments will change. For such items as dollar salaries, it is to be expected that fewer dollars will be converted, i.e., that bolívar expenditures will not increase by an amount proportionate to the change in the exchange rate. On the other hand, since purchases in Venezuela are now cheaper in dollar terms, the companies in procuring supplies may divert expenditures from imports to the domestic economy. Moreover, since the exchange rate is one factor taken into account by oil companies when making decisions about investment, the level of investment expenditures in Venezuela may be expected to rise.

FURTHER STEPS TO UNIFICATION OF THE EXCHANGE RATE

Although the decree of January 18, 1964 involved considerable progress toward the ultimate unification of the exchange rate, a number of further steps are necessary. These are (1) elimination of the subsidy arrangements for coffee and cacao; (2) removal of the subsidies on the 10 percent of imports now receiving the Bs 3.35 rate; (3) narrowing of the spread between the buying rate of the Central Bank and the commercial banks' selling rate to the public so that the rates are within the limits, permitted under the Articles of Agreement of the International Monetary Fund, of 1 percent on either side of a par value; and (4) legislation which changes the legal definition of the gold content of the bolívar and provides a basis for agreement with the Fund on a par value.

The subsidy for coffee and cacao is a particular instance of a general problem. Even at the new exchange rate for exports, the extent to which exports other than petroleum and iron ore will develop is open to serious question. These two products have great natural advantages, and for long periods in the past an exchange rate appropriate for substantial sales of these products and for balance of payments equilibrium has been inconsistent with the development of most other exports. The exchange rate of Bs 4.48 obtainable for proceeds of exports is, of course, much better than the rate of Bs 3.33 existing up to 1960, but many Venezuelan producers still regard it as inadequate and suggest that rates of Bs 7.00 or Bs 8.00 per U.S. dollar would be necessary to develop exports. It is difficult to see any rationale for the provision of such rates to obtain marginal export earnings.

In the particular case of coffee and cacao, in addition to the question of the need for any type of subsidy, there is the further issue of the form that the subsidy should take. Payment of a subsidy through the exchange system is not particularly convenient, since no exchange controls apply to transactions in commodities other than these two exports and the subsidized imports. Payment of the subsidy at the time that the goods cleared customs and payment on the basis of weight rather than the value of exports would produce simpler administration. Moreover, the subsidies should probably be devised to fit in with plans for the more rational allocation of agricultural land in Venezuela and with the improvement of the quality of the coffee and cacao exported.

A removal of the subsidies on the 10 percent of imports now receiving the Bs 3.35 exchange rate would involve difficult political decisions. It is unlikely that changing the exchange rate for these items from Bs 3.35 to Bs 4.5 would have any significant effect on the cost of living as a whole. The Central Bank has calculated that the effect on the price level would be less than 2 percent. Similarly, higher prices for the particular agricultural materials and capital goods included in the list of basic imports could not be expected to have any substantial effect on the use of such materials. The present arrangements have the disadvantage of providing an incentive for the overvaluation of imports, and the cost of the subsidies to the Central Bank involve a certain expansionary effect which will have to be taken into account in the formulation of overall monetary policy. One of the possibilities is that the authorities, in determining subsidies, could find some technique which did not involve the exchange system and which was exposed to less risk of benefiting the distributor rather than the consumer. Another possibility would be to adopt programs to promote domestic substitutes for these imports. Opportunities appear to exist in this direction, even though some of them might involve the need for at least temporary subsidies.

To avoid multiple currencies as defined by the Fund, the Venezuelan authorities will have to narrow the spread between the buying and selling rates to within 1 percent on either side of a par value. This could be achieved by a minor adjustment of either the buying or the selling rate. The only effect of any importance would be some loss of the exchange spread, but this would not be important, especially if the step were taken at the time that the consumer subsidies were eliminated.

Although the legal situation is not altogether clear, it appears that the Venezuelan authorities will need to revise the statute which defines the gold content of the Venezuelan bolívar at an amount which gives an exchange rate of Bs 3.0463 per U.S. dollar. Such a revision could be the occasion for making the provisions of the law defining the gold content for domestic purposes consistent with the provisions of the Fund's Articles of Agreement and Venezuela's membership in the Fund. This would clear up the last obstacle to the introduction of a new par value by Venezuela.

FLOATING VS PEGGED EXCHANGE RATES: THE CANADIAN EXPERIENCE*

There are few countries of the world today in which international considerations do not play an important part in domestic economic policy decisions. Over the postwar period many of the barriers to the flow of trade and capital have been removed or lowered and the international connections among domestic financial systems have been strengthened. Changes in financial policies can now have rapid effects on international flows of funds and recognition of this exercises an influence over the policies of countries large and small.

Moreover, all countries which buy and sell in markets abroad must ensure that policy is aimed at keeping their costs competitive if they are to earn the internationally-acceptable money needed to pay for imports. In this respect, countries are like individuals, being able to spend only what they earn or are able to borrow from others; (both can, of course, in the short run, also run down their external financial assets to the extent that they have them). Similarly, a nation's capacity to earn income or to borrow, like those of an individual, depend upon its skills, willingness to work and the efficiency with which it uses its resources. International lending and borrowing can be just as productive and useful as domestic lending and borrowing, but if carried on over a long period on a major scale relative to income can also create concern about the difficulties which may be associated with servicing a large external debt.

The fewer and lower the barriers and restrictions to the free flow of trade, capital and labour, and the more closely a nation is integrated into the international economy, the more necessary it is that international considerations play a part in all policy decisions. While membership in the international community sets some limits to the policies which can be pursued by individual countries, the net advantages derived from international specialization are very great. As with individuals, reductions in the degree of economic interdependence could lead only to higher production costs and a drastic reduction in the attainable standard of living.

Canada is *par excellence* an example of a country which is closely tied

---

* Extracted from Canada's *1964 Report of the Royal Commission on Banking and Finance,* Chapter 23, "International Financial Policy," Queen's Printer, Ottawa, 1964, pp. 479–492, 503–504.

in a variety of ways to the rest of the world, and its financial, trade and other links with the United States in particular make for a uniquely close relationship between the two countries. This close relationship is on balance of great advantage to Canada, but it does mean that changes in U.S. policies or investment attitudes which may not be of major importance in the huge framework of the U.S. economy can on occasion have very big effects on Canada and pose substantial difficulties for Canadian economic policy.

Given this high degree of economic interdependence, there is a sense in which all financial policy in Canada is to a greater or lesser extent international financial policy. There are, however, a narrower range of international issues including exchange rate policy, other policies to influence the balance of payments and policies connected with world payments arrangements, on which we shall focus our attention in the present chapter.

In the course of our discussion we shall be comparing the present exchange rate system with the flexible exchange rate which Canada has had in the past. The purpose of this analysis is to isolate fundamental factors influencing Canada's international financial policy and to assess the implications for general economic policy of the adoption of a fixed exchange rate. We wish to make it clear at the outset that we do not advocate any change in the existing exchange rate system: the fixed rate is at a level that seems appropriate and the system is working well.

THE CANADIAN EXCHANGE RATE BEFORE 1950

Over the decades, Canada has had considerable experience with both a fixed and fluctuating exchange rate. Prior to 1914, the Canadian dollar was fixed in terms of gold and, therefore, fixed in terms of all other major currencies. The international gold standard, which because of the then dominant position of Britain might more accurately be called the international sterling standard, was a workable arrangement, and the Canadian economy adapted to some very substantial changes in capital flows and trade within its framework. While in some respects it was like present exchange rate arrangements, the problems we confront and the means of dealing with them have changed, not least because of the increased responsibility for economic management which has been assumed by national governments. It was easier for governments to accept a fixed relation between gold and national currencies as the principal (and sometimes the only) objective of monetary policy when they were not expected to assume a major responsibility for national employment, productivity and prices.

For most of the period 1914–39, Canada had a fluctuating exchange rate. Canada went off the gold standard in 1914 and did not return to it until July, 1926: even then we remained on it only until January, 1929. As indicated in Chart 1, the fluctuation of the Canadian dollar was kept within narrow limits throughout most of the inter-war years, except during the periods 1919–20 and 1930–33. The fact that Canada was only on a fixed rate for two and a half out of twenty-five years could be taken as strong evidence of the difficulty of maintaining such a system in this country, but although this experience is by no means irrelevant, it is noteworthy that most other major currencies were also flexible for much of the period. Severe economic fluctuations and the inadequacies of the international payments system made the maintenance of fixed rates a world rather than simply a Canadian problem.

During the war years the value of the Canadian dollar was fixed at a 10 percent discount relative to the United States dollar and there was a comprehensive system of exchange control. In July, 1946 the Canadian dollar was revalued to parity with the American dollar, in part to insulate the Canadian economy from the rapid price increases following the removal of controls in the United States. This exchange rate was maintained for over three years in spite of serious balance of payments difficulties in 1947 and early 1948. Though the rate was appropriate in terms of price and cost relationships, the unexpectedly heavy drawings of the United Kingdom and European countries on Canadian reconstruction loans and other demands put upon an overburdened Canadian economy led to a decline in the Exchange Fund's holdings of gold and U.S. dollars from $1,667 million at the end of May, 1946 to $480 million at the end of November, 1947.[1] Emergency assistance was obtained from the United States Export-Import Bank and import controls and special excise taxes imposed. The reserves recovered fairly quickly and by the end of 1948 totalled just under $1 billion. In September, 1949 there was a 30.5 percent devaluation of sterling in terms of the United States dollar accompanied by devaluations on the part of many other countries. A decision was taken to devalue the Canadian dollar by 9 percent in order to protect Canada's competitive position and balance of payments. Following this devaluation, little change took place in the reserves for some months, but in the middle of 1950 a substantial speculative inflow of capital developed which added just under $500 million to the reserves in August and September. With two attempts at setting the exchange rate having yielded little success, the decision to free the exchange rate was announced on September 30, 1950.

THE FLEXIBLE EXCHANGE RATE 1950–1960

Immediately after the withdrawal of the official buying and selling rates, the Canadian dollar appreciated sharply. Following some weakness in the

---

[1] Had the exchange rate been flexible, it would undoubtedly have fallen sharply in 1947 and recovered in 1948.

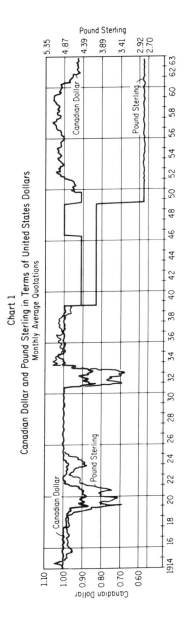

Chart 1
Canadian Dollar and Pound Sterling in Terms of United States Dollars
Monthly Average Quotations

first half of 1951 it resumed this movement in the latter half of 1951 and broke through parity with the U.S. dollar in March, 1952 to a premium of 4 percent in August. The total appreciation from September, 1950 was 14 cents but from mid-1952 to the end of 1960 the exchange rate stayed within fairly narrow limits—the total range of fluctuation amounting to about five and a half cents. Although the rate was flexible, it could not be described as unstable.

If there had been no major changes in the Canadian balance of payments during this period, the simplest explanation of this stability would be found in the economic conditions of the period. There were recessions in a number of major countries during these years, but they were much less severe than the prewar contractions, and not completely in phase. Thus, when cyclical declines occurred in the United States, the continued advance of the Western European economies, our second major market, provided a partial cushion for Canadian exports. The maintenance of favourable world economic conditions, and some fortuitously anti-cyclical movements in agricultural exports, is reflected in the basic stability of all exports shown in Chart 2. During these years also, as in others, the Canadian and American economies tended to move together and there was a similar parallellism in the economic policies followed by the governments of the two countries.

Chart 2
Canadian Merchandise Exports

Under these conditions it could be argued that there were unlikely to be major stresses and strains on Canada's balance of international payments and that stability of the exchange rate was precisely what might have been expected. This reasoning, however, assumes that no major shifts occurred in the Canadian balance of payments, and this was clearly not the case. Between 1953 and 1957, the Canadian current account deficit increased by over a billion dollars from $440 million to $1,455 million, declined by over

$300 million in 1958, increased by $370 million in 1959 and fell again by $260 million in 1960. These are large changes, and broad economic stability obviously is not the full explanation for the exchange rate stability of this period. To understand the forces at work some reference is required to the mechanism of adjustment under a flexible exchange rate.

Under balance of payments accounting, deficits on current account are necessarily matched by surpluses on capital account and vice versa. The question then arises as to how, with such limited adjustments in the international value of the Canadian dollar, the current and capital accounts were kept in balance. There are three possible explanations—first, that this was achieved through changes in the official reserves; second, that the factors determining the size of the current deficit and the capital surplus were such as to induce offsetting changes in these accounts without exchange rate movements; and third, that limited changes in the exchange rate affected the current or capital accounts or both in ways that quickly brought them into balance.

The official reserves were not used during the period 1953–60 to prevent persistent movements in the exchange rate. The policy of the Exchange Fund was one of correcting or preventing disorderly conditions rather than interfering with basic trends, and it intervened in the market only to prevent substantial movements in the exchange rate within any given trading day or from one day to another. There were, of course, occasions when this policy required the Exchange Fund to be a net buyer or seller continuously for several months. When a movement in the exchange rate became pronounced, however, there is no evidence that the Fund attempted to stop it. The limited part played by the Exchange Fund in the period 1953–60 is indicated by the fact that changes in the official reserves from month to month from December 1952 to 1960 were below $20 million in 59 of the 96 months, from $20 million to $50 million in 31, from $50 million to $100 million in five, and only exceeded $100 million in one of the months during the period. Over the period as a whole, the highest month-end reserve figure was only $233 million above the lowest holding recorded.

If official reserve operations did not play a major part, the second possibility is that changes in the capital account and the current account were related in such a way that a balance was achieved without the necessity of major movements in the exchange rate. Changes in these accounts do not just happen; they arise out of a set of economic conditions, and if these conditions were to produce capital account surpluses and current account deficits simultaneously they clearly provide part of the explanation.

An economy is ordinarily not the recipient of substantial foreign direct and equity investment unless economic prospects are favourable and long-term profit expectations high in relation to alternatives in other parts of the world. Similarly, the flow of long-term debt capital will be towards the country in which interest rates are high in relation to those offered elsewhere for securities of comparable quality. Profit expectations and interest rates are likely to move together since the rise in economic activity resulting from favourable economic prospects brings pressure to bear on financial markets and influences interest rates in an upward direction. An economy in which investment is particularly attractive in relation to other economies, therefore, will tend to have domestic interest rates higher than comparable rates abroad. Of course, the level of interest rates or, more generally, the state of credit conditions, will be influenced by the actions taken by the monetary and debt authorities, but it may be assumed that the authorities will broadly acquiesce in the tightening of credit conditions which occurs in a buoyant economy. Yet this very buoyancy is also likely to lead to a current account deficit. If the Canadian economy is expanding at a rapid rate, especially if it is growing faster than the economies of the United States and other countries and is at or approaching full employment, there will be a tendency for imports of goods and services to rise relative to exports and for a current account deficit to develop to balance the capital inflow, even without exchange rate changes.

The experience of the years 1953–60 tends to support these generalizations. This is a short period and as always there were random occurrences which tended to blur the outline. Nevertheless, it is clear that with the exception of 1960—when there were large capital inflows connected with take-over bids—direct investment tended to be higher during periods of expansion and lower during recessions.[2] Portfolio investment also responded significantly to economic and credit conditions in Canada. Simultaneously, the current account was affected in the opposite direction, with imports rising rapidly during periods of expansion and declining in periods of recession. Three main categories of imports show a strong cyclical movement; machinery and equipment, industrial materials and consumer durables. Fluctuations in the imports of machinery and equipment tended to reflect changes in domestic capital expenditure on these items, which have a high average import content. Imports of industrial materials reflected, with a slightly greater amplitude, corresponding swings in industrial production, while consumer durables imports appeared to be largely determined by cyclical movements in domestic expenditure on durable goods. Thus, over the period, capital account surpluses and current account deficits tended to be higher during periods of prosperity and lower during periods of recession.

If there were a perfect offsetting of long-term capital flows and the current account balance, one would expect a virtually stable exchange rate over the course of the economic fluctuations experienced in the period. In years of prosperity and restrictive monetary policy in Canada, however, the interac-

---

[2] Retained earnings of foreign-owned enterprises in Canada also tend to grow in periods of economic expansion, with higher dividend payout ratios occurring in recession years.

tion of heavy capital inflows and the current account deficit produced an appreciation of the Canadian dollar, while in periods of lower levels of activity our dollar tended to weaken. It is natural, therefore, to look to the exchange rate itself for part of the explanation of the balancing process. Indeed, this is precisely what a flexible exchange rate is supposed to do. If there is a tendency for the capital inflow to run ahead of the current account deficit, then pressure on the exchange market will lead to an appreciation of the Canadian dollar. An appreciation of the Canadian dollar will discourage exports and encourage imports of goods and thus increase the current account deficit. The opposite will occur if the capital inflow shows a tendency to fall short of the current account deficit.

We have already referred to this effect in our discussion of credit conditions and expenditure. Our inquiries suggest that the short-term effects of small changes in the exchange rate are likely to be fairly limited. Major changes in the exchange rate which are not quickly reversed are another matter. Canadian experience with such changes is not extensive, the most relevant experience being that resulting from the depreciation of the exchange rate in 1961 and 1962. The effects of this depreciation have been obscured by the imposition and removal of the import surcharges, the reduction in the tourist allowance and other factors which were already at work to improve our international competitive position. Early indications suggest that the effects are significant but that changes in the exchange rate take a considerable time to work their way through the economic system. During the period of 1953–60 the exchange rate moved within fairly narrow limits and changes in one direction were reversed before the effects were fully realized. Moreover, changes were often regarded as temporary and therefore as not justifying new production arrangements in Canada. We conclude, therefore, that the limited fluctuations of the flexible rate in the period 1953–60 did not have effects on the current account which were large enough to provide more than part of the explanation of the short-term balancing process. On the other hand, there is little doubt that the average level of the rate did have significant effects on the current account balance in the longer term.

The final possibility is that changes in the exchange rate had effects on the capital account and particularly on short-term capital movements. As we have pointed out elsewhere, small changes in the exchange rate may not have major effects on long-term capital movements. If the interest rate advantage which has been obtained by a Canadian borrower is sufficiently great to offset a change in the exchange rate of 10–15 percent over the term of the borrowing, short-term fluctuations in the value of the Canadian dollar will be of limited importance. On the other hand, small changes in the exchange rate can have a very considerable effect on the profitability of short-term capital transactions. For example, if under a flexible rate an investor anticipates correctly that the value of the Canadian dollar will decline by 1 percent in the course of the next thirty days, a purchase and resale of an American dollar asset would yield a normal interest return plus a profit at an annual rate of 12 percent on the investment. Such speculative flows serve to check the movement of the exchange rate.

A speculator need not go through these steps, but can instead enter into a forward contract with a bank to buy U.S. dollars. This does not involve a credit-worthy customer in putting up any capital, but allows him to sell the U.S. currency at a profit if the price rise materializes.[3] The transaction will nonetheless have effects on the balance of payments. If the bank cannot find a seller of forward U.S. dollars, it will cover its forward commitment by an equivalent purchase of spot U.S. dollars. As explained earlier, this is only an intermediate step; the bank will then seek someone in the market who is prepared to swap spot Canadian dollars and a contract to buy forward Canadian dollars for the bank's offering of spot U.S. dollars and a contract to buy forward U.S. dollars. In short, the bank must find someone who is prepared to hold U.S. dollars for the life of the contract—that is, someone who is prepared to move short-term capital to the United States. If the spot-forward differential is not sufficiently attractive to bring forth investors of this kind, then outright purchasers of forward U.S. dollars will have to be charged a price which will make short-term capital movements to the United States profitable. In either case, the upward movement in the exchange rate will be moderated by the consequences of the speculator's action.[4]

An outright purchase of forward U.S. dollars or forward Sterling is only one of the ways in which participants in the exchange market may react to a developing expectation that the Canadian dollar is likely to depreciate. Exporters receiving payments of U.S. dollars currently or in the future may decide to delay conversion in the spot or forward markets in expectation of receiving a higher price in the future. Similarly, those who have payments to make in the United States may choose to make these payments while the Canadian dollar is at a high level. Borrowers of long-term foreign capital may likewise decide to postpone their issues for the time being or defer bringing the proceeds back to Canada. If, therefore, under the influence of large-scale long-term capital movements the Canadian dollar appreciates for a period, the expectation may develop that the appreciation will be reversed. There will then be a tendency for an outward flow of short-term capital to develop and this will tend to inhibit further appreciation of the Canadian dollar.

This is not to suggest that all short-term capital flows in the period tended to moderate swings in the exchange rate. Tightening credit conditions in Canada were often associated with increased flows of unhedged short capital, particularly in the form of trade credit or other intercorporate indebtedness,

---

[3] It may, of course, involve him in a loss if the dollar moves the other way.
[4] The process described is reversed if speculation favours the Canadian dollar.

which tended to lead to further strengthening of the rate in such circumstances.

Nevertheless, stabilizing speculation of the kind described above appears to have contributed to the moderation of exchange rate movements during the period 1953–60. We found little evidence of what might be called "pure" speculation, that is, speculation which was unconnected with any other trade or capital transactions. We did find, however, that some of those who were participants in the exchange market in the ordinary course of business tended to take a view of the future movement of the exchange rate and act accordingly. It probably puts the point too crudely to say that many of these speculators were characterized by a "parity psychology" but the evidence suggests that when the Canadian dollar went to a significant premium in relation to the U.S. dollar, some participants in the market did not expect this rate to persist.

The explanation of the relative stability of the exchange rate during the period 1953–60 can therefore be summarized in the following terms. There were no depressions during the period in either Canada or the rest of the world. The major shifts which occurred in the Canadian balance of payments derived from favourable economic prospects in Canada which encouraged a flow of capital and at the same time led to a period of economic expansion which encouraged a sharp rise in imports. To a considerable extent, then, there were forces at work promoting a balance without the need for exchange rate changes. The average level of the exchange rate throughout the period exercised a significant influence on the current account, but the temporary fluctuations which occurred around this level appear to have had a limited short-term effect on trade in goods and services. Changes in the exchange rate did, however, bring forth stabilizing capital movements.

THE FIXED EXCHANGE RATE

While the foreign exchange rate was not formally fixed until May 2, 1962, there were fundamental changes in the flexible rate system a good deal earlier. In the budget of December 20, 1960, the Minister of Finance expressed concern over the impact which the inflow of foreign capital was having on the foreign exchange rate and announced a generalization of the 15 percent withholding tax on interest and dividend payments to nonresidents. This was generally considered to be a measure to restrict the inflow of capital and to reduce the price of the Canadian dollar in the foreign exchange market. It is also worthy of note that in each of the following six months official holdings of gold and foreign exchange showed successive increases; the additions from December 31, 1960 to June 30, 1961, totalled $256 million. In the budget speech of June 20, 1961 the Minister of Finance noted that the Government considered the existing international value of the Canadian dollar (monthly average in May just over U.S. $1.01) to be "unduly high" in the light of general economic conditions in Canada and expressed the following view on the appropriate level of the exchange rate:

> "No one can say today what the appropriate level of our exchange rate would be when our balance of payments is in a position better suited to our present economic circumstances. But the rate will certainly be lower than it has been of late, and it may well be appropriate for it to move to a significant discount. It will be government policy to facilitate such a movement."

In addition to the use of debt policies, this was to be done through direct intervention of the Exchange Fund in the foreign exchange market. The immediate effect of this announcement was a sharp depreciation of the Canadian dollar to just below 97¢ U.S. or a drop of about 3 cents. During the autumn the Canadian dollar showed renewed strength but in November and December it weakened again and from the end of October 1961 to June 22, 1962 the resources of the Exchange Fund were used to resist the decline in the value of the Canadian dollar.

In the early stages of the reserve drain, the authorities made concessions to the speculative pressure by allowing the value of the Canadian dollar to decline. As the loss of reserves accelerated in January and February a further adjustment of the rate was permitted, followed by an attempt to hold the Canadian dollar at around 95¢ U.S.

The behaviour of the rate in late February and March, and the decline in the reserve loss in March, suggest that this measure did lead to some abatement of the speculative pressures. In April, however, pressures were renewed and in addition to losses of $114.6 million from official holdings, the Exchange Fund entered into commitments to sell U.S. dollars forward amounting to $13 million. On May 2nd the Government announced a devaluation to 92.5¢ U.S., formal abandonment of the flexible exchange rate system and adherence to the International Monetary Fund system of maintaining the external value of the Canadian dollar within 1 percent on either side of the newly established par value of $1.081 Canadian for the United States dollar, with ultimate support points at $1.070 and $1.092.

The devaluation and adoption of a fixed rate was supported by a moderate upward adjustment of the yield on treasury bills. These measures were not sufficient to allay the speculative pressures. During May official holdings declined by a further $102 million and forward sale commitments rose by $72.6 million. The same pattern continued through the first three weeks of June. If we disregard the addition of $650 million of special international financial assistance, official holdings fell by an additional $334.1 million during June and through June 22 additional commitments were made to supply forward U.S. dollars to the extent of $154.4 million.

The measures announced on June 24, 1962, which successfully overcame the crisis, fell into two parts; a domestic "austerity" program and massive international support for the Canadian dollar. Import surcharges and a reduction in the duty-free allowance to returning tourists presented tangible evidence of direct action to reduce the current account deficit. A restriction on government spending, including a civil service wage freeze, gave evidence of direct action to limit the government deficit. A sharp increase in both short and long-term interest rates imposed additional restraint on the domestic economy and served to attract an inflow of capital. This was later supplemented by a long-term government issue of U.S. $250 million sold in the New York market. The international assistance took the form of drawings on the International Monetary Fund equivalent to U.S. $300 million and reciprocal currency swaps with the Federal Reserve System and the Bank of England totalling U.S. $350 million. In addition, a stand-by credit was arranged with the United States Export-Import Bank of U.S. $400 million. In the annual report of the Bank of Canada for 1962, the Governor pointed out that certain central banks in Western Europe had intimated that they were ready, if this were desired, to place additional funds at the disposal of the Bank of Canada. The magnitude of the international support provided and the rapidity with which it was arranged contributed to the restoration of confidence in the Canadian dollar and played an important part in reducing the burden of adjustment on Canada.

The measures initiated on June 24th had a rapid effect on the official reserve position. As pointed out in the budget papers of 1962, on June 24, 1962 the "spot" position of the official reserves had fallen to about $1,100 million and there were in addition substantial forward sales commitments outstanding. At the end of the year, the official holdings, excluding the remaining special international financial assistance of $300 million, had reached $2,239 million. As the reserve position improved through late 1962 and early 1963, most of the steps taken in June were reversed. The import surcharges were removed, and long-term interest rates—which had begun to decline in the late summer of 1962—were in the latter part of the year kept at levels only marginally higher than in the early months of 1962.

The Budget Speech of June 13, 1963 contained a number of tax and other proposals which could be expected to have an effect on the balance of payments. These included a 30 percent tax on the sale to nonresidents of corporations listed on Canadian stock exchanges and a similar tax on the sale of stock in such companies in amounts exceeding $50,000 a day by a single seller. In addition, special incentives were offered to the nonresident shareholders of companies beneficially owned by Canadians to the extent of 25 percent or more. These share-holders were given a reduction of withholding tax from 15 percent to 10 percent while nonresident shareholders in companies with less than 25 percent Canadian ownership were to have their withholding taxes increased from 15 percent to 20 percent. Manufacturing and processing companies with a minimum of 25 percent Canadian ownership were given the opportunity of writing off new machinery and equipment for tax purposes in two years, while companies with a lesser degree of Canadian ownership were not given this privilege. Subsequently, the 30 percent "takeover" tax was withdrawn, and the proposed changes in the withholding tax on dividends modified to entitle nonresident shareholders to a 10 percent rate if at least 25 percent of the outstanding voting stock was available for purchase by Canadians.[5] In addition, reference was made to proposed tariff changes—since implemented— with the objective of reducing "very greatly" net imports of automobiles and parts.

On July 18th, just over a month after the Budget, the United States Administration proposed an "interest equalization tax" designed to raise the cost to foreigners of borrowing or selling equities in the United States without the necessity of a general increase in long-term interest rates in the United States.[6] Representations by the Canadian Government led to an exemption for new issues of Canadian securities apparently on the understanding that such issues would not be used to build up Canada's foreign exchange reserves.[7] Canadian official holdings of gold and foreign exchange, which had remained at a high level during the first six months of 1963, fell in July by U.S. $110.9 millions (excluding a repayment of I.M.F. borrowings of $79.7 million) and declined by a further $31 million in August. On August 12 bank rate was increased to 4 percent from $3\frac{1}{2}$ percent but the reserves increased again thereafter and interest rates declined.

THE IMPLICATIONS FOR POLICY OF A FIXED EXCHANGE RATE

In thinking about Canadian economic policy for the future it is important to be clear on the way in which the adoption of a fixed exchange rate affects the choice of policies. There are some who feel that the system we had in

[5] These changes may lead to higher U.S. and other withholding taxes on Canada's growing equity investments abroad, although this will depend on the outcome of negotiations on internationally-agreed tax conventions.

[6] The proposed tax, when enacted into law, is to apply until the end of 1965 and date retroactively to the summer of 1963. It will not apply to foreign direct investment by U.S. residents or to the purchase by them of listed shares in foreign companies in which a majority interest is held in the U.S. and which trade mainly in the U.S. Nor will it apply to bank loans or borrowings of under 3-year terms. On borrowings longer than this, the tax scales up from 2.75 percent for under $3\frac{1}{2}$-year issues to 15 percent on issues with a term longer than $28\frac{1}{2}$ years. A number of technical exemptions are also proposed which relate to dealer inventories of foreign bonds resold to foreigners in 90 days, labour union investments, and insurance company foreign investments in connection with policy reserves in foreign countries.

[7] See, p. 14, House Ways and Means Committee Report, No. 1036, December 1963, U.S. Govt. Printing Office.

the 1950's permitted the pursuit of domestic objectives without the need for serious concern over the movements of the exchange rate: they thus expect the fixed rate to lead to a fundamental change in the orientation of economic policy, with international considerations receiving greater emphasis than domestic needs. There are others who feel that our room for manoeuvre under the flexible rate was not significantly greater than it is under a fixed rate and who therefore tend to argue that the two systems are in effect very similar. In fact, the truth of the matter seems to be somewhere in between: under no system is Canada free to ignore international considerations, but under a fixed rate system there is a more immediate and direct link with the international financial environment, a fact which is by no means always a disadvantage to Canada.

It is easy to see how even well-informed people can differ on these issues. There are many apparent paradoxes in the history of the Canadian flexible exchange rate. It was a flexible rate without explicit outer limits on its fluctuations, yet it was very stable after the initial adjustments of 1950–52. In part, this reflected the economic policies followed in Canada. This was also an apparent paradox since a flexible rate is supposed to tempt national financial authorities into policies which are excessively expansionist, but in Canada during 1958–60 restraining credit policies were maintained during a period in which unemployment averaged 6.7 percent. There was a third apparent paradox in the last phase of the flexible exchange rate experiment. When a decision was taken to use the resources of the government to force down the international value of the Canadian dollar it might have been expected that the government would be a large seller of Canadian dollars. Within a matter of months after this decision, however, the government in fact had to support the Canadian dollar by being a large seller of American dollars—indeed a seller on such a scale that the rate had to be fixed and emergency measures later implemented to maintain it.

Enough has been said earlier to indicate that these paradoxes are more apparent than real. The Canadian exchange rate did not need to be flexible over a wide range in order to perform its functions. Indeed, it is unlikely that a flexible rate which had fluctuated over a wide range would have achieved the degree of international acceptability which was accorded the Canadian rate and is vital to the workability of any exchange rate system. Moreover, wide swings in a fluctuating rate might have been difficult to contain. If the policies followed in Canada had led to the view that there was no reasonable limit to the likely moves in the exchange rate, speculative capital movements might have become violently destabilizing. If, for example, during a period when the United States authorities were imposing monetary and fiscal restraint, Canada had adopted a policy of extreme credit ease and very large government deficits, this might have set off a speculative outflow which would have carried the exchange rate below any level experienced in recent years. This might not have happened on the first occasion. A long record of prudent economic management is not dissipated overnight and a set of policies which diverged from this pattern might well have been regarded as a temporary aberration. If, however, it had become clear from repeated examples that prudence was not to be expected in the future, the reactions might well have become more violent—just as they would under a fixed rate system when the consequences fall on the reserves. The widespread and often vigorous opposition to flexible exchange rates voiced by experts outside this country is based on the disruptive effects of exchange rate changes of this kind. This, however, was not the kind of flexible exchange rate system we had in this country.

Indeed, the charge which reasonably can be brought against the flexible exchange rate is that the international value of the Canadian dollar was too stable in the face of a major change in the economic environment. A substantial premium on the Canadian dollar and large capital inflows were appropriate during the investment boom of 1955–57 but when economic conditions changed it was desirable that economic policy should be so ordered that there would be a fall in the international value of the Canadian dollar, the current account deficit and the capital inflow. Had credit conditions been easier, some of the capital inflow would not have occurred and the value of the Canadian dollar would have been lower: while the consequences would not have been immediate, the lower exchange rate would have stimulated employment, incomes and domestic savings. The policies in fact pursued were thus very different from those which might have been expected to result from the freedom sometimes thought implicit in a flexible exchange rate. Far from beggaring her neighbours Canada followed policies which in time led to such dissatisfaction with the level of the rate that an escape was sought through direct intervention in the exchange market.

The consequences of direct intervention were also less paradoxical than appears on the surface. If the government is known to be operating in the market with the express purpose of lowering the value of the Canadian dollar, this is likely to lead to considerable uncertainty among other participants in the market. Once expectations developed that a fall in the value of the Canadian dollar was likely to occur then, in the circumstances of the time, these expectations were very difficult to reverse and in fact were not reversed until emergency measures had been introduced.

The difference between the flexible and fixed rate systems is a matter of degree and not of kind. Under a flexible exchange rate, any country which is a responsible member of the international community and which is concerned with domestic price stability will find that there are implicit, if not explicit, limits to the variation of the exchange rate which is acceptable; movements in the exchange rate which result from policy changes therefore cannot be ignored. Under a fixed rate, attention first focusses on the reserves rather than the rate, but in both cases international limitations on domestic policy are effectively present.

Under a fixed exchange rate, monetary and debt policies have effects on domestic expenditure and on international capital flows, but since the exchange rate is fixed they do not at the same time have an influence over international trade through the channel provided by the exchange rate. The influence of monetary and debt policies on expenditure is correspondingly reduced. This has led to suggestions that under a fixed rate system the primary role of monetary and debt policies should be to influence the balance of payments, leaving to fiscal and other policies the primary responsibility for domestic stabilization. We have already had two examples, in the summers of 1962 and 1963, of increases in interest rates which were inappropriate from the point of view of the domestic economy but which were regarded as necessary in the light of the international payments position. This suggests that the choice of exchange rate systems may influence the "mix" of policies, although it does not mean that monetary policy must always be geared only to international considerations or that when it is, it is necessarily inappropriate from a purely domestic point of view.

The effects of a given mix of policies will also be different under a fixed-rate system, with fiscal policy having stronger effects. Fiscal deficits and surpluses affect the financing requirements of the government and thus influence credit conditions. Other things equal, fiscal deficits tend to raise interest rates and fiscal surpluses to lower them, and it is the task of the monetary and debt authorities to take these effects into consideration in achieving the credit conditions required in the circumstances. If this kind of accommodating action is not taken under a flexible exchange rate system, fiscal policy changes will encounter dampening effects. Thus the expansionary effects of a federal deficit will be reduced since if the federal deficit increases interest rates will rise, international capital inflows will increase and the resulting upward pressure on the Canadian dollar[8] will lead to adverse effects on our international trade in goods and services. A fiscal surplus, on the other hand, tends to lower interest rates, discourage the inward flows of capital and encourage a depreciation of the Canadian dollar; as a result, the contractionary impact of a Government surplus will be partly offset by effects on the current account of the balance of payments. Under a fixed rate system, effects of this kind influence the level of reserves rather than the exchange rate, and fiscal policy does not encounter offsetting effects working through the exchange rate and the current account of the balance of payments.

One would normally expect fiscal and other policies to be pulling in the

[8] There will also be some effects working in the opposite direction. Expansionary fiscal policy increases the demand for imports, thus increasing the demand for foreign currency. Moreover, the existence of a deficit may weaken confidence in the future value of the Canadian dollar with effects on the exchange market.

same direction unless international or other considerations dictated otherwise. However, the example given above is not too far removed from what actually happened in some of the years following 1957, and helps to explain why the relatively large federal deficits in this period, without the support of appropriate monetary and debt policies, did not produce the desired effect on domestic economic conditions. In any event, the reduced effectiveness of monetary policy under a fixed rate system and the enhanced power of fiscal policy under such a system means that the latter must be used more actively to achieve domestic objectives.

While the existence of a fixed exchange rate does have effects on the relative strength of the various instruments of Canadian policy, and can well influence the decisions on the "mix" of policies, it would be wrong to exaggerate the differences. As we have already pointed out, our enquiries indicate that the short-run effects on the flow of goods and services of moderate and temporary fluctuations in the exchange rate are quite limited, i.e. if policy changes are moderate and generally reversed within the period of a short-run cyclical fluctuation, the effects on trade will be relatively small. This in turn means that for policy changes of this kind, the difference between the relative capacity of the various instruments of policy is not greatly different under a fixed than under a flexible exchange rate system.

The issue, however, is not the relative effectiveness of the individual instruments of policy but the general question of the freedom of action of the financial authorities. The central question is not usually whether fiscal ease and monetary tightness is to be preferred to fiscal tightness and monetary ease, but rather whether a policy of general expansion combining fiscal deficits and monetary ease is consistent with the maintenance of a sound external financial position. If the exchange rate is fixed and if changes in exchange and import restrictions are ruled out, the authorities' freedom of action depends on holdings of official exchange reserves and the acceptable size of changes in them. If the exchange rate is at a level which leads to a continuous addition to the reserves and this is acceptable both domestically and internationally, the authorities will not feel unduly inhibited by balance of payments considerations. Similarly, if reserves are very high the authorities may be prepared to accept considerable losses before permitting balance of payments factors to weigh heavily in the determination of domestic policies.

Normally, the reserves will not be undergoing changes of a disruptive kind, and the authorities should have considerable freedom to pursue domestic economic objectives. If the domestic economy is soundly managed, it should be possible to handle even quite large swings in the reserve position, although such swings are not without their difficulties. If massive additions to reserves occur during a period of buoyancy, it is inappropriate to finance them through the banking system since this will add to the bank's liquidity, bring about an inappropriate easing of credit conditions and intensify inflationary pressure.[9] On the other hand, while an increase in interest rates might be appropriate domestically in such circumstances, it might merely add to the capital inflows. If these flows are expected to be temporary, there are a variety of devices—such as temporary liquid asset agreements with the banks, or sales of non-market securities to them—which can be employed to handle the domestic financing of the reserve changes.

If it becomes evident that the inflow reflects longer-term forces, the authorities will find it necessary to alter the "mix" of economic policies. Larger fiscal surpluses would be needed to provide the necessary domestic financing of reserves and to dampen business activity, since interest rates would have to be maintained at relatively lower levels to avoid adding to the capital inflow.[10] This assumes that the Canadian authorities are able to convince other governments that the reserve accumulations are not harming their international position and to persuade the Canadian public of the need to add to holdings of gold and U.S. dollars with a low rate of return.

Appropriate fiscal policies take on added importance under a fixed rate system, since if they are not used additional pressure will be put on domestic prices. Because price and cost increases are not readily reversible, increases will limit the authorities' ability to combat a subsequent recession because of a weakened international competitive position. Under a flexible rate system these adjustments can come about through upward movements in the rate which are subsequently reversed, although under either system the authorities must be concerned with containing domestic prices and costs to ensure that they do not necessitate continuous and cumulative depreciation of the currency, both internally and externally.

In the different circumstances of major reserve drains in periods of slack activity in Canada, the authorities may need to call on international assistance and bring about some increase in domestic interest rates. If the drain persists and interest rates must be maintained at higher levels than purely domestic considerations would call for, increased reliance must be put on fiscal measures to stimulate the economy and on other policies designed to bring about fundamental improvements in our relative costs of production.

It is sometimes argued that the difficulties with which a fixed rate system may occasionally confront the authorities can be overcome by making it an

[9] Such inflows do not present a comparable problem in periods of economic slack because an easing of credit conditions is then appropriate to both the domestic and international situation.

[10] If the present proposal to remove Canada's exemption from the U.S. interest equalization tax if our reserves become excessive is enacted into law, it might reduce foreign borrowing by Canadians in times of buoyant domestic conditions. It would thus reduce the capital inflows with which the Canadian authorities would normally have to cope when domestic credit conditions are restrictive. This temporary measure, however, is objectionable on other grounds, not least in that it may prevent Canada from accumulating sufficient reserves in such periods to defend the fixed rate in less favourable times.

"adjustable peg" which alters fairly frequently. Both economic logic and the existing international payments arrangements clearly indicate that a change in a fixed rate should be made if the disequilibrium is fundamental in nature. For example, a rate adjustment would be permissible and necessary if basic demand conditions for exports or imports were to alter in a major way, if the structure of Canadian relative costs and prices were to change substantially or if the character and amount of capital flows were to undergo massive and lasting shifts of a destabilizing nature. However, frequent changes in the fixed value of a major currency such as that of Canada cannot be made without creating serious uncertainties in domestic production, trade and capital flows. If it came to be believed that changes were likely to occur, then at the first hint of difficulties in either direction there would be widespread speculation on the Canadian dollar similar to that which took place in 1962.

If frequent changes in the exchange rate are ruled out, then there will be times when the rate is undervalued relative to existing conditions and other times when it is overvalued. Substantial changes in reserves will often provide the adjustment mechanism in such circumstances, but there is no denying that persistent gains or losses in reserves will limit the extent to which the authorities can follow policies to achieve their domestic objectives. Given the sensitivity of international capital flows, it may be possible to minimize these limitations by gearing monetary and debt policies to international considerations and by placing more reliance on fiscal and other policies to achieve purely domestic aims. Nevertheless, there are limits to this process and it is only realistic to recognize that international considerations will at times in the future, as they have in the past, exercise a decisive influence on the choice of policy at home.

While a flexible rate would appear to have some advantages in Canada's circumstances in that it provides for somewhat greater freedom and effectiveness of domestic monetary policy, its advantages should not be over-stressed. The flexible exchange rate was too high after 1957, in part because of domestic credit policies, but there is no certainty that more appropriate measures would have resulted in an exchange rate wholly suited to the structure of our relative costs and prices. If the view had been that the flexible exchange rate had not declined sufficiently, it might have been desirable to fix a lower rate, at least by 1960 when the disequilibrium in our international competitive position was generally evident. This would have made for greater certainty and facilitated the production adjustments in the export and import-competing industries that are necessary if the economy is to come closer to full employment levels.

The authorities cannot escape the consequences of their domestic policy actions on the international financial position under either exchange rate system, although a fixed rate system may bring the consequences of ill-advised steps more quickly and dramatically to public attention. However, when a low value is established under a fixed rate system so that the international consequences of domestic inflation are not immediately felt, poor performance at home will not immediately be reflected in exchange reserves; moreover, a fortuitous change in the current or capital accounts may temporarily mask the international consequences of domestic policy actions. What does remain beyond dispute is that under either exchange system the authorities can mismanage our affairs. Similarly, good economic results can be achieved under either system, although Canada's special position is likely to limit the domestic freedom of the authorities and may necessitate more exchange rate changes in the long run than would be needed by some other industrial countries. In the final analysis, it is not the exchange rate system in use but domestic policy designed to keep the economy efficient and adaptable which is the essential condition of achieving a sound and viable external financial position.

CONCLUSION

In our view the existing parity of 92½¢ U.S. is a good exchange rate for Canada and one which we hope can be maintained for a long time to come. Whether or not changes in the exchange value of the currency will be necessary in the more distant future will depend upon future developments, including changes which may be made in the world payments system. Under any financial arrangements, however, the Canadian economy will be subject to pressures arising from world trade and investment trends which will limit our independence of action. Our financial policies, particularly our monetary and debt policies, should never be carried out without regard to their international consequences and a fixed exchange rate will help to ensure that this is the case. Operation of the present system will involve substantial swings in our international reserves, and from time to time will require active foreign exchange market operations to counter speculative pressures. At the same time, it will mean that monetary and debt policies designed to achieve domestic objectives will have to be reasonably consistent with our short-run international economic position.

The best way for us to maintain a sound external financial position will still be to have a soundly-managed economy at home. While the burden of our external indebtedness is not excessive, we have pointed out that inappropriate financial policies can lead to the attraction of more foreign capital than is necessary or desirable in periods of slack in the economy. No doubt there will continue to be gross flows of capital in both directions and net drawings on foreign resources to supplement Canadian savings in boom periods, but we do not believe that the country needs to be heavily dependent on foreign financing at all times, especially when there are unused resources available in Canada. As in other aspects of policy, we are more likely to be successful in this aim if we take fundamental measures designed to improve the competitiveness and adaptability of the economy than if we deal only with the symptoms of the problem. In this task, constructive international cooperation to achieve high employment and price stability can play an important role, and Canada should take an active part in bringing about needed improvements to world payments and other facilities designed to achieve these goals.

ADDITIONAL READINGS

Alemann, Roberto T., "Monetary Stabilization in Latin America," *Journal of Finance*, May, 1961, pp. 167–175.

Alexander, Robert J., "Inflation in Latin America," *Indian Journal of Economics*, January, 1956, pp. 277–281.

Annual Report of Exchange Restrictions, International Monetary Fund, Washington.

Artus, R. E., "Canada's Floating Dollar," *The Banker*, September, 1960, pp. 581–588.

———, "Canada Pegs its Dollar," *The Banker*, June, 1962, pp. 362–369.

Collings, F. d'A., "Recent Progress in Latin America Toward Eliminating Exchange Restrictions," *IMF Staff Papers*, May, 1961, pp. 274–286.

Gilbert, Robert A., *International Investment*, New York: Simmons-Boardman, 1963.

Gudin, Eugenio, "Multiple Exchange Rates: The Brazilian Experience," *Economica Internationale*, August, 1956, pp. 501–509.

Matthews, Roy A., "Adjustment to a New Era: Canada's Devalued Dollar," *The Business Record*, June, 1962, pp. 8–11.

Outline of Exchange Controls in India, Reserve Bank of India, Bombay, 1960.

Sohmen, Egon, *Flexible Exchange Rates, Theory and Controversy*, University of Chicago Press, 1961.

Spiegel, Henry, *The Brazilian Economy, Chronic Inflation and Sporadic Industrialization*, Philadelphia: Blakiston Co., 1949.

Woodley, Wm. J. R., "The Use of Special Exchange Rates for Transactions with Foreign Companies," *IMF Staff Papers*, October, 1953, pp. 254–269.

FINANCING TRADE AND ECONOMIC DEVELOPMENT

chapter 6
Commercial Banking and Multinational Business

Commercial banks are normally first thought of, in relation to international business, as channels and sources for financing foreign trade. They provide the foreign exchange, handle the documents, provide the credit and transfer the funds as required to facilitate trade transactions. This was long the extent of the operations of the foreign departments of all but a very few U.S. commercial banks. But, with the growth of foreign investment by U.S. firms, greater demands are being made on commercial banks. In addition to their former functions, they are called upon to provide capital to help finance these foreign investments and to provide for their working capital needs. Some of these funds can be provided in dollars, but the U.S. company may wish to borrow funds in the country in which it is investing. This is particularly true, as is noted in Chapter 13, in countries where there are exchange controls and high rates of inflation. In such situations, the existence of a branch or subsidiary of the U.S. company's commercial bank can be of great assistance.

It becomes obvious that the more extensive the international operations of a U.S. company, the more extensive must be the organization of the foreign department of the commercial bank which wishes to hold that company's account. Thus, the post-war growth of U.S. foreign trade, which has involved a much larger number of companies, has brought about the establishment of foreign departments in many more banks. These foreign departments are often established even though, in themselves, they are deficit operations, for they are needed to hold and attract customers who want their bank to be able to carry out the increased international transactions directly, rather than through a correspondent of a New York bank.

In the same vein, the rapid growth of U.S. direct foreign investment has caused many commercial banks to follow these investments by their customers with the establishment of foreign branches or subsidiaries.

A very recent, and most interesting development in the overseas expansion of U.S. commercial banks, however, is a tendency toward aggressive investment. Some banks are no longer passively (and often reluctantly) responding to the needs of their domestic customers; rather, they are looking upon investment in an overseas branch in the same manner as the opening of another branch in their home state or city. The potential foreign branch or subsidiary is decided upon on the basis of long-run profit opportunity, taking into account the needs, the competitive situation and the risks involved. Thus, commercial banks are themselves becoming multinational businesses.

As will be seen in the readings, most U.S. banks have only recently begun to establish foreign branches. U.S. banks have less than 175 foreign branches altogether. This is about equal to the number of foreign branches of French or Canadian banks, while British banks have over 500 foreign branches. The existence of these branches of foreign banks can be of importance to a U.S. company. For example, if a U.S. firm has a subsidiary in Chile which is doing business with Italy, it can be advantageous to the subsidiary to utilize the services of a Chilean branch of an Italian bank.

The international businessman should be familiar, not only with the organization and operation of the international network of commercial banking, but also with the banking systems of each country in which he has operations or is contemplating an investment. He must know, for example (as discussed at at length in Chapter 2) the types of controls which the central bank is likely to impose on the system, so that he can anticipate the types and cost of credit which will be available to the subsidiary, and to its customers.

Obviously, because of space limitations, the following set of readings could not provide information about the banking systems of many countries. Instead, the readings provide the reader with a sense of the direction which commercial banking is taking in different areas of the world, and the forces which are determining these directions. The first article is a general review of these recent trends in several leading countries. The remaining articles take up the problem in greater depth in the United States, London, Western Europe, Latin America, and Africa.

BANKING ACROSS FRONTIERS*

These are difficult times for bankers trying to strike a neat balance between the conflicting virtues of prudence and enterprise demanded by their calling. The specialised compartments in which they have long worked are crumbling, at home and in the world at large, and new opportunities and new risks beckon equally. In this survey The Economist takes a close look at this process on a working level, and examines some of the wider policy implications.

Nowhere are present changes more striking than in the world's major financial centres. In the first article, below, a staff correspondent who has been visiting some of these describes a more truly international financial community that is springing into being under the stimuli of a world-wide money market in Eurocurrencies, the revival of Europe's international capital markets and, not least, the increasingly international nature of the credit demanded by giant industrial companies operating on a world-wide scale. Geographic barriers are breaking down as more banks abandon the long tradition of confining their direct dealings to the customers they know at home. Instead of channelling foreign business through their banking "friends," abroad, more of these are moving into foreign centres themselves, sometimes competing actively on the home ground of their hosts.

In an office deeply insulated from the turmoil of Frankfurt's traffic by pile carpets, veneered panelling, double doors and double windows, a German banker spends an hour itemising to a visitor, with great thoroughness, all of the manifold disadvantages and dangers of branching outside one's own country and thus invading the home preserve of one's foreign correspondents. Old banking friendships are turned to rivalries, new competition is needlessly created, the expenses are considerable, as much business is lost as gained, and all in all, what is the point of it? Surprisingly, this interview ends with the remark: "Of course when we see how active foreign banks are becoming here, we think we may change our own policy and start going abroad too."

This grudging ascendancy of temptation over distrust is doubly significant coming from a banker in Germany. Here, the memory of the expropriation of foreign branches and subsidiaries after each of two wars has thus far proved a large factor inhibiting new ventures abroad. Yet such conflicting reactions to the changes now stirring the banking world are widespread among bankers not only in Germany, but throughout Europe, and their fretful uncertainty is one measure of the impact these changes are making.

* *The Economist*, November 21, 1964, pp. 845–851.

This expansion now taking place does not amount to any movement proceeding on some grand, deliberate design. The process is an untidy one, motivated by considerations varying from bank to bank and country to country, and taking place piecemeal by a variety of methods. Yet however amorphous, it feeds on itself, acquiring a drive of its own. Those in for a penny go in for a pound; those holding back are increasingly assailed by doubts.

Merely keeping track of it all is difficult. The development of a truly international money market in foreign currency deposits now gives commercial banks an added incentive to follow their big industrial customers abroad by branching out in the main financial centres, and it exerts a particular attraction for American and Japanese banks. Investment and merchant banks, on the other hand, are tending to create foreign subsidiaries as they seek new footholds in an increasingly competitive international underwriting world. And banks spreading to the world's developing countries prefer yet another way, that of seeking partners to share the risks, which here frequently match the opportunities.

Of all the many forms of international banking expansion, the creation of foreign branches is by far the most controversial. However scrupulously a foreign branch refrains from poaching on the home preserves of its hosts, its mere existence takes business from them, because whenever a foreign branch is established, the parent bank transfers to it the business and deposits that previously went to its local correspondent banks. Yet this is not new and bankers have long come to accept the practice. What is setting the cat among the pigeons is that some foreign branches in Europe are now actively competing with local banks for local business, just as some recent arrivals in Hongkong and other Far Eastern centres are now competing with uncommon vigour for the customers of banks that have long been established there.

Here is a rude, unprecedented breach of hallowed banking custom. The invasion of sacred domestic preserves by foreign interlopers is a heresy offending the protectionist banker's deepest instincts. No wonder that some feathers have begun to fly.

Some of the fiercest competition is taking place in Brussels where the blame (or should it be the credit?) is for once placed mainly on the French rather than on the American branches. Here, the French are accused of having started the practice, some three years ago, of soliciting deposits from Belgian companies by bidding above the rate generally agreed among Belgian banks.

In a country where the loyalty of customers to their banks has never been particularly strong, a chaotic situation rapidly developed. Companies with idle funds acquired the habit of auctioning them off by telephoning each of the major banks in turn, "not just once around, but *twice*," in the words of one aggrieved Belgian banker. "What made me really angry," he

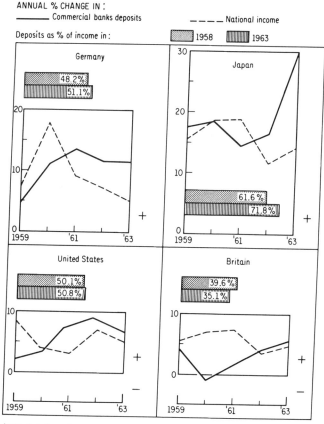

Where Bank Deposits Have Lagged

ANNUAL % CHANGE IN :
———— Commercial banks deposits   — — — — National income
Deposits as % of income in :   1958   1963

Germany   48.2%   51.1%

Japan   61.6%   71.8%

United States   50.1%   50.8%

Britain   39.6%   35.1%

Although in the past year or so the long fall in the ratio of bank deposits to national income has been checked in Britain, the rate at which they are expanding is slow compared with that in some other industrialised countries.

adds, "is when I offered to break the rate agreement and then found I didn't get the deposit anyway, because another bank had broken it even more flagrantly."

For the French, the obvious attraction, though now somewhat diminished by the recent rise in Belgian money market lending rates, is that these rates have consistently been at least a full point and at times three full points lower than in France over the past years, so that funds obtained in Brussels can be profitably lent at home.

In August this year, in an attempt to enforce stricter compliance, the Belgian Bankers' Association was given power to inspect members' books. As a result, greater nominal conformity is now reported, but potential depositors are offered instead, it is claimed, the inducement of some reduction in their banking charges. To the credit of the Americans, a subtler yet effective additional competitive element has been introduced in Brussels, consisting of no more (and no less) than an impression conveyed by Flemish-speaking clerks in a haughtily French-speaking city, that Flemish customers are as welcome as any others.

Undercutting in Germany

From Germany come equally vocal complaints of poaching by foreign branches. Here, the accusation is that some of these obtain money market funds at the prevailing interbank rate of 5 percent and then advance these to German borrowers at well below the agreed 7 percent which German banks are charging their customers.

It is this practice that has helped prejudice some of Germany's most eminent bankers so deeply against the Eurodollar market, for all the approval this market has now received from none less than the Bank for International Settlements and the Bank of England. "When I found a foreign bank that was doing this, I struck it off my correspondent list at once," said an angry German banker. "This upsets all the rules, to take my money at inter-bank rates and then use it to undercut me with my customers. We can combat this only by solidarity among ourselves." Logically, if the complaint exists, the solidarity doesn't, and if this needs any confirmation, it comes from the director of a smaller German bank, which deals mainly with individuals and smaller businesses. "Certainly I lend money at inter-bank rates to foreign branches here," he confesses cheerfully. "They don't compete for *my* customers."

Competition from foreign branches is not everywhere as dramatic as this, although "poaching" is alleged to take place also in Italy, in France (where it hits the *banques d'affaires* rather than the large, nationalised commercial banks) and in the Netherlands, where the growth of international banking competition is given as one of the reasons for this year's mergers of the four largest banks into two combines. In London, foreign branches have prospered largely by seizing opportunities that the clearing banks have been forced to neglect by their interest rate cartel, though the foreign banks' activity competes more directly in the Eurocurrencies market with that of the merchant banks.

In many instances, however, foreign branches still go to some lengths not to offend their hosts. British banks abroad have a universal name for gentlemanly behaviour, the City of London traditionally welcomes foreign banks, and its more than 160 international banking offices far outstrip the number in any other financial capital. The compliment is returned, and foreign banks in London generally do not solicit deposits from British firms, although they do accept such deposits when they are offered. Not long ago, when a visiting New York banker persuaded a British business man to switch his account to the London branch of the New York bank, it was the manager of the branch who gently turned down the account, steered the customer back to his original bank, reassured the London bank's management, and explained the City's ground rules to his visiting superior.

GINGERLY IN THE ALPS

In Switzerland, which has the reputation of giving invading bankers the coldest reception of any country, newcomers tread warily. One foreign merchant bank that opened a subsidiary there recalls that in spite of the most ringing assurances (scrupulously observed) that it would confine itself exclusively to the management of its own and its domestic customers' international investments, it was boycotted for five years by three of its former Swiss correspondents. "In that time, we did not get so much as a single foreign exchange order," says a spokesman for the victimised bank. The Banca Nazionale del Lavoro avoided such reprisals when it set up its wholly-owned affiliate, the Lavoro Bank, A.G., in Zurich in 1959, but it went beyond mere promises not to poach Swiss business by inviting Swiss banks to nominate three representatives to the affiliate's seven-man board—which the Swiss did.

The dust-up created by the practices of some foreign bank branches is very much larger than the number of branches that create it. Yet it is worth dwelling on, not because it makes entertaining bankers' gossip, or even because it has raised some very real resentment, but because there is a portent here. Foreign branches are costly; as more of them spring up not all will invariably find themselves able to show a profit merely by financing the foreign trade and enterprises of their own nationals. When once one of them breaches what have long been considered generally accepted ethics, the temptation for others becomes overwhelming. What matters then is not the resentment of the banks in the host country, but the strength of the weakest link in any united resistance they may try to offer. The little evidence there is so far suggests that the advantage lies with the invaders.

Not that the extent of the danger or the resentment should be exaggerated. Bankers are realists, and business relations are maintained wherever they happen to be mutually profitable. Even in countries like Germany, where some stiff new competition has arisen, German banks and foreign branches continue to conduct normal business with each other, which includes steering a customer to a sometime rival when that bank happens to be the one able to satisfy some special need the customer has.

Indeed, in Switzerland, for all its reputed hostility to outsiders, it is the

Swiss banks that regularly offer business to foreign branches. This comes in the shape of money market deposits, because Switzerland has no developed domestic money market, and Swiss banks are generally reluctant to place outside the country's physical borders, even for a few days, any sum exceeding their own stated capital. "Then, if we lose it all, we're still all right," explains a Swiss banker, adding, in response to his visitor's startled expression, "Yes, I know, all foreigners think it's mad. But by 1945, many Swiss banks were in a desperate position. We had liabilities at home and assets abroad, *and I assure you that if the war had lasted only another two or three years, some of us might have faced bankruptcy."* The memory of this bygone peril, so narrowly escaped, helps to dictate present policy.

WELCOME IN NEW YORK

If the reception in Switzerland is no longer as cool as once reputed (and perhaps it never was quite *that* icy) the welcome currently awaiting foreign bankers in New York seems positively ecstatic, by some accounts. Here, the Banca Nazionale del Lavoro had no need to attempt conciliation, partly, no doubt, because it is a relatively smaller animal in Manhattan than in Zurich. The Irving Trust Company sold Lavoro its old building in Rockefeller Centre, other American banking friends joined in helping the Italian bank through the formalities of setting up its branch (in July, last year) and helped, likewise, instruct in American banking ways some of the Italian personnel who were to staff it. No promises were required, and while the branch's business accounts are virtually all those of Italian companies or of companies trading with Italy, its personal savings accounts, recruited in the American fashion by sustained radio and television advertising, come mainly from Americans of Italian origin.

This kind of reception for a foreign bank by American bankers is not wholly altruistic, or even narrowly motivated by a desire merely to reciprocate hospitality extended by Italy, most notably to the Banca d'America e d'Italia, the Bank of America's affiliate with its 82 offices stretching from the thigh to the heel of the Italian boot. In recent years, American banks have set the pace in international expansion and have thus been anxious to create the freest possible atmosphere for it. One of their major contributions was the influence they successfully exerted four years ago to secure an amendment of New York state law so that foreign banks could establish fully-fledged branches in the city.

In branching abroad the large American banks are influenced by very special circumstances. For a start, their ability to branch at home is severely restricted. The ceiling on the rates they may pay on domestic deposits, imposed by Regulation Q, makes the Eurodollar market a particularly welcome source of additional funds for them, and it is this Eurodollar business that mainly accounts for the fact that the nine American banks in London increased their deposits more than threefold and their advances about fourfold in the four years to the end of 1963, thus helping to attract four more American banks to the City. There may sometimes be less direct profit in following American industrial giants abroad, since the foreign subsidiaries of these are often kept deliberately illiquid by their head offices and also frequently secure the credit they need at least partly from local banks. But there is certainly a long-term incentive to do so, if only the fear of losing such a customer to a rival bank that does provide world-wide services.

American banks, notably First National City Bank of New York, and Chase Manhattan, tend to Branch directly or through wholly-owned affiliates, into areas of Asia, Africa and Latin America by a method now widely eschewed by European banks, who prefer to spread their risks in the developing world by sharing them with other stockholders in joint ventures. But here, again, American banks are largely pursuing American international industrial concerns, and this expansion, though possibly less secure, is in some ways comparable to the move of European and British banks into the colonies in the late nineteenth century. It is looking very far ahead indeed to ponder where this new "American" approach might lead; but some connections have a habit of blossoming unexpectedly, and the more connections there are, the greater the prospect. Certainly, some banking ventures have assumed new importance through a combination of chance as well as design. Barclays DCO has grown into the world's biggest purely international bank by expanding energetically in the now independent states it originally entered when they were safely-held colonies; since the war, its branches in 40 African, Mediterranean and West Indian states have increased almost threefold to over 4,350, dwarfing in number the 100-odd overseas offices of First National City.

THE LURE OF CAPITAL MARKETS

If any remote visions of an unfathomable future ever pass even fleetingly through a banker's occasional daydreams, the sights of many are at present trained, among other things, on the prospects for a further freeing of international capital movements. The Treaty of Rome commits the members of the Common Market to remove restrictions on capital flows between each other by 1967, and the American interest equalisation tax is still, at present, due to expire at the end of next year, although there is no assurance that it may not be extended. Whatever may happen here, the outlook is that borrowers will continue to make relatively heavy calls on the international capital markets on both sides of the Atlantic, and this prospect is one consideration for investment banks and European general purpose banks that are contemplating branching into major financial centres where they are yet represented.

The lure of international underwriting is widely mentioned as one that may, at last, prod German banks into expanding abroad once more. This year, the German capital market will have raised some $250 million for international borrowers, six times the amount of the preceding year, ten times that of 1962, and by far the largest of any year since 1913. The appetite of German bankers has been whetted, as one of them put it. A significant straw, perhaps, is the Dresdner Bank's decision to open a first German representative banking office in New York in January. At present, German banks are represented abroad only by four relatively small overseas banks, the survivors of those expropriated after the last war (one of them by General Franco, no less); by the office of the Münemann investment bank in London; and by the Banque Franco-Allemande, which grew out of the Paris branch of a Saar savings bank, created when the Saar was in the Franc zone, and which is now owned by a large group of German savings banks.

European bankers do not, on the whole, seem keen to create foreign branches except in the largest financial centres at this stage. Indeed, there has been the occasional retrenchment, notably by the Dutch banks. Last year, the Nationale Handelsbank sold to Chase Manhattan its branches in Bangkok and Hongkong, while the Rotterdamsche Bank, which absorbed the Nationale Handelsbank, sold to First National City its half share in the Mercantile Bank of Canada.

Although an object of this year's merger of the Nederlandsche Handel-Maatschappij and De Twentsche Bank into the Algemene Bank Nederland, and the parallel merger of the Amsterdamsche and Rotterdamsche into the Amrobank was to create banks whose size would make them more competitive domestically and internationally, sheer bulk and the elimination of duplicated facilities was seen as the principal way of achieving this, rather than the operation of a far-flung foreign branch network. Indeed, one man who ought to know suggested that the Twentsche Bank may have seen its partner's more than 30 branches and affiliates in the Far East, Middle East, Africa, and Latin America as a liability rather than an asset, although here, the internationalists have apparently won over the doubters.

Britain's Way

British banks tend, on the whole, to side-step the dilemma between neglecting overseas opportunities and offending foreign banking friends, since their expansion is largely through wholly-owned subsidiaries. A sharper distinction is thus drawn between domestic operations and those abroad which are kept, not to overstate it, at half an arm's length. Moreover, subsidiaries provide one way around the strict interest rate agreements covering the domestic operations of the clearing banks.

International banking through subsidiaries owned by consortia is a relatively recent development for some of the European banks now spreading into the underdeveloped world (or, in other instances, retreating from it by retaining only a small share of previously wholly-owned colonial affiliates). The caution that dictates such action is not only that of some older hands, who recall the "drunken sailor days" forty years ago, when a heady vogue developed for participations in such seductive ventures as the Polish Electric Bank. Even when there is little danger of expropriation, the presence of some local participation helps insure against the forced financing of dubious projects favoured by the local government.

BANKING IN LONDON: COMPARING THE GAINS

	American Banks	Accepting Houses	British Overseas Banks	European Banks	Other Foreign Banks*	London Clearing Banks
Percentage increase June, 1963 to June, 1964						
Deposits ...	26	20	10	14	68	6
Advances ..	19	3	13	12	58	9
Percentage increase 1959/to June 1964.						
Deposits ...	274	257	108	95	...	20
Advances ..	338	319	202	117	...	69
Total Deposits:						
June, 1964	£769 mn.	£925 mn.	£1.4 bn.	£395 mn.	£657 mn.	£8.4 bn.
Dec., 1963	£670 mn.	£840 mn.	£1.4 bn.	£400 mn.	£460 mn.	£8.4 bn.
Total Advances:						
June, 1964	£583 mn.	£429 mn.	£607 mn.	£181 mn.	£475 mn.	£4.3 bn.
Dec., 1963	£528 mn.	£412 mn.	£560 mn.	£185 mn.	£330 mn.	£4.0 bn.

* Not available before 1962.

However, there are also disadvantages in this form of joint participation, however satisfactory it has proved in some cases. One complaint is that when there are numerous equal partners, matters are allowed to slide since none feels primarily responsible. Another, that the foreign trade financing originating from a jointly owned bank in a distant land tends to go rather more to those shareholding banks with men on the spot. What most of such complaints come down to is that when little is ventured, little is gained. This stricture is one frequently applied by European bankers to the novel but puzzling association formed last year by the Deutsche Bank, the Banque de la Société Générale de Belgique, of Brussels, the Amsterdamsche (now Amrobank) and the Midland.

The four banks in the group exchange some information, including products of research. Many bankers in Europe wonder what else they do, except that some bankers have noticed at least one member of the group handing out extra business to correspondents to reassure them that they will not be neglected. One banker, the object of such attentions, said that they had failed to reassure him; another observed, cynically, that banks often develop special friendships without exciting jealousy by loudly proclaiming the fact, as here.

INTERNATIONAL GROWTH: CHALLENGE TO U.S. BANKS*

The unparalleled growth in world trade and investment since 1950 has had a marked impact on the international activities of U.S. banks. The role of the American economy in, and its contribution to, this growth is impressive. Although the possibility that nations might revert to the restrictive trade practices and exchange controls of the Thirties and the immediate postwar period cannot be wholly ignored, the current emphasis is on programs and policies aimed at further increasing the volume of trade and investment.

It is against such a background that this article outlines recent trends in the international banking operations of U.S. banks, describes the history and structure of these operations, and relates them to the changing aspects of world trade and investment. The essential role that banking plays in international trade and investment is neither widely known nor thoroughly understood. It is hoped that greater awareness of the challenges and opportunities in the growing field of international banking will stimulate more U.S. banks to establish or expand their international activities.

I. THE SETTING

U.S. exports reached $21 billion in 1962, and imports more than $16 billion. Both have virtually doubled since 1950. U.S. long-term private investments abroad totaled $49 billion in 1961, about three times the figure of thirteen years ago.[1] Private foreign direct and portfolio investments in the United States almost tripled in a decade to reach over $21 billion at the end of 1961. Table 1 shows U.S. trade and investment since 1950, the average annual rate of increase, and the total increase through 1961.

The figures in Table 1 reflect largely the amazingly swift economic recovery of industrial Europe and Japan in the postwar period. With that recovery came a wholesale dismantling of exchange controls and many other artificial barriers to trade and capital flows. This not only permitted resumption of international investment, but gave rise to new phenomena—large-scale U.S. private direct investment abroad, and sizable foreign investment

---

* George S. Moore, *The National Banking Review*, September, 1963, pp. 1–14.
[1] Secretary of the Treasury Dillon testified on July 8, 1963, before the Joint Economic Committee of the Congress that private investment holdings abroad of Americans now exceed $60 billion.

TABLE 1

U. S. TRADE AND INVESTMENT
(Billions of dollars)

Year	Foreign Trade			Private Investment Abroad		
	Exports[†]	Imports	Total	Direct*	Portfolio	Total*
1950	10.0	8.9	18.9	11.1	5.7	16.8
1951	14.0	11.0	25.0	12.3	6.2	18.5
1952	13.2	10.8	24.0	14.0	6.3	20.3
1953	12.3	10.9	23.2	15.6	5.9	21.5
1954	12.9	10.3	23.2	16.9	6.7	23.6
1955	14.3	11.5	25.8	18.7	7.4	26.1
1956	17.3	12.8	30.1	21.7	7.9	29.6
1957	19.5	13.3	32.8	24.5	8.4	32.9
1958	16.4	13.3	29.7	26.5	10.3	36.8
1959	16.4	15.6	32.0	28.9	11.4	40.3
1960	19.6	15.0	34.6	31.8	12.6	44.4
1961	20.2	14.7	34.9	34.7	14.2	48.9
1962	20.9	16.4	37.3	n.a.	n.a.	n.a.
Avg. annual rate of increase	7%	6%	6%	11%	9%	10%
Increase, 1950-61	109%	84%	97%	212%	149%	191%

* excluding Cuba.   † excluding military.   n.a.–indicates not available.

Sources: Department of Commerce: Overseas Business Reports, April 1963; World Trade Information Service, March 1957; Survey of Current Business, August 1963; and Balance of Payments Statistical Supplement.

in the United States. These developments reflect the internationalization of business and the economic interdependence of the free world.

The removal of the elaborate war and postwar structure of financial and trade controls has made the international capital market freer than at any time since pre-1914, except possibly for a brief period in the Twenties. U.S. banks are not only participating in this freer capital market; they are also helping to bring it about in a number of ways.

There are many indications that world trade and investment are now entering a period of freedom of international movement that will rival or even outshine the "golden era" ushered in by the repeal of the British corn laws in the mid-nineteenth century. Although international trade and investment gains over the past decade may not be equaled in terms of rates of growth in the present decade, there are significant portents of continued gains in trade and investment flows among nations.

For example, in 1962, Congress passed the Trade Expansion Act, which authorizes the President to enter into agreements with other countries for reciprocal tariff reductions on broad categories of goods. Under this mandate, preliminary talks on tariff reductions between the United States and other free world countries got under way in Geneva in May 1963. While the outcome of these negotiations, which are scheduled to begin formally in the spring of 1964, is still some distance away, both tariff and nontariff barriers are likely to be reduced as a result of the "Kennedy round" of trade negotiations.

The future volume of world trade and investment will also be influenced by the efforts of the less-developed countries of the world to achieve faster rates of economic growth. Even if the ambitious plans for economic development by national, regional, and international agencies are only partially successful, these will inevitably bring further expansion in the two-way flow of goods, services, capital and people across national boundaries. The United Nations Trade Conference, scheduled for March 1964, will seek to extend the benefits of expanding trade and investment more swiftly to the less-developed countries. Its findings may have an important bearing on the long-term outlook for international trade, which could in turn affect the magnitude of the international operations of U.S. banks. Of course, the aspirations of all countries for expanded trade could be confounded, if countries become unwilling or unable to make necessary adjustments and, instead, raise barriers against one another.

II. THE GROWING ROLE OF U.S. BANKS

Historically, there has been a close correlation between high levels of international trade and investment on the one hand, and international activities of U.S. banks on the other. During the Twenties when trade and investment were expanding, U.S. banks expanded abroad. During the Thirties when world depression and the drive toward autarky contracted world trade and investment, there was a corresponding contraction of the international activities of U.S. banks. The same correlation is evident today, although the data selected for charting show only a portion of the international business conducted by U.S. banks.

Short-term (under one year) claims of U.S. banks on foreigners at the end of May 1963 totaled $5.2 billion, up $2.7 billion—a 100 percent increase—since the end of 1958, when external currency convertibility was restored in Europe and the United Kingdom (Chart 1). These short-term claims arise, for the most part, directly from the financing of international trade. They consist principally of (1) loans made to and acceptances made for foreigners; (2) drafts drawn against foreigners where collection is made by banks; and (3) foreign currency balances held by banks and their U.S. customers.

Short-term liabilities of U.S. banks to foreigners, including international agencies and foreign governments, are chiefly demand and time deposits and bankers' acceptances.[2] Since the end of 1958, these have increased $3.2 bil-

---

[2] U.S. Treasury bills and certificates are not liabilities of U.S. banks, and hence are not included.

Chart 1

Short-Term Claims on and Liabilities to
Foreigners Reported by U.S. Banks

Source: Federal Reserve Bulletin, July 1963.

Chart 2
Bankers' Acceptances of U.S. Banks Outstanding

Source: Federal Reserve Bulletin, July 1963

lion, or 33 percent, to a total of $13.3 billion at the end of May 1963 (Chart 1).

Bankers' acceptances drawn on and accepted by U.S. banks, primarily to finance international trade (Chart 2), increased $1.5 billion, or 125 percent, in the three years from 1958 through 1961 to a total of $2.7 billion,

Chart 3

Deposits in Foreign Branches of N.Y. Clearing House Banks

Source: New York Clearing House Association Statement (Weekly)

after which they leveled off. The increase during those three years reflects the greater use of dollar acceptances, mainly by Japan, in the growing trade relationships of the world.

Chart 3 shows deposits in foreign branches of the New York clearing house banks, which accounted for over 75 percent of all foreign branches of U.S. banks in 1962. These, too, have increased markedly.

The factors described above point toward an international interdependence unprecedented since the emergence of the nation-state. American banks have already responded to these dvelopments. With the dollar the leading international currency and the United States the world's largest exporter and importer of goods, services and capital, it is only natural that U.S. banks should gird themselves to play the same relative role in international finance that the great British financial institutions played in the nineteenth century. The fact that the Federal Reserve Board is in the process of revising Regulations K and M, which apply to the foreign operations of U.S. banks, is encouraging. To enable U.S. banks to play a leading role in international finance, they must be able to compete fully with the banks of other countries.

III. HISTORY OF U.S. INTERNATIONAL BANKING

To evaluate the changes now occuring in the international role of U.S. banks, it is helpful to glance briefly at the relatively short history of U.S. banks in world business.

These banks entered the arena of international finance much later than did the banks of most major European countries. Throughout virtually the entire era of what has been termed "the golden age" of *laissez faire* in the nineteenth century, the international banking field was left almost completely to the giant financial houses of Europe. Before enactment of the Federal Reserve Act in 1913, U.S. national banks had no authority to enter into foreign operations. Nor were they empowered to accept drafts arising from the import and export of goods and services. Several states permitted banks incorporated under their laws to establish foreign branches, but prior to 1914 the operations of such branches were confined to a few state banks and "private" (unincorporated) institutions. The earliest of these was opened in London in 1887. By 1914, only four incorporated U.S. banks and two foreign banking corporations were active in the operation of foreign branches, with a total of 26 branches overseas. Competition from experienced European banks operating internationally may have deterred U.S. banks from becoming more active, but in any event the focus of business of U.S. banks was on domestic trade and investments. As the composition of U.S. foreign trade broadened to include more manufactured goods rather than just food and raw materials, the need arose to finance trade in these products. In 1911 the National Monetary Commission reported the absence of U.S. banking operations in foreign countries as a major weakness in our financial structure.

The Federal Reserve Act of 1913 authorized national banks to accept drafts, and Section 25 of the Act authorized such banks to establish branches abroad under certain conditions and subject to approval by the Federal Reserve Board. Thus the fundamental banking law of this country for the first time permitted national banks to take advantage of the transformation of the United States from a debtor to a creditor nation. The onset of World War I rendered it virtually impossible for national banks to enter the international field, and it was not until the upsurge of international trade and investment in the Twenties that U.S. banks as a group became seriously involved in international operations. Even this period of comparatively free trade, however, did not stimulate as much interest in the international scene on the part of U.S. banks as does today's increased international business.

The recent expansion of international operations of U.S. banks has been manifested in a number of ways. The number of overseas branches of United States banks increased from 95 in 1950, to 145 at the end of 1962 (154 as of July 1963). U.S. banks which operate abroad exclusively through foreign correspondent banks, rather than through their own branches, are also handling more business than ever before. In addition, bank-owned Edge Act and Agreement corporations, whose foreign operations are described later, have increased from a total of 6 in 1955, to 26 at the end of 1962, and 32 at the end of July 1963. (See Table 2.)

Although these developments are impressive, they leave unanswered two

TABLE 2

INTERNATIONAL OPERATIONS OF
UNITED STATES BANKS

Year End	Foreign Branches	Edge Act & Agreement Corps.
1950	95	5
1955	111	6
1960	124	15
1962	145	26

Source: Information supplied by New York Federal
Reserve District (Unpublished).

significant questions: Are U.S. banks participating as completely as they might in international banking; and are they gearing their operations for further growth in world trade and investment?

Very few U.S. banks have direct branches abroad, even today. Eight banks operate 14 branches in London and four banks each operate a branch in Paris. Among U.S. banks, only First National City Bank, Bank of America, and Chase Manhattan Bank perform large-scale commercial banking through broad networks of foreign branches. Many banks abroad have older and well established overseas branch systems, the most extensive being those of Canada, which operate extensively in Latin America; British overseas banks which virtually encircle the world; and the following individual banks which specialize in geographical areas: The Standard Bank and Barclays Bank D.C.O. in Africa; Bank of London and South America in Latin America; Hong Kong and Shanghai Banking Corporation and Chartered Bank; and their respective affiliates in the Far and Middle East.

It should be noted, moreover, that most U.S. banks conduct their banking activities abroad through foreign correspondent banks rather than through their own branches supplemented by correspondent relationships. Many banks maintain overseas representatives to insure close liaison with foreign banks.

IV. INTERNATIONAL SERVICES OF U.S. BANKS

The response to expanded world trade which U.S. banks have already evidenced can be traced directly to the kind of services they perform in international banking. Since the days of the Hanseatic League, one of the primary functions of lending institutions has been to supply the financing for international trade and services. The basic function of banks in world trade today is still financing exports and imports by extending short- and medium-term credit. This is done through specially tailored methods, such as commercial letters of credit and bankers' acceptances. They also supply medium-

and long-term investment funds. But banks also extend services that are equally essential—the provision of information and know-how. Banks offer customers doing international business credit information and data on foreign markets, help locate potential partners, selling agents and customers, and assist in overcoming language and currency obstacles. In brief, banks bring buyer and seller together and create conditions under which the varying risks for credit and transfer of funds can be accepted by all concerned. Their services are offered to both American and foreign exporters and importers. In the area of overseas investment, businessmen often start by calling on the foreign department of a U.S. bank to obtain economic analyses of market opportunities, assessments of the various risks involved, introductions to potential foreign associates, and short- and medium-term loans.

The reliance of the Export-Import Bank on the commercial banking system to operate its new export insurance and export guarantee programs offers one illustration of partnership activity between government and private banking institutions. These programs perform a vital role in financing U.S. exports. Through them, the Eximbank assumes certain risks which private lending institutions would not be justified in taking. This greatly facilitates the financing of U.S. exports, thus helping us to compete more effectively in foreign markets by placing our exporters on an equal footing with those of Western Europe, where such insurance is well established. The Eximbank offers five types of export insurance or guarantee programs for the extension of short- and medium-term credit. Under four of these, jointly with the Foreign Credit Insurance Association (organized by over 70 private insurance companies), export credit insurance is issued to the U.S. exporter, enabling him to obtain financing more readily from commercial banks. Under the fifth, a guaranty is extended directly to the lending institution. All five programs insure against currency inconvertibility, import or export license restrictions, confiscation, and loss stemming from war or revolution. The programs also insure against certain commercial risks, such as insolvency or protracted default of the foreign buyer.

When a U.S. company sells its product to a foreign buyer under the Eximbank programs, the financial pattern is for the foreign buyer to advance up to 20 percent of the total costs; the American supplier to carry 15 percent of the financed portion; and a commercial bank to finance the remainder, or 85 percent of the financed portion, under Eximbank guarantees. Commercial banks also participate with the Eximbank in extending credit to foreign borrowers under its program of lending for specific projects.

In addition, the international services of U.S. banks are often called upon by international financial institutions. In fiscal year 1962, commercial banks participated in 22 development loans made by the World Bank. This compares with 13 such participations in the fiscal year 1957. Edge Act and Agreement corporations of U.S. banks have joined with foreign banks in partnerships with the International Finance Corporation to participate in financing industrial development banks and, along with the IFC, have provided equity capital for a growing number of industrial enterprises in the developing countries.

U.S. banks have also helped foreign governments to carry out financial stabilization programs. Upon reaching an agreement with the International Monetary Fund on the terms of an over-all stabilization program, foreign governments have on occasion approached U.S. banks for additional funds required beyond those extended by the IMF. Since the amounts involved have run into tens of millions of dollars, several banks have usually participated in the financing, which has taken the form of two-to-four-year term loans. One bank has usually taken the lead in organizing the consortium. In most cases, the foreign government has utilized the bank loans before drawing on IMF funds and has repaid the banks before the IMF was reimbursed.

Increased world trade and investment are rapidly altering and expanding the structure of U.S. international banking; more banks are organizing foreign departments; more correspondent relationships are being formed abroad; more branches are being opened; more Edge Act corporations are being established; and more foreign subsidiaries are being acquired.

V. Edge Act and "Agreement" Corporations

Important avenues through which national banks engage in international banking and finance are the so-called Edge Act and "Agreement" corporations. An amendment to Section 25 of the Federal Reserve Act, passed in 1916, authorized national banks, with permission of the Federal Reserve Board, to invest in corporations chartered either under United States or State law and engaged principally in foreign banking. State-chartered foreign banking corporations were eligible for such investments only where they entered into an agreement with the Board concerning the conduct of their operations. Such corporations have become known as "Agreement" corporations. Provision for federal incorporation of foreign banking and financing was not provided until 1919, under the Edge Act,[3] and such corporations came to be known as Edge Act corporations.

These amendments to Section 25 of the Federal Reserve Act were designed to provide greater flexibility to the overseas operations of U.S. banks. No less than 18 banking corporations were chartered, either by states under agreements with the Federal Reserve Board, or by the Board, between 1919 and 1929. But by the early Thirties all but two had been liquidated or ab-

[3] Senator Walter E. Edge of New Jersey sponsored this provision, Section 25(a) of the Federal Reserve Act.

sorbed by other corporations. Only recently have U.S. banks again taken the route of Edge Act and Agreement corporations to broaden their financial services and enhance their flexibility to participate in international transactions. As late as 1955, there were only six Edge Act or Agreement corporations. By July 1963, U.S. banks had formed 32 such corporations. Their growth has been spurred by the increase in the volume of international business and by the variety of financial transactions engaged in by foreign banks.

Both Edge Act and Agreement corporations are subject to the provisions of Regulation K of the Federal Reserve Board. Under that Regulation, two types of corporations have been established—banking and financing.

The *banking* corporation is empowered to engage in the entire range of U.S. banking activities overseas, with operations at home limited to those incidental to foreign business. In practice, U.S. banks have also utilized the Edge Act banking corporation provisions to acquire and hold stock in foreign banking institutions. The Banca d'America e d'Italia of Milan, for example, is a subsidiary of the Bank of America, New York, which is the Edge Act banking corporation of the Bank of America National Trust and Savings Association, San Francisco. The Bank of Monrovia in Liberia is wholly owned by the International Banking Corporation, First National City's Agreement banking corporation. Seventeen U.S. banks now have such Edge Act (or Agreement) banking corporations.

Edge Act *financing* corporations are chartered to make foreign investments other than in banks. The few financing corporations established in the Twenties and the Thirties were not very active. Revived interest in this approach to expand the international activities of U.S. banks did not occur until the mid-Fifties, and coincided with the postwar dismantling of exchange controls and the increased international flow of private investment. As of July 1963, fifteen U.S. banks had organized Edge Act financing corporations.

The Federal Reserve Board is currently in the process of revising its Regulation K, which applies to banking and financing corporations, to permit greater flexibility in their operations. This is particularly significant in light of the anticipated growth in international banking activities and the need for U.S. banks to compete effectively. The old Regulation requires that each equity investment made by an Edge Act or Agreement corporation be subject to the approval of the Federal Reserve Board, either under a limited general consent given to each corporation or on a case-by-case basis. It is anticipated that the revised Regulation K will permit corporations full flexibility to make equity investments, without the cumbersome procedure of approval, up to the limit permitted by the statute (10 percent of capital plus surplus). Such investments would, of course, remain subject to review by the Federal Reserve Board.

The total activities of Edge Act financing corporations are small compared with the U.S. share of world trade and investment. Current regulations could usefully be liberalized so that these corporations may play a wider role in providing equity financing for economic and industrial development purposes.

VI. ESTABLISHING INTERNATIONAL OPERATIONS

The three largest U.S. banks have sufficient business in certain trading areas abroad to handle transactions through direct branches, working in close harmony with correspondent banks in the particular countries involved. The decision whether or not to establish a new branch abroad requires the careful assessment of a number of factors additional to those considered in establishing a branch domestically. Analysis starts with the usual economic considerations that would be examined in domestic expansion—population, industry, transportation, volume of business activity, estimates of deposits, growth projections and the evaluation of existing and prospective competition. Important considerations are the volume of international trade and investment transactions that the branch could be expected to service, and the number and size of U.S. and other foreign firms located in the region of the country where the branch would be located. But beyond this, other more complicated factors must be assessed. These include the primary factor of political stability in the over-all investment climate. To this must be added the laws, regulations and banking customs of the country concerned. Highly important is the receptivity towards the establishment of a foreign bank displayed by national and local officials. A careful estimate is also made of the contribution that a branch of a U.S. bank could make to the economic objectives of the country. Finally, approval to establish a foreign branch must be obtained not only from the Federal Reserve Board, but also as a rule from the authorities of the country in which it is to be located.

The experience of large banks with direct branches abroad has made them aware that, to be truly international, financial centers such as New York City must welcome branches of foreign banks. To enhance the scope, liquidity and importance of New York as a world financial center, members of the New York Clearing House Association actively supported state legislation passed in 1961 permitting foreign banks to open branches in New York State. Ten foreign banks[4] have taken advantage of the State's new open-door policy. Table 3 lists the foreign bank branches in New York.

The operation of branches by foreign banks constitutes only a small percentage of foreign bank activity in the United States. In addition, over 20 foreign banks have agencies in New York City, with combined assets in excess

---

[4] Under New York State law, the two Puerto Rican banks are defined as foreign banks.

TABLE 3

FOREIGN BANKS WITH BRANCHES IN N. Y.
(As of June 1963)

Bank	No. Branches
Banco de Ponce (P.R.)	2
Banca Nazionale del Lavoro (Italy)	1
Banco Popular de Puerto Rico	1
Bank Leumi le-Israel	1
Bank of London & S. A. Ltd. (Br.)	1
Israel Discount Bank Ltd.	1
Netherlands Trading Society	1
Societe Generale (Fr.)	2
Swiss Bank Corp.	2
The Chartered Bank (Br.)	1

Source: Information supplied by New York State Banking Commission (Unpublished).

of $3 billion; and 30 other foreign banks maintain resident representatives in the U.S. The branches and agencies of foreign banks in the U.S. are not subject to Federal Reserve Board regulations dealing with such important matters as reserves and interest rates.

Canadian banks are especially well represented in the United States, with 28 offices. In addition to branches in Seattle, Washington, and Portland, Oregon, and 2 subsidiaries in California with offices in San Francisco and Los Angeles, Canadian banks own 5 trust companies located in New York City. New York is also the headquarters for seven Edge Act corporations owned by U.S. banks located outside of New York.

Should U.S. banks wish to add international activities to their domestic operations, they should be aware of special problems that the complexities of international banking bring. The most important is the difficulty of finding experienced personnel capable of surmounting the differences of language, geography, and laws and customs that international operations bring. Even U.S. banks with years of experience in the international field find that their biggest difficulty is the selection and training of personnel.

First National City Bank, for example, employs 8,000 people abroad in 33 countries. Less than 4 percent are American citizens assigned to foreign branches from the New York head office. Promising foreign nationals are brought to the New York City headquarters for extended periods of intensive training before returning to their own countries. Clerical as well as executive training programs identical with those conducted at New York headquarters are conducted in the overseas branches.

Among other special factors that arise in international banking are these:

(1) The problem of dealing in many currencies requires specialized knowledge of exchange rates and their movements. In some countries with unstable currencies U.S. banks must consider the risks and consequences of a possible devaluation.

(2) Many countries apply exchange controls over all or a part of their international financial transactions. Exchange controls limit foreign banking operations by impeding and sometimes preventing transactions involving foreign exchange. Rules and regulations of countries engaged in exchange controls are constantly changing. They are highly technical and must be lived with before they can be understood thoroughly.

(3) The possibility of expropriation is always present. U.S. banks at one time had important branches and interests in Czarist Russia, in mainland China, and most recently in Cuba. Unless accompanied by prompt and adequate compensation in convertible currency, which did not occur in the cases cited, the risk of expropriation inhibits overseas expansion. As a practical deterrent to such possibilities, the Hickenlooper amendment to the Foreign Aid legislation, requiring that U.S. aid be terminated in the event of expropriation without adequate compensation, is proving effective.

(4) The unavailability of credit information comparable to audited statements and registration statements of the SEC makes it difficult to evaluate a foreign credit risk. The general reluctance of foreign businesses to disclose information comparable to that which is readily available in the United States adds to the difficulty of judging creditworthiness abroad.

(5) Restrictive banking regulations limit U.S. banking operations abroad. U.S. banks operating branches abroad have suffered competitive disadvantages because they are subject not only to local regulations, but also to those of our own government.

Branches of national banks operating abroad are supervised by the Federal Reserve Board and subject to Regulation M. The provisions of Regulation M had, in effect, applied the same standards and structure to the operations of foreign branches of national banks as are applied to branches operated domestically. But laws, customs and practices for banking institutions vary widely from country to country. Until now the limitations of Regulation M have put foreign branches of national banks at a competitive disadvantage in some countries. European banks, including British banks, with large international commercial operations, have enjoyed a far greater latitude than have national banks in competing effectively within the laws and customs of the country in which a branch is located.

To correct this competitive disadvantage, the Congress in 1962 amended Section 25 of the Federal Reserve Act by enacting Public Law 87–588, "An Act to Improve the Usefulness of National Bank Branches in Foreign Countries." This amendment authorizes the extension to foreign branches of "such further powers as may be usual in connection with the transaction of the business of banking in the places such foreign branches shall transact business." Further powers newly authorized by law include authorization to (1) execute and deliver guarantees; (2) accept drafts on bills of exchange; (3) purchase and hold certificates of ownership issued by central banks; (4) buy and sell obligations of the national government of the country in which the foreign branch is located; and (5) take and record liens on real estate.

Effective August 1, 1963, the Federal Reserve Board revised Regulation M giving national banks these broader powers in operating their overseas branches. The extended powers to acquire and deal in certain securities will, under 12 U.S.C. 335, also benefit foreign branches of state member banks. Still termed "unnecessarily restrictive" by the Comptroller of the Currency, the revision nevertheless is a step in the right direction. To enable U.S. banks to compete effectively with foreign banks, both Regulations K and M must be liberalized to provide the same flexibility of operations as foreign banks enjoy.

VII. Conclusions

It would be easy to overemphasize the special problems and risks encountered in foreign banking. Actually, they are similar to those which must be faced and overcome successfully by all business corporations with global operations.

Despite the many issues in international trade and finance that have yet to be surmounted, the trends toward continued world growth are plain for all to see. These will continue to pose a challenge to U.S. banks. But they also present opportunities for broadening the services that U.S. banks can provide to the business community, to the nation, and to the free world. As American business increasingly looks outward for expansion, so U.S. banks will find international operations a profitable experience.

FOREIGN BANK ACTIVITY IN THE UNITED STATES*

Expanding trade and foreign investments and the importance of the dollar as an international currency are enlarging foreign banking requirements in the United States. The results: Foreign banks are opening branches in New York and foreign-controlled state-chartered banks are showing rapid growth in California.

Foreign international banks have been represented in the United States for a good number of years, but the advent of foreign branching promises a new era of even greater activity.

NEW YORK

Formerly allowing only agency offices, New York State banking laws were revised in 1960, and, effective January 1, 1961, foreign banks were allowed to open branch offices with full privileges to accept deposits and carry on a general banking business. This gave foreign banks rights which U.S. banks had enjoyed in branching abroad for some time, and followed reports that permission to open new U.S. branches was denied by some foreign countries because New York could not offer reciprocity.

To date, 12 banks headquartered abroad have opened New York branch offices: three from London, two from Israel and Puerto Rico, and one each from France, the Netherlands, Switzerland, Italy, and Lebanon. Banco da Lavoura de Minas Gerais S.A., Belo Horizonte, Brazil, has an application awaiting approval.

International Banks

In most instances, the banks involved are large, active international banks which have been doing business in world financial centers for many years. However, changing conditions and the opportunity to expand their banking services led to the conversion of agencies to branches.

As would be expected, most branches are heavily involved in international transactions and not directly competing with New York banks for domestic accounts. While these branches will certainly not turn away depositors

* R. Gerald Fox, *Bankers Monthly Magazine*, Sept. 15, 1963, pp. 46–60.

or savers, at the same time they are not actively soliciting personal accounts. Most such accounts come to the branches through their efforts to build international business.

Direct Appeal

This does not hold true for all branches, however. Offices of the two Puerto Rican banks, Banco de Ponce and Banco Popular de Puerto Rico, are directed primarily at the large Puerto Rican population in New York, estimated at some 750,000. Offering special services, including Spanish-speaking personnel, these banks have shown a significant increase in deposits since the branches opened in late 1961.

To a lesser extent, Bank Leumi le-Israel B.M. and Israel Discount Bank, Ltd., aim their appeal at the sizable Jewish community. While Bank Leumi, Israel's largest bank, is particularly active in international dealings, a relatively smaller percentage of transactions of these banks are directly involved in international trade and a greater attempt is made to obtain domestic deposits.

Facilities for Trade

Obtaining domestic deposit accounts, however, is not the primary reason for branching. In most European countries, trade accounts for a much larger percentage of Gross National Product than in the United States. Thus, with trade increasing, it is vital for major European and Mid-East banks to have the facilities to handle the necessary transactions. As Europe and the United States draw closer, such international banks must move actively into this country or risk becoming little more than a regional bank.

Also, with sterling and dollars the primary currencies, it is necessary to provide adequate facilities for transfer. Most of the banks now branching in New York are already represented with such offices in London. Since the bulk of reserves are often in dollars, it is essential to have a facility to transfer and trade dollars and dollar obligations.

Loan Activity

The percentage of loans and discounts directly involved in international transactions varies considerably among the branches. Israel Discount Bank estimates its foreign loans and discounts at 25 to 35 percent of the total. Discount Bank, of course, is more directly involved in domestic business and its domestic deposits have shown a rapid rate of growth.

On the other hand, banks such as The Chartered Bank and Societe Generale pour Favoriser le Development du Commerce et de l'Industrie en France, S.A. are much more active in international transactions. Chartered Bank for example, places the percentage of loans and discounts directly involved in foreign trade at approximately 70 percent. Fundamentally, Chartered Bank's branch acts as agent for branches throughout the world and provides services to its associated organizations, the Eastern Bank, Ltd., the Irano British Bank and the Allahabad Bank, Limited.

FOREIGN BANK BRANCHES (NEW YORK)

Bank	Home Office	Assets in Dollars (000)	Date Initial Branch Established
The Chartered Bank	London	$1,312,243*	August 1961
Bank Leumi le-Israel B.M.	Tel-Aviv	420,702	August 1961
Bank of London & South America Limited	London	1,017,218	August 1961
Banco de Ponce	Ponce, Puerto Rico	111,541	September 1961‖
Societe Generale	Paris	3,094,533†	November 1961#
Banco Popular de Puerto Rico	San Juan	220,229	November 1961
Israel Discount Bank, Ltd.	Tel-Aviv	239,078	April 1962
Nederlandsche Handel-Maatschappij, N.V. (The Netherlands Trading Society)	Amsterdam, Netherlands	674,747	June 1963
Swiss Bank Corporation	Basle	1,590,992*	June 1963**
Banca Nazionale del Lavoro	Rome	4,439,185‡	July 1963
Barclays Bank D.C.O.	London	2,366,713§	July 1963††
Intra Bank, Societe Anonyme Libanaise	Beirut, Lebanon	308,669	July 1963
Banco da Lavoura de Minas Gerais S.A.	Belo Horizonte, Brazil	204,421	‡‡

  * Total assets exclude liabilities of customers in respect of confirmed credits and guarantees.
  † Provisional figures.
  ‡ Includes annexed section.
  § September 1962 figures. All other figures are of December 1962.
  ‖ Two branches were opened in September 1961, a third in August 1963.
  # A second branch opened in May 1963.
  ** Two branches were opened in June 1963.
  †† A second branch was approved, but is not yet in operation.
  ‡‡ Application before New York State Banking Department.

Agency Decline

Since the advent of branching in New York, the number of agency offices has been slowly declining. Agency offices increased from 52 in 1955 to 74 at year's end 1960. That number has now declined to 64, although the increase in branches has left the total number of foreign bank offices in New York about unchanged.

Date	Number of Branches	Number of Agencies
December 31, 1955	0	52
December 31, 1960	0	74
December 31, 1961	6	70
December 31, 1962	7	68
August 31, 1963	12*	64*

* Not including one agency which has applied for branch status.

Of course, it is natural that an increase in branches would bring about a corresponding decline in agencies, with the exception of those foreign banks which previously had no agency office in New York. Under the New York State law allowing foreign bank branching, it is stipulated that a foreign banking corporation may not maintain both an agency and a branch. Only two branch offices had no representative in New York prior to their licensing: Banco Popular de Puerto Rico and Intra Bank, Beirut, Lebanon.

Opportunity Amid Competition

There can be no denying that foreign banks are taking some international business away from domestic banks. But while they offer a measure of competition, they are also helping to give a greater impetus to international activity. For one thing, the growth of foreign banking in this country has as its counterpart, greater domestic bank activity overseas. The liberalization of New York banking laws allowed foreign banks an opportunity to further their activities in the dollar market here, and improved domestic banks' opportunities to move into, say, the sterling market.

Revision of the banking laws, and the resultant competition, in the words of one New York banker, "definitely increased the stature of the international money markets." More active international competition leads directly to an improved international market.

Improved Relationship

A number of large New York banks also feel their correspondent relationships with foreign banks which opened branches have actually improved, rather than diminished as some overseas bankers had feared. Foreign branches commonly keep reserve accounts in domestic banks, and, on occasion, borrow from them. The technical bank practices, such as check clearing, also has allowed New York banks to obtain some additional business.

As a result, while the competition is greater, the branches have actually increased the business of some domestic banks, both directly, as noted above, and indirectly through area-wide stimulation in international activities.

In Chicago, some large commercial banks voice regrets that foreign bank branching is not allowed in that city. Notes one banker: "The tragedy is that all are going to New York." Most believe foreign banks would not affect customer relationships, but would give the Midwest a greater international awareness that would bode well for all concerned. There has been some support in Illinois for a proposed law allowing foreign branching, but opponents see it as a "foot-in-the-door" for domestic bank branching.

Although some 13 banks have either opened branch offices or made application for a branch, many foreign banks have taken no action. While most bankers look for additional branching activity in future months, it seems likely a substantial number of banks will make no effort to convert their agencies.

Of course, one of the primary prerequisites to establishing a branch office is the belief that the branch can generate enough business to make the venture worthwhile. Costs are high and taxes are substantial. Also, there is some fear of undermining a good correspondent relationship, although this does not seem to be borne out in actual practice. Some foreign banks feel New York State banking laws are too restrictive, although this too has diminished somewhat through a further liberalization of regulations.

As laws now stand, foreign banks are in a unique position in that they are not prohibited from operating branches in more than one state. It appears possible for such a bank to open branches in both California and New York, an opportunity not now open to domestic banks.

CALIFORNIA

In California, foreign banking growth has been of a different nature. With no foreign branching of the New York variety allowed, overseas banks have established separate state-chartered corporations to transact their international and domestic business. Recent growth has primarily consisted of establishing additional branch offices and in increasing assets and deposits.

Basically, foreign banking activity in California falls into three categories: foreign-controlled state-chartered banks, foreign banking corporations, and representatives of foreign banking corporations. Only the state-chartered banks are allowed to accept deposits and carry on a full banking service. At the present time, six foreign banks have established separate California banks, two each from Hong Kong, Japan and Canada (see accompanying table). While these banks have some domestic ownership, they are primarily foreign owned and controlled.

Foreign banking corporations are also licensed by the superintendent of banks. According to provisions of the regulation:

"A foreign corporation . . . may transact in this State the business of buying, selling, paying, or collecting bills of exchange, of issuing letters of credit, or receiving money for transmission by draft, check, cable, or other-

Foreign-Controlled Banks (California)

State-Chartered

Bank	Controlling Bank	Assets (000)
Bank of Canton	Bank of Canton, Ltd., Hong Kong	$ 25,757
Bank of Montreal (California)	Bank of Montreal, Canada	28,181
The Bank of Tokyo of California	Bank of Tokyo, Ltd.	104,585
The Canadian Bank of Commerce (California)	Canadian Imperial Bank of Commerce, Toronto	63,834
The Hongkong & Shanghai Banking Corp. of California	The Hongkong & Shanghai Banking Corp., Hong Kong	20,698
The Sumitomo Bank of California	The Sumitomo Bank Limited, Osaka	94,669

Foreign Banking Corporations

Corporation	Office	Head Office
Bank of Montreal	San Francisco	Montreal
The Bank of Tokyo, Ltd.	San Francisco	Tokyo
The Bank of Tokyo, Ltd.	Los Angeles	
Canadian Imperial Bank of Commerce	San Francisco	Toronto
The Hongkong & Shanghai Banking Corp.	San Francisco	Hong Kong
The Mitsubishi Bank, Ltd.	Los Angeles	Tokyo
The Sanwa Bank, Limited	San Francisco	Osaka, Japan

wise, and of making loans. A foreign corporation shall not accept deposits in this State."

Currently, six foreign banks have in operation seven such corporations. (The Bank of Tokyo, Ltd. has two.)

Seven additional foreign banks have obtained a license to maintain a representative office, or offices, in California (see accompanying chart).

Foreign Banks with Representative Offices in California

Bank	Home Office	Representative Office
Banco Nacionale de Mexico, S.A.	Mexico City	Los Angeles
Barclays Bank, Limited	London	San Francisco
First National Bank of Hawaii	Honolulu	San Francisco
The Bank of Nova Scotia	Toronto	Los Angeles
Bank Leumi le-Israel, B.M.	Tel Aviv	Beverly Hills
The Royal Bank of Canada	Montreal	Los Angeles
The Toronto-Dominion Bank	Toronto	Los Angeles

Growth in assets and deposits among several of the foreign-controlled banks has been substantial. In particular, the Japanese banks have seen assets soar in the past few years. The Bank of Tokyo of California, largest of the foreign-controlled but state chartered banks, registered a more than six-fold increase in resources since 1955. Assets in that year were just over $17 million. At year's end 1961, the total rose to $75.8 million and on December 31, 1962 stood at $104.6 million. Deposits rose from $15.3 million in 1955 to $77.1 million last December. The Sumitomo Bank of California, controlled by The Sumitomo Bank Limited, Osaka, Japan, showed an equally high growth rate. Assets rose from $17.5 million in 1955 to $94.7 million in 1962 while deposits jumped from well under $1 million to $74.4 million.

These California banks are actively seeking domestic deposit and savings accounts and concurrently their percentage of loans and discounts directly involved with international trade tend to be considerably lower than the New York branches of foreign banks. The Hongkong and Shanghai Banking Corporation of California provides one example. This British international bank subsidiary, established in 1955, showed total assets in 1962 of $22.8 million and deposits of $18 million. Interested in building up its domestic business in addition to maintaining its share of international trade, this bank estimates only about 15 percent of its loans and discounts are directly internationally-oriented. The Sumitomo Bank of California says approximately 75 to 80 percent of its loans and discounts are granted to domestic business. Also, the majority of the deposit accounts are domestic business firms and personal accounts.

Why do these foreign banks establish separate corporations? Of course, the opportunity for profitable business is a major reason. But M. Sasaki, president of The Sumitomo Bank of California voiced another important factor:

"Being a State bank, we can become better acquainted with the local business communities and the American people. Thus, in addition to international trade business, we can better promote friendship between the United States and Japan." This, in turn, can lead to greater trade and investment and more business for banks.

FOREIGN BANKS IN LONDON*

London has been important as an international trade centre since Roman times and as a financial centre since the thirteenth century, but London began to assume a special role during the French Revolution, when it was a safe refuge for French money, and during the Napoleonic wars afterwards it became the refuge for European capital as well. With the defeat of Napoleonic France and the decline of Spain and Portugal as maritime powers, Great Britain, with her vast and rich colonial Empire, her unchallenged rule of the seas and her industrial progress following the industrial revolution, emerged as the strongest military and economic power in the world, with London her foremost political, commercial and financial centre.

Businessmen were sent here to look after the transferred capital, but not unnaturally the world's most important commercial centre was also a magnet for other enterprising people and from the outbreak of the French Revolution until the beginning of Queen Victoria's reign there was a flow of foreign firms into London. Some of these were commercial, others were banking or financial concerns, but often the three characteristics were combined in the same firm. Their principal aims were: (i) the sale or the financing of sales of imported commodities; (ii) the purchase or the financing of purchases of products of the highly-developed British industries; and (iii) the issue of loans, very often for account of foreign states. It is only necessary to remember how the Rothschilds, the Hambros, the Schroders, the Sassoons, the Brandts, and others came at this period to realise the significance of the development.

IMPORTANCE OF STERLING

About the middle of the last century the aspect of interest, as far as concerns the present study, of the London financial market as well as of the overseas trade of the United Kingdom and the Empire was that London was pre-financing, financing, refinancing and post-financing almost exclusively in sterling. The clearing banks were purely domestic institutions, leaving any overseas business to the colonial companies, colonial banks, acceptance houses and other merchant banks. Imports and exports were generally dealt with against documentary drafts up to 180 days' sight on London or on important overseas cities. A large proportion of drafts was issued against documentary credits and authorisations to purchase. The usance drafts on London were discounted, as trade or banking bills, by the discount houses. Drafts

* O. Petit, *Supplement to Investors Chronicle*, March 30, 1962, pp. 37, 39.

payable on centres of the Empire as it then was, were negotiated either by colonial companies, by the recently founded colonial banks or by merchant banks dealing in colonial currencies. Negotiation of drafts payable in foreign countries and dealings in foreign exchange were performed exclusively by merchant banks.

Spread of Industrialisation

During the second half of the century industrial development spread to the Continent, the U.S.A. and Japan; and so far as Europe and Japan were concerned, their newly founded joint stock banks were often the promoters or the seconders of the new industries and therefore the purveyors of all types of financial aid.

The foreign banks had to utilise the London market to obtain sterling documentary credits for the import of raw materials by their customers and had to negotiate, at home, documentary letters of credit and authorisations to purchase, issued in sterling by British banks, relating to the export of national raw materials or products to Great Britain and her Empire. As was to be expected this business started through the intermediary of the London merchant banks, colonial banks and colonial companies, but because of its ever increasing volume and therefore increasing risks, the foreign banks began to consider the advisability of establishing offices in London themselves. They were assisted in that decision by the London money market, inasmuch as the discount houses were not only ready to receive money at short notice from, but also to discount the acceptances of the foreign banks.

Other direct and indirect benefits were considered before they decided to come—for instance, the possibility of dealing in foreign exchange, of immediately regarding the London branches or affiliations as customers of their own country's commercial concerns, of obtaining a share of the London business of their associated banks and correspondents spread over the world and of obtaining from the British banks a large share of their foreign business. In the last mentioned respect it may be said that in order to save expense and to avoid erroneous interpretation of instructions (often caused by exchange of correspondence written in different languages) British banks used to entrust their transactions to the foreign banks' London offices whenever that was possible.

An Unwritten Rating

One of the indirect benefits arose from the fact that London was, as it is now, the best information and observation centre of the world; but by far the most important indirect benefit was the appraisal of a foreign commercial bank by the money market, and this unwritten rating was of international importance. As mentioned before, the discount houses discounted the acceptances of a foreign bank and received the latter's short-term liquid resources. As foreign banks' acceptances are not admitted by the Bank of England for re-discount, they were either utilised as collateral for money received from other British or foreign banks or sold to them. The proportion between money placed in the market and the acceptances in circulation, the amount and the ease with which the acceptances were received by other banks, all gave an indication of the standing of that particular foreign bank and this standing had its practical expression in the rate of discount applied by the market. Many foreign banks enjoyed, as they do nowadays, such high standing that their acceptances could command the very prime rate.

The form generally adopted by the foreign banks for their London offspring was that of a direct branch but for particular reasons, such as the eventual participation of outside capital, the requirements of legislation at home, etc., an affiliated British limited company was sometimes established. The preference for a direct branch is obvious inasmuch as an affiliated company would, or at any rate should, have required the outright transfer of a capital proportionate to the importance of the parent bank instead of an elastic transfer of money according to the needs and to the prevailing rates of interest. Furthermore, the London money market would have been inclined to make its appraisal of the affiliated company, and of the parent institution only indirectly.

The flow of the foreign commercial joint stock banks into London started towards the end of the last century and by 1914, at the outbreak of the first world war, there were banks in London attributable to all important countries. The only nations not represented or who were only partially represented were the Scandinavian countries, the South American republics and the Austro-Hungarian Empire. Contemporaneously with the flow of foreign banks into London there had been the expansion abroad of specialised British banks and the complete or partial absence of Austro-Hungarian and South American banks stemmed from this. It should also be noted that the backbone of the commercial banking system of many South American countries was provided by affiliations of European banks already established in London. It is not so easy to explain the absence of Scandinavian Banks but, as far as I can see, it was due, (i) to the close economic and historical relationship between those countries and Germany ever since the time of the famous Hanseatic League, (ii) to their slight (with the exception of Sweden) industrial development, and (iii) to the Scandinavian origin of Hambros Bank.

Changing Methods

Soon after the first World War there was an important change in the methods of British overseas banking. By 1922/23 the process, which had started just before the war, was completed and all the clearing banks were fully engaged in all types of foreign business and foreign exchange dealings. Foreign banks therefore found easier access to the services and facilities of the London markets and had less need of local intermediaries. There were other changes, too.

The world economic crisis which started in 1929, the ensuing crisis of sterling, the crisis of the German balance of payments, the settlement by many important countries of their foreign trade through bilateral clearing accounts, were all factors harmful to the activity of the foreign banks in London and it was largely from prestige that only a few of them closed down between the wars. The German banks in London, liquidated by the British authorities during the war, never saw reason to re-open, however.

REPRESENTATIVES

After the second World War, notwithstanding the increasing competition of New York as an international trade and financial centre, London quickly regained the greater part of her importance. However, during the first ten years, the intransferability and inconvertibility of sterling, the ensuing delay in re-establishing a real exchange and arbitrage market, the policy of cheap money, and the wide service offered by the big British banks, did not much encourage foreign banks to open branches in London. Moreover, the two Italian banks, notwithstanding the revocation of their wartime liquidation, were content to send their representatives instead of reopening their branches in London.

The system of representatives started between the two wars. The services and facilities of the London market, as already explained, are now open to foreign banks more than ever before. With improved telephonic communications and the use of the Telex it is very easy now to deal in foreign exchange and to place money in London direct from abroad. Furthermore nowadays, and contrary to practice in the past, neither foreign nor British banks are, generally speaking, free to use a correspondent of their choice; the bank to whom an overseas transaction must be entrusted is specifically indicated by the customer.

If the need for a branch or an affiliation is no longer pressing, a representative can be useful. Not being engaged in banking work he does not require a large and expensive organisation; he can maintain contacts with correspondents and friends, he can settle incidents and above all he can provide the London market with any type of general and specific information it may require relating to his country. In turn he can convey to his bank any useful items of news which an important observation centre such as London will provide.

THE POST-WAR SITUATION

With the external convertibility of sterling, the re-establishment of a full exchange market, but above all with the relinquishment of the cheap money policy and the spreading of foreign industrial firms and factories in the United Kingdom, the opening of branches of foreign banks in London has been resumed. Broadly speaking, however, they are either banks of the in-dependent sterling area countries, or of countries with surplus capital, or of countries whose industrial activity has expanded in the United Kingdom, or banks with special interest in the so-called "Eurodollars" whose market is centred in London. It is also useful to know that many London branches and representatives of foreign banks have the whole of Europe as their zone of influence.

There appear to be at present in London about 45 branches or affiliations and 15 representatives of foreign commercial banks.

What of the future? Should Great Britain join the European Economic Community the importance of London could increase to an unprecedented level, but an essential condition, so far as I can see it, is the restoration of a full and lasting confidence in the currency. It would be sad if the continuing crisis of sterling were to undermine such a promising development.

COMMERCIAL BANKING TRENDS IN WESTERN EUROPE*

Spurred by rapid economic growth and even more rapid monetary growth, Europe's commercial banking industry has been expanding at a breath-taking pace during recent years. Since 1958 commercial bank deposits in the major countries have gained about 95 percent; bank credits have increased some 130 percent; and the number of bank offices has risen an estimated 25 percent over these years.

But at the same time as bank deposits multiply and bank office networks grow denser, banking competition is becoming increasingly intense, and the various financial institutions are showing a growing tendency to move into one another's traditional spheres. In Britain, for example, both hire-purchase finance houses and merchant banks are encroaching on some of the commercial banks' business. In Germany, the commercial banks find themselves vigorously competing with a greatly expanded savings bank system for both deposits and loans. And, in Italy, the nationwide commercial banks are facing savings institutions and regional banks that have grown large enough to lend to industry and engage in international transactions.

As a result of the new competition, the commercial banks have suffered a steady decline in their respective market shares. For instance, the German commercial banks' share of demand deposits fell from 48 percent in 1958 to 45 percent in 1963. In Italy, the commercial banks' share dropped from 70 percent to 68 percent, in Britain from 55 percent to 52 percent, and in France from 69 percent to 66 percent over the same five year period.

BROAD IMPLICATIONS

More important, however, than this direct impact on commercial banking are the implications of the new banking trends for the level of consumer demand and the pace of industrial investment in Western Europe.

The growing competition in retail banking has resulted in a rapid expansion of consumer finance at a time when automobiles and expensive appliances

* *Report on Western Europe,* The Chase Manhattan Bank, New York, February–March, 1965.

are coming within reach of the average household. Without this growing volume of consumer credit at reasonable interest rates, Europe's high level of consumer demand might be difficult to sustain.

The growing competition among banks in the area of industrial finance comes at a time when European industry is hard pressed for medium and long-term funds. Partly because of the narrowness of Europe's capital markets, a larger supply of capital funds from the banking system seems necessary for European industry to participate successfully in the costly automation race. Hopefully, the growth of personal savings and the steadily expanding volume of loanable term money will also tend to lower long-term interest rates in Europe, and thereby reduce the Atlantic interest rate differentials that are so detrimental to the U.S. payments balance.

These trends in Western Europe have important implications for U.S. companies with business relationships in Western Europe. Thus it is useful to take a closer look at recent developments in retail banking, business lending, and international finance.

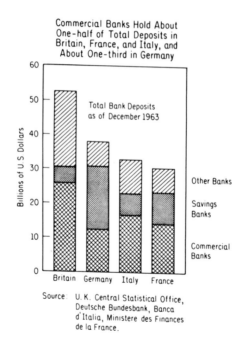

Commercial Banks Hold About One-half of Total Deposits in Britain, France, and Italy, and About One-third in Germany

Total Bank Deposits as of December 1963

Billions of U S Dollars

Other Banks

Savings Banks

Commercial Banks

Britain   Germany   Italy   France

Source: U. K. Central Statistical Office, Deutsche Bundesbank, Banca d'Italia, Ministere des Finances de la France.

RETAIL BANKING

Europe's new banking competition is getting its major boost from the expansion of retail banking and the unprecedented growth of savings deposits. Traditionally, European banking was based on a functional specialization where commercial banks catered mainly to corporate customers and specialized in international finance, and where savings banks collected small deposits and invested mainly in mortgages and government securities. But because of this traditional relationship, savings banks are now in a favored position to benefit from the rapidly growing retail banking market.

Moreover, as savings banks saw both savings and checking deposits bulge, they began to widen their operations by gradually moving into commercial banking. For example, savings banks are today making commercial loans with increasing skill, especially the regional or central savings banks with whom smaller local banks deposit surplus funds. In Belgium and Germany, such central savings banks compare in size with the large nationwide commercial banks, and in Denmark, Italy, and Switzerland a few large savings institutions have gained considerable prominence.

The competitive response of Europe's commercial banks to the savings banks' improving position has been a determined push for consumer retail business. Branch systems are being expanded rapidly, though Europe is already the most densely banked area of the world. In the United Kingdom, for example, there is now roughly one bank office for every 3,400 inhabitants, in Italy the number is 4,500, in France 3,800, and in Germany a mere 1,800. In contrast, U.S. banking density, including savings and loan associations, is one office for every 5,100 inhabitants.

The rapid pace of branching was accompanied by a general effort to extend the banking habit to wider sections of the population. Except for Britain, most continental countries still favor giro accounts—where payments are made by ordering one's bank to transfer funds to the account of one's creditor—over U.S.-type checking accounts. Partly for this reason, the use of cash as a means of payment is still considerable in most continental countries.

To change all this and to tap the potentially rich retail market, most of the large European banks are now actively soliciting personal checking and savings accounts, and many have entered the consumer loan field. This marketing offensive is being supported by increased advertising, though most of it has so far been of the institutional rather than the hard-sell variety.

Another response of Europe's commercial banks to the new competition in retail banking has been to form or acquire specialized financial institutions. Some British banks, for example, have become associated with hire-purchase companies, and German commercial banks have established mutual funds as well as instalment lending institutions.

The trend toward more aggressive retail banking has generally been most pronounced in those countries where the savings banks are competitively strongest, namely in Germany, Italy, Belgium, Denmark, and Switzerland—but less so in Britain and France. Yet the growth of personal deposits and the demand for consumer finance are pressing upward in all Western European countries, and only those banks that are able to satisfy the growing banking needs of the average wage and salary earners will stay ahead in the competitive race toward larger balance totals and better profits.

Business Lending

Parallel to the growth of consumer banking, new problems and competitive challenges have arisen on banking's wholesale front. The last decade has seen tremendous corporate expansions through internal growth, mergers, and acquisitions, both within and across the respective national frontiers. This expansion of industrial size requires larger single loan commitments, a development which has led to some bank mergers as, for example, in the Netherlands. It has also stimulated cooperation among financial institutions of different countries, a trend that is particularly pronounced in the areas of long-term lending, underwriting and investment counseling.

In addition to the need for an increase in the size of specific loans, European corporations require a larger volume of medium and long-term loans to meet the continuing heavy pace of industrial capital investments as well as the rising requirements of export financing.

Of course, the demand for medium-term bank loans has always been strong, and most continental commercial banks—though not in Italy—have traditionally done a great deal of medium-term lending. But competitive pressures to extend more term loans is growing steadily, and bank portfolios are showing it. For example, German commercial banks' medium and long-term loans (over one-half year) were 31 percent of total loans outstanding in 1955, 49 percent in 1960, and more than 65 percent in 1964. Similar shifts in commercial lending patterns, although to lesser extents, occurred in other continental countries. And even in Britain, where commercial banks hardly ever made exceptions to extending only self-liquidating loans, the banks are being pressed for term loans.

One reason why Europe's commercial banks find it difficult to resist pressures for longer term loans is the growing readiness of savings banks and insurance companies to extend such loans to private enterprise. Data showing the extent to which such institutions have entered the industrial lending field are hard to come by, but in Germany, loans of life insurance companies to the industrial sector rose by 143 percent between 1958 and 1963 (compared with a 63 percent growth of commercial bank loans); and in France, savings banks' loans constituted 20 percent of industry's outside financial resources in 1963, compared with 15 percent in 1958.

International Banking

Another important aspect of Europe's rising bank competition is the growing scope of international financial activity and the widening of banking opportunities that it entails.

There are at least three sides to this development. One has been the advent of nonresident convertibility in 1958, which enabled banks to make loans to foreign customers and to take advantage of existing interest rate differentials. Another has been the emergence of the Euro-currency markets through which many banks as well as large industrial concerns have gained easy access to foreign funds and to foreign deposit opportunities. And, finally, the over-all demand for international funds and services has increased greatly with the rapid increase in foreign trade and investment, and with the emergence of multinational corporations. These developments have contributed to a partial internationalization of banking, inside Europe as well as across the North Atlantic. The main effect of this has been the creation of banking alternatives for domestic corporations, which in turn has led to an over-all increase in bank competition.

The new competitive forces in European banking are powerful. They will undoubtedly require commercial banks to make further adjustments. But, more important, they will benefit the European economies by providing more consumer banking needed to support rising levels of incomes and expenditure. Moreover, the banks will be able to channel more funds into medium-term industrial credits to sustain Europe's rapid economic growth.

WHIRLING IN A LATIN AMERICAN SPIRAL*

A European banker recently returned from a year in Latin America describes some of the trials of banking in an area long on regulations, but short on stability.

It is normally unwise to generalise about Latin American countries, but one particular paradox appears to be common to the whole region. It is the determination of governments to prescribe minutely detailed regulations for every aspect of economic life, matched by an equal determination of their citizens to evade and frustrate the regulations so as to enjoy relative freedom in carrying on their business. This process is of course intensified when strict compliance with the regulations would logically cause bankruptcy.

Because of their sensitive central position in the financial system, the commercial banks in Latin America are particularly subject to their governments' passion for regulation. For example, in Brazil, the maximum rate of interest permissible on advances was fixed several years ago at 12 percent a year, after the speculative nature of many of that country's enterprises had forced up interest rates to a level that effectively precluded normally prudent concerns from using the banking system at all. Since the country's annual rate of inflation rose to over 80 percent last year and topped 140 percent early this year, the 12 percent interest ceiling has become risible. The result is that, to maintain their profits, the banks must impose extra charges, above the interest ceiling; thus they raise the effective interest by adding information fees, and commissions on transfers and guarantees.

This rule on interest has, together with other distortions caused by inflation, caused far-reaching changes in banking business in the inflationary Latin American countries—which means in practice most of them with notable exceptions like Mexico and Venezuela. Commercial deposits are maintained by firms at the lowest practicable levels, because the interest a bank is permitted to pay on such deposits is frequently insufficient even to offset the rate of depreciation of the currency. Similarly the interest ceiling has reduced the volume of overdrafts because of their comparatively long term—six to twelve months is usual. Banks have therefore to concentrate on essentially short-term operations such as the discounting of trade bills over one to three months and, a speciality of the foreign banks, foreign exchange operations.

The scarcity of deposits leads even the most reputable institutions into

* *The Economist,* November 21, 1964, pp. 868, 871.

Chart 1
Inflation in Latin America
Consumer price Index 1958 = 100 (All items)

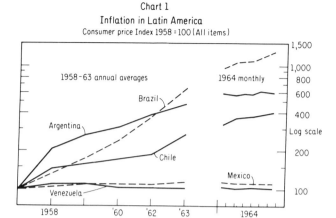

practices that would raise eyebrows in Britain. It is quite usual to induce a company to make a substantial term deposit by promising extra credit facilities to that firm in the future, or to an associated company in the present. The payment of interest on sight deposits, also unthinkable in Britain, is common practice in Latin America; it may be discouraged by the banking authorities, but recourse to it is necessary to maintain one's competitive position.

MANAGERS' COMMISSIONS

Further extraordinary practices are caused by the Latin American governments' predilection for credit squeezes in the private sector in an attempt to counter inflation—an attempt that rarely achieves its object because it is usually not accompanied by any effective restraint of public expenditure. But the response of the banks in Latin America to such pressure is not an evenly spread tightening of lending policy. The position is complicated by the common practice of paying a manager a personal commission on any facilities his bank may grant, one percent of the amount of the loan being a common amount.

It also happens that banks are closely integrated by common directorships with commercial and industrial concerns and this ensures at all times a class of powerful, preferred clients, despite recent attempts by the authorities of certain countries to curtail loans by banks to their own directors and chief executives, and their families.

Regulation of banking by the authorities is pervasive and ever-present, and the number of detailed regulations is so large that many banks maintain a legal section, manned by qualified lawyers, to deal with them. Compliance with the regulations is enforced by frequent visits from official inspectors; not, as in Britain, by the banks' own inspection departments acting as agents for the authorities. The banking system is supervised in most countries by an inspector of banks, who may be an official of the central bank, or may be independent of it and responsible directly to the minister of finance.

Because of rampant inflation in many important Latin American countries, particularly Argentina, Brazil, Chile, Colombia and Uruguay, it is usual to find specialised medium and long-term operations such as industrial, crop and mortgage loans, handled by official banks that specialise in these types of loan. Their inevitable losses are made up by the governments out of tax revenue, or by borrowing from the central bank. It will be possible to restore this type of business to the commercial banks only when reasonable monetary stability is achieved. Apart from these contractions of business, it is also found in the inflationary countries that banks, securities departments are unprofitable; in Brazil, for instance, securities are held almost entirely for capital appreciation as a hedge against inflation, and there is little profit to be made on commissions charged on interest payments, which are minuscule in relation to the cash value of the shares, especially as much extra paper-work is caused by the flood of new bonuses and rights issues on the market. In addition, the earnings of foreign exchange departments are reduced in certain countries by the existence of tolerated "parallel" markets for the purchase and sale of foreign drafts and banknotes, in which banks are forbidden to operate.

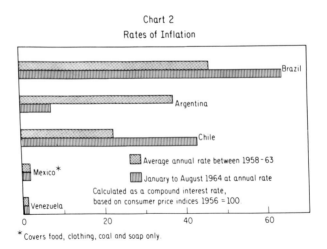

Chart 2
Rates of Inflation

Brazil

Argentina

Chile

Mexico*

Venezuela

▨ Average annual rate between 1958-63

▥ January to August 1964 at annual rate

Calculated as a compound interest rate, based on consumer price indices 1956 = 100.

0   20   40   60

* Covers food, clothing, coal and soap only.

BUREAUCRATS' SWEETENERS

The many foreign banks in Latin America are in a particularly unenviable position, especially in those countries where nationalist sentiments are strong.

It often happens that the friendly personal relations, always the most effective solvent of Latin American bureaucracy, which local banks enjoy with the authorities as a result of social contacts, are not so easily acquired by the foreign banks; it is also true that the offering by foreign banks of more concrete signs of regard to representatives of the authorities could result in much more serious consequences than for local banks. In certain countries foreign banks suffer from legal disabilities; for instance in Brazil they are not permitted to open more than one office in any one city. Also the traditional business of foreign banks, the financing of export crops, is extremely difficult in the inflationary conditions that plague so much of the region; this has led to a possibly unhealthy concentration on exchange business, particularly suited to the foreign banks because of their international connections and traditional expertise in that field.

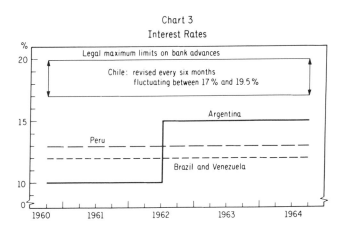

Chart 3
Interest Rates

MILITANT BANK CLERKS

In their internal administration, banks in Latin America continue mainly on traditional lines. Installation of computers proceeds only slowly, partly because of importing or manufacturing difficulties and partly because white-collar labour in most countries is still comparatively cheap. Automation is not yet economically profitable, and may not yet be economically desirable. Though it is estimated that about 70 percent of a bank's total expenditure in Latin America is for salaries, these are low by British standards, often being little above the standard for manual workers. This proletarianisation of bank staffs in turn accounts largely for the very large number of bank strikes, almost unknown in Europe. The labour situation is also made worse by the unsuitable hours worked by the majority of staffs in many countries (frequently of 6–7 hours without a break). These long shifts have been introduced to enable bank staffs to take up a second job in another part of the day; inevitably this lowers efficiency.

The impossibility of accurate business assessments in a continuing inflation, the often capricious and sometimes corrupt conduct of the authorities, the poor quality of much of the clerical labour available and the necessary concentration on short-term operations all tend to inhibit the healthy development of the banking system.

In developing longer-term financing services bankers in Latin America do have one model in the Inter-American Development Bank. Certainly private banks do not have the same freedom to insist on their own terms as this semi-official body, but they might profitably follow to the extent that they are able the development bank's general, very sensible practice, of investing mainly in projects in which local interests have shown confidence by investing their own money too.

However, the demand for banking services is increasing continually, in step with the progress being attempted in the countries of Latin America towards a modern industrial and commercial structure. Though operating conditions are far from satisfactory now, bankers hope that with a further development of Latin American economies, it will be possible to operate their businesses on somewhat more orthodox and comprehensive lines.

WHAT COURSE IN AFRICA?*

Emergent Africa offers bankers new opportunities; but they are seldom wholly free to pick and choose between the wheat and the chaff.

In Africa the rush of change sweeps with it the financial world, as every other. Over the past decade or so, existing banks have expanded rapidly and new ones have sprung into being, anxious to take advantage of the growing opportunities offered by the ambitious drive towards industrialisation and the diversification and mechanisation of agriculture now being attempted in large parts of the continent. But there are rapids to be negotiated here, and the choice of course is rarely entirely a banker's own.

Left to their own devices, private bankers would doubtless tend to follow their instincts and concentrate on their traditional, profitable, and relatively safe role of providing self-liquidating short-term financing and the provision of payment facilities for a growing volume of commerce and trade. But in a developing country they are, understandably, under considerable pressure to pay a subtle form of royalty for their presence, by providing also financing for the industrial ventures and development projects politically favoured by their hosts. Unlike an independent and distant development bank, a locally based, private banker cannot always insist that such projects must be clearly financially viable; unlike a foreign government he cannot chalk up intangible diplomatic advantage against financial loss. If he co-operates too freely, he risks his shareholders' money: if he co-operates too little, he risks mounting control and, possibly, nationalisation.

The big European commercial banks first established themselves in Africa in the 1890's. Among the pioneers were the National Bank of India, set up in Zanzibar in 1893, and the Bank of West Africa, formed three years later, and partly owned by Lloyds, the Westminster, National Provincial and Standard banks. The main function of these pioneering banks in Africa was to finance exports and virtually their entire clientele consisted of white settlers, mostly from Britain and France. The banks, too, were usually British or French, according to the colonial divisions of the time. To the end of the last war, this pattern scarcely changed, with relatively little increase in the number of banks and branches. Barclays DCO, for example, had nine branches in west Africa in 1926, and only seventeen in 1946.

It was only in the early 1950's, when the drive for economic development began in earnest, that the banks suddenly spread throughout Africa in

* A correspondent. *The Economist,* November 21, 1964, pp. 856, 859, 860.

large numbers. Barclays DCO alone has increased its west African branches almost tenfold since the war, and other big foreign banks have also expanded significantly. Moreover, with the advance of African nationalism, the Africans themselves began entering the financial field, in some cases by taking participations in local banks previously owned wholly by European interests. While in 1945 there were only about 15 indigenous banks in the whole of British East Africa, the Congo, Ghana, Morocco, Nigeria, Rhodesia and Nyasaland, Sudan and Tunisia, there are now well over 60. Throughout the former French colonies, one of the most important developments of recent years has been the establishment by the French Banque Nationale pour le Commerce et l'Industrie, the Belgian Banque Lambert, the Bank of America, and the German Commerzbank, of the Financial Corporation for Overseas Countries, a Swiss holding company controlling banks in ten African countries, among which are also the Congo (Leopoldville) and the former British colonies of Kenya, Uganda and Tanganyika.

At the same time the role of the banks has changed considerably since the war. Caught up in the great political and economic awakening of African life, the banks are now facing both problems and opportunities on a scale inconceivable to their predecessors. There has been a rapid extension of a money economy beyond the trading towns into the large, scattered agricultural areas in which most Africans still live. But most countries have begun to develop their own manufacturing industries, so that in Africa, too, the inevitable drift into the towns is now under way. Thus in addition to their long established business of financing exports, African banks are increasingly financing economies distinguished by a rapid growth of wage earning populations, often still illiterate, and they are also having to meet a demand for credit by a new class of African entrepreneur, using modern machinery and manufacturing methods, but with relatively large and risky capital requirements.

MONEY IN THE MATTRESS

In general, the banks seem to have adapted themselves to this new situation. The financing of trade has stayed mainly in the hands of the overseas banks, although their relative influence is now declining under pressure from their African competitors. The poor rural and urban communities are being served by a diverse but growing selection of post office savings banks, insurance companies and other financial intermediaries, owned partly by local and partly by overseas interests. The needs of industry are partly being met also by a new type of organisation in African banking, development banks, whose ownership is often divided between local and foreign private interests and the local government.

However there still are, at this stage of development, a large number of individuals who form a link between the local population and the banks—who borrow from the banks at official rates and re-lend at extortionate rates to those who cannot get financing in any other way, or don't know any better. Hoarding is also widespread, indicating that the banks have by no means fully won the confidence of the local populations. Even in South Africa, the most economically advanced African state, it is estimated that over £80 million lies hidden in mattresses, much of it by Africans.

In a purely commercial sense, where there has been a demand, African banks have usually been quick to supply the facilities required. However, the adequacy of the banking system in the African countries cannot be measured only by their ability to keep up with growing demands for self-liquidating commercial credits and the provision of payment facilities. The banks are also expected to play a positive role in economic development. And in this role, they are finding it more difficult to meet the demands made on them.

Ambitious Plans

All African governments have ambitious development plans with clear priorities for investment. They would like to see the banks use their resources to meet these priorities, in those areas and for those projects thought likely to do the most to further national economic growth. In Africa, this applies particularly to agricultural development. The banks, however, are ultimately responsible to their shareholders and are compelled to invest their money in the ways that are most profitable, at rates of interest commensurate with the risks they undertake and in projects that will show reasonable returns in the not too distant future. Thus, in the past, there has been a tendency for the overseas banks to invest their reserves in the main European centres in European-owned industries, which have more often than not remitted their profits abroad. The savings banks, also, have often been accused of holding an excessive proportion of their funds in real estate and "speculative" investments which yield high returns without necessarily contributing much to what is considered the nation's broad economic development. And even the development banks have found it difficult to dispose of their funds in profitable manufacturing enterprises at reasonable rates without too great a risk of default. The Industrial Bank of Sudan, for example, in its first year of existence found that it could grant only "three small loans for the manufacture of macaroni and air-coolers and for a car maintenance business."

African governments are trying to improve opportunities for investment and to steer the banking systems' investments closer towards national priorities. Increasingly, they are setting up central banks to provide greater control over the banking systems and today, 20 of the 36 principal African nations have their own central banks. Some countries, like Egypt and Syria, have tried to sidestep the whole problem of conventional monetary controls by simply nationalising all commercial banks. But a more usual approach so far has been to set up national development banks to finance those ventures in a national economic plan unattractive to or beyond the scope of the private banking system and the privately owned development banks. In Africa, such national development banks have often taken the form of agricultural credit institutions. Although agricultural development is one of the most urgent priorities for investment, the risks of giving agricultural credit are enormous, with defaults often running to about 20 percent of total credits, and privately owned banks understandably tend to avoid such excessive risks.

In an attempt to encourage and harness savings, African countries are now increasingly introducing government bond and treasury bill issues. The existence of stock exchanges in seven African countries is evidence of the efforts being made towards the establishment of domestic capital markets. And in several countries foreign banks are under considerable pressure or even compulsion to invest their money domestically rather than overseas.

The urgency with which African states are trying to create a bigger and better financial framework reflects the ambitiousness of their development plans. The greater the demands of the plans on the financial resources of each country, the greater the dangers of overstraining inadequate local resources. In Ghana recently, a system of forced savings produced major social disturbances. More commonly, inflationary pressures mount as countries begin to accumulate foreign debts, a situation often aggravated by the limited ability of African central banks to control the lending activities of the commercial banks.

FINANCIAL DIVERSIFICATION

On the other hand, time is short in the view of the new African governments, which are committed to rapid industrial growth. Their capital requirements are, therefore, large, and banks everywhere in Africa are under pressure to expand their deposits and increase the allocation of their investments in ventures favoured by the local governments.

As it seems probable that African development ambitions will increasingly outstrip domestic savings, demands for international financial aid will, predictably, grow. The recent discussions on the African Payments Union and the proposed formation of the African Development Bank may be the first steps towards the parallel objective of developing capital and money flows between the African countries themselves.

Yet given the present political climate in many of the African countries, direct government control over the banking systems seems likely to increase, especially where development plans prove too ambitious for private bankers, or totally beyond their capacity. But to the extent that banks do underwrite the rapid industrialisation envisaged, it is likely that they will take an increasing equity and managerial interest, and here, London's merchant banks may take a growing part.

As the drive towards industrialisation continues, and incomes rise, there is likely to be a further diversification of the financial structure, through the growth of intermediaries, such as acceptance houses, hire purchase companies, investment trusts and insurance companies. Moreover, commercial banks will probably increasingly seek deposits outside the main towns, in competition with the post offices, which receive the majority of small savings in rural areas. But much of this is looking well ahead, and just one obstacle to financial expansion is a serious scarcity of qualified staff. Here, foreign banks and the central banks of the developed countries can help not merely by providing financing, but also expertise.

One thing is certain: the opportunities in Africa are considerable. If African governments can produce relatively peaceful and balanced economic growth, if they do not try to go too fast, they will find banks anxious to play their part in the continent's development.

ADDITIONAL READINGS

Beckhart, Benjamin, *Banking Systems,* New York: Columbia University Press, 1954.

Covault, Ronald E., "Foreign Branches and Edge Act Corporations," *The National Banking Review,* December, 1963, pp. 247–254.

Cowan, Ed., "The Pace Quickens in U.S. Bank Expansion Abroad," *Burroughs Clearing House,* August, 1964, pp. 42–43.

Crafts, Prescott C., "The International Operation of American Banks," *Boston University Business Review,* Fall, 1962, pp. 12–17.

Gekker, Paul, "The Banking System of the USSR," *Journal of the Institute of Bankers,* June, 1963, pp. 189–197.

Joslin, David, *A Century of Banking in Latin America,* New York: Oxford University Press, 1963.

"Pep Pills for Canada's Banks," *Business Week,* May 2, 1964, p. 120.

Reimann, Guenter, and Wigglesworth, Edwin F., *International Guide to Foreign Commercial Banking,* International Reports, New York, 1961.

Sayers, R. S., *Banking in Western Europe,* Oxford: Clarendon Press, 1962.

"The Bank and the Banks," *The Economist,* November 23, 1963, pp. 815–841.

"U.S. Banks in Foreign Trade Financing," *Federal Reserve Bulletin,* April, 1955, pp. 1–11.

Williams, David, "Commercial Banking in the Far East," *The Banker,* June, 1963, pp. 418–426.

chapter 7

Financing East-West Trade, and Trade Between Socialist Countries

The question of U.S. trade with the Socialist countries has, for the past two years, been one of the most hotly debated issues in the U.S. international business community. The market for capital goods in those countries has increased significantly in recent years and has been exploited by several of the West European countries. In addition, the movement of some of the Socialist countries, particularly Yugoslavia and the Soviet Union, towards a consumer, market-oriented economy has opened up the possibility of additional substantial sales opportunities for U.S. firms. As a result, considerable pressure has been brought to bear on the U.S. government. The U.S. Chamber of Commerce and the National Foreign Trade Council have recommended a revision and relaxing of restrictive policies. A number of high-level government officials have consequently become outspoken in advocating a loosening of the strict and complex controls maintained by the U.S. government.

The commercial rapprochement between the Socialist and Capitalist countries has not been limited solely to trade. Another development, of interest to international businessmen, is the move toward investment in the Socialist countries. This investment is not of the usual equity type. Rather, it often entails the sale of a plant on medium or long-term credit (a portfolio investment), accompanied by a technical assistance agreement, and sometimes an agreement to purchase part of the output of the plant.

West European and U.S. companies which are selling on credit or are otherwise engaged in business within these socialist countries must be interested in a given country's balance of payments, the exchange rate of the currency and the operation of the banking system, as well as the means of financing trade. Hence, banking and finance within the Socialist countries is a relatively new field of interest for students and practitioners of international business.

One of the key institutions in the financing of East-West business operations has been the Moscow Narodny Bank, which was incorporated in London in 1919 for the purpose of financing trade between the Soviet Union and the United Kingdom. Its shares are owned by the Soviet government and by various cooperative enterprises in the Soviet Union. The bank's operations remained at a very low level, however, for many years, with assets reaching a peak of about $20 million in 1929 and not varying much above this until 1958. Since then, however, its activities have increased enormously. The year 1958 coincided with a change in bank management, banking policy and an increase in East-West trade. The bank began to compete with other British banks in general banking services, and entered actively into the London money market and foreign exchange market. Increased deposits, especially from foreign correspondents, helped to bring its assets up to $550 million in 1964. It has correspondent relationships with banks in most of the major countries, including the United States, and is thus able to serve most of the needs of companies engaged in trade or other business with the Socialist countries.

Other British banks have not hesitated to compete for this business. They are actively engaged in East-West financial transactions and, where the size of the transaction is too great for one bank, consortiums of banks plus insurance companies have been organized to provide the necessary financing. The same is true, but to a lesser extent, of the banking communities of other West European countries.

Most of the credits provided by the private banking community are insured by the trade credit insurance organizations of the respective governments. It is significant to note that the credit ratings of the Socialist countries, as reflected by the insurance premiums, are equivalent to those of "blue chip" companies in the West. Still, most of the credit is insured and is hence subject to the policies of the respective governments. These policies differ widely, however, and are a source of friction between the countries of the West. As noted in the readings, the U.S. law prevents the granting of all credit to the Socialist countries, although exceptions are made as required by foreign policy considerations. In most of the other countries, credits are permitted on terms up to five years. The British government has insured credits to the Socialist countries for periods of over five (up to ten) years. The current question is how soon other West European governments will break ranks (in violation of the Berne Union agreements) and permit their firms to offer longer credits, in competition with the British.

The first several articles in this chapter are concerned more with the magnitude and directions of East-West trade than with financing considerations. They are included, however, to give the reader some familiarity with the subject and an appreciation of the trends and policies which affect the specific subject of international finance.

The article on "The Finance of East-West Trade," however, narrows down to the specific topic of trade finance between the East and West, showing the role of trade agreements as well as of conventional means of trade financing.

The following article, by Oleg Kulikov, is more concerned with credit institutions in the Soviet Union and relationships between those institutions and the Soviet foreign-trade corporations. It also describes the arrangements for financing trade between Socialist countries, and the movement toward multilateral trade in Eastern Europe.

The latest step toward multilateral trade among the Socialist countries has been the establishment of the International Bank for Economic Cooperation (the Comecon Bank). The problems in establishing this bank and a description of its operations are covered in the last two articles. It is interesting and instructive to draw parallels and divergencies between this bank and the European Payments Union (which helped Western Europe to achieve multilateral trade and payments in the 1950's).

The last two articles raise another fascinating aspect of future trends in international finance. The rouble is a strong currency and is becoming transferable among the Comecon countries. As East-West trade grows, the rouble may soon achieve a degree of acceptance in the West and become a basis for financing East-West trade. Will the Soviet Union find it convenient to become a member of the International Monetary Fund? Will the rouble become one of the world's leading currencies? What effect would a powerful and fully transferable rouble have on the international monetary system?

UNITED STATES AND EAST-WEST TRADE*

Trade between the free world nations of the West and the Communist countries of Eastern Europe has increased markedly in recent years. Between 1952 and 1962, exports from the West to these Communist nations increased from $1.4 billion to about $5 billion, with U.S. exports accounting for less than 3 percent of the total. The Communist nations received 4.5 percent of free world exports in 1962, compared with 1.9 percent in 1952.

The steady increase in East-West trade has caused the United States government to re-evaluate its regulations on trade with Communist nations. At present, these regulations are designed to cope with specific problems in four major areas—the U.S.S.R., the Soviet-dominated countries of Eastern Europe, Communist China and the other Asian Communist countries, and Cuba.

In 1950, a total embargo was placed on all trade and financial transactions with China and North Korea because of their aggressive activities. This later was extended to North Vietnam for the same reason. The prohibition of all trade with Cuba, except for the U.S. export of nonsubsidized foods and medicines, is part of our attempt to isolate the Communist regime in that country and to counter its threat to this hemisphere.

The current review is largely limited to our policies on trade with Russia and the Soviet bloc countries of Eastern Europe—Poland, Czechoslovakia, Rumania, Bulgaria, Hungary, and East Germany. These policies date back to 1948 when the United States unilaterally prohibited any trade in strategic goods with these countries. At the onset of the Berlin blockade in 1949, Japan and all the NATO nations except Iceland joined us in forming the Consultative Group-Coordinating Committee (COCOM) which adopted trade controls on a list of strategic goods similar to that of the United States. In the atmosphere of the Korean War, this list was tightened so that there was a near embargo on almost all raw material and industrial equipment sales to the Communist bloc. In addition, after Korea, the United States denied most-favored-nation treatment to all of the East European nations, except Yugoslavia and later Poland. This made possible the re-establishment of tariffs on imports from these countries at 1930 levels which, in some cases, are as much as three times the tariffs on similar goods from West European nations.

* International Economic Review, The First National Bank of Chicago, March, 1965, pp. 1–5.

In 1954 the COCOM list of strategic goods was substantially reduced to include goods only of a clearly military or military-industrial nature. This list includes such items as highly advanced electrical or electronic equipment, special metals, some aviation equipment, a number of advanced chemicals, plastics, and atomic materials, certain machine tools and machines, and a few specialized scientific instruments.

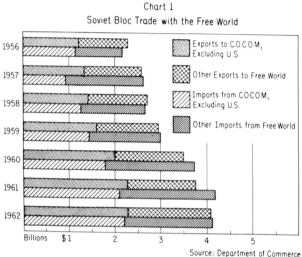

Chart 1
Soviet Bloc Trade with the Free World

Source: Department of Commerce

The Soviet bloc countries try to maintain a balance in their trade with the free world. Trade with the industrialized nations of COCOM has shown a surplus in the years since 1956, enabling the bloc countries to add to their limited convertible currency reserves.

With the revision of the COCOM list and the easing of Soviet pressures in Europe after the death of Stalin, many Western nations began to increase their trade with the East. Historically, the trade between East and West Europe was large. The traditional exports of Eastern Europe—agricultural products, minerals, and raw materials—found ready markets in the neighboring nations to the West. The Soviet drive for capital equipment in the mid-1950's was viewed by many West European countries as an opportunity to expand their trade, which is so much more vital to their economies than trade is to that of the United States. The widening of markets would enable their industries to take further advantage of the economies to be derived from large scale production. In 1962, the COCOM countries (excluding the United States), together with Austria and Sweden, conducted two-way trade with the bloc valued at over $5.1 billion.

The United States, on the other hand, continues to prohibit trade in many items not included in the COCOM list. The Export Control Act, as amended in 1962, gives the President the right to deny particular goods or technology to an unfriendly nation if it is deemed that they would aid the "military or economic potential" of that country to the detriment of our national security or welfare. All United States shipments to the Soviet bloc require an export license. In addition to those goods on the "Positive List" which require a license for export to any country except Canada, there are a great many other products which must be considered individually when application is made for license to export to the Soviet bloc countries.

However, goods which may be refused a license, and therefore are not exported from this country, are not necessarily kept from the Soviets. With the free flow of technology in the Western world, many of these products can be, and are, easily purchased from other nations.

Today, the major portion of the trade of the East European countries is still done within the Soviet bloc. Trade with the West, as well as intrabloc trade, is conducted on a bilateral basis, that is, agreements are drawn between two nations, covering the amounts and types of goods to be exchanged over a period of several years. There are several reasons for this use of bilateral agreements in dealing with the West. The leaders of the Communist nations attempt to keep extrabloc trade at the lowest level possible, because it introduces factors into the economy over which the State has no control. Since production targets and industrial development goals are established by the State and embodied in a detailed plan for economic development, only those goods which are necessary for the fulfillment of the economic plan are imported. Moreover, since Eastern Europe does not have a large supply of freely convertible reserve currencies, trade by agreement is essential. It enables the country dealing with the West to maintain a balance between exports and imports.

Exporters in West European nations have begun to extend medium-term commercial credits to the Soviet bloc nations to enable them to increase their imports from the West. The terms of these credits have, in large measure, followed the criteria of the Berne Union, formed in 1934 to prevent unfair trade competition on government-guaranteed credit terms. The members of the Union, the credit insuring or guaranteeing institutions of 18 nations, have agreed that, in general, medium-term credits should be limited to 5 years or less, with a 20 percent down payment required. Furthermore, the exporter must bear at least 15 percent of the risk. Lately, however, longer term credits have been made available to the bloc countries, notably by France and the United Kingdom.

Exporters in the United States are prohibited from extending credit to the Soviet bloc. Under the Johnson Act of 1934, certain financial transactions between private persons in the United States and foreign governments in default on their debts to the United States are banned. The only exceptions to these prohibitions are loans made by the Export-Import Bank of Washington and credits to nations which are members of the International Monetary Fund.

In order for United States exporters to compete with other countries in the East European markets, several major steps would have to be taken. First, the United States would have to reduce tariffs on imports from the East

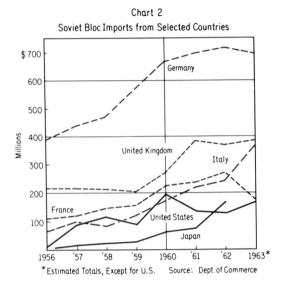

Chart 2
Soviet Bloc Imports from Selected Countries

*Estimated Totals, Except for U.S.   Source: Dept. of Commerce

Exports to the Soviet bloc by many major Western countries
have expanded rapidly since 1956 with industrial equipment
and machinery accounting for a significant portion of the
increases. On the other hand, U.S. exports, about 65 to 75 percent of which are agricultural products, have risen only slightly.

to competitive levels. Also, we would have to liberalize trade to the extent permitted by the other COCOM nations. Lastly, the Johnson Act would have to be amended.

Even if U.S. trade policy with the U.S.S.R. were modified, there is little likelihood that the volume of trade would reach substantial proportions in the near future. The main impetus to such trade traditionally has been from the U.S.S.R. because of its interest in our industrial equipment. There is a market in the U.S. for some standard Russian exports such as raw furs, manganese, chrome ores, platinum, crude drugs, and food specialties. But there is little demand here for the Soviet Union's traditional exports of agricultural products, timber, paper, fuels, ores, and other minerals. It has been estimated that our exports to Russia could be expanded from the 1960–1962 yearly average of about $30 million to about $150–200 million annually. However, there appears to be little likelihood of imports from the U.S.S.R. amounting to more than $50 million.

Another major obstacle to any significant expansion in trade would be Russia's limited ability to pay for increased imports. All extrabloc trade is conducted in convertible currencies or gold. In order for the Soviet Union to finance imports from the United States, it would have to use reserves earned on trade with Western Europe, sell gold in world markets to obtain dollars, or receive commercial credits from U.S. firms.

The outlook for U.S. trade with the nations of Eastern Europe is brighter.

Economic nationalism has become a characteristic of most of these countries. There is some disenchantment in these nations with their economic progress and, in particular, with the Committee for Mutual Economic Assistance (COMECON), which was formed to coordinate the development of the area. The controls imposed by the Committee over planning have likewise led it to fall into disfavor. Countries such as Rumania and Hungary resent the fact that they must act as farmers for the bloc at the expense of their industrial development. Moreover, shortages and production problems have appeared in some of the nations of the bloc which further delayed expansion. Thus, the East European nations are turning to the West for necessary goods and are finding that it is cheaper to buy in these markets. By selling to these countries, Western nations, including the United States, might help them to assert further their independence from Russia.

The approach of the United States to East-West trade differs significantly from that of the nations of Western Europe, and this is troublesome. The United States finds itself unilaterally adhering to policies which lose their effectiveness as our allies do not follow them. At the same time, the policy differences give the Soviet Union some leverage in pitting one nation of the West against another and thus permit the Soviets to promote rivalry and suspicion among the Allies. A united front would strengthen the position of the West as it enters into negotiations of such problems as patents, copyrights, royalties, licensing agreements, and the arbitration of trade disputes.

EAST-WEST TRADE—PRESENT TRENDS*

GENERAL WORLD STATISTICS

The socialist countries' total international trade in 1963 showed a continued rise, with imports increasing 8 percent and exports increasing 7½ percent relative to 1962. This was not markedly different from the progress since 1961; in 1962 imports were up 7 percent, and exports were up 9 percent compared with the previous year. (See Tables 1 (a) and 1 (b)).

TABLE 1 (a)

EAST-WEST TRADE STATISTICS
(Millions of dollars)

Exports from All Socialist Countries (f. o. b.)	1961	1962	1963
To whole world	16,934	18,591	19,980
Main nonsocialistic countries	3,384	3,598	4,018
Comprising:			
U. S. A.	150	148	136
Canada	28	26	38
West Europe	2,992	3,180	3,557
Including:			
E. E. C.	1,277	1,413	1,654
E. F. T. A.	1,167	1,170	1,257
Of which:			
U. K.	578	554	588
Australia and New Zealand	19	20	24
South Africa	7	6	9
Japan	194	217	253
All other nonsocialistic countries....	1,609	1,816	1,918
Other groupings:			
Middle East	446	498	469
Central Africa	120	110	110
Sterling Area countries in Asia	508	610	716
Other Asian countries	218	280	269
Whole Sterling Area	1,205	1,275	1,432
All Africa	416	462	496

Sources: As for 1 (b).

Their trade with nonsocialist nations, however, rose even more rapidly. Imports from the major nonsocialist countries, principally the United States of America, Canada, Western Europe, Australia, New Zealand, Japan, rose to $4,468 million, an increase of 11 percent over 1962, while imports from the

* *Moscow Narodny Bank Quarterly Review,* Autumn, 1964, pp. 27–36.

TABLE 1 (b)

EAST-WEST TRADE STATISTICS
(Millions of dollars)

Imports into All Socialist Countries (f. o. b.)	1961	1962	1963
From whole world	17,003	18,177	19,686
Of which:			
Main nonsocialist countries	3,788	4,038	4,468
Comprising:			
U. S. A.	328	316	390
Canada	395	291	430
West Europe	2,847	3,107	3,196
Including:			
E. E. C.	1,407	1,547	1,486
E. F. T. A..............	935	996	1,062
Of which:			
U. K.	390	390	439
Australia and New Zealand	240	170	311
South Africa	10	9	15
Japan	121	238	269
All other nonsocialist countries	1,472	1,444	1,638
Other groupings:			
Middle East	236	330	456
Central Africa	64	69	95
Sterling Area countries in Asia	390	443	499
Other Asian countries	139	165	173
Whole Sterling Area	1,089	1,082	1,380
All Africa	350	337	496

Sources: Official trade returns, U. N. Monthly Bulletin of Statistics, June 1964.

remaining nonsocialist countries (mainly in the form of primary products) rose even faster. Exports to the group of major nonsocialist nations rose by 12 percent, and to others by 4 percent. The socialist countries now transact some 31 percent of their trade with nonsocialist countries, compared with 69 percent with each other. The proportion of East-West trade has risen to 31 percent steadily since World War II. (See Table 2). On the basis of current statistics, the total of East-West trade is a twelfth of total world trade.

It goes without saying that the much improved political atmosphere which has proceeded during 1963 has facilitated the expansion of East-West trade, especially for Western European countries which accounted for 56 percent of this trade. The United Kingdom and France are now willing to grant credit to the socialist countries for much longer terms than was envisaged by the Berne Union, i.e. five years. The West German government has protested against this, but may well follow suit in the near future. In the United Kingdom, France, West Germany, and Italy, a number of large contracts have been signed, and others are being finalised. Exports from Western Europe to the socialist countries were $2,847 million in 1961, $3,107 million in 1962 and $3,196 million in 1963; a further substantial increase may be expected in 1964. Prospects are also bright for imports into Western Europe; U.K. import restrictions have been relaxed, and there are better possibilities for the sale

TABLE 2

PARTICIPATION OF SOCIALIST COUNTRIES IN EAST-WEST TRADE, 1963

	Value of Turnover (imports plus exports) in Million U. S. Dollars			Distribution of Turnover, %		
	World	Socialist	Non-socialist	World	Socialist	Non-socialist
All socialist countries	40,027	27,621	12,046	100	69	31
U. S. S. R.	14,331	10,086	4,246	100	70	30
Czechoslovakia (estimated from figures for first 9 months of year)	4,124	2,869	1,255	100	70	30
Rumania	1,989	1,319	670	100	66	34
Poland	3,751	2,380	1,371	100	63	37
Hungary	2,511	1,750	761	100	70	30
Yugoslavia	1,847	455	1,392	100	25	75
China and other Asian socialist countries	3,100	1,400	1,700	100	45	55
Cuba	1,330	800	530	100	61	39

Sources: Figures for the U. S. S. R. and Eastern Europe are taken from those countries' official sources. Figures for China, etc., are taken from the United Nations Monthly Bulletin of Statistics. Figures for Cuba are rough estimates made by us on the basis of statistics published officially by Cuba's trading partners. Figures for "all socialist countries" are derived from the Monthly Bulletin of Statistics, with adjustments for Yugoslavia and Cuba; they do not include trade between G. D. R. and F. G. R.

of Soviet and Rumanian oil in Western Europe. At $3,557 million, imports into Western Europe from the socialist countries in 1963 were 12 percent up on 1962, relative to a 6 percent increase in 1962 over 1961.

The six E.E.C. countries conduct slightly more East-West trade than the seven E.F.T.A. countries, and it is in the E.E.C. that the rapid growth of imports just referred to has been most marked.

Japan, in the course of its recent export drive, has come to take a greater interest in trade with the socialist countries, and, like the United Kingdom, has recently made long-term credit facilities available to the U.S.S.R. Her trade turnover with the socialist countries has risen from $315 million in 1961 and $455 million in 1962 to $522 million in 1963.

The outlook for East-West trade on the global scale has been brightened in recent months by numerous bilateral agreements to liberalise and extend trade. Most of these agreements have been between socialist and underdeveloped economies.

Among the advanced nonsocialist countries, the United Kingdom has been most energetic in government measures to stimulate trade with Eastern Europe. At the beginning of the year Mr. Edward Heath announced a new policy of liberalising imports of manufactured goods from socialist countries. On April 1, the first trade agreement to be drawn up under this scheme was signed with Czechoslovakia. On an undertaking that prices will not be below world price levels, most manufactured goods can now be imported free of quota restrictions. The next month a trade agreement with Hungary exempted a large number of commodities from quota restrictions. With Rumania, Bulgaria, and to a lesser extent Poland and the U.S.S.R., the problem is that the goods exported from these countries compete against the United Kingdom's imports from traditional sources, such as Denmark and New Zealand, whose interests the United Kingdom does not wish to damage. Quotas for Rumania in 1964 were no more liberal than the 1963 quotas; but the U.S.S.R. signed a moderately satisfactory protocol in April, which prolonged the existing five-year agreement for a further five years. "I am quite sure that trade between the two countries will increase in the future in every respect," said the Soviet Ambassador, Mr. Soldatov, speaking in Manchester on August 12. "We may even establish special branches of industry to satisfy your market and maybe you will do the same for us." Edward du Cann, British Minister of State, Board of Trade, said in June: "We believe that an expansion of trade plays an important part in encouraging the spirit of detente between East and West which all of us want so much."

The United States, which last year sold grain to the U.S.S.R., has now reached an agreement with Rumania providing for an increase in trade between the two countries.

There has also been some liberalisation of the embargo on the sale of "strategic materials" to the socialist countries by the Coordinating Committee on Export Controls. It is to be hoped that this embargo will be scrapped altogether in the next few years.

Canada, which has also embarked on East-West trade on a large scale by sales of grain, has concluded a very liberal agreement with Hungary on a most-favoured-nation basis. The two countries are to exchange trade missions.

Switzerland signed a protocol in June to liberalise extensively its trade with Poland, and to provide an improved system of settlements.

As to France, besides its extension of trade with China, the French banks have followed their British counterparts very closely in pressing for a relaxation of official restrictions upon credit facilities for socialist countries' imports. Their desire is to grant credit terms to the Soviet Union for the purchase of capital goods from French manufacturers, with repayment extended beyond the five-year period recommended by the Berne Union. Such an operation, however, requires the risk of default to be borne by the French government.

Government export credit insurance was granted by Belgium-Luxembourg to Yugoslavia and Hungary in 1963 with periods of repayment up to 8–9 years. The British government has authorised E.C.G.D. insurance cover for a deal involving £100 million, for sales of chemical plant to the U.S.S.R., which involve long-term credits. Japan is reported to be considering an extension of the maximum repayment period to 7 or 8 years.

The British "Financial Times" remarked editorially on August 13:

"If France decides to give long-term credit to Communist countries, there will be more competition for British exporters in this market. West Germany might well follow the French example so as not to be left out of the contest. . . . Italy would naturally follow suit. . . . It would then be America, not Britain, which was the odd man out in N.A.T.O. on the question of Soviet credits . . . If the credits are available, and the risks duly insured against, commercial trust is a good foundation for confidence between governments . . . Russia since the Revolution has proved to be a gilt-edged credit risk, and has never once defaulted on her financial obligations."

OVERSEAS STERLING AREA

Provisional figures for 1963 are now available from the British Board of Trade, showing trade between the Sterling Area countries other than the United Kingdom and the majority of the socialist countries, namely the U.S.S.R., Eastern Europe excluding Yugoslavia, and the People's Republic of China. (Table 3.)

TABLE 3

TRADE OF THE OVERSEAS STERLING AREA WITH THE SOVIET UNION,
EASTERN EUROPE AND CHINA, 1963
(Thousands of £)

	Exports to Soviet Union and Eastern Europe	Exports to China	Total Foregoing	Imports from Soviet Union and E. Europe	Imports from China	Total Foregoing
Total O. S. A.	204,446	114,474	318,920	157,348	168,154	325,502
Of which:						
Australia*	29,486	74,709	104,195	4,753	5,221	9,974
Burma	–	–	–	–	–	–
Ceylon	6,165	7,545	13,710	8,783	10,360	19,143
Ghana	–	–	–	–	–	–
Hong Kong	64	4,385	4,449	3,354	93,046	96,400
Iceland	5,831	–	5,831	6,963	10	6,973
India	69,345	–	69,345	79,629	101	79,730
Irish Republic	987	26	1,013	4,123	324	4,447
Jordan	–	–	–	–	–	–
Libya	–	–	–	–	–	–
Malaya	–	–	–	–	–	–
Singapore	–	–	–	–	–	–
New Zealand	1,251	1,764	3,015	1,274	746	2,020
Nigeria	–	–	–	–	–	–
Pakistan	6,328	4,608	10,936	3,492	2,103	5,595
Rhodesia and Nyasaland*	5,602	197	5,799	–	–	–
South Africa*	–	–	–	3,533	917	4,450

*Imports f. o. b. Exports include re-exports and are f. o. b. Imports are c. i. f. unless otherwise stated.

Source: U. K. Board of Trade.

Exports from the O.S.A. in 1963 totalled £318,920,000, an increase of 38 percent over the 1962 figures. India and Pakistan nearly doubled their exports, which amounted to £80,281,000; Australia and New Zealand's exports totalled £107,208,000, a rise of 27 percent. No major falls were recorded, except from Malaya and Singapore.

Imports from the socialist countries to the O.S.A. also showed an excellent rise; at £325,502,000 they were 22 percent higher than in 1962. India's increase was, however, only 4 percent, while Pakistan's figures revealed a drop of 7 percent. Australia and New Zealand showed a rise of 45 percent to £11,994,-000; markedly better than in 1962, but still a bare tenth of their exports. The Hong Kong figures revealed exports £1 million down at £4½ million, but imports £2.2 million up at £96 million.

On the whole the picture is a bright one, with total turnover up by 29 percent on 1962.

Only fragmentary information is available for 1964. Ceylon's trade with the socialist countries remains at a steady level, but elsewhere the picture is different. Figures from Hong Kong cover the period up to May, and a simple projection for the rest of 1964 suggests a fairly substantial increase for imports and exports compared with 1963. A similar calculation for Pakistan also indicates a sizeable increase for imports and exports. In the case of Australia, exports for the twelve months ending June, 1964, were 73 percent up on the preceding twelvemonth, while imports were 36 percent up.

These figures do not give a complete picture, but they certainly indicate that the brisk expansion of East-West trade undertaken by the Overseas Sterling Area in 1963 has continued, and indeed accelerated, into 1964.

THE UNITED KINGDOM IN EAST-WEST TRADE

Figures showing the United Kingdom's trade with the socialist countries during the first half of 1964 are now available (see Table 4) for comparison with those of the corresponding period of 1963. It will be noticed that while

TABLE 4

U. K. EAST-WEST TRADE, 1963-64
(Thousands of £)

	Imports 1963	Exports 1963	Imports Jan.-June 1964	Exports Jan.-June 1964	Imports Jan.-June 1963	Exports Jan.-June 1963
Albania	20.3	185.7	Nil	126.3	1.1	41.3
Bulgaria	3,654.1	2,143.4	1,932.1	1,023.1	1,784.8	1,083.3
Czechoslovakia	16,319.4	11,959.9	8,387.9	6,860.0	7,330.5	4,896.7
G. D. R.	7,532.2	7,997.4	4,667.3	3,722.5	3,850.2	3,791.6
Hungary	5,782.9	7,484.2	3,336.3	4,530.6	2,272.9	3,909.8
Poland	40,190.9	28,067.1	26,310.0	15,169.7	17,896.2	16,291.8
Rumania............	7,426.8	11,876.0	4,716.9	3,517.9	3,813.2	6,772.1
U. S. S. R.	90,960.6	63,871.4	33,278.6	22,489.7	34,489.5	36,642.5
Yugoslavia...........	15,086.6	17,485.1	9,675.2	12,192.8	7,666.7	9,183.3
China and Mongolia	18,529.3	13,356.6	12,027.6	9,138.3	9,537.6	4,557.7
North Korea	211.8	21.9	0.1	14.1	50.8	15.2
North Vietnam	26.1	36.5	23.5	10.6	9.9	19.0
Cuba...............	12,395.3	2,071.6	4,866.3	3,842.4	2,374.1	1,109.2
Total........	218,136.3	166,556.8	109,221.8	82,638.0	91,077.5	88,313.5

U. K. imports c. i. f., exports f. o. b. Exports include re-exports.

Source: U. K. Trade & Navigation Accounts, June 1964.

U.K. imports rose 20 percent from £91 million to £109 million exports dropped 6 percent from £88 million to £83 million.

The rise in imports was due mainly to the increased purchase of foodstuffs which has been a feature of U.K. external trade with nonsocialist countries too. There was also a rise of £1.5 million in imports of nonferrous metals, mainly aluminium and zinc from the U.S.S.R., and this too was also the pattern in U.K. imports from the rest of the world.

The drop in exports can be ascribed to the decline in re-exports of crude rubber to the U.S.S.R., which fell from £6.4 million to £1 million. There was also a noticeable decline in exports of iron and steel (sheet metal rather than bars or rods) which fell from £8.4 million to £2.1 million in the case of the Soviet Union, and from £1.2 million to £0.8 million in the case of Poland. The export of nonferrous metals to the U.S.S.R. also dropped by a million pounds.

TABLE 5

U. K. EAST-WEST TRADE PERFORMANCE IN FIRST HALF OF 1964

Country	U. K. Imports Jan.-June 1964 as % of Jan-June 1963	U. K. Exports Jan.-June 1964 as % of Jan-June 1963	U. K. Trade Turnover (exports plus imports) as % of Average in Jan. June 1963 and Jan.-June 1962
Bulgaria	+ 8%	− 6%	118.9 or + 19%
Czechoslovakia	+ 14%	+ 40%	120.6 " + 21%
G. D. R.	+ 21%	− 2%	105.9 " + 6%
Hungary	+ 48%	+ 16%	133.3 " + 33%
Poland	+ 47%	− 7%	116.0 " + 16%
Rumania	+ 24%	− 48%	102.6 " + 30%
U. S. S. R.	− 4%	− 39%	83.8 " − 16%
Yugoslavia	+ 26%	+ 33%	127.1 " + 27%
China and Mongolia	+ 26%	+ 101%	141.1 " + 41%
Cuba	+ 105%	+ 246%	190.6 " + 91%
Total of all above plus N. Korea, Albania and N. Vietnam	+ 20%	− 6%	101.9 " + 2%

Source: U. K. Trade & Navigation Accounts.

In Table 5 we have assessed the performance during the first half of 1964 on a percentage basis, by countries. On this showing, trade with China and Cuba showed particular improvement, while trade with the U.S.S.R. was disappointing. Cuban trade remains at a low absolute level, however; imports of sugar stood at £4.6 million (up on £2.2 million); imports of tobacco were a mere £217,550 (up on £143,091); exports of machinery (nonelectric) rose from £0.2 million to £1.1 million. Improvement in the Chinese trade were imports of textile fibres, which rose from £2.2 million to £4.1 million (silk doing rather better than wool), and of processed textiles, which rose from £1.3 million to £2.1 million (half of them being unbleached, woven cotton fabrics). U.K. exports of iron and steel to China rose by £2 million.

THE SOVIET UNION, THE COMECON, AND WESTERN TRADE*

At an economic conference in Prague some months ago a well-known Czech economist said that the problem of co-existence had been one-sidedly construed. In the socialist countries, he said, people "wish only to exert an influence on the capitalist world, while they do not wish to take any account of the capitalist world's influence on the socialist economy." People at the meeting went so far as to criticise socialism as an order of society. They argued that collectivisation or nationalisation could not be regarded as an end in itself. Foreign trade policy was described as completely irrational, inasmuch as "the trade was not in accordance with reality." At the present time prices in no way determined the course of foreign trade. They suggested that the law of supply and demand would have to be allowed to govern the consumer goods industries, and in the long run the entire economy.

Such severe criticism of the socialist economic order is perhaps not typical of the increasingly keen economic discussion which is taking place both in the Soviet Union and in its satellite states. But still it is a pointer to the new fashion in those countries, the new habit of unbiased economic discussion, the growing desire both to establish greater flexibility in the domestic economy and to broaden contact with the outside world.

Recently the Soviet Union has directed greatly increased trade policy activity towards the West, and indeed towards the whole of the outside world. The only striking exception is China, Soviet trade with that country having shown an exceptionally large decrease during the last few years. In 1959 China accounted for roughly one-fifth of the Soviet Union's total foreign trade; for 1963 the proportion can be estimated to be only 5 percent. A large part of the Soviet imports from China formerly consisted of food, and the loss of these supplies now has to be made good elsewhere. This does not imply that the big wheat deals with Canada and the United States can be entirely explained in that way. The serious crop failures in the USSR have probably been an equally important cause.

The Soviet Union's more tractable and more active attitude towards trade with industrial countries in the West can also be regarded as reflecting the significance which the Russians have attached, of late, to peaceful co-existence.

* Åke O. Liljefors, reprinted from *Ekonomisk Revy*, April, 1964.

Both Khrushchev and the Russian Minister of Foreign Trade, Patolitchev, have expressed the view that widening and deepening of the Soviet Union's economic relations with the outside world would be natural, and would be likely to contribute towards peaceful international progress. The journal of the Russian Ministry of Foreign Trade recently stated, in a prominent position, that all those who genuinely wish for peace, and for further international cooperation, are bound to feel alarm at the fact that trade between two great powers—the Soviet Union and the United States—has been practically taboo for 15 years. But apart from such general expressions of view there has also been definite evidence, in recent times, proving the desirability of increased trade with Western countries.

Less Autarky?

Even though the Russian's increased efforts to promote trade are largely based on motives of foreign policy, they can also be explained by internal economic developments in the USSR. One may perhaps venture to surmise that the Russian economy has now attained such a level of development that its leaders are prepared to cut down on their autarkic principles and to broaden trade with other countries—even, and perhaps not least, with countries outside the socialist bloc.

It also looks, when Russian statistics are studied, as though the Soviet Union is on the way to becoming more and more dependent on its foreign trade. It should of course be immediately emphasised that foreign trade is of relatively modest size in proportion to the whole economy's turnover, just as it is in the United States, but nevertheless during the last few years foreign trade has grown more rapidly than the national income. Thus between 1958 and 1963 foreign trade grew by nearly 65 percent, while the increase of the national income amounted to a little over 40 percent. Continuance of a similar faster growth-rate for foreign trade seems moreover likely in view of the programme for a rapid buildup of industry which the authorities are now trying to carry out in the Soviet Union.

Another reason why foreign trade may be expected to increase, even in relative terms, is that the general standard of consumption has now reached such a level that the need for imports seems certain to grow. There is quite naturally a conflict between the great capital development programme and the growing desire for consumption. And it is by no means impossible that, despite all the planning and rigidity in the Russian system, this conflict may have to be resolved by an increase of foreign trade—possibly even by a growing excess of imports. On the whole the Soviet Union has a respectable export surplus; in 1962 it exceeded 500 million roubles. But this was entirely due to the large favourable balance of trade with the satellite countries.

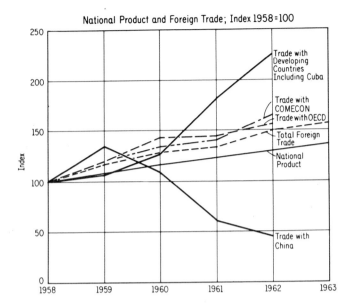

National Product and Foreign Trade; Index 1958=100

IMPORTS FROM THE WEST

Growing imports, for the purpose of rendering the desired economic growth possible, would presumably have to be obtained in large part from the industrial countries in the West. At the moment it is largely machines and technical equipment which Soviet Russia needs; and of such goods the countries in Western Europe are the chief potential suppliers, even though the division of industrial labour between the Comecon countries during recent years has greatly increased their capacity. But the satellite countries are engaged in such industrial and general economic development that they can hardly make any material contribution towards satisfying both the Soviet demand and their own capital requirements. On looking at the breakdown of Soviet Russia's imports by categories of goods one finds that growth in the importance of the group comprising machinery and industrial equipment has been relatively great during recent years. Between 1957 and the present time that group's share of the total imports would seem to have risen from 24 to over 30 percent.

There was a great increase in such imports both from the satellite countries and from the industrial countries in the West, but the increase was greatest in the case of the latter. In 1961 for example no less than 43 percent of the imports from the West comprised machinery and industrial equipment as compared with 32 percent in 1957. This increase is entirely explained by the growth in imports of equipment for the chemical industry. It is probable that just these imports will rise further in the next few years. Khrushchev has said that the chemical expansion programme in the Soviet Union requires the importation of industrial equipment both from the satellite countries and from the industrial countries in the West. For imports from these latter in the period between 1964 and 1970 a total sum of one billion roubles has been mentioned; and since it is unlikely that the satellite countries will be able to supply the whole of the deliveries forming the basis of that calculation, there will quite probably be much greater imports from the Western industrial countries.

In 1962 not quite two-thirds of Soviet Russia's foreign trade was with other countries within the communist bloc. Roughly 15 percent of the exports went to Western Europe, and 17 percent of the imports came from there. The country with which most trade is done is Finland; it is followed by Western Germany and the United Kingdom. Only in relation to the United Kingdom as can be seen from Table 1, has the Soviet Union any export surplus worth mentioning.

TABLE 1

**THE SOVIET UNION'S TRADE WITH CERTAIN
INDUSTRIAL COUNTRIES IN 1962**
(Millions of roubles)

	Exports	Imports	Total
Finland	162	194	356
Western Germany	121	184	305
United Kingdom	192	105	297
Japan	102	131	233
France	77	138	215
Italy	118	89	207
Benelux	80	72	152
Total	852	913	1765
Sweden	48	69	117

For 1963 no Russian data concerning the distribution of foreign trade between countries are yet available. But many of the countries mentioned in the table show in their statistics an appreciable decrease of Russian imports from them; in most cases, on the other hand, Russian exports to them have increased. It is still too early to say anything definite about the meaning of this trend. It is by no means impossible that the Russians, within the framework of their trade agreements, wanted to effect some shift in their future imports so as to counteract the strains on their exchange reserves entailed by their exceptional imports of grain.

Between 1961 and 1962 the Soviet Union's imports from the seven large suppliers mentioned in the table increased a good deal faster than the average for its total imports. What is more, the imports of machinery and equipment increased a good deal faster than the total imports; this applied both to those from Western industrial countries and to those from the Comecon.

TABLE 2

SOVIET IMPORTS FROM CERTAIN COUNTRIES
IN 1961 AND 1962

	(Millions of roubles)		Percentage Increase
	1961	1962	
Total imports	5,245	5,805	10.7
of which machinery and equipment	1,561	2,016	29.1
Imports from seven Western countries	716	913	27.5
of which machinery and equipment	354	444	25.4
Imports from the Comecon	2,740	3,229	17.8
of which machinery and equipment	1,121	1,459	30.1

In this context it has hitherto been assumed that a higher and rising standard of consumption in the Soviet Union—and of course the same also applies to the satellite countries—may lead to an increase of foreign trade, and in the first place to an increase of imports. Rising incomes, and to a certain extent also the growth of knowledge about the outside world, particularly as regards clothing and other kinds of consumer goods, cause the public to feel a desire for new goods. And as regards such desires people like, as consumers always do, to be able to satisfy them quickly. A more active consumer opinion may of course expose the planning system to disturbance. It has in fact been indicated in the Russian planning bodies that the demand for consumer goods is a confusing influence. So far as can be judged, there are only two possible ways to meet such an "unforeseen" demand for consumer goods, if the authorities are not to resort to stiffer regulations. One way would be to do the general planning with wider margins, that is to increase the "reserves against unforeseen demand;" the other, which is really the same thing, would be to let foreign trade become somewhat freer and to satisfy the new demand through imports.

IMPORT FINANCING

Both in the Ministry of Foreign Trade and in the Vneshtorgbank (the Foreign Trade Bank) it was admitted that the demand for imports will greatly increase. As to imports for the chemical expansion programme, it was said, these could be met through the possibilities which existed for an increase of exports by the industries concerned with both timber and oil. At the present time between 20 and 23 percent of the country's oil and oil products is exported, and it was stated that this proportion will probably be stepped up.

TABLE 3

EASTERN EUROPE'S FOREIGN TRADE BROKEN DOWN BETWEEN COUNTRIES
AND GROUPS OF COUNTRIES IN 1962
(Per mille)

	EXPORTS							IMPORTS						
	Bulgaria	Poland	Roumania	Soviet Union	Czechoslovakia	Hungary	Eastern Germany (1961)	Bulgaria	Poland	Roumania	Soviet Union	Czechoslovakia	Hungary	Eastern Germany (1961)
Albania	1	2	1		4		2	3	3	1		5		3
Bulgaria		15	14	64	28	14	37		17	18	60	31	13	30
Poland	42		49	84	92	64	92	31		37	87	70	58	46
Roumania	22	21		53	40	33	26	16	21		54	29	34	23
Soviet Union	502	345	420		378	356	403	564	306	394		377	363	483
Czechoslovakia	83	89	71	110		125	101	78	105	94	129		110	98
Hungary	21	39	47	58	57		44	19	36	39	60	67		47
Eastern Germany	104	71	57	195	105	95		86	125	59	166	110	102	
Eastern Europe, total	775	582	659	564	704	687	705	797	613	642	556	689	680	730
China	4	9	3	33	5	11	24	4	12	11	80	12	10	18
Mongolia		2	1	18	2		1		1	1	9	3		2
North Korea	1	2	3	11	3		2	2	2	2	14	3		1
North Vietnam		1	6	8	2		3		2	3	5	4		2
Asiatic communist countries, total	5	14	13	70	12	11	30	6	17	17	108	22	10	23
Cuba	25	12	7	53	23	10	12	16	10	6	36	23	8	5
Eastern bloc, total	805	608	679	687	739	708	747	819	640	665	700	734	698	758
France	17	15	34	12	9	12	5	14	14	22	24	13	28	13
Western Germany	37	51	63	19	31	49	97	28	33	85	32	30	43	89
Italy	24	24	38	19	15	25	6	18	16	50	15	14	23	8
Netherlands		7	7	6	9	11	10		5	5	7	10	14	10
Belgium–Luxemburg		6	12	7	6	4	7		3	6	5	10	8	9
EEC	78	103	154	63	70	101	125	60	71	168	83	77	116	129
Greece	7	5	6	3		6	3	4	3	3	3		6	3
United Kingdom	11	63	27	30	18	20	8	15	63	47	18	29	36	23
Sweden		20	4	8	6	7	7		11	7	12	7	6	8
Denmark		14		3	4		7		11	5	4	5		5
Norway		4	1	2	5		3		3	1	2	4		3
Switzerland		12	10	1		17			12	15	1		16	
Austria	12	20	18	6	13	31	12	28	16	19	10	17	32	9
Portugal		1	1						1	2				
EFTA	23	134	61	50	46	75	37	43	117	96	47	62	90	48
Finland		14	3	26	6	4	7		12	2	33	5	4	6
Iceland		1		1	1				1		2	1		
Spain		5	3		1				4	1		1		
Yugoslavia	16	19	5	10	11	20	17	8	21	9	7	10	10	12
Ireland		2												
Western Europe	124	283	232	153	135	206	189	115	229	279	175	156	226	198
Industrial countries outside Western Europe	1	31	7	18	12	3	8		71	8	32	12	1	6
Western industrial countries, total	125	314	239	171	147	209	197	115	300	287	207	168	227	204
Developing countries (outside Eastern bloc)	70	78	82	142	114	83	56	66	60	48	93	98	84	38

NOTE: A blank space in the columns means that information is lacking or that the amount is less than 1 per mille.

Even though the Soviet economy undoubtedly has an exceptionally great
export potential, and even though the Russians may be able rapidly to increase their exports of certain industrial products, it still seems inevitable
that the next few years' expansion of imports will in very great part have to

be financed on credit. During recent years the Russian gold and foreign currency reserves have undoubtedly been exposed to a quite considerable drain, which can hardly continue at the same rate. In addition Khrushchev recently said that it would be more expedient to increase the output of timber products, and to export more of them, than to expand the production of gold.

As a reflection of the new tendencies it may be pointed out that some important credit agreements have recently been concluded with certain Western industrial countries concerning deliveries of industrial products. The most remarkable case is that of the British credits, totalling about £100 million, to enable Russia to purchase equipment for chemical plants. These credits have been granted by insurance companies and banks with the benefit of a Government guarantee. In reply to a question Arefyev, Deputy Chairman of the Vneshtorgbank Managing Board, explained that the Soviet authorities want at least ten years' credit for imports of complete plants. At the same time they normally proposed to pay cash for imports "because that is cheaper than credits; but we never refuse credits when they are granted on favourable terms."

It may be supposed that very great and lasting expansion of the Soviet Union's trade with the capitalist world will by degrees lead to the Soviet authorities being forced to abandon principles of state control in foreign trade, or that at all events they may have to change those principles quite radically. At the moment, indeed, it is not very probable that people in Russia are already thinking on these lines. They are more likely to be making great efforts to solve the economic problems which they are facing, and to do so while maintaining the basic rules to which they have hitherto adhered. Spokesmen of the Ministry for Foreign Trade strongly emphasised the desirability of long-term trade agreements with Western countries. Such agreements, they argued, give both parties a feeling of increased security; besides this they of course assist the Russian planning. The increased activity in connection with trade must not yet be regarded as meaning any change of attitude towards the Soviet economic system. It is quite obvious that the big wheat deals, as well as some part of the increase in other trade, resulted from pressing necessity. That is so even though Russians have done a good deal of talking about the value of an increase in trade to both parties—preferably to the party trading with them—and have thus made a virtue of that necessity.

INTERNATIONALISED BANKING

One indication that broader economic links between the Soviet Union and countries outside the communist bloc may now be expected is that the Vneshtorgbank—which is a company with a capital of 300 million roubles, the owners of which include the Ministry of Foreign Trade, the Gosbank and the larger foreign trade organisations—does not appear to be entirely satisfied with its present organisation. Even though that organisation was reformed as recently as four years ago, reason has now been found to appoint a committee with instructions, is was said, to scrutinise the present structure of the Bank. In that connection the committee was to study how the large foreign banks operate in their business. The object is to find out whether any features in those foreign banks' working methods might be suitable for adoption by the Vneshtorgbank. Arefyev indicated that some adaptation might be conceivable, even though the basic conditions of course differed so greatly as between the Soviet Union and the West that no complete acceptance of Western methods would be practicable.

A further sign of increasing internationalisation of the Soviet economy is the foundation of the new Comecon bank, the International Bank for Economic Cooperation, which started business at the turn of the year. The most important and most immediate task for this bank is to operate a new system for multilateral settlement in connection with the member countries' external trade; this is to be done by means of a so-called transferable rouble. On the Russian side it has been pointed out that the new system represents a substantial improvement as compared with the previous system, which was virtually optional, being based on agreements reached within the Comecon "Chamber of Multilateral Settlements." Under the proposed new system each Comecon country must have a convertible account for each of the others; thus all the Comecon member countries have now been enabled to make use of their trade balances in relation to all the other members. It was stated that the total settlements under the new system during the first months of this year were considerably greater than corresponding transactions in the same months of last year. It is probable that new system will assist and stimulate trade between the Comecon countries. Besides operating the settlement procedure the Bank will be able to grant short-term credits so as to cover seasonal fluctuations in the member countries' external trade.

One important question is to what extent the Comecon bank thinks that countries outside the Comecon will be able to join the transferable rouble system. By this means it would of course be possible greatly to increase the flexibility of trade as between the Comecon bloc and the outside world. It was stated by Russian spokesmen, and it has also been pointed out by leading people in other Comecon countries, that such participation by non-Comecon countries in the clearing has not only been contemplated but is also desirable. Countries could take part in the clearing, they said, without applying for membership either in the bank or in Comecon. According to one statement Brazil has applied for admission to the system, and it was said that the member countries took a favourable view of this application.

The idea is, or perhaps rather was, that the bank shall also grant long-term credits; they would be granted not only to finance the member countries' joint capital projects but also to developing countries. In answer to a question, however, it was explained in the Comecon Secretariat at Moscow that it had not yet been possible to adopt any measures or take any steps in that direction. The reaction from the remaining Comecon countries to the idea of financing joint projects had not been particularly hearty. The allocation of such investments has indeed been one of the great sources of trouble affecting cooperation. It is therefore quite unlikely that this second task for the bank will become really important within any foreseeable future.

TRADING WITH THE PEOPLE'S REPUBLIC OF CHINA*

Trade with China is really in a category by itself. The possibilities of the market, the ups and downs it has seen since the war, the size of the country, and the total irrelevance of many of the rules of salesmanship make a promotion drive here or even an assessment of the position a difficult problem for the export manager or director. There are no possibilities for market surveys, there can be no advertising within the country, there is no contact with the end-user and yet despite this, sales are made.

Trading has reverted to an almost classical pattern of persuading first by correspondence and then perhaps in person a handful of capable and shrewd men that the goods we have are the best and that the price is right. In short, gimmicks are out. I asked a notably successful British businessman in this market how he accounted for his sales here. His reply was "Perseverance." That answer is I am sure valid for the sale of all types of goods, but in saying perseverance was the sole answer my informant was doing himself an injustice for he was discounting his own expertise which is essential in coping with the trading conditions here.

Those firms which are so experienced can testify that the entire foreign trade of the country is in the hands of some twelve Import-Export Corporations. As far as the British exporter is concerned the most important of these are the Machinery, Chemicals, Textile, Metals and Minerals, and the National Technical Import Corporation (complete plants). There are of course others, such as the Animal By-Products and the Tea and Native Produce Corporations which play an important part in Chinese exports to the United Kingdom.

THE STRUCTURE OF TRADE

The structure of Chinese foreign trade is such that all imports without exception must be ordered by one or other of the Corporations, whose officials will negotiate prices and terms and who will deal exclusively with the foreign manufacturer or his agent, if the manufacturer prefers to deal through an Export House. It is just not possible to deal direct with the end-user, or even to correspond with him and a company's sales will depend entirely

---

* *Board of Trade Journal,* (London), March 29, 1963, pp. 689, 690, 693, 694.

on their relationship with the relevant Corporation and the impression which they can make on it. The Corporations also have branch offices in several of the principal cities in China, particularly in Shanghai, Tientsin, Canton and Dairen. These sub-offices do make a number of purchases on their own account although these are often confined to a request for spares or for repeat orders.

The second point is that the relationship, even a good and successful one, with a Corporation is one conducted from a distance. It is impossible to have a sole or personal agent or indeed an agent of any kind in China; it is not in practice possible to advertise in Chinese newspapers or through the medium of the cinema or television or on hoardings although there are one or two magazines published in the United Kingdom and Hong Kong (including one printed in the Chinese language) which regularly reach Chinese eyes. Lacking therefore accepted means of contact with the potential customer, firms may on occasion feel a little detached and left with the feeling that if only they could do more to bring their products to the attention of the Chinese, then more sales would result. In order to obtain this closer contact, many firms are anxious to send out sales executives to China.

In the past the Chinese attitude towards this has been quite clearcut. Before any businessman received a visa he must receive an invitation from the relevant Corporation, and the Corporation will only do this if they have the intention to buy. A final sale will of course depend on terms and conditions but as a result of this selective granting of visas few business travellers to China leave empty handed. This has meant, however, that not all those persons wishing for a visa have been given one and many have accordingly felt disappointed.

Nevertheless the Chinese attitude is, given the circumstances here, reasonable, for they have maintained that there is no use in having numbers of businessmen coming to Peking when there is no real prospect of them making a sale. This, in the long-run, could do nothing to further commercial relations and it would certainly prove more expensive to the foreign firms than the present system. Happily however the growing number of British businessmen visiting Peking shows that the Corporations are treating requests for visas in a more relaxed manner than hitherto.

HARVEST SUCCESS A PRIME TRADING FACTOR

The number of businessmen given facilities to visit Peking depends of course on China's willingness to buy, which is itself directly connected with the economic state of the country. With about 70 percent of the nation's exports traditionally coming from the agricultural sector, the success of the harvest is of particular relevance to the country's foreign exchange position;

on it will depend the need for the purchase of cereals from abroad and also on Chinese export earnings.

Despite somewhat varied weather, the 1962 harvest was not unsatisfactory and this has placed China in a position where the Ministry of Foreign Trade have been able to state that there are now good prospects here for the British exporter. The Ministry's statement becomes even more convincing, when in order to encourage closer contact, and to give Chinese Corporations a better indication of the vast range of chemical, engineering and electrical goods, which we have to offer, the China Council for the Promotion of International Trade have said that they would welcome a series of small, specialized exhibitions to be organized in Peking during 1963 by United Kingdom firms. This should prove to be a very welcome opportunity for the British exporter either to make himself known in this market or if known already, to secure further sales.

The size of the Chinese market is such that any sales, however small, multiplied by 680 million become immensely impressive. Clearly this attitude could lead to over-optimism and to expectations that cannot possibly be fulfilled for many years to come. The Chinese Government themselves make no claims that the *per capita* income here, anywhere approaches that of the United Kingdom, but they can on the other hand reasonably point out that China has the ability to pay for a substantial and increasing number of imports from the West. In the first place China's exports are not confined, as is sometimes popularly supposed, to pig bristles and frozen eggs. In 1961 China earned a favourable balance of trade with Hong Kong alone of £58 million. In 1962 the figure will be very much larger. In 1961 her trade with the entire non-Communist world probably amounted to about £440 million with an overall surplus in her favour and this was a period when by China's own admission, economic conditions were by no means perfect.

CHINA IS A GOOD CUSTOMER

Trade with the United Kingdom has also been affected by internal economic conditions and as a result the 1962 figures were disappointing. Nevertheless in recent years China has been a good customer; in 1960 our exports amounted to over £31 million and British products enjoy an excellent reputation. There is also considerable respect for our technical knowhow and the "sale" of this, together with the attendant plant is something which could see a remarkable development within the next few years.

What are the Chinese likely to buy? There is no necessity, nor indeed any possibility, of conducting a market research programme here. The country's requirements are enormous and the position is not dissimilar to that in the United Kingdom following the war, when imports were controlled according to their importance to the national economy. Fortunately we have been given a clear indication of Chinese requirements. A series of statements by party and government leaders have emphasized that the modernization and mechanization of agriculture and the need to bring about a fundamental technical reform in that field, in a period between 20 and 25 years is the main task before the nation. 1.2 million tractors with the necessary infrastructure will be needed together with several hundred thousand hand-steered tractors and power-driven cable-drawn tractors; from 300,000 to 350,000 combine harvesters for grain and other crops, a similar number of trucks and 3.5 to 4 million machines for drainage and irrigation. The emphasis on agriculture does not of course just mean the need to purchase the above mentioned tools and machines to be used in the countryside; the whole of industry is affected. The Vice Minister of the chemical industry has stated that the target of the chemical industry is to build up a chemical industrial system with manufacture of chemical fertilizers as its centre, to keep up with the technical reform of agriculture and to assist in the development of the national economy.

He added that this also called for the construction of new plants to increase the manufacture both of chemical fertilizers and of highly effective insecticides; other priorities were the increased production of caustic soda, soda ash, nitric acid, sulphuric acid and other basic chemical materials and for further development of the organic synthesis of plastics, synthetic fibres and synthetic rubber. Finally the Minister stated that the investment allocated to the chemical industry especially for chemical fertilizer plants would be greatly increased. In addition considerable interest has been shown in synthetic fibre plants and many types of electrical machinery. Work on rural electrification is going ahead and heavy demands will be placed on the machine tool industry. Much of this can be supplied by China herself. But a certain percentage, within the limits of her foreign exchange earnings, will be purchased from abroad.

OPPORTUNITIES AT THE CANTON FAIR

No article on trade with China would be complete without some mention of the Canton Export Commodities Fair. This very capably organized Fair, is held twice yearly from mid-April to mid-May and mid-October to mid-November. Its primary function is of course to exhibit and sell Chinese goods and in the last Fair this aim was successful to the extent of some £51 million: but the Fair also provides an opportunity for the British business visitor, who is concerned with selling as well as buying, and even to those whose sole purpose is to seek rather than to make orders.

In a short time it provides an opportunity for the exporter to meet many senior officials from all the Corporations and visas are more readily granted for Canton than for Peking. For many firms it may not be worth, at least initially, sending out an executive purely to visit Canton, but if it can be fitted into a Far Eastern tour, then for an insight of what China has to offer and the extent to which she is prepared to buy, the Canton Fair offers a unique opportunity.

HOW CAN THE BRITISH MISSION HELP?

What can this Mission do to help the British businessman? Firstly, it is possible to give market prospects (although not of course a survey) for the goods which the British manufacturer has on offer. This information can only serve as an indication of what the Corporations may or may not wish to buy, and it is always easier to say what they are unlikely to want, such as luxury goods than to state with conviction that they will buy a certain product. To a newcomer to the market it is also possible to give some more detailed advice as to how to go about making a sale.

Secondly, we arrange with the Ministry of Foreign Trade who are always most helpful, that commercial magazines and technical works of reference supplied by us are circulated to the relevant Corporations, who in turn send them to the end-user. There is of course no reason why firms at home cannot send out magazines or sales literature, on a regular basis, direct to the Corporations, and this is preferable. Accordingly, the magazines distributed here tend to be those which cover the whole range of an industry rather than those representing individual firms but anything suitable that is sent out to us is passed on to the proper quarter.

Thirdly, under arrangements with the China Council for the Promotion of International Trade, we send to that organization suitable technical films which show some new industrial development or demonstrate a company's products. These films are not put up on public view but are shown privately, by the Chinese, to technical audiences. It is necessary to remember, however, that the films normally remain in Chinese hands for some time and if sent both ways by sea they will be out of the firm's hands for many months. The distribution of magazines and films or even merely the supply of addresses to which literature on sales or background information can be sent, is a particularly useful task when there is no normal medium of advertising.

Fourthly, we give all assistance that we can to British business visitors. We are of course delighted to see British businessmen out here and although the Corporations who will act as their sponsors are always excellent hosts, and, as those who have visited Peking know, are almost too hospitable, there are some things which we can do which may be a help or prove to be useful.

BRITAIN'S TRADING IMAGE IS GOOD

Finally, it is very pleasant to be able to say that the reputation of the British businessman in this market is high and our commercial image is a good one. There are still complaints about prices, less now than in the past, and in some categories of goods it is difficult to see how we can equal certain of our Far Eastern competitors. But by and large, trading conditions are now particularly favourable for the British exporter. The last nine months have seen a marked improvement in the economic state of the country and a continuation of this progress should again see China as a major importer of capital goods. The day is long past when it was said that the difficulty of business and of travelling to Cathay is so great and the route is so long and perilous that since those gentlemen twice made the journey no-one from Europe has dared to repeat it. Times have changed for the better since the days of Marco Polo, and the change has never been so marked as during the last fourteen years; those businessmen who now come are assured of a warm welcome; I have never met any who have regretted the journey.

"CHINA'S WESTERN TRADE; NO MORE RHUBARB"*

One hundred and seventy years ago with China still splendid in its isolation its emperor could write to George III that "We set no value on ingenious objects . . . and have no use for your country's manufactures." Recently, however, Communist China has come to place great value on such "ingenious objects" of the western world as chemical plants and industrial equipment, and to show considerable interest in western credit too. German exporters are complaining bitterly that since they are not allowed to grant credits to China, they are losing out on this growing trade.

This new trend in China's trade is a response to the heavy dose of Soviet economic pressure China received in 1960. It dovetails nicely with the new party line that China's salvation lies in modernising its agriculture and acquiring know-how from abroad by importing the most up-to-date equipment. Britain is well placed to meet many of China's needs—but so too are Japan and other western European countries. A Dutch trade mission is at this moment preparing to leave for Peking. Some political preference may be given to France, and to Italy, with its large communist party. In line with present political approaches, a French technological exhibition is to be held in Peking in September. France hopes to increase sales of cereals (wheat at present accounts for two-thirds of France's exports to China) but still more to expand sales of capital goods—locomotives, lorries, steel, precision instruments, chemical plant, and even Caravelles (China has already bought Viscounts from Britain).

In the last few months China has placed orders for seven chemical plants —three Italian, two Japanese, one Dutch and one British—at a cost of £33 million over the next five years. (There are more big industrial orders in the pipeline.) Five of the chemical plants are expected to form the core of a new chemical complex in the Szechwan basin—which appears to be one of the newly designated growth centres for Chinese agriculture.

Some would-be exporters of large-scale equipment to China have complained that the premium of about $4\frac{1}{2}$ percent demanded for guaranteeing medium-term supplier's credit to China is excessive. The rate for Russia is roughly $1\frac{1}{2}$ percent. Although it is true that China has a good credit rating in ordinary trade (barring the way it abruptly cut off trade with Japan in 1958) its economy is nevertheless unstable. Moreover, western countries have not

TABLE 1

TRADE WITH CHINA
(Millions of dollars: monthly averages)

	1960		1961		1962		1963 (9 months)	
	Imports	Exports	Imports	Exports	Imports	Exports	Imports	Exports
Britain	5.8	7.4	7.2	3.0	5.4	2.0	4.3	3.1
France	0.7	4.4	0.6	3.0	0.6	3.6	0.8	6.0
Germany	5.8	8.0	3.3	2.5	3.0	2.6	2.6	1.7
Italy	2.0	3.3	1.0	2.5	1.2	1.6	1.5	2.2
United States.	Nil	Nil	0.04	Nil	0.02	Nil	0.03	Nil
EEC.	12.3	19.9	7.2	9.3	7.4	8.8	8.6	11.1
EFTA.	8.7	10.9	9.4	5.0	7.4	3.2	6.6	4.6

supplied communist China with medium-term credit before. With no experience to go by the rates are high. The same thing happened when such credit was first offered to the Soviet Union. Nevertheless, there is unlikely to be any difficulty in offering China the same credit terms (10 percent on order, 10 percent on delivery and 80 percent over five years at $5\frac{1}{2}$ percent per annum) that prevail in trade with Russia.

Now that China has caught its breath after its calamitous slump of 1959–61 new trade patterns are already apparent. The Russians say that China's imports of their industrial machinery and equipment fell from over £200 million in 1960 to £10 million in 1962. This has worked to Britain's benefit. Britain's exports to China rose in the first eleven months of last year to $34 million compared with $20 million in the same period in the year before. True, these export figures are well below the best in Britain's trade with Communist China, which was in 1960 but Britain is now providing a higher percentage of China's industrial imports than ever before. This year three major British industrial exhibitions will be staged in Peking.

The era has long passed when Chinese mandarins harboured the illusion that westerners would meet an uncomfortable end if China refused them supplies of tea and rhubarb. Yet until now the Chinese communists have made little effort to meet the requirements of the international markets. Whatever the other disadvantages of the Russian market, selling was not one of them. For some time to come the mainstay of China's exports to Europe will remain agricultural products and the difficulty here is that China has not been a regular supplier. The Chinese are becoming increasingly aware of this problem. They doubtless realize that while China's present policies may help to meet a greater proportion of the needs of its growing industries the rate of growth envisaged will boost total import requirements.

THE FINANCE OF EAST-WEST TRADE*

While for world trade as a whole 1960 was a disappointing year, such was certainly not the case with East-West trade. This made very rapid progress, and reached a new record level. In the first half of 1960 the total East-West trade turnover rose by nearly 29 percent. Exports from the "West" to the U.S.S.R., China, and the East European countries rose by 36 percent in the first half of 1960 as compared with the first half of 1959. In the other direction, exports from these countries to the "West" went up by 21 percent. Taking the two together, the total turnover is now running at some $9,000 millions or £3,200 millions a year.

STERLING AREA'S SHARE

At present, three quarters of the total is accounted for by Western Europe and the Overseas Sterling Area. Of this, the share of the United Kingdom and Sterling Area together is about one-quarter, and the share of continental Western Europe about one-half. Among the remaining countries in the "West," substantial increases in East-West trade were scored in 1960 by a number of Latin American states and Japan.

The United Kingdom's East-West trade rose sharply in both directions during 1960. Exports (including re-exports) were up by 30 percent, compared with an overall increase of only 6 percent in British exports to all areas. Imports arose similarly by 21 percent, compared with an overall increase of 14 percent.

The outstanding feature in 1960 was the very large increase in exports to the U.S.S.R., which showed a rise of nearly 53 percent, as compared with 1959. Our exports of machinery, for example, rose from £12 millions to £19.8 millions, and exports of chemicals were more than doubled, from £2.9 millions to £6 millions. At the same time Britain increased its sales to China, and to every one of the East European countries with the single exception of Poland.

The increase in U.K. purchases from the U.S.S.R. was more modest, at 19 percent. This was spread over a number of commodities, including wood,

* Supplement to *Investors Chronicle,* March 17, 1961, pp. 27–28.

furs, nonferrous metals, petroleum products, etc. Britain also bought more from China and from each of the East European countries.

HELPFUL TRADE AGREEMENTS

This expansion in Britain's East-West trade follows the signing of new trade agreements with the U.S.S.R. and a number of the other countries concerned. These agreements are an example of the earnest wish of the British government and of the co-signatory government in each case to encourage a growth in trade between the two countries. They provide a general framework in which such a development in trade can take place. Where necessary they provide for the establishment of agreed quotas for the import into each country of particular classes of goods from the other country.

It should be emphasized that the agreements do not involve anything in the nature of barter arrangements. The trade itself is conducted on ordinary commercial lines between the business organizations in the two countries. It is these bodies which conclude and execute specific contracts in accordance with normal business considerations. In the United Kingdom, of course, the business organizations concerned are simply British firms which enter into East-West trade either as exporters or importers. In the U.S.S.R., China, etc., the organizations are the import and export corporations which are set up by the State to conduct foreign trade, which in these countries is a State monopoly.

The trade agreements concluded by the United Kingdom do not provide for any rigid overall balancing of the trade with any particular country, though the general spirit of the agreements is that there should be a two-way development. Specific quotas are often established, however, in respect of particular goods or classes of goods. This is where the goods concerned cannot be freely imported into the United Kingdom from the U.S.S.R. or the other country in question under Open General Licence from the Board of Trade. In such cases, if it is agreeable, the British government will open the way to trade in these goods by establishing quotas for their import during a given period, usually a year at a time. Within these quotas the government will issue the necessary import licences to British firms wishing to take up this opportunity.

The U.S.S.R., or other country concerned, reciprocates on its part by agreeing to license imports from the United Kingdom of stated British products to roughly the same value. Much of the trade, particularly in products traditionally exchanged between the United Kingdom and its "Eastern" trade partners does not, it should be added, require these special licensing procedures. It may be noted here that the export of certain goods from the United Kingdom to these countries is still forbidden or subject to license, on the grounds that they are of strategic importance.

USEFUL CONTACTS

The development of the United Kingdom's East West trade is considerably assisted by the fact that most of these countries maintain permanent Trade Delegations in Britain. These undertake pre-contract negotiations, and normally have the authority to sign contracts on behalf of the trade corporations. British businessmen have also found it worthwhile on an increasing scale to visit the U.S.S.R., China, and other countries to discuss trade matters. Highly successful specialized British trade exhibitions have already been held in Moscow. This year, a British Trade Fair will take place in Moscow in May, and a Soviet Trade Fair will follow in London in July.

One particularly interesting development has been the sale by British firms of complete manufacturing plants. Alongside of this, an important business is developing in the sale of technical know-how between the United Kingdom and the U.S.S.R.; this includes the purchase of Russian know-how by Britain.

FAMILIAR COMMERCIAL LINES

It will be clear from what has been said that the United Kingdom's East-West trade agreements do not involve any kind of bilateral government financing arrangements. Trade is conducted along familiar commercial lines, and its financing also follows the ordinary pattern. Thus, as in all international trading business, banks are called upon to act as the essential link between buyer and seller, in receiving and paying out money in accordance with the terms of the contract, and in providing finance in appropriate cases. For the most part the trade is conducted in sterling, though the basis is sometimes U.S. dollars.

At the U.K. end, traders can make use not only of the general banking facilities offered by London, but also of the specialized banks for East-West trade, namely the Moscow Narodny Bank, the Bank of China and the Zivnostenska Banka of Czechoslovakia. In the U.S.S.R., China and Eastern Europe the business is handled by the State central banks, or specialized foreign trade banks.

MOSCOW NARODNY BANK

Trade relations between the United Kingdom and the U.S.S.R. go right back to 1919, and it was in that year also that there was established in London the Moscow Narodny Bank, to assist in the development of trade between the two countries. This is a British registered company, its shares now being held by banks and trade organizations in the Soviet Union.

With the recent rapid development of Anglo-Soviet trade, and with the general all-round increase in the United Kingdom's trade with other "Eastern" countries, the scale of operations of the Moscow Narodny Bank has likewise undergone a great expansion. The 1959 balance sheet showed an increase in total assets from £8.6 millions to £54.8 millions, and there was a very marked growth in the balances held with the bank by its correspondents abroad, including particularly the banks in the U.S.S.R., and Eastern Europe. At the end of 1960 the paid-up capital was raised from £525,000 to £1,200,000.

United Kingdom imports from the U.S.S.R. and Eastern Europe may be divided broadly into primary commodities and consumer goods. The former are bought in bulk, and are usually the subject of documentary collections drawn on large merchants and nationalized industries in this country. Payment is made on presentation of the shipping documents. Consumer goods, such as watches, cameras, furs, etc., are usually imported by smaller firms, and in many cases financial accommodation is required. In extending such accommodation the Moscow Narodny Bank, or another London bank will be guided of course by usual banking considerations.

So far as U.K. exports to these countries are concerned, in the case of the bulk, traditional commodities, e.g. rubber, Documentary Credits are opened, for example through the Moscow Narodny Bank; but with increasing confidence, payment on a simple collection basis is becoming more frequent. United Kingdom exports of consumer goods and of certain other goods, which have begun to assume increased importance, are generally handled on the basis of sight credits. In such cases the seller in the United Kingdom may ask for bank accommodation to cover the short period between shipment and payment. Use is also made of the ordinary bank Acceptance Credit. Facilities of this sort may be provided to cover the import into Eastern Europe of certain goods from the United Kingdom, through the medium of term bills.

Another method of payment for U.K. exports which has a certain importance is settlement at a fixed date after shipment, under Guarantee from the State Bank of the importing country. The U.K. seller may approach his London banker for an advance against this Guarantee.

CREDIT FOR CAPITAL GOODS

A very high proportion of the United Kingdom's exports consists of expensive plant and machinery for factories in Eastern Europe. Credit may be required for a period of up to five years, and a London bank may be approached to provide such facilities. The contract will normally provide for certain initial cash payments, the balance of the contract being payable in installments thereafter. If it is agreeable, the London bank will advance to the U.K. manufacturer this balance, against suitable security, and will be reimbursed as the installments are duly paid. Such contracts are usually covered by Export Credit Guarantee Department Contract and Shipment Policies.

The 1959 balance-sheet of the Moscow Narodny Bank can be used to illustrate the role played by bank finance in the development of East-West trade. During the year the credit provided to customers of the bank under the headings of advances rose extremely rapidly from £1.3 millions to £29.7 millions. Alongside of this, at the end of the year, the bank showed a total of £2.3 millions of bills discounted on behalf of customers.

The prospects for the further development of East-West trade appear to be good. Certainly in terms of the economic needs of the United Kingdom and its East-West trade partners, there is large scope for further progress, and we are now only at the beginning of things in this field. Since finance goes necessarily hand-in-hand with the growth of trade, we can expect to see also a further expansion of the business of the institutions in the City of London which minister to the financial needs of this particular sector of international trade.

SOME ASPECTS OF THE U.S.S.R.'S INTERNATIONAL TRADE AND PAYMENTS*

The foreign trade of the Soviet Union has developed very rapidly since the war, and in 1960 it had trade relations with 81 other countries and in 1961 a total foreign trade turnover of 10,500 million roubles (approx. £4, 160 millions).

It is well known that the trade potential of a country depends on the level of activity of its internal economy, and in this connection it is worth noting that at the present time the U.S.S.R. is the second greatest economic power in the world. With a population of 220 millions the U.S.S.R. accounts for nearly one-fifth of the world's total industrial production, i.e., more than Great Britain, France, Italy, Canada, Japan, Belgium, and the Netherlands put together, these countries having a total population of 280 millions. This means that in the U.S.S.R. there are already great export and import possibilities. Now, however, the Soviet Union, in accordance with the new economic plan, is making great efforts to increase the volume of its industrial production by at least 6 times by 1980. If we bear in mind that 10–11 years ago the volume of industrial production in the U.S.S.R. was less than 30 percent of the industrial production of the U.S.A., and is now more than 60 percent, then it will be clear that the Soviet Union is not attempting anything unreasonable in trying to achieve this target.

The further development of the economy of the U.S.S.R. must lead to the growth of Soviet foreign trade, and will increase the trading importance of the Soviet foreign trade, and will increase the trading importance of the Soviet Union for many countries of the world. All this, of course, creates justifiable interest in Soviet foreign trade as well as centering attention on such questions as the U.S.S.R.'s international payments and the finance of Soviet foreign trade.

A STATE MONOPOLY

The main feature of the foreign trade of the Soviet Union is that it is a state monopoly, which is the natural consequence of the structure of the

* Oleg Kulikov, the Supplement to *Investors Chronicle*, March 30, 1962.

441

Soviet economy. This monopoly is exercised through special foreign trade organizations. The great bulk of the goods handled for export by these organizations is produced in state-owned manufacturing and other productive enterprises. On the import side, the foreign trade organizations supply imported goods to state-owned industrial enterprises and internal trade organizations which deal with the sale of imported goods to the general public.

The other main characteristic of the organization of Soviet foreign trade is that it is planned, the plan for foreign trade being part of the overall plan.

The trader in the West, therefore, who imports goods from or exports goods to the U.S.S.R., deals with foreign-trade organizations, whose financial standing is assured without any shade of doubt and who are absolute monopolists in the sphere of the Soviet foreign trade. The activity of these organizations is centrally planned; at the same time, however, these are in fact independent organizations with their own financial means, and they are responsible for commitments undertaken by them towards other Soviet organizations, as well as towards their foreign trade partners.

The above characteristics do not, of course, constitute a full description of the organization of Soviet foreign trade. But they help us to form a clear idea of the methods used by the Soviet Union with regard to international payments and the finance of foreign trade.

BANK CREDIT

Prior to 1961 credits given to Soviet foreign-trade organizations were extended exclusively by the State Bank of the U.S.S.R. (Gosbank). In January, 1961, however, Gosbank transferred this function to the Bank for Foreign Trade of the U.S.S.R. (Vneshtorgbank).

At the present time Vneshtorgbank is the only source of credit in the U.S.S.R. for the foreign-trade corporations. The other banks do not deal with the finance of foreign trade and there is no nonbank credit, i.e., no trade credit. These corporations conduct their export and import business almost entirely on the basis of bank credit. Vneshtorgbank is therefore able to insist on a strict financial discipline on their part.

"Export-credits" extended by Vneshtorgbank supply the foreign-trade corporations with the funds necessary to purchase goods, for export, from the Soviet enterprises that produce them. These credits are repaid by the corporations from the proceeds of their export sales.

"Import-credits" from Vneshtorgbank are used by the foreign-trade corporations to pay for goods purchased from foreign firms. These credits are repaid from the proceeds of the sale of these imported goods to Soviet enterprises.

In granting credits for foreign trade Vneshtorgbank follows the same principles as govern the granting of bank credit in general in the Soviet Union. Firstly, it acts in accordance with the current economic plan, which takes into account the export possibilities and import needs of the U.S.S.R., its foreign exchange reserves, and so on. Secondly, credits must be repaid within a strictly specified time. Thirdly, credits are extended only against security, and finally interest is charged on the credit.

METHODS OF PAYMENT

The U.S.S.R. is one of the leading countries in the sphere of international trade, and its foreign trade turnover is the fifth largest in the world, after the U.S.A., Great Britain, Western Germany, and France. Before the Second World War the U.S.S.R. in this respect occupied only the sixteenth place.

Of the Soviet Union's total foreign trade turnover in 1960, 7,100 million roubles, or nearly 71 percent was accounted for by its trade with Eastern Europe (Albania, Bulgaria, Czechoslovakia, German Democratic Republic, Hungary, Poland, and Rumania,) plus China, Mongolia, North Korea, and North Vietnam.

In that year the total trade between the U.S.S.R. and Czechoslovakia amounted to 1,200 million roubles, or about £475 millions. In the same year, for purposes of comparison, the trade between Great Britain and the Federal Republic of Germany was £366 millions, and that between Great Britain and France £230 millions. Trade between the U.S.S.R. and the G.D.R. in 1960, to take another example, was valued at 1,800 million roubles, or more than £710 millions. These comparisons are valid, since the values of exports and imports are in all cases based on world market prices.

The methods of payment employed by the U.S.S.R. in its dealings with Eastern Europe, China and the other countries listed above differ from those followed in its trade with the rest of the world. In trade with the rest of the world, the methods of payment are generally in accordance with normal international banking practice.

With Eastern Europe, China and other socialist countries, however, the payments techniques employed are substantially different. Here it should be noted, first of all, that the general organization of the foreign-trade system of these countries is basically similar to that of the U.S.S.R. Foreign trade payments between the U.S.S.R. and these countries, and between these countries themselves, are made through a clearing system. This clearing system operates on the basis of intergovernmental trade agreements. These trade agreements constitute guarantees on the part of the countries concerned to supply goods to each other in accordance with the detailed provisions of the agreements. In this respect they differ, therefore, from trade agreements of the type concluded, for example by the United Kingdom with another "Western" country, which commit the parties only to assisting the import and export of goods, e.g., by issuing the necessary licenses.

Implicit in the trade agreements between the U.S.S.R. and the countries of Eastern Europe, China, etc., is the principle that the payments arising out of these agreements should be balanced, usually at the end of the year. However, a certain amount of indebtedness is allowed in the clearing, which is not regarded as a violation of the basic principle of balanced payments. If the indebtedness of the country to the other exceeds this technical limit, however, this is then treated as a short-term credit given to the debtor country by its clearing partner, on which interest is charged. The clearing agreements do not provide for payment of a clearing indebtedness in gold or foreign currency; debts must be settled in goods.

MULTILATERAL CLEARING

Trade and payments agreements between the U.S.S.R. and the other countries are normally on a bilateral basis, but the planned nature of the trade also makes it possible to obtain the benefits of a multilateral clearing.

The clearing agreement signed in June, 1949, by the Soviet Union, in conjunction with Poland, Finland, and Czechoslovakia may be considered as a prototype of the present multilateral clearing in Eastern Europe. Under this agreement Finland agreed to supply standard houses, sawn goods and small ships, etc., to the U.S.S.R. to the value of 100 million roubles. The U.S.S.R. for its part agreed to supply consumer goods to Poland worth 80 million roubles, and goods to Czechoslovakia to the value of 20 million roubles. Poland agreed to supply Finland with coal to the value of 80 million roubles, and finally Czechoslovakia was to supply Finland with 20 million roubles of agricultural machinery and industrial goods.

In 1957 the U.S.S.R. and the East European countries agreed to establish a multilateral clearing system to be operated through a special Chamber. This did not cancel the bilateral agreements, but made them more flexible.

From what has already been said, it will be evident that the multilateralization of the clearings goes hand-in-hand with the development of coordinated international planning in Eastern Europe through the Council for Mutual Economic Aid.

Trade credit (the granting of credit by a foreign-trade corporation in one country to a corporation in another country) is not employed. Generally speaking these countries grant each other only direct, long-term government loans. As a rule the U.S.S.R. grants such credits for periods of five years or more, with a normal rate of interest of 2 percent per annum. As already indicated, short-term credits, are only granted in particular cases, by permitting an indebtedness in the clearing in excess of the technical limit originally laid down.

A New Instrument

Turning to the details of the payments techniques employed, in 1950 these countries began to use a new instrument and since 1955 this has been the main instrument used. This method is "Collection with Immediate Payment," or as it is sometimes styled, a "General Letter of Credit." The technique is as follows.

The exporter (e.g., a foreign-trade organization in Czechoslovakia) after shipment of goods to the importer (say a Soviet foreign-trade organization) presents to his bank, the State Bank of Czechoslovakia, the necessary set of shipping documents. The bank of the exporter, the State Bank of Czechoslovakia makes immediate payment to the exporter against the shipping documents and debits the corresponding amount from the clearing account of the bank of the importer, in this case Vneshtorgbank, to whom it immediately sends the set of shipping documents together with the notice of payment (payment advice). The bank of the importer, i.e. Vneshtorgbank, upon receipt of the above set of documents, credits the clearing account of the bank of the exporter (State Bank of Czechoslovakia) debits the account of the importer (the Soviet foreign-trade organization) and presents the shipping documents to the importer.

This method of payment is very quick and expeditious. The exporter ships the goods before payment is made, but receives payment immediately against the shipping documents. When the importer receives the documents, his payment has already been made. The exporter does not have to tie up his capital beyond the moment that the shipment is made, while the importer does not have to go to the trouble of opening a Letter of Credit, or of incurring bank charges against a credit.

Settling Disputes

This technique demands from all the foreign-trade organizations involved, an exact execution of their contractual obligations. But, of course, there may be cases when one or other of the foreign-trade organizations involved in a contract wishes to file a claim against its foreign partner, if it considers that the latter has not carried out the terms of the contract. In this instance the importer has the right to claim, within 14 working days from the day of the receipt of the shipping documents by the bank of the importer, the amount which was debited from his account. In order to do so he notifies his bank, giving the reasons for his claim against the exporter. When making his claim the importer can state that he refuses to accept the goods, and that all the expenses in connection with their export must be borne by the exporter.

If the exporter's bank establishes that the importer's claim is correct, and that this claim is merited by the terms of the contract between the importer and the exporter, then the bank will credit the account of the importer with the amount which was earlier debited. Simultaneously the importer's bank will debit this amount from the clearing account of the exporter's bank and will send to it a copy of the importer's claim. After this the differences between exporter and importer are settled between themselves, without the participation of the banks. Later, if the exporter admits that he has violated the terms of the contract or if an arbitrator rules that the exporter has violated the terms of the contract, then all the expenses incurred during the dispute will be paid by the exporter. If, however, it is found that the importer has refused to pay for the goods without having good grounds for so doing, then the importer will not only have to pay for the goods, but in addition will also have to pay a fine for the delay in payment. Two facts, then, stand out from the examination of the foreign trade and payments arrangements of the U.S.S.R. Firstly, these arrangements flow directly from the Soviet system of economic planning; and secondly, they are very simple and straightforward in operation.

TOWARD A TRANSFERABLE ROUBLE?*

While the West struggles with its own currency problems, the Soviet block is preparing for an important move of its own towards internal convertibility of currencies. But in the west, the experiences of the post-war years showed that progress towards real currency convertibility depended on freedom of trade. In the east, where trade is a state monopoly, it must involve inter-governmental planning decisions; and while Comecon provides the framework for such decisions, and a new International Bank of Socialist Countries is now to be established, progress may still be painfully slow.

Comecon, the council for mutual economic aid in Communist Europe, was established as early as 1949 in answer to the Marshall Plan and the freeing of trade and payments that it induced in Western Europe. However, though the volume of trade among members has been rising, a single "socialist market" is still far away. Among the major impediments are the absence of convertible or transferable currency and the habit of bilateral balancing; there is an obvious connection between the two.

The communist countries are accustomed to conduct their mutual trade bilaterally. Bilateral trade is the logical consequence of the planning system and the state monopoly of foreign trade. Where national economic plans are drawn up centrally, for the most part using the crude method of "material balances," and where the plans encompass and direct all economic activity in the country, the only practicable way of coping with foreign trade is to incorporate it into the central figuring of the domestic plan. Physical shortages and surpluses at home reveal what should be imported and exported. The simplest way to organize this is through bilateral agreements with individual countries, which ensure the delivery of the needed commodities and the disposal of surpluses, while avoiding the embarrassment of third countries demanding delivery of goods not provided for in the plan. At the same time, bilateral balancing can involve familiar artificial constraints. Some special arrangements for tri-lateral settlement in isolated cases existed as early as 1949 (e.g., between Russia, Poland, and Finland), but they were used on a very small scale. Alternatively, a country with a surplus could buy more of a particular commodity than it needed and re-export some of it, and so transfer its bilateral surplus. In this way, in 1950–51, Rumania sold Bulgarian to-

* *The Economist*, October 19, 1963, pp. 263, 264.

bacco to Czechoslovakia, Hungary, and East Germany in order to "transfer" the surplus earned with Bulgaria. But these arrangements did not involve Comecon as such.

The first multilateral trading agreement between Comecon countries was signed in Warsaw in 1957. But this agreement retained the system of bilateral settlements. The provisions stipulated that multilateral clearing would apply only to certain goods, mainly consumer goods, and that these goods could be cleared multilaterally only on the basis of an additional agreement and not automatically. Member countries were also given the right to transfer surpluses from bilateral to multilateral accounts, but again only by mutual agreement. As a result of such restriction on the use of "transferable currency," multilateral settlements have been very small.

Now a fully-fledged multilateral clearing system for Comecon countries is, on present plans, to be created on January 1, 1964, when the International Bank of Socialist Countries will begin operations and act as the agent for multilateral clearing in "transferable roubles." All member countries will hold their balances of Comecon currencies at the bank, and transferable roubles will simply be the unit of account in which intra-block settlements are made. In other words, if the Bulgarians earn a surplus of Polish zloty and wish to use them to buy goods in East Germany, the transaction will be cleared through the bank; no actual roubles will be transferred. But the activities of the bank will not be limited to multilateral clearing; it is also intended to play an important part in co-ordinating the foreign exchange dealings of members' own banks. Member countries will be able to use the funds in their accounts at the bank to finance their trade.

Temporary deficits within Comecon that are caused by seasonal fluctuations in imports and exports are to be financed by short-term credits from the bank. There will be some prearranged limit to the amount of credit that any one country can obtain, but there is still no firm decision about how this limit will be calculated. At present seasonal fluctuations in trade are offset by so-called "technical credits" agreed in advance by the bilateral partners. Technical credits are interest-free up to the agreed limit, but a rate of two percent is charged on any excess. This type of credit would be abolished with the introduction of multilateral clearing.

The funds at this Comecon bank's disposal will consist of its own capital, made up of subscriptions from member countries, in proportion to their relative share in mutual trade, and of the temporary surplus deposits of members in net credit in their Comecon payments. Apart from the use of these funds for short-term credits, it is conceivable that the bank may be used to finance capital investments, but it is still impossible to say whether much or anything will be done in this direction.

Some communist officials have suggested that countries should have the right to use these credit facilities only if their export commitments are being fulfilled, to ensure that export obligations take precedence over internal requirements. In another direction, the deputy chairman of the Bank of Bulgaria has suggested that the bank should eventually extend its activities to capitalist markets. Then the gold and foreign currency holdings of member countries at present scattered in accounts with capitalist banks would be concentrated with the Socialist bank. This would enable the bank to extend credits even for trade with the west—for which it would charge much lower interest rates than western bankers. However, this is little more than an idea for the longer term.

Introduction of the transferable rouble and multilateral clearing will itself demonstrate the need for further reform, as present illogicalities in economic relations within the block will become more obtrusive. For example, the cross exchange rates of member countries are out of line. This did not matter very much when there was no multilateral clearing, since a country could not transfer its surplus or deficit from one currency to another. But under the regime now envisaged countries could make unjustifiable gains from various forms of arbitrage—such as commodity shunting of the kind well known in the west in the semi-convertible fifties. In 1961, following the revaluation of the rouble, special exchange rates for "non-commodity transactions" were introduced and these for "non-commodity transactions" were introduced and these rates, which are mutually consistent, may form a convenient basis of new unified exchange rates.

Other anomalies may prove much less tractable; for example the basis of price used in mutual trade. At present, rough equivalents of world prices are used: these are averaged so as to avoid seasonal variations and five-year averages are used to counteract cyclical fluctuations. Domestic prices within communist countries bear very little relation to relative scarcities or use-values, being set according to other criteria; some are kept down by subsidies, and others allow for big profit margins. Unfortunately, the principles of pricing are not uniform in the Comecon countries, and anyway the exchange rates are set with very little regard to either purchasing power parity or to achieving balance between demand and supply. However, while for these reasons domestic prices are inappropriate indications of relative costs in communist countries, the pattern of efficient specialization within this isolated block may not be indicated by world prices either.

Not surprisingly, economists have urged that internal costs should be used as a criterion in decisions on trade. The Soviet government has established a working party "to study possible ways of utilizing home prices in trade between socialist countries." At present this working party calculates "corrective coefficients" for any pair of countries and for multilateral trade, amending relative prices and exchange rates to remove some of the grosser inconsistencies. Both in the Soviet Union and in the other Comecon countries much has been written, especially since 1961, on possible criteria of relative efficiency to determine international specialism between members. But, in spite of very complicated formulae, these articles for the most part suggest that the final solution lies in a comprehensive revision of the pricing policies of member countries—a process impeded in practice by lack of agreement among eastern economists about the theory and practice of prices in general. There have been some attempts to avoid the use of prices and of "corrective coefficients" by comparing—alas, only in absolute terms—the labour-time utilized in various commodities. No permanent solution to this problem has yet appeared and only stop-gap measures have been adopted.

In the West, once currencies are convertible, goods cross borders subject only to customs duty and occasional quantitative restrictions. A large number of firms take decentralized decisions, both on product specialization and investment, by reference to market conditions. In the communist world, where control over resource allocation is centralized, even the limited flexibility that separate enterprises have in dealings with one another does not apply to foreign trade. Even between communist countries, foreign trade deals are almost invariably the sole concern of a separate central ministry. This sets up bureaucratic barriers between enterprises and planning offices operating in similar and complementary branches of industry in different countries. The central planners of each country seek to fit trade into their separate national material balances, and to fit their investments, which will greatly influence the future pattern of trade into national estimates of future needs. It is realized today, from Mr. Khrushchev downwards, that specialization requires a supranational planning authority, with powers to lay down production programmes, to allocate resources, and to decide investment plans. Mr. Khrushchev publicly advocated such an authority in June, 1962. Only within such a setting could a system of multilateral trade and payments be effective.

But the creation of a supranational authority in Comecon raises a number of awkward problems. First of all, it is politically unpopular, both with the peoples and the leaders of the smaller countries. They recall their subordination to Moscow in Stalin's time and value their political autonomy, which would be greatly reduced if their economic life were controlled from outside. Secondly, the absence of rational or other agreed criteria for comparing costs would give rise to endless argument. Thirdly, even if such criteria could be found, the less-developed communist countries would refuse to accept the validity of the comparison as a guide to specialization, maintaining, as do underdeveloped countries in other parts of the world, that their comparative disadvantage is a temporary consequence of underdevelopment. This view seems to be particularly strongly held by the Rumanians, who fear that their ambitious plans for all-round industrialization would be held back if Comecon were given greater authority to decide on specialization. The Chinese have publicly accused Russia of "great-power chauvinism" (soon, perhaps "colonialism"?) for allegedly seeking to impose economic plans on its allies; and Russia is not in a position simply to issue orders.

The communique of the meeting of leaders of Comecon countries held in

Moscow in July revealed that Rumania had won at least a partial victory. The supranational planning authority, advocated by Russia in June, 1962, was abandoned for the time being. It was agreed instead that the plans of member countries would be coordinated for the period 1966–70 and that attention would be concentrated "on a few basic products like fuel, electrical energy, raw materials, the development of the chemical industry, machine building, electronics and other progressive branches." These, the communique added "will be developed on the principle of equality, with strict observance of sovereignty. . . ." An editorial on this meaning in the Soviet economic journal *Voprosy Ekonomiki* stressed that "self-sufficiency and autarky are alien to socialist countries." But in view of the failure of Comecon to move towards a closer integration through a supranational planning authority, one wonders how far the new multilateral payments framework in the proposed bank will in practice succeed in getting away from predominantly bilateral lines—or indeed, whether it will work at all.

THE INTERNATIONAL BANK FOR ECONOMIC COOPERATION*

The International Bank for Economic Cooperation started its operations on January 1, 1964. The legal basis for the establishment of the Bank was an agreement between the Comecon countries, signed on October 22, 1963, for a multilateral system of settlements in transferable roubles and for the organization of the International Bank for Economic Cooperation. The parties to the agreement are Bulgaria, Czechoslovakia, G.D.R., Hungary, Mongolia, Poland, Rumania and the U.S.S.R. The introduction of the system of settlements in transferable roubles and the creation of the Bank signifies the emergence of a new and relatively more perfect form of trade and financial relations between the socialist countries, which puts the payment relations of each particular socialist country on a multilateral basis.

Prior to this agreement, trade and payments between the socialist countries had been conducted on a bilateral basis. Settlements were conducted through bilateral clearing accounts, and the balance of these accounts in favour of one trading partner could not be utilized for payments to a third country. This forced countries to balance trade and payments bilaterally between each other, and tended to restrict the volume and value of trade.

The new system of multilateral settlements in transferable roubles, which was established according to the above-mentioned agreement, provides that:

(a) all settlements involved between member countries of the agreement are effected in a newly created international currency, namely, the transferable rouble, which has a gold content of 0.9874.2 grams of fine gold;
(b) each member country which has funds in transferable roubles on its accounts may use them freely for settlements with other members;
(c) each member country, when concluding trade agreements, envisages in general a balance of receipts and payments in transferable roubles with all other member countries within the calendar year.

The International Bank of Economic Cooperation aims at the promotion of the economic cooperation and development of the socialist countries as well as the expansion of the cooperation between these countries and non-

* *Moscow Narodny Bank Quarterly Review,* Winter, 1964.

socialist countries. The authorized capital of the Bank is established at 300,000,000 transferable roubles; the subscription quota of each member, which has been determined on the basis of the volume of exports in their mutual trade, is as follows:

People's Republic of Bulgaria	17 million roubles
Hungarian People's Republic	21 million roubles
German Democratic Republic	55 million roubles
Mongolian People's Republic	3 million roubles
Polish People's Republic	27 million roubles
Rumanian People's Republic	16 million roubles
Union of Soviet Socialist Republics	116 million roubles
Czechoslovak Socialist Republic	45 million roubles

Subscription payments to the capital may be effected in transferable roubles, in convertible currencies or in gold. The amount of the subscription payments will be paid back in the event of a country ceasing to be a member of the Bank. As other banks, the International Bank for Economic Cooperation has a reserve capital.

Legally, the International Bank for Economic Cooperation is a juridical person. In accordance with its statutes, the Bank is responsible for all its commitments, within the limits of the value of its own property, and is not responsible for the obligations of the member countries. On the other hand, the member countries are not responsible for the commitments of the Bank itself.

The control of the Bank is in the hands of the Council and the Board. The Council is the highest governing body and consists of the representatives of all member countries of the Bank, with a limit of up to three representatives from each country. All the member countries have equal rights and each country has one vote irrespective of the amount of its share. During the sessions of the Council the chair is taken by the representative of each member country in turn.

The Board of the Bank is the executive body and indirectly governs the administrative functions of the Bank. The Board is responsible and accountable to the Council of the Bank. The members of the Board are appointed by the Council on the basis of one representative from each country for a period of up to five years. The chairman and the members of the Board, when executing their duties, act as international executives, irrespective to which country they belong.

The staff of the Bank is selected from the citizens of the member countries of the Bank by agreement between the members of the Council and the Board. In this connection the banks of the member countries of the Comecon recommend their qualified specialists for the work in the International Bank.

In accordance with the above agreement, and in keeping with the statutes of the Bank, the latter is empowered to carry out the following main functions:

I. The organization and the maintenance of the multilateral system of settlements in transferable roubles in connection with both trade and other external transactions;
II. The crediting of foreign trade and other operations;
III. The attraction and holding of the members' free funds in convertible roubles;
IV. To accept on deposit, and on other accounts, gold, convertible currencies and other currencies, and to perform certain operations with these funds;
V. The crediting of enterprises and other undertakings in accordance with agreements between interested countries.

In accordance with its functions, the International Bank for Economic Cooperation carries out, as other banking institutions, various operations, namely payments, credits, deposits, and arbitrage operations, guarantees and so on.

To fulfill its functions the Bank is divided into three main parts:

A Credit and Planning Department.
A Foreign Exchange and Economic Department.
An Operational Department.

In addition to these, there are certain subsidiary sections, such as a Staff Division, a Secretariat, a Legal and a Maintenance Department.

The Department for Credit and Planning is concerned with all questions connected with the credit operations of the Bank, e.g. the drafting of credit plans, with studies connected with the granting and the repayment of credits, and with the organization of methods for settlements in transferable roubles.

The Foreign Exchange and Economic Department, as its name implies, is concerned with foreign exchange and gold operations and also with economic problems that confront the Bank. This department also deals with the establishment and maintenance for correspondent relations with other banks.

The Operational Department carries out the technical side of the Bank's work, handles payment and credit operations, and also undertakes accounting and statistical work.

Accounts in transferable roubles are opened with the Banks in the name of one of the banks of a member country under the authorization of the relevant government or central bank. In accordance with the Bank's statutes, all authorized banks of the member countries hold their funds for payments in transferable roubles.

The main form of settlement is by documentary collection, entailing immediate payment.

The bank of the exporting country dispatches all payments documents, together with documents dealing with the delivery of the goods, direct to an authorized bank in the importing countries. The exporting country presents daily to the International Bank a compound payment demand in accordance with which the International Bank debits the current accounts of the banks of the importing countries and credits, with these amounts, the account of the bank of the exporting country. According to the latest available information, the Bank has executed more than 50,000 transactions during the first half of 1964 and the volume of these transactions continues to grow.

In accordance with its statutes, the Bank may also carry out settlements in transferable roubles with other countries which are not members of the Bank. The latter settlements would be arranged by the Council of the Bank, in agreement with the interested countries.

The International Bank for Economic Cooperation may grant to authorized banks the following credits:

> (a) Settlement credits to cover temporary gaps between payments and receipts connected with the import and export of goods and services. These credits are repaid when the account of the borrowing bank is credited with free funds. The limit for a settlement credit is established by the Council of the Bank
>
> (b) Seasonal credits—which are extended in connection with the seasonal fluctuations of output and of export receipts. Such credits are issued for periods of up to one year.

The interest rate for these credits is fixed by the Council of the Bank, and at present the highest rate is 2 percent.

In some cases, by the decision of the Council, no interest is charged for settlement and seasonal credits.

The Bank is also able to grant credits for other purposes as well, for example, to cover the temporary excess of payments over receipts, due to the delay of the shipment of the goods; for the purpose of increasing the turnover and for equilibrating the balance of payments. However, so far there has been no use of these credits. As we mentioned before, the Bank can also credit the joint construction projects for the account of the interested countries.

In order to strengthen planning and payment discipline the Bank can restrict, or even discontinue altogether, credits to those banks which violate their payment obligations to the International Bank or to other Bank members.

It was stated above that one of the functions of the Bank is to carry out business in freely convertible and other currencies with the authorized socialist banks and with the banks in other countries. Currency transactions are carried out mostly in the form of the deposits for periods of up to three or six months. The Bank has quite successfully developed currency transactions with correspondent banks in various countries, e. g., the United Kingdom (included here is the Moscow Narodny Bank Ltd.), in France, Italy, Sweden and in Switzerland. At the present time the question of the establishment of correspondent relationships with the banks in Austria, Belgium, F.G.R., U.S.A., India, and Japan is under review. In the future the possibility of exchanging transferable roubles for gold and freely convertible currencies will be discussed.

It is quite clear that the role of the International Bank for Economic Cooperation will expand because the main aim of its activity is to constantly strengthen and develop the economies and foreign trade of the socialist countries. No doubt also that the Bank will develop in other directions, e.g. the statutes of the Bank provide for the possibility of opening branches and agencies and the possibility of accepting new members to the Bank.

ADDITIONAL READINGS

Altman, Oscar L., "Russian Gold and the Russian Ruble," *IMF Staff Papers,* April, 1960, pp. 416–438.

Annual Report, Moscow Narodny Bank, Ltd., London, 1964.

"Balance of Payments of the USSR, 1959–60," *IMF Staff Papers,* July, 1963, pp. 321–344.

East–West Trade: A Common Policy for the West, Committee for Economic Development, Washington, 1965.

Litvak, Isaiah A., *Trading with the Communists,* Canadian Institute of International Affairs, Toronto, 1963.

Mikesell, Raymond F. and Behrman, Jack N., *Financing Free World Trade with the Sino–Soviet Bloc,* International Finance Section, Princeton, N.J.: Princeton University, 1958.

Slawinski, C., "Financing of Foreign Trade in Poland," *Moscow Narodny Bank Quarterly Review,* London, Autumn, 1964, pp. 10–20.

"The Question of East–West Trade," *The Irving International Letter,* Irving Trust Company, New York, December, 1964.

chapter *8*

The International Financing of Economic Development

A few underdeveloped countries in the world have generated sufficient foreign exchange from oil revenues, so that foreign aid would have been superfluous. This did not, however, result in development, because other ingredients were missing. On the other hand, regardless of the amount and quality of technical assistance, training and planning which takes place, most underdeveloped countries need outside financial assistance to achieve satisfactory rates of development. The drive toward industrialization which precedes the "take-off" stage, requires the importation of very large quantities of capital equipment and engineering services, which are usually far in excess of the otherwise normal trade surplus of the country.

The flow of financial development assistance is derived from three major sources: (1) bilateral foreign aid, (2) multilateral organizations, and (3) private sources. The bilateral foreign aid component has been and continues to be the most important source. The multilateral organizations, such as the United Nations' agencies and the World Bank, are, however, becoming of increasing importance. On the other hand, private sources, which include direct investment, indirect investment, and trade credit with terms of over one year, have contributed a decreasing flow of funds to the developing countries.

The problem of financing private investment in the underdeveloped countries is the subject of a later chapter. This chapter is concerned with public, "official," development assistance, both bilateral and multilateral.

Why should the international businessmen be interested in this "official" foreign aid?

There are many dimensions in the community of interests between international business and foreign aid. In the larger dimension, foreign aid is a stimulus to the donor country's economy, to the extent that it results in increased demands for goods and services. Hence, the entire business community benefits from foreign aid in the same way that it benefits from an increase in defense expenditures. At the other end of the scale, still in the donor country, the exportation of a very significant amount of goods and services is of direct interest to the international business community which acts as a supplier. These exports are generally sold on a letter of credit basis (between the U. S. government and the exporter) and hence are not even a source of trade credit difficulty to the exporter, regardless of the foreign exchange position and exchange control policies of the recipient government.

Within the recipient country, to the extent that the total foreign aid receipts supplement export earnings, the country is better able to pay for imports other than those received as a component of foreign aid, and hence all exporters to that country benefit. In the largest and most important dimension, foreign aid advances economic development in the recipient country and thereby increases the demand for all goods and services. This provides an enlarged market for exporters in the donor countries. It also increases the attractiveness of the country as a place for new direct investment, and widens the market for existing subsidiaries.

It is not surprising, therefore, that the international business community is interested in continuation of foreign aid as a whole; particularly in the directions, policies, and trends of this aid, and the institutional arrangements through which the aid is channeled. The three readings in this chapter attempt to provide a basis for understanding these factors.

The first reading, on "Development Assistance Efforts and Policies," is excerpted from two OECD publications and provides a composite view of the volume and directions of foreign aid over the period from 1959 to 1963. It includes details on aid from the Socialist countries as well as from the members of the OECD. It will be noted that five countries (France, the Soviet Union, the United Kingdom, the United States, and Western Germany) supply over eighty percent of the financial development assistance. China has, however, offered considerable development assistance and should probably be included to make a list of six major donors.

This material reveals some statistics which are seldom given to the U.S. public. The usual comment on U.S. foreign aid efforts is that the United States has done so much for so long—why don't our West European friends begin to contribute their share? We find, however, that in 1962 and 1963, France provided foreign aid of an amount equal to 2.2 and 2.1 percent, respectively, of her gross national product; the United Kingdom gave 1.4 and 1.5 percent; West Germany gave 1.0 and 1.1 percent while the United States was giving 0.7 and 0.6 percent. In many international circles, there is a concensus that the industrialized countries should aim at a target of at least 1.0 percent of gross national product. Several countries have done so but the United States is not among them. The U.S. public may not be aware of these comparisons, but the international businessman should be, because his counterparts in other countries are.

The first reading often uses the term, "official bilateral assistance," but does not define it. The term is meant to include the following six elements: (1) contributions to international organizations, (2) bilateral grants, (3) bilateral loans repayable in lender's currency, (4) bilateral loans repayable in borrower's currency, (5) consolidation credits, and (6) commodity sale for nontransferable recipient's currency (almost exclusively done by the United States, under Public Law 480).

The second reading, extracted from a monograph by Alec Cairncross, is one of the very few existing analytical studies of the World Bank. While it was published seven years ago, because of its nature it is still a useful and applicable study. Some of its data is, of course, out of date, but can be updated by reading the latest annual report of the Bank.

Since the writing of this monograph, an important innovation of the Bank has been the establishment, in 1960, of the International Development Association (IDA). Its function is to meet a lending need not previously filled by the Bank. The IDA's purpose is to lend at long term and minimum interest. It is financially separate from the Bank but otherwise completely integrated with it. In effect, it is simply a special fund available to the Bank to be used in cases where a project is economically justified, and where the government is following sensible policies, but where the balance of payments situation of the country concerned makes it desirable that generous terms of payment be allowed.

All of IDA's loans must be repaid in convertible currencies, but the terms are usually such that repayments do not begin for ten years, and are spread over a further forty years. There is no interest rate—only a service charge of one percent per annum to cover administrative expenses. With such a rate of return on its funds, IDA is in no position to finance borrowings from the private capital markets. It thus depends upon contributions from the member-country governments to meet a present average annual loan commitment rate of about $300 million.

The World Bank and the IDA are the major sources of multilateral financial assistance for economic development. They are, however, the domain of the member countries (now numbering slightly over 100), which excludes nearly all of the Socialist countries. There are several other sources of multilateral aid, with a more restricted membership. One such organization is the Inter-American Development Bank. This, however, is only quasi-multilateral, in that although the Latin American member countries contributed to the initial capital, the United States is really the only "donor" country. The Inter-American bank is thus, in reality, only a means of channeling U.S. aid to Latin America in a manner which is more acceptable to the recipients.

The other major "restricted" multilateral source of development assistance is the Overseas Development Fund of the European Economic Community (EEC). The six EEC countries use this Fund as a means of channeling aid to the eighteen African countries which are associated with the Common Market. The Fund makes only grants, and has been disbursing funds in this manner at a rate of about $60 million per year.

The ultimate in multilateralizing development assistance is the Special Fund of the United Nations. Through this Fund the Socialist and Capitalist countries combine to disburse about $120 million per year.

Space limitations unfortunately prevent the inclusion of readings on each of these sources of multilateral development assistance. Also, no reading was included concerning the Export-Import Bank which, through its long-term project loans, is an important part of the total "official" development assistance of the U. S. government. Finally, only brief mention is made, in the first reading, of the role of the private sector in providing development assistance through medium-term trade credits.

Very little of an analytical nature has been published about the Export-Import Bank or about medium-term export financing. The reader is referred, however, to a recently published book by this author, entitled, *Financing Capital Equipment Exports,*[1] which includes a study of this important aspect of development assistance, and covers France, Italy, Japan, the United Kingdom, the United States, and Western Germany.

The last reading in this chapter concerns the techniques of development lending. At first glance, this may seem to be an odd reading to include in an international finance book written primarily for international businessmen and business students. Few (though some) students of international business will end up with jobs in the World Bank, or in other of the major sources of development loans. But, this article hits upon one of the major roadblocks to economic development—the preparation of loan applications for the consideration of some lending organization. It is important for the recipient organization to be aware of the criteria which will be used by the lender and to be able to develop and organize the data in the required manner. But, there is often a lack of qualified personnel in the developing countries to carry out this task. Therefore, the private U.S. firm which is interested in acting as a supplier for the project will be "one-up" if it can assist the loan applicant with this problem.

[1] Lee Charles Nehrt, *Financing Capital Equipment Exports: A Comparative Study with Policy Recommendations,* Scranton, Pa.: International Textbook Company, 1966.

DEVELOPMENT ASSISTANCE EFFORTS AND POLICIES

I. The Volume of the Assistance Effort

Before beginning the examination of the 1963 record, it may be helpful to express a few words of caution. It is quite clear that one should not rely too heavily upon the statistical record of each new year in order to judge the effort put forward to provide assistance or its effectiveness. Any new programme or even any considerable expansion of an old one may take several years before it enters into the actual flow of assistance. Individual projects or programmes may be of such a size that they greatly influence a donor's record in a particular year. Necessary actions by legislatures are sometimes seriously delayed and particular programmes may be retarded by unexpected developments in supplier or recipient countries. In addition, the calls made by the multilateral agencies on their sources of capital are not designed to provide a regular flow from year to year.

The statistical totals prepared by the Development Assistance Committee represent a summation of different terms and conditions, often with different motivations, but they do relate to specific forms of economic assistance. The D.A.C. definition which was discussed in some detail in the 1963 Report probably results in figures a little lower than those calculated under the definition adopted in the United Nations Conference on Trade and Development resolution on assistance targets, since that definition includes official loans and guaranteed export credits of more than one year while the D.A.C. definition includes only those of five years or more. To anyone undertaking a fresh tabulation there are various other items which might be added as well as the possibility of including some offsets. However, a particular effort has been made to make the figures consistent with those of earlier years, so that the record of change is less subject to controversy than the measure of level.

The 1963 record is presented below under three headings—official bilateral disbursements, multilateral flows, and the flow of private capital. In considering the record, it is important to keep in mind that donor countries have their own internal problems in connection with economic assistance to less-developed countries, particularly where there are no historical ties to bring

* Excerpted from *Development Assistance Efforts & Policies of the Members of the Development Assistance Committee*, OECD, Paris, 1964, and from, *The Flow of Financial Resources to Less-Developed Countries, 1956–1963*, OECD, Paris, 1964.

emotional justifications into play. In most cases development assistance is financed, directly or indirectly, through budgetary funds and thus has to compete with a multitude of important alternative claims. Several donor countries have to cope with problems of inflationary pressure and internal and external imbalances requiring restraints on budgetary expenditures from which, for political as well as economic reasons, foreign assistance cannot be fully exempted. Some donor countries are actually capital importers themselves. In addition, several D.A.C. countries include regions within their borders whose low per capita income makes them comparable with a number of less-developed countries.

In part, a limiting factor in some countries is the presence or apprehension of balance of payments pressures. While it can be argued that a transfer of domestic resources to a foreign country as a grant or a loan has no appreciable payments effect, the products of some countries have a large import component which cannot be disregarded and the level of commercial exports may also be affected. Some of the goods provided as assistance might otherwise be purchased and paid for by the recipient country. To the extent that balance of payments pressure is accompanied by tight capital markets or budgetary difficulties, these may operate as the limiting factor. Payments problems arise for the most part among the D.A.C. countries themselves and not vis-à-vis the developing countries, which are all too ready to spend their foreign exchange receipts on goods and services from the advanced countries. Thus the work being done elsewhere in the O.E.C.D. and in other agencies such as the I.M.F. in relieving trade and payments difficulties is of great importance for the future scale of development assistance.

While development assistance enjoys broad public support in many countries, several donor governments have had to face an increasingly critical public and parliamentary attitude with respect to increasing expenditures on external assistance. Clear demonstration that assistance funds are used effectively and that the receiving countries themselves are making a determined effort to help themselves will undoubtedly contribute to increased public acceptance of expanding assistance programmes. But the fact remains that the combination of political, economic, and humanitarian arguments relating to distant places must compete with the direct and immediate interest of the taxpayer. Nevertheless the record of our Members to date shows that these arguments in support of assistance have extraordinary vitality.

a. Official Bilateral Disbursements

By far the largest part of the flow of assistance to less-developed countries is based upon bilateral arrangements between donor and recipient. These are also the flows which most clearly reflect the policies and intentions of the donor countries, since their contributions to multilateral agencies depend primarily upon the requirements of the agencies and since flows of private capital can only be encouraged but not directed by the donor government.

The flow of official resources bilaterally as recorded by the D.A.C. consists of financial grants, grants in kind, technical assistance contributions, sales of surplus agricultural commodities against local currencies, and official net lending for maturity periods exceeding five years. Statistical tables in some detail are included at the end of part IV of this article, and a fuller description of the flow is given in "The Flow of Financial Resources to Less-Developed Countries, 1956–1963," an O.E.C.D. publication.

In 1963, total official bilateral net disbursements reached the level of $5,679 million, $345 million or 6.5 percent over 1962. The increase in these bilateral disbursements in 1963 was not shared equally by all Member countries, although nine of the twelve did record increases. In terms of actual amounts, the greatest increases over the previous year were shown by the United States, $236 million; the Federal Republic of Germany, $72 million; and Canada, $48 million. In percentage terms, the ranking was somewhat different among the countries recording increases, with Canada, Italy, and Norway more or less doubling their disbursements. The only reductions were those of France, $25 million, the Netherlands, $29 million, and the United Kingdom, $8 million. The decline in French disbursements is due to accidental factors, primarily to political events, notably in Algeria, and the completion of some of the major projects which had been undertaken in the overseas countries of the Franc Area. The decrease by the Netherlands was attributable to the discontinuation of bilateral assistance to Western New Guinea, which had amounted to $30 million in 1962, and to delays in reorienting the geographic distribution of the Netherlands' assistance programme.

The increase in bilateral net contributions took the form of a substantial expansion of the lending programmes of most Member countries. Net lending by all D.A.C. Member countries combined increased from $1,359 million in 1962 to $1,729 million in 1963. Total grants, loans repayable in local currency and sales for local currencies (the two latter primarily by the United States) decreased $25 million to $3,949 million in 1963, but still accounted for 69.5 percent of total bilateral disbursements. The increased share of loans in total bilateral disbursements reflects in part certain policy decisions that were taken in the United States several years ago and in part the fact that certain countries which have recently increased their assistance volume are doing this mainly through an expanded loan programme.

As in previous years, the sales of surplus agricultural commodities against local currencies, almost exclusively by the United States, constituted an important part of total bilateral assistance. Contributions under this heading reached a level of $989 million, about 17.4 percent of the D.A.C. total and more than 27.3 percent of United States official bilateral net disbursements.

Of particular note in the bilateral programmes are expenditures on technical assistance, which have continued to rise significantly. To a considerable extent, the increase in technical assistance expenditure results from rising costs of the services provided as well as of changes in the quality of those services. In some donor countries the statistics may also reflect the more complete coverage of expenditure data on technical assistance and closely related activities. There is sometimes a major difficulty of distinguishing technical assistance from capital support. Regarding the number of experts, training places, and other facilities, available data (which have improved but are still far from satisfactory) indicate a modest rise in 1963. The number of experts (including teachers, other experts and volunteers) financed under D.A.C. country programmes increased about ten percent above the level in 1962 to over 80,000 (of whom nearly one half were teachers) and the number of officially financed students and trainees accommodated also rose by about ten percent to around 40,000. Greater detail is given in Table 8.

As a proportion of the total D.A.C. flow of official long-term financial resources to less-developed countries, technical cooperation rose from about 13 percent in 1962 to 15 percent in 1963. This increase reflects the greater concern of donors both with the basic need for improving human skills in the developing countries and with the effective implementation of capital assistance projects. Disbursements by D.A.C. Member countries for bilateral and multilateral programmes of technical cooperation in 1963 totalled about $967 million, approximately one-fifth higher than in 1962. This follows a rise of one-quarter in 1962 over 1961. Disbursements for bilateral programmes accounted for some $848 million of the 1963 total.

These totals exclude an important category of expenditure on technical assistance which is not included in the flow figures, viz., the heavy subsidization of higher education in most Member countries which provides places for students and trainees from developing countries, in addition to giving direct government stipends. These subsidies have been estimated by the Secretariat as transferring at least $150 million annually to these students in recent years; better statistical coverage would probably increase this estimate significantly.

Nearly all D.A.C. donors reported increased technical assistance expenditures in 1963. There was a marked rise in the case of France (from $257 million in 1962 to $295 million in 1963) whose programme was second only to that of the United States ($368 million in 1963 including Peace Corps but excluding Educational Exchange Programmes), though it should be kept in mind that expenditures are difficult to compare between countries because of different levels of compensation and coverage. Smaller donors, e.g. Denmark and Norway, whose programmes largely consist of technical assistance, made notably greater efforts.

Some comment should be made about the difference in assistance efforts among the D.A.C. countries. It has been one of the purposes of D.A.C. to achieve a fair sharing of this massive contribution of resources among its Member countries. The Development Assistance Committee has never formally adopted a rigid standard for comparing relative assistance efforts such as the standard of one percent of gross national product suggested for the U.N. Development Decade and generally reaffirmed (using national income as the base) at the United Nations Conference on Trade and Development. In the Resolution on the Common Aid Effort adopted in 1961 by the Development Assistance Group it was agreed by all Members to work towards an expansion and more equitable sharing of the aggregate volume of resources made available to less-developed countries. Since that time, the volume of assistance has increased, but it cannot be said that the disparities have diminished. The two largest contributors continue to provide about 78 percent of the total official flow from Member countries, although their share of the D.A.C. gross national product is significantly less.

Many things should be taken into account in comparing the activity in this field of the various donor countries, such as level of per capita income, internal areas of underdevelopment, extent of capital importation, and commercial and historical relationships. Furthermore, recognition should be given to the proportions of grants and soft loans in the total, and the record of single years is subject to the influence of various temporary factors. As a very imperfect measure one may use the proportion which official and private assistance is of gross national product. In that case, the countries ranking highest are Belgium, France, and Portugal while Canada, Denmark, and Norway are at the bottom of the list. If one uses only official assistance as giving a somewhat better indication of assistance as directly determined by government policy, the list would be headed by the same three countries, but Canada would move out of the lower group and Italy would take its place.

In the Annual Aid Review, the Committee was pleased to note the gains made in a number of countries, but also had occasion to express the hope that these improvements would be vigorously continued and strengthened. It seemed that some countries had not yet succeeded in carrying their reasonable share of the burden. In some cases where there had been temporary difficulties affecting the volume of assistance, it was hoped that these difficulties would soon be overcome and the upward trend resumed. In some countries new types and areas of assistance activities have been launched recently, sometimes in addition to existing ones, and it will take time for these new programmes to become fully operational.

b. Multilateral Flows

Another substantial flow of assistance to less-developed countries takes place through the various multilateral agencies, which derive their funds either from governments or from sales of securities in the private capital markets. While these agencies cannot enforce demands for funds upon the national governments, the flow of funds to them is nevertheless in large part based on their requirements as determined by their members acting in concert and not individually.

Until 1963, the official flows plus the capital markets provided the international institutions with more funds than they disbursed and therefore substantial funds accumulated in their hands. This condition was in part the result of the creation and contribution of capital funds for new institutions such as the Inter-American Development Bank, the International Development Association and the European Development Fund, the fund created by the European Economic Community. The contribution of funds to these multilateral agencies reached a peak in 1961, when $811 million was contributed by D.A.C. Member governments and an additional $75 million was obtained from private capital markets in Member countries. Net official multilateral contributions fell to $602 million in 1962 while private contributions increased to $214 million. In 1963, the net official multilateral contribution dropped to $396 million with no fresh money reported to have been drawn from the private markets. The reduction is even more notable for the multilateral lending institutions since within the declining totals are contributions to multilateral technical assistance programmes which increased from $96 million in 1962 to $119 million in 1963.

The drop in 1963 is due to different factors independent of policy aspirations on the part of governments. In the case of the E.E.C. for instance, while it is true that amounts called upon by the European Development Fund in 1963 were very much lower than in 1962, the reason for this is that payments already effected under the First Convention of Association constituted a more than adequate reserve to meet all projects ready to be approved; also due to the delay in the ratification of the new Convention of Association, no new payment could be made under this head. On the other hand these payments are expected to reach a figure of $730 million over the 5-year period 1965–1969.

As compared with this substantial reduction in contributions since 1961, disbursements by these agencies have risen rapidly in recent years. Approximate figures are as follows for net disbursements by multilateral organisations to less-developed countries (i.e., gross disbursements less repayments of principal by less-developed countries).

NET DISBURSEMENTS
(Millions of Dollars)

1960 384   1962 583
1961 428   1963 776

It should be noted that less-developed countries themselves contribute financially to those multilateral organisations of which they are members. There is no way in which one can distinguish disbursements on an annual basis of D.A.C. Member countries' contributions from totals obtained by the financial institutions from all countries, but an estimate would suggest that the share of D.A.C. Member countries in recent years has been about 80 percent. In 1963, for the first time, disbursements have exceeded fresh contributions. This situation does not in any way reflect any policy decision on the part of the Member countries. Since disbursements are expected to rise still higher in 1964, it is evident that the supply of new funds will soon have to increase substantially. Various budget proposals for 1964–1965 indicate an expectation on the part of Member governments that these contributions will be resumed again on a substantial level.

c. The Flow of Private Capital

On the basis of the incomplete data available to date it appears that the flow of private long-term capital in all forms from D.A.C. countries to the less-developed areas may have decreased slightly in 1963. It should be noted that the data on the flow for private long-term capital is net, being corrected for disinvestment and other repatriation of principal. However, no adjustments are made in the case of capital losses by D.A.C. investors, whether by nationalisation or other causes, and no adjustment is made for counterflows of investments by residents of less-developed countries to D.A.C. Member countries.

There was an important shift in the composition of the total flow of private capital during the year. New direct investment increased by some $350 million in 1963 to an estimated total of about $1.7 billion. Portfolio investment and other net new private long-term capital lending fell by about $120 million. The changes in direct investment were primarily the result of relatively large fluctuations in only a few capital-exporting countries. Most of the increase was accounted for by United States investment in the petroleum sector in Latin America—largely a recovery from the heavy disinvestment in 1962—although there was also a sizable increase (almost $70 million) in the level of the Netherlands direct investment. Direct investment by France and Italy, on the other hand, declined sharply, primarily because of the completion of major oil development projects in North Africa and the Middle East.

There was no important new private investment in securities of multilateral agencies in 1963, in contrast to 1962 when seven D.A.C. countries reported transactions in this category equalling $214 million and the United States alone reported a flow of $160 million. It should be pointed out, of course, that private investment in these securities varies considerably from year to year, depending primarily on the periodic flotation of new issues rather than on the economic and political factors which normally affect other types of private capital movements. If one is measuring the direct flow of private capital to less-developed countries, this item would be disregarded and private flows would then have increased by about $198 million over 1962.

The increase in government guaranteed net export credits with maturities in excess of five years (only these longer-term credits are included by the D.A.C. in calculating the total flow of assistance to less-developed countries) was less than that in 1962 by about $36 million. At the same time, the net increase in credits with maturities of one to five years rose from about $227 million in 1962 to more than $248 million in 1963.

The bulk of the decline in long-term guaranteed export credits was accounted for by the Federal Republic of Germany, although there were also important reductions recorded for both Japan and the United States. These declines were only partially offset by an increase of about $50 million on the part of Italy and a smaller increase by France. Major increases with respect to guaranteed export credits with maturities of one to five years took place in the Federal Republic of Germany, the United Kingdom, and to a lesser degree, the United States. Data on changes in guarantees may not reflect the behaviour of total private export credits to less-developed countries, since there may be considerable amounts of private export credit which are not guaranteed and there is no necessary year-to-year correspondence between new guarantees issued and actual credit flows.

d. The Total Flow

The preceding sections have presented the individual components which make up the total flow of resources—official bilateral contributions, contributions to and from multilateral agencies, and private capital. As the data on private capital are still preliminary and incomplete, it is difficult to make any definitive statements about the exact amount of the total flow of resources during 1963. Nevertheless, because of the increase of official bilateral flows, the total net flow of official and private resources from D.A.C. countries for the purposes of economic development, despite the decline in flows to multilateral organisations, probably rose slightly above the level of 1962.

It has already been noted that the flow of assistance out of the D.A.C. countries varies from the flow into the less-developed countries because of the unequal flow to and from the multilateral agencies. Since expenditures by multilateral agencies are mostly for goods and services obtained from D.A.C. Member countries, the actual flow of Member non-financial resources to less-developed countries is more closely related to the disbursements by multilateral agencies than to the financial contributions made to such agencies. A summary picture on both bases is presented in Table 1. It should be noted that this table is based upon established D.A.C. definitions, with their inclusions and exclusions. The figures have been made comparable year by year so far as is possible. However, the data for 1963 are not fully complete and the estimates used for some part of the assistance by some countries are

TABLE 1

FLOWS OF ASSISTANCE (D.A.C. MEMBERS)

(Millions of dollars)

	1960	1961	1962	1963
A. Flows from D.A.C. Members				
Official bilateral	4,207	5,214	5,334	5,679
Official to multilateral agencies*	655	811	602	396
Private to multilateral agencies	77	75	214	−12
Private bilateral†	2,446	2,532	1,885	2,083
Total	7,384	8,632	8,035	8,146
B. Flows to Less-Developed Countries				
Official bilateral	4,207	5,214	5,334	5,679
Multilateral organisations* and‡	307	342	466	618
Private bilateral†	2,446	2,532	1,885	2,083
Total	6,960	8,088	7,685	8,380
Memo item:				
Government loans 1-5 years (net).	81	62	36	−27
Guaranteed export credits 1-5 years (net).	289	225	227	248

* Not including I.M.F.
† Not including guaranteed credits of less then 5 years, and flows from private nonprofit organisations.
‡ Figure represents 80% of total net disbursements, being the estimated share of D.A.C. Members.

subject to revision. The figures for the flow from multilateral agencies to less-developed countries given in the tables are 80 percent of the total such flow, being the part which can be roughly allocated to resources provided by D.A.C. Members.

In order to arrive at an estimate of the total flow of resources received by less-developed countries from all sources it is necessary to add to the D.A.C. net bilateral contributions (public and private) of $7,749 million the total disbursements of multilateral agencies of $776 million as well as public and private disbursements by all other industrial countries, including the Sino-Soviet countries. Though there are indications of some reduction in the Sino-Soviet flow, in the absence of better information, one may assume that bilateral contributions from all these added countries will remain at the same level as was estimated for 1962, namely $510 million. In this case, total resources received by less-developed countries in 1963 can be estimated at approximately $9,035 billion, $710 million more than a similar estimate for 1962. In other words, while the flow of resources from the industrial countries to the less-developed countries and the multilateral agencies showed only a small increase in 1963, the amounts actually received by the less-developed countries rose substantially. This increase was accompanied by a significant improvement in the export earnings of less-developed countries, particularly as a result of gains in the terms of trade. In addition, it should be noted that there is some flow among less-developed countries, not only of technical assistance, but of capital.

There are certain additional items which might also be included in the totals. The operations of the I.M.F. are completely disregarded in the figures for multilateral organisations. No estimate is included for the grant assistance provided by private nonprofit institutions. For 1963, the United States reported $229 million in this category, the United Kingdom upwards of $30 million and the Federal Republic of Germany $19 million. Furthermore, if one follows the UNCTAD definition, credits should be included which have a maturity of one year or more instead of the five-year requirement in the D.A.C. definition. Government and guaranteed credits of this type amounted to $221 million. In addition, there is an unknown amount of private export credit which is not guaranteed and not included in the figures. If such items were added, the total would approach the $10 billion mark.

e. New Official Commitment and the Pipeline

While disbursements are an important indicator of the actual resource flow in a given year, they are to a large extent the result of operations which were planned and set in motion in the past. Therefore they do not reflect current policy or current intentions. Having said this, it should be noted that there is a very large element of continuity in the flow of assistance. Projects seldom involve less than a year's time and assistance from donors and recipients tends to flow along established channels. New countries may be added to a donor's list and old ones may be dropped, but the main bulk of the assistance tends to continue along familiar lines.

While annual commitment figures come closer to indicating intentions, they are subject to appreciable random variations which should not be taken to reflect policy changes. Agreement on some large project which has been under negotiation for a long time may cause a sudden jump in a country's record. Two such projects, for example, reached the commitment stage for the Federal Republic of Germany in 1963 and thus caused a substantial increase in its commitments. In other cases, countries which enter into commitments only after funds are fully authorised or available may find it necessary to delay any formal commitment if legislation action is unduly delayed or capital markets are temporarily unfavourable.

Table 2 shows that the total of new commitments of bilateral official grants and loans by D.A.C. Member countries declined by 5.9 percent in 1963, less than the 1961 level. This decline of $418 million was in large part the net result of reductions on the part of the United States ($613 million), the United Kingdom ($118 million), and France ($54 million), offset by increases by the Federal Republic of Germany ($239 million), Italy ($68 million), and Canada ($64 million).

In no case of decrease was there any related policy decision in the coun-

TABLE 2

GROSS DISBURSEMENTS AND NEW COMMITMENTS
(Millions of dollars)

Year	Gross Disbursements	New Commitments	Apparent Additions to the Pipeline
1961	5,805	6,846	1,041
1962	5,667	7,143	1,476
1963	6,058	6,725	667

try involved to cut back its assistance operations. A considerable part of the United States' decrease is accounted for by a temporarily smaller volume of sales agreements signed under PL 480 (surplus commodity sales)[1] and the extraordinary delay in Congressional action which led to limitations on A.I.D. and Export-Import Bank commitments. In the United Kingdom's case it appears to have been a matter of timing between one year and the next. In the case of the Federal Republic of Germany the almost doubling of new loan commitments reflects the fact that, within the large volume of general prospective agreements that had been extended to less-developed countries in 1960 and 1961, an increasing number of firm commitments reached fruition as pre-investigation studies for new capital projects had been completed.

The comparison of the above commitments figures with the disbursements figures not only gives some indication of the probable future direction of volume figures, but also indicates the extent to which programmes and projects are accumulating in the pipeline. The size of the pipeline is significant because large amounts of committed but undisbursed funds give rise to the belief that additional assistance appropriations are not urgent, while a too small pipeline will eventually cause a drop in disbursements. The information available to the D.A.C. for several Member countries suggests that the total amount of funds in the pipeline presently corresponds roughly to the present annual rate of official gross disbursements.

The record of change in recent years is indicated by Table 2. The disbursements figures used are gross, since that is the volume record of total projects as they proceed at the disbursement point. The commitments figure is that of new commitments and probably should be somewhat reduced for some old commitments which were cancelled or put back on the shelf for further consideration. It immediately becomes clear that the addition to the pipeline in 1963 was much less than in the previous years, though still substantial. Having in mind the special circumstances of the United States' programme in 1963, the apparent shift is probably greater than might have been expected under more normal conditions.

Because of the universal appearance of substantial increases in the pipe-

---

[1] Recording of food sales raises difficult statistical problems. Present recording methods are being reexamined and this may entail revisions of these data at a later date.

line in 1961 and 1962, most Member countries and the I.B.R.D. have examined the problem with considerable care during the last year. Since the commitment figure covers disbursements to be made over several years, it is inevitable that any expanding programme will also expand the pipeline — more new projects being added to the list than old ones completed. In addition, any change in the general nature of projects is also a factor. There is evidence that certain types of commitment (e.g. budget support grants, non-project assistance for general import finance, certain industrial projects) are characteristically fast moving while others (e.g. multipurpose projects, irrigation projects, loans to development banks) may require a number of years for their implementation.

It is also true that disbursement rates vary considerably according to the recipient country involved. For example a major pipeline problem was faced by the European Development Fund during its early years of operation. At the end of 1962, though over $400 million were already committed, disbursements amounted to under $75 million. However, the situation recovered noticeably in 1963 due to a sharp increase in disbursements which almost doubled over the year. This speeding up can mainly be traced to an increase in technical assistance given to facilitate investment projects.

One cannot draw the conclusion that present implementation rates are necessarily satisfactory. There is clear evidence that the implementation of all types of projects generally requires appreciably less time in the more-developed countries than in less-developed countries. Among the reasons which have been suggested most often to explain slower action in less-developed countries are shortages of competent personnel and difficulties in the recipient country raising the necessary local currency financing for a project or providing agreed facilities. In addition, there have been delays in the placing of orders and contracts. In some cases, the delay is at the point of issuing the necessary licenses for import or foreign exchange permits or the taking of other regulatory steps essential to the effective implementation of projects. Many of these problems should be amenable to improvement through greater technical cooperation by donor countries, particularly through the provision of competent consultants. And in some cases the study of the problem has suggested that the delays may be laid at the donor's door where unnecessarily complex procedures have grown up.

The pipeline problem discussed in the preceding paragraphs must be clearly distinguished from the problem of reaching the commitment point in the first place. Frequently negotiations and preparatory work antecedent to the firm commitments are complicated and time-consuming. Occasionally there may be delays in reaching agreement between donors and recipients about the suitability of the project proposed as well as about the nature and financial terms and conditions of the assistance to be provided. The initial establishment of working relations between a donor and a new recipient may prove much more difficult than developing new projects where the parties are used to each other's practices.

While one can well be disturbed over unnecessary delays in implementation which expand the pipeline, it is most important to maintain it by an expanding inflow of new commitments. D.A.C. Members are increasingly financing pre-investment surveys and feasibility studies which may give rise to new projects. They may also provide help in drawing up projects; the process of evaluating projects in itself often implies a considerable amount of technical advice by the donor agency. Expenditures can only follow after the way has been properly prepared, and the 1963 record of commitments is on the low side if one hopes to ensure the growth of disbursements in later years. The efforts of donor governments and international agencies to help less-developed countries to identify opportunities for resource development and to assist in drawing up projects and executing them effectively and speedily should be stepped up in future.

II. THE GEOGRAPHIC DISTRIBUTION OF ASSISTANCE

The present pattern of the geographic distribution of assistance to the less-developed countries is the result of a complex of factors and circumstances. Clearly, it is not determined exclusively by purely economic objective criteria of relative needs and priorities. It is inevitable that historical, political, and commercial factors should continue to have an important influence on the distribution of each donor's assistance.

The overall geographic distribution of assistance resulting from these factors tends to change only slowly. A definite trend has been in evidence for some time wherein D.A.C. Members are individually extending their assistance to more and more countries, and recipients are dealing with an increasing number of donors. In a few cases of donors with small programmes there is a tendency to try to concentrate their efforts so as to have an identifiable responsibility or else to operate largely through the multilateral institutions; but these are the exception rather than the rule.

The trend towards geographical dispersion is most evident in connection with technical cooperation but it is also true of capital flows. For example the proportion of United Kingdom net bilateral assistance received by countries outside the Commonwealth rose from 7 percent in 1961 to 14 percent in 1963. The indications are that this tendency will continue. A similar trend is shown in the figures for Belgium and the Netherlands assistance to the countries with which they have special links. In the case of France policy decisions have been taken to increase assistance to countries outside the franc area, although these decisions have not yet had time to affect the figures of French disbursements. Assistance provided through the multilateral agencies has a very wide distribution, the number of countries receiving loans having greatly increased since the creation of the International Development Association.

In some instances, such as the consortia, the number of participating countries may be as high as fourteen. The D.A.C. records indicate that in 1960 there were 40 countries receiving assistance from four or more sources (including all multilateral organisations as a single source but not including members of the Sino-Soviet bloc). This tendency towards multiple sources of assistance in particular countries seems to have been most marked in Africa; not only have more donors become involved but those with relatively small programmes have increased their financial commitments.

The reasons for this tendency towards diversification of the geographic pattern of financial and technical assistance are of considerable complexity, but it is possible to mention some of the factors influencing it. The change in formal political ties between D.A.C. Members and particular groups of recipients has meant that the Member's attention has been less exclusively concentrated on the former dependent territories, while at the same time it has been easier for other donors to provide assistance to the newly-independent territories. In some instances, a major donor is eager to share its position of responsibility with other donors. Finally, to judge from the forms of assistance provided, it seems likely that the diversification of assistance is in part a reflection of actual or desired trade patterns. From the point of view of a recipient, interest in broadening its sources of assistance stems in part from the notion that independence requires limited dependence on any single foreign nation and in part from the belief that more donors will mean more assistance plus more room for flexibility of programme and bargaining on terms.

While further geographic diversification of assistance may be welcomed on the ground that it tends to widen the scope of the assistance available to individual less-developed countries, it may also lead to confusion and duplication of effort. Thus the trend towards geographical diversification increases the need for international coordination of aid, both globally and with respect to individual less-developed countries or regional groups of countries.

III. FINANCIAL TERMS AND CONDITIONS OF AID

a. Debt Burdens

The total volume of assistance discussed above is indicative of a flow of resources for development purposes but does not reflect various significant qualitative differences within the total. One of these differences relates to the terms on which the assistance is given. While either a grant or a loan may involve the same immediate transfer of capital, there is a substantial difference with respect to the long-run contribution made to economic development. Under the definitions used herein, loans on full commercial terms made by governments to less-developed countries are included as assistance. Since appropriate terms will vary from case to case, it is entirely proper that some part of the assistance flow be on "hard" terms. On the other hand, having in mind the obligations already accumulated in the past, the delayed impact of certain types of investment on productivity, and the difficulties of obtaining foreign exchange for debt payment under the balance of payments situation as it exists in many less-developed countries, it is clear that "soft" assistance is also needed. What is important is that the mix of terms should provide a total situation appropriate to the recipient country. It might be said that one of the goals of economic development which may be near for some countries but far away for others is to raise a country to the point where it can raise such capital as it needs on the world capital market.

In its Resolution on the Terms and Conditions of Aid, adopted on 3rd April 1963, the D.A.C. noted with concern the rapid increase in recent years of the external debt service liabilities of developing countries and recommended that the Members of the D.A.C. "relate the terms of aid on a case-by-case basis to the circumstances of each underdeveloped country or group of countries." It also recommended that the Members of D.A.C. "should make it their objective in principle to secure a significant degree of comparability in the terms and conditions of their aid, and so far as possible to eliminate or reduce discrepancies between them. While this would not necessarily entail standard terms and conditions from all donors, it would involve a liberalisation of the terms adopted by some Members, whether in their individual aid programmes or in concerted aid operations."

A certain amount of progress has been made in the past year in easing the terms on which loans are provided, though it is difficult to provide any single statistical measure. For D.A.C. Members as a whole the proportion of loans carrying interest rates of 5 percent and more fell from over 70 percent in 1961 to 40 percent in 1962 and to about 30 percent in 1963, while the proportion of loans at less than 3 percent rose from 19 percent to 40 percent during this period. Repayment periods of official bilateral loans have also continued to lengthen somewhat: the portion committed for 20 years or more increased from one-third in 1961 to over one-half in 1962 and 1963. Furthermore, the use of grace periods has increased substantially.

As against these improvements, the volume of loans increased in 1963 while the volume of grants and grant-like assistance decreased slightly. Grants and other assistance not requiring servicing in foreign currency accounted for roughly 70 percent of total official bilateral disbursements in 1963, but, as a proportion of new commitments, grants fell an additional few percentage points. In considering the effects of this relative shift towards more loans on the debt-servicing problems of developing countries, it has to be borne in mind that many of the countries where such problems are most serious are not recipients of, and therefore not affected by developments with reference to grants, but they do stand to benefit from the easing of loan terms.

Differences in the terms of assistance continued to prevail in 1963 among the different D.A.C. Members and often among the different loans made by the same lender. A rough measure of these differences is given in Table 3, which classifies the assistance given by each Member country into

TABLE 3

**THE RELATIONSHIP OF GRANTS AND SOFT LOANS
TO TOTAL OFFICIAL ASSISTANCE
FOR INDIVIDUAL D.A.C. COUNTRIES IN 1963**

Share	Total Official Assistance*	Grants[†] and Loans at Less Than 5 Percent[‡]	Grants[†] and Loans at Less Than 3 Percent[‡]	Grants[†]
	Million U. S. dollars	As percentage of total official assistance		
	1	2	3	4
Belgium	92.6	100.0	98.6	98.6
Canada	133.3	42.5	42.5	42.5
Denmark	15.9	93.7	93.7	93.7
France	892.3	92.7	86.3	81.2
Germany	696.0	72.1	54.7	27.7
Italy	128.4	19.0	17.2	17.2
Japan	280.3	33.5	31.9	31.9
Netherlands	41.8	78.0	64.8	64.8
Norway	22.0	51.4	49.1	49.1
Portugal	53.6	79.5	68.7	16.6
United Kingdom	500.9	71.2	69.2	52.4
United States	4,264.0	91.4	89.1	62.5
	7,120.7	83.6	79.3	58.5

* While in principle the table is on a commitments basis for certain items only gross or net disbursement data were available.
[†] Includes bilateral grants, reparations, loans repayable in recipients' currencies and net transfers of resources through sales for recipients' currencies. Data for Belgium and France are gross disbursements. Also includes grants and capital subscriptions to multilateral agencies on a disbursement basis.
[‡] For France, Norway and Portugal, interest breakdown has been estimated on the basis of 1962 data.

Source: Statistical Annex.

three categories which might be called "soft," "softer," and "softest"; namely, grants and loans at less than 5 percent, grants and loans at less than 3 percent, and grants only. While the classification relates only to the interest charge, adjustments for maturities and grace periods would not greatly change the general picture. While the variations reflect in part the credit position of different borrowers with whom the lenders may deal, they are affected in greater degree by differing policy positions.

During 1963, the average terms of United States assistance were eased somewhat further and grace periods of 10 years were accorded for well over one-half of the new lending. No further softening of the terms of its assistance is anticipated in the future. Canada has announced a programme of greatly easing terms to approximate those of I.D.A., but rates are still very high for Japan and Italy. Interest rates for French assistance seem to have softened but the granting of grace periods was the exception rather than the rule.

Nearly two-thirds of German official bilateral assistance in 1963 continued to be provided in the form of loans, loan commitments having almost doubled from 1962 to 1963. German lending rates are generally based on the type of project to be financed, e.g. relatively high interest loans are given for capital projects in manufacturing and mining and softer loans for non-commercial projects. In 1963, terms of German lending have been slightly eased. The average rate of interest on new loan commitments fell to 4.3 percent while the average maturity period rose to 19 years. Over half the loans committed carried grace periods of between 5 and 7 years.

For the United Kingdom, new loan commitments declined sharply from the level of 1962. Although many of the loans were at high interest rates, repayment periods are usually as long as 25 years with liberal grace periods; and a new provision for the waiving of all interest payments during the initial years of some loans was introduced in 1963 and represents a significant easing of terms.

Even if only a fairly limited part of the borrowing by a developing country from some of its donors is short-term and at high interest rates, this can markedly increase the debt service burden. Hence increasing harmonization of loan terms among the different suppliers of capital appears highly desirable. It is an unsatisfactory situation when some lending countries feel obliged to lend on lenient terms in order to ease the strains in the balance of payments of the borrowing country while at the same time other lenders contribute to these strains by continuing to lend on hard terms. And the countries which are now giving grants and soft loans are under pressure so long as other lenders are receiving hard terms for their capital. The difficulty for the less-developed country is usually a payments problem and in that case the function of interest payments as a device for selection and allocation can be achieved by appropriate charges within the borrowing country.

It already has been noted that guaranteed private export credits of one to five years have virtually doubled in the last two years, the greatest increase coming in 1963. Short- and medium-term suppliers' credits may increase the debt service burden in developing countries and hence create a situation which appears to need development loans on lenient terms. While export credits are a necessary element in carrying on foreign trade, they can be extremely burdensome if substituted for long-term loans. Present international action in the field of export credits aims at limiting "unfair competition" by preventing the lengthening of the terms of credits. Yet in the field of development lending, there is international agreement that it is desirable to lengthen the terms of loans in order to help countries with heavy external debt servicing burdens. The two contributions to debt burdens do meet in the balance of payments. The question is admittedly complicated. For example, in some countries, relatively short terms on export credits or the government guarantees make it easier to secure finance for less-developed countries from the banking system. Nevertheless, the rapid growth in short-term export credits makes it necessary to view the financial relations between the D.A.C. countries and the developing countries as an integrated whole, bearing in mind the accepted need for a sustained net transfer of resources to many of the developing countries. In addition, there are other miscellaneous flows of capital (bankers' swaps and capital flight) which are often unrecorded, but may have an important bearing on a country's economic situation.

Harmonization of the terms of assistance provided by different countries depends on a common understanding of the nature and degree of the debt servicing problems of the debtor countries concerned, and on a judgment as to what may be viable credit terms. The problem is not an easy one, and calls for the exercise of judgment, since neither diagnosis nor prescription can be reduced to formula. On this question, D.A.C. has greatly benefited from a study on the debt problem by the I.B.R.D., subsequently presented in revised and enlarged form to the U.N. Conference on Trade and Development. This study points out that neither the familiar "debt service ratio" nor any other simple formula can measure at all exactly the likelihood that a debtor country may be forced to choose between default on external debt service obligations and cutting back its imports to a degree which endangers the momentum of development. The study suggests a number of factors which must be taken into account: the expected future flow of capital, the future rate of growth in the country compared with its obligations, its ability to transfer, and the course of the accumulated burden of interest and amortization. In some instances, countries with good long-run prospects may face short-run difficulties because of a concentration of debt-payments in early years, typically due to large repayment obligations on relatively short-term debt. This situation may be compounded by the fact that short-term credit may tend to be used to a greater degree as the payments situation deteriorates. Essentially, this is a rescheduling problem, but it is one where the crisis might have been prevented by earlier appropriate action by debtor and creditors.

Of course, there are countries which can now be expected to pay normal rates for foreign capital and, as economic development proceeds, the list should grow. The basic task is to distinguish the problem situations described above from those where one can assume that capital inflow will in the long run make possible a substantial strengthening of the balance of payments. In that case, there may be no reason why the country cannot eventually meet interest charges at commercial rates on its accumulated external debt, provided that the requisite net capital inflow continues to be available in the meantime. It is particularly in the uncertain case that the capital-providing countries have a policy choice between applying lenient terms well in advance of the emergence of acute debt-servicing difficulties in order that these may never arise, and waiting to take remedial action until debt-servicing difficulties are imminent. This whole collection of problems is undergoing active consideration in the D.A.C. The assistance of the I.B.R.D. and the I.M.F. is most helpful on these matters.

There remains the question of the adequacy of present information on debt service burdens and external liquidity risks of developing countries. The figures on debt service obligations collected by the I.B.R.D. cover only public debt and debt under public guarantee in the debtor country (excluding debt to the I.M.F.), with an original maturity of more than one year. For many countries the debt recorded by the Bank appears to be the greater part of all external debt, but in others there are substantial amounts of private debt not under public guarantee and hence not recorded in the Bank's figures. Since it may be expected that much of this private debt is short-term, present projections of debt service obligations seem likely to understate the immediate balance of payments burden for some countries. Moreover, in assessing the immediate liquidity problem of many countries, more complete, systematic, and current information on short-term debt and commercial arrears would be desirable. Since there can be no doubt as to the increasing seriousness of the debt-servicing problem for many of the developing countries, it seems necessary to find ways of securing more complete data more rapidly in cooperation with the I.B.R.D. and other interested agencies.

b. The Problems of Aid Tying

One aspect of Members' assistance policies which is kept under regular review during the Annual Aid Review is that of aid tying conditions and procurement procedures. Unfortunately, during the last year there has been a further increase in the proportion of assistance subject to procurement restrictions. At the same time Governments have tried in various ways to reduce any harmful effects which may arise from such restrictions, e.g. by granting special waivers or by financing preferably those projects and commodities which they feel they can offer at competitive prices and quality. Programme assistance is likely to involve a flexibility of product choice on the part of the recipient. However, the provision of certain types of assistance such as surplus food and technical assistance are tied by their very nature. There is no doubt that a very large part of the assistance would continue in its present channels even if there were no requirements with respect to purchase. On the other hand, there would be no need for the aid-tying requirement if it did not on occasion substitute required channels for international competitive markets.

Some donor countries have been obliged to introduce and maintain procurement restrictions because of temporary or structural weaknesses in their balance of payments. In other cases, governments have pointed out that it is less difficult to obtain public support for expanding costly assistance programmes if it can be demonstrated that such expenditures will at the same time provide opportunities for expanding domestic employment and export business. Both business groups and trade unions may be aroused if they see assistance funds which are provided by their governments used to finance export orders of their foreign competitors.

It should be pointed out that there may also be certain other advantages if tying means a further acceptance by donors of full responsibility for the execution of given development projects by providing not only the necessary finance but also the equipment, consultants, engineers, etc. If the national prestige and reputation for efficiency and good workmanship are at stake donor countries will have added incentives to assure that the projects with which they are associated will be selected and carried out with maximum efficiency.

However, apart from short-run considerations of expediency it must be recognised that the present tendency towards an increasingly rigid connection between the geographic pattern of assistance and trade can have far-reaching consequences for the pattern of future world trade and payments. In 1963 total bilateral official gross disbursements by the D.A.C. countries to the less-developed countries corresponded to about 25 percent of D.A.C. exports to these countries. In addition, official guaranteed gross export credits amounted to another 20 percent of exports to less-developed countries. For certain commodity categories, especially equipment, these percentages are considerably higher. The bulk of the assistance disbursements are tied in one form or another, and the full play of international competition and comparative advantage is thus impaired. The increased diversification of aid sources, on the other hand, tends to increase flexibility. The recipient countries can themselves do much to mitigate the effects of tying by improving their procurement procedures and taking full advantage of the possibilities of international competitive bidding.

For economic and political reasons, it appears to be difficult for individual donor countries to make progress in isolation towards untying their assistance. A fresh move to reverse the present tendency of increased aid tying would be greatly facilitated if donor countries were to act jointly, even if comprehensive action had to be confined to those countries which do not have major balances of payments problems. To the extent that present aid tying does not have much effect on trade patterns, there could be little objection to permitting freer procurement. The D.A.C. would seem to be an appropriate forum for initiating action in this field whenever the time is opportune.

IV. ECONOMIC ASSISTANCE FROM SINO-SOVIET COUNTRIES TO LESS-DEVELOPED COUNTRIES [*]

Economic assistance from Sino-Soviet countries[2] to less-developed countries dates from 1954, when the Soviet Union established its first programme, although the first substantial disbursements were not made until 1956. Since then other Eastern countries, including China (Mainland), have established their own assistance programmes. By the end of 1963 total aid commitments by these countries had reached the cumulative total of $5.4 billion, mostly in the form of loans. Disbursements, however, lagged very considerably behind commitments, and the total amount of assistance actually disbursed during the period was only about $ 1.9 billion.

While disbursements of Sino-Soviet assistance have steadily increased throughout the period 1956 to 1962, reaching $390 million in 1962, and are estimated to have increased still further in 1963, commitments reached a peak of $1,165 million in 1960 and then fell away sharply to $507 million in 1962 and $319 million in 1963 (see Table 4).

The reasons for this fall are not clear but it may be due to the large backlog of unused credits, and in the case of China (Mainland), whose commitments dropped to almost nothing in 1962, to the economic difficulties which have beset that country in recent years. With regard to the other countries, however, there is no evidence that the recent decline in commitments indicates any sharp cutback in their long-term assistance programmes.

In its early stages Sino-Soviet assistance came almost exclusively from the Soviet Union, and as late as 1959 its share of the total was about 85 percent. In that year commitments by the Soviet Union reached a peak of about $ 900 million, but then fell sharply to an annual rate of about $ 300 million in 1961 and 1962. This fall was partly offset by an expansion of the assistance programmes of Eastern European countries and it is estimated that these now account for one-fifth to one-quarter of total Sino-Soviet commitments, on a cumulative basis, while Mainland China accounts for about 10 percent. Significant changes have also taken place in the geographical distribution of the assistance. Of the cumulative total of commitments up to the end of 1963, four countries, India, U.A.R. (Egypt), Afghanistan,and Brazil,

[*] *The Flow of Financial Resources to Less-Developed Countries, 1956–1963,* O E C D, Paris, 1964, pp. 54–57.

[2] The term "Sino-Soviet countries," for the purposes of this report, includes the U.S.S.R., Bulgaria, Czechoslavakia, Hungary, Poland, Rumania, China (Mainland) and the Soviet Occupied Zone of Germany.

TABLE 4

ECONOMIC ASSISTANCE TO LESS-DEVELOPED COUNTRIES
BY SINO-SOVIET COUNTRIES, 1954 to 1963*
(Millions of U. S. dollars)

	Commitments	Disbursements
1954	11	1
1955	149	3
1956	608	107
1957	227	87
1958	556	205
1959	894	161
1960	1,165	186
1961	957	294
1962	507	391
1963	319	(425)
Cumulative Total 1954/1963	5,393	(1,860)

* Excluding military aid.

Gross. Repayment figures are not available but in 1963 may have been up to $50 million.

together accounted for more than half. In 1963, however, another country, Algeria, accounted for about half of total commitments.

Sino-Soviet assistance is generally directed towards specific projects. More than half of these were concentrated in industry, particularly in the field of ferrous and nonferrous metals, engineering and metal-working industries. As example of this type of project is the Bhilai Metallurgical Works at Ankleshwar in India. Other projects involve power development and irrigation, such as the Aswan High Dam in Egypt and hydroelectric plant in Afghanistan, and transport and communication. Of total commitments extended by the Sino-Soviet countries between 1954 and 1962 about four-fifths were for projects in industry, power, transport and communication. Nonproject assistance has accounted for probably not more than 5 percent of total commitments, and the remainder has been for technical assistance programmes.

A high proportion of Sino-Soviet technical assistance consists of services connected with the construction and installation of industrial plant and the value of this assistance is usually included in the general credit arrangements. In addition, technical assistance is provided through the training of specialists, qualified managers and technicians under a number of programmes which are not related to specific projects. There is also an extensive programme for the training in the Sino-Soviet countries of personnel from less-developed countries.

Only about 6 percent of total Sino-Soviet commitments have so far been in the form of grants. The majority of loans by the Soviet Union carry an interest rate of 2.5 percent and are repayable over 12 years from the time of first disbursement or from the time of completion. However, there are also repayment schedules of up to 50 years. East European countries have often charged higher interest (up to 5 percent) and some of their credits have been for only 4 to 8 years. All loans are tied to deliveries from the donor countries and the products to be supplied, together with the associated technical assistance activities, are specifically listed in the credit agreement. Repayment is usually made in the form of local products, but most credit agreements also provide for settlement in convertible currencies if no satisfactory form of repayment in kind can be found. Although the usual formula for the valuation of both supplies and repayments is based on world market prices, deviations from this rule seem to have been frequent in the past. The exact prices used for valuation of the goods exchanged can obviously have a substantial effect on the real terms of the loans, and it is therefore open to question whether these are as advantageous as the nominal terms would make them appear.

Sino-Soviet countries also contribute to the United Nations technical assistance and relief agencies; none of the Sino-Soviet countries are members of the I.B.R.D. or its affiliated agencies. The Soviet Union became a member of the United Nations agencies in 1953 and has since been followed by the other countries, with the exception of the Soviet Occupied Zone of Germany and China (Mainland). Contributions, although rising, are relatively small and amounted to $ 6.3 million (net) in 1963. These contributions are normally in nonconvertible roubles and tied to procurement in the donor country.

TABLE 5

THE FLOW OF LONG-TERM FINANCIAL RESOURCES TO LESS-DEVELOPED COUNTRIES AND MULTILATERAL AGENCIES, BY MAJOR CATEGORIES, 1961-1963 (Disbursements)

(Millions of U.S. dollars)

	Year	Belgium	Canada	Denmark	France	Germany	Italy	Japan	Netherlands	Norway	Portugal	United Kingdom	United States	Total D.A.C. Countries
TOTAL OFFICIAL AND PRIVATE, NET (I + II + III)	1961	152.3	96.0	9.6	1,290.1	800.8	251.4	371.1	193.5	9.1	...	836.1	4,592	8,632.4
	1962	128.9	68.0	12.1	1,288.7	681.5	277.8	282.0	139.7	8.6	...	643.3	4,466	8,035.2
	1963	171.2	103.7	13.9	1,087.9	557.1	270.9	264.7	145.1	24.4	...	724.1	4,726	8,145.5
I. Total official, net	1961	92.1	61.5	7.2	943.3	589.2	65.8	214.2	69.3	9.0	29.6	450.3	3,493	6,024.5
	1962	79.8	54.4	7.4	972.1	427.0	67.0	165.2	90.8	7.0	37.2	417.7	3,610	5,935.7
	1963	90.2	99.1	10.2	857.9	421.0	63.0	171.5	37.7	20.7	47.1	412.9	3,844	6,074.9
A. Total bilateral, net	1961	69.5	45.1	0.7	870.0	303.0	50.0	202.8	30.4	1.3	21.6	410.0	3,208	5,213.8
	1962	64.6	41.9	0.7	855.9	324.6	34.9	158.0	46.7	1.3	37.2	377.1	3,391	5,333.9
	1963	74.7	90.2	1.1	830.9	396.2	62.6	159.3	17.8	2.4	47.0	369.5	3,627	5,678.7
1. Grants and grant-like contributions*	1961	70.5	48.5	0.7	786.7	111.5	32.5	67.8	21.7	1.4	3.0	207.0	2,583	3,944.5
	1962	65.6	26.2	0.6	756.7	109.2	34.5	74.9	24.6	1.3	3.1	211.7	2,648	3,974.6
	1963	75.8	51.4	1.2	696.8	141.4	24.8	76.0	9.9	2.4	8.8	209.1	2,651	3,949.3
2. Net lending†	1961	-1.0	-3.4	0.5	83.1	191.4	18.4	135.0	-1.3	-0.1	18.6	203.0	625	1,269.2
	1962	-1.0	15.2	-0.1	99.2	215.4	0.4	83.4	4.3	-0.1	34.1	165.4	743	1,359.2
	1963	-1.1	38.8	-0.1	134.1	254.8	37.8	82.6	7.9	–	38.2	160.4	976	1,729.4
B. Total multilateral, net	1961	22.6	16.4	6.0	73.3	286.2	14.9	11.4	38.9	7.7	8.0	40.3	285	810.8
	1962	15.2	12.5	6.7	116.2	102.4	32.1	7.2	44.1	5.7	–	40.6	219	601.8
	1963	15.5	8.9		27.0	24.8	0.4	12.2	19.9	18.3	0.1	43.4	217	396.2
1. Grants to multilateral agencies‡	1961	22.6	16.4	6.0	72.7	74.2	13.7	12.3	38.9	5.5	8.0	40.3	285	595.7
	1962	15.2	12.5	6.8	115.2	105.4	19.6	8.7	44.1	6.1	–	40.6	219	593.3
	1963	15.5	13.9	8.1	28.0	29.8	8.1	9.4	18.6	7.6	0.1	43.4	217	399.1
2. Other multilateral contributions§	1961	–	–	–	0.6	212.0	1.2	-0.9	–	2.2	–	–	–	215.1
	1962	–	-5.0	-0.1	1.0	-3.0	12.5	-1.5	1.3	-0.4	–	–	–	8.5
	1963	–	–	1.0	-1.0	-5.0	-7.7	2.8	–	10.7	–	–	–	-2.9
II. Private direct investment and other net lending	1961	29.5	34.5	2.4	312.3	153.6	(163.9)	110.3	114.4	0.1	...	376.4	1,099	2,396.6
	1962	28.1	(13.6)	4.7	306.8	150.1	(186.6)	83.1	31.7	1.6	...	211.9	871	1,899.2
	1963	(51.8)	4.6	3.0	208.4	107.4	(129.8)	79.9	98.3	3.7	...	(281.3)	(878)	1,846.7
III. Guaranteed export credits of 5 years and over, net	1961	30.7	–	–	34.5	58.0	21.7	46.6	9.8	–	–	10.0	-5	211.3
	1962	21.0	–	–	9.8	104.4	24.8	33.7	17.2	–	–	13.8	35	260.3
	1963	29.2	–	0.7	21.3	28.7	78.1	13.3	9.1	–	–	29.9	4	223.9
Memo items:														
1. Official loans 1 to 5 years, net	1961	–	–	–	–	26.1	19.5	7.2	–	–	14.2	-1.2	-5	61.7
	1962	–	–	0.9	2.4	22.8	42.9	2.9	–	–	3.6	0.3	-42	35.9
	1963	1.8	–	-0.5	3.6	2.7	46.4	2.0	–	–	4.1		-87	-26.6
2. Guaranteed private export credits, 1 to years, net	1961	15.6	-4.6	(6.6)	115.7	7.7	2.3	3.1	15.7	0.7	–	61.9		224.7
	1962	-3.3	5.0	12.8	112.8	-72.3	24.8	3.0	3.0	2.4	–	91.7	-13	226.7
	1963	8.3	17.9	-2.8	83.1	28.7	18.9	0.8		4.9	–	68.3	26	247.5

NOTES. a) Figures in brackets ( ) indicate incomplete information or preliminary estimates, in whole or in part, made by the Secretariat.

b) Data in this table, as in all tables in this report, are subject to further revision, particularly in respect to the year 1963.

* Includes loans repayable in recipients' currencies and transfers of resources through sales for recipients' currencies (net of resources realised by donor country by use of these currencies).

† Loans exceeding 5 years maturity. Also includes other government bilateral long-term capital.

‡ Includes capital subscription payments.

§ Including net purchases of loans and participations by Central Monetary Authorities.

TABLE 6

COMMITMENTS* OF BILATERAL OFFICIAL GRANTS & LOANS BY
D. A. C. MEMBER COUNTRIES TO LESS-DEVELOPED COUNTRIES, 1961-1963.

(Millions of U. S. dollars)

	Year	Belgium*	Canada	Denmark	France*	Germany	Italy	Japan	Netherlands	Norway	Portugal	United Kingdom	United States	Total D.A.C. Countries
Total official bilateral commitments	1961	71	96	1	913	402	64	308	40	1	58	474	4,418	6,846
	1962	66	61	..	918	432	60	265	39	4	60	577	4,660	7,143
	1963	77	125	7	865	671	125	268	22	4	54	458	4,047	6,725
Grants	1961	71	56	1	787	125	29	81	34	1	3	208	1,549	2,945
	1962	66	47	..	772	155	19	104	11	4	3	221	1,630	3,032
	1963	76	43	5	697	161	14	80	9	3	9	219	1,457	2,772
Loans repayable in recipients' currencies	1961	–	–	–	–	–	–	–	–	–	–	–	337	337
	1962	–	–	–	–	–	–	–	–	–	–	–	220	220
	1963	–	–	2	–	–	–	–	–	–	–	–	78	80
Net transfer of resources through sales for recipients' currencies	1961	–	–	–	–	–	–	–	–	–	–	–	1,024	1,024
	1962	–	–	–	–	3	–	–	–	–	–	–	1,175	1,178
	1963	–	–	–	–	3	–	–	–	–	–	–	913	916
Loans of more than 5 years' maturity	1961	–	40	–	126	276	35	227	6	–	55	266	1,508	2,539
	1962	–	14	–	146	274	41	161	28	–	57	356	1,636	2,713
	1963	1	82	–	169	508	114	188	13	1	45	238†	1,599	2,957
– 20 years and more	1961	–	–	–	63	89	–	–	6	–	46	235	545	984
	1962	–	–	–	39	101	–	–	28	–	46	340	1,144	1,698
	1963	1	–	–	17	110	–	–	11	–	45	188†	1,194	1,566
– more than 10, up to less than 20 years	1961	–	15	–	50	134	–	166	–	–	5	7	693	1,070
	1962	–	13	–	78	164	16	13	–	–	5	3	386	678
	1963	1	–	–	127	394	40	136	1	1	–	21	228	1,004
– more than 5, up to less than 10 years	1961	–	25	–	14	53	35	62	–	–	6	24	270	487
	1962	–	1	–	29	9	25	148	–	–	4	13	106	337
	1963	–	26	–	25	4	74	52	1	–	–	29	177	388
Memo item (not included in above): Loans for more than 1 to 5 years inclusive	1961	–	–	–	–	71	141	30	–	–	7	22	67	338
	1962	–	–	–	–	41	71	22	–	–	–	1	65	200
	1963	2	–	–	5	16	26	30	–	–	–	3	–84†	–3

* For Belgium and France gross disbursement data have been used.

† Includes $5.4 million "not defined."

‡ Negative figure results from recording new commitments less larger off-setting consolidation credit entries.

TABLE 7

THE TOTAL FLOW OF LONG-TERM FINANCIAL RESOURCES, BY COUNTRY 1956-1963

(Millions of U. S. dollars)

	1956	1957	1958	1959	1960	1961	1962	1963
Total official flow net*								
Belgium	20	20	23	79	101	92	80	90
Canada	29	48	92	60	75	62	54	99
Denmark	3	2	5	14	6	7	7	10
France	648	819	884	832	842ʳ	943	972	858
Germany	149	300	278	337	324	589	427	421
Italy	36	155	45	43	75ʳ	66	67	63
Japan	61	58	254	112	125	214	165	172
Netherlands	48	23	39	49	47	69	91	38
Norway	8	8	–	4	10	9	7	21
Portugal	3	3	1	17	37	30	37	47
United Kingdom	205	234	276	375	406	450	418	413
United States	1,996	2,083	2,388	2,310	2,817	3,493	3,610ʳ	3,844
Total D. A. C. countries	3,206	3,753	4,285	4,232	4,865ʳ	6,025ʳ	5,936ʳ	6,075
of which: Bilateral	2,987	3,396	3,927	3,887	4,210	5,214	5,334	5,679
Multilateral	219	358	357	345	655	811	602	396
Total private investment, including guaranteed export credits over 5 years, net	2,547ʳ	3,445ʳ	2,656ʳ	2,306ʳ	2,523ʳ	2,608ʳ	2,100	2,071
Total official and private, net	5,753ʳ	7,198ʳ	6,941ʳ	6,538ʳ	7,388	8,632ʳ	8,035ʳ	8,146

* Corresponds to item I, Table 1.

TABLE 8

THE FLOW OF LONG-TERM FINANCIAL RESOURCES TO LESS-DEVELOPED COUNTRIES AND MULTILATERAL AGENCIES, 1962 (Disbursements)

(Millions of U. S. dollars)

	Belgium	Canada	Denmark	France	Germany	Italy	Japan	Netherlands	Norway	Portugal	United Kingdom	United States	Total D.A.C. Countries
TOTAL OFFICIAL, NET (A + B)	79.8	54.4	7.4	972.1	427.0	67.0	165.2	90.8	7.0	37.2	417.7	3,610.1	5,935.7
A. Total official bilateral, net (I-IV)	64.6	41.9	0.7	855.9	324.6	34.9	158.0	46.7	1.3	37.2	377.1	3,391.0	5,333.9
I. Bilateral grants	65.6	26.7	0.8	756.7	107.7	34.5	74.6	42.4	1.3	3.1	211.7	1,365.0	2,690.1
of which: Indemnification and reparation payments	–	–	–	–	70.0	20.2	66.8	–	–	–	–	–	157.0
II. Loans repayable in recipients' currencies, net	–	–	–	–	–	–	–	–	–	–	–	414.0	414.0
III. Transfer of resources through sales for recipients' currencies (net of resources realized by donor country by use of these currencies)	–	–	–	–	1.5	–	–	–	–	–	–	869.0	870.5
IV. Government long-term capital, net	-1.0	15.2	-0.1	99.2	215.4	0.4	83.4	4.3	-0.1	34.1	165.4	743.0	1,359.2
Loans for more than 5 years, net	-1.0	15.2	-0.1	99.2	215.4	0.4	83.4	4.3	-0.1	34.1	165.4	743.0	1,359.2
1. Loans for more than 5 years, gross	–	20.4	–	136.9	244.8	14.9	115.1	5.2	–	34.1	142.8	743.0	1,336.6
a) loans for 20 years or more	–	–	–	38.7	29.3	–	–	5.2	–	34.2	165.7	955.0	1,692.2
b) loans for more than 10, up to less than 20 years	–	5.5	–	78.3	179.9	–	18.9	–	–	31.3	139.5	349.0	593.0
c) loans for more than 5, up to 10 years	–	5.5	–	19.9	35.6	14.9	–	–	–	1.6	2.2	458.0	744.4
2. Amortisation received on loans extended	1.0	14.8	–	19.9	35.6	–	18.9	–	–	1.3	24.0	148.0	354.7
3. Loans received or amortisation paid, net (outflows are shown +)	1.0	5.2	0.1	37.7	29.4	16.0	31.7	0.9	0.1	0.2	23.5	212.0	357.8
Other bilateral government long-term capital, net	–	–	–	–	–	+1.5	–	–	–	–	+0.6	–	+2.1
B. I. Total official multilateral contributions, net	15.2	12.5	6.7	116.2	102.4	32.1	7.2	44.1	5.7	–	40.6	219.1	601.8
1. Grants and capital subscription payments	15.2	12.5	6.8	115.2	105.4	19.6	8.7	44.1	6.1	–	40.6	219.1	593.3
of which: I.B.R.D.	–	–	1.8	24.3	7.8	–	–	7.1	2.4	–	–	–	43.4
I.D.A.	–	7.2	1.7	10.2	10.2	–	3.5	6.4	5.4	1.3	25.2	61.7	132.8
E.E.C.	13.5	–	–	77.0	77.0	15.4	–	27.0	–	–	–	–	209.9
U.N. Agencies	1.7	5.3	3.3	3.6	10.4	0.6	2.3	4.6	2.4	–	15.4	95.9	145.5
Other	–	–	–	–	–	–	–	–	–	–	–	61.5[†]	61.5
2. Purchases and sales of bonds, loans and participations with maturities of more than 1 year issued by:													
I.B.R.D.	–	–	-0.1	1.0	-3.0	12.5	-1.5	–	-0.4	–	–	–	8.5
I.D.B.	–	–	–	1.0	-3.0	4.3	-1.5	–	-0.4	–	–	–	0.3
Other	–	–	–	–	–	8.2	–	–	–	–	–	–	8.2
Memo items (not included in above):													
Official bilateral													
1. Loans extended for more than 1 up to and including 5 years, net													
2. Other transfer payments to and from private individuals and institutions (net)	–	–	–	2.4	22.8	42.9	2.9	–	–	3.6	3.3	-42.0	35.9
3. Interest payments received on loans for more than 1 year's maturity											1.7	-48.3	
C. Total private long-term, net	28.1	(13.6)	4.7	306.8	150.1	(186.6)	83.1	31.7	1.6	...	211.9	821.0	1,839.2
I. Direct investment, net	30.0	(5.0)	3.5[‡]	274.5[‡]	92.6	(126.5)	68.4	-12.2	0.8	...	200.2[‡]	567.0	1,356.3[‡]
1. New direct investment	-5.0	...	...	...	48.6	106.5	...	...	0.8	...	108.9	207.0	...
2. Re-invested earnings	35.0	...	...	...	44.0	(20.0)	...	...	0.8	...	91.3	360.0	...
II. Bilateral portfolio investment and other new lending[||]	–	...	...	1.2	21.3	57.9	42.2	14.0	32.6	0.8	4.5	94.0	268.5
III. Portfolio investment in multilateral agencies, net	-1.9	8.6	–	11.0	-0.4	17.9	0.7	11.3	0.8	–	7.2		214.3
D. Guaranteed private export credits, 5 years and over, net	21.0	–	1.3	9.8	104.4	24.2	33.7	17.2	–	–	13.7	35.0	260.3
Memo item: (not included in above)													
Guaranteed private export credits, 1 to 5 years, net	-3.3	5.0	1.1	112.8	-72.3	74.8	1.2	0.3	2.4	–	91.7	13.0	226.7

[†] I.D.B. Capital subscriptions.
[‡] Based on incomplete information.
[§] Excludes United Kingdom investment in petroleum.
[||] Includes bilateral securities, nonguaranteed export credits with maturities in excess of one (five) year(s) and other long-term assets. Complete information on export credits on a balance of payments basis is available for only a few countries. To ensure intercountry comparability the amounts recorded under C.II represent only nonguaranteed export credits, including the nonguaranteed part of guaranteed transactions, to the extent that they can be estimated.
[#] Includes United Kingdom direct investment in petroleum.

NOTE: Figures in brackets ( ) indicate incomplete information or preliminary estimates.

TABLE 9

THE FLOW OF LONG-TERM FINANCIAL RESOURCES TO LESS-DEVELOPED COUNTRIES AND MULTILATERAL AGENCIES, 1963 (Disbursements)

(Millions of U.S. dollars)

	Belgium	Canada	Denmark	France	Germany	Italy	Japan	Netherlands	Norway	Portugal	United Kingdom	United States	Total D.A.C. Countries
TOTAL OFFICIAL, NET (A + B)	90.2	99.1	10.2	857.9	421.0	63.0	171.5	37.7	20.7	47.1	412.9	3,843.6	6,074.9
A. Total official bilateral, net (I-IV)	74.7	90.2	1.1	830.9	396.2	62.6	159.3	17.8	2.4	47.0	369.5	3,627	5,678.7
I. Bilateral grants	75.8	51.4	1.2	696.8	139.2	24.8	76.7	9.9	2.4	8.8	209.1	1,358	2,654.1
of which: Indemnification and reparation payments	–	–	–	–	69.5	7.9	62.1	–	–	–	–	–	139.5
II. Loans repayable in recipients' currencies, net	–	–	–	–	–	–	–	–	–	–	–	306	306.0
III. Transfer of resources through sales for recipients' currencies (net of resources realized by donor country by use of these currencies)	–	–	–	–	2.2	–	–	–	–	–	–	987	989.2
IV. Government long-term capital, net	-1.1	38.8	-0.1	...	254.8	37.8	...	7.9	–	38.2	160.4	976	1,729.4
Government long-term capital, net	-1.1	38.8	-0.1	134.1	265.1	36.3	82.6	7.9	–	38.2	154.9	976	1,732.7
Loans for more than 5 years, net	1.3	40.7	–	168.5	299.1	59.0	118.0	9.3	–	38.3	181.6	1,193	2,108.8
1. Loans for more than 5 years, gross	1.3	–	–	16.8	65.3	–	–	8.0	–	35.9	151.0	831	1,109.3
a) loans for 20 years or more	–	19.5	–	126.7	180.4	24.0	46.2	–	–	1.4	2.6	253	653.8
b) loans for more than 10, up to less than 20 years	–	21.2	–	25.0	53.4	35.0	71.8	1.3	–	1.0	28.0	109	345.7
c) loans for more than 5, up to 10 years	–	–	–	34.4	34.0	22.7	35.4	1.4	–	0.1	27.2	217	376.6
2. Amortisation received on loans extended	2.4	1.9	0.1										
3. Loans received or amortisation paid, net (outflows are shown +)	–	–	–	...	–	–	...	–	–	–	+0.5	–	+0.5
				...	-10.3	1.5	...	–	–	–	5.5	–	-3.3
Other bilateral government long-term capital, net	–	8.9	9.1	27.0	24.8	0.4	12.2	19.9	18.3	0.1	43.4	216.6	396.2
B. I. Total official multilateral contributions, net	15.5	13.9	8.1	28.0	29.8	8.1	9.4	18.6	7.6	0.1	43.4	216.6	399.1
1. Grants and capital subscription payments	15.5	–	1.9	11.3	7.8	–	–	–	1.5	–	–	–	22.5
of which: I.B.R.D.	–	7.3	1.8	10.1	10.1	3.5	6.5	5.3	1.3	–	25.3	61.6	132.8
I.D.A.	–	–	–	–	–	–	–	1.9	–	–	–	–	15.4
E.E.C.	13.5	–	–	–	–	–	–	–	–	–	–	–	228.4
U.N. Agencies	2.0	6.6	4.4	6.6	11.9	4.6	2.9	11.4	4.8	0.1	18.1	155	
Other	–	–	–	–	–	–	–	–	–	–	–	–	–
2. Purchases and sales of bonds, loans and participations with maturities of more than 1 year issued by	–	-5.0	1.0	-1.0	-5.0	-7.7	2.8	1.3	10.7	–	–	–	-2.9
I.B.R.D.	–	–	1.0	-1.0	-5.0	-7.7	2.8	–	10.7	–	–	–	0.8
I.D.B.	–	–	–	...	–	–	–	–	–	–	–	–	–
Other	–	-5.0	–	...	–	–	–	1.3	–	–	–	–	-3.7
Memo items (not included in above):													
Official bilateral													
1. Loans extended for more than 1 up to and including 5 years, net	1.8	–	-0.5	3.6	2.7	46.4	2.0	–	–	4.1	0.3	-87	-26.6
2. Other transfer payments to and from private individuals and institutions (net)	–	0.8	...	...	154.3	–	...	–	–	–	1.7	124	280.8
3. Interest payments received on loans for more than 1 year's maturity	–	-1.3	...	...	-9.3	...	-5.7	-0.2	–	1.0	-58.4	-172	-247.9
C. Total private long-term, net	(51.8)	(4.6)	(3.0)	208.7	107.4	(129.8)	79.9	98.3	3.7	...	(281.3)	(878.2)	1,846.7
I. Direct investment, net	50.0	(25.0)	(3.0)	193.3+	88.9	(102.2)	76.7	57.3	0.4	...	(280.0)	(831.0)	1,707.8
1. New direct investment	–	...	(3.0)	–	48.9	82.2	–	–	0.4	...	...	461.0	...
2. Re-invested earnings	50.0	...	–	–	40.0	(20.0)	...	...	...	...	...	(370.0)	...
II. Bilateral portfolio investment and other new lending**	(–)	(12.0)	–	14.4	7.1	28.5	3.5	40.2	3.3	...	...	42.0	151.0
III. Portfolio investment in multilateral agencies, net	1.8	-32.4	–	1.0	11.4	-0.9	-0.3	0.8	–	...	1.3	5.2	-12.1
D. Guaranteed private export credits, 5 years and over, net	29.2	–	0.7	21.3	28.7	78.1	13.3	9.1	–	...	29.9	4.0	223.9
Memo item: (not included in above)													
Guaranteed private export credits, 1 to 5 years, net	8.3	17.9	-2.8	83.1	28.7	18.9	0.8	3.0	4.9	–	68.3	26.0	247.5

* Based on incomplete information.
  Includes bilateral securities, nonguaranteed export credits with maturities in excess of one (five) year(s) and other long-term assets. Complete information on export credits on a balance of payments basis is available for only a few countries. To ensure intercountry comparability the amounts recorded under C.II represent only nonguaranteed export credits, including the nonguaranteed part of guaranteed transactions, to the extent that they can be estimated.
  NOTE Figures in brackets ( ) indicate incomplete information or preliminary estimates.
  Source Contributions to the I.B.R.D., I.D.A., and I.D.B., agency submissions.

TABLE 10

INTEREST RATE STRUCTURE OF OFFICIAL BILATERAL CONTRIBUTIONS, 1963 (Commitments) *

(Millions of U.S. dollars)

COUNTRY	Total Official Bilateral Contributions	Grants[1]	Total Loans	INTEREST RATES OF OFFICIAL LENDING FOR MORE THAN 1 YEAR							
				Less Than 1% and Interest Free	1 to Less Than 3%	3 to Less Than 4%	4 to Less Than 5%	5 to Less Than 6%	6 to Less Than 7%	7% and more	Not Available
Belgium	78.9	75.8	3.1	1.8	–	1.3	–	–	–	–	–
Canada	125.2	43.6	81.6	–	–	–	–	–	81.6	–	–
Denmark	6.8	6.8	–	–	–	–	–	–	–	–	–
France	870.0	696.8	173.2	1.4	45.6	55.4	2.8	53.7	14.3	–	–
Germany	686.7	163.2	523.5	–	14.0	279.0	16.0	145.0	64.5	5.0	–
Italy	154.3	14.0	140.3	–	–	–	2.3	87.8	26.3	23.9	–
Japan	298.2	80.1	218.1	–	–	–	4.5	132.0	81.4	0.2	–
Netherlands	21.9	8.5	13.4	–	–	2.9	2.6	6.5	–	–	1.4
Norway	3.7	3.2	0.5[§]	..	..	..	..	..	..	..	0.5
Portugal	53.5	8.8	44.7[‡]	–	–	42.0	2.7	–	–	–	–
United Kingdom	460.1	219.3	240.8	6.6	50.8	9.8	1.6	144.4	–	–	27.6
United States	3,963.0	2,448.0	1,515.0	1,040.0	75.0	112.0	3.0	283.0	1.0	1.0	–
Total D.A.C. Countries	6,722.3	3,768.1	2,954.2	1,049.8	185.4	502.4	35.5	852.4	269.1	30.1	29.5

* For Belgium and France gross disbursement data have been used.
[1] Including grants, reparations, net loans repayable in recipients' currencies and net transfers of resources through sales for recipients' currencies.
[‡] For Portugal, interest rate breakdown is based on 1962 information.
[§] The terms of this loan have yet to be determined.

TABLE 11

DISTRIBUTION BY MATURITIES OF OFFICIAL BILATERAL LENDING, 1963 (Commitments) *

(Millions of U.S. dollars)

COUNTRY	Total Loans	More Than 1 to 5 Years Incl.	More Than 5 to 10 Years Incl.	More Than 10 to 20 Years Incl.	20 to 30 Years Excl.	30 to 40 Years Excl.	40 Years and more
Belgium	3.1	1.8	–	–	1.3	–	–
Canada	81.6	–	25.9	55.7	–	–	–
Denmark	–	–	–	–	–	–	–
France	173.2	4.7	25.0	126.7	16.8[‡]	–	–
Germany	523.5	15.5	4.0	394.0	110.0	–	–
Italy	140.3	26.3	74.0	40.0	–	–	–
Japan	218.1	30.1	52.1	135.9	–	–	–
Netherlands	13.4	–	0.9	1.4	11.1[‡]	–	–
Norway	0.5	–	–	0.5	–	–	–
Portugal	44.7	–	–	–	44.7	–	–
United Kingdom	240.8[§]	2.6	29.2	20.9	183.9[§]	4.2	–
United States	1,515.0	–84.0	177.0	228.0	171.0	35.0	988.0
Total D.A.C. Countries	2,954.2	–3.0[‖]	388.1	1,003.1	538.8	39.2	988.0

* For Belgium and France gross disbursement data have been used.
[†] May also include loans with maturities of more than 30 years.
[‡] Includes $1.4 million "not available".
[§] Includes $5.4 million "not defined".
[‖] Negative figure results from recording new commitments less larger offsetting consolidation credit entries.

TABLE 12 *

GEOGRAPHICAL DISTRIBUTION OF NET OFFICIAL FINANCIAL FLOWS[†] TO LESS-DEVELOPED COUNTRIES[‡] FROM INDUSTRIAL O.E.C.D. MEMBER COUNTRIES AND MULTILATERAL AGENCIES, 1960 TO 1963

	NET OFFICIAL CAPITAL FLOW (Millions of U.S. dollars)				POPULATION IN 1963 (Million)
	1960	1961	1962	1963	
Total Recipient Countries	4,559	5,544	5,792	6,317	1,511
Asia	2,245	2,221	2,373	2,756	910
India[§]	782	665	743	982	459
Pakistan[§]	253	266	397	502	99
South Korea	251	229	236	263	27
South Vietnam	192	167‖	180‖	221‖	15
Israel	104	107	114	132	2
Indonesia	61	106	119	116	100
Jordan	70	87	77	80	2
Formosa	107	115	80	74	12
Thailand	50	42	56	46	29
Iran	31	138	64	28	22
Other	344	299	307	312	143
Africa	1,464	1,651	1,710	1,650	281
French Franc Area South of Sahara[#]	314	364	431	422	40
Algeria and Sahara	405	433	393	295	11
Egypt (U.A.R.)	201	119	193	201	28
Morocco **	79	117	85	109	13
Congo (Leopoldville)	90	86	67	87	15
Tunisia **	62	87	65	74	4
Kenya [††]	21	65	51	56	9
Portuguese Overseas Provinces	35	35	41	53	14
Liberia	10	27	79	34	1
Tanganyika [††]	10	40	46	29	10
Libya	43	36	32	26	1
Uganda [††]	20	25	30	21	7
Other	174	217	197	243	128
America	335	877	945	1,140	226
Brazil	52	342	181	202	78
Chile	17	130	138	147	8
French Overseas Departments [‡‡]	73	73	104	130	1
Colombia	- 6	66	73	107	15
Mexico	16	64	52	86	38
Argentina	20	43	98	84	22
Venezuela	-5	-6	71	61	8
Bolivia	12	24	36	53	4
Other	156	141	192	270	52
Europe	354	548	468	471	90
Turkey	128	178	228	221	30
Yugoslavia	66	169	176	178	19
Greece	43	68	35	39	9
Spain	80	102	4	1	31
Other	37	31	25	32	1
Oceania	30	38	60	26	5
Unallocated	131	209	236	274	—

* Extracted from: The Flow of Financial Resources to Less-Developed Countries, 1956-1963, O.E.C.D., Paris, 1964.
† Net Official financial flows equal net bilateral official grants and loans received plus grants and loans received from multilateral agencies, less capital repayments and capital subscription payments to these agencies.
‡ Less-developed countries to which financial flow and population data apply are those countries listed in Annex B to: "The Flow of Financial Resources to Countries in the Course of Economic Development in 1956 to 1959, O.E.C.D.".
§ Grants of Canada and United Kingdom for the Indus Basin Development Fund amounting to $2.2 million in 1961, $8.6 million in 1962 and $18.5 million in 1963 have been divided evenly between India and Pakistan.
‖ French grants from 1961 onwards and French loans in 1963 to Cambodia, Laos and South Vietnam are not available separately. For the purpose of this Table it was assumed that South Vietnam received one half of the totals amounting to $10.6 million in 1961, $8.1 million in 1962 and $10.0 million in 1963.
Including French aid to all French Overseas Territories (Comoro Islands, New Caledonia, St. Pierre et Miquelon, Wallis and Futuna) amounting to $20.2 million in 1960, $24.6 million in 1961, $30.3 million in 1962 and $28.9 million in 1963.
** French grants to Morocco and Tunisia (amounting to $29.2 million in 1960, $28.3 million in 1961, $27.6 million in 1962 and $30.7 million in 1963) are not available separately. For the purpose of this Table it was assumed that two-thirds of the grants were received by Morocco and one-third by Tunisia.
†† Disbursements to and repayments by the East African Common Services Organization have been allocated for each of the years 1960-1963, on the following basis: 48 percent for Kenya, 30 percent for Tanganyika and 22 percent for Uganda.
‡‡ Including Reunion.
Population data are based on current United Nations Statistics complemented in some cases by Secretariat estimates.

TABLE 13 ·

TOTAL NET FLOW FROM ALL INDUSTRIAL COUNTRIES AND TOTAL NET RECEIPTS OF LESS-DEVELOPED COUNTRIES,
1959 – 1963

(Millions of U.S. dollars)

	1959	1960	1961	1962	1963
I. Official bilateral, net	4,200	4,499	5,635	5,830	6,154
From industrial O.E.C.D. countries	4,001	4,277	5,292	5,381	5,662
Grant and grant-like contributions	3,124	3,629	3,948	3,980	3,959
Bilateral loans (net)	877	648	1,344	1,400	1,703
From other industrial countries	38	36	49	57	67
From Sino-Soviet countries †	161	186	294	391	425
II. Private bilateral capital, net	2,545	2,838	2,975	2,216	2,469
From industrial O.E.C.D. countries	2,545	2,838	2,975	2,216	2,469
Direct investment and other new lending including reinvested earnings	2,229	2,375	2,482	1,662	1,903
Guaranteed export credits	316	463	493	548	566
From other industrial countries	..	..	..	..	..
III. Multilateral contributions, total net	576	890	983	901	385
From industrial O.E.C.D. countries	554	869	953	880	355
Official	348	664	842	633	386
Private	206	205	111	247	-31
From other industrial countries	15	16	24	14	24
Official	14	16	24	14	24
Private	1	–	–	–	–
From Sino-Soviet countries	7	5	7	7	6
Official	7	5	7	7	6
Total flow from all industrial countries (I + II + III)	7,321	8,227	9,593	8,947	9,008
IV. Disbursements to less-developed countries from multilateral agencies, net of capital repayments and subscriptions	289	283	253	412	654
Total receipts of less-developed countries, net (I + II + IV)	7,034	7,620	8,863	8,458	9,277

* Extracted from: The Flow of Financial Resources to Less-Developed Countries, 1956-1963, O.E.C.D., Paris, 1964, p. 26.
† Gross, Repayment figures are not available but in 1963 may have been up to $50 million.

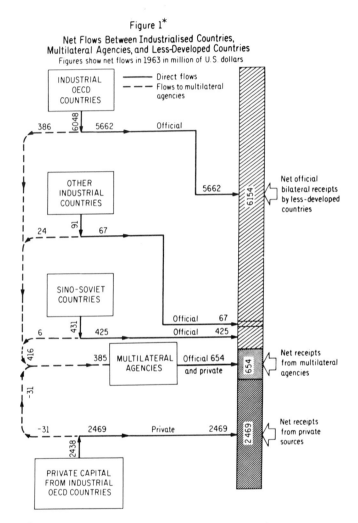

Figure 1*

Net Flows Between Industrialised Countries,
Multilateral Agencies, and Less-Developed Countries

Figures show net flows in 1963 in million of U.S. dollars

* The flow of financial resources to less-developed countries, 1956-1963,
OECD, Paris, 1964, p.27.

THE INTERNATIONAL BANK FOR RECONSTRUCTION AND DEVELOPMENT*

THE BANK AND THE FUND

Of the twins of Bretton Woods, the International Bank for Reconstruction and Development enjoyed far less of the limelight at its inception than the International Monetary Fund. At the preliminary conference at Atlantic City in June 1944, attention was concentrated on the Fund and at Bretton Woods the main source of controversy was the Articles of Agreement of the Fund, even when it was intended that similar provisions should apply to the Bank. The quotas on which so much of the discussion centred were worked out first for the Fund and later became the basis for subscriptions to the Bank—to the consternation of members who had sought high quotas in the Fund in order to establish drawing rights but were less anxious to make equal capital subscriptions to the Bank. At Savannah it was again the Fund that was the principal subject of debate; it seems to have been assumed that the same relations between management and executive directors would govern both institutions. The site chosen for the Fund automatically became the site of the Bank, which until 1958 shared the same building in Washington and continues to share the same library.

Yet in the first ten years of its existence it was the Bank rather than the Fund which most readily found a place for itself. The scope of its activities steadily expanded; it was never subject to the frustrations that inevitably beset the Fund when the burden of international reconstruction fell on the United States; its policies took increasingly firm shape; and its influence on world economic development grew progressively.

The membership of the Bank has throughout been identical with that of the Fund; Bank membership is, in fact, open only to members of the Fund. All the 44 countries represented at Bretton Woods subsequently joined the two institutions except the Soviet Union, New Zealand, and Liberia. Nearly all other countries of any economic importance outside the Communist bloc (except Switzerland) have been added to the list of members, which now totals 68. Poland withdrew in 1950 and Czechoslovakia was expelled

* Excerpted from Alec Cairncross, *The International Bank for Reconstruction and Development,* International Finance Section, Princeton University, 1959.

in 1953 for nonfulfilment of its obligations, leaving Yugoslavia the only Communist member. China's membership was continued in favour of Taiwan on an undertaking from the emigré government that it would pay the remaining (and major) part of its subscription as soon as possible, and the Chinese Executive Director retained his position as an appointed member of the Board.

Although the two institutions have led a more separate existence than was perhaps originally intended, they supplement one another and the future of the one is closely tied up with the future of the other. The Bank is concerned primarily with the flow of capital into long-term investment across national boundaries, the Fund with problems of international liquidity and short-term credit. But both institutions share a common interest in helping their members to reconcile economic balance and economic growth, in promoting economic and financial policies that pay regard not only to national but also to international interests, and in maintaining an international framework within which countries can make necessary adjustments in their economies without excessive strain.

THE FUNCTIONS OF THE BANK

The purpose of the Bank is implicit in its title. This emphasises an immediate and temporary function: that of assisting the restoration and reconstruction of productive capacity destroyed during the war. It also underlines a continuing and longer-range function: that of contributing to the development of economic resources and the growth of productive power and standards of living, particularly in backward or underdeveloped countries.

These functions were regarded at Bretton Woods as competitive; so long as the capital at the disposal of the Bank was limited and the claims of reconstruction were pressing, and indeed paramount, there could be no assurance that the Bank would have enough funds to discharge its obligations towards the less-developed countries. In the early years of the Bank there did in fact appear to be some antithesis between its functions. The first loans were made exclusively for the reconstruction of countries in Western Europe and it was only after a large proportion of the Bank's freely usable, paid-in capital had already been committed that any loan agreements were concluded with underdeveloped countries. But even at that stage the limiting factor in loans to those countries was not the inadequate resources of the Bank so much as the greater care that was needed in examining the projects submitted for financial support, and the delays that prolonged examination entailed. In any event, it was obvious that, sooner or later, reconstruction would come to an end and the needs of economic development would become the enduring preoccupation of the Bank. Marshall Aid hastened the transition and for many years the word "Reconstruction" in the Bank's title has been an anachronism.

The functions of the Bank can be not inadequately summarized by describing it as an international development bank. It is in the first place an *international* institution: a specialized agency of the United Nations operating as a cooperative venture in long-term foreign lending. It is, secondly, a *development* bank: not perhaps the exact counterpart at the international level of those development banks which it has done so much to encourage at the national level, since these have been devoted exclusively to industrial financing and have been privately owned; but, like them, engaged in promoting development by supplying long-term capital, and following an older tradition of development banks in financing a variety of large projects of special importance to the economies of member countries. Moreover, just as many development banks found themselves obliged to enter other fields of activity as they took a more comprehensive view of all that development implied, so the Bank, starting out as a lender on long-term, has been forced to take an increasingly wide view of its responsibilities.

As an international institution, the prime task of the Bank is to stimulate and support foreign investment. So far as this involves the use of the Bank's own resources, it must be able to mobilize capital from a variety of capital-exporting countries and lend the capital so mobilized to a variety of capital-importing countries. The wider the range of borrowers and lenders, the more truly international will the Bank become. It has in fact relied heavily on the United States for its funds and has found employment for those funds chiefly in the underdeveloped countries. But it is by no means simply a vehicle for channelling American investment towards the underdeveloped countries. It has raised a growing proportion of its funds outside the United States and it has always been willing to make loans to countries that would not normally be regarded as backward, or even underdeveloped. Every country aspires to economic development and nearly every country has a pressing need for extra capital. Developed countries, though generally lenders, particularly on long-term, very often import capital and may have good reasons for trying to borrow through an international institution. Similarly, underdeveloped countries, although normally importers of capital, at least on long-term, may at times be in a position to lend to the Bank or accelerate repayment of their loans from it. The Bank's international role, therefore, need not consist in raising capital in developed countries in order to lend it to underdeveloped countries. It may borrow from either group and lend to either group. It may even finance projects in countries from which it is currently borrowing; and it has in fact done so. For example, in a recent issue by private placement, the Bank found buyers for its bonds in no less than nine countries to which it had made loans during the year 1957–58. In May 1957 the Dutch Herstelbank borrowed $15 million from the Bank, although public issues of guilder bonds had been made in 1954, and again in 1955, by the Bank, and the Netherlands is a steady buyer of the Bank's dollar bonds.

As a development bank, the Bank is first and foremost a lender on long-term. From its standing as a lender, it has acquired authority in the exercise of other functions. It has built up a special expertise in the peculiar blend of engineering, economics and administrative skill necessary for the appraisal and supervision of large projects of construction. It has also a unique experience in the formulation of comprehensive programmes of economic development. This experience leads member countries to turn to the Bank not only for finance, but also for advice and guidance; while the Bank, in devising techniques by which it could put its experience at the service of member countries, has come to think of itself as a consultant quite as much as a financial institution.

The functions of the Bank extend, therefore, well beyond the series of loan transactions in which it engages. Not only does it, like other development banks, maintain a continuing relationship with borrowers throughout the life of each loan. It insists that the loans cannot be treated as isolated transactions and that the projects which they finance must be examined in relation to the rest of the development effort of the borrower. It constantly emphasises the value of a development programme into which the major projects are fitted. It aims also at identifying the economic and financial policies most conducive to development and the strategic factors upon which governments should be encouraged to operate. Thus the Bank has found itself involved in working out, if not a theory, at least a philosophy of development. This is not a philosophy which the Bank has ever articulated in any detail. But there are passages in its Annual Reports that recur to the same general themes: the limited value of additional finance if other, institutional factors are not propitious; the importance of good management both in the planning of individual projects and in the conduct of a nation's affairs; the need to encourage initiative, enterprise and the will to develop, and to avoid policies which, through weakness, vacillation or impatience, prevent the emergence of attitudes and institutions favourable to development.

THE BANK AS LENDER

By the summer of 1958 the Bank had made over 200 loans totalling nearly $4 billion. Its rate of lending, after a first burst of reconstruction loans in 1947–48, and a second, minor boom in 1950–52, remained relatively steady in the middle fifties at around $400 million but shot up in 1957–58 to a record total of $711 million. Most of the later loans have been made to countries which, on any normal definition, would be classed as underdeveloped. Thus, European countries, to which all the first loans were made, have not been large borrowers in recent years, with the important exception of Italy, itself in many ways underdeveloped. On the other hand, South-east Asia has come increasingly to the front as a borrower. India has emerged as the largest of the Bank's debtors and over the past two years has borrowed $240 million, or 20 percent of the total sum lent by the Bank during that period. Asia and the Middle East, which at one time occupied a relatively modest place in the Bank's lending operations, accounted for over half the value of the loans made in 1957–58 and showed every sign of continuing to absorb a high proportion of total loans. Four countries—India, Pakistan, Thailand, and Japan—borrowed between them over $350 million during the year and by June 30, 1958 had received loans totalling $772 million out of the aggregate for Asia and the Middle East of $948 million. Loans to Latin America totalled $798 million, Mexico, Brazil, and Colombia being the largest borrowers; but this total has mounted at a relatively slow pace in comparison with that for South-east Asia. Among the African countries, the main borrowers have been South Africa and the Federation of Rhodesia and Nyasaland, which borrowed $301 million by mid-1958 out of a total of $479 million for the continent. Australia, with loans totalling $318 million took second place only to India as a borrowing country. European countries, in addition to the reconstruction loans amounting to $497 million, had borrowed a total of $689 milion. In all, loans had been made to 47 member countries and territories by the Bank; but of these, 10 countries accounted for 60 percent by value of the total loans.

Has the Bank in its lending fulfilled the expectations that might reasonably be entertained in view of its origins and membership? Or, if not, wherein has the Bank failed in making loans to its members?

TABLE 1

LENDING OPERATIONS OF THE WORLD BANK, 1946-58

(Millions of dollars)

	Loans (gross of cancellations and repayments)	Disbursements	Sales of Loans	Repayments to Bank
1946-48	497	470	--	--
1948-49	153	56	28	--
1949-50	166	88	--	1
1950-51	297	78	5	5
1951-52	299	185	23	4
1952-53	179	227	14	2
1953-54	324	302	32	4
1954-55	410	274	102	124
1955-56	396	284	72	24
1956-57	388	332	57	26
1957-58	711	499	87	28
Cumulative to June 30, 1958	3,820	2,795	420	218

No critic of the Bank thinks that it should have done less, but a great many think that it should have done more. The scale on which it has lent may seem quite inadequate, for example, in relation to the needs of the underdeveloped countries. If the calculations of the United Nations experts who in 1951 estimated the capital requirements of those countries at $19,000 million a year are put in conjunction with the then rate of lending of the Bank—about $300 million a year—the contrast is overwhelming. But the calculations are now recognized to be largely meaningless, and there is little point in discussing what the "correct" figure should be. At the same time, the Bank has doubled its rate of lending and has concentrated more on the underdeveloped countries in Latin America, Asia, and Africa. Of the total inflow of long-term capital into those areas from outside, the Bank may be providing not far short of a quarter.

Nevertheless, even $700 million a year may seem an insufficient contribution to the development of those areas. How is it possible to reconcile the Bank's rate of lending with its dictum that as much money can be advanced as there is good reason to expect to see repaid?

First of all, there are good grounds for supposing that the real need for capital in many parts of the underdeveloped world has been grossly exaggerated. When one finds, for example, that real income rose by over 5.5 percent per annum in Latin America between 1945 and 1955 and that even per capita income rose nearly as fast as in Europe—3.5 percent per annum compared with 4.5 percent per annum—it is difficult to suppose that a vast inflow of capital would have made a great deal of difference. It might perhaps have helped to avoid bottlenecks in power and transport; but on the other hand it is arguable that, if the price of power and transport services had at least kept pace with the universal inflation, there would have been less need to borrow abroad to finance capital expenditure and less difficulty in offering adequate security to foreign lenders or investors.

Secondly, most of the underdeveloped world has enjoyed throughout the greater part of the postwar period highly favourable terms of trade. This has put it in a far stronger position to finance imports of capital goods without resort to foreign borrowing, especially where part of the higher export income was retained in the hands of the central government or its agencies. On the other hand, these high prices added fuel to inflationary fires that were already well stoked and the Bank has hesitated to make loans to countries that seemed to lack either the will or the capacity to keep inflation within measure.

Thirdly, some countries were unable to borrow more because they were simply not creditworthy. However, the Bank measures creditworthiness—and obviously there can be no single index that registers it, since political factors, trust in the good faith of the debtor, the efficiency of the administrative machine, the volatility of export earnings, the use to which borrowed funds are put, and so on, must all enter—there is some limit beyond which the Bank cannot safely go in lending to a given country if it is obliged to show prudence and a regard for the interests of the guarantors of its loans. It is not possible to say with any precision how far the efforts of the Bank to keep within a ceiling of creditworthiness have caused it to reject (or rather, turn aside, since it never formally rejects) loan applications. Even within the Bank there might well be disagreement about the influence of any notional ceilings on decisions to proceed with or discountenance a specific loan operation. But there are unquestionably countries to which the Bank will not lend because their creditworthiness is rated too low and others to which loans will be made only after more than usually rigorous examination.

Sometimes, when a very large project is involved, the Bank may be doubtful whether foreign exchange earnings will be sufficiently enlarged to enable the debt to be serviced and may, on those grounds, be unwilling to shoulder the whole responsibility without participation by other influential lenders or without substantial grants towards the cost. There are also cases where, if the Bank is not on the best of terms with an intending borrower, no new loans are likely to be made; but such cases often reflect the disappointment of the borrower over *past* failure to secure a loan, so that it is only the number of loan applications that is affected, not the number granted.

Two conditions governing the Bank's lending policy and limiting its loans arise directly out of its Charter. The Bank normally lends only against specific projects and confines its participation to financing the foreign exchange component, i.e. payments for imported equipment, technical services provided by foreigners, etc. Both of these conditions are open to criticism and both are subject to exceptions.

The first condition implies that a government with a large investment programme cannot come to the Bank and obtain from it funds to supplement its normal revenue and cover any deficit in the Budget. It has to submit projects one by one, justify each, and accept Bank supervision right through to their completion. This condition was introduced at Bretton Woods with a view to preventing unproductive borrowing. The Articles of Agreement make or guarantee loans in support of "programmes of economic reconstruction and the reconstruction of monetary systems including long-term stabilization loans"; and although no stabilization loans have ever been made, the loans to European countries were negotiated not in terms of specific projects but on the basis of the loophole left by the "except in special circumstances" clause that was finally inserted in the Charter. Other loans, although nominally made against specific projects, have seemed on occasion, to be only loosely connected with those projects, which were not contingent on Bank finance and appeared to be the subject of the loan contract almost by accident. The Bank has also made loans to Development Banks, which are able to feed in capital to local undertakings that are not specified in advance, although each loan made locally still requires Bank approval if it involves the use of Bank funds and is in excess of some agreed minimum. This last provision, if rigorously enforced, would represent the *reductio ad absurdum* of the specific-projects approach. It is hard to believe that the Bank can exercise really effective control over loans made by, say, the Ethiopian Development Bank.

An unkind critic would say that the whole idea of financing economic development project by project smacks of paternalism and a pedagogical outlook. The Bank is not willing to lend a country the money it thinks it needs because the money may be misused. The Bank wants not only to ensure eventual repayment, but also to see to it that the borrower will make the best use of the capital. It comes near to taking for granted that it is a more reliable champion of the borrower's best interests than the borrower himself.

This may seem presumptuous but it is very often true. The difference in competence in matters of economic development between the staff of the Bank and the administration of many underdeveloped countries is striking. What is more, the Bank's attitude is rarely resented, because many of the underdeveloped countries prefer to have technical assistance and foreign capital wrapped up together and supplied by the Bank. It is a measure of the success of the Bank in its dealings with the underdeveloped countries that they should place so much confidence in it, and accept almost without question the specific-projects approach to international lending. Yet the same countries complain both of the insufficiency of Bank lending and of the long interval that usually elapses before it is possible to complete arrangements for a loan from the Bank.

From the Bank's point of view the merit of the system is that it can offer the borrowing country much needed guidance on the elements of development policy. It can use each project as an object lesson in order to demonstrate how to plan and organize large-scale capital expenditure. This is true not only of the individual project that is being financed but also of the whole investment programme of the borrowing country. At the project level, the Bank has wide experience in finding suitable engineering consultants; in making sure that the scheme has been thoroughly examined, all the constructional and financial difficulties considered and the best alternatives reviewed before it is embarked upon; and in assessing the full social value that it may afford, directly and indirectly. At the national level, the Bank has always laid stress on its unwillingness to consider a project in isolation from the pattern of national development into which it is designed to fit. It has encouraged its members to prepare comprehensive investment plans, not because it believes in Planning with a capital "P," but so as to make sure that each Bank-financed scheme will fit into a consistent and systematic programme of action. It has found again and again that underdeveloped countries are taking no adequate thought for their future, or that their governments think it enough to have a shopping list of schemes with no internal consistency except perhaps their power to satisfy constituents or supporters up and down the country. The Bank attaches importance, therefore, to seeing the whole programme as well as confining its support to projects for which there is ample justification on economic and social grounds. It would be much more difficult to achieve the same leverage on the concrete, positive plans of member governments if general loans were made without reference to the details of the objects on which the money was to be spent.

From the point of view of the borrower, the system has obvious defects. It is impossible, for example, to raise money for various forms of social investment which the Bank rules out as unproductive; housing, schools, health services, and so on. The objection is not urged against roads although roads also are unproductive in the sense of yielding no revenue. The attitude of the Bank—on the whole, a justifiable attitude— is that governments are generally under stronger pressure to find capital for social purposes than for long-range economic development. If the Bank helps them to meet part of their total requirements, this should ease their difficulties in covering the remainder; but by limiting itself to so-called productive investment, the Bank can help to redress what might otherwise be a lack of balance in the general pattern of investment.

There is also a slowing down in the pace of lending. While some loans are concluded within a matter of months, others take literally years. This has meant that, in the early years of the Bank at least, it took a long time to work up steam and the sanctioning of loans lagged behind the submission of schemes. But after ten years, this effect can hardly amount to very much. The exhaustive scrutiny to which projects are submitted may delay the granting of loans, but it need not affect the peak rate of lending attained, provided member countries are not discouraged from feeding in new propositions by the uncertainty surrounding the old. The Bank assumes that countries seeking long-term capital can afford to wait, and indeed should wait, for loan approvals instead of rushing ahead without adequate preparation; and that if a country needs capital quickly for balance of payments reasons its proper recourse is to the Fund or other sources.

There is an obvious danger that the elaborate precautions taken by the Bank to ensure that it makes good loans may create some resentment among borrowers who have satisfied themselves in advance that their schemes meet all the criteria that the Bank could possibly lay down. There is a tendency in the Bank to erect project appraisal into a mystique when in fact it calls for no more than good organizing capacity, engineering experience and economic and financial insight. The combination of these may be rare but it is not unique. As the Bank educates its members in project appraisal and begins to receive a more sophisticated assessment of the schemes which it is asked to finance, it may be able to relax some of its present vigilance and give prompter approval.

While the Bank's insistence on project loans may be justifiable when the borrower is weak and inexperienced, it is irksome to countries that need no education in large-scale planning and administration. The system of rigorous supervision and control over disbursements that is an almost inseparable part of the project approach has been the subject of adverse comment by countries that have already devised effective instruments of financial supervision and feel that, having given adequate security for a loan, they should be dispensed from covenants and procedures that are both superfluous and harassing. Sometimes countries that have started out as critics of the degree of control exercised by the Bank have later expressed complete satisfaction with the procedures followed and have even found in them a model to follow; but the stronger and more experienced the borrower, the greater his difficulty in swallowing the system of investigation, appraisal, and supervision on which the Bank insists.

The second condition, that limiting Bank loans to the foreign exchange component in capital expenditure, could be a more serious handicap and more difficult to justify. One purpose of the limitation is to prevent borrowing countries from assuming too large a burden of foreign indebtedness in relation to their earnings of foreign exchange. But this already enters into the Bank's assessment of the creditworthiness of the borrower, and seems more relevant to the total external indebtedness that may safely be incurred than to the division between external and domestic sources of capital in each individual project. It is perhaps more reasonable to regard the condition as one intended to secure that the Bank is not normally called upon to promise more than about half the total capital and that local capital will play an effective part in any project financed by the Bank. If this is the right interpretation, there is some point in establishing a convention that the Bank's share should be governed by a formula that has an air of plausibility and can easily be applied. There is a further administrative convenience in that the Bank can supervise disbursements and release foreign exchange only against approved expenditures.

An over-scrupulous application of this condition would tend to discriminate against particular types of project and country. It would be natural, for example, for countries that were anxious to borrow as much as possible from the Bank to submit for its consideration the kind of project that had a large foreign exchange component, and they might be tempted to amend their investment plans so as to give preference to such projects over others which, if the condition did not apply, would be more attractive. Suppose, for example, that a country has a shortage of electric power and is faced with the choice between thermal, hydro, and nuclear generation. The cost in foreign exchange per unit generated may follow a different order from the total cost per unit including local currency outlays, and the total cost may itself depend upon the proportion of the capital supplied by the Bank at, say, 5 percent and the proportion supplied locally at an opportunity cost that may be twice as high or higher. The eventual decision may be in favour of nuclear power, with a high outlay on imported equipment financed with relatively cheap capital rather than on hydroelectric power involving a heavy expenditure of scarce local capital; yet if it were possible to borrow the whole of the necessary capital from the Bank, the decision might be reversed.

In the same way, some countries would be in a better position to take advantage of Bank lending than others because they would find it easier to put up, out of local savings, a supplement to the foreign exchange supplied by the Bank. A country so poor, or with so undeveloped a capital market or fiscal system that it could hardly take even the first steps in development, might badly want to borrow from the Bank but have great difficulty in matching the Bank's contribution with domestic savings. The countries likely to make most extensive use of the Bank would consequently be neither so rich that they had no need to borrow abroad, nor so poor that they could not meet the Bank's conditions.

The Bank has not, however, held rigorously to the position that it should supply no local currency but only foreign exchange. In the Fifth Annual Report it summarized its policy by laying down three conditions for the finance of local expenditures: "(a) if the project to be financed is of such economic urgency that the country's ability to undertake foreign borrowing—which is more or less limited in all cases—is better utilized in financing this project than in financing the direct foreign exchange costs of alternative projects; (b) if the local currency costs of the project cannot reasonably be met out of available domestic resources; and (c) if it is apparent that, unless foreign exchange is made available to the borrowing country to be employed for the import of either consumer goods or raw materials, the local currency expenditures involved in the project will lead to inflationary pressures."

These conditions are unexceptionable: but it is difficult to believe that, translated into action, they would make loans to cover local expenditure so extraordinarily rare, especially when any other kind of loan hardly existed up to fifty years ago. In an underdeveloped country almost any increase in capital investment heightens the danger of inflation and reacts on the balance of payments; it is quite arbitrary to single out the direct impact through imports of capital goods and distinguish it from the inevitable indirect impact through imports of consumer goods and raw materials. The shortage of capital from which such countries suffer normally finds expression in a physical shortage of specific equipment that can only be procured from abroad; but the shortage of capital is not limited to the lack of industrial equipment and does not arise merely from the absence of domestic capacity to produce that equipment.

The Bank has in fact made a number of "impact" loans, mainly to Italy, and has also, on occasion, made local currency loans, not attempting to determine the exact impact but financing a certain proportion of the total cost of the project. The first "impact" loans were to the Italian Cassa per il Mezzogiorno and received special justification on the grounds that, while the existence of a well-developed engineering industry in the north of Italy would make it unnecessary to provide for large foreign exchange costs, the indirect effect of expanding incomes on the balance of payments was likely to be particularly pronounced. Similarly, a recent loan to the Japan Development Bank for the finance of hydroelectric installations has been made to cover expenditures in Japan, not abroad, because Japanese industry is quite capable of furnishing the necessary equipment, but Japan has good reasons for trying to raise foreign capital.

The purposes for which the Bank has made loans are circumscribed by the conditions under which it operates. Two-thirds by value of the loans made so far (excluding reconstruction loans) have been for power and transport; and of the loans to industry nearly half has gone to iron and steel, leaving only $300 million for all other industries in thirteen years of operation. To some extent this reflects the inevitable concentration of the Bank on large loans; apart from steel, chemicals, and a few other exceptions, industry is, so to speak, a retail borrower while power and transport borrow wholesale. In part, it is the fact that the Bank supplies loan capital rather than equity capital that accounts for the pattern of its lending; public utilities in all countries raise most of their capital by the issue of bonds while industry relies heavily on share capital. In part, also, the concentration on public utilities does no more than reflect their enormous capital requirements in comparison with industry—a concentration that may be particularly marked in the early stages of industrialization.

Taking it all in all, the underdeveloped countries are wise to raise foreign capital in the form in which they can get it from the Bank, in large amounts and at low cost, rather than in the form of a large number of small industrial investments on which the private investor is likely to want a far higher return. Given the central place that industrialization takes in the process of economic development, however, neither the Bank nor the underdeveloped countries can neglect measures to speed up industrial growth with the help of foreign capital. If the scale of the Bank's lending for this purpose has so far been disappointing, this is due not only to the circumstances already mentioned but to two other factors of major importance. One is the reluctance of private firms to accept a government guarantee, with the loss of freedom of action that this implies, and the equal reluctance of governments to give guarantees to private firms for fear of charges of undue preference or of the subordination of public interests and projects to private. The second factor is the unwillingness of the Bank to finance manufacturing industries in government ownership.

A European observer, living in a mixed economy, cannot altogether share the ideological hostility of the Bank to public enterprise in manufacturing industry, although he may recognize its imperfections; and the Finance Minister—and still more the Central Bank—of an underdeveloped country may see inconveniences in relying too exclusively on private foreign investment for the development of new industries. These are large matters and cannot be fully discussed here. The Bank is much too intelligent to see the issues in black and white, and its bias rests as heavily on experience in the actual conduct of industry in underdeveloped countries as on the economic philosophy natural to Washington.

It may yet prove that, in seeking a way round these difficulties, the Bank has found a better and more economical way than direct investment of harnessing international capital to industrial development. In the past, it made quite incidental use of development banks as a channel for the financing of public utilities and agricultural development; more recently it has helped to set up development banks for the specific purpose of assisting industrialization. In doing so, it has insisted that they should not be the creatures of governments but should, as far as possible, be run either as private corporations or with representatives drawn from private industry on their Boards. It has, however, no absolute rule against providing finance through a government-owned development bank and has, for example, made loans to the Ethiopian Development Bank, which is a public institution, and to the Herstelbank, which is a mixed institution but under government control. Indeed, it would be absurd for the Bank to insist that money supplied against a government guarantee not only *should* but *must* be administered by a bank free from direct government control. There is no inconsistency in feeding capital to private industry through a government-owned financial institution and believing at the same time that industrial development is best left to private enterprise; and it would be difficult for an inter-governmental financial institution, feeding capital to private industry against government guarantees, to argue otherwise.

The major limitation on the Bank's lending is the simple requirement that its loans must be made on commercial terms. This is a requirement that the Bank has faithfully observed if we may judge from the fact that, so far, no Bank loan has ever been in default in more than a technical sense. The Bank took the view right from the start that it should charge each country the same rate of interest, irrespective of any difference in credit ratings, and it would obviously have created almost insuperable administrative difficulties to have adopted any other rule. The rate of interest payable is based on the rate that the Bank would itself have to pay currently if it were to make a bond issue of similar maturity in Wall Street. To this is added a 1 percent commission charge and ¼ percent to cover administrative costs. This yields a rate which, in recent years, has never been lower than 4 percent and never higher than 6.

These rates cannot be said to be unattractive so long as the trade of the underdeveloped countries is expanding. Each Annual Meeting sees an attack on the 1 percent commission charge; but the $100 million that it has so far brought in represents a very small liquid reserve against possible defaults on a total indebtedness over thirty times as large. The members of the Bank that are in a net creditor position can argue that they have had no dividends on their subscriptions and that the net income earned has contributed over twice as much to the Bank's reserve as the commission of 1 percent.

If one takes the view, as some economists do, that only massive capital investment can bring about rapid development of the underdeveloped countries, all this is largely irrelevant. If the underdeveloped countries cannot afford to borrow more because of the service charges involved, then these charges must be reduced. The Bank would then remain the agency through which loans were made, but the terms of the loans would be adapted to the capacity of the borrowing country to pay.

The Bank's attitude to this proposal has been that, whatever is done to help underdeveloped countries, its present relationships with those countries should not be disturbed. The Bank takes the view that capital is by no means the only stumbling-block to development and that it has been far more the lack of satisfactory projects and the lack of trained men to run them, that has prevented it from lending more. It would welcome grants or other help in supplementation of Bank loans and it is anxious to encourage a much larger volume of private loans against the credit of the borrower and aid offered by other countries individually or collectively.

SOME TECHNIQUES OF DEVELOPMENT LENDING*

I. INTRODUCTION

This paper sets forth some of the techniques of development lending which have been evolved by the World Bank in the preparation and administration of its loans for specific development projects in the less developed countries. Many of these techniques may be applicable in one form or another to other forms of development assistance (e.g. to *soft* loans or more generalized aid programs); but the paper does not attempt to cover the full range of problems arising in connection with financial aid to the underdeveloped countries.

The first step in the formulation of a program for conventional development loans to undeveloped countries is to establish the *creditworthiness* of the country concerned, i.e. its capacity to service external debt without imposing an undue strain upon its internal finances or its external balance of payments. When the limits of creditworthiness are reached, additional development assistance can be rendered effectively only if it is placed on a *soft loan* or outright grant-in-aid basis.[1] Whatever may be the repayment terms, development capital is almost always short in relation to the potential requirements of a less developed country. It is therefore a matter of vital importance to assure that the available funds are applied to the most productive uses and that development projects are executed with maximum efficiency. This paper describes ways of achieving these objectives. It should be emphasized that they do not and cannot provide a definitive body of techniques which can be applied immediately and straightforwardly in any situation. All underdeveloped countries have their own peculiarities which must be taken into account and a thorough knowledge of local conditions is essential. Moreover, statistical data are often incomplete, making more difficult the appreciation of economic problems and of the changes which are taking place in an economy. But even if all the necessary statistics are

---

*IBRD, *Some Techniques of Development Lending*, IBRD, Washington, 1960.

[1] For an analysis of the growth of the external public debt of the less developed countries from 1950–1958, see *Debt Servicing Capacity & Postwar Growth in International Indebtedness* by Dragoslav Avramovic (Baltimore, Md.: The Johns Hopkins Press, 1958) and *Debt Servicing Problems of Low-Income Countries, 1956–1958* by Dragoslav Avramovic & Ravi Gulhati (Baltimore, Md.: The Johns Hopkins Press, 1960).

available, judgment is required as well as technical analysis. The devising of policies for economic development and the selection of projects is not an exact science.

II. CREDITWORTHINESS

Creditworthiness must be considered both in connection with the project itself and in connection with the economic situation of the borrowing country. This is because the repayment of international loans requires both the accumulation of local funds and —except in certain so-called *soft* loans— their transfer into foreign exchange. If a country encounters severe foreign exchange difficulties, the repayment of all its external debt may be endangered even though the projects for which loans were originally made may have been sound.

The borrower will normally expect to use his own local currency to obtain the foreign currency needed for the service of the loan. If the project itself earns revenue, the creditworthiness of the borrower in local currency must be judged by an appraisal of the project and the financial situation of the borrower as is described later in this paper. If the project does not earn revenue directly, the servicing of the loan in local currency must depend upon some other source of revenue, usually tax revenue of the government or of a government agency. But the transfer of the debt service payment to the lender depends upon the availability of foreign exchange, which is itself determined by the country's general balance of payments situation.

Sometimes a project may itself earn foreign exchange directly, for example, by the development of a new mineral resource for export. In such a case it may be possible for the lender to obtain specific security by a lien on the foreign exchange earnings of the project itself. But in the majority of cases, even where the project does lead to increased exports, it is not possible to segregate specific foreign exchange income to provide security for the lender, and he must depend upon the adequacy of the country's foreign exchange earnings as a whole.

Clearly, therefore, the prospects for total export earnings are of major importance in assessing creditworthiness. It is true that a project may also improve the balance of payments by reducing imports rather than by increasing exports, and there is a legitimate place for this type of development. There is some danger, however, that in practice such projects may be fostered at too great a cost. Import saving projects entail in many cases some form of subsidy or tariff protection; this is a cost which must be borne by the rest of the economy including the export industries. It is therefore all the more necessary that projects of this kind should be carefully appraised since otherwise there is a danger that the direction of investment within the country will be distorted and the development of exports will be held back. In the long run, the expansion of exports is one of the most effective of all the stimuli to economic development, and the rising incomes which it brings provide the best incentive for the growth of local industries. In other words, economic development takes place most easily in a context of rising international trade; if a country's exports cease to grow, development in the rest of the economy will certainly be hampered and may even cease altogether.

In judging the ability of a country to service additional external debt the size and terms of the existing debt are clearly central factors. On the basis of comprehensive information about external debt a broad comparison can be made between the annual service payments which have to be made abroad and the growth of national income and foreign exchange earnings. Difficulties often arise, not so much from the size of the debt as from an overlarge proportion of it being at too short a term. In this event the annual burden of repayments may increase much more rapidly than foreign exchange income so that the country may eventually be forced either to reduce imports severely or—unless it is able to solicit emergency assistance—to default. It should be noted, on the other hand, that to incur long-term debt for sound development projects need not result in any substantial relative increase in a country's debt burden, if the country pursues sound foreign trade and exchange policies. Loans for productive projects will be matched by higher income and this should result in a stronger balance of payments position.

It is the level of *annual* service charges on external indebtedness which is the important magnitude. The lower the interest and the longer the term the greater the debt that can be serviced for the same annual charge. The terms on which development aid is provided are therefore of great significance. Whether for reasons connected either with the project itself or with the balance of payments, it is important that finance should be provided on terms which are not unduly burdensome. A great many development projects pay themselves out only over a long period of years but are frequently financed by short- or medium-term borrowings. These excessively short repayment terms may place serious strains upon a country's foreign exchange income, and destroy the flexibility which is required to meet vicissitudes in its external accounts. Some of the same effects may be produced in the financing of projects which governments should carry out, but which do not earn revenue to provide for debt service because the benefits accrue largely to the public. In such cases some or all of the debt burden falls within a short period upon the general budget, which is usually already overstrained with current governmental expenditures.

The behavior of a country's balance of payments is the result not only of the operation of independent economic forces but also of government policy. Since creditworthiness depends on the balance of payments, it depends also upon government policy to keep the demand for foreign exchange within the limits set by exports, invisible earnings and the proceeds of external borrowing and foreign aid. The consequences of inflation are well known; it stimulates imports and hampers exports and so may reduce foreign exchange holdings to a dangerously low level and lead to an accumulation of short- and medium- term external debt. If it continues, inflation can create a distortion of investment. In these ways, and others, inflation tends to increase the difficulty of servicing external debt.

The importance of avoiding inflation is, of course, familiar. It is as well to stress, however, that sound financial management in many underdeveloped countries demands more than the elimination of inflation. The ability of an economy to adjust to external changes is another essential element in creditworthiness. This applies particularly to countries relying for the bulk of their exports on one or a very few commodities or on those whose prices are subject to wide fluctuations. A fall in the demand for a country's exports normally sets in motion certain forces tending to restore a balance in its external accounts. However, it is generally also necessary for the government to take deliberate measures to adapt the economy to a lower level of foreign exchange income and hence an added responsibility is placed upon the government's economic and financial policies. It is in circumstances of this kind that the level of exchange reserves is of paramount importance since they can provide the vital element of time necessary for adaptive policies to take effect.

For all these reasons the financial policies of borrowing countries are of the utmost significance to lenders. If these policies are such as to endanger the repayment prospects of foreign loans, it is surely reasonable to require that the borrowing country institute measures designed to restore stability to its economy. It is not generally practicable to insist that all remedial measures which may appear necessary be completed before any further loans can be made, but it is desirable to obtain concrete evidence that the government is actually taking appropriate steps toward the re-establishment of stability.

Creditworthiness is not determined by economic forces alone; within fairly wide limits it is determined, also, by the intangible factor of the country's attitude toward its foreign debts. A country which shows a willingness to maintain debt service at the expense, if necessary, of sacrifices in consumption standards is plainly a better credit risk than a country which does not treat its foreign obligations with equal seriousness. To be sure, events have sometimes made defaults inevitable, but in such cases the attitude of the country toward its obligations, and the sort of settlement it has made or offered to its creditors, are valuable guides in judging credit for future loans. All lenders have, therefore, a direct interest in the creation and maintenance of satisfactory relations between countries and their external creditors. It is the normal practice of the World Bank, for example, to inform loan applicants who are in default on publicly-held external obligations that the Bank will be unable to assist them unless and until they take appropriate steps toward a fair and equitable settlement of their debts.

III. The Selection of Projects

Finance for development should be so directed as to make the maximum contribution to the growth of the recipient country. This is a broader objective than that which is uppermost in ordinary commercial lending. Not only must the funds be used to increase investment rather than consumption but the direction of investment as a whole must be such as to make the best use of available resources.

Ideally, therefore, development assistance should be accompanied by an appraisal of investment in all the different sectors of the recipient country. To carry out such a task adequately would be a major undertaking. Generally, however, it is possible to make some assessment of priorities in the different sectors of the economy so as to indicate where the most urgent projects may be found. In examining the different economic sectors it is useful to distinguish the basic services—transport, electric power, ports, etc.—from industry or agriculture. The problem of promoting economic development presents itself differently in these sectors; moreover, the former are frequently the responsibility of governments whereas the latter are traditionally the province of private enterprise.

As their name implies, the basic services are prerequisites for the growth of the other sectors. If one of them falls behind, a bottleneck is created, and in such a case the projects having a high priority are generally obvious. More difficult are those cases where it is thought that the expansion of certain basic services may itself stimulate other investment. A new road may well, for example, foster new industrial or agricultural activity. However, this process is by no means inevitable and the particular circumstances must be carefully studied. Instances in which the hoped-for growth has not materialized are far from unknown.

In an effort to ensure that each sector develops at the right pace and in the right way, many governments have drawn up development plans. The most important part of most of these plans is a program for public investment covering not only the basic services of an economic nature but also capital expenditure on education, health, and other social services. A program of this kind necessitates decisions by the government both on the size of the investment in the public sector which it is possible to finance and on which of the many desirable projects are to be included and which must be deferred. To take such a decision involves a careful estimate of the resources which will be available to carry out the program and an examination of the individual projects to see which of them will make the greatest contribution to the country's development.

One important problem in drawing up a public investment program is the balance between *economic* or *productive* projects and *social* projects which may be urgent and beneficial but which will not result in any immediate increase in the production of goods or services. And productive projects themselves may be either revenue-earning, such as power plants and railways, or they may be projects which, while they do increase the national income, do not produce a direct revenue to the government (such as flood control or roads). If insufficient emphasis is placed on projects in the former category, difficulties will arise in maintaining a balance in the current budget owing to rising current expenditures for the operation of the projects and for servicing debt incurred in their construction.

The task of encouraging development in the industrial sector is a more complex one than the provision of basic services. Obsolescence because of technical changes is usually more rapid; conditions for the purchase of raw materials and for marketing the finished product are usually more complex and variable; and hence the risks are greater and the demands on entrepreneurial ability are usually more exacting. The governments of less developed countries are rarely well advised to embark on industrial ventures. The numerous claims upon public funds for projects unattractive to private capital provide a strong practical reason for leaving competitive industry as much as possible to private enterprise. A clear delimitation between the spheres of public and private enterprise is one of the best ways of encouraging the investment of local capital in industry and the inflow of foreign private capital. Uncertainty about the intentions of government in this field can have an unsettling and therefore deterrent effect on enterprise. Furthermore, government participation in private industry always carries with it the possibility that decisions in government-controlled enterprises will be influenced by political considerations. Governments are by their nature subject to all kinds of pressures which it is undesirable to have carried over into the management of business enterprises. Finally, especially in the less developed countries, governments are very short of the kind of executive and administrative personnel required for the management of industrial enterprises. They usually have quite enough on their hands to supply the necessary supporting services for the private sector of the economy. If private initiative for the production of some important goods and services, or for the exploitation of some natural resources is not forthcoming, because the initial capital requirements are beyond the limits available to a private firm, then it may be preferable for the government to lend assistance through the provision of funds (e.g. through a Development Bank supported by the Treasury), or a guarantee, than to enter the field itself as an entrepreneur.

Since it is usually the small- and medium-sized enterprises which have most difficulty in finding long-term capital, a local institution which is closely in touch with conditions in the country is essential. Where these development banks exist, they also provide a channel by which foreign capital may be encouraged to enter the country. The World Bank has been active in promoting the establishment of such institutions on a basis of private ownership and administration, but usually with some government support.

Agricultural development is perhaps the most difficult of all. Here the problems of agricultural techniques, land use and land tenure, the need for agricultural extension work, etc., are far more important than the availability of capital. In some countries the problem of modernizing agricultural traditions which may go back for centuries requires what is tantamount to a social revolution. The demand for external assistance in the form of agricultural credit is usually limited, not because investment in agriculture is not beneficial, but because the necessary conditions for utilizing credit are lacking. Irrigation, flood control or land reclamation schemes, where they are possible, are exceptions, since they frequently require substantial capital outlays. Even here, however, most of the benefit goes to the farmers concerned, and the government rarely manages to obtain a return sufficient to provide the full service on the invested capital. Some part of the debt service must therefore be met from general tax revenue. No hard and fast line can be drawn as conditions vary so much from one country to another. In general, however, it could be said that the provision of basic services for agriculture, such as feeder roads to enable farmers to market their crops, irrigation, water supplies, and drainage are a proper concern of governments or public authorities while the provision of farm implements and the growing of crops or raising of stock are best left to individual farmers. Even here, however, governments frequently assist in establishing facilities for providing credit for the purchase of implements, perhaps through an agricultural development bank. Producers' cooperatives may in some countries be useful in enabling farmers collectively to do what they could not do individually. Marketing schemes and machinery pools are examples.

It will be clear from what has been said that there is no single test by which various alternative projects can be judged. In some cases, such as the expansion of a single industrial enterprise, a simple test of profitability may be sufficient, but in the field of public works and "infra-structure" projects, much more analysis is usually required. With this in mind the next section of the paper discusses some of the questions which arise in the appraisal of specific projects.

IV. THE APPRAISAL OF PROJECTS

In general, project appraisal has to answer three main questions, which involve the investigation of the project from six different points of view.

The first of these questions is: are the goods or services to be produced by the project needed by the economy for consumption or for export? In order to answer this question, the project must be investigated from the economic point of view.

The second question is: is the project properly designed and planned? To answer this question, the project must be examined from four different points of view, namely, the technical, the managerial, the organizational and the commercial.

The third question is: is the proposed method of financing the project appropriate, and (where relevant) are the earnings prospects satisfactory? This requires an examination of the project from the financial point of view.

The relative importance of these different aspects varies considerably according to the type of project involved, as is brought out in the following paragraphs, in which the six aspects are discussed in turn.

Economic Aspects

It is assumed that the sector of the economy in which the project belongs (agriculture, transportation, etc.) is of a priority which has already been established in a general review of the development needs of the economy. The economic examination of the project itself normally involves some kind of market study, the extent of which will depend on the type of project. In some cases, the study may be limited to a relatively confined area (for example, when a small power system is being considered), or at the other extreme, it may involve an analysis of the demand and supply prospects for a commodity on a world-wide scale (as for instance in the case of a large new source of iron ore).

The objective of the economic appraisal is to discover whether the project is able to earn a reasonable return on the capital which must be invested. The question of what rate of return is *reasonable* is not easy to answer, and the answer will vary from case to case. Where market forces operate freely it could be said that the new project should earn not less than the return from comparable enterprises in the country concerned. But in the case of projects which are subject to regulation because of their monopoly position (for instance, some public utilities and transport systems) this test tends to become indistinct, and resort must often be had to the application of pricing formulae to produce the desired results.

In addition to the direct return which a project may produce, there are a number of other ways in which it may contribute to economic development. One of these is the extent to which it would utilize resources, material or human, which would otherwise be idle or underemployed. Then there is the question whether the project would create conditions favorable for the establishment of related economic activities (for instance, industries supplying raw materials or processing the products of the project). The obverse of this question is the question whether the project could be successfully carried out only on condition that other developments, which were not directly a part of it, were also carried out (for instance, the establishment or expansion of a steel industry is only practical if there are adequate facilities to transport the raw materials and the finished products).

In the case of agricultural projects, an economic analysis may be required on several scales (that of the individual farmer, that on the project as a whole, and that of its effects on the whole economy).

An important aspect of the economic appraisal is a determination of the project's probable effects on a country's balance of payments, whether by way of generating increased exports or by way of import substitution. It is of course the net effect on the balance of payments which must be estimated, that is, account must be taken of possible need to import spare parts or raw materials, as well as debt service, etc. Nor should the indirect impact of the project on the balance of payments be overlooked.

In considering projects for highways or railways, particularly on a national scale, it may be necessary to compare the relative merits of different types of transportation (railways, highways, inland water transportation). Similarly, when considering projects for the development of energy sources, the relative advantages of different types of energy source may have to be examined.

Another important economic question is whether the success of the project will depend upon measures taken to protect it from competition. These may be of various kinds. The commonest type is the imposition of import duties or quotas, but there are other types of protection such as a limitation on the freedom of road transport in order to protect a railway system. Any protection should be embarked upon with care, although there are cases in which protection for a period can be justified on the classical *infant industry* grounds.

Where the project is a regulated monopoly it is necessary to investigate whether the regulatory supervision is such as to permit the sound operation and development of the project. In many cases external assistance, e.g. a loan from the Bank, will only be forthcoming if necessary changes are made in the management and regulations governing a project, as well as in its pricing policies, if these endanger the project's successful operation.

Technical Aspects

The technical side of the investigation concerns the appraisal work done by engineers and similar specialists.

One of the first things to be examined is the proposed scale of operation, which has to be viewed in relation to the results of the market study already referred to. This is of particular importance in the case of those industries which cannot be carried on economically except on a large scale (an integrated steel mill is an outstanding example). Technical appraisal will also include an investigation of the processes which it is proposed to use (and here technical obsolescence must be taken into account). It is necessary to confirm the availability of the different factors of production (raw materials, fuel, power, water, skilled and unskilled labor). The proposed location has to be considered in relation to the sources of the factors of production, to transportation, and to the markets where the products are to be sold. The layout of a project may also be very important, especially from the point of view of future expansion. The basis for the estimates of operating results must also be examined.

It is necessary to consider whether the engineering arrangements for a project are satisfactory. In many cases, especially where the type of activity involved is something new to a country, or where an organization undertakes a major expansion involving a change in the scale of its operation, it may be necessary to employ consultants to assist those responsible for the engineering arrangements. The scope of the consultants' work may need to cover one or more of the following functions: design, preparation of specifications, drafting of invitations to bid, analysis of tenders and recommendation for placing contracts, arrangements for the payment of suppliers and contractors and for the transportation of equipment, inspection and expediting of equipment, supervision of construction and installation, training or arrangement for the training of staff, and sometimes the supervision of initial operations. Where consultants are employed, it is necessary to be sure not only that the firm chosen has a good reputation and record, but also that their staff and organization are adequate.

This part of the appraisal also includes the investigation of the proposed construction schedule, which must cover all the different phases from design through installation, and must take into account the effect of seasonal variations in working conditions and so on.

The appraising engineers' work also involves the investigation of the assumptions on which the cost estimates have been calculated. The cost estimates must include adequate allowances for physical contingencies and for likely increases in the general level of costs during the construction period. Provision must also be made for interest on borrowed money during construction and for initial working capital. The cost estimates usually need to be broken down according to the amounts which will be spent locally and abroad, according to a time schedule and according to the different main elements of the project.

Each type of project has its own set of problems. There is, for instance, the question whether it is better, at a given stage in the development of an electric power system, to construct hydro plants which may combine large immediate investments with low running costs or to install thermal generating capacity, which has a lower immediate cost but a higher cost of operation. In preparing the answers to this question it is important to assume a realistic rate of interest. For hydroelectric projects, it is also necessary to check geological investigations for dam sites, and to examine hydrographical records, both in order to confirm the minimum amount of stream flow which can be relied on and to estimate the maximum amount of flood to be taken into account. The potential sedimentation of reservoirs must also be examined. In the agricultural field, one of the most important subjects for investigation is the adequacy of soil studies. In many agricultural projects, success will depend *inter alia* upon the education of farmers through extension services, and their willingness to adopt new systems of cultivation, *etc.* The system of land tenure is a question of particular importance in this respect.

There are some types of projects, particularly railroad and highway construction, in which the commencement of work need not be delayed until all the detailed engineering has been completed. In such cases, there may be a substantial margin of error in the estimate of the work to be done, and in particular of the amount of earth and rock to be moved. Allowances must be made for these uncertainties in estimating the cost.

Managerial Aspects

The appraisal of management presents peculiar difficulties. Of course, where a project is to be carried out by an existing organization much can be learned about the quality of management from a study of what has happened in the past. But it often happens that a management with a good past record may be inadequate to handle a greatly expanded operation. In particular, proper delegation of authority is sometimes difficult to obtain, and this may be due not only to unwillingness to delegate from the top but also to lack of executive ability on the second level.

The shortage of management experience and ability is one of the main difficulties standing in the way of economic development in many countries. This is compounded by the limited concept of the role of management in some countries, where it is not understood that management is much more than simply keeping a plant running. And there is often an unwillingness to employ foreigners in positions of management responsibility. One solution to this problem may be the partnership between local investors and an existing foreign organization. Another possibility is to have professional managing agents provide centralized management services for a number of different organizations.

There are, however, cases in which these solutions may not be practical, and in which the only reasonable assurance of adequate management is to import it. It may be possible to arrange for a management contract with a foreign organization, or it may be practical to employ individuals from abroad. One of the objectives of such arrangements should be that the foreigners train local people to take their places as soon as practicable.

A problem which often arises, and not only in countries which are called underdeveloped, is that of the management of government-owned enterprises. It is true that there are government enterprises which are managed efficiently; but others suffer from bad management, and in particular a lack of flexibility and of rapid decision. One possible way of solving this problem is to set up public corporations or autonomous agencies, but this in itself is no guarantee of good management, particularly when those in charge are appointed, or may be removed, for political reasons, and also where the arrangements provide for limited terms of office and militate against continuity of management.

Organizational Aspects

The organization of a project falls naturally into two phases, the organization required to bring a project to the operating stage and the organization required thereafter. The type of problem which has to be investigated here is the extent to which responsibility and authority should be centralized or delegated. This, of course, is intimately related with the scale of operations, and with their geographical extension.

One of the most important aspects of organization is the question of adequate internal controls. For management to function efficiently, an organization must be able to provide without delay information which is constantly checking performance against expectations and so bringing to light problems as they arise. It is, of course, equally important that an organization should be able to put the decisions of management into practice without undue delay.

As the scale of operation grows, functions previously combined in one part of the organization may need to be divided between separate parts. On the other hand, in certain types of projects, for instance those concerned with the development of ports and harbors, investigation may show that a number of different authorities are responsible for various aspects of what is essentially a single operation. In such cases it may be necessary to concentrate in a single authority all the functions which are integrally connected.

There are special problems of organization concerned with regulated industries, such as the electric power industry, the railroad industry, etc., in particular whether the mechanism for exercising the regulatory function (for instance, the tariff commission) is well designed to carry out its tasks, and whether it does so in practice. There are countries, for instance, where the laws provide for a rapid adjustment of permitted tariffs to compensate for types of increased cost which are beyond the control of management, but where in practice there is difficulty and delay in obtaining the necessary tariff increases.

Commercial Aspects

The commercial aspects of appraisal entail the investigation of the arrangements for buying the materials needed to construct the project and the arrangements for obtaining the raw materials, power and labor for the operation of the project and for marketing its product.

In the construction phase, the main objective is to see that the proposed arrangements will ensure that the best value is obtained for the money spent. This will normally mean that the arrangements should provide effective competition between potential suppliers and contractors. The best way to ensure this is usually international competitive bidding. It is, of course, true that there are exceptions to this. For example, it may be most economic to standardize on the basis of existing equipment in order to reduce both the investment in spare parts and the cost of maintenance; and sometimes competition may be inappropriate, as in the case of manufacture under license.

It is necessary to investigate whether those responsible for the project have the necessary knowledge and experience to reach the best decisions about the way in which the available money is to be spent. In many cases, they need outside help, which can be provided by consultants.

The investigation of this aspect of the project at the operating stage involves the proposed arrangements for obtaining raw materials, power, etc., and for marketing the products of the project. Among other things, this will involve investigation of the terms of purchase and sale, which will have an important bearing on the amount of working capital required.

Some of the most difficult problems in this field arise in connection with regulated industries, and in particular with the electric power industry. Two questions are generally at issue here. The first is whether the prices which the organization concerned is permitted to charge will give it adequate revenue. This question is discussed below in connection with the financial aspects of appraisal. The second question is whether the structure of rates charged is appropriate to the different types of traffic or customer concerned.

Financial Aspects

The financial investigation usually falls into two parts: that concerned with the amount of money required to bring the project into operation and with the sources from which this money is to be obtained, and that concerned with the operating costs and revenue and the prospective liquidity in the operating phase. In order to explain this approach fully, the main outline of the following paragraphs assumes a project which is to be carried out by an organization already engaged in operations, and already earning revenue. After the financial investigation of a project of this type has been sketched, the variations for other types of projects will be considered.

The first question is: how much money will be needed? Requirements will include some or all of the following items:

(a) cost of goods and services for the project itself
(b) allowances for escalation and contingencies
(c) interest on borrowed funds during construction

In addition account has to be taken of the financial position of the other activities of the enterprise, which during the construction of the project might make a net contribution to the requirements of the project or might give rise to additional cash requirements. Finally allowance has to be made for the working capital required when the project starts operations.

Many projects have got into difficulty because of a lack of adequate working capital. The estimation of working capital requirements has to be based on reasonable assumptions concerning the amount of stocks, raw materials, spare parts, etc.; the terms on which products are sold, which will indicate the amount of receivables to be financed; and the amount of funds necessary to take care of swings in payments and receipts, taking into account any seasonal variations in production or sales.

The sources from which it is planned to meet the financial requirements will normally include funds (depreciation and undistributed earnings) generated from operations. They may also include the proceeds of the issue of share capital, and part of the funds will normally be provided by borrowings at long-term, short-term, or both. In many projects, there may also be provision for public funds from central or local budgetary sources.

The importance of retained earnings as a source of finance in countries where capital is scarce and the rate of savings low must be underlined. It is recognized in many countries by existing tax legislation, but there are countries where regulated industries, particularly the electric power industry, have been unable to generate funds from operations to meet an adequate proportion of the costs of new construction.

The next step in the financial analysis is to prepare projections of two kinds:

(a) estimates of cash receipts and expenditures, from which it can be seen whether funds will be available at the right time to meet the expected requirements; and
(b) periodical balance sheets which show the financial situation of the organization during the construction period.

These projections, together with projections of earnings, then have to be carried on into the operating period to show the likely financial results of the operation. In these forecasts account must be taken of the time required to overcome initial operating difficulties and the rate at which the market may be able to absorb production. Corresponding calculations will have to be made of the growth in the amount of working capital required.

With these forecasts in hand, the investigator has to form various judgments. He has to satisfy himself that there will be no shortage of funds during the construction period and that the financial situation at the end of the period will meet the requirements of sound financial principles. He has to judge whether the expected revenue from operations represents a reasonable return on the capital invested, whether there is an adequate margin in the funds generated by operations to meet fixed financial obligations, and in many cases whether revenue will be adequate to establish reserves needed for sound operation and possibly for future expansion.

In the light of these judgments, the investigator should be able to say whether the proposed financing plan is sound, or whether some change is necessary. He should, in addition, be able to formulate the conditions upon which money should be made available for the project. The object of these conditions will be, among other things, to ensure that subsequent action on the part of the management will not jeopardize the soundness of the financial situation and prospects. This may involve placing limitations on future borrowing and on distributing cash dividends, *etc.* It may also be necessary to make arrangements for security, and for the provision of additional funds in case they are needed. With public utilities, it may be desirable to obtain an undertaking that adequate rates will be sought not only to meet the expenses of operation and financial obligations, but in addition to provide funds toward the cost of future construction.

There are various types of projects to which an analysis in the form described cannot appropriately be applied. This is true, for instance, of projects which do not earn revenue, such as highways (except toll roads), irrigation projects where no direct payment is made for the water, etc. Particular problems arise in the case of multipurpose projects, where the allocation of costs to the different functions which the project serves must always be to some extent arbitrary.

Where the benefits of a project (say for highways) cannot be measured precisely, estimates have to be made, for instance, of the decreased cost of road transportation, the increase in the amount of farm products which can be brought to market in good condition, the yield from new farming areas which may be opened up, etc. Moreover, it is generally necessary to assess separately the potential benefits at different levels, i.e., to the individual farmer, and to local or central government authorities. Even in the case of a revenue-earning project, such as an irrigation scheme in which a charge for water is made, a deficit on the project operation should be more than offset by increased revenue on growing production and commerce.

In this connection the habit of governments of not accounting separately for capital and current expenditures often obscures the real results of government enterprise. There are also cases where a government makes money available either at very low cost, or as equity on which no return is expected, for projects which earn revenue. If the revenue is not adequate to provide a reasonable return on the funds invested, it must be recognized that the recipients of the services or goods provided are being subsidized by the general taxpayer. On the other hand, there have been cases of industrial enterprises clearly unable to stand on their own feet, being started by private capital on the promise of a high protective tariff or a special tax regime. In such cases the general consumer or the taxpayer is providing a subsidy, not for the benefit of the private investor, but as the price for accelerating industrialization.

V. THE SUPERVISION OF PROJECTS

Experience shows that, at least for a lender, there are strong arguments against the method, at first sight attractive, of supervising a project by means of a resident representative. The main disadvantage of this type of supervision is the risk that the lender will unintentionally but inevitably become involved in management decisions which should be the responsibility of those running the project. On the other hand, there are risks involved in depending exclusively on written reports submitted by the borrower. Such written reports are certainly necessary for the efficient management of the project, and should therefore be readily available without the need for special procedures. It is, however, often the case that the management and organization responsible for the project are not sufficiently experienced or sophisticated to realize the importance of such reports or to be able to produce them, and consequently the lender may be obliged to specify the reports required. It is desirable to confirm the information provided by these reports by periodical visits to the project, which also provde an opportunity to discuss problems which have arisen or may be foreseen.

The kind of reports required will, of course, depend upon the type of project, but in general their function is to provide up-to-date information at reasonably frequent intervals which will show how the actual progress of the project compares with the physical and financial forecasts which were the basis for the decision to undertake it. This will apply both during the construction period and during the operating period, although, of course, the contents of the reports will be quite different in the two periods.

ADDITIONAL READINGS

Annual Reports, Export-Import Bank, Washington.
Annual Reports, IDA, Washington.
Annual Reports, Inter-American Development Bank, Washington.

Annual Reports, World Bank, Washington.

Avramovic, Dragoslav, *Economic Growth and External Debt,* Baltimore: Johns Hopkins, 1964.

—— and Gulhati, Ravi, *Debt Servicing Problems of Low-Income Countries, 1956–1958,* Baltimore: Johns Hopkins, 1960.

Baldwin, David, "The International Development Association: Theory and Practice," *Economic Development and Cultural Change,* October, 1961, pp. 86–96.

Friedman, W., *Methods and Policies of Principal Donor Countries in Public International Development Financing—A Preliminary Appraisal,* New York: Columbia University Law School, 1962.

Heilbroner, Robert L., "This Growing World: Economic Development and the World Bank," *Public Affairs Pamphlet No. 237,* Public Affairs Committee, Inc., New York, 1956.

International Flow of Long-Term Capital and Official Donations, 1951–1959, United Nations, New York, 1961.

Mikesell, Raymond F. (ed.), *U. S. Private and Government Investment Abroad,* University of Oregon, Eugene, 1962.

Morris, James, *The Road To Huddersfield: A Journey to Five Continents,* New York: Pantheon, 1963.

Paauw, Douglas S., *Financing Economic Development, the Indonesian Case,* Glencoe: Free Press, 1962.

Pincus, John A., "The Cost of Foreign Aid," *Review of Economics and Statistics,* November, 1963, pp. 360–367.

Policies and Operations of the World Bank, IFC and IDA, World Bank, Washington, 1962.

Stewart, Charles T., "Loans vs Grants," *Challenge,* January, 1964, pp. 4–10.

The International Bank for Reconstruction and Development: 1946–1953, Baltimore: Johns Hopkins, 1954.

The World Bank Group in Africa, World Bank, Washington, 1963.

The World Bank Group in Asia, World Bank, Washington, 1963.

The World Bank Group in the Americas, World Bank, Washington, 1963.

Thome, B., "The World Bank and Private Enterprise," *Skandinaviska Banken Quarterly Review,* April, 1961, pp. 33–38.

Wilson, Geoffrey M., "World Bank Operations," *The Fund and Bank Review,* June, 1964, pp. 15–25.

part C

FINANCING FOREIGN IN-VESTMENTS AND OPERATIONS

chapter *9*

Aspects and Trends in International Capital and Money Markets

Multinational firms, by definition, satisfy their capital needs from the optimum sources, taking into account the attendant risks and costs at any given time and place. This applies to short-term as well as to medium and long-term capital. It also applies to each operating entity of the company, individually, as well as to the parent company. Each subsidiary will have its own set of local conditions for raising capital, based on the tax laws, the characteristics of the money and capital markets, the exchange controls, the governmental controls on capital issues, interest rates, banking customs, etc. On the other hand, the parent company cannot give complete autonomy to each subsidiary to suboptimize the matter of raising capital. A central coordinating policy for capital acquisition is as important as that for capital expenditures. Only the central office is in a position to weigh the possibilities of intracorporate capital flows, and to measure the total corporate exposure to risks of devaluation, shifts of foreign exchange regulations and changes in interest rates in different markets. The international financial manager must, therefore, have a broad range of competence and understanding not only of the internal workings of the various money and capital markets in which his firm is operating, or to which he has access, but also to the interactions between the markets.

The markets for short-term funds have, in postwar years, become highly interdependent. This is true partially because advances in technology have made trading in foreign exchange highly efficient. But in addition, to facilitate international trade, the nations of Western Europe lifted controls on the movement of short-term funds at the earliest possible date. The countries then tended to rely upon monetary policy (as noted in Chapter 1) as a means of controlling undesirably large flows of short-term money. The early reductions of restrictions on short-term capital was made possible also, by the persistent deficits in the U.S. balance of payments.

These same deficits furthermore gave rise to a recent phenomenon, the Eurodollar. This new creature in international finance is of keen interest not only to U.S. banks and their overseas branches or subsidiaries, but also to multinational corporations which might find Eurodollars to be a source of less costly, short-term (and even medium-term) capital. Two of the readings in this chapter discuss the Eurodollar—its origin, its characteristics, its users and its effects.

A more recent question, however, is whether the disappearance of the deficit in the U.S. balance of payments will cause a dryingup of the Euro-dollar. Do Eurodollars depend upon these deficits, or, having established themselves as a desirable and useful tool in international finance, will their utilization persist?

While the deficit in the U.S. balance of payments tended to create an interdependence of markets for short-term funds, it initially had little effect on integrating the world's capital markets. It has, in fact, more recently had the effect of widening the separation between these markets. The separation and isolation of the various capital markets of Western Europe has continued not so much because of each country's balance of payments position, but because the markets tend to be too thin and too inefficient to handle foreign flotations as well as the domestic. One U.S. banker has confided, for example, that if its Belgian branch should attempt to unload even as little as $1 million of Belgian government securities at one time, it would disrupt the market and send prices tumbling. The branch consequently restricts itself to trading not more than about $100,000 per day.

Why are these capital markets so thin, resulting in governmental controls limiting access to them? It is partially a question of the amount of saving which takes place and the uses to which these savings are put. This aspect is discussed in some detail in the article by John D. Hogan. There is also a question of custom and related tax laws in many of the West European countries, as a result of which most of the rapid expansion of business enterprises is financed out of internal sources, that is, from depreciation and retained earnings. At the same time, most of the external financing tends to be done via bank credit, as opposed to public offerings of securities. In recent years, shrinking profit margins have often decreased internal sources of financing, and bank credit has not been able to make up the difference. The thin capital markets are thus strained to provide the additional expansion funds. Meanwhile, the private sector must compete with the capital needs of the government or government-owned enterprises, so borrowers must often queue up to secure access to the capital market. It is little wonder, then, that most governments maintained restrictions against foreign borrowers and that they sought more and more to make use of the highly efficient New York capital market, until they were cut off by the U.S. Government's interest equalization tax.

As mentioned earlier, one of the reasons for the thinness of the European capital markets is the preference of Europeans for keeping their assets liquid, or invested in real property. History, unfortunately, has too often proved them right. One of the recent innovations in international finance, to combat this situation and to widen and integrate the capital markets, has been the use of the "unit of account" as the denomination of security issues. The unit of account and its role are discussed in one of the following readings. Its use has had a mixed reception, a practical difficulty being that it is not readily understood by investors. Dollar issues are simpler and European investors are aware that the dollar's value has shrunk less than that of any other currency. As an official of Kuhn, Loeb & Company remarked, "It is the dollar sign which enables issues to travel far and wide, sometimes with administrative inconveniences, but nonetheless ultimately to reach investor portfolios in near and far-off places. The dollar has served as the essential integrating element in the functioning of the international capital market at a moment when this market had to adjust itself to new forces of fragmentation which were acting upon it."

Still, the dollar has lost some of its luster and a reorganization of the international monetary system may detract even more from its importance. The European unit of account may very well then be ready to step in as a supplement. The Luxembourg branch of Belgian's Kredietbank has, for several years, been accepting short-term deposits in European units of account so as to help create a market in the unit and to build a structural mechanism to handle loans. It has also lent these units to other financial institutions for relending at short-term, to multinational organizations which wish to take advantage of the slightly lower interest rate.

The unit of account may thus have important applications in the near future, for European companies with a multinational character. A Lyon-based company, for example, with subsidiaries in Madrid, Istanbul, Rome, and Copenhagen, could raise money for its needs in any one of many currencies through unit of account financing, without placing any undue pressure on the Paris market or an undesirable demand upon the French franc.

The last article in this chapter discusses the operations of the various European and Japanese stock exchanges, and traces the history of stock prices in these individual markets. A recent innovation not mentioned in the article is the action taken by the Japanese government, in 1964, to influence stock prices by direct support of the market. Thus, the Bank of Japan (the central bank) is making special, low-interest rate loans to securities firms to enable them to buy stocks to buoy the market, while the Ministry of Finance is making available an unlimited amount of credit to the Japanese Joint Securities Company, a private buying pool created to defend market prices. This company enters the market when the "average" slips below a certain index number. Is this an experiment which may be reenacted in other countries in the future?

RECENT INNOVATIONS IN EUROPEAN CAPITAL MARKETS*

In his foreword to a study of European capital markets prepared by the United States Treasury in late 1963, Secretary of the Treasury Dillon noted that many of the factors that have tended to limit the growth of these markets "are now receiving the attention of financial leaders in Europe," and that "progress toward improving the efficiency of these markets has begun." In particular, the Secretary noted that:

> Several possible means of promoting international security issues, thereby broadening the potential market and bringing together large aggregations of underwriting support and distribution facilities, are being actively explored. . . . New initiatives are being taken to eliminate barriers to foreign security offerings and to facilitate the use of the most developed markets within Europe as a kind of financial entrepôt for the use of borrowers and lenders of other nations.[1]

The current renewal of European interest in long-term lending, the increasing interdependence of European financial centers, and the movements of capital between those centers can be traced back to the return to convertibility of the major European currencies at the end of 1958. They were given added impetus by the progress in relaxing restrictions on capital transactions made by most European countries during the last few years. But the marked increase in the volume and types of foreign issues in European capital markets during the past year and a half—the subject of this article—was sparked by two more specific developments: in July 1963, President Kennedy proposed to Congress the imposition of an "interest equalization tax" on purchases of foreign securities by United States residents;[2] and at about this

* *Monthly Review,* Federal Reserve Bank of New York, January, 1965, pp. 9–15. John Hein had primary responsibility for the preparation of the article.

[1] "A Description and Analysis of Certain European Capital Markets," Paper No. 3 of *Economic Policies and Practices,* Materials Prepared for the Joint Economic Committee, Congress of the United States, 1964, p. xi.

[2] The tax—which was enacted in September 1964, retroactive to July 1963—applies to foreign stocks and bonds, both new and outstanding, purchased from nonresidents. It specifically exempts, however, securities of international organizations of which the United States is a member, governments of less developed countries, and corporations whose principal activities are in such countries. New Canadian issues are also exempt by special Executive Order. The tax is 15 percent on stock and other equity interests. On debt obligations (of three years or more) it ranges from 2.75 to

same time the British authorities were preparing the way for greater international use of the London capital market. These two developments had the effect of diverting new securities issues of industrial countries from the New York market, which had been heavily utilized by such borrowers. Concurrently, the international financial scene began to display some novel and noteworthy features, to be discussed here: the re-emergence of London as an important center for the underwriting of foreign issues; the growth of dollar issues placed outside the United States; the increase in foreign issues in Continental markets, especially Germany; the flotation of loans denominated in the so-called "unit of account"; the proposed flotation of different tranches of an issue in several centers; and increased international cooperation among financial institutions.

FOREIGN ISSUES IN THE LONDON MARKET

Participation by residents of the United Kingdom in foreign securities issues denominated in currencies other than sterling remains severely limited by present British exchange controls. But this has not prevented the City of London from expanding the scale of its brokerage and underwriting activities, frequently in close cooperation with European banking houses. Its highly efficient machinery has enabled it to bring together borrowers and lenders in the underwriting of foreign issues.

As far back as October 1962 the London financial community, with the encouragement of the Bank of England, began to consider ways and means of acting as middle-man between foreign borrowers and lenders. The objective was greater use of the City's capital market facilities without triggering substantial additional capital outflows from the United Kingdom to nonsterling countries. Loans of foreign-owned funds to foreign borrowers arranged in the London market have no adverse effect on the British balance of payments; in fact, they provide invisible earnings from the City's banking services, and quite possibly additional exports. Thus in early October 1962 the Governor of the Bank of England declared:

> The time has now come when the City once again might well provide an international capital market where the foreigner cannot only borrow long-term capital but where, equally important, he will once again wish to place his long-term investment capital. This entrepôt business in capital, if I may so describe it, would not only serve this country well but would

---

15 percent, according to the remaining maturity, and is so calculated as to increase by about 1 percentage point the interest cost to foreigners of obtaining capital in this market. The legislation does not extend to bank loans made to foreigners in the ordinary course of banking operations, but grants stand-by authority to the President to apply the tax to such loans of over one year, if he should find that they "are being used to circumvent the purpose of the legislation."

fill a vital and vacant role in Europe in mobilizing foreign capital for world economic development. It would be to the advantage of British industry in financing our customers.[3]

Specific moves in this direction were announced in the April 1963 budget, which included provisions for lowering the stamp tax on stock transfers and for the issuing of bearer, as well as registered, securities. The tax on bearer securities, previously set at 6 percent of the nominal value, was reduced to 3 percent of market value on securities issued by residents and to 2 percent on those issued by nonresidents. For registered securities, the rate was reduced from 2 percent to 1 percent (calculated at market value). Bearer issues had generally been prohibited since World War II, for exchange-control reasons.

These changes, which became effective in August 1963, and the general encouragement of foreign issues by the British authorities have resulted in a considerable expansion in the use of the London capital market by Continental European countries and Japan. Most of this activity has taken the form of dollar operations in which British financial institutions have acted as underwriters, gathering dollar funds owned by non-United States residents and putting them to work in longer term loans. (Previously, such funds might of course have been attracted into foreign issues floated in New York.) In a few cases, other nonsterling currencies have been used as well, and some issues have been denominated in sterling. (Countries belonging to EFTA—the European Free Trade Association, of which the United Kingdom is a member —have been given the right to raise loans in London in either sterling or foreign currencies.)

These foreign issues began in May 1963 with a private placing by the Belgian Government of $20 million in three-year bonds, the first loan not denominated in sterling placed in London since World War II; a second similar Belgian placement followed in December 1963. Meanwhile, another important issue occurred in July 1963, when a London merchant bank agreed to float —jointly with three banks in Belgium, Germany, and the Netherlands—a $15 million issue of a private Italian company engaged in operating and maintaining Italy's new national highway system. This issue attracted considerable attention as the first postwar nongovernmental (although government-guaranteed) issue in a foreign currency to be floated in London. The first postwar offering of sterling bearer bonds by a nonsterling-area country followed in August 1963 in the form of a £5 million refunding issue by the Government of Japan.

On the occasion of the Lord Mayor's dinner in October 1963—one year after the Governor of the Bank of England had called for the re-establishment of the City of London as a financial entrepôt—the Chancellor of the Exchequer

---

[3] Speech delivered at dinner given by the Lord Mayor to the Bankers and Merchants of the City of London, October 3, 1962.

praised the London market for its contribution to invisible earnings in Britain's balance of payments and declared that "for the future, foreign currency loans, i.e., those which are no drain on the reserves, are being allowed almost without restriction." The Chancellor thus indicated that the authorities were satisfied with the initial response of the City, but also that they were not yet ready to permit a further relaxation of controls over the outflow of British funds to the nonsterling world. This also meant that the proceeds of sterling loans raised by nonsterling-area borrowers were to be spent on purchases of goods and services in the United Kingdom, but such loans have in fact been negligible.

Since late 1963, British underwriters have arranged in the London market a fairly continuous series of nonsterling issues, all but one of which have been denominated in dollars.[4] In this connection it is worth recalling that London has an underwriting mechanism developed over a period of about 150 years and can provide quotation on Europe's largest stock exchange. Furthermore, various recent British steps, such as the resumption of bearer securities, should go a long way toward inducing international investors to make use of London's financial facilities. Finally, the London market has shown its ability to attract funds from a number of financial centers for investment in securities issued by borrowers with excellent international credit standing.

In the past year or so, British financial institutions have also participated in the sizable amount of dollar issues outside the United States that were arranged and underwritten by consortia headed by banks on the European Continent or by United States underwriters. Several of these issues have subsequently obtained quotation on the London Stock Exchange, and some have also been listed on the New York Stock Exchange, which permits the listing of certain foreign issues even when no distribution takes place to United States investors. New dollar issues outside the United States and underwritten by institutions in London and other centers rose from $35 million in the second half of 1963 to $330 million in January–June 1964 and amounted to an additional $180 million in the second half of 1964. About two thirds of this grand total of $545 million was arranged and placed in the London market. These bonds have generally been of 15 to 20 years' maturity, carrying a 5½ to 6½ percent coupon. The major borrowers have been governments, municipalities, and industrial firms of the Scandinavian countries, Finland, and Japan, with Japanese issues alone accounting for some $132 million or 24 percent of the total (see Table 1).

---

[4] The exception was a 60 million Swiss franc loan floated by the city of Copenhagen in October 1963. This issue met with objections by the Swiss authorities. Its denomination in Swiss francs was regarded as interfering with Swiss controls over domestic liquidity and new issues in the Swiss market, and as contributing—to an undesirable degree—to the use of the Swiss franc as an international currency. A $25 million loan by IRI, the Italian state holding company, in June 1964 could be subscribed to (and issued) in either dollars or German marks.

TABLE 1

UNITED STATES DOLLAR ISSUES IN EUROPE
July 1963 – December 1964

Borrower or Country of Borrower	Amount (Millions of Dollars)	Number of Issues	Comment
Japan	132.0	10	$22.5 million by city of Tokyo; remainder by private industry
Denmark	107.0	8	All by public sector or nationalized industries
Norway	92.0	7	All by public sector or nationalized industries
Italy	50.0	3	$25 million by state holding company; $15 million by national highway system; $10 million five-year issue by official long-term lending institution
European Coal and Steel Community	30.0	1	
Austria	28.0	2	$18 million by government; $10 million by nationalized steel company
Finland	26.0	3	All by private industry
European Investment Bank	25.0	1	
Belgium	20.0	1	Privately placed three-year government issue
Portugal	20.0	1	National government
Council of Europe	10.0	2	European Resettlement Fund
Israel	5.0	1	Private development corporation
Total	545.0	40	

Foreign Issues in Continental Markets

In addition to dollar issues arranged and placed on the European Continent, there has been a rise recently in foreign issues floated in certain Continental European markets and denominated in national currencies. The most noteworthy development in this respect has been the sharp increase in foreign issues in Germany. Such issues (all of which were denominated in German marks) rose to nearly $225 million equivalent last year, from only $40 million in 1963 and $25 million in 1962. As in the case of dollar-denominated issues placed in Europe, the bulk of the foreign loans floated in Germany was accounted for by Scandinavian, Finnish, and Japanese borrowers, with Japan alone taking $75 million or one third of the total (see Table 2). The remainder consisted of issues by international institutions, including

TABLE 2

FOREIGN ISSUES IN GERMANY IN 1964

Borrower or Country of Borrower	Amount (Millions of Dollar Equivalent)	Number of Issues	Comment
Japan	75.0	2	$50 million by government; $25 million by city of Osaka
Finland	47.5	4	$23 million by government; rest by long-term lending institutions
European Coal and Steel Community	25.0	1	
European Investment Bank	20.0	1	
Denmark	18.8	1	City of Copenhagen
Inter-American Development Bank	15.0	1	
Eurofima	12.5	1	Company established by sixteen European national railway administrations to finance rolling stock
Norway	10.0	1	City of Oslo
Total	223.8	12	

the Inter-American Development Bank. Again, as in the case of European dollar issues, these German mark loans generally are bonds of 15 or 20 years' maturity carrying a $5\frac{1}{2}$ to $6\frac{1}{2}$ percent coupon.

This record activity in the German market seems to have been stimulated not only by the United States interest equalization tax, but also by proposed German legislation. In order to curb the inflow of long-term capital and thereby alleviate the German payments surplus, the German authorities in March 1964 proposed a 25 percent withholding tax on nonresidents' interest income from German bonds. It was announced subsequently, however, that the tax—which has not yet been enacted—would not apply to income from German mark issues of foreign borrowers. This provision greatly stimulated demand for such issues, presumably to a large extent by foreigners (who during the second quarter sold sizable amounts from their German domestic bond holdings). It also enabled foreign borrowers to place their issues in the German market on somewhat more favorable terms than German borrowers could receive. In addition, the German authorities have proposed abolition of the $2\frac{1}{2}$ percent tax which foreign and private domestic borrowers currently have to pay on new issues; this should further facilitate the placement of foreign securities on the German market.

In France, where no issues by borrowers outside the franc area had been permitted since World War II, the authorities in November 1963 announced their intention to authorize the reopening of the capital market to foreign borrowers. Such issues (whose proceeds are to be spent largely in France) initially have been limited to international institutions. Accordingly, in December 1963 the European Investment Bank was able to place a 60 million franc ($12 million) issue with French insurance companies and other institutional investors. This was followed in July 1964 by a 150 million franc ($30 million) flotation of the European Coal and Steel Community. In Belgium— where until 1960 most foreign issues were those of the Congolese colonial authorities and of companies active in the Congo—the European Investment Bank in December 1963 made a further private placement of 400 million francs ($8 million).

Some European countries, such as the Netherlands and Switzerland, have of course long been substantial exporters of long-term capital. But the Netherlands closed its market to foreign borrowers in 1963, and except for two issues totaling 55 million guilders ($15 million) by the European Investment Bank and the European Coal and Steel Community the market remained closed in 1964 as well. This decision largely reflected the desire of the Dutch authorities to prevent the capital outflow and the upward pressures on domestic interest rates that might have resulted from foreign flotations. And in Switzerland, which maintains strict controls over all new issues, a heavy demand for capital by domestic borrowers led the authorities to adopt a somewhat stricter attitude toward foreign issues. As a result the 379 million francs ($88 million) of such issues authorized last year was noticeably below the 588 million francs ($136 million) permitted in 1963.

NEW TYPES OF FOREIGN ISSUES IN EUROPE

The search for ways to attract long-term funds into foreign issues led at one time to the flotation of bonds denominated in European "units of account." However, there have been only six such issues, totaling $68 million, and none has been floated since April 1964 (see Table 3). The issues, with maturities ranging between 15 and 20 years and coupons between $5\frac{1}{2}$ and 6 percent, were generally offered in Luxembourg, with a Belgian or Luxembourg bank heading the underwriting syndicate. United States underwriters participated in two issues.

Units of account, which were first used in the bookkeeping of the former European Payments Union,[5] are a composite of seventeen European curren-

---

[5] The European Payments Union was established in 1950 under the aegis of the Organization for European Economic Cooperation, and continued to function until the advent of convertibility at the end of 1958. It was designed to achieve transferability of the currencies of its seventeen members through monthly settlements of each member's current payments with the other members as a group. The net debtor or creditor positions resulting from the clearing were expressed in "units of account" (1 unit = 0.888671 grams of fine gold = US$1) and were settled partly in gold or dollars and partly by credits granted to or received from the Union.

TABLE 3

UNIT-OF-ACCOUNT ISSUES

Borrower	Amount (Millions of Dollar Equivalent)	Date	Comments
SACOR (Portugal)........	5.0 5.0	February 1961 May 1962	Partly state-owned oil refinery
Norges Kommunalbank (Norway).....................	12.0	January 1963	State-owned long-term credit institution
Imatran Voima (Finland)...................	5.0	July 1963	State-owned electric-power company
Cassa per il Mezzo-giorno (Italy)..............	18.0	October 1963	Official development fund for southern Italy
Banco de Fomento Nacional (Portugal)......	13.0	November 1963	Official development bank
Greater Copenhagen (Denmark)...................	10.0	April 1964	Seven Copenhagen municipalities
Total..............	68.0		

cies. They serve as a common denominator for issues floated in several markets and provide a limited guarantee against exchange rate changes for debtors and creditors with liabilities and claims in foreign currencies.

The unit of account is an entirely artificial yardstick that is used solely to measure the value of contractual loan obligations. It is not a means of exchange, but is designed to minimize exchange risks by keeping the value of claims and liabilities as constant as possible. As under the European Payments Union, each of the seventeen Western European currencies that are included—the so-called reference currencies—bears a fixed relationship to the unit of account through its own gold/dollar parity as communicated to the International Monetary Fund.[6] Since its appearance in early 1961, the unit-of-account formula has taken a number of different forms. It has always provided that the value of the unit would change only if the values of all seventeen reference currencies changed; however, under the terms of the more recent loan agreements at least two-thirds of these changes must be in the same direction. Under these conditions, the value of the unit—and hence of the securities denominated in these units—would be adjusted, after a lapse of two years, in the same direction and proportion as the currency among the two-thirds (or more) that had changed the least. The protection afforded by this complex formula is of course not absolute. It does not cover the

[6] Thus, one unit of account equals 0.357 pound sterling or 4 German marks or 4.937 French francs, and so on.

borrower if his currency is devalued, or the lender if his is revalued, vis-à-vis all the others.

Belgian bankers who are the original sponsors of this new means of financing—in particular Fernand Collin of the Kredietbank—readily admit that "the system is not simple and certainly not for people who are unfamiliar with monetary problems." The scheme "had to be complicated, because every possibility had to be foreseen—even those that will probably never occur,"[7] but it was hoped such a multicurrency unit would provide a means of weaning the Continental investor away from his preference for local issues (or for the hoarding of gold).

It is important to note that all unit-of-account issues have been floated by either nationalized companies or private companies in which the government is the main shareholder. Moreover, in four of the issues (the second through fifth in Table 3) payment of interest and principal is guaranteed by the government—which adds to the attraction that such issues may have for the lender. The borrower can probably raise funds in this fashion in larger amounts and on more favorable terms than in any one national capital market, but he can also incur commitments in foreign currencies that few private borrowers may wish to take on.[8]

An additional procedure that would permit foreign borrowers to obtain a larger amount of savings than could be tapped in any one Continental market has been proposed though not yet implemented. This is the so-called European parallel loan, which would involve the simultaneous flotation on different markets of different tranches of an issue, with each tranche denominated in the national currency of the country in which it is placed. This proposal was put forward in the fall of 1963 by Hermann J. Abs of the Deutsche Bank. In Mr. Abs' view,

> each individual loan could be raised within the limits of each country's financing capacity in different amounts varying between the equivalents of, let us say, $5, $10, $20, or even $50 million. In spite of their plurality, the European capital markets could then represent themselves as one market well capable of raising a total amount not falling short of that which the United States market could provide.[9]

---

[7] F. Collin, "Europe's Unit of Account," *Statist,* February 28, 1964, p. 635.

[8] Another type of bond issue that, in a very limited sense, can be compared to unit-of-account financing was offered in Europe in 1964. These are issues with an exchange option, which entitles the lender to request payment of interest and amortization in one or more currencies, including or excluding the currency in which the issue is denominated. The Finnish Government borrowed 40 million marks ($10 million) in Germany on this basis, with investors having the option of receiving payment in marks or dollars; and the city of Turin raised £4 million ($11 million) in London, with a repayment option in sterling or German marks. Although this issue was denominated in sterling, subscriptions had to be paid for in external sterling, i.e., sterling held by nonsterling-area residents, which for all practical purposes is like any other foreign currency for British investors.

[9] Hermann J. Abs, "Parallel Loans to Mobilize Continental Funds," *The Times* (London), March 11, 1964.

In such issues, the terms and conditions of all tranches would be as uniform as possible. Variations in the issue price would take account of differences in long-term rates in the different markets. Since this type of issue is largely designed to appeal to institutional investors—such as insurance companies and pension funds—that are limited to or prefer investment of their funds in securities denominated in their national currencies, the risk is reduced that investor demand would tend to concentrate on the highest-yielding tranche.[10]

CONCLUDING OBSERVATIONS

The recent growth in foreign issues in European capital markets suggests that Europe may eventually become again an important exporter of long-term capital. It will be recalled that prior to 1914 Europe played a key role in this respect and made a major contribution to the early development of public facilities (such as transportation) in Eastern Europe, the Western Hemisphere, and other then-underdeveloped countries. Subsequently, Europe's ability to function as a long-term capital exporter was curbed by a series of events—World War I and its aftermath, the economic disturbances of the 1930's, World War II, the needs of postwar reconstruction and, finally, the unprecedented investment boom in Europe itself. In the past year and a half, however, Europe has been able to increase markedly the volume of its foreign lending, partly as a result of the capital market techniques described in this article. These have the common characteristic of making it possible to mobilize the resources of several European financial centers at one time, with the issues expressed in dollars or in other currencies that have considerable investor appeal across national frontiers.

However, it is generally true that the net benefit of the international movement of capital will be more nearly assured if capital can move equally freely among different countries. To the extent that countries retain controls over foreign issues in their markets as well as over investor participation in issues abroad, the burden of providing capital internationally is shifted largely to other countries. And, in these countries, long-term funds may tend to flow out at times and in ways that create difficulties at home for the national authorities. In other words, the new types of financing described here, whatever their merits, cannot be considered a substitute for a more far-reaching development and strengthening of freer national capital markets. Although it is likely that recent foreign borrowings in Europe have attracted some long-

[10] A variant of this type of financing, actually used in two Belgian issues in 1960 and 1961, is an exchange-option issue in which the investor has the choice of subscribing in one of the currencies included in the option, in addition to the choice as to interest and amortization payments. Investors in countries whose currency is so included could then consider the bonds as denominated in their national currency.

term European funds over and above those that ordinarily would have participated in such issues in the New York market, the increased international capital flows within Europe have perhaps been stimulated more by the novel (and, to investors, attractive) features of these issues than by a genuine broadening of the individual European markets themselves.

Such a broadening requires the easing or removal of a host of inhibiting factors—legislative, institutional, and psychological—that still characterize various foreign markets. These factors not only tend to bar the flow or capital between countries, but also to limit the efficiency, growth, and diversification of domestic capital markets in general. Such factors, of course, vary in nature and degree of applicability from country to country. They include exchange controls, discriminatory treatment of foreign borrowers, strict regulations governing the composition of the portfolios of institutional investors (which often discriminate against foreign securities), various listing and trading restrictions on foreign issues that are stricter than those on domestic securities, and—on a more general plane—controls over new issues, the pre-empting of the market by the public sector, and official encouragement of specific types of financial investment. If the reform of national markets were to be accelerated, both their domestic activity and their internationalization might be furthered substantially.

As regards the United States, this country's balance of payments has benefited from the proposal and subsequent enactment of the interest equalization tax, which brought about a shift of new foreign issues by European and Japanese borrowers from the New York market to European financial centers. As a result, United States investors reduced their purchases of new European and Japanese issues from $326 million in the first half of 1963 to $110 million in the second half and to under $40 million in 1964; they continued of course to invest in issues of other borrowers, while United States banks substantially increased their loans to foreigners in general. It is clear that the proximate cause of any balance of payments relief obtained by the shift in borrowing to Europe has been the influence of the tax, rather than subsequent European adjustments. Moreover, the United States is still carrying a major share of the burden of providing long-term capital to the underdeveloped world. Steps that tend to make national capital markets in Europe more liberal and more genuinely "international" in their lending activities are therefore to be welcomed.

EURODOLLARS IN TODAY'S WORLD MARKETS*

Often called the forerunner of an international money market, trading in Eurodollars has developed to a high degree primarily because of greater currency convertibility and a desire to circumvent restrictive monetary actions.
The growth of the Eurodollar market has significance far beyond the sizable loans and investments of its participants: It has shown the ineffectiveness of monetary controls over international movements of currency in a sophisticated money market.

Probably no financial evolution in the past decade has attracted more attention than the Eurodollar. Monetary authorities and commercial bankers regard it with mixed emotions; exchange traders like it; central banks tolerate it; and financial writers hopelessly try to chart its ramifications and judge the size of the market. And all with good cause—because the market is new, flexible, complex, sometimes dangerous. and virtually limitless in potential application.

Eurodollars are demand balances in U.S. banks belonging to foreign nationals. No matter how often they are transferred from one foreign owner to another, they never leave the United States. The ownership might change once, twice, or many times—that is, one foreign owner might ask his U.S. bank to transfer the dollar balances in his current account to the account of another nonresident—but the dollars themselves never leave the country. The dollars can be used to purchase goods, make investments, finance receivables, purchase other currencies, repay loans or any other uses to which dollars may be put. The only difference between a Eurodollar deposit and any other deposit is that the original owner of the dollars no longer looks to the U.S. banks for repayment but to a foreign bank.

TYPICAL TRANSACTION

For example, assume that John Smith has an account at The First National Bank of Chicago. Mr. Smith does not need these funds for six months and seeks to invest them. He asks The First National Bank of Chicago how much it can pay for the funds. The reply is something less than 4 percent, the maxi-

* A. Robert Abboud, *Bankers Monthly Magazine*, Feb. 15, 1964, pp. 28–40.

mum permitted by law. Mr. Smith then asks an English bank how much it would be willing to pay for a six-month U.S. dollar deposit. The English bank replies 4¼ percent. Mr. Smith then agrees to place the deposit with the English bank in return for that bank's promise to repay the dollars after six months at an interest return of 4¼ percent. When the English (or foreign) bank agrees to accept the dollar deposit, this is called a Eurodollar.

Mr. Smith advises The First National Bank of Chicago to transfer the funds from his account to the account of the English bank. The English bank then transfers ownership of the deposit to an Italian bank at 4½ percent, which in turns lends the funds to an Italian importer at 5 percent, who, in his turn, instructs The First National Bank of Chicago to pay over the funds to a Chicago exporter to satisfy an outstanding indebtedness for goods shipped to Italy. After the expiration of six months, the Italian importer must acquire the necessary sum of dollars to repay the Italian bank, which in turn must repay the English bank and so down the chain until the funds eventually get back to John Smith. Once John Smith regains possession of the funds, the cycle is completed. The chain, of course, can be as long as there are successive borrowers who are willing to pay higher and higher rates of interest.

MONEY REMAINS AT HOME

In the example as quoted, the funds never leave The First National Bank of Chicago despite the movement from John Smith's account to the English bank, the Italian bank, the Italian importer, and the Chicago exporter in successive order. In practice, of course, the funds might move to a Boston or Philadelphia bank and be transferred from there to California or to New York, but they would never leave the United States. So long as a domestic bank holds the funds as agent for the foreign bank which in turn has the same deposit liability in dollars to one of its customers, it is a Eurodollar.

The term Eurodollar applies only because at the start of the chain John Smith placed a time deposit with an English bank rather than with The First National Bank of Chicago to obtain the higher rate of return. If the domestic bank had been willing and legally able to match the rate quoted abroad and the deposit were placed with the domestic bank directly rather than through the intermediary of a foreign bank, the term Eurodollar would not be appropriate, even if the depositor were a foreigner.

WHY THE MARKET EXISTS

The Eurodollar market probably got started about 1953. Some say that the two Russian banks in Western Europe, Moscow Norodny Bank Ltd., and

Banque Commerciale pour l'Europe du Nord, S.A., initiated the market to find a use for temporary surplus funds emanating from gold sales and additionally to obtain supplemental borrowings to finance imports. Others say that the London merchant banks started it to attract the large dollar balances previously maintained with the clearing banks by insurance companies at little or no interest. Most of the evidence points toward Brown Shipley & Co. Ltd., a London merchant bank, which not only wanted to attract the insurance funds but also to utilize the dollars over a broad range of highly profitable endeavors.

ENTER THE EURODOLLAR

During the early 1950s the hard currency shortage was acute and only the U.S. dollar carried universal acceptance. It was the practice of both governments and private institutions to maintain surplus positions in U.S. dollars almost exclusively. Year by year foreign liquid dollar holdings increased as the cumulative deficit in the U.S. balance of payments mounted. These dollars sought an avenue for profitable return, and some of the more astute European bankers provided such an avenue by introducing the Eurodollar.

Until about 1956, only a very few foreign banks participated. The early rates paid for 90-day Eurodollar deposits were 2 percent or about ½ percent above the rate paid by the U.S. banks. Although the U.S. banks gradually increased their rates, they were limited by Regulation Q. During the early 1950s, of course, the Regulation Q ceiling for time deposits of less than 6 months duration was 2 percent.

A HIGHER RATE

In January 1957 the ceiling was raised to 2½ percent and in July 1963 to 4 percent. At all times, the Eurodollar rates have exceeded the rates the U.S. banks have been either willing or permitted to pay (see Table 1). And due to the premium rates, plus the fact that the foreign banks offered more flexible terms, the market gradually grew, attracting funds of sophisticated investors seeking a marginally higher rate of return.

During the early period, Eurodollars were used for short-term sterling or French franc swaps. That is, the dollars were sold for sterling or francs, loaned to commercial borrowers, and repurchased at the end of the loan period. The borrower would pay interest on the sums borrowed plus or minus hedging costs. To the extent that the total costs of such borrowings were cheaper than normal commercial borrowings, the extra trouble was worthwhile. Generally, the Eurodollar dealers attempted to work on a 2 percent spread between the price paid for dollar deposits and the interest received from borrowers. Maintenance of the spread was feasible as long as the number of

TABLE 1

**U.S. TIME DEPOSIT RATE VERSUS
EURODOLLAR RATE FOR 90 DAYS
1953 – 1963**

(in percent per annum)

End of Month	Regulation Q Maximum 3-6 Months	Rates Offered by U.S. Banks 3-6 Months	Eurodollar Rates-London 90 days
December			
1953..................	2%	1-3/4%	2%
1954..................	2	1-3/8	2
1955..................	2	1-1/2	2
1956..................	2	1-1/2	2
January 1957.........	2-1/2	2	2-1/2
December			
1957..................	2-1/2	2	3-1/2
1958..................	2-1/2	2	3-1/4
1959..................	2-1/2	2-1/2	4-5/8
1960..................	2-1/2	2-1/2	3-7/8
1961..................	2-1/2	2-1/2	3-7/8
1962..................	2-1/2	2-1/2	4
July 1963..............	4	3-5/8	4-1/8
November 1963......	4	3-7/8	4-1/8

dealers remained small. Although infrequently at first, Eurodollars also were loaned to other banks but on somewhat tighter margins.

The practice of accepting deposits in foreign monies was not a new concept to European institutions. It was common during the 1920s and early 1930s when sterling constituted the universally accepted reserve currency. Hence, Eurodollar dealings in the 1950s quickly achieved widespread acceptance.

Central banks encouraged the market since it provided a vehicle to invest reserves and unutilized aid funds at higher rates of return than could be obtained in the United States. Fiscal authorities approved because it imparted movement to otherwise static dollar balances. Borrowers were delighted because it meant more funds were available at cheaper rates, (i.e., the local authority market in the United Kingdom largely grew on the basis of Eurodollars switched into sterling). And overseas financial institutions were pleased because it served to (1) alleviate liquidity pressures during periods of tight money, (2) provide additional earning resources (originally it was profitable just to buy U.S. Treasury bills[1]), (3) permit greater latitude in foreign banking since dollar loans, as opposed to sterling or other local cur-

---

[1] In the fall of 1956, Eurodollars cost 2 percent and 90-day Treasuries reached a peak yield of 3.28 percent in January 1957. The bills were then sold during a period of falling rates to yield even higher returns.

rency credits, were generally not subjected to exchange control restrictions. In short, Eurodollar trading developed to offset restrictive monetary actions. It diluted the impact of Regulation Q in this country. In Europe, it circumvented controls on foreign lending and measures designed to restrict domestic credit.

The Eurodollar should not be regarded as a temporary phenomenon. It is the logical consequence of concerted free-world efforts to make more and more currencies convertible. It may appear novel or even mysterious to Americans because of the name and the large number of U.S. investors presently committing additional funds to it. Yet as noted above, European banking institutions have been known to accept deposits in foreign currencies for many decades. It is only the name that is new. As for the mystery, there really is none. The practice is analogous to the Federal funds market in the United States.

EURODOLLAR MOVEMENT

In the post World War II period, the reserves of most European banks have typically included a large proportion of dollars. Introduction of the Eurodollar market has made it possible to trade these dollar reserves from areas of excess liquidity to areas of illiquidity, from areas of low interest rates to areas of high interest rates. Banks borrow Eurodollars to increase their lending capabilities if they are loaned up or if they are subjected to a credit squeeze because of monetary controls. Moreover, banks may appear on both sides of the market, both as borrowers and lenders. In the United States we do the same thing with Federal funds. The only difference is that we disclose our participation in our published statements under the caption "bills payable." Most foreign banks do not and therein lies one of the dangers.

EURODOLLAR TRADING

Today, approximately 10 years after the Eurodollar was created, almost all foreign banks participate to some extent. Although only a handful of merchant banks served as dealers during the early years, activity accelerated sharply during and after 1957, precipitated by the Suez crisis and the consequent flight from sterling which resulted in stricter exchange controls.

More and more, Eurodollar dealings have become the responsibility of the exchange traders. Whereas the original concept had been to obtain additional resources to assist the banks' customers in their commercial transactions, the practice was later broadened to include a trading criterion. That is, if it makes sense to borrow Eurodollars to buy U.S. Treasury bills at a profitable margin, then why not British or other foreign government obligations, assuming that the exchange exposure can be adequately hedged? And if it makes sense to do this, then why not lend to other prime banks at an incremental profit?

EVOLUTION

By borrowing deposits at one rate and lending out the very same funds at a marginally higher rate (i.e., $\frac{1}{4}$ percent) to a prime bank with little or no risk, profits may be increased with little or no danger. And if it is proper to borrow dollars and lend dollars, then why not borrow francs, guilders or marks and lend dollars? Or vice versa? It is relatively easy to cover the exposure by selling or purchasing dollars "spot" and reversing the transaction "forward." This is precisely what evolved. And what started out to be a dollar device has now become an international market of liquid short-term funds in any convertible currency.

It is said that some of the largest volume traders in the Eurodollar market are foreign branches of U.S. banks. These branches are principally borrowers, with their Eurodollar deposits (reportedly over $1 billion) exceeding their Eurodollar loans (estimated roughly at $200 million). The excesses of deposits over loans (about $800 million) are maintained in current accounts with U.S. head offices for use in the domestic market. Because foreign branches of American banks are exempted from the restrictions of Regulation Q, they can intercept the flight of short-term funds from the United States seeking a higher return and also can acquire other available convertible currencies—all of which may be used to purchase dollars for use by the head office.

TABLE 2

**PRIME RATES FOR SHORT TERM LOANS
IN SELECTED COUNTRIES***
1957 – 1963

(in percent per annum)

Date	June 1957	July 1960	Feb. 1962	Nov. 1963
Belgium	5-1/4%	6%	6-3/8%	6-1/4%
France	6-3/4	6-1/4	6	6-1/8
Germany	9	8-1/4	6	6-1/4
Italy	7-1/2	7	7-1/8	7-1/8
Netherlands	5-1/2	5	5-1/4	5-1/4
United Kingdom	5-3/8	6-3/4	6-3/4	4-1/2
United States	4	5	4-1/2	4-1/2

* Excludes compensating balance requirements in the U.S. and commissions and other charges in other countries. Foreign countries do not have as readily identifiable a prime rate as does the U.S. Rates are for local currency loans.

AN ATTRACTION

Although the prices presently paid for Eurodollar deposits are relatively high in that they exceed 4 percent, which is uncomfortably close to the U.S. prime rate of 4½ percent, the foreign branches of American banks quote the lowest rate of all the Eurodollar dealers. Still they attract a large percentage of the total volume—probably on the theory that if foreign dollar controls restrict repayment at maturity, the U.S. head office would make the money good. Since this is obviously impossible, the American banks do their best to rectify the misconception and even go so far as to ask their customers to sign statements relieving the head office of all liability.

The scope of the market is worldwide since almost every bank handling international transactions has some dealing with it. London and Paris are the principal markets, of which London is the more important. Although domestic U.S. banks may feed the market by providing funds, they cannot participate as dealers because of the interest ceiling imposed by Regulation Q.

THE PROFIT FACTOR

Because of the large number of dealers and the now multi-currency character of the market, the competition is keen and the margins ridiculously low—sometimes ⅛ percent or less. Banks paying 4¼ percent for deposits may relend these deposits for 4⅜ percent or even 4⁵⁄₁₆ percent. Moreover, some European currencies are so stable relative to the dollar that cross convertibility is easy and inexpensive.

Potential depositors may ask for rate quotations in several currencies such as dollars, sterling, frances or marks. Then by quickly computing the costs of conversion spot and forward, they select the most advantageous rate to the nearest thousandth of a point. On the other side of the market, potential borrowers ask for lending rates in several currencies and after making the same computations also select the most advantageous rate. The banks are thereby squeezed and some traders at least are becoming concerned about the generally declining margins.

NARROW MARGINS

Eurodollar traders are paying more for deposits and charging less for dollar loans than U.S. banks. This is justified on the theory that the Eurodollar operation requires no additional overhead, involves large sums with high volume, and includes little risk or exposure. Traders solemnly profess that deals are only made with prime-name customers and that all liabilities are fully offset by safe, liquid assets on a contra basis.

Yet the severity of the price competition may easily lead to questionable usages. One way to improve margins is to borrow short, perhaps three months, and lend long, one year. This is being done, and the Hugo Stinnes Bank failure in Germany is a recent example of possible consequences.[2] Other ways to improve margins are to lower credit standards or to finance borrowers otherwise hindered by credit controls. But barring extraordinary usages such as these, conventional Eurodollar trading, at least for the present, has become increasingly less profitable.

THE RISK FACTOR

Despite the profit squeeze, the market is well entrenched. The speed and convenience with which funds can be obtained and loaned make it popular. Because of the market, temporary excess funds or flash liquidity in any convertible currency may be quickly channeled to areas of currency shortages. Central banks use it to invest their dollar or other reserves. And commercial banks use it instead of correspondent credit lines in countries where interest costs are high. It is more profitable, for example, for European banks to finance their importers with Eurodollars than to employ the acceptance facilities of their U.S. correspondents. Similarly, the customers like it because Eurodollars can be obtained more inexpensively than local borrowings—a development which is wreaking havoc with local prime rate conventions and "gentlemen's agreements."

Originally, Eurodollars were only employed in foreign trade, i.e., by importers to pay for dollar purchases and by exporters for interim financing pending receipt of dollar receivables. Now, foreign prime-name customers are in the market to finance subsidiaries located in dollar areas and even on occasion for domestic working capital purposes. It is this latter usage that is causing resentment among banks in the high interest areas—particularly when the Eurodollars are provided by nondomestic institutions at rates that undercut the local prime.

A Number of Risks

Moreover, the market does not flourish without additional risks, some more remote than others. Because of the size, diversity and interwoven

---

[2] This old established bank which was actively engaged in import, export and arbitrage dealings was placed in the hands of a creditors committee in Oct. 1963 when it could not meet Eurodollar obligations owing to foreign creditors.

character of the market, it is difficult to quantify or even to identify these risks. Responsible European bankers, almost all of whom maintain an intimate knowledge of international affairs, recognize the existence of potential dangers and continually watch and change their credit availabilities. Some of the exposure may be noted as follows:

• Since inception the size and breadth of the market have spiralled upward and profit margins have declined. If the market continues to increase to make up in volume what may be lost in margins, the potential for trouble also increases in the event a major bank or creditor should fail.

• Responsibility for market operations appears to be largely in the hands of the exchange traders. To what extent individual traders may be subjected to surveillance by their respective managements is difficult to determine. Deposits are accepted without security and the funds often placed in other institutions without security. A transaction involving millions of dollars in deposits and loans may be consummated in a few minutes, all by telephone. Says one banker: "The exchange department is an empire unto itself and it is difficult for management to interfere except to express concern about the high volume. But the traders tell us that they can make money in Eurocurrencies with virtually no risk, so what can we do?"

Most other bankers are not quite so direct but appear to face the same dilemma. One lonesome voice says: "We feel that we have some of the finest exchange traders in the world but they are not credit men. Every transaction above a modest amount must be referred to management for approval. We will not permit inexperienced people to make loans nor credit to be extended without a thorough examination of the purpose." Unfortunately, this latter policy is presently a minority position. Credit is extended in great volume with few questions asked and without examining the underlying transaction. However, due to the Stinnes failure and other signs, the trend looks to be edging slowly toward the more conservative approach.

• The practice of borrowing short and lending long is accelerating. Some short-term borrowings are even being used for long-term capital expenditures —a development publicly criticized, even among the market's staunchest supporters. Borrowers argue that the short-term funds market will always exist at a price and that the only risk is the rate which might be charged. Yet, the continued availability of the short-term funds market did not save the Stinnes Bank.

• Eurocurrency transactions have made it more difficult to judge the solvency of foreign banks by their balance sheets. In many instances Eurocurrency deposits are merged with all other deposits and Eurocurrency loans are carried under the title "due from correspondents." Some institutions, like Hambros Bank, specifically segregate these transactions while others carry the asset or loan side of the operations under a caption similar to "advances." But this is not the universal practice and one must be careful not to be misled by liquidity ratios computed in the normal way.

• Similarly, growth and size calculations are apt to be misleading if the analyst makes no attempt to go behind the statement figures. When making comparisons, the apparently larger and more liquid institution may possibly be the more volatile if the bulk of its deposits and cash reserves are Eurodollars. Eurodollar deposits are the hottest of hot money. Each transaction typically involves a substantial sum. The deposit will remain or be withdrawn solely on the basis of rate consistent with some measure of safety. At the first sign of trouble, deposits will be withdrawn quickly and in quantity.

If the bank has employed these deposits in longer term investments (perfectly good but temporarily frozen), a liquidity problem evolves. The analyst must be careful to supplement his appraisal of the figures with accepted credit criteria—knowledge of the bank, its management and policies. This is not always done when placing Eurodollar deposits.

• Many Eurodollar transactions move through a long chain of banks before reaching the ultimate user. For example, an English bank may initially accept the deposit, transfer it at a higher rate to an Italian bank, which in turn would transfer it at a still higher rate to an Indian bank, and so forth. In most cases, the longer the chain, the riskier the credit, and the ultimate user may not have been an acceptable risk had he initially been the applicant. But, by the interposition of the intermediate banks, each of which assumes a small amount of additional risk, the loan is made. Moreover, it is not possible for the banks early in the chain to determine the country or the borrower where the credit will be finally reposed, which means political as well as financial exposure.

• Because of tightening margins it is difficult for banks subject to fixed legal reserve requirements to make a market in Eurodollars for inter-bank transactions. For example, both the English and Canadian commercial banks are required to maintain an 8 percent cash reserve against deposits in addition to other stringent liquidity requirements. If the cost of short-term funds to establish this reserve is 3 percent or more, the spread on each Eurodollar transaction must be at least $\frac{1}{4}$ percent (8 percent $\times$ 3 percent) just to break even. And as the cost of short-term funds increases, the spread must necessarily widen.

In the example cited earlier, the English bank accepted a Eurodollar deposit at $4\frac{1}{4}$ percent and then transferred it to an Italian bank at $4\frac{1}{2}$ percent. Today margins on inter-bank transactions are often less than $\frac{1}{4}$ percent, sometimes even $\frac{1}{8}$ or $\frac{1}{16}$ percent. As a result, the banks subject to fixed legal reserves mostly take in Eurodollars to lend to commercial customers where the margins are somewhat greater.

Dealers in inter-bank transactions are largely those institutions which are free to establish their own reserve and liquidity requirements and which can earn a return on these reserves in the short-term funds market. To cite one instance, the English accepting houses have no published conventional definition of liquid assets nor do they observe a common minimum ratio of liquid assets to deposit liabilities. Although the ratio of call money and discounts to deposit liabilities is relatively high (sometimes 40 to 50 percent) due to the nature of their business, these short-term assets do earn a fairly attractive return and do not constitute the handicap of a legal cash reserve which may earn nothing.

As for the overseas and foreign banks in London, there is no single definition of liquid assets or liquidity standard because their requirements and operating conditions vary widely. The branches of the American banks fall into this category. Neither the English monetary authorities nor our own Federal Reserve Bank require them to keep a fixed percentage of deposits as a cash reserve. However, a large proportion of their Eurodollar liabilities are kept on deposit with U.S. head offices which, in turn, must meet applicable requirements.

Some Canadian banks may also act as dealers because they accept Eurodollar deposits in their New York agencies, thereby obviating the need to keep fixed legal cash reserves in Canada. Because of their agency status, these New York offices are also not subject to legal cash reserve requirements in the United States. To be sure, they maintain proper liquidity standards but not necessarily in idle cash balances. A somewhat similar analysis could probably be made for principal Eurodollar dealers in other countries.

• Some Eurodollar transactions have unknowingly led to "back door credits" such as loans to "raiders," businesses trying to avoid central bank monetary restrictions, and borrowers circumventing margin requirements. They have also led to other questionable credits such as was the case recently with Ira Haupt, and the Allied Crude Vegetable Oil and Refining Co. Not only were foreign banks directly involved in Eurodollar loans to these firms but also to companies dependent on Allied as a principal supplier.

• If one depository in the chain of Eurodollars fails to pay at maturity, the next depository in line must make good the funds out of other resources. But this domino effect is not as serious as the initial impact which would result if a major European bank and principal Eurodollar dealer failed. In some banks, the volume of Eurodollar or Eurocurrency transactions may be equal to four times capital and reserves. These deposits include large obligations to many banks and one or two major bank failures at the same time would create losses for dealers throughout the world. The traders consider this prospect highly remote since they foresee no possibility of a 1930 type of depression.

• As things now stand, present European confidence is so high that many Eurodollar transactions are not hedged by commercial borrowers. Normally a Frenchman, Dutchman or other national borrowing dollars for a short term would hedge these dollars against his own currency. At present, however, many Europeans consider their own currency at least as strong as the dollar and, therefore, feel no compulsion to buy dollars forward. This is causing the market to expand almost without limit and if the dollar should suddenly strengthen versus the European currencies, unhedged commercial borrowers could encounter serious difficulties.

In short, Eurodollar trading involves a number of risks. But each risk considered alone appears to be either remote or nominal. Only when all of the potential risk is considered together does the weight of the exposure warrant concern.

The Bank for International Settlements is presently engaged in a study of the market that reportedly was prompted by worried bankers, some of whom are urging the Bank to supervise the market. Along with indications that central banks are more closely regulating the flow of Eurodollars into the market, are other reports that the Federal Reserve Board requested U. S. banks to see that their foreign deposits are not used as a substitute for long-term lending.

SIZE OF THE MARKET

It is virtually impossible to measure the volume of Eurodollar trading because of the difficulty in defining the market. Does the market include only dollars or should other Eurocurrencies convertible into dollars also be counted? Should the measurement be limited to deposits accepted by the first foreign bank or should it also include deposits all along the chain (i. e. from the English bank, to the Italian bank, to the Indian bank, and so on)? Estimates of market size vary widely as do criteria for calculation. The most popular estimate appears to be about $4 billion but there seems to be no practicable way to determine its accuracy. If anything, the market probably exceeds this amount.

To some extent, the scope of the market is artificially limited by exchange and capital controls in many European countries. When and if these controls are relaxed, the demand for dollar loans and deposits could substantially increase.

A CONTINUING MARKET

Eurodollar trading is well entrenched and barring extraordinary circumstances such as the repeal of Regulation Q, an increase in American short-term interest rates, a decline in European interest rates, or abolition of all exchange controls governing European currencies, the market will probably never disappear. As long as European and other foreign banks are either willing or able to pay higher rates for short-term funds than the American banks, dollars will continue to flow abroad during periods of excess liquidity in the United States and to return during periods of tighter money. Individuals and corporations with idle funds available will always seek to invest these funds at the highest possible return. When business activity picks up and additional resources are needed to finance expansion, the funds are brought back home.

The existence of the Eurodollar market aggravates our balance of payments problem, particularly during periods when U.S. interest rates are low. Short-term funds pour abroad and every additional dollar that passes into the hands of a foreigner represents a potential claim on our gold supply. On the other hand, because of the market's existence, large holders of dollars are less compelled to seek conversion into gold since Eurodollars provide a vehicle to invest these dollars profitably. The effect on our balance of payments is therefore double-edged.

IMPACT OF THE MARKET

Development and growth of the Eurodollar market has had and will continue to have an impact on the U.S. banks and monetary system in several ways:

• The market grew as a direct result of monetary controls imposed in the United States and exchange controls imposed in Europe. The consequence has been to dilute the influence of these controls, thereby reducing their effectiveness. Basically, Eurodollars represent the natural evolution of a long desired and expected international money market. Certainly, the device has led to abuses in lending practices, partially because the trading criterion is sometimes wrongly applied and responsibility for investments improperly delegated, but the concept is sound. Cross convertibility and movement of funds from areas of excess liquidity and low interest rates to areas of credit scarcity and high interest rates are worthy objectives. Consequently, the market will always exist in one form or another.

Someday, we may have Amero-sterling or Amero-francs reflecting deposits in U.S. banks of European currencies. But this is not the point. Of more significance is the conclusion that controls, unless they are total, just cannot work in a sophisticated money market. We can restrict American participation in the Eurodollar market altogether but we cannot restrict it partially. If we wish to impose a total embargo on the foreign movement of U.S. dollars, American participation in the Eurodollar market will cease to exist. But partial controls, no matter how ingenious, can always be circumvented.

A better approach would be to abolish Regulation Q, if not totally, at least with regard to foreign transactions; to encourage absolute freedom in money market affairs, spur economic activity domestically to improve the investment climate, and raise interest rates to a closer parity with Europe. The higher the rates, the wider the margins must be for the foreign banks to break even (due to reserve and liquidity requirements) and the more difficult it will be for them to slip in between U.S. deposit and lending rates.

• As long as Regulation Q remains effective with regard to foreign transactions, only those American banks with foreign branches (since Regulation Q exempts foreign branches) can participate in the evolving and increasingly more important international money market. The regulation effectively gives these banks an unnecessary monopoly position.

The argument that the Regulation Q ceiling has always been higher than the American banks were willing to pay is not persuasive. First, if the ceiling has always been high enough to permit higher rates when and if the American banks wanted to pay them, then what purpose does the ceiling serve? Secondly, since almost all the U.S. banks with foreign branches are active solicitors of Eurodollar deposits, the conclusion must necessarily be that some banks at least are willing to pay higher rates for foreign funds and that they can find profitable investments for these deposits.

It is unsatisfactory to argue that any U.S. bank is free to open a foreign branch if it so chooses because the economics of the matter are that it is just not practicable, especially if the primary purpose is simply to attract Eurodollar deposits.

• The Eurodollar market will almost certainly attract an increasing number of domestic and foreign borrowers as long as foreign banks are not forced to pay a rate nearly equal to or greater than the U.S. prime rate for dollar deposits thereby making it difficult for them to undercut the rates charged by U.S. banks for loans.

This is not an impractical objective because the market approached this condition in December 1963. When Eurodollar lending rates tried to go up in response, some borrowers came back to borrow in the United States. This tended to impose a ceiling on the rates foreigners were willing to pay to obtain additional deposits and temporarily inhibited market growth. Otherwise foreign importers who would normally utilize U.S. acceptance facilities will almost certainly substitute part of these borrowings in favor of cheaper Eurodollars. This will tend to reduce the volume of a hitherto profitable asset for American banks.

Domestic customers may also tend to do the same with regard to their borrowings, for not only will these customers pay lower rates but, in addition, they need not maintain compensating balances. The tendency of domestic borrowers to tap the Eurodollar market will probably be greatest during periods of tight money. The German banks have already suffered this experience and complain that the customers they lose first are the prime customers. Banks in other countries such as Italy, Netherlands, France, Norway, Denmark, the United Kingdom and elsewhere have been partially protected by regulations prohibiting domestic companies from borrowing foreign currencies without official permission.

As the application of these restrictions wanes, as it now appears to be doing, the banks in these countries, like the German banks, may also have cause to complain since Eurodollar loans typically cost less than local currency loans. To date, the resources of the market have been limited. But as it grows, it may give the American banks greater anxiety as well as increased competition for their prime and biggest customers.

• The interest equalization tax is no solution but a penalty. The proceeds of the tax do not go to the banks but to the Government. Moreover, the price a bank can or may be willing to pay for funds depends on the interest structure generally and not on premium rates in a few minority situations. The solution to the problem is to make it possible for the U.S. banks to pay competitive rates for dollar deposits. Other controls to limit foreign dollar investments will not work unless the controls are total.

A Logical Outcome

There is little doubt the Eurodollar market is here to stay. It is a logical consequence of a developing world economy comprised of competitive markets, not only for goods but also for money.

The primary benefits of the market are that it encourages cross convertibility of currencies and an economically motivated flow of funds from areas of supply to areas of demand. In addition, it provides foreign central banks with a monetary weapon, like our open market operation, to ease or tighten local credit availability plus an outlet to profitably employ dollar reserves which might otherwise be wholly or partially converted into gold.

To be sure, the market is fraught with certain risks, largely due to the narrow margins and the manner in which credit is extended. But these are risks of administration which should be remedied over a period of time. The basic concept is sound.

If there is one lesson to be learned from the Eurodollar market, it is probably the realization that partial controls in a sophisticated multinational money market are largely ineffective. Either the controls must be total or they will be circumvented.

Today, financial transactions in North America, Japan, and Europe are closely interrelated. Some domestic American banks are presently accepting deposits in Canadian currency. In the years ahead, these and other domestic banks will probably accept deposits in European currencies. This will then complete the evolution of a truly international money market of which the Eurodollar is the harbinger.

CREDIT CREATION THROUGH EURODOLLARS?*

Do the various Eurocurrency markets that have sprung up in recent years actually create credit on an international scale? Or do they merely transfer credit already created from one taker to another? This question has increasingly been engaging the attention of central bankers. In practice the answer must turn largely on institutional attitudes. But as an aid to clearer thinking in this complex field Mr. Geoffrey Bell sketches out a theoretical framework to demonstrate that the Eurocurrency markets could, under certain conditions, create credit by a process analogous to the working of a domestic banking system.—EDITOR.

This article seeks to examine whether or not the Eurodollar market "creates" credit. Much has been written about the "double-counting" or "chaining" of credit in the market, and this is often contrasted with the "pyramiding" of credit that occurs in a domestic banking system. These distinctions, however, may be less significant than the similarities between some aspects of the Eurodollar system and domestic banking. It is argued here that the Eurodollar market, by the process of intermediation, can increase the flow of international credit and can thus affect total world demand in a meaningful sense. Moreover, the market could, under certain conditions, act in the same manner as a domestic banking system and from a given flow of dollars from the United States, increase the total stock of world dollar liquidity by some multiple. This thesis is, in fact, an extension to the field of international finance of the discussion about the respective actions of banks and nonbank financial intermediaries in the domestic economy which in this country was sparked off by the Radcliffe Report. It should be emphasized that even though the following discussion is presented in terms of "dollars" the analysis applies to any currency that is traded systematically outside its country of origin— for example, Eurosterling or Euro-Swiss.

Before examing the problem of credit creation it may be useful to review briefly the Eurodollar market and its origins.[1] Eurodollar operations are a particular form of banking whereby banks outside the United States, chiefly European, accept dollar deposits and lend dollars, typically for short periods. The market is, essentially, an international short-term money market, although loans are occasionally made for medium-term periods.

---

* Geoffrey L. Bell, *The Banker,* Aug. 1964, pp. 494–502.
[1] For a fuller description, see "U.K. Banks' External Liabilities and Claims in Foreign Currencies", Bank of England *Quarterly Bulletin,* June, 1964.

The original impetus for its development has been ascribed to the desire of several East European banks to leave their dollar working balances with correspondents in Paris and London rather than in the United States.[2] A further impetus was given to the expansion of the market in 1957 when the U.K. authorities imposed restrictions on the use of sterling for the refinancing of foreign trade credits for nonresidents and banned sterling acceptance credits covering trade between countries outside the sterling area. British banks then substituted dollar facilities for the prohibited sterling credits, obtaining the requisite balances in the European dollar market. The introduction of nonresident convertibility in Western Europe at the end of 1958 also aided the market since it enabled nonresidents to exchange European currencies into dollars without restriction. European banks were then able to accept deposits in nondollar currencies, switch into dollars (with forward cover) and use these funds in the market.

Although the introduction of convertibility and the relaxation of exchange and other selective controls have helped to stimulate the market's development, the main economic reason for its continuance is the spread between borrowing and lending rates in the United States domestic money market—which enables European banks, by working on narrower margins, to outbid U.S. banks for dollar deposits and loans. The European bank offers a time deposit (in dollar terms and usually for maturities of between 1–12 months) in return for receiving a spot claim on the United States. The deposit-holder therefore has a liquid asset bearing a higher rate of return than is available in the U.S. market. This means that the crucial variable in the determination of the flow of funds into and out of the market is the interest-rate sensitivity of dollar holders. The greater this sensitivity, the smaller becomes the rate differential on deposits of similar maturities between European and United States banks necessary to induce a given flow of funds.

The supply of dollars to the market comes, to a large extent, from countries experiencing, or which have experienced, balance of payments surpluses with the United States. American residents also invest in the market, both directly and, probably more usually, via Canadian banks. The demand for dollars in Europe comes from a variety of sources, mostly in the private (nongovernment) sector. Most are ultimately lent to nonbank customers. The majority of funds are probably used to finance international trade—in preference to acceptance credits because of lower interest charges and because of the convenience of borrowing (given both the wide range of maturities available and the ready supply of funds in the market); some, however, are used domestically after switching into local currencies (the switching being undertaken either by the operating bank or by the commercial borrower).

In addition to lending to nonbank customers, a substantial amount of

[2] See Alan Holmes and Fred Klopstock: New York Federal Reserve Bank *Monthly Review*, November, 1960.

dollars are used in interbank transactions. As dollars can be loaned or borrowed for various maturities, they are an excellent medium for banks to adjust their liquidity positions. In these operations the market is closely analogous to the Federal Funds Market in the United States. Often banks are trading on both sides of the balance sheet, lending and borrowing.

MECHANICS OF CREDIT CREATION

In the following paragraphs the process of credit creation in the Eurodollar market is illustrated by the use of balance sheets for a United States bank and for one or more European banks. Two models of credit creation are discussed. The first is concerned solely with interbank lending, in order to make clear how the double-counting of dollar deposits takes place. The second, and more significant, concerns lending to nonbank customers. In practice no complete distinction can be drawn, since many accepting banks on-lend dollars to both types of borrowers; however, for the purposes of exposition it is helpful to make such a distinction. The term "high-powered" dollars is used to denote the liabilities of United States residents, which can be used as a medium of exchange. "Secondary" dollars denote the dollar-denominated liabilities of European banks, which are liquid assets to the holders (since they are time deposits) but cannot be used as media of exchange. The "United States bank" is a proxy for the entire U.S. banking system, Eurobank I is the first generation of European banks that accept dollar deposits, Eurobank II the second deposit-accepting generation and Eurobank N serves as the generalization for any succeeding generation.

As a starting point, let us assume that a private resident of the United States transfers a demand deposit at a U.S. bank to a European bank in exchange for a time deposit at that bank. This leaves the U.S. banking system unaffected: demand deposits remain at the same level, merely the pattern of ownership has been changed. The money supply of the United States (defined as currency plus demand deposits) is also unaffected, since foreign-owned demand deposits are included in the definition of money supply. The balance sheets of the United States and European banks are as follows:

PHASE I

U.S. Bank		Eurobank I	
Liabilities	*Assets*	*Liabilities*	*Assets*
Demand deposits		Time deposits	Demand deposits
—100 U.S. resident		+100 U.S. resident	+100 U.S. bank
+100 Eurobank I			
Net change 0		+100	+100

Thus, by transferring a demand deposit to a European bank, an additional supply of dollar-denominated deposits has been created. Since the liability of the European bank can be regarded as a liquid asset to the holder, the world supply of dollar-liquidity has been expanded by this transaction.

The European bank will be anxious to convert its U.S. demand deposit (which is a noninterest bearing) into an interest-bearing asset by on-lending at a rate higher than the rate paid on its time liability. It is assumed in the following table that the bank on-lends the whole amount to another European bank. (As is noted later, this is an unrealistic assumption but it is a useful one to make at this stage of the argument to demonstrate the basic principles involved.) The reason why Eurobank I, and not the U.S. resident, lends to Eurobank II, is that the bank can command a higher rate of return on time deposits than can a private depositor. This transaction continues the chain of secondary dollar creation.

PHASE II

U.S. Bank		Eurobank I		Eurobank II	
Liabilities	*Assets*	*Liabilities*	*Assets*	*Liabilities*	*Assets*
Demand deposits			−100 U.S.	+100 deposit	+100 U.S.
−100 Euro-bank I			Demand	Euro-	Demand
+100 Euro-bank II		+100 Time	deposit	bank I	deposit
		deposit			
		Euro-			
		bank II			
___		___		___	___
Net change 0			0	+100	+100

Thus, Eurobank I, in the same manner as the U.S. resident who made the initial injection of dollars into the market, has converted a demand deposit into a time deposit. The result of this has been to bring into existence another $100 of dollar-denominated time deposits. Therefore, from an initial $100 of demand deposits (or "high-powered" dollars), $200 of liquid assets have been created, with the total supply of U.S. demand deposits remaining unaffected.

This process of creating dollar-denominated time liabilities can go on indefinitely so long as the European banks lend directly to one another, since there will be no leakages in the system. The high-powered dollars will be continually re-deposited in the system; hence an almost infinite volume of time deposits (secondary dollars) could be brought into existence.[3] But this is clearly an unrealistic assumption. If, as it is more reasonable to assume,

---

[3] Theoretically, the creation of secondary dollars could be $100 (the original deposit) × N (the number of banks in the system).

each lending bank retains some proportion of high-powered dollars in reserve, and consequently on-lends only a proportion of the total demand deposit, then a definite limit will be set to the creation of time liabilities. More specifically, the limit will be $100 $\dfrac{1}{(\text{reserve ratio})}$; thus if each bank maintains a liquidity reserve of 10 percent the total creation arising from the depositing of the initial $100 could not exceed $1,000.

The creation of secondary deposits described above, it should be noted, is essentially financial, since it is appropriate to regard banks as nonspenders —which therefore have no influence on the income-generating process. The model does, however, illustrate the process that has led to confusion about the size of dollar liabilities in the market. In a domestic banking system such inter-bank deposits are netted-out in summing aggregate deposits. The number of banks operating in the Eurodollar market, however, is not clearly defined and there are no systematic statistical reporting procedures. As a result, the netting-out of deposits cannot be effected so certainly as in the domestic banking system; given that interbank lending is substantial, the total amount of dollar liabilities of European banks is inflated by extensive double-counting.

Lending to a Commercial Customer

Now let us consider the more significant case where Eurobank I, after borrowing an initial supply of high-powered dollars on-lends, not to Eurobank II, but to a commercial customer. It is assumed in the following model that borrowing takes place because domestic banks are fully lent and therefore normal credit channels are not open. The first stage in the process is exactly as in the table on page 556. The next page is outlined here:

· PHASE II

U.S. Bank		Eurobank I		Commercial Borrower	
Liabilities	*Assets*	*Liabilities*	*Assets*	*Liabilities*	*Assets*
—100 Eurobank I		—100 U.S. Demand deposit		+100 Euro-bank I	+100 U.S. Demand deposit
+100 Commercial borrower			+100 Commercial loan		
Net change 0		0		+100	+100

At this stage the high-powered dollars have disappeared from the Eurodollar market and since such dollars are necessary to a further creation of secondary dollar liabilities, the process of secondary creation is ended. But this is unlikely to be the end of the story, since the commercial customer presumably borrows in order to spend—either on imports or in the domestic market. He has a choice either of spending the dollars directly or of converting them into another currency and spending that. Let us assume that the dollars are spent by a European on importing goods from the United States (this is a particular case of the general principle but will clarify the process of multiple credit creation). This means that the ownership of the demand deposit in the United States is transferred to the account of an American exporter. The total supply of U.S. bank deposits (and hence bank assets) will remain constant so long as the exporter does not use his new deposit to pay off a bank loan. The action of the European importer, in buying goods from the United States, however, has increased spending in the United States and has, therefore, tended to raise incomes in that country. Thus the Eurodollar market, by facilitating spending, has enabled U.S. national income to rise through the stock of money (i.e. currency and demand deposits) has remained constant—in other words, the operations in the Eurodollar market have raised the income velocity of deposits in the United States.

The American exporter will presumably spend some proportion of his new deposit on goods and services and keep some part idle (in the form of a liquid asset). If he spends, the income generating process will continue, while if he leaves the funds in the form of a demand deposit in a U.S. bank the process will stop (NB—bank deposits in the U.S. are still constant and therefore banks cannot expand their balance sheets). Let us assume that the exporter spends $80 and keeps $20 idle. However, instead of leaving the $20 with a U.S. bank, he deposits in Eurobank II: the effects of this are shown in the accompanying table. The $20 is a new deposit of high-powered dollars to Eurobank II and therefore the bank is in a position to lend dollars.

PHASE III

Eurobank I			Eurobank II	
Liabilities		*Assets*	*Liabilities*	*Assets*
+100 U.S. resident Time deposit		+100 Commercial loan	+20 Time deposit U.S. resident II	+20 Demand deposit
+100		+100	+20	+20

Thus, from an initial deposit of $100 in Eurobank I, by a U.S. resident, the Eurodollar market has created $120 of credit. From the $20 of new demand deposits in Eurobank II, some proportion may return into Eurobank III and so continue the process of credit creation. Thus a single injection of new spending in the economy is translated into a stream of spending when the holder of the "new" deposit makes it available to a European bank rather than leaves it in a U.S. bank, i.e. income velocity continues to rise.

The principle of multiple credit creation through the Eurodollar market is not affected if the original dollar borrower uses the funds to finance trade with a third country or switches into another currency. So long as the original demand deposit in a U.S. bank is not used to pay off a loan in the U.S. banking system or to purchase gold from the United States, the deposit will continue to exist and therefore some proportion may be re-deposited in the Eurodollar system. The act of spending the dollar loan will, in these cases, give rise to income-generation outside of the United States.

RETURN FLOW OF FUNDS

As outlined above, the key assumption that is necessary for a multiple creation of credit in the Eurodollar system is that some proportion of the original loan be re-deposited in the system. This in turn depends on the interest-rate sensitivity of dollar holders and the level of minimum money balances in an economy—which determines the volume of idle balances that could be activated by employment in the Euromarket. The decision whether or not to deposit in the Eurodollar market will depend on the rate of return on time deposits in that market as compared with alternative assets. Since the market has attracted substantial amounts of dollars, it is not inconceivable that "new" dollar holders have deposited some proportion of their balances there.

Admittedly in practice, the return flow—on which the scope for credit creation fundamentally depends—is likely to be small. If, however, central banks are introduced into the analysis, the possibility of a substantial return flow is increased. It is known that central banks have been large scale lenders to the system[4] (although they have been withdrawing lately) and it is by no means inconceivable that a part of these dollars were originally borrowed from the Euromarket. Thus a central bank may acquire dollars as a result of switching into local currency by Eurodollar borrowers: unless it takes offsetting action, this increase in its reserves will form the basis of an increase in domestic liquidity. In this, however, the Eurodollar market plays no new rôle—precisely the same effects would have arisen from an inflow of U.S. dollars or, under the classical gold standard, from an inflow of gold. Where the market may play a new and active part is in providing another medium for the investment of the central bank's dollars. If the central bank simply deposits them in New York the credit-creating process, domestic and international, is terminated; if, however, it prefers (because, say, of the higher interest rates obtainable) to leave them in the European market the

---

[4] See Annual Report of Bank for International Settlements, June, 1964, Chapter V, pp. 132 and 133.

possibility of a further creation of international credit arises through the on-lending of a European commercial bank.

Thus, even though the Eurodollar market performs the functions of an intermediary, it is possible for the participating banks to expand their balance sheets by making loans, as in a domestic banking system. The main difference is that the return flow of funds domestically is greater. This is mainly because a domestic holder of bank deposits can use his deposit for making current purchases, while the holder of a Eurodollar deposit cannot. If, however, Eurobanks could be assured of a substantial return flow (perhaps as an incentive they might pay interest on demand deposits), there is no theoretical reason why the banks should not offer demand deposits with a dollar-denominated chequing facility. To the deposit holder, the deposit would be a perfect substitute (assuming that the cheques were generally acceptable) for a deposit in a U.S. bank; and the banks by making loans would, in fact, be creating a medium of exchange and acting exactly as a domestic banking system. But, even though the Eurodollar market does not at present create a medium of exchange, it should be stressed again that the market increases liquidity—and hence the probability of spending—exactly as when a financial institution interjects its "intermediation" into a domestic system.

WESTERN EUROPEAN CAPITAL MARKETS AND U.S. CAPITAL OUTFLOW RESTRICTION*

The events since President Kennedy's proposal last July for an interest equalization tax have been profoundly different from the expectations with which the new balance of payments policy was launched. A reluctant acceptance of some form of capital outflow restriction quickly took form in the financial community as a result of the record $5.1 billion second-quarter deficit rate. A limited discussion of methods alternative to the tax took place, the most frequently mentioned being a capital issues committee; but resignation to the tax prevailed and questions were confined to the degree of effectiveness that the tax might have in restricting foreign issues in the United States market. The answer was swift in coming: the threat of the retroactive tax produced an abrupt reduction in capital borrowing in the third quarter and brought a much-reduced deficit.

A descriptive survey of the chief capital markets of Western Europe—their depth, flexibility, and degree of public control—is presented here in the hope that the basis for capital outflow control can be clarified. The question of the effectiveness of the tax in achieving its temporary objective seems to have been answered. It is difficult to answer a second question that has been raised as the aggravated deficit has improved; that is, Should the United States as a matter of principle interfere in the free transfer of capital? This question is not trivial and to justify the new policy of restriction it must be shown that the long-run interests of the United States and Europe are being served as well as the short-term interest of the United States. The argument presented here is that capital requirements in both industrially developed and developing countries are large in relation to the savings being mobilized to finance them; that free and open access to United States capital markets by the industrially advanced countries, unless accompanied by efforts to develop their own capital markets, is inimical to the development of sufficient capital fi-

* John D. Hogan, *Quarterly Review of Economics and Business,* Summer, 1964, pp. 65–78. (This paper was prepared before the study, "A Description and Analysis of Certain European Capital Markets," was published by the Joint Economic Committee in January, 1964. The author did not have available to him the current data prepared by the Treasury Department for the Joint Committee on the Economic Report. The original paper was delivered December 29, 1963, at the meetings of the Allied Social Sciences.)

nancing sources to meet future Free World demands; and that a policy of creating doubts about the free and open status of United States capital markets by temporarily inhibiting that status may have desirable incentive effects in the offending countries.

Capital markets are most often understood to be sites where bond and share sales are effected to obtain funds for fixed investment. While the end-use of savings is an important aspect of capital markets and fulfills the reason for their existence, the *intermediation mechanism* by which savings are accumulated is equally important. A complex of financial institutions, including savings banks, building and loan associations, and life insurance companies, perform two vital functions: they exchange relatively *nonliquid* assets (savings accounts, savings shares, life insurance contracts, and so on) for liquid assets (demand deposits and currency), and they channel savings of disparate economic units that operate at a current surplus into central pools where they may be employed by economic units that operate at a current deficit. This process is carried on with widely varying effectiveness, even among industrially developed economies. The pooling of savings is essential to the formation of capital, and efficient capital markets are, therefore, strong precursors of economic growth.

The performance of a capital market is judged by both quantitative and qualitative standards. An effective capital market possesses depth and flexibility. It can accommodate frequent security issues of large amounts—$50 million by today's standards—and adapt quickly to changes in demand for and supply of funds. As secondary markets, capital markets provide an important liquidity source to the saver-lender who, being assured that he can exchange his nonliquid assets for cash, is willing to reduce the risk-premium he would otherwise demand of the borrower. Finally, and this characteristic is implied in the requirements for depth and flexibility, market forces (as opposed to personal forces) are the preferred rule over the market. Given that a capital market is deep and flexible, that it affords liquidity to holders of nonliquid assets, and that it is ruled by market forces, the supply-of-funds side of the capital investment process tends to be highly favorable. A large proportion of surplus funds tend to find their way to the market by way of intermediary institutions. The interest rate cost of funds and the net rate of return on capital assets (marginal productivity of capital) in which the funds are employed will, moreover, tend to be separated by a minimum point spread.[1]

The industrially advanced economy, if it lacks strong capital markets, can opt among several alternative methods of financing capital formation. Sav-

---

[1] A broad point-spread between the interest rate charged by lenders and the marginal productivity of capital to borrowers, the "financial spread," is a major obstacle to capital formation in underdeveloped countries. See Moses Abramovitz, "Economics of Growth," in Bernard Haley, ed., *A Survey of Contemporary Economics*, Vol. 2 (Homewood: Irwin, 1952), pp. 164–65.

ings generated within corporations, in the form of depreciation balances and retained earnings, can be encouraged by tax policy. Or the government sector may operate its accounts on a surplus basis and provide transfers or loans to deficit units for fixed investment purposes. These choices and others similar to them have the drawback that they shift decision-making away from competitive markets with presumed lamentable consequences, chiefly the courting of misallocation of capital. Decisions not to develop capital markets, but to circumvent them, probably exact their price in ways obvious or subtle that are ultimately inimical to economic growth.

CAPITAL OUTFLOW AND THE U.S. BALANCE

The United States balance of international payments recorded an average annual deficit ("regular balance") during the period 1958–63 or $3.0 billion. Private capital movements averaged $3.5 billion over the same period, of which $1.2 billion was long-term portfolio investment. Substantial increases in the rate of capital outflow, especially purchases of foreign securities, took place in 1962 and 1963. The trend of purchases of new foreign security issues in the New York market during the first half of 1963, shown in Table 1,

TABLE 1

UNITED STATES PRIVATE NET LONG-TERM INVESTMENT IN FOREIGN ISSUES,
1960 – 1963

(Millions of dollars)

Type and Country of Purchase	1960	1961	1962	1963 I	1963 II	1963 III
By type:				Seasonally adjusted annual rates		
Private long-term capital, net	2,114	2,143	2,495	4,016	3,604	1,928
Purchases of foreign securities	750	876	1,131	2,092	2,200	648
New issues.........................	573	523	1,076	1,900	1,944	852
Outstanding issues, net........	177	353	55	192	256	(-)204
Other	1,364	1,267	1,364	1,924	1,404	1,280
By country of purchase:				Unadjusted annual rates		
Purchases of foreign securities..	750	876	1,131	2,216	2,328	512
Western Europe.....................	133	266	195	336	776	68
Japan.................................	n.a.*	79	124	188	320	228
Canada..............................	241	327	379	1,328	1,044	204
Other.................................	n.a.	204	433	364	188	12

* n.a. Not available.
Source: U.S. Department of Commerce.

could not have been anticipated from the trend of preceding data and was attributable to an abrupt increase in purchases of securities offered by Canada and Western Europe.

A change in United States policy was proposed by the President within the month following the determination that an accelerated program of foreign security offerings was aggravating the balance of payments deficit. The boldest departure from prevailing practice in the six-point program released July 18, 1963, was the interest equalization tax. Other recommendations in the program were within the pattern of policies formulated during the preceding two years—tying foreign aid to United States exports, reducing overseas expenditure, obtaining a stand-by credit with the International Monetary Fund, and expanding exports. Early in the second session of the 88th Congress, the Ways and Means Committee of the House of Representatives approved a bill (H.R. 8000) which substantially endorsed the President's request for an excise tax to be applied to purchases by Americans of new and existing foreign securities, the tax to impose on foreign sellers the equivalent of 1 percent additional interest cost and to be operative through 1965.

INTERNATIONAL COMPARISONS IN FINANCING OF INVESTMENT

Saving Levels

The surplus funds generated by an economy and the relative contributions of the several sectors to the surplus total provide basic measures of the funds available to finance capital formation. Some insight into the strength of capital markets can be gained from intercountry savings data alone. Table 2

TABLE 2

SAVING IN MAJOR COUNTRIES, AVERAGE, 1950-59

(Percentage of gross national product)

Country	Gross Saving			Deprecia-tion	Net Saving
	Total	Domestic	Foreign		
Norway	29.7	27.1	2.7	9.9	17.2
Australia	28.4	26.1	2.3	5.9	20.2
Japan	27.5	28.7	(-) 1.2	7.6	21.1
West Germany	23.2	26.3	(-) 3.1	9.1	17.2
Italy	20.8	19.5	1.3	8.9	10.6
France	18.6	18.4	0.2	9.3	9.1
United States	18.0	18.6	(-) 0.6	8.7	9.9
United Kingdom	14.7	15.2	(-) 0.5	8.0	7.2

Source: United Nations, World Economic Survey, 1960.

presents gross saving and net saving (gross saving less depreciation) data for major countries during the decade of the 1950's. The range of gross saving among countries is wide, but the range of net saving is wider still. This reflects the importance of depreciation and, by implication, tax policy with respect to depreciation.

The relative importance of the several sectors in the gross savings of major countries is shown in Table 3 for the 1950–59 period. Some limitations apply to the "enterprise" sector because this category includes public and

TABLE 3

GROSS SAVING IN MAJOR COUNTRIES BY SECTOR, AVERAGE, 1950-59

(Percentage of gross national product)

Country	Gross Domestic Saving		
	Government	Enterprise	Household
Norway	7.3	13.6	6.2
Australia	5.5	10.6	10.0
Japan	5.9	12.6	10.2
West Germany...........	7.7	10.5	8.1
Italy *	2.3	– 19.1 –	
France....................	3.9	11.1	3.4
United States...........	2.5	10.8	5.3
United Kingdom........	2.2	11.4	1.6

* These figures refer to annual averages for 1955-59 only; the domestic saving ratio is therefore different from that in Table 2.
   Source: United Nations, World Economic Survey, 1960.

private corporations and (in some countries) nearly all household depreciation. The variability of the household sector among countries as a source of saving is, nonetheless, clear from the table;[2] and the government sector, even if all public corporations are included, also shows wide variability. Enterprise saving shows less variability in relation to gross national product (GNP) than the saving of the other sectors. The differences in public policy which underlie the narrow range of enterprise saving are implied in Table 4, which shows uses of corporate net income in major countries.

TABLE 4

LEVEL AND USES OF CORPORATE NET INCOME, MAJOR COUNTRIES, AVERAGE, 1950-59

Country	Net Saving*	Direct Taxes	Net Saving*	Direct Taxes	Net Saving*	Dividends
	Percentage of GNP		Percentage of Corporate Income Before Taxes		Percentage of Corporate Disposable Income	
Japan	4.0	3.5	47.0	40.9	79.3	20.7
United Kingdom..............	5.0	5.1	33.4	39.2	54.6	45.4
France	4.3	2.1	31.4	34.4	47.9	52.1
West Germany................	1.8	3.1	31.0	54.3	68.1	31.9
United States.................	1.9	5.3	20.8	49.5	41.2	58.8

* Depreciation and retained earnings.
   Source: United Nations, World Economic Survey, 1960.

The conclusion to be drawn from Table 4 is that public policies in major countries have encouraged widely differing levels of corporate saving. At the extreme, Japan has provided very high levels of corporate net saving by keeping direct tax burdens moderate and by permitting high depreciation and earnings retention rates relative to other countries. Combinations of tax and earnings distribution policies result in high corporate net saving rates in Germany, moderate rates in the United Kingdom and France, and low rates

   [2] Household saving as a percentage of gross national product was, for the period 1950–59, an annual average of 10.2 in Japan, 10.0 in Australia, 8.1 in West Germany, 5.3 in the United States, 3.4 in France, and 1.6 in the United Kingdom.

in the United States. In Germany and Japan corporate tax rates were reduced on earnings reinvested, and rapid write-off of new equipment was encouraged. Both Japan and Germany have, as a recent policy, decreased direct taxes on corporations from the average rates shown in the table. The implication is that public policy tends to promote internal enterprise savings where the capital markets and financial institutions lack the capability to supply prevailing needs for investible funds. Development of strong financial institutions is a long-term operation, whereas capital financing needs are current. To corroborate this hypothesis other data relating to the volume of capital issues and the variety and strength of financial institutions are required.

Security Issues

Security issues data provide relative measures of capital market activity among countries. The annual volume of issues over recent years is shown in Table 5.

TABLE 5

SECURITY ISSUES IN MAJOR COUNTRIES
(Percentage of gross savings)

Country	Gross Security Issues	Net Security Issues
West Germany (1959-61)..........	13.8	12.0
France (1958-60)....................	15.1	11.0
United Kingdom (1958-60).......	32.4	11.3
United States (1957-61)..........	47.4	19.5

Sources: Organization for Economic Cooperation and Development; Board of Governors of the Federal Reserve System; and International Monetary Fund.

Gross security issues in relationship to gross savings are much larger in the United States and the United Kingdom than in France and Germany, and in the United States, net security issues are also larger. Net security issues expressed as a percentage of fixed capital formation indicate the extent to which real investment relies on the capital market. These data and other data which permit comparison of the relative importance of the capital market are shown in Table 6. Among the countries compared, the United States and the United Kingdom have high percentages of net securities issues relative to fixed capital formation; the percentages for West Germany and France are low. The numbers of securities quoted on the exchanges are much larger in the United States and the United Kingdom than in the other two countries.

The United States and the United Kingdom are countries with moderate savings levels but highly developed capital markets fed by a variety of financial institutions. Data presented earlier suggest the superior development of the two countries over West Germany and France in terms of savings entering the capital markets and the dependency of fixed capital formation on

TABLE 6

NET NEW SECURITY ISSUES RELATED TO CAPITAL FORMATION,
MAJOR COUNTRIES, 1962

(Millions of dollars)

Factor	France	West Germany	United Kingdom	United States
Net new issues	2,005	2,957	3,256	23,111
Shares	806	549	717	2,212
Bonds...............................	1,198	2,408	2,540	20,899
Gross Fixed capital formation....	12,005	21,400	12,953	73,360
Net new issues as percentage of gross fixed capital formation .	16.7	13.8	25.1	31.5
Number of securities quoted......	2,800 *	1,825 †	9,134 ‡	7,659 §

* Paris Exchange only.
† Frankfort Exchange only.
‡ London Exchange only.
§ New York Stock Exchange only. Stocks only.
Source: Bank of England, Quarterly Bulletin, July, 1963.

the markets. As a consequence, the United States and the United Kingdom possess markets of greater depth and are able to absorb frequent large new private issues of $50 million or more. The Continental markets cannot do so and government or nationalized industry issues are the only borrowers in West Germany and France capable of raising frequent amounts in excess of $50 million.

The consequences to an economy of a comparatively thin capital market are significant. Interest rates will tend to be higher than in markets of greater depth because lenders discount the risk of holding a less liquid asset. The borrowing costs associated with the issues also tend to be higher. Borrowers must be prepared to risk markets that may not be capable of absorbing their issues and then turn to alternative financing, usually short-term bank credits. Since capital needs are compelling, public policy tends to compensate for undeveloped capital markets by providing government transfers or grants and encouraging internal generation of savings by enterprise.

Capital markets can be described in terms of flexibility as well as depth. A comparison of markets in terms of flexibility and vigor requires description of institutions unique to each country. A brief discussion of the United Kingdom, West Germany, and France follows.

Anatomy of European Capital Markets

United Kingdom

The London market is second only to New York in terms of its depth and the vigor of its financial institutions. Issuing houses are the institutions chiefly concerned with new issues of securities. They act as sponsors and underwriters of new issues and place them with many different financial institutions, chiefly insurance companies. The position of the insurance companies is pivotal in the market, since they underwrite at least half of total new issues. Investment and unit trusts and building societies all participate strongly in the intermediation of savings.

Nationalization of basic industries in the United Kingdom is generally thought to have inhibited the growth of the private issues market because funds for the nationalized industries are obtained through offerings of gilt-edged government securities. Table 7 shows the levels of gross investment in recent years and the sources of investment financing. The division of gross fixed investment between the public and private sectors has remained relatively stable. At 15 percent of GNP, the investment level in the United Kingdom is not high by Continental European standards and the market has not been burdened to finance it. The household sector was a growing source of savings until 1962, owing in large part to life insurance and pension fund

TABLE 7

CAPITAL INVESTMENT AND ITS FINANCING, UNITED KINGDOM, 1959-61

(Millions of pounds)

Year	Gross Fixed Investment		Financing Gross Investment			New Security Issues, Net	
	Public	Private	Household Saving	Enterprise Saving	Other*	Shares	Bonds
1959	1,582	2,165	990	2,070	687	262	164
1960	1,650	2,469	1,565	2,330	224	338	145
1961	1,729	2,691	2,035	1,915	470	438	184
1962	1,844	2,546	1,795	– 2,595 –		257	309

* Includes borrowing, government grants and loans, and so on.
Sources: National Economic Development Council and Bank of England.

growth and the expansion of unit trusts. Net security issues have increased steadily, but leveled off in 1962. As a percentage of fixed capital formation, however, new issues in the United Kingdom are twice the volume in West Germany and France.

The level of interest rates in the United Kingdom tends to be higher than that in the United States, but equal to or slightly below the West German and French rates. Costs of public security issues[3] to the borrower are considerably lower in the United Kingdom than elsewhere, except the United States. Costs to the purchaser of securities are equal to those in Continental markets except for Switzerland and the Netherlands.

The United Kingdom can be described in summary as possessing a capital market and associated credit markets which are effective mobilizers of funds. In terms of depth and flexibility, the London market is inferior only to New York. The market has remained vigorous and competitive in spite of a substantial shift of emphasis from the private to the public sector. Probably the

[3] Initial taxes, fees, commissions, and so on. See Bank of England, *Quarterly Bulletin,* June, 1963, p. 115, for a schedule of initial costs of public issues for major countries.

market can meet the investment financing needs of the United Kingdom and the prevailing borrowing of Commonwealth nations for an indefinite period.

Continental Capital Markets

The markets which are most important in this comparison are those in West Germany and France. Other markets of considerable importance exist on the Continent, notably in Amsterdam, Zurich, and Milan. The number of securities quoted on the Amsterdam stock exchange, for example, equals the Paris Exchange and exceeds the Frankfort Exchange. Funds from various European countries are channeled to the Amsterdam and Zurich exchanges, which have a long tradition of international lending, at present under strict regulation.

Capital needs to fulfill growth targets are urgent in West Germany and France. In spite of high saving levels, funds to finance fixed investment are in relatively short supply. A brief discussion of recent experience in the two countries will reveal widely differing adaptations to the problem of insufficient funds in the market. Germany has relied primarily on enterprise internal savings; France has mounted an ambitious national planning experiment and relied primarily on government and paragovernment institutions.

The West German capital markets have been unable in the postwar period to renew their traditional prewar role in financing investment. This is in part the consequence of the great strength developed in the commercial banking system[4] although the government's role in the markets has also increased. The public does not acquire large amounts of nonliquid financial assets, especially securities. Moreover, financial institutions such as insurance companies are not net purchasers of securities.

Gross security issues are only 4 percent of GNP,[5] less than half the level of the prewar years. Fixed-interest securities in circulation are 18 percent of GNP in comparison with 55 percent in the United States.[6] Few issues of securities currently in circulation were issued prior to the 1948 currency reform. Since 1950, however, the volume of securities has increased fiftyfold and the last few years have seen a doubling of the 1958 volume. Turnover on the major stock exchanges (there are eight) is frequently as few as 100 shares a day. Securities markets are thin and therefore susceptible to manipulation. Interest rates are high and costs of flotation—2.5 percent of the par value of stocks and bonds—also tend to be high.

---

[4] Commercial banks in West Germany, as in Switzerland, function as investment *and* commercial credit institutions. Banks act as underwriters of securities and all securities trading is effected through them. Interlocking directorates between banks and corporations add to the banks' importance.

[5] Deutsche Bundesbank, *Monthly Report,* October, 1963, p. 101.

[6] *Ibid.,* p. 103. The federal debt in West Germany is a negligible amount. If the U.S. long-term debt were subtracted from the U.S. fixed interest security total, the proportion would be 32 percent of GNP.

TABLE 8

NET SAVINGS SUPPLIED, BY SECTOR, 1958 AND 1961*

(Percentage of total)

Source	1958	1961
Households..............................	34.0	29.1
Enterprises..............................	54.3	34.4
Government..............................	22.1	27.9
Social insurance	6.1	10.0
Foreign.................................	- 16.5	- 1.4
Total.................................	100.0	100.0

* Includes capital transfer.
   Source: Deutsche Bundesbank, Statistisches Bundesamt, Statistisches Jahrbuch, 1962.

The net saving levels achieved in West Germany in recent years have been high in relation to GNP. Table 8 shows the division of net saving among sectors. Government saving is the largest part of the total when social insurance funds are included.[7] Household saving in the form of securities acquisition is only 15 to 20 percent of net savings. Savings accumulated in cash and demand deposits are approximately 10 to 15 percent of net saving and another 50 to 60 percent goes into saving deposits. Substantial inducements to accumulate savings deposits have operated in West Germany. Small savings deposits, for example, have qualified for a 25 percent bonus if held for five years.

Financial institutions have not developed the intermediation role familiar in the United States. As a group, financial institutions are not net acquirers of securities. Insurance companies, for example, in spite of constantly receiving 10 percent of net personal saving, have less than 25 percent of their assets in securities and hold less than 10 percent of all fixed-interest securities.[8] United States companies have more than half of their assets in securities and hold perhaps three-fourths of all corporate and foreign bonds.

The consequence of large amounts of savings being channeled to the Land governments, where they are employed chiefly in social capital programs, and the failure of financial institutions to develop a vigorous role in the capital markets has been the abandonment of the investment finance function to the banks (short-term notes) and the enterprises themselves. Table 9 shows the means by which investment has been financed in recent years.

Some 50 to 70 percent of the funds for net investment has been obtained through direct (short-term) credits in recent years, largely through banks and insurance companies. The comparable United States figure is 20 to 25 percent. Retained earnings are not a larger source of investible funds than

[7] The chief government surplus is accumulated by the Länder, which retain 61 (formerly 65) percent of the income tax, not by the federal government.
[8] Statistisches Bundesamt, *Statistisches Jahrbuch* (Stuttgart and Mainz: Kohlhammer, 1962), pp. 403 ff. and pp. 413 ff.

TABLE 9

FINANCING OF NET INVESTMENT, 1959-61

(Billions of deutsche marks)

Year	Net Investment	Sale of Securities		Direct Credits		Retained Earnings	Others
		Fixed Interest	Shares	Govern-ment	Financial Institutions		
1959	40.5	8.7	2.7	4.8	20.3	19.0	(-) 15.0
1960	51.6	4.5	5.3	3.4	21.1	22.5	(-) 5.2
1961	56.0	9.0	4.5	5.6	34.5	19.3	(-) 16.9

Source: Deutsche Bundesbank, Monthly Report.

the United States, but the stage of West German economic development makes its dependence on this source precarious.

The requirements of the West German economy for investment funds are based on investment growth of 6 to 7 percent in equipment and 8 to 9 percent in residential and public construction.[9] The rise in production costs and a continuous labor shortage have created these needs. Consequently, the need for investment funds will become more urgent during the next few years and the policy of generating internal funds for investment and borrowing abroad will probably not be adequate to supply the country's needs.

The problems of supplying investment funds are similar in France to those just outlined for West Germany. An adequate saving rate exists but savings are not channeled in large amounts to capital markets to finance investment. An ambitious planning experiment envisages investment growth of 7 percent a year in comparison with the 5.6 percent level of 1956–61. Concern with the capability of the capital market and related financial institutions to finance this program led to the appointment in 1962 of the Lorain Committe by the Minister of Finance to study the question; it reported in May, 1963.[10]

Sources of gross saving are given in Table 10 for 1959–61 with a forecast of 1965 needs.

The government sector is understated in the table because probably one-half to two-thirds of enterprise saving is attributable to government or para-government bodies. An estimated 25 percent of saving is government saving. Household saving, though large, is chiefly used to acquire liquid assets. More than 50 percent of household asset accumulation has been in the form of cash in some recent years and another 25 percent is typically held in time and saving deposits.[11] Life insurance and pension funds represent less than a tenth of household asset accumulations, one-fourth the United States figure.

The sources of funds to finance gross investment are given in Table 11.

Public funds are the largest source of capital funds in France. The special

[9] Federal Minister of Economic Affairs, *Report on Economic Trends in 1962 and Prospects for 1963* (Bonn: 1963), p. 12.

[10] *Rapport par le Comité Charge Detudier le Financement des Investissements* (Paris: 1963). Hereafter cited as the *Lorain Report.*

[11] *Ibid.*, pp. 9 ff.

TABLE 10

SOURCES OF GROSS DOMESTIC SAVING, ACTUAL 1959-61 AND FORECAST 1965

(Billions of francs)

Source	1959	1960	1961	1965
Enterprise sector	24.97	28.20	29.38	39.50
Household sector......	17.58	21.25	20.93	29.60
Government sector	6.37	7.16	7.88	7.60
Total	48.92	56.61	58.19	76.70

Source: Lorain Report, p. 7.

organizations lumped with insurance companies and financial markets are government or paragovernment bodies such as the Caisse des Dépôts et Consignations, the Crédit National, the Caisse des Marchés de l'Etat, and the Caisse Centrale de Crédit Hôtelier. Some of these special organizations act to permit banks to make effective five-year (medium-term) loans which the banks are otherwise forbidden to do. This is accomplished by rediscounting paper with the Caisse des Dépôts et Consignations (the ultimate repository of funds of a large number of other institutions). The Caisse des Dépôts, after securing the the Caisse des Dépôts et Consignations (the ultimate repository of funds of a large number of other institutions). The Caisse des Dépôts, after securing the countersignature of the Crédit National or Crédit Foncier, may rediscount the paper with the Banque de France. Capital funds managed by the Caisse des Dépôts et Consignations amount to about 45 billion francs. Government bodies are almost exclusively the arbiters of the uses to which the funds of this large organization are to be put. Consequently, more than 40 percent of the gross investments of the Caisse des Dépôts et Consignations are used for social capital (roads, schools, public services, and so on).

The Crédit National and the Crédit Foncier are both stock companies who shares are widely held by the public. These bodies make long-term loans (typically 15 to 20 years at 6.75 percent including taxes) to industry and commerce. The government appoints the general managers and two other

TABLE 11

SOURCES OF CAPITAL TO FINANCE GROSS INVESTMENT, 1961 AND 1962

(Percentage of gross investment)

Source	1961	1962*
Public funds	24.1	23.6
Special organizations, insurance companies, and financial markets......................................	23.7	25.5
Medium-term bank credits............................	13.2	12.2
Other sources	39.0	38.7

* Preliminary.
Source: Lorain Report, p. 16.

managers of each bank. A board of directors is elected by the shareholders. Any loan in excess of 2.5 million francs and bond issue in excess of 1 million francs must be approved by the Commissariat for the Plan. Thus, tight control is exercised over these and other special organizations.

The government itself is a large supplier of capital. Medium- and long-term investment finance amounted to 7.5 billion francs in the 1961 budget.[12] These resources are channeled into the economy (chiefly nationalized industries) by the Fonds de Développement Economique et Social. In 1962 gross investment in France was 61.1 billion francs, of which 14.4 billion francs (23.5 percent) was financed from public funds; of this amount, 2.9 billion francs (20 percent) was channeled through the FDES account, with 2.2 billion francs going to nationalized enterprises.[13]

Government borrowing is confined to the short- and intermediate-term market and averages about 3 percent of the gross national product. Treasury bonds (2.75 percent one-year maturity to 4.34 percent five-year maturity) are exempt from the income tax. These bonds are sold to the public by preference but also to the banks.

The relatively large amount of medium- and long-term credit extended by the banking system is similar in magnitude to that in West Germany. Two peculiarities of the French market help explain some part of the high bank credit level: No mortgage market, as such, exists in France, and consumer credit has not developed to the extent common in other industrial countries. Household construction is financed largely by extension of medium-term credits. The enterprise sector also depends heavily upon short- and intermediate-term credits and the proportion of these forms of liability is twice the United States level.[14]

Financial markets in France are inflexible and thin. Large amounts of savings are hoarded because of unwillingness of the French people to invest in nonliquid assets and for lack of the institutions to channel them into the market. Recent efforts have been made by the government, on recommendation of the Lorain Committee, to persuade the household sector to acquire nonliquid assets. To this end public promotional campaigns, development of open-end mutual funds, encouragement of public offerings of stock, and tax incentives have been adopted. The revitalization of the securities exchanges has been approached by reducing the requirement that 50 percent of life insurance reserves be invested in government securities, encouraging stock issues rather than bond issues as a source of funds, and permitting issue of preferred shares with reduced voting rights to prevent dilution of control in closely held corporations.

---

[12] Including 1.2 billion francs for consolidation of special construction credits.

[13] Ministère des Finances, *Statistiques et Etudes Financières,* Supplement (Seizième rapport annuel du Conseil national du crédit), August, 1962, pp. 897 ff.

[14] *Lorain Report,* pp. 90–91.

THE IMPLICATIONS FOR U.S. POLICY

This outline of Continental European capital market operations would seem to support two inferences: the markets have not developed to the level necessary to finance the expected investment levels, and the need for funds will become increasingly stringent. In this context the increase in resort to the New York market by European borrowers could be and was interpreted by the Treasury as evidence of an intention to obtain an increased amount of funds from the United States. This interpretation was made by the Administration last July and repeated in the President's 1964 Economic Report.[15]

The description of Continental European capital markets presented here also lends support to the point of view which urges caution in attributing the outflow of United States capital to higher interest rates abroad and the logical conclusion that United States long-term rates must rise to meet the competition.[16] Factors such as flotation cost and ease of entry into the United States market are important to European borrowers, probably more important than interest differentials. The level of United States rates, moreover, ought not to be required to meet an inevitable higher level established in markets where risk premiums result from nonmarketability.

THE POLICY ALTERNATIVES

The requirements of a policy to prevent aggravation of the United States payments deficit by long-term capital outflow are simple in the near-term perspective: the flow must be reduced without penalizing the developing countries and without long-run deleterious effects on developed countries with inadequate capital sources. Such a policy was proposed to apply immediately, to be selective, and to be temporary.

Only the United States throughout the postwar period has made its capital markets freely available. It is the practice in every other country to have machinery in being or on a stand-by basis to thwart unusual debits that would arise out of capital movements. In France no foreign issue has come to

[15] *Economic Report of the President* (Washington: U.S. Government Printing Office, 1964), pp. 125 ff.

[16] Philip W. Bell, "Private Capital Movements and the U.S. Balance-of-Payments Position," in U.S. Congress, Joint Economic Committee, *Factors Affecting the United States Balance of Payments*, 87th Cong., 2nd Sess., 1962, p. 395. Other discussions of this question are contained in Benjamin J. Cohen, "A Survey of Capital Movements and Findings Regarding Their Interest Sensitivity," in U.S. Congress, Joint Economic Committee, *The United States Balance of Payments*, 88th Cong., 1st Sess., 1963, p. 192, and in Peter B. Kenen, "Short-Term Capital Movements and the U.S. Balance of Payments," in U.S. Congress, Joint Economic Committee, *The United States Balance of Payments*, 88th Cong., 1st Sess., 1963, p. 153.

market since 1951 and in the Swiss market, usually considered free, the government is the final arbiter of foreign issues.

Two options have been discussed in the financial press that might be expected to fill the needs of capital outflow policy—the interest equalization tax and a capital issues committee. A preference for the tax seems justified on a number of grounds. It preserves the market's arbitration of the worthiness of an issue. It is an additional cost compatible with existing costs of issue flotation in other countries. Flexibility can be maintained by exemption tied to self-policing of issue offerings (as proposed with respect to Canada and Japan). It can be made retroactive. It can be applied for a stated period without disruption of normal market processes.

In contrast, a capital issues committee *must* circumvent the market arbitration of capital allocation. The Radcliffe Commission report[17] was critical of British experience with issue control, citing, among other reasons, the frightening away of "marginal issues," the necessity of citing detailed reasons for negative decisions, the tendency for "advisory" decisions to be rubber-stamped by the government as fiat, and the promotion of traffic in professional dressing-up of issue applications so that they would pass the committee. A determination between the tax and an issues committee is, however, not a black and white choice. Either might be effective.

With respect to the fact of requiring *some* form of capital outflow control, several observations are pertinent. The apparent upward trend in the use of United States capital markets by industrially advanced countries is inimical to efforts mounted to bring improvement to the United States payments balance. If a conflict of capital control policies exists between the United States and Western Europe, the danger to the United States and the Free World of failure to reduce the deficit would seem to outweigh the inconvenience to European countries of having to seek other sources of finance and develop their own capital sources. Some beneficial effects may ensue from creating doubts in Continental Europe as to the continuity of the access it may expect to enjoy in the New York market. Possibly Germany and France may be stimulated to develop their own capital markets. Finally, the low-cost benefits of the New York market, while admittedly attractive, are not necessarily a freely available international subsidy and there is ample room for some cost-based control consistent with a free-trade philosophy.

[17] *Report of the Committee on the Working of the Monetary System* (London: H. M. Stationery Office, 1959), pp. 163 ff. and pp. 332 ff.

THE EUROPEAN CAPITAL MARKETS*

The high rate of economic growth in Europe during the past fifteen years was due in large part to a high level of investment in new productive capacity. The role which the European capital markets played in this development may be suggested by a few facts:

- The market value of all outstanding securities in the Common Market in 1962 was roughly $120 billion—which is less than 13% of the United States volume.
- Yet in 1962, total issues of new securities in the EEC were $8.3 billion, or about 42% of the U.S. total.
- Moreover, this represents an increase in new issues of more than 100% during the last five years.
- Further, European capital needs were supported by an inflow of private long-term capital from the United States of more than a billion dollars in 1962.

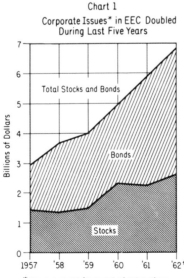

Chart 1
Corporate Issues* in EEC Doubled
During Last Five Years

* Nongovernment issues net of redemptions
in 6 EEC countries.
† 1962 partially estimated.
Source: EEC - All. Stat. Bulletin.

* *Report on Western Europe,* The Chase Manhattan Bank, New York, April–May, 1963, pp. 1–4.

Until recently, only a small share of Europe's long-term capital funds came from formal capital markets. High business profits in Europe have been the major source of industrial capital funds. But business profits have been shrinking during the last years, and more and more companies have found it necessary to seek additional capital by floating new bonds and stocks.

This raises the question of what the role of European markets will be in meeting future needs. This is of great importance to American companies operating in Europe because it will affect where and on what terms they will be able to satisfy their investment requirements.

A second problem arises from the large outflow of long-term capital to Europe that has occurred because of the higher interest rates and greater profits that have been made in that area. This has produced a continuing strain on the U.S. balance of payments. For this reason, growing concern has been expressed about the adequacy of the European capital markets. Thus it is useful to examine more closely the institutions—and the dimensions—of these markets.

THE MARKETS ARE SMALL

A broad definition of the term capital market would include that whole set of financial institutions which help to channel the financial savings of a country into real investments. Another definition, more narrow than the first, refers only to the issue and exchange of marketable securities. It is the latter type of markets for bonds and stocks in Europe which are alleged to be too small and relatively undeveloped, and about which the following paragraphs will be concerned.

One measure of the scope of the capital market is its absolute size. Rough estimates of the value of securities outstanding in Europe are taken from calculations of the par value of private bonds and of government bonds held by the public, plus the market value of shares outstanding. By this measure, the total value of listed securities outstanding, government and private, in all of Western Europe today approximates $300 billion.

The countries in Europe with the largest volumes of marketable securities are Britain—$153.6 billion, Germany—$36.6 billion, Italy—$35.7 billion, and France—$33.3 billion. The comparable figure for the United States is $925 billion at the end of 1962. The magnitude of this difference is somewhat surprising, considering the fact that the gross national product of the United States is just double that of Britain, France, Germany, and Italy together.

Yet the relatively small volume of securities in Western Europe is easy to explain. The financial aftermath of World War II—inflation, devaluation, and currency reform—reduced sharply existing debt in Europe. Continuing inflation discouraged the acquisition of fixed-interest securities, and low levels of per capita income, together with a huge pent-up demand for housing and durable consumer goods, left relatively few funds for investment in newly issued shares. Furthermore, profits were high and little incentive existed for companies to finance expansion from outside sources.

As a result of changing conditions, however, a more significant volume of new issues has appeared in recent years on the various capital markets of Europe.

NEW ISSUES ARE INCREASING

In 1962, all new public and private issues, net of redemptions, in the EEC countries totalled $8.3 billion, or about 42% of the comparable United States figure. And though the government sectors of the European economies include the railroads and various public utilities, net issues of corporate securities in Europe were nearly as large as the U.S. volume. The total for the EEC, Britain, and Switzerland was 85 percent of the respective U.S. market in 1962.

This is a good showing—and reflects a phenomenal growth in volume of new corporate issues in Western Europe. In the European Economic Community alone, new corporate bonds and stocks, net of redemptions, issued in 1962 had a market value of $6.8 billion—an increase of over 100 percent since 1957. During the same period, net issues by corporations in the United States decreased slightly.

There can be no doubt that the European capital markets have responded quickly and at an unprecedented pace to the rising demand for investment funds. At the same time, it is evident that the demand for funds has ex-

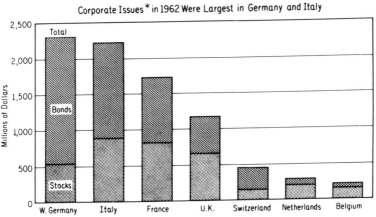

Chart 2
Corporate Issues* in 1962 Were Largest in Germany and Italy

*Nongovernment issues net of redemptions (partially estimated)

Sources: EEC-All.Stat.Bulletin, Midland Bank Review, Schweizerische National Bank-Monatsbericht

ceeded the supply that could be generated through regular capital markets. Two facts illustrate this:

First, business investment in excess of depreciation in plant and equipment in the EEC countries has been increasing rapidly and is now larger than that of the United States. Even after allowing for the different methods of measuring aggregate depreciation in the various countries, the comparison is striking. In 1961, when investments in the United States levelled off, net investment reached about $10 billion in the United States as against an approximate Common Market total of $20.6 billion.

Yet the volume of new private issues in that year was larger in the United States, some $5.8 billion for the EEC as against $8.8 billion for the United States. Much of the difference in Europe was made up through "short-term" bank borrowing.

Second, certain leading European companies and public authorities have been able to raise additional capital at reasonable rates by floating new issues in the New York market. The net outflow of U.S. private capital to Western Europe in the form of new issues, direct investments, long-term loans, and portfolio investments amounted to $1,052 million in 1962. The inflow from Western Europe of such funds was a mere $163 million.

Thus the European financial markets present a picture both of very rapid growth and of continuing capital scarcity. The growth is evidenced by the fact that new corporate issues have been rising faster than net investments. The scarcity is evidenced by the comparatively large share of investment funds obtained from short-term and medium-term bank credit.

A favorable omen for continued growth is the rapid expansion of personal savings in the major European countries. In Germany, for example, personal savings rose from $4.9 billion in 1957 to $6.8 billion in 1961. In time, the financial institutions are certain to channel a larger portion of these funds into the capital markets.

Another hopeful factor is the slow but steady improvement of the institutions of the European capital markets, although one must realize that developments of recent years took place in a number of separate national markets rather than in a single large economy.

THE MARKETS ARE SEPARATE

Whereas New York is the center and ultimate clearing point for most new issues in the United States, there is no equivalent financial center in Western Europe. There the stock exchanges are primarily national in character, and even today the number of listings of foreign securities in London, Paris, or Frankfurt is small.

This national separation of markets is still more apparent in the flotation of new issues. London, which used to be a primary source of long-term capital for the entire world, nowadays serves Commonwealth countries primarily. In 1962, Great Britain permitted the flotation of a single nonsterling loan: a $5.5 million issue by the Government of Iceland. Not a single issue of a country outside the Franc Zone was floated in Paris last year nor in any other year since the end of World War II, and the only foreign loan floated in West Germany in 1962 was a $25 million bond issue by the City of Osaka.

Government controls constitute still another limitation affecting foreign capital issues in most European countries. These controls are designed to channel capital into domestic needs at interest rates lower than would prevail in free markets.

The Netherlands and Switzerland are the only European countries where foreign securities are regularly floated, although on a relatively small scale. In these countries interest rates are lower and total borrowing costs compare favorably with those prevailing in the New York market. In part, this is because new issues require a government license, and total foreign issues are limited by a predetermined quota.

Chart 3

VOLUME OF NEW SECURITIES IN SELECTED COUNTRIES
ACTUAL PROCEEDS, NET OF REDEMPTIONS, IN 1961

(Millions of dollars)

	National* Government	Other Public Auth.	Total Government	Corporate Bonds	Stocks	Total Corporate	Foreign Securities	Total New Issues (Net)
Belgium and Luxemburg	101.0	317.3	418.3	16.6	106.0	122.6	–	540.9
France	-151.9	24.3	-127.6	862.8	656.2	1,519.0	–	1,391.4
Germany	512.0	466.0	978.0	1,016.1	823.9	1,840.0	3.0	2,821.0
Italy	216.4	18.4	234.8	1,156.4	666.8	1,823.2	24.0	2,082.0
Netherlands	73.5	48.6	122.1	34.2	48.6	82.8	119.3	324.2
United Kingdom	-590.0	64.1	-525.9	313.0	1,151.4	1,464.4	154.6	1,093.1
Switzerland	-8.9	8.1	-0.8	222.9	83.3	306.2	196.7	502.1
8 European Countries	152.1	946.8	1,098.9	3,622.0	3,536.2	7,158.2	497.6	8,754.7
United States	-3,300.0	4,700.0	1,400.0	5,100.0	3,700.0	8,800.0	600.0	10,800.0

* Change in public holdings of marketable debt having a maturity of one year or more.
Sources: EEC – All. Stat. Bulletin, Midland Bank Review, Statistique et Etudes Financiere, Monatsbericht der Deutschen Bundesbank, Schweizerische National Bank – Monatsbericht, Finance Accounts of United Kingdom, B.I.S. – Annual Report.

In West Germany, on the other hand, there is a minimum of capital market controls and the effective bond rate last year was close to 6 percent which, together with a 2.5 percent tax on new issues, made the German capital market unattractive to foreign borrowers.

INTEGRATION PROCEEDS SLOWLY

The Treaty of Rome stipulates the eventual removal of all restrictions against capital movements among the six countries of the EEC. This important liberalization is expected to become fully effective by 1967. It does not necessarily mean that the European capital markets will be open to all would-be borrowers—it implies only free access of the member countries to each other's markets.

The removal of legal restrictions will be a great step forward, though it may not by itself assure effective integration of the European capital markets. Integration is complicated by the divergent banking structures in the member countries. In Italy, industrial long-term capital is supplied in large amounts by government lending agencies. In addition, the large deposit banks with nation-wide branch systems are all nationalized. Investment banking in France essentially involves the making of long-term loans. New capital issues, on the other hand, are mainly distributed by nationalized nation-wide deposit banks. In the Netherlands and Germany a few very large banks dominate the capital markets, operating as investment bankers, deposit bankers, and security brokers all in one.

This great divergence of banking institutions and underwriting practices in the EEC countries means that integration of the capital markets in Europe will be a rather slow process, though much depends on the future pace of overall economic integration.

The lack of integration is illustrated by the fact that almost all underwriting consortia formed in Europe today involve banks of one country only. However, one recent issue (a new bond of the Municipal Bank of Norway) proved to be an exception. The bonds in question were denominated in 17 European currencies, thereby insuring the lenders not only against devaluation, but also allowing them to benefit from a possible future appreciation of any of the seventeen currencies in which redemption may be demanded. This method could be employed in the future—but would likely require the prior consent of the central banks involved.

IMPLICATIONS FOR AMERICAN BUSINESS

Despite these favorable signs, it is unlikely that American firms will find it profitable to issue securities in Europe in the near future. At present, only Switzerland and the Netherlands offer long-term funds on terms comparable with those in the United States. With the establishment of freedom of capital movements within the EEC, any free Netherlands funds are likely to be absorbed by the other Common Market countries. This leaves Switzerland, where a substantial volume of foreign securities are floated each year. However, the Swiss authorities seem to favor corporate borrowers that operate in Switzerland itself. At any rate, the Swiss volume of foreign flotations is not likely to increase.

Subsidiaries of American companies in Europe will most likely continue to obtain capital funds in Europe—from retained earnings and depreciation, and from bank loans. However, the meager possibilities of issuing securities in continental financial centers mean that part of U.S. subsidiary capital will continue to be raised in the United States.

CONCLUSION

Over the near future, it seems likely that Europe will remain an area of relative capital scarcity compared with the United States, and that investment funds will tend to flow chiefly from the United States to Europe.

As the European capital markets become broader and deeper, however, and as the institutions serving them become more integrated, the cost of channeling savings into investments should decline. It may then become easier to float major issues in Europe, and, as a secondary result, the demands on the U.S. capital market should become relatively smaller.

THE UNIT OF ACCOUNT*

At the beginning of January, a loan expressed in units of account was placed, on behalf of the Norges Kommunalbank, very successfully in a number of Western European countries. Two similar loans had previously been issued in 1961 and 1962.

The unit of account is not a modern invention. As long ago as the late Middle Ages, units of account were in use, such as the well-known Mark-Banco of Hamburg and the Florin-Banco of the Amsterdam Exchange Bank. An example nearer to the present day is the currency of account of the Bank for International Settlements, Basle, the unit of which is equivalent to the 1914 Swiss gold franc.

Various international institutions, such as the European Payments Union, the European Monetary Agreement, the European Coal and Steel Community, the European Economic Community and the European Investment Bank also make use of the system when drawing up their balance sheets, even if the units of account used differ from one institution to another.

DEFINITION

A unit of account is not a full-fledged currency, in that it is not a means of payment or an instrument of exchange. The unit of account is a yardstick, serving to determine the value of obligations entered into, with the aim of maintaining the value of the respective liabilities and claims as constant as possible.

The very nature of the unit of account, i.e., to serve as a measure of value for contractual obligations, points to the inference that various such units may exist. The creation of a unit of account, indeed, rests on the basis of an agreement between parties. Thus, in 1950, a unit of account was set up by the seventeen countries of the European Payments Union, with a gold fineness of 0.88867088 grams.

This unit of account, which is sometimes called the Epunit, was employed for accounting purposes among the 17 central banks of the Union. The actual payments were effected in gold, U.S. dollars or some other national currency agreed upon by the creditors.

In the case of the three loans floated so far, the unit of account has been that of the former European Payments Union. Since this unit had already

* Reprinted from the *Weekly Bulletin of the Kredietbank,* February 23, 1963.

been officially used by the central banks and their respective governments for the purpose of establishing contractual obligations, it was obvious that the utilization of a similar unit of account by private institutions could encounter no objection of principle on the part of the authorities.

As this unit of account is based on gold and as the seventeen currencies —known as reference currencies—to which it is linked also have, directly or indirectly, a gold value, there exists a fixed proportion between each currency and the unit of account.

The gold value of the unit of account, referred to above, will remain unchanged as long as all the base parities (i.e., the proportion between the unit of account and the currencies of the 17 countries at the date when an agreement has to come into effect) shall not have been altered.

The present base parities of the reference currencies are:

IUA = 26.000 Schillings (Austria).
IUA = 50.000 Francs (Belgium).
IUA =   6.907 Kroner (Denmark).
IUA =   4.937 Francs (France).
IUA =   4.000 Marks (Federal Republic of Germany).
IUA =   0.357 Pound (United Kingdom).
IUA = 30.000 Drachmas (Greece).
IUA = 43.000 Kroner (Iceland).
IUA =   0.357 Pound (Ireland).
IUA = 625.001 Lire (Italy).
IUA = 50.000 Francs (Luxemburg).
IUA =   3.620 Guilders (Netherlands).
IUA =   7.143 Kroner (Norway).
IUA = 28.749 Escudos (Portugal).
IUA =   5.173 Kroner (Sweden).
IUA =   4.373 Francs (Switzerland).
IUA =   9.000 Pounds (Turkey).

Modifications to these base parities may, under certain conditions, set in motion the machinery whereby the unit of account will be given a new value. A distinction should be made between the following cases:

(a) if this modification occurs for all the reference currencies in the same direction and in the same proportion, the gold value of the UA will be altered in the same direction and in the same proportion;
(b) if in the same direction but in different proportions, the gold value of the UA will be altered in the same direction and in the same proportion as the reference currency (currencies) which has (have) been altered the least, in relation to its (their) base values;
(c) if in different directions, then the gold value of the UA will be altered in the same direction and in the same proportion as the reference currency (currencies) which has (have) been altered the least, in relation to its (their) base values.

Should it happen that the proportion of the alternation of the reference currency which has been devalued the least is equal to the proportion of the alteration of the reference currency which has been revalued the least, then the gold value of the UA will remain unchanged.

TECHNICAL ASPECTS

It is sometimes contended that the unit of account would amount to a gold clause in disguise. A gold clause confers upon the currency in which the obligation is expressed an unchangeable gold value. It is in most cases formulated in such a way that the payment of interest and principal has to occur in the gold currency of a specific country. The weight and content of this currency are defined at the time of the issue. The actual payment will usually occur in national currency, but in that case it will be in an amount permitting of the purchase of the gold currency.

The very definition of the unit of account indicates that its gold fineness is not constant. It may, depending upon the variations of all reference currencies, increase or decrease; indeed, after the conclusion of a contract; whereby an original base parity was established for each reference currency, these currencies may be devalued or revalued either successively or simultaneously, which means that finally modifications occur to the gold value of the unit of account.

The conversion of the unit of account into one of the reference currencies is carried out in each case by reference to the base parities of the currency in question. The unit of account is sometimes mistakenly interpreted as being a kind of multiple currency clause. The latter, in one of its most widely-used forms, entitles the creditor to request payment of the interest and redemption of the debenture not only in the currency of the loan, but also in one or more other currencies, to be determined beforehand, as well as in accordance with a previously established unchangeable parity. This means that the obligation of a loan of this type is expressed in various national currencies, at the choice of the lender. Consequently, the debtor's burden is increased in the case of revaluation of one particular currency, while on the other hand he derives no benefit from a revaluation of his own currency. Whenever his own currency is devalued, he will pay more, without benefitting from the devaluations of the other currencies.

With a multiple currency clause, when all currencies are devalued but in different proportions, the obligations fluctuate in the same proportion as the currency which has been devalued the least. This is also the case with the unit of account.

If there is a general revaluation, the obligations will, in the case of a multiple currency clause, vary in line with the currency which has been revalued the most. In the case of the unit of account, however, the obligations will vary in the same proportions as the currency which has been revalued the least.

Moreover, the obligation in units of account is much more stable, as it only changes after the 17 currencies have been altered. In the case of the multiple currency clause, it is sufficient for one currency to change in order to cause the obligation to undergo an alteration.

By the way of summary, it may be said that in the case of the multiple currency clause, the debtor bears the risk of other currencies as well as that of his own currency; in the case of the unit of account, however, his obligations do not change as long as his own currency remains unchanged.

In the case of revaluation or devaluation of one or more, but not of all national currencies, the base parities are adjusted, as indicated above in the definition of the unit of account. The financial servicing will thus not necessarily be transferred to the country carrying out the revaluation, as the value of the unit of account remains unchanged.

For example, the base parity of the DM, prior to the revaluation of March 1961, was DM 4.20 = 1 UA. This meant that the creditor who held a coupon of 1 UA obtained DM 4.20. After the revaluation he would still, under a multiple currency clause system, have obtained DM 4.20. With the unit of account system, whereby the base parity is adjusted, the creditor will receive only DM 4.

If in these two cases the creditor had wished to sell his DM for Belgian francs, then he would have obtained:

prior to the revaluation: $4.20 \times 11.904 = $ fr. 50;
after the revaluation: $4 \times 12.50 = $ fr. 50.

On the other hand, had the DM been devalued, so that the base parity had become DM 4.50 instead of DM 4.20 per UA, while other currencies remained unchanged, then the creditor, in the case of a multiple currency clause, would obtain only DM 4.20 (devalued) at the time of payment of coupons or redemption of the debenture, and would thus refrain from requesting this currency. Under the unit of account system, he will receive DM 4.50 (devalued) and hence, when selling the DM for Belgian francs, he will obtain:

prior to devaluation: $DM\ 4.20 \times 11.904 = $ fr. 50;
after devaluation: $DM\ 4.50 \times 11.111 = $ fr. 50.

The examples given here show clearly that the unit of account system, while offering a safeguard against devaluation, to the advantage of the creditor, also acts as a brake on speculation which would be to the disadvantage of the debtor.

The unilateral nature of the multiple currency clause leaps to the eye, i.e., that it may prove very expensive for the debtor, especially if a reference currency is revalued in relation to his own national currency. Indeed, he no longer depends solely on what happens to his own currency, but shares the fate of each of the reference currencies.

With loans in units of account this is not the case. As long as the national currency remains unchanged, the debtor does not pay more in his own currency for the financial service of the loan.

The unit of account thus constitutes a fair distribution of risks as between debtors and creditors, by ensuring that the claim retains its original value as long as possible — i.e., as long as at least one reference currency remains unchanged.

For individual savers and for institutional investors which manage the former's savings, the system of the unit of account offers obvious advantages by reason of its stability. For reinsurance companies it provides an extremely favorable solution for the currency spread of their risks. Changes in the geographical location of risks are no longer bound to involve a corresponding adjustment in the portfolio.

The operations in units of account are spread over several countries. On the one hand, this will contribute towards the development of a Western European financial market and on the other, to the levelling-off in rates of interest. Bonds in units of account will indeed circulate beyond the frontiers of a country with a high rate of interest to another with a low rate of interest. By means of this arbitraging, an equalization of the price of money will be promoted.

The system of the UA itself can also act as a restraining influence on the flight of capital for monetary purposes. It is a well-known phenomenon that capital of this kind returns when an adequate degree of safety is guaranteed. An investor who subscribes to a loan in UA obtains a number of advantages inherent in loans expressed in foreign currencies, without being subjected to the limitations of such loans. The principal and interest can also be collected in a particular country, and it is thus not necessary to go abroad in order to obtain the advantages of the strongest currency.

The recent loan in units of account has undoubtedly contributed to draw the attention of wide circles to this system, which is from all points of view an original and also a fair method of establishing international obligations between parties.

THE EUROPEAN STOCK MARKETS *

The European stock exchanges have a very long history. The Paris Bourse has its origins in a money changer's market which operated on a bridge over the River Seine back in the Middle Ages. The Belgian Stock Exchange is also of Medieval origin. The Hamburg Exchange dates from 1558, and Amsterdam's from 1608. The new quarters which will house the London Stock Exchange will be located at the same site—bounded by Threadneedle, Throgmorton, Bartholomew, and Old Broad Streets —where the exchange has flourished for almost 300 years.

There is no unified stock market for all of Europe. Rather, there are a number of national markets, with a proliferation of smaller markets within most countries. Each country has its own particular organization.

The securities market in the United Kingdom is the most highly developed in Western Europe. In size, number, and value of transactions, the London Stock Exchange surpasses any other European exchange. Although there are some twenty local stock exchanges in the country, the market for securities in the United Kingdom can be described as a single market with headquarters in London. In this respect, it is similar to the U.S. market, which is centered in New York despite the seventeen regional exchanges in the United States.

On the Continent, France, Belgium, and the Netherlands have centralized security markets. On the other hand, decentralized stock exchange systems prevail in West Germany, Switzerland, and Italy. West Germany has eight separate exchanges with Frankfurt and Dusseldorf being the most active, followed by Hamburg and Munich. Switzerland has seven. Zurich accounts for about two-thirds of the Swiss security business and is the leading continental market. In Italy there are ten exchanges in operation, of which Milan is the most important, followed by Rome, Turin, and Genoa.

One important characteristic of some European exchanges is the role played by the banks. In Belgium, France, and Italy, the functions of commercial and investment banking are separated by law as they are in the United States. In the United Kingdom, there is by tradition a similar distinction although there is some overlapping of the two functions. On the other hand, in the case of Western Germany and Switzerland, the large commer-

* *International Economic Review,* The First National Bank of Chicago, December, 1964, pp. 1–5.

Chart 1

NET CHANGE IN OUTSTANDING STOCKS

(Millions of dollars)

	1956-58 Annual Average	1959-61 Annual Average	1962	1963
Belgium	$ 134	$ 124	$ 154	$ 106
France	525	598	808	847
Germany	367	440	377	255
Italy	304	606	973	403
Netherlands	97	35	127	19
Common Market Total	$1,427	$1,803	$2,439	$1,630
Switzerland	$ 58	$ 244	$ 420	$ 355
United Kingdom	$ 392	$ 980	$ 728	$ 560
United States	$3,600	$4,000	$2,400	$1,000

Source: Bank for International Settlements.

While the total market value of all securities in the Common Market and the United Kingdom is estimated at only about one-third of that in the United States, new offerings of stocks in these countries between 1956 and 1963 have amounted to some 70 percent of the total in the U.S.

cial banks engage in investment banking. They act as dealers and brokers for customers' accounts and also conduct trading operations for their own accounts. Moreover, the banks participate in underwriting the greater part of the new issues.

Other differences exist between the various markets. In the London Stock Exchange, a broker only buys and sells securities for the public. A jobber, on the other hand, unique to the London market, operates as a principal, buying and selling securities on his own account and dealing with brokers. In effect, the jobber establishes the price. On the Continent, the tasks of determing the price and of matching buying and selling orders rest directly with either brokers or stock exchange officials.

The transfer of securities also varies. In the United Kingdom and Italy, nearly all shares must be in registered form. On the other continental markets, however, the shares usually are in bearer form. Each market also has its own settlement rules. In most continental countries transactions usually are settled in cash within one to four days. If a transaction is not for cash but on account, the settlement date may vary from two weeks as in London and Brussels, to the end of the month as in Paris, or to the end of the following month as in Zurich and Milan.

One accustomed to dealing in the stock market in the United States would find that there are many other dissimilarities between the U.S. and European exchanges. For example, reliable figures on the volume of trading and price quotations of securities, reported regularly for the U.S. stock exchanges, are not readily available in London. In Italy, trading in large blocks of shares is not generally handled on the floor of the stock exchanges but is done privately, often in great secrecy. In Germany, many security transactions between banks are made in private so that the published volume of the exchanges may be quite different from the actual volume of shares traded. Recently, in the United States a so-called "third market" has developed where a substantial volume of listed securities is traded in large blocks and is not included in the volume totals reported by the stock exchanges.

There are about 12,000 different issues listed on the London exchange in contrast to the 1,500 or so listed on the New York Stock Exchange. However, the European financial centers have no over-the-counter market as exists in the United States. Instead, the counterparts of those securities which the United States generally appear in the over-the-counter market are listed and traded on the floors of the various European exchanges.

Basically, in almost all cases, the stock market in the U.S. is broader and enjoys much wider public participation than European markets. In addition, the disclosure of financial data of publicly held shares is much greater than in Europe.

Prices on the European stock exchanges have roughly paralleled those of the United States during the postwar period. The 1950's was a period of moderate general growth in share prices followed, in subsequent years, by rapid advances and steep declines. Important differences exist, however, which dispel somewhat the popular assumption that the European price patterns are rigidly linked to New York. First, share prices in some European markets increased more rapidly, and in other markets more slowly, than they did in the United States. Second, prices began to decline in the European stock markets several months earlier than in the U.S. exchanges. Third, this declining "bear" market, in most cases, has lasted longer and has been much more severe in Europe than in the United States.

The general advance in share prices in most Western European exchanges from 1950—the year in which Western European countries reached, and in many cases surpassed, prewar production levels—through 1958 reflected primarily the postwar surge of business activity. Except for the phenomenal share price advances experienced by Western Germany (323 percent) and France (308 percent), the price rise of the U.S. stock market (169 percent) topped the increases of the major European exchanges. The U. S. advance was more than three times as large as the increases in the Netherlands and the United Kingdom, about two and one-half times that of Switzerland, double the rise in Belgium, and a few percentage points above the one in Italy.

During the next period, roughly 1959–61, a number of broad economic and political factors, both domestic and international, stimulated a sharp rise in share prices on all major European exchanges. This strong advance,

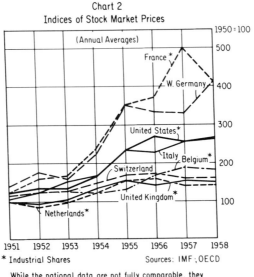

Chart 2
Indices of Stock Market Prices

(Annual Averages)

1950 = 100

France *

W. Germany

500

400

300

United States*

Italy
Belgium*

200

Switzerland

United Kingdom*

100

Netherlands*

1951   1952   1953   1954   1955   1956   1957   1958

* Industrial Shares   Sources: IMF ; OECD

While the national data are not fully comparable, they
provide a good approximation of the behavior of the
various markets.

or "bull" market, got under way in 1959 (late 1958 in the case of Germany) against a background of substantial easing of credit in most European countries. Stocks became particularly attractive as business profits increased. There was a strong rise in economic activity, and at the same time, the balance of payments position of most European countries improved steadily. These factors, together with the gradual dismantling of external payment controls, the advent of currency convertibility, and the formation of the Common Market, engendered optimism among investors.

It was during this period that the major European exchanges developed closer links which led to the cross listing of the stocks of major European firms. In 1960 the first trades in German and Italian stocks took place on both the Paris and Amsterdam exchanges. Moreover, American investment in European securities rose sharply. Between 1959 and 1961, Americans bought about $500 million of European stocks. This volume had a considerable upward impact on prices, due primarily to the thinness of European markets.

Another important factor accounting for the rise in stock prices during this period was the general broadening of stock ownership in Europe. This was done by channeling an increased volume of small savings into stock investments. For example, mutual funds, a much more recent phenomenon in Europe than in the United States, developed quite strongly in the late 1950's. Tax incentives favoring stock ownership were introduced in several countries. Moreover, in Austria and in Germany, the governments stimu-

Chart 3
Indices of Stock Market Prices
(Quarterly Averages)

1950 = 100

Since 1958, U.S. stock prices have fluctuated less widely than in Europe.

lated the interest of small investors by the sale of capital stock in government-held concerns (the so-called "people's shares"), such as the public sale of Volkswagen and Preussag Mining shares in Germany.

The sharp rises in share prices gradually undermined investors' preferences for equity investment and led the way to a decline in stock prices about the middle of 1961. The same speculative excesses which later, in May, 1962, generated the sharp downward adjustments in the United States stock exchanges were abundantly evident in Europe as well. However, while the stock market in the United States regained its losses by 1963 and went on to new highs, most European exchanges so far have failed to regain the peak levels reached in the 1959-61 period.

During the past two years or so, something of a paradox seemingly has developed in Europe. Most European investors have demonstrated little faith in the idea that common stock investments constitute a hedge against inflation. Since the end of 1962, in those countries where the cost of living and the general price levels have been rising the most, stock prices have staged a considerable and worrisome decline. In Italy, for example, where inflationary pressures have been the strongest, stocks are near a five year low. Share prices are down about one-third in France, and in Switzerland, the averages are forty percent below the postwar highs reached in the first quarter of 1962.

There are a number of reasons for the "bearish" state of most European markets. First, a restrictive credit policy has prevailed in most European countries in the last two years or so. This has had a dampening effect on equity investment. Second, the profit margins of most European firms have been narrowing due to rising costs, particularly for labor, and intensive foreign competition. Third, the adjustments that most companies have had to make in the process of European integration have been difficult and costly. Fourth, political influences, such as the "opening to the left" in Italy, and the nationalization of important industrial sectors, as for example the electric utility industry in Italy, have shaken the confidence of the investing public. Finally, the U.S. proposal in July, 1963 of an Interest Equalization Tax on purchases of foreign securities has had the immediate effect of curtailing, at least temporarily, new U.S. portfolio investment in Europe.

Despite these general contracting influences, each market remains, in effect, a special situation and already some important year-to-year advances have been registered by the German, British, and Dutch exchanges. Moreover, with the apparent successes of the anti-inflationary policies in Italy, France, Switzerland, and Belgium, a new impetus toward a general rise in share prices seems likely.

ADDITIONAL READINGS

Altman, Oscar L., "Foreign Markets for Dollars, Pounds and Other Currencies," *IMF Staff Papers,* December, 1961, pp. 313–352.

Campbell, P. A. T., "The Canadian Money Market," *The Bankers' Magazine,* July, 1963, pp. 11–17 and August, 1963, pp. 95–102.

Einzig, Paul, "European Capital Markets," *The National Banking Review,* June, 1964, pp. 569–576.

———, *The Eurodollar System,* New York: St. Martins, 1964.

Elman, Lee M., "Move Toward the Development of a European Capital Market," *Export Trade,* December 16, 1963, pp. 10–13.

Johnson, Norris O., *Eurodollars in the New International Money Market,* First National City Bank, New York, 1964.

Kenen, Peter B., "Towards an Atlantic Capital Market," *Lloyd's Bank Review,* July 1963, pp. 15–30.

"Problems of Financial Integration," *The Atlantic Community Quarterly,* Fall, 1963, pp. 438–447 (reprinted from the Annual Report of the Compagnie d'Outremer pour l'Industrie et la Finance, Brussels, March, 1963).

Segre, Claudio, "Foreign Bond Issues in European Markets," *Banca Nazionale del Lavoro Quarterly Review,* March, 1964, pp. 41–89.

Statistical Analysis of Publicly Offered Foreign Dollar Bonds, Institute of International Finance, New York University, 1958.

The Capital Market in Japan, Institute of International Finance, New York University, 1962.

The Euro-Dollar Market, International Reports, New York, 1963.

Wilson, J. S. G., "The Internationalization of Capital Markets," *The Three Banks Review,* June, 1964, pp. 3–24.

chapter *10*

Money and Capital Markets in Underdeveloped Countries

As indicated in the introduction to Chapter 7, multinational business has a direct interest in the development of the underdeveloped countries. Any aspect which furthers the industrialization of a country will increase its attractiveness as a market for goods manufactured elsewhere, or as a location in which to invest. Two of the major factors restraining rapid industrialization are the lack of a local capital market and the lack of a local money market.

The first two readings of this chapter find that without an active capital market, it is difficult to mobilize and allocate the existing capital resources of a country for the effective development of the economy. Without such a market, available funds tend to go into commerce and real estate rather than into industrial enterprises. Without such a market also, it is difficult for a given industrial project to attract the investment of more than one wealthy family group, while an operating capital market can gain the support of more sources of capital and at the same time spread the risk of the venture. An effective capital market can, furthermore, attract the savings of many small investors. This is particularly important to a foreign company which wishes, for financial or political reasons, to obtain local equity capital but wants the ownership sufficiently distributed so that it is passive as a voice in management.

An interesting example of this situation is the Cummins Engine Company[1] investment in India. The Indian government insisted upon a majority ownership by Indians. The company found an Indian partner who had sufficient capital to finance only twenty percent of local capital requirements, so forty percent of the shares of the Indian venture were offered to the public. The name of Cummins was sufficiently well known so that the issue was oversubscribed by 5000 percent. This resulted in an allocation of the shares per subscriber and a very broad spread of ownership. Without the effective primary market, the shares might have ended up in the hands of only a few investors and become a source of difficulty.

[1] This company is a manufacturer of diesel engines, with headquarters in Columbus, Indiana.

It is, therefore, important for the international financial management of a firm to be able to recognize the stage of development of the capital market of a country where the firm plans to invest so as to determine what role the market can play in the investment financing. It is also important for the company to work with the governmental authorities of the country which has no such capital market, to help them to nurture the growth of the market. The foreign investor is in a particularly favorable position to interest small savers in investing in industrial shares, and to demonstrate to local entrepreneurs the benefits of widespread rather than family ownership.

The next chapter is devoted to the overall role of development banks. The second reading in this chapter, however, is restricted to the role that development banks can play in fostering a capital market. The individual private investors certainly can do little unless the governmental authorities favor and work for the establishment of a capital market, and unless an institution such as a development bank is available to assist in the effort.

The third reading in this chapter, extracted from a work by Peter G. Fousek, discusses the development and use of money markets. The fostering of a money market depends, even more than in the case of a capital market, upon the stimulation and active encouragement of the government. The major purpose of a money market is to act as an instrument of monetary policy. But, as the reading points out, the existence of a money market also benefits the commercial banks and industry, permitting a more efficient use of funds. In fact, as noted in the article by J. S. G. Wilson, an underdeveloped money market can benefit commercial banks and businesses without serving as an effective instrument of monetary policy. It is, therefore, important for the foreign investor to be well aware of the status of development of a money market to effectively plan cash flows in a subsidiary in an underdeveloped country.

A PHILIPPINE CASE STUDY: PROBLEMS IN FINANCING ECONOMIC DEVELOPMENT: THE NEED FOR AN EFFECTIVE CAPITAL MARKET*

It is the argument of this paper that without an active and dynamic *capital market*, capital resources cannot be mobilized and allocated efficiently for development purposes in a developing economy. The absence of such a capital market arises from the lack of efficient institutional machinery to mobilize and allocate capital. As long as such machinery is lacking, it is inevitable that large amounts of capital will be devoted to low priority uses.

A vigorous capital market is just as important for development financing as a central bank is for commercial financing. By acting as a "banker's bank" and "a lender of last resort" a central bank can help prevent commercial banks from tying up their assets and endangering their cash positions and lending abilities. An effective capital market does approximately the same thing in financing the development of an economy.

Such a market must be more than a "one-shot affair" in which a development loan or a stock issue can be initially floated. It must include a secondary market as well, where existing obligations can be bought and sold. Otherwise, an underwriting institution becomes "locked in" to its original investment and cannot finance new ventures. Moreover, without a secondary market, it is more difficult for new money to be drawn into productive investment. The absence of a secondary market, in short, is one of the principal reasons why less developed economies are continually lacking development capital.

THE EXISTING PHILIPPINE CAPITAL MARKET

The capital market in the Philippines is divided between an equity market and a market for public and private debt instruments. The market for equity shares is very limited. Although about 90 issues are listed on the

* H. K. Charlesworth and Richard W. Hooley, *International Development Review*, September, 1963, pp. 25–29.

stock exchange, not more than 60 are actively traded, even in the broadest sense of the term. Several different types of equities are traded on the Exchange, including shares of commercial and industrial enterprises, mining shares and oil shares. Since oil deposits in commercial size have yet to be found, none of the oil companies listed on the exchange can show earnings or dividends and these shares can be omitted in considering the investment potential of this market. The balance—representing share of commercial, industrial and mining companies in varying degrees— can be considered as constituting the available supply of investment (as distinguished from purely speculative) instruments. Table 1 shows the peso volume of transactions in these securities.

TABLE 1

PESO-VOLUME OF TRANSACTIONS IN COMMERCIAL, INDUSTRIAL AND MINING SHARES ON THE MANILA STOCK EXCHANGE (1951-60)

(Million pesos)

Years	Peso-Volume of Transactions Manila Stock Exchange	Peso-Volume of Transactions Deflated by Turnover Index*
1951	38.2	38.2
1952	27.0	41.5
1953	21.8	33.0
1954	26.2	38.9
1955	129.5	33.4
1956	208.8	56.1
1957	89.3	47.0
1958	193.5	27.5
1959	169.0	20.0
1960	41.0	26.8

* Turnover Index: $\dfrac{\text{Quantity of shares traded, year N}}{\text{Quantity of shares listed for trading, year N}}$ $\dfrac{\text{Quantity of shares funded, 1951}}{\text{Quantity of shares for trading, 1951}}$

Source: Manila Stock Exchange.

The data in Table 1 show that the total peso volume of transactions in equity shares (after adjustment for speculative turnover) for the past three years is equal only to about 5 percent of household savings in financial assets as measured in 1960.[1] Not only is the equity market deficient in its capacity to absorb household savings, but the trend of its development in recent years indicates its capacity is not likely to grow under present conditions.

The market for long-term debt instruments is also limited, and is divided between a public (government) debt and a private debt market. Although National Government (Public Works and Economic Development)

---

[1] It has long been assumed that the Philippine economy did not produce enough savings to fund a flourishing capital market. Recent research indicates that the level of gross domestic savings is much higher than has been shown in national income accounts and approaches 16% of GNP (14% if consumer durables are not included). In 1960, Philippine households registered savings of approximately P550 million in nonphysical assets—i.e. bank deposits, life insurance, pension funds etc.

bonds have been listed on the Manila Stock Exchange for some years, the record shows only a few isolated transactions over the entire period. Nor is trading in these bonds to be expected. Until recently interest rates on government bonds (4 percent per annum) were held below the general level of yields prevailing on alternative debt instruments because holders can always find a ready buyer in the Central Bank at par. Because the Bank supports the market for government debt instruments, a secondary or general market for such instruments is virtually nonexistent. Issues of long-term corporate bonds and notes are relatively rare, and most of what has been successfully floated has been issued by a few utility companies. Although a few corporate bond issues are listed on the Manila Stock Exchange, trading in these items is also virtually nil.

As for the private debt market, it is difficult to measure the amount of investment (i.e. long-term) credit which the commercial banks have extended for industrial expansion. In many instances lines of credit were extended or renewed to permit the borrower to refund a short term loan over a longer period of time. The economic nature of the loans suggests that most were medium-time credits. The credits were extended on a short-term demand basis with no guarantee by a commercial bank that it would not call the loan within the contracted period of the credit facility. However, a commercial bank would state that it would try to consider sympathetically requests for extension of the loan, and in effect this is what has happened.

Commercial loans by the commercial banks for industrial expansion purposes reflected not only a judgment of a prospective borrower's entrepreneurial ability and asset position, but also whether or not the Central Bank would permit a letter of credit to be opened for the import of the raw material, equipment, technical "knowhow", etc. It is probably true in most cases that the potential borrower's possession of a license to buy foreign exchange was as important in obtaining bank financing as his entrepreneurial ability or his asset position. In any case the commercial banks have become heavily involved in industrial investment, granting medium and even long-term credits which have tied up their loanable funds and reduced their ability to finance loans of a purely commercial nature.

Unable to find adequate investment outlets in corporate securities or in public or private bonds, household savings have been channeled into other areas. Table 2 presents a breakdown of sources and uses of funds for household savings in the form of financial claims for the calendar year 1958. The major uses of household savings are three: (1) short-term credits to business, (2) real estate investment, and (3) equity investment in business enterprises. The first two categories absorbed 44 percent of household savings in 1958. Although an equal share went into business equity investment, most of this was directed toward proprietorships and partnerships. *Only 15 percent of household savings was transferred to the corporate sector in the form of ownership of common stock.*

TABLE 2

ESTIMATED SOURCES AND USES OF HOUSEHOLD SAVINGS IN
THE PHILIPPINES IN THE FORM OF FINANCIAL CLAIMS, 1958

(Million pesos)

Sources		Uses	
Currency in circulation..........	47.5	Short-term credits to business	114.3
Bank deposits *.....................	124.1	Long-term credits to business	3.7
Net insurance premiums........	139.5	Equity investments in business	232.6
Pension funds and		a. Corporation...... 79.8	
personal trusts	13.0	b. Partnership and	
Mutual funds........................	4.4	Proprietorship 152.8	
New Security Issues		Real estate investment †	119.1
acquired directly..............	205.6	Hoarding............................	64.4
		Government bonds................	‡
	534.1		534.1

* Includes the net increase in postal savings deposits.
† Includes real estate developed as well as the net increase in mortgage loan financing by intermediaries during the year.
‡ Less than .1.
Sources: Savings by source from Hooley, Savings in the Philippine Economy, 1951-1960; uses of savings developed from data on uses of commercial bank loans and capital investments in new security issues in The Statistical Bulletin; investments of insurance companies from Insurance and Finance Journal, 1960.

The data in Tables 1 and 2 and the above discussion provide the basis for some preliminary inferences concerning the absorptive capacity of the Philippine equities market. On the one hand in 1960 Phillippine households held a potential P550 million available for investment either in the equities or debt market. However, the equities market after deflation for excessive turnover registered an annual volume of approximately P27 million for that year as shown in Table 1.

As for the long-term debt market, the volume of corporate debt securities (debentures, finance paper) placed has far exceeded the (deflated) total of Manila Stock Exchange transactions for 1960. However, a large part of this is refunding, so that the net flow of funds into this sector of the capital market also has been relatively small. In any event, it is abundantly clear that the existing structure of the capital market is incapable of absorbing more than a small fraction of household savings as claims on financial assets. As a result of this low absorptive capacity, that part of household savings which is not devoted to hoarding or financing real estate development reaches the corporate sector more often than not in the form of short-term credits. At the present time, for example, about one-half of the assets of domestic insurance companies are invested in real estate and another one-fourth in policy loans.

WHY THE CAPITAL MARKET IS INEFFICIENT

The question arises as to why the existing Philippine capital market has failed to promote a more productive allocation of domestic savings. The answer is complex and springs both from certain basic characteristics of the

Philippine economy and society and, more directly, from the monetary policies of the Central Bank.

Among the socio-economic factors which inhibit a successfully functioning capital market, one of the most important is the key role of a relatively few wealthy old families. For example, most large equity holdings are held by such family groups or by large institutions such as PhilAm Life. The general public to date has not been either actively associated or interested in equity capital. A major reason is that the wealthy families normally refuse to offer their proven holdings to the public for sale. An important exception has been the offer of San Miguel Brewery stock to the general public. The success of this offer was due in large part to the company's proven earnings and to the excellent management it enjoyed. (In this connection, it is interesting to note that to increase the volume of turnover on the Manila Stock Exchange by 50 percent, one need only offer for trading another San Miguel issue.)

Moreover, success in underwriting new issues often depends on the purchase of substantial amounts by one or more of these large financial "blocks." In this instance, the Philippine equity market is similar to the New York market for specific issues, (e.g. utility bonds) where a large part of an issue is taken by a few financial intermediaries. If the big financial institutions in the Philippines arbitrarily decided to play a "waiting game" after the offerings, they can ruin an underwriter. This is not so true in the United States, where the willingness of the general public to purchase securities establishes a freely competitive market in most types of new issues.

In many cases, therefore, successful underwriting in the Philippines requires that the underwriting firm obtain a commitment for a large part of the issue from one of the "financial groups" before offering it publicly. For example, in underwriting an issue of P1 million for a new TV station, floating of the new issue was successful despite an unfavorable market, because the Manila Times Publishing Company agreed to purchase one-half of the total offering. When this became general knowledge, the public eagerly absorbed the other half.

On the other hand, many times projects require the support of resources greater than any one family is willing to risk. But because one family is already interested, and has in this sense a priority, other families often decline to join in financing the venture. As a result, many worthy ventures never come to fruition. What is more, large financial institutions and families of wealth usually decline to reveal their investment aims. They rarely seek to shift from low yielding securities to higher yielding securities given comparable quality. This creates an insensitive secondary market, and this in turn impedes the formation of a new issue market. In short, the psychology of many of the old established family financial groups is basically antithetical to the foundation of an efficient mechanism for allocating scarce resources on criteria of productivity.

Another important factor in the sluggishness of the Philippine capital market is that the functions of an investment counselor are highly personalized. Such securities as are traded are often purchased on the mere suggestion of the counselor. This places the counselor in a very strong position, because independent judgment is often not exercised by his client. The close personal nature of this relationship is in contrast to the more impersonal relationship between counselor and client existing on the New York market. In New York independent judgment on the client's part is exercised, and he may disagree or agree with his counselor's suggestions. In Manila, the highly personalized character of the client-counselor relationship inhibits the counselor from basing his judgment solely on economic and financial grounds. Rather, he must continually be aware that it is his personal judgment, not that of his client, which often determines the final decision. Caution and hesitancy are therefore encouraged, and many worthwhile new ventures or innovations never see the light of day.

Finally, the Philippine economy and the private enterprise sector in particular are by their very nature commercially rather than industrially oriented. This inhibits the formation of capital, and restricts the offer of new good issues on the securities market. The Filipino businessmen more often than not conceive of their profit as arising out of trading and speculation rather than from increasing production or beginning a new business enterprise. To be sure this business characteristic has been disappearing, particularly since World War II, but it is still important in the Philippine business community, and will likely continue to be so for some time. An example of this orientation is found in the textile industry where profits from investment in some plants and equipment were realized before the plant was erected and the machinery installed.[2]

THE ROLE OF THE CENTRAL BANK

The monetary policies of the Central Bank have also greatly impaired the effective functioning of the Philippine capital market. The equity market is highly volatile and easily subject to pressure from speculative funds, as is clearly pointed out in Table 1. If no funds are available because of a tight monetary or fiscal policy, equity prices fall drastically. Equity prices therefore do not reflect the economic worth of the issue, but mainly the degree of speculation existing in the market. For example, in the first quarter of 1960,

[2] This could be accomplished by applying to the Central Bank for dollar financing for new equipment and purchasing used but serviceable equipment at a discount from the United States. The savings would be deposited in foreign banks abroad and the investors would have their investment liquidated before the machinery arrived in the Philippines.

a prominent Philippine investment broker attempted to sell issues amounting to P1 million to the general public. Unfortunately, the public purchased no more than P100,000, and as a result other financing arrangements had to be made with the banks. The principal reason for the failure to sell this issue was the tight money policy adopted by the Central Bank after underwriting negotiations were begun. A tight money policy in the Philippines can virtually wipe out all demand for new issues, so that the new issue market temporarily ceases to exist. This is what occurred between 1960 and 1962.

The imposition of foreign exchange controls also had much to do with stunting the growth of the financial mechanism. Under controls, the state set up its own bureaucratic machinery to allocate dollar resources. The Central Bank's role in this resource allocation has been a direct and primary one, and the money market became only a mirror of Central Bank policy. As a result alternative institutional machinery to perform the allocation was truncated. Although foreign exchange controls have now been lifted, an efficient allocative mechanism for such resources still does not exist.

Moreover, just as Central Bank support of Government bond issues hindered the growth of the secondary debt market, so did the Bank's foreign exchange control program hamper the growth of a secondary market for equity issues. Priority of investment was determined primarily by the Central Banks arbitrary allocation of foreign exchange rather than by a market mechanism where price (i.e. the yield on an investment) was the determining factor.

TECHNICAL PROBLEMS OF UNDERWRITING

There are in addition a variety of technical problems which make the floating and underwriting of new securities or new issues difficult. Underwriting of security issues is by its very nature subject to declining average costs, because most underwriting costs, such as negotiating contracts and investigating the economies and financial feasibility of a proposed venture are fixed in nature. Under present conditions, the preferred size of issues is probably not in excess of P1 million. Underwriters' commissions average approximately 7–9 percent of the issue. Assuming a P1 million offering, the gross underwriting commission would amount to about P70,000. But the latter amount is small recompense for the enormous risks and preparatory work that must be accomplished in any sound underwriting.

Fees for auditing and legal work, moreover, could easily account for one-third of the gross commission. Most of the remainder is exhausted in administration, salaries, etc. As a result, most issues offered in the Philippines are underwritten on a "best effort" basis with the underwriter acting only as a lead broker, and not performing his true economic function of guaranteeing to the enterprise a minimum amount of funds.

Other technical underwriting problems include:

(a) The relative lack of any historical data on the earnings record of firms seeking new capital; this makes the pricing of a new issue very difficult.

(b) Absence of "experts" employed either by investment houses or by large financial institutions who can independently conduct an investigation into the economic and financial feasibility of a proposed issue. For example, executives of a Philippine iron mining company pointed out to the authors that the lack of "expertise" in the Philippines prevented the company from seeking financial support to expand its operations from either the capital market or from such financial institutions as Insular Life and the Philippine American Insurance Companies (Phil-Am Life). Insurance companies prefer real estate investments, because they have "experts" who know and understand the nature of the real estate market; by contrast, lack of knowledge and understanding about iron ore mining operations increases the risk to the insurance companies and inhibits them from investing in such enterprises.

(c) The difficulty of obtaining accurate and honest accounting data on which to base cost estimates necessary for correctly pricing a new security issue. Before one can accept the accounting data made available by many firms seeking to market a new security issue, it is necessary to make a careful check of company records and accounting procedures. The underwriting firm offering a new venture must be very careful that the firm whose security it is presenting to the market has not been bled by nefarious business practices. The firm cannot risk its reputation and therefore is necessarily cautious about backing new undertakings.

THE ROLE OF A PRIVATE DEVELOPMENT BANK

To prevent the misallocation of capital funds and overcome underwriting problems, the capital market must be widened and deepened by bringing more investors into the market, by expanding the variety of "instruments" suitable for investment, and by offering positive measures to overcome the financial, institutional and psychological difficulties experienced in underwriting. This can be accomplished through the agency of a private development bank.

The bank should view its relation to the capital market as the principal agency to absorb the initial risk in financing new investment ventures. If the bank would play this role properly, it could become the cornerstone on which an expanded and dynamic Philippine capital market could be erected. To fulfill this role, the bank would have to choose good venture risks, design appropriate instruments for financing, find markets for the securities and choose the appropriate time to make a public offering.

The most critical problem facing the private development bank is the marketing of securities, because if the development bank is unable to market either the debt instruments or equity securities of the new venture, it will become "locked in."

To avoid this danger the private development bank must be prepared to select a few venture projects initially, hold them, and permit them to attain some maturity. After a passage of time, say several years, the bank should be able to pass the reduced risk on to other financial institutions such as insurance companies. The insurance companies in turn should be willing to accept the risk involved because it would be of a lower order compared to the initial risk which the bank assumed.

Again, after a period of several years and a further proving of the success or failure of the original investment venture, the financial institutions should be capable of passing the risk on to individual investors through sale in the capital market. The development bank and the financial institutions therefore would occupy a relationship somewhat similar in nature to the underwriting relationship found in the United States between an investment house and an insurance company.

Given the performance of the entrepreneurial function by a development bank, there is every indication that the financial institutions which now exist in the Philippines can and will assume their "rightful function" if the investment "instruments" they are asked to underwrite carry varying degrees of risk. The institutions which could make up the capital market in the Philippines, aside from the private development bank, are as follows:

(a) Life insurance companies, e.g., Phil-Am Life and Insular Life.

(b) Other insurance companies, such as the Filipinas Guarantee Company and the Universal Insurance and Indemnity Co.

(c) Private pension funds.

(d) Mutual funds.

(e) Assets controlled by the Trust Departments of the commercial banks.

(f) Social Security System and the Government Service Insurance System.

(g) Large family holdings, such as Soriano and Co., Madrigal, Ayala and Araneta.

The above institutions could become the nexus around which a flourishing and growing capital market can be built, because they have the funds to absorb the intermediate risk between the development bank and the industrial private investor. Some indication of the extent of their investment resources is given by an examination of the investment portfolio of the two life insurance companies, i.e. Phil-Am Life and Insular. At present, of their total investable funds, only about 12 percent (amounting to about P 70 million) goes into equities. Moreover, each year from premium income alone about P100 million is available for new investment. It should be the aim of a flourishing and expanding capital market to increase the flow of funds from such institutions initially to 25 percent and eventually to 50 percent of their total investment portfolios.

The danger of a development bank becoming "locked in" may also be reduced by offering to the borrower long-term notes bearing a serial maturity. For example, a ten-year serial note would mature at the rate of 10 percent each year. Such notes should become a large part of the bank's development lending policy, and would assure the bank a revolving fund of liquid capital to support new venture issues. In turn, these ten-year serial notes could be convertible into stocks. This would also enhance their market utility.

In the formation of a private development bank, personalities and character will play an important part. Very careful consideration must be given to the choice of directors for the development bank. An unsmirched reputation of the Board of Directors is required to assure the success of such a bank, because in great part the bank's reputation will be immediately determined when the board of directors is announced. The names will be critically analyzed. Associations with other business or banking firms and political connections will be noted. If the names cannot bear close scrutiny, the bank's reputation will be questioned even before the first loan is granted.

Therefore, to minimize possible conflict between interests, and to assure the general public that the bank is completely impartial in its judgment about financing a new venture, the directors must be carefully chosen and all their outside investment holdings or other financial interests be made known to the bank when they are appointed. Moreover, the bank must be aware that it cannot permit its equity to be held predominantly by any one family or group. If the development bank is identified too closely with any particular family, the excluded families will not be interested in the bank, will not offer their resources to the bank, and will not bring good venture risks to the bank for its financing.

Finally, the bank must recognize that investors in the Philippine capital market, in common with investors in other capital markets, operate on the principle of "follow the leader." In the United States one of the principal institutional investors and a recognized leader in that capital market is the Metropolitan Life Insurance Company. If the "Met" decides to purchase a new issue, the word quickly gets around, and other investors are more likely to purchase because the "Met" did. Such a leader does not exist at present in the Philippine capital market. However, such a leader is vital and necessary if the market is to become active and expansive, and if capital is to be correctly allocated. A well organized and well run private development bank could perform this function in the Philippine capital market.

SUMMARY

In the Philippines, as in many developing countries, the problem of allocating scarce capital resources primarily arises from the absence of a dynamic capital market, in particular a secondary market where already issued securities can be successfully traded and financial resources "unlocked." Unable to find attractive investment outlets in the corporate sector, because the capital market is so thin and narrow, household savings are channeled into first, real estate; second, short-term credits to business; third, equity investment in noncorporate business enterprises.

The imperfections in the present Philippine capital market which prevent the development of a secondary market arise from socio-economic forces, from monetary policies of the Central Bank, from problems of economies of scale, and from technical problems concerning the floatation of new securities.

To prevent the misallocation of capital funds, the capital market must be widened and deepened by bringing more investors into the market, by expanding the variety of suitable investment instruments and by offering positive measures to overcome financial, institutional and psychological difficulties experienced in underwriting. This can be accomplished through the agency of a Philippine development bank which can absorb the initial risk in financing new ventures as well as perform the necessary underwriting functions. Once a development bank has accepted the initial risk of promoting a new venture, the bank must hold the venture's equity or debt instruments for a period to permit the instruments "to ripen," and thereby reduce their risk to other purchasers. After this period of proving the initial worth of the venture, the bank can sell the instruments to other financial institutions, such as insurance companies, who should be willing to purchase the issue because of the reduced risk. In turn the insurance companies after a further maturing of the issue under their ownership, should be able to pass it on to an individual investor through sale in the capital market. In this manner, a development bank can play a catalytic role in the creation of a dynamic capital market because it reduces the risk of the initial venture, stimulates the creation of an active secondary market, and provides the market with securities which investors desire.

METHODS OF FOSTERING
A CAPITAL MARKET*

In the characteristic underdeveloped country, the prospects for the rapid development of a capital market are limited. The volume of private voluntary savings is relatively low to begin with, and is at any given income level not likely to be altered significantly by institutional innovations or new savings media. But the proportion of savings that may be redirected to more productive uses is in most countries quite large. The immediate objective of efforts to develop a capital market is to provide the incentives and means for the investment of savings in new ways, which will make financing more readily available for productive projects requiring more funds than entrepreneurs can readily provide. The ultimate goal is the expansion of the country's possibilities for self-sustaining economic growth.

The contribution of development banks to this end differs from country to country. The Industrial Development Corporation of South Africa (IDC), for example, was established in a country in which there were both well-developed financial institutions and savers accustomed to holding at least a portion of their savings in some form of negotiable securities. The Industrial Development Bank of Turkey (IDB) could only look forward to the capital market developments which the IDC was able to take for granted. Nevertheless, each institution has contributed to the development of capital market functions in its country, the IDC by underwriting and sales from portfolio, the IDB by sales of its own shares to the public.

Most development banks can similarly assist in the growth of a capital market. They can help directly to bridge the gap between savers and investors by selling their own obligations to the public. They can engage in portfolio sales. They can underwrite the issue of new securities. Besides pooling savings, banks can also attract direct investor participation in their own financing, thus providing still another means for channeling liquid savings to worthwhile investments. In all these ways thay can contribute to gradual changes in attitudes toward direct investment in industrial securities.

But a bank cannot achieve these results unless it designs its policies accordingly. Its investment criteria must be such that investors who contemplate participating in projects, whether directly or indirectly through purchase of the bank's own securities, feel satisfied that the projects are soundly

* Excerpted from Shirley Boskey, *Problems and Practices of Development Banks,* Baltimore, Md.: The Johns Hopkins Press, 1959, pp. 103–113.

conceived and well managed and have reasonable prospects of being profitable. Perhaps the single most important way in which a development bank can lower investor resistance to committing funds to it, or to its projects, is to win public confidence in the objectivity and quality of its investments. In Puerto Rico and South Africa, investor confidence has developed to the point where the development bank's willingness to invest usually attracts private funds to the project, sometimes in a volume which makes the bank's financing in the end unnecessary. In countries with less developed financial media, and inadequate legal and institutional protection for the private investor, it may be some years before development bank approval will of itself make full private financing of projects possible. But the goal has been shown to be feasible.

Where the nucleus of a private capital market exists, development banks have been concerned to support and not impede the growth of this market in their search for profitable projects and in the formulation of operational policies. Banks are commonly required by charter to satisfy themselves, before approving an application, that financing is not available through other channels, and this is generally their policy, even in the absence of charter requirement. Applicants may be required to produce evidence of unsuccessful efforts to obtain financing elsewhere. The Industrial Finance Corporation of India (IFCI), for example requires an applicant to go the market for at least part of its financing needs. However, the chances for favorable consideration are not prejudiced if good reasons are shown for an inability to obtain outside financing. IFCI is even more strict in this regard when an enterprise returns for a second loan, especially if the enterprise has been declaring a good dividend for some years.[1]

PLACEMENT OF INDUSTRIAL SECURITIES

Banks can broaden investor participation in industry by selling investments from their portfolio. Each sale enlarges the supply of marketable securities and, if new buyers are attracted, enlarges the base for future sales of this kind. At the same time, bank funds are released for new investments which may one day also be added to the market supply of securities. Portfolio sales represent both the culmination and the beginning of a cycle of activities in which the bank participates, as a developer first of securities and later of markets for these securities once they have become seasoned.

Portfolio sales also provide a means for the banks gradually to dispose of enterprises which they themselves have established. Shares may be sold

---

[1] Bank managers who encourage applicants first to exhaust all other financing possibilities must be sure that there is no conflict between the bank's interest policy and its desire to help develop a capital market.

in small lots, the venture becoming a partnership between the bank and private investors. Further sales may be made from time to time, gradually reducing the bank's interest to a minority, and in the end the whole venture may come to be privately owned. The policy of selling gradually may also be followed with respect to shares of client enterprises. The Industrial Credit and Investment Corporation of India sells shares of its portfolio gradually and in small quantities to avoid depressing their price, in the interests of the enterprise and other investors in it.

In this connection, it may be noted that some government banks are slow to part with their share interests. They have an understandable reluctance to dispose of successful investments and to be left with those which are unable to attract the private investor. Sometimes they find it difficult to obtain what they consider a fair price, sometimes they fear criticism were they to sell a bloc of shares to a particular group or individual. Particularly to meet the latter problem, and because the market is small, the Corporacion de Fomento de la Produccion of Chile, a public bank, offers shares in small lots at the current market price, generally by private sale to existing shareholders in proportion to their holdings.

Portfolio sales are only one aspect of the ordinary financing activities of the bank. But they are sufficiently important to warrant pointing each stage of the financing process to this end. The necessary condition for marketability is the established success of the enterprise and reasonable prospects for its future. The quality of the initial investment and a willingness to hold the investment until it becomes seasoned, perhaps for three or four years, is thus basic to any efforts the bank may make to sell securities from its portfolio. The form of the investment is equally important. In countries with a history of inflation, such as Turkey and Chile, equities may be the only readily marketable security. Where savers are willing to buy bonds, provided they are of fairly short maturity, some banks try to set up their loans to permit separate sale of the early maturities. Nacional Financiera of Mexico, for example, has been able to sell 5–10 year bonds but not 20–25 year bonds. In Ceylon, there are no purchasers for long-term loans, even with the development bank's guarantee.

Placement of industrial securities with the public by the underwriting of new issues has been much less common than portfolio sales in underdeveloped countries. Most development banks have had little, if any, underwriting experience. In underdeveloped countries lacking financial intermediaries with substantial resources and a fairly broad securities market, underwriting has been largely, although not exclusively, restricted to situations in which the bank has also assisted the enterprise directly.

In any event, the practice of underwriting in the less-developed countries is rather different from the practice in New York or other financial centers. Underwriters in Wall Street, for example, perform essentially a marketing function. They intend and expect to dispose of all the securities they underwrite and consider the operation unsuccessful if they are left with any substantial amount. But in the less-developed countries, underwriting, at least as practiced by the development banks, combines marketing and investment functions. The Industrial Credit and Investment Corporation of India (ICICI), for example, tries to attract as much private interest as possible, but does not agree to underwrite unless it is prepared and willing to keep the full amount of the issue in its portfolio.[2] ICICI will agree to underwrite even if it has no assurance, perhaps not even a reasonable expectation, that the entire issue can be placed. To the extent that private capital is attracted, ICICI feels it has performed a useful function, even though it retains in its portfolio a large part of the issue. Actually the enterprise whose securities are underwritten, as well as the private purchasers, may often prefer that the development bank retain some interest.[3]

Though the activities of underwriting and selling from portfolio place the bank in different relationships to clients, the selling problems are similar. It may be difficult to sell the securities of closely-held companies not listed on any securities exchange. The fact that the development bank has approved the securities may inspire confidence and facilitate sales. But the bank may be placed in a position in which, to preserve its own reputation, it must support these securities in the market, especially where the market is narrow. If the securities were to fall in price, the success of future sales could be severely prejudiced. A bank which enters the market to support an issue may thus find that it has acquired a majority interest in the enterprise, with all the attendant problems of management and control. Most banks accordingly are very cautious about underwriting, especially where the enterprise is not well-known and established.

The Industrial Development Corporation of South Africa (IDC) once underwrote an issue which was four times oversubscribed. Unfortunately, within nine months the price of the shares had dropped by half. IDC offered to buy back at the issue price all the shares sold, with the result that it acquired a 52% interest in the enterprise, which it took over and managed. It was five years before the enterprise began to be profitable and its shares could again be sold on the market.

Another obstacle to placing industrial shares with the public is that generally, only the securities of seasoned enterprises are marketable. But when

---

[2] Of 22 underwriting operations completed by May 1959 in respect to ordinary and preference shares and debentures totalling Rs. 68 million (equivalent to U.S. $14.3 million), ICICI actually took up 26% of the aggregate underwriting commitment. A very few issues required no subscription by ICICI, several required complete subscription, and most required that ICICI take up more than half.

[3] The Industrial Finance Corporation of India, which is not authorized to make equity investments, is required to dispose of any shares it acquires as a consequence of an underwriting or foreclosure, within seven years.

the enterprise has proved itself, the sponsors understandably want to reap the rewards of having taken the original risks. A development bank may seek to acquire shares for later public sale by conditioning its financing on an option to underwrite subsequent share issues or, in the case of a loan, by insisting on conversion rights.[4] However, if the original risk-takers insist on a right of first refusal, they may effectively prevent the bank from carrying out this plan.[5]

What can be done in this situation depends largely upon local circumstances. Company law in the Union of South Africa prohibits the grant of rights of first refusal where shares of an enterprise are both publicly-held and quoted (although the bank may agree to inform the shareholders in advance of any projected sale). Some banks, the Puerto Rico Industrial Development Company and the Nacional Financiera of Mexico, for example, decline to give first refusal rights. Others grant them occasionally. First refusal rights are generally a matter for negotiation with the client. Sometimes, although the right has been given, banks have been able to persuade existing shareholders not to exercise it.

SALES OF INDUSTRIAL SECURITIES WITH THE BANK'S GUARANTEE

The advantages of placing industrial securities directly with the public are clear. Developing a willingness to hold securities is an ultimate goal of efforts to develop a capital market. This may be accelerated through the sale of clients' securities with the bank's guarantee. The investor thereby obtains the additional protection of a direct claim upon the bank's resources in case of trouble. From the standpoint of the institutional investor, a security of this kind would have a great attraction. But it may seem less desirable from the standpoint of the bank, since widespread porfolio sales with the bank's guarantee might well narrow the market for its own obligations.

---

[4] The Industrial Development Corporation of South Africa has on occasion obtained an option to take up shares against unpaid installments of loan principal or for cash.

[5] The reluctance of enterprises to permit public offerings of their shares may be overcome by statutory incentives, which the development bank may advocate even though it cannot itself offer them. For example, Puerto Rico is considering extending the period of tax exemption for enterprises which sell a certain proportion of their shares to the local investing public, and giving special inheritance tax treatment to estates which hold local corporate industrial issues.

[6] The International Finance Corporation has almost invariably given the sponsors or the enterprise itself a right of first refusal as to all or a part of its interest. It always gives its partners an assurance that it will not sell to parties to whom its partners can properly object.

SALE OF THE BANK'S OWN OBLIGATIONS

Some banks have issued their own obligations to the public. This avoids many of the difficulties inherent in selling industrial securities directly. The investor need not appraise the merits of particular enterprises. He need decide only whether he has sufficient confidence in the management of the bank and in its investment decisions to commit to it any part of his savings. Some banks have arranged for redemption of their obligations at face value and for a minimum guaranteed return, thereby adding to the appeal of the obligations by endowing them with liquidity, safety and an attractive yield. It should, however, be noted that sale of the bank's own obligations does not necessarily broaden the market for industrial securities, particularly where the obligations carry special guarantee and redemption privileges. This is essentially a device for enlarging the bank's resources, i.e., for channeling funds through the bank to industry. The bank itself is the capital market instrument.

Only a few of the banks which participated in the International Bank conference had, by then, issued their own obligations.[7] These included the Industrial Development Corporation of South Africa and the Industrial Finance Corporation of India, whose bonds carried a government guarantee. The Industrial Development Bank of Israel has had two successful issues of 6% debentures and has plans for a third, to carry a participation in profits as well as fixed interest. The debentures already issued are secured by a floating charge on the assets of the bank, and are linked to the price of the dollar, with an option (exercisable within a fixed period) to convert this linking to a link to the cost-of-living index.

The Industrial Development Corporation of South Africa once sold its obligations to raise funds for a specific project, rather than to add to the total of its general investment resources. This device might be useful in other countries as a means of attracting the savings of the probable beneficiaries of a given project, who are likely to have a special interest in its success. It could at the same time have the important incidental effect of helping to develop investor interests and attitudes that may later be receptive to other securities sold directly from the bank's portfolio.

A practice of the Nacional Financiera of Mexico is also of interest. About 1940 Financiera began to offer participation certificates to the public issued against a fund of shares and bonds held by Financiera. At first these represented a form of time deposit redeemable nominally on 90 days' notice, in practice at sight. They did not carry any property rights to the securities backing them. The certificates now represent co-ownership of a designated block of securities in Financiera's portfolio, composed half of industrial equities

---

[7] Only one, the Corporacion de Fomento de la Produccion of Chile, lacked authority to do so.

and half of fixed-yield obligations. Thus the certificates provide a variable return. Five years after issue, the certificates are callable in the underlying securities or in cash at par. By putting both blue chip and new shares into each package, Financiera has tried to establish a market for new securities. It is Financiera's policy, when asked to lend to a family enterprise, to try to persuade the enterprise to accept equity participation instead; the device of the certificates is used to broaden the ownership base.

The cases cited suggest that in many countries the issue of development bank obligations tailored to local situations might well make an important contribution to the growth of a capital market.

PARTICIPATIONS

Since the average investor is not in a position to appraise the technical, financial and managerial aspects of an enterprise or project, often the best way to encourage him to invest in industry is to provide him with an opportunity to participate in such an investment together with a development bank.[8] This presupposes, of course, that investors have confidence in the bank's judgment. It is an equally necessary condition that the bank have established a wide network of contact with potential investors. To this end, some banks have sought to keep potential investors within the country regularly informed of their activities and of new investment opportunities.

Participation by foreign investors has not been very widespread. In Turkey the balance of payments situation has hampered the efforts of the Industrial Development Bank in this field. Other banks have been able to accomplish somewhat more. The Corporacion de Fomento de la Produccion of Chile has established a special committee to invite foreign participation in attractive projects, and has made contacts through its New York office and in Europe. At the time of the International Bank conference, about $150 million in foreign participations had been approved. The Industrial Development Corporation of South Africa has attracted a substantial degree of participation by foreign enterprises.[9] But development banks in general are not well equipped to discover potential participants or to take the initiative in developing leads. This was one consideration which led to the establishment of the International Finance Corporation. Development banks have, however, encouraged foreign investment in other ways: directly, by selling their own ob-

---

[8] Private institutional capital often participates in International Bank loans in this way.

[9] The Government Development Bank for Puerto Rico has made large investments in Puerto Rican industry in participation with institutional investors from the mainland United States, and assists in attracting private external financing through its contacts with financial institutions and investors in the United States.

ligations abroad, and by giving information and advice to existing and potential foreign investors; and indirectly, by sponsoring favorable exchange and fiscal regulations.

Development banks may likewise participate in financing by other banking institutions. But of the banks which took part in the International Bank conference, only the Government Development Bank for Puerto Rico (GDB) and the Industrial Development Corporation of South Africa had done so. The GDB has established an advisory committee of prominent local bankers and businessmen for the purpose, among others, of assisting in coordinating its lending activities with those of the commercial banks. It expects this to lead to an increase in the number of its participations with the commercial banks, which have been interested in purchasing short-term portions of GDB's portfolio.

An active capital market will not, of course, follow automatically upon establishment of a development bank. The real question is whether the bank can do anything to make a beginning. The experience recounted at the International Bank conference suggests that banks not only can take, but have taken, significant first steps in this direction.

The International Bank's own experience with finding local capital for industrial projects has convinced it of both the importance and potentialities of activity in this field. For example, the government of Pakistan sought an International Bank loan for a paper mill for which the government had supplied all the equity. The Bank, being reluctant to lend because of the plant's governmental ownership, first persuaded the government to offer shares to the public, with the result that 70% of the equity is now in private hands. Again at the International Bank's urging, shares in a natural gas transmission company in Pakistan were offered publicly; three-quarters of the equity is now held by private investors in Pakistan and the United Kingdom. In both instances local "informed" sources had predicted that the issues would not be fully taken up and in both the issues were oversubscribed, many small investors being among the purchasers. A public offering of shares in a textile plant in Ethiopia was likewise a success, notwithstanding a general belief that there was little private capital available for industrial investment. The response of small investors to the second issue of the shares in the Turkish development bank has already been mentioned.[10]

___

[10] Other instances of a growing receptivity on the part of small savers to industrial investment could be cited. For example, it has been reported that the first share issue by a public company in Nigeria, in the spring of 1959, was substantially oversubscribed, with almost 1,200 of total applications being for only 10 shares, the minimum number for which application could be made.

THE DEVELOPMENT OF
MONEY MARKETS*

The increasing reliance on monetary policy in much of the world in recent years has emphasized the importance of fostering short-term money markets. Central banks have long endeavored, of course, to develop active local money markets, and since the war steps in this direction have been taken by numerous foreign countries—those with relatively developed financial systems as well as those with less developed ones. The rapid broadening of the Canadian money market has been the most notable example of these efforts in the last few years. Other foreign markets—with the exception of London—remain relatively narrow, but a number of them have gained much in scope and flexibility since the war.

FUNCTIONS OF A MONEY MARKET

The developing of money markets may seem a rather technical matter that mainly concerns the commercial banks. In reality, however, it is of much wider importance, even when, as here, the money market is defined in a narrow sense. In this narrow sense, the money market may be defined as a center for organized dealings in monetary assets which provides the liquidity needed by lenders and at the same time satisfies the short-term requirements of borrowers.[1]

A well-functioning market of this kind has important advantages not only for a country's commercial banks, but also for other financial institutions, businesses, and individuals, and for the economy as a whole. For the commercial banks, such a market makes possible a rapid and relatively inexpensive evening-out of their reserve positions, by helping to match off among the banks the excesses and deficiencies of reserves that result from shifts of deposits from one bank to another in the normal course of trade. It also enables the banks to employ a part of their reserves in income-earn-

* Excerpted from: Fousek, Peter G., *Foreign Central Banking: The Instruments of Monetary Policy,* Federal Reserve Bank of New York, 1957, pp. 82–84, 98–100.
[1] For a more extensive discussion of the various definitions of the money market, as well as for a description of the United States market, see *Money Market Essays,* by Harold V. Roelse and others, Federal Reserve Bank of New York, March 1952 (fourth printing, November 1954, currently out of print but being revised), and Robert V. Roosa, *Federal Reserve Operations in the Money and Government Securities Markets,* Federal Reserve Bank of New York, 1964.

ing assets, since it assures the liquidity of such secondary reserves. As a result, the banks are able to operate on a narrower margin of nonearning assets. A developed money market, moreover, provides a convenient outlet for the short-term investment by corporations and other nonbank investors of surplus funds over and above the cash balances maintained on deposit in the banks. Such a market also tends to facilitate short-term borrowing by business firms and others in the form of marketable instruments such as bankers' acceptances, commercial paper, finance company paper, or loans collateralized by stock exchange securities.

A flourishing and flexible money market not only leads to a more economical allocation and more intensive use of short-term capital but also, by supplying temporary financing for the holding of securities, facilitates the ready shifting of liquid assets that is essential if there are to be smoothly functioning markets for securities in general. By providing diversified, competitive facilities that reach into all other markets for credit and capital, a developed money market helps to assure the channeling of funds into the uses most needed for the expansion of the economy, and facilitates the most efficient utilization of domestic savings.

A developed money market also makes a major contribution to the effectiveness of monetary policy. It provides a sensitive barometer of monetary conditions generally, and is a natural point of contact between the central bank and the financial sectors of the economy. A market with a broad distribution of short-term government securities, for example, is able to absorb transactions of reasonable size without undue price fluctuations, and thus makes an effective and flexible open market policy possible. Such a market also helps to spread the intended effects of central bank open market operations throughout the economy. The widening of the market may increase the influence of open market operations in another way: the fact that secondary reserve assets can be readily shifted among the banks makes it possible for the banks to operate with smaller excess reserves and with relatively stable cash ratios, rather than with widely fluctuating excess reserves; and the maintenance of stable cash ratios in turn provides an effective base for open market operations. As a result, the changes in bank reserves effected through central bank open market operations can substantially and promptly affect the availability of credit from the commercal banks.

Since an efficient money market operates for the most part with a relatively narrow margin of excess bank reserves, the need frequently arises in the normal course of day-by-day fluctuations in money payments for resort to central bank credit. The discount rate thus acquires a positive influence on commercial bank lending policy. This is true, moreover, whether the actual use of the central bank's "discount window" is by the commercial banks themselves, as in the United States, or whether that use is limited to intermediaries, like the discount houses in the United Kingdom. At the same time, because the commercial banks can rely on the market as a "buffer" for the adjustment of their positions, the central bank becomes truly a lender of last resort, and excessive injections of central bank credit can be avoided. The influence of the central bank is likely to be further enhanced by a decline in the commercial banks' dependence on secondary liquid assets held in foreign centers as the banks increase their dependence on the local market.

Finally, a money market in which all suppliers and users of liquid funds actively participate will necessarily provide facilities in which the government's own short-term financing requirements can be met more efficiently. It reduces the need for direct central bank loans to the government, and thus minimizes the kind of threat that historically has been the most serious cause of undesirable expansion in bank reserves and the money supply. A developed money market can also help accommodate short-term swings in the government's borrowing requirements without the risk of creating sharp changes in the commercial banks' liquidity, such as would make the banks extremely short of liquid assets at one time and unduly liquid at another.

THE POSTWAR EXPERIENCE

A country's money market is naturally a product of its local institutions, and the fact that certain markets have grown up in a particular fashion does not imply that others necessarily must do the same. Nevertheless, the foregoing survey of recent foreign experience reveals, amidst a great variety of national settings, some common lines along which the development of short-term markets might be expected to proceed.

A short-term loan market, often centering on loans against the collateral of marketable obligations such as Treasury bills, is a feature of almost all money markets. In countries where such a market exists on an interbank basis it tends to spread to include other participants.

In some countries, where conditions were otherwise suitable, the monetary authorities have taken the initiative toward the establishing of a short-term loan market and have succeeded in obtaining the cooperation of banks and securities dealers in the development of such a market. In other countries, they have been able to encourage it by permitting money market loans to be included in commercial bank liquidity ratios where such ratios have been introduced, by helping to ensure the liquidity of the underlying collateral, or by establishing semiofficial intermediaries that would pool idle funds and hold other liquid or shiftable assets. Where such intermediaries function, however, experience has shown the advantages of introducing a flexible rate policy fairly promptly. Otherwise, such arrangements may retard progress toward a more effective market and may even become merely a syphon for drawing funds into government obligations, thereby stifling instead of encouraging competitive forces.

While call money markets fulfill some of the money market's functions, many countries have found it desirable to proceed to the establishment of a market for commercial or Treasury bills. Even though the commercial bill has generally declined in importance, a few countries have concentrated on this form of short-term paper in developing their markets, both because they have considered it a useful form of short-term financing and because the alternative of establishing a Treasury bill market may have posed special problems. In such endeavors much help has been obtained from the activities of semiofficial intermediaries that ensure secrecy for the originating bank, and from the operations of central banks that help to assure the liquidity of such instruments. While the revival of the market in bankers' acceptances and commercial paper has shown signs of becoming important at various times in the postwar period, this development has not yet become a factor of major significance on a world-wide scale.

Since World War II, the Treasury bill has generally been the preferred basis for the establishment of a bill market. In their efforts to establish such markets, central banks have on occasion faced the possibility of unduly sharp increases in time deposit rates by the commercial banks. For a Treasury bill market to succeed the central banks therefore have some times had to persuade the banks that any increased competition of Treasury bills with their time deposits as an outlet for short-term funds need not, on balance, be harmful to their interests. More important perhaps, the central banks have found the cooperation of the Treasury necessary. Where the Treasury has gradually increased the volume of bills, evened out the flow of maturities, and enlarged their variety, it has contributed a great deal to a broadening of the market. In this endeavor the issue of bills by regular tender, rather than on tap at rates fixed by the Treasury, has been found preferable; in particular, the determination of issue rates by tender has helped to give the market a certain amount of flexibility even from the start. The removal of restrictions limiting the ownership of Treasury bills to any one category of holders has often been considered a necessary first step for a widening of the distribution of bills. Beyond that, the readiness of the central bank to buy and sell such bills has been useful in stimulating active trading. In some instances the central banks have given special inducements by posting purchase prices close to each tender rate, but, as the markets have widened, the central banks have found it advisable to withdraw these more or less automatic facilities in order to avoid undersirable distortions or "pegs" in the market.

Finally, the existence of market intermediaries holding money market securities, making markets in them, and seeking out idle short-term funds from all parts of the economy has generally proved of great help in the development of money markets, even though it may not always have been found essential. These intermediaries have been either semiofficial institutions or private firms. Where private, they have been either firms already in existence, which had been operating in other markets such as those for long-term government securities or for foreign exchange, or new firms established with or without official encouragement. In any case, provision for such dealer-intermediaries to have access to central bank credit in some form has been found almost essential to their smooth functioning as a helpful part of the money market.

The development of broad and flexible money markets, as recent experience shows, is a slow and often difficult process. A country's economy must first expand and diversify, and a money market must not merely be able to draw upon a well-organized banking system; it must also be able to draw on a supply of short-term funds from nonbank sources interested in a relatively low return in exchange for high liquidity. Nevertheless, central banks and governments have had considerable success in developing money markets since World War II. The development of these markets has in turn helped the various countries to adapt their financial resources to their own needs for liquidity and investment, and has provided facilities through which the selection among alternative uses of funds could be resolved in greater degree by reliance upon competitive market forces.

THE NEW MONEY MARKETS*

Some time ago, monetary economists were inclined to ask whether central banks were universally necessary. Today, they would probably agree that, once a country effectively becomes part of the modern world, some form of monetary regulation is desirable. The establishment of a central bank is perhaps the most obvious way of ensuring that such regulation will be implemented with some semblance of expertise and—one hopes—in as objective a manner as is consistent with the maintenance of relatively harmonious relationships with the country's fiscal authorities. Admittedly, there are times when, because of the relative poverty or small size of a country, a central bank may seem to be rather an expensive luxury. Even then—and on the basis of quite a modest start in terms of personnel—it can be expected to contribute usefully to the development of institutions (such as commercial banks and industrial and agricultural finance corporations) that will considerably assist in any programme that might be launched to further economic progress.

Nevertheless, it would be wrong to deceive ourselves. Many central banks were undoubtedly established primarily as status symbols—a concomitant of economic autonomy and the related freedom from the more obvious restrictions that derive from foreign influence. Latterly, the emphasis has shifted somewhat and possession of a money market has in some instances tended to become the new status symbol. The appropriate question to ask today, therefore, is not whether a central bank but whether a "money market" is universally necessary.

Is a Market Necessary?

At the outset, it is desirable to define what precisely we mean by a "money market."[1] It will be a market that facilitates the borrowing and lending of short-term funds (say, up to periods of two to three years) and is usually concentrated in a particular centre (sometimes in two or more related centres). In all its dealings, it will be guided by the purely commercial considerations of price and profit, whether the parties be concerned with the borrowing and lending of money or the buying and selling of short-dated

* J. S. G. Wilson, *Lloyds Bank Review*, April, 1962, pp. 31–45.
[1] This and related questions are discussed at greater length in a complementary article, "The Structure of Money Markets," *Banca Nazionale del Lavoro Quarterly Review*, March, 1961.

securities, such as Treasury bills, commercial bills (or similar instruments), and short-dated government bonds. If a market grows up in this image, it will be a "money market." More frequently, however, such a market will not yet exist (at least not in a developed form) and the proposal will then be to *establish* a "money market." If this is the objective, there are a number of additional questions that must be put in order to determine whether a money market is "necessary." It is only on this basis that a sensible decision can be reached in any particular instance.

The first of these questions concerns the nature of the economy that any proposed money market would have to serve. Is it, for example, one that depends for its prosperity to a large extent on exports—possibly only on one export commodity, or at most on a small group of such commodities? If it does, the economy of that country will be very much at the mercy of its "terms of trade" (the movement of export prices in relation to import prices). Holdings of foreign exchange and regulation of their expenditure by the central bank could be one means of providing a cushion against violent fluctuations in export incomes; but if there are marked annual variations in external earnings, will it be possible to develop a domestic money market? There may well be no regularly revolving fund of cash and other liquid assets available to the economy on the basis of which to organize such a market.

Second, it is pertinent to enquire into the prevailing institutional arrangements in the country concerned. There is not much point in trying to establish a "money market" unless a relatively well developed banking system already exists. It is not only important that the managements should be experienced and already subscribe to the accepted conventions of sound banking practice; the institutions on which a money market is to be based must also be known for their integrity. When dealings are to be primarily in short-dated assets, and many must necessarily be based on agreements that are entered into orally, integrity is a *sine qua non*.

This does not mean that the existence of doubtful institutions will necessarily preclude the development of a money market, but it must impede the complete integration into a single system of the several types of banking and other monetary institutions. Alternatively, as in India, the practices of certain institutions (in this case of the "indigenous banker") may be unacceptable to the central bank and this may bar the path to fuller integration. Furthermore, if in these circumstances a money market is to exist at all, the central "organized" sector must be large enough to provide a sufficient demand for the types of services that can be supplied in a "money market." (Again, India provides an appropriate example). Yet, even where there already exists a minimum number of sizeable banks of unquestioned integrity (e.g. in South Africa) but there are no suitable indigenous institutions on which to build, the introduction of "money market" institutions such as discount houses will obviously require the provision of specialist expertise.

Third, what useful purpose could a "money market" serve? From the point of view of the commercial banks, it should be able to provide an investment outlet for any temporarily surplus funds they may have available. If the several banks operate rather dissimilar types of business, they may well be able to accommodate each other by organizing a "call loan market"; but if their business is liable to be affected by similar seasonal influences, money will be easy or tight for each of them at the same time, and the problem then becomes one that can most easily be resolved by the provision of special facilities at the central bank. Alternatively, the government may decide to mop up seasonal surpluses (e.g. by issuing Treasury bills for the purpose). For this system to be attractive to the commercial banks, however, there must also be a willingness to release funds during the period of seasonal stringency, either by central bank rediscount of Treasury bills at market rates or by means of a government switch to ways and means advances from the central bank (substituting an overdraft at the central bank for government borrowing on the basis of a Treasury bill issue).

Basis Must be a Revolving Fund

Hence, for a money market of some kind to exist, there must be a supply of temporarily idle cash that is seeking short-term investment in an earning asset. There must also exist a demand for temporarily available cash either by banks (and other financial institutions) for the purpose of adjusting their liquidity positions, or by the government, when it chooses to finance itself by adding to the floating debt or by issuing short-dated bonds. If the banks and similar institutions are to employ such short-term borrowed funds with any degree of confidence, however, they must expect the supply of these funds to be reasonably regular (as must governments that borrow against short-dated securities, such as Treasury bills and bonds). In other words, there must in some sense be a revolving fund of cash. Otherwise, financial institutions in particular dare not become dependent on outside sources and must maintain their own internal liquid reserves, necessitating a rather higher cash ratio and they would otherwise need.

Whether such a revolving fund is likely to exist depends (*a*) on the extent to which we are dealing with an export economy, and (*b*) on the degree of diversification in its exports: since a seasonally balanced distribution of exports will produce a continuous inflow of external earnings and of bank cash to offset the demands for cash that relate to financing the movement to the ports of the original exports and the subsequent further financing of the imports that ultimately have to be paid for from the proceeds of these exports. Furthermore, if the economy were relatively self-sufficient, and depended for its prosperity to only a minor extent on exports, the cash flows would be influenced for the most part by internal considerations and the stringencies caused by lags in payments need not create any embarrassment. That is to say, if it is only the domestic economy that requires finance, the funds that accrue from borrowing and selling must remain available somewhere in the economy, even when they are passed on by spending or lending. In this context, a "money market" has an obvious task to perform: to seek out the funds wherever they may be and to channel them into the hands of the institutions that require them.

The difficulty is that the market houses that could perform this function may not yet exist. There may be temporarily surplus funds in existence (e.g. in the hands of big industrial and commercial enterprises) but there is no institutional mechanism to make available such funds for employment elsewhere in the economy and also to ensure that the funds can be recalled as and when required, to be replaced by other temporarily surplus funds from similar sources. There is as yet no means of ensuring that these funds will "revolve."

Hence, if the prospect of making a profit out of this situation fails to attract private enterprise, then there may well be a case for a public authority to take the initiative and by setting up a suitable institution (e.g. the National Finance Corporation in South Africa) to provide an earning outlet for such funds as well as facilities for their withdrawal as and when required. Once the necessary stimulus has been provided, private enterprise may well follow the lead given by the authorities. On other occasions (e.g. in Canada) it has been possible to encourage private enterprise itself to supply the desired facilities, while on occasion (e.g. in Australia) it was private enterprise that forced the pace and the authorities were ultimately obliged to recognize the existence of a market and to provide it with the lender-of-last-resort facilities without which such a market cannot approach its full potential.

Against this background, it is now appropriate to consider briefly some of the experiences in setting up new money markets within the framework of rather different environments and, for this purpose, it is proposed to cite as examples the development of money market institutions in Canada, South Africa and Australia, and to contrast this with the type of solution sought in India.

CANADA: OFFICIAL INITIATIVE

Canada and South Africa are the leading examples of countries in which the development of money markets has been officially encouraged and assisted.

The Canadian experience in particular emphasizes what can be done in quite a short space of years, given the necessary underlying conditions that favour the emergence of such a market, plus the wholehearted support both of the government and the central bank.[2] Although the establishment of a "money market" in Canada is essentially a post-war phenomenon, one of the essential steps was taken as far back as 1934, when arrangements were first made to sell Treasury bills by tender. Gradually, both the number of issues and the total volume outstanding were increased, but trading in Treasury bills continued to be largely between the chartered banks and the Bank of Canada. Dealers may have done a little business in bills, but only on a commission basis for customers. They never carried inventories.

It was during the second world war that dealers began to take Treasury bills more seriously and only towards the end of the war that they even thought of carrying a small inventory. The big step forward came in January, 1953, with the introduction of a weekly tender and the grant of "limits" to certain dealers by the Bank of Canada. This permitted them to secure accommodation on the basis of a sale of short-dated government securities (including but not confined to Treasury bills), subject to an agreement to repurchase and at rates cheaper than those charged by the chartered banks. By this means, it was hoped to increase nonbank holdings of Treasury bills and to build up dealer experience of the relevant techniques.

By April, 1954, the Bank of Canada felt the dealers were ready for the next step. The way was prepared by a revision of the Bank Act in 1954 that replaced the traditional 10 percent cash ratio with a legal 8 percent minimum based on monthly averaging. This made it easier for the banks to adjust their cash positions and also freed a large volume of reserves for lending to dealers on a day-to-day basis, in amounts and at rates that enabled the latter to carry inventory at a profit. From the banks' point of view, day-to-day loans were a highly liquid earning asset, which facilitated the fullest possible employment of their funds, since they were committed for no more than a day at a time.

In order to encourage the dealers to carry as much inventory as was consistent with the available supply of day-to-day money, and as a means of underwriting the experiment, the Bank of Canada stood prepared to act as "the post of last resort." Not being specifically authorized to lend to dealers, the Bank arranged to make accommodation available to certain dealers as a privilege, up to negotiated limits on the basis of a sale and repurchase agreement, whenever it proved impossible to raise sufficient money elsewhere with which to carry inventory, the cost of this accommodation being calculated as the difference between the prices at sale and repurchase.

[2] For the detailed story see J. S. G. Wilson: "The Canadian Money Market Experiment", *Banca Nazionale del Lavoro Quarterly Review*, March, 1958.

Since the rate charged was equivalent to Bank Rate, it was in the nature of a penalty.

Initially, the dealers' chief difficulty was to find customers for the bills they carried in inventory. But gradually they established retail outlets by selling bills to business corporations (often on a "buy-back" basis and latterly terminable by either party on demand). They were further assisted by the Bank of Canada's wire transfer arrangements that ensured speedy delivery of securities at whichever of the Bank's nine agencies (i.e. branches) might be stipulated, and, if necessary, in separate parcels.

After February, 1957, it was also possible to borrow securities from the Bank. The chartered banks, too, were tending to use the dealers to an increasing extent in order to sell or buy money market assets with appropriate maturities. At the same time, since the banks remained in the Treasury bill tender, they could adjust their bill portfolios without resorting to the dealers —simply by varying their intake of new bills. Moreover, a big barrier to the stimulation of greater dealer interest was partially removed when the chartered banks first reduced and, in March, 1957, radically modified their over-certification charge,[3] thereby encouraging an increase in the turnover of loanable funds.

It was on this basis that both the tender and the market for Treasury blls and bonds was steadily expanded. Although only the chartered banks and 14 money market dealers can tender for Treasury bills, outside parties can either arrange for a bank or dealer to tender on their behalf or obtain their requirements later in the market for issued bills. When it comes to new issues of Government of Canada bonds, there are in all some 300 dealers who act as "primary distributors." Indeed, as the money market grew, it extended its activities into prime commercial paper,[4] finance company paper, and the short-term bills and notes of provinces and municipalities.

THE SOUTH AFRICAN CASE

In South Africa, too, the short-term money market was only established in the years after the second world war. Again, growth has been rapid. A National Finance Corporation had been set up in 1949 with capital subscribed both by the private financial institutions and the Reserve Bank, the Board reflecting this shareholder interest but also including a Treasury representative. The Governor of the Reserve Bank is Chairman.

By establishing this institution, the authorities hoped, first, to reduce the

[3] See Wilson, *ibid.*, pp. 29–33.
[4] Most of this paper is offered by large commercial corporations with seasonal requirements and it is purchased by parties with a temporary surplus of liquid resources.

large volume of short-term central bank advances to the government and, second, to provide an outlet for some of the large current account balances that appeared to be available but which were not being invested in Treasury bills or other government stocks. These moneys might now be placed on deposit with the NFC, which would then invest them in government paper. Initially, the liquidity of the NFC was guaranteed by the Reserve Bank.[5]

In the first instance, it was excess domestic current account balances (e.g. those of the big corporations) that it was attempted to tap, though the banks also placed money on deposit. To cushion the banks against the immediate effects of this transfer of funds, their required minimum cash reserves were temporarily reduced. For a time, bank deposits with the NFC tended to fluctuate quite considerably, even though cash reserves were often well above the required minimum, but from 1953 onwards excess balances were steadily reduced.

In more recent years, the evidence suggests that the banks have been using both NFC facilities and the call money market with increasing freedom as a means of adjusting their cash positions. Moreover, the Corporation's own total deposit liabilities have become much less volatile as a result of compensating movements in the balances of other depositors, which include the big mining houses.

When the NFC was first launched, there were many who were decidedly critical of its proposed rôle. It was regarded very much as an adjunct of the Reserve Bank, which in a sense it was, and there was a tendency to think of it as little more than an engine for siphoning off surplus short-term funds for the purpose of expenditure by the government. That would seem to have been far too uncharitable an interpretation and the setting up of the NFC should more properly be regarded as an experiment that broke new ground and pointed the way to the development of a true money market.

In particular, the successful operations of the NFC in due course encouraged private enterprise to take the plunge in expanding money market facilities, when towards the end of 1955 Union Acceptances Limited was set up to develop an acceptance and discounting business. Two years later the discount business was transferred to a separate company, with the original institution acting as managers for the new discount house, the latter's business being modelled on the London practice of borrowing money at call in order to finance a portfolio of commercial and Treasury bills and of short-dated government bonds. In addition, it stood prepared to retail bills to institutions seeking investment for temporarily surplus funds.

The success of these two houses attracted other companies into the field, such as the Central Finance and Acceptance Corporation, the Accepting Bank for Industry, and the Philip Hill Acceptance Co. Finally, a separate

---

[5] By 1955, the NFC felt sufficiently well established voluntarily to surrender these statutory privileges.

discount house was established, specifically to take over the discounting business formerly undertaken by these three merchant banks. At the same time, the development of a true money market must wait upon the emergence of more impersonal relationships between accepting and discount houses. At the moment, the links between particular institutions are too direct.

On the official side, too, important changes have been taking place. In June, 1958, Treasury bill rates that had been "administered" (though changed periodically with some reference to market conditions at home and abroad) became subject to a competitive weekly tender, with the NFC's call money rate fluctuating in sympathy, thereby imparting for the first time a measure of true flexibility to the rate structure. Subsequently, in 1960, the Reserve Bank also freed the prices of short-dated bonds, thus encouraging an expansion in discount house bond dealings. Further, by withdrawing its undertaking to sell and discount Treasury bills at preferential rates, the Reserve Bank clearly indicated that the money market was now to be both the main source of bills and the place where they could be converted into cash. But the Bank also began to develop a closer liaison with market houses, which it was prepared to help at times of severe strain, and "smoothing out" operations became more frequent. Nevertheless, for a market to operate with complete confidence, these must be given a continuing character in order to eliminate excessive fluctuations in the availability of funds.

THE MARKET IN AUSTRALIA

The Australian economy offers an example of a relatively developed country still subject to strong seasonal influences that have obvious effects both on bank liquidity and on the flow of cash. Seasonality is due partly to the concentration of government revenue receipts in the April–June quarter and partly to seasonal production and sale of the several primary commodities that still furnish much of Australia's export income. There is in consequence a demand both for outlets to absorb temporarily surplus cash and for some means of tapping sources of liquidity during periods of monetary stringency.

Prior to 1959, the means of investing money for short periods were rather limited. The traditional outlet in Australia was the "fixed deposit" accepted by the trading banks for terms of from three to 24 months. Latterly, however, the rate paid on such deposits had ceased to be competitive with alternative outlets, such as the issue of short-term debentures by hire purchase finance companies.

This latter facility began to be offered (soon by other enterprises as well) in 1950, but trustees and public authorities were unable to employ this technique because of legislative restrictions. Hence, a means had to be devised to meet the needs of investors who wanted the security of government paper but whose funds were unlikely to be available long enough to justify an outright purchase. Also government securities with only a few months to run to maturity were not normally available in large amounts. This need was met by the "buy-back" facilities that certain stock exchange dealers in Sydney and Melbourne were prepared to offer to their customers. Moreover, by selling securities subject to an agreement to repurchase, as well as by the more normal borrowing of funds at short-term, these dealers were able to build up sizeable portfolios.

Yet it was not until February, 1959, by which time there already existed an "unofficial" market of quite appreciable size, that the central bank began to provide lender-of-last-resort facilities to "authorized dealers" in the short-term money market. Nevertheless, operation in the money market was subject to observance of minimum capital requirements, maximum portfolio limits (and, by implication, a limit on their lines of credit at the Reserve Bank), the restriction of money market investments to Commonwealth Government stock with a term not exceeding three years, the provision of margins against loans and the daily reporting of their positions. Moreover, when the dealers borrow from the Reserve Bank, this must be done for specified minimum periods (though dealers may also rediscount money market securities with the Bank). Nine such dealers have now been authorized.

The funds on the basis of which the dealers hold their portfolios have grown considerably over the past three years and are largely borrowed at call. Initially the trading banks were the chief source, but they are now subject to limits on the amount they can place in the market and have been overtaken by other lenders—savings banks; public authorities; insurance, finance and pastoral companies; and business houses with temporarily surplus funds, such as derive from tax or dividend provisions, or the proceeds of new issues prior to their expenditure, or from peak retail sales as at Christmas. So far, lender-of-last-resort facilities, though obviously a basic requirement for the successful operation of the market, have been used only for short periods.

At all times, and provided the parcels are of sufficient size, the dealers stand prepared to purchase or to sell money market securities, or to provide the facility of a "buy-back." For the most part, the sources of money market securities remain direct purchases of government bonds (from the public or the banks) and subscriptions to new government loan offers, which now usually include a three-year security. The dealers could have no interest in Treasury bills at the present fixed rate of 1 percent (these are held by the banks), but the range of available securities was widened to some extent with the issue in November, 1959, of three months Seasonal Treasury Notes (rediscountable at the central bank), originally on a fortnightly but now on a daily basis. These must be redeemed by the end of each financial year (June 30th) and no new issue may be made before the following September. In addition, the dealers have been able to supplement their supplies since

1959 by purchases from the Reserve Bank, now a significant source. Since there are no brokerage or similar charges on these transactions, rate competition has full play.

There can be little doubt that the emergence of an "official" money market in Australia represents a major gain. It has secured for the dealers access to the central bank when they have need of accommodation and enabled the Reserve Bank to regulate the market's rate of growth. The latter has been necessary to ensure a smooth transition to a more active government securities market, as well as to develop the requisite technical expertise and to accumulate experience.

Nevertheless, even at this stage, there are some changes that might be made with advantage. Thus, the absence of a complete spectrum of regularly maturing securities denies the dealers the opportunity to provide all customers with the range of services they require. "Buy-backs" are an incomplete substitute for Treasury bills and, where regular runoff in some volume is desired over a period, they may not meet the needs of some customers at all. There can be little excuse (apart from the recalcitrance of the Treasury, which has a vested interest in low rates) for the refusal to make Treasury bills available to dealers at market rates, thereby preparing the way for the institution of a weekly tender and imparting greater flexibility and consistency to the rate structure as a whole. In addition, the banks would then be able to secure more readily the specific maturities they require for their liquid assets porfolios.

So far, the major benefit that the market has conferred relates to the improved marketability of government securities and the extra funds that are being funnelled into the public sector; but there are great dangers in becoming too dependent on the longer-dated money market issues close to the three-year limit, the holding of which is being largely financed by specifically short-term loans to dealers. Much better to be open about it and to finance a floating debt by means of tender issues of Treasury bills. It would be easier then, too, for the central bank to operate in the market for the purpose of smoothing out flows of cash. If this is to be done, however, it is important that the banks' call loans should be included in LGS ratio (cash, Treasury bills, and other government securities to deposits), since only movements in this ratio will reflect fully the proximate effects on the banks of open market activity.

THE INDIAN BILL MARKET

In the banking field, one of the main problems in India—over a period of many years—has been the need to provide seasonal finance for the movement of crops and their export to overseas countries. Formerly, the scheduled banks supplemented their loanable funds to meet seasonal needs either by the sale of securities to the Reserve Bank, or by borrowing from it against government securities, or—in the case of the exchange banks—by transferring funds from London. Nevertheless, and despite the fullest resort to the call loan market in India, financial stringency regularly developed at the height of each season and money often became very expensive.

For these reasons, the Reserve Bank actively canvassed the possibility of creating a "bill market" in India and a scheme was launched on an experimental basis in January, 1952. Its specific purpose was to relieve seasonal stringency by granting accommodation to banks in the form of loans repayable on demand and against the security of a demand promissory note executed by the bank, but supported by the usance promissory notes of the bank's customers. In other words, the banks were asked to split their customers' loan, cash credit, or overdraft accounts into two parts, the first being covered by a demand promissory note to permit the borrower to vary the amount of his indebtedness in accordance with fluctuating requirements and the second representing his minimum borrowing requirements over a period of (say) three months, which was converted into a promissory note with a usance of 90 days.

Initially, "bill market" finance was made available at $\frac{1}{2}$ percent below Bank Rate and there were other concessions. The scheme was extended progressively to supplement the supply of loanable funds during the busy season. It soon became an accepted part of the money market mechanism in India. This, together with the subsequent necessity to restrict credit, led to the withdrawal of the original concessions. Even the amounts advanced in this way were restricted from June to September, 1960 (this was replaced later by a system of penalty rates on scheduled bank borrowings from the Reserve Bank). In any event, the emphasis of the scheme had now shifted more particularly to the financing of exports.

The value of the "bill market" scheme was that it took into account the preference of the Indian business community for advances of the "cash credit" type and combined the advantage (to the borrower) of this kind of advance with the advantage (to the lending bank) of a discountable bill, thereby providing a mechanism specifically suited to Indian conditions. Yet, the scheme as such has done nothing to develop an integrated money market. Furthermore, such money market arrangements as India possesses have remained largely unchanged over quite a period of years. The interbank call money market assists to some extent in evening-out the flows of cash, but on the whole the liquid positions of the several banks tend to move in one direction or the other at much the same time, depending on the season. Likewise, because of the highly seasonal character of banking business in India, bank holdings of government securities are also liable to wide fluctuations, tending to be high during the slack season and to run down when the banks have need of funds in the busy season.

In the circumstances, only the Reserve Bank itself can effectively provide the necessary buffer. But there is a bigger problem in India than accommodating seasonal swings in bank liquidity—or, indeed, of expanding the supply of credit to meet the requirements of a rapidly developing economy—and that is the problem of providing an effective basis for the complete integration of the so-called "organized" money market and the indigenous markets of the bazaars.

If this is to be achieved, there would seem to be a strong case for seeking such a basis in the wider employment of an indigenous credit instrument such as the *hundi*, the most appropriate form for the purpose being the usance *hundi* made out in promissory note form, payable so many days after date and executed by a merchant, trader, or manufacturer in favour of an indigenous banker (usually a Multani), who lends money against it.

Frequently, no value will have been received, but this is accepted practice in India. Often, the *hundi* will then be endorsed and discounted through a *hundi* broker with a scheduled bank up to agreed limits. Usually, the Multani will have limits with several banks, which fix them on the basis of the usual criteria (integrity, size of resources, and known limits with other banks). Thus, the discounting *shroff* is an intermediary between the big joint stock banks and the small indigenous commercial borrower, about whose creditworthiness the former would not usually have any detailed information. These facilities are now being made available on a much wider geographic basis than formerly and, if the authorities would only make such *hundis* (when supported by the endorsement of a scheduled bank) eligible for rediscount at the Reserve Bank, this would provide an appropriate basis on which not merely to expand further the use made of this instrument but also to establish a truly integrated bill market in India fully adapted to the needs of the local environment.

MONEY MARKETS AND CENTRAL BANK CONTROL

Finally, from the point of view of central bank control, what are the implications of the types of money market structure discussed in this article? In all these countries, except India, there already exists a fully integrated banking system. The banks have also established continuous relationships with the new money market houses. Hence, the effects of any action taken by the authorities will tend to work through the whole of the financial structure and, by this means, influence activity in the country at large.

In India, the central money markets are developed, but the links with the indigenous sectors, though improving, still require some strengthening. For this reason, the effects of any operations in the central money markets may not filter through as rapidly as may be desired to (for example) the rural sector of the economy. In addition, the development of a more active short-term money market would enable the authorities to supplement the methods of direct action (e.g. variable minimum reserve requirements and directives) by operating more frequently in the open market and allowing market forces to spread their effects far and wide. On the whole, this is likely to permit smoother adjustments, so that opposition to changes in the emphases of policy is less likely to be provoked.

In the absence of a true money market and of a fully integrated banking system, direct action is the only practicable method open to a central bank. Furthermore, when facilities exist that make possible the ready adjustment of liquid assets positions, and when these are supported by the activities of a lender of last resort, commercial banks will tend to develop more predictable patterns of behaviour and this will of itself render them more amenable to effective central bank control. The authorities will also be able to evoke responsive action by exerting no more than a minimum amount of pressure.

It is on these grounds that the present writer would encourage the growth of new money markets and, indeed, where the emergence of appropriate institutions has proceeded rather too slowly, even their artificial creation. For those who would otherwise wait on natural growth, perhaps the success of the Canadian and South African experiments will persuade them to venture more boldly.

MONEY MARKETS OF SOUTH-EAST ASIA*

Money markets are often classified as developed or undeveloped according to their degree of institutional specialization. The greater the proliferation of financial intermediaries the more "developed" is the money market. On this count London is the most developed money market in the world. But the degree of institutional specialization within a market is often a reflection of the diversity of demands for financial assets. The money markets in London and New York satisfy primarily the needs of rapidly changing and increasingly complex economies, but they also serve a wider purpose. Both are international money markets and meet the demands of foreigners in providing an outlet for surplus funds and also in creating short-term assets in response to foreign demands for accommodation. London acts both as a borrower and as a lender on international account, New York mainly as a borrower; and the difference in organization and development in the two markets can be partly explained by this difference of emphasis.

Money markets in underdeveloped countries, however, are often highly specialized in the sense that the functions they perform are limited. Local money markets are often little more than markets where first-line cash reserves are held and traded between the banks. This trading can take the form of dealings in foreign exchange as the banks concerned are often international or local banks that have heavy commitments to meet in the international money markets. In such cases the settlements between banks can, therefore, take place through one or other of the international money markets. Further, short-term local investment opportunities are frequently either not available or not acceptable to the banks in the light of their current operations. Local money markets, as a consequence, have often been developed by the commercial banks as a means of expediting their international financial transactions. This is not surprising when it is recalled that the main function of the banks in areas such as Malaya and Singapore is to provide finance for international trade and that most banks have continuing financial commitments to meet in London.

The development of a money market should be judged, therefore, by its adequacy in meeting current demands made upon it, rather than by its institutional structure. What might seem undeveloped, or even inadequate,

* David Williams, *The Banker*, July, 1963, pp. 484–491.

when compared with the stage of institutional development in London might prove to be adequate when taken in a local context.

The Singapore money market should be regarded in this light: it is institutionally rudimentary but functionally adequate given the present orientation of the banks towards financing international trade. The important question that arises, however, is whether Singapore can remain the leading money market in South-East Asia in the face of the development of a money market in Kuala Lumpur and the changing functions of the banks. The future development of the Singapore market lies most promisingly in encouraging it to serve more directly the internal needs of the Malayan economy. But this is likely to call for a major readjustment of the practices of existing financial institutions and the development of new credit instruments and perhaps of new financial institutions as well. This article outlines first the present money market structure in South-East Asia, and then goes on to discuss some of the difficulties likely to be encountered in attempts to "develop" the market.

CLOSE LINKS BETWEEN THE CENTRES

Over the past four years a small but active money market has grown up in Kuala Lumpur. This development has coincided with the establishment (in January, 1959) and growth of the Central Bank of Malaya (Bank Negara Tanah Melayu), with a rapid increase in the number of commercial banks operating in Kuala Lumpur and, finally, with the growing industrial and administrative importance of the town as capital of the Federation of Malaya. This market is, however, virtually an appendage of the Singapore market and is closely integrated with it. Funds move freely between Singapore and Kuala Lumpur; exchange control does not exist and no commission charges are levied on the movement of funds between the two centres. Interest rates rarely diverge between the two centres except, in extreme cases, for late "night" money. This is partly a consequence of almost perfect arbitrage between the two markets, but it is also a consequence of agreement between the Malayan Exchange Banks' Association in Singapore and the Central Bank of Malaya (in consultation with the Federation commercial banks) on maximum rates of interest allowed on deposits and minimum rates charged for loans. The rate agreed for fixed deposits, the key rate in the whole structure, also determines the Treasury bill rate in both centres. Interest rates are also kept closely together because some of the important commercial banks in the Federation have their head offices in Singapore or regard their Singapore branch as their effective head office. Further, it is often easier to borrow than lend in Kuala Lumpur and surplus funds tend to be invested in Singapore. Kuala Lumpur can thus frequently adjust its cash position simply by altering the flow of funds to Singapore.

An important factor that helps to determine the structure of agreed rates in both centres is the banks' assessment of their need for deposits in the light of the demand for credit (there is, normally, at least a 2 percent spread between fixed deposit rates and minimum lending rates). The Central Bank, of course, considers the broad structure of rates in the light of the state of the economy as a whole. Over the last few months the Central Bank has shown, for the first time, an open bias towards a regime of low rates. In the final resort, however, the level of rates ruling in London underpins the Malayan rate structure. If the interest rate differential between Singapore and London becomes sufficiently wide, capital movements occur that tend to pull rates in Singapore closer to those in London. The rate pattern that seems to have emerged over the past few years is a maximum spread between rates in Malaya and London of 2 percent in favour of London but a minimum rate of 4 percent in Singapore for fixed deposits. For the past year Malayan fixed deposit rates have equalled London Bank rate (i.e. 2 percent above London clearing banks' seven-day deposit rate), but there has been no obvious switching of funds to London. Local commercial bill rates are, of course, directly determined by the London discount rate for commercial bills.

Both money markets are almost purely interbank call money markets. Banks do not accept deposits at call except from other banks (from the public they accept fixed deposits for periods of three, six, nine or twelve months) and they do not lend at call or short notice outside the banking system in Kuala Lumpur, though a few of the banks in Singapore now make small loans to some of the leading stock and money brokers. The bulk of lending in the Kuala Lumpur market is made on an overnight basis, i.e. for repayment the following day unless specifically renewed; some funds are placed on a three- or four-day basis, but loans for seven days or over are unusual. A few banks place call deposits with those larger banks with whom they have special relationships, but the bulk of such surplus funds is placed in Singapore. At least four of the 21 banks that operate in Kuala Lumpur do not deal in the local market; a further three banks each deal with only one other bank. The majority of the remainder tend to deal with particular groups of three or four other banks. The amount of nonbank lending in the market is small; the banks deal directly and do not use other intermediaries. The foreign exchange market, so crucial to the net cash reserves of Singapore, is unimportant in Kuala Lumpur.

In Singapore, interbank loans are made at call, or for three or seven days. Exceptionally, interbank loans are made for up to one month, and some banks lend to others by placing funds with them on deposit account. The Chinese banks, as in Kuala Lumpur, are the main lenders in the local market and the nonBritish foreign banks are the chief borrowers. The British banks sometimes act as lenders in the call market and also provide special overdraft facilities for a few important banks. On the other hand, they also take deposits from some of the local banks and, indeed, until quite recently ¼₄ percent commission. The remainder of the funds is placed through direct contact with a bank or group of banks.

Though all banks in Singapore agree in principle to deal through brokers, probably not more than 60 percent of the funds placed in the interbank market are handled by money brokers. These include most of the ten stockbroking firms, six of which also act as foreign exchange brokers. They charge ¼₄ percent commission. The remainder of the funds is placed through direct contact with a bank or group of banks.

Interbank rates are determined bilaterally and the spread of rates within, but not between, the two centres is surprisingly large. This presumably reflects the different credit rating of the banks, as some of them—in both centres—consistently pay more for interbank borrowing than others. Interbank rates seem to fluctuate within a range of ⅜ percent either side of the agreed rate for fixed deposits. The interbank rate is in fact closely governed by the rate offered by the banks to the public for fixed deposits, which itself is fixed partly with an eye on the level of rates ruling in London.

Both centres have small Treasury bill markets, but commercial bills never appear on the open market, though some of the small Singapore banks occasionally discount bills directly with the larger banks. Treasury bills are available on tap from the Central Bank in Kuala Lumpur and though their supply is limited—the maximum permissible issue is M$150 millions—the bills are held by most of the banks and by a few outside institutions. There is, however, only restricted dealing in Treasury bills. The banks hold the bills as investments (since they are on tap the banks can match their needs exactly) and a few banks hold them as part of their statutory capital requirements. Further, the banks hold large balances in Singapore because these can provide liquid funds more easily, and less revealingly, than can the discounting of bills at the Central Bank. In any event, the Central Bank does not encourage rediscounting of Treasury bills, arguing that it does not have the resources to provide such facilities. This is partly because the note issue, no part of which is fiduciary, is in the hands of a Currency Board and backed with foreign—predominantly sterling—securities. The Central Bank does not publish a Bank rate, but charges a discount commission of between ⅛ and ¼ percent above the ruling Treasury bill rate. The bank will also provide "buy-back" facilities for Treasury bill dealings with the commercial banks.

In Singapore, bills are available on tender from the office of the Accountant General, which also provides rediscount facilities—so far unused by the banking community. The banks tender directly for bills—only seven of the 32 banks operating in Singapore regularly hold bills—but they can be, and sometimes are, resold to private institutions through the money brokers. There are, however, no institutional arrangements outside the banking system to deal extensively in commercial bills.

An outstanding characteristic of the money markets in Kuala Lumpur and Singapore is the great degree of stability in the interest rate structure. There are relatively few occasions when the demand for even overnight money pushes rates extravagantly above the levels normally ruling. There is, too, only a very slight seasonal movement in the demand for cash. The main exports of Malaya—rubber and tin—are not seasonal crops and imports do not fluctuate widely. Seasonal factors probably cause a swing of less than 5 percent in the demand for cash; that change is due mainly to the Chinese New Year, which normally falls in the first week of February and inflates the demand for cash because all outstanding debts are then cleared.

Interest rates can remain firm even though surplus funds overhang the market; similarly, a sharp increase in the demand for funds does not usually lead to an immediate rise in rates. The excess or deficiency in the supply of funds is offset by the placing or withdrawal of funds from other money markets. This technique of inter-money-market lending is the basis for the observation that the market is usually "all one way." Kuala Lumpur places its surplus funds in London and, predominantly, in Singapore. Singapore, in turn, uses London as its money market. Indeed, Singapore's net indebtedness to the Federation is almost completely offset by its creditor position *vis-à-vis* London. Funds are much more readily transferred between Kuala Lumpur and Singapore than between Singapore and London. Indeed, if the money brokers in Singapore are unable to place surplus funds, those funds are simply held over until the next day and attempts are made to place them again. By contrast, surplus funds in Kuala Lumpur are immediately transferred to Singapore.

INTERBANK DEALINGS IN STERLING

The surpluses will not, however, remain indefinitely in the Singapore market. Sooner, rather than later, they will be converted into sterling and invested in London. This transfer will depend, of course, on how long the funds are expected to be "surplus," and on whether they are required to meet commitments in London. The relative market rates in London and Singapore will be of crucial importance. However, the most significant determinant of the speed with which the local surplus funds are invested in London will be the sterling-Malay dollar exchange rate as determined in the interbank market for sterling in Singapore.

There are no restrictions on dealings in sterling in Singapore. The sterling exchange rate varies ⅛d either side of par—2s 4d per Malay dollar.

These limits are set by the Currency Board, which is required to redeem Malay dollars in sterling at 2s 3⅞d and to release them for sterling at 2s 4⅛d. The banks' dealings with the public attract a commission of ⅓₂nd percent at the so-called merchant rate. The extreme limits of fluctuation of the exchange rate are, therefore, 2s 3²⁷⁄₃₂d and 2s 4⁵⁄₃₂d.

The interbank market for sterling is, in fact, the heart of the Singapore money market. All the banks keep accounts in London to meet commercial commitments there, and most of them keep a substantial part of their liquid assets in London, partly to enable them to meet local demands for legal tender notes. Interbank debts can be paid and liquidity ratios adjusted through transactions in sterling. The fact that sterling is demanded both for commercial purposes and for capital transfers accounts for the high turnover in the market; this probably amounted to about £1,000 millions during 1962.

The sterling market is dominated by two British banks—the Chartered and the Hongkong and Shanghai Banking Corporation. These are the great sellers of sterling—which accounts for about 85 percent of the foreign exchange turnover in Singapore—and the Chartered Bank, in effect, fixes the interbank sterling rate. There is no marked seasonal movement in exchange rates, though there is a sufficiently regular variation in the exchange rate to make exchange profit an important consideration in bank operations. At the peak period—late October to early February—the local supply of cash is supplemented by bank sales of sterling to the Currency Board, which will deal only in minimum amounts of £10,000 and at the top limit of the exchange rate of 2s 4⅛d. In late spring and early summer the local notes flow back to the market and, if they cannot be sold for sterling in the interbank market, they will be redeemed (literally, by taking notes to the Currency Commissioners in minimum amounts of $100,000 million) for sterling in London at 2s 3⅞d. The market is cleared of funds at the foreign exchange limit and interest rates in the interbank market are, as a consequence, stabilized.

LINES OF DEVELOPMENT

The Kuala Lumpur money market is virtually subsidiary to Singapore and it would be wrong to suggest that Kuala Lumpur could quickly displace Singapore as the leading money market of the area. As noted earlier, the growth of the market is largely a consequence of the political separation of the Federation from Singapore and the establishment of the Central Bank there. With the formation of Malaysia (expected this year) the two regions will become reintegrated and the Central Bank will, in fact, operate directly in the Singapore market, though its head office is likely to remain in Kuala

Lumpur. The Central Bank will, however, add considerably to its problems if it attempts to assist the development of both money markets simultaneously.

The most interesting feature of the Singapore money market is that the volume of liquidity is determined as much by the state of the foreign exchanges as by the level of interest rates in London and Singapore. Surplus money is not automatically taken off the market nor do movements of interest rates necessarily reflect changes in liquidity. This rigidity, however, also reflects institutional inflexibility, which is apparent in Kuala Lumpur as well. The brokerage system is, as yet, not fully accepted by the banks themselves. Hence arbitrage in the market is not complete. Further, little opportunity has been taken to extend the call loan market to include the brokers as principals, as well as agents, and thus enable them to base call transactions on their stock market operations. A widening of the call market seems to be a desirable first step in increasing the facilities of the Singapore market to the local banks. Though it is unlikely that a call market will grow around a bill market (the London pattern) it is possible that the early New York pattern (a call loan market based on the stock exchanges) could be adopted in Singapore. Indeed, the volume of bills—commercial and Treasury—is insufficiently flexible to absorb temporary increases in surplus funds. At the moment, however, there are too few local outlets to utilize fully surplus bank funds and provide banks with sufficient liquidity to meet future short-term commitments locally and abroad.

POINTERS FOR POLICY

The shortage of local bills is the heart of the problem of development of the Singapore money market—as, of course, it is in other money markets of the world. Moreover, the local banking system holds the bulk of the foreign exchange reserves of Singapore and Malaya in the form of sterling assets in London. The development of the local money market will depend on the extent to which these reserves, if repatriated to Singapore, can be used as profitably and as safely at home as they are abroad.

This implies a specific rôle for the market in meeting local short-term financial needs more directly than hitherto. Frequently, development of a local money market takes the form of the creation of a bill market. Funds that were formerly kept abroad can then be invested at home and adjusted in the light of local needs for liquidity. A local bill market, however, unless it deals in international assets, does not necessarily meet the needs of those institutions heavily engaged in international trade and incurring commitments in foreign financial centres.

In the evolution of money markets these days, Treasury bill business usually takes the lead owing to the need for Governments to increase their borrowing to expedite economic development. In effect, the Government borrows external reserves for internal financial purposes. Reserves formerly held by the commercial banks in international assets are exchanged for Government Treasury bills. Whether the centralization of reserves, with the consequent obligation of the central bank to discount Treasury bills to allow commercial banks to meet foreign exchange commitments as well as local cash needs, will lead to more effective control over the local banking system is a debatable point. The substitution of the Treasury bill market for the foreign exchange market as the heart of the money market is, however, certain to involve the Malayan monetary authorities in important changes in exchange rate policy—both in allowing a free sterling market and in maintaining a relatively wide spread of the Malay dollar-sterling exchange rate.

The development of a Treasury bill market will not necessarily benefit the commercial banks; indeed, the likely contraction of the interbank sterling market might in fact be a real loss to the banks. The majority of the commercial banks in Malaya and Singapore are interested mainly in financing foreign trade. The bulk of their profits derive from international commerce and foreign exchange dealings. Local Treasury bills are generally less profitable to the banks than commercial bills; interest rates tend to be lower and, more important, no exchange profit can be made on the transaction. In addition, there are the problems associated with the conversion of locally-held liquid assets to meet obligations incurred abroad and (more remotely perhaps) with the possibility that local banks might one day find themselves holding larger amounts of Government paper than they would wish.

The greatest difficulty in establishing an active local Treasury bill market in Singapore, however, seems to be the complete lack of tradition in dealing in bills locally. Bills are generally regarded as short-term investments and are held to maturity. Competition among the banks for short-term paper is so intense that it would need a revolution in attitude to permit interbank dealings in bills. Under these conditions there is little chance of any substantial growth of financial intermediaries or bill brokers.

THE CASE FOR BILLS

Professor Silcock, formerly of Singapore University, has gone further than recommending the establishment of a Treasury bill market. He has called for the growth of a local commercial bill market, arguing that "An effective market in local bills would enable the central bank to manipulate interest rates by making money abundant or scarce through its own purchases and sales. It would also diminish the reliance on trade credit which limits the freedom of action of many local traders."[1] But there seem almost insuperable obstacles to the establishment of such a market. First, in many countries—particularly in the underdeveloped territories—credit needs tend to be of longer duration than is usual in bill financing. Six months or more, rather than three months or less, is a more normal credit need in newer developing territories. Secondly, there is the possibility that bills would be used for financing transactions that would not be self-liquidating. Thirdly, it might prove impossible to develop the habit of local discounting especially if, as is likely, much local commercial bill financing would displace the use of the bank overdraft to meet temporary financial needs of borrowers.

The problem of the future development of the Singapore money market can be put quite shortly. It is basically the transformation of a money market at present geared to the financing of foreign trade by means of the interbank market for sterling (and its appendage, the interbank call loan market) to a market more concerned with domestic finance and fostering central bank control over the banking system through the development of local bill markets. It is not clear, however, that the establishment of a local bill market in Singapore could be achieved without a drastic change in the liberal monetary and economic policies traditionally pursued in Singapore. It is also debatable whether central banks require a money (bill) market as an aid in implementing monetary policy.

ADDITIONAL READINGS

Doodha, Kesari D., *Stock Exchanges in a Developing Economy*, Bombay: University of Bombay, 1962.

Johar, Bajindar Sungh, "Cost of Capital Issues in India," *The Indian Journal of Economics*, January, 1961, pp. 241–248.

Low, A. R., "The Short-Term Money Market in New Zealand," *The Bankers' Magazine*, April, 1963, pp. 277–283.

MacLeod, John D. S., "Australian Money Markets Expand," *The Bankers' Magazine*, June, 1964, pp. 397–403.

Nevin, Edward, *Capital Funds in Under-developed Countries*, London: Macmillan, 1961.

Olakanpo, O., "The Money Market in Nigeria," *The Bankers' Magazine*, September, 1963, pp. 167–176.

Palmer, G. F. D. and Dickman, A. B., "South Africa's Expanding Money Market," *The Banker*, October, 1961, pp. 694–701.

Pitout, C. V., "Short-term Money Market in South Africa," *The Bankers' Magazine*, December, 1961, pp. 387–396.

Ross, Carl D., "The Mexican Stock Market," *Financial Analysts Journal*, May–June, 1962, pp. 57–60.

---

[1] Professor T. H. Silcock, "Merdeka in the Money Market," reprinted from the *Singapore Free Press Banking Supplement*, November 5, 1959, in *Readings in Malayan Economics*, ed. T. H. Silcock, Singapore: Eastern Universities Press Ltd, 1961.

"Saving in the Philippine Economy," *Economic Bulletin For Asia and the Far East,* September, 1962, pp. 1–22.

"Stock Exchange Development," *Statistical and Economic Review,* June, 1962, pp. 1–26.

"The Money Market in the Federation of Rhodesia and Nyasaland," *The Bankers' Magazine,* December, 1962, pp. 401–407.

The New Issue Market and the Stock Exchange—A Study in the Theory and Working of the Securities Market in India, Indian Institute of Social Welfare and Business Management, Calcutta, 1961.

chapter 11
The Role of Development Banks in International Finance

For many years investment banks in the industrialized countries have played somewhat the role of development banks. They have, through investment on their own account or through private placement of shares, financed the establishment or expansion of ventures which might otherwise have had difficulties in raising the necessary capital. But one must distinguish between them and the "development bank," for the investment bank operates in an economic environment which is entirely different—an environment where well established capital markets exist, and where there is a large middle and upper class with savings and investment habits favorable to investment in industrial enterprises.

The development bank, however, is a post-World War II phenomenon which is located in an underdeveloped country and which, in spite of the economic and cultural climate, is attempting to speed up the process of industrialization. Because it is operating in a climate which is unfavorable to industrialization, its lending and investing policies are necessarily different from those of the investment banks of industrialized countries. It is a specialized institution which has grown up to meet the new circumstances of the postwar period. It is, on the one hand, an institution for the channeling of investment funds from the industrialized to the developing countries, while on the other hand it is a means of channeling savings from within the developing countries away from their traditional patterns and into productive enterprise. It provides capital and services of a type which the commercial banks of those countries could not be expected to furnish, and which are vital, in the absence of a developed capital market.

As a focal point for the channeling of the international flow of funds, the development bank is of particular interest to governments which are furnishing foreign aid, and is of great importance to such international financial institutions as the World Bank and the Inter-American Development Bank (which is not a "development bank" in the same sense). The development banks are of growing importance to private financial institutions in the industralized countries. For example, Edge Act subsidiaries of U. S. commercial banks have found that equity in development banks is a valuable type of investment, which often supplements the activities of their bank branches or subsidiaries in the same country. Insurance companies are beginning to consider shares in development banks as an addition to their portfolios.

The first reading in this chapter is extracted from a book by Shirley Boskey. This book, which is one of the most complete studies of development banks, discusses in some detail their purposes and types, their sources of finance, their loan and investment policies, and the relationships with their clients. The second reading is by William Diamond, who has also written a comprehensive study of development banks. In this article, however, he expounds the philosophy that a privately-owned development bank (often called a development finance company) is a better instrument for the purpose than a development bank which is owned or dominated by the government. The third reading is a resume of the current interest which the general business communties in the industrialized countries are showing in development banks and development finance companies.

We see, therefore, that there is a broad spectrum of interest in development banks. In addition, the multinational firm has a very direct interest in them. The development bank may well be the only, or one of the few, sources of equity capital and of long and medium-term loan capital. And it may be acting as a commercial bank, providing short-term working capital as well.

It is thus very important for the financial management of a multinational firm to be familiar with the development bank in each country where the firm is operating. Among the questions which are of concern are: (1) Is it a privately-owned bank or is the management responsible primarily to the government? (2) What types of industry will it finance? (3) Does it provide equity as well as loan capital? (4) Does it provide short as well as medium and long-term capital? (5) What are the maximum and minimum size loans it will offer? (6) To what extent does the bank require mortgages or representation on the board of directors of a firm to which it makes a loan or provides equity funds? (7) What are the relationships between the development and the commercial banks? (8) Will the bank be useful in lending to ancilliary industries which will have to grow to support the multinational firm's initial investment?

PROBLEMS AND PRACTICES
OF DEVELOPMENT BANKS*

A. Purposes and Types of Development Banks

This book is concerned with a relatively new kind of investment institution. Institutions established principally or solely to provide long-term financing for industry have long been known.[1] The development bank, intended not only to provide capital for the private industrial sector, but also to mobilize savings, enterprise and skills for productive investment in that sector, is largely a post-World War II creation.

The last fifteen years have seen the less-developed countries swept by a determination to accelerate the pace of their economic development. This determination has been manifested by an increasing emphasis on industrialization, and by the hope that industrial expansion can be speedily achieved.

However, progress has been impeded in most countries by the lack or inadequacy of various ingredients of industrial development. The first impediment is a shortage of capital for industrial investment. In the more advanced countries industrial expansion was achieved in large part through self-financing and, in the early stages of industrialization, at a slow pace. The less-developed countries, spurred by the rapidity of their political advancement during recent years, feel it a necessity to achieve their economic growth at a faster pace. But their resources do not permit the accumulation of earnings sufficient to finance a rate of growth satisfactory to them. Some capital usually does exist in the form of private savings but not enough, and only a small part of those savings is in any event readily available for investment in industry; wealth is traditionally invested in land or commercial enterprises.

The second ingredient of industrial development which is generally lacking is an effective mechanism for channeling into productive investment a sufficiently large proportion of such savings as exist. The absence of a capital market means in turn that there is little familiarity with investment financing techniques. Finally, many countries suffer from a limited initiative on the part of the industrial community—a disinclination to seek out and to venture into new areas of activity—and from limited or no opportunity to

---

* Excerpted from Shirley Boskey, *Problems and Practices of Development Banks,* Baltimore, Md.: The Johns Hopkins Press, 1959, Chaps. 1, 2, 6, 7.

[1] See William Diamond, *Development Banks,* Baltimore, Md.: The Johns Hopkins Press, 1957, pp. 19–40.

become acquainted with and to profit by technological advances achieved abroad.

To help in overcoming these obstacles and in supplying the missing ingredients, the institution known as a development bank has been devised. Some eighty are now functioning all over the world in the less-developed countries which are members of the International Bank.

A number of these banks have been established with the assistance of the International Bank, and in some cases the Bank has provided the foreign exchange needed for their operations.

A principal reason for the International Bank's original interest in development banks was that they offered a practical solution to the difficulties the Bank encountered in financing small private industrial projects directly. Where the projects were many and the amounts sought were small, the Bank could not afford to undertake the detailed technical and creditworthiness appraisals which are a normal preliminary to a loan. Moreover, effective appraisal of such projects called for a greater knowledge of local conditions and the business standing of the sponsors than the Bank possessed or could readily acquire. More important, it was not feasible for most private enterprises to obtain, and many were reluctant to accept, the government guarantee required by the Bank's charter when a loan is made to a nongovernmental borrower. However, these difficulties were avoided or surmounted when the borrower was a local financial institution, which could readily obtain a government guarantee, could select the most promising enterprises for financing out of the proceeds of the Bank's loan, and could undertake the necessary technical and financial appraisals.

Considerations such as these accounted for the initial appeal of development banks as vehicles for International Bank assistance to private industry. Experience has furnished broader grounds. The success of these institutions in stimulating new investment in and by the private industrial sector, and in making available new skills and enterprise as well as capital, has proved their value as instruments of economic development in their own right.

Because each bank is a response to the particular needs of the country which it serves, and to the political, economic, and social environment in which it functions, there is considerable variety among them, particularly in scope of activity.

Most are public institutions, owned and managed by the government. Several are owned jointly by government and private capital, the latter generally having a minority interest. A few are privately owned and controlled.

Some development banks play a major role as financing institutions; for others, providing finance is of less significance. A few are a source of capital for government undertakings as well as for the private sector. Most assist industrial enterprises exclusively; some will also finance large-scale commercial agriculture, or agricultural undertakings integrated with a manufacturing operation. Within the industrial sector, normally only manufacturing or processing enterprises are eligible for assistance, but a few banks are prepared to finance service industries or housing projects. Many concentrate on medium- and large-scale industry; some have been created expressly to cater to the needs of small exterprises.

Most banks are free to provide funds in whatever way seems most appropriate: by equity participations, or loans, or some intermediate form of investment. Some, however, are not authorized to invest in shares.

Many development banks provide their clients with various kinds of technical assistance—engineering, accounting or management advice—on projects they finance; some will advise on a project even if they are not financing it. Other institutions offer no technical assistance, even to clients, beyond that incident to effective administration of their investment.

Some banks investigate promising new investment opportunities, bringing them to the attention of private businessmen. Many of these banks enter the industrial arena directly, establishing enterprises and arranging for their operation until such time as private capital can be induced to take them over.

Some banks engage in activities designed to promote a capital market, actively seeking to broaden the base of industrial ownership by selling investments from their portfolios, by underwriting industrial issues, or, more indirectly, by issuing their own securities.

A few banks have been made responsible for general economic programming for the country.

This great variety among existing banks indicates that no single model is suitable to all, perhaps not even to any two, countries. The design of the bank must be drawn in the light of its purposes and of the economic, social and political environment in which it is to function.

Thus the first group of issues confronting the sponsors of a new bank has to do with the bank's purposes. Is it to be only a financial institution? Is it to offer extensive technical assistance services, or engage in promotional activities, doing research or establishing industries itself? Will it provide only loan funds, or risk capital as well? Is it to concentrate on large and medium-scale enterprises, or on small concerns, or is its assistance to be given without regard to the size of the enterprise? The answers to these and related questions are important in determining not only the design of the bank, but also whether it must be a government institution or can be established with private capital.

In some situations government finance and direction are obviously called for; for example, where the bank is to operate entirely in the public sector, channeling public funds to public enterprises or executing and operating public projects such as highway construction, power development or public works.

But even where the object is assistance to the private sector, it may not always be possible to attract private capital to the bank without an unreasonable degree of government subsidy. This is likely to be the case, for example, where the primary objective is to provide finance for enterprises which are pioneering and promotional in character. Enterprises of this type may be expected to prove profitable in the long run, but are not likely to show returns soon enough or large enough to be considered satisfactory by private shareholders. Moreover, because there are likely to be other more immediately attractive investment opportunities, private investors would probably be reluctant to assume the risk that the experimental ventures might never be profitable. A public institution can more easily await delayed returns from new industries, and it is in a better position to keep an enterprise going for other than investment considerations.

It may also be difficult to induce private investors to subscribe to the equity of a bank intended to cater primarily to the long-term capital needs of small enterprises, which normally have little industrial experience and frequently are one-man ventures. This type of financing is inherently risky, and it is difficult for the development bank to arrange to invest on terms which would compensate it for the risk. For reasons discussed later, the bank will probably find that its financing must take the form of loans. An institution which is to engage primarily in loan financing, and whose borrowers will be numerous and small, can look forward on the one hand to high costs of investigation and administration, and on the other hand to returns not only fixed but relatively small. Here again there is a case for a public institution. Being free, as they usually are, from pressure to make large profits, public banks can contemplate with greater equanimity the prospect of fixed and low returns, and can more readily assume the administrative costs of many small loans to small clients.

Where the environment is inflationary and the demand is for long-term credits, it may likewise be difficult to establish a private bank. Owners of capital hesitate to lend directly at long-term when the value of money is declining, and may therefore not be willing to do so indirectly, by investing in the equity of an institution whose principal activity will be providing loan capital.[2]

If, on the other hand, the purposes of the bank and the environment in which it is to function are such that it appears feasible to organize a privately-owned and managed institution, there are substantial advantages in doing so. Experience indicates that in appropriate circumstances, a private development bank, properly organized and staffed, can be a particularly effective mechanism for promoting industrial growth.

It should be recognized at the outset that a private bank normally can-

---

[2] Investment in the bank's shares will have a greater appeal if they offer an opportunity to hedge against inflation—that is, where it is contemplated that the bank will make index-bound loans, or loans with a gold or dollar clause, or will invest heavily in industrial equities.

not be established on a sound financial basis unless the government is prepared to extend generous financial support. Returns satisfactory to private shareholders cannot be expected in the absence of substantial government financing on terms which make that assistance in essence a subsidy. But the fact that the private institution is not part of the machinery of government, and that its management is selected by and responsible to private shareholders, means that it will in many cases be better able than a public institution to make investment decisions objectively, without being subject to political pressures. Moreover, as compared with a public bank, a private institution is likely to have considerable freedom to engage and dismiss staff, and to establish administrative and fiscal procedures appropriate to its purposes and needs. The ability thus to function on a businesslike and efficient basis will in turn increase the bank's effectiveness in stimulating investment activity in the private industrial sector.

It would, of course, be wrong to suggest either that public banks are necessarily susceptible to political influence or that private banks are necessarily immune to any kind of influence. It would be equally unfair to suggest that a public bank cannot, by its nature, be efficient.

Many public banks have achieved a high degree of independence of the government proper. But the closer the link to government through ownership and management, the greater the likelihood of government influence on investment decisions.

Similarly, there are some highly efficient public banks. The experience of a number of others suggests that accountability to the head of a government department or to the legislature may be less effective in keeping an agency up to the mark than a responsibility owed to private shareholders. If a government enterprise consistently operates at a loss it may well become the subject of a legislative inquiry, but should it merely be less profitable than was expected, it may function undisturbed for years. The shareholders in a private enterprise, on the other hand, insist upon a satisfactory return on their investment, and they also expect the investment itself to increase in value. For a private development bank, this means not only that investments must be sound but that the institution itself must be efficiently and economically operated.

It has already been noted that there are only a few development banks in which the entire share capital, or a majority interest, is in private hands, and which are under private control and management. But the number of such banks has been increasing steadily. In July 1959, there were six in active operation in the less-developed countries which are members of the International Bank: the Industrial Development Bank of Turkey, the Industrial Credit and Investment Corporation of India, the Development Finance Corporaton of Ceylon, the Agricultural Industrial and Real Estate Credit Bank of Lebanon, the Pakistan Industrial Credit and Investment Corporation, and the Industrial Finance Corporation of South Africa. The Industrial Development Bank of Israel is under private control, although its initial capital has come largely from public sources.

Several other private banks have recently been established or are expected to come into being soon. The China Development Corporation, organized in the spring of 1959 (but not yet in operation), is under private control, although the government is a shareholder. Another "mixed" bank under private management has just been established in the Federation of Malaya. The Industrial and Mining Development Bank of Iran opened its opened its doors in October 1959. A privately-owned development bank was established in Thailand in late 1959 as successor to a government institution. Announcement has been made of a development bank for the Northern Region (Syria) of the United Arab Republic, with 69 percent of the shares being offered for public subscription. The National Investment Corporation of Tunisia, established in April 1959 with the government holding a majority of the shares, plans to increase its capital and is inviting subscriptions by small private shareholders; if the offering is fully taken up, the government will become a minority shareholder. A proposal to reorganize a government bank in Peru, to bring in private share capital and to place control in private hands, has been accepted in principle by the government. In several other countries, plans for private development banks are under active and serious consideration.

It was this evidence of the growing popularity of the private development bank as a vehicle for stimulating industrial development that led the International Bank to believe that it would be useful to set forth in some detail the experience of existing private banks.

B. The Bank's Finances

Capital Structure

MAGNITUDE OF RESOURCES. The International Bank is often asked how large the resources of a development bank ought to be. There is no categorical answer to this question, no formula to determine the "proper" magnitude of a given bank's capitalization. The bank ought to have sufficient capital to enable it to make an impact on industrial development, and to earn enough for expenses, the accumulation of adequate reserves and, in the case of a private institution, payment of a satisfactory dividend. On the other hand, resources should not be so large that they greatly exceed what appears reasonably necessary for the fulfillment of the bank's purposes. Overcapitalizations, in the sense of having a great deal more funds than are needed to do the job—whether this is providing finance and technical assistance or establishing industries—may give rise to strong pressure to do too much too early and too fast.

Whatever the desirable capitalization figure from the standpoint of the bank's effectiveness, the actual resources at its disposal will in the last analysis be determined by practical considerations. Where the bank is to be a public institution, account must be taken of the implications for the national budget; i.e., what can be afforded without resort to inflationary means of financing. When a private bank is in view, an estimate must be made of the amount of private savings that can be tapped.

RELATIONSHIP BETWEEN DEBT AND EQUITY. Later in this chapter there is reference to the fact that institutional subscribers to shares of a development bank are usually motivated by other than purely investment considerations. Nevertheless, it is generally necessary to assure them of at least a modest return on their investment, and noninstitutional potential investors may have to be persuaded that the bank's shares offer prospects of returns comparable to those which could be expected on alternative investments.

Private development banks have had to be given special privileges—in most cases an opportunity to earn a profit on long-term, interest-free government advances. To the extent that share capital is supplemented by conventional loan funds, the earning power of the shares is further increased: the higher the proportion of borrowed funds to share capital, the greater the potential earning power of the latter. But if the portion of total resources to be put up by shareholders is too small, the possibility of obtaining further capital by way of loans may be prejudiced. Prospective lenders will not lend unless they are satisfied that there is a sufficiently large equity cushion to protect their interests. In any case, since the share capital stands behind the bank's obligations, it is to the interest of the shareholders that borrowings remain safely below the level at which a substantial loss on the bank's investments might cause a default and wipe out the equity.

Still other factors are relevant. Borrowed funds impose fixed charges.[3] Equity capital imposes no fixed charges, but at the same time it may be more costly in the long run. If the bank is a success, it is likely that a larger total sum will be paid out as dividends than would have been paid out as interest on an equal amount of loan capital obtained on conventional terms. To the extent of the difference, the amount of funds available for reinvestment—and new earnings—will be reduced.

These considerations have little significance for a wholly government-

---

[3] Loans made to development banks by the International Bank and the United States Development Loan Fund, referred to later in this chapter, are in the form of a line of credit, interest being charged only on the amount withdrawn and outstanding from time to time.

owned bank which is not under pressure to earn large profits for its share-holders and which looks to the government for all of its resources. But they may be important, even for a public bank, if it is contemplated that the bank may sometime wish to borrow from other sources, perhaps through issuance of its own obligations.

The relationship between debt and equity in the bank's capital structure also has implications for the bank's investment policies which should not be overlooked. In determining the proportion of its resources which it can pru-dently employ to purchase equities, the bank must be mindful of the need to have sufficient funds in liquid or readily realizable form to meet its fixed obligations. A bank capitalized heavily with borrowed funds would probably be reluctant to invest heavily in equities, and might even accept only the more conservative loan proposals. Therefore, it may be said that if it is the primary purpose of the bank to provide risk capital, the bank's own capitalization should not contemplated a relatively high proportion of loan capital. On the other hand, a preponderance of local capital would not be inappropriate for a bank expected to make few or no equity investments.

Taken together, these considerations can translate into a variety of debt-equity ratios in practice. There is no single "correct" ratio. The International Bank suggested a 3:1 ratio for the banks in Turkey, India, Pakistan and Iran, which it helped to establish. To encourage subscriptions to an increase in share capital, the ratio for the Turkish bank was later raised to 4:1, after the bank had established itself as a going concern. A 3.51:1 ratio is pre-scribed in the second loan agreement between the Investment Credit Corpo-ration of Austria and the International Bank. The government advances to the Industrial Credit and Investment Corporation of India, the Pakistan In-dustrial Credit and Investment Corporation, the Investment Credit Corpora-tion of Austria and the Industrial and Mining Development Bank of Iran are considered to be equity for purposes of the debt-equity ratio: in the event of liquidation, the Indian, Pakistan and Austrian government advances would rank for repayment not only after debts but also after the share capi-tal, while the Iranian government advance would rank *pari passu* with the share capital. Thus the banks have ample scope for borrowing.

The Industrial Development Bank of Canada, a public bank, and the Commonwealth Development Finance Company, a "mixed" bank, are also by charter subject to a 3:1 ratio. Another "mixed" bank, the Industrial Fi-nance Corporation of India, may borrow up to ten times the amount of its paid-in capital and reserves. Unless the shareholders approve, outstanding borrowings of the Industrial Development Corporation of South Africa, a public institution, may not exceed three-fourths of the issued capital.

It may be noted that the actual debt-equity ratio may change substan-tially where the bank has borrowed abroad and the local currency is ther-after devalued. The value of the equity would be reduced in relation to the amount of the loan, and the safety of outstanding foreign debt may be imperiled.

Sources of Equity Capital

With respect to the financing of public banks (whether wholly government-owned or "mixed," with the government holding a majority interest), it suffices to note here only that what corresponds to the share capital of a private bank may, in the case of a public institution, be provided in various ways.

Funds may come as annual appropriations, or Treasury advances, or a lump sum allocation which may or may not take the form of a subscription to share capital. In Yugoslavia, publicly owned enterprises are required to contribute to the public development bank's lendable resources, annually, the equivalent of a fixed percentage of their assets. Certain tax proceeds are earmarked for the development bank, a technique followed in other countries as well. Financial and investment companies and insurance companies and stock exchanges in Mexico are required to subscribe to shares of the Nacional Financiera (in which the government holds a small majority) in amounts corresponding to a specified proportion of their capital and reserves.[4]

A number of issues relating to sources of share capital for private banks warrant discussion. Their equity has, of course, come principally or wholly from private sources; foreign as well as domestic investors have subscribed. As noted earlier, governments have taken minority participations in a few banks. And some have received government assistance in a form which, while not conventional equity, is sufficiently similar to justify describing it together with subscriptions to shares.

DOMESTIC.   A private development bank may, in theory at least, look to two different groups of domestic private investors: institutional and individual. Commercial banks and insurance companies were initial subscribers to the capital of the Development Finance Corporation of Ceylon, the Industrial Credit and Investment Corporation of India, the Industrial Finance Corporation of India and the Pakistan Industrial Credit and Investment Corporation.[5] Institutional investors are usually motivated by patriotism and principle, on the one hand, and on the other by the belief that the bank will perform a useful function for the economy in general, and may in consequence be of more or less direct benefit to their particular business interests. On occasion institutional support has been forthcoming only after special inducements (tax concessions or a government-guaranteed dividend) or government pressure. Commercial banks, industrial firms and trade associations

---

[4] In some other countries (e.g., Haiti), particular types of business entities are required to make compulsory loans to the development bank, or to deposit funds with it.
[5] In some cases it has been necessary to enact special legislation to qualify the bank's shares for institutional investment.

took up the entire initial share capital of the Industrial Development Bank of Turkey, but first it was necessary for the government to offer a guaranteed minimum dividend and, in the case of the commercial banks, to exercise some persuasion.

Individual investors are harder to attract than institutions. It is likely to be particularly difficult to attract individuals when the bank is to finance small or developmental projects or to lend in an inflationary economy. However, in some situations private capital may be more responsive: where other investment opportunities are not considerably more attractive; where, for lack or inadequacy of a market mechanism, the investor is not aware of other opportunities; or where the known alternatives are considered less safe than investment in the bank's shares. Government sponsorship may reassure the small saver. And even though private investors may hold back at the start, they may in time become more cordial. There were no individual subscribers to the initial share capital of the Industrial Development Bank of Turkey, but a capital issue four years later was oversubscribed, and many of the subscribers were individuals.

Where it seems that an appeal to both investor groups may prove successful, there are several considerations to be weighed before approaching either. Operations are probably facilitated when a few institutional investors hold all the equity. As noted above, these subscribers are likely to have acted largely for noninvestment considerations. The extent and immediacy of the bank's profitability are therefore not likely to be of principal concern to such shareholders. They will probably be content, in the main, if the bank appears to be serving its purpose and if they receive a reasonable dividend. The individual shareholder, in contrast, is more likely to have a lively interest in the yield and safety of his investment, and to be satisfied only if returns are substantial, prompt and regular. He will be inclined to be impatient with investment policies which do not achieve this result.

However, while there are advantages from the standpoint of administration in a few large institutional shareholders, such an arrangement may be politically unacceptable where substantial government aid is to be extended. The government may be severely criticized for supporting and helping to finance a private bank in which the equity is to be narrowly held within the business community or by other wealthy groups. Moreover, widespread ownership achieved through a public offering of shares can engender widespread interest in, and support of, the bank's activities. This may be particularly helpful in the years during which the bank will be a pioneering institution, engaged in a kind of financing new or little known in the country.

When the Industrial Credit and Investment Corporation of India was established, an effort was made to reconcile these conflicting considerations by allocating 40 percent of the shares for private placement with large industrial groups and financial institutions within India, at the same time reserving 30 percent for individual investors. More than half the applications received for the public offering were for fewer than 20 shares.[6] The balance of 30 percent was allocated to foreign institutional investors. Similarly, 60 percent of the initial issue of shares of the Pakistan Industrial Credit and Investment Corporation was sold in Pakistan, one-third by public offering, and the rest by private placement with banks, insurance companies and leading industrialists.[7]

Widespread share ownership has sometimes been advocated as a solution to the problem of how to prevent any single group of shareholders from acquiring voting control. It must be recognized, however, that even if shares are widely offered at the start, it is difficult to prevent a subsequent concentration of voting power. To attempt to do so by charter provisions (for example, by limiting the number of shares which one person may hold or by reducing voting rights per share as an individual's shareholdings increase) may adversely affect the marketability of shares. Moreover, formal restrictions would not hinder groups of individuals from coming together for the purpose of acquiring control. Recognizing this difficulty, the Industrial Credit and Investment Corporation of India and the Pakistan Industrial Credit and Investment Corporation agreed, as a condition of receiving government advances, that their directors' powers with respect to registration of share transfers would be so exercised as to prevent "any one person or company or group of affiliated persons or companies" from acquiring effective control.

FOREIGN. Foreign capital participation offers a development bank a number of possible advantages. It may help to insulate management against local political pressures to make or decline to make particular investments, thereby strengthening the bank's independence. It may promote a flow of external capital to local industry and provide a point of contact with capital markets in the industrialized countries. It may facilitate the importation of technical skills in industrial production and management. Finally, the evidence that overseas capital regards the bank's shares as a good risk may give confidence to potential domestic investors and lead them to invest their own funds.

Foreign banks and insurance companies doing business in the country are likely shareholder prospects. Being an integral part of the economy they, like their domestic counterparts, are often disposed to participate for other than purely investment reasons. Their subscriptions are usually facilitated by the fact that they can pay for their shares in local currency. British, Indian, and Pakistani banks, and British and Canadian insurance companies were among the initial subscribers to the capital of the Development Finance

---

[6] The shares were of Rs. 100 each (U.S. $21 equivalent), at par.

[7] In May 1959 PICIC had 675 shareholders, all but 56 being Pakistani nationals. Domestic shareholders consisted of 383 private individuals, 203 industrialists and businessmen, 9 banks, 8 insurance companies and 16 business houses and other institutions.

Corporation of Ceylon. British banks and insurance companies subscribed to shares of the Pakistan Industrial Credit and Investment Corporation and the Industrial Credit and Investment Corporation of India. Among the 13 commercial banks which subscribed to the initial share capital of the Industrial Development Bank of Turkey were several foreign banks doing business in Turkey.

It has been harder to enlist nonresident investors. These must pay for their shares in foreign exchange, thereby assuming an exchange risk. The larger the portion of the bank's funds out on loan and drawing only a fixed return, the greater is that risk. Nonresident foreign investors are therefore likely to participate only if they too are to some extent influenced by noninvestment considerations. For example, they may hope to obtain profitable future business in the country and may believe that early association with the bank will put them in an advantageous position with respect to developments in the industrial field. Or they may count upon assistance from the bank or the government for their own ventures. Whatever the particular considerations influencing them, nonresident investors are likely to want assurance that they may remit any profits they may realize.[8]

GOVERNMENT. An equity subscription by the government which carries full voting and dividend rights, as in the China Development Corporation or the Industrial Finance Corporation of South Africa, is in principle no different from a subscription by private investors. But the potential earning power of the private equity can be increased if the government's shares carry no dividend rights, as in the case of the Industrial Bank of Peru, or if the government accepts deferred shares which are not eligible for dividend until the privately held shares have earned a specified return.

[8] In PICIC (Pakistan) the nonresident foreign investors are: from the United States, the International Basic Economy Corporation (IBEC), other Rockefeller interests, the Bank of America, Transoceanic Development Corporation (Canada) and Henry J. Kaiser Company; from the United Kingdom, the Commonwealth Development Finance Company (CDFC), Imperial Chemical Industries, Associated Electrical Industries, English Electric Company and General Electric Company; and 12 Japanese foreign exchange banks.

In the ICICI (India) the nonresident foreign investors are: from the United States, the Bank of America, Rockefeller interests, Olin Mathieson Chemical Corporation and Westinghouse Electric International Corporation; from the United Kingdom, besides the CDFC, Associated Electrical Industries, English Electric Company, General Electric Company, Guest, Keen and Nettlefold, and Gray Dawes and Company.

In the IMDBI (Iran) nonresident foreign investors are: from the United States, Lazard Freres & Co., Chase International Investment Corporation, IBEC, and The First Boston Corporation; from the United Kingdom, Lazard Brothers & Co., Lloyds Bank, Midland Bank, English Electric Company, and Simon Carves; from France, Lazard Freres & Cie., and Banque de Paris et des Pays Bas; from Belgium, Societe Financiere de Transports et d'Entreprises Industrielles (Sofina); from Germany, Sal Oppenheim Jr. & Cie., and Deutsche Bank; from the Netherlands, Amsterdamsche Bank, Nederlandsche Handel-Maatschappij, and Hollandsche Bank-Unie; and from Italy, Banca di Credito Finanziario (Mediobanca), Societa Generale per l'Industria Mineraria e Chimica (Montecatini) and Fiat.

There have been several general references, earlier in this book, to government contributions to the initial capital of several private banks. Governments gave such assistance to the Industrial Credit and Investment Corporation of India, the Pakistan Industrial Credit and Investment Corporation, the Development Finance Corporation of Ceylon and the Industrial and Mining Development Bank of Iran, in the form of noninterest-bearing 30-year advances, repayable in equal annual installments after a 15-year grace period. The Investment Credit Corporation of Austria received a government loan carrying interest at 1 percent, for a term of 60 years, with a 20-year grace period. The loan arrangements provide for the funds to be advanced in full at the outset of operations (except in the case of the Austrian and Iranian banks), and permit them to be invested on short term until required for financing operations.[9] These loans are from a financial standpoint quasi-equity, in that they carry no or token interest, have very long grace periods and rank after (or, in the case of the Iranian advance, *pari passu* with) the share capital in the event of liquidation.[10] For this reason the charters of the Indian and Pakistan banks provide, as noted earlier, that the advance shall be treated as equity for purposes of the prescribed debt-equity ratio. The loan agreements between the International Bank and the Iranian and Austrian institutions contain a similar provision. The charter of the Ceylon bank does not prescribe a debt-equity ratio.

Sources of Loan Capital

DOMESTIC. Development banks, both public and private, have borrowed from the government on a conventional, fixed-interest loan basis. Some have borrowed from the public by issuing their own obligations. Raising capital through bond issues has often been difficult, particularly in inflationary economies. When the Industrial Development Bank of Turkey was created, it was expected to help in promoting a capital market by selling both its shares and its obligations. But while shares have been in demand, there have been no public borrowings; the obligations would not have sold unless they paid interest at a higher rate than the bank charged its borrowers. On the other hand, the first public debenture issue of the Industrial Development Bank of Israel was fully subscribed within two hours.

The Industrial Finance Corporation of India (IFCI) has had considerable success in selling its obligations, both by public issue and through nego-

---

[9] The Government of Iran agreed to put the specified amount at the disposal of the bank "upon the bank's request and as required." The loan from the Austrian government was made one year after the bank started operations.

[10] The governments of India, Pakistan and Ceylon reserved the right to force the banks into liquidation should the capital be impaired by as much as 30 percent. The government advance being junior to equity on liquidation, any losses will be met out of the advance in the first instance; the shareholders' interests will not be affected unless the total of losses should exceed the amount of the advance.

tiation with banks—a success doubtless attributable principally to the fact that its obligations carry a government guarantee. IFCI paper is eligible for rediscounting with the Reserve Bank of India, so that there is little practical difference between such obligations and government bonds. The Government Development Bank for Puerto Rico has issued securities against its own credit, and has likewise had no difficulty in selling them. Although the securities are not guaranteed by the government, the fact that the bank is government-owned has certainly been a factor in the success of the issues.

FOREIGN. The International Bank, the U.S. Development Loan Fund (DLF), and the U.S. International Cooperation Administration have been the principal sources of foreign loans to development banks.

The International Bank has made loans of foreign exchange to a number of development banks. The loan proceeds are re-lent as approved by the International Bank from time to time. The Bank has authorized some of its development bank borrowers to re-lend up to a stated amount without obtaining its prior approval. For example, the Industrial Development Bank of Turkey may re-lend the proceeds of its loan without prior International Bank approval for projects requiring no more than $50,000 in foreign exchange. Under the terms of the second International Bank loan to the Industrial Credit and Investment Corporation of India, the latter may re-lend up to $100,000 for any one project without prior International Bank approval, to an aggregate of $1 million. International Bank loans, being repayable in foreign exchange, give rise to an exchange risk problem; this has in some instances caused delay in drawing on a loan.

The DLF, like the International Bank, is a source of foreign exchange loans for development banks. DLF is not required to insist upon a government guarantee, and moreover has the authority to permit repayment in local currency. Where repayment in local currency is permitted, however, the loan is denominated in dollars, thereby providing for maintenance of value; repayment must be made by the borrower at the rate of exchange prevailing at the time of repayment. Thus DLF loans, like International Bank loans, involve an exchange risk. As a general rule, this risk has been passed on to the ultimate borrower. DLF normally lends only for foreign exchange costs, but has on occasion agreed that a portion of the loan proceeds may be used for local currency expenditures. It has permitted development bank borrowers to re-lend as much as $250,000 to individual borrowers, without obtaining its approval. The Industrial Development Bank of Turkey, the Pakistan Industrial Credit and Investment Corporation and the Industrial and Mining Development Bank of Iran have this authority.

The ICA has made loans to development banks out of U.S.-owned local currencies received in payment for surplus agricultural commodities sold under the provisions of the Agricultural Trade Development and Assistance Act of 1954 (Public Law 480, 83rd Congress), or under provisions of the

Mutual Security Act of 1954.[11] The Industrial Development Bank of Israel, the Industrial Credit and Investment Corporation of India, and the Industrial Finance Corporation of India, for example, have received loans of such U.S.-owned local currencies. Such loans have generally been repayable in local currency or in dollars, at the borrower's option; until recently, the interest rate for dollar repayments was one percentage point below that applicable to repayments in local currency.

Other Sources of Funds

AGENCY ARRANGEMENTS. Two private banks, the Industrial Development Bank of Turkey (IDB) and the Industrial and Mining Development Bank of Iran (IMDBI) have been made agents for the management of public funds, on a fee basis. The IDB administers the Marshall Plan Private Enterprise Fund for an annual fee of 3 percent, retained from the 7 percent interest charged on loans out of the Fund.[12] The Government of Iran has agreed to turn over to the IMDBI certain loan portfolios, to be managed for fifteen years. For its services, the bank will receive an annual commission of 3 percent of the face amount of the loans (exclusive of any loan as to which principal or interest has been in default for more than three months). Like the government advances to the Indian, Pakistan, Ceylon and Iranian banks, these agency arrangements add appreciably to earning capacity, without cost (except the cost of administration), and provide a source of immediate income. They have the important added advantage that the development bank assumes no risk of loss on the loans it makes or administers as agent.

INVESTMENT OF IDLE FUNDS. During the bank's initial period, when it is finding its way, income is likely to be low in relation to costs. It will therefore probably be necessary to consider what provision, if any, can be made to add to income through the investment of temporarily idle funds.

The purchase of securities or the making of short-term commercial loans are theoretically possible sources of income. The feasibility of the first depends on the availability of securities sufficiently marketable and safe. The second raises the question of the advisability of a development bank's entry into the field of commercial banking. In some countries there are no govern-

---

[11] These funds are sometimes incorrectly referred to as "counterpart" funds. Counterpart funds proper are deposits of local currencies made pursuant to the United States' requirement that foreign governments set aside in a special account the commensurate value in local currency of certain U.S. dollar aid. Such counterpart funds are the property of the local government, although they may be expended only with the approval of the United States. The government advances to the Industrial Credit and Investment Corporation of India, the Pakistan Industrial Credit and Investment Corporation and the Investment Credit Corporation of Austria, referred to earlier, were made out of counterpart funds. The Industrial Development Bank of Turkey received a counterpart credit in 1959.

[12] Before the Fund's resources were fully invested, the IDB received a flat annual fee plus a percentage of loans outstanding.

ment securities which the bank can purchase and no corporate securities which seem liquid and safe enough for the purpose. Commercial banks may object to competition from the development bank in the field of short-term commercial lending. In any event, difficult administrative problems may be created by an attempt to combine two types of financing, calling for different kinds of portfolio management and different staff qualifications.[13]

C. INVESTMENT TERMS

Size of Investment

Charters normally do not limit the size of individual investments.[14] None of the banks which participated in the International Bank conference is held to a lower limit by its charter. Only two are subject to an upper limit, and each of these limits is flexible. Except with the approval of the Ministry of Finance, the Industrial Finance Corporation of India may not lend more than a specified amount on its own authority without a government guarantee, or make more than three loans to any one borrower. The charter of the Government Development Bank for Puerto Rico provides that it may not lend to any one borrower an amount which is greater than 10 percent of the bank's capital and surplus; in exceptional circumstances the limit may be 25 percent.

However, many banks have as a matter of policy adopted financing limits. An upper limit helps to ensure a minimum acceptable diversification of investments. An announced lower limit may stave off a flood of applications for projects on which the probable returns would not meet the cost of investigation and supervision.

Actual limits vary widely. Some banks define their self-imposed limit as a proportion of their capital. The Industrial Credit and Investment Corporation of India, for example, normally limits its commitment in any one undertaking to 10 percent of its original share capital and its government advance. Other banks will lend no more (or no less) than an absolute sum. The accompanying table illustrates for several banks the range of investments actually made; in some cases actual investments are larger or smaller than "normal policy."

[13] The Industrial Development Bank of Turkey puts its idle funds to use by making short-term working capital loans, but regards this kind of lending as an exception to its normal policies.

[14] Regulations appended to the law which is the charter of the Agricultural, Industrial and Real Estate Credit Bank of Lebanon limit the amount of any single agricultural loan, depending on its term and whether the borrower is an individual or an agricultural or cooperative society.

SIZE OF INVESTMENTS ACTUALLY MADE*

	Minimum	*Maximum*
	(U.S. $ equivalent)	
Industrial Finance Corporation of India†	10,500	6,300,000
Industrial Credit and Investment Corporation of India	67,410‡	2,100,000
Pakistan Industrial Credit and Investment Corporation	21,000	2,250,000§
Government Development Bank for Puerto Rico	300	4,000,000
Puerto Rico Industrial Development Company	250	10,000,000
Industrial Development Corporation of South Africa	5,600	3,500,000
Development Finance Corporation of Ceylon	18,000	420,000
Banco Nacional do Desenvolvimento Economico of Brazil	11,770	23,500,000
International Finance Corporation	140,000	2,450,000

* As of May 1959.

† Single loans of less than the equivalent of $210,000 are normally made only to enterprises in States lacking a State Finance Corporation, or to supplement a loan previously made to the enterprise. Loans exceeding $2.1 million to a single enterprise or to enterprises under common management require government approval.

‡ ICICI has decided to reduce its normal lower limit from the former $105,000 equivalent to $21,000, to make possible financing of small imports of miscellaneous equipment, and loans for new projects in selected fields offering opportunity for high returns and foreign exchange savings from investments in small units of equipment.

§ The loan for $2.25 million was exceptional; with that exception, PICIC's maximum has been $525,000.

PROPORTION OF CAPITAL REQUIREMENTS. A policy of providing no more than a stated proportion of an enterprise's total capital requirements has the consequence of limiting the size of individual investments. Generally banks are not prepared to invest more than the owners of the enterprise are themselves willing to put up. Thus the banks normally finance no more than 50 percent of total capital requirements.

There are variations about this norm. For example, the Industrial Development Corporation of South Africa normally finances up to about one-third of an applicant's capital requirements, although it has on occasion financed 50 percent. The Banco Nacional do Desenvolvimento Economico of Brazil normally limits its participation to 60 percent of the cost of a private project, but may provide all the capital for a government project. The International Finance Corporation expects the private investors to put up at least half the required capital in the case of a new enterprise. For expansion of an existing enterprise it will consider providing a higher proportion of the new investment, but nevertheless requires that the total private investment in the expanded enterprise exceed the amount of its own investment. The proportion which the Government Development Bank for Puerto Rico lends depends on the assets to be financed: it finances 60 percent of the value of land and buildings, but only 50 percent of the value of equipment. The Corporacion de Fomento de la Produccion of Chile has financed from 5 percent to 90 percent of a project's total cost.

Variations in lending limits also result from the fact that "total capital requirements" are not calculated in the same way by all banks. As discussed further below, to some banks "50 percent" means half the capital requirements, exclusive of working capital. Other banks include working capital under appropriate circumstances. Some consider only the project being financed, whether the firm is new or established; others, like the Caisse Centrale of France, the Pakistan Industrial Credit and Investment Corporation and the Industrial Finance Corporation of India, take into account both existing and to-be-acquired assets when financing an expansion scheme, and finance up to one-half of the total.

Notwithstanding these variations, the requirement that the applicant put up substantial matching funds is general.

FINANCING WORKING CAPITAL. Most banks distinguish between permanent and temporary working capital requirements. They generally feel that the latter should be financed at short term by commercial banks. But where the scale of operations is being permanently enlarged, permanent working capital requirements are generally considered to be as appropriate an object of long-term financing as the acquisition of fixed assets.

There are, however, differences in the readiness of banks to finance working capital and the ways in which they do so. Some banks, like the Industrial Development Corporation of South Africa (IDC), finance permanent working capital as a matter of course. Where an enterprise's operations require that substantial inventories or stocks of raw materials be on hand at all times, IDC takes these needs into account in determining total capital requirements. Nacional Financiera of Mexico finances permanent working capital where it is also lending for fixed assets, if funds for working capital are not otherwise available. The Corporacion de Fomento de la Produccion of Chile distinguishes between established and new enterprises for this purpose; it normally does not provide funds for working capital needs to the former, but may in the case of new ventures. The Industrial Finance Corporation of India (IFCI) takes account of working capital requirements only exceptionally, when an applicant can clearly demonstrate that he cannot finance them through the commercial banks on the security of goods in process, spare parts and raw materials which IFCI exempts from its mortgage charge for this purpose.[15]

Other banks, like the Banco Nacional do Desenvolvimento Economico of Brazil, the Pakistan Industrial Credit and Investment Corporation and the Caisse Centrale of France, prefer not to finance working capital needs directly. Where funds for permanent working capital cannot be raised else-

[15] When IFCI's willingness to provide capital up to 50 percent of the total value of the assets and to exempt the stated items from its mortgage charge is made known, commercial banks are generally ready to provide the additional funds required to make up the necessary working capital. If they are not, this suggests to IFCI that perhaps the applicant should be made to raise more capital than originally contemplated from its own resources or from the money market.

where, these banks on occasion provide such funds indirectly, by financing a somewhat larger proportion of fixed asset capital requirements than is their normal practice.

These differences in attitude toward working capital financing reflect a variety of views. One is that permanent working capital is properly financed by the owner's equity: that the funds of the entrepreneur which are released by the development bank's fixed asset financing should be used to meet permanent working capital needs. A related view is that any working capital which the enterprise itself cannot supply should properly be provided by the commercial banks. The Industrial Finance Corporation of India has found that companies which enjoy the full confidence of the commercial banks and which therefore need not ask it for working capital financing are likely to be more reliable; it has found the disciplines imposed by the commercial banks helpful in this respect. On the other hand, the Pakistan Industrial Credit and Investment Corporation, although of the opinion that permanent working capital normally should be put up by the applicant, with seasonal requirements financed by commercial bank credit, feels that enterprises can become too dependent on commercial banks; accordingly it has decided not to adopt a firm rule for its own financing.

Form of Investment

Though some charters authorize only conventional fixed-interest loans, most permit loans, equity investments or loans convertible into equity.[16] Article 5 (i) of the charter of the Development Finance Corporation of Ceylon may be taken as an illustration. It authorizes the bank to "provide finance in the form of long-term or medium-term loans with or without security, or by purchasing or subscribing for shares or other securities, or by acquiring any other interest."

Banks generally try to tailor their financing to the applicant's requirements. But other considerations are also relevant. The fact that one bank's portfolio consists predominantly of equities while another's may be almost wholly in loans reflects the combined result in a particular situation of the variety of factors discussed below.

SOURCES OF THE BANK'S FUNDS. Banks are generally reluctant to purchase equities with borrowed funds, even where the terms of the loan do not preclude such use of the funds. Thus the equity portion of a bank's resources (including surplus and reserves) normally approximates the limits

---

[16] Of the banks which participated in the International Bank conference, the Government Development Bank for Puerto Rico and the Industrial Finance Corporation of India are not authorized to make equity investments. The International Finance Corporation may not invest in capital stock or shares, but the loans it makes are not conventional fixed-interest loans; they combine certain features of both debt and equity.

within which the bank may prudently make equity investments. The more conservative banks limit their equity portfolio to a fraction of this total, sometimes even to their earned surplus.[17]

ECONOMIC ENVIRONMENT. Under persistent inflationary conditions, the real value of debt is so quickly eroded that lending at long term without some protective provisions is tantamount to making a gift. To protect its capital, a bank operating in such an environment can be expected to emphasize equity investments. Protection of capital is not the only reason for the preference for equities. To spread the benefits of financial assistance as widely as possible and to help widen the channels through which savings can be directed to industrial investments, development banks generally try to revolve their funds as quickly as possible. In an inflation-oriented community, one of the few ways to accomplish this is by the sale of equities from portfolio. No private investor will put funds into ordinary long-term debt obligations in the face of virtually certain continued steep increases in the price level.

Various devices have been adopted to protect against inflation where financing must be provided in loan form. One is to insist upon conversion rights. The Caisse Centrale of France requires accelerated amortization of a long-term loan if the borrower's gross sales rise above a stipulated figure (the forecast of gross sales made at the time of granting the loan). The Corporacion de Fomento de la Produccion of Chile lends only with a dollar clause. Bonds carrying profit participation rights when profits pass a certain level provide similar protection.[18] So do loans with escalator clauses, tied to some specified index of prices.[19] The Industrial Development Bank of Israel, for example, makes loans linked to the price of the dollar or to a cost-of-living index.

PREFERENCES OF THE BANK. There are reasons apart from the economic environment for a preference for equity investments or loans with conversion rights. At the outset of operations, when the bank is concerned to build up reserves, meet administrative expenses, service borrowed capital and pay divdends on its share capital, the regular and immediate income generated by a loan portfolio has a greater appeal than the delayed and uncertain returns on equity investments. The Industrial Development Bank of Turkey deliberately avoided equity investment in its early years, believing it too risky for a private bank in the initial phase of operations.

---

[17] Note that the long-term, interest-free government advances made to the private development banks in India, Ceylon, Pakistan, Iran and Austria may, for this purpose, also be considered as having some of the characteristics of "equity."

[18] The Industrial Development Bank of Turkey does not lend on these terms, believing that a profit-sharing provision would violate the 7 percent legal interest ceiling.

[19] It was the view of the banks at the International Bank conference that it was not possible fully to protect against inflation through the interest rate. See the discussion of interest policy later in this article.

But once the bank is a going concern, equity investments have many advantages. They enable the bank to share in the profitability of successful enterprises, thereby adding to the bank's income, providing a cushion against possible losses on other investments and demonstrating the attractiveness of industrial financing. By selling equity out of its portfolio, the bank can help to spread share ownership and develop a capital market.

Equity investments may have tax advantages for a bank which is not tax-exempt.[20] The Pakistan Industrial Credit and Investment Corporation, for example, is subject to a tax of 60 percent on its profits, but dividends on share holdings and capital gains realized from the sale of equity investments are tax-free. Similarly, in South Africa, interest payments are taxable to the recipient, but dividends on preferred shares are not.

PREFERENCES OF THE CLIENT. The form of investment is not always the bank's choice alone. The attitude of the applicant enterprise toward outside participation must be taken into account.

There has been considerable resistance to the surrender of share capital. Businessmen are frequently reluctant to share their ownership, because this usually means that they must disclose the details and secrets of their operations. And even if they are prepared to accept the development bank as a partner, they may be concerned that the bank's shares may be sold to rival interests or other persons they would not want as partners. The Pakistan Industrial Credit and Investment Corporation has found that some entrepreneurs would rather pay more to borrow funds elsewhere than share equity with it.

Resistance has perhaps been strongest where sizeable financing is sought from a government bank. Private firms often do not want government equity participation, fearing government interference in management.[21] Foreign firms have been particularly sensitive on this score. Even government-controlled firms may be reluctant to surrender equity. The Commonwealth Development Finance Company of the United Kingdom once considered investing in an enterprise in which a colonial government was the largest shareholder. However, the colonial government was unwilling to surrender any of its shares, preferring to reserve them for eventual sale to local interests.

Of course the situation may sometimes be otherwise: the bank may be

[20] The private development banks which participated in the International Bank conference are subject to income tax. The Development Finance Corporation of Ceylon pays a tax of 45 percent; the tax paid by the Industrial Credit and Investment Corporation of India is about the same. The income of wholly government-owned banks is usually tax-exempt. However, the Nacional Financiera of Mexico and the Industrial Finance Corporation of India, in both of which the government holds a majority interest, pay a tax of about 43 percent and about 51 percent respectively, on gross profit. The Industrial Bank for the Northern Region (Syria) of the United Arab Republic, in which the government and the Central Bank are to have only about a one-third interest, is to be tax-exempt during its first six years.

[21] And government banks may be anxious to avoid creating the impression that funds are available only to enterprises willing to accept the government as a partner.

asked to take at least a token interest as evidence that the enterprise has its blessing. This has been the experience of the Caisse Centrale of France of France and the Puerto Rico Industrial Development Company.

Tax consequences may affect not only the bank's but the enterprise's preference for one or another form of new financing. For example, where interest on debt is a business expense deductible from gross earnings, it may be less costly for a firm to expand by borrowing than by issuing new shares.

All these considerations are applicable to loans with conversion rights. If the bank is to supply a substantial portion of the requisite total capital, so that control as well as participation in the direction of the enterprise is involved, it may be particularly difficult to obtain conversion rights. Some banks compromise by taking conversion rights for only a portion of their loan, by accepting nonvoting shares, or by giving existing shareholders a right of first refusal before they sell their shares to outsiders.[22] Where the absence of voting rights would limit the marketability of the shares, the enterprise may agree that a purchaser of the nonvoting shares from the bank may exchange them for voting shares.

FINANCES OF THE ENTERPRISE. Within the context of all these considerations, the question of the most appropriate capital structure for an enterprise is clearly of primary importance in determining the form in which a bank can best provide financing. Equity is probably the most appropriate form of financing for a new enterprise, but this is the riskiest form of investment for the bank and, until the enterprise becomes seasoned, the hardest to sell. Moreover, for the reasons already given (reluctance to accept a partner, and tax considerations), the enterprise itself may prefer to borrow. Thus loan financing may coincide with the initial preferences of both the enterprise and the bank.

But if more capital should later be needed for expansion, both the enterprise and the bank may then prefer the bank's investment to be in the form of equity. The enterprise would have a broader base on which to borrow from other sources, and the bank would be enabled to share in the growing enterprise's profits. In this situation, initial financing by way of convertible debentures has been found particularly appropriate. The Industrial Development Corporation of South Africa has normally made this kind of investment in a small or new enterprise, sometimes taking conversion rights for as much as 50 percent of its investment.[23]

---

[22] This does not further the objective of helping to foster a capital market, and at least one bank, the Puerto Rico Industrial Development Company, does not give first refusal rights for this reason. On the other hand, it is a standard provision of investments by the International Finance Corporation.

[23] IDC also finances established enterprises by way of convertible debenture, but then normally takes 20 percent–25 percent conversion rights. In these cases it is motivated by income and profit considerations: upon exercise of the conversion right it obtains tax-free income in the form of dividends, and shares which it may be able to sell for a tax-free capital gain. The Pakistan Industrial Credit and Investment Corporation

Where the corporation laws do not permit authorized but unissued capital, a bank making a convertible loan must arrange in advance for the requisite increase in the enterprise's share capital when the conversion rights are exercised. Some banks obtain an assurance from the borrower that there will either be a new capital issue at that time or require one of the large shareholders to grant an option on some of his shares to the bank. Where unissued capital is permitted, banks insist that at the time the loan is made there be outstanding and remain reserved a sufficient number of unissued shares against which the conversion right may be exercised.

Once the form of an investment has been determined, the bank must make a number of related decisions about the investment contract. In the case of loans, the principal questions, to which the balance of this chapter is addressed, concern the rate of interest, the amount and type of security to be pledged and the allocation of the foreign exchange risk where the bank is lending foreign exchange.

Interest Policy[24]

Banks ordinarily try to set their loan charges to cover administrative expenses and the cost of borrowed funds, plus a margin for reserves and for profit to the share capital. For purposes of a preliminary calculation, the minimum share margin may be taken to be the minimum dividend that the bank feels it must pay to keep shareholders' funds voluntarily invested in its shares and to preserve the possibility of expanding its equity base in the future.

The cost of capital to the development bank may vary over time, not only with changes in interest rates, but also with changes in the proportion of borrowed funds obtained from such different sources as the government (perhaps as an interest-free advance), other local lending institutions or the public, and lenders such as the International Bank or foreign governments. Nevertheless, capital costs are fairly well fixed for the bank at any moment of time.

On the other hand, there are a number of factors influencing a bank's interest policy which may be changed by decision of the bank. What items are to be included in the administrative costs to be covered out of income? If the bank is to engage in research activities and make the results available

---

also finances established enterprises by way of debentures, of which 25 percent–50 percent are convertible into tax-free cumulative preference shares.

The International Finance Corporation, wherever practicable, obtains share options, subscription warrants or some other form of rights to acquire shares at a predetermined price. These rights may be sold to and exercised by a private purchaser. The Corporation expects to realize capital profits through such sales, thus building up reserves and its resources for reinvestment.

[24] The specific rates cited in this section do not in all cases reflect changes which may have occurred during the latter part of 1959.

to its clients and perhaps to offer other technical assistance, on what basis are these services to be priced? Are research facilities to be made available at cost, at some nominal rate, or without charge? Should lending rates be set at a level which will encourage applicants to exhaust all other financing alternatives before approaching the bank? Does the bank, like the Industrial Development Corporation of South Africa, prefer to accumulate funds for investment out of earnings rather than by enlarging its capital, and therefore charge "the market" rate? Or does it regard itself as a source of cheap money and, like the Development Finance Corporation of Ceylon, attempt to stimulate industrial development by charging the lowest possible rates commensurate with its solvency as a bank? These are all matters of policy to be resolved before loan charges can be determined.

In practice, the basic arithmetic of lending rates has often consisted of adding two to three percentage points to the cost of money to the bank. The rate charged by the Pakistan Industrial Credit and Investment Corporation (PICIC) on rupee loans has been 6 percent–6½ percent, or 2½ percent above the cost to it of rupee funds. On foreign exchange loans out of the proceeds of its loan from the International Bank, PICIC's rate has been 7 percent–7½ percent, to which is added in some cases a commission based on the volume of the borrower's sales, bringing the effective rate to 8½ percent–10½ percent. Against this is the 5¾ percent interest PICIC pays the International Bank and the 5 percent interest charged on its loan from the Development Loan Fund.[25] The Industrial Credit and Investment Corporation of India has charged 6½ percent on rupee loans, 7 percent for foreign exchange loans, as against the 4⅝ percent it pays on its first International Bank loan.[26] The Industrial Finance Corporation of India started off with 5 percent; the rate has risen to 6½ percent, as against 4½ percent paid on its borrowings. When the cost of money to the Nacional Financiera of Mexico was 5 percent– 6 percent, it charged private borrowers 9 percent. It lends foreign exchange borrowed abroad at a 2 percent mark-up, and makes a similar charge when guaranteeing foreign borrowing by a client. The Development Finance Corporation of Ceylon charges 5 percent (6 percent with a 1 percent rebate for timely repayment), having in mind that long-term government obligations sell for 3 percent.

The level of lending rates cannot, of course, be fixed by independent decision of the bank. There are externally determined limits beyond which it may not be able to go. In many countries there is a legal ceiling on interest rates. The 7 percent rate of the Industrial Development Bank of Turkey, for

---

[25] The references are to the first loans from the International Bank and DLF, respectively. The second loan from the Bank carries a flexible rate of interest, and the second DLF loan carries interest at 5½ percent.

[26] Its foreign exchange loan rate has subsequently risen to 7¾ percent, plus a ¼ percent fee charged once, when the loan contract is signed.

example, is the legal maximum. The government of India must approve the interest rate adopted from time to time by the Industrial Finance Corporation.

A less readily identifiable but more fundamental restraint is the effect that loan charges may have on the demand for loans. That demand is not determined exclusively by the bank's interest rate. It may be stimulated by the availability of non-financial services and advice, and by the "certificate of soundness" that the bank's financing may represent in the community. Moreover, the bank may be the only source of long-term finance. On the other hand, the demand may be inhibited by the requirement that applicants disclose certain information about their enterprises, a requirement which, in the case of public banks, may make businessmen fear unwelcome investigation by tax collectors and other government officials. Tax laws may make the actual cost to the borrower somewhat different from the nominal cost of borrowing.

But with due allowance for all these considerations, there is always a level of cost beyond which a borrower will not be prepared to borrow. In some cases, the project is not expected to be sufficiently profitable to justify the loan charge. More often, a reluctance to borrow from the development bank is due simply to the fact that funds can be obtained more reasonably elsewhere—perhaps from commercial banks, or from insurance companies or equipment and materials suppliers—even if at shorter term.

A development bank does not normally wish to take business away from existing financing institutions; if it must obtain its business this way there is a reasonable presumption that no development bank is needed. This might suggest that interest rates should be set somewhat higher than the "market cost of capital," especially since the bank will be providing services and a kind of financing not available elsewhere. The market rate may be difficult to define in a country with limited financing facilities, but the going rate at which commercial banks are prepared to provide funds for varying terms under given conditions provides one convenient point of reference.

In fact, however, most of the development banks which participated in the International Bank conference charge rates somewhat lower than "the market." They try to assure that they do not compete with other sources of finance by requiring applicants to produce evidence of unsuccessful efforts to obtain financing from those sources, or by restricting their activities to types and maturities of financing which other institutions are not prepared to provide, at least to the full amounts sought.

Such rate policies are often a reflection of the fact that the development bank has been able to obtain funds more cheaply than private borrowers. Interest-free or low-cost government advances have already been mentioned; some banks may borrow with a government guarantee. The extent to which the benefits of this "cheap capital" are passed on to clients depends, of course, on whether the bank intends to be a high- or low-cost lender. It also depends on the extent to which it wishes to attract participation in its loans, to sell from its portfolio or to borrow on the collateral of its portfolio. Other investors are not likely to be interested in participating in or purchasing development bank loans at "promotional" rates below the "market rate" which they can earn elsewhere.

Banks which charge less than the "market rate" for loans must examine closely the extent to which the solvency of applicant enterprises is based on the availability of this "cheap capital." If the enterprise's prospects depend entirely on obtaining low-cost funds, there are good grounds for questioning the economic merits of the project. Moreover, it is important that the bank should not come to be regarded as an institution through which the government subsidizes uneconomic enterprises.

Where an extremely high market rate reflects a shortage of capital, the development bank may consider it important to try to bring about a reduction in the level of interest charges by taking the lead in adopting a rate slightly below the prevailing one. Again, a private development bank which has received government financing on very favorable terms will probably not wish to invite public criticism by charging a high rate of interest for the use of its low-cost or interest-free funds.

For the banks at the International Bank conference, considerations such as these led to the adoption of rates ranging from the 5 percent of the Development Finance Corporation of Ceylon to the 12 percent charged by the Corporacion de Fomento de la Produccion of Chile. Most of the rates fall between 6 percent and 8 percent.

Some banks, such as the Industrial Credit and Investment Corporation of India, the Industrial Finance Corporation of India, the Development Finance Corporation of Ceylon, the Pakistan Industrial Credit and Investment Corporation and the Industrial Development Bank of Turkey, have adopted one rate charged uniformly to all borrowers of local currency.[27] The reason for the preference for a flat rate is generally a belief that flexible rates might expose the bank to pressures and charges of favoritism. At the same time, it may be said of a single rate that if it is set at an appropriate level for borrowers with a good credit standing, it necessarily embodies an element of subsidy for the riskier projects.

Other banks have a spread of rates, the difference between the maximum and minimum figure being commonly about one percentage point. Within this range, loan charges are fixed on the basis of such factors as the type of enterprise, the size and term of the loan, the nature of the security and sometimes the nature of the borrower. The Nacional Financiera of Mexico,

---

[27] Borrowers from the Industrial Finance Corporation of India and the Pakistan Industrial Credit and Investment Corporation have had to agree to accept a higher rate should the bank's rate rise during the life of the loan.

for example, charges government borrowers one percentage point less than private borrowers. The Government Development Bank for Puerto Rico gives a preferential rate (6 percent) to industrial borrowers, one-half percentage point below the rate on loans to hotels, tourist restaurants, supermarkets and commercial centers, and one percentage point below that for other commercial loans. The Economic Development Financing Organization in Greece charges 8 percent, except that hotels and tourist enterprises generally pay only 6 percent, and an even lower rate applies to certain types of large projects, especially during the early stage of operation. The Caisse Centrale of France charges 4½ percent when the loan carries conversion rights, 5½ percent otherwise; on 10-year loans the rate increases by ½ percent every year after the fifth year. For longer loans made for projects requiring heavy capital expenditure, the rate ranges from 3 percent to 5 percent without intermediate increases.

The riskiness of the enterprise is likewise a consideration. If the rate does not include a premium for unusual risks, the profit margin may be so narrow that the bank cannot build up an adequate reserve against losses. However, some banks feel that they cannot adequately compensate for the risk assumed in new ventures by charging these ventures only 1 percent more than established enterprises. When they wish to differentiate among borrowers as to risk, they demand conversion rights and sometimes additional security.

Loan charges tend to be highest in inflationary economies where market interest rates are also highest. The Corporacion de Fomento de la Produccion of Chile charges 12 percent, with the rate rising to the legal maximum (currently 16.39 percent) for overdue loans, against a prevailing commercial bank rate of 14 percent.[28] It is contemplated that the interest rate of the China Development Corporation may be 15 percent–16 percent.[29] It appears to be the general view that in most circumstances it is not possible fully to protect against inflation through the interest rate, and that it is necessary to rely upon the other devices noted earlier in this chapter.

Commitment Charge

Practice with respect to commitment charges on the undisbursed portion of a loan varies widely. The Corporacion de Fomento de la Produccion of Chile, the Banco Nacional do Desenvolvimento Economico of Brazil and the Development Finance Corporation of Ceylon make no commitment charge.[30] The Puerto Rico Industrial Development Company generally does

[28] As noted earlier, CORFO protects itself against inflation by lending with a dollar clause. Moreover, precisely because of inflationary conditions, most of its investments are in equities.

[29] At the time the development bank was established, the commercial banks charged about 20 percent; private lenders charged between 26 percent and 40 percent.

[30] Funds of the Ceylon bank are in local currency and investments of the funds can be readily realized. Moreover, the bank has overdraft facilities with a local commercial bank.

not but has power to do so. No commitment charge is applicable to peso loans by the Nacional Financiera of Mexico, but any commitment charges paid by the bank on its foreign exchange resources are passed on to borrowers.

The Industrial Development Bank of Turkey and the International Finance Corporation charge 1 percent, with no exceptions.[31] The Government Development Bank for Puerto Rico charges a 1 percent commitment fee but waives it where the delay in drawing is caused by circumstances beyond the borrower's control; this is also the practice of the Industrial Finance Corporation of India. The Pakistan Industrial Credit and Investment Corporation charges one-fourth of 1 percent per three months on the highest amount standing to the credit of the loan account in that quarter.

The Commonwealth Development Finance Company of the United Kingdom has tried three techniques. On small investments it may collect a lump sum at the time the loan agreement is signed. Sometimes it charges 1 percent between signing and disbursement. In one case it agreed with the borrower on three disbursement dates, and required commitment charges to be paid only if drawings should be delayed beyond those dates.

Security Policy[32]

While charters usually authorize unsecured loans, it is general practice to try to obtain the maximum security (although "character" loans for small amounts are not unknown). Even where the physical assets of an enterprise have very little resale value because, for reasons of location or design, they are not readily convertible to other purposes, a mortgage has its uses. The existence of the power of foreclosure may serve to reinforce the bank's influence over policies of an enterprise in difficulties. If that influence can be exercised sufficiently early, difficulties may be anticipated and the viability of the enterprise, the true security for the loan, may be protected.

Varying degrees of coverage are sought. The Nacional Financiera of Mexico habitually receives a mortgage on the entire industrial unit in the case of a loan for fixed assets. In the case of a loan for working capital, it has a lien on all inventories, including raw materials in process of production. The Banco Nacional do Desenvolvimento Economico of Brazil, the

[31] On foreign exchange loans, the Turkish bank also charges existing enterprises a commission of 1 percent per annum on the principal outstanding (to cover the cost of technical assistance and project study and supervision) ; the bank asks for founders' shares, in lieu of a commission, when lending foreign exchange to new enterprises.

[32] The policies set forth in this section, based upon information supplied by the banks concerned, in some cases reflect provisions of general local law or customary practice within the country and are not peculiar to the development bank. Moreover, while legal terms and concepts are necessarily used in the discussion of security policy and policy toward enterprises in difficulty, the summary in the text should not be taken as an authoritative statement of the requirements of local law or as a comprehensive description of the legal techniques employed.

Industrial Credit and Investment Corporation of India, the Industrial Finance Corporation of India and the Industrial Development Bank of Turkey demand collateral valued at twice the amount of the loan.[33] The Pakistan Industrial Credit and Investment Corporation requires collateral equal to the amount of the loan. The Corporacion de Fomento de la Produccion of Chile requires collateral equal to the amount of the loan plus the aggregate of interest charges. The Development Finance Corporation of Ceylon requires collateral valued at more than the amount of the loan, the margin being determined by the type of asset pledged and the credit standing of the borrower. The Industrial Development Corporation of South Africa has no uniformly applicable requirement in this respect.

The amount of security demanded sometimes depends on the nature of the borrower. Government projects may be required to put up less security than private borrowers, and companies with widespread share ownership less than closely-held family concerns. In some countries, a good personal guaranee may be the preferred type of security, because of the difficulty of executing foreclosure judgments in the local courts. Where the borrower is a private company, particularly a family concern, the Development Finance Corporation of Ceylon and the Pakistan Industrial Credit and Investment Corporation require, in addition to other security, the personal guarantee of the directors of the enterprise for the full amount of the loan. The Industrial Development Bank of Turkey sometimes requires the personal guarantee of the shareholders in a family concern. The Industrial Development Corporation of South Africa sometimes requires that the life of the manager or proprietor of a small business be insured for its benefit, where the company's success depends essentially upon that individual. The Industrial Finance Corporation of India normally insists on the personal guarantee of two or more of the prominent directors of the concern and of the managing agency concern if there is one.

There are also differences in the types of assets acceptable as security. In view of the practical limitations of mortgages on fixed assets located outside an established industrial center, the Caisse Centrale of France in such a situation prefers some other type of security, such as personal guarantees or liens on movables. Since most banks are not normally engaged in operating enterprises, they find it important to ensure that they will acquire good title, readily saleable, if they must foreclose. In some countries this consideration leads to a refusal to accept land as security, where the land is held in the name of a clan or family or, even if held by an individual, where it may have been granted under restrictions on alienation. However, most banks accept liens on land, as well as on buildings, machinery and equipment; liens on inventories are sometimes taken.

Banks which lend for permanent working capital of course accept mova-

[33] The Industrial Credit and Investment Corporation of India also accepts bank guarantees of the full amount of the loan.

ble assets as security. The Pakistan Industrial Credit and Investment Corporation seeks to obtain a lien on all the firm's assets movable and immovable, even when lending only for fixed assets. The Caisse Centrale of France sometimes requires a borrower to assign to it accounts receivable. As long as a loan from the Caisse is outstanding, the Caisse is the channel for payments to the borrower on receivables. It may withhold an appropriate amount if the borrower is deliquent in servicing the loan.

The Industrial Finance Corporation of India, in contrast, does not accept a mortgage on movables, raw materials or spare parts; only land, buildings and machinery are eligible as security. But, as is not unusual in India, it insists on a lien covering not only all existing eligible assets but all those which may be acquired while any part of its loan remains outstanding. This lien is supported by a prohibition against the creation of any new debts or liens without prior permission.[34] The bank has taken over existing debentures when it could, so that it may have a first lien.[35]

A bank cannot take a mortgage on all of an enterprise's assets and expect it to obtain financing from other sources. Where borrowers are expected to finance their working capital needs with commercial banks, there must be sufficient unencumbered assets to secure this additional financing. The Pakistan Industrial Credit and Investment Corporation (PICIC) which, as noted above, prefers to take a comprehensive mortage initially, later releases movables to enable the borrower to obtain working capital credit from a commercial bank approved by PICIC. An alternative procedure, employed by the Development Finance Corporation of Ceylon, is for the development bank to retain a lien on all the enterprise's assets and then to give its own guarantee as security for a working capital loan from a commercial bank.

Some development banks, for example the Puerto Rico Industrial Development Company, occasionally lend on the security of property unrelated to the business of the enterprise, such as the borrower's house. The Industrial Development Corporation of South Africa, however, feels that if it must look beyond the assets of the enterprise itself for security, the enterprise is not economic and the bank should not finance it.

The comprehensiveness of security requirements reflects, at root, the way the bank views its relationship to its client. Where a bank supplements other sources of financing and is only one among creditors, it is likely to be less encompassing in its requirements than where it is the sole or major creditor and regards itself, as does the Industrial Finance Corporation of India, as the "perpetual guardian" of its client.

Book values are generally used in valuing assets offered as security.

[34] Permission to borrow is freely granted, except that the bank rarely consents where the loan is to be secured by a second mortgage on the enterprise's assets, unless the second creditor is an institution unlikely to cause difficulties for the bank.
[35] The Industrial Development Corporation of South Africa, on the other hand, does not try to take over existing mortgages because this would benefit only the former holder of the mortgage, not the borrowing enterprise.

Where the firm is new, these tend to be equal to actual costs. In the case of established firms, fixed assets are taken at their depreciated book value rather than current market value. The use of book values or historical costs is the more conservative practice in countries where, as a result of rising prices, book values understate market values and replacement costs. But where book values seem excessively low, some banks, like the Industrial Finance Corporation of India, call upon independent assessors to value the assets.

Loans in Foreign Exchange

Banks which are capitalized entirely in domestic currency are not confronted with the special problems associated with lending foreign exchange. They have only local currency to lend. Borrowers who need foreign exchange may use the proceeds of their bank loan to buy foreign exchange at the going rate from either the market or the exchange authorities; their repayment obligations to the bank remain in local currency. Neither the bank nor the borrower is affected by any change in the exchange rate.[36]

But the banks which have borrowed abroad directly and have foreign exchange obligations to repay are confronted with a dilemma to which no wholly satisfactory solution has yet been found. The bank cannot prudently assume the risk of depreciation in the rate of exchange. If it did, a devaluation of any magnitude in the national currency could seriously impair its capital, especially if the devaluation occurred while the bank was new and had not yet been able to accumulate adequate reserves.[37]

The most obvious way for the bank to protect itself is by passing the risk on to the borrower, requiring that a loan in foreign exchange be repaid in foreign currency. The borrower is normally in the best position to assume the risk. Where devaluation is a consequence of inflation, the cash flow generated from operations is likely to increase sufficiently to cover increased service payments, in the absence of price controls. Moreover, it is generally agreed that as a matter of principle the risk should be borne by the borrower. If the enterprise had borrowed foreign exchange directly from abroad, it would have had to bear the risk. If the government should assume the risk, the borrower whose project had imported components would receive a subsidy. Enterprises with the largest investment in imported machines and equip-

---

[36] Where the government has borrowed abroad to help capitalize the bank, so that some part of the bank's capital has in fact originated abroad, no exchange problem arises for the bank unless the government's foreign currency repayment obligation has been transferred to it.

[37] The Industrial Development Bank of Turkey estimated at the International Bank conference that a 10 percent devaluation of the lira would mean a loss of one year's profits; a 25 percent devaluation would mean the loss of its accumulated profits and reserves; and a 75 percent devaluation would mean the loss of its share capital as well.

ment would thus receive preferential treatment and, where the exchange risk is substantial, a distorted investment pattern might be encouraged.

It is not always possible to follow this principle. The country may have no exchange controls, so that foreign exchange can be purchased against local currency in the market. Or, while there may be controls, import permits may not be difficult to obtain, and the proceeds of a local currency loan may be readily convertible into foreign exchange. In these circumstances borrowers are naturally unwilling to borrow foreign exchange directly from the development bank if they thereby assume an exchange risk—at least unless this risk is offset by a substantial differential in the interest rate.[38]

If the risk is not, or cannot practicably be, passed on to the borrower, the government or the central bank has sometimes been willing to carry it. The government of Pakistan agreed to safeguard the Pakistan Industrial Credit and Investment Corporation (PICIC) against any foreign exchange loss arising out of the first International Bank loan to PICIC. The loan must be drawn down within a four-year period, and the term of the government's guarantee is similarly limited.[39] The Ethiopian government in effect bears the risk for borrowers from the Development Bank of Ethiopia.[40] In Turkey, by agreement between the government, the Central Bank and the Industrial Development Bank (IDB), the risk on the International Bank loan to IDB was assumed by the Central Bank, for a fee which IDB has passed on to its borrowers.[41]

If borrowers can obtain foreign exchange from other sources without assuming an exchange risk, and if no other provision is made for covering the risk, there is danger that the development bank's foreign exchange resources may be immobilized. This was initially the experience of the Industrial Credit and Investment Corporation of India (ICICI) on its first loan from the International Bank. ICICI refused to bear the exchange risk; borrowers would not do so as long as they could readily purchase foreign ex-

[38] Banks have often found themselves in competition with foreign suppliers' credits, offered at a lower rate than they can afford to charge.

[39] But the guarantee continues to apply throughout the life of any transaction engaged in during that period. At the end of the period, the government and PICIC will consult on the need for continuing arrangements regarding the exchange risk. PICIC was at first required to obtain government approval of each foreign exchange loan it proposed to make; more recently, blanket approvals have been given for investment in certain types of industries.

For the second International Bank loan to PICIC, the exchange risk will not be assumed by the government; it will be passed on to borrowers from PICIC. The exchange risk under the two DLF loans is passed on to the ultimate borrower.

[40] In this case it was the government which incurred the foreign exchange obligation in the first instance. The government borrowed from the International Bank and invested the proceeds of the loan in the equity of the development bank.

[41] The Central Bank did not assume the risk on loans made by IDB prior to the date of the agreement; on these loans (17 in number) the risk is borne by the borrowers from IDB. Moreover, the exchange risk agreement does not apply to loans for imports from the United States.

change from the Reserve Bank against rupees; and no provision had been made for the government to accept the risk. As a result, the International Bank loan was not drawn upon until such a severe shortage of foreign exchange developed that the government restricted imports to those goods for which foreign financing had been arranged. Since financing by ICICI out of its International Bank loan was considered to be within the category of foreign financing, enterprises which wished to obtain import licenses for machinery and equipment were anxious to borrow foreign exchange from ICICI even though that meant assuming the exchange risk.

Even if the government or the central bank is willing to provide insurance against the exchange risk, a difficult problem remains. Where the bank has borrowed abroad at one maturity, and has re-lent the proceeds at another and shorter maturity, repayments will accrue at a faster rate than the bank's own service obligations, and a balance will accumulate until the bank pays off its foreign debt, unless the foreign lender and the local government permit prepayment. If this balance can be kept in foreign exchange, no foreign exchange risk will be incurred; but if under applicable exchange regulations the balance must be held in local currency and the exchange rate should depreciate, the bank will suffer a loss.

The bank can protect itself against the risk arising from different amortization schedules if the schedule of repayments on its foreign exchange debt coincides with repayment on its own loans of foreign exchange. But in most cases the bank cannot know, at the time it arranges to borrow foreign exchange, what the purpose, size and timing of its investments of these resources will be.

The International Bank is considering an arrangement for future loans to development banks designed to take care of this situation. The development bank's loan account would be credited with the requisite sums ("installments") as and when investment projects for which the bank proposes to use funds provided by the International Bank are approved by the latter. No overall amortization schedule would be specified for the loan, except that repayment would have to be completed by an agreed date. Instead, an amortization schedule would be agreed upon for each installment at the time of crediting the installment to the loan account. Each such schedule would be based on the schedule of repayments agreed upon by the development bank and the ultimate borrower of the foreign exchange.[42] For such an arrangement to be fully effective, borrowers from the development bank should be permitted to prepay only if the bank itself may prepay to the International Bank. Alternatively, the ultimate borrower should be required to maintain the foreign exchange value of any amount prepaid, if the exchange rate should depreciate before the development bank's payment to the International Bank falls due.

[42] The International Bank's 1959 loan to the Investment Credit Corporation of Austria embodies these features.

Other Investment Terms

Most development bank financing contracts include a number of provisions designed to assure the most effective use of the funds provided and the maintenance of standards of financial behavior by the borrower. Some of the more usual ones are noted here; several are discussed in other chapters.

DIVIDEND LIMITATIONS. A number of banks prohibit the payment, or limit the amount, of dividends except with their approval. The Industrial Finance Corporation of India, for example, holds its borrowers to a 6 percent dividend, unless it approves a higher figure.

ISSUE AND SALE OF SHARES Existing shareholders are frequently required to undertake to provide additional capital in given circumstances, and to agree that they will not dispose of their shares without the bank's approval.

LIMITATIONS OF CAPITAL EXPENDITURES AND ON BORROWING. Limitations are frequently imposed on further borrowing and on the capital expenditures which may be incurred without the bank's consent. Some banks also prohibit loans or guarantees other than in the normal course of business without their consent.

LIMITATIONS ON PLEDGES OF ASSETS. The International Finance Corporation fortifies its unsecured loans by requiring the borrower to agree to give no mortgages or pledges of assets without equivalent security being given to the Corporation. Some banks require that their clients first obtain their consent to further liens.

PREPAYMENT. Borrowers from the Industrial Finance Corporation of India may not prepay without the bank's consent, but no premium is charged when prepayment is permitted. Borrowers from the Caisse Centrale of France may prepay without special permission or premium, except where an option to convert is involved.[43]

ACCELERATED AMORTIZATION. The Government Development Bank for Puerto Rico reserves the right, in the case of loans collateralized by machinery or equipment, to require that 50 percent of the borrower's net profits remaining after payment of debt service be devoted to repayment of its loan. The Caisse Centrale of France, as noted earlier, applies an automatic acceleration formula to all loans for more than 10 years. After the fifth or sixth year, the

---

[43] The Government Development Bank for Puerto Rico imposes a premium of 5 percent of any amount prepaid to any first mortgage holder other than the bank. The purpose of this stipulation is to protect participants in a bank loan or purchasers of a loan from the bank.

Caisse requires that the amount of each installment paid by the borrower be increased by one-half (sometimes one-third) of the amount by which its gross sales exceed the gross sales forecast when the loan was made. Gross sales, rather than profit, are the measure because it is easier to determine the volume of sales.

OTHER TERMS.   It is commonly required that the borrower's properties be insured. Some banks require the borrower to refinance excessively heavy short-term indebtedness, and to consult before embanking on a new project. Banks sometimes require to be consulted on proposed managerial changes. Sometimes they place limits on compensation of directors and managers.

D. RELATIONSHIP TO CLIENTS

Participation in Management

In contrast to development banks empowered to promote new industrial fields by establishing and operating industrial enterprises, those which are primarily financial institutions are seldom authorized to assume direct management responsibility, except to protect an investment in jeopardy. Management calls for skills so different from those employed in project or credit-worthiness appraisals or in loan administration that banks which are authorized to undertake management do so infrequently and very reluctantly. Some have decided as a matter of policy not to exercise this authority at all. Even those which may manage enterprises in an emergency generally try to find other solutions.[44]

Notwithstanding unwillingness or lack of authority to participate directly in management, banks seek to keep informed of the progress and policies of their clients. They also want a convenient mechanism for offering technical and policy guidance. Some ask for a seat on the board of client enterprises as a means of accomplishing these objectives without involvement in operational responsibilities. The proposal is not always acceptable: enterprises unwilling to disclose details of their operations have been known to decline financing conditioned on board membership. Public banks in particular have encountered this attitude, related to the disinclination of private enterprises to accept a public institution as a partner. It is not only equity investments which raise the question of policy on board representation: some banks condition their lending on the right to appoint a director. The Industrial Finance Corporation of India, for example, always insists on—although it does not always exercise—the right to appoint two directors.

[44] The policy of normally taking only minority participations is related to the reluctance to accept management responsibility.

In deciding whether to insist on board representation, as general policy or in a given case, banks weigh several considerations. Board membership keeps the bank informed of an enterprise's progress, but may result in involving it in the enterprise's affairs to a much greater extent than it considers desirable. The enterprise's management may be encouraged to negotiate with the bank nominee rather than directly with the bank; this is particularly likely where the nominee is a senior official of the bank. Sometimes management tends to refer every decision to the bank through its nominee. If the bank is a public institution, board representation may result in drawing the government into intracompany disputes. Some banks have therefore concluded that they can more effectively keep themselves informed, and can more satisfactorily guide and influence their clients' policies, by a device other than board membership.

The decision may be influenced by considerations other than the wish to be kept informed of developments. A public bank, for example, may conclude that private investors should be encouraged to operate without any interference from government, and may therefore normally refrain from seeking board representation.

If the bank does decide to appoint a director, it faces the problem of selecting a nominee. Designation of a staff member is perhaps the most effective way to keep informed, but this approach presents some problems. One has already been referred to, that the enterprise's management may regard the nominee as a channel for negotiation with the bank. Another is that the enterprise's board may from time to time have to make decisions on matters reviewable by the bank under the terms of the investment contract. A third difficulty, for an active bank, is that its senior officials may come to find an undue proportion of their time taken up by meetings of the boards of client enterprises.

Various approaches to these difficulties have been taken. Sometimes nominees are instructed to make plain that they do not speak for the bank and to suggest, should the management seek to negotiate through them, that the bank be approached directly. The Industrial Finance Corporation of India (IFCI) instructs its nominees not to vote on any matter which may later come before it. For example, they do not vote on proposed sales of assets, since assets normally cannot be sold by a borrower without IFCI's prior consent. The IFCI nominee may, however, join in the discussion of such matters.

Some banks, while always exacting the right to appoint a director, exercise it selectively, finding that this sufficiently eases the burden on their staff. The Industrial Finance Corporation of India exercises its right of appointment only in certain circumstances: when it has made a large loan, when the nature or some special feature of the project makes a close check desirable, or when an enterprise appears headed for difficulty. The Industrial Development Bank of Turkey appoints a director only when making equity investments and then only when it has more than a 15 percent interest. When appointment is put on a selective basis it is generally found desirable to make clear to the business and investment community that appointment does not necessarily indicate that the enterprise in question is risky, in difficulty or, on the contrary, extremely successful. This poses a delicate problem of public relations.

Some banks, the Industrial Finance Corporation of India, Nacional Financiera of Mexico and the Industrial Development Corporation of South Africa for example, occasionally appoint businessmen, industrialists or retired civil servants. The Puerto Rico Industrial Development Company (PRIDCO), which insists on the right to board representation only where its investment is substantial and the risks associated with the enterprise are greater than average, exercises the right rarely, and then does not select its own officials. The Caisse Centrale of France, which invests overseas, gives local persons a voice in management by drawing its nominees from the local community. Appointment of persons not associated with the bank not only helps to ease the burden on staff but avoids the difficulties of subsequent bank review of a decision in which a bank official has participated. Nevertheless the Corporacion de Fomento de la Produccion of Chile, which insists on board representation in proportion to its share of the client's equity, has on occasion designated members of its own board to represent it; so has the Development Finance Corporation of Ceylon.

It is very important that the bank be represented by men of high calibre, if the bank hopes to guide its clients' policies. Some banks take pains to impress upon their nominees that their duties and obligations vis-à-vis the enterprise are no different from those of the other directors, and that decisions should be made with the interest of the enterprise primarily in mind. The Industrial Finance Corporation of India, which does not normally seek to influence clients' policies through its nominee directors, has made it a practice, where proposed nominees are not officials of the bank, to submit their names to clients to be sure that the choice is acceptable.

As already noted, board representation is not the only way banks keep themselves informed of clients' affairs. The Pakistan Industrial Credit and Investment Corporation also receives all documents sent to board members and minutes of board meetings. Nacional Financiera of Mexico appoints an agent, usually an accountant, whose principal responsibility it is to keep Financiera informed of the client's financial status. The Caisse Centrale of France makes use of a similar device (although not in enterprises in which foreign capital has participated). The Banco Nacional do Desenvolvimento Economico of Brazil usually arranges for representation on an enterprise's auditing committee; this committee is appointed by the enterprise's shareholders and has access to its books.

Bank staff member nominees are usually required to turn over to the bank any directors' fees they may receive from the enterprise. Nominees who are not associated with the bank are generally permitted to retain directors' fees. However, the Industrial Development Corporation of South Africa (IDC) sometimes requires nonofficial nominees likewise to turn over any fees received, in which event IDC compensates them itself.

Provisions of Investment Contract

Investment contracts normally include provisions designed to further the common interest of the enterprise and the bank in assuring the most efficient use of the funds provided. The extent of these safeguards usually has some relation to the nature and size of the investment.

The borrower is commonly required to furnish periodic reports, technical, financial and operational. The information sought is intended to make it possible to appraise the progress of construction and the course of expenditure in relation to original work schedules and cost estimates, where funds have been made available for new facilities, and to keep generally in touch with the activities of the enterprise after those facilities are in operation. Banks try not to impose unduly burdensome reporting requirements, while at the same time assuring sufficient detail and frequency to serve their purpose. The right of periodic inspection is also normally specified.

It is usual to require enterprises to maintain adequate accounting records and to have those records checked by independent auditors. The enforcement of such provisions is often very difficult, particularly where the requirement is substantially at variance with business mores. In many of the less developed countries it is common for enterprises to keep several sets of books and to present to outsiders, including the government, information which amounts to considerably less than a full and accurate disclosure of their financial condition and operating results. Public development banks which have tried to reform these practices have met with particularly strong resistance because of their government association.[45] Nevertheless, the widespread share ownership which development banks seek to foster requires that minority shareholders be assured of reasonably complete and accurate information about the enterprise's operations. Publicly available and reliable financial information is an essential of a capital market.

In some countries there are no independent public auditors; this adds to the difficulties. In Turkey, the Industrial Development Bank (IDB) had to assign its own staff to help clients inaugurate and maintain accurate financial records. Although it did not charge for the service, it met with considerable resistance at first. When auditing was made a condition of IDB financing, however, clients ceased their objectives. IDB feels its insistence has

---

[45] The Industrial Finance Corporation of India has experienced no difficulty in this matter, possibly because its loan agreements give it the right to an independent audit and inspection, at the client's expense, by an agency of the bank's choice, if and when it deems this necessary.

materially aided in raising accounting standards in Turkey. A contribution in this field can be among the most useful achievements of a development bank.

It has of course sometimes been the case that a shortage of accounting personnel has made it difficult for the bank to meet its own needs. At least one bank, the Industrial Development Corporation of South Africa, itself trains employees with good academic qualifications and above average ability for accounts work. Sometimes it is practicable to arrange for auditing by a foreign firm.

Disbursements

It is common practice to supervise the use of loan proceeds. Disbursements are customarily made in installments, paid out at specified intervals or upon satisfactory documentary evidence of expenditures incurred for specified goods and services. The Government Development Bank for Puerto Rico disburses only after the borrower presents acceptable evidence that the equipment or machinery being financed is properly installed and operating or that the buildings being financed are constructed. During the period between approval of the loan and the installation of machinery or construction of buildings, the borrower is given a commitment letter on the strength of which interim financing can be obtained from a commercial bank. The Industrial Development Bank of Turkey sometimes pays the borrower's suppliers, rather than the borrower directly.

As noted in an earlier chapter, the borrower is generally required to provide a specified minimum proportion of the necessary funds; some banks insist that all or part of the borrower's share be put up before they will themselves disburse. The Corporation de Fomento de la Produccion of Chile, for example, usually requires that the borrower first put up at least 30 percent of its share. Where the Industrial Development Bank of Turkey has reason to believe that a borrower is overcommitted and may not be able to put up its share, it requires the whole of the commitment to be met before it will disburse. The Caisse Centrale of France requires borrowers to begin disbursing their own funds before it disburses its own. The Industrial Finance Corporation of India requires borrowers to open a special account; it then arranges that withdrawals are so made that the stipulated proportion between the amounts to be contributed by each party is maintained.

Loan Supervision

Normally banks do not merely control the rate at which funds are withdrawn; they also scrutinize the execution and operation of the project being financed. Sometimes such supervision is broad in scope and the scrutiny very detailed. On the other hand, where the client enterprise is large and has had a long history of successful operation, there is a tendency to put supervision on a routine and minimum basis. The funds and staff at the bank's command may be limiting factors.

The objective of such supervision is to keep the bank informed of progress, and to provide an opportunity for advice in anticipation of difficulties and for assistance if trouble nevertheless arises. The procedures vary from one institution to another. The reporting requirement has been referred to earlier. In the case of new enterprises, or during the initial period of a loan, reports are generally required each month; for established enterprises, or in the latter stages of a loan if all is going well, semiannual reports may suffice. It is generally thought desirable to conduct inspections once a year at a minimum, more frequently in the case of risky or new enterprises or where difficulties have arisen. However, some banks have insufficient staff to meet even a yearly inspection schedule.

The internal arrangements for assigning responsibility for loan supervision vary greatly. The Industrial Development Bank of Turkey deals with the problem in two stages. The engineering department takes principal responsibility during the construction stage, visiting the project site, checking on installation of machinery, etc. The financial department is called upon only when necessary at this stage, unless the project is relatively large, in which case it participates from the start.[46] When the project begins operations, primary responsibility shifts to the financial department, which conducts two inspections a year; at this stage the engineering department participates only if necessary. A special coordinator of supervision is responsible for planning an inspection schedule for all projects; the schedule calls for a routine visit every year to all but the very smallest plants.

Supervision by the Industrial Finance Corporation of India is organized on a regional basis. Regional managers of the bank are responsible for routine inspections; if difficulties appear, the central internal audit branch conducts a special inspection. The latter also does spot-checking on the work of the regional managers. Enterprises report to the regional manager monthly for the first six months; thereafter reports may be put on a semiannual basis. The enterprise submits balance sheets twice a year. If the expected progress is not made, the enterprise is visited by a financial inspector from the bank's staff, a technical expert borrowed from a department of government, or a private consultant.

The Caisse Centrale of France leaves inspection to its local representatives; these address themselves only to the financial aspects of the enterprise or the project.

The Industrial Development Corporation of South Africa (IDC) has adopted still another procedure. Its "after-care program" is closely linked to the initial project investigation. IDC has three investigation sections: production;

---

[46] It is of course essential that the financial department be kept informed of any changes in the project plans which may have major financial implications.

financial; and commercial and economic. A group comprised of one staff member from each section is responsible for evaluating the proposal and recommending IDC action. Which of the groups supplies the coordinator depends upon the type of problem which, on the basis of initial assessment of the project, seems likely to be the most serious. The same group is automatically responsible for subsequent supervision. The theory of this arrangement is that the members of the group which recommended the project will feel a certain responsibility toward it, and that their early and continued association with an enterprise will facilitate understanding of whatever problems may arise. The group tries to visit each enterprise as a rule once a year, more often if difficulties arise, less frequently if the enterprise is successful.

Most of the banks at the International Bank conference carry out supervisory activities at their own expense. Nacional Financiera of Mexico, however, charges clients for all supervision, even if conducted by its own staff. The loan contracts of the Industrial Finance Corporation of India (IFCI) stipulate for periodical inspection entirely at the borrower's expense, except that no portion of the salary of an IFCI official is charged to the borrower.[47] The Development Finance Corporation of Ceylon, which relies on the staff of the Ceylon Institute of Scientific and Industrial Research for supervision of its investments, requires its clients to pay the Institute's fees.

[47] Private technical consultants are paid a fee; a government technical expert receives travel expenses and per diem.

THE ROLE OF PRIVATE INSTITUTIONS IN DEVELOPMENT FINANCING*

The philosophy of the World Bank family, in dealing with development finance companies, is that it is possible to combine profit making with a development orientation. And not simply possible. If a development finance company is providing financial, technical and entrepreneurial services which are in demand and not being adequately supplied, then it is service-oriented in the best sense of the term. The prospect of, indeed the need for, profit makes it possible to provide these services, to mobilize capital, both at home and abroad, and to take the risks which investment entails. The combination of profitmaking with an orientation towards providing services crucial to economic development is, indeed, the fundamental justification lying behind assistance from the World Bank group to a development finance company.

The kind of company which we prefer to deal with is one which is national both in identity and outlook, vigorous in the promotion of productive investment, yet prudent in the conduct of its affairs. It seeks to promote industrial and other development on business principles in the interest of the sound economic growth of the country. It performs a valuable function by identifying promising fields for investment and helping to bring together the factors of production. By becoming an active and important element in a country's capital market, it helps mobilize domestic savings and, in combination with technical knowhow, directs them into productive activities. At the same time it becomes a channel through which foreign and international capital and skills can flow into the national economy, reaching enterprises too small to be able alone to attract foreign capital and technology.

Not all private financing companies fit these criteria. But some do, and many can; and when they do, they become powerful instruments for the promotion of industrial development.

TWO CRUCIAL FUNCTIONS

Let me illustrate two crucial functions of private development finance companies. The difficulty of finding capital bears very heavily on new large-

*William Diamond, *International Development Review*, March, 1965, pp. 10–13.

scale enterprises and on relatively small- or medium-sized companies making that crucial jump to large-scale production. The needs of such enterprises are usually specific and evident. They need equity capital, not only for fixed assets, but also for the permanent working capital necessary to start production or to achieve and sustain higher levels of production. Private development finance companies can provide that equity. They can also, in the process of doing so, seek to arrange wide distribution of that equity. There are few tasks more important to the economic and political welfare of the developing countries, particularly in Latin America, than the widespread distribution of ownership of enterprise. Let me give you two examples of how private development finance companies in Latin America are working to provide equity capital and to distribute ownership.

The first case is that of Forjas de Colombia, in which two Colombian financieras—working with IFC—are helping to promote and finance the establishment of a new industry of high economic priority. The story goes back to 1961 when a group of private Colombian investors, principally from the Bucaramanga area, were drawn to the possibility of setting up a forge plant. The project appeared attractive for a number of reasons. Colombia is a heavy importer of forgings, and the creation of this new industry will save a significant amount of foreign exchange. Moreover, a forge plant seems a logical development in the metal-working industry emerging from the existence of the Paz del Rio steel mill.

The group engaged a German forge expert to make a basic study of the feasibility of the project. His analysis convinced them that they should go ahead and, after reviewing several offers, a contract for the design and construction of the plant as well as for machinery and equipment was placed with the important German engineering concern of Rheinstahl, which also took a substantial share interest. However, it became clear very soon that the capital required for the project was more than the original group could provide. They decided to approach other sources, starting with the Corporación Financiera Colombiana of Bogota and Corporación Financiera Nacional of Medellín, with whom they had connections. Subsequently, other investors—both Colombian and foreign—were brought in; and the government gave its blessings in the concrete form of special privileges of various kinds and of an equity investment by the Instituto de Fomento Industrial.

IFC was invited into the picture by the financieras in late 1963 to provide the missing portion of share capital. IFC appraised the project (in the company of the financieras) and liked what it saw: a project of high priority in Colombia with prospects of suitable financial return, to be carried out and operated by capable and experienced sponsors and management. However, it became clear that the financial plan was not adequate, and that the project needed additional equity financing. A new financial plan was accepted by the promoters of the enterprise and, as a result, it was possible to go ahead early this year with plans to complete the more than $14 million of financing needed to carry out the project. Of this amount, $6.5 million is being provided in the form of share capital. $4.0 million had previously been subscribed by private individuals and industrial and financial institutions, including the two financieras. As a result of the reappraisal, IFC agreed to take up $1 million Forjas stock; the two financieras, together with IFC, are underwriting the placement of another $1 million; and the newly formed ADELA is subscribing to $500,000.

This underwriting arrangement represented something new in Colombia. It was a true underwriting, perhaps the first true underwriting of a public issue of capital stock in that country. Other publicly-owned Colombian companies have, as a rule, relied on placing their stock privately, generally by offering rights to their shareholders; and so-called "underwritings" have in fact been "best-efforts" arrangements which carry no commitment and leave the company in doubt about whether it will have all the finance it needs. In this case, the financieras and IFC guarantee to place the shares, both inside and outside of Colombia, or themselves to take up what has not been placed in a specified time. The sponsors of Forjas can now proceed in the knowledge that their financing is assured.

THE ROLE OF THE FINANCIERAS

I do not want to overemphasize the role of the financieras in this important operation, but I do want it fully appreciated. The financieras did not conceive the project; that was done by the promoters of Bucaramanga; but the financieras very early recognized the important economic contribution which this project could make to Colombia and decided to support it, despite the risks involved in establishing a new enterprise in a new field of industry. They backed up their decision with substantial investments in share capital.

The financieras then played an important part in interesting other investors, including investors in Germany, and the IFC. In the course of studying the project with IFC, they helped transform its financial plan and put it on a sounder basis. By participating in the underwriting, they are not only assuring that this important project can go ahead, but are pioneering a new type of financial service in Colombia. Finally, the shares they earlier subscribed, as well as the shares they have now underwritten, together constitute a pool of shares which one day, some sooner and some later, will be held by the Colombian public. For it is the policy of each of these financieras to work actively to widen the ownership of and market for industrial securities and to revolve its portfolio to a reasonable extent, when it can do so on a profitable basis, in order to assist in the growth of the capital market in Colombia.

This case also illustrates a point about IFC policy, to which I should like to refer. We prefer to work together with, rather than independently of, domestic financing institutions. If a well-run development finance company exists in a particular country, especially if it is one in which the World Bank family has a financial interest, our policy is to work with it, in joint investments. We would refer applications that came to us to that company. And we would expect that company to come to us to participate in a project which is too large for it to handle alone or if for some other reason our presence would serve a useful purpose.

Expanding Existing Production

The Forjas case involves promoting a new enterprise. Development finance companies can also assist in expanding capital markets to meet the equity needs of existing companies. A company may be able to finance its expansion from its own earnings or by offering rights to its shareholders. But one day it may find that its needs outrun such resources and that it must seek additional funds from the public—from domestic or foreign investors or both. Such a situation occurred in the case of Compañía Fundidora de Fierro y Acero de Monterrey, the largest privately-owned steel company and the second largest producer of steel in Mexico. Here again is a case in which IFC collaborated, but this time with a development finance company in which it does not have a financial interest.

Fundidora is an old and well established company (it was founded in 1900) which in recent years had experienced a sustained rate of growth matching that of the Mexican economy. In 1954, it started a modernization and expansion program to increase its capacity from 200,000 to 500,000 ingot tons of steel. This required close to $100 million. In the last stage of this program, in 1962, Fundidora lacked something over $5 million which were needed in the form of equity. The company's bankers, the Banco Nacional de México, and its investment sudsidiary, the Crédito Bursátil, felt that a sum of this magnitude could not be obtained at that time from the existing shareholders. They felt that in the circumstances prevailing in Mexico early in 1962, it would not be prudent to try to raise additional equity by an offer of subscription rights without an underwriting syndicate prepared to subscribe any stock not taken up by shareholders and recognizing that it might have to hold much of the stock it took up for some time to come. They also felt that outside participation in that syndicate was essential.

Accordingly they approached IFC, which decided to invest $1.1 million. It also joined forces with Crédito Bursátil to underwrite a rights offer to raise the remaining $4 million. The IFC obtained three sub-underwriters in the United States and Switzerland to share its commitments. Despite the fact that conditions in the capital market in Mexico were not propitious and that there was abroad a monetary hesitation about Mexico, the underwriting was a complete (and, incidentally, an unexpected) success.

This story has a sequel. By early 1963, Fundidora had completed one expansion program, but by late 1963, its operations were approaching capacity because of the rapid increase in Mexican demand for steel. Therefore, it decided to proceed without delay with another round of expansion, aimed at raising output from 500,000 tons to 750,000 tons a year. It needed more than $55 million in order to complete this program, of which $12.5 million would have to be raised publicly in the form of equity capital. Market conditions in 1964 promised to be as favorable as they had been unfavorable for the earlier underwriting in 1962.

Nevertheless, in view of the size of the offer, it was again considered prudent to form an underwriting syndicate. Accordingly, IFC joined Crédito Bursátil again in a syndicate to carry out the biggest underwriting operation ever attempted by a private concern in the Mexican market. The American and Swiss companies that had joined IFC in 1962, joined again in 1964, but this time 7 Mexican institutions joined Crédito Bursátil. Moreover, while in 1962 Crédito Bursátil took only 25 percent of the underwriting commitment, it took 50 percent in 1964. Today, it is a matter of record that the underwriting was a complete success and that over 99 percent of the issue was subscribed almost immediately.

What was the importance of these underwritings? What did the Crédito Bursátil, working with the IFC, achieve? In the first place, of course, an important enterprise received the funds it needed to carry out important expansion programs. Secondly, the underwritings showed that Mexican investors—who by tradition have preferred fixed-income securities—can be persuaded to support well-conceived share offers, even very large ones. As a result of the 1962 underwriting, the number of Fundidora's shareholders increased from 700 before the underwriting to 2,500 afterward, evidence enough of the existence of an important potential source of industrial financing, which the right kind of institution can tap if it comes forward with the right kind of proposal. Further, the underwriting helped establish investment banking contacts abroad for Fundidora and showed that a company geared primarily to serving the domestic market in a developing country can prove attractive to foreign investors.

FIVE CONTRIBUTIONS OF FINANCE COMPANIES

I have dwelt at some length on these cases because they illustrate certain functions which the service-oriented development finance company can perform in the pursuit of its objectives.

Firstly, promotion of new industrial enterprise. The Forjas case illustrates the entrepreneurial role of a development finance company, which needs to be able to pick up a good and important idea, help transform it if necessary to satisfy sound economic, engineering and financial standards, and help arrange the finance the project needs.

Secondly, provision of equity. In both cases, adequate loan funds were available; what was missing was the equity capital necessary for a sound financial plan. The development finance companies involved were prepared to take the risk of investment in share capital.

Thirdly, broad distribution of ownership. In both cases one technique adopted to provide equity was by true underwriting—by seeking to mobilize capital from the widest possible public, both at home and abroad, thus stimulating the capital market. This required particular courage in view of the thinness of that market. In the Forjas case, the financieras run the risk of having to hold on to the shares until the project is in operation and proves its profitability. In the Fundidora case, the underwriters ran the risk of momentarily unfavorable circumstances abroad and of an unusually large flotation for the home market.

Fourthly, mobilization of private savings. Except for the IFC contribution, the capital required in both cases has come from private savings, and represents an important contribution of private savings to industrial investment.

Fifthly, introduction of foreign capital. In both cases the financieras brought foreign financial institutions into the picture, to meet the needs of the particular cases. More importantly, they established permanent banking contacts abroad for the enterprises concerned, and gave the foreign institutions concerned a financial involvement in the countries.

Not all private development finance companies are prepared to or can act in this way. They fear the risks of equity investment, especially in new enterprises and in enterprises which they do not control; and they fear freezing their resources. These fears reflect dangers which are real. But they are not always as great as is sometimes thought.

The risks are not so great if they involve the shares of well-designed and timely projects, for which the economy of the country provides a basis and which give promise of profits commensurate with the risks incurred. In many countries an investing middle-class public is emerging, prepared to acquire seasoned industrial shares. In Peru, the shares of Lima Light and Power move actively, despite the very thin market for shares. In Colombia, Coltejer has more than 25,000 shareholders and Bavaria more than 60,000. A development finance company which is ready to take the risks of investing in equity, which is able to hold on until those shares prove profitable, which actively seeks to educate the public in the advantages of industrial ownership and to broaden the distribution of the shares it acquires may find the risks of liquidity less than is supposed. Its task of selling in due course, in order both to renew its own resources for new investments and to broaden ownership, will be facilitated to the extent that it has won public confidence in its own performance, that is by the profitability and safety of its investments.

I would submit that these functions can most advantageously be carried out by a private company. The classical relationship between an enterprise and its investment banker is one of great and continuing intimacy, particularly where share capital and the ownership it represents are involved. That kind of intimacy is often impossible between a private enterprise and a government bank. Where it is possible, it may be unacceptable to both sides, governments will not normally want to be involved in the ownership of private securities; private entrepreneurs, however much they seek government support, may not want government participation in ownership.

The examples I have given would not have been possible, nor are the objectives they were meant to illustrate be capable of achievement, in countries where the general climate is not conducive to private investment. A development finance company, public or private, designed to mobilize savings and channel them into private investment and to broaden the ownership of private securities will be crippled or helpless in an atmosphere of monetary instability or of political uncertainty or in the presence of that myriad of factors that work to undermine investor confidence. A development finance company cannot provide, in the nation's company law, for adequate protection of minority shareholders; it cannot alone lead the business community to understand the importance of independent public accountants; it cannot create conditions which will lead a citizen to save rather than spend. Government has the principal responsibility for creating the right climate and conditions for taking entrepreneurial risks and for promoting the expansion of industry.

In the last analysis a development finance company can do little to broaden the capital market, unless the broadening of the capital market is a conscious objective of government policy. It is an objective that can be met only if government encourages the flow of private domestic and foreign capital into industrial ventures, supports the establishment of private financieras and builds public confidence in capital markets. It is no coincidence that, for the most part, those countries of Latin America, where industrial progress has been most rapid and where expansion of the private sector has achieved most in raising living standards, are also countries in which active capital markets have begun to develop.

THE POORER NATIONS FIND A NEW BOOTSTRAP*

From Latin America to Nigeria, the private development bank, aimed at promoting as well as financing ventures, has become a valuable tool in broadening the overall economy.

Private Development Banks

Private development banks—institutions that help promote as well as finance business and industrial ventures—are the newest banking fashion in the underdeveloped world.

Over the past few years, they have been sprouting in places like Malaysia, the Philippines, Nigeria, and Morocco. Currently, a rash of private development banks is breaking out in Latin America, where many of them are setting up shop with equity capital from U.S. companies and loans from the U.S. Agency for International Development (AID). Colombia now has eight of these "financieras," as they are usually called; Central America has at least four, and even backward Bolivia has one.

Double Opportunity

Alliance for Progress officials, under fire from Congress for paying too little attention to private enterprise in Latin America, see in the development institutions a convenient funnel for putting money into private business, and a means of making available scarce management help to new enterprises. U.S. commercial banks, which are allowed to invest in foreign development banks through their affiliated Edge Act corporations, see in the financieras a chance to participate in fast-growing Latin business ventures, while cementing relations with Latin clients.

Oil companies operating in Latin America, worried about attacks on foreign capital and on the private enterprise system itself, are putting money into development banks in the hope of improving the overall business climate.

I. Status Symbol

The new financieras are the latest manifestations of development schemes that go back at least a couple of decades. Government development institu-

* *Business Week*, March 14, 1964, pp. 63, 64, 68.

694

tions, such as Mexico's powerful Nacional Financiera, date back before World War II. A private development bank was set up in Turkey in 1950. It was aided by loans from the World Bank and Turkey's central bank. Local financial and industrial interests set up Industrial Credit & Investment Corp. of India in 1955, and Pakistan Industrial Credit & Investment Corp., Ltd., in 1957. U.S. and European companies participated in both.

But now, private development banks are becoming a status symbol among emerging nations, much as steel mills were in the years following World War II. In the Ivory Coast, one is being set up with help from Chase Manhattan Bank, Lazard Freres, and AID. In Latin America, AID is lending private financieras large chunks of money, at interest as low as 2 percent and on terms as long as 20 years.

Two Needs

Behind the current fashion is a real need in developing countries for both financing and expert management assistance for new enterprises.

Many aspiring entrepreneurs in developing countries can't get money for worthwhile business ventures because they can't provide adequate feasibility and engineering studies, financial analysis, market projections, and other data as a basis for attracting loans and equity capital. Private development banks provide some of these services themselves, in addition to buying shares or providing loans for the projects. In some cases, the banks actually initiate business ventures by doing the preliminary studies, then go out and look for an entrepreneur to take them over.

Setting up Plants

One of the most successful, the Corporation Financiera Colombiana de Desarrollo Industrial (Cofinanciera, for short), was set up by leading commercial banks in Bogota. It is financing fertilizer factories, metal-working plants, and agricultural projects aimed at diversifying Colombia's exports and reducing its dependence on coffee. Manufacturers Hanover Trust, through an Edge Act affiliate, holds stock in the bank and a seat on its board. In one project, Cofinanciera negotiated a line of credit in the U.S. to be used, in turn, for loans to farmers developing 25,000 acres of new banana lands. United Fruit Co. agreed to buy the farmers' crops at a guaranteed price.

In Peru, Peruano Suiza de Fomento de Inversiones, S.A. (Peruinvest), with Morgan Guaranty International Banking Corp. as a minority stockholder, has been building up its business by extending short-and-medium term loans to industrial, agricultural, and fishing companies. It sells the paper generated by these loans, with Peruinvest's own guarantee, in the U.S., Europe, and even Buenos Aires. Now Peruinvest is starting to provide equity financing to new and expanding ventures, while the Inter-American Development Bank (IADB) is lending Peruinvest $750,000 to be re-lent to Peruvian industries.

Venezuelan Group

In Venezuela, Cia. Shell is the biggest stockholder in C. A. Venezolana de Desarrollo (Cavensa), a financiera in which Gulf Oil Corp., First National City Bank, Chemical Bank New York Trust, Manufacturers Hanover Trust, and a number of Venezuelan companies also hold shares. The International Finance Corp. (IFC) and the Venezuelan government development bank are minority stockholders. Cavensa is also hoping to get some loan money from AID.

II. BOOSTING THE TAKE

Borrowing money and re-lending it at high rates in capital-short economies is the secret of the private development banks' success. In Latin America, commercial banks are often unable to attract deposits because they are limited by law to interest rates as low as 4 percent. But financieras may borrow at 12 percent, and charge as high as 36 percent for factoring operations. They thrive in an inflationary situation: "The more the inflation, the more they thrive—in a sickly sort of a way," says one U.S. banker.

For longer-term loans, development banks can borrow money from AID, the World Bank, or in some cases from their country's central bank, and re-lend it at a spread of 5 percent or 6 percent. In Pakistan, the private development bank got a no-interest loan from the Pakistan government. The Private Development Corp. of the Philippines, set up last year with participation of 18 U.S. and foreign companies, got a $7-million local currency loan from AID, subordinated to equity shares, from funds generated by U.S. surplus food sales.

Leverage

These loan funds are often four or five times greater than the development bank's own capital resources, and profits from re-lending this money can provide a tremendous "leverage" to boost the bank's take.

Turkey's highly successful private development bank paid dividends up to 12 percent, in addition to plowing back earnings into its operations.

Bolivia's new private development bank, Banco Industrial, S.A., has that kind of leverage in the shape of a $2.5-million AID loan, added to $600,000 of capital put up by local businessmen. The bank got additional technical assistance from AID, from IADB, from Mexico's Nacional Financiera, and even from Colombia's Cofinanciera. Confor, Inc., Canadian export financier, has opened a $10-million line of credit for the new slightly overwhelmed little Bolivian bank, which is making its first loans to a sugar mill and a brewery in the boom town of Santa Cruz.

III. A SOLID BASE

There is some concern that this growing flow of international loan money may tempt local businessmen, eager to turn a quick profit, to set up financieras on shaky foundations. One optimistic Central American group tried unsuccessfully to raise $1-million of equity capital—in order to qualify for a much larger AID loan—by offering to sell $100,000 worth of shares to a U.S. bank, if the bank would lend them the remaining $900,000. But so far, there haven't been any major failures among Latin development banks.

Many of the development banks face a more subtle problem, in trying to decide just what they are in business for. Actually, development banks range from the strictly government banks like Mexico's Nacional Financiera and Venezuela's Corporacion de Fomento (CVF), to the strictly private financieras. Somewhere between are "government-oriented" banks like Cavensa in Venezuela, controlled by private capital but with CVF and IFC participation.

Conflicting Motives

Political pressures on the government banks sometimes influence their investment decisions, with disastrous results, even though there are some official banks such as Nacional Financiera and Chile's CORFO that have done excellent jobs. Banks like Cavensa, though privately controlled and set up with the intention of making a profit, also are aimed at contributing to the nation's economic development. When it comes to a decision between alternative investments, they may be torn between the two motives.

One banker calls this dilemma the "IBEC syndrome"—after Nelson Rockefeller's International Basic Economy Corp., which lost heavily in its early attempts to prove that private capital could make a profit while lowering food costs in Venezuela. Standard Oil Co. (N.J.) may face something of the same problem with its Creole Investment Corp. in Venezuela and Inversiones Esso de Colombia, both set up with the aim of strengthening confidence in private enterprise in Latin America.

Bright Prospects

Despite these problems, officials of lending agencies and U.S. bankers alike see a good future for private development banks. In some countries, development banks are helping to build up local capital markets by underwriting stock issues and setting up mutual funds. Colombia's Cofinanciera is helping the government with its economic development planning.

To date, the World Bank, AID, and other international agencies have channeled some $500-million into private projects around the world, through loans and stock subscriptions in private and quasi-private development banks. U.S. banks, though their Edge Act investments in development banks are still small, are looking at them as a means of expanding their overseas operations.

Morgan Guaranty, for example, is interested in overseas development banks mainly as a means of generating business and extending the help that it can give its customers. In Mexico, Morgan Guaranty has an interest in Crédito Bursátil, S.A., which three years ago floated a $4-million issue—the largest public equity sale in Mexico's history—for Union Carbide Mexicana. Development banks also help uncover direct investment opportunities overseas, and serve as local watchdogs over such investments. In Peru, for example, Morgan Guaranty International itself bought shares in a company that makes equipment for the fishing industry, after Peruinvest had made loans and equity investments in the firm.

First National City Bank, with a worldwide branch banking system of its own, is in a somewhat different position. Citibank's Edge Act affiliate is mainly interested in acquiring a large enough interest in development banks so that it can have a voice in management.

ADDITIONAL READINGS

Benedick, Richard Elliot, *Industrial Finance in Iran,* Harvard Graduate School of Business Administration, Cambridge, 1964.

"Development Banks of the World," *Business International,* August 14, 1964, p. 7; August 21, p. 7; August 28, p. 6; September 4, p. 6; September 18, p. 7; October 9, p. 7; October 16, p. 6; October 23, p. 7.

Diamond, William, *Development Banks,* Baltimore, Md.: The Johns Hopkins Press, 1957.

"Learning to Lend," *Economist,* January 2, 1965.

Mora, Getulio, S. J., "Private Development Banking: Problems and Suggested Remedies," *Economic Research Journal,* September, 1963, pp. 99–102.

Private Development Finance Companies, International Finance Corporation, Washington, 1964.

Some Techniques of Development Lending, World Bank, Washington, 1960.

chapter *12*
Financing Direct
Investments Abroad

When a company decides upon an overseas investment, it need not rely upon its own funds. There are many sources to supplement the investor's funds, some domestic, some international, and some within the country where the investment is to be made — the host country. Most of these sources have been mentioned in earlier chapters, or are discussed in the readings in this chapter. It may be helpful, however, for purposes of the discussion which follows, to mention some of the more important sources.

While one does not immediately think of U.S. commercial banks as sources of funds for overseas investment, it is important to remember that all investments require a certain amount of working capital. Consequently, short-term loans from commercial banks are an important part of the financial package. Also, the Edge Act subsidiaries of U.S. commercial banks have become important sources of equity capital, as well as sources of medium and long-term loans.

In answer to the demand, a number of nonbanking financial institutions have sprung up as sources of capital for foreign ventures. To mention a few, the ADELA Investment Company, Transoceanic Development Corporation, Lambert & Company, International Mining Corporation, International Basic Economy Corporation, Five Arrows Securities Company, Deltec Corporation, Chesapeake Industries, and American Overseas Finance Company all have offices in New York City. Another domestic source, often of key importance, is the medium-term credit (up to five years) which is often available from the companies which are to furnish the capital equipment needed for the project. Along this same line, the U.S. Export-Import Bank often supplements the credit of equipment suppliers, or finances the entire export credit as a medium or long-term project loan. Or, the Agency for International Development (AID) may similarly finance the export credit.

Where capital equipment for the project is to be supplied by a manufacturer from some West European country, or from Japan, one finds that medium-or long-term credit is equally available in these countries.

The first reading in this chapter, by John G. McLean, identifies (in Exhibit I) a number of international institutions which act as sources of foreign investment finance. All, however, are sources of trade credit (similar to the Export-Import Bank) except for the International Finance Corporation (IFC). The role of this institution as a source of loan and equity capital for overseas investment is described at length in one of the readings which follow. Its total investments to date have been relatively modest, but a proposal to quadruple its capital is pending and will greatly increase its importance.

Within the host country itself, the investor has recourse to commercial banks for short-term credit, to development banks for equity capital or medium- to long-term loans, to the local capital market if one exists, and, if not, to individual private investors or to the government itself.

A key source, which is not discussed in the readings, is the availability of "Cooley" loans in the underdeveloped countries. These Cooley funds, which are administered by the Agency for International Development, consist of local currencies received by the U.S. Government as payment for surplus foods sold to the host government. They may be utilized as medium- or long-term loans to branches or subsidiaries of U.S. firms. In mid-1965, a total of over $100 million of such funds were available in twenty different countries.

Given all of the above mentioned sources, how does the investor decide which to utilize? What criteria can he apply to enable him to put together the best financial package?

If the investment is to be made in a West European country whose currency is convertible, and if the investor has sufficient funds, the solution seems simple. Why not a fully-owned, equity investment, in dollars, using the company's own funds? The criteria which must be examined are those of cost, legal structure, fiscal legislation, and risk. The investor may be able to borrow Eurodollars at a lower cost than the alternative investment value of his own funds. On the second point, the legal structure of a country may be such that many financial advantages accrue if the investor has a local partner. The article on "Financing Foreign Operations: Spain" is indicative of this. The fiscal legislation of the host country, and of the United States, may penalize the declaration of dividends. Hence the investor may wish to have a minimum of equity, supplying most of the funds as a loan from the parent. Finally, there is an element of risk even in investing in a West European country. Most U.S. firms with investments in the United Kingdom have, when the value of the pound was in doubt, had to pay a high price to cover their dollar exposure. The same situation occurred during 1964 in regard to investments in Italy. It could happen in a number of other countries. One must, therefore, even in Western Europe, consider the possibly higher cost of investing host country currency versus the risk of exposure when that currency is under pressure.

The criteria become more complicated when considering financing an investment in an underdeveloped country with exchange restrictions, a fairly rapid rate of inflation and the probability of a future devaluation. To minimize exposure, all funds should be raised within the host country (although it may be cheaper to finance the investment with dollars and cover the exposure with a series of swap arrangements). On the other hand, an investment will generally entail the importation of capital equipment and other foreign exchange expenditures. Different industries have different ratios of foreign exchange to local currency costs. Exchange controls will generally require that the investor provide at least enough dollars to cover the imports of equipment and services, which may be thirty to eighty percent of investment cost.

With regard to this dollar portion, how much should be equity and how much loan? This depends partially upon the tax laws, costs, and foreign exchange regulations. If the investor has insufficient funds to supply the equity portion of the dollars, what type of partner should he seek? Does he want one which will not exercise a voice in management? Does he want the involvement of the International Finance Corporation, which may add prestige to his investment vis-à-vis the host government? If the investor has insufficient funds to supply the loan portion of the dollars, does he wish to sustain the delays which may be entailed in utilizing the resources of the Export-Import Bank, the Agency for International Development or one of the international financial institutions, or would it be preferable to utilize slightly higher cost credit from commercial banks and equipment suppliers?

As to the portion of the investment funds to be supplied by local currency, does the investor *want* a local partner, for political (public relations) reasons or to utilize local business know-how? Should this partner be a private party, the government, or the local development bank? Is it preferable to have the local equity dispersed, and if so, what is the feasibility and cost of selling stock to many small stockholders? If a local partner is not needed, are there local sources of loan capital? If so, are the interest costs greater than dividend costs would be with a local partner, particularly when one includes the income tax implications of interest payments versus dividends? Are there local sources of medium-term loans (Cooley funds or a development bank) or will it be necessary to rely upon short-term credit from local commercial banks, with the possibility that the source may dry up at a critical time?

All of the above criteria and questions must be considered when determining the financial sources to be utilized in a foreign investment. The resultant financial package should, then, optimize long-run profits. An additional factor, not considered above, is the possibility of insuring the investment against losses of various kinds. The third reading in this chapter, "The AID Guaranty Program," describes this possibility. This presents a very real problem, however, of weighing the costs of the insurance premiums against the risk of loss.

The two readings on financing foreign operations in Spain and in the

CACM are included to give the reader a feeling for the availability and cost of financing in foreign countries, and the conditions under which it might be available.

Finally, the last reading, "The Peace by Investment Corporation," is included as a visionary thought-provoker. Is such a corporation a feasible project? Is it desirable? What are the problems involved in implementing it? What would be the results (or repercussions) if it were successfully implemented? It is interesting to note that although the Senate bill proposing the establishment of this corporation was never moved out of committee, it has had a significant effect. The ADELA (Atlantic Community Development Group for Latin America) Investment Corporation is an outgrowth of the idea of the Peace by Investment Corporation. Its stockholders are a group of major U.S. and European industries and financial institutions and its aims are to make direct, equity investments in new or expansion projects in Latin America.

It becomes apparent that lack of capital should not be a barrier to foreign investment. One needs only to complete a study which demonstrates the feasibility and profit potential of the project, and prepare the documentation needed for consideration of each source of finance. Often, the investor (promoter) need not even carry out extensive studies. Many of the institutions, as illustrated by the reading on the International Finance Corporation, will, if interested, complete a detailed feasibility study and put together the financial package needed to make the investment. On the other hand, the more thoroughly the investor has prepared his prospectus for a loan or for additional equity investment, the more likely he is to find them, and with less time delay.

FINANCING OVERSEAS EXPANSION*

The need and the will for foreign ventures are well established. The real question is "How?"

About three years ago my company "went overseas." Before that time our operations were limited primarily to the United States and Canada, although we had also engaged in oil exploratory activities in a number of foreign countries. In 1958 we discovered a major new source of crude oil supply in Libya. Shortly thereafter we embarked on an aggressive program of expansion in Western Europe, looking toward the development of markets for our production.

As a consequence, it has been my good fortune in recent years to be involved in perhaps 15 different overseas ventures—acquisitions of companies, negotiations of contracts, project proposals, construction of new plants, and similar matters—in some 10 different foreign countries. Nearly all of these deals have been protracted, complex, and troublesome. In the course of them, I have met many foreign businessmen—some extremely skillful, some extremely difficult, and some whom I hope I shall have as friends for the rest of my life.

From these experiences, I have developed some convictions and impressions, and learned a few things the hard way, about:

- The activities of U.S. industries overseas.
- The sources of investment capital for industrial ventures abroad.
- The problems involved in carrying out foreign projects.

The purpose of this article is to present some ideas on these matters which I hope may be of interest to others who are going, or are about to go, "abroad."

VANISHING BOUNDARIES

American industry has today a new role to play in the world of business affairs. It is no longer a "minor player" but a "major player" on the international business scene. On this score, I have three observations to offer.

1. *The industries and business managers of this country are entering a new era—an era of transition from domestic to international business affairs.*

* John G. McLean, *Harvard Business Review*, March–April, 1963, pp. 53–65.

For the past 100 years or more the main thrust of the industrial effort in this country has been toward the establishment of strong, efficient domestic industries with modest capacity for exporting goods abroad. In the years ahead our industrial effort will take on a new direction. We shall become increasingly engaged in the establishment of manufacturing plants, selling operations, and other business activities in foreign areas. We shall become a nation of international industrialists, merchants, traders, and financiers.

As evidence of the trend of our times, consider the following:

• In the period from 1950 to 1961, our merchandise exports increased from $10 billion to $21 billion a year and our merchandise imports from $9 billion to almost $15 billion a year.

• In the decade from the end of 1951 to the end of 1961, our private assets and investments abroad grew from $21 billion to $56 billion.

• Between the years 1952 and 1961, our plant and equipment expenditures abroad increased from $1.7 billion to $4.2 billion a year, and our dividends from foreign investments and other income receipts abroad grew from $1.7 billion to $2.7 billion a year.

• Congress has recently enacted the Trade Expansion Act of 1962 which, if carefully administered, should further stimulate and accelerate the expansion of our international business activities.

The transition we are making is not a new thing in the history of business affairs. In earlier centuries, a similar transition marked the experience of many other nations with highly developed business societies. Interesting analogies may be found in the experience of Babylon, Egypt, and Crete around 2000 B.C.; in the experience of the Phoenicians a millennium later; in the development of the Greek and Roman Empires; and in the truly remarkable international trading activities developed by the Florentine and Venetian merchants shortly after the Italian Renaissance. Further, we should note the experience of England and other European nations after the Industrial Revolution in the early 1800's. These countries first developed great industrial societies at home and then went abroad to find new markets, new sources of raw materials, and new investment opportunities. More recently still, we see the European Common Market countries, first rebuilding their internal economies, and then embarking on a bold new effort to lay aside the barriers to international trade.

The economic, political, and social circumstances in all these situations were, of course, in many ways different from those prevailing in the United States today, but the results for the business manager were essentially the same. He left the familiar environs of his native land and went abroad—and that is what is happening to the U.S. businessman today.

2. *It is highly important that our industries, business managers, and our investment capital should move into foreign countries, and particularly into those countries which have a lesser degree of industrial development than we do.*

The ten most highly industrialized nations of the Free World, whom I suppose we might regard as our natural friends and allies, have about 18 percent of the world population. These same countries have a national income equivalent to about $1,250 per capita a year. The remaining countries of the world have 82 percent of the population and a national income equivalent to about $125 per capita a year. Many of the people in these countries fight a grim, terrible battle from the day they are born until the day they die—a battle to get enough food to stay alive.

The long course of history demonstrates all too clearly that this is a kind of imbalance which mankind, and society generally, will not tolerate for long. Recall the repeated, and eventually successful, attacks on the Roman Empire by the Visigoths, Vandals, and other "have-not" tribes from the North; the Viking invasion and destruction of the Carolingian Empire; the French Revolution: and the Russian Revolution. Consider then the surging unrest throughout the world today—especially in Africa, South America, the Near East, the Middle East, and the Far East—where multitudes of people are suddenly awakening and demanding a better way of life in our time. And remember that the "have-nots" of this age outnumber the "haves" by at least five to one.

It seems to me, therefore, that we must find means of redressing the economic imbalance between the so-called "have" and "have-not" nations, or some day we may be confronted with a struggle between them which could make the present conflict between the Free World and Communist countries seem mild in comparison!

I realize that these opinions open up a large and very difficult topic. Let me withdraw from it by simply stating that I see no means of bringing about a better balance between populations and national incomes except through the movement of investment capital and management know-how from the countries that have them to those that have not. The alternative— hoping that the latter countries will develop capital and know-how internally from their own resources—is probably impractical and too slow a process in the light of the evolutionary social changes taking place almost every- where one chooses to look in the world today.

I also believe that the movement of American capital and management know-how abroad is an essential element in our Cold War with Communism. To win that war three things are needed:

> (a) We must have indisputable military superiority. But in the long run military strength alone will not be sufficient.
>
> (b) The uncommitted and have-not nations must be drawn perma- nently into our economic orbit with the enduring ties that spring from mutually profitable business relationships.
>
> (c) We must offer and carry to the other nations of the world an ideology, a culture, a way of life that is at least tolerable to, if not acceptable by, them.

3. *The transition of our industries from the domestic to the international field is taking place for some very sound business reasons.*

For convenience, I divide these reasons into two categories—profit opportunities and competitive necessities:

¶ With regard to the profit opportunities,[1] we may note that many industries in this country expanded very rapidly in the period following World War II. They have now established more-than-ample producing capacities and have saturated the available domestic markets with their products to a fairly high degree. Future rates of growth in many cases will be determined largely by population expansion.

Abroad, the situation is quite different. Sufficient productive capacity is frequently lacking, consumption is expanding more rapidly, and consumer wants and requirements have been satisfied to a much lesser degree. For example:

— In the United States, there is one automobile for every 3 persons; in the countries of the Common Market, one for every 11 people; in Latin America, one for every 78 people; in Africa, one for every 95 people; and in Free Asia, one for every 467 people.

— In the United States, there is one television set for every 3.2 people; in the Common Market countries, one for every 13 people; in Latin America, one for every 48 people; in Africa, one for every 790 people; in Free Asia, one for every 102 people.

— A similar situation exists with respect to refrigerators, washing machines, and many other consumer and industrial products. As a result, a steadily increasing number of American businesses are finding excellent growth prospects and rewarding profit opportunities from participation in foreign industrial development.

¶ With regard to the competitive necessities, some industries are finding their traditional export markets preempted by the growth of efficient, indigenous producers.[2] The development of local industries abroad has in some cases made it impossible from a competitive and economical standpoint to continue shipments from this country; and the manufacturers so affected have been forced to establish plants abroad to retain their business. The automobile, chemical, office machine, and oil field supply industries provide examples.

We should also note the increasing tendency of our stronger foreign competitors to challenge us for our *domestic* markets by establishing manufacturing operations in this country. Foreign interests now have about $7.5 billion of direct investments in the United States (in addition to $12 billion in U.S. securities), and the earnings from such investments are currently running at a rate of more than $400 million a year. Examples of the trend are the recent acquisition of the Underwood Corporation by Olivetti Corporation of America and the purchase of a substantial stock interest in the Howe Sound Company by Pechiney.

[1] See Raphael W. Hodgson and Hugo E. R. Uyterhoeven, "Analyzing Foreign Opportunities," *Harvard Business Review,* Vol. 40 (March–April, 1962), p. 60.
[2] See Dennis J. O'Connell and John J. Benson, " 'Sourcing' Abroad for Domestic Profit," *Harvard Business Review,* Vol. 41 (March–April, 1963), p. 87.

In the light of these and many related facts, we can only conclude that business competition in the future will be waged with increasing disregard for national boundaries.

EXPORTING CAPITAL

Thus far, I have been describing some of the reasons why U.S. industries and U.S. business managers are, and should be, going abroad. The United States today has the greatest aggregation of investment capital, industrial machinery, and management know-how that the world has ever known. Our accumulations of these resources far surpass those of any other nation. However, at the same time there are vast areas of the world, containing the great majority of the world's population, where these resources are disturbingly scarce. To my mind, therefore, the investment capital and management know-how should flow from the United States to foreign areas in a steadily increasing volume until a better equilibrium is established. We come then to the question: How well equipped are our financial institutions to facilitate the flow of capital into foreign areas? I have two observations about this question.

1. *The financial institutions and markets of this country are not yet well equipped to support the movement of our industries into the international field.*

Our financial institutions are, of course, well organized to provide short-term funds and the routine commercial banking services in support of trading operations. Their capacity to provide intermediate- and long-term funds for investments in plant facilities, however, is an entirely different matter. (I am speaking here about investments which look to the foreign venture itself for security rather than to parent company guaranties. Prime U.S. corporations can, of course, borrow almost unlimited funds for use abroad if they provide guaranties.)

Institutional Funds

The major accumulations of private investment capital in this country are in the insurance companies and various types of pension and trust funds. Few, if any, of these organizations are disposed, or in a position, to make any significant part of their reserves available for capital investment abroad. To be more specific:

¶ Insurance companies located in New York State, for example, are permitted by state law to invest only 1 percent of their assets in foreign investments outside Canada. In addition, certain types of foreign investments may qualify under the "basket" clause, which permits investment of up to 2 percent of assets in certain special, usually higher risk, categories. The restraints on foreign investments in other states are different but are usually of the same order of magnitude. In addition to these technical limitations, most insurance companies have strong, self-imposed limitations on investments overseas. Generally speaking, the rates they charge their clients and the entire structure of their businesses presuppose relatively low rates of return from investments that are exposed to low degrees of risk.

Accordingly, the insurance companies have no strong incentives—and are not organized and equipped—to face the risks and seek the rewards that lie abroad.

¶ Essentially the same considerations apply in the case of pension and trust funds. Estimates by representatives of these institutions suggest that, taken altogether, U.S. insurance companies and pension and trust funds do not have more than perhaps $200 million committed to truly foreign (nonguaranteed by parents) industrial projects.

Investment Banks

U.S. investment banking institutions are beginning to show a very active interest in financing industrial projects abroad. Most of them will admit, however, that to date they have arranged the financing of only a few foreign projects and have put almost none of their own funds into such ventures. Their activities consist largely of advising corporations contemplating foreign projects and of contacting institutions and individuals, domestic and foreign, who might be interested in financing such projects.

Commercial Banks

Commercial banks may lend to foreign borrowers under generally the same conditions as to U.S. borrowers. But the function of a commercial bank is to make funds available for short-term, relatively low-risk operations, and loans for foreign ventures must pass the same rigid bank examinations as do domestic loans. Most commercial banks, therefore, have not been in a position to do very much toward facilitating the flow of U.S. capital overseas.

Edge Act Subsidiaries

One of the most encouraging developments of recent years has been the establishment by the commercial banks of international subsidiaries under the Edge Act of 1919. This legislation was designed to allow funds from United States sources to participate in the reestablishment of Europe after World I and to provide funds for export financing.

Little was accomplished under the Edge Act until certain clarifying regulations were issued by the Board of Governors in January 1957 (Regulation K). Under the new regulations, a commercial bank may establish (a) a foreign banking corporation which engages chiefly in commercial banking activities, and/or (b) a foreign financing corporation which engages chiefly in investment banking functions. At the present time, there are about ten commercial banks with both types of subsidiaries and about four commercial banks with one type but not the other. The great majority of these subsidiaries have been established in the last two years.

Financing corporations set up under the Edge Act are particularly interesting because they are engaged in the long-term financing of truly foreign ventures. They are permitted to charge interest rates commensurate with the risks involved and to take special "kickers," such as equity participations or warrants to buy common stocks. They have funds of their own to invest and can arrange for the participation of other investors on either a "commitment" or "best efforts" basis. They offer exactly the kind of service as industrial company needs in developing a financial program for a venture abroad.

Unfortunately, the dozen or so Edge Act companies now in existence have limited facilities and an aggregate capitalization of only about $40 million. To date, they have arranged only a few hundred million dollars of financing for foreign ventures. In the future, however, there is reason to believe and hope that their operations will be greatly expanded.

2. *Because of our lack of well-developed facilities for channeling private capital into investment opportunities abroad, the task of financing our industrial expansion in foreign countries has fallen too heavily on the national and multinational agencies in Washington.*

I shall not attempt to describe the activities of these agencies in any detail. The general nature and scope of their activities are indicated in Exhibit 1. Suffice it to say that their resources run into the billions, and they are in a position to provide a very wide range of financing services for projects in the less industrialized countries of the Free World. During recent years, the bulk of U.S. capital flowing overseas has passed through these agencies rather than through private financing channels.

I view this situation with some apprehension for two reasons: (a) It suggests to me that our private financial institutions may be passing up one of the greatest challenges and opportunities that will come their way in this decade. (b) I fear that we may unwittingly be letting another important segment of our business affairs drift into government hands and may thus, by default, be taking another step in a socialistic direction.

I do not mean to disparage the programs of the national and multinational lending agencies. Many of these programs are well administered and vitally important in the world of today. It appears to me, nevertheless, that the efforts of these agencies should be concentrated primarily on three things:

(a) The providing of funds for projects which are in the public or quasi-public works category and are not normally of interest to private capital (e.g., schools, hospitals, research programs, roads, dams, harbors, and agricultural reclamation).

Financing Direct Investments Abroad

EXHIBIT I. AGENCIES WHICH HELP FI*

	EXPORT-IMPORT BANK	AGENCY FOR INTERNATIONAL DEVELOPMENT (AID)			INTERNATIONAL MONETARY FUND (
	U. S. Dollars	U. S. Dollars[1]	Foreign Currencies: Special Loans	Investment Guarantees	Currencies of Member Countries
PURPOSE	Aid in financing; facilitate U. S. foreign trade.	Assist in developing economic resources and productive capabilities of less developed countries and increase economic cooperation, trade and private investment.	Assist in development of less developed countries and expand markets for U. S. agricultural products.	Encourage, facilitate, and increase the participation of private enterprise in furthering the economic and social development of the less developed countries.	Promote international monet' eration and encourage stabili viding resources to meet balance-of-payments problem other means.
RESOURCES	$7 billion of which $1 billion is capital stock subscribed by U. S. Treasury; $6 billion borrowing authority.	Annual appropriation ($1.1 billion for FY 1962) supplemented by long-term commitment authority ($7.2 billion for FY 1962-1966).	Up to 25% of proceeds of sales of U. S. surplus agricultural commodities in each country.	Annual appropriation. Currently $1 billion for specific risks; $90 million for all risk; and $10 million for pilot housing in Latin America.	Resources consist of gold an of member currencies a $14.85 billion. The U. S. $4.125 billion.
NATURE OF LOANS	• Project loans. • Exporter credits. • Medium-term comprehensive guarantees or insurance. • Short-term comprehensive insurance.	• Loans to foreign governments. • Loans to private U. S. and foreign firms. • Loans to intermediate financing institutions.	• Loans to U. S. firms, their subsidiaries and affiliates abroad for business development and trade expansion. • To U. S. or foreign firms to expand foreign markets for U. S. agricultural products.	Guaranteed investments include equity, loans, licensing arrangements, contributions in kind, or any combination of these.	Member's purchases from IM rencies of other members equivalent amount of the mem currency. Member's purchase rency from the IMF must be repurchases.
WHO CAN APPLY	• U. S. or foreign firm, or friendly foreign government. • U. S. exporter. • U. S. banks; or exporter directly until cover becomes available at Foreign Credit Insurance Association. (FCIA) • U. S. exporter at FCIA.	• Foreign governments. • U. S. firms and firms in recipient countries. • Development banks, savings and loan associations, and other relending institutions.	• U. S. firms only. • U. S. and local firms.	U. S. citizens and firms; U. S. chartered corporations "substantially, beneficially owned by U. S. citizens" and their wholly owned subsidiaries on new investment in friendly less-developed countries with which the U. S. has all over-all guaranty agreement.	Member governments
GUARANTEES	• May guarantee payments of project loan financed by private sources. • Up to 85% of credit and political risks. • Up to 85% of credit risk; up to 95% of political risk.	Not applicable.	Not applicable.	• Guarantees of new investment against specific risks (expropriation, inconvertibility, loss due to war, revolution, or insurrection). • All risk guarantees. • Guarantees of investment in private pilot or in demonstration housing projects in Latin America.	Not applicable.
MATURITY	• 8 to more than 20 years according to nature of project. • 1 to 5 years (exceptionally 7 years). • Up to 180 days. Special cases up to 1 year.	• In general, up to 40 years, including 10-year grace period; in special situations, substantially shorter terms. • Flexible; grace periods in some cases; economics of project a major consideration. • Flexible to permit revolving credits, including grace periods in some instances.	Based on nature of project but generally not exceeding 10 years.	Normally up to 20 years.	Members undertake to repurch in a period not exceeding 3 t
CURRENT INTEREST RATES OR FEES	• Minimum interest 5¾%. • Minimum interest 6%. • Fees vary by market and term of credit.	• Generally ¾ of 1%, but varies under special circumstances. • Based on nature of project, generally 5¾%. • Based on local rates and nature of sub-loans.	Based on local rates and nature of project.	• Current rate is ½ of 1% on liability for each risk actively covered; on "standby" coverage, ¼ of 1%. • Under consideration, probably 2%.	Service charge of ¼ of 1%, p est on purchases in excess increasing with length of time outstanding and amount p with lowest rate 2% per annum
CURRENCY OF REPAYMENT	U. S. dollar.	U. S. dollars.[1]	Foreign currency loaned.	Not applicable.	Gold or convertible curren
WHERE PROCEEDS MUST BE SPENT	In the U. S.	Primary emphasis on U. S. procurement.	Locally.	Not applicable.	Not limited to U. S. procur
RELATIONSHIP TO OTHER SOURCES OF FINANCING	Does not compete with private capital.	Must take into account whether financing is obtainable on reasonable terms from free-world sources.	None.	Not applicable.	Cooperates with and acts member countries, treasuries banks, stabilization funds, fiscal agencies.
DECISION-MAKING BODY	Board of Directors with advice of National Advisory Council (NAC) on international monetary and financial problems.	Administrator of AID with advice of NAC.	Administrator of AID with advice of NAC.	Administrator of AID with advice of NAC.	Board of Governors or, as of the Board of Directors; U. S. instructed by NAC.
LEGAL AUTHORITY	The Export-Import Bank Act of 1945, as amended.	The Act for International Development of 1961, Section 201.	PL 480, Sections 104(e) and (g).	The Act for International Development of 1961, Sections 221-224.	Articles of Agreement, and th Woods Agreement Acts.

[1]AID also extends grant assistance for development and support of economics. In some circumstances, Supporting Assistance may take the form of local currency repayable loans.

[2]IMF's contribution to economic development efforts, while important, is indirect direct.

SOURCE: Foreign Commerce Weekly (now International Commerce), May 14, 1962, pp. 886-887.

IGN TRADE AND INVESTMENT

TERNATIONAL BANK (IBRD) — Currencies of Member Countries	INTERNATIONAL FINANCE CORP. (IFC) — Dollars	INTERNATIONAL DEVELOPMENT ASSOCIATION (IDA) — Currencies of Member Countries	INTER-AMERICAN DEVELOPMENT BANK (IDB) — Currencies of Members (Principally Dollars)	INTER-AMERICAN SOCIAL PROGRESS TRUST FUND — IDB Administered Trust Fund (Dollars)	
e development of productive fa- and resources in member es.	Further economic development by encouraging growth of productive private enterprise in less developed member countries.	Promote economic development in member countries by providing finance on terms not possible under IBRD, of which IDA is an affiliate.	Contribute to accelerating process of economic development in the member countries.	Provide capital and technical assistance to support efforts of Latin American countries to achieve greater social progress and balanced economic growth.	PURPOSE
subscriptions of member coun- $20.4 billion of which approx- $2 billion is in and $18 is callable. U. S. subscription $5 billion of which $5.7 billion able, if required by the Bank to is obligations.	Capital subscription of member countries of $96.4 million, and proceeds of sale of investments.	Proposed initial subscription of $1 billion, of which $916 million is subscribed. U. S. subscription is $320.3 million. Review of resources required every five years with a view to replenishment.	Authorized resources of $959.5 million (U. S. share $450 million) of which $813.2 million is for ''Ordinary Operations'' and $146.3 million is for ''Fund for Special Operations''. $431.6 million of callable capital to meet defaults on Bank's securities of which U. S. share is $200 million.¹	$394 million appropriated by the U.S.²	RESOURCES
to member governments to other or private entities if guaranteed member government.	Investment in productive private enterprises. May now subscribe to their capital stock. Guarantee of member governments not sought.	Credits to member governments or territories.	Loans to member governments or political subdivisions of such members and to public and private entities in those countries from the Bank's resources for ''Ordinary'' and ''Special'' operations.	Loans in fields of land settlement and use, low income housing, community water and sanitation, and, to a limited extent, higher education.	NATURE OF LOANS
r governments, private and public titles guaranteed by member ent.	Private firms operating in the less developed member countries on projects which contribute to the development of the private sector, offer promise of returns, and for which adequate financing from private sources is not available on reasonable terms.	Member countries, and their territories.	Member governments and their agencies and subdivisions; private local firms (or firms owned jointly by local interests); public or private relending agencies.	Governments, public institutions, private borrowers, co-operatives.	WHO CAN APPLY
r partial guarantees of loans by lenders for purposes noted if such loans are guaranteed by ser government. Guarantee auth as not been exercised.	Not applicable.	Not applicable.	May guarantee in whole or in part loans by private investors. Guarantee authority has not been exercised.	Discretionary.	GUARANTEES
Generally 15 to 25 years.	Generally 5 to 15 years.	All credits so far extended for 50 years, with 10-year grace period and graduated authorization.	• 10 to 20 years in ''Ordinary Operations.'' • 10 to 50 years in ''Special Operations.''	Generally 15 to 30 years.	MATURITY
currently - based on cost of to Bank, plus 1% commission % for administrative expenses.	Currently about 7% for loans. No fixed interest on equity participation.	¾ of 1% service charge; no interest.	• Currently 5¾% for ''Ordinary Operations.'' • For ''Special Operations,'' about 4% repayable in currency of borrower; higher in certain cases where funds are for relending.	Generally 1¼% to 2¾% payable in local currency plus a ¾ of 1% per annum service charge, payable in dollars.	CURRENT INTEREST RATES OR FEES
Currencies loaned.	Currencies invested - usually U. S. dollars.	Currency loaned, or other foreign exchange as appropriate. Has power to accept local currency but no indication power will be used.	• For ''Ordinary Operations'' in currency lent. • For ''Special Operations,'' in whole or in part, in currency of borrower.	Largely in the currency of the borrowing country.	CURRENCY OF REPAYMENT
t limited to U. S. procurement.	Not limited to U. S. procurement.	Not limited to U. S. procurement.	Not limited to U. S. procurement.	Limited to procurement in U. S. and member countries.	WHERE PROCEEDS MUST BE SPENT
t lend where private capital is ble on reasonable terms.	Cannot lend where sufficient private capital is available on reasonable terms.	Cannot lend when private capital is available on reasonable terms.	Cooperates with other sources of financing. Takes into account the ability of borrower to obtain private loans on terms which the Bank considers reasonable.	Must take into account whether assistance can be obtained from national or international agencies or private sources on reasonable terms.	RELATIONSHIP TO OTHER SOURCES OF FINANCING
of Governors or, as delegated, oard of Directors; U. S. Director cted by NAC.	Board of Governors or, as delegated, the Board of Directors; U. S. Director instructed by NAC.	Board of Governors or, as delegated, the Board of Directors; U. S. Director instructed by NAC.	Board of Governors or, as delegated, Board of Directors; U. S. Director instructed by NAC.	IDB as trustee; IDB Board of Directors; U. S. Director instructed by NAC.	DECISION-MAKING BODY
es of Agreement and the Bretton Agreement Act.	Articles of Agreement and the International Finance Corporation Act.	Articles of Agreement and the International Development Association Act.	Agreement establishing the Inter-American Development Bank and the IDB Act (PL 86-147).	The Social Progress Trust Fund Agreement and the Act authorizing Inter-American Social and Economic Cooperation program.³	LEGAL AUTHORITY

e basis of current membership. Authorized resources originally contemplated $1 billion was reduced to $959.5 million when Cuba did not become a member of IDB.

des $100 million administered by AID for grants and for loans for health and education;

and $6 million to the Organization of American States for technical assistance in public administration and other fields.

³Agreement signed on June 19, 1961 between the U. S. and IDB.

(b) The development of broad and effective programs of investment insurance against political risks in foreign countries (e.g., risks relating to currency convertibility, expropriation, and wars and insurrections). The assumption of the *commercial* and *business* risks, however, should be left to the private investor.

(c) The "gap-filling" role of providing some part of the funds for private projects—either in the form of debt or equity capital—when a modest amount of such funds may be needed to complete the financing of an otherwise private venture.

The rest of the job of bearing the risks and of financing U.S. industrial expansion abroad should be handled insofar as possible by *private* investors and by *private* financial institutions. One of the astonishing political paradoxes of today lies in the fact that our government is urging the expansion of the national and multinational lending agencies to promote the flow of capital abroad, and at the same time imposing additional tax burdens on private business ventures overseas. Indeed, government officials in some quarters are discussing the possibility of restricting the investment of capital abroad by private companies!

THE PASA PROJECT

Turning now from the general to the specific, let us look at an actual case example illustrating problems and opportunities of the types just outlined. The example that follows is one I am personally familiar with. It concerns Petroquimica Argentina, S.A. (PASA), a project for the manufacture of synthetic rubber and other petrochemicals in Argentina. The project is being undertaken by five U.S. companies (Continental Oil Company, Cities Service Company, United States Rubber Company, Fish International Corporation, and Witco Chemical Company, Inc.). Details with regard to the nature of the venture and the program of financing employed are contained in Exhibits 2-4.

Motives in Going Abroad

The PASA project illustrates some of the business reasons which prompt U.S. industries to go abroad. In this case, profit opportunities rather than competitive necessities were the chief motivating factors:

> Argentina has experienced a rapidly expanding automobile industry. Automobile tires are manufactured locally, but all of the rubber has been imported from foreign sources. Meanwhile, Argentina has been developing its oil and natural gas resources. As shown in Exhibit 2, a recently completed, 1,200-mile pipeline brings natural gas and natural gas liquids to the San Lorenzo area, about 230 miles northwest of Buenos Aires, where the PASA plant will be located. (The geographical chart is

EXHIBIT 2

DESCRIPTION OF PASA PROJECT

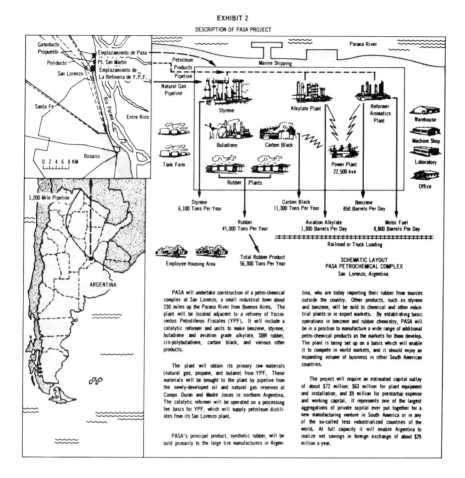

SCHEMATIC LAYOUT
PASA PETROCHEMICAL COMPLEX
San Lorenzo, Argentina

PASA will undertake construction of a petro-chemical complex at San Lorenzo, a small industrial town about 230 miles up the Parana River from Buenos Aires. The plant will be located adjacent to a refinery of Yacimientos Petroliferos Fiscales (YPF). It will include a catalytic reformer and units to make benzene, styrene, butadiene and aviation grade alkylate, SBR rubber, cis-polybutadiene, carbon black, and various other products.

The plant will obtain its primary raw materials (natural gas, propane, and butane) from YPF. These materials will be brought to the plant by pipeline from the newly-developed oil and natural gas reserves at Campo Duran and Madre Jonas in northern Argentina. The catalytic reformer will be operated on a processing fee basis for YPF, which will supply petroleum distillates from its San Lorenzo plant.

PASA's principal product, synthetic rubber, will be sold primarily to the large tire manufacturers in Argen-tina, who are today importing their rubber from sources outside the country. Other products, such as styrene and benzene, will be sold to chemical and other industrial plants or in export markets. By establishing basic operations in benzene and rubber chemistry, PASA will be in a position to manufacture a wide range of additional petro-chemical products as the markets for them develop. The plant is being set up on a basis which will enable it to compete in world markets, and it should enjoy an expanding volume of business in other South American countries.

The project will require an estimated capital outlay of about $72 million; $63 million for plant equipment and installation, and $9 million for prestartup expense and working capital. It represents one of the largest aggregations of private capital ever put together for a new manufacturing venture in South America or in any of the so-called less industrialized countries of the world. At full capacity it will enable Argentina to realize net savings in foreign exchange of about $29 million a year.

shown as we presented it to the Argentineans, with some of the terms in Spanish.)

Fundamentally, it makes good economic sense to use the newly developed, indigenous raw materials for the manufacture of rubber and other chemicals. The finished products can be offered at prices which will provide some savings to local industries and yet enable the sponsors to earn an interesting financial return.

In addition, the PASA project establishes an industrial beachhead in two major fields of chemistry (benzene and rubber) and has great potential for future growth and expansion.

Economic considerations are not the only ones that have influenced top management. The project has strong sponsorship; the five parent companies have financial resources to meet contingencies and an abundance of technical and managerial know-how in the projected fields of endeavor. Moreover, Argentina is rich in economic and social resources, produces ample food for its people, and has a population which is 92 percent literate. Notwithstanding the current disturbances, its political leaders in recent years have demonstrated their firm desire to develop a strong system of private capitalism and free enterprise.

In sum, the PASA situation has *intrinsic* economic merit; it offers far more than a transient profit potential.

Gains for Host Nation

The PASA project also illustrates the economic benefits which a host country can derive from industrial investments by U.S. companies.

Argentina is in the throes of transition from an agricultural to an industrial economy and is experiencing the usual difficulties of capital accumulation. In recent years, it has had substantial deficits in its foreign exchange position. The PASA project will involve a capital investment of about $72 million and will represent one of the largest aggregations of private capital ever arranged for a new manufacturing venture in Latin America. About $15 million of the plant construction costs will be expended for labor and materials in Argentina, and, after the plant is in full operation, it will enable Argentina to realize a net gain in its foreign exchange position of about $29 million a year.

In the course of our negotiations with Argentine government officials,

EXHIBIT 3

CUMULATIVE BALANCE SHEET OF FOREIGN EXCHANGE

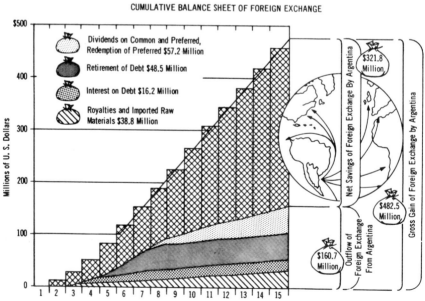

Years Since Beginning of Construction

we found it necessary and desirable on many occasions to demonstrate the impact of our project on Argentina's foreign exchange balance. To this end, we eventually developed a series of colored charts in Spanish to show the money flowing in and the money flowing out throughout the project life. One of the summary charts from this series is shown in Exhibit 3.

In addition to benefiting Argentina's fiscal situation, the PASA project will provide employment to about 700 nationals and a means of transmitting to the country a broad accumulation of managerial know-how and technical skills in several different fields.

Financial Teamwork

From a financial point of view, the PASA project is interesting because it illustrates a situation in which private institutions and the national and multinational lending agencies have played well-balanced roles. The project was financed basically from private sources, but the national and multinational lending agencies have made a vitally important *supplementary* contribution. Details of the financial arrangements are shown in Exhibit 4. The salient features follow:

¶ One group of private industrial companies, the five sponsors, agreed to supply $18.5 million in the form of common and preferred stock. These companies also provided the management skills and technical know-how required for the undertaking.

¶ A second group of private industrial companies, the vendors of materials and equipment, agreed to supply $30 million by taking Class A debentures (vendors' credits) of five- to seven-year maturity in partial payment for their goods.

¶ The Chase International Investment Corporation (an Edge Act subsidiary of The Chase Manhattan Bank) and Lazard Freres & Co. agreed to supply and find purchasers for an aggregate of $18.5 million of Class B debentures of ten-year maturity, partially on a "commitment" and partially on a "best efforts" basis. Chase and Lazard each purchased some of these debentures for their own account and found 17 other investors in North America and Western Europe who agreed to purchase the remainder.

¶ The International Finance Corporation (a multinational lending agency) purchased about $3 million of the Class B debentures to close out the issue when it became clear, in the face of a deteriorating investment climate in Latin America, that the entire issue could not be placed with private investors.

¶ The Agency for International Development (a national lending agency) has provided convertibility insurance to the U.S. holders of all classes of securities. Also it will, when possible, provide expropriation and war-risk insurance. In view of the current financial and political difficulties in Argentina, this insurance has become exceedingly important. Furthermore, it is highly doubtful that the PASA venture could have been arranged without such assistance.

EXHIBIT 4

PASA – PLAN OF FINANCING

Proposed Capitalization	U. S. Dollar Equivalents
6% to 8% Five to Seven Year Class A Debentures (Suppliers' Credits)	$30,000,000
Working Capital Loans	5,000,000
7½% Five to Ten Year Class B (U.S. Dollar) Debentures	18,500,000
Total Debt	$53,500,000
7½% Preferred Stock to be Purchased by Sponsoring Group	$13,500,000
Common Stock to be Purchased by Sponsoring Group	$ 5,000,000 (85%)
Additional Common Stock to be Subject to Warrants Accompanying Class B Debentures	882,000 (15%)
Total Initially Authorized Common Stock	$ 5,882,000 (100%)
Total	$72,882,000

Description of Class B Debentures

Amount: $18.5 Million. To be sold to Chase International and Lazard Freres Investor Group.

Interest Rate: 7½% a year.

Commitment Fee: 1% a year on unused balances from the effective date of commitment.

ICA Insurance: PASA will provide ICA convertibility insurance for American investors prior to first drawdown and expropriation insurance if and when available.

Maturity: Final maturity ten years from date of drawdown. Ten equal semiannual payments of principal to commence five and one-half years after date of issue.

Dual Pay: Foreign holders may elect to receive principal and interest in U. S. dollars or Swiss francs (at a final exchange rate of $0.2322 per Swiss franc). Elections to be made prior to February 14, 1970, or five years and 45 days after last drawdown, whichever comes first.

Redemption: Redeemable in whole or in part at no premium on 20 days notice.

Warrants: Class B debentures will receive detachable warrants to purchase a total of 15% of PASA's common stock at par at any time within ten years after date of last drawdown of Class B debentures.

Sinking Fund: After Class A debentures are retired, 50% of PASA's net cash flow will be applied to accelerate payment of Class B debentures, provided that no payments shall be made which would reduce working capital below required levels.

¶ A consortium of commercial banks is expected to provide $5 million of short-term money for working capital as the final element in the financial structure.

Our decision to draw our funds primarily from private sources eventually produced two unexpected benefits:

(1) By using private funds, we avoided any drain on Argentina's lines of credit or allotments of funds from the various monetary agencies in Washington. Because Argentina has many other needs for capital, its officials were very appreciative of this aspect of our financial arrangements.

(2) An element of competitive strategy was involved. We had many business competitors in Argentina who from time to time sought authorization to undertake part or all of our project for their own account. In most cases, however, these competitors postulated financial programs which included loans from the Export–Import Bank in Washington. As a matter of policy, the Export–Import Bank was unwilling to extend financial assistance to these firms as long as PASA was in a position to carry forward its program with private financing.

Special Provisions

From a purist standpoint, the anomaly in the PASA financing program is the $30 million of vendor credits. Some vendors told us bluntly that they were not in the business of lending money and objected to our request that they, in effect, provide five- to seven-year financing for the venture. We used this source of capital simply because (a) we saw no other means of obtaining the necessary funds from private sources, and (b) we knew that, under the pressure of intense competition, many vendors in Western Europe and in the United States (sometimes with government assistance) were accustomed to granting such credits. Our need to use them—and the vendors' need to grant them—reflected the lack of well-developed private institutions for financing foreign ventures, an important point mentioned earlier in this article.

As for the Class B debentures, this placement was a long and difficult task. The terms and conditions of the debentures originally provided:

- A commitment fee of 1 percent.
- An interest rate of 7½ percent.
- A stated maturity of ten years from date of drawdown with provisions for accelerated amortization if the projected cash flow is available, which should result in an average maturity of six or seven years.
- Warrants to buy 15 percent of the common stock at par any time in the ten-year period following the last drawdown.

Initial discussions with a small group of major prospective buyers indicated that it would be extremely difficult, if not impossible, to place the entire $18.5 million with these conditions only. Accordingly, we added one additional "sweetener"; namely, we gave the bondholders the option of receiving payments of interest and principal in Swiss francs or U.S. dollars. (The right was later made available to the foreign bondholders only.) This option may be exercised and changed from time to time up to the end of the five-year period following the last drawdown. With this feature, and the assistance of the International Finance Corporation, the Class B issue was finally closed.

We have been asked many times why the sponsors—at least three of whom are very large—did not simply guarantee their pro rata share of the debt in order to facilitate the financing arrangements. I do not know what prompted the other companies, but in the case of my own company (Continental Oil) the answer is clear. In the foreign field, we like to see "each tub stand on its own bottom," insofar as is possible. We are ready to put up a certain amount of equity capital for foreign ventures and to provide management and know-how. For the rest of the funds, we like to find financial associates who will put their money along with ours and take the risks along with us. If we undertook to guarantee the debts on all the foreign ventures in which we are engaged, we might soon have a greater exposure than was prudent. Moreover, by limiting our financial obligations in this manner, we can go into more different ventures and spread our activities over a wider field than would otherwise be possible.

The Perils of PASA

One of the most important lessons of the PASA project is a fairly general one. A venture of this kind calls for much more than a sound conceptual basis. A good deal of persistence, drive, and top-management commitment is needed to cope with the full range of problems and difficulties involved in financing and carrying out an industrial project abroad.

The history of PASA has been the history of one "insurmountable" problem after another—obstacles raised by the Argentine government; attacks by competitors; obstacles raised by the U.S. Government; obstacles raised by the sponsors, bankers, or vendors; difficulties with the Argentine and U.S. legal codes; technical, engineering, and patent problems; and, finally, very serious internal political strife in Argentina. Four years elapsed between the conception of the original idea and breaking of ground for plant construction in the fall of 1962, and three more years will pass before the plant is on stream.

We have been particularly impressed with the sensitivity of the U.S. and European capital markets to adverse political developments in Argentina. During the 2½-year period that the PASA financing has been in process, we have witnessed Castro's antics in Cuba, the political upheaval in Brazil, and the ouster of the Frondizi regime in Argentina—not to mention the lesser difficulties in Chile, Peru, and Venezuela. Each of these events has had a significant chilling effect on the investment climate in Latin America and has accentuated our difficulties in holding our financing arrangements together. Reaction to the Castro regime in Cuba is a case in point. Robert L. Garner, retiring president of the International Finance Corporation, estimated in 1961 that at least $500 million of private capital had been held back from investment in Latin America because of events in Cuba.[3]

From our experience with PASA, I am convinced that foreign ventures

[3] Address at the Annual Meeting of the Board of Governors of the International Finance Corporation, Vienna, Austria, September 21, 1961.

of this type require a certain stubbornness of purpose—even bullheadedness, perhaps—on the part of the sponsors. Thus far, we have been able to circumvent or overcome PASA's problems, one by one, simply because a small group of people have become dedicated to the project and are determined not to give it up as long as the *long-run* economic outlook for the venture remains sound.

One of my colleagues has likened PASA to the old-time movies of "The Perils of Pauline," where the heroine got into one horrifying predicament after another from which she was always extricated at the last moment. PASA has been like that. It has been an interesting—but ulcer-producing—kind of experience, and there are still a good many hurdles yet to be cleared in the road ahead. For example, a condition precedent to each successive drawdown of the Class B debentures is that no event shall have occurred and no situation shall exist in Argentina or elsewhere which in the judgment of Chase and Lazard so adversely affects the affairs of PASA as to make it inadvisable for the purchasers to make additional purchases of the debentures.

CONCLUSION

By way of summary and conclusion, I have three points to emphasize.

First, the business managers of this country should welcome the new era of international business which we are now entering. It offers us new challenges and new opportunities, and we should meet them with spirit and enthusiasm. Moreover, I believe that through the development of close and profitable business relationships with the businessmen of other countries, we can do much toward bringing about a better understanding among the peoples and nations of this troubled world.

Second, the commercial and investment banks of this country should develop with all possible dispatch better means of channeling private investment funds into foreign ventures. Whether we like it or not, U.S. investment capital *is* going to go abroad. It is better for it to do so, insofar as possible, through the normal channels of the private financial institutions than through national or multinational monetary agencies.

Third, major plant investments abroad must be viewed as long-run ventures and must be made in the light of long-run considerations. The investor should take it for granted—particularly in the less industrialized countries—that the economic and political winds may from time to time blow against him. He should be prepared to hold to his course as long as the fundamental conditions that prompted him to make his investment decision remain unchanged.

EDGE ACT AND AGREEMENT CORPORATIONS IN INTERNATIONAL BANKING AND FINANCE*

With the steady rise in international trade and investment, United States banks have been expanding their foreign activities. As a consequence, there has been considerable growth in the international departments of United States banks, and the banks have also made increased use of additional possibilities for doing business abroad. Among these possibilities are the so-called Edge Act and Agreement corporations. By now, twenty-three banks and bank holding companies operate a total of thirty-six such subsidiaries.

Edge Act and Agreement corporations are United States corporations carrying out international banking and financing operations, some of which —notably equity investment abroad—the parent banks themselves are not permitted to undertake under existing laws and regulations. The corporations' actual functions range from acting as holding companies to rendering a wide variety of international banking services; and they include also the financing—through term loans and equity participations—of industrial and financial projects in both developed and underdeveloped countries. Furthermore, under strictly prescribed conditions and incidental to their main purpose, the corporations do a limited business in the United States.

BACKGROUND[1]

The origins of Edge Act and Agreement corporations go back almost half a century—to a time when a broader scope for private American financial activity abroad appeared desirable. In 1916, section 25 of the Federal Reserve Act was amended so that any national bank with a capital and surplus of $1

---

* *Monthly Review*, Federal Reserve Bank of New York, May, 1964, pp. 88–92. (George H. Bossy had primary responsibility for the preparation of this article. Edna K. Reynolds and Robert Ritchie provided technical assistance.)

[1] For a fuller description, see F. M. Tamagna and P. B. Willis, "United States Banking Organization Abroad," *Federal Reserve Bulletin*, December 1956, pp. 1284–99; Richard A. Wiley, "Edge Act Corporations—Catalysts for International Trade and Investment," *The Business Lawyer*, XVI, July 1961, pp. 1014–29; and T. M. Farley, *The "Edge Act" and United States International Banking and Finance* (mimeographed) New York: Brown Brothers Harriman & Co., May 1962.

million or more was authorized to invest, singly or jointly, up to 10 percent of its capital and surplus in a corporation chartered under Federal or state law to conduct "international or foreign banking" activities. Each corporation was required to "enter into an agreement" with the Board of Governors of the Federal Reserve System as to the type of activities it would undertake and the manner in which it would conduct its operations. The wording of this provision gave rise to the name Agreement corporation.[2]

As an additional inducement to the expansion of the foreign business of the United States, Congress passed a law in December 1919 (sponsored by Senator Walter E. Edge of New Jersey). This act added section 25 (a) to the Federal Reserve Act, a section that authorized the Board of Governors to charter corporations "for the purpose of engaging in international or foreign banking or other international or foreign financial operations . . . either directly or through the agency, ownership, or control of local institutions in foreign countries." The stock of these corporations, which have come to be called Edge Act corporations, is also eligible for bank ownership. The corporations must be capitalized at a minimum of $2 million.

The activities of Edge Act corporations are thus governed by the Federal Reserve Act, and by the related Regulation K of the Board of Governors which was first issued in 1920 and has since been periodically revised. The primary purpose of the latest revision, effective September 1, 1963, was to enable Edge Act corporations to operate more effectively in financing international trade and commerce.[3]

NUMBER OF EDGE ACT AND AGREEMENT CORPORATIONS*
1956–64

End of Year	Edge Act Corporations	Agreement Corporations	Total
1956	3	4	7
1957	4	3	7
1958	5	3	8
1959	6	3	9
1960	10	5	15
1961	11	5	16
1962	22	4	26
1963	30	5	35
1964 (March)	31	5	36

* Numbers exclude corporations organized but not yet open for business on dates given. There were two such corporations at the end of 1963 and one at the end of March 1964.

[2] Since the Banking Act of 1933, these provisions have been applicable to state member banks of the System as well; and both national and state member banks have, or have had, such corporations. All Agreement corporations have been state chartered.

[3] An authoritative description of the major changes may be found in a Board of Governors press release dated August 23, 1963.

After a short period of moderate operations during roughly the first decade following World War I, Edge Act and Agreement corporations were relatively inactive until the midfifties, although there were a few significant exceptions. Since the late fifties, on the other hand, their number has grown markedly. As shown in the accompanying table, most of this recent growth has been in Edge Act rather than in Agreement corporations.

PRESENT USES AND FUNCTIONS

The uses and functions of Edge Act and Agreement corporations are influenced by two main factors—the scope granted by laws and regulations and the needs of their parent banks. Between January 1957 and September 1963, an Edge Act corporation was required by Regulation K to operate either as a "banking corporation" or as a "financing corporation." While the activities of the two types of corporations could overlap to a modest extent, banking corporations had a much wider range of banking powers than did financing corporations. In particular, they could accept deposits, which financing corporations could not do. On the other hand, the equity investments of banking corporations were limited to the stock of corporations engaged in banking or closely related activities. Financing corporations—which operated solely on the basis of parent bank funds plus retained earnings—were empowered to invest in foreign concerns not engaged in banking (and only in these).

The latest revision of Regulation K eliminates the formal distinction between the two types of corporations and considerably modifies the substantive distinctions. A United States bank thus has now more freedom to have *one* Edge Act subsidiary engage in both banking and financing operations. Nevertheless, there are still certain restrictions. For example, a distinction is drawn in the present regulation on the basis of whether or not a corporation is "engaged in banking" (i.e., has aggregate demand deposits and acceptance liablities exceeding its capital and surplus). If it is, the corporation's commitments to any one person are not permitted to exceed 10 percent of its capital and surplus, whereas the limitation is 50 percent if the corporation is not "engaged in banking." For reasons such as this, and because of the recent date of the latest change in the regulation, the corporations' activities still tend to reflect the prior distinctions. Thus, of the total of thirty-one Edge Act corporations active as of March 31, 1964 (as shown in the table), fourteen would previously have been considered banking corporations and seventeen financing corporations. This background, together with the availability of the Agreement corporation device, accounts for the fact that a number of banks have several subsidiaries. (Agreement corporations are limited to the powers exercised by Edge Act corporations engaged in banking.)

In terms of a rough distinction between the former banking and the former financing corporations, those active in banking either do a variety of business typical of that of the international department of a commercial bank or function as holding companies for equity investments in foreign banks. In some cases, they fulfill both functions. The former financing corporations have tended to operate in a different area, with investments in the stock of nonbank financial concerns, development corporations, or commercial and industrial firms.

Edge Act corporations have, for example, enabled banks with head offices outside New York City to operate in that key location for foreign banking operations (since an Edge Act corporation does not have to be established in the same city as the owning institution). Such a corporation may, for instance, hold demand and time (but not savings) deposits of foreign parties; issue or confirm letters of credit; finance foreign trade by extending loans and advances, by creating bankers' acceptances, or by making other credit facilities available; receive items for collection and offer other services to customers, such as remitting funds abroad, purchasing and selling securities, or holding securities for safekeeping; issue certain guarantees; act as paying agent for securities issued by foreign governments and certain foreign corporations; and engage in both spot and forward foreign exchange transactions.

In their capacity as holding companies, Edge Act corporations can own the stocks of foreign banking subsidiaries and affiliates (which member banks cannot own directly). This fact accounts for the existence of a number of Edge Act corporations (and of several Agreement corporations, which can serve the same purpose). A foreign banking subsidiary may be more advantageous than a branch, or it may actually be a necessity for doing business in a given country. Certain countries—e.g., the Union of South Africa—prohibit nondomestic banks from opening branches in their territory. A United States bank wishing to operate in such a country can do so by establishing a subsidiary, the stock of which would, however, have to be held through an Edge Act or Agreement corporation. In other instances— Brazil, Italy, and Liberia—such corporations have been the channel through which United States banks have acquired an interest in well-known foreign banks.[4]

Edge Act corporations have also been the instrument through which, as previously noted, United States banks have acquired equity interests in foreign nonbanking concerns.[5] Such investments, to be sure, are subject to prior specific consent of the Board of Governors under certain circumstances

---

[4] Edge Act corporations themselves may also establish branches or agencies abroad, although prior approval of the Board of Governors is required for the establishment of the first branch or agency in a particular foreign country.

[5] Since September 1963, of course, *all* Edge Act corporations have been permitted to hold both banking and nonbanking equity investments.

—as is the acquisition of stock in foreign banks.[6] Furthermore, such equity investments are only a fraction of the total assets of all Edge Act corporations, albeit a significant one of those formerly considered financing corporations. At any rate, equity investments in nonbanking concerns, and the combination of loans and equity acquisitions in "packages," give the activities of a number of Edge Act corporations a distinct characteristic, well worth exploring in some detail. The remainder of this article is therefore devoted primarily to the portfolio management of Edge Act corporations in those cases in which they go beyond short-term commercial banking and holding company functions. (This covers mainly the former financing corporations but also includes a number of the former banking corporations. Agreement corporations are at present mainly used as holding companies for foreign subsidiaries and affiliates.)

FINANCING THROUGH EDGE ACT CORPORATIONS

Recipients of Financing

Two broad classes of nonbank borrowers from Edge Act corporations may be distinguished—specialized foreign financial institutions, and commercial and industrial firms. As regards foreign financial intermediaries, Edge Act corporations have in numerous instances helped in the financing of foreign official or semiofficial development corporations through purchases of shares. These institutions, as the Edge Act corporations often do themselves, help finance slowly maturing enterprises in their early stages. By channeling funds to development institutions, an Edge Act corporation can avoid the detailed studies and investigations that might render small investments unprofitable. Edge Act corporations have also participated in foreign finance companies. Such companies may, for instance, be engaged in the financing of private purchases of consumer durable goods, including some manufactured in the United States. In a few cases, the portfolios of Edge Act corporations also include investments in the stock of foreign securities underwriters.

[6] Specific consent is *not* required when the stock acquisition (a) is incidental to an extension of credit to the foreign corporation (in making loans to foreign enterprises, Edge Act corporations frequently acquire an equity participation) ; (b) consists of shares in a foreign bank, but does not bring the Edge Act corporation's holdings of the voting stock of the foreign bank to or above 25 percent; or (c) is "likely to further the development of United States foreign commerce," provided the purchase of the stock of any one foreign corporation does not exceed $200,000.

It should also be noted that Edge Act corporations, like all United States investors, would of course be subject to the proposed interest equalization tax on purchases of securities issued by foreign borrowers in developed countries. (This tax, proposed by the Administration in July 1963, has been passed in the House of Representatives but is still to be considered by the Senate.)

In most instances, however, Edge Act corporations finance foreign commercial and industrial borrowers directly through loans and equity participations. While such financings do not normally involve the acquisition of control, the Edge Act corporation is seldom a passive partner. The primary purpose typically is to supply capital to promising foreign enterprises at an early or other important stage. Thus, the Edge Act corporation may be dealing with a newly launched business or with a firm planning, or engaged in, a major expansion, modernization, or reorganization. Negotiating and carrying through such ventures call for ingenuity and enterprise.

Industrial and Geographical Distribution

The loans and equity investments of Edge Act corporations cover a broad spectrum—manufacturing, mining, and service industries; and, while the financing of public utilities is rare, there is one instance of a gas pipeline interest of an Edge Act corporation. Manufacturing industries are perhaps the most frequent borrowers, but a certain specialization within that broad category can be detected. Thus, Edge Act corporation financing, at least in the less developed countries, is often directed toward manufacturing enterprises that process a country's resources of primary materials—concrete products from cement, chemicals based on oil, paper mills, cotton textile mills, and even steel mills where there is coal and iron ore.

Edge Act corporations appear to have no particular preference with regard to the geographical distribution of their porfolios. They will, of course, be deterred from financing in countries considered politically unstable, or those in which attitudes and policies are inimical to foreign investment. Apart from such obvious considerations, however, the location of loans and investments appears to be chosen only on the basis of business criteria. In terms of the value of equity investments alone, the portfolios of Edge Act and Agreement corporations at present appear to be distributed roughly as follows: Europe, about 40 percent; Latin America, approximately 20 percent; Canada, almost 20 percent; Africa, about 10 percent. The Far East accounts for almost one half of the remainder.

Initiating an Operation

Financing decisions of Edge Act corporations call for special skills in appraising not only technical matters but also the "human element" in the foreign business and political environment. Since in many cases it would be difficult—for lack of a market—to pull out should the project not be giving satisfactory results, the initial investigation and evaluation must be thorough.

The project is almost invariably initiated abroad, with the foreign concern in need of capital making contact with the Edge Act corporation or

—more frequently—its parent bank. The initial proposal usually contains a fairly detailed description of the project, supported by documentation. Further data may be requested from the foreign party as the Edge Act corporation begins to look more closely into the proposal, and the officers of the Edge Act corporation or the parent bank may go abroad for personal study and negotiation. On the strictly technical side, the degree of reliance on the studies of the foreign applicant may be heavy in the case of well-established foreign firms.

The investor, as already suggested, will wish to find out a good deal about the foreign company's financial structure, management and organization, indebtedness, past history, the market outlook for its products, and its competitive position. This may well lead into studies of the host country's economy, growth, and policies, which in turn may necessitate some study of international trade and finance as they affect that country. All of these efforts are designed, of course, to add up to an informed appraisal of risks and earning prospects, which in turn becomes the basis for a firm decision.

SIZE OF FINANCING.   Once the soundness and potential profitability of the project have been established, a decision is required on the size and type of a commitment and on possible partnership arrangements. The decision will vary not only from one project to the next, but also according to the role of the Edge Act corporation within the banking organization to which it belongs. On the whole, the minimum size of an individual financing that might interest on Edge Act corporation is smaller if the parent bank has a large network of foreign branches and representatives. For a bank without local representation, the costs of study and evaluation can be high and therefore worthwhile only for a relatively large potential financing. As regards the maximum size of an individual operation, one limitation—previously noted—is that an Edge Act corporation's commitments to any one party cannot exceed 50 percent of its capital and surplus (10 percent if engaged in banking). The size of such capital and surplus in turn reflects parent bank policy.

Most Edge Act corporations probably will not normally consider requests involving less than $100,000, and some even place the preferred lower limit as high as $1 million. But actual commitments have occasionally fallen well below these minimum levels, and they frequently range upward into several millions.

PERIOD OF FINANCING.   Edge Act corporations tend to extend loans over a broad range of short and intermediate maturities. As to equity investments, the corporations usually seek to disengage themselves within five to ten years. The size of an Edge Act corporation is a factor in the maturity structure of its portfolio. Most such corporations naturally consider their capital as a revolving fund—new investments being made with the proceeds of the liquidation of previous ones. The larger corporations tend to make somewhat longer loans than the smaller ones, because their more numerous and bigger commitments generate larger return flows from which frequent new financings can be undertaken. Smaller corporations prefer to restrict their time horizon to shorter periods in order to avoid situations in which they might be out of the new-project business—unless, or course, the parent bank injects new capital.

In liquidating equity holdings, Edge Act corporations frequently avail themselves of prenegotiated resale agreements (discussed later). In some instances, the foreign partners make efforts to develop a local market for such securities.

REMUNERATION. The negotiation of the amount and form of its remuneration tends to be an intricate operation for an Edge Act corporation, since the circumstances of individual financings tend to differ widely. Equity participations frequently are a method of compensating for risks exceeding those ordinarily taken on loans. (Sometimes an Edge Act Corporation makes an equity investment while the parent bank grants a loan.) When both a loan and an equity investment are involved, the potential returns from the financing will typically be appraised as a whole rather than separately. For example, relatively low interest on the loan portion can be offset to some extent by a higher equity interest for the Edge Act corporation. Besides the possible dividend income, the equity portion of the investment may, of course, result in a capital gain—often a very important consideration. Should no present or foreseeable market for the shares exist—as is true in many instances—the Edge Act corporation may enter into an agreement with the firm's local shareholders for the sale at predetermined future dates of its holdings to them. The sale price is determined according to any of a number of formulas, which usually contain a provision for ascending values of the shares.

The Edge Act corporation often receives some additional shares or cash as a bonus to compensate it for the efforts expended in bringing together various partners—including technical assistance and third-party capital—in an enterprise it helps to finance. The work done in initiating and negotiating such partnerships frequently entails the devising of an intricate financial structure.

ASSOCIATES IN FINANCING. Most Edge Act corporations consider local partnership of the highest importance and often believe it advisable that the local partners hold majority control. Technical management, on the other hand, is frequently supplied from abroad.

With the exception of investments in subsidiaries, Edge Act corporations are unlikely to be the sole or principal capital-supplying partner in large projects. Other private United States or foreign investors, as well as United States or international government lending agencies, are frequent participants. Such mixed investments are often made in conjunction with the International

Finance Corporation (IFC)—a 76-member subsidiary of the International Bank for Reconstruction and Development (World Bank). The IFC is authorized both to grant loans and to make equity investments in private enterprises located in developing areas, and thus undertakes operations frequently quite similar to those of Edge Act corporations. To date, most of the investments made jointly by Edge Act corporations and the IFC have been in the fastgrowing field of development corporations. In a recent financing, for instance, the Private Development Corporation of the Philippines sold shares totaling $6 million equivalent to the IFC, to ten Edge Act corporations and one Agreement corporation, to three other United States private investors, and to four banks in other countries; in addition, the Philippine institution received loans from the World Bank and the Agency for International Development (AID) of $15 million and $7 million, respectively.

The participation of a governmental agency, however, does not entail a guarantee of the Edge Act corporation's investment. If such a guarantee is desired, the Edge Act corporation may apply to the AID. The AID has an insurance program for new private United States investments in underdeveloped countries that covers three types of risks: inconvertibility, expropriation, and damages due to war or civil disturbances. Edge Act corporations are steady users of this facility.

OUTLOOK

Edge Act corporations, as has been shown, are a highly adaptable instrument of international finance and enhance the range of activity of United States commercial banks. An intensified use of such corporations therefore may be expected whenever the general conditions for expanded international trade and financial operations are favorable. This was the case in the early 1920's when Edge Act and Agreement corporations first blossomed. It has been the case again since the late fifties following the end of the postwar reconstruction period and the relaxation of exchange controls. In order to participate fully in the recent growth of international commerce and investment, United States banks "rediscovered" the Edge Act instrument.

A substantial further increase in Edge Act (and possibly also in Agreement) corporation activites may thus, in a broad sense, depend upon the future growth of international trade and investment. Currently, of course, economic transactions among the industrialized countries are continuing to rise. Furthermore, quite a few newly emerging nations are seeking to avail themselves of the managerial and financial capabilities of the industrialized countries through private as well as through public channels. There is a distinct possibility, therefore, of a continued rise in the activities of Edge Act corporations and hence in their role in United States Foreign economic relations.

THE AID GUARANTY PROGRAM*

There are few, if any, Government programs in which the policy aims of the United States and the interests of the international business community are served better, and at less expense to the taxpayer, than the investment guaranty program of the Agency for International Development (AID).

The purpose of the guaranty program is to encourage the movement of private U.S. capital and know-how into the less developed countries by insuring investors against *political* losses from specific *political* risks, and in the case of high-risk investments especially important to the development of the host country, against all *business* risks as well. The guaranties are backed by the full faith and credit of the United States.

Since the program began 17 years ago, AID has issued over 1,250 guaranty policies totaling more than $2.2 billion to insure private U.S. investment overseas against the specific political risks of inconvertibility, expropriation, and war, revolution, and insurrection. Almost $1.8 billion of this is currently outstanding. (AID has collected $21 million in fees for these guaranties and paid out only $70,000 in claims. Even this small amount, paid on convertibility guaranties, gave the U.S. Government title to the blocked foreign currencies, which were later sold at a profit.) The extended risk program, which guaranties against both political and business risks, is relatively recent, and investors have had little experience with it as yet.

ELIGIBILITY AND AVAILABILITY

The criteria for eligibility are as follows: (1) The investor must be a U.S. citizen, or a U.S. corporation that is at least 51 percent U.S.-owned, or a wholly owned subsidiary of such a corporation. (2) The investment must be in a new project, which may include the expansion or diversification of an existing enterprise. AID will not entertain an application for a guaranty after the investment has been made or an irrevocable commitment to invest has been given. (3) The application must have the specific written approval of the host government. (4) The investment must be one that promotes trade, contributes to economic development, increases production, raises standards of living, or improves technical efficiency in the host country, and that does *not*

* *The Irving International Letter*, Irving Trust Company, New York, March, 1965.

have a significantly adverse effect on the United States. (5) The investment—except for those in housing—must be in countries that have signed agreements with the United States (*see* Table I).

At present, 64 developing countries, plus the underdeveloped overseas dependencies of Denmark, France, the Netherlands, Norway, and the U.K. participate in the program. Brazil signed an investment guaranty agreement only last month. National pride, however, has kept a few developing countries out of the program. Agreeing to participate would imply, in their eyes, that private foreign investments in their countries *need* protection.

TABLE 1

WHERE AID GUARANTIES ARE AVAILABLE

Against Inconvertibility & Expropriation	Against War Risk	Against Extended Risk	Against Inconvertibility & Expropriation	Against War Risk	Against Extended Risk
Afghanistan	*		Liberia	*	*
Argentina	*	*	Malagasy, Republic of	*	*
Bolivia	*	*	Malaysia, Fed. of		
Brazil *	*	*	Mali	*	*
Central African Republic	*	*	Mauritania	*	*
Chile	*	*	Morocco	*	
China, Republic of	*	*	Nepal	*	*
Colombia	*	*	Nicaragua	*	
Congo (Brazzaville)	*	*	Niger	*	
Congo (Leopoldville)	*	*	Nigeria		
Costa Rica			Pakistan		
Cyprus	*	*	Panama	*	
Dominican Republic	*	*	Paraguay		
Ecuador	*	*	Peru †		
El Salvador			Philippines		
Ethiopia			Portugal		
Gabon	*	*	Senegal	*	*
Ghana			Sierra Leone	*	*
Greece	*	*	Somali Republic	*	*
Guatemala			Spain		
Guinea	*	*	Sudan	*	*
Haiti			Tanganyika	*	*
Honduras			Thailand	*	
India			Togo	*	*
Iran			Trinidad–Tobago	*	
Israel	*	*	Tunisia	*	*
Ivory Coast	*	*	Turkey		
Jamaica	*	*	U. A. R. (Egypt)		*
Jordan	*	*	Uruguay *		
Kenya	*	*	Venezuela	*	*
Korea	*		Vietnam	*	*
Laos	*	*	Yugoslavia ‡		

Convertibility and expropriation guaranties are also available for underdeveloped overseas dependencies of Denmark, France, Netherlands, Norway, and, for convertibility only, of the United Kingdom.

*   Agreement not yet ratified.
†   Expropriation risk not covered.
‡   Limited applicability.

The size of the investor and the amount of capital required by the project are not major considerations. There is no maximum or minimum dollar amount for individual contracts: AID has signed guaranty contracts for as little as $1,000, while others have run to tens of millions of dollars. Almost every corporation, large or small, that has invested in underdeveloped countries in recent years has taken out guaranties for some investments.

The investment may be made in cash, provided it is in dollars or another convertible currency, or it may be in the form of machinery, services, patents, processes, or techniques. The investment may be an equity investment or a loan. Even royalties and fees to be paid under a licensing agreement may be insured.

SPECIFIC-RISK GUARANTIES

Inconvertibility

In the event remittance of earnings or repatriation of capital is blocked or made too costly by the host government, the inconvertibility guaranty assures the investor that he may secure 95 percent of the U.S. dollars that he would have obtained in exchange for local currency at the exchange rate current at the time he attempted the transaction. It does not protect him against the effects of devaluation.

Expropriation

This guaranty covers losses from straightforward nationalization and may in certain cases include breach of contract by a foreign government, unsatisfactory compensation for a lawful expropriation, or such measures as excessive taxation or regulation that may effectively destroy the value of an investment.

War, Revolution, and Insurrection

This guaranty covers destruction of or damage to tangible property resulting from hostile acts by national or international organized forces. Tangible property for the purpose of this coverage does not include accounting books, deeds, securities, money, and similar valuable property which a company could lose in war.

Fees are the same for all countries. For each of the three risks covered, AID charges 0.5 percent per annum on the "current amount" of investment that the investor wishes to cover, and a standby fee of 0.25 percent on the "standby amount"—the maximum amount to be covered by the contract minus the "current amount." The maximum coverage for inconvertibility or expropriation on an equity investment is 200 percent. This allows coverage of a reasonable portion of retained earnings. The maximum coverage on a loan can be the total value of principal plus total interest payable over the life of the loan in the case of an expropriation or inconvertibility guaranty. Coverage of war risk is 100 percent of the depreciated value of the investor's share in tangible property.

Guaranties are transferable, with the consent of AID, if the investment is sold to an eligible party. They are limited to 20 years and cannot be renewed. Contracts may be terminated by the guarantied party at any time.

AID's procedures in administering the specific-risk program have been greatly improved in recent months. It is now in the position of having to wait for 90 percent of current applicants to take the next step in the procedure that leads to a signed contract. During the third quarter last year, for example, six times as many contracts were mailed as in the same period in 1963.

EXTENDED-RISK GUARANTIES

The extended-risk program of AID was designed principally to interest banks and investment institutions in high-priority projects in underdeveloped countries where a high degree of risk is involved. It can also cover a manufacturer's investment in such a project. AID has authority to insure up to 75 percent of such investments against all risks except fraud or misconduct on the part of the investor.

After a thorough review of the program, AID issued a new policy paper last December which indicates that it will use it more flexibly and aggressively in the future. In most cases, AID will offer prompt payment upon default, as opposed to the previous policy of payment after one year. It is prepared to have its guaranty apply 100 percent to later maturities, with the 25 percent risk borne by the investor concentrated in the early maturities. This 25 percent can be insured against the specific political risks under the specific-risk program.

The cost of an extended-risk policy has been reduced from 2 percent to 1.75 percent per annum. The maximum coverage for a single contract is $25 million. Congress has authorized $300 million for this type of guaranty, and the Administration has asked for additional authority.

To encourage social improvement and housing industries in developing countries, Congress has also authorized an extended-risk housing guaranty program. This guaranty protects home mortgage loans made by private U.S. institutional lenders to demonstration housing projects. It covers up to 90 percent of the loan plus accrued interest, with the assurance of prompt payment in the event of default. A number of U.S. insurance companies, banks, and pension funds have insured housing loans in this way. The program has been aggressively used in Latin America as an important feature of the Alliance for Progress—so much so, that AID suspended accepting new applications in May of last year, when it had received more than enough to use up its $250-million allocation of funds. Smaller amounts are still available for housing projects in Africa and Asia, and applications are welcome.

EFFECTIVENESS OF PROGRAM

Would there be substantially less U.S. private investment today in the developing countries if these guaranties were not offered? Probably, if only because the participating countries have to sign prior agreements with the U.S. Government, and hence are more likely to respect the rights of U.S. investors. The way the program has picked up steam, and the rate at which new applications have been pouring in—about $5-billion worth are pending—give ample evidence that the business community finds the guaranties particularly helpful.

Expropriation in Cuba and elsewhere in the developing world account for this recent interest. Guaranties were available for Cuba before Castro took over, but no U.S. companies had insured themselves there, or they had made their investments before the program came into effect. Investors are being more cautious now, and are seeking to cover most of their new capital outlays in developing countries wherever the coverage is available. If another Cuban situation should occur tomorrow in an important country, AID would be faced with a very large bill, and might have to go to Congress for an appropriation to supplement its $250-million reserve fund. This is why AID, sometimes criticized for showing a profit in its guaranty program, has steadfastly refused to lower its fees for specific-risk coverage.

The AID investment guaranty program has been a success by whatever standards one uses. It has encouraged a significant flow of new private investment to the developing countries. With the streamlined administration of the specific-risk program and the recent major changes in the extended-risk program, it should be even more useful to companies investing in these countries in the future.

INTERNATIONAL FINANCE CORPORATION*

The International Finance Corporation (IFC) is another *international* investment institution. It is an offshoot and close affiliate of the World Bank, having been organized by members of the Bank in 1956 primarily to finance private enterprise in developing countries. A need for IFC arose because the World Bank's pattern of financing—hard currency, fixed-interest loans requiring a government guaranty—was often unsuitable for new or expanding private enterprises in these areas. Accordingly, the Corporation's precepts and policies are designed to permit financing on more flexible terms and without a government guaranty.

IFC financing generally takes the form of investment in capital shares, sometimes in combination with a direct loan, or with loans which have equity or other special features. A primary objective of the Corporation is to attract other investment funds into ventures in which it has an interest. Accordingly, it helps investors find additional sources of financial and industrial capital, including local funds.

Under certain conditions U.S. capital goods firms may desire IFC participation when they invest in manufacturing or assembling facilities overseas. IFC's participation can be particularly useful for firms relatively inexperienced in overseas operations. The Corporation is highly respected in many countries and its investment in an enterprise may often encourage experienced private investors doing business in the region to join the less experienced firm, contributing management know-how as well as capital to the venture.

There may be occasions when a capital goods supplier is aware that his sales are financed by IFC money and he may, in fact, be in touch with an enterprise from the early stages of a particular IFC-financed project. However, suppliers cannot rely upon public announcements concerning IFC investments in seeking out sales opportunities. Typically the source of supply has been determined before an investment is announced. It is the responsibility of the management of the enterprise in question to assure, among other things, that equipment of adequate quality is available on competitive terms. Since IFC normally wishes to be assured in this and other matters before proceeding with an investment, it follows that

*Excerpted from *Financing U.S. Exports and Overseas Investment*, Machinery and Allied Products Institute, Washington, 1964.

the equipment to be purchased, including its source, is typically decided upon by the time the investment becomes generally known.

At present IFC invests mostly in industrial projects whose products are important to the economic development of the country in which the project is located. To qualify for IFC investments, a country must be an IFC member or overseas territory of a member, and also normally must be a so-called developing area (see below). The Corporation's investments have ranged from some $300,000 to around $4 million in firms with capital of at least $500,000 after financing. The average investment is $1.25 million. The Corporation's present authorized capital is $110 million. It made 11 commitments totaling $18 million for the financing of private enterprises in 10 countries in fiscal 1963. IFC financing does not represent more than one-half of an enterprise's capital.

POLICIES

Position in the International Financial Field

IFC acts as a catalyst, attempting to introduce sound industrial investment opportunities to financial and industrial investors who provide the managerial talent necessary. IFC does not infringe upon private financial institutions fulfilling a comparable role. It will take part in the financing only when other funds cannot be found in sufficient amount and on acceptable terms, or when its participation is necessary to bring in other investors. Also IFC does not undertake management responsibilities in the enterprises in which it invests nor does it take up directorships except in the case of industrial finance companies.

Although the Corporation makes long-term investments, it expects to sell them when the enterprise matures and they become attractive to private investors. This practice enables IFC to assist more ventures than would be possible if it held certain investments over the long run to maximize its profits. Nevertheless, IFC strives to make a good return on each of its investments in order to maintain its capital, offset any losses, and build a reputation as a sound and successful investor.

Eligibility of Investment Proposals

DEVELOPING AREAS. IFC as a practical matter almost always invests in the developing areas of its member countries and their territories. Projects in the United States, Canada, Japan, and Western Europe—except for Greece, Austria, Ireland, Finland, and the southern part of Italy—are rarely considered. In the developing areas of the free world, Australia and all

Latin American countries except Uruguay and Cuba are members.[1] Most Asian and African countries are either members or overseas territories of European members of IFC.

TYPES OF PROJECTS. At present IFC considers industrial projects and development finance companies as the proper outlets for its limited capital. Accordingly, it will not invest in hospitals, housing, hotels, etc., or in facilities for luxury products or services. Even when private capital has been involved, the Corporation has not invested in projects such as agricultural development, or transportation and communication facilities. It will, however, finance agriculture as a peripheral activity to an industrial enterprise. For example, a sugar mill could grow its sugar and a pulp and paper manufacturer could have timber reserves.

With respect to mining, IFC will not finance exploration although it would consider a mining venture where reserves are proven and reasonably well blocked out, and the qualities of the ore have been determined.

USE OF FUNDS. IFC will invest in new enterprises or in the expansion or modernization of existing firms. It requires that its financing represent a net addition to investment since it will not engage in refinancing or in replacing existing investment. Otherwise, IFC funds may be used for any purpose, including permanent working capital.

SPONSORS. An investment proposal may be brought to IFC by local investors in eligible countries, corporations in capital exporting countries interested in investing in a developing country, or by the government of a developing country interested in finding private capital to undertake a specific industrial project. While sponsors can be nationals of a nonmember country, a project to be eligible must be proposed for a member country or territory.

When an enterprise is partly owned by a government, IFC may invest in it provided the enterprise is still fundamentally private in character. In addition, IFC generally avoids investment in holding companies although it is willing to participate with them in investing directly in one of their industrial enterprises.

Finally, it should be noted that IFC will, in an appropriate situation, provide equity financing to an enterprise in conjunction with financing from other agencies such as Eximbank, AID, the World Bank, and private financing institutions. Its investments in development finance companies are typically accompanied by loans from the World Bank.

SIZE OF INVESTMENTS. Ordinarily, IFC is not prepared to make investments of less than $300,000, or to invest in projects with capital of less

---

[1] Cuba withdrew from membership in 1960.

than $500,000 after financing. Besides the relatively high expense of administering numerous investments in small projects, such firms rarely attract the type of outside investment IFC seeks to encourage. On the other hand, IFC has no maximum for its investments, although to date the most invested in a single enterprise is slightly more than $4 million.

Operating Policies

Before investing in an enterprise IFC investigates a proposal thoroughly. While this is obviously necessary in order to invest prudently, the practice has two important side benefits. It enables IFC to evaluate an investment proposal for its sponsors, often to point out flaws or deficiencies in their plans, and to assist them, where appropriate, in solving the problems which are discovered. Secondly, other investors can be induced to invest on the strength of IFC's investigation and participation.

In evaluating a proposal for investment, IFC considers the same factors which concern private investors. Among other things, it investigates the sponsors of the project; determines the qualifications of the management; reviews studies of markets, costs, profit estimates, and technical feasibility; and checks on the availability of materials as well as transportation and other service facilities. Capital cost estimates in particular are closely scrutinized since there is a tendency to underestimate such requirements.

PROJECT INVESTIGATION. Where possible, IFC relies on its own personnel to investigate proposed projects. Often, however, outside consultants are needed, and the cost of their fees is shared with the enterprise provided IFC makes an investment offer. Only when IFC rejects a proposal does it absorb all of these costs. Auditing and local attorney fees are borne by the enterprise.

Not all projects proposed to IFC receive its thorough investigation at once. This practice would be too costly, considering the many proposals which lack adequate documentation. While IFC may be able to indicate the eligibility of such projects, it cannot decide on their merit until additional data are made available and details worked out.

MANAGEMENT OF AN ENTERPRISE. Since IFC will not participate in the management of firms in which it invests, it makes certain that these firms have good general and technical management personnel. If they do not, IFC may try to help in finding satisfactory management in the form of an industrial partner (see page 741).

LOCAL AND FOREIGN INTERESTS. Where foreign sponsors are involved, IFC prefers investments that include local interests. In these situations,

IFC looks to the foreign investor to contribute foreign exchange, in dustrial experience, technical know-how, and perhaps even broad international commercial experience. Local interests create goodwill towards an enterprise in its community and can help solve many marketing and legal problems. Also the fact that there are local shareholders tends to reduce the likelihood of political and press attacks on the profits of foreign-controlled firms.

GUARANTIES. IFC does not seek a government or parent-company guaranty for any of the business risks it assumes when it invests.

TARIFF PROTECTION. In selecting projects, IFC avoids enterprises that will rely on excessive tariffs or import quota restrictions. Although it feels that reasonable protection is warranted for new industries, it believes extreme protective measures can leave an enterprise competitively vulnerable should such measures be reduced or eliminated. Tax incentives are preferred to protection.

TERMS OF INVESTMENT

Until September 1961 IFC was prohibited from making equity investments. In order to live with this prohibition and still make IFC's holdings sufficiently attractive to be marketable at a later date, the Corporation normally required, in addition to fixed-interest loans, some additional income related to profits, or a long-term option on the stock of the enterprise, or both. Even with these equity characteristics, however, IFC often found it difficult to use its capital efficiently and to attract adequate private capital in accordance with its objectives.[2]

An amendment to the charter of the Corporation granting authority to make equity investments was ratified by the requisite number of member countries and became effective in September. It was stipulated in the amendment that the Corporation "shall not assume responsibility for managing any enterprise in which it has invested and shall not exercise voting rights for such purpose or for any other purpose which, in its opinion, properly is within the scope of managerial control." IFC can vote its stock in the event of bankruptcy or a change in the capital structure or any other matter that involves the protection of its basic security.

IFC's financing is tailored to suit the individual case. It now typically takes the form of investment in capital shares, sometimes in combi-

[2] For a detailed statement of the IFC position on this matter, see "International Finance Corporation," Hearing before the Committee on Foreign Relations, United States Senate, July 31, 1961.

nation with a direct loan, or with loans which have equity or other special features. The Corporation is also now able to underwrite capital shares. IFC commitments to purchase new stock issues pending their sale to the public and assistance in their distribution should facilitate the development of capital markets in the underdeveloped countries.

IFC naturally insists upon a good capital structure. While it has pointed out that there can be no set formula in terms of the debt-equity ratio, a review of investments to date shows that equity has exceeded 50 percent of total capital in most (although not all) cases. Also IFC will not contribute more than half of an enterprise's capital. Where IFC is financing the expansion or modernization of an enterprise, it may provide more than one-half of the capital to be supplied for that purpose, but its total investment will not represent more than one-half of the enterprise's total capital, and, in fact, the Corporation prefers to invest as little as possible itself. IFC investments average about one dollar for every three and one-half contributed by private investors.

Provisions

REPAYMENT TERMS. The loan portion of an IFC investment characteristically is long term with final maturities ranging from about 7 to 15 years. In many cases IFC loans are for longer terms than can be obtained from private sources.

It is IFC's general practice to take unsecured obligations which frequently have lowest priority among the enterprise's debt issues. In addition, amortization and interest payments typically do not begin until a few years after the loan is made. This moratorium helps new enterprises begin their operations on a profitable basis.

INTEREST, PROFIT PARTICIPATION, AND DIVIDENDS. Where direct loans are made, interest is at a moderate fixed rate, usually 6 or 7 percent, although rates charged have been as high as 10 percent. To supplement its interest income on loans and to make its securities more marketable, IFC has in the past sought an arrangement by which it realized additional earnings when the enterprise became profitable. The arrangement has been normally either an additional interest charge contingent upon a certain level of earnings, or an option on shares of capital stock. Formerly, not being able to hold capital stock, IFC had to sell equity options and convertible debentures in order to realize the gain on these assets. Now, however, it can exercise the option and then sell the stock acquired.

IFC loans usually are expressed in United States dollars, and amortization and fixed-interest payments are also normally in dollars. However, IFC's profit-sharing income typically has been in the currency earned by the enterprise. IFC's equity investments are denominated in the currency of the country where the venture is situated and dividends are, of course, paid in the local currency.

DISBURSEMENT AND COMMITMENT FEE.   Once a loan agreement is signed the borrower may have the funds as he wishes, either in a lump sum or according to the schedule of his choosing. However, IFC charges a commitment fee of 1 percent per annum on the undisbursed portion of an investment.

OTHER CURRENCY.   While its capital is in dollars, IFC is prepared to accept repayment partly in local currency provided the currency is relatively stable and the investment terms compensate for the additional risk.

RIGHT OF FIRST REFUSAL.   When making an investment IFC usually gives the sponsors of the enterprise a right of first refusal to purchase all or part of IFC's interest in the enterprise. Moreover, IFC will not sell out to parties to whom its investment partners could properly object on business grounds.

PROGRESS REPORTS AND AUDITS.   IFC requires certain progress reports, generally quarterly, and the right to consult the management on policies and practices of mutual interest. In addition, IFC requires a periodic audit in acceptable form by qualified public accountants, and expects to receive a report on the results of their examination.

OPPORTUNITIES FOR U.S. CAPITAL GOODS MANUFACTURERS

IFC investments in less developed countries can be of assistance to U.S. capital goods manufacturers for a variety of operations in those areas. The possibilities in this regard encompass IFC investment in manufacturing subsidiaries abroad (including joint venture enterprises), in foreign licensees, and in local customers. The latter may be purchasers of engineering and technical services as well as equipment. The discussion and illustrative examples below expand on these possibilities.

Investment Opportunities

LOCATING MANUFACTURING FACILITIES OVERSEAS.   As noted earlier, IFC participation can at times bridge the gap of inexperience for a U.S. firm locating manufacturing facilities in a developing country. The Corporation's position in the international field facilitates its dealing with local nationals and their institutions; its advising on local laws, regulations, and customs relating to investment and to commerce; and, often of most importance, its finding local investors to participate in an enterprise.

Some investors seek IFC participation in an enterprise believing that there are intangible benefits to be gained. These are largely in the form of better treatment from the host government and from public authorities responsible for import licenses, currency exchange, etc. While there is some validity in such opinions, IFC does not seek any preferential treatment.

INDUSTRIAL PARTNERSHIP. When local investors sponsor an industrial project, IFC may suggest that they select an industrial partner experienced in that industry to assist them in the technology and in training local personnel. In fact, IFC insists on an industrial partner whenever it feels that local enterprise lacks adequate specific industrial experience and technical know-how for the product it proposes to manufacture. To help local investors find a partner, IFC suggests a number of eligible firms—European and Japanese as well as U.S.—but leaves the investors with the choices of whom to contact and what arrangements to make. Any American company considering a joint venture in a particular area of the world may write IFC providing information as to its interests, its product, and its general qualifications. If it meets what are felt to be necessary qualifications, it will be added to a list of eligible firms.

Industrial partnership usually involves an investment, although a technical assistance agreement alone is possible. The role of an industrial partner is illustrated in the case of a $14.5 million synthetic nitrogenous fertilizer plant in Peru sponsored by several groups of Peruvian business interests. IFC made an original investment commitment of approximately $4 million. The industrial partner is a large well-known Italian chemical and metals company. In connection with its minority interest, the Italian firm handled the design, equipment procurement and installation, layout, and break-in of the plant; is training Peruvian employees in its operation; and has assumed the responsibility of running the plant for several years. The top management of the fertilizer company are Peruvians with the exception of the plant management. The Italian company, however, has the controlling voice on the board of directors for the first few years.

Sales of Capital Goods

In arranging credit for an overseas purchaser of capital equipment, a U.S. manufacturer naturally thinks of the Export-Import Bank. In certain situations he might consider IFC too, although IFC does not finance export sales as such. As noted, it is an investment institution which assists firms on a long-term venture capital basis. Nevertheless, this very approach can be more useful to a purchaser whose enterprise is more in need of long-term capital than medium-term equipment financing. Moreover, if the exporter can instigate IFC financing for his customer without participating in the investment himself, he avoids the Export-Import Bank's participation requirement on exporter credits. Finally, the exporter may find in certain circumstances that loan capital will not be made available to a prospective customer company because of an excessively high debt-equity ratio. In such cases IFC equity financing, in lowering the ratio, may overcome this objection.

Before financing will be made available, however, the enterprise must of course appeal to IFC as a worthwhile investment opportunity. In addition, IFC will require sound management plus technical know-how and industrial experience in the specific operations planned. It should also be noted that IFC seeks firm commitments to assist the enterprise in breaking in its operations and training personnel.

Some firms seek to keep themselves informed concerning financing extended to foreign enterprises or governments with a view to placing bids where equipment of their own type is in demand. While this procedure may be useful in the case of AID and certain other agencies, this is not normally the case with IFC loans. Typically, by the time a particular IFC investment is publicly announced the sources of supply have already been arranged. This stems from the fact that the agreement is usually not finally consummated until IFC is satisfied with the conditions under which the financing is to be made available and this includes approval of the quality and price of goods to be purchased. Since an announcement is properly held up until an agreement is reached, it is too late for a prospective supplier to act. It follows that U.S. companies must normally apprise themselves of pending IFC-financed projects through their contacts in the country in question or through other sources, and then make direct contact with the prospective entrepreneurs.

Examples of IFC Investment

As of June 30, 1963, IFC had commitments to help finance or underwrite stock of 62 enterprises in 24 countries. These include producers of machine and foundry products in Mexico, rolled steel products in Pakistan, electrical equipment in Brazil, and high speed twist drills in Mexico. IFC-financed enterprises also produce automotive parts, ceramic tile, cotton textiles, building materials (concrete, cement, and bricks), copper, lumber, and mill products, pulp and paper, and rubber products, among other items.

MAGRINI MERIDIONALE.   In 1960 IFC financed a $960,000 investment in Magrini Meridionale S.p.A., an Italian firm located near Naples. This is the wholly owned subsidiary of Magrini S.p.A. of Bergamo, Italy, a long-established manufacturer of electrical control apparatus. The subsidiary took over the company's production of low-voltage and medium-voltage circuit breakers which have been manufactured under license from Westinghouse Electric Corporation since 1947. In this connection it might be noted that in 1960 Westinghouse also acquired a minority interest in the parent company, Magrini S.p.A., through purchases of capital stock.

Besides IFC's $960,000 loan investment in Magrini Meridionale S.p.A., the parent company contributed the equivalent of $960,000 in Italian lire as equity capital, and a local development institution, ISVEIMER, loaned lire equivalent to $1,600,000. The ISVEIMER loan was amortized; one-half in U.S. dollars and one-half in Italian lire in four equal annual installments. IFC's loan does not carry any fixed-interest charges; instead it provides for 6 percent interest contingent upon the availability of profits and surplus. IFC also shares in dividends, and has the right to convert its notes into common stock. All of IFC's earnings will be distributed in lire.

FEMSA. Early in 1962 IFC invested $3 million in FEMSA, the leading Spanish manufacturer of automotive electrical equipment. The investment consists of a loan of $2.5 million and the purchase of 30 million pesetas (approximately $500,000) in common shares, amounting to approximately 13 percent of the company's share capital. This was the first IFC investment which included the purchase of capital shares as part of the initial commitment and was also IFC's first investment in Spain.

FEMSA, a family business, needed capital to undertake an expansion of a size that could not be financed by its retained earnings. The company was unable to borrow long-term capital domestically in the amount needed and a public issue of stock did not seem practical. IFC was able to make a loan appropriate to FEMSA's capital structure and to provide the remaining funds required by purchasing, at a reasonable price, the company's capital shares. This strengthened the company's equity position and was the first step towards broadening the company's ownership.

Bankers International Financing Company, Inc., New York, participated in the investment to the extent of $300,000, representing 10 percent of the loan portion and 10 percent of the equity. Subsequently, the Dresdner Bank, Frankfurt, purchased a participation equivalent to $148,500, being the balance of the first maturity of the IFC loan.

IFC's investment is helping FEMSA to undertake the expansion of its plant in Madrid and to construct a new factory at Treto, in the Province of Santander.

FUNDIDORA. In the early summer of 1962 in Mexico IFC engaged in its first underwriting. IFC formed a syndicate with Credito Bursatil, S.A., A Mexican investment house, to underwrite an issue of capital shares of the largest private steel company in the country, FUNDIDORA. The underwriting assisted the company to obtain financing to complete a program to expand steel production from 200,000 to 500,000 ingot tons annually. Handelsfinanz A.G., Zurich; Kuhn, Loeb & Co., Incorporated, New York; and Morgan Guaranty International Finance Corporation, New York, joined IFC as participants, taking up about one-third of the IFC underwriting commitment. The offering to the shareholders totaled the equivalent of about $4 million.

FUNDIDORA manufactures a wide range of steel products and, together with its subsidiaries, forms a vertically integrated steel operation largely self-sufficient in raw materials and able to process a substantial part of its production into an advanced stage. For the last 45 years, FUNDIDORA has had a record of profitable operations. The company undertook its program to increase steel ingot capacity and to enter into the production of flat steel about six years ago at a cost estimated at almost $100 million. Financing has been provided through previous capital increases, retained earnings, and substantial borrowings.

FUNDIDORA shares are listed on the Mexico City stock exchange and are held by an estimated 700 shareholders, mostly local. The company is closely associated with Banco Nacional de Mexico, S.A., the largest Mexican private bank.

The new issue, composed of 458,333 shares, was offered to shareholders, on a basis of one for six already held, for a period of about two weeks starting June 20, 1962. That part not subscribed was to be taken up the syndicate and immediately offered for sale to investors in Mexico, Latin America, Canada, and Europe. IFC's commitment in the syndicate, together with its participants, was 75 percent; Credito Bursatil's was 25 percent. The underwriting was one of the largest ever undertaken in Mexico.

In addition, IFC agreed to purchase outright 128,000 shares of FUNDIDORA common stock for about $1.1 million.

BNDE.   Early in 1963 the International Finance Corporation financed an expansion of the Banque Nationale pour le Developpement Economique (BNDE), a development bank in Morocco. This was the first time that the World Bank and IFC had engaged in a joint financing and was the first of a number of combined operations under which the Bank provides loan funds and the IFC provides share capital for industrial development banks in the less developed countries.

The World Bank loaned the Moroccan Bank the equivalent of $15 million in foreign exchange and the IFC invested 7.5 million Moroccan dirhams (equivalent to U.S. $1.5 million) in common stock of BNDE, representing three-quarters of a new stock issue. BNDE is devoting a major portion of its resources to financing private industrial enterprises.

The Bank is owned by both Moroccan and foreign investors. Although the government was initially the main shareholder it sold a large portion of its shares to other investors and is now in a minority position.

GENERAL OBSERVATIONS

As discussed above, IFC's financing services can be made available to overseas investors and to capital equipment suppliers in certain instances. Two thoughts might be added to the previous discussion. First, IFC's paid-in capital of less than $100 million leaves it heavily dependent upon participating industrial investment. This need has been met quite successfully, however, with each $1 of IFC investment having been matched by over $3 from other investors. Second, since the Corporation is a comparatively young institution, and inasmuch as its authority to undertake equity investments was granted only two years ago, its pattern of financing is still evolving. However, it appears that future investments will tend to be a combination of simple interest loans and equity investments. While the use of the stock option or variable income techniques will not be nearly as common as before the charter amendment, they will continue to be used if warranted in a particular situation. In this connection, it should be emphasized that the equity investment authority has served more to broaden the flexibility of IFC than to provide it with a substitute technique.

FINANCING FOREIGN OPERATIONS: SPAIN*

Industrial financing—both short and long-term—is in very limited supply in Spain. While the mushrooming economy is spawning new institutions and total investment funds are rising rapidly, demand for money is growing even faster. The Government is trying to assure enough credit for high-priority activities, but it also is attempting to curb a credit expansion that may fan inflationary flames.

CORPORATE FINANCING PATTERNS

Most of the foreign subsidiaries in Spain are financed initially by the parent company and then by the plowing back of their comparatively high profits.

Companies that have chosen the joint-venture route have found almost invariably that their Spanish partner had excellent banking connections and that working capital loans were no problem. This is hardly surprising in view of the widespread control over industry exercised by the Spanish banks. The 5 largest control as much as 75 percent of Spanish industry, according to some estimates. Many of the 100 percent foreign-owned companies have chosen internal or parent financing and, occasionally, loans from banks in their home country, in preference to the fairly expensive local loans. Foreign borrowing is encouraged by the Government, which does not allow foreigners to borrow locally to buy into existing Spanish companies. Moreover, it limits the local borrowing of firms with 25 percent or more foreign ownership to ½ of their paid-in capital. Higher proportions are permitted on a case-by-case basis, but then the Ministries of Finance and Commerce usually require matching funds from foreign sources.

To balance the restrictions, the Government often offers incentives: it may forgive up to 95 percent of the taxes normally levied on loans from foreign banks or international finance organizations. These concessions also apply to local loans in sectors important to national development. In addition, the loans the Government considers essential may be granted interest rates 3.5 or more percentage points below the usual.

To break up the widespread control exercised by the large banks, the

*Business International, January 17, 1964, p. 6 and January 24, 1964, p. 6.

746

1962 Bank Reform Act requires the separation of normal commercial banking activities from the investment and underwriting functions. The major mixed banks are expected to form separate industrial banks to handle this part of their present business.

MONETARY STRUCTURE

Under the Bank Reform Act, the bank of Spain was nationalized and placed under the control of the Ministry of Finance. It is a true central bank, with responsibility for currency and monetary policy (the "Central Bank" is a key private commercial bank). At the time, the privately held shares of the national credit agencies were purchased by the Government, and the Medium and Long-Term Credit Institute (MLCI) was established as a liaison with the Bank of Spain.

The savings banks are required to invest 65 percent of their increase in deposits in public securities, which heretofore usually meant in the paper of the government-owned holding company INI. Regulations are now being rewritten to enable the savings banks to provide more credit to farmers and small commercial and industrial enterprises.

SHORT-TERM CREDIT

In the absence of a well-developed public bond and share market, Spanish private banks have played for many years the major role in channeling savings into industry through credits and direct investment. The banking reform initiated in 1962 will bring about a gradual separation of the functions of commercial banking (short-term credit) and investment banking (industrial promotion, long-term credit, equity participation, and assistance in public share and bond flotation).

Previously, most banks handled both activities. Some of them have already begun to reorganize according to the new legal requirements, with almost all choosing the commercial bank form. Under the new law, commercial banks cannot hold more equity than the total paid-in capital plus reserves. Holdings above this level must be disposed of within 5 years, but the Finance Ministry may extend this deadline.

COMMERCIAL BANKS

Commercial banks provide mainly credit lines of not more than 18 months (firms with good banking connections—and few are without—can generally count on extending the lines indefinitely). The standard practice is for the borrower to draw overdraft funds accordinng to his needs, paying interest only on the amount actually drawn plus a 0.25 percent commission on the largest overdraft outstanding in the quarter. In theory, the overdrafts must be covered within 2 weeks, but in practice the banks like the business and overlook extended procrastination. The prime rate for short-term credits is 5.5 percent plus 0.5 percent commissions, but the actual cost (including extra charges) is closer to 8 percent, and sometimes more, depending on the risk, the nature of the operation, and similar factors. Interest on term loans is about 7 percent. Other credit needs are often satisfied by discounting ordinary trade bills (at 5 percent or more, depending on quality) or finance bills not tied to trade transactions.

There are no foreign banks or branches in Spain, but The Bank of America, Chase Manhattan, and Manufacturers Hanover maintain representative offices in Madrid.

The "Big 5" commercial banks, which account for 65 percent of private deposits and have offices in most important cities in Spain, are:

▶ Banco Espanol de Credito (1961 total assets $2.6 billion, capital and reserves $48 million).

▶ Banco Hispano-Americano (1961 assets $2.2 billion, capital and reserves $45 million).

▶ Banco Central (1961 assets $1.4 billion, capital and reserves $30 million).

▶ Banco de Bilbao (1961 assets $.7 billion, capital and reserves $31 million).

▶ Banco de Vizcaya (1961 assets $.7 billion, capital and reserves $31 million).

MEDIUM AND LONG-TERM CREDIT

Medium and long-term credit is becoming the province of the government-owned credit institutions, subject to the control of the Medium and Long-Term Credit Institute, which must also authorize all private bank loans whose duration exceeds 18 months (or 3 years in the case of the new private industrial banks). The key official credit institutions, for industrial borrowers:

▶ The Mortgage Bank (Banco Hipotecario), still the easiest and quickest source of long-term loans (2–20 years, or longer). Its charge is 5.5 percent, plus 0.6 percent p.a. commissions, to which must be added another 2 percent for taxes and stamps when signing the mortgage, and a similar amount when the mortgage is ended. The upper limit of loans is generally 40 percent of the true market value of the mortgaged property. The Mortgage Bank made new loans of $50 million in 1962, of $42 million in the Jan.1–Oct. 10, 1963 period.

▶ The Industrial Credit Bank (Banco de Credito Industrial), which concentrates on medium- and long-term loans—mainly to medium-size firms—for modernization, reorganization, or new equipment.

The ceiling on individual loans is $670,000 (most loans are under $330,000), covering up to 70 percent of project cost (but not more than 50 percent of the total investment in the company), and eligibility is restricted to firms whose paid-in capital is not over $1.7 million, in business at least 3 years, and not listed on a stock exchange. Duration of loans ranges from 5 to 15 years, but in practice the maximum maturity is around 8 years. Collateral requirements are generally a real estate mortgage, sometimes a private bank guarantee, with the real cost of the loan (including commissions, taxes, and stamp duties) about 8 percent. Two criticisms often leveled by local businessmen are the lengthy delay in negotiating loans and the bank's desire to be "too well informed" of the borrower's business. Private banks can be of great assistance in cutting down the red-tape and in providing 18 month "bridge-over" credits (with authorization of the subsequent Industrial Bank credit virtually automatic).

The normal procedure is for petitioner to open negotiations with a short note describing his industry and his needs. If the bank finds the loan feasible in principle, a full description of the company must be forwarded within 3 months, covering patents, licenses, plant and equipment workers, costs, accounts receivable and payable, accounts for the previous 2 years, and future plans, along with 0.5 percent of the loan as a deposit. If the credit is rejected, only part of this deposit will be returned.

A World Bank mission recommended in 1962 that the Industrial Bank be more venturesome in assuming risks of lending to enterprises with good business prospects even if they cannot meet the normal collateral requirements. The most evident recent change in the Bank's credit policy, however, is a stricter discrimination in favor of the firms whose projects fall in line with the goals of the Development Plan. Other public banks for specialized purposes:

▶ The Banco Credito Local supplies funds for housing and local public construction projects. It provided $36 million in loans in 1962, $20 million to October 10 in 1963. Along with the savings banks, the Banco de Crédito Local can muster combined credits of $1.7 billion.

▶ The Banco de Credito Agricola will provide up to 70 percent of project cost (with a limit of $670,000, which may be raised under special circumstances) for investment in agriculture, forestry, and related industries. There is a similar bank for fisheries. Loans are normally 12 years, extendable to 14, at 3.75–5 percent. Loans were $56 million in 1962, $106 million to October 10, in 1963.

▶ The Banco de Crédito a la Construccion, a relative newcomer, will finance up to 70 percent of cost of new construction equipment at 5⅝ percent for up to 5 years, 5⅞ percent for longer loans (which require special approval). Loans were $97 million in 1962, $52 million to October 10 in 1963.

▸ The Hotel Credit Plan has been set up to offer 30-year credits at 5.25 percent for tourist buildings that fit government tourist planning.

Official credits totaled $240 million in 1961, $285 million in 1962, and about $470 million in 1963. Priority goes to firms in regional development areas (BI, 11/29/63).

INDUSTRIAL BANKS

The industrial banks, (separated from commercial banks by the Bank Reform Act) are expected to create and finance new enterprises. They must have at least $1.6 million paid-in-capital and not more than 50 percent of their stock held by another bank. The banks can receive sight and term accounts and make loans over 2 years (over 3 years requires MLCI approval). They cannot engage in regular commercial banking except with firms in which they have a large interest.

In general, a bank that reclassifies will have 5 years to adjust its portfolio to the requirements of the law (industrial share holdings may not exceed 3 times capital plus reserves, it cannot own over 50 percent of any firm, or have more than 10 percent of its total resources in a single firm). It can continue its present operations for 10 years, with the proviso that not more than 20 percent of its resources can be used for transactions with firms in which it does not hold any stock.

Since the industrial banks are a new arrival on the financial scene their impact remains to be assessed. The ones formed by the end of 1963 are:

▸ Banco de Desarrollo Económico Español (Bandesco) with $3.3 million capital. Its backers are Banco Espanol de Credito 45 percent, Banco Guipuzcoano (an affiliate of Credito) 5 percent and the International Finance Corporation, Banca Commerciale Italiana, Barclays Bank, Deutsche Bank, Morgan Guaranty, and Rothschild Freres with 8.3 percent each.

▸ Corporación Español de Financiación Internacional (Cefisa) with $1.65 million capital shared equally by Lehman Bros., Banque de Paris et des Pays Bas, Banco Urquijo of Madrid, and London's J. Henry Schroder, Wagg, & Co.

▸ Banco Industrial de León (Banile) with capital of $3.3 million from the León Savings Bank and private Spanish businessmen. It is a regional bank with headquarters in León and a branch in Madrid.

▸ Banco de Fomento is 25 percent-owned by Banco Central, 50 percent by Banco stockholders, and 25 percent by the former stockholders of Hispano de Inversiones, an investment company absorbed by the industrial bank.

▶ Unión Industrial Bancaria with $21 million capital, formed by Banco Atlantico, headquartered in Barcelona.

▶ Compañía Financiera Hispana-Internacional with $5 million capital supplied 50 percent by Banco Central de Madrid, 50 percent by a group of 8 European banks led by the Dresdner Bank of Frankfurt.

▶ Banco Urquijo, formerly a mixed bank with long experience in promoting foreign investments in the $50,000–1 million range, has elected to become an industrial bank and has until 1973 to change over.

STOCK AND BOND FINANCING

Partly because of the tight control of industry by the banks, and partly because of a formerly stagnant economy, there has been little development of stock and bond markets. There are, of course, "national" stock exchanges in Madrid, Barcelona, and Bilbao, and several regional exchanges (all tightly regulated by the Government), but it is estimated that little more than 5 percent of the value of Spanish industry is represented by issues traded on the exchanges.

Interest in the exchanges is growing, but the market was sluggish throughout 1963 owing to an excess of new issues that could not be absorbed. Current estimates are that it will be at least 5 years before there will be a sufficient accumulation of savings and sufficient development of the exchanges to make this a valuable source of financing.

EXPORT CREDIT AND INSURANCE

Spain is making efforts to encourage exports, both to offset a rapid rise in imports typical of a country in the early stages of economic development and to foster a rapid growth of domestic industry. The program of export credits and insurance, still in its infancy, could become a powerful export incentive and a major source of capital.

Export credit has been available from the Industrial Credit Bank since 1962 (and in theory from the Banco Exterior de España and the private banks since 1963) under the over-all supervision of MLCI. Credits may be granted for exports for construction of ships or capital goods for export, and for working capital for production of export goods.

Credits are available to all manufacturers and to export agents with prior-year exports of over $170,000. The maximum credit available is 20 percent of the prior year's exports. On any given transaction it may not exceed 80 percent of the sale price (since a buyer must pay 20 percent in cash, this may cover all of the deferred payment). In general, credits are granted for up to one year, but they may be extended (some ship yards have received 5-year credits). Charges are 5 percent of the credit plus 1 percent of the value of the shipment. Export credits are not granted without insurance.

EXPORT CREDIT INSURANCE

The Compañía Espanola de Segurus de Créditos y Caución (CESCC) was originally formed in 1928, but it did not manage to get into business until 1960 and has operated in an experimental fashion since. Nonetheless, it insured $45 million in export credits in 1962.

CESCC is a private company with shares held by 48 insurance companies, the Banco Exterior, and the private Consorcio de Compensación de Seguros. CESCC covers commercial risks, and the Consorcio the political risks, in separate contracts.

CESCC and the Consorcio offer 3 types of policy:
▶ The "global" policy covers all shipments to all destinations.
▶ Individual policies covering specific contracts with more than 2 years deferment of payments.
▶ "Risk of manufacture" policies cover cancellation between the signing of the order and the date of shipment (seldom used).

Usually, commercial risk will not be covered unless political risk has been. Services can be covered as well as goods. Coverage is usually available up to 80 percent of the deferred payment but when total export credits exceed $3.3 million the coverage may be raised to 85 percent, with permission of the Finance Ministry.

Because of limited actuarial experience, rates are set empirically on the type of operation, customer, and geographic area. For global contracts, they may range from about 0.25 percent to 0.8 percent of total exports. Rates on individual contracts appear to fall in the range of 4–5 percent of the amount covered.

In 1962, CESCC covered commercial short-term (normally up to 6 months, exceptionally to a year) risks of $5 million, long-term (1–5 years, but usually 2) risks of $40 million. During the first 11 months of 1963, the figures were $9 million short-term and only $3 million long-term, mainly on machine tools and electrical equipment.

FINANCING FOREIGN
OPERATIONS: CACM*

Facilities in the 5 countries that have joined in the Central American Common Market (CACM — Costa Rica, El Salvador, Guatemala, Honduras, and Nicaragua) have traditionally been grossly inadequate for financing activities other than agricultural production for export. In recent years, however, CACM countries have recognized the need for institutions capable of financing manufacturing firms, the most important effort along this line being the Central American Bank of Economic Integration (CABEI).

All 5 CACM members have similar banking systems and strong currencies, and, in 1961, they formed a Central American Clearing House to clear intra-regional payments. The several currencies are computed on their relation to an accounting unit, the Central American peso, at par with the U.S. dollar. Approximately 75 percent of the visible trade among the 5 countries is currently cleared through this mechanism. Early in 1964, the Central Banks started to harmonize their credit and monetary systems in preparation for a monetary union. The 5 Central Banks, in addition to performing the normal central-bank functions, act as commerical or even development banks.

SHORT-TERM CREDIT

The commercial banks (see Table 1) are the main source of short-term credit in CACM, but the development banks and corporations and the Central Banks (except in Nicaragua) also provide funds of this type to productive enterprises. But the total amount of money available is very small. In 1962, the Guatemalan banking system lent Q17.9 million, and most of that went to farmers and importers. Despite the shortage of funds, there seems to be no serious discrimination against affiliates of foreign firms.

The usual rate of interest is 10 percent, but it ranges from 8 percent to 12 percent. Maximum rates are set in each of the 5 countries (usually 12 percent), with specific ceilings on different types of loans. For example, in Honduras, production loans face a maximum of 11 percent if less than L1,000, of 10 percent if between L1,000 and L2,500, and of 8 percent if larger than L2,500. However, additional fees are almost always charged: a 1 percent commission

*Business International, February 21, 1964, pp. 6–7.

TABLE 1

CAPITAL SOURCES IN CACM – THE LEADING BANKS

Costa Rica	El Salvador	Guatemala	Honduras	Nicaragua
Currency Colón – C6.6:$1	Colón – C2.5:$1	Quetzal – Q1:$1	Lempira – L2:$1	Córdoba – C7:$1
Commercial Bank Reserve Requirements 20% sight 10% time	20% sight 20% time	35% sight 10% time	27% sight 5% time	28% sight 28% time
Development Banks* Banco de Costa Rica (46.4) Departmento de Crédito Rural of the Banco Nacional de Costa Rica	Instituto Salvadoreno de Fomento Industrial (INSAFI) (5.1) Federación de Cajas de Créditos (agriculture)	Instituto de Fomento de la Producción (INFOP) (8.6) Banco Nacional Agrario (1.8)	Banco Nacional de Fomento (18)	Instituto de Fomento Nacional (INFONAC) (18.9) Banco Nacional de Nicaragua (51.0)
Commercial Banks* Banco Nacional de Costa Rica[1] (53.6) Banco de Costa Rica (45.9) Banco Anglo-Costarricense (23.6) Banco Lyón	Banco de Comercio (31.2) Banco Salvadoreno (27.2) Banco Agricola Comercial (22.8) Banco Capitalizador (21.6) Bank of London & Montreal First National City Bank[1]	Banco del Agro (34) Banco Agricola Mercantil (17) Banco de Occidente (14) Bank of America Bank of London & Montreal	Banco Atlántida (28) Banco de Honduras (7) Bank of London & Montreal	Banco de América[§] (15.4) Banco Nicaraguense (13.3) Banco Caley Dangnall Bank of London & Montreal

* Assets in $ millions are indicated in parentheses, where available.

Footnotes:
[1] Costa Rica's commercial banks are state-owned, except Banco Lyón.
[‡] Scheduled to open branch in 1964.
[§] Not affiliated with the US' Bank of America.

for opening a current-account credit, 0.5 percent for discounts or collections, and 1 percent for supervision.

Medium and Long-Range Credit

Until recently, the only local source of more than 1-year credit was the commercial banks, which occasionally lent up to 5 years against real estate. The total volume of this type of credit in Guatemala as of Sept. 30, 1963 was Q797,870 on 1-3-year terms to 250 borrowers and Q2.9 million on more-than-3-year terms to 732 borrowers.

In the past few years, "financieras" have been springing up, which provide 5-6-year loans, mainly for housing projects and construction. Savings and loan institutions are also developing in El Salvador, Honduras, and Nicaragua.

But by far the most important new source of capital in the area is the Central American Bank of Economic Integration (CABEI). Founded in 1961, its head office is in Tegucigalpa, and its president is Dr. Enrique Delgado. Authorized capital is $20 million, of which half has been paid in by the 5 member countries in equal parts. In addition, CABEI has received

$21 million in grants from the U.S. Government and loans from the Inter-American Development Bank, almost half of which is earmarked for housing.

CABEI's primary responsibility is to promote the balanced economic integration of the member countries. It concentrates on private industrial and agricultural development, but also assists key public works (such as the $97,000 grant for a study on linking the Río Lempa and Yojoa-Río Hondo hydroelectric complex in Honduras and El Salvador). It may make loans, participate in equity, and even act as go-between among governments. CABEI may not make loans to refinance obligations incurred previously, but part of the loan may be for working capital purposes.

Although CABEI does not require government guarantees for loans to private borrowers, it generally seeks collateral of 150 percent of the principal lent, either as a mortgage or other type of lien. The minimum loan is $25,000 and the maximum is 60 percent of the cost of the project. It also may take up to 25 percent of the equity. It is more inclined to lend to joint ventures, but wholly foreign companies are not ruled out.

Loans can be made in any of the currencies held by the Bank for terms adapted to the nature of the project. Grace periods of up to 2 years are not abnormal. The annual interest rate charged by CABEI is 6.25 percent for U.S. dollar loans, 7.25 percent for local currency loans, and 7–7.5 percent for loans in other currencies. CABEI is represented in each of the countries by the local development bank or corporation.

Typical of the CACM national development banks is INSAFI in El Salvador, created in 1962 to replace an earlier institution. INSAFI receives funds via term deposits and savings accounts, govenment funds, stock and bond issues, revenue from its properties, and foreign loans. As of June 30, 1963, it had received $4.5 million from AID for relending to small and medium industries. INSAFI has opened an office in New York to seek foreign capital and assist prospective investors.

Nicaragua's INFONAC, created in 1953, has a capital of C50 million provided by the Government, as well as funds from other sources, including C10.6 million from savings deposits, C13.8 million from its own bond issues, and C58.2 million in credits obtained abroad (as of Dec. 31, 1963). INFONAC has granted about 40 percent of its credit to industrial development. It recently took 10 percent of the equity in a $280,000- 400,000 shrimp operation with Booth Fisheries of New Orleans. It also maintains an office in New York City.

In Honduras, the Banco Nacional de Fomento acts both as a commercial bank and a development agency of the Central Bank. As a commercial bank, it receives all kinds of deposits and engages in all usual banking operations. As a development bank, it makes a variety of loans, the terms of which are governed by the rules of the Central Bank.

Costa Rica's Central Bank is, in effect, another source of medium- and long-term money. Since 1952, it has had a program to assist the commercial banks in financing imports of capital goods. The program has been financed by $5-million loans from the World Bank and the Inter-American Development Bank and a C56 million credit from the Chase Manhattan Bank, of which C10 million is earmarked for the manufacturing sector.

Other sources of medium- and long-term capital include wealthy families and aggressive local entrepreneurs who often form groups or syndicates for joint ventures with foreign firms. Among the leaders of these groups in Costa Rica are Jaime Solera, Rodrigo Madrigal, and Mario Esquivel; in El Salvador, Francisco de Sola, Alfonso Alvarez, and Antonio Belismelis cluster around the Banco de Comercio and Compañía de Inversiones; and in Nicaragua, Eduardo Montealegre of the Banco Nicaragüense, his brother Jorge Montealegre, and Edmundo Tefel are prominent.

Mortgage banks, such as El Salvador's Banco Hipotecario and Guatemala's Crédito Hipotecario Nacional (which provided almost 30 percent of Q113 million credit availabilities in the country as of December 1962) are also important sources of long-term credit, especially for building loans. Similarly, insurance firms, especially the local ones, provide an important source of long-term credit, when adequate guarantees are offered.

Stock and Bond Financing

Although none of the CACM countries now has a stock exchange, local and foreign firms have secured capital by placing shares through banks.

In Costa Rica, Industria Nacional de Cemento placed 6 percent of its $15.5 million equity with some 3,200 local investors. Shares were sold for $15 on an installment plan calling for a $4.50 cash payment and the balance at $0.50 per month.

In Guatemala, American & Foreign Power (AFP) offered a package of $800,000 through local banks, but after more than 3 years it has still not been completely subscribed.

In Costa Rica, AFP fared much better with a $2-million public offering of roughly 10 percent of the local subsidiary's capital. AFP handled the sale itself.

In El Salvador, a firm has just been established with a C100,000 capital to operate a stock exchange under the name of Bolsa de El Salvador, which is expected to start operations in March 1964. And CABEI has announced plans to create a CACM-wide stock market which it hopes will provide capital for about 80 percent of local and foreign firms investing in regional projects.

THE PEACE BY INVESTMENT CORPORATION*

The basic purpose of the Peace By Investment Corporation, proposed to be established by Act of Congress, is to provide the machinery and means for accomplishing about 2 billion dollars annually of private capital flow from the United States to underdeveloped areas of the Free World (which would comprise about one-fourth of an 8 billion dollar projected total annual private capital flow from the United States) during the longer-range period following an "interim" period of seven years from the establishment of the Corporation. The establishment of the Peace By Investment Corporation would enable it also to provide the means for a private capital outflow to the underdeveloped areas averaging about one billion dollars (out of a projected total annual average overseas private capital flow from the United States of about 5 billion dollars) during the "interim" period.

EQUITY INVESTMENT IN UNDERDEVELOPED AREAS

The main function of the Peace By Investment Corporation—an American corporation—would be to serve as an equity investment agency. As such, it would make available funds of a private capital nature, to assist in the financing of economic development projects and private business in underdeveloped countries deemed to contribute to the sound economic development of the country in which any project is located. It would finance directly, make loans, and engage in the purchase of securities. It would deal with governments and other official instrumentalities, and deal also with private ventures of a representative and sound character. Its purpose would be, as soon as feasible, to transfer undertakings and the securities representing them to local management and/or ownership.

As a necessary condition of such funds, the Corporation would have to find that such project met sound economic criteria. The Corporation would also be required to obtain the views of the country in which the affected enterprise would be located. A further criterion of assistance would be that loan financing or equity assistance would not take the place of funds which

* Extracted from, Benjamin A. Javits, and Leon H. Keyserling, *The Peace by Investment Corporation*, International Committee for Peace by Investment, Washington, D.C., 1961.

757

otherwise would flow readily for the same purpose. Findings would also be necessary that the investment program in general was consistent with the policy of the United States to maintain maximum employment, production, and purchasing power within the domestic economy; that the program in general was consistent with promotion of a satisfactory balance of payments position for the United States; and that the program in general was in accord with the general international economic and political policies of the United States.

INVESTMENT TRUST AND INSURANCE FUNCTIONS

In support of this major purpose, the Peace By Investment Corporation would also be authorized, as an investment trust, to purchase minor stock interests in enterprises in the United States already in being under effective management and engaged substantially in investment in underdeveloped countries, to the extent that such purchases were clearly desirable in conducting the financial functions of the Corporation on a sound and prudent basis. This would enable payment of dividends from the start.

In further support of its major purpose, the Corporation would be empowered to establish an insurance system, on an actuarially sound basis, to protect all or part of its outstanding overseas investments against loss arising from any cause, including but not limited to political or military events.

The Corporation would be empowered to establish a second and distinct insurance system to protect against loss for specific causes, not including mismanagement, all or part of the outstanding investments of private investors other than the Corporation in any overseas undertaking eligible for financial assistance by the Corporation. This insurance feature would help to encourage the far-flung development of investment in underdeveloped areas.

MAIN SOURCE OF FUNDS: CLASS B STOCK

The Corporation would obtain capital funds for its operation basically by offering its Class B capital stock for public sale, predominantly to small investors in the United States, and elsewhere to the extent feasible, at a price yielding $5 per share to the Corporation. Not more than 500 million shares of this type of stock, totaling 2½ billion dollars, could be sold in any one year, not more than 1½ billion shares, totaling 7½ billion dollars, could be sold so long as the Corporation remained an agency of the United States, and not more than 3 billion shares could be sold in the aggregate. This would result ultimately in a maximum of 15 billion dollars worth of Class B stock.

INITIAL CAPITAL FUNDS: CLASS A STOCK AND OTHER OBLIGATIONS ISSUED FOR PURCHASE BY THE TREASURY

To provide initial and temporary capital funds for its operations, the Corporation would be authorized to issue Class A stock of a hundred shares of par value of one million dollars per share, totaling 100 million dollars. This Class A stock would be subscribed to by the United States Government through the Secretary of the Treasury. The Corporation would also be authorized to obtain initial and temporary capital funds for its operations by issuing obligations to the United States Treasury. Such obligations would be authorized to be issued only during the first six years from the first date of issue, and only while the Corporation remained an agency of the United States. Such obligations could not be issued in excess of 125 million dollars in any one year, nor could the total amount outstanding in the form of such obligations exceed 600 million dollars at any time. Such obligations would be interest bearing and would have varied maturities not in excess of 20 years, with provision for retirement before maturity.

PROTECTION OF CLASS A STOCK, AND OF OTHER OBLIGATIONS ISSUED BY THE TREASURY

The proposal contemplates that one-fifth of the proceeds of the sale of the Class B stock be earmarked in a special fund for the retirement of the Class A stock which would have to be retired in full within six years or less from the date of original issue of Class B stock. The special fund would also be earmarked for retirement of the other obligations held by the Treasury. If the special fund were not sufficient to retire all of the obligations held by the Treasury while the Corporation remained an agency of the United States, such obligations would thereafter bear interest at the rate of 4 percent, and would of course remain subject to retirement in accord with their maturity terms. The special fund would be invested in interest-bearing obligations of the United States, or in obligations guaranteed as to principal and interest by the United States.

MANAGEMENT OF CORPORATION DURING INITIAL PERIOD AND THEREAFTER

Until the Class A stock was completely retired (within a period of six years from the initial issuance of Class B stock), and until in the judgment of the Secretary of the Treasury there had been a sufficient retirement of other obligations held by the Treasury to justify transition to a private corporation, the Corporation would be an independent agency of the United States, and such Class A stock would be the only stock of the Corporation having any voting power so long as any of it remained outstanding. During this period, the Corporation's management would consist of a Board of Directors of fifteen members, consisting of a President and Executive Vice-President appointed by the President of the United States, and five members appointed from private life by the President of the United States, all with the advice and consent of the Senate; four members appointed by the President of the United States from various United States agencies concerned with international economic development; and the Secretaries of State, Treasury, Commerce and Labor, serving ex officio. This would facilitate coordination of effort. So long as the Corporation remained an agency of the United States, its basic obtaining of funds would be subject to careful supervision by the Secretary of the Treasury.

Upon final retirement of the Class A stock, and upon retirement of a sufficient amount (as determined by the Secretary of the Treasury) of the other obligations held by the Treasury, the exclusive voting power of the Corporation vested in its Class A stock would be transferred to the Class B stock. At this stage, further legislation would be proposed, in order that the Corporation subsequently would function under private ownership and management.

The Peace by Investment Corporation Bill

On May 25, 1961, the Peace by Investment Bill was introduced in the Senate of the United States, by Senator Jacob K. Javits (R-N.Y.) Cosponsors included Senators J. Glenn Beall (R-Md.), Vance Hartke (D-Ind.), Senator Claiborne Pell (D-R.I.) and George A. Smathers (D-Fla.). A facsimile of the opening portions of the bill is shown in Figure 1.

Goals for Public Investment Overseas

During recent years, public and long-term private investment have flowed from the United States overseas at an average annual rate in the neighborhood of 4 billion dollars. About a quarter of this has been public investment; the net outflow of long-term private investment has averaged in the neighborhood of 3 billion dollars a year (excluding reinvested earnings).

Practical goals for lifting this flow of capital from the United States to other countries cannot be derived primarily by looking at the needs in these other countries. For these needs are almost limitless. Instead, these practical

Figure 1

87TH CONGRESS
1ST SESSION **S. 1965**

IN THE SENATE OF THE UNITED STATES

MAY 25, 1961

Mr. JAVITS (for himself, Mr. BEALL, Mr. HARTKE, and Mr. SMATHERS) introduced the following bill; which was read twice and referred to the Committee on Foreign Relations

A BILL

To establish a Peace by Investment Corporation, and for other related purposes.

1   *Be it enacted by the Senate and House of Representa-*

2 *tives of the United States of America in Congress assembled,*

3   GENERAL PURPOSES

4   SECTION 1. The recent establishment of the "Peace

5   Corps" reflects growing realization that governments and

6   diplomatic relations alone cannot bring enduring peace, with-

7   out the consolidation and expansion of people-to-people rela-

8   tionships. Economic relationships are fundamental to human

9   relationships, and private economic endeavors are inseparable

10   from systems of human freedom. This measure is designed

11   to establish and expand people-to-people relationships in the

    I

goals must take into account also the needs and potentials of the American economy. In the case of public outlays for overseas use, other considerations must also be recognized.

There is now a growing consensus that our public outlays for overseas economic assistance should be raised to an average of at least 2 billion dollars a year, or more than double the recent average level. These public outlays underpin private expansion. To date, such outlays have been channeled through the Export Import Bank, the Development Loan Fund, the International Cooperation Administration, and also through international agencies such as the International Bank for Reconstruction and Development, the International Finance Corporation, and the Inter-American Development Bank. Proposals are now under consideration which, if enacted, would alter the structure of domestic and international agencies handling United States funds (and other funds) flowing overseas.

Seven-Year or "Interim" Goals for Private Investment

Practical goals for overseas private investment might well be set in terms of an "interim" target for the next seven years, and a longer-range target for the years thereafter.

Taking into account the basic stimulative effect of expanded public overseas economics assistance, a practical "interim" target on the private front might well be to lift the net outflow of long-term private funds from the recent annual average of about 3 billion dollars to an annual average of about 5 billion during the seven years ahead. About one half of this 2 billion increase might be achieved through various channels already established, and the other half might be achieved through the Peace By Investment instrumentality described in detail earlier in this article.

Thus, the public and private effort combined should result, during the "interim" seven-year period ahead, in an annual overseas investment flow of about 7 billion dollars, contrasted with about 4 billion averaged during recent years.

This "interim" program should be directed primarily toward improving the foundations and instrumentalities for a much larger longer-range program thereafter.

The Longer-Term Goal

The public investment element in this longer-range program might well be contemplated in the neighborhood of 2 billion dollars a year, representing no expansion of the projected rate during the "interim" period.

But the longer-range goal for the private phase of our overseas investment, after the "interim" period, should be in the neighborhood of an annual average of 8 billion dollars a year. About 6 billion dollars of this might well flow through customary channels, in contrast with a 3 billion dollar average in recent years and the 4 billion dollar customary channels goal for the "interim" period. And about 2 billion of the 8 billion could flow through the new Peace By Investment mechanism. Thus, the longer-range program contemplates an average annual overseas flow of private and public capital from the United States in the neighborhood of 10 billion dollars, or about $2\frac{1}{2}$ times the average annual rate during recent years.

MODERATE SIZE OF THE GOALS

Even if this 10 billion dollars a year were spread fairly evenly among the underdeveloped countries of the Free World, this would represent a public and private investment on our part equivalent to about 7 dollars per capita per year, taking into account the growth in population. This demonstrates the extreme modesty of the goals from the viewpoint of the need overseas.

In an adequately expanding American economy, public overseas outlays for economic assistance, in an amount of 2 billion dollars annually, would be only 0.4 percent of our current total national production, and less than 0.3 percent of what our total production should be by 1965.

A total private capital outflow, averaging 5 billion dollars a year during the next seven years, would represent a considerably smaller portion of our total national production than our private overseas investment averaged during the 1920's. And if the American economy expands as it should, an annual private capital outflow of even 8 billion dollars would be only about one percent of what our total national production should be before 1970—a ratio lower than during the 1920's.

While it is beyond the scope of this study, note should be taken of the fact that American leadership in this phase of world development will tend to expedite and augment the flow of capital from other highly developed areas to less developed areas. This may seem strange to those who, unfortunately, hold to the limited concept that trade or investment opportunity for one country may be gained only at the expense of another. But the new technology and the desire of peoples everywhere for improved living standards are so immense that, in a sufficiently expanding world economy, there will be room for all peoples in all countries greatly to enlarge their investments, their trade, and their standards of living. In fact, the world of today and tomorrow presents only the alternatives of mutual progress or mutual destruction.

THE NEW ADMIXTURE OF PRIVATE AND PUBLIC INVESTMENT

In the "interim" or seven-year period ahead, with a total flow of combined public and private overseas investment about 75 percent above the recent rate, the private portion would be about 2½ times the public portion. And in the longer-term view, with a public and private outflow about 2½ times that during the most recent years, the private portion would be about 4 times the public portion.

These trends would be entirely consistent with the nature of our own economic needs, and with the evolving economic characteristics of the Free World, especially the underdeveloped areas. The public portion in the long run, while adequate to its purposes, would stabilize at a rate representing a rapidly decreasing portion of our total national production in a growing economy. This would release more of our domestic public resources, to provide for the national defense and to promote the common welfare. The private outflow from the United States would expand much more rapidly even than our total national product. This would provide needed stimulation to our domestic economy in the short-run, and in the longer run would expand both our domestic prosperity and our world trade in an expanding world economy.

The Underdeveloped Areas Have the "Absorptive Capacities"

There are also those who believe that a vast expansion of our overseas investment would be in excess of the "absorptive capacities" of those countries most in need of such investment.

It is true that the absorptive capacities of some of these nations have not been very large, in the very early stages of their economic development. Moreover, their economic and political willingness to absorb United States capital has been unfortunately limited by the temporary and improvised nature of our private and public plans for making it available. It has been further discouraged by our occasional unwise efforts to impose unrealistic conditions, which assume that we know best because we are richer, or which assume that other lands and peoples with other histories can follow the exact economic pattern which we have been following in the United States.

But if these difficulties are overcome—and they should be—it is a monstrous misreading of the capabilities of other free peoples to think that they could not absorb and use well a total inflow of capital from the United States which, even at the peak of the proposed program, would average only about eight dollars per capita per year for all the people and all the lands which might benefit by this inflow. Further, our managerial, financial, and technical skills, if organized for peace on a cooperative basis, even half as thoroughly as they have been organized in support of a world-wide war effort, are clearly sufficient to help lift enormously the absorptive capabilities of the recipient countries. History in general, and especially history during the half century prior to World War I, demonstrates that, if a flow of capital from highly developed to underdeveloped countries is effectively started and effectively encouraged, the economic development it engenders tends to move forward at a very rapid rate—beyond the most fanciful expectations even of those who had the vision to commence the process.

HOW THE RECIPIENTS CAN REPAY OUR LOANS

Ultimately, there is also the question of the capacity of the recipient countries to service loans, and to make principal repayments as they fall due. To do so, their sales of goods and services in world markets must earn for them a sufficient volume of foreign exchange. As applied to the United States, what are the prospects in this direction? Can the recipient areas, including the lesser developed areas, be expected to sell enough to us, directly or indirectly, to earn the needed foreign exchange? If the Free World cooperates and prospers as it should, the prospects for this are excellent.

United States merchandise imports, which averaged about 4 billion dollars a year in the 1920's, and then fell to an average of only about 2 billion dollars a year in the 1930's, rose rapidly in the period after World War II to an average of 6.7 billion dollars a year during the period 1946–1950, to almost 11 billion a year during the period 1951-1955, and to 13.7 billion a year during the period 1956–1960. Even after allowing for price increases, the real volume was about 80 percent higher during the period 1948–1960 than during the period 1921–1930.

If we grow to an economy of 680 billion dollar size by 1965, our merchandising imports, at the 1959 price level, would total about 20 billion dollars, if these imports maintained their recent 3 percent ratio to our total national product. But this ratio was more than 6 percent in the closing years of the last century, and about 4½ percent in the mid-20's. If a very conservative 3½ percent ratio were established and maintained, merchandise imports would be about 24 billion dollars by 1965. By 1980, if our total output continues to advance at about 5 percent a year, our total national product would be in excess of 1.4 trillion dollars, in 1959 prices. Under these conditions, our merchandise imports, at a 3½ percent ratio to our total national production, would rise to about 50 billion dollars a year. Students of the import problem incline to the view that the volume and value of American imports will rise in step with, or somewhat more than, the rise in our total national production.

We must take account also of very recent developments throughout the Free World. The increasing economic cooperation of the nations of Western Europe, with our encouragement, can if built upon provide a foundation for an enormous expansion of Free World production and Free World trade. This would affect us in many favorable ways. It would increase both our imports and our exports, without changing the preponderantly domestic nature of our immense economy.

But the very fact that this cooperation is largely limited to the more advanced free nations, and thus bypasses the teeming hundreds of millions of people in the underdeveloped areas, intensifies the urgency of our leading the way toward bringing these underdeveloped areas within the compass of the Free World's economic advance. If we do not bring them to our side, they will most assuredly be forced to look increasingly in other directions— to the economies of Russia and China. And the totalitarian states are willing to fill the void, and are becoming able to do so.

ADDITIONAL READINGS

Financing Foreign Operations, American Management Association, New York, 1958.

Loomis, John E., *Public Money Sources for Overseas Trade and Investment,* BNA Inc., Washington, 1963.

McDaniels, John F., (ed.), *International Financing and Investment,* Dobbs Ferry, N. Y.: Oceana Publications, Inc., 1964.

Mock, Edward J., "Financing Overseas Subsidiaries and Evaluating Their Earnings," *Business Topics,* Summer, 1964, pp. 31–37.

Remba, Oded, "Public Finance and Private Enterprise in the Middle East," *Middle Eastern Affairs,* December, 1959, pp. 382–394.

Robinson, Harry J., *International Private Investment: A Guide to Prospectus Preparation,* Stanford Research Institute, Menlo Park, California, 1960.

Sources and Methods of International Financing, American Management Association, New York, 1961.

Srivestava, S. S., "Extent of Auto-Financing in Major Indian Industries," *The Indian Journal of Economics,* October, 1960, pp. 183–189.

Woodland, Don L., "Foreign Subsidiaries of American Commercial Banks," *University of Houston Business Review,* Winter, 1963, pp. 1–80.

part **D**

OTHER FINANCIAL ASPECTS OF MULTI-NATIONAL BUSINESS

chapter *13*

Taxation of Multinational Business

The tax laws of the United States and of the various foreign countries have a pervasive effect on the decision making of U.S. firms which are considering investing, or have already invested, overseas. These laws affect, first, the decision of whether or not to make a foreign investment. Secondly, they help to determine the location in which the investment is to be made. Thirdly, they are a major factor in deciding whether a foreign subsidiary will reinvest its profits or declare dividends. Lastly, they affect the decision on whether to bring these dividends back to the United States, or to reinvest them abroad. It becomes obvious that the tax manager and the financial manager of a firm must work very closely and that the latter should have a clear grasp of the implications, if not the details, of the pertinent tax laws. He should also, of course, be aware of the forces which act to change these laws and of the directions in which they might be changed.

United States tax laws affecting foreign-earned income remained basically unchanged during the decade of the 1950's and until the Revenue Act of 1962. Various forces were, however, at work during the period to bring about a change. Initially, efforts were being made to encourage an increase in foreign investments as a means of exporting U.S. technology and to provide the rest of the world with additional dollars. However, the formation of the European Economic Community triggered a very large increase in such investments and coincided with the undesirably large gold outflows from the United States. Consequently, by the 1960's many of the proposals for changes in U.S. tax laws were aimed at restricting foreign investment, or, at least at reducing the flow toward Western Europe and redirecting more of it toward the underdeveloped countries.

All of these proposed changes presupposed that U.S. tax laws have a significant influence on the volume and direction of foreign investment. It is not certain that this is true. A study conducted by E. R. Barlow and Ira T. Wender[1] found that ". . . the role of United States taxation in investment decisions has been minor in the past and changes in United States taxes cannot be expected to have a significant effect upon the attitudes of the executives responsible for investment decisions." These authors felt, however,

[1] A detailed report on this study is contained in a book by these men, *Foreign Investment and Taxation*, Harvard Law School, Cambridge, 1955.

that although changes in the *level* of taxes may not change the viewpoint of existing or potential investors, a change in tax laws which had a dramatic appeal could be effective. They subsequently proposed that the law be changed to permit the creation of a special class of domestic corporation called a U.S. Foreign Business Corporation. Such a corporation could engage in exporting, foreign licensing of patents and services, and foreign investment. It would pay no U.S. income tax on its profits until they were distributed as dividends to the parent company. It would, in effect, permit a domestic "tax haven," similar to those based in Switzerland, Panama, Bermuda, the Netherlands, etc., which multiplied between the years 1958 and 1962. However, it would not require the establishment of an office overseas. Consequently, every U.S. company involved in exporting could afford to establish such a corporation and then, as the profits accumulated (free of U.S. taxes) the company would be pushed into examining potential foreign investments as a use for the otherwise idle money.

The proposal of Messrs. Barlow and Wender was only one of a number of proposed changes in U.S. tax law. The end result, however, was the Revenue Act of 1962. A number of the readings included in this chapter are selected to enable the reader to understand the factors which led to this act and which might consequently lead to future changes. The first, by Thomas E. Jenks, discusses the basic principles behind U.S. tax policy. It is followed by a reading by Lawrence D. Hollman which includes a discussion of several of the proposals which were competing with the government's proposals. The article, "Taxing U.S. Investments Abroad" is a critique of the bill submitted to Congress by the administration, while the speech by Representative Thomas B. Curtis gives the reader a feeling for the forces at work during Congressional consideration of the legislation.

The result of all of this discussion was the Revenue Act of 1962. This law permitted U.S. firms to continue to invest in operating subsidiaries in Western Europe and to reinvest the profits in those subsidiaries without their being subject to U.S. taxation. It did, however, emasculate the pure tax-haven company. Consequently, if, for example, a German subsidiary now declares a dividend to a Swiss tax-haven corporation, that dividend is immediately subject to U.S. taxes, even though the Swiss corporation does not remit those dividends to the U.S. parent. This provision, and the conditions under which its application can be partially avoided, caused many multinational firms to change their organizational structure. The law continues to affect the organizational planning of multinational firms and of firms which are just venturing into the international field. It also is a major determinant in the flow of profits between foreign subsidiaries and back to the U.S. parent. The article by Edward B. Bartoli provides an analysis of the foreign income provisions of the Revenue Act of 1962 and contains examples of how the Act affects different types of international operations.

In some countries the tax on dividends is much higher than on reinvested profits, while in other countries the opposite is true. This, and the many other differences in tax laws, affect not only the decision of whether a subsidiary will declare a dividend, but also the decision of where to make the initial investment. These differences in tax laws and their effect on investment location are discussed in the two articles "How Taxes Compare" and "Choice Between Alternative Countries for the Location of an Enterprise."

Finally, what changes in tax laws can be foreseen which are of interest to the financial manager of a multinational corporation? The article by Carl S. Shoup discusses the question of whether the European Common Market countries might align their tax laws. The last article, "Importing a Tax from Europe," indicates a possible effect of the current intensive study of fiscal legislation abroad. The United States may decide to copy some good ideas discovered abroad. At that point, not only the firms engaged in foreign investment, but every company in the country will be affected by foreign tax laws.

U.S. TAX POLICY: BASIC PRINCIPLES *

In 1954, the Treasury Department placed before Congress a proposal to reduce the U.S. tax rate on certain types of foreign income from 52 percent to 38 percent. The form of this proposal caused a bitter controversy, and the proposal was dropped in conference, with the suggestion that the Treasury study the problems further and attempt to work them out.

In the debate which ensued, no common agreement could be reached, either with the Treasury Department or among business groups engaged in foreign operations, as to what form relief should take or who should be benefited thereby. Moreover, the attention focussed on the problem developed strong opposition to granting any additional tax relief to foreign-source income. Both the Mills Subcommittee on Tax Policy, which held hearings in 1956, and Professor Stanley Surrey of Harvard Law School, in an article published the same year in the Columbia Law Review, appear to hold this view. Suggestions have also been made for restricting present Code provisions or adding new ones unfavorable to the foreign taxpayer.

A good place to start, therefore, is with the basic concept of taxing U.S. citizens and U.S. companies on their foreign-source income. The arguments against reducing or eliminating the full U.S. tax on such income appear to run as follows.

- The United States has, from the beginning of its income tax, asserted jurisdiction to tax its own citizens and corporations on all income from all sources, including foreign sources.
- This jurisdictional principle is correct, since there is no valid distinction between a dollar earned in the United States and a dollar earned abroad, and all citizens with equal incomes should contribute equally to the support of the Government.
- All stable, highly industrialized countries with substantial foreign investments follow the same basic principle.

Let us consider these propositions individually.

THE JURISDICTIONAL PRINCIPLE

It will not be disputed, as a legal matter, that the United States has the right to tax any income of any citizen "from whatever source derived."

* Thomas E. Jenks, excerpted from *The Taxation of Business Income from Foreign Operations*, American Management Assn., New York, 1958, pp. 30–38.

The Sixteenth Amendment says so, and there are no theoretical limits on the exercise of sovereignty. However, the existence of the power and the exertion of that power are two different things.

Even a cursory examination of the Internal Revenue Code will demonstrate that no such principle has been observed in taxing foreign income. Consider the following examples of congressional intent:

1. The foreign-earned income of individual citizens is exempt from tax, provided they are bona fide residents of a foreign country, or are present there for a specified period (I.R.C., Sec. 911).

2. The foreign income of foreign corporations is not subject to U.S. tax, even though they are resident in the United States, until such income is remitted through dividends (I.R.C., Sec. 881–882). Under the stated jurisdictional principle, management and control by U.S. citizen-owners would be sufficient to support a tax on the stockholders. There is an exception for foreign personal holding companies (I.R.C., Secs. 551–557), but this exception, based on tax avoidance, emphasizes the deliberate departure from the citizenship principle in the normal case.

3. Income derived from sources within the possessions of the United States, by either citizens or defined U.S. corporations, is likewise exempt from U.S. tax until remitted to the stockholders (I.R.C., Sec. 931–933). In some cases this amounts to complete exemption, since U.S. corporations operating in the possessions may be liquidated by a parent company taxfree.

4. The source country is recognized as having the primary right to tax the income of U.S. citizens and corporations derived therein, by the foreign tax credit (I.R.C., Secs. 902–904). This can be explained, in terms of the basic jurisdictional principle, as enforcing a "tax neutrality" among U.S. enterprises operating abroad. Nevertheless, the foreign tax credit obviously operates to reduce the rate of U.S. tax. As one critic of the U.S.-Pakistani Treaty put it (in another context), the finance minister of each foreign country sets the effective rate of U.S. tax.

5. A corporation deriving income from sources within the Western Hemisphere may receive a special deduction equal to 14 percentage points on the present 52 percent rate (I.R.C., Secs. 921–922). There is a direct-rate reduction on certain foreign-source income.

In the light of these provisions, can it be said that Congress has, in fact, asserted its authority to tax foreign income of its citizens on a parity with U.S. income? The foreign tax credit provisions go back to 1918; the possession income section to 1921. At the very least, such provisions evidence an uneasy congressional conscience about the basic proposition.

JUSTIFICATION OF THE PRINCIPLE

Nevertheless, the principle of equal taxation of U.S. and foreign income has been warmly defended, as being equitable and in accordance with the "ability to pay" doctrine of progressive taxation.

The theory of all taxation is that it is imposed for the support of government in return for benefits and protection afforded the taxpayer. Without having exhaustively examined the literature, I suspect that the English doctrine of taxing extraterritorial income arose in the days when Brittania ruled the waves. With a great colonial empire under the guns of the Royal Navy, there can be little doubt that Britain provided substantial protection for its foreign investors. There were no problems of source taxation or inconvertible currencies in those days. Great sums were spent through the Foreign Office for the development of the colonies, and the justice of collecting taxes from the British beneficiaries is apparent.

By the time the United States had acquired an income tax, doubts as to the wisdom of this policy had arisen. The Supreme Court had sustained an excise tax levied on the foreign-built yacht of James Gordon Bennett used entirely outside the United States, while he was both a U.S. resident and a citizen (232 U.S. 299 (1914)). For a period in which he was domiciled in France, however, application of the tax was denied on grounds of statutory interpretation (232 U.S. 309). The question thus avoided was subsequently decided in Cook v. Tait (265 U.S. 47 (1923)), holding that the income tax could be levied on rents from Mexican real estate received by a nonresident citizen. The rationale of this decision was that government, by its very nature, confers benefits on the citizen and his property wherever found, and taxes are the price he pays for them. Later, in New York ex rel. Cohn v. Graves (300 U.S. 308 (1936)) the Supreme Court elaborated this reasoning in sustaining a state income tax on out-of-state income. The state, it said, afforded protection to the person who receives the income, his right to receive it, and his enjoyment of it after receipt.

None of these arguments sounds very impressive in the light of present world conditions. Many countries now insist that a foreign investor, as a condition of his investment, abandon his citizenship rights and agree to subject himself to local law as if he were a national. Even where such express stipulations are absent, there is less and less our State Department can do to protect our private financial interests abroad. The days of "dollar diplomacy" are over. Nor can our Government do much to enforce the right to receive income, in the face of blockage, multiple currencies, and devaluation. Protection of enjoyment of the income, if received, may be a good argument for remittance taxation, but hardly supports equal taxation of income at its foreign source as if it were the same as U.S. dollars.

I would not push this argument to the point of saying that a U.S. citizen or a company organized in the United States derives no benefits and receives no protection from the fact of citizenship. But it does seem obvious that income earned abroad receives substantially less benefit and protection from our Government than income earned in the United States. Foreign income is earned under an entirely different set of economic circumstances and is exposed to many hazards not encountered in this country. This is not to say that we should tax a "risky" business at a lower rate than a "safe" business. Risk is something an investor weighs before he makes an investment. My point is that the Government has little to do with earning, protecting, or preserving foreign income, and has a lesser claim to tax it than domestic income. Perhaps it would be more precise to say that the Government has a valid claim to tax such income, but only at a lesser rate.

The "ability to pay" argument is subject to the same weakness. Until the foreign profits have been converted to dollars and are available in the United States, the incomes cannot be equated. Perhaps a dollar earned in Canada is the same as a dollar earned in the United States. But it is certainly untrue that a company possessing a dollar expressed in Argentine pesos has the same ability to pay as a company having a U.S. dollar. Either it has no present ability to pay, if the dollars are blocked, or it has a lesser ability to pay, depending on the hazards which must be overcome before the equivalent amount in dollars can be put in the bank. There is no adequate measure of the ability to pay until the incomes are put on an equal footing.

APPLICATION OF PRINCIPLE IN OTHER COUNTRIES

It has also been asserted that only the countries with little or no foreign investment have exempted extraterritorial income of their nationals from tax—and, conversely, that highly industrialized countries with large foreign investments all tax foreign income of their citizens.

This is a correct statement only if it is understood as meaning total exemption from income tax. Virtually every country taxing extraterritorial income accords it preferential treatment of some kind. The British Royal Commission, in its 1953 Report, summarized this conclusion as follows:

> For one reason or another (and we are conscious that the reasons may be various), profits earned abroad appear to receive a preferential treatment for purposes of tax, even in countries which still subscribe to the general principle of taxing the world income of their residents. Of the countries covered by the survey, there is none except West Germany which uniformly taxes the external profits of its residents by the same measure as it applies to profits arising within its own territory. The methods of giving a differential in favour of external profits and the details of the variations are not important for our present purpose. There may be a simple exemption of such profits from taxability, as in Australia, South Africa, or Switzerland, subject or not to the condition that they bear tax in the country where they are made. There may be exemption of corporate profits, if external as in Canada, or of dividends drawn from a foreign subsidiary or trade investment, as in the Netherlands. There may be a percentage deduction in the assessment of certain external profits, as in the U.S.A. (where) "Western Hemisphere" profits are reduced by a deduction of 27 percent. There may be a reduced

rate of tax for external profits, as in Belgium, where the rate is one-fifth of the home rate. Finally, Sweden, while retaining the same principle as the United Kingdom, favours the making of double-taxation agreements in a form which has the effect of wholly exempting the external trading profits of corporations resident in Sweden from Swedish taxation.

On the basis of this study, the United Kingdom decided that it, too, should grant preferential treatment on external profits.

U.S. TAX POLICY:
LEGISLATIVE PROPOSALS*

In addition to those proposals already discussed in the preceding article, a number of other measures are now being considered or discussed. These include proposals for tax-sparing provisions in current tax treaties with underdeveloped countries, a proposal for tax concessions for certain types of foreign income from operations in underdeveloped areas (these sources to be certified by an independent agency), several less-significant proposals under the Technical Amendment Bill of 1957, and several potential proposals to restrict the use of "tax haven" operations and Western Hemisphere trade corporations.

PROPOSALS FOR TAX-SPARING PROVISIONS

In his Economic Report to Congress in January 1957, President Eisenhower stated:

> At present, foreign tax inducements to attract capital are in some situations nullified by not allowing credit in determining United States tax liability for income taxes waived by the country in which the investment is made. The investment of private funds abroad would be facilitated by tax treaties which, subject to appropriate safeguards, recognize the laws of other countries designed to attract new investment.[1]

On July 1, 1957, the Secretary of State signed a double-tax convention with officials of Pakistan (1957-32 I.R.B. 29) which incorporated the President's suggestion in the guise of what has been termed at various times "tax sparing," a "credit for ghost taxes," and the "phantom tax credit." If this treaty incorporating the tax-sparing provision is approved by the Senate, other treaties are expected to be consummated which will contain similar relief provisions for foreign-source income. Potential tax treaties with Peru, Chile, Uruguay, Mexico, and Cuba all have been mentioned as possible vehicles for incorporation of the tax-sparing provision.

Arguments for the Tax-Sparing Provision

This tax-sparing provision in the U.S.-Pakistani Treaty has been the subject of recent controversy, particularly in hearings before the Senate Foreign

---

* Laurence D. Hollman, excerpted from *The Taxation of Business from Foreign Operations*, American Management Assn., New York, 1958.
[1] Economic Report of the President, January 23, 1957, p. 55.

Relations Committee concerning the treaty.[2] Testimony by the proponents of the provision illustrate both its purpose as a reflection of U.S. tax policy and also the extent to which it may benefit U.S. corporations. The rationale of both the Treasury and State Departments in proposing tax sparing, as expressed in the hearings, has been threefold:

1. The provision is designed to facilitate the promotion of the economies of underdeveloped countries by providing an incentive for private U.S. investment in the treaty country. Since the United States taxes foreign-source income of American companies, even though abating tax by the credit device, the tax concession of the foreign country is nullified unless credit is also given for taxes imposed but then waived. The sparing device is proposed as the suitable vehicle to achieve this end. In effect, this device, as incorporated in the U.S.-Pakistani Treaty, permits the United States to extend tax benefits selectively to those areas and under those conditions which will further its own economic policy. Thus, the prime thrust of the provision is the promotion of our own foreign economic policy through means other than direct governmental aid. Ancillary to this rationale is the fact that American concerns will be put on an equal footing with local concerns of the foreign country involved and with investors from other countries, some of which already permit recognition of the tax incentive laws of the country in which investment is to be made.

2. While the provision in the U.S.-Pakistani Treaty admittedly will be a minor incentive to American business because of the limitations imposed on the concession itself, tax sparing has great symbolic value and emotional appeal to the foreign country, since these countries heretofore have viewed with regret the workings of the U.S. tax which deprive their concessions of any application vis-a-vis U.S. operations in them.

3. The provision, by being of benefit to the underdeveloped countries with which the treaties are consummated, permits us to bargain with those countries for a quid pro quo in negotiating foreign tax conventions. To date, the United States has been generally unsuccessful in negotiating tax conventions with underdeveloped states. Officials of both the Treasury and State Departments claim their lack of success arises from the fact that, while agreements to avoid double taxation should have mutual and reciprocal advantages for both participating parties, this is not true in the case of the so-called "underdeveloped" countries, since the flow of business income is almost entirely from such countries to the United States. Consequently, in the absence of an agreement, some income may be taxed by both the United States and the underdeveloped country, without adequate credit being given by the United States because such income is not foreign-source income under the U.S. view. In order to remove such discrimination and to correct

[2] Hearings, U.S. Senate Committee on Foreign Relations (85th Cong., 1st Sess.), July 30, 1957,—August 9, 1957.

what the United States deems other inequities in the taxation of foreign business income by foreign countries, it becomes necessary to offer the underdeveloped country something beneficial in return. Accordingly, the tax-sparing device was selected as the appropriate means by which the United States would give up something in return for concessions from the foreign country.

From the American company's point of view, the tax-sparing provision offers to it what a number of nongovernmental proponents of the provision have stated is an inadequate device to promote private U.S. investment abroad. In many cases, the provision means little in the way of increased benefits to American companies which now are operating in or will operate in Pakistan because of the limitations of the Pakistani incentive there. However, from the point of view of the tax-sparing proponents the provision is important and praiseworthy, probably for the precedent it establishes—a precedent which would compel incorporation of the provision in other treaties, with perhaps even broader possibilities of tax relief.

Objections to the Tax-Sparing Provision

Despite the laudable motives of the provision's proponents, both in and out of the Government, a number of objections have been raised to it, primarily by Professor Stanley Surrey of Harvard Law School in the Senate hearings. Since these objections are illustrative not only of the problems concerned with the tax-sparing provision but of problems concerned in any legislative measure to provide relief for foreign-source income, it seems worth while to recapitulate some of them here.

1. The provision is objected to because it provides preferential tax treatment for foreign income earned in Pakistan as against income earned in the United States, or income earned in other foreign countries. This argument appears fallacious to me, since it presupposes that no distinctions now exist in the treatment of foreign income.

2. It is contended that, if tax sparing were extended to other countries—and all indications are that it will be, if it is approved in the U.S.-Pakistani Treaty by the Senate—then the rate of U.S. tax on foreign income would vary, depending upon the rate established by the finance minister of each foreign country with whom we consummate a treaty incorporating tax sparing.

3. It is argued that most U.S. investors can now take advantage of a foreign country with which we consummate a treaty incorporating tax corporate vehicle to conduct business in that country. Since the early earnings of a foreign subsidiary generally are retained and reinvested in the foreign country, no U.S. tax would be imposed on the subsidiary's income. Only if a branch, or a foreign subsidiary whose earnings are repatriated immediately

to the United States, is used does the concession enacted by the foreign country lose all its value. I believe this contention has considerable merit if a foreign subsidiary is used but loses its force if a branch operation becomes preferable.

In this context, there would appear to be some clarification needed in the tax-sparing provision's application to the foreign tax credit available to a U.S. corporation receiving dividends from its Pakistani subsidiary. Since Treasury officials have stated that the provision's scope is not limited to foreign-branch operations alone but extends to foreign subsidiaries as well such a clarification would not be inconsistent with Government policy.

4. Countries with a stable, moderate, or low tax rate cannot and will not be benefited by tax sparing; instead, it is argued, countries with more erratic tax structure—with high rates and tax concessions—will be the only ones to benefit by tax sparing. Thus, tax sparing discriminates among underdeveloped countries and encourages high rates of tax in foreign countries desirous of getting U.S. investment. This appears to me the most telling point in opposition to the provision.

5. The contention is made that tax sparing creates discrimination among U.S. corporate taxpayers in Pakistan itself. Those U.S. businesses investing in physical plant in Pakistan will be preferred over those which license knowhow or export essential items to Pakistan, since the latter groups are not benefited by tax sparing. Again, I believe this to be a vital defect in the provision's scope, since technical agreements and certain exports may be more important to Pakistan's economic well-being than capital investment by U.S. companies.

6. The objection is made that only the largest American companies will be the beneficiaries of tax sparing, since only they will have the capital and manpower necessary to invest abroad. While it appears to me that small business might be able to benefit from tax relief on the export of goods or of technical expertise, the limited opportunities available to these groups under the benefits of tax sparing provide a further element of discrimination.

7. Finally, the argument is presented that, even if we accept the premise that tax incentives are needed to promote our foreign economic policy, tax sparing is not the best solution. Even some of the proponents of tax sparing admit that it will not seriously encourage U.S. capital investment in a foreign country. If this is so, will not tax sparing be merely a windfall to U.S. businesses, increasing their profits at the expense of the U.S. Treasury? In addition, to the extent that tax sparing may encourage investments in foreign countries, such investments may not be desirable, either from the foreign country's point of view of from ours. Therefore, should not the United States be the country to decide what incentives are desirable, since it is to be the country that must make the incentive effective?

In the light of these many objections—some of which I consider quite forceful—to the tax-sparing provision of the U.S.-Pakistani Treaty, the Senate Foreign Relations Committee has referred the provision to the Senate Finance Committee for consideration. The hearings themselves indicate that at least some members of the Foreign Relations Committee now are opposed to the provision, and that certain members of the Senate Finance Committee likewise will do battle against it. Thus, despite the fact that the Treasury, the State Department, the chief of staff of the Joint Congressional Committee on Internal Revenue Taxation, and various private groups representing U.S. industry are behind the provision, even the proponents of the provision believe that its approval by the Finance and Foreign Relations Committees and its confirmation by the Senate are in serious doubt.

THE KUST PROPOSAL

Another tax proposal aimed at encouraging private U.S. investment and trade in underdeveloped countries by means of a more favorable U.S. tax rate on foreign income earned in those countries was presented and discussed at the International Industrial Development Conference in San Francisco in October 1957. This proposal, prepared by Matthew J. Kust, a Washington attorney with extensive experience in underdeveloped countries, relies on the syllogism that U.S. private investment and technical assistance are essential to further our foreign economic policy, that such investments and assistance are presently deterred by a matrix of unfavorable conditions and circumstances, and that, therefore, positive legislative steps must be adopted to induce U.S. business to employ its capital and technology in the underdeveloped areas. The approach of this proposal is to provide income tax concessions as the necessary stimulant to secure a positive response from domestic business.

Nature and Scope of Concessions

The technical aspects of the proposal are as follows. The tax concessions would be administered under a certification procedure similar in form to the "necessity certificate" procedure which the Office of Defense Mobilization has followed in permitting rapid tax amortization of emergency facilities. The agency suggested as best equipped to administer the program is the State Department, which allegedly already has the information and expertise required to make the necessary administrative determinations. At any rate, the administering agency would be entrusted by statute with broad discretion to determine the amount of tax rate concession, including complete exemption, needed to accomplish private investment in, or consummation of technical agreements with, underdeveloped countries on a case-by-case and country-by-country basis.

Such concessions would be applicable not only to income from direct private investment but also to income from loans and equity investments. The concessions for technical-assistance agreements would extend not only to income from the licensing of know-how but to income from the rendering of technical services, the training of foreign personnel, and installation and construction work, and they would also extend more broadly than is now possible to personal-service remuneration.

Finally, concessions would be available to income derived from export sales or leases of certain capital goods and certain agricultural and industrial requirements to the qualifying countries. In general, the items sold or leased for which concessions could be granted would be machinery, equipment, tools, certain raw materials, fuels, fertilizers, chemicals, and certain essential commodities such as hospital equipment, drugs, and research or educational materials. In the case of these transactions, certification for tax concessions would take place by publishing lists, subject to periodic change, of the qualifying commodities to be sold or leased to each underdeveloped country. Also subject to the concession (but by special certification) would be sales and leases of industrial components pursuant to technical collaboration or similar agreements with parties in the underdeveloped countries desirous of manufacturing a basic article in that country.

In the case of investment and technical agreements, the concessions, once granted, could not be reduced or minimized until expiration of the period for which they were granted, nor would they be open to attack or question by the Revenue Service. Neither rules to determine source of income nor extensive statutory definitions would be necessary, since the agency determination as to each individual case or as to qualifying exports would substitute for these rules. While the proposal requires no specific term for which a concession could be granted for investment or technical agreements, a 20-year period is suggested. As to the countries defined as "underdeveloped" (or, as the proposal's authors prefers to term them, "underindustrialized"), the provision contemplates that concessions would be granted to all countries of the non-Communist world outside the United States except Western Europe, Canada, Australia, New Zealand, and the Union of South Africa. However, flexibility is suggested in this area also, so that marginal countries such as Italy and Japan might be included or excluded as our foreign economic policy dictates.

On the negative side, the concessions would only be available to income from prospective transactions; no retroactive transactions could benefit. In addition, income from the sale or lease of most consumer or other non-capital goods would not be entitled to the concessions.

In summary, the degree of tax concessions would vary from country to country and within a particular country with regard to different business activities, as the administering agency determined to what extent such concessions were necessary to stimulate private U.S. investment and assistance. In this manner, the proposal's author believes a flexible tool of foreign economic policy would be established.

Advantages of the Proposal

Considering the Kust proposal in the context of the objections made to the tax-sparing provision, I believe that the former is considerably better suited to our foreign economic policy by providing a more general and equitable stimulus to private U.S. investment and trade abroad. Some of the specific merits of the proposal are as follows:

1. It would eliminate the inherent control exercised by foreign countries in tax sparing. The United States alone would be the party to determine how, to whom, and to what extent incentives should be given to encourage private investment abroad. Since, under both proposals, the United States is the party foregoing revenue, it would seem to be the suitable judge of the relief to be granted its own taxpayers.

2. The Kust proposal would not discriminate against countries not granting tax concessions and would not encourage higher foreign taxes and erratic tax structures, since it is a peculiarly U.S. device.

3. While tax sparing would discriminate against licensors of know-how and exporters, the Kust proposal applies to all possible groups doing business abroad, and in this context would permit smaller concerns to enjoy the fruits of tax relief.

4. Although some discrimination would appear to be most difficult to avoid under any proposal suitably aimed at encouraging foreign investment, the Kust proposal applies to all underdeveloped states, while tax sparing initially will apply to Pakistan alone and only gradually to certain other selected countries.

5. Perhaps most important, the Kust proposal would provide an effective incentive for U.S. investment abroad, while tax sparing—as attested to by some of its proponents — might not serve this purpose. Thus, the Kust proposal would promote better foreign relations with other countries by improving their economies, while tax sparing has been described as only a symbolic gesture of our desire to aid underdeveloped countries.

6. By being merely prospective in its application and by encouraging greater business activity, the Kust proposal would result in a minimal loss of existing tax revenue. (It should be observed, however, that only a minimal revenue loss will result from tax sparing under the U.S.-Pakistani Treaty model, as well.)

Disadvantages of the Proposal

I do not mean to infer by the views above that the Kust proposal is not subject to valid criticism. Substantively, it discriminates tax-wise between new U.S. investment in underdeveloped countries and already established U.S. investment there, as well as between investment in underdeveloped countries and investment in the United States, Western Europe, and certain other foreign industrialized areas. However, since a generalized rate reduction of foreign income has not been possible to attain (and, indeed, as previously indicated, may be undesirable), and since our foreign economic policy requires some means to stimulate the economies of underdeveloped areas, an element of discrimination would appear unavoidable.

Again, discrimination among U.S. taxpayers is possible under the plan, as where U.S. concerns desire a concession for the same investment in the same locale. The only solution here is that administrative practices must be depended upon to grant the most equitable treatment possible to all applicants.

Administrative discretion is still another problem. The Office of Defense Mobilization quite recently testified to the difficulties encountered in exercising its discretionary authority to grant necessity certificates. Clearly, agency powers of considerable flexibility are necessary if the proposal is to operate satisfactorily, and the best answer to this problem would appear to be reliance on the competence and equitable evaluations of the qualifying agency.

A Balanced Evaluation

I believe that the objections to tax sparing, on balance, outweigh its advantages. In addition, approval of tax sparing by the Senate would, I believe, be detrimental to any chance for enactment which the Kust proposal or similar measures may have. While the Kust proposal has not yet been formally introduced in Congress, it is expected that this will occur in the next congressional session. Because of the breadth of its purview and the enumerated advantages I believe it possesses over tax sparing, it is my opinion that, if it is necessary to be selective, this proposal deserves first consideration.

It would appear to be our national policy now that only where foreign economic policy requires selective tax relief for foreign income is such relief likely. Thus, the Government's support of tax sparing and its failure to propose any broader relief for foreign income (such as the proposal for reduction of tax by 14 percentage points) indicate verification of this conclusion.

TAXING U.S. INVESTMENTS ABROAD*

In his tax package President Kennedy recommended overhauling the tax treatment of income earned by Americans abroad. Secretary Dillon presented the proposals before the House Ways and Means Committee and pressed for prompt enactment.

The principal and most controversial proposals would make a far-reaching change in the long-established tax treatment of profits earned abroad by American firms operating through foreign subsidiaries. At present, such earnings are taxed in the country where the subsidiary operates and then again in the United States when they are distributed to the parent company in the form of dividends. Earnings retained abroad are not subject to U.S. tax. It is now proposed that the United States should tax earnings retained abroad by foreign subsidiaries in "economically advanced" countries. Profits earned and reinvested in "developing" countries would continue to be eligible for what the Administration proposals call the "privilege of tax deferral" (postponement). The tax burden on dividends from both areas would be increased by technical changes.

The idea is not only to enlarge U.S. tax revenues, but to make overseas investment in advanced countries less attractive to American industry. Thus it introduces a new concept of public policy. Ever since the United States, which was benefited for many decades—and still is—by foreign investment in its own development, became in turn a capital generating and exporting country, it has been believed that U.S. investment abroad helped other countries by building up their production, stimulating their economic growth, and increasing their trade. Similarly, it helped the United States by expanding markets for U.S. products, building U.S. assets abroad, and providing a flow of income back to the U.S. investor. Economic history is filled with lessons of these mutual benefits. The history of Great Britain, whose investments helped build other countries and whose overseas assets in turn aided immeasurably in her fight for survival through two world wars, is a dramatic example.

The benefits of the flow of capital over international boundaries, which indeed is as natural as the flow of water from one level to another, have seldom been questioned in principle, though to be sure there has been much

* *Foreign Information Service Bulletin*, First National City Bank, New York, June 5, 1961.

controversy on nationalistic or other narrower grounds. In these days of widespread government grants and aids, there seems special reason not to discourage the investment of private capital, which brings a return flow of income in support of the balance of payments and tax revenues, and which ought to be encouraged and expanded to lighten the burden the government programs lay on the taxpayer.

The new proposals therefore raise fundamental questions. One argument advanced for them is that they would reduce private capital outflows and bring about increased remittances to this country, thus helping to overcome the balance of payments deficit and win the "battle to safeguard the dollar." Another is that the change would make the tax system more equitable. The basic issues include not only these points, but how economic growth, production, trade, and capital formation everywhere would be affected.

"BATTLE TO SAFEGUARD THE DOLLAR"

Implicit in the use of the balance of payments argument is an assumption that private capital investment is at least *a* bad boy, if not *the* bad boy, in the U.S. balance of payments problem. This, however, is contradicted by readily available figures.

Despite the implications that American corporations have been hiding income in "tax havens" abroad, the fact is that data of the U.S. Department of Commerce show that American corporations do bring home, for inclusion in U.S. income tax returns, large and growing amounts of earnings. Remittances of income, year after year, are larger than the outflow of new funds going into plants abroad—so-called direct investment.

As Chart 1 shows, annual outflows of long-term capital for direct investment increased from $0.5 billion in 1951 to a peak of $2.1 billion in 1957, declined to $1.1 billion in 1958 and rose to $1.5 billion in 1960. Remitted income on private investment abroad runs to larger amounts, exceeding $2 billion in each of the last five years. Over the past decade, income on private foreign investment has exceeded the outflows of long-term capital for direct investment by $7.8 billion. Income on foreign investments is—next to exports—the largest single source of income in the U.S. balance of payments.

Moreover, the comparison of capital outflow and remitted income understates the benefit of overseas investments to the balance of payments. The establishment and operation of an overseas plant typically means larger exports of U.S. machinery and other supplies. The U.S. Department of Commerce reports that the value of machinery and equipment exported from the United States for the use of American enterprises abroad in 1957 amounted

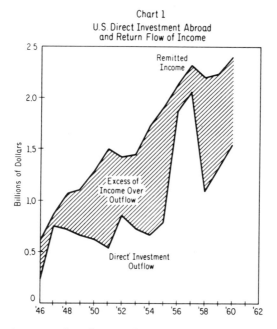

Chart 1
U.S. Direct Investment Abroad
and Return Flow of Income

to $1 billion—about one fourth of U.S. machinery exports in that year. The Department is currently conducting another survey which, it is hoped, will be available early in June. In addition to machinery exports, there is a huge and steady export of components and other supplies.

Mr. Stanley C. Allyn, Chairman of the Board of the National Cash Register Company, has said:

> Following World War II, we strategically located overseas plants in highly developed countries which offered a broad home market and good prospects for exporting. By investing in such overseas plants, we were able to build up and support a marketing organization abroad which is also selling our newest and most complex Dayton-made products. As a result, our exports from Dayton have increased more than 10 times over the prewar years, and more than three times in the past 10 years. They are now at the highest level in our history.
>
> I think it is significant that these increased exports from our Dayton factory are not our low-price products, but rather our more sophisticated electronic and electro-mechanical machines. Without our plants abroad to meet overseas competition in simpler machines, we could not have maintained the marketing organization to sell our higher-price American-made products.

Investments and operations of U.S. corporations abroad constitute one of the strongest foundations to the U.S. balance of payments, both through remittances of profits and through sustenance of export volume.

EARNINGS RETAINED ABROAD

The new proposals would penalize particularly foreign subsidiaries that customarily plow back earnings. Retained earnings are a common and necessary source of capital for expansion, abroad no less than at home. The growth and competitive potential of U.S. subsidiaries would be seriously impaired if they were to be required to pay both the foreign and the U.S. taxes on these earnings while their competitors paid only the foreign tax.

For the decade 1951–60, retained earnings are estimated by the Department of Commerce at some $9 billion. For the same period, new long-term funds supplied from the United States amounted to $11.4 billion. In the aggregate, therefore, U.S. direct investments climbed about $20 billion—to reach an estimated $32 billion at the end of 1960.

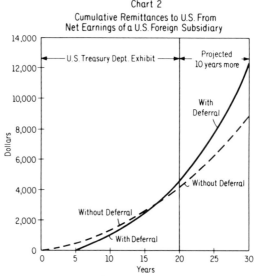

Chart 2
Cumulative Remittances to U.S. From
Net Earnings of a U.S. Foreign Subsidiary

Initial investment $1,000; annual rate of earnings before taxes 20%; foreign tax rate 20%; U.S. tax rate 50%. Reinvestment of all after-tax earnings for first 5 years, and reinvestment of half after-tax earnings for next 25 years.

Earnings reinvested abroad generate profits the remittance of which bolsters the balance of payments. Secretary Dillon, in his testimony on May 3, presented a theoretical example showing that, under the assumptions stated, remittances will be larger for 17 years if income is fully taxed when earned, rather than if the U.S. tax is deferred.

It is interesting to see what happens in the theoretical example *after* 17 years. If the entire income is subject to U.S. tax when earned, there is obviously a smaller amount of after-tax profit available for reinvestment.

If, on the other hand, U.S. tax is "deferred," more capital is reinvested, so that total investment—and, hence, remitted income—increases much more rapidly. While the Secretary recognized that remitted income would rise "over a long span of years," the fact is that at the end of only thirty years total remittances amount to 39.3 percent more if there is "deferral" than without it.

The moral is crystal clear: Don't kill the goose that lays the golden eggs. Or, to use another analogy, a farmer can build up his bank account by re- fusing to purchase seed. His saving is only a temporary one, however, and disappears when there is no crop to harvest.

TAX EQUITY

The Administration further takes the position that, by failing to subject currently to U.S. tax the entire earnings of foreign subsidiaries, our legisla- tion favors foreign earnings in preference to domestic earnings. The Adminis- tration calls this "tax deferral" and has said such deferral is a "privilege." Others have called it a "subsidy."

Such words overlook the fact that the subsidiaries compete, not in the United States, but in other tax jurisdictions. Equal treatment of taxpayers is, of course, an eminently desirable principle. The question, as put by Repre- sentative Hale Boggs, is: "Equal to what?" Surely, the proper comparison must be with the corporations abroad with which foreign subsidiaries com- pete. American income taxes are more severe than those of most foreign countries; thus, the effect of increasing the severity of U.S. taxation applica- ble to income earned abroad is to put American business under additional handicaps in the world markets.

The intent of the proposals is to achieve "tax neutrality" as between American enterprise operating at home and in "economically advanced" countries abroad. But foreign operations are conducted in an entirely differ- ent tax climate. Foreign countries typically collect far greater proportions of their revenues by turnover, excise, stamp, and capital taxes for which no credit is allowed against the U.S. tax. Accordingly, attaining mathematical equivalency of income tax rates between a foreign subsidiary and a U.S. corporation does not assure equality of tax burden. On the contrary, the new tax proposals would frequently impose a heavier tax on U.S. business abroad than upon domestic corporations.

Finally, the new proposals disregard the fact that business abroad operates outside the full protection of U.S. laws and is exposed to greater risks and losses as from confiscations, nationalizations, devaluations, and barriers to remittances of profits home. There are countries, even in Europe, where earnings continue to be blocked by exchange controls; it would be inequitable to tax book profits which are not, in fact, available in dollars for satisfying U.S. income tax liabilities.

"Tax deferral" is not a privilege; still less is it a subsidy. The present law simply recognizes the fundamental principle that income is not taxable until received.

DISTINCTION BETWEEN "ADVANCED" AND "DEVELOPING" COUNTRIES

The purpose of the proposals is to make investment in "economically advanced" countries less attractive to U.S. business. On the other hand, the tax "deferral" for income from U.S. investment in the "developing" countries is presented as "helpful" in fulfilling the Free World's "strong obligation" to assist in the development of these economies.

In the Western Hemisphere Trade Corporation Act, under which corporations operating predominantly in the Western Hemisphere are entitled to a 14-point reduction in the corporate tax rate, we already have a distinction in tax laws applicable to overseas income. This is something geographically precise, whereas the proposed distinction between "advanced" and "developing" countries would be based on changing judgments and perhaps political attitudes toward particular countries. The criteria for distinguishing between these two types of countries have not been officially stated; the Treasury has merely published a list of 29 countries considered "ineligible for deferral," including not only areas like Europe, Canada, and Japan, but also a miscellany of territories like the Bahamas, Bermuda, and Hong Kong.

In fact, all countries, whether "advanced" or not, are "developing." A country like Italy is "economically advanced" in the north and "developing" in the south. All countries can mutually profit from competition of business enterprise operating internationally, regardless of which nation issues the charter of incorporation. A given foreign subsidiary may be designed to carry on business in several countries in varying stages of economic development. A subsidiary based in Europe may do most of its business in Africa.

Generally, an American company venturing abroad for the first time will choose a fairly well-developed country where business practices are somewhat similar to those at home. Success there leads to a willingness to consider greater risks in other overseas areas, with earnings generated by foreign subsidiaries in "advanced" countries turned over for investment in younger nations.

The global operations of U.S. business are so interrelated and interwoven that any attempt to discourage expansion in the "advanced" economies cannot help but retard expansion in the "developing" areas, thus defeating the very purpose the Administration is attempting to achieve.

TAX INCENTIVES ABROAD

Other countries have long recognized the special risks, as well as national advantages, in overseas investment. France, Italy, the Netherlands, and Switzerland impose virtually no tax on profits derived from foreign branches and have easier rates on dividends from qualified foreign subsidiaries. Belgium reduces the proportional tax on foreign profits to a fraction of the regular rate. In Germany, the tax authorities can extend special treatment (up to complete exemption) to income generated by business activities abroad that are of interest to the German economy. France, Germany, and Sweden have negotiated tax treaties with other countries which provide that their citizens will be totally or partially exempt from taxation on income realized from investments in treaty countries.

In the United Kingdom—known for its stiff taxation—tax deferral was extended in 1957 to so-called Overseas Trading Corporations on profits derived from foreign branches. A similar plan for U.S. corporations (the Boggs bill), supported by all branches of the Eisenhower Administration, passed the House by a narrow margin a year ago, but failed to be approved by the Senate Finance Committee. Another noteworthy feature of British taxation is the generosity of tax credits on dividends received from overseas. Under the new British budget the government would be authorized to include in tax treaties with other nations a clause giving a United Kingdom resident credit for a tax waived by the country where an investment is made— so-called "tax sparing." In other words, credit is given for taxes even though they are not required to be paid. The purpose is to avoid nullification, by the British tax system, of incentives given by another country. In the United States, "tax sparing" clauses have been inserted into tax treaties negotiated in the past two or three years with certain less-developed countries, but none of these treaties has been ratified.

"TAX HAVENS"

The Administration also aims at ending the use of "the tax haven device" by American companies. There are practical difficulties in the way of enforcement of U.S. tax laws beyond the national boundaries though the improved reporting techniques authorized by Congress last year should help.

But to condemn the use of holding companies chartered under the laws of such countries as Switzerland and Panama is to overlook the useful and important economic functions which they serve. These countries do not tax foreign income realized by their citizens, including corporations chartered under their laws. Like Delaware charters for domestic holding companies, Swiss charters offer convenience for international holding companies which, to carry on business, must have subsidiaries chartered and taxed under laws of different countries. A Swiss holding company makes it possible to channel earnings from an established subsidiary in one foreign country into new investments in another foreign country without the imposition of U.S. tax. It is a pity that U.S. laws do not permit a U.S. holding company to do the same— in other words, operate as a tax entity without taxation on sheer transfers of capital within the enterprise as a whole.

As the President of Pfizer International, Mr. John J. Powers, Jr., so pertinently remarked, "to the extent that headquartering in a 'tax haven' country may have saved the payment abroad of foreign income taxes, it has automatically increased the U.S. income tax payable when dividends are brought home. 'Tax havens,'" he added, "are looked upon by many foreign governments with appreciation rather than suspicion, as evidence by the fairly widespread practice of foreign exchange conscious governments of approving transfers of foreign industrial holdings to Swiss-based companies."

The idea that American corporations accumulate hoards of cash in foreign subsidiaries to avoid U.S. income tax is a delusion. The dominant practice is to remit the maximum of profits consistent with the capital needs of the foreign subsidiary. In fact, as overseas banks and branches of American banks can attest, foreign subsidiaries are heavy borrowers of local currencies to support their working capital positions and reduce exchange risks.

What Needs to be Done

Certainly our tax laws are in need of repair, specifically including taxation of income from overseas investments. But the point of view should be one of encouragement which recognizes that private investment abroad strengthens America's place in the world.

Over the past several years, the Congress has devoted much careful study, in the hearings on the Boggs bill, to the tax treatment of income from investment abroad. In particular, it has sought to devise a method of taxation applicable to U.S. corporations almost wholly engaged in foreign operations that would enable U.S. business to go abroad under the American flag and compete with business abroad on something approaching tax equality.

American business wants neither subsidies nor penalties but only equitable tax treatment that gives fair opportunity to go abroad and market American ingenuity and know-how. The U.S. balance of payments and tax revenues will benefit; but the greatest gain will be in the political and economic strength and cohesion of the Free World.

FOREIGN INCOME PROVISIONS OF THE "REVENUE ACT OF 1962," AND WHERE WE GO FROM HERE *

As a member of the tax and tariff writing House Committee on Ways and Means the past several months have found me rather busy dealing with legislative subjects concerned with foreign commerce and international finance. On the few occasions that respite was found from the demands of that Ways and Means Committee activity, then my assignment to the Joint Economic Committee found me dealing further with the subjects of foreign commerce and international finance from the aspects of basic philosophy and practical administration. Hence, I feel a community of interest with you as members of the National Foreign Trade Council.

More recently I have been engaged in a chore which biennially confronts a Congressman who stands for reelection—I have been back home trying to convince my constituents that I have single-handedly solved most of the domestic and world problems and those few that happen to remain can best be handled in the next two years by a man of my capability, patriotism, experience, integrity, and trustworthiness. The foregoing is not a paid political announcement, but there is always the possibility that in an audience of this size there might be someone present from St. Louis County and the seasoned campaigner never misses a bet.

Having come to you directly from the hustings and the opportunity this gives to learn the current thinking of the people, it can be reported that you and I are not alone in our interest in foreign trade and foreign affairs. Indeed, I find encouragement in the greatly increased interest that our citizens are devoting to these important concerns. This expanded interest will hopefully lead to greater knowledge and understanding of the issues involved which inevitably will contribute to improved policy and strengthened execution relative to our international objectives and commitments. Improved public interest and awareness of the issues concerning our foreign economic and

* The Honorable Thomas B. Curtis, M.C. Senior Republican, House-Senate Joint Economic Committee Member, House Ways and Means Committee, St. Louis County, Missouri, Address at the Tax Session of the Forty-Ninth National Foreign Trade Convention, the Waldorf-Astoria Hotel, New York City, Wednesday, October 31, 1962, 3:00 p.m.

foreign political affairs can only serve to contribute to our security and influence.

It is my task this afternoon to discuss with you some considerations involving the foreign income aspects of the Revenue Act of 1962 and to speculate on where we go from here. I will discharge this task briefly and in a nontechnical fashion beginning at this point.

In April 1961 the Administration sent to the Congress certain tax recommendations set forth in a Presidential Message. I once described that tax package as a "muddled hodgepodge of dangerously bad tax policy" that constitutes a "virulent assault on American free enterprise." Regretably in the important foreign income areas of the bill the changes that were made subsequent to that expression of view fall considerably short of providing meaningful amelioration of the shortcomings of the original proposals.

It will be recalled that the original tax package proposed a complex investment credit on net capital additions made with respect to domestic plant and facility. This credit as initially conceived was going to be discriminatory in its application and its availability to small business. The revenue loss of 1.8 billion dollars stemming from the investment credit was to be fully offset from a revenue pickup of 1.8 billion dollars brought about by a series of substantive tax modifications including the reimposition of a full double tax on dividends by repeal of the dividend credit and exclusion, changes in the taxation of cooperatives and certain mutual institutions, withholding on dividends and interest income, and sweeping revisions in the taxation of so-called foreign income of American taxpayers. In advocating these substantive changes the proponents used such terms as "loophole," "equity," "neutrality," and other phrases that all too often are used these days taxwise to beguile rather than to explain.

A major part of the Administration's 1961–1962 tax program dealt with the tax treatment of foreign income. These foreign income provisions were designed to impose greater tax burdens on American overseas operations and operators. Curiously, the reasons given by the proponents for the suggested changes included these expressions—"changing economic conditions at home and abroad," "greater equity in taxation," and "balance of payments" strains.

To my way of thinking and according to my economic reasoning these expressions are reason for doing just the opposite to what the Treasury proposed. Instead of changing our tax laws to impede the ability of American enterprise to compete in world markets, we should have adopted changes designed to abet our international commercial engagement. Indeed, the changing economic conditions referred to find foreign owned competitors receiving more favored tax treatment from their respective home governments and making inroads in markets of American owned producers who are handicapped by tax policies that are more onerous in their impact. The balance of payments argument in support of the proposed changes completely ignores the facts that American ownership of enterprise abroad returned to the U. S. annual income that was many fold greater than investment outgo. The tax equity argument just did not bear examination and need not be belabored here.

Literally hundreds of persons and protests were heard in opposition to the foreign income provisions of the tax package during the Congressional hearings held on the tax bill. These objections came not from special pleaders who sought to perpetuate unwarranted special privilege; the protests came from academicians, professional people, and businessmen expert through training and practical experience in the world's commercial affairs. They foresaw in these tax proposals a dangerous commitment to economic retreat and stagnating isolationism. These expert views were steadfastly disregarded by the Administration. The Treasury Department adhered to position of increased taxation on foreign operations and as the bill, H. R. 10650, was recently signed into law the Treasury Department had obtained its way to a significant degree.

Parenthetically, I should at this point explain that the Revenue Act of 1962 was not *all* bad. In fact the measure as it emerged from Conference Committee received my support because on balance it accomplished some worthwhile purposes. As I have stated the investment credit was made more equitable in its availability; the provisions of the bill affecting the taxation of cooperatives, mutual financial institutions, and mutual casualty insurance organizations constituted an important step in the interest of achieving tax equity. Excluded from the bill were the Treasury recommendations for dividend and interest withholding and for the repeal of the dividend received credit. The Treasury recommendations for the treatment of business expenses were extensively modified to make the provision more nearly conform to a workable approach.

Thus, except for those amendments affecting foreign income, it can be said that H. R. 10650 had significant merit. I return now to further discussion of the foreign income provisions.

As the bill became public law, twelve of the twenty sections of the bill dealt with foreign income. The substantive scope of these twelve sections might be said to range from changes in the taxation of overseas annuity income to the current taxation of income *not* repatriated and consequently not earned by a U.S. taxpayer and to the unilateral negation of obligations we had previously assumed in tax treaties with certain of our free world allies.

At the time the Revenue Act of 1962 was reported by the House Committee I filed separate views in which I commented on the foreign income provisions of the bill in part as follows:

> These Treasury-espoused tax changes affecting foreign income threaten the ability of American private enterprise to compete and share in world trade. These changes would tax American industry and com-

merce on veritably phantom income—income that has never been received
—under arbitrary and unprecedented tax concepts forcing a retrenchment in the role of American business in domestic and foreign trade.
. . . To the extent that there is a tax-induced decrease in the role of the
private sector of our Nation's economy in the development of the
emerging countries, there will be increased dependence on less effective
government-to-government aid at a vastly greater cost to the U.S.
taxpayers. . . .

Unfortunately, the benefit from the enactment of the gross-up and
controlled foreign corporation proposals at the expense of American
enterprise would not be restricted to European Common Market producers. The "foreign-owned" competitors of American overseas companies include the increasing economic activities under the control of
Iron Curtain countries. The policies implicit in the foreign tax provisions
of this bill indicate a shocking unawareness of the benefit the Communist
countries would derive from curtailed American overseas economic
endeavors as a consequence of added U.S. tax encumbrances. . . .

The Treasury argument completely disregards the very substantial
contribution to a favorable balance of payments position that is made by
U.S. exports stimulated solely by American investment overseas; these
are exports that make American jobs for American workers.

Another important factor that must be considered in making a
judgment with respect to the Treasury foreign income proposals pertains
to the benefits that are derived from American management and control of overseas operations. . . . To the extent that American investors
shift from investment in U.S. controlled and operated subsidiaries to
minority positions in foreign controlled and operated companies, we
would lose the export benefits we derive from American management
preferences for U.S. manufacturers and the advantages we derive in
"know-how," patents, and secret processes. In addition, we would lose
the national defense benefits from American control of foreign business
activities. Also, the shift from investment in U.S.-controlled foreign
subsidiaries to investments in foreign-controlled enterprises would constitute a serious blow to American persuasion and prestige in international affairs. . . .

The existence of U.S.-controlled overseas companies does not result
in the "export" of American jobs. The business of such a company will
continue to exist abroad—either as an American-owned or a foreign-
owned business. The jobs are there and they are overseas. The issue is
whether the employers will be the American-controlled overseas companies or the foreign-owned competitor companies. Removing the
American flag from an overseas company will not automatically remove
a factory's production, or the market demand for it, from the world
market. Any vacuum will be quickly filled by a foreign-owned company.
Instead of resulting in the export of jobs the U.S. control of overseas
companies accounts for substantial merchandise exports to, or developed
by, U.S. foreign subsidiary companies.

I concluded by saying

The Treasury proposals to change the tax rules for doing business
abroad will unreasonably penalize those business entities on which

America relies to perform vital and enduring foreign policy objectives. Such an approach would make U.S. business activity abroad less welcome and would encourage foreign nations to impose discriminatory taxes on foreign subsidiaries of American corporations. These consequences are contrary to our international commitments and to our national interest. . . .

Our national tax policy must not be based on unwise and unjustifiable expedients seeking a piecemeal reform of our Federal tax structure which may give rise to widespread and irreparable damage to our economic well-being. The excellence of our American free enterprise system and the urgent needs of our economy require that we avoid tinkering with our Federal tax structure.

Such were and are my comments on the foreign income provisions of the Revenue Act of 1962. My quoted comments originally applicable to the House Bill are applicable also to the underlying philosophy in the Senate Bill and in the Bill that emerged from Conference. It is true that the Conference Report applied the gross-up only to income derived from developed countries, but it is also true that the concept on which the gross-up must be predicated—that the foreign tax credit accurately measures foreign taxes paid—just does not conform to reality. It is true that the Conference Report provides an escape valve for a so-called controlled foreign corporation from the application of new Section 12 but it is also true that the escape valve has added unbelievable complexity to the law and discriminates in favor of established businesses and against new businesses. However, the conference bill does afford some degree of flexibility and maneuverability for a taxpayer that were not present in the House bill. But the Conference bill goes far beyond striking merely at any alleged loophole.

If thus far you have inferred that I am seriously concerned over the foreign income provisions of H. R. 10650, then I am succeeding in getting my message through. My concern arises from my conviction that the tax philosophy inherent in these proposals is clearly bad business for America. It is tax philosophy that overlooks the fact that in the period 1950–1960 earnings returned to the United States from overseas investment amounted to 20.5 billion dollars—considerably more than our overseas investment. It is tax policy that disregards the fact that in 1960 American managed foreign subsidiaries were the reason for the export of 2.7 billion of American made goods—six times the imports sent back to this country from these subsidiaries. It is tax policy that threatens the major favorable factors in our balance of payments namely, the earnings and exports generated by foreign investment. It is tax policy that seeks to increase the already intolerable tax advantage realized by foreign competitors in competing with American owned business abroad. In short it is tax philosophy and policy that are bad for American business, bad for the Treasury, and bad for the American people.

Now a word about where we go from here.

The first thing we must now concern ourselves with in regard to the tax treatment of overseas income is the promulgation of regulations pursuant to the tax changes in the 1962 Act. In Section 12 alone we find express delegation to the Secretary to "prescribe" and "determine" in 32 instances and 12 of these involves issues of major policy. I do not know when the regulations may be forthcoming but their pendency and their issuance are events of major significance. It is a matter of first importance that persons concerned with the subject of foreign income taxation pay careful attention to the development of these regulations.

In responding to the question of where do we go beyond the issuance of regulations—I foresee no major changes in the foreign income area being proposed by the Treasury Department in connection with the promised 1963 tax recommendations. Future correction of errors and oversights in the 1962 law may be necessary but that is all. Similarly, I foresee no significant liberalization in the taxation of foreign income. A bit of a hedge on this assurance of no major change must be offered to the effect that if our balance of payments position worsens we may find renewed attempts to promote the Treasury position of across-the-board current taxation of unrepatriated earnings.

It is likely that a tax message will be forthcoming from the Executive urging certain tax changes but this message will be devoid of recommendation affecting in any major way the present provisions of law pertaining to foreign income.

Principal public interest in the 1963 message centers on the promised tax rate reduction and its prospects for Congressional action.

On that subject I would urge caution and restraint in developing expectations for tax cuts next year. I make this observation entirely apart from any impact that foreign affairs may have on our budget posture. In this recently completed Session of Congress appropriations exceeding 100 billion dollars were approved. It now seems certain that the budget for next year will exceed this unprecedented level. The current fiscal year threatens a deficit in excess of 8 billion dollars. The rigors of balance of payments, gold outflow, and the need for avoiding any further debasement in the dollar argue forcefully against a program of sustained deficits. These rigors make tax reduction urgent but require that the event be realized under the stringent ground rules of a budget in balance or at least with our spending proclivities under manageable control. Thus, it is that tax reduction which may possibly seem likely in January will likely fade as a prospect in February and March under the hard reality of the fiscal facts of our National life.

Despite my expression of doubt over the prospects for sound improvement in the provisions of our tax structure dealing with foreign income, I urge that the members of the National Foreign Trade Council persevere in seeking such an objective. Only in this way can we achieve improved equilibrium in our balance of payments and enhanced opportunity for American private exterprise to make its maximum contribution to the fulfillment of our national objectives.

I would close with this thought:

> Private capital, carrying with it management techniques and abilities, not only contributes directly to economic growth; it also provides the picture of our free-enterprise system in action. . . . In short, if the free world is to stay free, if the spark of international economic progress is to be fanned into glowing health, there must be greater activity by private investors.

Those are not my words. They are the expression of opinion on August 27, 1960, by the then Under Secretary of State, Douglas Dillon.

UNITED STATES TAXATION OF INTERNATIONAL BUSINESS*

The constitutional and statutory reach of U.S. income tax law extends to income from "whatever source derived." The only legal limitation on U.S. taxation of international business is the constitutional law prohibition that the imposition of the tax must be reasonable and not arbitrary or confiscatory. The broad reach of these fundamental principles of international taxation are restricted by commonsense limitations on U.S. taxing power. The necessity for reciprocal mutual accommodation with the tax systems of other nations and the practical inability to lay and collect taxes on some foreign transactions have led to restraint on the part of the United States in taxing international business. The object of this article is to set out a simple outline of the extremely complicated provisions of the Internal Revenue Code as amended in 1962 and the regulations promulgated by the Treasury that apply to the international business operations of United States and foreign corporations and individual U.S. citizens.

UNITED STATES CORPORATIONS

U.S. citizens, wherever they are, are subject to U.S. tax law. Under certain conditions, however, the income earned abroad by our citizens is exempt from U.S. taxation, either in whole or in part. But corporations, as such, or their subsidiaries or branches doing business abroad are not entitled to the exemptions allowed by the Code to individuals. Thus, the general rule for corporations is that the entire world-wide income of a corporation organized within the United States is subject to U.S. income tax. It must be immediately apparent that under this rule a U.S. corporation might pay double taxes: one to the foreign country in which it is doing business, and one to our government. The foreign tax credit was introduced many years ago into U.S. tax law to mitigate this problem.

Foreign Tax Credit

A U.S. corporation is allowed to credit against its U.S. income tax the amount of income tax (or tax in lieu of income tax) which it pays to the foreign country or possession of the United States which is the source coun-

* Edward B. Bartoli, reprinted from *Business Topics*, Summer, 1964, pp. 55–62.

try of the income in question. The credit is allowed in full only if the foreign tax rate is less than the U.S. tax rate as applied to the same income. Thus the United States collects income tax to the extent of the difference between the lower foreign tax rate and the higher U.S. tax rate (subject to the limitations discussed below). Taxes other than the income tax are deductible but not creditable.

There are two types of credit:

1. DIRECT CREDIT. Here, if the total world-wide income of a U.S. corporation were $200 and a foreign country imposed a $40 income tax on the income arising within its borders, the corporation can credit the $40 directly against its U.S. income tax. If the U.S. tax on the entire income is $60, the credit would be $40. This would leave a net tax of $20 to be paid to the United States. The direct credit is designed for taxes imposed directly on the U.S. taxpayer corporation. If the tax is imposed on a subsidiary or sub-subsidiary, a *derivative* credit can be used.

2. DERIVATIVE CREDIT. This allows a U.S. corporation to credit foreign income taxes imposed on its foreign subsidiaries or sub-subsidiaries. The credit is allowed where the U.S. corporation receives a dividend from its subsidiary or subsidiaries. It is not allowed for a distribution received in the liquidation of the subsidiary (where the capital gains tax applies) unless the distribution is of earnings accumulated after 1962, and the distribution is taxed as ordinary income. The derivative credit can be used by a U.S. corporation if it owns 10 percent or more of the voting stock of its foreign subsidiary, or if its foreign subsidiary owns 50 percent or more of the voting stock of a sub-subsidiary. Under the Revenue Act of 1962, there are two methods of computing the derivative credit.

a. If the foreign subsidiary is in a developed country, the foreign tax is used to *gross up* the amount of income subject to U.S. tax. Assume a U.S. corporation receives a $100 dividend from a foreign subsidiary in a developed country. The total profit of the foreign subsidiary was $150, and it paid an income tax of $40 to the foreign country. The $40 is added to the $100 dividend to *gross up* the income subject to the U.S. income to $140. The tentative U.S. tax would be $67.20 (48 percent of $140). Credit is then allowed for the $40 income tax paid to the foreign country. The net U.S. tax payable is $27.20. The total U.S. and foreign tax is $67.20.

b. If the foreign subsidiary is in a less developed country there is no *gross up* of U.S. income. In the example above the amount of income subject to U.S. income tax is $100. Credit is then allowed on the relation between the dividend paid and the entire profits. Here the dividend is

66 percent of the profit so the credit allowed is 66 percent of the income tax paid (66 percent of $40) or $26.40. Tentative U.S. tax is 48 percent of $100 or $48. After the credit of $26.40 is subtracted, the net U.S. tax is $21.60. The total U.S. and foreign tax on the $150 world-wide income is $61.60.

There are two limitations on the foreign tax credit:
a. The *per-country limitation* limits the credit to the amount of the U.S. income tax that would have been imposed on the income from sources in the foreign country. The formula shown in Example A is used to compute the per-country limitation.

EXAMPLE A

$$\text{U.S. tax on entire income} \times \frac{\text{taxable income from the foreign country}}{\text{taxable income from all sources}}$$

The credit for each foreign country would be the lesser of either the income tax paid to that foreign government or the per-country limitation. Thus, if a U.S. corporation has $100 of U.S. income, $110 of foreign income in A, and $120 of foreign income in B, the total income is $330. If it paid $60 income tax in A and $40 income tax in B, the limitation on credit for tax paid to *each* foreign country, would be computed as in Example B.

EXAMPLE B

Credit for country A = $52.27

$$\$158.40 \ (40\% \text{ of } \$330) \times \frac{\$110 \ (\text{foreign income from A})}{\$330 \ (\text{total income})}$$

Credit for country B = $56.65

$$\$158.40 \ (48\% \text{ of } \$330) \times \frac{\$120 \ (\text{foreign income from B})}{\$330 \ (\text{total income})}$$

Thus the U.S. corporation is limited to a $52.27 credit of the $60 tax paid to A but it can credit the entire $40 tax paid to B because this amount is under the $56.65 per country limitation applying to B. The total credit is $92.27.
b. After December 31, 1960 a binding election can be made to take the *overall limitation*. This limitation is based on the amount of U.S. tax on the total foreign source income. In the above example, the U.S. tax on the entire foreign income (48 percent of $200) would be $110.40. This is the overall limitation, and the entire $100 of foreign income tax paid could be credited. The difference from the per-country limitation is that here the limitation is computed on an aggregate basis.

If a credit for foreign taxes is limited because of either of the above limitations, the amount of tax paid in excess of the limit allowed as a credit may be carried back two years and forward five years and used against unoffset foreign income from those years.

The Revenue Act of 1962 added a *special limitation* in which the taxpayer must segregate certain types of interest income in computing the maximum tax credit where the interest is investment income and the tax rate on interest is lower under foreign law than the tax rate on business income.

FOREIGN CORPORATIONS

Foreign corporations are subject to U.S. income tax only on income that has its source in the United States. If the foreign corporation is engaged in a trade or business in the United States, it is a *resident* corporation and is treated in general in the same manner as a domestic corporation for tax purposes. Deductions are allowed only if they are connected with U.S. business, and no foreign tax credit is allowed. A nonresident foreign corporation, which is one not engaged in a trade or business in the United States, pays a flat tax on 30 percent of income received from sources in the United States (except interest on bank deposits). This rate may be reduced by an existing tax treaty with the nation of incorporation.

A foreign corporation is engaged in business in the United States if it carries on regular and continuous business activities. Mere investment activities are not considered engaging in business.

The foreign income of a foreign corporation is not taxed under U.S. law even if the corporation is wholly owned by U.S. shareholders. The tax is applied when the U.S. shareholders receive a distribution of earnings from the foreign corporation, or when a gain is realized on the sale or exchange of the stock or upon liquidation of the foreign corporation. This *deferral* concept of taxing income of a foreign corporation having U.S. shareholders has been limited by the Revenue Act of 1962. Deferral is withdrawn in several situations.

Section 1248 of the Revenue Act of 1962 states that when a controlled foreign corporation is liquidated or its stock sold by a 10 percent or more U.S. shareholder, the shareholder must pay ordinary income tax on post-1962 earnings on which the U.S. tax has been deferred. Under prior law, capital gains rates were applied to a sale of stock or liquidation of the corporation. The Act also provides that distributions in kind by a foreign corporation to a domestic corporation will be treated as a dividend equal to the *greater of* the basis or the fair market value of the property. Under prior law the dividend was limited to basis of the property.

"Foreign personal holding company" sections of the Code impede a foreign corporation from being used to own portfolio investments. The law here only applies to foreign corporations controlled by five or less U.S. shareholders. The U.S. shareholders are taxed on "undistributed foreign personal holding company income." In general this refers to passive investment income. The U.S. shareholder is taxed as if he received the income and gave it back to the corporation as a contribution to capital. Sixty percent or more of the gross income must be passive income for the corporation to classify as a foreign personal holding company. The Revenue Act of 1962 has applied these rules to foreign insurance companies whether they are widely or closely held.

The Revenue Act of 1962 imposes the income tax on "U.S. shareholders" of "controlled foreign corporations" to the extent that the foreign corporation has "Subpart F income" (income derived from insurance of U.S. risks on foreign base company income) or invests its earnings in U.S. property. A controlled foreign corporation is a corporation in which U.S. shareholders own more than 50 percent of the stock on any day of the taxable year. The share can be held directly or indirectly through foreign entities. U.S. shareholders are U.S. citizens who own 10 percent or more of the stock of a controlled foreign corporation either directly or indirectly. Stock ownership is determined by voting power. Subpart F income includes passive or tax haven income. Tax haven income is income earned by a foreign corporation from a trade or business having no connection with the country of incorporation and involves the shifting of income from a related party (usually another subsidiary). Profits or commission from sales, fees, services, or rentals are included here. An exception is allowed for foreign base income where the organization of the controlled foreign corporation in a particular country does not have the effect of substantially reducing the income, war profits, or similar taxes of the corporation. A further exception is applied to income from qualified less-developed country investments.

Two other exceptions are allowed where a domestic corporation receives a "minimum distribution" from a foreign subsidiary or subsidiaries and for foreign corporations operating "export trade corporations." In these cases the deferral concept is retained.

Special Corporations' Tax

Special deductions and exemptions are also allowed for foreign corporations qualifying as Western Hemisphere Trade Corporations and corporations operating in certain U.S. possessions.

Western Hemisphere Trade Corporations are given a 14 point reduction in corporate income tax. A deduction is allowed in figuring taxable income computed by multiplying taxable income (computed normally) by a fraction with 14 percent as a numerator and 48 percent (the sum of the corporate normal tax and surtax in effect in the taxable year) as a denominator. This places the tax rate at 15.6 percent for income up to $25,000 with a top limit of 34 percent (instead of 48 percent) for income in excess of $25,000. To qualify as a Western Hemisphere Trade Corporation all of the corporation's business must be done in North, South, or Central America; at least 95 percent of the gross income of the corporation must be derived from sources outside the United States; and 90 percent or more of the corporate income must be derived from the active conduct of a trade of business. As a further requirement there must be "economic penetration" of the foreign country. As a practical matter this requires using a foreign-based subsidiary. Royalty income from licensing, or other passive income from investment, does not qualify as income from a trade or business.

In Section 931 of the Code, certain corporations operating in the possessions of the United States are exempted from U.S. income tax if the corporation gets 80 percent or more of its gross income from within the possessions of the United States and 50 percent or more of its gross income from the active conduct of a trade or business in such possessions. The income must not be received in the United States or this will destroy the exemption.

INDIVIDUALS' TAX

As a general rule a citizen of the United States is subject to U.S. income tax law whether he resides in the United States or abroad. The foreign tax credit explained above also applies to individuals. But income earned abroad by U.S. citizens who qualify as "bona fide residents" of a foreign country or citizens who can establish "physical presence" in a foreign country for a set period of time is exempt from taxation to a limited extent. These exemptions do not apply to employees of the U.S. government, corporations, residents of Puerto Rico and Virgin Islands, and aliens. Special rules apply for citizens deriving income from possessions of the United States.

To come under the exemption for the bona fide residents rule, a foreign country includes any territory under the sovereignty of a country other than the United States. Also the income in question must be from "sources without the United States," which is defined as the place where the services which produce the income are performed. The place where the money is paid is irrelevant. The income itself must be *earned* income in the sense that it is compensation paid for services rendered by the taxpayer.

If the citizen is a bona fide resident of a foreign country or countries for an uninterrupted period which includes an entire tax year and the citizen has earned income which is attributed to the period of residence, a limited amount of the earned income is tax exempt. It is also necessary that the income be received no latter than a year after the year the services are performed, and the income must not be paid by the U.S. Government or its agencies. The question of whether a citizen is a bona fide resident of a foreign country is a question determined by the Internal Revenue Service from the fact of each case submitted by the taxpayer.

If the citizen fails to qualify for the exemption as a bona fide resident abroad, he may still qualify for a tax exemption if he is physically present in a foreign country. Physical presence is established if, during a period of 18 consecutive months, he is in a foreign country or countries for 510 full days. The presence required need not be exclusively for employment purposes. The requirement for 510 days presence is absolute and nothing short of that time will qualify. The income subject to the exemption must be *earned* income from personal services rendered outside of the United States. The income must not be paid more than a year after the year it is earned and must not be paid by the U.S. Government or its agencies.

The bona fide residence rule concerns itself with the type of residence established, the intentions of the taxpayer about returning to the United States, and nature and purpose of the stay in a foreign country. The physical presence rule is concerned solely with the taxpayer's being on foreign soil for the requisite length of time.

A citizen who qualifies for the tax exemption under the physical presence rule is exempt from United States tax on income earned abroad up to $20,000 annually. A citizen who qualifies as a bona fide resident abroad is exempt from United States tax on income earned abroad up to $20,000 during each of the first three years of residence abroad and on income up to $35,000 per year for all subsequent years. This amount is reduced to $25,000 by 1964 amendment to the code (effective 1-1-65). The income tax applies to all income in excess of the exempted income and only deductions from nonexempt income are allowed.

Where the qualifying period under either rule does not include a full taxable year, the taxpayer gets an exemption for only a partial year. He must prorate the exemption for the number of days in the qualifying period.

Tax Treaties

The United States has entered into tax treaties with approximately 21 countries. Since the United States Constitution gives treaties of the United States the status of "supreme law of the land" it is important to examine the effect of these treaties on the taxation of international business.

The basic reason for the existence of tax treaties is to avoid multiple taxation. They try to divide corporate income and personal income in an equal way so that each country party to the treaty gets its basic share, but the taxpayer does not suffer by having to pay the tax of both countries on the same income. The object is to avoid the oppressive effect of multiple taxation on the growth of international business.

The U.S. tax treaties cover U.S. corporations and the income and property of the branches and permanent establishments of U.S. corporations and citizens abroad. Therefore, if a U.S. corporation sets up a foreign branch operation which qualifies as a "permanent establishment" abroad, the tax treaty between the United States and the foreign country should be examined for its effect on the income tax of the corporation. If the U.S. corporation sets up a foreign subsidiary, it would be a national of the foreign country for purposes of any tax treaty with the United States and would acquire all rights under the treaty as a foreign national.

Tax treaties do have a great effect on U.S. taxation of U.S. corporations because they generally have a saving clause reserving to the United States the right to tax its citizens and domestic corporations as if the treaty had not come into effect. But they can affect the taxes due a foreign country from U.S. corporations. Some contain clauses which exempt a U.S. firm from foreign tax for the industrial and commercial profits of a U.S. corporation which does not have a "permanent establishment" in the foreign country. A tax saving can also be involved if the treaty has a clause which in effect eliminates the payment of foreign taxes which exceed the applicable U.S. tax rate.

In any event, consideration of the tax implications of international business is not complete unless the taxpayer examines in detail the effect of applicable tax treaties.

CONCLUSION

Legality or illegality is not the whole substance of the taxation of international business. Tax advantages do exist as an incentive to enter international business. This is the present policy of the U.S. Government because of the beneficial effect of exports by U.S. exterprises on our balance of payments difficulties. But tax advantage is not the whole of it. There are many practical considerations that must accompany a decision to enter international business, and the tax aspects are just one consideration. One may ignore the tax implications of branch operations to achieve flexibility of control of the business enterprise. Local political or commercial acceptability may dictate entering a foreign market by local incorporation as a subsidiary even though this may not be the most favorable tax posture. In short, this article is designed to give the businessman a capsule view of the basic rules of U.S. tax law as applied to international business so that any judgments that must be made in relation to international business can qualify as *educated* judgments when restricted to the tax area.

HOW TAXES COMPARE*

In the copper-roofed Town Hall of Stockholm is the effigy of an unfortunate little human being, crouched on all fours—his back supporting the larger statue of an ancient ruler of the city. Nobody knows who the heavily burdened man is, but Stockholmers like to quip: "It's the Swedish taxpayer."

This cowed figure could well stand as a cenotaph to the Unknown Taxpayer in most Western lands today. For, virtually all industrialized economies are carrying sizable tax burdens, ranging from one-fourth to one-third of gross national product.

Yet in any one country specific taxpaying groups might argue who the cringing man really represents. If the total load is much the same, the structure of tax systems means it can be felt in vastly different ways from one country to another—and the structure can have different effects on the economy.

Key Differences

A comparison between the United States and the mature economies of West Europe suggests these general conclusions:

■ If you're rich, you might be able to hold onto more of your wealth under European income-tax treatment than under the U.S. system. But if you're making under $50,000 or so and trying to become a capitalist, you doubtless have a better chance of doing it in the United States than in most European countries. Economically, this situation may make Europe more favorable to development of venture capital, but it also may be the reason the United States gets a much greater flow of funds from middle-income earners into the capital markets.

■ Apart from the income tax, European governments also tend to favor the man with money by a heavy reliance on indirect taxes, such as those on retail sales. This shifts much of the tax burden onto middle- and low-income groups who spend relatively more of their income. In some countries, particularly France and Italy, it offsets the relatively lighter taxation of personal and corporate income.

For the economy as a whole, the sizable indirect taxes sometimes are rejiggered to encourage or discourage consumer spending. But a high level of indirect taxes weakens the "automatic stabilization" effect of government budgets, by which a business upswing brings in more revenue—tending to

* *Business Week*, August 25, 1962, pp. 52–66.

balance the economic cycle. A weaker stabilizer may be good in a recovery, since America's high tax rates tend to choke off a recovery too early. But in a downturn, a weak stabilizer is not desirable.

■ If you're worried about modernizing or expanding your plant, you would find it easier to generate the funds in Europe—even though the total tax bite on a European company may not be any less than on a company in America. Most Europeans can still write off their investments faster than Americans, despit recent liberalization of U.S. depreciation rules [BW Jul. 14'62,p25]. Moreover, European businessmen can negotiate all sorts of special tax-free reserves that add to the cash flow of their business.

These devices in themselves may not act as a direct incentive to investment, but they obviously make it easier for industry to finance expansion and modernization.

■ You might be goaded into more rapid modernization in Europe than in America, too. That's because many European countries—with the notable exception of Britain—rely more heavily on payroll taxes and employer-paid social security, which put a premium on investment in labor-saving machinery. Whether this spur is any greater than the high wage rates in the United States is another matter, but it's certainly true in the strict context of tax devices.

■ If you're exporting, your European competitors have a decided tax advantage over you in most world markets. Partly, this stems from the competitive strength that comes from more rapid depreciation. The French, in fact, give faster write-offs to manufacturers in proportion to the size of their exports.

More directly, however, European exporters get a tax break through rebate, or outright exemption, on indirect taxes. The United States does exempt some export products from excise taxes, but because indirect taxes are far more significant in Europe the exemption means more there.

Ancient Rule Forgotten

Some 2,000 years ago, a Hindu law book known as the Code of Manu laid down an oft-repeated rule of thumb on tax burdens: "A king who in times of distress taxes even the fourth part of the crops is free from guilt if he protects his subjects to the best of his ability."

By this standard, few mature nations today are free from guilt. This is indicated by Chart 1, which shows the share of GNP taken by total tax collections—federal, state, and local, including social security charges—in 21 nations. Starting with United States at 26 percent and running up to West Germany's 34 percent, nearly all the Western industrialized nations exceed the old rule-of-thumb limit.

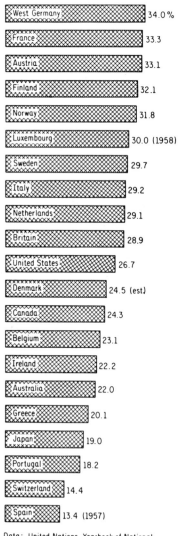

Chart 1

The Tax Burden

Share of GNP Taken by National,
State, and Local Taxes, 1959

West Germany 34.0%

France 33.3

Austria 33.1

Finland 32.1

Norway 31.8

Luxembourg 30.0 (1958)

Sweden 29.7

Italy 29.2

Netherlands 29.1

Britain 28.9

United States 26.7

Denmark 24.5 (est)

Canada 24.3

Belgium 23.1

Ireland 22.2

Australia 22.0

Greece 20.1

Japan 19.0

Portugal 18.2

Switzerland 14.4

Spain 13.4 (1957)

Data: United Nations, Yearbook of National
Accounts Statistics; United Nations
Statistical Yearbook; U.S. Treasury

Dividing the Load

But the way the load is spread is perhaps more important than its size. The pattern of tax collections (national, state, local, and social security) in Table 1 indicates some of the variations in structure. Admittedly, this is not a true picture of tax incidence, which would take into account the unknown degree to which various business taxes are shifted to consumers. But collections at least show who foots the bill in the first instance, and perhaps where the intentions of governments lie.

Rather surprisingly, U.S. corporations shoulder a smaller share of this nation's total burden than do those in Germany, France, Belgium, and Holland. Britain is the only major European nation in which corporations carry a lighter load than U.S. companies. Most of the countries that place a substantially lighter burden on business are small, like Switzerland, and, ironically, include such Socialist lands as Denmark and Sweden [BW Jul.14'62, p72].

I. Impact of Depreciation

But there's a considerable difference in the form of taxation on business, as Table 1 suggests. The U.S. tax structure puts a heavier penalty on the use of capital through the larger burden of direct taxes—mainly profits and

TABLE 1

HOW THE TAX BURDEN IS SPREAD – COUNTRY BY COUNTRY

(Percentage of total tax collections at all levels of government by source, 1958)

	Direct Taxes on Income, Wealth, Payroll						Indirect Taxes (Excise, Sales, etc.) on Individuals and Corporations
	Individuals			Corporations			
	Income, Wealth Taxes	Social Security Charges	Total	Income, Wealth Taxes	Social Security Charges	Total	
Sweden	46%	7%	53%	11%	3%	14%	33%
Denmark	43	5	48	6	–	6	46
Netherlands	31	7	38	10	19	29	33
Austria	30	7	37	7	15	22	41
Britain	26	7	33	15	6	21	46
W. Germany	18	15	33	10	14	24	43
Belgium	21	9	30	9	19	28	42
France	11	6	17	7	23	30	53
Portugal	10	6	16	21	15	36	48
Spain	10	5	15	17	14	31	54
Ireland	12	2	14	9	3	12	74
European Average	23	7	30	7	11	23	47
United States	35	6	41	16	8	24	35

For all countries, 1958 is most recent year of breakdown on social security charges.

NOTE: Similar breakdown on Italy is not available, but ratio averages 48.5% from indirect; 16% direct taxes on corporations and individuals; 29% in social security charges on business; 6.5% in social security charges on individuals.

DATA: National Institute Economic Review, Britain.

Business Week

property taxes. Here again, Britain is closer to the U.S. situation, with only a slightly smaller share of the burden falling in direct taxes on its business. Leading Continental countries get a considerably smaller share of revenues from direct business taxes.

But that's not because corporate tax rates in Europe's major countries are appreciably lower than the U.S. 52 percent rate. In Britain, the rate is 53.75 percent; in France, it's 50 percent; and in Germany on undistributed profits, it's 51 percent. That being so, why does virtually the same rate mean a substantially smaller direct tax burden on corporations in, say, France and Germany?

Partly, it reflects the fact that the heavy social security charges and substantial indirect taxes are written off as costs, thus reducing income subject to the profits tax.

Special Reserves

Mainly, however, it's due to more generous depreciation allowances, tax credits for new investment, and special taxfree reserves for such "contingencies" as price rises on raw materials. The full impact of special reserves is only hinted at in handbooks of foreign taxation, because in most cases they are negotiated with the tax collector. In France, for instance, a company balance sheet may list six or seven classes of special reserves, some of which may have been established on the company's promise to invest the funds during the next year. Swedish companies can set aside 40 percent of profits any time they want, as long as they deposit nearly half the reserve in frozen government accounts, which obviously curtails their usefulness.

The impact of depreciation is more measurable. Total depreciation funds (including investment credits) as a percent of GNP run close to 9 percent in France and Germany, 8 percent in Britain—compared to a scant 4 percent in the United States. These ratios emphasize the contribution that depreciation funds have made to the financing of new investment in postwar Europe. But there's a practical reason for it: Unlike the U.S., European capital markets have been unable to provide the funds for industrial growth, and companies have been forced to rely to large extent on internal financing.

Case Study

Nowhere is the effect of depreciation on internal financing more apparent than in the case of Continental steel producers. In a study for Britain's Iron & Steel Board, Sir Robert Shone, now head of Britain's national planning board, shows that British steel companies are in an unfavorable tax position vis-a-vis Continental producers. For Business Week, he has extended his computations to American steel companies—which turn out to be in an even less favorable position than the British (Table 2).

TABLE 2

WHAT DEPRECIATION CAN DO TO CASH FLOW

(Disposal of gross earnings of steel companies, annual average 1955-59)

	Britain 15 Companies		Continent 52 Companies		U.S. 30 Companies	
	Per Ingot Ton	Percent of Gross Earnings	Per Ingot Ton	Percent of Gross Earnings	Per Ingot Ton	Percent of Gross Earnings
Depreciation	$4.75	20.3%	$10.78	50.4%	$8.10	26.0%
Retained profits (Incl. allocations to fixed asset reserves)	7.40	31.7	2.52	11.8	6.60	21.0
Total cash flow	$12.15	52.0%	$13.30	62.2%	$14.70	47.0%

DATA: British Iron & Steel Board   Business Week

These are the points in Shone's findings: Figured in dollars per ingot ton, U.S. steel companies retain a smaller share of gross earnings (47 percent) than U.K. companies (52 percent)—and substantially less than the Continental companies (62 percent). For the Continent, the big difference lies in depreciation, which accounts for 50.4 percent of gross earnings, compared to 26 percent for U.S. companies. Depreciation for British companies, however, is less than in the United States though taxes take a smaller share of gross earnings than in this country.

Taxes as a share of steel's gross earnings, according to the Shone study, are 32.6 percent in the United States, 26.4 percent in Britain, and 18.2 percent on the Continent. But this does not show the effect of indirect and payroll taxes deducted from taxable income.

It's worth noting, too, that although U.S. steel companies retain a smaller percentage of gross profits in their business, the actual amount retained (in dollars per ingot ton) is larger than in the other countries—because total gross earnings are considerably higher. This suggests another reason why European companies have been forced to rely on depreciation to maintain a high level of investment.

Sales Tie-in

Moreover, Continental countries may have carried depreciation further in steel than in most other industries. In its effort to encourage growth of this basic industry, France ties the rate of steel depreciation to sales, varying by product. For example, a company can take annual depreciation equal to 8 percent of Bessemer sales, 4 percent of ferromanganese sales, 20 percent of iron ore sales. One result: In 1959 the Big Four French steel producers, according to one expert, took depreciation totaling over $112-million, leaving reported net income aggregating only $6.5-million.

Even so, normal depreciation practice for other European industries is far more beneficial than it is in the United States. In the first three years of the average life of all depreciable assets (except buildings), French businessmen recover 58 percent of the cost; Germans recover 49 percent (recently changed from 58 percent); Britons can get back up to 66 percent, depending on the industry; and Swedes get up to 65.7 percent. In contrast, under the Treasury's new guidelines, Americans can recover an average 41 percent in three years, which is some improvement over the 34 percent prevailing before the change went into effect July 12. With the new average life of 12 years for all U.S. assets, it still takes an American six years to recoup 66 percent of cost.

The Treasury's proposed investment credit of 7 percent after taxes would bring the United States more in line with West Europe. But the proposal already has been weakened greatly, except for investments up to $25,000, by the Senate Finance Committee. If this version passes Congress, it would leave U.S. depreciation considerably behind the usual European treatment.

Endless Variety

The great variety of depreciation rates and initial investment credits in Europe defies enumeration.

The declining-balance method of depreciation is widely used, as it is in the United States, but the rates are more flexible. In declining-balance depreciation, the cost of an asset is written off more rapidly in the early years of the service life, as opposed to equal installments under straight-line depreciation. Just how rapidly the cost is written off in the early stages depends on the coefficient. In the United States, this is limited to twice the straight-line depreciation rate. In Europe, there is more variation. In France, for example, the longer the useful life of an asset, the higher the coefficient.

But perhaps the most simple and liberal depreciation system is Sweden's. It permits a five-year write-off on all machinery and equipment, with the amount to be taken in any single year almost at the discretion of the company, within liberal limits.

Several countries, too, boast a proviso that would appeal to American companies that are losing money: If the depreciation allowance is not covered by profits in any one year, it can be taken in succeeding years.

Export Incentive

The French, who have often been called the most imaginative innovators in the field of taxation, use depreciation to encourage exports. If a company's eports reach 20 percent of its total sales—or, if the company simply "undertakes" to reach that figure—it can increase its depreciation by an amount equal to the ratio of exports to sales. Thus, if exports account for 30 percent of sales, a company can increase its depreciation allowance by 30 percent. The system applies only to straight-line depreciation, but some companies still find it more advantageous than the new declining-balance method.

II. BUSINESS TAXES

Liberal depreciation treatment, then, fosters internal financing of investments and offsets the effect of relatively high corporate tax rates by reducing taxable income. But this does not necessarily mean European companies are more pampered when it comes to taxation than American companies. When you tot up payroll taxes, indirect taxes, municipal profits taxes, and capital levies, the total tax bite on any one European company may be just as hefty as on a comparable American company if figured on the basis, say, of percentage of sales.

Steel Study

One industry where this question has been studies is steel. Total taxes as a percent of sales in 1960 for steel companies in several countries were compiled recently by the International Metalworkers at Geneva. For U.S. steel producers, taxes were 7.7 percent of sales; in France, 11.5 percent; in West Germany, 7 percent; in Belgium, 7.3 percent; in Britain, 5.5 percent; and in Sweden, 4.4 percent.

In light of the considerably more favorable treatment of corporate profits taxation—as compared with the United States—it is surprising to find a similar, or heavier, tax burden in Germany, Belgium, and France. This is only one industry, of course, but three far-flung U.S. companies in other industries, too, report there's "some doubt" that the total burden on their several European subsidiaries is much different from the burden on their U.S. companies.

But even if the load, company for company, is about the same, the form taken by these other taxes can have different effects.

Offsetting Factor

Payroll taxes, for one, may largely offset lower income taxes on business in many countries. In France, Germany, Belgium, Holland, and Italy, most of the direct revenue collections from corporations come from social security contributions and other payroll taxes (Table 1).

French employers pay social security and other compulsory charges, such as housing allowances, averaging 44.5 percent of their payroll—and sometimes it runs to 50 percent. Italian employers pay an average 47.8 percent of their wage bill in social security. German employers are better off, but still face payroll charges of about 16 percent. In the United States, the average is only 4.5 percent.

Even if wages are lower in Europe than in the United States, these enormous payroll charges are a considerable incentive to modernize plants to minimize labor costs. Britain, whose industry bears a social security burden closer to that of U.S. industry, has been keenly aware of this incentive on the Continent. In fact, Britain enacted a payroll tax last year, partly to discourage adding workers in boom times—which strains an already short labor supply. But trade union opposition to the tax was so strong that it has never been applied—and there's talk of repealing it.

Turnover Tax

Indirect taxes, too, offset the lighter profits tax in some countries. This is particularly true of the French production tax—a tax on the value added by manufacturer. Basically, the "TVA," as it's called, is a turnover tax that is noncumulative—in contrast to a general sales tax whose total effect is multiplied as it is added on at each stage from raw material to retail customer. In effect, the French manufacturer subtracts the value of all his purchases of materials from the value of his own sales and applies the tax to the difference.

For the company that cannot pass it on, it's a sizable tax bite. The current rate is close to 20 percent, but because it is included in a company's sales figures, it is in effect a tax of close to 25 percent. But economists contend that in most cases the TVA is shifted to the buyer in the form of higher prices. Moreover, it is deductible for income-tax purposes, and it's even included in the value of depreciable assets. Thus, its real burden on profits is unknown.

For the French government, the TVA yields as much, and sometimes more, than both personal and corporate income taxes combined. Partly because of this, and also because of its noncumulative effect, it's being considered for eventual adoption by all Common Market countries in lieu of other types of indirect taxes.

Evasion Preventive

The heavy reliance on indirect taxes in France, as well as in Italy and other Latin countries, has developed not so much from the economic merits of this type of tax as from its collectability. Tax evasion is notorious in these nations—and to some extent it must distort the picture of the real burden on business. Corporations are known to keep separate books for the tax collector, and the tax bill is often negotiated. Unincorporated businesses often show no books at all, and taxes are sometimes assessed on the basis of floor space, number of machines, and other indirect signs of financial status.

In personal taxation, too, evasion of income taxes has forced a heavy reliance on indirect taxes. Because of inaccurate reporting by taxpayers, income taxes in France and Italy are often assessed according to the outward signs of wealth. The French taxpayer, for instance, must declare the number of rooms in his house, the number of horsepower in his car, and whether he has a maid, a pet, or a piano. If his income seems out of line with these indexes, it can bring the assessor down on his head.

Consumer Taxes

In Britain, the burden of indirect taxation falls on the consumer through the purchase tax, which can go as high as 50 percent on autos and other durables. The government has the authority to move the rates up or down by 10 percent to aid in leveling off the business cycle. Rates vary widely by commodities, but they average out at about 20 percent across-the-board. A move is under way now to cut top rates and raise the lower rates gradually to bring the purchase tax to a single rate of about 20 percent. This, however, might lessen the influence of changes in the tax on consumer spending.

Business circles in Britain, mainly sparked by the powerful Federation of British Industries, are eying the use of indirect taxation on the Continent, particularly the French system. A recent FBI report suggested that the government consider shifting some of the burden of business taxation from a direct to an indirect basis.

The export incentive aspect of indirect taxation particularly has perked the ears of Britons. The French, for instance, exempt export sales from the sizable TVA. The Germans have a turnover tax, payable on all domestic sales, including intercompany sales, of 4 percent. Because its effect is compounded, the German manufacturer gets a rebate of 6 percent on his export sales, and this may be more than he has actually paid in turnover taxes.

Local Levies

Thus, the total tax burden on European industry on the national level counts many taxes whose effect are different from direct income taxation. But other taxes have the same effect. In Sweden, companies pay a deductible local income tax of 14 percent in addition to the 40 percent corporate rate imposed by the national government. This, in effect, raises the corporate rate to 48 percent. Germany also has a deductible municipal profits tax that goes as high as 15 percent.

In another way, leading European countries favor capital by greatly reducing double taxation on corporate dividends and profits. A stockholder gets a tax credit of 24 percent for dividends in France and 38.75 percent in Britain. In the United States, the deduction is only 4 percent.

Germany taxes a corporation on its distributed profits at the rate of 15 percent, compared to the rate of 51 percent on undistributed profits—similar to a system tried in the United States in the late 1930s. Although this is a definite incentive to distribution, it doesn't lower the corporate tax burden as much as the difference in rates would suggest. Because local profits taxes and capital assets taxes limit the amount available for distribution, a company ends up with a total direct tax bill of 65 percent even if it distributes 40 percent of those profits that are available for dividends.

III. How Individuals Fare

As in business taxation, personal income taxation in Europe tends to favor the reinvestment of capital by currying the rich. But, contrary to some myths about European taxes, in most countries they do not necessarily encourage the accumulation of capital by those who do not already have it. Many fortunes have been built in post-war Europe—mainly through corporations, for which reinvestment is easier. But the European tax odds are against the man who wants to save enough to start his own business, or the average executive who wants to build an estate for his family. For the tax rates on middle- and low-income groups are quite harsh.

Where Americans Stand

Collectively, Americans rank only below the Scandinavians in the share of their total tax burden paid in direct personal taxes (Table 1). But individually, Americans are not taxed so heavily as most Europeans—except in the very highest income brackets. This apparent conflict is partly due to the fact that incomes are higher in America; therefore lower rates produce more revenue.

The rich American is considerably worse off than his counterpart in Europe, not only because the U.S. top rate of 91 percent is the highest in the world, but also because there are probably more loopholes for wealthy Europeans.

This generalization, however, does not apply to landed wealth, since high estate taxes, with few loopholes, in such countries as Britain and Sweden often force inheritors of large holdings into bankruptcy.

Legal Dodge

High-paid Britons can escape taxes on a part of their income by giving part of it on a regular basis through a "deed of covenant" to other persons, who likely would be in a lower tax bracket. Also, the deeded income can be put into a trust for minor descendants as a way of avoiding estate taxes.

Capital gains treatment, usually considered a boon to wealthy Americans because of the reduced rate (25 percent maximum), is an outright loophole in Britain and France—especially for investors in the stock market. In France, such gains by individuals are not taxed at all, and in Britain they are taxed (at ordinary rates) only on securities held less than six months and on land held less than three years. But losses cannot be balanced against gains, as in America. And if the tax collector can consider stock trading—or real estate trading—as integral part of an investor's livelihood, the gains are taxed as ordinary income. Also, gambling gains are not taxable—unless it's practiced as a profession.

Nontaxable Benefits

Hidden-income benefits for executives—deductible to the corporation and not taxable to the recipients, abound in Europe. Among them: company-owned villas and apartments, chauffeur-driven cars, and expense-account travel for executives' wives. French companies can pay an indemnity for expenses, which amounts to under-the-table income. British executives can get sizable deferred income in the form of pensions; in a recent case such tax-free benefits added 40 percent to the executive's salary.

The "golden handshake" is a British dodge by which a man obtains tax-free compensation if he's fired. It has become so popular under the rash of mergers that Parliament finally set a limit on the tax-free amount. But the managing director of an acquired company recently got a golden hand-shake worth $70,000—then immediately went to work as head of a division of the acquiring company.

Middle-Income Treatment

But top tax rates in most European countries slash deeply into what Americans would consider middle-income territory—a fact that's seldom pointed out in comparisons of "maximum marginal" rates. A single Briton starts paying the 88.75 percent maximum rate on taxable income above $42,000 —a point where the U.S. marginal rate of 69 percent. Except for the range be-tween $12,000 and $17,000, the single American is at a lower marginal rate than the Briton until he reaches $100,000, when the U.S. rate of 89 percent applies.

Even France, which boasts some generous offsetting factors, applies its top rate of 65 percent on a single man's income over $12,000; the U.S. mar-ginal rate on this is 43 percent. Sweden's top rate of 65 percent applies at $29,000, where America's rate is a shade less at 62 percent. The glaring ex-ception to all this is Germany, where the top rate of 53 percent applies when taxable income reaches $27,000; the single American is already paying a marginal rate of 62 percent at this level. In all cases, split-income treatment for married couples works in favor of the American. In fact, in Sweden and Britain, taxation can penalize the working, middle-class wife.

U.S. Comes Out Ahead

The fact that Europe's top rates are lower than America's also obscures the fact that European rates below this point tend to be higher all down the line—with the notable exception of France. In Britain, too, there's an exception in the range of $12,000 to $17,000 where the flat rate of 38.75 percent on single persons is lower than the U.S. rates.

All this takes into account only national or federal rates. The income tax in New York and a few other states may make the U.S. comparison less favorable, but in most cases Americans still have an advantage. That's true especially in the case of Sweden, where there's a uniform 14 percent municipal income tax. And the sizable indirect taxes in France and Germany undoubtedly mean the total tax bite on middle incomes there is heavier than the total burden from all taxes that Americans in the same group are subject to.

Take the sales manager of an engineering firm near London, with an income of $9,000 and four dependents. His income tax bill is 21 percent of gross income, while the tab for a similar American is only 12 percent. In fact, a recent study of tax incidence in the United States indicates that an American at this income level pays about 23 percent of his gross income in taxes of all kinds —direct and indirect at all levels of government, including an imputed portion of corporate taxes that may be shifted into prices.

The Base

The tax base in Europe also is broader than it is in the U.S. That's because exemptions and deductions are less (except in France), which means low income groups in most European countries pay taxes at levels where Americans would not be taxed. Thus, in Sweden 54 percent of the population pays income taxes; in Britain, 36 percent, and in the United States only 26 percent (though more Americans actually file non-taxable returns).

These comparisons on the basis of official exchange rates are distorted, of course, by differences in the cost of living. But if you take actual percentage of gross income paid in income taxes and social security charges by a standard, four-person family, and convert incomes on an exchange rate that adjusts for the cost of living, you still come up with a favorable picture of American taxation on middle and low incomes (Chart 2).

On this basis, the U.S. taxpayer fares better than the German until he earns about $68,000—above which point he's taxed more heavily than the German. He's better off than a comparable Swede until his income is over $200,000. And he's taxed less than the Briton all along the line.

Chart 2

Who Pays the Most

American families pay less than those in Britain, Germany, and Sweden — until they reach high income levels.

[Chart shows percent of gross income paid in taxes by a family with two children. Tax includes national and local income taxes and social security charges, except for U.S. state income taxes.]

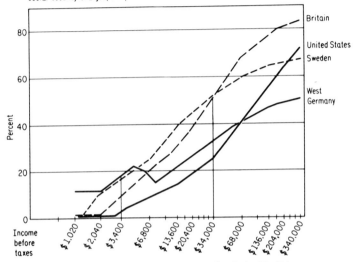

Data: Logarithmic chart, with pounds converted to dollars, from National Institute Economic Review, Britain.

IV. Beneficial Exchange

The great variety of tax devices that one finds from one country to another obviously have sprung from the historical needs of each country. Thus, it would be a mistake to judge one system good and another bad. For one thing, comparative taxation is a toddling new field in which little has been reduced to common denominators, and the effects that can be seen are at best signposts.

Even so, there are lessons to be learned. The U.S. Treasury recently turned to Europe for ideas on its proposed investment credit and on treatment of foreign-source income. The British have drawn on American experience to make recent changes in capital gains taxation. French production taxes are now being studies both in Britain and in Common Market countries.

Areas for Study

Currently, the Brookings Institution in Washington is studying the effects of taxation on economic growth; in the next year or so it will take a hard look at European experience. But some European countries with great tax incentives to business investment have not grown so fast as others. Thus, close examination may indicate that such provisos only facilitate financing, while the actual incentives lie elsewhere—in budgetary policies, in cooperative relations between government and business, or in pent-up consumer demand.

One area that perhaps warrants further study is this: America has developed the greatest capital markets in the world, while the once-great capital markets of Europe have declined to a position of chronic dearth, particularly in long-term funds.

To what extent has taxation contributed to this? To what extent has Europe's large social security spending (and the concomitant tax burden) curtailed the role of insurance companies and other large savings institutions in the capital markets? And to what extent has taxation prevented Europe from developing a shareholding public anything near America's 17-million stockholders? An intensive exploration of these questions might well bear lessons for the Europeans—and also might suggest a direction for reinforcing the American tax system.

Thus, examination of tax systems on both sides of the Atlantic may prove mutually beneficial. And, as competition grows between America and its largest trading partner, Europe, there is sure to be an increasing exchange of ideas in the field of taxation.

CHOICE BETWEEN ALTERNATIVE COUNTRIES FOR THE LOCATION OF AN ENTERPRISE*

I. INTRODUCTION

The present epoch is not only an epoch of national economic expansion but also, to a very significant extent, an epoch of expansion across national frontiers. If the attention is turned only to Europe—apart from the part which is under Communist control—it can be observed that American corporations especially have established numerous branch offices and subsidiary corporations all through Europe.

America's opposite party, Russia, is also starting to penetrate within the area, viz. it has a Belgian corporation manufacturing motor cars. Furthermore, Asiatic countries, notably Japan, are finding their way into the European market and are either establishing or planning to establish sales organizations and manufacturing plants in Europe.

Finally, the European corporations themselves are—especially under the stimulus of the Common Market Treaty and EFTA arrangements—also fanning out into the other European countries.

It is obvious that if the management of a corporation has decided to create an organization in another country a host of factors have to be evaluated, such as marketing possibilities, banking facilities, transportation costs, labor costs, etc. One of the significant factors which has a bearing on the choice of the location of the new enterprise is the tax factor.

This article intends to describe in a general way how the tax aspects may influence the decision to choose a specific location. It focusses thereby not so much on the actual results but on the method to be used.

Main Functions of an Enterprise

An enterprise usually has several functions. In the first place it will often manufacture certain products. In the second place it will act as a trader, i.e., it will either purchase raw materials, use them for manufacturing

* *European Taxation*, September 15, 1963, pp 143–148.

or processing and then sell the finished product, or, where no manufacturing or processing takes place, it will act solely as a dealer. Finally, many enterprises have as an additional or as their sole function the holding of incorporeal values; stocks, bonds, patents and similar rights.

In principle these three functions which we will call the manufacturing function, trading function and holding function could be performed by one organization, either a branch office or subsidiary corporation, or by two or three different organizations located in one, two or three different countries. This will depend on the final decision which is made.

The question whether a branch office or a subsidiary corporation is preferable may also depend on tax factors. This problem will be discussed in the next section (Section II).

A discussion of the tax problems connected with the three functions as listed above is given in Sections III, IV and V.

II. Branch Office or Subsidiary Corporation

Before dealing with purely tax factors it is observed that in many cases it may be virtually impossible to carry out activities in a foreign country through a branch office.

This may be due to *inter alia*:

> the legislation of the country concerned which may prescribe that certain activities may only be carried out by a domestic corporation (this was the case in Sweden before 1956);
> the chauvinistic attitude of the customers, who may only want to deal with a domestic corporation;
> the need for local capital, which might be difficult to obtain for a foreign corporation;
> the size and the nature of the activities, which might require obtaining capital by issuing securities.

Taxes, however, may also play a certain role, since in some cases taxation of a branch office is more favorable than taxation of a subsidiary corporation or vice versa. This is illustrated in the two following examples.

EXAMPLE 1. A Dutch corporation carrying on a business through a branch office within Belgium will be subject to the Belgian "impôt des non-résidents" at a flat rate of 35 percent on its Belgian income. This income will be exempt from Dutch income tax by virtue of Article 4 of the Belgian-Dutch tax treaty and Article III of the Final Protocol belonging to that treaty.

If this Dutch corporation has a subsidiary corporation in Belgium the situation is as follows: Profits of this subsidiary which are not distributed are subject to the Belgian "impôt des société" at a rate of 35 percent on that part which exceeds B.frs. 5,000,000 ($100,000). The first B.frs. 5,000,-000 is taxed at a lower rate of 30 percent.[1] In this respect a subsidiary corporation is only slightly more favorable than a branch office. Distributed profits, however, are subject to a 30 percent "impôt des sociétés" plus a dividend withholding tax at the rate of 18.2 percent. Therefore, if profits before income tax are assumed to be 100, only 70 can be distributed to the Dutch parent corporation. This 70 is again reduced by 18.2 percent (or 12.74 units), so that ultimately 57.26 is received by the Dutch parent, meaning an effective tax burden of 48.74 percent. These dividends are exempt from Dutch corporation income tax (Article 10 Corporation Income Tax Ordinance 1942).

The conclusion therefore is that in this case having a branch office is more advantageous than having a subsidiary corporation if it is assumed that the profits are distributed. For nondistributed profits the difference is fairly small.

EXAMPLE 2. A United Kingdom corporation carrying on a business through a branch office in Germany will be subject to the following income taxes on its German income: "Körperschaftsteuer" at a flat rate of 49 percent and "Gewerbesteuer" at a flat rate of 15 percent.[2] Since the "Gewerbesteuer" is a deductible item for the "Korperschaftsteuer" and for itself, the "Gewerbesteuer" can be roughly assumed to amount to 13.5 percent, meaning that the total German income tax burden is 62.5 percent. According to Article XVI of the Germany-United Kingdom tax treaty the German taxes may be credited against the United Kingdom profits and income tax, meaning that no additional United Kingdom tax will be due, since the combined rate of U.K. income tax and Profits tax is only 53.75 percent.

If, however, the activities in Germany are carried on by a German subsidiary corporation the rate of the German "Körperschaftsteuer'" is 51 percent on undistributed profits and 15 percent on distributed profits. In the latter case there is a German withholding tax on the dividends at a (reduced) rate of 15 percent. Article VI German-United Kingdom tax treaty. Further we take into account the "Gewerbesteuer" levied on the corporation's income (average is assumed to be 13.5 percent). This tax is a deductible item for the "Körperschaftsteuer".

The effective rate of the "Körperschaftsteuer" and the "Gewerbesteuer" together varies from 33.8 to 57.7 percent, depending on the amount of profits which are distributed.

This is computed as follows: Assume that all profits after tax (x) are distributed. If total profits before tax are called P then $P = x$ (profits after

---

[1] A still lower rate is applied if the nondistributed profits are less than B.frs. 1,250,000. This will be disregarded here.

[2] The basic rate is 5 percent. The municipalities, however, are entitled to apply a multiplication factor, which is usually 3. See 2 Eur. Tax. 154 (1962).

tax) $+ 0.15x$ (15 percent "Körperschaftsteuer" on distributed profits) $+$ 0.51 ($P - x - 0.135P$) (51 percent "Körperschaftsteuer" on nondistributed profits less the "Gewerbesteuer") $+ 0.135P$ ("Gewerbesteuer").

This is true since total profits must be equal to distributed profits plus taxes.

$$P = x + 0.15x + 0.51P - 0.51x - 0.06885P + 0.135P$$
$$0.42385P = 0.64x$$
$$x = 0.662P$$

Income tax ("Körperschaftsteuer" + "Gewerbesteuer") $+ 0.338$ or 33.8 percent.

If no profit at all is distributed the "Körperschaftsteuer" is 51 percent on profits less 13.5 percent "Gewerbesteuer" or 44.11 percent. Combined with 13.5 percent "Gewerbesteuer" this makes a maximum rate of 57.66 percent.

Assuming that all profits are distributed, the total German income tax will be 33.8 percent plus 15 percent dividend withholding tax on the remaining 66.2 percent of profits, or 43.7 percent. In this case since total United Kingdom tax amounts to 53.75 percent there will be 10 percent additional United Kingdom tax.

The conclusion is that if all profits are distributed, having a subsidiary corporation is more advantageous than having a branch office. On the other hand if all profits are retained, a branch office is somewhat more advantageous.

Note that this example can only be used for a rough comparison, since we have disregarded the German "Vermögensteuer" (which is levied on the corporation's net worth) and that part of the German "Gewerbesteuer" which is also imposed on the corporation's net worth. These taxes, however, will be the same for a subsidiary as for a branch.

Another reason why there sometimes exists a significant difference between a branch office and a subsidiary corporation is that special tax advantages may be offered to either of the two forms of organization. For example, a number of Swiss cantons offer special advantages to Holding companies and Domiciliary companies, provided they are incorporated in Switzerland.[3]

Finally it must be noted that in some cases it may be advantageous to avoid having a branch or subsidiary corporation at all in the foreign country. This will notably be the case if the tax rates in that country are higher than in the country where the business is a resident and it is indeed possible to trade within the foreign country without attracting tax. This will need some explanation. Many countries, including Belgium, Germany, Switzerland, Austria and the Netherlands, will only tax business income if the business is carried on through a permanent establishment (branch) in that country.

[3] See 2 Eur. Tax. 29 et seq (1962).

Therefore if in such a case a trade is carried on within the particular country without having a branch the income earned will not be taxable. It must be noted that having a "permanent representative" i.e. an agency which has either the authority to negotiate and conclude contracts, or holds stock, will often be considered as having a permanent establishment.

III. MANUFACTURING CORPORATION

The location of a manufacturing corporation will *inter alia* be determined by local labor costs, cost of energy and transportation, cost of raw material and finished product.

Tax wise, the following are primarily significant:

import duties in the customer countries
income taxes in the country of location.

A. Import Duties

The most significant recent development is the creation of custom unions. Such a union has already been attained by Belgium, the Netherlands and Luxembourg (Benelux Convention of February 3, 1958) meaning that no tariffs are imposed on merchandise moving from one of these countries to the partner countries and that a common external tariff is levied. The same goal has been set for the Common Market countries and although it will take some years to achieve, at present the tariffs between the member countries of the Common Market are already significantly lower than between these member countries and nonmember countries.

Therefore it may be advantageous for a corporation of a nonmember country which has a considerable part of its customers within the Common Market to establish a plant within the Common Market, because then the relatively high external tariff is levied on the relatively low value of imported raw materials and vice versa the relatively high value of the finished product will only be taxed with the relatively low inner tariff. Obviously a similar advantage is offered by the Benelux countries.

B. Income Tax

Many countries offer special incentives to investment. This may be done in various ways, *inter alia* by:

the granting of an investment allowance, whereby an amount may be deducted from taxable income in addition to the depreciation allowances e.g. in Luxembourg, the Netherlands, and the United Kingdom;

granting a total or partial tax holiday (e.g. in the southern part of Italy, in Ireland (for specified activities at Shannon airport), and in Luxembourg; exempting profits from export industries (e.g. Ireland);

the granting of accelerated depreciation such as in Denmark, France, the Netherlands, and the United Kingdom.

How these favorable tax provisions may affect a decision in a special case will be illustrated in the following example.

EXAMPLE 3. A German corporation wishes to enter the Benelux market and since, by virtue of the Benelux convention, no tariffs are imposed on merchandise imported from one Benelux country to another it decides to establish a subsidiary corporation in one of those countries which will manufacture a certain product. The investment will be relatively heavy—assume $3,000,000 in fixed assets and $2,000,000 for other depreciable assets—so that any investment incentives will be welcomed. It is further assumed that the investment must be replaced within 10 years and that the annual profits after deduction of all costs, but before taxes are $400,000, i.e. during the life of the invested assets an amount of $4,000,000 will be earned.

The German corporation has learned that the rates of income tax in Belgium, the Netherlands and Luxembourg are respectively 30 percent, 45 percent and approximately 45 percent (combined rate of corporation income tax and business income tax), while in Luxembourg a net worth tax is also levied on the corporation's net worth at a flat rate of approximately 1 percent (combined rate of net worth tax and business tax on net worth).

This seems to indicate that Belgium is the most favorable country for the location of the business, followed by the Netherlands, and finally Luxembourg, but the corporation wishes a more thorough investigation, which will prove that the above assumption is not true.

The following computation is made.

BELGIUM

Total profits (10 years period)	$ 4,000,000
Corporation income tax 30 percent (minimum rate if all profits are distributed)	$ 1,200,000
Available for distribution	$ 2,800,000
Dividend withholding tax 18.2 percent	$ 509,600
Received by the German parent	$ 2,290,400
German corporation income tax and business tax (assume 40 percent, which is about the minimum rate) on $ 2,800,000 (grossed up amount) is $ 1,120,000 less Belgian tax of $ 509,600 makes[4]	$ 610,400
Net income after taxes	$ 1,680,000

[4] There is no tax treaty between Belgium and Germany, therefore the German national rules apply, which provide for a credit against tax (Article 34c Income Tax Law). Such a treaty is under negotiation, however.

LUXEMBOURG

Total profits (10 years period)		$ 4,000,000
Investment allowance 20 percent of $ 3,000,000	$ 600,000	
Special exemption (8 year's period) 25 percent of 8 × $ 4,000,000 (annual profit)[5]	$ 800,000	
Total deduction	$ 1,400,000	

Taxable amount $ 4,000,000—$ 1,400,000 or $ 2,600,000.

Corporation income tax + business tax on income 45 percent on $ 2,600,000	$ 1,170,000	
Net worth tax + business tax on net worth 1% of 10 × ½ × $ 5,000,000[6]	$ 250,000	
		$ 1,420,000
Available for distribution		$ 2,580,000
Dividend withholding tax 10 percent [Article 13 (4) German-Luxembourg treaty]		$ 258,000
Received by the German parent		$ 2,322,000
No tax in Germany by virtue of the German-Luxembourg tax treaty [Article 20 (2) treaty]		$ ...,...
Net income after taxes		$ 2,322,000

NETHERLANDS

Total profits (10 year's period)		$ 4,000,000
Investment allowance 10 percent of $ 3,000,000 = $ 301,987. $ 300,000.		

Taxable income $ 4,000,000 — $ 300,000 = $ 3,700,000.

Corporation income tax 45 percent on $ 3,700,000		$ 1,665,000
Available for distribution		$ 2,335,000
Dividend withholding tax 10 percent [Article 13 (4) Dutch-German tax treaty]		$ 233,500
Received by the German parent		$ 2,101,500
No tax in Germany [Article 20 (2) Dutch-German tax treaty] ..		$ ...,...
Net income after taxes		$ 2,101,500

[5] This special exemption of 25 percent of the annual profits is granted on request by the Minister of Finance. It is given for a maximum period of 8 years. Cf. our article Tax incentives in Luxembourg, 2 Eur. Tax. 171 (1962).

[6] Since the assets which were originally invested will depreciate we have assumed that during the 10 years period on the average ½ of the invested capital is present.

The conclusion is that—with the figures assumed in the above example—it is not Belgium but Luxembourg which is the most favorable country for the German business.

IV. SALES CORPORATIONS

A sales corporation has fewer regional ties than a manufacturing unit. In many cases—especially for products which have a world wide market—it may be possible to have a sales corporation in a particular country to deal in merchandise which never enters the country of location but is exclusively traded between third countries.

It is obvious that it may be advantageous for a manufacturing corporation which is established in a country with relatively high tax rates to create a sales corporation or establish a sales department in a country with lower rates. In such a case part of the profit may be shifted to the sales organization and thus be subject to a lower rate.

A country which offers particular advantages for foreign controlled international sales corporations is Switzerland, where some cantons subject only a fraction of the profits of such corporations to income tax, or apply a special reduced tax rate.[7]

> EXAMPLES ARE: Canton of Vaud where only $\frac{1}{5}$ of the profits are taxed (but at the maximum rate of 25 percent). Canton of Zug imposes income tax on $\frac{1}{4}$ of total profits (maximum rate 6.6 percent).
> Canton of Geneva levies tax at a reduced flat rate of 7 percent.
> Canton of Luzern reduces its rate to a flat 4 percent.
> Note, however, that to these taxes must be added the federal income tax (maximum rate 8 percent).

It may be remarked here that in some cases even a subsidiary sales corporation may be considered to be a permanent establishment of its foreign parent. This will be the case, for instance, if the sales corporation has the authority to negotiate and conclude contracts for its parent or if it holds stock for the latter. In such a case not only the profits of the subsidiary sales corporation will be subject to tax in the country concerned but also the profits of the parent which are derived through the subsidiary.

Another major problem between the parent corporation and its subsidiary is billing. The prices must be established as if the parent were dealing at arm's length with its subsidiary. Since this problem, however, is not so much connected with the location of a corporation, we only mention it without discussing it at length.

---

[7] Cf. 2 Eur. Tax. 32 (1962).

V. Holding Companies

In many cases part of the function of a corporation is to hold controlling stock in other corporations, or to hold stock and bonds for portfolio investment or to hold patents in order to exploit the licenses.

These three types of holding company will be discussed below.

A. Holding Companies for Controlling Purposes

Special exemptions for dividend income received by this type of holding companies exist in a number of countries such as Austria, Belgium, Denmark, France, Germany, Luxembourg, the Netherlands, Norway, Sweden, Switzerland, and the United Kingdom.

Austria, Germany, Norway, Sweden, and the United Kingdom, however, only exempt dividends received from domestic corporations, although sometimes by virtue of treaty provisions foreign dividends may also qualify for an exemption.

With respect to Denmark a special approval of the Ministry of Finance is needed to qualify for the exemption.

It must be emphasized, however, that many countries impose a withholding tax on dividends paid by a resident corporation to a nonresident stockholder. Therefore, a holding company, even if it is exempt from corporation income tax in its country of residence may have to bear the withholding taxes which are imposed on the dividends in the countries from which the income originates. In this connection tax treaties may be significant since they usually provide that those withholding taxes are to be levied at a reduced rate or not at all.

Therefore a country such as Luxembourg, although it has very favorable tax provisions for holding companies, is often at a disadvantage since it has concluded relatively few tax treaties, and some of these exclude holding companies from the treaty.

Again many countries which favor holding companies levy a net worth tax instead of income taxes, e.g. Luxembourg and Switzerland.

The following example will illustrate that the Netherlands—since it both exempts dividend income of holding companies and does not levy a net worth tax—is in many cases the best location for a holding company. It must be noted, however, that each case should be investigated separately, since it might well be that in other cases another country comes out as the best solution. France, for instance, offers advantages to holding companies which are very similar to the Dutch provisions.

EXAMPLE 4. An English corporation wishes to set up three manufacturing corporations, one each in France, Italy, and Greece. It has been decided to create a holding company on the continent which will collect the profits of the operating corporations and which if necessary will finance the existing or newly to be created operating corporations.

This construction has been chosen because of the strict English exchange provisions which make it impracticable to remit the profits to the United Kingdom.

Three different countries will be used for an example to see to what extent they are suitable for the location of a holding company viz: Luxembourg, the Netherlands and Switzerland.

We assume that each subsidiary corporation is 100 percent owned and distributes a dividend of $ 50,000 annually, and that the net worth of the holding company amounts to $ 2,000,000.

Holding Company in Luxembourg

French withholding tax on dividends at the normal rate of 24 percent, since the France-Luxembourg tax treaty does not allow a reduction of French withholding tax in this case	$ 12,000
Italian withholding tax 15 percent (there is no tax treaty between Italy and Luxembourg)	$ 7,500
Greek withholding tax 38.25 percent (there is no tax treaty between Greece and Luxembourg)	$ 19,125
Luxembourg annual net worth tax 0.16 percent (the dividends are exempt from income tax)	$ 3,200
Total tax	$ 41,825

Holding Company in the Netherlands

French withholding tax not due (Article VIII Dutch-French tax treaty)	$ ..,...
Italian withholding tax not due [Article VII (2) Dutch-Italian tax treaty]	$ ..,...
Greek withholding tax 38.25 percent (no tax treaty between Greece and the Netherlands)	$ 19,125
Dutch income tax in practice levied approximately 0.5 percent	$ 655
Total tax	$ 19,780

Holding Company in Switzerland

French withholding tax not due (Article 10 French-Swiss tax treaty)	$ ..,...
Italian withholding tax—15 percent (no tax treaty between Italy and Switzerland)	$ 7,500
Greek withholding tax—38.25 percent (no tax treaty between Switzerland and Greece)	$ 19,125
Swiss net worth tax in, say, canton of Ticino—0.125 percent (the dividends are exempt from income tax)	$ 2,500
Total tax	$ 29,125

The conclusion is, therefore, that the Netherlands would be, in this particular case, the most suitable country of location.

B. Holding Companies for Portfolio Investment

In some cases it will be advantageous for a corporation to create a special subsidiary corporation whose only purpose is to administer portfolio investments.

In this respect Liechtenstein, Luxembourg and Switzerland offer favorable provisions, especially if the portfolio consists of securities which are of many nationalities.

The Netherlands also has favorable provisions, but for the exemption to be applicable the stock of the portfolio investment holding company must either be quoted on a Dutch stock exchange or the company must distribute at least 60 percent of the income annually, which makes the provisions somewhat difficult to apply.[8]

C. Patent Holding Companies

For this type of holding company only a few countries have favorable provisions. In Liechtenstein they can be brought into the category of "domiciliary companies" if they receive income exclusively from foreign sources.[9] In that case they are exempt from the income tax and are subject only to a small net worth tax.

In Luxembourg the special provisions for holding companies also include patent holding companies, so that they may be exempt from the normal tax and are only subject to a small net worth tax instead.

Although Switzerland has much less favorable provisions for holding companies—since the Federal income tax will be due—than the other two countries it might be worth while to keep this country in mind also, since it has concluded many more tax treaties than Liechtenstein or Luxembourg. Just as is the case with dividends this may mean a considerable saving in withholding tax which would otherwise be due in the country from which the royalties originate.

We will illustrate this in the following example:

EXAMPLE 5. Assume that a Dutch corporation wishes to contribute its patents to either a Luxembourg or Swiss patent holding company and to accumulate other profits in the holding company. The royalties are paid by United States and United Kingdom licensees, and the annual amounts are $ 100,000 from both countries. The value of the patents is $ 2,000,000.

---

[8] See 1 Eur. Tax. 10, page 5 (1961).
[9] See for the definition of domiciliary company 3 Eur. Tax. 132 (1963).

Luxembourg Holding Company

Royalties from the U.S.: withholding tax 30 percent (the American-Luxembourg treaty does not apply to Luxembourg holding companies, art. XV) .... $ 30,000
Royalties from the U.K.: withholding tax 38.75 percent (no treaty between Luxembourg and the U.K.) .... $ 38,750
Luxembourg net worth tax 0.16 percent .... $ 3,200

Total tax .... $ 71,950

If the royalties are distributed to the Dutch parent there is no Luxembourg withholding tax, but in the Netherlands the usual dividend exemption will not be granted since one of the conditions for such an exemption has not been fulfilled, i.e. the Luxembourg holding company is not subject to a normal income tax.

The Dutch parent corporation will therefore ultimately receive the dividends of $ 200,000 less $ 71,950 = $ 128,050. After Dutch tax of 45 percent there remains a net amount of $ 70,450.

Swiss Holding Company

Royalties from the U.S. no withholding tax (Article VIII American-Swiss tax treaty) .... $ ..,...
Royalties from the U.K. no withholding tax (Article VII Swiss-United Kingdom tax treaty) .... $ ..,...
Swiss Federal income tax (according to the tax table) .... $ 11,200
Swiss Federal and cantonal net worth tax (no cantonal income tax) say 0.12 percent .... $ 4,000

Total tax .... $ 15,200

If the profits are distributed on a later date to the Dutch parent a withholding at the reduced rate of 3 percent is due (Article 9 Dutch-Swiss tax treaty), but the dividends will be exempt from Dutch corporation income tax since the profits from which they have been paid have been subject to an income tax. Thus the net amount the Dutch parent corporation ultimately receives is $ 200,000 less $ 15,200 = $ 184,800 less deduction of 3 percent withholding tax of $ 5,514 = $ 173,256.

It is obvious that the Swiss holding company is much more advantageous than the Luxembourg holding company in this particular case.

It must be noted that in many cases existing patents are transferred to a patent holding company. It is obvious that in most cases this will mean that a profit will be realized on those patents, since the tax administration of the country where the parent corporation is located will demand that the transfer be effectuated at arm's length basis. It seems therefore wise to take this into account in planning a patent holding company, since the tax on those profits may amount to a considerable sum. A possibility to avoid this taxation is to have the patent holding company develop the patent itself, i.e. perform the research itself.

TAX COORDINATION IS THE NEXT STEP*

One might suppose that when the six countries of the European Economic Community completely abolish customs duties on goods traded among themselves, internal barriers to commerce will have disappeared. Quite the contrary! Border controls will still be needed unless the Six drastically reform their tax systems. EEC cannot become an economic entity, permitting the unencumbered movement of trade, capital and labor, unless the Six complement their customs union with a tax union.

Border controls will be necessary even after customs duties have been completely abolished because all EEC countries levy a general tax at varying rates on sales of goods and services at every stage of production and distribution.

Each EEC country exempts its exports from these sales taxes while imposing a "compensatory tax" on imports. The import tax is designed to eliminate the competitive advantage that would otherwise accrue—for instance, to Renault cars in the German market since they are exempted from the French sales tax upon export to Germany, while Volkswagens sold in Germany are subject to the German sales tax at various stages of production and distribution.

The prevalence of different excise duties on tobacco and liquor also requires border controls. Moreover, capital might concentrate in those EEC countries which levy the lowest income taxes. The disparity in income tax rates might also stimulate artificial migration of labor.

Finally, differences in social security systems may also induce workers to migrate to that country whose system is most advantageous. Contributions paid by employers and employees differ considerably among the six countries, as do benefits for old age, unemployment and family allowances.

All these considerations have made the need for a tax union increasingly apparent. Government officials and fiscal experts, in their gropings for a realistic solution to the problem, have not been able to rely on past experience or precedent. In 1953 the Coal and Steel Community explored the effect of sales taxes imposed by member countries upon the commodities under its authority. And the Benelux countries (Belgium, the Netherlands and Luxembourg) made limited adjustments in their general sales taxes. In neither in

* Carl S. Shoup, *Challenge*, October, 1963, pp. 4–7.

stance, however, were vast revenues involved, nor was a drastic overhaul of existing tax structures required.

EEC made its first major attempt to solve the problem of a tax union in 1960, when it appointed a Fiscal and Financial Committee, under the Chairmanship of Prof. Fritz Neumark of the Goethe University in Frankfurt. The committee, consisting of experts from the six EEC countries and myself, as an "outside" representative, suggested measures to harmonize the various systems. The recommendations of the committee are embodied in a 150-page report published by EEC in French and German and recently translated into English.

The goal, concluded the committee, should be to harmonize rather than unify the existing tax systems. The tax structure of each nation reflects its own particular social, political and economic realities and cannot be replaced suddenly by a new system. Even if all EEC countries employed the same types of taxes, tax rates could not possibly be uniform. No one set of tax rates could yield the different amounts of revenue required by the various governments of EEC countries.

For instance, annual per capita income varies greatly among the Six, ranging from $598 in Italy to $1,441 in Luxembourg (the figures, taken from the Neumark report, are for 1959). Per capita tax revenues vary in about the same proportion, from $119 in Italy to $295 in Luxembourg, or, if social security contributions are included, from $169 in Italy to $420 in Luxembourg.

Of course, tax revenues as a percentage of GNP (1959) fall within a narrower range, from 18 percent in Belgium to 25 percent in West Germany (the German percentage includes state taxes). If social security contributions are included, the percentages are substantially higher. Belgium is once again at the bottom of the scale with 24 percent, while West Germany is at the other extreme with 34 percent. France, incidentally, which is reputedly unable to tax herself, collects about as large a percentage of GNP in taxes as West Germany.

Tax harmonization as a goal is harder to achieve than a customs union. A customs union requires construction of a common external tariff in place of differing tariff schedules hitherto imposed by the several countries. Tax harmonization, in contrast, must achieve a certain degree of uniformity without going the whole way. The problem thus becomes one of a delicate balance in determining just how far the process of coordinating tax systems should go.

The temptation to initiate tax reforms for their own sake compounds the problem. The Neumark committee clearly did not consider tax reform within its sphere of competence, but it found that two reforms were essential to the harmonization of EEC systems. One deals with the general sales or turnover tax and the other with the personal income tax structure.

All EEC countries except France levy a turnover tax. (The French impose a value added tax which will be discussed later.) With some exceptions (agri-

Chart 1

ECC Government Revenues As Percent of
Gross National Product 1955-61

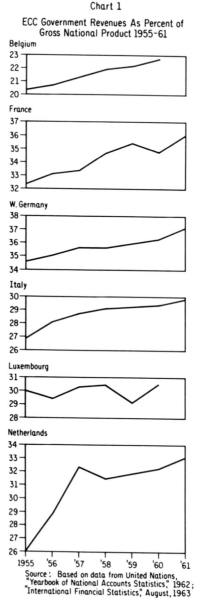

Source : Based on data from United Nations,
"Yearbook of National Accounts Statistics," 1962;
"International Financial Statistics," August, 1963

cultural products in all EEC countries and retail sales in Belgium and the Netherlands are exempted), the turnover tax is levied on every sale at rates that usually range from three to four percent. These levies, which may be repeatedly collected at various stages of manufacture, as well as on the wholesale and retail sales, are known as "cascade taxes."

The turnover tax, it is argued, more heavily penalizes small producers than large integrated corporations. Since the tax is imposed on sales, it rests lightly on vertically integrated concerns which produce their own raw materials, do most or all of their own manufacturing and perhaps even sell the finished product directly to the consumer through retail outlets which they own. On the other hand, the small independent firms that buy and sell to each other are placed at a disadvantage by the turnover tax which is collected each time a sale takes place.

The Neumark committee concluded that tax coordination cannot be achieved among the Six unless turnover taxes are eventually replaced by a value added tax system similar to that prevailing in France. The French tax is applied to manufacturing and wholesaling firms on the value that each firm adds to the commodities it processes or handles.

Let us assume, for example, that a manufacturer sells a car for 10,000 francs, before taxes. He computes a tentative tax of 25 percent, or 2,500 francs. He subtracts from that tentative tax the 25 percent tax previously passed on to him when he purchased tires, glass, paint, fenders and other materials going into the car. He pays the balance; this is the tax on the value his firm has added to the car. The same is done by manufacturers at each level of production.

Unlike the turnover tax, the value added tax is "neutral" in that it places an equal burden on both integrated manufacturers and small producers. Ultimately no more is collected in taxes whether one, three or 20 sales take place during production and wholesaling. (The value added tax, however, is not imposed on farm products such as bread and milk, or on other exempt items such as newspapers.)

The French tax on value added marks a great advance in indirect taxation. While at present it is only used in France, if the recommendations of the Neumark committee are followed, it will become the mainstay of the fiscal systems in EEC countries.

Why did the committee think that the replacement of the turnover tax by a value added tax, which at first sight looks simply like an internal tax reform, was necessary to harmonize the tax structures of the various EEC nations? Partly because adoption of the value added tax would make possible an accurate computation of export exemptions and compensating import taxes. Furthermore, this tax would have less of an influence on trade and commerce among member nations than the prevailing turnover tax. One of the Common Market's major aims is to free the movement of goods, labor and capital from the impact of disparate taxes.

The first of these reasons is perhaps the most important. When a German exporter, for instance, sells merchandise to a Dutch firm, he is exempted from the four percent German turnover tax. In addition, the German government grants him a tax rebate, a repayment of the turnover tax that had been levied during the earlier stages of manufacture or handling in Germany. More or less arbitrary estimates are used to determine the repayment to the exporter, since the precise amount of turnover tax previously paid is impossible to compute.

The Netherlands, in turn, levies a compensating import tax on the German goods. The compensating import tax, unlike customs duties, equalizes the tax burden on foreign and domestic products. But since the turnover tax makes it impossible to determine the exact amount to be assessed in compensatory taxes, more or less arbitrary levies are imposed. This gives rise to the claim that countries use the compensatory tax to protect domestic industries.

An advantage of the French value added tax is that amount levied can be exactly computed. If a record of tax paid on value added is entered on invoices all the way down from the earliest stages of production, the cumulative tax paid by the time the article is exported can be easily determined. It is somewhat more difficult to compute accurately the compensation import tax, but it is still easier than under the turnover tax.

But even if all EEC countries adopt the French value added tax, border controls would still be required in order to insure that excessive export refunds are not granted or import compensating taxes avoided. Yet economic union remains imperfect as long as border controls (i.e., fiscal frontiers) persist. Some tax specialists believe that controls can be maintained at the factory and warehouse instead of the border. It remains to be seen, however, whether this is really practicable.

A true solution, at least in the economists' view, would require an even more drastic change in existing tax structures. The value added tax could be revised to eliminate exemptions for exports and compensating taxes on imports. Thus, instead of taxing commodities depending on their *destination* (that is, whether they are to be sold on the domestic or foreign market), they would be taxed on the basis of *origin* (that is, they would be subjected to the tax of the country in which they are produced).

To oversimplify somewhat, suppose a commodity, produced in country A, which levies a four percent sales tax, is exported to country B, which levies a three percent tax. Under the present system, country A exempts exports from its four percent tax through the export exemption and refund. But country B imposes a three percent import compensating tax on the imported commodity. This places the imported commodity on an equally competitive basis with goods manufactured in country B.

If the origin principle were adopted, the commodity would be subjected to the four percent tax of A (country of origin), but would not pay the three percent tax levied by B (importing country) on domestic products. Thus the commodity which had been subjected to a four percent tax of country A would compete in country B with domestic products which had been subjected to a three percent sales tax. Under such a system, border controls would become unnecessary, but competitive advantages would be drastically altered. The result might be a major shift in the pattern of trade.

The disruption might not be severe if EEC nations allowed their currencies to fluctuate freely on the international market. Upon the abolition of export exemptions and import compensating levies, the exports of country A, which imposes a higher tax rate, might decline. The resulting adverse balance of payments might compel country A to devalue its currency which, in turn, would restore the competitive position of its products even though they continued to be taxed at a higher rate than products of country B. But such a course is not attractive, since the EEC nations do not wish the international exchange rates of their currencies to fluctuate.

Consequently, the country-of-origin principle would require uniform sales tax rates in all EEC countries. In fact, the Neumark committee recommended adoption of uniform sales taxes as the ultimate long-range goal.

The other reform proposal of the committee concerned personal income taxes. Until a few years ago, Belgium, France and Italy levied a two-stage personal income tax: a general progressive income tax was imposed on top of flat-rate taxes levied on different sources of income—one "schedular" tax on wages, another on interest income, and so on. Corporations paid a schedular tax, and dividend income was subjected to the progressive income tax.

The complexity of the personal income tax structure in France, Belgium, and Italy made it almost impossible to calculate accurately the comparative tax burdens' in these three countries or to compare them to the tax liability in Germany, Luxembourg and the Netherlands, which collect a uniform progressive income tax. Some time ago France shifted to a uniform personal income tax system, and recently Belgium initiated a similar change. Italy, however, shows no intention of replacing the older two-level system.

The Neumark committee recommended that all six EEC countries adopt a simple graduated income tax system. The committee, however, did not propose that personal income tax rates be made uniform throughout the Common Market. Differing fiscal needs and economic resources of the several countries make it impossible to institute uniform taxes and tax rates.

Once internal barriers are abolished, to what extent would the existence of diverse taxes and tax rates cause workers to seek employment where taxes are lowest? This question is extremely difficult to answer, since, at present, labor mobility is not great enough to make this problem pressing. Moreover, countries imposing higher income taxes may provide a higher level of government service for education, public health, and so on. Varying tax burdens, however, may also reflect differences in military expenditures.

Capital moves fairly readily from one EEC country to another in search of maximum returns after taxes. Thus if capital flows among EEC nations are not to be distorted, corporate taxes must be harmonized. But this cannot be achieved by merely equalizing corporate tax rates in various countries. The true burden of a profits tax depends on depreciation schedules, the accounting system used to calculate changes in inventory and other technicalities which are not reflected in the tax rate. At present, corporate income tax rates of EEC countries do not differ greatly, but depreciation rules and the treatment of distributed profits as compared with undistributed profits vary considerably.

A Columbia University research project in the School of International Affairs is now attempting to determine equivalent real tax rates in the six countries under a uniform system of depreciation accounting. The data gathered thus far indicates differences that are, if anything, even greater than the Neumark committee suspected. Nevertheless, the committee was aware that various features of the corporate income tax structures required more extensive harmonization than personal income tax rates.

One important area which the committee's recommendations did not cover were EEC's social security systems, which are currently undergoing transformation. Some countries had a series of separate funds for various specific purposes (such as old age, disability, hospitalization) which were jointly financed by employers and employees. Now, however, the trend is for all the funds to be amalgamated in a single social security system. This point is of particular importance since social security contributions constitute a much larger percentage of total wages in most EEC countries than in the U.S. or Britain. In fact, in some EEC countries the contribution or payroll tax is as much as 50 percent of a worker's wage.

The nontransferability of social security benefits is a special but related problem. For instance, if a worker moves to another country when he retires, he may be unable to collect his social security benefits. The worker may also forfeit accrued benefits if he moves from one country to another in search of employment. Obviously, EEC countries must agree to some reciprocity of social security benefits if labor mobility is not to be hampered.

The problem of tax harmonization among EEC countries is unique and cannot be equated with the U.S. experience. The U.S. has 50 different state tax systems that have become more or less harmonized, as well as congeries of local tax systems. But they are overshadowed by the federal internal revenue structure.

The EEC countries, in contrast, must coordinate their national and, in some instances, local tax systems without the cushioning effect of an overall community-wide tax structure. They must coordinate six extremely complex, sophisticated, highly developed tax systems that are products of distinct national economic and social forces. They must do so in the face of tax rates that absorb a larger percentage of gross national product than U.S. federal, state and local taxes combined. The magnitude of the task is only now becoming apparent and, as harmonization proceeds, many new problems will undoubtedly be uncovered.

Furthermore, some of the problems that can already be identified require policy decisions beyond the realm of public finance—for instance, social security questions that have social as well as economic implications. If the community is enlarged, these problems will be magnified and multiplied. This may be the case even if new members have only associated status, as Greece has at present.

Ultimately EEC may develop into a federation. Then, as part of the taxing power is transferred to a community-wide political authority, the problem of harmonizing the tax systems will become less acute. Conversely, progressive fiscal harmonization among the Six may give an added push to federalism.

Uniform rates in certain taxes might place one or more EEC nations in such a difficult fiscal position that they would raise other tax rates. This, in turn, might accelerate the outflow of labor and capital. As the tax base dwindled, still higher taxes might be required until the economy progressively deteriorated. Although such a development seems unlikely in the near future, the Neumark committee warned that some kind of intercountry financial compensation or fiscal aid may be required in the foreseeable future.

The economic advantages accruing from the integration of EEC fiscal systems may ultimately exceed the obvious advantages of the customs union which is by now more than half accomplished. The EEC's progress toward tax harmonization will be watched with keen interest by common markets and free trade areas in other parts of the world.

IMPORTING A TAX FROM EUROPE*

Congress is about to explore the 'value added' tax, popular in Common Market countries, as a possible substitute for part of the corporate tax. The size, shape, and timing of future cuts in excise taxes will be argued next week before the House Ways & Means Committee. The subject of the hearings is the $13-billion-plus of excises collected by the federal government each year—and which of the taxes should be reduced, dropped entirely, or kept as is.

But also on tap will be the U.S. debut of something called "the value added" tax—a sales tax that is almost unknown here, but is becoming the predominant corporation tax of the European Common Market countries. The case for the value added tax—as an alternative to all or part of the corporate income tax, or as an alternative to some of existing excises—will be advanced by Dr. Dan Throop Smith, Harvard professor who was a top Treasury official during the Eisenhower Administration. Smith made a special trip to Europe last month to get last-minute assessments of the tax in England (where it was recently rejected) and in the Common Market countries (where it is being more widely adopted).

Chmn. Wilbur Mills is starting off his excise hearings with a two-day educational session by Smith and other experts. The value added tax is the only "new tax" that gets a mention in Mills' announcement of hearings. After the experts have their say, the remainder of the hearings will be devoted to pleas by specific industries for relief from their specific excise.

I. WHAT IT IS

The value added tax actually is a sales or excise tax based not on the total price at which a manufacturer sells his product, but on the gross receipts or sales of the company minus cost of goods purchased from other businesses. Thus the tax is based on the total amount of wages, salaries, rent, interest, and profits. As a simple example; if the factory price of a car is $1,200 and the cost of materials, tires, parts, glass, is $700, then the manufacturer pays an excise on $500, instead of on $1,200.

But the value added tax would be paid similarly by all other manufac-

* Reprinted from *Business Week*, June 13, 1964, pp. 136, 138, 140.

844

turers, those who make glass, sheet metal, fabrics, paints, nuts and bolts, and by those who produce the raw materials out of which such parts and materials are made. Because of the broad base this implies, even assuming exemptions for a great many products or industries, a low rate would produce large revenues. But the burden would be imposed generally at all stages of production rather than concentrating the tax—as our present excises do—on the price charged by the final manufacturer (as in autos) or by the retailer (as in furs, jewelry, and the like).

Richard E. Slitor, a Treasury expert, says a 1 percent value added tax (always assuming wide exemptions) could bring in about $2.5 billion. That would be equal to the amount brought in now by five points on the corporate income tax. Thus, Slitor suggests, a 2 percent value added tax could finance reductions in the corporate tax rate from the 48 percent effective on 1965 income, down to 38 percent—the rate that prevailed in the years between World War II and Korea.

Generally, this is what the proponents of the value added tax have in mind—substituting the tax for a portion of the corporate income tax. It is also suggested that its adoption is a way of eliminating the present excises on specific products by substituting this more general tax that would spread the burden more evenly across all producers.

Rising interest in the value added tax has shown up in inquiries to Washington tax experts and the Congressional committees. Private tax experts have already been holding conferences:

- Last fall, the Tax Institute of America had a special meeting on the subject at which Smith, Slitor, and others analyzed the virtues and vices of the tax.
- Published in mid-June will be a book on the Role of Direct and Indirect Taxes in the Federal Revenue System—the results of a conference last fall held by the Brookings Institution and the National Bureau of Economic Research.
- The Committee for Economic Development and the U.S. Chamber of Commerce are now taking "good hard looks" at the value added tax, along with other tax matters.

CED, in backing corporate and individual tax reductions a couple of years ago, didn't specifically recommend the value added tax, but said that "serious attention should be given the establishment of a broad-based, low-rate federal excise tax to provide additional revenues and relieve the burden of income taxes."

II. Pros and Cons

Dr. Smith described the tax to the Ways & Means Committee last year as one that "is a tax on costs and profits with a deduction for costs of items purchased from companies that have already been subject to the tax. The significance of it is that it gives, in effect, tax neutrality between costs and profits . . . you do not have any tax subsidization of extravagant expenditures as happens with the corporate income tax. If one saves on costs . . . the tax is the same as it was before. Or if one reduces profits by expending on a new item of cost, again the tax is the same as before."

Opponents of the value added tax, including labor and the Treasury Dept., want no shift away from the U.S. reliance on income taxes. They see the value added tax as shifting more of the tax burden to individuals, as against corporations, and as a sure way of boosting the price level—as any excise tax must do.

This gives rise to the argument whether the corporate income tax in many cases isn't also passed along to the consumer by companies that have some power to set their prices—and keep them—where they think they ought to be. As Smith and others point out, the corporate income tax can be described as a tax upon efficiency. The companies that make profits pay the tax, those that are inefficient and just break even just don't pay at all for the use of the resources of the country.

Opponents counter that it would impose a new tax burden on new businesses which may not become profitable for a number of years, and should be encouraged, as a matter of national policy.

Smith's suggestion to the Ways & Means Committee was to give the value added tax a try:". . .put in a very low rate of value added tax, which would bring in as much revenue, for instance, as 10 percentages points on the corporate tax." After getting some experience with it, he said, we might "ultimately have the total burden on business divided equally between a corporate income tax and a value added tax."

III. For Social Security?

However, the tax changes of the last two years have weakened this argument about the burden of the corporate income tax. The liberalization of depreciation allowances, the 7 percent investment tax credit, and the corporate income tax reduction to 48 percent (on next year's income) has had the same effect in increasing the rate of return on capital investment as cutting the corporate rate by 18 to 23 percentage points, according to George Terborgh, of the Machinery & Allied Products Institute. Under such conditions, "lowering the tax burden on corporations" isn't likely to win a lot of converts among the tax-writing legislators in the immediate future.

However, some government officials say, there's another twist being given to the value added tax; academics are talking about it as an alternative to higher social security taxes. The argument for this is that as the social security payroll tax approaches 10 percent it is already providing an incentive for employers to invest in labor-saving machinery rather than in labor; whereas the value added tax would be neutral, since it taxes all costs and not labor alone.

This is the kind of suggestion that gives second thoughts to some of the experts who like the value added tax. They would be dead set against it except as a substitute for the corporate income tax. "As an added tax," one suggests, "it would be another source of revenue for the spenders."

IV. SPREAD IN EUROPE

Regardless of what happens here, the spread of the value added tax over Europe is something that will plague our exporting businesses and government negotiators for years to come. Internal Revenue Commissioner Mortimer Caplin has raised the question of whether the United States is relying too heavily on income taxes — "particularly as compared to the practices of the other nations of the world."

Caplin, who is leaving IRS next month, points out that "80 percent of this country's revenue comes from income tax; less than 12 percent from excise taxes," whereas in Europe excises bring in from 40 percent to 60 percent, mostly from turnover or value added taxes.

As the Common Market countries harmonize their tax systems, for instance, the Netherlands, which collects about 58 percent in income taxes, would raise more from excises while reducing its income tax burden.

The French type of value added tax seems to have the inside track, Caplin said, rather than the German, which is a turnover tax pure and simple—a 6 percent excise levied on the full price of the goods each time there is a transaction. Already, the German government has taken steps towards switching to a value added tax in place of its turnover tax. When this happens, the average tax on U.S. exports to Germany will jump from the present 6 percent to 10 percent—over and above the duty on the item.

Here's how the tax works, taking the French as an example. An exporter ships an auto to France, for which he paid $2,000, and, say, $250 freight and insurance. The duty now being renegotiated downward during the Kennedy Round at Geneva is 25.2 percent, or $567. But on top of this new total of landed cost plus duty—$2,817—the French then apply their 25 percent value added tax paid on the car. Suppliers whose parts went into the making of the car also get rebates for the value added taxes they paid that went into the exported product.

United States negotiators at Geneva aren't negotiating on this, but are urging the Europeans to make the shift in a manner posing the least amount of difficulties for U.S. exports. Studies of the value added tax are being made in Europe, taking into account the fact that the percentage scale of the tax burden on corporations in Europe and the United States seems to be about the same, regardless of the different manner in which the taxes are levied.

One sharp setback for the value added idea, however, comes from England, where a government committee turned it down flatly as an alternative to the present reliance on out-and-out sales tax. "The report of the committee on turnover taxation" in March found that the value added tax would not help exports or the growth of the British economy, and would be more burdensome administratively than the purchase or sales tax. The committee also rejected the value added tax as a substitute for the corporate income tax. The committee said in so many words that businessmen would seek to recover a value added tax by raising their prices, while removal of the "profits tax" would not tend to reduce prices.

ADDITIONAL READINGS

Barlow, E. R., and Wender, Ira T., *Foreign Investment and Taxation*, Englewood Cliffs, N.J.: Prentice-Hall, Inc., 1955.

Cohen, Mark I., "Common Market Operations of Controlled Corporations Under the Revenue Act of 1962," *The Tax Executive*, July, 1963, pp. 253–272.

Connolly, John L., "Foreign Depreciation Methods," *Taxes*, March, 1962, pp. 174–195.

Fayerweather, John, "A Principled Approach to Overseas Taxation," *Business Topics*, Autumn, 1961, pp. 49–59.

Graves, Thomas J., "Problems in the Allocation of Foreign Income," *The Tax Executive*, July, 1964, pp. 284–292.

Hoefs, Richard A., and Bunge, George H., "Tax Considerations in International Business Under the 1962 Revenue Act," *Journal of Taxation*, November, 1963, pp. 294–299.

Morton, Senator Thurston R., "Proposed Taxes on Income Earned Abroad by American Business Firms," *Congressional Record*, Speech, September 15, 1961.

O'Connor, Walter F., "U. S. Taxation of Earnings of American-Controlled Foreign Corporations," *Taxes*, September, 1964, pp. 588–613.

Rado, Alan R., *U. S. Taxation of Foreign Investment*, International Bureau of Fiscal Documentation, Amsterdam, 1963.

Richman, Peggy, *Taxation of Foreign Investment Income*, Baltimore, Md.: The Johns Hopkins Press, 1963.

Taxation and Operations Abroad, Tax Institute, Princeton, 1960.

Wales, Robert W., "Tax Policy in Relation to Foreign Business Income," *Taxes*, December, 1962, pp. 961–973.

Wender, Ira T., "Tax Planning for International Operations under the Revenue Act of 1962—A Case Study," *Taxes*, December, 1963, pp. 835–858.

chapter *14*

Accounting, Controlling, and Reporting in International Finance

The foreign subsidiary of a U.S. company must keep a set of books in accordance with the laws of the country in which it is operating. If it is in a country with a significant rate of inflation, it will most likely have to keep a separate set of books to determine its actual local profits or losses. These profits or losses must, at the same time, be reported back to the parent company in a manner which is meaningful to the management (as well as to the stockholders). This requires the translating of financial results from local currency to dollars on a basis which reflects the effects of the exchange controls and exchange rates of the country involved. The above mentioned problems are the essence of accounting in international operations, and they must often be accomplished with personnel who have been trained in widely differing methods of accounting and in environments where accounting practices and the role of the accountant is far different from that in the United States.

Here are several examples of the differing roles of the accountant. We find that in Finland, the certified public accountant's responsibility is to examine the records and report to the annual stockholders' meeting an analysis not only of the company's balance sheet and operating statement, but also of its management. He must, in effect, decide whether the actions of management were such as to best accomplish the company's function in accordance with prevailing law and good business practice. In France, on the other hand, the equivalent of the certified public account (*l'expert comptable*) does not even perform the audit function. It is done by a *Commissaire aux Comptes* who may not even be a member of the accounting profession and who need only examine the balance sheet (given him by company management) and observe physical verification of assets.

Accounting practice and local law in Sweden permits the company to set up a reserve for possible future decline in value of inventory. At the discretion of management, this may be as much as sixty percent of the year-end inventory. And, in Brazil, we find that deductions for depreciation are limited to movable property, no allowance being permissible for depreciation of buildings or other improvements to real property.

These differences in regulations and practices do not, however, present any great difficulties. Parent companies generally send their own audit personnel out to each subsidiary to examine the books on behalf of central management and of the stockholders of the parent company. Also, some multinational companies require all of their subsidiaries to follow the same accounting methods as prescribed for the U.S. parent so that accounts and product costs can be compared between different countries. Then, any deviations from prescribed practices which are needed to comply with local regulations or practices are made locally by working paper adjustments. The first reading in this chapter, by H. H. Oppenheimer, discusses in much greater detail the differences in accounting practices and regulations, and the problems which these differences cause in consolidating financial statements of the subsidiaries with that of the parent.

A more vital problem in international accounting is that of the effect of inflation and the accompanying exchange controls, multiple exchange rates and periodic devaluations. It is important for the student of international finance to have a clear grasp of the effect of these on the financial accounting of a subsidiary. The article by John J. Miller contains a hypothetical business transaction which shows the effects of a devaluation upon profits, depending upon the actions taken, by several different firms, prior to a devaluation. The articles by George C. Watt and S. R. Sapienza contain an explanation of the question, "How can it be that a subsidiary may show a significant profit in terms of local currency, but must report a loss to the parent company after having translated operating results into dollars?" And, more vitally, they discuss the actions which a firm might take to avoid such a translation loss.

The last article, by John Verroen, gives an overall view of how a major company, ITT, has organized its international financial operations to deal with the problems mentioned above. Of particular interest is the method of measuring and limiting "exposure" of subsidiaries to exchange losses in case of currency depreciation or devaluation.

Many companies, like ITT have learned to operate profitably under conditions of rapid inflation and devaluation. Unfortunately, too many U.S. firms have an unreasonable fear of such an operating environment. The financial managers and accountants are habituated to the U.S. environment, with a very low rate of inflation and no concern of devaluation. Their business sense and training do not prepare them to react correctly to the situations existing in many of the underdeveloped (and some of the industrialized) countries. The readings in this chapter demonstrate, however, that there are operating methods to deal with such an environment. These operations require different accounting methods, different credit policies, different cash flows—a new approach to corporate financial planning. But, it is possible to operate under what, to a novice, seems to be an unbearable financial climate, and still make a dollar profit for the U.S. stockholders.

REPORTING UNDISTRIBUTABLE FOREIGN EARNINGS*

Foreign accounting principles differ in various respects from American principles for statutory and practice reasons. Therefore the consolidation of foreign and domestic financial statements creates problems of reconciliation of differences in principles and of resultant adjustments. In this article the author discusses major problems and his personal concept of their treatment, particularly those involving restrictions on surplus and their disclosure.

With the continuing upsurge in American overseas investment, financial reporting for foreign operations is constantly assuming increasing importance. The easing of exchange restrictions has, however, brought into sharper focus many complex foreign trade accounting problems of long standing. One of these concerns the distinction between distributable and undistributable foreign earnings and the adequacy of current reporting practices with respect to disclosure of the undistributable or restricted foreign earnings. This article is devoted to an examination of that problem and the expression of certain conclusions which, it should be noted, do not necessarily reflect the views of any firm with which the author has been associated. It is also necessary to point out that the problem presented is but one aspect of the much broader question whether significant differences still exist between domestic and foreign operations which would preclude the inclusion of foreign accounts in consolidated reports. Consideration of this broad question suggests the need for a reappraisal of Chapter 12 of the AICPA's Accounting Research Bulletin No. 43 which deals with foreign operations.

CONSOLIDATION POLICY AND PRACTICE

Accounting Research Bulletins

Because of war conditions and exchange restrictions, Accounting Research Bulletin No. 4, which was issued in December, 1939, stated that "accounting must take into consideration the fact that most foreign assets stand in some degree of jeopardy, so far as ultimate realization by United States owners is

* H. H. Oppenheimer, CPA, *The New York Certified Public Accountant*, February 1962, pp. 99–106.

concerned." Disregarding the somewhat changed conditions, Chapter 12 of ARB No. 43, which superseded ARB No. 4 in 1953, is couched in similar language and also states that "careful consideration should be given to the fundamental question of whether it is proper to consolidate the statements of foreign subsidiaries with the statements of United States companies. Whether consolidation of foreign subsidiaries is decided upon or not, adequate disclosure of foreign operations should be made."

Thus, while suggesting the need to weigh carefully the individual circumstances which may have a bearing upon any decision to consolidate foreign subsidiaries, the bulletin fails to provide any objective criteria to determine the circumstances under which it is either proper or improper to do so. In this connection, only one substantive change was made in ARB No. 43. While ARB No. 4 stated that it was a "safe rule" to include foreign earnings only to the extent received, ARB No. 43 now indicates that it is "sound procedure" to include in the accounts of American companies, in addition, foreign earnings to the extent that "unrestricted funds are available for transmission" to the United States. It should also be noted that Accounting Research Bulletin No. 51, issued in August, 1959, and dealing with consolidated statements, is silent on this question except for a reference to Chapter 12 of ARB No. 43.

Consolidation Practice

Since the issuance of ARB No. 43, foreign currencies have, of course, stabilized and exchange restrictions have been eased in many countries. These changes have been recognized in actual reporting practice, which is attested to by the trend towards consolidation of foreign and domestic accounts. The 1960 AICPA survey, *Accounting Trends and Techniques*, reviewed 381 companies with foreign subsidiaries. Of these, 145 companies consolidated all foreign and domestic companies. Of the remaining companies, 230 prepared only partial domestic and/or foreign consolidations and, of these, 49 companies generally made no distinction between domestic and foreign subsidiaries *per se*, while 57 companies excluded all foreign subsidiaries, and another 58 companies stated that subsidiaries in certain geographical locations were excluded from consolidated statements. The remaining companies either gave various other reasons for excluding foreign subsidiaries from consolidation, or did not state their policy in this respect.

It is apparent, then, that considerable support exists for the practice of consolidating foreign operations with domestic accounts. While it cannot be said that such consolidations will be realistic in all circumstances, at least the exclusion of all foreign subsidiaries, *ipso facto*, from consolidations is no longer warranted. Since most European currencies and quite a few in other parts of the world are now externally convertible, and since transmission of profits to the United States is frequently possible, the propriety of consolidating foreign subsidiaries should not be open to question is most cases.

One of the basic criteria in determining consolidation policy is, of course, the degree of parent company control. At times, export and import restrictions may have a significant effect on parent company control. However, more frequently, commercial transactions between a parent company and its foreign subsidiaries located in the major trading centers of the world can take place relatively freely. In such cases, the parent exercises the usual rights incident to stock ownership, except for the transmission of profits to the United States, which may be restricted.

The mere existence of such exchange restrictions on the transmission of foreign profits to the United States does not, however, constitute *prima facie* evidence of a significant impairment of working control. True, the parent company's normal right to receive foreign dividends has been abrogated, but that would appear to be academic if there were not any intent to exercise that right in any event. In other words, if a major portion of the foreign earnings would be reinvested in the foreign country even in the absence of transmission restrictions, then the fact that transmission restrictions exist does not *ipso facto* impair working control and, hence, should not preclude consolidating the foreign accounts with those of the domestic parent company.

While each situation must be decided on its own merits, we may conclude that from the viewpoint of consolidation policy there often is no essential difference between foreign and domestic operations.

STANDARDS OF DISCLOSURE IN CONSOLIDATIONS

Uniformity of Domestic and Foreign Principles and Standards

Having concluded that it may be entirely proper to consolidate foreign subsidiaries where parent company working control has not been effectively impaired, we must address ourselves to the specific problem of determining whether or not a need exists to accord foreign retained earnings special treatment insofar as disclosure in financial statements is concerned. In view of the conclusions already reached, it would be utterly illogical to argue that foreign earnings *per se* merit any special disclosure treatment in consolidated financial reports once the propriety of consolidating foreign and domestic earnings has been established in any given case. On the contrary, a consolidation presupposes that generally accepted accounting principles and standards of reporting as practiced in the United States have been consistently applied to foregn and domestic operations alike.

In following accounting and reporting practices for foreign operations which ostensibly are, or should be, in consonance with the AICPA pronouncements, we must, however, be cognizant of the fact that there are certain features inherent in foreign operations which have not specifically been dealt with in any official AICPA pronouncements. Until certain of these official pronouncements are amplified in this respect, it is incumbent upon us first to search for the intent behind accepted accounting principles and reporting standards, and then to apply the same basic concepts to both foreign and domestic situations. Unless such an approach is followed, the consolidation of foreign subsidiaries could render consolidated reports materially misleading. Adopting this crucial standard, let us now proceed to examine the seemingly simple problem of disclosing restrictions which limit the availability of dividends.

RESTRICTIONS ON THE PAYMENT OF DIVIDENDS

Reporting Standards for Surplus Restrictions

Reporting standards have always taken into consideration the needs of stockholders who are vitally interested in the extent to which earnings may be available for dividends. In the Institute's publication entitled *Generally Accepted Auditing Standards* reference is made to the fact that fairness of balance sheet presentation requires disclosure of restrictions on dividends. Accounting Terminology Bulletin No. 1 is perhaps even more explicit on this point in stating that ". . . there should, so far as practicable, be an indication of the extent to which the amounts have been appropriated or are restricted as to withdrawal."

In domestic accounting we find, for example, that restrictions on dividend availability may be imposed by bond indentures, corporate charters, state laws, and perhaps by voluntary actions of the board of directors. By one method or another disclosure is commonly made, as is evidenced by the fact that out of 600 companies reviewed for 1960 in *Accounting Trends and Techniques*, 391 companies disclosed various restrictions. By far the largest number of restrictions related to long-term debt indentures or agreements, but it is noteworthy that only three cases pertained to certain restrictions peculiar to foreign operations which, in essence, are no different than any domestic legal restrictions on the availability of retained earnings for dividends.

Application of Reporting Standard to Foreign Operations

As previously indicated, the test of what constitutes a "restriction" should be the same for both domestic and foreign accounts, particularly where they are consolidated. The criterion is simply the availability of retained earnings for withdrawal. The term "withdrawal" is, of course, understood to connote a cash (or property) distribution in the form of dividends; and from the viewpoint of a United States parent company, "cash" is understood to mean U.S. dollars. It follows that the physical withdrawal of foreign currency earnings necessarily involves the sale of foreign currencies for dollars, either prior or subsequent to the transmission of funds to a United States bank for the account of the domestic parent company.

Inasmuch as the right of transmission of funds to the United States may be abrogated or curtailed by foreign governmental regulations, the withdrawal of foreign earnings is susceptible to a restrictive factor which is not present in domestic operations. The fact that we are dealing here with a matter peculiar to foreign operations, which has not been specifically considered in official pronouncements or other texts, in no way invalidates the conclusion that this constitutes a cause of surplus restrictions.

Similarly, the intent of the disclosure criterion quoted above would also be applicable with equal force to other facets of foreign operations. For example, domestic laws of the various states may contain statutory restrictions as to dividend declaration. Although conceptually quite different, foreign statutory limitations have the same restrictive effect from the viewpoint of disclosure in financial reports. In short, in order to ascertain whether foreign retained earnings are subject to restrictions we must be cognizant of the following considerations:

1. Exchange remittance restrictions
2. Other restrictions imposed by law and regulations
3. Restrictions arising from conforming foreign accounting practices with U. S. practices
4. Problems of currency translation

FOREIGN RESTRICTIONS ON DIVIDENDS

Exchange Restrictions

As has already been indicated, the presence of exchange restriction on the transmission of foreign earnings is not necessarily incompatible with sound consolidation theory and practice. With the continuing need to reinvest earnings abroad for expansion, an abridgment of the normal right to transmit foreign subsidiary profits to the United States frequently does not necessarily constitute an impairment of parent company control. Some therefore argue that it is not necessary to call attention to surplus restrictions that are due to foreign exchange regulations if it is possible to utilize the foreign earnings for plant expansion. Such an assertion is, in the author's opinion, incongruous because it confuses the dividend payment right with the investment of funds attributable to retained earnings.

To demonstrate the fallacy of the argument for the omission of a surplus restriction disclosure where foreign earnings are reinvested, let us consider an analogy in the domestic accounting field: Suppose a domestic subsidiary has considerable retained earnings all of which are unavailable for dividends by reason of stipulations in a bond indenture. The subsidiary therefore reinvests the earnings in new physical facilities. Generally accepted standards of disclosure would dictate that the surplus restriction be disclosed in the financial statements of the subsidiary as well as in consolidated reports. The reason for such mandatory disclosure is easy to detect; it is based on the obvious fact that, in the absence of the bond indenture, dividends could be paid out and plant expansion could be financed by borrowings, if necessary.

Now, let us substitute a foreign company for the domestic subsidiary and replace the restrictions in a bond indenture with exchange restrictions on the transmission of foreign profits to the United States; we are compelled to conclude that the domestic and foreign situations are, in essence, identical. The existence, and presumably also the magnitude, of restrictions on retained earnings must, therefore, be divulged in financial reports when foreign exchange restrictions limit the payment of cash dividends. In a number of countries, the question of dividend remittances can only be determined on an individual basis for each company.

The Effect of Investment Laws

The subject of profit transmission to the United States is closely linked with various foreign investment laws. Capital registered under these laws usually secures a repatriation guarantee, that is, the proceeds on liquidation of such investments may be remitted to the United States. In addition, profits derived from such investments are often accorded preferential treatment with regard to taxation and transfer to the United States. This special treatment of capital, profits, or both, is usually limited to investments made prior or subsequent to a specific date, and often applies only to certain industries essential to the local economies. At times, a distinction is also made between investments made in the form of foreign exchange, i.e., cash in dollars, and those made in the form of equipment or other tangible property.

Another consideration involves the fact that profits from registered investments may sometimes qualify for preferential exchange rates upon remittance to the United States, while profits derived from other operations in the same country can only be remitted at a less favorable free market exchange rate. Then too, there are a number of countries which impose restrictions only on the repatriation or return of capital investments, but permit the free transfer of dividends. Since there must be a presumption that foreign investments will ordinarily not be liquidated, restrictions on the transfer of capital *per se* are not pertinent to this discussion. Similarly, we may generally also dismiss foreign requirements for specific permission to transfer profits. Usually, such official authorization is merely a matter of formality, and permission will be readily granted. However, where experience of individual companies indicates otherwise, disclosure of exchange restrictions is, of course, necessary.

Most of the major trading currencies are now fully convertible, or nearly so. Early in 1961, Belgium, France, Germany, Ireland, Italy, Luxembourg, the Netherlands, Peru, Saudi Arabia, Sweden, and the United Kingdom formally accepted the obligations of full convertibility under the International Monetary Fund's Articles of Agreement, and a number of Western Hemisphere countries, among them Canada, Mexico, Panama, and the United States, had done so in earlier years.

The formal acceptance of the full convertibility principle by these countries has entailed the virtually complete elimination of currency restrictions for current trade payments, although some of these countries have retained certain limitations applicable to capital transactions. Generally, however, these countries and others such as Austria, Denmark, Norway, Portugal, and Switzerland permit the transfer of profits freely with only minor exceptions of practical consequences. While some of these countries require prior approval of exchange control authorities, this is as a rule, freely granted. By way of contrast, there were eleven member countries of the International Monetary Fund in which multiple currency practices prevailed early in 1961, and, in many of these profit remittances may be completely blocked, at least for certain companies not entitled to preferential treatment because their activities are not considered essential to the local economies.

It will be noted, therefore, that the application of exchange regulations must be constantly observed, both with respect to individual countries and from the viewpoint of individual companies, bearing in mind that changes in laws and regulations attributable to economic or political developments may sometimes have a profound and sudden effect on dividend remittability. From the viewpoint of an American stockholder, however, it makes little difference whether withdrawal of earnings is wholly or partly precluded because of exchange restrictions or for some other possibly more important reasons such as those examined below.

Statutory Reserves and Dividend Limitations

One of the most familiar restrictions arises from the operation of foreign corporate laws. This refers, of course, to the so-called "Legal Reserves," sometimes also referred to as "Statutory Reserves." Such reserves cannot be utilized for the payment of dividends. They are as a rule created out of earnings and therefore constitute restricted surplus. Occasionally, contributed capital in excess of par value may also be designated as a legal or statutory reserve. In addition, certain countries also limit the dividend declaration out of otherwise unrestricted earnings. The complex legal requirements in force in Denmark provide an excellent illustration of both types of restrictions.

In that country, a minimum statutory reserve equal to 10 percent of share capital must be created. In order to establish this reserve, corporations must transfer to the reserve 10 percent of the annual profits after depreciation and after covering prior losses, but before taxes. When the reserve is equal to 10 percent of capital stock, an additional 5 percent of annual profits must be added to the reserve until such time as a maximum reserve, equal to 25 percent of capital, has been established. Furthermore, no dividends may be paid until the foregoing annual transfers from profits to the reserve have been made. In addition, dividends may not exceed 6 percent of capital in any year until the statutory reserve has reached the minimum level of 10 percent of capital. Moreover, between September 1957 and August 1958, a law was in effect which required a 10 percent reduction in declared dividends of companies that had paid more than 6 percent of share capital in the previous year.

While these Danish laws are perhaps more complex than many others, restrictions of this nature are very common. Legal reserves must be established in such countries as Mexico, Belgium, former Belgian Congo, Germany, Switzerland, Italy, Greece, Turkey, Norway, Sweden, Spain, Portugal, France, and many of the African republics which have been economically tied to the French franc currency area. In most cases, the legal reserves are based on percentages of nominal capital stock, but in a few isolated cases the base may include, in addition, certain specified liabilities. Some laws also make provision for utilization of the reserves to extinguish accumulated deficits in other surplus accounts.

The transfer of the annual earnings to surplus, legal reserves and other accounts, as required by law, and dividend declarations, must also be approved, in many countries, by stockholders at a duly constituted meeting. This generally gives rise to the following possibility: the transfers to legal reserves and other accounts, as required, may not be made in the applicable year but rather in the year approved. In this event the legal reserves would be understated and the unrestricted retained earnings overstated.

The dividend limitations which fall outside of the requirements for legal reserves are not nearly as widespread. Such other limitations exist, for example, in the United Arab Republic where they are coupled with a system of compulsory investments in government securities. Among notable exceptions to the list of countries which enforce legal reserves and other dividend restrictions, we must include the Netherlands, the United Kingdom, and most other countries which follow the British accounting and legal systems. It is, therefore, particularly noteworthy that consolidated reports of British and Dutch companies frequently state the amounts of statutory reserves applicable to subsidiaries located outside of those countries.

Since reference has been made to consolidated reports, it is also pertinent to note the following statement contained in Accounting Research Bulletin No. 51: "Occasionally, subsidiary companies capitalize earned surplus arising since acquisition, by means of a stock dividend or otherwise. This does not require a transfer to capital surplus on consolidation, inasmuch as the retained earnings in the consolidated financial statements should reflect the accumulated earnings of the consolidated group not distributed to the shareholders of, or capitalized by, the parent company." In this connection, it should be pointed out that such capitalized post-acquisition earnings of both domestic and foreign subsidiaries are analogous to the legal reserves discussed above; in each case, there is implied an intent to restrict the withdrawal of earnings permanently.

While no issue is taken with the premise that capitalized post-acquisition earnings of a subsidiary represent accumulated retained earnings to the consolidated group, it must be recognized that such capitalization is a legal act, initiated by the subsidiary's board of directors, which effectively limits the amount of dividend distribution to the parent company permanently in much the same way as a legal reserve. By way of contrast, exchange remittance restrictions are at least susceptible to economic conditions which may lead to their eventual relaxation or removal. It follows that capitalized post-acquisition earnings as well as legal reserves constitute, in some respects, more important restrictions than regulations precluding the transfer of earnings. Regardless of the degree of permanency involved, however, with the removal of many exchange restrictions, legal reserves and other elements comprising total accumulated earnings now require separate emphasis.

EFFECT OF DIVERSE FOREIGN ACCOUNTING PRACTICES

It will be appreciated that differing economic, social, or political developments, as well as local foreign customs, bookkeeping, tax or other regulations result in a great variety of foreign financial and accounting practices. For instance, it is often customary for foreign boards of directors to restrict surplus voluntarily in order to gain certain tax benefits, or with the specific objective of forestalling stockholders' demands for increased dividends. Apart from the fact that foreign companies sometimes portray these surplus appropriations erroneously as liability reserves, they are no different from many surplus restrictions which we may encounter in the United States.

We will often find more fundamental departures from generally accepted American practices. In such instances, the foreign accounts must be restated so that they will conform to practices in this country. The required adjustments generally are not reflected in the official books or reports of the foreign companies and, at best, a memorandum entry might be made in the accounts. Obviously, we cannot undo foreign laws by workpaper or memorandum adjustments made solely for the purpose of conforming the foreign books to our standards. If follows that we cannot alter the amount of surplus which a foreign company may declare as dividends under local laws and regulations.

In view of this, a consolidation adjustment for an understatement of foreign net worth generally results in restricted surplus, since such surplus *legally* does not exist under foreign laws. Conversely, adjustments reducing the official foreign net worth will not give rise to a corresponding reduction in the amount of dividends which could legally be declared. In reducing the stockholders' equity, however, the free or unrestricted surplus on an American basis would have to be reduced, so that dollar surplus would be less than the amount which the foreign company could legally distribute. A distribution of the entire foreign surplus would then give rise to a return of capital on an American accounting basis. It may be well to cite some specific examples of these diverse accounting practices, bearing in mind that these practices are subject to constantly changing foreign laws and differences in their interpretation.

Overstatement of Net Assets

While unfavorable distortions of net worth appear to be much more prevalent, some foreign accounting practices may result in a hyperbolical misrepresentation of stockholders equity from the American viewpoint. One such practice is the failure to reflect amortization of leasehold improvements of depreciation of certain classes of buildings. Other depreciation reserves may also be inadequate where accounting records must conform to tax laws and regulation which often circumscribe depreciation rates. In these cases, procedures may differ for each enterprise and, consequently, the applicable foreign laws and private plans must be reviewed on an individual basis.

This is also the case with respect to the omission of liabilities. In some foreign countries it is not customary to make periodic accruals for estimated liabilities under formal or compulsory pension, retirement, or separation benefit plans. It may be found that these and other payroll fringe benefits are handled on a cash basis, or that accruals are made only when earnings permit.

A significant departure from sound practice may be encountered in Denmark where current income taxes may be accounted for on the cash basis.

Another feature arises under German law which expressly permits the omission of the "Capital Levy" liability from the balance sheet, provided adequate footnote disclosure is made of the present value of this liability. The reference here is to a tax on net assets at June 21, 1948, the date of the German Currency Reform and, to a lesser degree, to a tax on profits resulting from the conversion of Reichsmark to Deutsche Mark. This tax is payable in equal quarterly installments until 1979, calculated to include interest at 4½ percent. Although the liability cannot be escaped, prepayment will result in the saving of interest. Of course, German companies have the option to record the present or discounted value of this liability in their accounts, but this does not seem to be the prevailing practice. This then is just another illustration of the fact that no direct counterpart exists in the United States for certain foreign laws and practices. Consequently, experienced judgment is required, and where we conclude that net worth has been overstated, the correction will usually entail a reduction of unrestricted retained earnings.

Assuming for a moment that a foreign company's accumulated earnings are fully extinguished by an American adjustment correcting for an over-statement of net worth, it would still be possible for the foreign company to declare a dividend under local laws. From the viewpoint of United States parent company, however, such a dividend constitutes a return of capital.

One notable exception should, however, be made to the general rule that a correction for an overstatement of foreign net worth results in a reduction of unrestricted surplus. This exception pertains to conditions where the failure to record a tax liability is simply a by-product of an understatement of asset values. Before we can deal with this deviation from the general rule which is related to the tax allocation principle, it is desirable that we discuss foreign practices whereby the net assets are materially undervalued.

Undervalued Current Assets

Foreign procedures which have the effect of understating net assets in-clude the arbitrary write-down of inventories. In Sweden, for instance, in-ventories may legally be understated by as much as 60 percent. Stated another way, the balance sheet value may be as low as 40 percent of fair valuation computed in accordance with American concepts. Other countries have com-parable laws, although the extent of the write-downs and the disclosure prac-tices in local foreign reports will vary. In Sweden, Finland, and Denmark the inventories *per se* are usually understated and the intent seems to be to equalize profits from year to year for tax purposes thereby achieving results comparable to those under the carry-back provisions of the U.S. tax laws. French companies frequently disclose a "Reserve for Renewal of Inventories" as a separate item in the financial reports. We may also encounter other unac-ceptable costing procedures.

It must be realized that these practices are sanctioned under local tax laws and that they are primarily devices to equalize taxable income from year to year. Furthermore, in many foreign countries fiscal or taxable income must by law be identical to book income; no distinction whatsoever is made between tax accounting and orthodox accounting for any other purpose. This point cannot be emphasized too strongly, for a diminution of taxable income by whatever means results in a corresponding reduction in legal income under applicable local statutes. Hence, the true retained earnings represented by hidden inventory reserves are in actuality frequently not available for dividend distribution under foreign laws.

While it is common practice to correct the foreign accounts preparatory to consolidation for such understatement of asset values, the increment attributable to the correction is usually not identified as "restricted retained earnings." A proper restatement of the foreign accounts where these conditions are present should, of necessity, take into consideration that, *ipso jure*, dividend restriction exists. An accounting correction cannot negate this restriction no more than it could produce a dividend remittance from a foreign company which has no accumulated surplus according to the applicable foreign law.

The effect of accounts receivable valuation reserves in some instances is no different than in some instances is no different than the inventory practices just described. For example, German companies are permitted to write off certain collectible loans, for tax purposes, provided such loans are receivable from designated public and private companies. Upon repayment of the loans taxable income results, but in the interim net assets are understated and earnings legally available for dividends are correspondingly reduced. The adjustment to reflect the true net assets will therefore give rise to restricted surplus. A similar situation exists in Brazil where local tax laws permit bad debt provisions which may be considerably in excess of reasonable estimates based on past collection experience.

Undervaluation of Property

We turn next to an examination of various foreign accounting procedures related to property, which generally have their origin in foreign tax or related economic laws. Obviously, these laws are subject to frequent changes, but as a rule they are not cancelled retroactively so that the year of asset acquisition is often the controlling factor. This makes it necessary that we concern ourselves not only with current laws, but also with laws which may no longer be applicable to current capital expenditures. From a review of these laws emerges the fact that many countries, among them, Austria, Belgium, Denmark, Germany, Finland, France, Italy, Luxemburg, the Netherlands, Norway, Portugal, Sweden, the United Kingdom, India and certain other British Commonwealth Countries, and Indonesia, currently permit accelerated depreciation for tax purposes in order to achieve counter-cyclical economic stabilization, or to spur long-run increases in investments. These depreciation provisions contain many different features and are, at times, applicable only to certain assets or to underdeveloped or industrial regions.

Certain unique characteristics of these foreign laws may be mentioned here to illustrate the wide divergence of methods by which accelerated depreciation is accomplished. For example, in France and certain countries within the franc monetary area, the gain on the sale of fixed assets may be carried on the balance sheet, instead of being credited to income. This gain is referred to as "Plus-Value to be Reinvested" and may be applied as a reduction of the cost of assets subsequently purchased, provided the re-investment takes place within a specified time. Thereupon, this credit balance is applied against the cost of new assets acquired and this results in lower depreciation charges in future periods. Then, in order to derive maximum tax advantages, French companies will frequently utilize the gain for the purchase of land, thereby perpetuating the understatement of fixed asset values.

In Finland, accelerated depreciation is often closely tied to the operation of so-called "Investment Funds." Under the applicable laws, 50 percent of profits may be set aside annually in order to establish these funds, which at this point simply constitute restricted retained earnings. While a tax deduction is obtained for the amount appropriated for these funds, the tax saving is deposited with a governmental agency, and is subject to refund only when the Investment Funds have been utilized for fixed asset expenditures. The assets to be purchased must, however, meet with the approval of the official agencies. After the acquisition of the property, the appropriated surplus, instead of being restored to free surplus, is applied as a reduction of the depreciable value of the assets acquired. This, in effect, constitutes accelerated depreciation. Furthermore, the reduced book value of the new assets may also be depreciated on a fast basis.

More straight-forward methods of accelerated depreciation may be accomplished by either liberal depreciation rates or incremental allowances in the first or early years of asset life, the latter method being commonly referred to in English parlance as "Initial Allowances." This should not be confused with "Investment Allowances" which need not concern us in this context, since they represent additional tax deductions over and above 100 percent of the original asset cost. Such "Investment Allowances" therefore, are not fast depreciation methods, but simply another device whereby the economy may be stimulated and tax relief may be obtained which has been employed in the United Kingdom, for example, sometimes in addition to the fast write-off or "Initial Allowances" and at other times in lieu of such accelerated depreciation.

The diversity and range of these foreign tax laws notwithstanding, there is no essential or inherent difference between domestic and foreign practices involving a rapid write-off of plant and equipment. Material distortions created by accelerated depreciation for tax purposes must be corrected when presenting financial statements to stockholders. This is generally done, not only in the United States, but also in a few other countries, notably the Netherlands and the United Kingdom where a distinction is made between "generally accepted accounting practices" and "tax accounting." However, in many other countries where the stockholder and legal basis of accounting must be in accord with the tax basis, the accelerated depreciation element decreases the net worth and therefore the amount legally available for dividends. In restoring such accelerated depreciation to net worth for U.S. reporting purposes, we must therefore recognize that retained earnings created by such an American accounting adjustment represent a form of restricted surplus which cannot be remitted to the American parent company since it is nonexistent under the foreign laws.

Property Appreciation

Certain highlights of foreign accounting practices have been presented above in order to illustrate that American accounting adjustments cannot nullify the effects of current foreign laws and official regulations which are currently in effect. If we accept this thesis, then we must also apply it to laws which permitted the revaluation of property at some time in the past, notwithstanding the fact that such laws may have lapsed. This is so, because once an upward revaluation of property has been reflected on the books in accordance with permissive governmental regulations, the appreciation element reflected in the asset accounts, and hence in the net worth accounts, will usually not be rescinded by the lapsing of a statute. The extinction of additional asset values attributable to such an asset appraisal can usually take place only by the process of charging depreciation on appreciation to the income account.

Superficially, it might appear that this subject does not merit consideration even though a number of foreign countries, including Belgium, Germany, France, Italy, Norway, Brazil, Mexico, and Australia have in the past permitted asset revaluations. At first glance, the argument could be advanced that from the American viewpoint the true historical cost, translated at the exchange rate prevailing at date of asset acquisition, governs, and that consequently any local currency appreciation should be ignored. As far as it goes, this reasoning is perfectly sound, even when it is permissable under foreign laws to declare dividends out of appraisal surplus; for the absence of a corresponding dollar value for the local currency appraisal surplus would compel us to construe such a dividend as a return of capital.

Usually, therefore, both the upward revaluation of property and the related appraisal surplus which are recorded on the books of a foreign company are ignored when expressing financial statements in dollars, but there is one exception. This occurs when a foreign company transfers appraisal surplus into a capital stock account. Such capitalization obviously precludes the periodic transfers from earned surplus to appraisal surplus for charges equivalent to depreciation on appreciation which are reflected in the income account. When the assets are fully depreciated, the foreign books will then continue to reflect a charge to earned surplus for the appreciation element, which will be offset by a credit to capital stock for the capitalization. Earned surplus will thus have been frozen into the capital structure for foreign legal purposes in much the same manner as in the case of a stock dividend. From the dollar viewpoint this will ultimately give rise to a surplus restriction in consolidation, and this end result should be anticipated immediately upon capitalization of the appraisal surplus on the books of the foreign company.

IMPACT OF TAXES

The principle of tax allocation, or tax rectification as it is known in British parlance, certainly is not new but this subject has attracted considerable attention since the revision by the AICPA in July 1958 of Accounting Research Bulletin No. 44 entitled "Declining-balance Depreciation." After extensive study and public hearings, the Securities and Exchange Commission also affirmed this principle with the issuance of Accounting Series Release No. 85 in February 1960. Since the soundness of the principle is no longer open to question, it follows that it should be applied with respect to the accounts of foreign subsidiaries. In fact, many companies in the United Kingdom and the Netherlands recognized deferred taxes in their accounts even prior to the American pronouncements cited above. However, as we have already noted, the accounts of companies located in other countries often require restatement to reverse the effect of accelerated depreciation. In such cases, a concurrent adjustment will then be required for the accrual of deferred income taxes equal to the tax reduction arising from accelerated depreciation. It will be recalled that restricted surplus is created in correcting an understatement of fixed assets, since such an American accounting adjustment can in no way undo the official local law which recognizes only the reduced asset value and therefore precludes dividend distribution out of surplus represented by the fast depreciation element. If follows, therefore, that a fair and realistic treatment for the accrual for deferred income taxes would be to apply the net worth reduction inherent in such tax adjustment against the restricted surplus created by the correction for the related accelerated depreciation. In essence, then, the dividend restriction applies to the after-tax increment in net worth arising from adjustments to correct the undervaluation of foreign net assets.

Furthermore, the tax allocation principle should also be extended to other situations where restricted earnings arise by reason of adjustments made solely for American accounting purposes, as for example in the case of hidden inventory reserves. Here, it should be observed that Accounting Series Release No. 85 contains the following pertinent statement: "It is the Commission's view, however, that comparable recognition of tax deferment should be made in all cases in which there is a tax deduction resulting from deducting

costs for tax purposes at faster rates than for financial statement purposes."
Subsequently, in response to an inquiry by the American Institute of Certified
Public Accountants, the Commission made public a letter stating that the sen-
tence quoted above was not intended "to make mandatory the use of deferred
tax accounting beyond the requirements of generally accepted accounting
principles." (See Accounting Series Release No. 86.)

Although none of these official pronouncements contains specific references to the diverse foreign practices, it is quite clear that the proper matching of costs and revenues constitutes one of the fundamental requirements of
generally accepted accounting principles. Accordingly, if American accounting
adjustments are required to properly reflect foreign income before taxes, the
necessary adjustments for deferred income taxes should also be recognized
at least where material amounts are involved. In short, in correcting for the
understatement of foreign net worth for one reason or another, a concurrent
adjustment would seem to be necessary to reflect a deferred liability for
any significant tax consequences of the understatement.

Beyond this, the principle of tax allocation might be extended to situations where it is necessary to restate the foreign accounts for the overstatement of net worth. For instance, where sound accounting requires the accrual of certain costs which will be recognized on the foreign books and tax
returns only in subsequent accounting periods, it would seem entirely appropriate that we accrue for the costs as well as for a deferred tax debit if
the amounts are significant. In such situations, the after-tax effect of the necessary corrections for an overstatement of net assets would be applied against
retained earnings which are otherwise not restricted by local laws. As stated
previously, dividends remitted out of local earned surplus for which no dollar equivalent exists by reason of the after-tax correction will then constitute
a return of capital from the dollar viewpoint. In practice, however, such return
of capital dividends which would be perpetuated by an American accounting
adjustment will not arise very frequently, since considerable portions of local
currency profits are usually not remitted in the form of dividends due to the
need for reinvestment, exchange restrictions, and managerial decisions.

On the other hand, the tax allocation theory does not apply to situations
resulting in definite tax savings as contrasted with temporary or long-range
postponements. Yet, it would be logical to apply this theory in connection
with potential American or foreign taxes which may become payable on the
undistributed earnings or subsidiaries. This point was recognized in Accounting
Research Bulletin No. 51 which states that taxes on distribution of subsidiaries' earnings should be reflected in the year in which such earnings are included in the consolidated income. This requirement is, however, qualified.

Firstly, the bulletin states that it applies "where it is reasonable to assume
that a part or all of the undistributed earnings of a subsidiary will be transferred to the parent company in a taxable distribution . . ." Secondly, it does

not apply "where the income has been, or there is evidence that it will be, permanently invested by the subsidiaries . . ." The capitalization of earnings or a transfer to legal reserves would certainly seem to be indicative of a permanent investment of earnings. However, it is not clear from the wording of the Bulletin whether, for example, a simple intention to expand plant facilities, and therefore not to declare dividends, would obviate the need for accruals of taxes potentially due on the transfer of earnings to the parent company. In such circumstances, a company may, of course, voluntarily earmark surplus thereby seeking to avoid the accrual of such taxes.

Yet, this question cannot be considered in a vacuum. Having once decided that profit transmission restrictions are no bar to consolidation, we have, in effect, contended that parent company working control is not impaired by virtue of the intent to utilize unremittable profits for reinvestments abroad. It has been argued in the preceding sections that under these circumstances a dividend restriction should be recognized in consolidation to the extent profits remittances are precluded by exchange controls. Advocating disclosure of such surplus restrictions in no way invalidates the propriety of consolidation, but rather supports the practice of consolidating the foreign accounts. In essence, therefore, by the disclosure of the exchange restriction we are simply saying that foreign earnings can be effectively and profitably reinvested abroad, and, that being the case, we are evidently relieved of the obligation to accrue for potential taxes, since no accrual is required under the terms of ARB 51 "where the income has been, or there is evidence that it will be, permanently invested by the subsidiaries."

It will be seen, therefore, that adoption of the principles espoused in this article may have a material effect on compliance or non-compliance with the intent of ARB 51. In the author's opinion, this pronouncement requires further clarification, particularly as to its applicability in the context cited above, but also in the domestic area. As the Bulletin points out, prospective taxes would be mitigated by foreign tax credits, but there is no doubt that significant amounts may be involved in many cases, particularly when subsidiaries are located in "tax haven" countries. We simply cannot ignore the existence of a potential tax liability and, at the same time, imply that all earnings are available for dividends. Conservatism would seem to dictate that prospective United States and foreign taxes should at least be accured on all unrestricted earnings.

Translation Procedures

The subject of determining distributable foreign surplus would not be complete without some consideration of the effect of certain balance sheet currency translation procedures. As has been indicated in the preceding sections, it should be a cardinal principle that the presentation of retained earnings in consolidated financial statement without further description or qualification is indicative of the fact that all such earnings are, in fact, legally and practically available for dividends. When we deal with foreign accounts, however, it is seldom true that the entire dollar value of the retained earnings can be remitted in the form of dividends. Even if none of the restrictions already described exist, it will often be found that it is impossible for the American parent company to receive dividends equivalent to the dollar value assigned to the surplus of a subsidiary.

This conclusion can be illustrated by the fact that fixed assets are generally translated at exchange rates prevailing at the date of asset acquisition. If a currency devaluation occurs, no devaluation loss is recognized in dollars with respect to fixed assets. Consequently, after a devaluation it is possible for the dollar net worth and therefore dollar surplus to be greater than the dollar equivalent of local currency amounts translated at post-devaluation exchange rates. It follows that dollar surplus arrived at in the conventional manner contains or is comprised of remittable earnings, i.e., local currency retained earnings at post-devaluation exchange rates, and what may be called a "deferred exchange loss applicable to fixed assets" which will be absorbed by future depreciation charges at historical exchange rates.

The latter element clearly represents unremittable retained earnings, notwithstanding the fact that the fixed assets values as such may be more realistically depicted in dollars when translated at the historical exchange rate in view of the fact that the foreign currency replacement cost presumably will be higher after a currency devaluation. Thus, we see that there are certain restrictions on the availability of dividends which are inherent in the customary mechanics of translating foreign currency accounts into U.S. dollars. The ordinary reader of consolidated financial statements cannot be expected to be aware of these technical accounting procedures and, in the absence of full disclosure, may wrongly assume that all of the foreign earnings could be remitted to the American parent company and be in turn distributed to American stockholders.

CONCLUSION

We have established in the foregoing sections that the earned surplus of foreign companies may not be avilable for dividend distribution to an American parent company due to (1) foreign legal requirements, (2) exchange restrictions, (3) the effects of restating the foreign accounts in conformity with generally accepted principles as understood by the accounting profession in the United States, and (4) due to the interplay of currency translation procedures. In ascertaining these surplus restrictions, we should consistently follow domestic principles and disclosure practices which are generally adaptable to situations encountered in foreign trade accounting. In this connection we should particularly observe the irrefutable fact that no restatement of the foreign accounts can effectively negate the provisions of foreign law and regulations applicable to the declaration of dividends, nor do American accounting concepts in connection with translation procedures in any way influence or govern the availability of surplus for dividend distribution. Rather, the actual availability of retained earnings for withdrawal should be the deciding factor in balance sheet disclosure practices.

The author is fully in accord with the practice of consolidating foreign accounts provided, among other conditions, that parent company working control is not impaired by exchange restrictions, that realistic exchange rates can be determined and applied and, above all, that the doctrine of consistency is strictly adhered to in consolidation so that the same principles and disclosure practices govern for both domestic and foreign accounts alike. A stockholder of a United States parent company cannot be expected to be familiar with the many technical features which preclude transmission of profits to the United States. Yet, he is vitally interested in the availability of earnings for dividend distribution, and since he is entitled to this information in accordance with accepted reporting standards, there is no reason why such standards should not be consistently observed with respect to foreign operations.

Misleading inferences may be drawn from both financial reports that exclude all foreign subsidiaries *per se* from consolidation as well as from reports that consolidate all foreign subsidiaries but without disclosure of the restrictions as to dividend availability. It is the author's thesis that, unless such restrictions are indicated in the consolidated reports, the consistency principle will have been violated thereby causing considerable doubt as to the propriety of foreign and domestic consolidation. Accountants must take an unequivocal position about dual standards in reports of American companies and for their foreign subsidiaries.

DEVALUATION OF FOREIGN CURRENCIES*

World War II created special conditions under which American business was able to rapidly expand and develop its export trade. With Europe's manufacturing facilities destroyed or obsolete, U.S. companies found it necessary to organize foreign subsidiaries and branches to cope with the increased volume. For many companies this export trade has become a highly important part of total operations. International operations, however, created new risks and unique problems for American business. Among the new risks, the most prominent is the risk of devaluation of foreign currencies. As dollar reserves are depleted by the increased purchases of American goods, foreign governments arbitrarily establish new, lower rates of exchange for foreign currencies in relation to the U.S. dollar. This paper discusses the effects of devaluation on various financial positions and the problems of continuing post-devaluation operations.

For illustrative purposes, three hypothetical businesses operating in a foreign country with a peso monetary unit will be used. It will be assumed that each business imports a single product from a U.S. supplier with the following exchange rates, costs, and selling prices:

	Before Devaluation			After Devaluation		
	Pesos		U.S.$	Pesos		U.S.$
Exchange rates	4	=	1	8	=	1
Cost per unit	8	=	2	16	=	2
Selling price per unit	12	=	3	24	=	3

A different financial position will be used for each importer to demonstrate the effects of devaluation under various conditions:

Importer A: Dollar debt to U.S. supplier
Importer B: No dollar debt to U.S. supplier
Importer C: Local borrowings before devaluation to pay U.S. dollar debt

In each case, the effect upon operations of a selling price increase will be contrasted with no selling price increase. To eliminate unnecessary details, all balance sheets and profit and loss statements have been stripped to the basic elements and all items of income and expense are assumed to have been settled in cash between balance sheet dates.

* John J. Miller, *The Controller*, August 1956, pp. 366, 368, 369.

Under the above conditions, the financial statements of each of the three importers before devaluation would have appeared as follows:

BALANCE SHEET BEFORE DEVALUATION

	Pesos	Commodity Units	U.S.$
Assets—Inventory	4,000	500	1,000
Liability—Due U.S. supplier	4,000		1,000

If all merchandise were sold before devaluation, the profit and loss account would appear as follows:

PROFIT AND LOSS BEFORE DEVALUATION
Exchange Rate P/4 to U.S. $1.00

	Pesos	Commodity Units	U.S.$
Sold for	6,000		1,500
Cost of inventory	4,000	500	1,000
Profit	2,000		500

When the business cycle is completed and the P/6,000 is collected and reinvested in inventory, the balance sheet would appear as follows before devaluation:

	Pesos	Commodity Units	U.S.$
Assets:			
Inventory	6,000	750	1,500
Liability and Surplus:			
Due U.S.A. supplier	4,000		1,000
Surplus (Profit as above)	2,000		500
Total	6,000		1,500

The effect on the financial condition and profit and loss of each importer will now be shown when merchandise is sold after devaluation.

IMPORTER A
DOLLAR DEBT TO U.S. SUPPLIER
BALANCE SHEET

	Before Devaluation Pesos 4 = U.S. $1.00			After Devaluation Pesos 8 = U.S. $1.00		
	Pesos	Commodity Units	U.S.$	Pesos	Commodity Units	U.S.$
Assets:						
Inventory	4,000	500	1,000	4,000	500	1,000
Liability:						
Due U.S. supplier	4,000		1,000	4,000		1,000

No profit or loss occurred in U.S. dollars upon the devaluation at this point because there were no sales. The imported inventory is always equal in value to its dollar cost.

Now assume that all 500 units of commodity are sold after devaluation.

		Exchange Rate now P/8 to U.S. $1.00				
		Old Price P/12			*New Price P/24*	
		Commodity			*Commodity*	
	Pesos	*Units*	*U.S.$*	*Pesos*	*Units*	*U.S.$*
Sold for	6,000		750	12,000		1,500
Cost	4,000	500	1,000	4,000	500	1,000
Profit (loss) on sale	2,000		(250)	8,000		500
Loss on remittance of original $1,000 debt to U.S. supplier	4,000			4,000		
Net profit (loss)	(2,000)		(250)	4,000		500

No dollar equivalent has been given to the P/4,000 loss on remittance of the $1,000 debt to the U.S. supplier. This loss has been provided for in U.S. dollars by retaining the original dollar identity of the dollar debt. The debt is U.S. $1,000. It cannot be any more or any less in dollars.

Again assuming that the business cycle is completed and the original P/4,000 plus profit or loss are reinvested in inventory to continue in business, the balance sheet would appear as follows:

		BALANCE SHEET				
		After Sales with No Price Increase			*After Sales with a Price Increase*	
		Commodity			*Commodity*	
Assets:	*Pesos*	*Units*	*U.S.$*	*Pesos*	*Units*	*U.S.$*
Inventory	-0-	-0-	-0-	4,000	250	500
Liability and Surplus:						
Loan	2,000		250	4,000		500
Surplus (deficit)	(2,000)		(250)			
Total	-0-	-0-	-0-	4,000		500

Importer A reflects the problem of importers with unpaid debts in dollars at time of devaluation. An importer in this position must obtain enough local currency from sales to pay for replacement of merchandise which now costs him 16 pesos per unit instead of 8 and also to pay his predevaluation dollar liability at a rate of 8 pesos per dollar instead of 4 pesos per dollar. This dollar element is reflected in the profit and loss statement in this example as loss on remittance. In this case, P/4,000 of proceeds from sales had to be applied to pay this loss.

The importer who does not raise his selling price but continues to sell his products at P/12 per unit exchanges 500 units of commodity for P/6,000 which will not pay his liability to the supplier. He is forced to borrow P/2,000 to pay his liability and has no merchandise to resell. He can continue in business only if he gets additional capital and raises prices. A competitor who has no dollar liability can keep prices depressed to force this importer out of business.

This importer must double his prices to come out whole. He would then earn enough in local currency to pay the additional cost of P/4,000 necessary to liquidate his dollar debt of U.S. $1,000 and also have a profit of P/4,000 to purchase 250 units of commodity at the new cost of 16 pesos or U.S. $2.00 per unit. He could continue in business on capital provided by the selling price increase; however, he would be at the mercy of competitors who had no dollar liabilities. Importers with no dollar liabilities have an advantage over competitors with dollar debts.

IMPORTER B
No DOLLAR DEBT TO U.S. SUPPLIER
BALANCE SHEET

	Before Devaluation Pesos 4 = U.S. $1.00			After Devaluation Pesos 8 = U.S. $1.00		
		Commodity			Commodity	
Assets:	Pesos	Units	U.S.$	Pesos	Units	U.S.$
Inventory	4,000	500	1,000	4,000	500	1,000
Surplus	4,000		1,000	4,000		1,000

This case is identical to the balance sheet of Importer A; no profit or loss is shown in U.S. dollars on the conversion from local currency at this point. Inventory has not changed because it is represented by 500 units of commodity which have a U.S. dollar value of $1,000 in spite of what happened to the rate of exchange. A loss can occur only if the selling price at which subsequent sales are made cannot produce enough local currency to replace the merchandise sold.

The tabulations submitted below show what happens to the financial condition with the sales at old prices and at increased prices.

	Exchange Rate now P/8 to U.S. $1.00					
	Old Price P/12			New Price P/24		
		Commodity			Commodity	
	Pesos	Units	U.S.$	Pesos	Units	U.S.$
Sold for	6,000		750	12,000		1,500
Cost	4,000	500	1,000	4,000	500	1,000
Profit (loss)	2,000		(250)	8,000		500

Again assuming the completion of the business cycle and the reinvestment of the proceeds of sales in inventory to continue in business, the financial condition would appear as follows:

	After Sales with No Price Increase			After Sales with a Price Increase		
Assets:	*Pesos*	Commodity *Units*	*U.S.$*	*Pesos*	Commodity *Units*	*U.S.$*
Inventory	6,000	375	750	12,000	750	1,500
Surplus:						
Opening balance	4,000		1,000	4,000		1,000
Profit (loss)	2,000		(250)	8,000		500
	6,000		750	12,000		1,500

Importer B portrays the situation of those importers with no liability in U.S. dollars but who are still faced with the problem of continuing operations without impairing their net worth. If the merchandise is sold without a selling price increase in local currency, capital will be lost. If 500 units of commodity were sold at the old selling price, the importer would find that he gave up his 500 units worth U.S. $1,000 for P/6,000. When he tried to replenish his inventory, he could buy only 375 units with his currency. In other words he would lose 125 commodity units or U.S. $250. This occurs in spite of what appears on his books to be a profit of P/2,000 which, if taken at face value, should be worth U.S. $250. Judged from the local currency position, this importer would appear to have a net worth of U.S. $1,250 if the U.S. $250 equivalent in local currency profit were added to his opening U.S. dollar worth. If this man continues in business with no increase in price, he will gradually lose all his capital and be forced out of business.

The importer who raises his selling price makes a profit in dollars that he would have enjoyed had he made his sales before devaluation. He would then recover enough in local currency to replace his original stock of 500 units of commodity and to increase it to 750 units all worth U.S. $2.00 each. To arrive at this position, the selling price must be doubled. This is a drastic increase in price. Whether or not such drastic increase in price can be made is a commercial problem which must be solved by an appraisal of the market.

IMPORTER C
LOCAL BORROWING BEFORE DEVALUATION TO PAY U.S. DOLLAR DEBT
BALANCE SHEET

	Before Devaluation Pesos 4 = U.S. $1.00			After Devaluation Pesos 8 = U.S. $1.00		
Assets:	*Pesos*	Commodity *Units*	*U.S.$*	*Pesos*	Commodity *Units*	*U.S.$*
Inventory	4,000	500	1,000	4,000	500	1,000
Liability:						
Loan	4,000		1,000	4,000		500
Surplus:						
Conversion gain					-0-	500
Total	4,000		1,000	4,000		1,000

This case is different from Examples A and B in that there is a profit of $500 after devaluation in converting the balance sheet to U.S. dollars without a corresponding profit in pesos. No peso profit or loss is shown through the usual profit and loss accounts. This profit was not earned through normal operations; it was the result of a change in values due to a change in exchange rates. This importer has his 500 units of commodity which are worth U.S. $1,000 in spite of an increase or decrease in exchange rates. The amount of loan is now equivalent to only U.S. $500 because he will not be required to put up any more than P/4,000 to pay it off. The importer who was indebted P/4,000 in the form of $1,000 debt in U.S. dollars before devaluation in Example A was forced to put up P/8,000 to pay off his predevaluation debt after devaluation occurred. The importer in this case is in a very favorable position competitively. His post-devaluation operations will not be burdened with the additional cost of remittance of dollars for predevaluation debt. All he is required to do to come out whole is to recover enough local currency to replace his merchandise. The profit and loss accounts will appear as follows, that is, the same as Importer B.

		Exchange Rate now P/8 to U.S. $1.00				
	Old Price P/12			New Price P/24		
		Commodity			Commodity	
	Pesos	Units	U.S.$	Pesos	Units	U.S.$
Sold for	6,000		750	12,000		1,500
Cost	4,000	500	1,000	4,000	500	1,000
Profit (loss)	2,000		(250)	8,000		500

The balance sheet, after the business cycle is completed, would appear as follows after paying off the loan from the proceeds of sales:

	After Sales with No Price Increase			After Sales with a Price Increase		
		Commodity			Commodity	
Assets:	Pesos	Units	U.S.$	Pesos	Units	U.S.$
Inventory	2,000	125	250	8,000	500	1,000
Surplus:						
Opening balance	-o-		500	-o-		500
Profit (loss)	2,000		(250)	8,000		500
Total	2,000		250	8,000		1,000

If this importer did not increase selling prices but borrowed locally before devaluation to pay his dollar debt, he would be able to earn enough local currency to pay off his loan. In addition, he would have enough local currency left over to buy 125 units of commodity to start him off on a new cycle. This importer will eventually be forced to raise prices because he cannot long continue to sell for P/12.00 per unit and purchase for P/16.00 per unit.

If this importer doubled his prices, he would gain enough local currency to obtain an equity equivalent to 500 units of commodity or U.S. $1,000. His future sales would permit him to earn the equivalent of U.S. $1.00 on each sale or the same amount as before devaluation. This importer would then be in a most favorable position. However, he would not have to double his prices to replace his original inventory. His selling price increase could be more moderate. This is an enviable position if prices are under government control and increases in prices are delayed for some time after devaluation. The importer in this position can continue to operate while awaiting approval of a price increase based on increased dollar cost and still keep his capital intact. If this importer is well supplied with merchandise paid for with borrowed funds, he can operate with depressed prices for a longer period. His competitors would then wither away selling at prices which would provide insufficient local funds to pay for both the increased cost of merchandise and predevaluation dollar debts.

CONCLUSION

The preceding paragraphs demonstrate the relationship of selling price levels to post-devaluation operations. Selling price increases in most foreign countries cannot be made at the will of the importer. Many countries maintain price controls on all commodities and most countries have price controls on some commodities. The existence of price controls is a factor which must be considered in planning post devaluation operations.

The local currency financial position can be planned to reduce the impact of devaluation by taking into account risks in any particular market. The two basic problems are:

1. Budgeting and planning a balanced stockpile of inventory before devaluation to put the foreign operation in a position to survive any post-devaluation adjustment period.
2. Introducing local capital to eliminate dollar liabilities before devaluation occurs.

Selection of local participation in capital could take the form of outright bank loans, issuance of bonds, or any one of the several forms of capital stock. Selection of the form in which local capital is to participate will depend on availability and cost. An element to consider before selecting a form of capital stock is the participation in management that might be required by purchasers.

This paper deals only with devaluation. There is the possibility of appreciation in values of foreign currencies, which has occurred in some instances during recent years. The conclusions would be reversed in case an appreciation in value of a currency were in prospect.

MANAGEMENT ACCOUNTING PROBLEMS IN FOREIGN OPERATIONS *

INTRODUCTION

To the Stateside accountant the most interesting and perhaps baffling phase of accounting for foreign operations is the actual translation of local currency financial statements into U.S. dollars. The purpose of this paper is to indicate some of the basic accounting problems arising in this area from the fluctuation of foreign currencies in relation to U.S. dollars.

HOW FOREIGN CURRENCY PROFIT CAN BECOME U.S. DOLLAR LOSS ON TRANSLATION

The Paradox

One of the most difficult obligations the accountant faces is to explain to U.S.-educated operating management how a foreign subsidiary can report a respectable profit in local currency and how in the accountant's translation procedures this may result in a U.S. dollar loss for the period. Two factors contribute to cause this paradox, which usually follows a sharp decline in the exchange rate:

1) Depreciation for the year is translated into U.S. dollars at stronger rates of exchange prevailing when the assets were acquired, while local currency selling prices have not been increased following a weakening of the local currency, to compensate for this continuing depreciation charge brought forward from prior year's expenditures, as shown in the following table:

(Amounts taken from Exhibit I, p. 879)

	Local Currency	Percent of Sales	U.S. Dollars	Percent of Sales	Exchange Rate
Sales	4,800,000		1,093,750		Average for year .2279
Depreciation	1,200,000	25	300,000	27½	Historical .2500

* George C. Watt, excerpted from the *1960 Institute on Private Investment Abroad*, 1960, pp. 493–512.

2) Apart from operations, the loss on the net assets of a financial nature (*i.e.*, other than physical assets) that occurs when a currency weakens in relation to the dollar and is charged to the U.S. dollar profit and loss statement.

Paradox Illustrated

An illustration of the financial statements after the first year of operation of a foreign subsidiary is attached as Exhibit 1, and an explanation of the loss on the weakening of the foreign currency in relation to the U.S. dollars that year is attached as Exhibit 2. The transactions for the year reflected in those two exhibits are summarized in the following table:

ANALYSIS OF TRANSACTIONS

Cash from sale of foreign subsidiary's capital stock to its U.S. parent	LC 6,000,000
Cash from foreign bank loan	1,200,000
Spent for fixed assets	(3,600,000)
Spent for material	(2,760,000)
Spent for labor	(1,200,000)
Receipts from sales	4,800,000
Dividend	(275,000)
Cash—closing balance on Exhibit 1	LC 4,165,000

Balance Sheet Illustrated

It will be observed on Exhibit 1 that at the end of the year the net assets of a financial nature (cash and bank loan payable) are translated at the ex-

EXHIBIT 1

FIRST YEAR OF OPERATION OF A FOREIGN SUBSIDIARY

	Local Currency	U.S. Dollars Per L/C Unit	U.S. Dollars	
Assets at End of Year:				
Cash	4,165,000	.1563	$ 651,000-	(1)
Materials inventory	960,000	.2083	200,000	(2)
Fixed assets	3,600,000	.2500	900,000	(3)
Allowance for depreciation	(1,200,000)	.2500	(300,000)	(3)
Total	7,525,000		$1,451,000	
Liabilities and Net Worth At End of Year:				
Bank loan payable in local currency	1,200,000	.1563	$ 187,500	(1)
Income taxes payable	250,000	.1563	39,000	(1)
Capital stock	6,000,000	.2500	1,500,000	(4)
Retained earnings (deficit)	75,000		(275,500)	(5)
Total	7,525,000		$1,451,000	

(continued)

EXHIBIT 1 (cont.)

FIRST YEAR OF OPERATION OF A FOREIGN SUBSIDIARY

	Local Currency	U.S. Dollars Per L/C Unit	U.S. Dollars	
Income Statement For The Year:				
Sales.................................	4,800,000	.2279	$1,093,750	(6)
Cost of goods sold:				
Purchases of materials.........	2,760,000	.2174	600,000	(6)
Less—Closing inventory	960,000	.2083	200,000	(2)
Cost of materials used.........	1,800,000		400,000	
Wages paid........................	1,200,000	.2100	252,000	(6)
Depreciation	1,200,000	.2500	300,000	(3)
Total	4,200,000		952,000	
Income from operations before taxes......................	600,000		141,750	
Taxes on income.................	250,000	1563	39,000	(1)
Income from operations after taxes......................	350,000		102,750	
Loss on foreign exchange, Exhibit II			323,250	(7)
Net income (loss).................	350,000		(220,500)	
Dividends...........................	275,000	.2000	55,000	(8)
Balance carried to retained earnings (loss)	75,000		($ 275,500)	

(1) Rate prevailing on closing date for period—.1563.

(2) Average rate prevailing during period of accumulation—.2083.

(3) Historical rate, i.e., rate prevailing at time fixed assets were acquired—.2500.

(4) Historical rate—.2500. This was the investment made on January 1, by the parent company buying 6,000,000 Pesos for U.S. $1,500,000 and delivering the Pesos to the subsidiary in return for Capital Stock of a total par value of 6,000,000 Pesos.

(5) See (7) below.

(6) Each month's total translated at average rate for that month. These rates are omitted from the illustration, but the average rate of the year is shown to assist readers in following the illustration.

(7) Since a decrease in dollar net worth has occurred, a loss on foreign exchange has been sustained. The amount of this loss is the figure necessary to adjust income from operations to the change in net worth shown by the balance sheet. The loss on foreign exchange is charged against operating income for the year to arrive at the dollar net loss.

(8) Rate prevailing at the date the dividend was paid—.2000.

* * * * *

Attention is invited to the fact that if the exchange rate of .2500 had not changed during the year to .1563, then the original investment of LC 6,000,000 translated at $1,500,000 would have produced LC 350,000 income translated at .2500 or $87,500 rather than a loss of $220,500 shown in the illustration.

change rate on the last day of the year. Physical assets still under the control of management decisions are inventory (to be sold at prices to be set by management) translated to U.S. dollars at the average exchange rate prevailing during the period of accumulation, and fixed assets (to be used to create a product that can be sold in the local economy) translated to U.S. dollars at rates prevailing at the time the fixed assets were acquired.

EXHIBIT 2

FIRST YEAR OF OPERATION OF A FOREIGN SUBSIDIARY
ANALYSIS OF LOSS ON FOREIGN EXCHANGE FLUCTUATION

		Exchange Loss or (Gain)
Cash—opening balance.............................	LC 7,200,000	
Bank loan payable—opening balance............	(1,200,000)	
Loss from change in rate from .2500 to .1563—net current items "exposed"........	6,000,000	$562,200

Difference between local currency profit plus depreciation (i.e., cash flow) translated at the year-end rate of .1563 and the similar dollars in the income statement (i.e., sales less costs excluding depreciation):

Profit..............	LC	350,000	$102,750	
Depreciation.....		1,200,000	300,000	
Totals.............		1,550,000	402,750	

Translated at closing rate of .1563.........		1,550,000	242,350	

Loss on Pesos added in cash flow compared to income statement......................	$160,400	1,550,000	160,400

Reduction of above losses by investment prior to year end in:

Fixed assets, LC 3,600,000 invested at .2500 compared with .1563, if Pesos had been held until year end......................	(3,600,000)	(337,350)
Inventory, LC 960,000 purchased on the average at .2083 compared with .1563, if Pesos had been held until year end........	(960,000)	(50,000)
Dividend, LC 275,000 paid at .2000 compared with .1563, if Pesos had been held to year end...	(275,000)	(12,000)
Closing balance of net current items (details shown below)......................	LC 2,715,000	$323,250 loss

Cash...............................		LC 4,165,000	
Less—Bank loan payable....	LC 1,200,000		
Income taxes payable	250,000	1,450,000	
As above.........................		LC 2,715,000	

Since (1) selected exchange rates were applied to each item of the balance sheet except "Retained earnings" and (2) the local currency weakened during the year, the dollar amount of "Retained earnings (deficit)" is "forced" into the U.S. dollar balance sheet. Actually, the Income Statement for the year shown on Exhibit 1 immediately below "Retained earnings (deficit)" accounts for the "forced" dollar amount.

Income Statement Illustrated

In the simple illustration of the income statement on Exhibit 1, "Sales, Purchases, Wages," were translated at the average exchange rate of the various months the transactions took place. Depreciation on the other hand was expressed in dollars at the same exchange rate as the gross fixed assets being depreciated which were acquired before the weakening in the exchange rate. This, you will recall, is the first explanation that the accountant offers to operating management. In the illustration, sales prices in local currency did not increase in line with devaluation, for on translation, sales yielded the equivalent of $1,093,750 not $1,200,000 (if expressed at the rate when fixed assets were purchased), while depreciation continued at the exchange rate prevailing when the fixed assets were acquired.

Loss on Foreign Exchange Illustrated

The U.S. dollar Income Statement had to absorb the "Loss on foreign exchange" of $323,250 illustrated on Exhibit 2. This, you will recall, is the second explanation that the accountant offers to operating management. This was also the more important explanation in this particular illustration.

The "loss on foreign exchange" is a measure of the treasury function of the business. Companies operating abroad should attempt to maintain a balanced position so that net assets of a financial nature (as distinguished from physical assets such as inventory and fixed assets) are kept to the minimum. As can be seen from Exhibit 1, this subsidiary carried too much cash for the size of the operation, and so when the local currency weakened the loss analyzed on Exhibit 2 was unduly large. This must have been a painful explanation to make to management. True, it cannot be completely avoided in many cases, but it can be minimized by astute treasury action.

TREASURY FUNCTION IN MINIMIZING POSSIBILITY OF LOSS FROM WEAKENING OF FOREIGN CURRENCY

What are some of the treasury actions that can minimize "exposure" to the loss that can occur when a foreign currency weakens in relation to the U.S. dollar?

At all times:

1) Remit promptly to the U.S. parent or U.S. supplier for goods payable in U.S. dollars. If cash balances permit, remit well in advance of sale or even the landing of the merchandise.

2) Purchase dollars for local currency and declare and remit dividends promptly (say at least quarterly). Waiting for the books to be closed at the end of the year to declare dividends is an unnecessary risk. In some countries interim "provisional" dividends must be made subject to later stockholder approval at the annual meeting following the close of the year, but this should not prevent early remittance of a substantial part of the total annual dividend.

3) Remit excess cash as a return of capital, if local currency profits are not available for a dividend declaration.

When it is apparent that devaluation is imminent:

4) Borrow money locally to finance working capital requirements (or even acquisition of fixed assets if possible). While the interest expense may be high in foreign countries, it is deductible for income tax purposes and it may be a lot less expensive than investing parent company dollars that, as local currency, will be subject to devaluation.

5) If cash is expected to become excessive in the near future upon collection of a large account, purchase forward exchange commitments at fixed rates, provided the differential is not excessive in relation to the risk of devaluation.

6) Cash in excess of normal requirements may be used to purchase fixed assets that will not lose their intrinsic value, when the need for them is clearly indicated in the not-too-distant future. Excessive cash may also be used to purchase goods for resale. Some protection is obtained by holding goods rather than money on the basis that the items may be resold subsequently at higher local currency prices.

EXAMPLE OF A DIFFICULT SITUATION: ACCOUNTING FOR IMPORTATIONS INTO BRAZIL FOR U.S. DOLLAR FINANCIAL STATEMENTS

As to countries that exercise control of imports by preference exchange rates (encouraging importation) or by penalty exchange rates (discouraging importation) the translation of local currency financial statements into U.S. dollars can produce misleading results unless certain supplementary information is considered. This supplementary information is required to balance in U.S. dollars the trade account payable by the foreign subsidiary in U.S. dollars at a preference or penalty rate, with the translation to U.S. dollars of local currency, cash, and other assets which will be required to settle the trade account payable to the parent.

Perhaps one of the most difficult situations exists in Brazil.[1] When certain goods are to be imported into Brazil the local company must bid at official "auctions" for exchange certificates. Assume that a foreign subsidiary bid and obtained for cruzeiros 1,400,000 exchange certificates entitling it to remit 5,000 U.S. dollars to its parent company in the United States. Since the free market rate was 125 cruzeiros to the U.S. dollar (.008) at that time, the equivalent of 11,200 U.S. dollars were bid for the exchange certificates which gave the foreign subsidiary the right to buy $5,000 of merchandise from the parent at the official rate of 20 cruzeiros to the U.S. dollar (.05). This is, indeed, a complex penalty rate situation.

[1] George C. Watt, "Accounting for Importations into Brazil for U.S. Dollar Financial Statements," *The Price Waterhouse Review,* Winter 1959.

EXHIBIT 3

An Example of Translating Cruzeiros into U.S. Dollars Without Developing Foreign Exchange Gain or Loss in U.S. Dollars upon Acquisition of Exchange Certificates for the Importation of Merchandise into Brazil.

BALANCE SHEET

SHOWING BEGINNING AND ENDING BALANCES OF A FOREIGN SUBSIDIARY ORGANIZED IN 1958 AND THE ONE PURCHASE TRANSACTION FOR THE YEAR

	Local Currency	Rate	U.S. Dollars
Assets			
Cash at beginning of 1958	3,000,000	.015	45,000
Buy agios when current rate was .008 in weekly auction entitling the purchase of U.S. Dollars 5,000 at the official rate....	(1,400,000)		
Cash at ending rate...............................	1,600,000	.007	11,200
Add — Available preference on 100,000 (.05–.007) Note 1			4,300
Total cash at end of 1958	1,600,000		15,500
Inventory:			
Dollar item purchased for:			
Official rate....................................	100,000		
Free rate (Exchange Certificates on hand)...	1,400,000		
Note 2...	1,500,000	.008	12,000
	3,100,000		27,500
Liability and Capital			
Account payable to parent for imports (Note 3)...	100,000	.05	5,000
Capital stock	3,000,000	.015	45,000
Earned surplus (deficit)			
Loss on foreign exchange (see explanation below)......................................			(22,500)
	3,100,000		27,500

EXPLANATION OF LOSS ON FOREIGN EXCHANGE

	Local Currency	Rate	U.S. Dollars
Opening current items...........................	3,000,000	(.015) .007	($24,000)
Less—Portion of loss absorbed in inventory	1,500,000	.008 (.007)	1,500
Loss on foreign exchange			($22,500)

Notes:

1. Alternatively this dollar amount may be reflected as a deferred item in the current position.

2. A test of market follows on the next page.

3. On payment no gain or loss will be incurred as the entry will be:

	Cruzeiros	U.S. Dollars
Debit — Account payable.............	100,000	5,000
Credit—Cash	(100,000)	(700)
Credit—Cash item or deferred item		(4,300)

Note that the following is the year-end situation, from the foreign subsidiary's point of view, for merchandise purchased from the parent for a contract price of $5,000.

	Cruzeiros		U.S. Dollar
Exchange certificates (agios) held for goods not yet landed	1,400,000	.008	$11,200
Payment required when goods are received (official rate)	100,000	.008	800
Cost of importation	1,500,000		$12,000

(Parent has shipped and billed $5,000. In effect, the foreign subsidiary has paid an import tax—via exchange controls—of $7,000.)

The illustration appearing as Exhibit 3 assumes that the foreign subsidiary began business at the beginning of 1958. At that date the parent company bought capital stock with a par value of cruzeiros 3,000,000 for which it remitted 45,000 U.S. dollars (rate .015 or 66⅔ cruzeiros to the U.S. dollar). The rate steadily declined throughout 1958 to .007 or 140 cruzeiros to the U.S. dollar. The only transaction of the year was to arrange for the importation of merchandise from the parent company before the end of the year. Note that a cash item of $4,300 with no cruzeiro equivalent was developed to prevent the reporting of a loss of $4,300 simply because merchandise was purchased and the supplier-parent remained unpaid at the year end.

There are, of course, other methods of accomplishing the objective of not reporting U.S. dollar profit or loss on the importation of certain items into

EXHIBIT 4

MARKET VALUE TEST OF CLOSING INVENTORY

The total inventory shown on Exhibit 3 should not be carried at the end of the period in local currency or dollars in excess of an amount equivalent to the estimated sales realization reduced by estimated selling and other local expenses necessary to complete the sales. After the above computation has been completed the following "market test" should be made:

	Local Currency	Rate	U.S. Dollars
Sales realization (estimated)....................	(2,500,000)		
Less—Estimated selling and other related expenses..	500,000		
Net realization at year-end rate................	(2,000,000)	.007	A (14,000)
Cost per balance sheet of foreign subsidiary			B 12,000

Thus, cost is not in excess of market by $2,000 (A–B)

In the event this test discloses that estimated net realization at the close of an accounting period is less than cost, the inventory should be written down to the estimated net realizable value.

In consolidation, the profit of the parent company, say $500, should be eliminated. The inventory item in its consolidated financial statements should not be reduced to the parent's cost of $4,500 but should be reduced to $11,500, the consolidated cost of having the article available for sale in Brazil.

Brazil. The illustration shown as Exhibit 4 has the practical advantage of permitting the translation of the inventory at the rate of exchange in effect on the date of the accumulation. The translation of the inventory at the year-end rate would not have disturbed the illustration, as the cash item of $4,300 is the essential calculation required to prevent reporting a loss of that amount in this situation. If a loss were erroneously reported, however, there would be an erroneous gain of equal amount reported in the following year.

INFLATION AND FOREIGN INVESTMENTS *

How can a U.S. parent company properly determine the operating results of a foreign subsidiary operating under inflationary conditions?

The inclusion of foreign subsidiaries in consolidated statements has become increasingly evident in recent years. One might say that many foreign subsidiaries after long absences are being "readmitted to consolidation." While this might indicate improving world-wide economic conditions, exclusion from consolidation still occurs because of exchange conditions, trade factors, and the possibility of expropriation.

Many U.S.-owned subsidiaries, located in countries such as Brazil, Argentina, and Chile, are insulated, because of exchange problems, from their parents. These companies continue to operate, and, hopefully, they will one day be brought back into consolidation with the U.S. parent. Important economic factors, such as inflation, plague such countries and the U.S.-owned subsidiaries operating overseas under these conditions. Many years may pass before conditions return to "normal," or at least to a condition of stability on a different plane. In the interim, the accounts become less meaningful under the impact of inflation.

If inflation has eroded the significance of the accounts of such a subsidiary, what factors need to be considered in attempting to translate these accounts into U.S. dollars? Even if consolidation is not imminent and is not the objective, can such accounts be recast so as to give management a better evaluation of this subsidiary's financial status? How can a U.S. parent properly determine the operating results of a foreign subsidiary operating under such conditions? This paper uses the eight-year experience, 1953–1960, of a St. Joseph Lead subsidiary, Compania Minera Aguilar, S.A., located in Argentina to illustrate the problem and indicate a possible solution.

The President of St. Joseph Lead highlighted the problem in this manner: "As it is difficult to determine the U.S. dollar value of the peso, the financial statements are again being submitted in pesos."[1] This was in 1951, when the latest round of inflation was in its incipient stages. Thus, the current problem is equally if not more difficult than in 1951.

---

* S. R. Sapienza, *Financial Executive*, April 1963, pp. 27–31.
[1] St. Joseph Lead Co., Annual Report to Stockholders, 1951, p. 7.

COMPARISON OF ECONOMIC FACTORS RELATING TO THE U.S. AND ARGENTINA

The study of inflation within Argentina necessitates the use of some measuring devices that will adequately describe Argentina's situation.

Table 1 shows the economic factors that reveal price changes.

TABLE 1

VARIOUS INDICES OF ARGENTINA AND THE U.S. 1951-1960

(1953 = 100; except wholesale prices in Argentina where 1956 = 100)

Argentina	1960	1959	1958	1957	1956	1955	1954	1953	1952	1951
Wholesale Prices....	439	380	163	124	100					
Cost of Living	590	464	217	165	132	117	104	100	96	69
Wages...................	608	435	277	196	148	130	116	100	92	74

United States	1960	1959	1958	1957	1956	1955	1954	1953	1952	1951
Wholesale Prices....	109	109	108	107	104	100	100	100	101	104
Cost of Living........	111	109	108	105	102	100	100	100	99	97
Wages...................	129	125	120	117	112	106	102	100	94	90

While there might be many arguments as to the inclusion or exclusion of items in the various indices, the selection of a base year, or the reliance on a particular index, it is quite clear that Argentina has suffered a considerable inflationary trend when compared to the U.S. The amount of inflation in Argentina compared to the United States between 1953–1960 is in the approximate order of 6 to 1. Accordingly, companies located in Argentina, caught up in this inflationary spiral, have the impact of this price rise inherent in their accounts.

The American Institute of Certified Public Accountants has advocated that significant changes in the value of a country's currency may dictate adjustment in the dollar amounts that the foreign subsidiary contributes to a consolidation.[2] Whether or not a "significant" change has occurred is always a matter of judgment.

Since the translated amounts of current assets and current liabilities would automatically tend to follow any new rate of exchange, the fixed assets, long-term debt, and stockholders' equity remain as areas that might not be adjusted unless the adjustment in the exchange rate is considered significant. Often companies avoid this problem by not consolidating a subsidiary, in a country such as Argentina, or by partially consolidating such a company, or by only recognizing dividends when remitted to the United States. Management's problem remains: How do they evaluate a company operating in a country with an unstable exchange rate even though consolidation of accounts is not practiced?

---

[2] See Chapter 12, *Accounting Research and Terminology Bulletins.*

TABLE 2

EXCHANGE VALUES OF ARGENTINA
PAPER PESOS PER U.S. DOLLAR

	Rate		
Year	Official*	Free	
1960	82.7	82.7	Adopted a single
1959	83.3	83.3	fluctuating rate.
1958	18.0	70.0	
1957	18.0	37.0	
1956	18.0	37.5	
1955	18.0	36.1	
1954	7.5	14.0	
1953	7.5	14.0	
1952	7.5	14.0	
1951	7.5	14.5	

Source: International Monetary Fund, *ibid.*, pp. 46-47; pp. 42-44.

* Argentina had multiple exchange rates in the years 1951-1954.
The rate used is the buying rate for years 1951-1954.

Table 2 reveals the changing values that Argentina pesos have experienced in recent years:

Table 2 indicates an essential element in this discussion; that is, the prices in Argentina have exerted sufficient pressure on the official rates to force them up from 7.5 pesos to the U.S. dollar to 82.7 pesos for each U.S. dollar. It must be admitted that the pressure from prices is not the only factor to be accounted for in setting an official rate; but it is an important factor. The balance of payments (or foreign exchange market) is the immediate determinant of exchange rates.

Since translation of Argentina pesos to U.S. dollars might normally follow the official rate, it is evident that amounts translated at an "old" rate (1951–54) hardly represent the existing situation today—a significant deterioration has occurred. Fixed assets, long term debt, and stockholders' contribution, if so translated, would be unrealistic. In the face of such a situation, how does a company evaluate the financial status of a subsidiary working in this environment?

For purposes of this exposition, we shall use data for Compania Minera Aguilar from 1953 through 1960. The year 1953 has been selected because the price indices given above use 1953 as the base year and because Argentina's current inflation starts about that time.

COMPANIA MINERA AGUILAR, S.A.

This subsidiary was organized by St. Joseph Lead Co. in 1929. During the period under discussion, 1953–1960, St. Joseph Lead has not consolidated Compania Minera Aguilar (non-consolidation goes back to 1951), showing this investment at the nominal amount of $1 and recognizing actual cash received from earnings of Compania Minera Aguilar as dividend income.

The balance sheets given in Exhibit 1 represent the financial position at the dates given. From this comparison, it would appear that the stockholders' equity has been erased and supplanted by a deficit. Much of this condition turns on the classification of one item under the caption "reserves," a special appropriation amounting to $16,395,000 for rehabilitation of machinery, that if placed in stockholders' equity would make a net credit balance of approximately $7,232,000. More will be said of this special appropriation later.

Suffice it to say, this subsidiary shows a shrinkage in assets of about 50 percent from 1953–1960, using the official rates indicated. This reduction occurs because official rates used in translating the accounts do not take into consideration the extensive reduction of purchasing power in the exchange rates of pesos per U.S. dollar. The refusal to consolidate this foreign subsidiary

EXHIBIT 1

COMPANIA MINERA AGUILAR, S.A.
COMPARATIVE BALANCE SHEETS
As of Dates Indicated
(U.S. dollars)

	December 31	
	1960	1953
Current Assets	$ 7,695,000	$21,372,000
Investments	1,253,000	911,000
Mining Property, net, cost	78,000	117,000
Land, Bldgs., net, cost	4,547,000	2,193,000
Other Assets	216,000	484,000
	$13,816,000	$25,077,000
Current Liabilities	$ 1,139,000	$10,092,000
Reserves	21,840,000	5,472,000
Stockholders' Equity	(9,163,000)	9,513,000
	$13,816,000	$25,077,000

Source: These figures have been derived from the St. Joseph Lead Co., Annual Statements 1960 and 1953.

The rates used in translating for 1960 balances are:

Item	Translating Rates
Current assets and current liabilities	83 pesos per U.S. $.
Investments, Mining Property, Land, Buildings, Other Assets, Reserves	Balances from 1953 at 7 pesos per U.S. $. Additions to 1953 balances at rates prevailing for the years when changes occurred.
Stockholders' Equity	Residual Amount

The rates used in translating for 1953 balances are all peso amounts at 7 pesos to one U.S. $, except Stockholders' Equity which is a residual amount.

indicates management's concern that any inclusion of the accounts in a combined statement would not be useful. Still, management must try to judge as best it can what the peso balances really mean.

RELATION OF PRICES WITHIN A COUNTRY TO EXCHANGE RATES

The exchange rate is an official statement of what a sovereign nation, perhaps in consultation with the International Monetary Fund believes its own currency to be worth in terms of other currencies. Thus the Argentina government has seen fit to restate its official peso exchange rate(s) many times over the years, as have other countries. There is often a considerable difference between these rates so stated by a government and the price structure within country, that is, the changes in local price structure of a country are not necessarily expressed sympathetically and automatically in the current exchange rates. Exchange rates that adjust between gold exchange points are gone. Actually, Argentina was seldom on the gold standard but experienced, instead, fluctuating rates. Exchange rates administered by governments are, and have been for some time, the policy of many nations.

If a company in the U.S. holds shares in another company in Argentina, any attempt to understand what happens in the Argentinian company in terms of U.S. dollars requires "going through the exchange," so to speak. This simply means translating Argentina peso—to U.S. dollars. The U.S. executive thinks and acts in terms of U.S. dollars.

Argentina is a good example of the situation in which a country's exchange rates do not mirror its internal price structure. Using the data cited in Table 1, this point can be demonstrated. The two indices selected are wages and cost of living mainly because they go back to 1953 (1953 = 100) and, more important, they give a reasonable clue to the internal price structure of Argentina. A comparison of 1960 wages in Argentina with those in the United States reveals:

$$\frac{\text{Argentina}}{\text{U.S.}} \frac{608}{129} = 4.71 \text{ or } 471\%$$

This indicates that money wages rose approximately 4.71 times more in Argentina than those in the United States from 1953 to 1960.

Turning to the 1960 cost of living in the two countries, this appears:

$$\frac{\text{Cost of living in Argentina}}{\text{Cost of living in the United States}} \frac{590}{111} = 5.32 \text{ or } 532\%$$

Again we see a relatively greater rise in cost of living in Argentina over that in the U.S. between 1953 and 1960, approximately 5.32 times as calculated.

A rough approximation might be that prices rose, generally, five times as much in Argentina as those in the U.S. from 1953–1960. This calculation rests heavily on the belief that 1953 really was a representative year, and that, therefore, 1960 can be represented adequately by price indices and changes therein that rest on the year 1953. The merits of this point are not argued here; the only case made is that inflation was relatively greater in Argentina than that in the United States. A measure of this greater degree of inflation is roughly in the order of five times.

How did the official exchange rates fluctuate? Table 2 shows that a rate of approximately 7 pesos per U.S. dollar prevailed in 1953. If this rate moved in tandem with the relative price structures of the two countries. (Argentina and the U.S.) the exchange rate in 1960 would be:

Peso Rate   Measure of Relative
in 1953   Price Changes
7            $\times$ 5
Estimated Rate for 1960 Based on Purchasing
Power Changes Between 1953–1960
$= 35$ in 1960

Actually the official rate in 1960 was 82.7 pesos per U.S. dollar. Therefore, a comparison of these two rates approximates the ability of the peso to buy more internally than "through" the exchange.

1960 Rate
1960 Rate Adjusted $\dfrac{82.7}{35} = 2.36$
For Price Changes

or a measure of the peso's ability to buy more locally than in the United States.

Expressed another way, the peso in 1960 possessed approximately 236 percent more purchasing power within Argentina in 1960 than in the U.S., as compared with 1953.[3]

Direct investments are made in foreign countries to give a return to the U.S. investor. The balances so invested are not "moved through the exchange," except figuratively when statements are made, or actually for conversion of earnings. Generally accepted accounting principles place reliance on official exchange rates for statement purposes. Translation of balances overseas usually is accomplished by applying such official rates to account balances to determine financial position and earnings. With the above-noted discrepancy in purchasing power inherent and apparent in exchange rates, it follows that

---

[3] This paper concentrates its attention on "official" rates and thus avoids "free" rates. The reason for this treatment is that an investment made in a foreign country is more often than not at "official" rates and transactions stemming from such an investment are usually at official rates.

any attempt to assess how a company located in Argentina is doing, looking at it from a U.S. point of view, is likely to miss the differences in relative purchasing power if reliance is placed on official rates only.

This is not to suggest that parent companies in this predicament overlook this difference in purchasing power. There is a real possibility, however, that they do not quantify this difference and they do not have, therefore, the best expression of values overseas.[4]

THE CRUX OF THE PROBLEM

A foreign subsidiary is set in a local environment that may isolate it, for practical purposes, from the exchange rate(s). Many, if not most, of its transactions may be local in nature. While it is true that many foreign subsidiaries will have close and frequent business relationships with a U.S. parent, many also deal with the parent only in terms of dividends and working capital needs, once established. A large portion of assets are never intended to be converted to U.S. dollars. Therefore, any translation of such amounts might be better stated if expressed in terms of local purchasing power simply because this is where the balances will be used.

Exhibit 2 is a comparison of Compania Minera Aguilar at December 31, 1960, using what might be termed conventional translating rates, and rates adjusted for purchasing power follows:

Column 2, left, tends to soften the impact of the straight translation using conventional techniques and official rates exhibited in Column 1. This is so because the purchasing power factor is introduced to mitigate the influence of the official rates expressed in Column 1, thereby coming closer to a better statement of Compania Minera Aguilar's dollar purchasing power. As can be seen, Columns 2 and 3 show a reduced difference in totals, as against the shrinkage that Column 1 indicates occurred. In terms of purchasing power, there has been a reduction in the total asset position from 1953–1960, and the stockholders' equity is about the same in 1960 as it was in 1953. While this tends to indicate no change has occurred, the point should be made that peso profits were made from 1953 through 1960 and dividends were paid to St. Joseph Lead in six of the eight years.

LOCAL ATTEMPTS TO COMPENSATE FOR INFLATION

The government of Argentina has attempted to compensate, in part, for inflationary conditions. They recognize that long-lived assets recorded at cost

---

[4] Some of this discussion rests, in part, on an unpublished master's paper by Richard B. Klein.

EXHIBIT 2

COMPANIA MINERA AGUILAR, S.A.
COMPARATIVE BALANCE SHEET
As of December 31
(U.S. dollars)

	(Column 1)	(Column 2)	(Column 3)
	1960		1953
	OFFICIAL RATES [a]	ADJUSTED RATES [b]	ALL PESOS 7 = 1 U.S. $
Current Assets	$ 7,695,000	$13,007,000	$21,372,000
Investments	1,253,000	834,000	911,000
Mining Property, (net) Cost	78,000	17,000	117,000
Land, Bldgs., etc., (net) Cost	4,574,000	4,308,000	2,193,000
Other Assets	216,000	213,000	484,000
	$13,816,000	$18,379,000	$25,077,000
Current Liabilities	$ 1,139,000	$ 2,701,000	$10,092,000
Reserves	21,840,000	6,089,000	5,472,000
Stockholders' Equity	(9,163,000)	9,589,000	9,513,000
	$13,816,000	$18,379,000	$25,077,000

Source: These figures have been derived from the St. Joseph Lead Co., 1960, and 1953 Annual Reports.

(a) See Exhibit 1 for an explanation of translating rates.

(b) The rates used in translating for 1960 balances on an adjusted base are:

	Translating Rates
Current assets and current liabilities for local use	35 pesos per U.S. $

Example: Current assets in pesos $\frac{321,476,392}{35} = \$9,185,000$

Investments, Mining Property, Land, Buildings, and other Assets	35 pesos per U.S. $

Example: Land, Buildings, Property and Equipment in pesos
$\frac{150,773,997}{35} = .\$4,307,828$

Current assets reserved for purchases in the U.S.	83 pesos per U.S. $

Example: Current assets in pesos $\frac{317,217,498}{83} = \$3,821,000$

Reserves for local commitments	35 pesos per U.S. $

Example: Reserves in pesos $\frac{80,326,872}{35} = \$2,268,000$

Reserves for foreign (U.S.) purchases	83 pesos per U.S. $

Example: Reserves in pesos $\frac{317,217,498}{83} = \$3,821,000$

Stockholders' Equity	Residual Amount

gradually are assigned to income over an extended period of years. While the peso amounts of depreciation express an allocation of original cost, these amounts do not compensate for the rather rapid rise in prices within Argentina through 1953–1960. The Argentinian government has attempted to alleviate the extra burden of taxes that results from rising profits calculated with peso costs that are rapidly outdated.[5] The present law, No. 15272, became applicable beginning January 1, 1960.[6] The essence of this law is to allow a reduction in the taxes on ordinary profits and excess profits while increasing slightly the tax on capital (because of the revaluation). The net effect should be a reduction in taxes.

SPECIAL APPROPRIATION

Compania Minera Aguilar has attempted in its own way to compensate for this rapid price rise and the stringent exchange position that has prevented proper external purchases of supplies for maintenance of equipment. Each year since 1951, Compania Minera Aguilar has appropriated from annual earnings varying amounts that ranged from 20 percent to 40 percent of net income before the appropriation.

The St. Joseph Lead reasoning is best expressed in the 1951 Annual Statement:[7]

> The impossibility of obtaining sufficient permits for foreign exchange and the resultant lack of spare parts, mine and mill supplies are having a very adverse effect on this operation (Compania Minera Aguilar), as does the shortage of rail transport. Unless steps are shortly taken to rehabilitate the underground, milling and power equipment, and to complete the development work long deferred by the lack of drill bits, dynamite and miscellaneous mine equipment, the Aguilar output will be further curtailed, with serious effect on the output. . . .
>
> Because of the ultimate heavy rehabilitation expense and the greatly decreased value of the peso, it was believed necessary to set aside from the 1951 earnings a special reserve of pesos to cover the replacement and rehabilitation of fixed assets.

This appropriation of earnings was not allowed for tax purposes. Also, the U.S. public accounting firm (Haskins and Sells) took exception to this practice and has consistently repeated its exception in its opinion concerning the financial statements each year since 1951. The exception rests on the point that such an appropriation is more commonly made out of retained earnings and not current income. From an initial appropriation of 12,778,026 pesos in 1951, Compania Minera Aguilar has accumulated 317,217,498 pesos through 1960.

[5] Argentinian laws 13,393 and 14,060 allowed increased amortization on assets required after 1927 in order to compensate, in part, for the rising costs of replacement. Decreed Law No. 4,610 granted larger percentages than the aforementioned laws.

[6] Revalucion de Activos—Ley No. 15,272 (The reappraisal of assets—Law No. 15,272). The author has avoided any effects of this law in 1960 figures by reversing the reappraisal stemming therefrom, including any income effects.

[7] St. Joseph Lead Co., Annual Report to Stockholders, 1951, p. 7.

These 317,217,498 pesos are included in the 1960 balances under the caption "Reserves." This amount, in line with the public accountant's opinion, might well be included under "Stockholders' Equity." If official dollar exchange rates existing in the year of each appropriation are used to translate these pesos into dollars, the 317,217,498 pesos become $16,395,000. This dollar amount, of course, is questionable as an expression of dollar equivalent of these pesos. Thus, in Column 2 of Exhibit 2, an adjusted amount of $3,821,000 (the total of $6,089,000 includes other reserves) is used as the purchasing power equivalent of the pesos reserved for maintenance, or 317,217,498/83. This is the better figure because if such maintenance occurs the assets will undoubtedly be secured in the U.S.

MANAGEMENT IS FACED WITH AN UNUSUAL PROBLEM

The interesting aspect of this special appropriation is that it represents management's concern over the exchange problem. While an attempt has been made to offset rising costs of maintenance, the earlier appropriations are eroded year-to-year as prices rise. Thus, appropriations have to rise through the years as they did except for 1960, in order to maintain an annual increment to the reserve of approximately the same amount of purchasing power. Whether such a procedure is successful rests on the future course of inflation within Argentina. Balances so segregated lose their significance, unless adjusted for purchasing power changes, as rapid inflation occurs and the task becomes one of running increasingly faster in order to stand still.

EARNINGS

Compania Minera Aguilar has been profitable in terms of pesos in each year since 1950. Total profit from 1953–1960 has been 917,000,000 pesos. Of this amount, the author has estimated that from 1953 through 1960 approximately 431,000,000 pesos have been converted into U.S. dollars at varying rates, summing to $7,883,000. This would mean that St. Joseph's Lead has received about 82 percent of the 1960 stockholders' equity in the form of dividends in U.S. dollars, using the stockholders' equity in Column 2 of Exhibit 2. Based on the 1960 stockholders' equity (excluding reserves) the percentage return if spread over eight years is a little more than 10 percent return per annum or 6 percent return per annum if based on the stockholders' 1960 investment (including reserves for foreign purchases). This, of course, does not consider U.S. taxes that might be applied against the dividened income received here in the U.S. after giving due weight to offsetting foreign tax credit.

CONCLUSION

Exhibit 2 shows a negative stockholders' equity if official rates are applied. The uselessness of these figures makes it imperative that new ones be developed to state the stockholders' equity and any return thereon better. The position taken here is that some weight be given to the internal price changes of Argentina in reporting to management. Official exchange rates do not give an accurate portrayal of the situation. It might be argued that no one can recast the accounts where inflation has occurred so rapidly. This avoids the issue; but the problem for management remains because Compania Minera Aguilar is a viable company and its operations need to be followed. The officers of the parent need to have a better expression of the subsidiary's operations than is obtained in the statements for stockholders.

The technique suggested here is not limited to inflationary situations, as above. The operations of an international organization involves use of funds in many areas—inflationary and deflationary. The maximization of purchasing power available is a critical problem in international operations and every means possible must be used to achieve this result.

HOW ITT MANAGES ITS FOREIGN EXCHANGE*

International Telephone and Telegraph Corporation, which sells its products in 115 countries, has 100 subsidiary companies in 49 countries. It is thus vitally concerned with currency fluctuations abroad, particularly in areas where there are consistent and considerable inflation and frequent devaluation of the local currency, which results in a reduction of income in U.S. dollars as well as an erosion of the investment made in local currency.

The principles outlined in this article are applied on a worldwide basis, but the locale emphasized is Central and South America, where the company has extensive assets and where currency devaluation is a constant problem. This is how we have organized to meet it.

HEADQUARTERS PRACTICES

Our company has created a committee at our headquarters in New York for the purposes of continuously determining our corporate approach toward foreign exchange problems and of advising management on specific foreign exchange situations. This committee is composed of the area executive, the treasurer, the tax director, the comptroller, and his specialized assistant.

Our headquarters practice concerning foreign exchange administration emphasizes:

I. Assurance of maximum awareness in local managements of the effects of devaluation and inflation on the dollar income. This awareness results in the continuous anticipation of problems and in the avoidance of losses and unpleasant surprises. It also results in recognition of opportunities to take advantage of special situations and opportunities for profits, remittances, tax advantages, etc.

II. Simplification of the procedures and instructions regarding reporting and forecasting of the effect of devaluation in our financial statements and in our forecasts, plans, and budgets.

III. Authorized procedures for executive determination of exchange rates to be used for the translation of financial statements.

IV. Maintenance of an early warning system of potential problems and

---

* John Verroen, *Management Services*, January–February, 1965, pp. 27–33.

immediate consultation and cooperation to find the best possible solution under the circumstances.

V. Establishment of reasonable limits on maximum credit to be given to clients who pay in local currency.

VI. Formal consideration and decision concerning additional investments in local currency assets, taking into account the dollar return on additional investments.

Local Management Awareness

It is usually confusing to the second level of local management to think in terms of dollars rather than of local currency. This management level is inclined to consider dollar exchange losses as a "conversion" loss of the local currency whose results are not under their control. This tends to put an additional burden on the top management of the local company, which must accept the primary responsibility of safeguarding the dollar value of the investment and producing a reasonable dollar return on that investment.

Some basic decisions reached by headquarters are pertinent to the handling of the valuation of the assets of the local companies. Besides the items which by their nature are fixed in dollars, such as the accumulated investment in the equity and dollar receivables and payables, the following assumptions are made:

Fixed Assets Retain Their Historical Dollar Values

This assumption is in accordance with the customary practice of U.S. companies operating in other countries and is generally valid on a long-term basis, although temporary distortion sometimes offsets the results of a given fiscal year. The internal inflation may not fluctuate simultaneously with the devaluation, particularly in countries with runaway inflation and artificially established "official" exchange rates. The accounting profession usually ignores the short-term differences (which may show up when insurance revaluations are made), because in the long term the monetary value of land, buildings, machinery, and equipment increases as the real purchasing power of the currency declines.

Inventories Retain Their Historical Values, Subject to the Rule of Cost or Realizable Values, Whichever Is Lower

This is an assumption *not* universally used by U.S. companies abroad. We have found considerable benefits from this assumption; We no longer have large unrealistic gross profits which are offset by large and hard to explain exchange losses. This is a technique that is winning additional professional support.

Simplified Reporting

We try to have a pragmatic approach to all budgeting and forecasting with the intent of reducing the time spent on calculating in detail the effect on the financial statements of highly tentative devaluations.

Companies submit a five-year business plan in June each year using imagination and showing appropriate initiative. This plan is based on an exchange rate which at the time of preparation is forecasted for the end of the current year. This rate is used throughout the five years.

A yearly exposure statement is made for the total company and an estimate is made of the potential exchange gains or losses at the forecasted exchange rates. This gain or loss is distributed over the year and by product line and is shown on one line in the income statement.

After review of the business plan and tentative approval or rejection of major projects, a budget is prepared and submitted before November 30.

For this budget the exchange rate used is the one in effect when the budget is prepared, usually on or around September 30. This rate is usually not far from the one used in the business plan.

In the budget, quarterly exposure statements are submitted for the total company and the exchange gain or loss is calculated at the forecasted exchange rates. This gain or loss is spread equally over the three months and allocated by product line.

The actual monthly financial statements are translated at the current exchange rate in effect at the end of the closing day, except that the income statement is converted at the accumulated monthly average exchange rate. This means that the cumulative income statement, say, for June, is translated at the arithmetical average of the exchange rates at the end of each of the six months. The rates used are those at which remittances can be made (actually or theoretically).

Even if exchange rates are being artifically stabilized by official sources and a devaluation is imminent, we do not normally accrue in the accounts for any future possible exchange losses in our monthly financial statements.

Monthly Telex reports on the performance of the month and the forecast for the remainder of the year are made at realistic forecasted exchange rates so that our latest forecast reflects our best appraisal of what we think revenues and income are going to be in dollars.

Approval of Exchange Rates

The comptrollers of the companies abroad consult the company comptroller and treasurer on the exchange rate to be used for business plans; budgets, and year-end financial statements.

Alertness

The local management exposes in weekly letters any area of potential dangers of impending devaluation. Contacts with local bankers, finance men, and government officials are maintained to get accurate and up-to-date evaluations of the monetary situation.

The comptroller, treasurer, and area management staffs also keep up to date on any financial information affecting foreign currencies from reports, banking relationships, magazines, etc.

Local Currency Credit

Sales from one country to another are usually made in dollars and with all available guarantees.

Credit for sales in local currency by local companies is left to the judgment of local management, which seeks advice from area management on major items. However, in the area reviews of quarterly statements, budgets, and business plans, a discussion of credit terms is usually made and certain limits may be imposed on local management, depending on the amount of exposure and the economic outlook.

Dollar Investments

We have a very positive approach to expansion and usually we do not hesitate to make investments to get additional business.

Although we do not specifically take the gross capital employed into account for pricing our sales of manufactured products, we expect to get a reasonable income from royalties, management fees, and dividends and a contribution to research and development costs.

MANUFACTURING SUBSIDIARIES

The managements of subsidiary companies in countries where devaluation occurs have the primary responsibility of following the headquarters practices and protecting the dollar income as well as investment.

The following areas require specific attention:

> I. Selling prices
> II. Financial executive
> III. Local receivables
> IV. Local currency statements
> V. Exposure
> VI. Cover

Selling Prices

The most effective way to offset exchange losses is to make more local currency profit on sales. This may be attempted by increasing selling prices to the extent that exchange losses or the costs of cover against exchange losses are offset. However, if the net income is reinvested in local currency assets, then the exposure is increased. Therefore, prompt remittances of dividends, royalties, management fees, etc., become of vital importance. Reinvestment must be studied as carefully as new investments (as our experience has indicated). We recognize that the resistance from local competition and from consumers against price increases is reduced more and more in those countries where devaluation is repetitive and high inflation has become a way of life. One of our companies charges the high "protection" interest cost separately to its customers rather than including it in the selling price. This reduces sales taxes and encourages the customers to pay cash. We record these interest charges as "other income" since our gross margin is shown more accurately by excluding these inflationary interest charges.

Financial Executive

The pressure for continuous price increases, for obtaining more local financing, for keeping costs up to date, and for special financial reporting creates the need for a high degree of sophistication in the financial staff, and the hiring of an internationally oriented treasury executive to supplement the comptroller is often required even in smaller companies.

The purchasing function also demands special attention aimed at keeping the investment in inventories down because of the higher carrying cost. More effort has to be spent in obtaining longer credit terms and fixed price arrangements from suppliers.

Local Receivables

Since inventory is handled on a dollar acquisition cost basis, the major pertinent element in local currency assets is usually "accounts receivable," and the exchange losses from this investment may be significant. This would indicate that the credit should be kept at a minimum level. However, we see that in inflationary countries the sales to consumers depend more on credit terms than on the basic price, and a dealer must carry a large investment in consumer financing. In turn, the manufacturing companies need to give more credit in order to maintain a sales volume. This, of course, brings the tendency to increase the investment in receivables, and this becomes one of the major problems.

In our company, the local management has been made responsible for the daily solution of this problem except that by means of the yearly budget approval some general restrictions are imposed.

In Brazil, the discounting of receivable paper is still possible. However, these discounts are subject to full recourse and our account is charged back within a few days after collection has failed. Therefore, we do not report these discounts as a deduction from receivables but rather as a source of local bank loans, particularly since additional receivable paper has to be given for collection in order to obtain discounts.

Local Currency Statements

For a greater awareness of the effect of devaluation, the statements in local currency issued for internal use by the second management level include some items which are not necessarily recorded in the local books:

In the cost and expense statements, a separate line is added for "additional dollar depreciation." This item brings the cost in local currency in line with the dollar statements. The amount is determined by taking the historical dollar depreciation provision and translating this into local currency at the rate of exchange currently used for the income statement. The excess of this amount over the actual local currency provision (including depreciation on appreciated fixed assets, where applicable) is then shown as additional dollar depreciation.

The individual product costs are adjusted semiannually, based on an index figure. Currently we are deriving this index from the increase in the cost of living and from the exchange rate applicable to imported materials. Individual product costs are checked and adjusted on a cycle basis and by selecting the principal cost factors only.

During the in-between months, a monthly cumulative index figure is applied to product or statistical costs in order to have more local currency statements that are more representative.

The amount of any change in the costs of inventories is applied to an inventory reserve account and is subsequently amortized over the estimated carrying times. The translation of inventories to dollars in the income statement takes places on a monthly "first-in, first-out" basis on the total net charge to cost of sales.

The monthly local statements of costs and expenses of each cost center show budget figures for the month and year to dates. As our budget is made on the convenient presumption of stability in currency conditions and the effect of devaluation is shown in a single item, the budget figures need adjustment to give effect to the rate of devaluation as assumed in the budget.

With the three items above, local management has a means of measuring operations in local currency which will be in rough agreement with the ultimate data in the dollar financial statements.

Exposure

The local management keeps track of the position of the exposure to exchange losses by monthly exposure statements showing the local currency assets (excluding inventories) and local currency liabilities.

When an exposure position exists, the possibilities and extent of probable devaluation are immediately considered and all available sources of information are consulted. Conditions are evaluated and the possible means of coverage determined (e.g., forward exchange contracts, swaps, local loans for investment in inventories and for purchase of other assets retaining dollar value). The circumstances and related recommendations are then submitted to the exchange committee for policy determination. These proposals also indicate the cost of forward contracts, etc., the possible benefits to be derived, and the period for which such coverage is required.

If it is decided that the potential losses are less than the cost of coverage and the risk should be taken, we do not provide for the potential exchange losses, but we do revise the earnings forecast for the remainder of the year.

The exposure statements, as mentioned above, are summaries of local currency assets and liabilities. For local management a very realistic loss is incurred when dollar debts are paid because it requires more local currency to pay off a dollar debt. This may be rather confusing to those who have not gone through actual translations of financial statements into dollars. It is essential to see that dollar assets and liabilities are stable and that the local currency items are the variables. Therefore, the foreign exchange loss incurred when dollar debts are paid is actually the result of the deterioration of the international buying power of the local currency assets. Consequently, if we determine the exposure (in dollars) of the local currency net assets, we have systematically and currently included the local currency exchange losses applicable to future international remittances.

A simple illustration of one transaction and its effect on exchange exposure may be helpful.

(a) Assume that a company borrows $1,000 in the U.S. and brings the money into a foreign country, exchanges it and collects P.10,000.

(b) Assume further that this is held in cash, receivables, or any other local currency asset.

(c) When a balance sheet is prepared, it is found that we have a local currency exposure on the payment of the dollar debt in the amount of $1,000 and at the same time a dollar exposure on the local currency asset of $1,000.

(d) A potential loss exists which can be measured either by calculating the amount of local currency now needed to pay the debt or by calculating the dollar worth of the local currency asset.

(e) Let us go one step further and assume that the peso is devalued from P.10 to the dollar to P.12 to the dollar.

(f) The local books still show the peso cash at P.10,000 but must provide for an exchange loss of P.2,000 in order to update the payable to its present dollar equivalent. In dollars the cash is now worth only $833, and the debt to be paid is $1,000, so there is a loss of $167, which again is the present equivalent of the loss above of P.2,000.

(g) Thus, when we think in terms of dollars, it is only necessary to establish the net local currency assets in order to determine the amount of exposure to exchange loss.

Cover

Routine procedures are set up and reviewed periodically to minimize the investment in net local currency assets. These procedures include the following:

Increasing dollar funds and decreasing local currency funds by keeping excess funds or emergency funds in dollar accounts.

Increasing dollar receivables (including export receivables and local contracts with maintenance of value) and reducing the local currency receivables. This can be done by prompt billing and mailing of invoices, by reducing credit terms of local currency sales, by increasing collection efforts to reduce past due accounts, and by discounting trade paper, without recourse if possible.

Increasing local currency payables—by getting longer and more favorable terms, by cooperating with suppliers in getting bank credits, etc.

Keeping dollar debts current, particularly to associated companies, since they are settled by use of local currency assets.

Increasing local loans and swaps. When the cost becomes exorbitant, we determine whether the gross profit from additional business volume still warrants the high cost of borrowing. It usually does.

Reducing inventories if the realizable selling prices are not expected to increase simultaneously with the devaluation.

When remittances cannot be made currently and therefore a forced reinvestment occurs, making profitable use of these reinvestments.

Making simultaneous exchange transactions if remittances can be made legally but the cash is lacking. This establishes the dollar debt (to an intermediary bank, if deemed advisable) and often makes the exchange loss actually incurred deductible for taxes even though it does not decrease the exposure.

It is clear that our attempts to protect ourselves against inflation and devaluation clash with the similar attempts being made by others. Moneylenders demand higher interest, customers want longer credit, suppliers give less credit and increase prices in anticipation of cost increases, and labor steps up its demands for higher wages and more frequent adjustments.

The reader will realize that management in developing countries has to cope with a multitude of problems nonexistent in the United States, and the above by no means reflects the whole story of the financial problems. In some countries there are multiple exchange rates, and different rates are therefore applicable to the various assets, liabilities, and income items. In other countries one has to cope with frozen rental income on fixed assets.

Some of our companies are developing an emergency defense program to minimize the demand of dollars from the parent company at the time that investment of additional dollars is least desirable. This program includes deferring payables, sales taxes, etc., even if penalties are due; suspension of purchases, travel expense and advertising; etc. In addition, we expect in due course to accumulate a general emergency fund by contributions from all companies in developing countries, so as to avoid devaluation shocks which are in fact the risk factor which caused the relatively high profit margins in prior periods.

COMMUNICATIONS SUBSIDIARIES

The foreign exchange problems of our communications companies have certain special aspects:

1. Collections of receivables are becoming more difficult in the communications business due to trade customs and the practice of competition, except for telephone companies, where these problems are usually restricted to government receivables.

2. Although the rates chargeable for communications business are usually legally regulated and tied to gold francs (or gold pesos), we find that there is usually a fairly long lapse of time between the time of devaluation and the approval of higher rates. This is not shown as an exchange loss anywhere but is expressed in a reduction of revenues. Prompt and vigorous claims for revision of the rates has become a necessary tradition and is essential to a healthy operation.

3. Books have to be kept in gold pesos or gold francs in order to keep track of the allowable return on assets employed.

4. Our radio companies charge at rates based on gold francs as fixed by international convention. However, we collect in local currency and cannot change the rates at will.

In Argentina, for instance, we can increase charges only when the average exchange rates fluctuates more than 10 percent compared with the previous six months. Changes are made effective May 15 and November 15 with government approval.

In Brazil, the charges are based on average daily official exchange rates for the three months up to the tenth of the month prior to the date of change. Changes are made quarterly.

In Chile, we change monthly, based on the official exchange rate upon notification to the government. Charges for telegraph services are changed only when the exchange rate changes by more than 20 percent, dependent on government authorization, which may take two months.

5. We have not been very successful in selling shares to the public as a means of getting local financing for communications companies; many local restrictions exist, varying in each country, to prevent such financing.

Obviously, we must earn a reasonable return on our assets if we are to induce the investing public to support our activities in foreign countries. This is right and proper. However, we believe that we make a vital contribution to the business activity of developing countries by furthering local assembly and manufacture. We train and employ thousands of local people and we are eager to expand local communications in accordance with the desire and the ability of local government. We are very proud of our long association with the internal development of Latin America and expect to make a continued contribution to the inevitable growth of its economies.

ADDITIONAL READINGS

Applying Financial Controls in Foreign Operations, International Management Assn., Special Report No. 2, New York, 1957.

Brandt, Robert F., "One World of Accounting," *Journal of Accountancy*, July, 1962, pp. 68–71.

deLeeuw, H. D., "Some Aspects of Auditing in the International Field," *The Accountant*, March 30, 1963, pp. 385–391.

Engelmann, Konrad, "Accounting Problems in Developing Countries," *Journal of Accountancy*, January, 1962, pp. 53–56.

Epley, Stewart, "Using Liquid Funds Overseas," *The Controller*, February, 1962, pp. 56–59.

Epps, Max I., "Realistic Accounting Under South American Inflation," *Journal of Accountancy*, January, 1961, pp. 67–74.

Hepworth, S. R., *Reporting Foreign Operations*, University of Michigan, 1956.

Management Accounting Problems in Foreign Operations, National Association of Accountants, Research Report No. 36, New York, 1960.

Maynard, Brian A., "Overseas Branches—Interesting Accounting Problems Met in Practice," *The Accountant*, July 3, 1954, pp. 6–13.

Mueller, Gerhard G., "The International Accounting Problem," *The Accounting Review*, January, 1963, pp. 142–147.

Parker, W. E., "Changes in the Purchasing Power of Money," *Accountancy*, January, 1963, pp. 8–13.

Puente, J. Irizarry y., "Currency Depreciation in Latin America—Its Character and Effect on Foreign Tax Payers," *Taxes (The Tax Magazine)*, January, 1955, pp. 52–67.

Salgado, Ignacio Perez, "Accounting Reports in Chile," *The Accounting Review*, January, 1963, pp. 142–147.

Smith, St. Elmo, "Accounting for Overseas Operations," *The Canadian Chartered Accountant*, November, 1961, pp. 455–460.

von Amerorgan, F., "Dutch Accounts," *Accountancy*, June, 1963, pp. 497–500.

Wilkinson, Theodore L., "Can Accounting be an International Language," *The Accounting Review*, January, 1964, pp. 133–139.

Index

Accounting
  recommenations of AICPA, 851
  survey of practices of multinational companies, 852

ADELA Investment Corp., 702

Advance deposits on imports, 286–289

Agreement Corporations, 371–373

AID investment guaranties; *see* Foreign investment guaranties

Algeria, central bank, 91–99 *passim*

Australia, money market, 628–630

Balance of payments, U.S.; *see* U.S. balance of payments

Bank for International Settlements (BIS), 263–264

Banking laws affecting foreign bank activities in U.S., 377–383 *passim*

Barlow, E. R., 769, 770

Bernstein plan, 220, 221, 225

Bernstein report, 140–142

Bretton Woods, 492, 493, 498

Burundi, central bank, 91, 93, 95, 96

Cameroon, central bank, 91

Canada
  floating exchange rate, 167
  money market, 624–626

Canadian exchange rate history, 329–330

Capital markets
  data on corporate issues in various countries, 566, 567
  data on security issues in various countries, 567–568
  functions, 563, 564
  hindrances, 600–602
  relation to central banks, 602, 603
  relation to savings levels, 565, 566, 599, 600
  in Western Europe, 562, 568–574, 577–582, 589–594

Capital transfer restrictions, 279, 299–301

Central bank discount rate, U.K., 269

Central banking
  bank-government relations, 93, 94
  credit controls, 96, 97
  discount policies, 67–76
  instruments, 65, 66
  new central banks, 91–100
  open-market operations, 80–90
  relationship with money market, 94–96
  vs. capital markets, 602, 603
  vs. money markets, 619, 632, 633

CFA (French African Community) currency, 98

Chad, central bank, 91

China
  foreign aid, 481–483
  trade structure and data, 428, 429, 435
  trade with the U.K., 430–433

City of London, foreign banks, 384–388

COCOM, 407–410 *passim*

Comecon, 411, 447
  multilateral trade financing, 444, 445, 448

Comecon Bank, 406, 444, 452–456

Commercial bank lending abroad, controls by U.S. government guidelines, 189–194

Commercial banking
  Africa, 399–403
  Belgium, 354–366, 389–393 *passim*
  Germany, 353, 356, 357, 389–393 *passim*
  international activity of U.S. banks, 363–376
  Latin America, 394–398
  role in multinational business, 351, 352
  Switzerland, 357, 358, 389–393 *passim*
  U.K., 360–362
  U.S., 358, 359

Congo (Brazzaville), central bank, 91

Congo (Leopoldville), central bank, 91

Consolidation of accounts of multinational corporations, 851–854

Convertibility, non-resident, 274, 275

Cummins Engine Co., 595

Cyprus, central bank, 91–99 *passim*

Dahomey, central bank, 91

Devaluation
 effect on accounting procedures, 870–882
 relationship to cost of living indices, 148, 150
 relative to miscellaneous governmental policies, 152, 153
 of U.S. dollar, 145–154, 163–165 *passim*

Development Assistance Committee (DAC), 461

Development banks
 capital structure, 651–654
 investment policies, 614, 615
 lending and investment terms, 661–680
 purposes and types, 646–651
 relationship to IBRD, 646, 647
 relationship with clients, 680–686
 role in international finance, 644, 645
 sources of capital, 654–661
 vs. capital markets, 604–606, 608–615 *passim*

Development finance companies, 687–698

Discount rates, central banks, 67–76

Dollar gap, 104

East-West trade
 financing, 438–440
 importance to U.S. businessmen, 404–406, 407–411
 with sterling area, 416, 417, 436
 with U.K., 417, 418, 430, 437
 U.S. government regulations, 407
 volume, 408, 410, 412–418 *passim*

Edge Act Corporations, 371–373, 708, 709, 715, 720–728

Equatorial African Central Bank, 91–99 *passim*

Eurodollars
 as means of credit creation, 556–561
 as source of investment capital, 525, 526
 definition and origin, 539–541, 554
 future, 553
 interest rate, 541–545 *passim*
 risk to investor, 546
 size and impact of market, 550–553
 utilization, 539, 543, 555

European Payments Union, 406

Exchange controls, history, 273–275

Financieras; *see* Development finance companies

Flexible exchange rates; *see* Floating exchange rates

Floating exchange rates
 Canada, 10, 328–348 *passim*
 effect of, 10, 11, 147
 solution to U.S. balance of payments problems, 161–174

Foreign aid
 bilateral aid data, 462–465, 484–487
 distribution, 473, 474, 489
 interest to businessmen, 457, 458
 loan criteria, 506–510
 multilateral aid data, 465–467
 project selection and appraisal, 510–521
 role of private captial, 467, 468
 from Socialist countries, 481–483
 terms and conditions, 474–481, 488
 total flow
  from all countries, 490, 491
  from DAC, 468

Foreign banks
 in London, 384–388
 in U.S., 377

Foreign dollar issues
 in continental markets, 532–534
 on London market, 530–531

Foreign exchange
 brokers, 7
 professional risk takers, 16, 19
 role of commercial banks, 7, 19, 20
 speculators, 17, 18
 traders, 20
 U.S. market, 7
 uses, 7
 volume of trading, 8

Foreign exchange market, role of, 12, 13

Foreign exchange reserves, effect of gold supply, 253, 254

Foreign exchange restrictions, effect on accounting procedures, 855, 856

Foreign exchange trading
 long position, 21, 22, 23, 24
 short position, 25

Foreign investment by U.S. firms, 113, 115
 as adjunct to foreign aid, 467, 468
 controls by U.S. government guidelines, 189–199
 effect on U.S. balance of payments, 148, 149, 175–183
 in U.S., 112, 114
 U.S. taxation, 175

Foreign investment guaranties, 729–733

Foreign securities, purchases by Americans, 185

Foreign tax credit, 800

Foreign trade of the U.S., 116

Forward cover
 definition, 46
 use of, 47–52
 volume, 52–55

Forward exchange
 role of, 46
 supply and demand, 33–38

Forward exchange rate, central bank intervention, 56–58

France, capital market, 573, 574, 577–582 *passim*, 589–594 *passim*
Frank—Radcliffe plan, 221, 222, 225
French franc zone, 98

Gabon, central bank, 91
Germany
  capital market, 570–572, 577–582 *passim*, 589–594 *passim*; revaluation of D-mark, 24, 25, 39–42
Gold
  price of, 258, 259
  private use, 249–251
  world supply, 236, 247–252
Gold exchange standard
  description, 205, 206
  operation, 242–244
  weaknesses, 206, 211
Gold points, 58, 59
Gold pool, 118, 264–265
Gold reserves of U.S., 105, 107, 108, 109
Gold supply, effect on international liquidity, 155–160
Grossing up, 801
Group of Ten, 265–266
Guidelines by U.S. government to affect U.S. balance of payments, 189–199
Guinea, central bank, 91

Hedging, 24
Hot money, 212

Import surcharges in U.K., 268, 282–286
India, money market, 630–632
Inflation
  cover, 905, 906
  effect on financial management, 887–897
  exposure, 903–905
  indices of Argentina and U.S., 888, 889
Inter-American Development Bank, 459
Interest equalization tax, 562, 565
  effect on U.S. balance of payments, 184–188
Interest rate arbitrage
  definition, 14
  effect on U.S. balance of payments, 118
  general considerations, 26–28
Interest rates
  effect on U.S. balance of payments, 184–188 *passim*
  government securities, 77, 78
International Bank for Economic Cooperation; *see* Comecon bank
International Bank for Reconstruction and Development (IBRD)
  functions, 493–495

IBRD (*continued*)
  history and membership, 492, 493
  lending policies and procedures, 496–505
International Development Association (IDA), 459
International Finance Corporation (IFC)
  examples of investments, 742–745
  lending and investment policies, 734–738
  terms of investments and loans, 738–740
International liquidity, 208–214
  definition, 231, 232
  means of increasing, 238, 239
  measuring, 234–237
  vs. gold supply, 253, 254
International Monetary Fund (IMF), annual meeting, 262
International monetary system
  history, 201–203, 241, 242
  needs, 216–218
  reforms suggested, 219–230, 246
Ivory Coast, central bank, 91

Jamaica, central bank, 91–99 *passim*

LAFTA, 277
Lebanon, central bank, 91–99 *passim*
Lederer, Walter, 176
London, as source of capital, 1, 2
London capital market, as underwriter, 529–531
London gold market, 257–261

Malagasy, central bank, 91, 92, 93
Mali, central bank, 91–99 *passim*
Mauritania, central bank, 91
Money markets
  Australia, 628–630
  Canada, 624–626
  definition, 621
  functions, 616–618
  India, 630–632
  purpose and method of operation, 622–624, 634
  South Africa, 626–628
  South East Asia, 634–642
Morocco, central bank, 91
Moscow Narodny Bank, 404, 405, 438–440 *passim*
Multiple currency practices; *see* Multiple exchange rates
Multiple exchange rates, 278, 280, 281, 290–294, 311–314

Niger, central bank, 91
Nigeria, central bank, 91

Official free market rate, Venezuelan experience, 304–306, 307
Overseas Development Fund, 459

PASA project, 712–719
Peace by Investment Corporation, 757–766
Philippines, capital market, 597–607

Quantitative trade restrictions, 277, 294–299, 305

Radcliffe Committee hearings, 9, 10
Regulation K of the Federal Reserve Board, 371–373 *passim*, 721
Regulation Q of the Federal Reserve Board, 551, 552
Revenue Act of 1962
 criticism, 785–799
 explanation, 800–807
Roosa, Robert, proposals on international monetary reforms, 159
Roosa bonds, 142
Rouble as international currency, 406, 447
Rueff, Jacques, 240
Rwanda, central bank, 91, 94

Senegal, central bank, 91, 92
Short-term capital flows
 charted, 115
 effect on U.S. balance of payments, 135–137
Socialist countries, intra-bloc trade, 424, 444, 445
Somali, central bank, 91–99 *passim*
Sources of finance for international trade and investment
 CACM, 753–756
 general, 711
 Spain, 746–752
South Africa, money market, 626–628
South East Asia, money markets, 634–642
Speculation in foreign exchange
 Canada, 336
 U.K., 368–371 *passim*
Spot exchange, 31–38
Sproul, Allan, 187
Stamp plan, 221, 222, 225
Sterling crisis, 267–271
Sudan, central bank, 91
Swap, 14
Swap arrangement, official, 269, 270

Taxation of business operations
 common market policies, 836–843
 comparison between countries, 808–818, 824–835 *passim*

Taxation (*continued*)
 effect on choice of investment location, 823–835
 general effect, 175
Taxation of multinational business activity by U.S. government
 historic, 772–776
 Kust proposal, 781–784
 proposed changes, 777–784, 785, 786
 tax havens, 791, 792
 tax sparing, 779–781
 tax treaties, 806, 807; *see also* Revenue Act of 1962
Taxation of personal income, comparison between countries, 818–821
Togo, central bank, 91
Triffin plan, 222–226, 245
Turnover tax, 816, 837–839 *passim*

Underwriting in underdeveloped countries, 603–606 *passim*, 609–614
Unit of account
 as recent innovation, 527, 534, 584
 data on use, 535–537
 definition, 584–586
 methods of use, 586–588
United Kingdom
 capital market, 568–570, 577–582 *passim*, 589–594 *passim*
 pressure on pound sterling, 42, 43, 44
United Nations Special Fund, 460
Upper Volta, central bank, 91
U.S. balance of payments, 101
 analysis, 121–136
 effect of
  foreign aid, 146, 176
  foreign investment, 175–183, 786–789
  sales of foreign securities in U.S., 184–188 *passim*
  wage rates, 146
 floating exchange rate as solution, 161–174
 foreign capital issues in U.S., 564
 government guidelines, 189–199
 methods of calculating, 139
 reserves, 123
 solutions, 145–154
 special transactions, 121, 122
 vs. domestic economic policy, 153, 154, 163
 vs. gold supply, 155–160
U.S. Department of Commerce, study of effects of foreign investments, 177–178
U.S. Treasury, study of effect of foreign investment, 180–183
USSR
 foreign aid, 481–483
 foreign trade
  data, 419–423

USSR (*continued*)
  financing, 423, 427, 442–446
  organization, 441, 442

Value-added tax
  introduction into U.S., 844–848
  method of operation, 847, 848

Value-added tax (*continued*)
  status in the common market, 839–842
    passim
Wender, Ira, T., 769, 770
West Africa, central bank, 91–99 *passim*
World Bank; *see* International Bank for
  Reconstruction and Development

Zolotas plan, 221